HUMAN RIGHTS IN THE TWENTY-FIRST CENTURY

Human Rights in the Twenty-first Century

A Global Challenge

Edited by

KATHLEEN E. MAHONEY

Professor of Law, The University of Calgary, Alberta, Canada

and

PAUL MAHONEY

Head of Personnel, Council of Europe, Strasbourg, France

MARTINUS NIJHOFF PUBLISHERS

DORDRECHT / BOSTON / LONDON

Library of Congress Cataloging-in-Publication Data

Human rights in the 21st century : a global challenge / edited by
Kathleen E. Mahoney and Paul Mahoney.
p. cm.
Includes index.
ISBN 0-7923-1810-2 (acid-free paper)
1. Human rights. I. Mahoney, Kathleen E., LL. B. II. Mahoney,
Paul. III. Title: Human rights in the twenty-first century.
K3240.6.H8775 1992
341.4'81--dc20 92-15848

ISBN 0-7923-1810-2

Published by Martinus Nijhoff Publishers,
P.O. Box 163, 3300 AA Dordrecht, The Netherlands.

Sold and distributed in the U.S.A. and Canada
by Kluwer Academic Publishers,
101 Philip Drive, Norwell, MA 02061, U.S.A.

Sold in the U.K. and Ireland
by Kluwer Law, part of Kluwer Publishing Ltd.,
1 Harlequin Avenue, Brentford,
Middlesex TW 8 9EW, UK.

In all other countries, sold and distributed
by Kluwer Academic Publishers Group,
P.O. Box 322, 3000 AH Dordrecht, The Netherlands.

printed on acid-free paper

Printed in the Netherlands

Table of Contents

Preface

These are extraordinary times. As the end of the millennium approaches, incommensurable feelings of optimism and dread are in the air. History will record this period as the time the Soviet empire disintegrated, the map of Europe was redrawn, new independent states emerged, the roots of South African apartheid were severed and major, unintended changes occurred to the environment because of new technologies and economic growth. Significant points of reference are shifting, but as yet, no one knows when they will stabilize. Still unfolding are struggles for supremacy between forces of democracy and inward-looking nationalisms; a fragile global ecosystem and the much vaunted but highly elusive new world economic order. Woven into this matrix of power relations are challenges to gender, race and class inequities perpetrated by institutions with inherent patriarchal, racist and classist tendencies. The tensions these struggles create cause fear and uncertainty for many people but for those who work in human rights, there has never been such a moment of unique opportunity to introduce the future to the present. Human rights activists, scholars, institutionalists and reformers now have an unprecedented opportunity to develop new values, mechanisms and strategies to guide and shape the future. The contributors to this volume try to do just that.

Seventy-two of the seventy-five papers and eighteen comments in this collection originate from an international human rights conference convened in a peaceful mountain setting in Banff, Alberta Canada. About three hundred participants from thirty countries attended the conference which was built around the complementary themes of "interdependence" and "solidarity". The purpose of the conference was to precipitate dialogue and debate on a wide variety of topics amongst people of widely different backgrounds, perspectives, values, experiences and insights. Women and representatives of disadvantaged and dispossessed groups, often absent from meetings of this type, were present in equal numbers with institutionalists, reformers and "movers and shakers" within the human rights community.

A spectrum of actors are involved, to a greater or lesser degree, in the human rights debate: first-hand witnesses of human rights abuses, grass roots militants, native people, non-governmental organizations, concerned academics, journalists, politicians, judges, civil servants, representatives of human rights institutions (national and international), the small voices, the official voices of reason, angry voices. Together these disparate groups make up a "human rights community", the unifying force being that each group feels its mission to be the futherance of what it regards as human rights. The Banff conference endeavoured to bring together that community – or some members of it.

The pluralistic mix of participants is reflected in both the content and style of the papers. Some are personal and profoundly disturbing; others are analytical, descriptive and occasionally even optimistic. Still others are deeply critical and reconstructive. In the early planning stages, there was some concern expressed that the differences of opinion amongst the participants were potentially so great that they would be unbridgeable. Nevertheless, we felt that if positive, inclusive, forward-looking social change is to occur, a progressive and more inclusive conversation must begin. We believed communication across divides of cultures, races, gender, professional and social backgrounds, religions and regions would identify and deal with barriers to progress better than any single perspective alone could. The aim pursued was to seek enlightenment as to the way forward through confronting in dialogue groups that are perhaps unaccustomed to meeting one another. It was our view that once such a process of dialogue was in place, more global, realistic approaches to shared problems and challenges would evolve.

To a large extent, our goals were achieved within the microcosmic context of the conference. While undoubtedly full agreement about ultimate remedies remains utopian, the open communication, the process of learning and sharing, the identification of common objectives and purposes, nevertheless emphasized the multi-dimensional nature of human rights and the layered responses that are required in order to start building foundations for consensus.

Hopefully the book will be of value at two levels: first, the wide range of topics are discrete units on their own. Chapters on discrimination, state and non-state violence, science and technology, economic, social and cultural rights, the environment, refugees, development and dispute resolution, provide independent analysis of topical, key issues by leading writers or practitioners in the particular subjects covered. Secondly, the collection of papers taken together reveals common themes, traits and core values which transcend categorization. The thematic consistency that emerges emphasizes that social progress, development, the environment and equality and human dignity are increasingly intertwined and mutually dependent; that ever closer relationships and interaction between communities inside and outside national boundaries are required if our fragile planet and its inhabitants are to survive into the next century and beyond.

There is a related recognition in the papers that legal responses to problems are themselves social actions. While on the one hand, laws are required to articulate change and set the course for the implementation of such change, on the other, they can have a detrimental effect if they fail to question the nature and quality of assumptions and philosophies which inform them.

There is no pretention in the collection of papers presented in this volume to provide a matrix for resolution of the problems of human rights in the twenty-first century. The starting point of principle has been that no one perspective has the monopoly of correct answers. A variety of perspectives, sometimes conflicting, is offered in the hope of lighting up what threatens to be a dark path ahead. Some of the major differences of opinion in the book are revealed in the structural analyses the authors provide. They make clear to the reader how contingent and incomplete our answers – indeed even our questions – really are. Contributors, whether they be feminists, grassroots reformers or human rights "insiders", talk about social, legal and institutional change in a way that deals with some of the most fundamental questions and premises of human rights. They consider questions of legal and political philosophy, principle and context, priorities and pragmatism. They critically examine tacit assumptions about how the world works, about values and customs, and about right and wrong. The authors search for and discuss serious alternatives, questioning the constructive nature of power and analyzing it from different world views. They teach us about different axes of power – that hierarchies can benefit some people, but they can disadvantage others in multiple ways. We learn that categories of disadvantage cannot be separated from one another. Gender, for example, cannot be separated from race, or race from class. They operate synergistically, and are mutually constitutive.

The feminist papers in the collection are particularly noteworthy for their structural critique. On a wide variety of topics they expose how existing human rights standards and laws – and the philosophies underpinning them – not only fail to protect women properly, but often actively disadvantage them. The overwhelming conclusion to be drawn is that sexism is as pervasive in the human rights as it is in all institutional structures. It is important to note, however, that the feminist analysis goes beyond so-called womens' issues. The "bottom-up" contextualized approach they take revolutionizes traditional equality theory across the board. The kinds of questions feminists ask go beyond comfortable abstract rationalism into the messy complexity of reality. The answers they propose make for a more open, flexible, experiential and interdisciplinary understanding of rights. But not only do the feminists lay bare one of the failures of traditional human rights analysis, their approach mandates the equal participation of marginalized groups in the conversation even if – or perhaps more accurately, particularly if – that means creating new methodologies and structures to make it happen.

A related but different critique is offered by papers which could be described as "grassroots" in orientation. Their emphasis is on the failure of governments and international institutions to integrate and implement rights in day-to-day existence, particularly as they pertain to environmental, social and economic needs of disempowered and disadvantaged people. They argue that without the effective implementation of social, economic and cultural rights, poverty and global inequities will destabilize the entire world. They posit that it is impossible to separate economic development issues from environment and human rights ones. Global poverty – itself a human product not a naturalistic phenomenon – is a major cause and effect of violence, hunger, ill health, environmental degradation, population growth and inequality of opportunity. In order to address these problems, greater international co-operation, understanding and commitment to action of individuals, voluntary organizations, businesses, institutes and governments are necessary so that more equitable access to resources and education to manage those resources are assured. Authors argue that tribal and indigenous peoples must be recognized and traditional rights and life-styles protected. Similarly it is advocated that the status of women must be improved through allowing them control over their fertility, improving their education and health, and enhancing their abilities to earn money through their own labour and the equitable valorization of such labour, quite apart from generally granting them proper participation in the processes and structures of decision-making in society. Above all, an integrated approach is stressed as opposed to a fragmented one. There is a recognition that what happens somewhere, at once happens everywhere. Global systemic poverty is a seamless net of causes and effects interwoven locally, regionally, nationally and globally. Policies regarding population, food security, genetic resources, energy, industry and human settlements must be developed holistically, guided by human right principles and values.

Papers written by human rights "insiders" emphasize and are concerned with human rights law and legal methods of protection for citizens, both within states and across them, without purporting to suggest that this aspect of the "human rights approach" represents the whole story. The relationship and balance between competing rights and society are investigated on a variety of different levels, including analyses of existing international and regional instruments and judicial decisions.

Visions and ideas for reform proposed in the papers range from improving present structures to radical and even revolutionary change. But regardless of the degree and scope of change suggested, there is a clear consensus that it must occur quickly.

A century ago, or even half a century ago, social change was slow enough that legal responses to it could safely take decades. Today, in our much touted "postmodern world", some change occurs so rapidly that assumptions presently held may not be valid within a matter of a few years. At the same time, scientific advances in mind manipulation techniques, genetic engineering, reproductive technologies and mass communications, and the increased ability of the computer to invade privacy, raise even more moral, legal and ethical issues that contributors to this volume grapple with. It is obvious from many of the papers that the traditional study of human rights has not kept pace with science and technology and that legal skills underlying the evolution and articulation of human rights must be integrated with those of economists, sociologists, feminists, philosophers, scientists, engineers, and grassroots activists.

If the challenge of stimulating new visions is to succeed, the message in this book is that we must be prepared to unpack structures which set standards and paradigms for human rights. Hierarchial, mechanistic and instrumental approaches are evidently no longer the best way to organize ourselves. Provocative thoughts of a social order based on solidarity rather than status challenge readers of this volume in every chapter. The long established liberal moral values that to a large degree have informed our understanding of human rights, are under fire. The extreme value liberals place on individualism is questioned in light of the increasingly obvious interrelatedness and interdependence of human existence.

Arguably the authors in this book, regardless of perspective, place a higher value on mutual responsibility and connection than they do on individualism. As a common moral imperative, connectedness with others and a sense of community ranks ahead of individual autonomy and independence. They stress attachment and the formation of relationships. They say responsibility is tied to those relationships. They explain aggression, violence and discrimination as a failure of connection. As an organizing principle to sustain and create human communities, this notion of mutuality could take us into the next century with a sense of hope.

Whether the ideas this book disseminates will become a point of departure for human rights in the twenty-first century or accepted wisdom in another era remains to be seen. But if one believes that progress lies in directions not yet taken, the book contains some road maps for all sorts of unexplored possibilities in the evolution of human rights. It provides some basis for an alternative ethos. Much more needs to be done. But it is, we believe, a start, a call for change and a stimulus for action. The various authors, whatever the divide between them in terms of spirit and approach, concur that agreement on general slogans such as the *need for solidarity* and the *indivisibility, interdependence and global character of human rights* is too easy: it masks the difficulty of what is meant by these concepts in real-life situations of disempowerment, oppression and misery. Is the closing report by Richard Devlin justified in its erudite pessimism as to the capability of the "human rights community" as a whole, and not merely one or two enlightened strands of it, to respond to that difficulty? This will be for the reader to judge after reading, or dipping into, the array of papers published in this volume.

Kathleen E. Mahoney
Calgary

Paul Mahoney
Strasbourg

Table of Cases

Abbreviations

YBECHR = Yearbook of the European Convention on Human Rights
CD = Collection of Decisions of the European Commission of Human Rights (1960-1974)
DR = Decisions and Reports of the European Commission of Human Rights (1975 to date)
EHRR = European Human Rights Reports
ECtHR = European Court of Human Rights
ECmHR = European Commission of Human Rights

Acknowledgements

First and foremost, we must thank our contributors. Their scholarship is an inspiration, their patience through this long process, a blessing. Our collaboration has been productive and we have learned a great deal from them.

But of course, many other people contributed to the work of the Conference and published proceedings – by intellectual means, by financial means and by organizational support. We are sincerely grateful to everyone who made such contributions. Kathleen Mahoney's particular gratitude is extended to the Conference advisory committee members: Rosalie Abella, Irwin Cotler, Alexandre Kiss, Virginia Leary, Peter Leuprecht, Paul Mahoney, John McLaren, Dinah Shelton, Lynn Smith and Bill Warden. The support staff at the Faculty of Law at The University of Calgary deserves special mention for their consistent support through both projects, especially Karen Argento, Bev Powell and Tammy Donovan. The University of Calgary Conference Office, especially Margaret-Anne Stroh, performed at their usual best as did our travel co-ordinator, Shirley Welter and our Calgary Bar volunteers, Linda Taylor and Ron Holdsworth. The Council of Europe, The University of Calgary Faculty of Law and the International Institute of Comparative Human Rights Law lent their moral, organizational and intellectual support from the very beginning and without the generous financial support and confidence of first the Alberta Law Foundation and then the Law Foundations of British Columbia, Ontario, Saskatchewan, Manitoba and the Northwest Territories, the Conference could not have taken place. The Global Fund for Women, the Secretary of State for Canada, the Canadian International Development Agency, and the International Centre for Human Rights and Development also provided essential funds for travel and translation services for delegates. Calgary Law firms, Macleod Dixon, Code Hunter and MacKimmie Matthews also lent additional, much appreciated financial support, as did The University of Calgary and the Students' Union at the University.

The editors are particularly grateful to the Department of Justice of Canada for the funding to publish these proceedings. Karen Argento can never be adequately thanked for her unflagging dedication to the enormous task of typing, organizing and marshalling the papers. Terry Meyers, a student volunteer reader provided comments and insights which helped to bring this long journey to publication to a conclusion as did other student helpers at the Law Faculty, including David Dzidzornu, Rose-Marie Cassis, Andre Cyr, Jacqueline Devlin, Monika Grosselfuenger, Sandra Hildebrand, Rena Krasnow and Marilyn Loewen.

The problems of editing across the Atlantic, between Calgary and Strasbourg, were also greatly eased by the understanding and encouragement of the publishers, Martinus Nijhoff, in the person of Alan Stephens. To him we owe a special statement of appreciation.

Finally, our deepest thanks must go to those closest to us. Our families including our spouses, Parvin Mahoney and Bryan Mahoney, and our children – Stefan, Leila and Alexander as well as Bryan Jr., Meghan, Brendan, Tara and Conor, continue to be patient, understanding, helpful and encouraging, even though they never get paid and seldom get recognized for the enormous contributions and sacrifices they make for us.[1]

[1] The European part of the editorial team (PJM) would like to add that although two Mahoney's are presented as co-editors the major portion of the work and the inspiration came from the Canadian part (KEM).

Editor's Note

The book is divided into six sections: Section I: Interdependence and Solidarity: Is the Human Rights Approach Relevant; Section II: Discrimination: The Need to Respect Equality and Diversity; Section III: Violence: The Need to Respect Human Life and Dignity; Section IV: Evolution of Human Rights into New Areas; Section V: New Threats to Human Rights Through Science and Technology – The Need for Standards; Section VI: Achieving Human Rights Goals. Each section is itself divided into constituent chapters, but begins with a general overview paper setting the common theme running through the topics treated in the different chapters. For readers' ease, each overview paper (and thereafter each chapter) is preceded by an introductive summary picking out the essentials of the subject-matter(s) dealt with. Some of these introductive summaries are based on the introductive speeches delivered by the relevant (session or panel) chairs at the Banff conference; others have been prepared anew by the editors.

SECTION I

Interdependence and Solidarity: Is the Human Rights Approach Relevant?

ROLV RYSSDAL*

Introduction

The opening chapter addresses the question, "Is the Human Rights Approach Relevant?" The area for our inquiries is vast: the varied and in many respects frightening human rights challenges facing our world in the coming century.

In the formulation of the basic premises, there is little dispute amongst the authors. Human rights are "indivisible" and "interdependent"; "solidarity" at all levels is needed if it is not to be just the strong and privileged who are able to benefit from the full enjoyment of their fundamental rights; and the onus for securing human rights is "global", not one that can be confined to one's own community or localized within the different continents or national borders.

All seem to agree on the necessity to protect, in real terms and for everyone, not only the classic civil and political rights but also, and even more, economic, social and cultural rights. Efforts have to be made not to exclude those left behind by the ever accelerating pace of change in our modern world, not to exclude the sick – it is high time to reflect on the human rights implications in this context – and not to exclude ethnic or other minorities, and, of course to fight the old evils of racism and sexism.

The "human rights approach" is not limited to enacting a legally defined catalogue of rights and setting up institutional machinery to enforce those rights. It is much broader. Contributors to this chapter and indeed to the entire volume, from their varied backgrounds and different origins, elucidate the potential as well as the drawbacks of the human rights approach in relation to the topics under consideration.

National laws and practices and international instruments on their own are not enough to adequately safeguard human rights. We also need education, trust, voluntariness and honesty. We need the responsible behaviour of all concerned. Mr. Justice Brennan of the U.S. Supreme Court has stated, "A judge who operates on the basis of reason alone risks cutting himself off from the wellspring from which concepts such as dignity, decency and fairness flow". In our struggle for better protection of human rights in the twenty-first century

* President of the European Court of Human Rights, Strasbourg, France; formerly President of the Norwegian Supreme Court.

K.E. Mahoney and P. Mahoney (eds.), Human Rights in the Twenty-first Century, 3–5.

we should be careful to avoid the danger of cutting ourselves off from the wellspring of such concepts.

In the first paper of the section, Irwin Cotler discusses the power of human rights law as a revolutionary change agent. He argues that the revolutions of the late 1980's and early 1990's are anchored in, and inspired by international human rights law, the internalization of human rights and the humanization of international law. He frames his article around the dramatic events of 1989–90: the dismantling of the Berlin Wall, the fall of the Politburo in Czechoslovakia and the release of Nelson Mandela, making the point that the power of human rights ideas in the present age is unprecedented but must be nurtured and protected or the revolution will be lost. In some areas of the world, violations continue unabated, particularly against women, children, racial minorities and indigenous people. To maintain the momentum of the human rights movement and to ensure that the human rights doesn't pass people by, strategic advocacy impelled by solidarity and interdependence is essential. He sets out a framework for the transformative, revolutionary role he envisages for the international human rights movement, emphasising the relentless, ongoing struggle that the achievement of human rights requires.

The second paper by Catharine MacKinnon criticizes the conceptual underinclusiveness and inadequate definition of human rights. Using the example of violence against women, she demonstrates through actual accounts of the torture of women how both national and international law and policy fail to meet human rights standards when violence is sex-based and "private". She argues that atrocities perpetrated against women are sex equality violations. Viewed that way, equality guarantees in national constitutions and international covenants could be used to address violence against women and illuminate human rights with the realities of women's condition.

In the third paper, Michael Czerny says that human rights represent a minimum that everyone should be able to take for granted. He argues that when human "rights" are inflated beyond their minimum, they lose their relevance to most of the world's population and merely masquerade as another form of individualistic, western-style liberalism. Writing from the perspective of the world's most impoverished, he says the starting point of human rights must be to privilege the rights of the poor. He believes this preferential option is essential if human rights are to address the real conditions, circumstances and history in which people live.

Joe Thloloe writes from the personal experience of apartheid. He describes how interdependence, solidarity and the world-wide condemnation of the human rights abuses in South Africa helped to force the South African government toward reform and emphasizes the importance of continued sanctions. Like Michael Czerny, he sees little benefit in human rights as abstract concepts. Academic debates about social and civil rights are meaningless to South African citizens oppressed by systemic apartheid, violence, poverty, low wages and inaccessible education. He says before peace and stability can be achieved, human rights must be as real and concrete as their violations are.

In the final paper of the section, Marc Bossuyt discusses the strengths and weaknesses of international human rights systems. He describes the normative and institutional progress in human rights systems since World War II particularly the relative success of the European Convention and its control machinery. On the other hand, he decries the politicization of human rights and lack of adequate funding for the international human rights institutional framework. He emphasizes the importance of recognizing the juridical differences between civil and social rights. If this distinction is "watered down", he argues, civil rights will be weakened without any advance in the implementation of social rights.

IRWIN COTLER*

Human Rights as the Modern Tool of Revolution

I. Introduction

In the struggle for human rights and human dignity in our time – in the promotion and protection of human rights as a modern tool of revolution – international human rights law is both inspiration and anchor, while the Mandelas, and the Havels, are metaphors and messages of this revolution. More importantly, perhaps, this struggle for human rights and human dignity is very much our struggle – the struggle for ourselves. For in what we say, or more importantly in what we do, in our deeds more than even our words, we make a statement about ourselves as a people – indeed, we make a statement about ourselves as people.

For we are today at a critical, historical juncture in the global struggle and responsibility for human rights – the anniversary of what has been called the "Year of the People – the Year of the Revolution". Tragically as well, it is the anniversary of the murder of the Jesuit priests of El Salvador who died for no other reason than they took human rights seriously.

For it is just a year ago – the Year of the People – that things that were thought impossible not only happened, but in some instances have already been forgotten – or are in danger of being forgotten.

- where, for example, in Poland, Hungary, Czechoslovakia and East Germany the power of the people prevailed over the power of the state and the Party.
- where hundreds of millions of people now exercise the franchise who could not do so just one year ago or less.
- where the re-unification of Germany, considered unthinkable just a year ago, is now a reality.
- where, as Gorbachev put it, more has been achieved for human rights in the Soviet Union in 1500 days than in the last seven decades.
- where Namibia has been liberated from South Africa; Nelson Mandela has been liberated from a South African prison; and the ANC, unbanned, and no

* Professor of Law, McGill University, Montreal, Quebec, Canada.

K.E. Mahoney and P. Mahoney (eds.), Human Rights in the Twenty-first Century, 7–20.

longer illegal, now negotiates the dismantling of apartheid with the South African government.

A human rights revolution – or revolution made possible by human rights – the whole dramatized in three vignettes:

In 1989, Eric Hoeneker, the then Communist party chief of East Germany, mockingly said to a group of people in prison for their struggle for human rights, "the Berlin wall will last for 100 years". At the end of 1989, not only had the Berlin wall been dismantled, but Eric Hoeneker was in prison.

Second vignette: On November 17, 1989 the Czech militia were beating demonstrators in the streets. Vaclav Havel was in danger of being imprisoned. One week later, November 24, the Politburo in Czechoslovakia had fallen. I remember it well because I happened to be visiting Dr. Andrei Sakharov in his apartment in Moscow at that time. The phone rang and it was Francesco Janouch – a founder of Chapter "77" and close associate of Havel – who was calling to tell Andrei Sakharov of the dramatic developments. Janouch held the phone so that Sakharov could hear a quarter of a million Czech citizens celebrating in Wenceslas Square. Sakharov, the man who alone had stood up against the Soviets in 1968 when they invaded Czechoslovakia now said to Janouch, "I feel 21 years younger tonight". And he then turned to Mikhail Chlenov, a leading Soviet human rights activist who had accompanied me, and spoke to us of the power of ideas – of the idea of human rights – of the Helsinki Final Act as the "Human Rights Manifesto" of the Revolution – of how the Soviet Union had tried to convert this Helsinki Final Act into a "prosecutor's club" – and of how those who struggle for human rights will ultimately prevail over those who seek to repress human rights.

And it was Sakharov, characteristically enough, who then went on to begin the struggle for the repeal of Article 6 of the Soviet Constitution which granted the Communist Party monopoly power; who rose in the Congress of People's Deputies to move its repeal only to be rebuffed by Gorbachev himself, who characterized Sakharov's proposal as "rubbish" as he cavalierly waved Sakharov off the podium; and who died tragically on December 14, 1989, some two months before he could witness the repeal of Article 6, and the beginning of democratization and political pluralism in the Soviet Union.

And the third vignette: The release of Nelson Mandela after twenty-seven years in a South African prison on February 11, 1990 – exactly four years later to the day that Natan Sharansky had been released in 1986; two political prisoners who had emerged as metaphors for human rights in our time – and whose lives, and fate, had somehow become intertwined one with the other. For one may not remember – or even have known – that South African President P.W. Botha had offered in December 1985 to release Mandela if the Soviet Union released Sharansky. The Soviets released Sharansky but Mandela remained in prison. Then Botha offered to release Mandela if the Soviets released Sakharov – which they subsequently did in October 1987 – but Mandela still remained in prison. Now Mandela has finally been released – and one of the most dramatic moments I witnessed when I was in South Africa this past May 1990 was to watch Mandela negotiating on behalf of the ANC with the South African government. Again, the power of the powerless, of ideas, of human rights advocacy – of rights as the basis for revolution.

II. The Rise of the International Human Rights Movement and Its Impact

This, then, was the year of the people, the power of the powerless, the year of the revolution, the velvet revolution, "without force or lies", as Czech playwright Anton Chechov had put it, and as Havel was so wont to quote him. And, most importantly, a revolution anchored in – and inspired by – the power of an idea – human rights – an idea emerging as the "secular religion" of our times; and of international human rights law – the internalization of human rights and the humanization of international law – as the revolutionary change agent of the [human rights] revolution.

As the former Procurator-General of the Soviet Union, Alexander Soukharov, put it in a January 1988 discussion with a then "unprecedented Human Rights Mission to the Soviet Union",[1] "What you are witnessing today in the Soviet Union is a revolution, the likes of which has not taken place since 1917. If you want to understand this revolution, you have to understand the revolution in the law. For law is the agent of the revolution in the Soviet Union – of the movement to a "Rule of Law" State."

In describing this "jurisprudential revolution" in the movement of the Soviet Union to a Rule of Law State, Soukharov continued that, "today individuals can do everything, except that which they are expressly prohibited from doing by law. Before, individuals could do nothing except that which they were expressly permitted to do by law". When advised of Soukharov's comments, Andrei Sakharov, in his inimitable wit and wisdom, responded as follows: "Soukharov has it wrong. Previously, individuals could do *nothing*, even that which they were expressly *permitted* to do by law."

This notion of law – of human rights law – as a revolutionary change agent finds dramatic expression in the compelling and prescient work of Father Robert Drinan, distinguished human rights scholar and advocate – and author two years ago of *The History and Hopes of the Human Rights Revolution*. In the words of Father Drinan, "the elevation of human rights to the international level is one of the most dramatic events in the history of international jurisprudence. It will have consequences and implications that even the most sanguine observer of human rights cannot now foresee." This was written one year before the year of the people, the year of the revolution.

It is perhaps not surprising then, that during the first ever public hearings on human rights in the Soviet Union in June 1990 – itself a revolutionary event –

[1] *On Speaking Terms: An Unprecedented Human Rights Mission in the Soviet Union*, Vienna, International Helsinki Federation for Human Rights, 1988.

this Year of the People was characterized as "Human Rights' Finest Hour"; that the revolution in law, it was said, had indeed made the human rights revolution possible. But, argued the human rights representatives from each of the Republics, the time had come to "move on" – to move from the arena of human rights to the arena of political and economic reform; that the human rights movement – the Charter "77s" – the Helsinki Groups, had served their purpose; that former dissidents and political prisoners had become Presidents and political leaders; that Yuri Orlov, who in 1978 had been sentenced to seven years imprisonment and five years in exile for seeking "to know and act upon his rights" – for taking the Helsinki Final Act seriously – was now, in June 1990, a guest of the KGB in the Soviet Union; that two former political prisoners in the 80's – Sergei Kovalov and Lev Timofev – were now co-chair of these public hearings, while some of their "jailers" sat among the assembled to hear them.

There was almost a sense in these hearings that human rights "had spent its force"; that, ironically enough, human rights was being marginalized by the very revolution that it inspired; that the real issue now was the political struggle for self-determination – the politics of independence – in each of the Republics; that, only when independence had been secured, could one go back to thinking about rights.

Indeed, I was confronted with the "fall-out" of the Year of the Revolution on a personal level. For I was asked by my family to take a sabbatical on the grounds that the human rights struggle had indeed been won. That all the political prisoners whom I had been representing all these years in the Soviet Union, in South Africa, and Latin America had been released; that the Refuseniks on whose behalf I had been advocating had been permitted to leave the Soviet Union; that "closed borders", the metaphor for the Soviet Union's denial of the right to emigrate, had been turned on its head, and the right to leave was now being institutionalized as a matter of law; that not only had Mandela been liberated from a South African prison, but that apartheid itself was being dismantled; that democracy was on the march in Latin America, in Central and Eastern Europe, in the Soviet Union; that suspected Nazi War criminals were being brought to justice in Canada and elsewhere; that the doomsday clock – recording the 80's march towards an apprehended Nuclear Armageddon, had been moved back from 3 minutes to midnight, to 12 minutes to midnight, and was now largely irrelevant. That, in a word, the human rights agenda had been secured – the human rights struggle had been won. Or as my children put it to me, the real test of human rights was always to ask the question, "Is it good for children?". And the time had come, as they put it, to spend a sabbatical with my children.

But, as I said to my family then – though not in rebuttal of the maxim that the test of human rights is indeed whether it is good for children – that we retreat from human rights at our peril, or at the peril of our case and cause. That while history may acknowledge Gorbachev as the man of the decade – as the mid-wife or mother of the human rights revolution – as a Hegelian world historical figure in the human rights revolution, there was another and even more compelling hypothesis: that it was the courageous men and women of the human rights movement – the Helsinki Monitors for example – who not only put their livelihood but their lives on the line, and who are no less responsible for the inspiration and impact of the human rights revolution – and are no less relevant today.

III. Continuing the Human Rights Revolution: A Framework for the Future

We run the risk now of not only betraying the revolution but losing it – if the human rights movement abandons the revolution, or we abandon the human rights movement. For it is the revolution in human rights law – invoked and inspired by the human rights movement – by the Vaclav Havels and the Charter "77s" – that made possible the revolution in Central and Eastern Europe, the Soviet Union, and elsewhere. For traditional international law eschewed any relationship to human rights, let alone to human rights law as a tool in a global human rights revolution.

In general, traditional international law purported only to govern relations between nation-states; it did not regard individuals as having any international legal rights – they were considered objects rather than subjects of international law; it denied any juridical standing to NGO's; it excluded the invocation and application of international human rights law in domestic courts, nor did it foresee, let alone authorize, individual representations to international bodies; it did not comprehend, let alone commit itself to a human rights foreign policy, nor did it provide for domestic remedies for international human rights violations; it denied any state responsibility for the violations of the rights to its own citizens, let alone consider developing any procedure for international redress. In a word, human rights was to be regarded as a matter that came within the "domestic jurisdiction" of each State – a principle which effectively denied other States, and the international community, the right to intervene on behalf of individuals.

But the post World War II explosion in international human rights law – the internationalization of human rights, and the humanization of international law – turned this traditional international law theory on its head. Accordingly, international human rights law would now be premised on the notion that every state has an obligation to protect not only any aliens within its midst, but its own citizens. Individuals, then, are not objects, but subjects of international law with rights and remedies that are justiciable in both domestic and international fora. NGO's have recognized standing and status, and may appear as intervenants in domestic courts invoking international human rights law, or as Petitioners – or on behalf of Petitioners – in international fora.

In a word, Human Rights Law was no longer to be regarded as a matter of "State Sovereignty", or an "internal matter" immune from international scrutiny and sanction. The world community had both a right and a responsibility to protest and seek redress for violations of human rights.

Moreover, not only had there been an explosion in international human rights law, but a dramatic development in the creation of international human rights *remedies*.

Accordingly, the international human rights movement now had a plethora of strategic advocacy initiatives at its disposal, including, for example:

- holding State Parties accountable for any human rights violations under the "Reporting" mechanisms set up pursuant to international human rights treaties;
- making representations to the U.N. Human Rights Commission under the "1503 Procedure" respecting any "consistent pattern of gross violations of human rights";
- making, since 1980, submissions that focus on the nature of the abuse or "theme oriented representations" – rather than just "country-oriented" submissions – and involving such concerns as Disappearances, Summary or Arbitrary Executions, Torture, and Religious Intolerance;
- making oral or written statements as accredited NGO's before a host of U.N. human rights agencies;
- making representations on behalf of individuals who are victims of violations by a State Party of its undertakings under, for example, the International Covenant on Civil and Political Rights, whenever domestic remedies have been exhausted, and the State Party has ratified the Optional Protocol authorizing such representations (itself a revolutionary measure);
- submitting Petitions to specialized agencies of the U.N. such as the International Labour Organization or U.N.E.S.C.O., whenever a violation takes place of the undertakings of a State Party to these Conventions;
- invoking international human rights law in a domestic proceeding – as with the prohibition against torture under customary international law – to buttress a cause of action in the domestic arena; or, as took place more recently in Canada, invoking international human rights law, such as the International Convention on the Elimination of all Forms of Racial Discrimination, in support of the constitutionality of domestic legislation prohibiting racial incitement against vulnerable minorities;
- institutionalizing a human rights foreign policy that conditions economic and military assistance on the human rights record of the prospective beneficiary state;
- making representations pursuant to the various processes and proceedings under the Helsinki Process, thereby securing redress and relief for victims of human rights violations by State Parties to the Helsinki Final Act.

And so, whether the matter involve the USSR's denial of the right to emigrate; or South Africa's apartheid and institutionalized racism; or Iraq's crimes against peace; or the United States' violations of international refugee law; or Israel's impugning of international humanitarian law; or Canada's treatment of indigenous peoples; or Romania's suppression of the Hungarian minority –

whether the human rights violator be a totalitarian government or a democratic one – all are responsible and accountable to this international human rights legal regime.

But even as we proclaim – if not celebrate – the human rights revolution, one cannot ignore its Dickensonian character – that 'tis the best of times, but also the worst of times'. For while 1989 was the Year of the Revolution for many in Europe, Africa, and Latin America, violations in China, Asia, the Middle East and elsewhere continue unabated. Assaults on rights of vulnerable peoples, be they indigenous people, racial minorities, aggrieved women, or powerless children, continue to abound. The hungry in Brazil, the homeless in Africa, the refugees in Asia, the imprisoned in the Middle East, can be excused if they consider that the "human rights revolution" has somehow passed them by.

Indeed, viewed from the optic of the victim, international human rights law may well invite the not uncynical rejoinder that, as Bentham once said of international law itself, that it is so much "nonsense on stilts" – rights without writs, rhetoric without remedy, semantics without sanctions. I would submit however, that it is no less prejudicial to the case and cause of human rights to wax cynical about it as to be complacent about it, i.e. it is no less prejudicial to assume that the struggle can never be won, as to assume that it has already been won.

The role of the human rights movement – anchored in the explosion in human rights law and remedy – must, therefore, be one of strategic advocacy, impelled by the imperative of solidarity on the one hand, and the interdependent universe we inhabit, on the other; and that strategic advocacy must be seen as being empowered by – as it itself empowers – the people – and the idea of human rights – as tools of revolutions towards the twenty-first century. The following advocacy functions may offer a framework for this transformative role.

IV. The Advocacy Role of the International Human Rights Movement

(1) Fact Finding and Human Rights Monitoring

One of the most important, indeed crucial, advocacy functions – and indispensable to the promotion and protection of human rights – is the investigation, documentation, exposure, and denouncing of violations of human rights and the violators themselves; in a word, what is involved here is "the mobilization of shame against human rights violators"; where monitoring, as Professor Mullerson has said, "is the very essence of human rights"; and where exposure is the ultimate sanction against human rights violators – the notion that "the whole world is watching".

Accordingly, whether we are speaking about the dismantling of apartheid in South Africa, or human rights repression in China, or war crimes in East Timor, the evidence is compelling that this fact-finding function is crucial to the promotion and protection of human rights. Indeed, governments themselves have become increasingly dependent on the fact finding of non-governmental human rights organizations; while the inter-governmental machinery, such as the U.N. Commission on Human Rights, or the U.N. Human Rights Committee under the International Covenant on Civil and Political Rights, would be "virtually incapacitated"[2] in the absence of NGO briefs, petitions, documentary evidence, legal analysis, and written and oral interventions.

The Sandra Lovelace case,[3] which resulted in a decision by the U.N. Human Rights Committee that Canada had breached its undertakings under the Covenant – and which in turn resulted in Canada acknowledging that it was "embarrassed" by the decision and was moving to repeal the offending Article 12(1)b from the *Indian Act* – was virtually carried by NGO's, or lawyers working with NGO's; while the relationship between members of the U.N. Human Rights Committee, and the NGO's themselves, has been described, by members of the U.N. Human Rights Committee itself, as being "exemplary".[4]

(2) Legislative/Advocacy Role

It might seem paradoxical to attribute a "legislative" role to Non-Governmental Organizations; but increasingly, and in the international arena in particular, NGO's are playing a formative role in the initiation, drafting, interpretation, and application of international human rights agreements and standard-setting generally[5]; and so, whether it be the involvement of the International Commission of Jurists in *International Covenants on Civil and Political Rights*, and *Economic Social and Cultural Rights*; or the work of the World Jewish Congress and church-based NGO's in the *International Convention on the Elimination of all Forms of Racial Discrimination*; or whether it be the work of Women's Rights Groups in the initiation and enactment of the *Convention on the Elimination of Discrimination Against Women*; or Children's Rights Groups in the initiation and adoption of the

[2] See for example, David Weissbrodt, "The Contribution of International Non-Governmental Organizations to the Protection of Human Rights", in Theodore Meron, *Human Rights in International Law: Legal and Policy Issues*, Volume 2, Oxford: Clarendon Press, 1984, p. 403–438.

[3] Under Section 12(1) of the Canadian *Indian Act*, a status Indian woman who married a non-Indian male would lose her Indian status and all the rights and privileges relating thereto – together with her children – in consequence of this marriage; yet if a status Indian male married a non-Indian woman, he would not only retain his Indian status, but the non-Indian woman would also acquire Indian status. Clearly, the *Indian Act* prescribed different consequences for Indian females and males as a result of their respective marriages to non-Indians. Indian women had challenged the validity of this provision as constituting a denial of equality before the law, but the Supreme Court of Canada had upheld this provision in the *Lavell* case. As Canada had ratified the Optional Protocol under the International Covenant of Civil and Political Rights, Ms. Lovelace was authorized to petition the U.N. Human Rights Committee respecting Canada's breach of its undertakings under the Covenant. Both the initiative for the complaint, and its representation, involved NGO work.

[4] See note 2, *supra*.

[5] See for example, Howard Tolley, Jr., "Popular Sovereignty and International Law – I.C.J. Strategies for Human Rights Standard Setting", in *Human Rights Quarterly*, 11 (1989), p. 561–585.

recent *Convention on the Rights of the Child* – the NGO's have played an important legislative role.

(3) The Public Advocacy Role

The international human rights movement has exercised an increasingly important and creative role in both shaping the public agenda and framing the nature of rights discourse, through the identification and articulation of areas and issues requiring international attention. Accordingly, whether it be the exposing of the plight of abused children, or asserting the plight of indigenous people, or the horrors of involuntary disappearances, or insisting on the minimum standards for detainees, NGO's have put these claims – and claimants – on the domestic and international agenda.

And so it was the Helsinki Monitoring Groups in the Soviet Union – and the Chapter "77s" in Eastern Europe – most of whose members were arrested, imprisoned, or exiled – who made the issue of human rights a compelling priority on the international agenda in general, and East-West relations in particular; it was the International Women's Rights Action Watch that highlighted the global pattern of violence against women; it was the anti-apartheid groups in the United States, Canada and Europe who promoted the "Sanctions regime" against South Africa; it was the "minority rights" NGO's that highlighted the plight of endangered minorities; and it was the NGO's representing indigenous peoples who brought their case before the court of world public opinion.

(4) Humanitarian Assistance to Victims of Human Rights Abuses

NGO's are playing an increasingly important, if not, indispensable role, in rendering a variety of forms of humanitarian assistance to victims of human rights abuses and their families, including, for example, tracing disappeared persons; visiting detainees in prison; securing humane conditions of confinement; and providing material and moral assistance to their families and the like. This humanitarian assistance may involve not only representations to the human rights violator government, but to one's own government, to other governments, to inter-governmental bodies, and to international organizations.

(5) The Legal Representation to Victims of Human Rights Abuses

This is, admittedly, a difficult and somewhat complex role, but a particularly compelling one. For it not only helps to secure redress for the victims of human rights violations, but it serves a number of collateral functions at the same time, including, for example, the mobilization of shame against the violator regime; preparing documented testimonials to the innocence of the accused; organizing a critical mass of human rights advocacy, such as, for example, writs for Amparo (Habeas Corpus) in Latin and Central American jurisdictions, or the Petitions to the Procurator-General of the U.S.S.R. in the matter of political prisoners; Petitions to inter-government fora, such as the U.N. Human Rights Committee (where appropriate); utilizing the I.L.O. or U.N.E.S.C.O. Petition procedure; or the complaints procedure of the Helsinki process.

As well, as set forth earlier, NGO's now have standing to use a spectrum of procedures under International Human Rights Law such as the reporting mechanisms under the Covenant; the 1503 procedure respecting "consistent patterns of gross violations of human rights"; the Optional Protocol to the International Covenant on Civil and Political Rights; the U.N. Center on Human Rights; the complaints procedure re Working Group on Disappearances and the like.[6]

(6) Human Rights Education

This educational process involves "conscientization", as some in the human rights movement call it – or "sensibilizer" as the French put it – creating a Culture of Human Rights – and respect for the "right to be different".

This may include education as much at the non-formal as at the formal level, involving consultations, workshops, seminars, and including special training courses for women, trade unionists, leaders of indigenous organizations, church-groups and the like. While this role is especially important in a period of repression, it is no less important during a period of transition to democracy, such as is presently occurring in the Soviet Union, Eastern Europe, Latin and Central America, and Asia. The initiation of Centers for Human Rights in Poland and the U.S.S.R. are excellent case studies of this role.

(7) Expressing Solidarity

This role involves not only providing a *moral/physical* lifeline to victims and their families, but also to the *indigenous* human rights NGO's who may be putting not only their organizational status but their lives on the line, as well as to those who provide a moral support system to those isolated and vulnerable individuals and groups. In particular, it may involve developing links with local human rights lawyers and advocacy groups who have a special role in the promotion of democracy and human rights in their countries. For example, the U.S. – based Lawyers Committee for International Human Rights has often acted as a liaison between indigenous groups and the American Bar Association, the U.S. Congress, and inter-governmental organizations such as the U.N.

Accordingly, even though human rights struggles are fought and won in the national arenas, the international NGO support system provides not only promotion of, but protection for, the indigenous human rights struggle; it gives the local NGO's an international voice, while amplifying their voice at home.

(8) Delivery of Services

This function involves less the juridical protection of victims and their families than it does helping them to realize a broad spectrum of economic, social and cultural rights, as well as civil and political rights.

[6] See for example, H. Hannum (ed.) *Guide to International Human Rights Practice*, University of Pennsylvania Press, 1984.

This is particularly true in the Third World where NGO's are sometimes better able to deliver services than are the governments themselves. I am referring here to essential, if not indispensable services, such as assisting victims in a disaster relief situation or situation of famine; providing assistance to refugee populations; offering skill training to underprivileged groups; giving courses in human rights education to military police; and providing legal assistance to those who cannot afford it.

(9) The Promotion of Human Rights and Democratic Development

Human rights advocacy groups are not mass-based organizations, nor are they political organizations in the sense that they seek political power for themselves; but they may be seen as "politically" engaged in that the struggle for human rights is often not only a struggle to curb *abuses* of power but also to promote the *democratic* exercise of power.

And so, NGO's have an important role not only as monitors of the election process but in developing institutional mechanisms for the protection and preservation of the electoral process itself. Again, the experience and role of Helsinki Monitoring Groups in Eastern Europe and the Soviet Union even in the "Years of Stagnation" provide ample testimony of the ability of people "to know and act upon their rights", and to thereby advance the process of democratization and the Rule of Law.

A shared international commitment to building a "Rechstaat" – or Rule of Law State – in this "Common European Legal Space", for example, will require a set of articulated principles and related institutions that form the core of a Rule of Law State, such as the Independence of the Judiciary; for law itself, as the experience of some of these C.S.C.E. states has shown, and as former political prisoners know only too well, can become an agent of repression. The Copenhagen Conference on the Human Dimension of June 1990 – and the road to the Moscow Conference in September 1991 – can provide an opportunity for NGO's to use their "legislative role" for the articulation and implementation of "Rule of Law" Principles – and related institutional frameworks – if a true "Rechstaat" is to emerge.

(10) The Constitutionalization of Rights

A corollary to – and support system for – the development of the Rule of Law and the process of democratization is the constitutionalization of rights in a Rights Charter. This holds true whether one speaks of constitutionalization in the "democratizing" C.S.C.E. States, or a Charter of Rights for a post-apartheid, non-racial, constitutional democracy in South Africa. The recent, Constitution-building exercise in Czechoslovakia, where a "constituent assembly" of scholars gathered together to consider a prospective Rights Charter for Czechoslovakia, had the atmosphere and resonance of, as one of the invited American scholars put it, being "present at the creation" – of both the 1789 American Constitutional process as well as the 1990 Czechoslovakian one; while Canadian scholars in particular have been active in the "constitutionalization" process in South Africa.

In this connection it might be instructive to note that the *Canadian Charter of Rights and Freedoms* may be a more relevant "Rights" model for the emergent democratic Federation of Czechoslovakia, or for a proposed Bill of Rights for Israel – than the American model which is usually held out – and not uncharacteristically by Americans – as being *the* model. For the Canadian model – and experience – may contain both historical and institutional features that are more responsive to the Czechoslovakian or Israeli legal and political culture, including, *inter alia*, a parliamentary system; no absolute separation of Church and State; a multi-cultural heritage; and a theory of minority and group rights and the like.

(11) Development of a Code of Conduct Respecting Rights of Minorities
In the words of Edouard Shevardnaze, ethnic hostility is a "gathering storm"; the anniversary of the Year of the People – the Year of the Revolution – may become as much a cause for lament as a cause for celebration.

Accordingly, NGO's have an important task in not only articulating the basic principles of a Code of Conduct respecting the rights of minorities, but of working for, and monitoring the implementation of, such a Code. Indeed, the role of NGO's here is nothing less than creating a "community of conscience" from NGO "coalitions of conscience".

For the dialectics of Glasnost have given birth to a host of xenophobic, racist and anti-semitic organizations in the U.S.S.R. and Eastern Europe, requiring thereby appropriate mechanisms – legal and institutional – to control incitement to racial hatred. In this connection, it might be instructive to note that Canada and the U.S.S.R. co-sponsored a Proposal respecting the combatting of hate propaganda at the recent Copenhagen C.S.C.E. meeting in June 1990. NGO's such as the Canadian Helsinki Watch Group had previously proposed such an initiative; and in Copenhagen the NGO's supported the joint Canada – U.S.S.R. co-sponsorship of this Proposal, lobbied for its adoption among participating States, and will now monitor its implementation.

(12) The Ratification of International Human Rights Treaties
It is important to get States who have yet to ratify the International Covenants to do so with all deliberate speed; and to get both those who have yet to ratify the Covenants, as well as those who have, additionally, to ratify the Optional Protocol to the Covenant. In this connection it is encouraging to report that the U.S.S.R. has indicated that it will soon ratify the Optional Protocol – a further example of the "domestication" by the Soviet Union of International Human Rights Law; while Israel has indicated that it is exploring the possibility of ratifying *all* the major Human Rights Treaties, which ought to augur well not only for the internationalization of human rights within Israel, but the humanization of international law as it applies to the Occupied Territories.

(13) Advocacy of Social Safety Nets

Many of the economic proposals recommended – or even being adopted by – the newly-emergent democracies in Eastern Europe and the Soviet Union – be it a market economy, or removal of subsidies, or price reform, are going to result – and have resulted – in serious economic dislocation and social grievance. This economic dislocation and social grievance in turn is feeding, and being fed by, the inter-ethnic conflict and exploding national antagonisms. Accordingly, it is important that appropriate consideration be given for social safety nets – networks of medicare, social security, and unemployment insurance; in a word, human rights NGO's have a particular role to play in ensuring that Western nations do not make an automatic transplant of notions and institutions – such as a market economy – that are themselves anchored in a particular political culture and experience, without seeing that this transplant may not result in greater injury and instability.

(14) Center for Prevention and Resolution of Conflict

NGO's have traditionally been more crisis-oriented, and have often functioned as crisis managers. What are now needed are Distant Early Warning Systems for rights abuse, so as to detect – and prevent – the development of conditions that may explode in "killing fields", as, for example, what happened in Burundi in 1988. For no had ever addressed the "root causes" that had produced the original "killing fields" in Burundi in 1972.

Finally, there will be a host of challenges for NGO's in the Post "Cold War" – or New International Order – such as:

- the protection of human rights in the "democratizing" states of Eastern Europe, where the dialectics of Glasnost and Perestroika have unleashed their own anti-democratic demons and assaults on human rights.
- the "accountability" of former human rights violator governments and officials, i.e. those responsible for the "disappeared", political killings, arbitrary detention, torture, etc. Is it enough that the violations be documented and the violators exposed?, or should those responsible be brought before the courts? What new law reforms – and institutions – may be necessary? Should, for example, involuntary disappearances be regarded as a crime against humanity?
- the inclusion of human rights norms in the decision-making criteria of international financial institutions.

(15) Human Rights NGO's and Their Mandates

At present a disproportionate number of NGO's deal with matters pertaining to political and civil rights, while the cause of economic, social and cultural rights appears to be under-represented among the NGO's. Accordingly, while there are a host of NGO's for such causes as political prisoners (AI), independence of lawyers and judges, prison conditions, freedom of the press and the like, most Western-based NGO's have not taken up such issues as toxic waste dumping in the Third World; or industrial pollution by multi-national corporations; or the rechannelling and revolving of Third World Foreign debt; or the transfer of weapons of mass destruction to the Third World whose economies are further impoverished through such purchases; or the internationalization of social welfare rights and the like.

V. Conclusion

We end in effect where we began. The struggle for human rights and human dignity – as Havel and Mandela have put it – separately but in solidarity – is really initially and ultimately the struggle for ourselves. And in this struggle, each one of us can and does make a difference – each one has a role to play in the indivisible struggle for human rights and human dignity in the interdependent world. And if ever one becomes tired or fatigued – complacent that the struggle has been won, or cynical as to whether it can ever be fought – let us remember that one person, Vaclav Havel invoking the Chekhov maxim "without force or lies" – speaking truth to power and in solidarity with the powerless, stood up against the whole Czech system and prevailed; that one person, Nelson Mandela, symbolizing the "power of the powerless", in solidarity with the international human rights regime and the power of the anti-apartheid movement, is bringing about the dismantling of apartheid and the building of a post-apartheid, non-racial, just democratic society. That one person, one Swedish non-Jew by the name of Raoul Wallenburg, saved more Jews in the Second World War than any single government. It is a staggering datum – but it happens to be true. People who stood up and shattered the conspiracy of silence – who broke the well of indifference.

This then must be the task for the human rights movement wherever it may be. To speak on behalf of those who cannot be heard. To bear witness on behalf of those who cannot testify. To act on behalf of those who continue to put not only their livelihood but their lives on the line. To stand up and be counted, and not look around to see whoever else is standing before a judgment is made to do so. For in a world of growing indifference, characterized by the culture of narcissism and of the politics of appeasement, there are increasingly few who are prepared to stand up, let alone to be counted.

At times such as these, as the French put it, and as I have said elsewhere – Qui s'excuse, s'accuse – whoever remains indifferent indicts himself or herself. But as the Havels, and the Mandelas, and the Salvadorean Jesuits, and the millions of others around the world in solidarity with them put it – if we stay the course, if we struggle for human rights day in and day out – and not just as an exercise in cocktail advocacy where we walk around with a placard one time a year to show our commitment to human rights – if we stay the course in the trenches of human rights day in and day out – then the struggle for human rights will prevail.

CATHARINE A. MacKINNON*

On Torture: A Feminist Perspective on Human Rights

Torture, with accompanying disappearance and murder, is widely recognized as a core violation of human rights.[1] Inequality on the basis of sex is equally widely condemned, and sex equality affirmed as a core human rights value and legal guarantee, both nationally and internationally.[2] My question is, given these two facts, why is torture on the basis of sex in the form of rape, domestic battering, and pornography not seen as a violation of human rights?

The purpose of this paper is to illustrate the way the realities of women's condition illuminate what must be included within the concept of human rights unless it is implicitly assumed that women are a lesser form of human life. My argument is that law and policy – national as well as international – and society must be held to human rights standards when torture, violence, assault and other forms of inequality are sex-based, just as much as when they are based on anything else.

Internationally, torture has a recognized profile.[3] It begins with abduction, detention, imprisonment, and enforced isolation; it progresses through the infliction of extreme physical and mental abuse; it may end in death. For torture to work, the absolute power of the torturer must be established. Life and death turn on his whim, a fact torture victims must believe absolutely and utterly. The victims are beaten, raped, shocked with electricity, nearly drowned, tied, hung, burned, deprived of sleep, food and human contact. The atrocities are limited only by the torturer's taste and imagination, plus any value the victim may be seen to have alive or unmarked. Verbal abuse, humiliation, and making the victim feel worthless are part of the necessary degradation.

* Professor of Law, University of Michigan, Ann Arbor, Michigan, USA.

[1] Convention Against Torture and Other Cruel, Inhuman, or Degrading Treatment or Punishment, UN Doc A/RES/39/46, (10 Dec. 1984).

[2] Universal Declaration of Human Rights, General Assembly Resolution 217A(111) (10 Dec. 1948); the Convention for the Elimination of All Forms of Discrimination Against Women, No. 34/180, General Assembly 34th Session (18 Dec. 1979) has been ratified by 103 states parties as of February 18, 1991. Many nations have explicit sex equality provisions in their constitutions. See A. Blaustein, *Constitutions of the Countries of the World* (1991).

[3] Amnesty International, *Torture in the 80's* (1984), London, Gerald Duckworth & Co. Ltd., p. 18–26.

K.E. Mahoney and P. Mahoney (eds.), Human Rights in the Twenty-first Century, 21–31.

Often torture victims are selected and specifically tortured as members of a social group, as described in Jacobo Timmerman's extraordinary account of his torture as a Jew in Argentina.[4] Torturers also exploit human relationships for their potential to inflict mental suffering; a man will be forced to watch his wife being raped, for example. Victims are forced to drink their own urine, to eat their own excrement. Sometimes drugs are forcibly administered which alter personalities and make bodily or mental control or even self-recognition impossible. Torture is a process toward death. Often one is killed. Even when one is not, events move and escalate in that direction. At any point, one could be killed.

There is also international consensus on what torture does to a human being. It is recognized that people break and change under such extreme pressure, studied under the rubrics of brainwashing, post-traumatic stress and the Stockholm Syndrome. Long-term consequences to survivors are both mental and physical. Many victims disassociate to survive and find the response hard to reverse. What one learns about life from being tortured, and what one has to do to survive it when others do not, makes being alive unbearable for some. Suicide can result even years later.

It is also generally recognized that the usual purpose of torture is to control, intimidate, or eliminate those who insult or challenge or are seen to undermine a regime. Torture is thus imagined to be political, although it often seems that its political overlay is a facilitating pretext for the pure exercise of sadism, which is a politics in itself.

When these things happen, human rights are deemed violated. These recognitions delineate a standard for acknowledging atrocities.[5]

With this framework in mind, consider the following accounts. "Linda Lovelace" was the name I bore during the two and one half year period of imprisonment beginning in 1971. Linda "Lovelace" was coerced through physical, mental and sexual torture and abuse, often at gunpoint and through threats on her life to perform sex acts, including forced fellatio and bestiality so that pornographic films could be made of her."[6] Ms. "Lovelace" then describes

[4] J. Timmerman, *Prisoner Without a Name, Cell Without a Number* (1981), New York: Alfred A. Knopf.

[5] This language, and much of the following analysis, was inspired by Andrea Dworkin's brilliant essay, "Pornography: The New Terrorism", *Letters From A War Zone: Writings 1976–1989* (1989), New York: E.P. Dutton, pp. 199-200.

[6] Declaration of Defendant-Intervener Linda Marchiano, *Village Books, et al. v. City of Bellingham*, (Marchiano Affidavit) para. 2 No. 88–14701 (unpublished) (W.D. Wash., Feb. 9, 1989).

The publisher has asked me to explain the unaltered use of raw and direct language– the language of the victims of sexual abuse themselves– in this article. Few hear the voices of victims of sexual abuse unmediated. This should end. Only unspeakable language currently exists for women's violations. Academic euphemisms cover them up. To make these accounts pretty is an insult and a lie. The realities are not pretty; nobody makes them pretty for the women who live through them. Elevated discourse creates distance. Only words like these begin to place the reader close to what happened, including a reader to whom it has happened. The comfort of distance also makes action less likely. These accounts *should* be hard to take. Surviving them was unbearable.

encountering Chuck Traynor, a pimp, as follows:

[W]hen in response to his suggestions I let him know I would not become involved in prostitution in any way and told him I intended to leave he beat me up physically and the constant mental abuse began. I literally became a prisoner, I was not allowed out of his sight, not even to use the bathroom, where he watched me through a hole in the door. He slept on top of me at night, he listened in on my telephone calls with a .45 automatic eight shot pointed at me. I was beaten physically and suffered mental abuse each and every day thereafter. He undermined my ties with other people and forced me to marry him on advice from his lawyer. My initiation into prostitution was a gang rape by five men, arranged by Mr. Traynor. It was the turning point in my life. He threatened to shoot me with the pistol if I didn't go through with it. I had never experienced anal sex before and it ripped me apart. They treated me like an inflatable plastic doll, picking me up and moving me here and there. They spread my legs this way and that, shoving their things at me and into me, they were playing musical chairs with parts of my body. I have never been so frightened and disgraced and humiliated in my life. I felt like garbage. I engaged in sex acts for pornography against my will to avoid being killed. Mr. Traynor coerced me into pornography by threatening my life first with a .45 automatic eight shot and later with an M 16 semi-automatic machine gun which became his favorite toy. I was brutally beaten whenever I showed any signs of resistance or lack of enthusiasm for the freaky sex he required me to act like I enjoyed. The lives of my family were threatened. Each day I was raped, beaten, kicked, punched, smacked, choked, degraded or yelled at by Mr. Traynor. Sometimes all of these. He consistently belittled and humiliated me. I believed Mr. Traynor would have killed me and others if I did not do what he demanded of me. I didn't doubt he would shoot me. I made myself go numb as if my body belonged to someone else... Simple survival took everything I had.

I managed to escape on three separate occasions. The first and second time I was caught and suffered a brutal beating and an awful sexual abuse as punishment. The third time I was at my parents home and Mr. Traynor threatened to kill my parents and my nephew if I did not leave immediately with him.

The physical effects of this are still with me. During my imprisonment my breasts were injected with silicone which has since broken up and has been dangerous and painful. All of the surface veins of my right leg were destroyed because I used it to protect myself from the beatings. My doctor told me that because of the abuse, it was unsafe for me to have another child so I had an abortion when I wanted to have the child. It took a long time to even begin to deal with the mental effects. A person can't be held prisoner for two and one half years and the next day trust society, trust the people who have put me there and just go on with the life that you once thought was yours.[7]

[7] Ibid., para. 7–11, 15, 22–23.

Now consider this account.

My name is Jayne Stamen. At one time I thought there was no one who could help me to get away from my husband. There wasn't a day that went by I didn't think was my last as he totally lost control. He slept with a gun beside him every night as he promised he would kill me and then shoot himself if I didn't submit to his obsession of slavery and bondage and beatings during sex. I was raped 11 times between March '84 and November '86. I had four broken hands during my marriage, caused by my husband. I was put into the hospital in traction for two weeks due to a beating by him. I walked with a walker several months after that. When I was raped by Jerry, I was always tied to my bed. Tied where my legs were spread apart. He tied me with nylon cords and extension cords. I even got tied up while I was sleeping at times. He would then penetrate me with objects such as his rifle or a long necked wine decanter or twelve inch artificial rubber penises. He would shave all of the hair off my private area as he said he wanted to "screw a baby's cunt". He would slap me while I was tied, call me all sorts of horrible names. I broke my arm on two occasions trying to get away from him. When he would watch porno movies on our VCR, he would tell me to do exactly what the women in the movies had done to the men. I would tell him to forget it and then he would continue to slap me around until he'd get so angry that I was afraid he'd beat me so hard he'd kill me. At times he'd grab a large knife he kept in the drawer beside our bed and he'd hold it to my face or breasts and tell me to do as he said or he'd cut me up. If I didn't act like I was enjoying pleasing him he'd threaten me again and then replay the scene he wanted acted out from the movies. I had no place to run as I never had any money of my own. He cut off the phone which was my only contact with the outside world. He would make me visit him when he finished his mailman routine and give him a blow job on the public street while people were passing by. I really wanted to die.[8]

Now consider this composite account of the systematic violation of a woman named Burnham by a man named Beglin, her husband. Beglin was watching an X-rated movie on cable TV in the family room. He entered the bedroom, threw her on the bed and bound her. He ripped off her clothing and began taking photos of her. He then sexually assaulted her. Crisis centre workers and an emergency room doctor testified that photos of her wrists and ankles were marked from being tied to the bed by ropes. He forced her 68 different times to have sex with neighbours and strangers, while he took photographs. She was forced through assault and holding their child hostage to stand on the corner and invite men in for sex and to have sex with the dog. He beat her so that she was nearly killed. She testified to episodes of torture with a battery charged cattle prod and an electric egg beater. She was asked about photographs in an album showing her smiling during the sexual encounters. She said that her

[8] Jayne Stamen statement, Feb. 14, 1988.

husband threatened her with violence if she didn't smile while the photographs were taken.[9]

In the accounts by these women, *all the same things happen* as happen in the Amnesty International accounts of torture, except that they happen in homes in Nebraska or in pornography studios in Los Angeles rather than prison cells in Chile or detention centres in Turkey. But the social and legal responses to their experiences are not the same. Torture victims are not generally asked, "How many like you are there?", as if it is not important and we do not have to worry about it if it happened only to you, or a few like you. Torture is not generally attributed to some sick individual and dismissed as exceptional. With torture, one doesn't hear that maybe the increase is just an increase in reporting, as if a constant level of such abuse would be acceptable. Billions of dollars are not made selling pictures of what is regarded as torture, nor is torture as such generally regarded as sexual entertainment. Never is a victim of torture asked, didn't you really want it?

A simple double standard is at work here. What fundamentally distinguishes torture, understood in human rights terms, from the events these women have described is that torture is done to men as well as to women. Torture is regarded as politically motivated not personal; the state is involved in it. I want to ask why the torture of women by men is not seen as torture, why it is not seen as politically motivated, and what is the involvement of the state in it?

Women comprise half the human race. Almost universally, women are battered, raped, sexually abused as children, prostituted, and increasingly live pornographic lives in contexts saturated more or less with pornography.[10] Women do two-thirds of the world's work, earn one-tenth of the world's income, and own less than one-hundredth of the world's property.[11] Women are more likely to be property than to own any. Until very recently, women have not even been allowed to vote, and still are not in many places. Women's reproductive capacities are systematically taken and used. While the rate and intensity of these atrocities and violations vary across cultures, they are never equal or reversed on the basis of sex. This is done to women as women, by men as men.

Selected examples show this in detail. In the United States, 44% of all women at one time or another are victims of rape or attempted rape; for women

[9] This account is drawn from the following sources: *Los Angeles Times*, May 19, 1981; *Costa Mesa Daily Pilot*, May 29, 1981; *Los Angeles Herald Examiner*, May 30, 1981; at A-1; *Sun-Star* (Merced, Calif.), May 29, 1981; *Sun-Star* (Merced, Calif.), May 27, 1981; *Times-Delta* (Tulare County, Calif.), June 6, 1981; *Sun-Star* (Merced, Calif.), May 28, 1981; *Sun-Star* (Merced, Calif.), June 5, 1981; *People v. Burnham*, 222 Cal. Rptr. 630 (Ct. App. 1986), (rev. denied, May 22, 1986).

[10] International League for Human Rights, *Human Rights Abuses Against Women: A Worldwide Survey* (1990), excerpts from the U.S. State Department's 1990 Country Reports on Human Rights (1990). L. Heise, "The Global War Against Women", *Utne Reader* 45 (Nov./Dec., 1989). No data is kept on the prevalence of pornography.

[11] United Nations, The State of the World's Women 1979, quoted in B. Weston, R. Falk, and A. D'Amato, *International Law and World Order* (1980), pp. 578–580. See also M. Waring, *Counting For Nothing: What Men Value and What Women are Worth* (1988).

of colour the rates are substantially higher.[12] In 1988, 31% of murdered women were killed by husbands or boyfriends.[13] In egalitarian Sweden, one woman is battered to death every week to ten days.[14] Recent dramatic increases in the rate of reported rape are being debated in Sweden; the debate is whether the increases are "real" or "merely" reflect an increase in reporting. Where women are chattel, or have only recently even legally emerged from the condition of being chattel such as in Japan, what can rape mean? If a woman exists to be sexually used, to what sexual use is the proper man not entitled? Sweden, the United States, and Japan are all saturated with pornography. In the United States, women simply disappear on a daily basis. They disappear from their homes, they disappear from supermarkets, sometimes we find them in ditches or floating down rivers, sometimes we dig up their bones along with those of ten or fifteen other women ten or fifteen years later. Serial rapists and serial murderers, who are almost always men, target women virtually exclusively.

Why isn't this political? The abuse is neither random nor individual. The fact that you may know your assailant does not mean your membership in a group selected for violation is irrelevant to your abuse. This abuse is systematic and group-based. It defines the quality of community life and the distribution of power in society. It would seem that something is not considered political if it is done to women by men, especially if it is considered to be sex. Then, it is not considered political or even violent because what is political is when men control and hurt and use other men, persons who are deserving of dignity, on some basis men have decided is deserving of dignity, like political ideology. So their suffering has the dignity of politics and is called torture.[15] Women as such are not seen as deserving of dignity, nor does the sexuality that defines us have any dignitary standards, nor is women's belief in our own dignity given the dignity of being regarded as a political ideology. The point is that the definition of the political is an unequal one, determined on the basis of sex such that atrocities to women are denied.

A reason often given or implicit in considering atrocities to women not human rights violations, politically or legally, is that they do not involve acts by states. They happen between non-state actors, in civil society, unconscious and unorganized and unsystematic and undirected and unplanned. They do not happen by virtue of state policy. International instruments (and national constitutions) control only state action.

[12] D. Russell, *Sexual Exploitation* 35, (1984); Wyatt, The Sexual Abuse of Afro-American and White-American Women in Childhood, 9 Child Abuse and Neglect (1985) p. 507. See also Senate Judiciary Committee Majority Staff Report, "Violence Against Women: The Increase of Rape in America" 1990, 102 Cong. 1st Sess. (March 21, 1991).

[13] U.S. Department of Justice, *Crime in the United States* (Uniform Crime Reports), August 6, 1989, p. 13.

[14] *Yearbook of Juridical Statistics*, Statistics Sweden, 1989 as cited in R. A. Elman and M. Eduards, "Unprotected by the Swedish Welfare State: A Survey of Battered Women and the Assistance They Received," (unpublished) (1990) at p. 1 (1989).

[15] Exceptions being, for instance, gay men who can be seen to be feminized by this process – and so are not exceptions at all because their abuse as gay is not seen as political either.

But the state is not all there is to power. To act as if it is produces an exceptionally inadequate definition for human rights when so much of the second class status of women, from sexual objectification to murder, is done by men to women prior to express state involvement. If "the political" is to be defined in terms of men's experiences of being subjected to power, it makes some sense to centre its definition on the state.[16] But if one is including the unjust power involved in the subjection of half of the human race by the other half – male dominance – it makes no sense whatsoever to define power exclusively in terms of what the state does. The state is only one instrumentality of it. To fail to see this is pure gender bias. Usually, this bias flies under the flag of privacy, so that those areas which are defined as inappropriate for state involvement, where the discourse of human rights is irrelevant, are those "areas in which the majority of the world's women live out their days."[17] Moreover, the fact that there is no single state or organized group expressly dedicated to this pursuit does not mean that all states are not more or less dedicated to it on an operative level or that it is not a deep structure of social, political, and legal organization.

Actually, though, the state is deeply and actively complicit in all the abuses mentioned. Linda "Lovelace" describes her escape from Mr. Traynor: "I called the Beverly Hills police department and told them my husband was looking for me with an M 16. They told me they couldn't be involved with domestic affairs. When I told them his weapons were illegal, they told me to call back when he was in the room."[18] She testified before a grand jury in an obscenity case involving one of the films made of her. The jury looked at the films and asked her how she could have ever done that. She said because a gun was at her head. They did nothing.[19] Linda Marchiano later became actively involved in an attempt in the United States to have an ordinance passed that would have made it possible for her to bring a civil action against the pornographers for everything they did to her and to remove the pornography of her from distribution.[20] This ordinance, a sex equality law, was invalidated by the courts as a violation of freedom of expression, even though the Court of Appeals that invalidated it recognized all of the harms pornography did to women and agreed it actually did those harms. This court held that pornography must be protected as speech in spite of its harm to sex equality – indeed, *because* of these

[16] Note this definition also does not include racist atrocities such as lynching unless it was done under colour of law, or class-based oppression.

[17] Burrows, International Law and Human Rights: The Case of Women's Rights, in *Human Rights: From Rhetoric to Reality*, (1986), p.82. It is worth noting that the Convention of the Elimination of all Forms of Discrimination Against Women makes no public/private split in its guarantees and requirements. See also E. Rhoodie, *Discrimination Against Women: A Global Survey* (1989), p.92. ("This [public/private] dichotomy is deeply engrained in the laws of some countries and thus the law plays a critical role in maintaining gender stratification."

[18] See note 6, *supra,* at para. 17, p. 7.

[19] See note 6, *supra,* at para. 21, p. 8.

[20] *Public Hearings on Ordinances to Add Pornography as Discrimination Against Women*, Minneapolis, MN., Dec. 12, 1983, pp. 45-57.

harms, inasmuch as the value of the speech for purposes of protection was measured by the harm it did to women and to their equality.[21] When this result was summarily affirmed by the U.S. Supreme Court, the United States government legalized an express human rights violation on the view that the harm which pornography causes is more important than the people it hurts.[22]

If someone took pictures of what happens in the prison cells in Turkey, would they be sold as protected expression and sexual entertainment on the open market? In the United States, that is unfortunately something of a rhetorical question if the victims are women. In most other countries, the answer is less clear, so far. Yet the pornography of Linda continues to proliferate worldwide.

Jayne Stamen wrote the account I read you from the Nassau County Correctional Facility where she is currently imprisoned. She was convicted of manslaughter in Jerry's killing by three men she supposedly solicited. Evidence of "battered women's syndrome" was excluded from her trial, to the accompaniment of judicial remarks such as "I'm not going to give any women in Nassau County a license to kill her husband" and "Jerry Stamen is not on trial here but Jayne Stamen is."[23] Can you imagine a murder prosecution against a torture victim who killed a torturer while trying escaping? If you can, can you imagine Amnesty International ignoring it?

In the *Burnham* case, the conviction for marital rape which the wife won at trial was overturned on appeal because of the failure of the judge below *sua sponte* to instruct the jury that the husband might have believed Ms. Burnham *consented*.[24] No standard beyond which it is obvious that a human being is violated. No realization that people break under torture. No realization that anyone will say anything to the torturer to try to get it over with. When women are tortured, when we break, we are said to have consented, or the torturer could have thought we did. Pictures of our "confessions" in the form of pornography follow us around for the rest of our lives. Few say, well that isn't who she really is, everybody breaks under torture. Many do say, *he* could have believed it, even if he forced her to do it; some women are like that.

This is the *law* of pornography, the *law* of battered women's self-defense, the *law* of rape. Why isn't this state involvement? Formally, it is very close to

[21] *American Booksellers Assn. v. Hudnut*, 771 F.2d 323, 329 (7th Cir.) (1985) ["Depictions of subordination tend to perpetuate subordination. The subordinate status of women in turn leads to affront and lower pay at work, insult and injury at home, battery and rape on the streets. In the language of the legislature, "[p]ornography is central in creating and maintaining sex as a basis of discrimination. Pornography is a systematic practice of exploitation and subordination based on sex which differentially harms women. The bigotry and contempt it produces, with the acts of aggression it fosters, harm women's opportunities for equality and rights [of all kinds]. Indianapolis Code 8 16–1(a)(2). Yet this simply demonstrates the power of pornography as speech."]

[22] *American Booksellers Assn. v. Hudnut*, 475 U.S. 1001 (1986) (summarily affirmed).

[23] Personal correspondence from Jayne Stamen to author, March 11, 1988.

[24] *People v. Burnham*, see note 9, *supra*.

the recent case of *Velasquez-Rodriguez* against Honduras,[25] in which a man was violently detained, tortured and accused of political crimes by a group that was allegedly official but was actually an unofficial but officially-winked-at, death squad. He has never been found. What was done to him was legally imputed to Honduras as a state under international law largely because the abuse was systematically tolerated by the government. The abuse of women I described does not pretend to be official. But the cover-up, the legitimization, and the legalization of the abuse is. It is done with official impunity and legalized disregard. The abuse is systematic and known, the disregard is official and organized, and the effective governmental tolerance is a matter of policy.

Legally, the pattern is one of national and international guarantees of equality coexisting with massive rates of rape and battering and traffic in women through pornography effectively condoned by law. Some progressive international human rights bodies are beginning to inquire into some dimensions of these issues under equality rubrics – none into pornography, some into rape and battering.[26] Still, rape is more likely to look like a potential human rights violation when it happens in official custody.[27] A woman's human rights are deemed violated because the state was an instrumentality of the rape. The regular laws and their regular everyday administration are not seen as official state involvement in legalized sex inequality.[28] The fact that rape happens is regarded by some far-thinking groups and agencies as a violation of a *norm* of sex equality. But the fact that the *law* protects rapists and is written from their point of view, is officially regarded as a violation of the *law* of sex equality, national or international, by virtually nobody.

[25] Inter-American Court of Human Rights, Series C, No. 4. *Velásquez-Rodríguez v. Honduras* (Judgment of July 29, 1988) (1989) 28 ILM 291.

[26] See, e.g., Directorate of Human Rights, Council of Europe, Information Sheet No. 24 (Nov. 1988– July 1989) Appendix XXXII, Declaration on Equality of Women and Men (16 Nov. 1988). CEDAW, General Recommendation 12 (8th Sess.), Report of the Committee on the Elimination of Discrimination Against Women on its 8th Session, UN Doc. A/44/38 (1989) 81 (reading in a Convention an obligation to take steps to address violence against women. Efforts to eradicate violence against women within society and the family, "Report by the Secretary-General", UN Doc. E/CN.6/1988/6 (1987). Regarding pornography, see Directorate of Human Rights, Council of Europe, Information Sheet No. 24 (Nov. 1988–5 May 1989); Recommendation No. R (89) 7 (principles on distribution of violent, brutal, or pornographic videos).

[27] See, e.g., Prepared Statement of Amnesty International USA, Hearings on Human Rights Abuses Against Women, Hearing before the Subcommittee on Human Rights and International Organizations, Committee on Foreign Affairs, U.S. House of Representatives, March 21, 1990. ("[S]ome governments do not consider rape, sexual assault and sexual abuse as serious a crime as other types of physical assaults. This is particularly alarming when the perpetrators of the rape are government officials charged with the protection of the public... id., at 6.)

[28] But see U.S. State Dept. Cable, "In recent legislative report language, the Senate Foreign Relations Committee observed that government tolerance of violence and abuse against women appears to be widely practised and tacitly condoned in many parts of the world. Noting that such abuse is a violation of human rights as defined in existing legislation the Committee called on the Department to pay special attention to these abuses in the cruelty reports." International League for Human Rights, *Human Rights Abuses Against Women in a Worldwide Survey* (May, 1990). See note 10, *supra* at Appendix 2.

High on my list of state atrocities of this sort is when the rape law permits a defense of mistaken belief in consent. This permits the accused to be exonerated if he *thinks* the woman consented, no matter how much force he used. This is the law in Canada, New Zealand and the United Kingdom, as well as some parts of the United States, including in California where the *Burnham* case was adjudicated. Another example is abortion being unconstitutional, as in Ireland. A further example is the affirmative protection of pornography in the United States, through the case mentioned in which Linda "Lovelace" participated. Of course, the United States, an international outlaw of major proportions, is not bound by most of the relevant international agreements, not having ratified them. But other countries where the pornography of her, and others like her, is trafficked, are. I would also include in this list of state atrocities, the decriminalization of pornography, first in Denmark then in Sweden. Those were official state acts, however beside the point of the harm to women their prior pornography laws were. No pornography laws at all is open season on women with official blessing.

Why are there no human rights standards for tortures of women as a sex? Why are these atrocities not seen as sex equality violations? The problem can be explained in part in terms of the received notion of equality which has served as a fairly subtle cross-cultural template for the legal face of misogyny. The traditional concept is the Aristotelian one of treating likes alike and unlikes unlike. Mostly likes alike. In practice, this means that to be an equal, you must be the same as whoever sets the dominant standard. The unlikes unalike part has always been an uncomfortable part of equality law, really an exception to it, so that affirmative action, for example, is regarded as theoretically disreputable, and logically problematic, even contradictory. The Aristotelian approach to equality, which dominates worldwide, never confronts several problems which the condition of women exposes. One is why don't men, particularly white upper class men, have to be the same as anyone in order to get equal treatment? Another is, men are as different from women as women are from men. Equally different. Why aren't they punished for their differences like women are? Another is, why is equality as well satisfied by equalizing down as up? In other words, if equality is treating likes alike and unlikes unlike, if you get somebody down in the hole that the unlikes are in, in theory that is just as equal as elevating the denigrated to the level of the dominant standard.

The upshot of this approach is what is called in American law, the "similarly situated" test, and is used in one form or another around the world wherever law requires equality.[29] As I understand it, applied to women, it means if men don't need it, women don't get it. As men, men do not need effective laws against rape, battering, prostitution, and pornography, so not having such laws for women is not an inequality, it is just a difference. Implicit here is that these abuses are part of the sex difference, the permitted treating of unalikes unalike.

[29] In some places, there are various ingenious methods for cushioning its impact or qualifying its abuses, but it remains the main rule.

Because there are few similarly raped, battered, or prostituted men around to compare with, such abuses to women are not subjected to equality law at all. Where because of sex inequality, the reality of women's condition is extreme in its lack of similarity to men's, the view is that the law of equality does not properly apply.

I think sex inequality is not simply a distinction to be made properly or improperly, as in the Aristotelian approach. It is fundamentally a hierarchy, in this instance, a two-tiered hierarchy. On this level, it is not abstract but substantive and produces systematic subordination, as in the situations of the women I have discussed.[30] The Canadian Supreme Court recently has come closer than any court in the world to beginning to recognize this fundamental nature of inequality and, under the new *Charter of Rights*, is engaging in a world leadership on the subject in an attempt to rectify it.[31]

This means that to act consistent with equality guarantees is to move to end sex inequality through law. Wherever the law reinforces gender hierarchy, it violates legal equality guarantees in national constitutions and in international covenants as well.

Understanding inequality in this hierarchical context makes the torture of women because of sex an obvious human rights issue rather than a subtle one, obscure only because of its pervasiveness. The jurisprudence of human rights must rethink the relation between law and society in these terms. We need to look at laws that prohibit what women need for equality, such as restrictions on abortion. We need to look at unenforced laws: those that exist but virtually nothing is ever done with them, such as the law against battering, which can make violence women's only survival option. This violates women's human rights. We need to look at the wrong laws: the laws that don't fit the violation, have nothing to do with what really happens to women, such as the law of self-defense, the law of rape, and the law of obscenity in most places. They violate women's human rights. All these are affirmative state acts or positive omissions. To go deeper, we also need to look at those areas where there are no laws at all for the harms women experience in society because we are women, such as most of the harms of pornography. Women are human there, too. Women's human rights are being violated there, too.

If, when women are tortured and disappear because we are women, the law recognized that a human being had her human rights violated, the term "rights" would begin to have something of the content to which we might aspire, and the term "woman" would, to paraphrase Richard Rorty, begin to be "a name for a way of being human".[32]

[30] This critique is discussed more fully in my "Reflections on Sex Equality Under Law", 100 *Yale Law Journal* (1991), p. 1281.

[31] *Andrews v. Law Society of British Columbia* [1989] 1 S.C.R. 143; *Regina v. Turpin*, [1989] 1 S.C.R. 1296; *R. v. Lavallee* [1990] 1 S.C.R. 852, but cf. *R. v. Hess*, [1990] 2 S.C.R. 906.

[32] R. Rorty, "Feminism and Pragmatism", 30 *Michigan Quarterly Review* (Spring, 1991), p. 234, C. MacKinnon's central point, as I read her, is that 'a woman' is not yet the name for a way of being human...".

MICHAEL F. CZERNY*

Liberation Theology and Human Rights

I. Introduction

I was born in what used to be called the Second World; grew up, was educated and trained in the First; and now live and work in the Third – in the tiny country of El Salvador, whose only claim to world attention has been the decade-old agony of civil war through which it is living, indeed dying. I write [speak] out of deep concern that, as the Second World is slowly joining the First, the Third World is rapidly assimilating to the Fourth, and soon our conflict-ridden globe will end up with no world at all.

"Human Rights" considers the non-negotiable essentials which are necessary in order that life may be life. "Liberation Theology" reflects on life as a gift of God's love and on the divine imperative to defend this gift as passionately as possible. The present paper offers some reflections on how human rights and liberation theology might shed some light on each other.

II. Human Rights

Human Rights[1] comes out of the liberal heritage or tradition. At its best, human rights enjoys a universal basis and expresses desires common to all peoples of

* Michael F. Czerny, S.J., former director of the Jesuit Centre for Social Faith and Justice in Toronto, is Vice-Rector for Social Outreach, and Director of the Human Rights Institute, Central American University (UCA), San Salvador.

[1] An introductory bibliography on human rights may include:

Frank Newman and David Weissbrodt, *International Human Rights*, Cincinnati: Anderson Publishing, 1990.

B.G. Ramcharan, ed., *Human Rights: Thirty Years after the Universal Declaration*, The Hague: Nijhoff, 1979.

Paul Sieghart, *The International Law of Human Rights*, Oxford: Clarendon Press, 1983.

UNESCO, *Human Rights: Comments and Interpretations.* A Symposium edited by UNESCO, introduction by Jacques Maritain, Westport, Connecticut: Greenwood, 1973.

United Nations, *Human Rights: A Compilation of International Instruments,* New York: United Nations, 1978.

K.E. Mahoney and P. Mahoney (eds.), Human Rights in the Twenty-first Century, 33–39.

the world.[2] Where the weakness of liberalism prevails and where economic and social Darwinism is the only real law of the land, human rights becomes "a hidden way of protecting what has been achieved or what could be achieved by the more powerful,"[3] merely another market place of so-called free competition.

Another danger is that the splendid achievement and constant developments in human rights remain at the level of a false universality, abstract and absolute. This occurs to the extent that human rights is discussed and even put into practice at a distance from the real conditions, circumstances and history in which people live.

Human rights can be effective if, and only if, we are clear about their starting point, their subject and their goal. The starting point is the struggle between life and death. The subjects of human rights are those who are oppressed, the great majorities, the repressed minorities. The goal is their liberation.

Taking my current homeland as a case study: El Salvador covers an area of 21,041 square kilometres, the size of Israel or the state of Massachusetts. Out of its small but over-crowded population, some nearly two million people "manage": they live with the sort of security which one might call middle class, and a small pocket within it enjoys great wealth and luxury. Another two million live in "technical" poverty, that is, with all the work they do they are barely able to assure the minimum basket of basic goods and services, nothing more and often less: the poverty of day-to-day survival. And finally a third, another two million live in absolute poverty, unable to earn the minimum basket of goods and services.[4]

Yet El Salvador is internationally notorious, not for its poverty, but for the civil war in which state terror – the systematic violation of human rights in order to control the population – has formed an integral element of counter-insurgency strategy. Why is life less than life in El Salvador? Obviously because of this war in which more than 75,000 lives have been lost since 1980. Everyone hopes that it may end soon, but many fear that the war is El Salvador's last link to the world and, once it is over, the country will sink into the oblivion of an indistinguishable poverty in which all human rights are abused indiscriminately. For the radical reason why life is less than life in El Salvador, is because

---

Karel Vasak, ed., *International Dimensions of Human Rights*, 2 volumes, Westport, Connecticut: Greenwood, 1982.

[2] V. Ramaswamy, "A New Human Rights Consciousness," *IFDA* Dossier 80 (January/March 1991), pp. 3–16. Human rights comes out of the particular history of one part of the world. To impose it, in its original restricted form, on the rest of the world, would be a form of treason.

[3] Ignacio Ellacuría, S.J., "Historización de los derechos humanos desde los pueblos oprimidos y las mayorías populares," *Estudios Centroamericanos*, 45:502 (agosto 1990), p. 590.

[4] The Latin American Economic Council (CELA) predicts that in the year 2000, the population of Latin America will be approximately 500 million persons, divided into the same three classes: roughly one third will manage in relative "middle class"; another third will struggle in average or technical poverty; and a final third will suffer critical or absolute poverty.

of the prevailing poverty which gave rise to the war in the first place.

TIME magazine's business section, in this case a reliable source, predicted in 1989 that 80 per cent of Latin America was heading towards a poverty characterized simply as "Bangladesh." And yet in all the Americas, only Haiti is listed by the United Nations Development Programme as belonging to the world's forty-four poorest countries![5] That means that on a world scale, El Salvador's dreadful poverty is far from the worst. Ominously all trends suggest that the Third World is deteriorating in the direction of poverty la Bangladesh.

Both technical poverty and especially absolute poverty generate the cycle which obtains in every circumstance of major human rights violations: the cycle of exploitation, misery, protest, repression, violations and, often, violence in response. This poverty, which is the fate of such vast numbers of people, needs to be turned into the priority in human rights and development, and the starting point of our reflection. Such a premise does not suggest that poverty is the only problem. It does not advocate tolerance for the violation of other rights (for example, freedom of expression or private property) not directly connected to poverty. But it does mean that poverty is *the* starting point and thus *the* priority.

Human rights is only a minimum. Lawyers, philosophers and practitioners perhaps tend to inflate human rights into a world view, a way of life, a vision, a mystique. Human rights may become any of these, but as the American Catholic Bishops explain:

> *Human rights are the minimum conditions for life in community.* In Catholic teaching, human rights include not only civil and political rights, but also economic rights. As Pope John XXIII declared, all people have a right to life, food, clothing, shelter, rest, medical care, education and employment. This means that when people are without a chance to earn a living and must go hungry and homeless, they are being denied basic rights. Society must ensure that these rights are protected.[6]

Human rights thus is a legal and constitutional minimum which, after all, people should *not* have to worry about and a minimum which, were this a more just world, should not have to be the subject of law and coercion.

Of human rights, therefore, the fewer the better. Let the declarations whither away. Let the conventions and treaties become obsolete. Let the courts go out of business. The best future for human rights would be, to become such a real, effective minimum that everyone could take them, literally, for granted. Let us not inflate human rights into a maximum which, it turns out, is only

[5] UNDP, *Human Development Report* 1990, New York: Oxford University Press, 1990, p. 185.

[6] United States Catholic Conference, *Economic Justice for All: Pastoral Letter on the Catholic Social Teaching and the Economy of the United States*, Washington, D.C.: National Conference of Catholic Bishops, 1987, paragraph 17. Italics in original.

another masquerading form of individualistic, western-style liberalism.[7]

Privileging the rights of the poor brings human rights back to the minimum they ought to be: a minimum for all! The rights of the poor do not turn into injustice for the few. The rights of the poor do not turn into the exploitation, the persecution, the torture, the disappearance, the summary execution of the few. The rights of the poor cause no conflict within the hierarchy of human rights, or between generations of human rights.[8] On the contrary, the rights of the poor form the basis for an inclusive human community.

Human rights translates the human condition into those fundamental, essential, non-negotiable and enforceable terms which are necessary in order that life might be life, that is, in order that life might begin, grow, develop and flourish in all its dimensions. Otherwise premature and unjust death holds sway. Human rights is the least we can – and must – do for the sake of life itself. This is the minimum.

III. Liberation Theology[9]

Discourse on human rights must begin with the right to life, *the* right precisely of the poor. "This is the basic intuition in Latin America with regard to human rights. To see them in the perspective of the right to life of the poor, and not the

[7] Human rights reduced to liberalism assumes that "liberty has as its proper subject each individual; it is each person who can be free, and freedom is predicated formally only of individual persons. Liberalism and individualism thus seem to be mutually inclusive." Ignacio Ellacuría, S.J., "En torno al concepto y a la idea de liberación," *Implicaciones sociales y políticas de la teología de la liberación*, Madrid: Escuela de Estudios Hispanoamericanos: Instituto de Filosofía, 1985, p. 99.

[8] "Hierarchy" refers to the priority which certain rights take over others, for example, the right to life over the right to property. "Generations" refers to the historical emergence, first of civil and political rights (late eighteenth century), then of economic, social and cultural rights (early twentieth century), then people's rights (e.g., self-determination) and finally rights of humanity (e.g., a life-sustaining environment) in the late twentieth century.

[9] An introductory bibliography on liberation theology may include:

Philip Berryman, *Liberation Theology: The Essential Facts about the Revolutionary Movement in Latin America and Beyond*, New York: Pantheon Books, 1987.

Leonardo Boff and Clodovis Boff, *Introducing Liberation Theology*, trans. Paul Burns, Maryknoll, N.Y.: Orbis Books, 1988.

Roger Haight, S.J., *An Alternative Vision: An Interpretation of Liberation Theology*, New York: Paulist Press, 1985.

Alfred Hennelly, S.J., *Liberation Theology: A Documentary History*, Maryknoll, N.Y.: Orbis Books, 1989; and *Theology for a Liberating Church: The New Praxis of Freedom*, Washington, D.C.: Georgetown University Press, 1989.

Penny Lernoux, *Cry of the People*, Garden City, N.Y.: Doubleday, 1980, and *People of God: The Struggle for World Catholicism*, New York: Viking Press, 1989.

Arthur McGovern, S.J., *Liberation Theology and Its Critics: Toward an Assessment*, Maryknoll, N.Y.: Orbis Books, 1989.

Paul E. Sigmund, *Liberation Theology at the Crossroads: Democracy or Revolution*, New York: Oxford University Press, 1990.

other way around..."[10] In Christian terms, Archbishop Oscar Romero emphasized the same point more than ten years ago when he said, "In my country cruel death is an everyday occurrence. The poor are being murdered. Peasants (campesinos) are being tortured, day in and day out, with the most extreme violence. What must be defended is the minimum. God's maximum. Life."[11]

The relationship between human rights and liberation theology is the relationship between this minimum and this maximum.[12] For from God's point of view, life is *the* gift, it is everything. Life is *the* expression of God's love. God's gift to the poor is life.

Perhaps the best-known and most-quoted theme of liberation theology is the preferential option for the poor. Only God can really exercise a preferential option for the poor, and yet treat all with justice and with love. Only God has the infinite love to love the poor preferentially but not exclusively, and to treat each man and woman on earth as His unique and beloved child. God loves the poor, not because they are good, but because they are suffering and because He is good and merciful. Only God has the unlimited imagination to foresee how the systemic violations of the rights of the poor (over two-thirds of the world's people) will give way to societies of justice, security and peace.

The fact that we on our own cannot imagine, the fact that we on our own cannot reconcile, the fact that we on our own cannot muster enough love and mercy, does not exempt us from the task that God gives us, which is to struggle to defend the rights of the poor.

The Judaeo-Christian tradition establishes human rights on this absolutely fundamental basis. The *torah* demands that people "choose life" over death.[13] The architectonic value of the Bible is *sedeq*, justice, which includes *mishpat* ("right") and *sedaqah* (an act of compassion or deliverance). But *sedeq* and *mishpat* are not mathematical justice-in-law. Rather, they mean "setting things right again." They have to do with proper relationships between human beings,

[10] "The Divine Element in the Struggle for Human Rights," in Jon Sobrino, S.J., *Spirituality of Liberation: Toward Political Holiness*, trans. Robert R. Barr, Maryknoll: Orbis Books, 1988, note 44.

[11] Ibid. For the meaning of Archbishop Romero's life and the significance of his death for human rights and liberation theology, see James R. Brockman, S.J., *The Word Remains: A life of Oscar Romero*, Maryknoll, N.Y.: Orbis Books, 1982, and *Romero: A Life*, Maryknoll, N.Y.: Orbis Books, 1990. See also Oscar Romero, *Voice of the Voiceless: The Four Pastoral Letters and Other Statements*, Maryknoll, N.Y.: Orbis Books, 1985.

[12] "The fact that philosophy or theology does not talk about the violation of human rights, diminishes the importance of this question and at the same time makes their violation easier; the fact that the institutional Church does not do it, brings about the same result. If on the other hand philosophy and theology took human rights as a relevant issue of social praxis (a redundant expression), they would give this historical reality a relevance which would otherwise remain concealed, to the benefit of the dominant groups or class." Ignacio Ellacuría, S.J., "Función liberadora de la filosofía," *Estudios Centroamericanos* 40:435–436 (enero-febrero 1985), 58.

[13] Deuteronomy 30:15–20. Without mentioning "human rights" in the modern sense, the Hebrew and Christian scriptures nevertheless ground these rights in the physical, psychological, social and spiritual dimensions of human nature.

which are the conditions for *shalom*, namely, peaceful community. *Sedeq* and *mishpat* refer precisely to the deliverance of the oppressed, those who are denied their rights. The supreme virtue of the Judaeo-Christian tradition is that love (*hesed*) which puts *sedeq* and *mishpat* into practice by defending the innocent victims of injustice and restoring them to the community.

To assure human rights (*mishpatim*) means to set social relations right (*sedeq*) again. This utopian proposal, which is both imaginative and realistic, places the emphasis, as did the ministry of the prophets and Jesus, on the need for new social relations throughout society: in their day, at the village, district and country level; in our day, at the local, municipal, regional, national and international levels. But Gustavo Gutiérrez, the father of liberation theology, has stressed that structural change, including the taking of political power, is not sufficient for true liberation, which includes development and democracy. Human beings need to become *new persons*, just as much as new economic and political *relations and institutions* are required. Human relationships between men and women, between generations and races, between producers and consumers, between poor and rich nations, need to be set right again.

This is how liberation theology reflects upon the divine maximum and tries to bring the human minimum into harmony with God's will. Liberation theology counteracts the liberal temptation to reduce human rights to individual rights and justice to mathematical equality. The biblical option or preference may be summed up in the following practical criteria:

> The needs of the poor take priority over the wants of the rich. The freedom of the dominated takes priority over the liberty of the powerful. The participation of marginalized groups takes priority over the preservation of an order which excludes them.[14]

Liberation theology calls getting social relations right again, whereby the needs, the freedom, the participation of the poor take precedence over the prerogatives of the status quo. Thus the light of Jewish and Christian revelation and, by extension, the light of all divine revelation is shed on these horrendous facts of life (that is, death) for the majority of humankind in the Third and Fourth Worlds.

Liberation theology makes sense out of what seems contradictory and impossible, namely, what seems surely beyond all human strength and resources. In this way it also clarifies the task of human rights work. Human rights workers and organizations are called to take up the defense of the right to life, even though it brings them into confrontation with the powers of this world and with the forces which tend to annihilate life.

In conclusion it seems appropriate to recall the violent deaths of six Jesuit priests and their two co-workers at the Central American University (UCA), who were murdered on November 16, 1989, by members of the Salvadoran

[14] David Hollenbach, S.J., *Claims in Conflict: Retrieving and Renewing the Catholic Human Rights Tradition*, New York: Paulist Press, 1979, p. 204.

Armed Forces. The martyrs of the UCA believed in human rights and opted preferentially for the poor majority. Living their faith to the full, they inevitably confronted the powers-that-be and finally paid the ultimate price. Their martyrdom enshrines the values and commitments which this essay has sought to present.

One cannot speak about human rights without speaking about a vocation and a mission. In the Christian tradition and in many others too, to lay down one's life for the life of the poor can be expressed in one word only – Love. The defense of the life of the poor is love. The defense of their life, at the risk and the price of one's own, is love to the divine limit.

JOE THLOLOE*

Human Rights and the South African Context

You have probably never heard of a little township called Bekkersdal. It is a small place about 50 kilometres west of Johannesburg. I am also sure that you have never heard of Mavis and Cornelius Montshiwa. They, in turn, know nothing about this very important conference. They probably have never heard of the Universal Declaration of Human Rights and other instruments for the promotion of human rights.

When this year started, Mr. and Mrs. Montshiwa had two sons, aged 22 and 18, and a daughter aged 13. Six months ago their first born was murdered in Bekkersdal because he refused to join a political party. Two weeks ago, their second son was killed because he joined the "wrong" political party. The younger boy was a member of the Azasm. It is the youth wing of the Azanian People's Organization. The story is that members of the ANC-supporting Bekkersdal Youth Congress attacked him, stabbed and clubbed him to death. He was buried last Saturday.

We have a tradition in the black community of holding a vigil the night before we bury somebody. Prayers are said, friends and relatives say all the good things about the dead person. The Friday before the burial, the friends and relatives of Michael, the dead boy, were at the Montshiwa home, holding the vigil under a canvass tent. In the middle of the night youths came, attacked the mourners and left two dead.

By the time I left home, at least 25 people, mostly youngsters, had been killed in six days of violence between members of different political organizations. Today, Saturday, the African National Congress, the Pan Africanist Congress and the Azanian People's Organization are holding talks to end the violence in this tiny township. What is of interest to us here, however, is that Mr. and Mrs. Montshiwa have lost two sons. They are victims of apartheid in two ways: directly, because apartheid has still has not been dismantled, whatever some people might say, and indirectly because of what apartheid has done to its victims, turning them into seemingly mindless killers.

* Deputy Editor, Sowetan Newspaper, Johannesburg, South Africa.

K.E. Mahoney and P. Mahoney (eds.), Human Rights in the Twenty-first Century, 41–45.

Let's talk a little about apartheid, which is an Afrikaans word for "apartness". Many people see it as a vertical line that separates blacks from using the same toilets as whites, for instance, or using the same buses as whites. They see it as the line that keeps people of different skin colour from marrying one another. The people who hold this view are the ones who are now jumping with joy and suggesting that apartheid is either dead or dying, simply because the Separate Amenities Act has been scrapped or because the Mixed Marriages Act has been repealed. But for the people like the Montshiwa's, apartheid is still alive and very, very far from dead.

When we sit at conferences like this one and talk about human rights, we should not forget that we are dealing with abstractions, with theories that are difficult for the man in the street to grasp. He understands violations of human rights in concrete terms and reacts to them from his gut, not his intellect. Mrs. Montshiwa would have loved to see her children well educated, with a promise of a much better life than she has had. I'm remembering at this point what Professor Bossuyt says about social and civil rights in his paper in this chapter. But no, instead her two boys had to drop out of school eventually and were killed. The academic theories about why this happened are not important to her.

Let me discuss some figures. In the academic year 1987–1988 the South African Government spent 595 rand on the education of an indigenous African child; it spent almost three times that, that's R1,508, on that of a child they classified as coloured; R2,015 on a child they classified as Indian; and R2,722 on that of a white child – which is five times what it spent on an indigenous African child.

This is what apartheid is really about. It is a horizontal stratification of society according to race. It is a hierarchy of power, with whites at the top and the indigenous African at the bottom. All the statistics that measure power in society reflect this hierarchy: whites at the top, Indians immediately under them, coloureds in the third layer, and the indigenous African at the bottom of the heap.

Allow me to highlight another set of figures – the annual per capita income, just to emphasize this point. The average income of whites in 1987 was R14,880; that of Indians was R4,560; coloureds, R3,000; and that of the indigenous African, R1,989 – less than one seventh of what whites earn.

Mrs. Montshiwa gets angry that her children are not as educated as white children and that they earn less than whites. This will continue because it is a self-sustaining system: those with better education will get better jobs and can afford even better education for their children. She gets angry because she and her children have to continue carrying water and wood for whites. It is the concrete material deprivation that she feels and reacts to.

Let us shift our attention a little, away from Mrs. Montshiwa, and hear what academics and intellectuals have to say. Mr. Justice P. J. J. Olivier, a judge of the Supreme Court of South Africa, headed a law commission that investigated and made recommendations to the Government on human rights in the country. On page 181 of its working paper 25, the commission concludes:

> "In view of our system of parliamentary sovereignty and denial of a testing right for the courts on the basis of fundamental human rights, the courts are severely hampered as regards to the protection of individual and group rights in the face of legislation which curtails these rights."

The commission also noted that treaties signed and ratified by South Africa do not become part of our law until such time as they are given statutory sanction by legislation. The only human rights document to which the South African Government is signatory is the Charter of the United Nations. But its provisions have never been promulgated as law. Now for the important quote from the report:

> "There is therefore no international charter, document, convention or manifesto relating to human rights in South Africa which has statutory force and can be enforced by the courts."

Thus, the courts have watched helplessly as the National Party robbed South Africans of their human rights. Let me quickly say that the report of the commission raises the possibility – at this point it is no more than a possibility – of a return to the rule of law and of the passage of a Bill of Rights to protect human rights in our land. South Africa today stands at an important crossroads, with the possibility of democracy triumphing.

When the National Party took over the Government in 1948, racial discrimination already existed. The National Party merely systematized it and enshrined it in the statute books. I will not go into the litany of crimes committed by the National Party. The oppressed and exploited black communities, on the other hand, did not just lie down and die. They fought back. The international community also did not shrug its shoulders; it intervened with passion.

In the past 30 years there have been three important periods of revolt against the National Party. The first one was between 1960 and 1963. The second was in the years of 1976 and 1977. The more recent one was between 1984 and 1986.

In 1960 the Pan Africanist Congress called on all black males over the age of 16 to leave their passbooks at their homes, go to the police stations nearest to them and demand to be arrested because they were not carrying their passes and were no longer prepared to carry them.

Led by Robert Mangaliso Sobukwe, the first president of the PAC, we marched to the police stations to be arrested. We were tired of carrying the badges of our oppression. We were tired of being hunted down by police in our Motherland simply because we did not have the "right" to be in urban areas. We were tired of being allowed into the urban areas only for as long as we were employed and useful to white society. And we were tired of being sent back to the "homelands" to die of old age and poverty. Thousands went to the police stations on March 21, 1960 and were arrested.

At Sharpeville, south of Johannesburg, the police panicked and shot at the crowd that was demanding to be arrested. Sixty-nine people died and hundreds were injured.

The Government declared a state of emergency and more people were arrested, this time without being brought to the courts. The pass laws were suspended for a while and the PAC and the ANC were banned. It became illegal to be a member of those organizations or to propagate their ideas. The international community was outraged by the killings at Sharpeville and the Western Cape and to this day March 21 is observed as the International Day for the Elimination of Racial Discrimination.

Capital fled the country, the value of the South African currency dropped, and these were the beginnings of economic sanctions against South Africa. This was a pattern that was to be followed faithfully in subsequent years: first there is internal defiance of the government, which then reacts violently, using the police and the army; then the international community expresses its outrage by imposing sanctions against South Africa. This pattern was repeated in 1976 and 1977 and again between 1984 and 1986. I believe that it is this combination of internal and external pressures that has finally forced the South African government to start talking of reforms and negotiations. The economy was collapsing and South Africa could no longer afford to stand alone as a pariah, shunned by all.

I think we have come full circle now, to the theme of this particular session, "Interdependence and Solidarity: Is the Human Rights Approach Relevant?" South Africa would not have reached this important fork in the road if it was not for the support shown by the international community for the victims of apartheid. The road ahead is tough. Apartheid is not dead yet. Substantive negotiations between the Government and the oppressed have not started yet.

We have often heard that State President F. W. de Klerk is a man of integrity and sincerely wants to democratize South Africa. But we should remember that we are not dealing with an individual, however sincere he might be. We are dealing with Afrikaner nationalists, first of all, and the white community as a whole. Anything could go wrong in the process – and each one of us knows that negotiations is a game of power. The weaker you are, the less likely you are to get a deal favourable to you.

The spontaneous revolts in the black townships, the economic sanctions against South Africa and the armed struggle conducted by the liberation movements are weapons that are used by the oppressed. If sanctions are lifted before there are even substantive negotiations, the black community is likely to emerge from the talks with a bad deal that will require us to resume the struggle for liberation again. At that point, it will be that much more difficult to reimpose sanctions if they have been lifted. And it will be even more difficult to gather people back into a fighting mode. We have already had bad deals during the talks about talks. We cannot afford more.

Let me return once more to Mrs. Montshiwa. In order to understand her anguish fully it is important that we keep looking at both sides of this issue. When the political organizations were banned in 1960 and other years, they continued their work underground, fighting a guerilla war. We all know that armies are not democratic, even the armies of the oppressed. They adopted autocratic styles of the people they wanted to overthrow. There was no time to grow a culture of democracy. And to make matters worse, all the concessions that the oppressed have won up to now were won through force.

Now, as these organizations emerge from the shadows, they do not have a tradition of open debate. Article 19 of the Universal Declaration of Human Rights is very quickly forgotten. But as South Africa cautiously moves forward, the liberation movements have to be reminded that the struggle for liberation will have been worthless unless a culture of respect for human rights replaces the dying Afrikaner culture.

So far, the international community has not been very helpful in this area. We have seen governments and other parties outside South Africa pouring money and other support into only one of the liberation movements. They are not encouraging open debate.

The Montshiwas and their children need to be given the choices they deserve. Mrs. Montshiwa will fully understand the meaning of Article 19 of the Universal Declaration of Human Rights the day she stands up to announce her preferences without fear. The challenge to theoreticians and activists alike is to provide a framework that will ensure that Mavis's voice has a meaningful impact on the public life in South Africa and around the world, even when she is speaking from her humble position.

We, on the *Sowetan* newspaper are trying to make that day dawn. We have started a campaign called *Democracy in Action*, to make readers understand that liberation without freedom of expression is meaningless. We ran a series of articles on the freedom of expression after nearly 800 people were killed in township violence earlier this year. A high point in this campaign was reached on October 19, the 13th anniversary of the banning of the *World*, a predecessor of the *Sowetan*. Several political and cultural organizations were also banned on that day in 1977. This year we hosted an all-day seminar involving the leading black political organizations and trade unions. We realize that this is just the beginning of a long struggle.

MARC BOSSUYT*

International Human Rights Systems: Strengths and Weaknesses

The issue of "social rights" is probably at the heart of the question "Interdependence and solidarity: Is the human rights approach relevant?". Indeed, over and over again the interdependence of civil and social rights has been stressed and many believe that social rights are the legal expression of the necessary solidarity among all human beings. The basic question is, however, to what extent the human rights approach is relevant in the field of what is called "social rights". Before addressing this question, the strengths and weaknesses of the international human rights systems will be reviewed.

1. The Strengths of International Human Rights Systems

If one looks at the international human rights system in perspective it is quite clear that the progress made in less than half a century is tremendous. With the sole exceptions of humanitarian intervention, the minimum standards of treatment of foreigners and the protection of minorities – which were the rare examples of a very limited degree of international concern for the protection of some vulnerable groups – it is fair to state that nothing came even close to an international system of protection of human rights before the founding of the United Nations.

The vivid memory of the massive and gross violations of human rights which took place during the Second World War induced non-governmental organizations to press for the inclusion of respect for human rights and fundamental freedoms in the UN Charter. As a result, when becoming Members of the United Nations, States pledge themselves to take joint and separate action for the achievement – *inter alia* – of universal respect for, and observance of, human rights and fundamental freedoms. Despite the absence of a precise definition and implementation machinery, this provision

* Professor of International Law, University of Antwerp, Former Chairman (1989) U.N. Commission on Human Rights.

K.E. Mahoney and P. Mahoney (eds.), Human Rights in the Twenty-first Century, 47–55.

constitutes the legal basis of the obligation of all UN Member States to respect human rights.

The UN Commission on Human Rights devoted the first twenty years of its existence to filling the two gaps just mentioned: absence of definition and implementation machinery. By 1948 the Universal Declaration of Human Rights had already been adopted by the General Assembly. On the basis of the Universal Declaration, numerous conventions were elaborated on the regional as well the universal level.

Undoubtedly, the most important are the International Covenants on Human Rights (1966), preceded by the International Convention on the Elimination of All Forms of Racial Discrimination (1965) and followed more recently by the Convention on the Elimination of All Forms of Discrimination Against Women (1979), the Convention against Torture and Other Cruel, Inhuman or Degrading Treatment or Punishment (1984), the Convention on the Rights of the Child and the Second Optional Protocol on the Abolition of Capital Punishment (both of 1989). On the regional level, mention should be made of the European Convention on Human Rights (1950), the American Convention on Human Rights (1969), and the African Charter of Human Rights and Peoples' Rights (1989).

All the above noted international conventions have enumerated and defined – generally in very similar wording – the rights and freedoms States should respect. Consequently, the world now has universally accepted standards in the field of human rights and in several States, individuals under their jurisdiction may invoke these rights or freedoms before the national Courts. Indeed, to the extent that their definition is sufficiently precise to enable the courts to apply the norms established[1] – as is the case with civil rights and fundamental freedoms – the judiciary will enforce them even if they contradict other legal provisions. In several countries this is not mere theory but present-day reality.

As a result of continuous internationalization, the protection of human rights still belongs *primarily* but no longer *exclusively* to the domestic jurisdiction of States. This is particularly true for States which are parties to an international convention on human rights, but it can also apply to any Member State of the United Nations. All States parties to an international human rights convention are entitled to insist that other States parties respect the human rights obligations they have undertaken.[2]

Besides the impressive normative progress, significant institutional progress has been made, both on a conventional basis and on the basis of the UN Charter itself. The greatest progress has been made on the regional level. For example, the success of the European Court on Human Rights in Strasbourg lies in its power to hold that measures taken by the authorities of a State party to the

[1] Cf. Bossuyt, Marc, "The direct applicability of international instruments on human rights (with special reference to Belgian and U.S. law)", *Revue Belge de Droit International*, (1980), pp. 317–320 et ss.

[2] M. Bossuyt, "Human Rights and non-interference in domestic affairs", *ICJ-Review*, (1985), Geneva, International Commission of Jurists, pp. 45–52.

European Convention are in conflict with the obligations arising from it.[3] As more and more States have become members of the Council of Europe and parties to the European Convention, more and more States have recognized the jurisdiction of the Court and the competence of the Commission to receive individual petitions. This has resulted in more cases being referred to the Court, which in turn finds more violations and grants more frequent satisfaction to injured parties.

The same level of achievement has not yet been attained by younger systems of regional or universal protection but it is likely that similar developments are to be expected. An encouraging development is the activities of the Human Rights Committee under the (First) Optional Protocol to the International Covenant on Civil and Political Rights. A growing number of States parties to the Covenant have become parties to the (First) Optional Protocol, recognizing the competence of the Human Rights Committee to receive individual applications, the cornerstone of any efficient system of international protection of human rights.

The Human Rights Committee takes a less restrictive approach in the admissibility phase than the European Commission. Of great importance is the interpretation given by the Human Rights Committee to article 26 of the International Covenant on Civil and Political Rights. This article[4] prescribes equality before the law, equal protection of the law and the prohibition of discrimination – not limited to the rights enunciated in the Covenant but extended to any field regulated and protected by public authority.

As more lawyers become aware of the potentiality of article 26 (as interpreted by the Human Rights Committee in the cases of *Broeks*[5] and *Zwaan-de Vries*[6], and in its general comments adopted on November 9, 1989)[7], a considerable increase of the caseload of the Human Rights Committee may be expected, particularly with respect to complaints against States parties to the European Convention, which lacks a general prohibition of discrimination.

Progress has also been made in organs directly derived from the UN Charter.[8] The adoption of Resolution 1503 in 1970 by the Economic and Social Council marked an important step. The confidential procedure established by this Resolution to examine individual allegations of "a consistent pattern of gross and reliably attested violations of human rights" is not always effective. But at the time of its adoption no conventional system of individual appli-

[3] M. Bossuyt and Y. Vanden Bosch, "Judges and Judgements: 25 Years Judicial Activity of the Court of Strasbourg", *Revue Belge de Droit International*, (1984/1985), pp. 695–712.

[4] M. Bossuyt, "The Principle of Equality in Article 26 of the International Covenant on Civil and Political Rights", in A. de Mestral, *The Limitation of Human Rights in Comparative Constitutional Law*, (1986), Cowansville, Quebec, Y. Blais, pp. 269–288.

[5] Report of the Human Rights Committee, A/42/40, pp. 139–150.

[6] Ibid., pp. 160–169.

[7] Ibid., A/44/40, Annex VI.

[8] M. Bossuyt, "The Development of Special Procedures of the United Nations Commission on Human Rights", *Human Rights Law Journal*, (1985), pp. 179–210.

cations existed. Several dozen situations of gross violations of human rights which otherwise could not have been dealt with at the international level have been dealt with using this procedure. Moreover, many situations ultimately the subject of public procedures were first scrutinized under this confidential procedure.

The so-called "country-oriented" public procedures have also developed considerably in the last two decades. Starting at the end of the 1960's with Working Groups on Southern Africa and the Israeli-occupied territories, those procedures evolved slowly in the 70's with Chile and Equatorial Guinea and more rapidly in the 80's first with Bolivia, El Salvador and Guatemala and later also with Afghanistan, Iran and Romania. Over the years, those procedures have progressively encountered less opposition and are now often extended by consensus.

Most promising, however, are the "thematic procedures" which focus special attention on particularly grave violations of human rights, such as disappearances (1980), summary and arbitrary executions (1982), torture (1985), and religious intolerance (1986). Compared with the Resolution 1503 procedure, the thematic procedures have the advantage of not being confidential (the thematic reports are public), less selective (several dozen countries are mentioned in each thematic report) and more rapid (the Special Rapporteurs have introduced appropriate mechanisms for making urgent appeals).

In summary, it may be said that the international machinery to deal with human rights violations has developed significantly in recent decades. In particular, the United Nations has greatly expanded its capacity to exercise pressure on governments violating human rights.

2. The Weaknesses of the International Human Rights Systems

Governments are the main violators of human rights, but are also the best placed for guaranteeing respect for human rights. This paradox constitutes one of the weaknesses of the system. Many procedures, particularly those available to the UN Commission on Human Rights, depend mainly on governments to become properly operational. Certainly, non-governmental organizations play an essential role. They generally provide the indispensable information on human rights violations and try to convince governments to take initiatives. But only governments may table resolutions in the UN Commission on Human Rights and only governments have voting rights. Governments are political organs and the Commission composed now of 43 – and soon 53 – governments is an eminently political body. Consequently, politicization of human rights is an inherent weakness of the UN Commission's work.

Not long ago international relations were dominated by security and commercial considerations. Human rights concerns were almost invisible. But lately, they have acquired more importance, particularly since Jimmy Carter, a former president of the United States, promoted human rights as a major objective of foreign policy. Nevertheless, whenever human rights concerns enter into conflict with security or commercial considerations, the latter are generally on the winning end.

Consequently, it is the strong conviction of the writer that only when human rights are treated as an independent element of foreign policy,[9] do they have a fair chance of being dealt with in an even-handed and credible manner. After all, concern for human rights does not as a matter of principle require the breaking of military alliances or commercial relations with countries not respecting human rights. It requires loud and clear protest whenever human rights are violated, regardless of the military and commercial links which may exist with the country in question. A government which fails to do so will damage its own reputation both with its own citizens and with the peoples who are victims of human rights violations.

Another main weakness of the international human rights system is lack of funding. No system for the protection of the human rights can function without a minimum of resources. Compared with the resources for other concerns, the resources needed for enabling an international mechanism for the protection of human rights to function are minimal. Even this minimum is not made available. With less than 0.7% of the UN budget, the UN Centre for Human Rights which is the indispensable Secretariat for human rights activities falls definitively below that minimum.

The financial crisis provoked by the continued withholding, by the United States of its financial contribution has had disastrous consequences for the United Nations as a whole, but more particularly for the UN Centre for Human Rights. If no remedy is soon found, the system will break down and the progress made in the field will be jeopardized.

Resources are needed, not only to back up the Secretariat, but also to initiate programs of human rights assistance. For too long, development assistance has been seen as a pure technical matter without sufficient attention being given to the human rights dimension. Development assistance misses the point if it does not improve the living conditions and the human rights of the peoples of the developing countries. Speeches lamenting deplorable human rights conditions in developing countries are empty if there is no willingness to respond effectively to the requests from the governments concerned for assistance to provide the minimum institutional machinery necessary for guaranteeing the rule of law.

Respect for civil rights and fundamental freedoms does not require huge financial resources. Some costs are required to provide the minimum institutional framework but compared with the resources mobilized for maintaining peace and security and for sustaining economic development, the resources

[9] M. Bossuyt, "Human rights as an element of foreign policy", *Bulletin of Human Rights*, (1989), Geneva, United Nations, pp. 27–33.

needed to assist developing countries in the field of human rights are very modest.

A final weakness is the confusion over the very notion of human rights caused by gliding too easily over the differences between civil and social rights.[10] Civil rights require from the State essentially – but not exclusively – an abstention. Consequently, they must be observed immediately, totally and universally. On the contrary, social rights require an active intervention from the State. As a result, they may be implemented progressively, partially and selectively. It is precisely because observance of civil rights merely requires abstention that States have no excuse for not respecting the human rights of everyone within its jurisdiction. On the other hand, because the implementation of social rights requires an active intervention by the State to the extent of its available resources – a State can be allowed to set priorities in the realization of social rights.

This is also the reason why the control of the observance of civil rights can be entrusted to judicial bodies, while the control of the implementation of social rights is left to administrative or political bodies. Indeed, in spite of the often very general and vague formulations of civil rights, a judge – national or international – is able to decide whether or not civil rights have been observed in a specific case and, particularly for the international judge, whether in the context of a specific case national laws do or do not secure the civil rights of all persons under the jurisdiction of the respondent State. On the other hand, without further elaboration by national or regional legislation, no judge is in a position to rule whether in a specific case a State has fulfilled its obligations in the field of social rights, because – depending on the available resources – it is up to each State to decide which social rights should be implemented first and which citizens should be first entitled to the benefits of those rights. National political authorities and not international judicial bodies have to establish those priorities.

The trend over the last few years has been to downgrade the juridical differences between civil and social rights. We all have heard over and over again, particularly in United Nations fora, that civil and social rights are interdependent and indivisible. We have often heard the rhetorical question: "What is the importance of freedom of opinion for someone starving of hunger?". As if acknowledging the existence of juridical differences between civil and social rights would entail the downgrading of the importance of the improvement of the social conditions of peoples.

Men and women have a variety of aspirations. Many are legitimate and a just society should do all it can to meet them. Some can be fulfilled by ensuring international legal protection. Law, however, is not an instrument that can guarantee the fulfilment of all human aspirations. Whether a human aspiration can be protected by law has nothing to do with its importance, nor even its

[10] M. Bossuyt, "La distinction juridique entre les droits civils et politiques et les droits économiques, sociaux et culturels", *Revue des Droits de l'Homme*, (1975), pp. 783–820.

legitimacy, but with its content. Several aspirations are of the utmost importance and perfectly legitimate, but are not suited for legal protection and should not be labelled as human rights. Nothing is more important in life than happiness. But to recognize a right to happiness as a human right would be meaningless.

Respect for human rights in its traditional sense imposes on the State a number of prohibitions, such as the prohibition against torture and slavery, the prohibition against depriving someone arbitrarily of his/her life or liberty, the prohibition against interfering in someone's privacy or in his or her freedom of opinion, expression, association, assembly and circulation. Any well organized State can always, through the proper functioning of its judicial apparatus, ensure for everyone under its jurisdiction the respect of all those civil rights or fundamental freedoms. When fundamental freedoms are violated, a properly functioning judicial system will be capable of putting an end to the violation by the State.

The same is not possible in case of violation of social rights. It is hard to imagine that when there is insufficient food or insufficient housing for everyone – someone who is hungry or freezing from the cold will obtain satisfaction by invoking before a court, a right to food or a right to shelter enshrined in an international convention. Only to the extent that the necessary resources are available and within the limits of appropriate national legislation can a judge be of any avail in such matters. Without specific national legislation spelling out the conditions under which someone is entitled to food, housing, education, health care, etc., a judge – national or international – cannot ensure the implementation of social rights enunciated in an international instrument. In contrast, a judge can, even in the absence of a specific national legislation, verify the observance by a State of any fundamental freedom guaranteed in an international convention.

As a matter of principle, the absence of economic resources is no valid excuse for the non-respect of civil rights. Even in a poor country, there is no need to torture, to proceed to summary executions and arbitrary detentions, to prohibit peaceful assemblies or freedom of movement. Nevertheless, the fact that the map of the less developed countries and the map of countries where human rights are frequently violated coincide to a large extent is itself no coincidence. Economic prosperity does not automatically bring about respect for human rights, but it certainly creates more favourable conditions for observance of human rights. Technical assistance in the field of human rights is highly desirable in order to help developing countries which lack even the minimum infrastructure of a well-trained and equipped judiciary and police force indispensable for ensuring respect for the rule of law.

The tendency in recent decades to minimize the juridical differences between civil and social rights should be questioned. Under the pressure of socialist countries and developing countries, more and more emphasis has been given to social rights. Quite often this emphasis is stressed by those States to conceal their failure to secure civil rights. The recent political changes taking place in the socialist countries and in some developing countries have made it clear that playing down the importance of civil rights was a ploy by certain regimes to justify manifold violations of human rights. At the same time their people did not enjoy superior welfare conditions. It is striking that in those countries where the people can now express themselves freely, the previous emphasis on social rights is rejected as old fashioned rhetoric and propaganda.

There is no need to qualify any legitimate and important aspiration as a "human right". Law is certainly not the only instrument for improving the well-being of humankind. Qualifying some legitimate aspirations as internationally guaranteed "rights" despite the finding that they are unfit for judicial determination creates only an illusion of progress, leading to distrust in the effectiveness of international human rights law. A careless utilization of the terms "rights" and "human rights" weakens the whole concept of human rights.[11] Of course, anyone may call a "human right" whatever he or she likes (it even proves what a tremendous impact the concept of human rights has had), but would it not be better to limit the term "human right" to its specific technical meaning?

Confused legal terminology weakens the very concept of human rights. In the absence of judicial enforcement, only the appearance of legal protection is given. In any case, it is not strengthening the international legal machinery that will improve the socio-economic conditions of humankind, but rather the pursuit of an efficient economy coupled with a fair social system.

The United Nations human rights concept is not determined by the justiciable character of rights. Rather, the view was that progress could be gained from the sheer force of human rights as an unassailable concept. It was felt that it would be helpful to declare as "human rights", several legitimate aspirations of humankind in the hope that States would feel obliged to fulfil them.

When one remembers the controversies that have raged over the precise scope of the obligations of States with respect to those (social) rights, the question may be asked whether it would not have been more useful to define the obligations of the States at the national and international level rather than to enunciate the rights of the individual.

Be that as it may, the notion has been abandoned that human rights are minimum guarantees of (legal) rights which everyone not only *should*, but also *can*, enjoy through justiciable enforcement – once the State under whose jurisdiction the individual comes is a party to an international human rights treaty commitment. A further dichotomy has been created between "legal rights" and "human rights". It has always been obvious that not all rights secured by a national legal system are internationally guaranteed human rights. The international human rights concept has developed to the point that not all

[11] See also Shestack, Jerome, "The Jurisprudence of Human Rights", in T. Meron, *Human Rights in International Law: Legal and Policy Issues*, Oxford University Press, Vol. I, pp. 69–113.

human rights – even when they are internationally proclaimed – are judicially enforceable rights.

There is always the danger that some could believe that the obligations of States to recognize civil and political rights are as vague and controversial as in the field of social rights. Another danger could be the impression created that legal mechanisms are appropriate to provide humankind with all the benefits that social rights are supposed to bring about: work, education, food, health, shelter and so forth.

Now, some legal human rights commentators are trying to turn to agronomical or medical problems. Human rights bodies are devoting part of their scarce time and resources to discussing issues of development, of foreign debt, of economic and monetary import without generally succeeding (up to now) in obtaining that the authorities competent in those fields devote the necessary attention to the human rights impact of their decisions.

Whatever may have been the arguments favouring the broadening of the human rights concept to non-justiciable rights, it is difficult to see what useful purpose can be served by watering down the juridical differences between civil and social rights. Any confusion in this matter weakens the concept of civil rights without advancing in any way the implementation of social rights.

SECTION II

Discrimination: The Need to Respect Equality and Diversity

Introduction

Rosalie Silberman Abella authors the thematic overview for Section II of the volume. Her paper encapsulates not only the underlying motivation raised in the specific chapters on gender, race, religious, ethnic, health and disability discrimination, its emphasis on human rights as an ever changing process and ideal rather than as static ideology challenges the reader to consider the issues in an open-minded, generous and visionary way.

The interdependent nature of rights is discussed as well as the social partnership that the author's definition of human rights requires. She emphasizes the importance of developing policy strategies which seek to eliminate discrimination wholesale rather than dealing with one group at a time, establishing a kind of pecking order among or within the disadvantaged. In her discussion of civil liberties and human rights, Ms. Abella makes the point that civil liberties, while a good beginning, have largely provided only the illusion of fairness and equal treatment. Human rights require more. Unlike civil liberties, she argues that human rights more emphatically emphasize individuals in their relationship to one another. Civil liberties require protection from the State, but the realization of human rights, in many cases requires the State to act on behalf of the disadvantaged. She argues that unless we come to terms with the sometimes dichotomous relationship between civil liberties and human rights, appropriate remedies to address issues of exclusion will never be developed or implemented and society as well as individuals will be the poorer for it.

K.E. Mahoney and P. Mahoney (eds.), Human Rights in the Twenty-first Century, 59.

ROSALIE SILBERMAN ABELLA*

From Civil Liberties to Human Rights: Acknowledging the Differences

1. Introduction

Affiliation with the human rights movement attracts easier adherence when the magnet is a simple one, when the human rights cry screams against the slaughter of religions, the disenfranchisement of races or the outright exclusion of genders. When the injustices are palpable and easily articulated.

But, we have by now in many countries, entered a sophisticated era of competitive anxieties when many injustices seem to have been sufficiently cauterized so as to appear cured, when the obvious has been replaced by the subtle, and when the patience of the majority appears to have surrendered both to a complacent *status quo* and to a temperamental economy. The magnet is now prismatic. Human rights has achieved political maturity of expression, but its implementation remains in adolescence.

There is no doubt that in our lifetime and certainly in Canada, an enormous amount of progress has earned our gratitude. This generation has produced many more human and legislative instruments than we could have imagined either possible or necessary. The Charter, Human Rights Codes, Employment and Pay Equity Legislation being just a few – and under their auspices we have successfully eradicated innumerable barriers. But while the successes are obvious, they are far from complete. Human rights is a process, an ideal not an ideology, and it demands flexible vigilance because its gains are never irreversible.

2. Solidarity and Human Rights

Human rights is about fairness, a commodity much valued in the cultures of civilized countries, but more easily embraced than implemented. As a concept, it inspires platitudinous articulation, but one person's platitude may be another person's dignity. No one objects to fairness. Its charisma lies, in fact, in its

* Chair, Ontario Law Reform Commission, Toronto, Canada.

K.E. Mahoney and P. Mahoney (eds.), Human Rights in the Twenty-first Century, 61–69.

objective simplicity, a perceived simplicity whose rhetoric is all too often so self-serving and made-to-measure, that it appears to be "one size fits all."

It is an undisputed synonym to "being humane", and humane is what we all want to be. But however seductive its objective appeal may be, it can never be properly applied unless it is understood that it is anything but objective. What is fair to an Anglophone may not be to a Francophone; what is fair to a white male may not be to a black female; what is fair to an atheist may not be to a 7th Day Adventist; and what is fair to any of them may not be fair to someone who is a disabled or aboriginal person. Each clamours for tolerance, each represents thousands more, each invokes the rhetoric of human rights, and each grows increasingly frustrated. The social contract comes under magnified scrutiny and the lens grows opaque, clouded by the terpsichorian movement of other issues competing for global policy attention, leaving human rights too often as a perpetual runner up in a race it should be umpiring.

How then to find solidarity in the tangled web of remedial pleas? How then to so define the issue that the web weaves a whole cloth rather than the tatters of good intentions.

The common ground is empathy. As more and more of us approach, and even achieve respectable levels of security, more and more of us should be looking over our shoulders to see whom we have left behind and why. And we should be looking through their eyes, because discrimination, whose eradication is the object of human rights, is in the eyes of the disadvantaged beholder.

While it is true that the plateaus are getting crowded, and that there will always appear to be less room than comfort suggests, we must all be reminded that our own comfort is fragile if the levels below us are at least as crowded. I am one of those who believe that absolute fairness, or equality, or peace, or absolute anything, is likely unattainable. But that does not mean that they are not worth pursuing. The fewer we have in our midst who feel a sense of arbitrary exclusion, the closer we are to civility. The quest is in the reduction of unfairness, and the way to achieve it is to strive towards the seemingly unattainable absolute of fairness, to make room for others, and even to facilitate their ascension to levels above our own. If the footpaths are strewn with victims of insensitivity, they will repay us. If on the other hand the path is clear, and heterogeneous, and optimistically travelled, those we promote will lead us in turn with enlightened nobility.

It is called generosity. There are thousands lined up around the block who have paid their admission and cannot understand why they are not being allowed into the theatre. It is trite to observe that indifference breeds indifference, but it is less trite to experience its costs.

"We cannot afford it" is only one side of a ledger, and it melts before the undisputable morality on the other side of the ledger that says "we cannot afford *not* to". Cost/benefit analyses suffer from being more easily amenable to demonstrating measurable immediate costs than ineffable future benefits. We are, I fear, at a social crossroads in our efforts to retain the fairness we prize ourselves on espousing. Without aggressive attention, we could easily allow the gains and goals to atrophy, overwhelmed by confusion and overtaken by false confidence.

Leaving aside for a moment the argument that centres on the inherent justice of promoting a genuinely egalitarian society, there is a less metaphysical inspiration, and that is the cost of neglect. Not merely the economic cost, but the cost to democratic values themselves. History is full of countless examples of the social upheavals generated when the disadvantaged can no longer be placated or mollified. Not for long can any democracy suppress the legitimate aspirations of those who no longer tolerate or understand their exclusion. And so we can either scramble to keep the lid on, or we can spend the same energy to figure out what causes the pot to boil and what we can do to turn down the heat. The first approach suggests complacent impatience; the second suggests visionary realism. We can either reverse exclusion, or wait to be reversed. How then to protect the gains and promote the values? We could do worse than starting with education.

We are as wise as what we know. By that I do not mean to define knowledge as merely the accumulation of facts which can be regurgitated when appropriate. I mean by knowledge a compendium of sensibilities, informed by facts, by sensitivity, by curiosity, and by experience. We are not omniscient and cannot know or experience all things, but we can be taught what questions to ask. The answer to any question about human behaviour is probably "it depends". Understanding what it depends on, is a function of what variables we are prepared to consider determinative. The ultimate question in human rights is "is it fair?" The answer may well be "it depends", but on what will we place reliance in deciding the solution? That depends on what we know.

Do people know that many have been arbitrarily excluded from the economic, social and political mainstream? Do they know why? Do they care? They cannot care unless they are taught that there is a problem, that it has victims, and that they have a stake in its resolution. Have they been trained to probe, to challenge, and above all, to empathize? Do they see education as a lifetime pursuit, or is it the mere acquisition of documentary proof that a standard of qualification has been achieved? Do they appreciate the vulnerability of young minds to insidious nuance, or do they judge educators by their simple capacity to transfer facts?

Does the media ascribe to the public a thirst for intelligent analysis, or does it cater to a perceived lowest common denomination of intellect? In other words, is education an exhortation to be our best selves, or is it just one in the taxonomy of public entitlements we wish to discharge with moderate competency. With all due respect to transportation, fiscal policy, the environment or any of the other indispensable amenities we have come to presume to be part of the House of Good Governance, the teaching of tolerance – the essence of a good education – is the foundation, whose solid structure is the best defence against the hurricane winds of regressive ideologies.

Without a thoughtful public, the House will be a hotel for transients, alternating members of the public welcomed from time to time by expediency, none of whom can claim ownership or even its possibility with any certainty. We must have a clear sense of who we are and where we want to go, and we cannot do it unless we are grounded in education, fortified by knowledge, and protected by wisdom. If we do not know who and what we are, how can we possibly make the changes fairness demands?

Human rights is after all about change. It is about new membership to old clubs and it is sometimes about changing the club.

I accept that change is difficult, that it is easier to enunciate the need to accommodate others than it is to do it. And when I try to rationalize to myself why it is that so many resist the expanded tolerance and access human rights preaches, I explain to myself that it is because we are all fearful of change and of the introduction of people and issues whose claim may be meritorious, but whose impact is uncertain. And while I find it a legitimate explanation for tentative reluctance, I hasten to add that I do not find it a legitimate excuse for ultimate inaction or for the kind of fear that allocates entitlement or lays exclusive claim to pieces of the social pie.

We cannot forget that everyone has entitlement to fair access to the whole pie. If the pie is not big enough, let us work towards expanding it. If it is not nourishing enough, let us change the recipe that has been handed down from generation to generation. Neither the merit principle, the economy, nor productivity are jeopardized by an opening of the minds and systems of any country to a pluralistic competition. All three, in fact are enhanced. We all lose by denying options to those who would contribute, a loss outrageous in principle, unforgivable in context, and cowardly in retrospect.

Unless the issue of human rights is defined as a social partnership, we risk the poignant spectacle of disadvantaged groups competing with one another for primacy, arguing the urgency of their disadvantage over and even within each other, when there need be no competition between them at all.

(1) Interdependence of Rights

Here many issues converge and require explanation. The first is to understand that when one group is disadvantaged, all are in peril. A society, for example, that permits discrimination on the grounds of sexual orientation is a society that permits discrimination, period. And if it exists for any, it is capable of existing for many. The groups who find themselves disadvantaged by discrimination are interdependent in their mutual needs for tolerance. The idea of a pecking order among or within the disadvantaged is neither productive nor acceptable when each shares the burden of arbitrary economic, social and political disadvantage. The emphasis must be on policy strategies that seek to eliminate discrimination wholesale, not one group at a time. Different groups require different approaches, I agree, but all of them must be designated beneficiaries of the assault on intolerance.

This does not mean, however, that all disadvantage is a human rights issue. I think it is time to acknowledge boldly that while the Charter of Rights and

Freedoms has had the positive impact of constitutionalizing the rights we always thought we had in Canada, it has nonetheless also generated a "rights" frenzy that seeks to put every claim of right on the same moral plateau. The rights to smoke or to keep pets in an apartment are not human rights issues, and we need apologize to no one for asserting that not all rights are created equal. Some are more equal than others. The attempt to equate the needs of white able-bodied males, for example, to their female counterparts, misses the point of human rights. White able-bodied males have not suffered historic generic exclusion because of their gender. Their female counterparts have. There may be many among white able-bodied males who have been treated unfairly, but not, on the whole, because there have been assumptive barriers to their access. Those disadvantaged among an otherwise advantaged group are no more the indicators of the presence of discrimination than are those exceptions in otherwise disadvantaged ones. Exceptions do not prove the point, history does. The arbitrarily disadvantaged must be seen to have a prior claim on remedial responses. The elimination of discrimination is the pursuit of equality and the pursuit of equality is the reduction of the disadvantage that stems from discrimination. And the proof of the reduction is not the extent to which we endorse all claims with equal righteous vigour, it is the extent to which, over time, those who were inappropriately under-represented take their representative place throughout the systems and institutions of a country, through good times and bad. It would go no small way to satisfying the concerns of the disadvantaged to give them the same opportunities to experience, equitably, the slings and arrows of outrageous economic fortune as those who are currently advantaged. They are ready to assume the burdens, but first they must be accorded the benefits.

(2) Acknowledging Difference

And this leads to the second issue, the extent to which we acknowledge that the only way to reduce disparities based on group differences is to acknowledge those differences. It is the fact of these differences that have historically inspired exclusionary systems, institutions and attitudes. Many differences ascribed to groups are as mythical as the excuses used to justify them. But other differences are genuine and immutable. These are the differences that should be respected and accommodated. Accidents of birth or heritage do not argue for the retention of a hegemonic vision. They argue for an expanded one that breaks the exclusionary monopoly and permits all who are willing, capable and entitled to compete fairly for access to and in the hierarchy of opportunities, in spite of and based on, those differences.

Changing the rules of the competition may change who gets the rewards, but if the new victors are people who ought to have been among the old ones, we are not being unfair. We are catching up. However benignly intentioned the former competition many have been, its impact was far from benign. And it is the impact, not the motive, that indicates whether the game was fairly played.

(3) Assimilation versus Integration

And this leads to the third and final issue, the issue of assimilation versus integration. Because not all people are, should be, or can be the same, it is hard to see how the objective measure of equality can be assimilation. What is easy to see, however, is the seductive appeal that assimilation offers. Its carrot is the mainstream, and membership is premised on homogenization. If this means conformity to values of civility and tolerance, assimilation is devoutly to be wished. But if it means, as it usually does, obliterating racial, cultural, linguistic, religious or gender differences, let alone pride in any of them then it is neither realistic nor equitable. Access to the mainstream must be based on those differences, and integration, not just assimilation, must be seen as the social goal. An integrated community is one whose members feel that their unique participation is both desired and desirable; an assimilated one denies participation to those who seek to assert the relevance of their differences. Descartes may have said, "I melt, therefore I am." But a melting pot denies the validity of how differences may impede equality. To be the same is not to be equal. To be equal is to be treated as an equal based on relevant differences. And to be treated as an equal is to be free from discrimination, from those traditional and erroneous assumptions that ascribe merit rather than acknowledging it.

3. Civil Liberties and Human Rights

To really understand human rights in a democratic context we must examine the historic role of the individual in the democratic hierarchy and to understand that while civil liberties and human rights are theoretical siblings, they are different both in their objectives and what they are prepared to sacrifice in their pursuit. Our tradition of human rights grows from the civil libertarian roots watered by Locke, Hobbes and Mill and pruned by the nineteenth century. It was a tradition whose centre was the individual and whose crucible was the relationship between the individual and the State. It was a theoretical root whose soil was theoretical equality. Its branches were individualism and each person had the right to be treated like every other person; its gardener was a State whose functions were presumed to be restricted to those occasions when one person violated the rights of another; and its guardian was a legal system deemed to be neutral in its equal application of the law. It was, in short, a philosophy that respected the autonomy of individuals and their rights to equal treatment. It was *laissez-faire*, and to an extent, *lese majesty*. In protecting the individual from unwarranted interventions from the State, it provided the illusion of fairness and the romantic rhetoric of access. In fact, it was neither always fair nor accessible.

What it was, was a good beginning. Different countries are in different stages of rights development, and all must begin with a commitment to civil liberties, but they are just the beginning. Human rights start where civil liberties end. And by end I do not by any means consign civil liberties to historical oblivion. I merely point out a source of potential confusion. The issues in human rights are not only about the civil liberties' emphasis on individuals in their relationship to the State, they are more emphatically about individuals in their relationship to one another, relationships that invoke the State's intervention and assistance, and request different treatment to narrow the gap. While there are some rights as individuals we protect from the state, in human rights there are rights we, as individuals who are members of a group, ask the State to promote.

What we have come to recognize is that treating likes alike, for all its facial neutrality, destroys the possibility of neutrality. Neutrality implies impartial application, but of what value is impartial application if it yields partiality? Process is only one side of the equation. The other is substance. And having accorded all individuals the same right to be free from the same State restrictions, we find that the impact of this universal standard is disparate treatment. Procedural sameness may lead to substantive inequality.

We find, at least, that equality is not a synonym for sameness, and that to presume that every individual is the same for all purposes, is to create the greatest presumptive barrier to equality. If equality can be defined as the reduction of inequality, we must come to grips with how to narrow the gap.

The civil libertarian emphasis on the individual is not a sufficiently broad framework in which to understand or analyze human rights. Human rights is no less about equal individuals but it is also about each individual's equal right to be free from discrimination. It is about individuals as members of a group, a group whose individuals experience disadvantage because they are members of that group. If we continue to focus on individuals, the claim of each individual is equal to the claim of every other individual. The claim of a non-white is equal to that of a white, the claim of someone who is blind is equal to the claim of someone with sight. This misses completely the issue of diversity and the hierarchy of historic disadvantage. If we want to include the widest possible number of individuals in the distribution of social amenities, we must appreciate that they were excluded not simply as individuals equally free to pursue legally sanctioned objectives, but as individuals whose group affiliation created physical and psychological prophylactics to access and outcome. Unless we come to terms with the sometime dichotomous relationship between civil liberties and human rights, we will be in policy *rigormortis* over remedy. If we allow ourselves to be chained to the pedestal of civil liberties, we will keep other tough issues under house arrest. The other tough issues are pluralism and diversity. Their benefit however is to individuals. And their benefactor is the State, the very State which is the civil libertarian's nemesis. The libertarian individual seeks freedom from association; the egalitarian group seeks freedom for association. Affirmative action may be a group remedy that impairs one individual's guaranteed access, but it is also a remedy that provides other individuals access they never had. Feminism may offend one individual's world view but it is also a philosophy that helps explain why for a whole gender of individuals, their views were impaired. The requirement to retrofit a building with wheel chair ramps may impose a financial burden on an individual landlord or employer, but for other individuals it means the elimination of a burden. If choices sometimes have to be made, and they do, human rights argues that the choices be on behalf of the arbitrarily disadvantaged group not the temporarily inconvenienced individual. To integrate individuals, we must sometimes integrate their groups, and integrating their groups may mean imposing on other individuals and restricting their autonomy.

Inclusion of those who were previously excluded may require and usually does require active interference with someone's right to decide whom to hire, promote, fire or make way for, but as unfair as it may seem to the individual who seeks to preserve autonomous judgment on these issues, it is the only way to reduce inequality. Education is critical, a good economy helps, a stable political environment helps, but in the end, these factors are conducive only of the possibility of an improved attitude over time. They do too little to alter behaviours, and while attitudes may open doors, only behaviour lets people in.

In all aspects of societal membership, the rules should be so designed that membership is not only reflective of pluralism and diversity, but systems are so designed and changed that those results are induced. The issues are very different for different groups, but each should be presumed to have the same entitlement: to have their uniqueness acknowledged and accommodated from their perspective, and not to be arbitrarily excluded or disadvantaged because of it; that choices be genuinely available, either to assimilate or to integrate; and that the primary strategy be a focus not on all individuals equally, but on those individuals whose group membership has impeded their participation and representation.

Individualism if necessary, but not necessarily individualism. The vigorous protection of civil liberties, but not necessarily the vigorous protection of all of their theoretical assumptions. Where we can make common cause we should, but if we cannot resolve the debate with mutual comfort, need we defer to 18th and 19th century theories that served well the need to create true democratic models, but serve less well the wider democracies we have become? While I said that I see no need for disadvantaged groups to compete with each other, I see no reason why any democracy should be embarrassed to embrace the primacy of their collective needs over those less needy of remedial attention. Human rights is a remedy for exclusion. It argues that there is a difference between social evolution and social Darwinism. One accommodates, the other neglects. One narrows the gap, the other tolerates it. Disadvantage occurs for different people for different reasons and each disadvantage is entitled to its own policy response. But where and only where the disadvantage comes from a denial of equality, or its tautology the impact of discrimination, is the disadvantage entitled to attract the legitimate vocabulary and policy of human rights attention.

4. Conclusion

Equality and its handmaiden human rights are about fairness, an ethereal objective. But it is also a realistic vision. To have the benefit of diversity is to have the benefit of heterogeneous input – human, intellectual, economic, cultural and political. It is to appreciate that the social orchestra, conducted by democracy, sounds best when it is harmonious. The sounds blend, they do not merge. It is a symphony, not a concerto. All the players expect to contribute to the melodious whole, and are interdependent on one another for support. It is a sound based on understanding the unique value each different instrument brings to the whole orchestra. It is a sound we must never stop trying to achieve.

As the second millennium closes, we should open the next determined that early in its chronology, we will have together assisted in creating a truly harmonious millennium.

SECTION II(a): EXCLUSION OF WOMEN FROM EQUITABLE PARTICIPATION

CHAFIKA SELLAMI-MESLEM*

Introduction

The exclusion of women from equitable participation is one of the major problems to the advancement of women in every forum, be it in the areas of politics, employment, or social services. It is of the greatest importance to achieve equitable participation, particularly at the decision making levels in order to remove discrimination against women. If women continue to remain outside the network of decision making nothing will change. Despite the progress and actions since the UN Decade for Women, women's issues are still considered marginal in many instances. The achievement of the goals of the Decade imply that equitable participation in all aspects of life is required to remove the roots of discrimination.

Each of the papers in this section deal with the issue of the exclusion of women from one of the identified areas, that is, human rights, politics, justice and employment. In her paper, Shelley Wright analyses the contents of the Convention on the Elimination of all Forms of Discrimination Against Women which leads her to state that it is absolutely necessary to find an accurate definition of women's rights as part of human rights to ensure their effective implementation. She states that women's rights are marginalized in all major international instruments and the fact that they are put into a specialized Convention enhances their "ghetto effect". Moreover, the weak implementation process and the lack of enforcement mechanisms hinder its effectiveness. She suggests effectiveness would be enhanced by extending the duration of annual sessions of the Committee, adding a Protocol to allow the hearing of petitions of individuals and non-governmental organizations and allocating more resources. The paper concludes that as long as the perception of women's role as reproducers and caretakers is not changed, human rights will never be human.

Mona Makram-Ebeid concentrates on the situation of women in the Arab world in the political sphere. She observes that the twentieth century brought considerable changes to the role and status of Arab women, changes they themselves helped to produce. Women's role in Arab society is linked with the

* Division for the Advancement of Women (DAW), Vienna, Austria.

K.E. Mahoney and P. Mahoney (eds.), Human Rights in the Twenty-first Century, 71–73.

political, social and economic crises it faces. Depending on their political and social values, governments in the Arab world respond to women's participation in politics in diametrically opposite ways: some offer them the right to vote, seats in Parliament or other material benefits such as education or guaranteed employment in order to add them to the list of regime supporters; others relegate women to their "traditional roles", denying them all political participation in order to get the support of the conservative, fundamentalist forces.

She concludes that the Arab family today is not totally traditional as it was a century ago, but neither is it totally modern in the western sense. The political landscape of the Arab world is being transformed by rapid social change. It is in a state of transition in structure, functions and values. Although in the minds of many, politics, economics and religion in the Arab world are still men's issues, this is not true in reality. Women have been and continue to be involved in politics, business and religion. Although the fundamentalist movements want to stop it, the process of change cannot be halted.

Ms. Makram-Ebeid's position is consistent with the Forward-looking Strategies, the Convention on the Elimination of All Forms of Discrimination against Women and the Convention on Political Rights for Women. All state that the basic principle of full participation of women in all spheres of life includes their participation in politics. There is a close reciprocal relationship between the general advancement of women and their participation in politics.[1] One of the recommendations made in September 1990 by the Expert Group Meeting on Equality in Political Participation and Decision making organized by the Division for the Advancement of Women was that political parties should, as an interim measure, establish substantial targets, such as quotas or similar forms of positive action to ensure women's candidacy for office and participation in political party posts.[2]

In the same year, the Commission on the Status of Women in the first review and appraisal of the implementation of the Forward-looking Strategies acknowledged that the number of women in decision making positions in intergovernmental and non-governmental organizations should be increased. They further recommended that Governments, political parties, trade unions, professional and other representative groups should each aim at targets to increase the proportion of women in leadership positions to at least 30 percent by 1995 with a view to achieving equal representation between women and men by the year 2000.[3]

Norma Wikler confronts a well-known but to-date, largely unaddressed problem. The paper "Exclusion of Women from Justice: Emerging Strategies for Reform" is about injustice arising through unequal treatment and unequal opportunity in the legal system of the United States and some of the efforts that

[1] Report of Expert Group Meeting on Equality in Political Participation and Decision making (EGM/EPPDM/1989/1), para. 5.

[2] *Ibid.*, para. 22.

[3] Economic and Social Council resolution 1990/15, recommendation VI.

have been made to ameliorate this problem. Her paper specifically deals with gender bias in judicial decisions. Even if laws are not discriminatory and women understand them and have complete understanding of and access to the court system, justice will be denied them if their treatment in courts is subject to gender bias on the part of the judge. The author also deals with the important question "How does a society maintain desirable judicial independence while also creating mechanisms which allow social reformers to impart to the judiciary new information and ideas that are essential to impartial and equitable judging?" One of the solutions she suggests is that judges with the help of "outsiders" formulate their own plans to elicit change within the justice system, beginning with possibly the biggest task of demonstrating that gender bias exists and that gender bias creates injustice. She describes the National Judicial Education Program in the United States (NJEP) which adapted this model. She concludes her paper by relating growing interest in the topic of gender bias in the judicial system. Canada has taken many steps toward creating data collection systems and judicial education programs similar to those of the NJEP.

As a group, women are generally ignorant of their rights. This increases their susceptibility to legal systems which are already biased against them because of male–defined norms and the use of sexist stereotypes. One of the recommendations of the thirty-fourth session of the Commission on the Status of Women concerns the development and implementation of programmes to improve women's awareness of their rights. This requires education at all stages in their lives, and access to educational facilities, media, and other means. Programmes such as these would complement the judicial education programmes recommended by Norma Wikler.

In the final paper of the series, Marilyn Waring discusses the exclusion of women from employment and opportunity and the invisibility of women's labour by today's economic definitions. She elaborates on attributing a monetary valuation to unpaid work, productive and reproductive and to including it in national income accounts. She argues that making women's work visible would influence policies and concepts as well as question values.

Despite the fact that much has been written on this question since 1975, a solution has yet to be found. It is certain that as long as women's domestic work at home, in family enterprises and in the fields together with their reproductive role remain unremunerated, their economic value will be denied and their real contribution to the economy not recognized.

All the questions that were raised in the papers, accurately emphasized the obstacles that remain to the realization of equality between men and women. Advanced ideas and new perspectives keep the debate open and oblige the international community to double its efforts in order to accelerate the process of the advancement of women.

SHELLEY WRIGHT*

Human Rights and Women's Rights: An Analysis of the United Nations Convention on the Elimination of All Forms of Discrimination Against Women[1]

1. Introduction

The United Nations Convention on the Elimination of all Forms of Discrimination Against Women (the "Women's Convention") was adopted December 18, 1979 by a nearly unanimous resolution of the General Assembly.[2] As of late 1990 the Convention has been adopted by over 100 nations, representing the majority of peoples from all cultural, religious and linguistic backgrounds throughout the world. Significant exceptions are the United States of America which signed the Convention in 1980 but has failed to ratify it, and India. Some nations' adoption of the Convention have been made with reservations to certain provisions that arguably undermine the object and purpose of the Convention, thus reducing if not nullifying the commitment to the protection of women's rights as described in that document. It should be noted that under Article 28(2), reservations "incompatible with the object and purpose of the present Convention shall not be permitted."[3] The effect and

* Faculty of Law, University of Sydney, Sydney, Australia.

[1] Much of the material on which this paper is based was gathered for the Annual International Law Seminar held at the Australian National University in 1989 and for a subsequent One Day Seminar on "Gender and International Law" which was hosted by the Centre for International and Public Law, the Faculty of Law at the Australian National University in Canberra and by the International Law Association (Australian Branch) Committee on International Law and Gender.

[2] 130 votes in favour, none against, ten abstentions as cited in I. Brownlie, *Basic Documents on Human Rights* (1981), Second Edition, at p. 94. G. A. Resol.34/180; 34 UN GAOR Supp.(No.46) at 193; UN Doc A/RES/34/180 (1980); 19 ILM (1980), p.33. The Convention was preceded by a Declaration on the Elimination of Discrimination Against Women which was adopted unanimously by the General Assembly on November 7, 1967; see Brownlie, (4R) First Edition, at p.183 for the text of this Declaration. The text of the Convention, ratifications and accessions, reservations and objections to reservations which is used in this article is from R.B. Lillich, "International Human Rights Instruments: A Compilation of Treaties, Agreements and Declarations of Especial Interest to the United States" (1986), [Looseleaf as updated].

[3] For general principles governing reservations and objections to reservations to Conventions in international law see the Vienna Convention on the Law of Treaties, Articles 19-23, 8 ILM (1969), p.679 and *Reservations to the Convention on Genocide Case* (Advisory Opinion of the International Court of Justice) [1951] ICJ Rep 15.

K.E. Mahoney and P. Mahoney (eds.), Human Rights in the Twenty-first Century, 75–88.

significance of reservations appear to be purely technical issues of international legal doctrine but in fact, represent a much deeper problem.[4]

The United Nations has been committed to sexual equality, at least as a matter of rhetoric, since the drafting of the Charter in 1945. The Preamble reaffirms "faith in fundamental human rights, in the dignity and worth of the human person, in the equal rights of men and women and of nations large and small . . ." Article 1(4) states that the promotion and encouragement of respect for human rights "without distinction as to race, sex, language, or religion" is a basic purpose of the United Nations.

The UN Commission on the Status of Women was set up under the auspices of the Economic and Social Council of the United Nations in 1946 to investigate the position of women.[5] In 1972 the UN General Assembly proclaimed 1975 to be International Women's Year. In June and July of that year the United Nations sponsored a Conference in Mexico City to discuss women's issues. Documents adopted by this Conference included "The Declaration of Mexico on the Equality of Women and their Contribution to Development and Peace" and a "World Plan of Action".[6] The General Assembly approved the action plans proposed by the Conference, including two regional plans focussing on Asia and Africa, and declared 1975 to 1985 to be the UN "Decade for Women". From 1972 to 1979 the Commission on the Status of Women through a Working Group drafted the present Women's Convention which was adopted by the General Assembly in December, 1979.[7] In 1980 and 1985 two further Conferences were held in Copenhagen and Nairobi to evaluate the progress of action to improve the status of women and to set out further strategies up to the year 2000.

Despite the work that has been done throughout these 15 years of activity, it is difficult to see any significant improvement in the position of most women in the world. It is arguable that in some areas, such as reproductive control or paid work, the status of women in some areas has actually declined since the commencement of the "Decade for Women".

[4] For a full discussion of the nature and extent of reservations to the Women's Convention, see below, and also see Rebecca Cook, "Reservations to the Convention on the Elimination of All Forms of Discrimination Against Women", 30 *Virginia Journal of International Law* (1990), p. 643.

[5] ECOSOC Res.48 (IV), March 2, 1947; see L. Reanda, "Human Rights and Women's Rights: The United Nations Approach", 3(2) *Human Rights Quarterly* (1981). p. 11.

[6] Discussed briefly in J. McKenna, "Address Given at the Fourth Annual International Symposium" from the Symposium on Women's Rights in International Law, 9 *Whittier Law Review* (1987), p. 407; see also N. Kaufman Hevener, *International Law and the Status of Women* (1983).

[7] See Cook, note 4, *supra*.

2. Definition of Women's Rights

There appear to be a number of major historical and theoretical barriers to the accurate definition of women's rights as part of "human" rights, including their effective enforcement. These might be summarized as follows:

1. The historical construction of modern human rights from norms and institutions designed by men to serve men's interests.
2. The cultural construction of women's reproductive role and the continuance of this role within the family.
3. The division of rights into discrete categories and definitions such as "civil", "political", "economic", "social", "cultural" or "peoples'" rights which do not reflect the reality of women's lives.

3. Human Rights As Men's Rights

With the exception of international documents and instruments directed specifically towards women, such as the Women's Convention, the language of human rights is resolutely and utterly male. The rights which are guaranteed are the "Rights of Man" or "Mankind" or "les droits de l'homme".

The exploration of the problem of masculinist language in the law has been made on a number of different levels by both Anglo-American and continental European, particularly French, feminists. Very little has been made of language within international law, probably because the problems of language diversification and translation are already so great.[8] The effect of masculinist language exacerbates a serious problem in characterising human rights as inclusive of women. Women are, linguistically, and on consequent deeper levels of thought and action, consistently marginalised in the "mainstream" international instruments. Only where women are dealt with in their "own" conventions, committees and other international fora are issues relevant to them discussed. The other major human rights instruments, although paying lip-service to the ideas of equality and non-discrimination including sexual equality, are consistently expressed, described and interpreted as they relate to men's experiences.[9]

The problem is also historically and politically important in relation to human rights, in that, at the time "Les droits de l'homme et du citoyen" and the Bill of Rights were being drafted and incorporated into the revolutionary constitutions of France and the United States, women were specifically excluded from most market oriented economic and all political institutions.[10] It

[8] See note 6, *supra*, for a brief discussion of this problem.

[9] The one convention not specifically geared towards women which to some extent avoids the use of masculinist language is the most recent Convention on the Rights of the Child, Adopted by the UN General Assembly on 20 November 1989, entered into force 2 September, 1990.

[10] See J. Landes, *Women and the Public Sphere: in the Age of the French Revolution* (1988), for a discussion of the position of women and the existing public and private discourses of 18th century France.

has been argued that this exclusion was extended and exacerbated to the point of virtual "slavery" for most women (and "real" slavery for many others) within European and, to a lesser extent, North American and Australasian societies after the success of the bourgeois political and economic revolutions of the 1780's and 90's.[11] When masculinist language is used within human rights law, it is based on a history of the exclusion of women. The words "les droits de l'homme" or "the Rights of Man" meant and still largely mean "men's" rights, "les droits des hommes", not "women's" rights. The claimed gender neutrality of modern international law instruments disguises this background and distracts our attention away from the marginalisation and exclusion of women through the period when modern political and economic rights were being defined and limited. Nor does the problem appear to have been identified or resolved in instruments which attempt to redefine human rights outside their Euro-centric origins, such as in the African Charter on Human and Peoples' Rights ("Banjul Charter").[12]

The Women's Convention is the major international instrument dealing specifically with women.[13] The very existence of this and other "women's" conventions indicates the failure of human rights law generally to adequately deal with women's issues. "Women's" rights as opposed to "human" rights are ghettoised into their "own" convention, which nevertheless reproduces many of the assumptions found in "human" rights generally. Other mainstream instruments or institutions, such as the Human Rights Committee under the International Covenant for Civil and Political Rights, the UN Commission on

[11] See E. J. Hobsbawm, *The Age of Revolution: 1789–1848* (1962), for a largely masculinist history of this period and B.S. Anderson, and J.P. Zinsser, *A History of Their Own: Women in Europe From Prehistory to the Present* (1988), Vol.II which provides a welcome wealth of information on women's history in Europe from the 15th to the 20th centuries; See also E. Kennedy, and S. Mendus (eds.) *Women in Western Political Philosophy* (1987) and the works of C. Pateman, particularly *The Disorder of Women* (1989) for a feminist critique of the philosophical assumptions on which these revolutions were based; and See K. Alford, *Production or Reproduction? An Economic History of Women in Australia 1788–1850* for a particularly Australian perspective.

[12] Adopted by the Organisation of African Unity, June 27, 1981, entered into force October 21, 1986: 21 ILM (1982), p.58.

[13] See also the Inter-American Convention on the Granting of Political Rights to Women (1948), Convention for the Suppression of the Traffic in Persons and of the Exploitation of the Prostitution of Others (1949), Convention on the Political Rights of Women (1952), Supplementary Convention on the Abolition of Slavery, the Slave Trade, and Institutions and Practices Similar to Slavery (1956), Convention on the Nationality of Married Women (1957), Convention Against Discrimination in Education (1960), Convention on Consent to Marriage, Minimum Age for Marriage, and Registration of Marriages (1962), the General Assembly Declaration on the Elimination of Discrimination Against Women (1967) and numerous "protective" conventions on women from the International Labour Organisation as discussed in Hevener Kaufman, note 6, *supra*, and "An Analysis of Gender Based Treaty Law: Contemporary Developments in Historical Perspective" 8(1) *Human Rights Quarterly* (1986), p.70; See also M. Halberstam, and E. Defeis, *Women's Legal Rights: International Covenants an Alternative to ERA?* (1987).

Human Rights and other organs set up under the Economic and Social Council consistently fail to deal with human rights violations against women.[14]

The basis of the Women's Convention is equality, or the principle of non-discrimination on the basis of sex. The Preamble, the first four articles, and nearly all the substantive rights contained in Parts II, III and IV of the Convention are explicitly designed to eliminate "discrimination against women" and ensure the "equality of men and women". Article 1 defines "discrimination against women" as:

> . . . any distinction, exclusion or restriction made on the basis of sex which has the effect or purpose of impairing or nullifying the recognition, enjoyment or exercise by women, irrespective of their marital status, on a basis of equality of men and women, of human rights and fundamental freedoms in the political, economic, social, cultural, civil or any other field.

Articles 2 and 3 outline in more detail the requirement to take steps to eliminate discrimination against women "in all its forms" and to advance women's "full development". Article 4 allows the adoption by States Parties of "special measures" creating temporary inequality in favour of women "aimed at accelerating *de facto* equality between men and women" and protecting maternity. Such "special measures" are deemed not to be discriminatory, but (with the exception of protecting maternity) "shall in no way entail . . . the maintenance of unequal or separate standards" and "shall be discontinued when the objectives of equality of opportunity and treatment have been achieved." Parts II, III and IV set out substantive political, civil, economic and social rights to be applied without discrimination to women as well as men. These rights reiterate, for the most part, the substantive rights contained in other mainstream "human" rights instruments.

4. Equality As the Basis of Women's Rights

The problem of equality as the basis for theorizing about "women's" rights contains some major difficulties. I can only briefly summarize some of these problems here.

1. Equality, particularly where, as in the Women's Convention the ideal is "sameness" with men, accepts the validity of a male standard as "human" and indirectly silences or subverts the value of specifically female experiences, such as maternity, which men do not directly share. Thus the concrete reality of the lives of half the human race is marginalised and denigrated and a major part of most women's experience, maternity and child care, is marginalised as requiring "special measures".

[14] Reanda, note 5, *supra*, at p.12.

2. Where equality attempts to validate the "difference" of women, as in the work of some American psychologists and, in an entirely different context, French linguistic and psychoanalytic theorists, the effect can also be marginalisation and trivialisation of women's realities.[15] As Catharine MacKinnon points out, "difference" tends to ignore the underlying power imbalance out of which women's experiences are constructed. Women are arguably "different" in the existing sense because of sexual oppression. There is no adequate means of knowing what is "female" because the "feminine" is presently defined by men to serve men's interests.[16]

Difference as a basis for equality tends to be reductive and hence unrealistic in adequately reflecting or dealing with women's or men's experiences. It's as if we can either be men (or "the same as men") or mothers ("different from men"). Somehow what might be fully human for many women and men is silenced or portrayed as suspect or abnormal; for example the experiences of lesbians and gay men who defy simple gender dichotomies, or the complicated intersection of race, class and cultural contexts in relation to the rights of women and men. This is particularly acute in an international law context where cultural differences and the existence of diversity of traditional and other practices fragments the search for simple equality. The Women's Convention incorporates "difference" only in a very narrow sense as the existence of maternity and childcare.

3. A third way in which "equality" can be discussed is in terms of dominance and submission, or power imbalance.[17] Sexual inequality is entrenched within existing social structures and the social construction of sex, sexuality, reproduction and gender are responsible for the continuing oppression of women. MacKinnon identifies sexual harassment, rape, incest, pornography and abortion as key areas for identifying the sources of women's inequality. It is arguable that this is still too narrow in that it focuses on the extreme end of sexual coercion. A more subtle approach would look at the whole range of

[15] See the work of C. Gilligan, especially *In a Different Voice: Psychological Theory and Women's Development* (1982). Numerous attempts have been made in Anglo-American feminism to come to terms with "French feminism" and the exploration of "difference". Perhaps the best introduction to this diverse range of "feminisms" in English is Elizabeth Grosz, *Sexual Subversions: Three French Feminists* (1989); See also D. Stanton, "Difference on Trial: A Critique of the Maternal Metaphor in Cixous, Irigaray and Kristeva", in J. Allen and I. Young (eds.) *The Thinking Muse: Feminism and Modern French Philosophy* (1989); T. Moi (ed.) *French Feminist Thought: A Reader* (1987).

[16] See in particular C. MacKinnon, *Toward a Feminist Theory of the State* (1989). Luce Irigaray makes a similar point from a very different perspective in her earlier work; See in particular *Speculum of the Other Women* (1974) and *This Sex Which is Not One* (1977) (both books translated for Cornell University Press in 1985).

[17] See especially the work of C. MacKinnon, ibid., for a critique of MacKinnon's work; and C. Smart, *Feminism and the Power of Law* (1989), for a not altogether successful attempt at a different analysis of power based on the works of the obtrusively masculinist work of Michel Foucault; See I. Diamond and L. Quinby (eds.) *Feminism and Foucault: Reflections on Resistance* (1988); See also the acute critique of the use of Foucault by feminists in N. Fraser, *Unruly Practics: Power, Discourse and Gender in Contemporary Social Theory* (1989).

cultural constructions of sexuality and reproduction, of "femininity" as revolving around various forms of reproductive control both coercive and apparently non-coercive.

The Women's Convention, alone amongst international instruments dealing with "human rights", attempts to address some of these problems. Article 14 highlights the role of rural women and their important contribution to the economic survival of their families, allowing an interpretation of rural women's work which steps outside the existing boundaries of "femininity". Article 16 attempts to redress problems of inequality for married women in ways which highlight the usual standard of subservience and submission which most married women suffer. Article 5 states:

> States Parties shall take all appropriate measures:
> (a) To modify the social and cultural patterns of conduct of men and women, with a view to achieving the elimination of prejudices and customary and all other practices which are based on the idea of the inferiority or the superiority of either of the sexes or on stereotyped roles for men and women;
> (b) To ensure that family education includes a proper understanding of maternity as a social function and the recognition of the common responsibility of men and women in the upbringing and development of their children, it being understood that the interest of the children is the primordial consideration in all cases.

The difficulty with these provisions is that the standard for comparison is still male against which "inferiority" or (rarely for women) "superiority" can be evaluated. The subtle nature of the construction of ourselves as male or female is portrayed in simple terms as "prejudices" which the State can remedy by passing "appropriate measures". Common responsibility for child rearing is described as a matter for "education" rather than for radical social or economic restructuring and the primordial nature of concern for children over all other considerations subtly reproduces the sanctity of "maternal instincts" and the primacy of child care no matter what the consequences for women in a world where, as a matter of practical reality, women remain the primary care-givers.

5. Construction and Protection of Women's Reproductive Role

Marilyn Waring, in her ground breaking work, *Counting for Nothing*,[18] outlines six basic facets of reproduction which she claims are crucial to the continuing inequality of women within modern economic and political spheres. These include biological reproduction, reproduction of the labour force, reproduction of the relations of production, reproduction of the relations of reproduction, reproduction of social relations between women and men, and

[18] M. Waring, *Counting for Nothing: What Men Value and What Women are Worth* (1988).

the categorisation and institutionalisation of those who may or may not reproduce.[19]

An examination of the centrality of reproductive control and the protection of traditional values through the description of the "family" as the "natural and fundamental group unit of society" in most human rights instruments effectively reproduces female subservience within the private sphere and makes the list of "human" rights useless to most women.[20] An examination of the Women's Convention through Waring's six-faceted description of reproduction is revealing both of the strengths and weaknesses of our "own" convention.

(1) Biological Reproduction

"Maternity" is specifically mentioned as allowing the adoption of "special measures" for its "protection" in Article 4(2). Likewise in Article 12(2), States Parties are required to provide "women appropriate services in connexion with pregnancy, confinement and the post-natal period" and "adequate nutrition during pregnancy and lactation". Waring states that "[w]ithin economics, its [maternity's] only visibility is as welfare". Rights to "family benefits" and "social security programmes" are mentioned in Articles 13 and 14 and "maternity leave", "childcare" and protection against dismissal for pregnancy from the workplace are described in Article 11(2). Unlike most other human rights instruments,[21] the Women's Convention expressly addresses the issue of biological reproduction, but does not appear to contradict Waring's observation that such reproduction has no value in economic or other terms, but is rather the subject of "special measures", "protection" or "welfare" benefits which reproduce not only the position of women as beneficiaries of special attention whenever they perform their "natural" role, but also reinforces the paternalistic nature of the State.

(2) Reproduction of the Labour Force

To fulfill the needs of existing male dominated economic and political structures it is necessary, according to Waring, to control human (read

[19] Ibid., at pp. 153–154.

[20] Universal Declaration of Human Rights (1948), GA Resol.217A (III), UN Doc.A/810, at 71, Article 16(3); See S. Wright, "Economic Rights and Social Justice: A Feminist Analysis of Some International Human Rights Conventions", Conference Paper presented at the One Day Seminar on "Gender and International Law", note 1, *supra* to be published in the *Australian Yearbook of International Law* (1992).

[21] See however the International Covenant on Economic, Social and Cultural Rights (1966) which specifically mentions "[s]pecial protection" for "mothers during a reasonable period before and after childbirth" including paid maternity leave in Article 10(2) and "provision for the reduction of the still-birth rate and of infant mortality" in Article 12(2)(a); GA Resol.2200 (XXI), 21 UN GAOR Supp. (No.16) at 49, UN Doc.A/6316.

women's) fertility. I would suggest that this also includes the construction and control of human sexuality, both masculine and feminine. Enforced heterosexuality ensures the submergence of freedom of sexual preference preventing the expression of sexual choice and individual control of fertility, not only by lesbians and gay men, but by everyone.

The technological control of reproduction both to encourage fertility (such as in vitro fertilisation) or reduce it (such as the Pill) are expressions of the Western preference for scientific control of fertility, rather than through religion, the State or other cultural institutions. Religious prohibition of abortion and contraceptives, the "privatisation" of sexual morality in Western human rights discourse, or coercive techniques of birth control either to encourage or prevent pregnancies (such as in Ceaucescu's Romania or the People's Republic of China) are further examples of the varying range of activities exercised through various cultural bodies which restrict or prevent women's free choice in relation to their own fertility or sexuality. It is not particularly significant whether the prevailing institutional ideology is towards high fertility (as in Islamic or Catholic countries where contraceptives and abortion are banned) or towards low fertility (through coercive sterilisation programs such as in China or India or as in the West where some degree of personal control over fertility is allowed through "privacy" rights that tend to lead to fewer births). The point is that through these and other less obvious practices, women are denied even the most basic rights of control over their own bodies. An extreme example of such control is female genital mutilation. Other examples might include child marriages; the legal condonation of rape within marriage or effective social acceptance of most forms of sexual assault generally; standards of female sexual morality that deny women freedom in many or all areas of activity including especially paid employment; polygyny; purdah; and legal rules in relation to illegitimacy, promiscuity, sexual assault, sexual harassment, sexual preference, pornography and trafficking in women and children.

Article 16 of the Women's Convention provides:

1. States Parties shall take all appropriate measures to eliminate discrimination against women in all matters relating to marriage and family relations and in particular shall ensure, on a basis of equality of men and women:

a. The same right to enter into marriage;
b. The same right freely to choose a spouse and to enter into marriage only with their free and full consent;
c. The same rights and responsibilities during marriage and at its dissolution;
d. The same rights and responsibilities as parents, irrespective of their marital status, in matters relating to their children; in all cases the interests of children shall be paramount;
e. The same rights to decide freely and responsibly on the number and spacing of their children and to have access to the information, education and means to enable them to exercise these rights;

f. The same rights and responsibilities with regard to guardianship, wardship, trusteeship and adoption of children, or similar institutions where these concepts exist in national legislation; in all cases the interests of the children shall be paramount;
g. The same personal rights as husband and wife, including the right to choose a family name, a profession and an occupation;
h. The same rights for both spouses in respect of the ownership, acquisition, management, administration, enjoyment and disposition of property, whether free of charge or for a valuable consideration.

2. The betrothal and the marriage of a child shall have no legal effect, and all necessary action, including legislation, shall be taken to specify a minimum age for marriage and to make the registration of marriages in an official registry compulsory.

This provision, as well as others, has given rise to a considerable number of reservations and objections to reservations.[22] The reservations to Article 16 and associated provisions are arguably at the heart of difficulties with the rights enumerated in this Convention. Egypt, in its reservation to Article 16 and Article 9(2) (with reference to the nationality of children), probably sets out most clearly a major stumbling block in balancing traditional values and the emancipation of women.

The instrument of ratification by the Government of Egypt confirms the following reservations in respect of Article 9, 16 and 29 [with reference to arbitration of disputes under the Convention], already made upon signature...

Article 16

Reservation to the text of Article 16 concerning the equality of men and women in all matters relating to marriage and family relations during the marriage and upon its dissolution. This must be without prejudice to the Islamic Sharia provisions whereby women are accorded rights equivalent to those of their spouses so as to ensure a just balance between them. This is out of respect for the sanctity deriving from firm religious beliefs which govern marital relations in Egypt and which may not be called in question and in view of the fact that one of the most important bases of these relations is an equivalency of rights and duties so as to ensure complementarity which guarantees true equality between spouses and not a quasi-equality that renders the marriage a burden on the wife. This is because the provisions of the Islamic Sharia lay down that the husband shall pay bridal money to the wife and maintain her fully out of his own funds and shall also make a payment to her upon divorce, whereas the wife retains full rights over her property and is not obliged to spend anything for her keep. The Sharia therefore restricts the wife's rights to divorce by making it contingent on a judge's ruling, whereas no such restriction is laid down in the case of the husband.[23]

[22] The reservations and objections discussed here are those entered as of June, 1988 listed in Lillich, note 2, *supra*. See also Cook, note 4, *supra*.

[23] See Lillich, ibid., at 220.13.

Other states which have made reservations for apparently similar reasons include Bangladesh, Iraq, Jordan, Mauritius, Tunisia and Turkey. In addition, Brazil, South Korea and Thailand felt themselves unable to accede to Article 16, although they are not influenced by principles of Islamic law. Malawi, also not primarily an Islamic country, made a general reservation to the whole of the Convention: "Owing to the deep-rooted nature of some traditional customs and practices of Malawians" although this reservation has recently been withdrawn.[24]

A few countries entered objections to these reservations, specifically citing them as going to the "object and purpose of the Convention" including West Germany, Mexico and Sweden.[25] It is interesting that a major concern of Sweden in particular, but also of Mexico, is in relation to the possibility that the basic nature of international law will be undermined by States who enter into contractual obligations, in the form of multi-lateral conventions, and then reserve their right not to implement certain provisions of those conventions which arguably go to the heart and focus of the obligation as a whole. What is not stated in the objections by Mexico or Sweden is why reservations in relation to the rights of married women are so crucial to the rights of women generally.

Article 16(1)(e) is one of only three mentions of any explicit recognition of women's right to control their own fertility, at least after marriage, in any major human rights instrument. The other reference to a right of women to control their own fertility is access to "information and advice on family planning" as provided for in Articles 10 and 14 of the Women's Convention. Instead of sanctifying the family as the fundamental group unit of society, the Women's Convention took the important step of outlining rights for women that enhances their control over reproduction of the labour force through control of their own fertility at least within marriage, but which, not surprisingly, is seen as unacceptable to many States.

(3) Reproduction of the Relations of Production

This topic is dealt with in Article 11, which attempts to outline basic rights of equality for women in the workplace; Article 14, which discusses the position of rural women; and less directly, in Article 10, which sets out rights to equal educational opportunities. Waring states that this form of reproduction is characterised by ghettoising women who engage in "productive" (rather than reproductive) labour into exploitative, low paid or unpaid labour.[26] This ensures the continuing devaluation of "housework" as unpaid labour and its invisibility as work. It also results in problems with development in relation to rural women as the work that most women do is not seen as "productive" and is therefore ignored by development policies formulated within Western

[24] See Cook, note 4, *supra*.

[25] For the text of Mexico and Sweden's objections to reservations see Lillich, note 2, *supra*, at 220.28 and 220.30.

[26] See note 18, *supra*, at p.154.

patriarchal notions of women's position within marriage and the family. These issues have received a much greater attention in existing international literature on women's rights than some other areas, possibly because women in "relations of production" may be more visible, or at least potentially more visible, as engaging in activities which men also perform. The "invisibility" of much of women's productive, as well as reproductive, work is partially attributable to the maintenance of the distinction between the public and private spheres. This is particularly important in the construction of modern human rights which are predicated on the Western liberal democratic maintenance of this distinction in a sharp form. This often prevents or distorts the capacity for provisions such are contained in the Women's Convention in affecting the advancement of women within productive relations. Productive work is seen as men's work and is relatively "public". Women's work is characterised as closely related to or made problematic by their primary roles in reproduction rather than production, which is seen as "private". The public/private dichotomy can be a useful means of analysing the relative ineffectiveness of provisions such as Articles 10, 11 and 14.[27]

(4) Reproduction of the Relations of Reproduction

Women's rights in this area can be seen in Articles 5(b) and the "common responsibility of men and women in the upbringing and development of children"; Article 6 "to suppress all forms of traffic in women and exploitation of prostitution of women"; and again in Article 16 in relation to married women's rights. It is in this area that the cultural institutions (included in Waring's fifth and sixth facets) denying women freedom in any meaningful form are perhaps most intransigent and least amenable to eradication through instruments such as the Women's Convention. So deeply entrenched are most aspects of the reproduction of the relations of reproduction, that they are rarely questioned, but are rather perceived as "normal" or "natural". Heterosexual marriage, or the nuclear family, are major institutions maintaining this fourth facet. The Women's Convention does not, perhaps cannot, significantly undermine this last aspect of women's oppression.

6. The Fragmentation of Rights

The third major theoretical difficulty in describing "human" rights as including "women's" rights is the division of rights into discrete categories which may or may not adequately reflect *men's* realities, but which rarely have much meaning

[27] See in particular H. Charlesworth, "The Public/Private Distinction and the Right to Development in International Law", Conference Paper presented at the One Day Seminar on "Gender and International Law", note 1, *supra*; Charlesworth, Chinkin and Wright, "Feminist Approaches to International Law", published in 85 *American Journal of Internatoinal Law*, vol. 85, pp. 613-645 (1991).

in relation to *women's* lives. Most women, because of their lack of access to public spheres of power, will be relatively poorly served by traditional civil and political rights. This is exacerbated by the usual characterisation of these rights as individual rights. Women, in their usual role as care-givers, are not individuals in the same sense as men perhaps can be. Individuality denotes autonomy, something which women are rarely seen as possessing or able to possess. Yet the newer category of "peoples' rights", which departs from the notion of individual rights, rarely addresses itself to the specific needs of women who must be at least 50% of most population groups, if not "peoples" in and of themselves.

Perhaps the category of rights which might be of greatest applicability to women are economic, social and cultural rights. Within "mainstream" human rights instruments there is greater attention paid in this type of right to the needs of women than in the more traditional delineation of civil and political rights. The International Covenant on Economic, Social and Cultural Rights does at least mention some women's needs.[28] But economic and social rights are rarely contained in instruments with effective enforcement mechanisms. Rather they are seen as aims to be achieved through progressive development rather than as existing rights giving rise to claims and obligations now.

The Women's Convention itself is characterised in this way with no enforcement mechanism and a relatively weak implementation process of reporting by States Parties and the making of suggestions to the Economic and Social Council.[29] The effectiveness of this Convention could be improved by a greater allocation of resources to the work of the Women's Committee set up under the Convention,[30] by the extension of time within which the Committee may meet,[31] and possibly by the addition of a Protocol allowing the Committee to hear petitions by individuals, groups and non-governmental organisations as exists under other human rights conventions.

7. Conclusion

Although the Women's Convention does have the effect of marginalising women's rights and confining them to the ghetto of a specialized treaty, these rights were not any more central in human rights prior to the Convention and were unlikely to become so in the absence of our "own" instrument. Conventions and other sources of international law specifically addressed to women go some way to fill in a large gap left by traditional "human" rights law.

[28] See note 21, *supra*; See also Article 7 on "equal pay for equal work".

[29] Articles 18, 20-22 and 24 which is worded more strongly than the equivalent provision in the International Covenant on Economic, Social and Cultural Rights, Article 2.

[30] For a discussion of other human rights instruments using a similar range of historical and theoretical perspectives see Shelley Wright, "Economic Rights and Social Justice: A Feminist Analysis of Some International Human Rights Conventions".

[31] Article 17.

This alone provides adequate reason to continue to work within the Women's Convention.

It remains however something of an absurdity that one half of the human race and such rights that they may have of both a politicial and an economic or social nature, should be dealt with by one Convention while other human rights instruments fail to adequately address women's issues. There is an urgent need to put economic, social and cultural rights as they affect women, children and men at the top of the international agenda instead of close to the bottom. Until major problems of poverty and underdevelopment of women, social ostracisation and political powerlessness, and the maintenance of women's primary role as reproducers and caregivers are dealt with, "human" rights cannot be fully "human".

MONA MAKRAM-EBEID*

Exclusion of Women from Politics

1. Introduction

Women's appearance on the political scene and their participation in the political and parliamentary decision making process is undoubtedly one of the major "silent revolutions" of this century. Yet the visible and public exercise of power by women is controversial in major societies, especially in Arab and other Muslim countries.

It has been clear since the early days of the debate over modernization that one of the main problems with which the Arab world has had to cope was the role and status of women.[1] The twentieth century has seen considerable change in the tone and content of the debate and the composition of these roles. The intensity of the debate suggests considerable ambiguity rather than broad consensus. One of the reasons for this is that women have not been mere recipients of that change, they have helped produce it. The issue of women's roles in Arab society is a complex one, exacerbated by and linked to the political, social, and economic crises facing the Arab world.

All Arab states to some degree are meshed in three inter-related problems each associated with the process of change and to issues pertaining to women. One is political. It involves the on-going crisis of legitimacy of the political order and efforts by the leaders of it to establish or maintain independence in the face of external threats. Central to this crisis is the attempt by both government and opposition forces to recruit traditional political elites as well as new elements to their side. Depending on the nature of their political projects, States have variously challenged, accommodated or abdicated to local/communal patriarchal interests, with important consequences for family legislation and more general policies affecting women.

Another concern is the social crisis brought about by the dislocation and cognitive dissonance resulting from rapid social change. Whether change is

* Sociologist, Member of Executive Board, Egyptian Organization of Human Rights, Cairo, Egypt; Member of Parliament since December, 1990.

[1] Amin, 1893 and 1990.

K.E. Mahoney and P. Mahoney (eds.), Human Rights in the Twenty-first Century, 89–94.

induced and directed or the result of forces over which national leaders have little understanding or control is irrelevant. The important fact is that one of the major features of rapid social change is the alteration in the role of women in the Arab world. Key elements in this process of change are issues of population growth and internal migration either from the countryside to the city or external migration from country to country. Such wholesale movements bring about numerous ancillary changes, including those involving women. Changes involve new conflicts over new roles, some of which are clearly political in nature.

A third crisis is the economic one. Inflation, unemployment and underemployment, low worker productivity, balance of payments problems and budget deficits loom large. Here too, women change roles. This is often due to forces over which they have little control. They are driven into the job market by inflation, desertion or widowhood and must find work outside the home regardless of social structures to the contrary.

In all three of these "crisis zones", gender issues are vital.[2] Furthermore, they are connected.

2. The Political Crisis

With respect to the legitimacy of the domestic political order, governments in the Arab world often seek to bolster support by using women. They may for example, seek to add women to the list of regime supporters by offering them concrete rewards such as the right to vote, seats in Parliament, or other material benefits such as education or guaranteed employment. Egyptian leaders Nasser, Sadat and Mubarak have all used these tactics, as have Ghaddafi in Libya, whose personal guards are women and Saddam Hussein in Iraq where many women now serve in Parliament. On the other hand, leaders also try to shore up support among conservative forces by advocating or implementing politics which keep or put women "in their place". This means in the home, subservient to men, disenfranchised and not competing with men for jobs. Saudi Arabia is a case in point.

Opposition forces now play the same game as governments. They either seek the support of women or try to legitimize their claim to power based partly on their program or platform on women. Thus, in the core argument over legitimacy, women are either new political constituents to be courted, or hapless victims of efforts to secure the backing of conservative, mainly Islamist conservative elements.[3]

[2] Earl L. Sullivan, *Women in Egyptian Public Life* (1986). Offers a very useful discussion of this general issue.

[3] Ibid. Also see Bouthaina Shaaban, *Both Right and Left Handed: Arab Women Talk About Their Lives* (1991), p. 18. She argues that in Syria, official women's unions, even those on the left of the political spectrum are more interested in winning women recruits and defending partisan positions than in feminist issues.

A few examples from Arab and Muslim countries serve to illustrate how issues pertaining to women are linked to all three areas. Egypt is presently witnessing the most severe setback in the participation of women in political life. Out of 444 candidates in the November parliamentary elections, the ruling National Democratic Party endorsed the candidature of only four women, less than one percent of the total number. But first let us go back a few years. The Egyptian woman's struggle to achieve significant status in any sphere of life has been fraught with obstacles. One of these is the fact that Egypt is a traditionally conservative and male dominated society. This barrier to be one of the most difficult to overcome. With respect to establishing a role for women in the political and parliamentary decision making process, the interruption of the democratic process and parliamentary system which started in 1866 proved to be another stumbling block. The achievements the feminist movement gained during Egypt's liberal experiment between 1919–1952, when women's rights were linked to broader social and political issues, left their imprint until today. In fact, the period which started in 1935 with the Feminist Union endorsing the principle of full political equality, did not end until 1956 when the new constitution gave women the right to vote. This was partly due to pressures exerted by a then very "active women's movement called "Bint al Nil" (Daughter of the Nile) whose goal was to obtain political and constitutional rights for women.

The first political action to achieve this objective came in February 1951 with a demonstration which led to the seizure of Parliament by more than a thousand women amidst the cries of "Down with parliament without women"; "this Parliament does not represent the whole nation"; "women's place is next to yours". Yet although women were granted suffrage in 1956, Nasser's authoritarian regime did not encourage the creation of democratic civil societies in which women's gender interests could be autonomously represented, and all feminist organizations were outlawed.[4]

Another important date was 1979 when women were given guaranteed seats in all of Egypt's elected assemblies. These elections saw 200 female candidates enter the competition. In addition to the 30 reserved seats, three women ran against men on party lists and won. Two more were appointed. As a result, women constituted nine percent of the Peoples Assembly, a proportion that competed favourably with some of the most progressive Western countries. Their success, however, was not overlooked and in 1983 an attempt was made by leaders of the ruling party to get rid of the 30 reserved seats. This was met with vigourous back-room bargaining by Egypt's women parliamentarians. Consequently, in the 1984 multi-party election, the first since 1952, women were allowed to become candidates either by competing for one of 30 seats or

[4] In Iraq, the General Union of Iraqi Women, although it has provided genuine benefits for women in education and employment opportunities, has prevented any independent women's movement from developing.

by being placed on a party list. Thirty-three women were elected, all but one of them from the ruling party.

In 1987, the "women only" seats were cancelled under the pressure of extreme conservative elements. The official version of this change was that the introduction of participation quotas was unconstitutional, bending the principle of equality whereby all citizens are eligible. As a result, only fourteen women were elected and four were appointed.

In 1990, a new amendment to the electoral law replaced the proportional representation system by the majority vote. Out of 1300 candidates only five women re-entered the competition. It was suggested that the government feared a fierce competition from opposition parties, particularly Islamic militants, and deemed it safer to give priority to locally, well established male notables.

In the Sudan for example, the fundamentalist regime of General Bashir is determined to end the advancement of women which became so noticeable in recent years. With so many Sudanese men working abroad, women in recent years have come to play an increasingly important role in all aspects of Sudanese life. But if the government has its way, women will be confined to two areas of public employment: elementary school teaching and nursing: two areas of employment deemed "suitable" for them.

A major objective of Sudan's fundamentalism is to indoctrinate and coerce the female populace so as to remove a major threat to the regime's power. This has less to do with Islam than it does with the fear that women, increasingly released from the shackles of tradition, will insist upon the totality of their rights. In a similar vein, militant fundamentalists in Pakistan derive strength from the military establishment that has openly favoured them. The "Islamization" package introduced by General Zia ul Haq gave legal sanctions to crude forms of sexual discrimination, which Pakistani women's organizations loudly protested.[5]

Islamists have exploited democracy to make gains through elections in Jordan and Algeria. No amount of fundamentalist apologetics can fudge the fact that, as currently interpreted, their brand of Islam discriminates against women. In Jordan's first parliamentary elections in 23 years, Jordanian women entered the November 1989 electoral campaign with 12 candidates out of 635. While liberal parties supported them, they were virulently attacked not only by male fundamentalists, but also by conservative women who form 90 percent of the female electorate. Intimidation took the form of "intellectual terrorism". The most notorious case was that of Tougan Feycal, a woman journalist who incurred the outrage of Islamic conservatives who publicly accused her of

[5] The author participated in a 40-member team international delegation sponsored by the National Democratic Institute that observed the 1990 Pakistani elections. See also, Deniz Kandiyote, "Women, Islam and the State" (1991). *Middle East Report*, November-December, p. 10.

writing blasphemous articles and "corrupting the sacred scriptures".[6] In an article entitled "They Insult Us and We Vote for Them" (21/9/89) she defended women's rights answering the attacks levelled at women's mental inadequacies as cited in the Qur'an. They proferred a death penalty against her and she had to appear before the court. However, such intolerance triggered the anger of many sectors of the society and a movement of solidarity was organized around her; the press condemned this new "Salman Rushdie affair" and a group of academics and jurists took the case to the Jordanian sovereign who intimated that there should be no exploitation of religion for political reasons. In early November, the court cleared her case. In Algeria, fundamentalist acts of intolerance included a number of attacks on "single women", i.e. those divorced, widowed or unmarried. Even the donning of the Islamic garb, head scarf and long dresses, proved insufficient to meet their exigencies. The passivity of the authorities towards such infringements was estimated by some as being a ploy to attract those frightened by the excesses of the FIS Islamic Salvation Forces (i.e., triggered violence) to rally round the FLN (the governing party) providing a much needed reinforcement of their ranks.

3. Conclusion

The political landscape of the Arab world is being transformed by rapid social change and coming to terms with that dynamic process is one of today's most challenging issues. Thus, the Arab family today is not totally traditional as it was a century ago.[7] But nor is it totally modern in the Western sense: rather it is in a state of transition in structure, functions and values. Women epitomize this transition. Conventional wisdom suggests that politics, economics, and religion are men's issues in the Arab world while women are confined to the private realm. This may be true in the *mentality* of many, if not most, people and helps to explain why issues pertaining to new and more public roles for women are so controversial. But it is factually an inaccurate description of day-to-day relations. Women have been and continue to be involved in politics in Arab states and communities, both in the private and increasingly in the more public worlds of politics, business and religion. Through the mechanism of linkage politics, issues pertaining to women are tied to issues of legitimacy, independence, economic wellbeing, social cohesion and increasingly, democracy. The global wave of transition to democracy has caught up with the Arab world and authoritarian rulers who have adopted limited moves toward liberalization so as to appease the opposition or strengthen the support of their own regimes often find out that they have set off a process of change that

[6] See "Noun" a quarterly (unlicensed) magazine published by the Arab Women's Solidarity Association, an organization committed to promoting women's equality and eliminating gender based discrimination. It was ordered dissolved in June 1991 by Egyptian authorities.

[7] See note 5, *supra*.

cannot be halted. In the resulting restlessness and confusion, people take out their resentment on those who are "different".

Obviously some explanations have to be given for the political gains made by Islamic fundamentalism that have occasioned the myth of its inevitable advance. Few of these gains are due to the inherent strength of militant Islam. In several Muslim countries, regimes have suppressed the secular political movements that would be the real competitors of the fundamentalists. Such has been the case in Algeria and Tunisia, in Egypt and the Sudan, in Jordan, Bangladesh and Malaysia. The regimes, unwittingly, have cleared the political field for the militants and in the recent Jordanian and Algerian elections the fundamentalists benefitted from the fact that many non-Islamic voters, 70 percent of the electorate in Jordan and 35 percent in Algeria, either did not bother to vote or deliberately boycotted the elections. Furthermore, in Algeria for instance, husbands still have the right to cast their wives' votes. However, woman's role in society incorporates within it the West versus East dichotomous relationship.[8] To the extent that the greatest resistance to the Western cultural model is found in the religious organization of private space of relations between the sexes, the very contours of the process of secularization are drawn around the issue of women's status as a battlefield to fight Western influence and clearly reveals the cultural and societal challenge that is at stake.

[8] In Egypt, Islamist groups have frequently attacked the opening of the country to the West through condemnation of the loose morals of women who wear Western-style clothes and adopt secular behaviour. On the other hand, see the article by Fahmy Haweidi (Islamist writer) 20 November, 1990 (in Al Ahram semi official Egyptian daily reproduced in 'Islam and Women Drivers') Middle East International 7 December, 1990 p. 24 where he argues that recent developments in the Gulf may force a redefinition of the existing sexual division of labour.

NORMA WIKLER*

Exclusion of Women from Justice: Emerging Strategies for Reform

1. Introduction

On the eve of the French Revolution, the poet Robert Burns wrote:

> While Europe's eye is fix'd on mighty things
> the fate of empires and the fall of kings;
> while quacks of state must each produce his
> plan, and even children lisp the Rights of
> Man; amid this mighty fuss just let me
> mention, the Rights of Women merit some
> attention.[1]

Two hundred years later, Burn's words are still appropriate. Since 1985, however, a movement has been underway to move women onto the world's human rights agenda.[2] As this process accelerates, increasing attention will be directed to the exclusion of women from all forms of justice – social, economic and legal.

The exclusion of women from legal justice is a universal problem which poses a formidable challenge to those concerned with human rights in the twenty-first century. Regardless of the culture or the social structure of the country, women's subordinate status in society is reflected in and reinforced by the courts, as it is with all other social institutions. Race, ethnicity, age, and social class may also be the grounds for systematic denial of justice for both sexes. But women's exclusion deserves special attention, for gender compounds the discriminatory effects of these other factors, rendering women as a group more vulnerable than men.

* Professor of Sociology, Sociology Board of Studies, University of California, Santa Cruz, and a Judicial Consultant, 110 Bleecker Street, 11–E, New York, New York 10012.

[1] Burns, "The Rights of Women", as cited in Seldes, *The Great Thoughts* (1985), at p. 60.

[2] J. Chapman, "Violence and Human Rights: New Directions for the 90's", 13 RESPONSE, (1990), p. 1. Chapman credits the 1985 Nongovernmental Tribunal of the United Nations Conference held in Nairobi at the end of the United Nations Decade for Women as the catalyst for this movement.

K.E. Mahoney and P. Mahoney (eds.), Human Rights in the Twenty-first Century, 95–108.

One of the current approaches linking women's rights to human rights identified by Charlotte Bunch, is the creation of new legal mechanisms to counter sex discrimination, with accompanying efforts to make existing legal and political institutions work for women and to expand the state's responsibility for violation of women's human rights.[3] The topic of this paper fits squarely into this category. After setting forth a framework for an overall strategy for securing women's legal rights, I will describe and analyze a unique judicial reform movement in the United States and Canada that attempts to secure equal treatment for women and men in the courts by eliminating judicial gender bias (or sexism) through education and institutional reform.

(1) Components of a Strategy for the Realization of Women's Legal Rights

The four critical components necessary for the realization of women's rights are: (1) the legal framework; (2) legal literacy; (3) access to the courts; and (4) fair treatment in the courts.[4]

The legal framework refers to the content of law. Clearly, if the laws themselves are sex discriminatory, or if they are inadequate in terms of the scope of their protective reach, equal justice inside of the courts is impossible. Legal literacy is also essential. If women do not understand the law or the functioning of the courts, they cannot act on their own behalf to realize their legal rights or to redress injustices against them. But progressive laws and knowledge of one's rights are meaningless if access to the courts is obstructed. Common barriers to access include lack of affordable legal services, as well as the behaviour of gatekeepers to the justice system, such as the police in cases where women are victims of violence. Geographic distance to the courts and their limited hours of operation, along with lack of child care facilities may also be formidable barriers to access. Fair treatment for women in the courts requires that the behaviour of judges, as well as lawyers and court personnel, not reflect gender-based myths, biases or stereotypes. If any of the four components – the legal framework, legal literacy, access to the courts and fair treatment in the courts – is inadequate, the result will be the exclusion of women from justice.

(2) Fairness in the Courts: The Role of the Judge

Judges are the most powerful players in the drama of the courtroom. The degree of judicial independence, legal tradition and the culture of the country all affect the nature and extent of discretion accorded to judicial officers. In almost every country, however, judges and other adjudicators of disputes exercise discretion in the interpretation and application of the law. Within the

[3] Bunch, "Women's Rights as Human Rights", 12 *Human Rights Quarterly* (1990).

[4] For a cogent, somewhat different conceptual framework of issues and strategies for achieving women's equal justice, see Schuler (ed.) *Empowerment and the Law: Strategies of Third World Women* (1986), pp. 13–40.

zone of judicial discretion personal sex biases and beliefs of judges come into play. Regardless of how progressive laws may be, their intent will be undermined if judges adhere to traditional sex stereotypes about the "true nature" and "proper roles" of women and men. Not only in fact-finding and decision making do judges wield power, they also control court procedures and set the tone for interactions among other participants in the courtroom. Sexist comments and remarks demeaning to women from the bench, from counsel or from others in the courtroom, can also result in unequal justice for women and men.

In most countries, the core norms of an established judiciary are fairness and impartiality. But the fact that judges, like other citizens, have been socialized into sexist societies in which women hold subservient and inferior status, makes the actualization of these norms problematic. Consciously or unconsciously, with or without biased intent, gender-based myths, biases and stereotypes are likely to be expressed in judicial behaviour with serious consequences for women's legal rights.

If the role of judges is so important to the realization of women's legal rights why until recently have they remained immune from efforts of reform? In the United States and Canada, and in many other countries as well, part of the answer lies in the wall society places around judges and the courts. The insularity of the judiciary is intentional, a matter of social design, and largely it is desirable. The theory behind it is that judging, unlike legislating, is supposed to answer to relatively timeless and non-localized norms of fairness and procedure, rather than to the push and pull of the political process and the fads and enthusiasms of the moment. Thus, it is held that judges must maintain their distance in order to be protected not only from the individuals pushing reform agendas, but even from the reformers' aims and ideas.[5]

The advantages of this arrangement for the processes of justice are apparent, but it also has its drawbacks. While institutional insulation may protect judges from inappropriate political interference, it also removes them from reformers' information and ideas, which may be essential to impartial and equitable judging due either to judicial inexpertise, or to systematic biases which judges may share with the larger society. If judges do not change as social attitudes and conditions change, their traditional values, beliefs and perceptions may operate to prevent groups and individuals from achieving equality.[6] Since the life experiences of the typical male middle-aged or older judges are unlikely to challenge sex stereotypes and beliefs, a direct judicial educational program, which challenges these stereotypes and replaces myths with facts about women's lives, is necessary.

Recent reports from networks of women's legal rights advocates and practitioners around the world have identified judicial behaviour as a key

[5] N. Wikler "Water on Stone: A Perspective on the Movement to Eliminate Gender Bias in the Courts", 26 *Court Review* (1989), p. 6.

[6] K. Mahoney, and S. Martin (eds.) *Equality and Judicial Neutrality* (1987), at p. iii.

problem area.[7] Until recently, however, strategies for realizing women's legal rights have focused on the first three components mentioned above: law reform, legal literacy and access to the courts. Not until 1980 was there a systematic effort undertaken in the United States to ensure fair treatment in the courts through educating judges about gender bias and implementing court reforms. The next section of this paper describes and analyzes this unique judicial reform movement.

2. THE ORIGINS, DEVELOPMENT AND CONSEQUENCES OF THE MOVEMENT TO ELIMINATE GENDER BIAS IN THE COURTS IN THE UNITED STATES[8] .

(1) Background to the Reform Effort

The late 1960's and the decade of the 1970's was a period of intense legislative reform in the United States, which brought about many progressive laws in areas of domestic violence, rape reform and family law, as well as in federal legislation which barred sex discrimination in employment and education. Those seeking equal justice placed great hope in the efficacy of these laws to realize their goal. Yet as the decade wore on, the limits of law reform as a means of securing women's rights became increasingly clear to the growing number of women lawyers litigating in the courts. They were in a position to observe first-hand that laws are not self-executing; judges breath life into them through the exercise of judicial discretion in fact-finding and decision making. When judicial behaviour is guided by the judges' own sex-based biases and stereotypes, even the most enlightened legal reforms may be rendered meaningless.

For example, despite new progressive laws in domestic violence, women litigators, along with social science and legal researchers, who had begun to study gender bias in the courts, noted that the casual response of the judiciary to the plight of battered women denied the law's protection to these victims.[9] Some researchers interpreted this finding as evidence that echoes of the

[7] Since the Nairobi Women's Forum in 1985, the Women's Law and Development Program of the Overseas Education Fund, a non-profit organization based in Washington, D.C. has developed regional organizations in Asia, Latin America and Africa dedicated to promoting women's legal and economic rights. A recent series of three books describe the issues they face and the strategies they use to confront them. See Schuler (ed.) *The Asia Pacific Forum on Women, Law and Development: Its Origins, Issues and Vision* (1990); Schuler (ed.) *Action for Change (Latin America, Asian and African networks)* (1990); and Schuler (ed.) *Women, Law and Development in Africa* (1990).

[8] The common working definition of gender bias in the courts is: behaviour or decision making of participants in the justice system that is based on or reveals (1) stereotypical attitudes about the nature and roles of women and men; (2) cultural perceptions of their relative worth ; or (3) myths and misconceptions about the social and economic realities of both sexes. See Schafran and Wikler, *Operating a Task Force on Gender Bias in the Courts: A Manual for Action* (1987), at p. 2.

[9] N. Wikler "On the Judicial Agenda for the 80's: Equal Treatment for Women and Men in the Courts", 64 *Judicature* (1980), p. 203, at p. 206.

common law view of a wife as her husband's property continue to linger in the minds of some judges and attorneys. Similarly, studies documented that despite the extensive legal reforms brought about by the anti-rape movement, the persistence of judicial myths regarding male and female sexuality and attitudes towards the "proper" women's roles served to punish rape victims by defining rape (and spousal abuse) as "victim-precipitated crimes".[10]

In juvenile law it was observed that although the "crimes" that females were accused of are categorized as less serious and harmful to society than those of males, girls were more often held in longer periods of detention and were less likely to be placed in community programs than boys.[11]

But, it was the looming disaster in family law which most disturbed those concerned with equal justice. American social scientists studying the consequences of changes in divorce laws in the 1970's began to document how state courts were unwittingly contributing to the feminization of poverty through seemingly minor day-to-day decisions in divorce cases. In the United States, a new underclass of women and children was coming into being through inadequate support awards, which were then inadequately enforced. Researchers traced these inequities directly to the misinformation on the judges' part about the social and economic realities for women and men.[12]

(2) Creation of the National Judicial Education Program to Promote Equality for Women and Men in the Courts (The NJEP)

The urgent need to educate judges about their biases and misinformation had become apparent to female litigators and social scientists alike, but the pathway to this goal remained obscure. Implementing this idea would encounter formidable barriers, since it would require a breach in that wall surrounding the judiciary. For ten years the idea of a national judicial education program about gender bias sat on the back burner of the NOW Legal Defense and Education Fund, a legal advocacy group for women based in New York. Neither judges, judicial educators nor the potential funders approached by the organization were receptive to this idea. Waiting for the time when the project might be feasible, the Fund spent its energy shoring up the documentation of judicial gender bias, in part through court watching projects and through publicizing the problem through the media.

From a sociological perspective, it seemed that in 1979 the moment had come when there was a way through the impasse.[13] A number of factors combined to make the timing of such a program auspicious. The most important was the formation in 1979 of the National Association of Women Judges and its subsequent decision to become a co-sponsor of the NJEP. This meant *bona fide*

[10] Ibid.

[11] Ibid., at p. 205.

[12] Ibid. at p. 207.

[13] The author was the Founding Director of the NJEP; Lynn Hecht Schafran, Esq. has served as its Director since late 1981.

members of the judicial community, whose experiences ranged beyond that of male judges, were ready to work with non-judges to bring the necessary information to their colleagues.

The efforts of the NJEP were further facilitated by the endorsement of leading mainstream judicial organizations. They gave their support for a variety of reasons. Some judicial leaders recognized that a serious problem of gender bias did indeed exist; others were less convinced of the need, but worried about the mounting scrutiny of the judiciary by the public and the press, which was increasingly reporting judges' sexist comments, particularly in rape and spousal assault cases. Another powerful motivating factor among judicial leaders was their fear that if they did not demonstrate their willingness to engage in self scrutiny and *internal reform*, outside forces such as women's rights groups would generate increasing pressure and external review.

The NJEP's primary purpose was to develop curricular materials for judges, which would examine the effects of gender on the interpretation and application of substantive law and on courtroom interaction. These materials would then be introduced into official state and national judicial educational programs, with judges trained by the Program serving as the primary instructors.[14]

The first presentation on judicial gender bias focused on gender disparities in sentencing and in the standard of living after divorce. When first presented to a group of eighty new (male) judges in 1980 the responses were overwhelmingly negative. Clearly, judicial gender bias would be a sensitive, even explosive, subject for judges to examine, requiring a special pedagogic approach.

(3) Educating Judges about Gender Bias in the Courts

Judicial gender bias takes several forms and it is critically important to identify and differentiate them.[15] The basic form is the assumption that women conform to a single profile or small range of profiles, regardless of individual differences. The second is the pervasive tendency to regard men as more credible than women. A third source of bias consists simply in the ignorance and misinformation of many judges about the economic and social realities of most women.[16] Male identification with males is a fourth element of gender

[14] There is wide variation in the nature and extent of judicial education provided for U.S. state court judges. Most states provide some training for both new and experienced judges; and many states also send judges the national programs outside of the state. The Federal Judicial Center in Washington, D.C. is responsible for training Federal Court judges throughout the United States.

[15] For a full discussion of the forms of judicial gender bias, the nature of judges' resistance to education on this subject and effective pedagogic strategies to overcome such resistance, see N. Wikler, "Educating Judges About Gender Bias in the Courts", in Crites and Hepperle (eds.) *Women, the Courts and Equality* (1987).

[16] For example, the judges' decisions on property settlement and support awards in divorce cases may depend crucially on the judges' personal estimates of the facts in these matters. Yet little in a judges' life experiences or education may have taught him or her what a divorced woman's employment or remarriage prospects really are, or what it actually costs to raise children.

bias, though it is difficult to demonstrate. Finally, some of the gender bias in judges' decisions may represent a backlash against feminism. The judge may feel that women are best protected under traditional arrangements and be disinclined to offer the law's protection to women, who he sees as insisting on different roles.[17]

Courses for judges, then, must be designed to correct these and other similar forms of gender bias. In the United States, we have found that presenting judges with specific evidence of these forms of bias and their damaging effects on women can provide the impetus for judges to adopt practices more closely in keeping with the legal ideal of equal treatment. To be effective, the educational material needs to be technical, specific and directly related to judicial activity.[18] The choice of instructors is also crucial. Judges have more credibility in judicial education than non-judges, and male judges more than female judges. Therefore, in judicial education on gender bias it is important to include both male and female judges as instructors, even when expert legal or social science scholars participate in teaching these courses.

During its first two years of operation, the NJEP's progress was uneven. Doors opened only after strategic planning and much negotiation and persuasion. There were periodic setbacks; approaches rebuffed, invitations rescinded, sessions that did not go well. Judges and judicial educators manifested a variety of forms of resistance to the material on gender bias. The most consistent was the denial that such problems occurred in that particular judges' jurisdiction, even if it was acknowledged that such problems might exist in other states.

(4) The Task Force Phase

The NJEP's early recognition of the need to develop state-specific data for effective judicial education led to a crucial event which transformed this educational effort, which had been created and directed by non-judges, into a unique internal judicial reform movement that would dramatically change the American state judiciary by the end of the decade.

The task force phase of the movement began when a woman judge asked the chief justice of her state for assistance in gathering state specific data on gender bias for a judicial education program in her state. In response to her request,

[17] See note 15, *supra*, at p. 235.

[18] The design of the second NJEP course, "Judicial Discretion: Does Sex Make a Difference?" reflects this approach. In the first segment of the course judges worked in small groups to analyze hypothetical cases focusing on rape as an illustration of the role of sex stereotypes and attitudes in judicial decisions in criminal law cases. The second segment examined the impact of the judges' attitudes toward changing women's roles in women lawyers, litigants, witnesses, court personnel and judges. The final part used statistical data from governmental and recent legal and social scientific research to show (through hypothetical cases) how the lack of enforcement of child and spousal support awards combined with job discrimination against women to create gross disparities between spouses after divorce.

Chief Justice Robert N. Wilentz created the New Jersey Supreme Court Task Force on Women in the Courts with a mandate "to investigate the extent to which gender bias exists in the New Jersey judicial branch, and to develop an educational program to eliminate any such bias."[19] The Task Force was comprised of 32 trial and appellate judges, lawyers, law professors, judicial educators and community leaders from all parts of the state. The substantive law areas investigated included domestic violence, damages, juvenile law, matrimonial law and sentencing. A variety of data collection methods were employed, such as reviews of case law, regional meetings with attorneys throughout the state, analyses of statistical materials from state and federal agencies, and a state-wide survey of all attorneys and judges regarding their experiences and perceptions of gender bias in the court.[20]

At the end of its first year the Task Force released its findings at the state's annual judicial college. An uncomfortable group of judges listened as the Task Force's general conclusion was reported:

> Although the law as written is for the most part gender neutral, stereotyped myths, beliefs and biases were found to sometimes affect decision-making in the areas investigated... In addition, there is strong evidence that women and men are sometimes treated differently in courtrooms and professional gatherings.[21]

The following day, an article entitled, "Panel in Jersey Finds Bias Against Women in the Courts" appeared on the front page of the *New York Times*.[22] This publicity made it easier for women judges and lawyers in other states to press their Chief Justices for similar efforts. The highest courts in New York and Rhode Island established their own task forces in 1984. Others soon followed. As of February 1991, gender bias task forces have been established by the Chief Justices (and in a few instances, by the state bar associations) in approximately thirty-five states.

The non-judges, who had been instrumental in launching and guiding the movement, recognized that while external pressure to educate judges about gender bias coming only from women's groups and the press might elicit some response from the judiciary, the effects would likely be fleeting. Lasting reforms would require the development of an *internal* judicial reform movement advanced by judicial leaders calling upon members of the profession to make their judicial behaviour consistent with the core institutional norms. By creating a special gender bias task force required to report to the State Supreme Court, New Jersey's Chief Justice Wilentz effected this change. Judicial gender

[19] L. Schafran "Documenting Gender Bias in the Courts: The Task Force Approach", 70 *Judicature* (1987), p. 280, at p. 282.

[20] Ibid.

[21] "New Jersey Supreme Court Task Force on Women in the Courts, First Year Report (1984)", 9 *Women's Rts. L. Rep.* (1986), p. 129.

[22] Hanley, "Panel in New Jersey Finds Bias Against Women in the Courts", *NY Times*, (November 22, 1983), at p. 1, col 1 (front page).

bias was transformed from a problem "for women" into a problem "of the judiciary".

The second turning point in the U.S. effort came in 1986 when the Conference of Chief Justices (an association comprised of the ranking judges from all 50 states) included for the first time a program on judicial gender bias. This act further "legitimated" the topic as one of direct concern to all judges. Subsequently in 1988, this same group of judicial leaders endorsed the task force phase of the movement by passing a formal resolution urging each chief justice to establish a task force devoted to the study of gender bias within each state's judicial system.[23]

3. Implementation of State Task Forces on Gender Bias

(1) The Structure and Operation of the Task Forces

Since the task forces on gender bias are the primary vehicles for bringing about the inclusion of women into the justice system in the United States, I will provide some details about their structure and operation.[24] Typically, members include trial and appellate judges, judicial educators, lawyers, law professors, bar leaders, community leaders, legislators and social scientists. Although the precise wording of the mandates may differ, the charges are similar: to investigate gender bias throughout the state's judicial system (usually for a period between 2–4 years), to prepare written reports of their findings and to recommend reforms.

Task forces employ a broad range of legal and social scientific information gathering techniques such as surveys of judges, lawyers and court personnel, reviews of case transcripts and written judicial decisions, group discussions with judges, practitioners, court personnel and sometimes incarcerated women, reviews of relevant research, confidential meetings with lawyers and lay persons, as well as empirical studies on topics of special concern. The substantive areas investigated generally include gender bias in divorce – child and spousal support, as well as custody – domestic violence, sexual assault, and the general treatment of women in the courts in their diverse roles as lawyers, litigants, witnesses, jurors or judges. Task forces have also studied gender bias in the sentencing of juvenile and adult offenders, the status of female court employees, civil damages, prostitution, and employment discrimination.

[23] Resolution XVIII adopted by the August, 1988 Conference of Chief justices also calls for the creation of special task forces in every state on racial bias and minority concerns. For the text of the resolution, see 26 *Court Review* (1989), at p. 5. As of February 1991, task forces on race bias and minority concerns have been established in 14 states.

[24] The similarity in the structure and functions of the task forces can be attributed to the widespread use of a comprehensive manual prepared by the first and second directors of the NJEP. See L. Schafran and N. Wikler, *Operating a Gender Bias Task Force: A Manual for Action*, Washington, D.C. Women Judges' Fund for Justice (1987).

(2) Findings of the Task Forces

Thus far, task forces in fourteen states have issued final reports, which all support the general finding of the 1986 Final Report of the New York Task Force on Women in the Courts:

> "Gender Bias against women litigants, lawyers and court employees is a pervasive problem with grave consequences. Women are often denied equal justice, equal treatment and equal opportunity."[25]

What is most impressive about these reports is that they reveal that the problems are generally the same everywhere. The task forces as a whole generate a consistent picture of the forms of gender bias which permeate the American state's court system. They confirm the studies which were done in the 1970's and they corroborate state and national data currently being assembled by academic researchers.[26] These investigations do much more, however. Task force inquiries add specific detail about the nature, extent and consequences of gender bias. For example, task forces in every state found that after divorce, the standard of living of mothers and children plunges severely while that of the father usually improves. One of the main reasons for this, task forces discovered, was that in property division and alimony awards (rarely granted), and in family businesses including family farms women's unpaid work as homemakers is devalued or ignored.[27] Similarly, damage awards in personal injury cases showed a devaluation of women's unpaid labour.[28]

The task force reports also brought new or insufficiently examined forms of gender bias to light. For instance, a critical issue in every state was the court system's general distaste for family law matters, manifested by its inferior status among other departments and functions of the courts, and by the inadequate allocation of judicial resources.

(3) Outcomes

Undoubtedly, the task forces have been successful in identifying problems. There is also evidence that they are helping to ameliorate them. As court systems begin to implement the myriad of their recommendations, progress in reducing gender bias has been made on several fronts, including legal and

[25] Unified Court System Office of Court Administration, "Report of the New York Task Force on Women in the Courts". 15 *Fordham Law Review* (1987). (This report is published with commentary.)

[26] A list of the final reports of the task forces and persons to contact to obtain them can be secured from Lynn H. Schafran, Director, NJEP, NOW LDEF, 12th floor, 99 Hudson Street, New York, New York 10013.

[27] L. Schafran "Overwhelming Evidence: Reports on Gender Bias in the Courts", *Trial* (1990), at pp. 28–29. For other discussions of task force findings, also see L. Schafran, note 8, *supra*, and L. Schafran, "Gender and Justice: Florida and the Nation", 42 *Florida Law Review* (1990), p. 181.

[28] Ibid., at p. 30.

judicial education, and administrative and legislative reforms. As a result of the task forces, more and more states are adding specific prohibitions against gender-biased behaviour to codes of judicial conduct. They are also adding standards and rules of court, instituting statistical data collection systems that will allow for on-going monitoring of gender bias issues, gender neutralizing court documents and correspondence, and improving the work environment for court personnel. In addition, the task forces' work promotes equal justice by stimulating change in bar associations, by facilitating inquiries about bias against minority groups and by creating state and national public awareness of judicial gender bias through its contact with non-legal organizations and the media.

Thus far, there has been only one systematic evaluation of the work of a task force. It attempted to assess how well the task force's recommendations were implemented and its impact in reducing gender bias in the state's court system. In the report of the investigation that Lynn H. Schafran and I conducted in the state of New Jersey, we concluded that after six years of work, "The Task Force's greatest accomplishment in the state is also its most subtle; creating a climate within a court system in which the nature and consequences of judicial gender bias are both acknowledged to exist and understood to be unacceptable in the New Jersey Courts".[29]

Facing up to a problem is not the same as eliminating it, however. But in the context of the judiciary's need for insulation and the traditions of judicial education, this is a significant accomplishment. In less than ten years since the term "judicial gender bias" was introduced in the United States, well organized and dedicated groups have been constituted by the profession's leaders to scrutinize the problem, design solutions and monitor compliance with reforms. This institutional reform movement is still in progress; indeed, its work has hardly begun. Nevertheless, the claim can be made that by directly addressing the problem of women's fair treatment by judges in the courts, the previous gap in the overall strategy for women's legal rights, described earlier in this paper, has begun to be filled.

(4) The Effort in Canada to Educate Judges about Gender Bias in the Courts

Canadian judges were first introduced to the topic of gender bias in the courts during a national interdisciplinary conference convened in 1986 by law professors Kathleen E. Mahoney and Sheilah L. Martin. Although few judges had accepted invitations to attend the conference held in Alberta, Canada called "The Socialization of Judges to Equality Issues", those who attended learned about the educational efforts underway in the United States to

[29] N. Wikler and L. Schafran, "Learning from the New Jersey Task Force on Women in the Courts: Evaluation, Recommendations and Implications for Other States", *Washington, D.C. Women Judges' Fund for Justice* (1988), at p. v.

eliminate gender bias in the judicial system and heard speakers advocate similar initiatives in Canada.[30]

Although the Canadian effort began more than a half decade after the effort in the United States, it appears to have met with less resistance from the judges and generated more support from the media. Mahoney and Martin provide an explanation in their book of the conference proceedings, *Equality and Judicial Neutrality*. "Before the issue of judicial gender bias had been raised, the Canadian Charter of Rights and Freedoms, with its strongly worded equality guarantees for every individual, had already focused public attention and scrutiny on the judiciary. Women, along with other disadvantaged groups, had begun to look increasingly to the judiciary to fulfill the Charter's promise of social equality and individual liberty."[31]

The first systematic undertaking by judges to educate themselves about gender bias issues commenced in 1989 when the Canadian Western Judicial Education Centre included a full day on the subject in its annual workshop. In 1990 and 1991 the program expanded to two days. Feminist legal scholars and social scientists served as the primary instructors for these courts.[32] The rich body of Canadian feminist legal scholarship, which burgeoned during the 1980's, has facilitated the development of curricular materials for judicial education by providing sophisticated analyses of gender bias in Canadian law. Further documentation has been provided by reports that demonstrate how gender bias operates in the application and interpretation of the law, particularly in family law and in criminal law.[33]

A turning point in the Canadian effort to educate both the legal and judicial communities came in 1990 when then Madam Justice Bertha Wilson, sitting on the Supreme Court of Canada, delivered the 1990 Betcherman Memorial Lecture at Osgoode Law School. Her bold speech entitled, "Will Women Judges Really Make a Difference?", challenged the notion of inherent judicial neutrality, by asserting that judges' personal opinions and predispositions have shaped the content of certain areas of existing Canadian law from a distinctly male perspective and that they continue to affect decisional outcomes in court.[34] Justice Wilson identified the need to challenge stereotypes about women in sharp terms saying, "Some aspects of the criminal law in particular cry out for change since they are based on presuppositions about the nature of women and women's sexuality that in this day and age are little short of

[30] This conference also dealt with many other topics such as judicial insensitivity to native culture, problems in human rights legislation, and philosophies of equality and judicial activism.

[31] S. Martin and K. Mahoney, note 6, *supra*.

[32] In 1991 the Western Judicial Education Centre secured a grant to develop model materials on gender bias in the courts to be made available throughout the country.

[33] An example is the study commissioned by the Manitoba Association of Women and the Law. Brown and Penner, *Gender Equality in the Courts* (1988).

[34] B. Wilson, "Will Women Judges Really Make a Difference?", 28 *Osgoode Hall Law J.* (1990), 507 at p. 515.

ludicrous."[35] She also called for remedial action similar to that taken in the United States. This address sparked heated public debate and controversy within the judiciary. It also gave great visibility and impetus to the movement to eliminate gender bias in the courts.

In contrast to the United States, Canadian women judges have not formed a national organization and have not, as a group, played a central role in the effort. However, they are individually becoming increasingly involved in judicial education on the subject. Unlike the United States, Canadian government officials have involved themselves with the problem of gender bias in the courts. In 1990, a national committee of federal and provincial Attorneys General in Canada was created to develop strategies for improving the treatment of women in the justice system. The committee convened a national conference on this topic in June 1991, whereat strategies for change to be implemented by the Minister of Justice were developed.

While judicial education programs on gender bias are appearing across the country, Canadians have not created task forces, but this may come to pass.[36] Recently, the Minister of Justice of the Northwest Territories appointed a special advisor on gender equality in the justice system to consult with professionals in the system and to convene community meetings throughout the territories.

(5) Equal Justice for Women and Men in the Courts: The Global Challenge

Since equal justice is a human rights issue that transcends national borders, the North American experience in judicial reform of gender bias has relevance to many other countries. Because of cross-cultural variations in social contexts, legal frameworks, the structure and organization of judiciaries and many other factors, different countries that attempt such judicial reform will necessarily follow different paths. One of the challenges for the 1990's will be to find ways to make the experiences and expertise gained in the United States and Canada accessible to women (and men) around the world who perceive the need to sensitize judges, other adjudicators of disputes and lawyers about the sources and manifestations of gender biases in the courts.

The "internationalization" of the movement to eliminate gender bias in the courts has already begun. An international organization of women judges, which has equal justice as a central goal, is in formation.[37] Women's organizations in Africa and Asia have begun to study the effects of court decisions and judges' conduct on women's rights and well-being. In Brazil, an

[35] Ibid.

[36] Press Information 90–207, Yellowknife NWT. December 13, 1990.

[37] Fifty women judges from thirty countries on four continents attended the 1989 annual meeting of the National Association of Women Judges. There they learned about the findings and perspectives of the gender bias task forces. Several judges have subsequently begun to raise these issues within their own judicial systems.

activist lawyer has initiated a similar process,[38] and in the United States and in Canada, a judicial education project on fairness in judicial processes is being developed in co-operation with human rights groups, scholars, judges in South Africa and Costa Rica, with a view to expanding the program to other countries once an International Centre for Fairness in Judicial Processes is established.[39]

Progress can be hastened in the realization of women's legal rights by bringing the exclusion of women from justice into the human rights arena of concerns. As Bunch has stressed, "Human Rights is one of the few moral visions ascribed to internationally... Further, it is one of the few concepts that speaks to the need for trans-national activism and concern about the lives of people, globally".[40] Now, as on the eve of the French Revolution, the rights of women merit more attention.

[38] *International Women's Right's Action Watch*, 3 The Women's Watch (1989), reported on the studies in Africa and Brazil. Dr. Margaret Schuler (personal communication, February 14, 1990) described the current study in six Asian countries.

[39] The Project is sponsored by The Faculty of Law, The International Centre and The University of Calgary Group for Research and Education in Human Rights. The author is currently working with Professor Kathleen E. Mahoney in the development and implementation of the Project.

[40] See note 2, *supra*, at p. 2.

MARILYN WARING*

The Exclusion of Women from "Work" and Opportunity

1. Introduction

"They" say that national income accounts should include everything that passes through the market. "They" say that even if an activity is unpaid, if there is a recognizable market equivalent for carrying out that activity, then it ought to be included. "They" established a boundary of production, deciding that all "economic activity" on one side of the boundary is to count, and that everything on the other is excluded. The one major international single exclusion is the word "housework". Nowhere is "housework" defined, so that it becomes the generic term for everything that women do in an unpaid capacity.

"They" say that "primary production and the consumption of their own produce by other than non-primary producers is of little or no importance".

And while all of this occurs, "they" sign international covenants outlawing slavery. "They" teach us that slavery involves the appropriation of the unpaid work of others. "They" seem to see no linkages between this and their definition of "work".

I wonder who "they" are, and what their motives could possibly be.

2. What Is Work?

Consider Tendai, a young girl in the Lowveld in Zimbabwe. Her day starts at 4:00 am when, to fetch water, she carries a 30 litre tin to a bore hole about 11 kilometres from her home. She walks bare foot and is home by 9:00 am. She eats a little and proceeds to fetch firewood until midday. She cleans the utensils from the families morning meal and sits preparing a lunch of sudsa for the family. After lunch and the cleaning of the dishes, she walks in the hot sun until early evening, fetching wild vegetables for supper before making the evening trip for water. Her day ends at 9:00 pm after she's prepared supper and put her

* Professor, University of Waikato, Hamilton, New Zealand.

K.E. Mahoney and P. Mahoney (eds.), Human Rights in the Twenty-first Century, 109–117.

younger brothers and sisters to sleep. Tendai is considered unproductive, unoccupied and economically inactive. According to the International Economic System, Tendai does not work and is not part of the labour force.

Kathy, a young middle class Australian housewife, spends her days preparing food, setting the table, serving meals, clearing food and dishes from the table, washing dishes, dressing her children, disciplining children, taking the children to day care and to school, disposing of garbage, dusting, gathering clothes for the washing, doing the laundry, going to the gas station and the supermarket, repairing household items, ironing, keeping an eye on, or playing with the children, making beds, paying bills, caring for pets and plants, putting away toys, books and clothes, sewing or mending or knitting, talking with door-to-door sales people, answering the telephone, vacuuming, sweeping and washing floors, cutting the grass, weeding, cleaning the bathroom and kitchen, putting her children to bed. Kathy has to face the fact that she too, fills her time in a totally unproductive manner. She is economically inactive. Economists record her as unoccupied and not working.

Ben is a highly trained member of the US military. When last spoken to he was regularly descending to an underground facility, where he waits with a colleague, for hours at a time for an order to fire a nuclear missile. So skilled and effective is Ben, that if his colleague were to attempt to subvert an order to fire, Ben would, if all else failed, be expected to kill him to ensure a successful missile launch. Ben is in paid work, he is economically active. His work has value, and contributes as part of the nuclear machine to the nations growth, wealth and productivity. That's what the International Economic System says.

Mario, is a pimp and a heroin addict in Rome. He regularly pays graft. While Mario's services and his consumption and production are illegal, they are, none the less, marketed. Money changes hands. Mario's activities are part of Italy's hidden economy. In a nation's book-keeping not all transactions are accounted for, but by the end of any year, it's impossible to measure the black market. So many nations, including Italy, regularly impute the minimal value for the hidden economy in their national accounts. So Mario's illegal services and production and consumption activities are recognised and recorded as work. That's what the International Economic System says.[1]

Since 1949, at least eight conventions and declarations directly affecting the rights of woman have been adopted by member-states of the United Nations. These include the suppression of traffic in persons and exploitation of prostitution, equal remuneration for work of equal value, political rights of women, nationality of married women, protection of women and children in emergency and armed conflict, participation of women in promoting international peace and the 1979 Convention on the Elimination of All Forms of Discrimination Against Women.

Supervision of these declarations and conventions, along with the Inter-

[1] M. Waring, *If Women Counted. A New Feminist Economics* (1988), Harper and Row, San Francisco.

national Covenant on Civil and Political Rights and the International Covenant on Economic Social and Cultural Rights, is assigned to a group of persons nominated by their nation-states, voted upon by nation-states, who, it is said, then serve "in their personal capacities" examining reports submitted by nation-states. These groups seldom have any power to impose sanctions or censure a State Party in any manner.

The omission of women from consideration in the key international covenants is glaringly obvious when you have learned how to read them unfettered by blinkers. One of the most glaring tools which continually enslaves more than half of the human species is focused in the inadequate international patriarchal concept of "work".

3. The Boundary of Production

When I consider the right to work, I am interested in the right for women's productive and reproductive functions and activities to be recognized as work. It is quite clear that 'work' is any activity culminating in a service or product which one can buy or hire someone else to do, even if pay is not involved.[2] The system which proscribes these rules, the United Nations System of National Accounts (UNSNA) is quite explicit in that definition, and so is the ILO, up to a point. *Housework* is specifically excluded from the definition of work – and nowhere is housework defined – so that housework becomes the generic term for *everything that women do in an unpaid capacity*. This is not because of any lack of flexibility in the international system defining work. In fact, the boundary of production may be shifted with ease by statisticians and policy makers in any country.

The boundary is often shifted when an undeveloped country recognizes black market activities or work by rural women as economically productive but then realizes that the figures may boost their GDP to a point where their 'undeveloped' status could be in jeopardy. As a result, the country adjusts the boundary of production in order to keep its GDP down and its ability to access concessionary loans viable. On the other hand, if you consider a place such as Thailand, which may be seeking additional loans from the World Bank or the IMF, the boundary of production will be neatly shifted to include the entirety of prostitution, pornography, female sexual slavery, trafficking in drugs, trafficking in children and anything else that demonstrates an income generating capacity sufficient to repay the loan. The boundary of production is also flexible enough to adjust to tribal behaviour in countries such as Kenya.

[2] "If an activity is of such a character that it might be delegated to a paid worker then that activity shall be deemed productive". Margaret G. Reid, *Economics of Household Production* (1934), New York: Wiley. "Material wealth that is not the spontaneous product of nature, must invariably owe its existence to a special productive activity, exercised with a definite aim, an activity that appropriates particular nature-given materials to particular human wants." Karl Marx, *Capital* (1967), New York, International Publishers, Vol. 1:42.

For instance, when the men of a tribe carry water even though it is unpaid, the carriage of water is considered a productive and economic activity. This is explained by the proposition that if the men were not carrying water they would otherwise be engaged in an economic activity. However, in a different tribe when women carry the water it is considered housework, and so it does not count as work.

Such is the flexibility of the boundary of production in the right to work. What most women would like is not only recognition of the fact that they do the majority of work on the planet, *and that it is work*, but a lot of them would like the right not to do so much of it.

4. The Enslavement of Women through Their Exclusion from Work

Just how do U.N. Conventions deal with this situation? Can we find a rationale? Keeping the daily working activities of Tendai and Kathy clearly in our minds let us look at the following from the Universal Declaration of Human Rights.

Article 23

1. Everyone has the right to work, to free choice of employment, to just and favourable conditions of work and to protection against unemployment.
2. Everyone, without any discrimination, has a right to equal pay for equal work.
3. Everyone who works has the right to just and favourable remuneration ensuring for himself and his family an existence worthy of human dignity, and supplemented, if necessary, by other means of social protection.
4. Everyone has the right to form and to join trade unions for the protection of his interests.

Article 24

Everyone has the right to rest and leisure, including reasonable limitation of working hours and periodic holidays with pay.

('Everyone', that is, except women in unpaid productive and reproductive work. These rights for "everyone" are repeated in the International Covenant on Economic, Social and Cultural Rights.

Article 7

The States Parties to the present Covenant recognize the right of everyone to the enjoyment of just favourable conditions of work which ensure, in particular:

(a) Remuneration which provides all workers, as a minimum, with:

(i) Fair wages and equal remuneration for work of equal value without distinction of any kind, in particular women being guaranteed conditions of work not inferior to those enjoyed by men, with equal pay for equal work;
(ii) A decent living for themselves and their families in accordance with the provisions of the present Covenant;

(b) Safe and healthy working conditions;
(c) Equal opportunity for everyone to be promoted in his employment to an appropriate higher level, subject to no considerations other than those of seniority and competence;
(d) Rest, leisure and reasonable limitation of working hours and periodic holidays with pay, as well as remuneration for public holidays.

When you think about it then, this work, undefined housework, falls very quickly into another article of international covenants. But because it is called housework, we dare not call it slavery. In 1934, George Scelle wrote:

> "The struggle against slavery, the protection of the bodily freedom of individuals only begins in international law when it is clearly demonstrated that slave labour has economic drawbacks and that the progress of modern technology allows it to be replaced. Whenever human manpower has not been replaced, slave labour and forced labour still exist despite all efforts made to proscribe it. This proves that a moral conviction even if of a general character does not override the necessities of economic life in the formation of legal rules."[3]

Slavery is defined as the right to appropriate the unpaid labour of others. Housework is the appropriation of the unpaid labour of others. Whether it occurs in the exchange of bride wealth or in the exchange of dowry, it occurs. It occurs in rural areas of India, of Nepal, of the Philippines, of Bangladesh, of Thailand, and in too many places where young rural girls are taken to the city and sold, supposedly as maids. The sale of girls into prostitution is yet another form of slavery which includes rape and forced participation in the production of pornography. Such slavery is blatantly displayed in the brothels of Bangkok, where naked, twelve year old girls, identified only by numbers, can be seen chained on catwalks and sold to well-dressed European, Asian and Thai men, carrying Gucci bags. Further proof of this slavery was found when a Bangkok brothel burned down in 1984. Skeletons of six girls aged between 12 and 16 were found chained to the bed in the ashes. The sale of children overseas is well documented, whether it is in Romania or South Korea. The situation in Romania was discovered due to the recent political upheaval, while slavery in South Korea was exposed prior to its hosting the 1988 Olympic Games. The country ceased such trade during the Olympics as it feared exposure in the international media.

[3] G. Scelle, Precis de Droit des Gens (Paris, 1934), ii 55. Cited and translated by A Cassesse, *International Law in a Divided World* (OUP 1986) p.53.

This enslavement is not something that is restricted to the (so called) developing world. Consider the rights of women in the division of matrimonial property along with the rights of women and the awards of maintenance in Western countries. Courts award maintenance payments for the purchase of clothing or the purchase of food and then miraculously expect clothing to be washed, ironed, darned, or food to be processed and to arrive on the table. Apparently no work whatsoever takes place in the purchase, processing, the furnishing and the continued maintenance and repair of items for which maintenance is awarded. By ignoring women's work, Courts enshrine the right to appropriate the unpaid labour of others.

The exclusion of women's unpaid production and reproduction from the definition of 'work' has further consequences. In developed countries, such a narrow definition generally excludes women from private disability insurance, compensation in accident compensation schemes, tax credits for child care expenses (if child care services are available), unemployment insurance, holidays, retirement pensions or 'pay as you go' superannuation schemes. It also renders women invisible in policy decisions on everything from transportation routes to support services.

It is instructive to examine man-made human rights instruments. The Universal Declaration of Human Rights addresses slavery in Article 4 directly and indirectly. Article 4 states:

Article 4

No one shall be held in slavery or servitude; slavery and the slave trade shall be prohibited in all their forms.

This is also the first sentence of Article 8 of the International Covenant on Civil and Political Rights. It also states:

> "2. No one shall be held in servitude", and "3(a) No one shall be required to perform forced or compulsory labour". There is a caveat in Article 8 3(c)(iv) which states that the term "forced or compulsory labour" shall not include "any work or service which forms part of normal civil obligations".

Perhaps some patriarchs would attempt to argue that 'housework' is a civil obligation, despite their concern at other times to highlight the public-private sphere and confine women and 'housework' to the private realm. Just to ensure that the home is the castle where "he" remains King, articles on enslavement should be read in conjunction with Article 17(1) and Article 23(1):

Article 17

1. No one shall be subjected to arbitrary or unlawful interference with his privacy, family, home or correspondence, not to unlawful attacks on his honour and reputation.

2. Everyone has the right to the protection of the law against such interference or attacks.

(I have heard this statement used to defend marital rape);

Article 23

1. The family is the natural and fundamental group unit of society and is entitled to protection by society and the State.

This assertion in Article 23 is highly debatable, particularly while the word 'family' remains undefined. But non-definition in international law is clarified by the use of the "norm". That is, the insertion of the word 'patriarchal' before the word 'family'. Based on global percentages however, the patriarchal family is no more the 'norm' than it is 'natural' or 'fundamental'. Undoubtedly, it is 'fundamental' to patriarchal power, but those of us who care about female sexual slavery and the abuse of children are familiar with the fact that more than two-thirds of violent exploitation of women and children occurs within this "norm" of the patriarchal family.

So 'privacy' protects patriarchy. Riane Eisler has important insights to offer here. Our first lessons in human rights are learned in the 'private' sphere. She explains how:

> "Certainly the right to privacy...is an important civil right. But the right to protection from government interference in certain areas of personal choice and action...is a *personal* right. With whom to speak and associate, with whom to have intimate relations, whether or not to conceive, whether or not to carry a pregnancy are *not* family rights. They are individual rights even though they may involve personal choices or actions that characteristically take place within the family. Moreover, personal relations in families have always been socially regulated. For example, the killing of one brother by another in the privacy of their home is regarded as a crime in both tribal and modern codes of law.

Clearly a person's right to make certain private decisions should be free from governmental interference. But that is not the same as immunizing family decisions – or more specifically, the decisions of those who wield power in a family – from public scrutiny and regulation. In short, *the protection of personal rights is not synonymous with non-interference with actions within the family – and in fact there may be a direct conflict between the two.*[4]

[4] R. Eisler, "Integrating the Private and Public Spheres: Toward a New Partnership in Human Rights", unpublished, (1990).

5. Perpetuation of the Patriarchal State

It is in the so-called 'private' sphere that most of the 'work' of the world occurs, even though it is defined by the U.N.S.N.A. as 'leisure'. It is inside the home that most of the worlds' forced labour occurs, despite the general acceptance "that freedom from forced labour (in other words, prohibitions on slavery) is building on customary international law".[5] It is overwhelmingly men from this 'natural' and 'fundamental' family unit who are the "clients" of women held in female sexual slavery. It is not an accident, as Andrew Byrnes reports, that "various anti-slavery conventions (including those which cover trafficking and forced prostitution) have a weak, almost non-existent supervisory and enforcement mechanism".[6]

In the international forum, the hope that women may have any right of appeal in our demand for rights has a very hollow ring. Multi-lateral institutions are appointed by the same people who give us nation-states. In some countries they literally are the uncles and brothers of Presidents and Prime Ministers. In others they are the people who have contributed most heavily to the last election campaign. Women's issues are assigned to CEDAW[7], a committee where only nation-states are allowed to report on the situation of their women. We cannot take a class action to the International Court of Justice. Class actions are not available for complaints brought to the Human Rights Committee. I.L.O. conventions operate on a tripartite system of employers, workers and nation-states, but attendees are always overwhelmingly male. Women, who do most of the work most of the time are unwelcome because they are not "workers".[8] Women may have some hope due to the fact that States are privileged in the system, ratification of conventions is voluntary and can be agreed by States alone. But as yet, the representative democratic state is a dream. Once again, the descriptive 'norm', is employed, for this is the patriarchal state.

Patriarchy has been defined as "any kind of group organization in which males hold dominant power and determine what part females shall and shall not play, and in which capabilities assigned to women are relegated generally to the mystical and aesthetic and excluded from the practical and political realms, these realms being regarded as separate and mutually exclusive."[9]

[5] S. Adelman, "International Labour Standards and the Third World: The Need for a New Theoretical Approach", Report of the Ninth Commonwealth Law Conference, p. 568.

[6] A. Byrnes, "A Feminist Analysis of International Human Rights Law", Paper presented at the Conference on the Role of Consent and The Development of International Law at the End of the Twentieth Century, p. 15.

[7] United Nations Committee on the Elimination of Discrimination Against Women.

[8] With the exception of those women whose economic lives mimic men (and co-opted women academics) the majority of the worlds' women live lives too busy and various to be simply encapsulated by notions of "public" and "private" worlds.

[9] J. Rifkin, "Towards a Theory of Law and Patriarchy", *Harvard Women's Law Journal* (1980), vol. 3., p. 83.

Regardless of the form the patriarchal state takes, democratic, military, or religious fundamentalist, it makes the laws.

According to Austin Turk, there are five kinds of power that accrue to those who control the established legal system:

1. Physical force, which may be used to restrain dissidents;
2. Economic power, which supplies a system of rewards and punishments to the benefit of those who control the system;
3. Political power, whereby certain 'political structures' and their norms are supported instead of others, thus constituting a method of control.
4. Power to influence the ideological environment, which helps promote unquestioned compliance and acceptance as inevitable and desirable; and
5. Diversionary power, which helps mask real sources of inequality and the key ingredients that centralize power by getting some people involved in minor law suits and political movements.[10]

It is men, individually and collectively, who abuse their powers with impunity. Domestic violence and marital rape are frequently sanctioned by the state so that women are "restrained". Labelling women's work as "unproductive unoccupied economically inactive leisure" ensures that economic benefits are distributed only to those workers who are in the paid work-force, who happen to be overwhelmingly male.

Supported by brothers in political power, patriarchy controls language, media, education, and custom. The ideology of women as a second-class is thus easily perpetuated and entrenched. Occasionally, the patriarchal state allows challenges to its powers, but in the sphere of "work and opportunity" such challenges inevitably focus on creating opportunities for women to do what men do (actions for equal pay, affirmative action, comparable worth, mothers in the military) rather than on the fundamentals.

However cleverly phrased, construed or defined, whatever the explanation or subtlety of convention or statute, the reality in women's working lives is clear. It suits men, individually and collectively, to ensure a slave caste. The conspiracy of the brotherhood of politicians and economists and judges and diplomats, ensures its perpetuation.

[10] A. Turk, "Law as A Weapon in Social Conflict", *Social Problems* (Feb, 1976) 23, No. 3, p. 276.

Bibliography

A. Cassesse, *Human Rights in a Changing World* (1990), Polity Press, Oxford.

M. Fineman and N. Thomadsen (eds.) *At the Boundaries of Law* (1991), Routledge, New York.

W. Hazon, *The Social and Legal Status of Women*, (1990), Praegar, New York.

M. Waring, *If Women Counted* (1988), Harper and Row, San Francisco.

SECTION II(b): EXCLUSION OF ETHNIC, RELIGIOUS, AND RACIAL MINORITIES FROM EQUITABLE PARTICIPATION*

Introduction

The section Exclusion of Ethnic, Racial and Religious Minorities from Equitable Participation, includes four papers addressing widely different cultural realities which nonetheless demonstrate strong similarities because of discrimination against minorities.

Irwin Cotler addresses antisemitism in the Soviet Union. He argues that it is a unique, distinguishable brand of discrimination because Soviet Jewry, unlike other minorities, experience all the dynamics and policies of exclusion. He explains current antisemitism as a composite of historical and contemporary conditions and constituents, of themes and theories of which all must be appreciated in order to comprehend the depth and complexity of the problem. He describes various faces of antisemitism: historical, socio-economic, "environmental", popular, ideological, intellectual, theological and cultural. He holds out hope that in a changing Soviet Union perhaps the dialectic of encounter inspired by revolutionary transformation will move the Jew from the politics of exclusion into the politics of inclusion together with other racial and religious minorities. Otherwise, he believes the exodus of Jews from the Soviet Union will continue.

Abdullahi Ahmed An-Na'im discusses the broad question of how to maintain equality and equitable participation despite the existence of different and often competing bases of solidarity. He uses the example of Christianity, Islam and traditional African religions in five countries of Subsaharan Africa. He applies his thesis to the present situation of inequitable exclusion of minorities in the Sudan.

Edward Taihakurei Durie describes aboriginal rights from the Maori experience. The historical development of the Maori and their struggle to uphold their independent sovereignty is not dissimilar to that described in Chief Mercredi's paper but the recognition of them as a people in the Treaty of Waitangi has created a more favourable situation than Canadian native people have experienced. Unlike aboriginal rights in Canada, Maori rights are seen to flow from their circumstances as a group, where their culture has dignity and

* Summary prepared by the editors.

K.E. Mahoney and P. Mahoney (eds.), Human Rights in the Twenty-first Century, 119–120.

where Maori as a people can advocate the greater recognition of group rights as an antidote to the deleterious impact of the emphasis given to individual rights. The operation of the Waitangi Tribunal, its strengths and weaknesses as an implementing device, are also discussed.

Ovide Mercredi describes what it is like for an aboriginal person to grow up in a dominant society which not only excludes but rejects his indigenous culture. This discussion leads to an explanation about the need for constitutional recognition of collective rights of Canada's aboriginal peoples.

IRWIN COTLER*

Antisemitism, Pogroms and Human Rights in a Single Party State

1. Introduction

The state of Soviet Jewry today is a case study in the politics and policies of exclusion in the Soviet Union. Admittedly, there are other minorities and groups that are the object of a politics of exclusion. But antisemitism in the Soviet Union, both historically and presently – let alone the question of "pogroms" – is a unique, distinguishable brand of the politics of exclusion. Indeed, Soviet Jewry is not only a case study of the politics of exclusion; but a special kind of politics – and set of policies – appear to have been invented for, or even reflected by, the case of Soviet Jewry; and while some of the factors or dynamics of the politics and policies of exclusion apply to other minorities, only Soviet Jewry is the object – or expression – of them all. In a word, not only is the case of Soviet Jewry a prototype of the politics of exclusion and human rights violations in the single party state of the pre-Gorbachev Soviet Union, but in some paradoxical, dialectical fashion antisemitism continues as a metaphor for the politics of exclusion and human rights violations even as the Soviet Union emerges into a Rechstaat or "Rule of Law" state.

In Chapter 1, I wrote of the "Velvet Revolution" in Czechoslovakia, which took place in 1989, the "Year of the Revolution" in Central and Eastern Europe, and one might say, of the revolution in the Soviet Union, which emerged as the "mother of revolutions" in Eastern and Central Europe and elsewhere; while the revolutionary transformation in the Soviet Union can be said to be having a revolutionary impact on the state of the Soviet Jews.

Indeed, to appreciate the state of Soviet Jews today and the nature of their exclusion or inclusion, one must examine the state of the Soviet Union today inhabited by Jews; and one dramatic expression of the revolutionary "fall-out" of the Soviet Union for Soviet Jews is that some one hundred and thirty thousand Soviet Jews have already been permitted to emigrate thus far in the year 1990 alone. This empirical datum takes on dramatic proportions when one compares it with the fact that in 1986, just four years ago, less than 1,000 Soviet

* Professor of Law, McGill University, Montreal, Quebec, Canada.

K.E. Mahoney and P. Mahoney (eds.), Human Rights in the Twenty-first Century, 121–132.

Jews, *914 to be exact*, were permitted to emigrate in that entire year. In other words, one hundred and thirty times as many Jews have been permitted to emigrate thus far in 1990, as were permitted to emigrate in 1986. The rate now is abut 20,000 per month. So in each month in 1990, some twenty times as many leave as did in the entire year of 1986.

Moreover, there are no longer any prisoners of Zion, as Jewish prisoners of conscience were called. Most of the refuseniks[1] – even long-term refuseniks who have been denied exit visas for ten years or longer on grounds of possessing alleged state secrets – have been permitted to leave. There has been a veritable explosion of Jewish cultural and religious organizations throughout the Soviet Union. Jews are increasingly free to exercise their religion, teach and study Hebrew, and give expression to their Jewish sensibility. Israeli-Soviet relations are moving towards the full establishment of diplomatic relations, most recently on a consular level. And for the first time in 45 years, there is a Soviet-International Joint Commission of Inquiry on the Fate and Whereabouts of Raoul Wallenberg, the "lost hero of the Holocaust" who "disappeared" in the Soviet Union in 1945, and who was an unmentionable in the Soviet Union until as recently as two years ago.

And so the question might naturally be asked: if everything is so good, why is it that everything is also deemed to be so bad? Why is it that Perestroika, a metaphor for reform in the Soviet Union, is now being accompanied by reference to the other "p" – the dreaded "p" word – pogrom? And why the persistence of antisemitism when the Soviet Union is moving from a single party state to a multi-party democracy based on the rule of law?

A snapshot of antisemitism in the Soviet Union today is a composite of conditions and constituents, of themes and theories of both a historical and contemporary character that together give expression to this very complex phenomenon. What follows below is an attempt to identify and delineate these factors or dynamics, which together comprise the politics and policies of exclusion – and antisemitism.

2. Varieties of Antisemitism

Some of the features or components of the different varieties of antisemitism in the Soviet Union, as set forth below, could probably be applied to other

[1] The term for those Soviet Jews whose application to emigrate was denied on arbitrary or capricious grounds, resulting often in the prospective emigrant losing his job, and even rendering him liable to imprisonment. For example, Soviet "refusenik" Josef Begun lost his job for applying to emigrate, and was then charged with parasitism for not having a job, a case-study in Catch-22 Gulag Justice. In some instances, the "refusenik's" status led to even more serious charges, as in the case of "Prisoner of Zion" Natan Sharansky. He was charged and convicted of both the charges of treason and anti-Soviet slander and agitation. The writer acted as Counsel for both Mr. Begun and Mr. Sharansky. A comprehensive account of the plight of refuseniks – and political prisoners in the Soviet Union – appears in my Petition to the Soviet Procurator-General on behalf of Begun and Sharansky.

religious and racial groups that suffer exclusion. The distinguishable factor, however, as indicated above, is that Soviet Jews, alone amongst all national minorities in the Soviet Union, are the victims of all of the dynamics that make up the politics of exclusion – and antisemitism.

(1) Historical Antisemitism

The first such factor or dynamic is the special character of historical antisemitism. To understand antisemitism in the Soviet Union today, one must return to antisemitism in its historical roots. Indeed, the very word "pogrom" is itself an outgrowth, an expression of the attacks against Jews in the latter part of the nineteenth and earlier part of the twentieth century – the word that came to symbolize the beatings, the killings, the vandalism against Jews; while the "Pale of Settlement", the restricted area in which Jews were allowed to live but from which they could not emerge or live elsewhere, became a prototype for the politics of segregation; and the "Protocols of the Elders of Zion", the classic antisemitic forgery, had both its birth and massive circulation in the Soviet Union itself.

Finally, and ironically, there was theological antisemitism, which took on a particularly virulent expression in Czarist Russia and in the times of Alexander III, when the Jews were blamed for being "Christ killers". This led Andre Sakharov to later remark, in a pithy sentence about which volumes could be written, both respecting classical, historical antisemitism and the more contemporary brand of the 60's and 70's, that "antisemitism in the Soviet Union has been raised to the level of a State religion in a godless society". This godless society, then, particularly during the period of Czarist Russia, had its own theological dimensions. For the Jews were seen not only as an "accursed people who had crucified the Saviour", but also as the killers of Russian Emperor Alexander II. The "Christ-killers had killed the 'Little Father' (Alexander II)" was the common belief. As his son Alexander III (1881–1894) himself put it, "in the depth of my soul I am always happy when they beat the Jews".[2]

In a word, throughout Soviet history – whether it be Czarist Russia or Stalin's "War against the Jews",[3] or in the state supported antisemitism of the sixties and seventies, the common thread was the notion of the Jew "as the enemy of the people", the "poisoners" of the Russian well – a racist politics of exclusion which leads to the second dynamic.

(2) The Politics of Soviet Federalism and Independence

While Soviet Jews like other Soviet citizens applauded the "Year of the Revolution" in Central and Eastern Europe, they feared that in the Soviet

[2] Referred to in "Russians Against Jews", *Atlantic Monthly*, October 1990, at p. 42.
[3] The title of the authoritative work by L. Rappaport, Macmillan, 1989.

"Revolution" the power of the people would not prevail over the power of the State and the party without – to use Havel's words – "force or lies". For in the Soviet Union, in their view, there is no people, no Soviet, no Union – no people or polity as found in Poland or Czechoslovakia; rather, Havel's "Velvet Revolution" as metaphor and message would be replaced by a Hobbesian notion of a group of warring nationalities – of "a war of all against all" in which Soviet Jews believe they will be the ultimate if not the first victims. For Soviet Jews, the "political meltdown" may result in a situation in which they are the only "Soviets" – or where for the Russians they are Soviets and for the Republics they are Russian – either way they are the classic *l'etranger*, and the victims of somebody's politics of exclusion.

(3) The Dialectics of Nationalism and Antisemitism in the Soviet Union

The volatility in the Soviet Union was present even before the "Year of the People" in Europe. Political, economic and particularly nationalistic fissures were breaking out all over. The Soviet Union was an explosion waiting to happen – and Soviet Jews found themselves caught up in a pincer movement between these imploding fissures, these explosive nationalistic currents. For what must be realized is that the politics of independence and separation is not just a political dynamic but a nationalist one – that the independence/secessionist movement is not just a separatist one in political terms, but a nationalistic one in ethnic terms.

And just as the Jews are caught in a pincer movement in the politics of independence, so are they caught in the crossfire of the politics of ethnicity. For when one reads of the ethnic hostilities between the Azeries and Armenians what the reports do not mention is that there are 30,000 Jews in Baku who find themselves in a crossfire between the warring ethnic groups, and so communities of Jews, and not just individuals, seek the right to emigrate; and when one reads about the ethnic hostility in June 1990 between the Uzbeks and the Kirgizians, there is no mention of the vulnerable Soviet Jewish minorities in both Uzbekistan and Kirgizia which found themselves in this kind of pincer movement.

Similarly, when there was an ethnic explosion in the Fergana Valley in April 1990, or a "pogrom" in Andhizian, in Eastern Uzbekistan in May 1990, or one in Dushanbe in Tadzhikistan in June 1990, while the primary targets were not intended to be Jews, "Soviet Jews" found themselves the innocent by-standers in the ethnic cross-fire. As Mikhail Chlenov, a noted Soviet ethnologist put it,[4] the Jews are also victimized because they look like Armenians, just as the Armenians are victimized because they look like Jews; while for Jews the ethnic politics of exclusion are particularly menacing. For Soviet Jews are almost the

[4] M. Chlenov, remarks to the founding Conference of the Federation of Jewish Communities and Organizations in the USSR, December, 1989; Professor Chlenov, a noted Soviet ethnologist, was elected Co-Chair of the Federation, otherwise known as the "VAAD".

only national minority in the Soviet Union that does not have any kind of physical security that a territorial homeland would provide.

(4) Socio-Economic Antisemitism

This leads to a fourth dynamic, what might be called socio-economic antisemitism. In a word, the political meltdown in the Soviet Union is being accompanied, if not preceded, by an economic meltdown. Whatever be the index of measurement – be it the conventional economic indices of inflation, unemployment, balance of payments, deficits and the like, or economic indices peculiar to the nature of the Soviet Union economy – it is clear that the Soviet economy is unravelling throughout the Soviet Union. For example, 50% of the grain never reaches the market because the transportation system breaks down; and if it does reach the market it does not get distributed because of the breakdown of the delivery system. At the same time, inflation is now running at about 100%; the GNP is estimated to be some 20% less this year than last; price rises are rampant – the economy in effect, is in a "free fall". Who is to blame? If one reads in and out of different parts of the Soviet press and populace, it is the Jews. The evidence? Well, the only part of the economy that appears to be working are the cooperatives, and the Jews are popularly perceived to be in charge of the cooperatives. Just as the Jews have organized for their own economic betterment, so it is said, they have also organized the economic unravelling of the Soviet Union.

(5) The "Misery Index" and "Environmental" Antisemitism

Nor does it end there. For these features of socio-economic antisemitism can also be seen in the antisemitic fall-out relating to the condition and perception of the quality of life in the Soviet Union. If one looks at today's erosion in the overall quality of life there is, for the Soviet citizens of whatever nationality, a kind of pervasive misery index. For example, thirty percent of the rural hospitals do not have indoor toilets, forty percent do not have hot running water, and fifty percent do not have syringes – the whole symptomatic of the breakdown of the health care system in the Soviet Union.

Indeed, whatever the measure, the "misery index" is growing. And once again, Jews are being singled out. For if the misery index is growing, someone – some "otherness" – Jews – must be "responsible" for that growing misery; while by their visible emigration, Soviet Jews are seemingly prepared to allow the other Soviet people to bear the burden of this misery, a factor accounting for the laying of charges of "treason" and "parasitism" against the Soviet "Prisoners of Zion" of the 70's and 80's.

A growing part of this corrosive misery index – and its attending assault on human dignity – involves the increasing recognition of pervasive environmental pollution. Industrial areas have become so polluted that even the heavy industry can no longer be located in those areas – while Chernobyl has become the classic metaphor for environmental contamination. On this front, Soviet Jews again find themselves in a unique form of "double jeopardy".

On the one hand, 130,000 Soviet Byelorussian Jews inhabit the more immediate orbit of the Chernobyl reactor. These Byelorussian Jews have carried out a study of the incidence of disease – particularly amongst children in the Byelorussian sector – and have found a tragic increase in the incidence of disease amongst members of groups living in that sector. That alone would be cause enough for worry, and accounts for the impulse to emigrate among Byelorussian Jews; indeed, at the founding Conference of the Federation of Jewish Communities and Organizations in the U.S.S.R.[5] just a little less than a year ago today, a group representing the Byelorussian Jewish leadership spoke at the Conference of the need for an airlift of this community. But what is unique to Soviet Jews – and where the "double jeopardy" occurs – is that while all Byelorussians – including the Jews – are victimized from the radioactive "fall-out" of the Chernobyl reactor, only the Jews suffer the "fall-out" from the politics of blame.

Similarly, when the Armenian earthquake occurred, there were those who said that the Jews were to blame, because the seismologists who were Jewish did not warn the rest of the population about the earthquake that was to take place. The politics of blame, exclusion and antisemitism.

(6) The Dialectics of Glasnost

While at times the situations described above appear almost as caricatures, they reflect a very painful reality – a reality anchored in the sixth dynamic, namely, the dialectics of Glasnost. For under Glasnost, every disaster is increasingly a matter of public knowledge, which is good, but many are deemed to have a Jewish footprint, which is not. Everyone seeks to identify who is to blame; and for many of these disasters a Jewish signature is imputed. What is occurring, then, is a kind of rolling public indictment of Soviet Jews. For as Glasnost unravels the crimes of the past and exposes the wretchedness of the present, somebody must be blamed. The search for a scapegoat is bound to have wide appeal, and the Jews are there to provide the scapegoat, the whole nurtured and anchored in the roots of historical antisemitism and the politics of exclusion.

"Why blame the ... Jews", asked last month's article (October, 1990) in the *Atlantic Monthly* on Soviet antisemitism. Because, it continued, "if you ask Russian Jews this question, most will stop and look at you with a mixture of incredulity and scorn. Why? Why? We're in Russia, aren't we, they finally answer. Antisemitism is traditional, endemic, as Russian as kasha with mushrooms".[6] The battle-cry from Czarist years, "Be Zidof Spacie Russia" – "Beat the Jews and save Russia" – emerges once again as part of the dialectics

[5] Ibid., Statement and Study by L. Guttman, on behalf of Byelorussian Jewry, to the Conference.

[6] See note 2, *supra*, at p. 40.

of Glasnost – inhabiting now the streets and marketplaces of the present Soviet Union.

(7) Popular Antisemitism

The emergent and increasingly popular public antisemitism in the Soviet Union may be seen as a seventh dynamic. Admittedly, Soviet State sponsored antisemitism has been receding in the age of Gorbachev. In other words, the organized, orchestrated, State-supported, and State-sanctioned antisemitism that was characteristic of antisemitism in a single party State in the pre-Gorbachev days has considerably lessened. Nonetheless a new phenomenon of increasingly popular antisemitism in the workplace and in the marketplace is appearing, the codeword for which is "Pamyat". But while Pamyat may be the most visible of the extremist antisemitic fronts, it is not necessarily the most dangerous form of this new popular antisemitism.

Indeed, even Pamyat itself is somewhat a misnomer, for while it is the most widely publicized of the extremist groups, many other "Pamyats" are beginning to assert themselves. For example, in March 1990 five extremist Russian nationalist groups formed a coalition under the umbrella of "The Russian Orthodox National Patriotic Front, Pamyat". Their doctrines can perhaps best be expressed in the following three themes espoused at their recent press conference.[7]

1. Jews are responsible for all the tribulations of the Russian people over the last 73 years.
2. The main task for the renaissance of the Slavic Aryan peoples is the elimination of overt and covert Zionism in Russia and the world at large.
3. This struggle is supported by official Soviet organs and healthy forces in the KGB, the MVD, the army and the presidential council (this refers to Valentin Rasputin and Veniamin Yarin, two extremist Russian nationalists appointed by Gorbachev).

In a word, while "Pamyat" has acquired a certain notoriety in the West as well as in the Soviet Union because of its virulent and public antisemitism, it should be seen not as an organization but as a code word – or shorthand – for an assemblage of extremist and xenophobic nationalist groups which have cropped up in the Soviet Union. Indeed, there are now believed to be dozens of such organizations with millions of adherents.

Moreover these organizations are seeking, and finding, recruits amongst the veterans of the Afghan War, disgruntled Party apparachniks, members of the demobilized military, (who lost Eastern Europe), extremists of the Russian Orthodox Church, and the economically aggrieved; while the Tsarist "Black Hundreds" – the forerunners of Pamyat at the turn of the century – are increasingly looked to as some form of spiritual ancestor.

[7] Statement at Press Conference of the "Russian Orthodox National Patriotic Front, Pamyat", in Moscow on March 21, 1990.

(8) Ideological and Intellectualized Antisemitism

An eighth phenomenon may be called ideological and intellectualized antisemitism. In a word, what is most disturbing – and dangerous – about the Pamyat phenomenon in general, or extremist and xenophobic antisemitism in particular, is not just the virulent and public character of the antisemitism; but rather the anchorage of that antisemitism – and its legitimation – amongst the intellectual and cultural elites.

In other words, Soviet cultural life today consists of an array of sentiments, beliefs, and grievances whose outstanding feature – as Boris Paramonov put it in a recent issue of *Partisan Review*,[8] happens to be antisemitism. According to Paramonov, the historic varieties of antisemitism in the Soviet Union were never really a featured expression of the Soviet cultural elite; yet today there is a growing – and alarming – "culture" of antisemitism from which the "Pamyats" of the Soviet Union draw sustenance and legitimacy. And so it is, then, that amongst the Masters of Contemporary Russian Writers such as Victor Astafiev, Vasily Belov, and Valentin Rasputin,[9] one can find those responsible for legitimizing this new cultural antisemitism – a cultural-intellectual antisemitism which links up with – and energizes – the popular antisemitism. A classic case-study is Igor Shafarevitch, whose work "Russophobia" is the intellectual bible of this old/new cultural and popular antisemitism. The generic theme of Shafarevitch's work is the notion of the Jew as "the enemy of the people"; the specific characterizations include the following:

1. Notion of the Jew as *l'Etranger* – an alien, corrupting influence
2. The Jew as *Parasite* – feeding off the Russian people
3. The Jew as *Agent/Source* of an international conspiracy for world domination of which the Russian people are the main victim.
4. The Jew as *Privileged Benefactor* manipulating the victimized Russians
5. The Jew as *"enemy of the people"* responsible for all the evils of Russian people/history

What is important here is that Shafarevitch is not your common street demagogue, or Pamyat villain. He is a serious ideologue, and intellectual, a distinguished mathematician and member of the U.S.S.R. Academy of Sciences, and a founder of the Committee for the Defense of Human Rights in the Soviet Union. It is the legitimation given by Shafarevitch that gives Pamyat antisemitism respectability – and influence; and it is Shafarevitch who has spoken of Pamyat as being a "Patriotic Front" that is to be supported and promoted.

When you add to this the dozens of publications with millions of readers giving expression/exposure to the Shafarevitches of the Soviet Union, then you

[8] Boris Paramorov, "The Culture of Soviet Antisemitism", *Partisan Review*, May, 1990, pp. 194–200.

[9] Ibid., page 197; See also, B. Keller, *New York Times Magazine*, January 28, 1990.

have a critical mass of intellectualized/cultural antisemitism of which the publications *Nash Sovremenik*, *Molodin Guardia*, and *Literatura Russia* are the most important.

(9) Theological Antisemitism

It is somewhat ironical that in a country where religion was the "opiate of the people", there should emerge the dynamic of theological antisemitism – and becoming even, as Sakharov put it, "a State religion in a Godless society".

But the emergence of the Jew as "Christ killers" is both anchored in Russian/Czarist history as it is in the contemporary politics of the Soviet Union. Indeed, a recent poll showed that 800,000 Muscovites believed not only that the Jews killed Christ but that the Jews must now be held accountable for that killing.

(10) Islamization and the Culture of Antisemitism

In the Muslim republics of Central Asia, Jews historically felt safe and secure, with very little of the antisemitism that characterized relations, for example, in the Russian Republic. But a growing inter-Republican ethnic hostility in Central Asia, and inter-group hostility within Republics, is once again resulting in the Jews being caught in the ethnic crossfire. Interestingly enough, the Jews of Andhizan, relying on good relations between Jews and Moslems in Central Asia, put a Star of David on their homes when the killing broke out in Uzbekistan to *protect* themselves in the ethnic rioting. They believed that the Moslems would not assault them. But the inter-ethnic hostility has taken on a dynamic of its own, and the Jews are once again the vulnerable bystander, if not intruder.

Moreover, just as the Russian nationalist sees the Jew as the agent of Capitalist Imperialism (or Communism, or both) the Islamic nationalist increasingly sees the Jew as the agent of Russian imperialism – or Communism – or both. And so while the "imperialism" may be different, the Jew is still the enemy of the people – and the object of the politics of exclusion.

(11) The Political Uses of Antisemitism

This is one of the most disturbing – and dangerous – of the dynamics of the politics of exclusion in general, or the dynamics of antisemitism in particular. In a word, the xenophobic Russian nationalism of the New Right blames the Jews for the bringing about of Communism, while the old Communist Russian Left blames the Jews for the downfall of Communism. Either way, the Jew, once again, is the "enemy of someone's people".

(12) Empirical Data Regarding Antisemitism

Clearly, antisemitism would be particularly dangerous if it found support in the popular vote, and the beginning of that would be a growing expression of antisemitism in public opinion. In that regard, some of the recent data, albeit somewhat limited, is nonetheless disturbing.[10]

For example, a recent study of 500 new Soviet immigrants in Israel conducted in August 1990 showed that 69% of these immigrants had experienced some form of antisemitism. Of some 467 incidents of antisemitism reported in this study, 5% were direct physical assaults; 56% involved verbal assaults and distribution of antisemitic materials; 15% concerned harassment of children; and another 15% vandalism of property.

Similarly, a public opinion poll conducted in Moscow found that one in four Soviet citizens harboured antisemitic attitudes.

Nor can Soviet Jews take comfort from democratic movements in Eastern Europe. For a burgeoning antisemitism appears to be finding expression even in Central and Eastern Europe – including a new phenomena of antisemitism in countries without Jews, such as Poland – posing a danger even to the development of democratic institutions in these countries.

3. Countervailing Dynamics

It would be remiss not to mention the countervailing dynamics, namely the combatting of antisemitism that is also part of the age of Glasnost, Perestroika and Gorbachev.

For example, on July 24, 1990, for the first time in 70 years, the Soviet Union instituted a prosecution for antisemitic conduct against one Smirnov-Ostashvilli; and in October 1990 he became the first person ever tried and convicted under the Soviet law prohibiting incitement to racial hatred.

Also, for the first time ever in the history of international human rights agreements, at the Copenhagen Conference on the Human Dimension in June 1990, the Soviet Union co-sponsored a proposal with Canada that specifically condemned antisemitism in addition to condemning xenophobia, chauvinism and other racist conduct. Articles condemning antisemitism have appeared in Soviet papers alongside articles expressive of antisemitism; and unprecedented demonstrations condemning Pamyat and antisemitism have taken place in the streets of Moscow.

Nor should one ignore the fact that there is very little antisemitism amongst the mainstream independence and national movements – such as, for example in the Baltic republics or in the Ukraine. In both these areas one finds almost exemplary relations between the Jewish minority and the nationally based majority in these Republics.

[10] Study conducted by Anti-Defamation League in August, 1990.

In many ways, antisemitism – and the condition of Jews in the Soviet Union – may well be a "weather-vane" of the state of human rights and a politics of inclusion in a democratized Soviet Union. Some of the unanswered questions – or questions to be kept in mind as verification measures for this weather-vane, are as follows:

- Will a culture of human rights or democracy prevail over antisemitism – which democracy had ironically set free – or will antisemitism threaten democracy itself?
- Will the Russian Orthodox Church be part of the new religious sensibility – or will extremists foster an old/new theological antisemitism?
- Will antisemitism be nurtured as a form of "protected speech" under a Soviet version of the U.S. First Amendment Doctrine, or will Soviet Law – which is similar to Canadian and European anti-hate legislation – be invoked and applied against antisemites in the Soviet Union?
- Will the Politics of Ethnicity sublimate ethnic grievance, or will inter-ethnic violence claim the Jew as victim?
- Will the political meltdown – and politics of independence – lead to a new/safer multi-national mosaic, or will it result in a Hobbesian War of all against all?
- Will the dialectics of Glasnost and freedom of information develop a Jewish footprint for every disaster, or will truth prevail in the marketplace of ideas?
- Will there be a politics of inclusion as expressive of the process of democratization, or will the political uses of antisemitism become the new politics of exclusion?

4. Conclusion: Soviet Jewry and the Politics of Inclusion

Are Soviet Jews in physical danger today? For the most part, no. Admittedly, many Soviet Jews remain apprehensive about the danger of a pogrom but the evidence does not suggest that this is "a clear and present danger". It is true that during the last year there were a spate of horror stories about different types of violent murders of Jews because they were Jews. However, it turned out upon investigation that some never happened, and some happened but not because the victims were Jewish. The kind of brushfire rumour that went across the Soviet Union about impending pogroms, and which had its apex last spring, fortunately did not prove to be true. This is not to understate the dangers, particularly to vulnerable communities in some of the Central Asian republics; but one must be very careful about making accusations that are not true, lest the real ones not be believed.

Are the gates of emigration in danger of closing? Both Yeltsin and Gorbachev proclaim that they are democrats and would not close the gates. Indeed, Gorbachev would not likely close the gates because his whole reform is contingent upon the economics of Perestroika, and this in turn is contingent upon technology and credits from the West. For Gorbachev, then, Soviet Jewry is a minor domestic issue in the Soviet Union, but it is a major issue in Soviet-American relations. It is sufficiently a marginal domestic issue that Gorbachev does not need to add it to all his present woes – both international and domestic.

Will most of Soviet Jewry leave? Historically, the sociology of Jewry is such that unless there is a gun pointed at their head, Jews will stay where they are. In 1989 enough Soviet Jews began to believe that they were being caught in a crossfire, even if the gun was not pointed specifically at their head, and so they began to assert their desire to leave, which became a kind of emotional contagion. The Soviet emigration movement became, in effect, not a movement of individuals and families but of entire communities – an emigration movement which began to take on the characteristics of an "exodus". But there are still enough Soviet Jews who believe that they can not only weather the gathering storm, but that they can actually develop a Jewish *geseilshaft* in the Soviet Union.

If Perestroika is a metaphor for the changing, if not revolutionary, transformations of the Soviet Union today, then, in the context of the dialectics of encounters inspired by this revolutionary transformation, pogrom can be a metaphor for the apprehended state of Soviet Jewry. But perhaps the dialectics of encounter we are witnessing will move the Jew from the politics of exclusion into the politics of inclusion together with other racial and religious minorities in a changed Soviet Union.

ABDULLAHI AHMED AN-NA'IM*

Cross-Cultural Support for Equitable Participation in Subsaharan Africa

1. Introduction

The exclusion of religious, ethnic or racial minorities from equitable participation in the political process of their countries is one of the major global challenges facing the human rights movement. At the heart of this challenge is the tension between the nature and implications of solidarity, on the one hand, and the demands of equality and equitable participation, on the other.[1] Solidarity is usually taken to be inherently exclusive of the "other", in that the perceptions of one group's interests are necessarily antagonistic and irreconcilable with the those of other groups. Action in pursuit of group interests, it is normally assumed, can only be at the expense of the interests of other groups. Yet in an increasingly interdependent and interactive world, this exclusive view of solidarity cannot and should not be maintained. The challenge facing the human rights movement is how to maintain equality and equitable participation despite the existence of different and often competing bases of solidarity.

This paper focuses on the role of religious identity as grounds for exclusion from equitable participation in Subsaharan Africa, without in any way suggesting that it is peculiar to this part of the world.[2] For illustrative purposes some brief references are made to Uganda, Kenya, Malawi and Zambia.

* Ariel F. Sallows Professor of Human Rights, College of Law, University of Saskatchewan, Saskatoon, Saskatchewan, Canada. I am grateful to Shelley Cooper-Stephenson for editorial assistance in preparing this paper.

[1] Equality and equitable participation are complex concepts which cannot be discussed in detail here. See generally, Warwick McKean, *Equality and Discrimination Under International Law* (1983), Oxford: Claredon Press. For an example of a debate on equality in a particular constitutional and political context see, Peter Westen, "The Empty Idea of Equality," *Harvard Law Review* (1982), vol. 95, 3, pp. 537–96; Kent Greenawalt, "How Empty is the Idea of Equality," *Columbia Law Review* (1983), vol. 83, pp. 1167–85; Peter Westen, "To Lure the Tarantula from its Hole: A Response," Ibid., pp. 1187–208; Peter Westen, "The Meaning of Equality in Law, Science, Math and Morals: A Reply," *Michigan Law Review* (1983), vol. 81, pp. 604–63 and Erwin Chemerinsky, "In Defence of Equality: A Reply to Professor Westen," Ibid., pp. 575–99.

[2] See generally the two studies prepared for the U.N. Sub-Commission on Prevention of Discrimination and Protection of Minorities by Arcot Krishnaswami, *Study of Discrimination in*

K.E. Mahoney and P. Mahoney (eds.), Human Rights in the Twenty-first Century, 133–148.

Conclusions are drawn through a case study of the situation in the Sudan. These issues are discussed in the context of particular nation States, despite the arbitrariness of political boundaries and weakness of the State in post-colonial Africa – and perhaps because of that.

While it is unwise to over-generalize about majority/minority relations because of the wide variety of minorities and the contexts within which they interact with majorities,[3] in this paper sharp distinctions are not drawn between religious and ethnic or racial minorities in Subsaharan Africa, because ethnic identity often includes a religious factor.[4] In the case of Asians in Kenya and Uganda, for example, it may not be possible to distinguish between religion and other factors which contribute to the identification of an excluded population and the rationalization of their exclusion.[5] Moreover, general similarities between historical and present status of minorities defined by these inter-related identity features in many parts of the world exist, including in Subsaharan Africa.[6]

The thesis in this paper consists of three elements.

First, all religious and ethnic groups within the nation State should strive for, and be allowed to realize, different and overlapping levels of solidarity, from the broadest universal level to national and sub-national levels. Each level should seek to accommodate the legitimate demands of other levels of solidarity. The fundamental criterion for defining the legitimate demands of each level of solidarity is the principle of reciprocity (also known as the "golden

---

the Matter of Religious Rights and Practices (1960), New York: United Nations, (U.N. Sales No. E.60.XIV.2); and Elizabeth Odio Benito, *Elimination of all Forms of Intolerance and Discrimination Based on Religion or Belief* (1989), New York: United Nations, (U.N. Sales No. E.89.XIV.3). For documentation of this problem and legal responses to it in many parts of the world see the series of reports prepared by Angelo Vidal d'Almeida Ribeiro, Special Rapporteur for the U.N. Commission on Human Rights on the implementation of the 1981 Declaration on the Elimination of All Forms of Intolerance and of Discrimination Based on Religion or Belief. E.CN.4/1986/37, E/CN.4/1987/35, E/CN.4/1988/45, E/CN.4/1989/44, and E/CN.4/1990/46.

[3] F. Heckmann, "Toward the Development of a Typology of Minorities," in C. Fried (ed.) *Minorities: Community and Identity* (1983), Berlin, Germany: Spinger-Verlag, pp. 9–23.

[4] Robert G. Wirsing, "Dimensions of Minority Protection," in Wirsing (ed.) *Protection of Ethnic Minorities: Comparative Perspectives* (1981), New York: Pergamon Press, p. 7. Cf. O. Patterson, "The Nature, Causes, and Implications of Ethnic Identification," in Fried (ed.) *Minorities: Community and Identity*, See note 3, *supra*, pp. 25–50.

[5] The case of the East African Asians illustrates the complexity and interplay of ethnicity and religion with economic and political factors leading to the exclusion, indeed physical expulsion in this case, of a minority. Space does not permit a detailed examination of this case. See generally, Dharam P. Ghai and Yash P. Ghai (ed.) *Portrait of a Minority: Asians in East Africa* (rev. ed., 1970), Nairobi: Oxford University Press; Michael Twaddle (ed.) *Expulsion of a Minority: Essays on Ugandan Asians* (1975), London: The Athlone Press; and Yash Tandon *Problems of a Displaced Minority: The New Position of East Africa's Asians* (1984), London: Minority Rights Group.

[6] See generally, Minority Rights Group, *World Directory of Minorities* (1990), Essex, U.K.: Longman, Chicago: St. James Press. African minorities are discussed on pp. 216–83.

rule"). By this is meant that each group must concede to the other(s) what it claims for itself. The implementation of this principle will ensure equality and equitable participation for all religious, ethnic or racial groups and safeguard collective and individual human rights.

Second, religious and ethnic or racial identity is too deeply embedded in local cultural traditions to be disregarded in human rights discourse in these countries. The internal terms of such identity should be transformed in order to accommodate the legitimate demands of the other. This can be done within the framework of local cultural traditions by drawing on generally accepted values and by working with existing institutions. The establishment of different yet mutually-inclusive levels of solidarity should be undertaken through culturally legitimate means, with due regard to local conditions. This dynamic and flexible process would allow for a variety of approaches within the framework of the principle of reciprocity. The pursuit of internal cultural legitimacy should also take into account the perspectives and resources of other relevant cultural traditions. In other words, a cross-cultural approach to promote mutually inclusive levels of solidarity should be sought.

Third, although voluntary compliance with the principle of reciprocity must be the objective, a degree of "pressure" may be necessary to induce voluntary compliance. The pursuit of equality and equitable participation is a struggle drawing on several resources, in both the domestic and international spheres. Domestic pressure should mobilize relevant cultural and cross-cultural resources in support of different, yet mutually-inclusive levels of solidarity. The political, economic and social costs of denial of reciprocity and exclusion of religious or other groups from equitable participation should be highlighted as the interests of the majority are also jeopardized by denial of the rights of minorities.[7] The international sphere of the struggle should include monitoring, documentation of, and protest against human rights violations. Governments of other countries should be encouraged to pressure offending governments to comply with reciprocity principles. Both the domestic and international efforts should seek to adjust the relative bargaining positions and power relations of the victims and perpetrators.

2. Historical Background and Context

The three most relevant religious traditions in Subsaharan Africa are Christianity, Islam and what is commonly referred to as the traditional African religion(s).[8] Traditional religions are the oldest and previously the most pervasive in the region. Until recently it was commonly assumed that little could

[7] Robert G. Wirsing, "Dimensions of Minority Protection," in Robert G. Wirsing (ed.) *Protection of Ethnic Minorities: Comparative Perspectives*, pp. 3–4.

[8] See generally, Geoffrey Parrinder, *Africa's Three Religions* (1976), London: Sheldon Press. The term traditional religion refers to preliterate belief systems, sometimes called animism,

be known about them, with any reasonable degree of certainty.[9] It has also been commonly assumed that traditional African religions by nature, were primarily local or clan (tribal) belief systems, operating within the context of highly personalized traditional, social and political organization.[10] There may have been similarities or common themes and features among some of them, especially those of adjacent or physically close communities.[11]

More is known about these traditions now. With forthcoming developments and refinements of appropriate methodology, a comprehensive and systematic understanding of their continued role and influence will likely soon evolve. At this point, however, one must be careful in making broad generalizations about their content and impact on political and social institutions and practices,[12] especially in relation to present-day communities living under the totally transformed contexts of the modern nation State. But the available literature seems to indicate that within the historical context traditional religions were an integral part of a living, comprehensive cultural system that encompassed all fields of human activity.[13] Their primarily local or clan focus would lead one to expect that there was little articulation of the norms which regulated inter-religious relations. As part of the integrated cultural system as whole, however,

---

fetishism or polytheism, which had no scriptures of their own, no ancient texts and no old expressions of faith. Ibid., p. 8. For a general explanation of African traditional religions and critique of terms and classifications applied to them in earlier Western scholarship see B.I. Sharevskaya, *The Religious Traditions of Tropical Africa in Contemporary Focus* (1973), Budapest: Center for Afro-Asian Research of the Hungarian Academy of Sciences, pp. 13–66.

[9] Some African scholars challenge the common belief in the impossibility of reconstructing a history of the traditional religion. See, for example, Review of Parrinder's *Religion in Africa®*. This book has been republished as *Africa's Three Religions*, cited above by B.A. Ogot, in *African Historical Studies* (1970), vol. III, no. 1, pp. 182–83. On methods for the reconstruction of early religious history see T.O. Ranger and I.N. Kimambo (ed.) *The Historical Study of African Religion* (1972), Berkeley and Los Angeles: University of California Press, pp. 27–70. This book contains several studies of specific traditional African religions. See also Charles Edward Fuller, "Native and Missionary Religions," in Stanley Diamond & Fred G. Burke (ed.) *The Transformation of East Africa* (1966), New York, London: Basic Books, pp. 511–35.

[10] In relation to the peoples of Zambia between the 16th to 18th centuries, for example, see A. Roberts, *A History of Zambia* (1976), New York: Africanan Publications, pp. 72–79 or London: Heinemann Educational Books.

[11] These themes and features have been explored by some writers to develop notions of regional and territorial cults. See, for example, R.P. Werbner (ed.) *Regional Cults* (1977), New York: Academic Press; and J.M. Schoffeleers, (ed.) *Guardians of the Land: Essays on Central African Territorial Cults* (1979), Gwelo: Mambo Press.

[12] It may have been true certain cults did cut across ethnic and regional boundaries as argued by some scholars. K. Asare Opoku, "Religion in Africa during the colonial era," in A. Adu Boahen (ed.) *General History of Africa, Volume VII: Africa under Colonial Domination 1880–1935* (1985), Paris: UNESCO; London: Heinemann Educational Books and Berkeley: University of California Press, pp. 514–16. But that would not change the fact that traditional African religions in general were local and fragmentary.

[13] Ibid., pp. 508–11. See generally Parrinder, *Africa's Three Religions*, pp. 88–96; and Matthew Schoffeleers, "The History and Political Role of the M'Bona Cult among the Mang'anja," in Ranger & Kimambo, *The Historical Study of African Religion*, pp. 73–94.

one would expect them to have reflected both the antagonism and coexistence that characterized the general relationships between adherents of different religions.[14] The terms of these relationships would have been dictated by the exigencies of varying degrees of rivalry and competition over scarce resources and the demands of communal or clan security.

Of the five countries focused on in this study, Islam is significantly present in Kenya and Uganda, and to a lesser extent in Malawi and Zambia, but it is the dominant religion in the Sudan.[15] There appears to be a striking difference between the way Islam has been conceived and the impact it has had, and continues to have, on inter-religious relations in the Sudan on the one hand, and in the remaining four countries on the other. Even in relation to the Sudan, there are significant differences in perceptions of Islam, including the Islamic view of inter-religious relations, during different phases of recent Sudanese history. Traditionally, Islam in Subsaharan Africa (including the Sudan, except under the two totalitarian phases of the first Islamic state of 1885–98 and the second Islamic state of 1983 to the present) tends to be more social than political, and rather tolerant and accommodating of other religions. However, as discussed below, Islam can also be presented and practiced as a totalitarian political ideology which oppresses and excludes non-Muslims. The reasons behind these differences and their relevance to the subject of this paper must be understood.

It must first be noted that the Islamic tradition encompasses a broad spectrum of perspectives, ranging from a strictly legalistic, doctrinal approach, which claims an organic link between religion and politics, to the highly personal mystic (*sufi*) perspective, which emphasizes the authenticity of private religious experience.[16] In contrast to the material and rigid nature of the first approach, the second is more spiritual and adaptive in orientation.[17]

Unlike North Africa where it initially came through military conquest, Islam spread into Subsaharan Africa primarily through the efforts of *sufi* masters and preachers. It interacted and coexisted with pre-existing traditional African religions for centuries.[18] These two features constitute one of the main underlying causes of the social and tolerant nature of Subsaharan Islam in

[14] David Parkin, "Politics of Ritual Syncretism: Islam Among the Non-Muslim Giriama of Kenya," *Journal of the International African Institute* (1970), vol. XL, 3, pp. 217–33.

[15] I.M. Lewis, "Introduction," in I.M. Lewis (ed.) *Islam in Tropical Africa* (1966), Oxford: Oxford University Press, pp. 9–15; Yusuf Fadl Hasan, "The Penetration of Islam in the Eastern Sudan," Ibid. pp. 144–55; George Shepperson, "The Jumbe of Kota Kota and Some Aspects of the History of Islam in British Central Africa," Ibid., pp. 193–204; and David S. Bone, "Islam in Malawi," *Journal of Religion in Africa* (1982), vol. XIII, 2, pp. 126–38.

[16] For a survey and critique of modern Islamic reform reflecting this diversity see Abdullahi Ahmed An-Na'im, *Toward an Islamic Reformation: Civil Liberties, Human Rights and International Law* (1990), Syracuse: Syracuse University Press, chapter 3.

[17] See for example, Azim Nanji, "Modernization and Change in the Nizari Ismaili Community in East Africa – A Perspective," *Journal of Religion in Africa* (1975), vol. VI, 2, pp. 121–39.

[18] See Lewis, "Introduction," in Lewis (ed.) *Islam in Tropical Africa*, pp. 20–75; and I.J.S. Trimingham, "The Phases of Islamic Expansion and Islamic Culture Zones in Africa", Ibid., pp. 127–39.

general. The possibility is ever-present, however, that the strictly legalistic approach might gain support among the local Muslim population (for a variety of reasons that cannot be detailed here), causing them to seek the establishment of a totalitarian Islamic State to the exclusion of non-Muslims in the area. This is what happened during the nineteenth century through the so-called *jihad* movement of West Africa which reached the present day Sudan and led to the establishment of the first totalitarian Islamic (Mahdist) State in the history of the country.[19] Since the early 1980's a second cycle of totalitarian Islam appears to be gaining momentum in the Sudan. Such a shift from accommodation to exclusion, however, is unlikely to materialize where Muslims are unable to exert hegemony over the non-Muslim population.

Two conclusions can be drawn, therefore, in relation to Islam and the question of religious exclusion. First, there is a choice within the Islamic tradition between exclusion and accommodation. This is important for facilitating the cultural legitimacy of the transformation of religious solidarity among Muslims, in order to accommodate other levels of solidarity. One does not cease to be a Muslim by accommodating non-Muslims and according them their right to religious solidarity. Second, this culturally legitimate transformation of Islamic solidarity is more likely to be achieved under power relations where Muslims are not in a clearly homogenous position.

The history of Christianity in Africa as a whole is long and complex, but its significant presence in Subsaharan Africa dates only to the late nineteenth century colonial era.[20] Although much has been done since de-colonization to indigenize and legitimize Christianity as a local religion,[21] some problems may still persist. In particular, Christianity's history of close association with the colonial State undermined the principle of separation of church and State[22] and

[19] On the *jihad* movement see M. Last, "Reform in West Africa: The Jihad Movements of the Nineteenth Century," in J.F.A. Ajayi and M. Crowder (ed.) *History of West Africa* (1974), Vol. II, London: Longman, p. 1–29; M.G. Smith, "The Jihad of Shehu Dan Fodio: Some Problems," Ibid., pp. 408–20. See generally, P.M. Holt, *The Mahdist State in the Sudan 1881–98* (1970), Oxford: Oxford University Press.

[20] Asare Opoku, "Religion in Africa during the colonial era," pp. 512–13; Steven Kaplan, "The Africanization of Missionary Christianity: History and Typology," *Journal of Religion in Africa* (1986), vol. XVI, 3, pp. 166–86. For a brief history see Parrinder, *Africa's Three Religions*, pp. 101–36. In relation to the region in question see generally Fuller, "Native and Missionary Religions"; and Robert I. Rotberg, *The Rise of Nationalism in Central Africa* (1966), New York: Basic Books, chapter 1.

[21] Asare Opoku, "Religion in Africa during the colonial era," pp. 529–37. See generally, Edward Fasholé-Luke, *et. al.*, *Christianity in Independent Africa* (1978), Bloomington, IN: Indiana University Press; and Aylward Shorter, *African Christian Theology – Adaptation or Incarnation?* (1977), Maryknoll, NY: Orbis Books.

[22] See generally, for example, Holger Bernt Hansen, *Mission, Church and State in a Colonial Setting: Uganda 1890–1925* (1984), New York: St. Martin's Press; and Renison Muchiri Githige, "The Mission State Relationship in Colonial Kenya: A Summary," *Journal of Religion in Africa* (1982), vol. XIII, 2, pp. 110–25.

probably continues to do so. Separation may not be easy to achieve notwithstanding the European and North American models. The process of separation must be indigenized and sensitized to local African circumstances and cultural traditions. In order to develop working African models of the relationship[23] a process of trial and error will be necessary as it was in Europe.

Another source of tension relates to doctrinal and institutional aspects of European Christianity. On the one hand, Christianity in Europe was the first officially-established religion and later became the religion of the State and the establishment. As such it tended to be conservative and supportive of the *status quo* both internally, within the institutional hierarchy of the church, and externally, in its relationship with the State. Yet the fundamental doctrine of Christianity can be and has been interpreted as protest or even as revolutionary ideology, as evidenced by Christian religious protest in colonial central Africa and recent liberation theology of Latin America.[24]

Finally, it should be noted that Christianity can be as intolerant and uncompromising as Islam. This is clearly reflected in its history of antagonism to other religions including Islam, and among different Christian denominations[25] in Subsaharan Africa. Christian missionaries also had a negative attitude towards African religion and culture and were determined right from the start to stamp them out.[26] Such a heritage can hardly be conducive to equality and equitable participation for religious groups. In fact, this heritage has tended to generate antagonism and counter-exclusion.

Moreover, while a religious group may claim Christian doctrine in support of its protest ideology, State and establishment Christianity can be used to justify and rationalize the persecution of members of that group and the denial of their equitable participation. As in the case of Islam, however, the existence of competing interpretations of Christianity provides possibilities for re-examination of the meaning and implications of religious solidarity, thereby enhancing the prospects of accommodation and inclusion of religious minorities. The importance of adjusting bargaining positions and power relations among Christian, as well as between Christian and non-Christian groups in order to develop mutually-inclusive levels of solidarity must be reiterated.

[23] For a treatment of these issues in a specific African context see, F.B. Welbourn, *Religion and Politics in Uganda 1952–62* (1965), Nairobi, Kenya: East African Publishing House.

[24] See note 19 *supra*, Rotberg, *The Rise of Nationalism in Central Africa*, chapter VI, pp. 135–155.

[25] Fuller, "Native and Missionary Religions," pp. 523–26.

[26] Asare Opoku, "Religion in Africa During the Colonial Era," p. 526.

3. Majority/Minority Relation and the Exclusion of Religious Groups

There are some controversial and unresolved issues relating to objective and subjective components of the definition of majority and minority.[27] For example, should these terms be defined in numerical, sociological or political terms? To what extent do members of each group have to be aware of, and act according to, the status of their group in relation to other groups for the majority/minority relationship to operate? Space does not permit dealing with these and other issues except to specify that this paper is concerned with a political majority that is seeking to exclude the minority or minorities from equitable participation.

Many internal and external factors contribute to the determination of the existing or possible future majority/minority relationship. Some of these factors would be peculiar to certain situations while others are encountered in different situations. The majority/minority relationship in a given situation is often described in terms of demands by (aspirations and expectations of) the minority and reactions to them by the majority.[28] This sort of inquiry should include examination of other issues, such as the capacity of the minority to formulate demands, the nature of the demands actually made, and strategies pursued by the minority as well as the possibilities of their success – all in relation to the particular context. The situation can also be described from the other side of the coin, that is to say, in terms of demands, policies and actions of the majority against or in relation to the minority, and the latter's reaction to them.

It has been suggested that acceptable options for majority/minority relations should be adjudged in accordance with the standard of "humane incorporation". According to the authors of this standard, acceptable options should

> provide minorities with genuine opportunities for humane incorporation: *incorporation* in that members of every minority should be fully able, if they wish, to enjoy the shared status of equal citizens available to all without discrimination; *humane* primarily in that members of each minority should be fully able, if they wish, to enjoy also the special identity of membership in their own community. This standard of humane incorporation requires a practical synthesis of pairs of principles that pull in opposite directions: incorporation into the majority culture and preservation of the minority culture, a universality across the whole society and a particularity within constituent groups.[29]

[27] Warren Weinstein, "Africa", in Robert G. Wirsing (ed.) *Protection of Ethnic Minorities: Comparative Perspectives*, p. 215.

[28] A.D. Murray, *et. al.*, "Minority Demands, Majority Reactions?" in Fried (ed.) *Minorities: Community and Identity*, pp. 193–217.

[29] H. Shue, Rapporteur, "Humane Incorporation: The Shape of Acceptable Options for Relations Between Majorities and Minorities," in Fried, (ed.) *Minorities: Community and Identity*, pp. 283–84.

The authors explained feasible options in relation to foreign groups (e.g., migrant workers) as well as domestic ones, and the appropriate criteria for selecting between or mixing these options. In their view, these criteria are historical conceptions of citizenship, and philosophical conceptions of community, namely, the ideal of social democracy and the value or right of self-determination. The first philosophical conception (the ideal of social democracy) refers to the idea that if a government is to provide the requisite level of economic and social security, then it must limit the number of people toward whom it bears these responsibilities. This argument could justify the exclusion of migrant workers, notwithstanding long residence in the country. The second philosophical conception is the value of self-determination of communities: the right of a political community to shape its own character.[30] This criterion is relevant here because the exclusion of indigenous religious and ethnic minorities is often rationalized as necessary for the exercise of the right to self-determination by the majority.

The standard of humane incorporation does not provide immediate resolution of all issues of majority/minority relations. It is not enough to say that universality across the whole society and particularity within constituent groups must somehow be balanced without offering guidance on how that balance can be achieved. One possible guiding principle is to make a distinction between the public and private domains – allotting equal participation to public affairs and shared identity with one's minority to private affairs. Some Muslim and Christian groups, for example, may not accept this distinction, and may believe that they should act as Muslims or Christians at least in some public affairs. This may be necessary in order to preserve their religious identity in the private domain. In any case, the public/private dichotomy does not necessarily resolve basic practical issues of majority/minority relations. For example, is education a public, private or mixed matter, and what are the policy implications of its classification?[31]

Nevertheless, the standard of humane incorporation provides a useful framework for arbitrating some fundamental aspects of majority/minority relations. It can provide a sufficient basis for judging clear cases of inequality and inequitable exclusion of religious groups. Even in difficult border-line cases, the basic rationale of the humane incorporation can be helpful in mediating competing claims to self-determination. It is important to establish that there are limits to what the majority may reasonably do and that those limits are indicated by notions of reciprocal recognition of majority and minority rights. To recognize another group's right to self-determination necessarily implies respect for a minimum level of equality and equitable participation in the enterprise of the nation State.

The principle of humane incorporation appears to be designed to deal with the usual type of problems of majority/minority relations which arise when

[30] Ibid., pp. 285–91.
[31] Ibid., pp. 295–98.

minorities are excluded from equitable participation or otherwise denied the benefits of equality. But how can it be useful in cases where a religious minority, such as the Jehovah's Witnesses in Malawi and Zambia, is being forced or pressured to participate in the political process against its will, or in violation of the tenets of its faith? How does the standard of humane incorporation apply to situations where a minority demands to be left alone rather than to be allowed to participate?

Jehovah's Witnesses, the members of an American-based millenarian religious sect known as "Watch Tower Bible and Tract Society," have suffered harassment and persecution by governments in many parts of the world.[32] Of the five countries focused on in this paper, Jehovah's witnesses face most serious persecution and hardship in Malawi and Zambia, but they are also vulnerable to similar treatment in Kenya and Uganda.[33] Although the movement has long lost the overtly political and rebellious image it had during the first half of this century, Jehovah's Witnesses are perceived by African political leaders to be subversive precisely because they refuse to participate in the political process. They are accused of "attempting to undermine national unity and sabotage development".[34] They are also seen by many African politicians as obstacles to the building of stable one-party regimes, indeed as competitors of the ruling political parties. As an easily identifiable, socially conspicuous and politically defenseless minority, Jehovah's Witnesses sometimes serve as useful scapegoats for the failures of governments. Since they concentrate exclusively on their evangelical work without contributing to national services in education and health, it has been suggested that African governments may feel that little is lost by persecuting them.[35]

The standard of humane incorporation speaks of genuine opportunities to enjoy shared status of equal citizenship, not compulsion to do so. It "indicates which kinds of opportunities ought to be protected, not which kinds of opportunities individuals ought to choose".[36]

As such, this standard should apply to protect the minority's right not to participate in the political process, if it so wishes, as well as protecting it against inequitable exclusion. This right not to participate in the political process however, does not exempt members of the minority from other obligations of citizenship such as the duty to pay taxes and to conform with the laws of the land which respect their right to exclude themselves. They cannot object to these

[32] The level and severity of such harassment and persecution range from concentration camps in Nazi Germany to banning by Canada and Australia during the Second World War because of the Witnesses' pacifist teachings. Tony Hodges, *Jehovah's Witnesses in Africa* (rev. ed., 1985), London: The Minority Rights Group Report No. 29, p. 3.

[33] Ibid. pp. 4–6 and 9–10. See also Bryan R. Wilson, "Jehovah's Witnesses in Kenya," *Journal of Religion in Africa* (1974), vol. v, 2, pp. 128–49.

[34] Ernie Regehr in *Christian Century*, 7–14 January 1976, as quoted in Hodges, "Jehovah's Witnesses in Africa," p. 9.

[35] Hodges, "Jehovah's Witnesses in Africa," p. 9.

[36] Shue, Rapporteur, "Humane Incorporation: The Shape of Acceptable Options for Relations between Majorities and Minorities," p. 284.

obligations on the ground that they did not participate in their imposition, because it was their choice to abstain from such participation.[37] This variation on the principle may be called the "standard of humane non-incorporation".

Although the case of a religious minority resisting inclusion is different from that of one suffering exclusion, the promotion of culturally legitimate and mutually inclusive levels of solidarity through the principle of reciprocity – the thesis of this paper – can be helpful in both types of situations.

4. The Promotion of Equality and Equitable Participation in Subsaharan Africa

It is logically possible to promote the development of different, yet mutually-inclusive levels of group solidarity within the nation State. This is because nobody identifies with the same group or opposes the same set of "others" all the time.[38]

At the domestic level, the legitimacy of the notion of different yet mutually-inclusive levels of solidarity should be established through internal cultural discourse and cross-cultural dialogue. People should be shown that their own cultural tradition sanctions this notion, and that others will also accept and honor it. This process must be undertaken simultaneously within all relevant cultural traditions. For example, it must be undertaken within both the Christian and Islamic traditions in general, and within those traditions in the context of the particular country in question. As one aspect of the concept of cross-cultural support for equitable participation, both Christians and Muslims must seek ways of enhancing the notion of multiple yet mutually-inclusive levels of solidarity from within their own traditions. At the same time, they must be able to refer to and rely upon similar efforts to do the same within the other tradition.

The universal cultural legitimacy of the principle of reciprocity is crucial for the success of this domestic level. Since members of the majority claim the right to maintain their group identity without sacrificing their right to equality and equitable participation, they must concede the same rights to the members of the minority. This principle is compelling because it is recognized by all cultural traditions and it is sanctioned by the knowledge that those denied reciprocal recognition of their rights will resort to whatever means are available to them in order to redress the situation. Members of the minority must have the full and equal opportunity (not the obligation) to enjoy the status of equal citizens, while being able to enjoy also the special identity of membership in their own

[37] The principle of this case is similar to that of exemption from military service on grounds of pacifist or religious beliefs. While operative only in relation to the type of obligation of citizenship objected to on grounds of faith or belief, the exemption would not apply to non-military national service or other general duties.

[38] S. Wallman, "Identity Options," in Fried (ed.) *Minorities: Community and Identity*, pp. 69–78.

community, because the majority claims both aspects of the standard of humane incorporation for its members.

Underlying this domestic level of the struggle for equality and equitable participation are the dynamics of power relations and relative bargaining positions. An appeal to the majority's sense of justice and to the dictates of the principle of reciprocity is necessary, but may not be sufficient, to accord the minority equal rights to national and group identities even though it is in the majority's self-interest to respect the rights of minorities. The majority may be made to see this through domestic political discourse before the minority is forced to resort to drastic action to enforce its rights. But given the reality of the weakness of minorities in normal situations, part of this burden of adjusting power relations and relative bargaining positions may fall on external forces. This is the role of the international human rights movement.

The basic difficulty at the international level of action is the tension between national sovereignty and self-determination and the need to support oppressed and persecuted minorities.[39] Admittedly there are dangers and problems with "foreign" intervention in the domestic affairs of other countries, but lack of concern and action in the face of serious human rights violation is unacceptable. It is not within the scope of this paper to discuss in detail ways and means of implementing sufficient safeguards for international action in support of human rights, but much of the resentment and suspicion of international action can be dispelled if sufficient sensitivity to the cultural integrity of the community being criticized is displayed. Such criticisms are sometimes labelled "cultural imperialism," indicating that external values and standards are being imposed on the target community. To the extent that external criticisms are shown to be emanating from values and norms shared by the community in question, the label of cultural imperalism would not be valid.[40]

If even culturally sensitive criticism is not enough to change attitudes and policies,then action in support of the human rights of excluded minorities in the form of political pressure and economic sanctions is legitimate in order to influence the behavior of offending governments.[41]Since each situation has its own circumstances and dynamics, methods and tactics should always be selected and constantly evaluated in accordance with the requirements of practical efficacy in the given situation.

[39] See generally, Richard Falk, *Human Rights and State Sovereignty* (1981), New York: Holmes and Meier Publishers.

[40] See generally Abdullahi Ahmed An-Na'im, "Problems of Universal Cultural Legitimacy for Human Rights," in A. An-Na'im and F. Deng (ed.) *Human Rights in Africa: Cross-Cultural Perspectives* (1990), Washington, D.C.: The Brookings Institution, p. 331; and Abdullahi Ahmed An-Na'im, "Toward a Cross-Cultural Approach to Defining International Standards of Human Rights: The Meaning of Cruel, Inhuman or Degrading Treatment or Punishment," in A. An-Na'im (ed.) *Human Rights in Cross-Cultural Perspectives* (1992), Philadelphia, PA: University of Pennsylvania Press, p. 19.

[41] For the practice of Scandinavian countries in this regard see generally, Katarina Tomasevski, *Development Aid and Human Rights* (1989), London: Pinter Publishers.

The concept of inter-group bargaining can be useful in understanding and adjusting majority/minority relations.[42] Such bargaining can be tacit or direct, conscious or partly unconscious, and should be related to the international environment as well as the domestic scene.[43] Inter-group bargaining can relate to establishing the principle and mechanisms of bargaining itself, as well as to specific policies and governmental decisions. The international dimension is relevant to all these levels and types of bargaining situations.

There are limits to the availability and effectiveness of inter-group bargaining, however. For example, the majority or dominant group is unlikely to bargain if it thinks that it can achieve or retain hegemony through forcible domination, assimilation or extermination of the minority or by forcing it to leave, as happened with the Asian minority of East Africa.[44] Adjusting power relations and relative bargaining positions is only part of the struggle for equality and equitable participation for religious minorities, not the sole and conclusive answer to the problem. Its success or failure depends on complex and interrelated factors which should be discussed in relation to a specific situation.

5. Equitable Participation for Non-Muslims in the Sudan

The present situation in the Sudan is a useful case-study for the application of the thesis of this paper because it represents both the complexity and urgency of the issues. Inequality and inequitable exclusion of minorities is clearly a major part of the underlying causes of the civil war which has raged intermittently in that country for decades and claimed hundreds of thousands of lives. Whole communities have been uprooted and displaced and massive human rights violations committed.[45] But religious exclusion can neither be singled out as the sole cause of the conflict nor disentangled from historical, ethnic, cultural and other causes and factors contributing to a complex web of developments and events.[46] Nevertheless, the religious factor is highlighted because its independent role and contribution to other causes of the conflict are becoming

[42] See generally, Donald Rothchild, *Racial Bargaining in Independent Kenya: A Study of Minorities and Decolonization* (1973), London, New York, Nairobi: Oxford University Press.

[43] Ibid., pp. 7–13. In chapter 13 of this book, Rothchild discussed how Kenya made extensive concessions to secure continuing support from international capitalism.

[44] Ibid., pp. 13–17.

[45] For a recent comprehensive record and documentation of massive human rights and humanitarian problems arising from this conflict, see generally, Africa Watch, *Denying "The Honor of Living": Sudan, a Human Rights Disaster* (1990), New York and Washington: Human Rights Watch.

[46] On the causes and development of this protracted conflict see M. O. Beshir, *The Southern Sudan: Background to Conflict* (1968), London: C. Hurst; Oliver B. Albino, *The Sudan: A Southern Viewpoint* (1970), London: Oxford University Press; Dunstan M. Wai (ed.) *The Southern Sudan: The Problem of National Integration* (1973), London: Frank Cass; and Abel Alier, *Southern Sudan: Too Many Agreements Dishonoured* (1990), Exeter, England: Ithaca Press.

increasingly more important. A brief sketch of recent history and developments is necessary to put issues in perspective.

Although the Sudan is characterized by a very high of degree of ethnic, religious and cultural diversity throughout the country, its population can be broadly divided into the Arabized Muslims of the north and African non-Muslims of the south.[47] Historical, geographical, social and economic factors (aggravated by the British colonial policy, which neglected the south and restricted movement and integration between northern and southern Sudan until the late 1940s) also contribute to this north/south dichotomy in the country. The recent northern drive to deny non-Muslims equality and equitable participation has created a serious and immediate obstacle to peace, stability and development in the country.

The first phase of the civil war in the Sudan lasted from 1955 to 1972, when it was settled through what is known as the "Addis Ababa Agreement", which granted the south regional autonomy within a unitary country.[48] That Agreement was implemented through the *Regional Self-Government Act* of 1972 which was entrenched in the Constitution of 1973. By the late 1970s, however, the Government of former President Numeiri started to adopt a policy of Islamization designed to transform the Sudan into an "Islamic" republic.[49] That policy culminated in the wholesale enactment, in 1983, of legislation based on historical Islamic law (*Shari'a*) in violation of the Addis Ababa Agreement and the 1973 Constitution.[50] To eliminate opposition to Islamization from the non-Muslim southern Sudanese, Numeiri took a series of measures between 1979 and 1983, including dissolutions of the southern Regional People's Assembly and Governments and the division of the region into smaller provinces. This combination of developments led to the resumption of the civil war in the southern Sudan, on-going since 1983.

In April 1985, Numeiri was overthrown by a civilian uprising which encouraged the military to seize power and establish a transitional government until power was handed over to civilian leadership. One year later, general elections were held, mainly in the north, because the security situation did not permit elections in most parts of the south. The civilian governments of Prime Minister Sadiq al-Mahdi failed to end the civil war or implement its electoral promise to repeal the *Shari'a* laws of 1983. Civilian rule was overthrown by the military *coup d'etat* of 1989. This latest *coup* is generally believed to have been

[47] Most southern Sudanese profess traditional African religions, but the educated and modern political leaders are generally Christians. The shorter term "non-Muslim" is used here because it indicates that non-belief in Islam is the operative element of religious exclusion.

[48] See generally, M.O. Beshir, *The Southern Sudan: From Conflict to Peace* (1975), London: C. Hurst.

[49] Numeiri did not start the quest for an Islamic sate in the Sudan, but his government was the first to translate that vague aspiration of northern Sudanese into concrete policies and practical measures. See Abdullahi Ahmed An-Na'im, "The Elusive Islamic Constitution: The Sudanese Experience," *Orient* (1985), vol. 26, p. 329.

[50] On the scope and speed of this legislative *coup* see Carey N. Gordon, "The Islamic Legal Revolution: The Case of Sudan," *The International Lawyer* (1985), vol. 19, p. 793.

sponsored by the National Islamic Front, which was the primary force behind Numeiri's policy of Islamization. In any case, it is clear that this military regime is more committed to *Shari'a* and the establishment of a totalitarian Islamic state than any government in the country's history since the Mahdist state of the last century.

An Islamic State under *Shari'a* is inherently exclusive of non-Muslims. *Shari'a* confines citizenship to Muslims with a limited degree of communal autonomy in private matters and certain guarantees of personal safety and property for non-Muslim believers or *Dhimmis*.[51] *Dhimmis* are not entitled to hold any elected, executive or judicial position which involves exercising authority over Muslims. This status of *dhimma*, (tolerated or protected communities) is not available to those who profess traditional African religions because *Shari'a* does not recognize them as believers.[52] Thus, all non-Muslims under a *Shari'a* State in the Sudan will be denied equality and equitable participation, but the specific negative consequences are much more serious for believers in traditional African religions, the majority of southern Sudanese.

As I have argued elsewhere, the only way to resolve the present conflict and lay the foundations of peace, stability and prosperity in the Sudan is through the establishment of a genuine national consensus on the principles of constitutionalism which guarantee equality and equitable participation for all Sudanese, without distinction on grounds such as religion, race or gender.[53] In terms of the first element of the thesis of this paper, that is the development of different yet mutually inclusive levels of solidarity, all Sudanese must strive for and be allowed to realize their respective distinct religious, ethnic, cultural identity, while retaining their full rights to equality and equitable participation at the national level. The standard of humane incorporation requires the Muslim majority to grant members of the non-Muslim minority equal citizenship with equal opportunities to enjoy their own religious identities.

The second element of cultural legitimacy for these different but mutually inclusive levels of solidarity must be sought in the traditions of all Sudanese in a process of internal discourse and cross-cultural dialogue. In relation to the northern Islamic tradition, which is particularly important here because of its present dominance in national politics, there are sufficient resources which can be used to provide the requisite cultural legitimacy. As indicated earlier, there is a long and rich history of accommodation and cooperation between Muslims and non-Muslims in this part of the world. Moreover, there is sufficient Islamic theological and legal bases for this accommodation and cooperation.[54]

[51] On these aspects of *Shari'a* and their constitutional implications see Abdullahi Ahmed An-Na'im, *Toward an Islamic Reformation: Civil Liberties, Human Rights and International Law* (1990), Syracuse: Syracuse University Press, chapter 4.

[52] Those recognized by Shari'a itself as believers, known as People of the Book or *dhimmis* (mainly Christians and Jews).

[53] Abdullahi Ahmed An-Na'im, "Constitutionalism and Islamization in the Sudan," *Africa Today* (1989), vol. 36, p. 11.

[54] See generally, Abdullahi Ahmed An-Na'im, *Toward an Islamic Reformation*.

Unfortunately, the present military regime in the north, and civil war in the south, are unlikely to permit this process of internal discourse and cross-cultural dialogue to take its course. Moreover, the dynamics of antagonistic and violently hostile majority/minority relations are not conducive to constructive discourse and dialogue. The third element of the thesis, namely international action to adjust power relations and relative bargaining positions within the country, might be helpful in overcoming these obstacles. Political, diplomatic and economic pressures should be brought to bear on all sides to the conflict so as to encourage and facilitate the achievement of peace and democratization, which are necessary for internal discourse and dialogue in order to realize equality and equitable participation for all Sudanese, Muslims and non-Muslims alike.

E. TAIHAKUREI DURIE*

The New Zealand Maori and the Waitangi Tribunal

The thesis of this paper is that New Zealand's Treaty of Waitangi promises Maori what human rights conventions have yet to, the recognition of Maori as a separate and indigenous people with rights accruing to them in those capacities. Despite recent advances under the Treaty however, through the courts and the Waitangi Tribunal, the maintenance of Maori rights remains overly susceptible to political expedience and, in the absence of constitutional protections, there is need to develop appropriate international human rights sanctions.

1. Maori Status

Whakarongo te taringa ki te hau raki e pupuhi nei, i takea mai i Hawaiki nui...

Listen to the north wind blowing from the great Hawaiki...

The New Zealand Maori descend from South East Asian voyagers who peopled the Pacific some 3,500 years ago, spreading across as many miles of ocean until in the last millennium, Aotearoa (New Zealand) was settled too.

The Maori are an adventurous race whose penchant for history and genealogy has fashioned their strong sense of identity and destiny as a people. They recount the ancient voyages as though they were yesteryear, recalling to mind that the winds that brought the Maori to Aotearoa made their country a part of the Polynesian homeland. Polynesia, or "many islands", belies the customary view that conceptualizes the islands as one home, Hawaiki, and the people as belonging to one family, the family of Hawaiki – or Hawaii, Savaii or Havaiki, as it is variously called.[1]

Theirs is a developed sense of place and belonging, encapsulated in their description of themselves as *tangata whenua*, the people of the land. The concept pervades the Pacific, through *"whenua"* is *"vanua"* in Vanuatu, as

* Chief Judge of the Waitangi Tribunal, Wellington, New Zealand.

[1] For this perception of Maori as a part of the Polynesian family see Sir James Henare in *The Polynesian Heritage Trust* (1984).

K.E. Mahoney and P. Mahoney (eds.), Human Rights in the Twenty-first Century, 149–159.

"tangata" is *"kanaka"* for the Kanaks of New Caledonia. The feel for a historical belonging to the land of one's birth is emphasized in the Maori metaphorical manner of speaking. *"Whenua"*, or land, means also after-birth, or that which one is born out of.

From belonging comes identity, an identity here established against daunting odds across vast ocean expanses. It is said then, by one tribe, with reference to the place of its origin in Hawaiki:

E kore au e ngaro; he kakano i ruia mai i Rangiatea.

I will never be lost; I am the seed sown from Rangiatea.[2]

From this understanding of themselves as a people, Maori claim dual status in the modern State, now dominated by persons of another kind, as citizens on the one hand, and as a distinct group with inherent self-governing rights on the other.

What is the authority for such an opinion? Sir Monita Delamere has responded:

Ko te mana kei a tatou ano, he iwi hoki tatou.

The authority is in ourselves, we are a people.[3]

Sir Monita expresses the historic Maori position that as a matter of *mana*, their independent status as a people should be upheld. If the constitutional structures of the State cannot cope, it is primarily a problem for the State, that it should be so out of harmony with reality.

So also no natural order can decline the admission of Maori to the family of peoples that comprise humankind. If Maori lack full entry to the family of nations as well, that is a problem for its institutions that they cannot then claim to represent humanity.

It is as a people that Maori should be acknowledged, though at the domestic level they stand according to their numerous kin group associations. Such divisions do not deny a Maori identity when dealing internationally. Despite the western image of Maori led by hierarchical hereditary chiefs within defined tribes, there are in fact few other peoples of greater republican persuasion where the main authority is vested in local family units. Consequentially however, there is no limit on the extent of collectivization.

2. The Significance of the Treaty of Waitangi

The British annexation of New Zealand in 1840 was preceded by a Treaty secured over several months with the leaders of the numerous tribes. It is called the Treaty of Waitangi, after the place where the first meeting was held.

[2] From Ngati Raukawa, which includes the author, and who descend from Hoturoa, captain of the Tainui canoe that left from Rai'atea in the Cook Islands about 1350. The soil carried from there is now at Rangiatea church in New Zealand.

[3] Sir Monita Dalamere, Maori elder and Waitangi Tribunal member, in *Hui Manawhenua*, brochure for an indigenous peoples' gathering in New Zealand in February 1990 to mark the 150th anniversary of the Treaty of Waitangi.

By this treaty it was intended Maori would cede sovereignty, and in return, the Crown would protect them in the ownership of those lands and fisheries they wished to keep, ensuring as well full rights of citizenship.

The Treaty is remarkably brief, and quite properly so considering the cross-cultural circumstances. Its brevity indicates that it is directed to principle rather than detail, and that, like many Oriental transactions, it is founded not on legalism but on a philosophy of good faith.

There is much evidence of the Imperial Government's sincerity, influenced as it was by the humanitarian movement of the times. With or without annexation the settlers were coming, and experience had shown the deleterious impact on the natives in the absence of proper controls.[4]

That same evidence fleshes out the Treaty's bare bones. They describe, for example, an intention to regulate land buying to ensure that each tribe retained a sufficient land endowment for its likely future needs.

Accordingly, though the Treaty may be variously seen, it was not the sham some settlers contended it to be.[5] Assuming for the moment a western perspective, it may rather be seen as illustrating an early commitment to internationally accepted standards. It acknowledges the international law that no country may take the territory of another without agreement, and the common law rules for indigenous peoples expounded in North American courts in the preceding 1830's.[6]

This needs emphasis. Some Commonwealth opinion has predicated a shift to an international common law, as the courts turn increasingly to the standards prescribed by the international community.[7] This must question whether the international norm setting process will displace the need for such treaties as that of Waitangi within a State's domestic law.

Many would welcome that prospect, since the status of the Treaty is not secure and its opponents portray it as archaic and imprecise. There is however, another view of the Treaty by the other party to it, and it is presumptuous to consider a cross-cultural treaty from the opinion of one side only. The Maori

[4] Annexation was influenced by the Report of the Aborigines Committee of the House of Commons, 1836, sought by humanitarian and evangelical lobbyists. The report emphasized the dangers of uncontrolled colonization for aboriginal people. The British Government's concerns are spelled out in the instructions for a Treaty from the Colonial Office, 14.8.1839.

[5] The Treaty was described as a sham by prominent settler, E. G. Wakefield. Others gave similar descriptions.

[6] For an opinion that the Treaty expresses the common law doctrine of aboriginal title and a review of the North American decisions. See P. G. McHugh *The Aboriginal Rights of the New Zealand Maori at Common Law* 1987 Thesis (Ph.D), University of Cambridge.

[7] The development of an international common law is presaged in England by Sir John Donaldson MR in *DST v. Racknoc* [1987] 2 *All ER* 769, 777–9, in New Zealand by Sir Robin Cooke in *Dynamics of the Common Law*, the opening paper to the 9th Commonwealth Law Conference 1990, and possibly by Professor Weeramantry of Australia in a paper to the same conference.

In *NZ Maori Council v. Attorney-General*, [1987] 1 NZLR 641, 655–656, Sir Cooke further considered that "...the Treaty (of Waitangi) is a document relating to fundamental rights; (and) that it should be interpreted widely and effectively and as a living instrument taking account of the subsequent developments of international human rights norms;..."

view casts doubts on the efficacy of any moves to displace the Treaty within the foreseeable term. It has become the talisman of their cause, and is seen to require the recognition of their status as a necessary antecedent to the definition of their rights. It is, for them –

3. The Peoples' Treaty

The Treaty of Waitangi has enormous significance for Maori. There is little point in talking with them of human rights if there are no prior obeisances to it. It is more than symbolic. It is *he kawenata tapu*, or sacred covenant[8], and any challenge to it may be read as an unfriendly act.

Why? The answer is that the Treaty is seen as having acknowledged and affirmed their status as a people; not only because of the words used, but because the event itself provided confirmation of their polity. That recognition in 1840 has not since been given. From then to today, both nationally and within the representative institutions of the world, their recognition as a people, with rights accruing to them in that capacity, has been lacking.[9] The historical development of the Maori has rather been characterized as a battle to uphold their independent sovereignty against every endeavour to subdue it.[10]

Talk of Maori sovereignty was treasonable to earlier generations of Caucasian settlers. Maori were declared rebels and their lands confiscated. It is less threatening today and new attitudes abound, but for Maori the Treaty remains the only document that specifically acknowledges their particular status. Human right norms also abound now, but none is seen to give to Maori the recognition the Treaty provides, and there are no international covenants to which they as a people have been called upon to subscribe.

But did the Treaty of Waitangi in fact give this recognition? The standard western view is that any such recognition was momentary, for while the

[8] The late Sir James Henare, a notable Treaty proponent of recent times, regularly referred to his forebears' description of the Treaty as a sacred covenant. That opinion was adopted in a resolution of some 1000 Maori at the Ngaruawahia treaty *hui* in 1984.

[9] That perception may soon change. New Zealand has now ratified the Optional Protocol to the International Covenant on Civil and Political Rights with effect from August 1989. Articles 1 and 27 of the Covenant give some recognition to the rights of peoples within a State, and the Protocol would appear to enable Maori to make claims as Maori to the Human Rights Committee. At present, however, Maori appear more interested in the revised ILO Convention 169 on Indigenous and Tribal Peoples in Independent Countries (though the Convention, and the preceding Convention No. 107, have never been ratified in New Zealand) and in the Drafts for a Universal Declaration on the Rights of Indigenous Peoples proposed by the United Nations Working Group on Indigenous Populations.

[10] See for example, MPK Sorrenson, historian and Tribunal member, in *A History of Maori Representation in Parliament*, appendix to the Report of the Royal Commission on the Electoral System (1986), Govn't Printer, Wellington, NZ.

independent sovereignty of Maori was acknowledged from 1836, in 1840 the Treaty took it away.[11]

That is not the Maori understanding. How Maori viewed the Treaty at the time it was signed is necessarily speculative but it has not generally been seen by them as ceding sovereignty. Such record as exists of what Pakeha thought Maori to have said, points naturally to a range of opinion and expectations.[12] From the Maori text however,[13] read in light of the culture and the people's subsequent conduct, it is doubtful Maori saw themselves as ceding sovereignty, or of understanding what that culture-laden concept meant.[14] It seems rather Maori saw themselves as affecting an alliance in which the queen would govern for the maintenance of peace while Maori would continue as before to govern themselves.[15] Certainly it seems doubtful, having regard to the Maori character, that Maori would have accepted any Treaty that was thought to diminish their own *mana* or status.

Courts and politicians now characterize the relationship as a partnership, denoting the joining of distinct persons in common enterprise for mutual benefit.[16] This is closer to the Maori view of the Treaty as an alliance. Such a concept was unthinkable earlier, since the maintenance of State sovereignty, in the sense of absolute, ultimate power, was seen as essential. Future discussion on the relationship between Maori and the Crown need no longer be restricted by fundamental legal views on sovereignty however, as increasingly State sovereignty is constrained by the reality of world economics, political and economic alliances, ratification of United Nations conventions and the introduction of domestic constitutional instruments. The concept of a

[11] Maori leaders executed an 1835 *Declaration of Independence*, following which the Colonial Office acknowledged their independent sovereignty in 1836. It made the Treaty a pre-requisite to annexation.

[12] Recorded Maori views at the many signings are collated by Claudia Orange in *The Treaty of Waitangi* (1987), Allen and Unwin NZ Ltd.

[13] There are English and Maori texts of the Treaty and one is not an exact translation of the other. The Maori version was probably based on an English draft then modified to fit Maori expectations. It received little official attention in the past, but (with one exception) was the text that was taken about the country and signed, and is the text on which Maori have relied. The Tribunal is required to consider both texts, the Governor relying on the English version.

[14] The Maori text gives a right of national governance *(kawanatanga)* to the Crown on an undertaking to uphold the independent authority *(rangatiratanga)* of Maori.

[15] The classic Maori position was expressed by Paora Te Ahura in 1857 with reference to the establishment of a Maori King – "The [Maori] King on his piece, the [English] Queen on her piece, God over both and love binding them to each other." See *New Zealander* 6.6.1857.

Maori may also have expected however that they would govern not just themselves but settlers resident in their districts – see *Rigby-Koning Report to the Waitangi Tribunal* (1990) in the Muriwhenua Land Claim.

[16] The Treaty relationship between Maori and the Crown was characterized as a partnership by the Court of Appeal in *NZ Maori Council v. Attorney-General* [1987] 1 *NZLR* 641 following historical evidence from Claudia Orange. The Waitangi Tribunal used similar descriptions in *Manukau Report* [1985] 8.3 and *Te Reo Maori Report* (1986) 4.2.8.

partnership has since been adopted in numerous Government publications and policies, and there are now some statutory utterances in support of it too.[17]

Not all Maori are enamoured of these opinions of course and there is a continuing debate. The point here, however, is that the Treaty is seen as providing more than a bagatelle of individual rights. It gives instead the recognition of Maori as a people, and, by virtue of their prior occupation of the land, a special relationship with the State beyond that which might be claimed by other citizens. Though it is less explicit, still it provides for Maori that which is but a proposal with the United Nations Working Group on Indigenous Populations. It further creates a situation in which Maori rights are seen to flow from their circumstances as a group, where their culture has dignity on that basis, and where Maori as a people can advocate the greater recognition of group rights, as an antidote to the deleterious impact of the current emphasis given to individuals. Unless and until human rights catch up, the Treaty will likely maintain priority in the hearts and minds of Maori.

It does not follow that there should be a Treaty rights–human rights contest, for the Treaty's vulnerability suggests the maintenance of one may depend on the influence the other can provide.

4. Post-Treaty Changes

The Treaty lost profile in New Zealand at the time that the Maori numerical superiority was reversed (in the mid 1850's). It was also then that Britain passed responsibility for self-government to the colony.[18] War was the immediate result, and, with it, native land confiscations.[19] The allotment of the remaining lands in dispersed parcels fragmented the people's former solidarity.[20] Amalgamation policies, well known to indigenous people throughout the world, followed quickly, and were continued into current times. Nonetheless, a massive State machinery for cultural displacement did as much to evidence the resilience of the native order as it did to achieve its purpose.

[17] Treaty of Waitangi Ammendment Act 1988, No. 233, s.2.

[18] At 1840 there were probably about 2,000 British and 100,000 Maori. By 1858, Maori were outnumbered 59,000 to 56,000, disease reducing one, migration swelling the other. In 1896, after the wars, Maori were estimated at 42,000 but numbers have consistently increased since. Maori are now 294,000 or about 12% of the population. Non-Maori are overwhelmingly of British stock.

[19] The main wars were 1860–1867. Confiscation of the lands of "rebel" tribes was provided for in the New Zealand Settlements Act 1863.

[20] Native land legislation from 1862 to the present day has so insisted on title individualization that now no Maori land is held in the communal ownership customarily preferred. Maori were generally opposed but unable to stop the process. The object was stated plainly in Parliament "...to destroy, if were possible, the principle of communism which ran through the whole of their institutions, upon which their social system was based, and which stood as a barrier in the way of all attempts to amalgamate the Maori race into our social and political system" [1870 IX NZPD 361]. It also helped the sale of Maori land, removing the tribal veto that had been the bulwark to settler land acquisition.

The historical process exposed the fragility of the Treaty without special sanctions. For well over 100 years, Maori pleaded their treaty-based cases to no avail, before every judicial, political and popular forum available. The courts held the Treaty had no legal status without Parliamentary ratification, and Parliament was unwilling to intervene.[21]

A remarkable feature of the last decade is that the Treaty has been resurrected from its former obscurity as a declared "legal nullity", and has taken a position of pre-eminence in national affairs. Jurists and politicians now describe it as a document of fundamental constitutional importance. It has been depicted as the most important document in New Zealand's history, as that which marks the foundation of our modern State and as that which gives legitimacy to the Government's right to govern.[22]

This change of heart may be due to the growing awareness of human rights principles as well the work of the Waitangi Tribunal. Equally significant, New Zealand's new Treaty consciousness has been taken to the schools and the general public, due in large part to the centrality given to the Treaty by the 1990 Commission, a body established by the Government to co-ordinate New Zealand's sequi-centennial celebrations.

Despite all that however, the incorporation of the Treaty into particular statutes and its acknowledgement in modern court decisions, the Treaty's position remains vulnerable. The reality is that it is not entrenched in the domestic law, and an attempt by the then Minister of Justice in 1985 to incorporate the Treaty into a Bill of Rights failed for want of public support. The need for the international acknowledgement of the rights of indigenous peoples in colonized countries is still very much apparent.

5. Current Position and the Waitangi Tribunal

The statutory provisions for the Waitangi Tribunal represent the New Zealand Government's resolve to recognize the distinctive position of the indigenous New Zealanders.[23] It falls short of the recognition given aboriginal tribes in entrenched and constitutional documents in Canada and the United States, but the Tribunal has had an impact nonetheless. Shortly it will be considered why that might be so.

The Tribunal was founded in protest. Demonstrations in the 1960's and '70's drew attention to the extent of Maori land losses and grievances. An erudite

[21] The authoritative case is *Te Heuheu Tukino v. Aotea District Maori Land Board* [1941] 60 *NZLR* 590 (Privy Council).

[22] For the Treaty as NZ's most important historical document, see, e.g., Sir Robin Cooke, President of the Court of Appeal, 'Introduction', 14 *NZULR* (1990), 1, p. 1–8; as the foundation of our modern State, see Minister of Justice White Paper on a Draft Bill of Rights presented 1985; and as legitimizing the Government's right to govern, see Prof. F. M. Brookfield inaugural lecture on appointment as Dean of the Law Faculty, Auckland University, 1985.

[23] See Treaty of Waitangi Act 1975, No. 114.

Maori leadership spoke also of the destruction of the tribal economic base and of the impact of enforced change on cultural maintenance and social stability. Once more, the Treaty was argued as authority for an alternative order where two societies stood alongside.

The protests engendered some public sympathy, which, in coalescence with a growing concern with the low Maori socio-economic status, was sufficient to goad the Government to promise some relief.[24] In 1975 it established the Tribunal, with its authority at that time limited to reporting on claims that the Treaty was not being honoured in current or proposed government policies and laws. It was not empowered to deal with those old land claims that were the main source of unhappiness.

With limited powers of recommendation only, few claims were put to the Tribunal in the first eight years. Change came in 1983 when the Tribunal reported on a complaint of prejudice to a tribe's fishing grounds from certain major industries that the government was promoting.[25] Its findings that the Treaty promised Maori a priority of consideration in areas of conflict and cast a duty on the Crown to actively protect their interests, led to conclusions that the Crown had failed to live up to its treaty obligations, and to recommendations for major scheme changes.

Those recommendations won public acclaim. Aided by the coincidence of interests with environmental and economic lobby groups, the recommendations were adopted by the Government, and though it had earlier been sceptical of the Tribunal's role and of any priority of treatment for indigenous people.

A new Government the following year professed greater sympathy for Maori claims, now linked in many minds to environmental matters, and to opine that the findings of such an independent and expert body as the Tribunal ought generally to be followed. More claims came in, moving beyond environmental concerns to aspects of central and local administration, and to such matters as national policies affecting the status and promotion of the Maori language.

Through the handling of these claims the Tribunal came to acquire a better image. In 1985 its membership was increased and its jurisdiction extended to enable it to deal with those outstanding old claims that had been the main source of Maori grievance.

[24] In socio-economic terms Maori rank as underprivileged – more than twice as likely to be unemployed or totally welfare dependent and only half as likely to own their own homes. Those earning earn less (80% the national average). Only 4% Maori men are self-employed compared with 21% non Maori men. 63% Maori as cf. 28% non Maori leave school without formal qualifications and Maori are less than 1% of those in professions or major business.

While the number of non-Maori indicted in the courts doubled between 1961 and 1984, the Maori increase was six-fold, and Maori now comprise nearly half the prison population.

Maori land holdings have been substantially eroded, less than 5% the total land area. Much is on poorer country, about 7% being undevelopable. The spread of ownership is uneven so that some tribes are landless, contributing to a substantial move to towns. Maori in urban areas were in 1936–11.2%, and in 1981–79%.

[25] *Motunui Report*, Waitangi Tribunal, 1983.

Several factors contributed to the enhancement of the Tribunal's standing. It appeared the power of recommendation should not be underestimated, at least when supported by a balanced assessment of exhaustive research and an honest endeavour to find practical solutions. There is also a sense in which the reporting and recommendatory role has an advantage. Effectively the public, not opposing legal counsel or a court of review, becomes the Tribunal's target audience, leading to reports in suasive rather than legal style, and hopefully, increasing public awareness of the issues and of the data base on which decisions must be made.

It has assisted further that the Tribunal is comprised of both Maori and Caucasian members, in roughly equal numbers, each holding professional or leadership positions. Matters about the Treaty, history and current policy thus fall to be determined by representatives of both Treaty partners. Accordingly, in portraying both Maori and Pakeha perspectives on any issue, the Tribunal has promoted the growth of a bicultural national development, exposing Maori culture, practice and history to an increasingly receptive white audience. A move to biculturalism is now encouraged and provided for in schools and in the public service.

It follows further that the Tribunal adopts both Maori and western protocols in the conduct of its inquiries, never assuming that only Anglos have laws and legal processes. The claimant's case is usually presented on traditional *marae*, the proceedings following customary laws under conduct of the Tribunal's Maori members. Likewise the general public may be heard in public halls, and the Government response and legal argument in courtrooms so that all are heard by the rules and in the surroundings of their choice.

Significant too is the Tribunal's quasi-judicial character and its relationship with the general courts in the development of a treaty jurisprudence. This embraces more than the fact that the Tribunal is presided over by judges and that a number of retired judges and lawyers are included in its membership. The Tribunal is structured as a Commission of Inquiry, able to organize research to lay the facts bare and to promote bicultural understandings about them. Although it cannot make binding orders, except in a special class of case,[26] it makes important findings of fact and interpretation. Those findings, arrived at judicially and open to challenge in a court of review, are an essential step in the disposal of complex historical and cross-cultural issues. They serve to settle matters that might otherwise remain in contention, just as the Tribunal's reports ensure that the facts, the range of opinions and variety of options for the provision of redress are fully and sensitively described and made known.

The general courts are also involved indirectly through interpolating the Treaty, examining the public interest, and directly where Parliament has required consideration of the Treaty in the implementation of specific

[26] Where a claim is proven, the Tribunal may order that Crown land or forest assets sold after 1986 be reclaimed for Maori ownership – see Treaty of Waitangi (State Enterprises) Act 1988, No. 105 and Crown Forests Assets Act 1989, No. 99.

statutes.[27] The courts have significantly influenced the public Treaty debate, lending weight to the Tribunal's operations. Nonetheless, though they have the power the Tribunal lacks to make final orders, the opportunities for judicial intervention are more limited than in Canada, for example, where claimants have recourse to a Charter of Rights and Freedoms. They have also used final orders sparingly, no doubt aware of the practical exigencies, and instead, through injunctions and the retention of a supervisory role, have sought to goad the parties to realistic settlements.[28]

6. Current Issues

An essential feature of the court and Tribunal role is that the resolution of native claims is related to the delivery of justice and the maintenance of a fair society. That may be an assumed position in some countries, but not so in New Zealand where, until recently, those matters were dealt with solely at a political level, very much to Maori prejudice, and settlements were effectively on a take it or leave it basis. Time has proven graphically that justice for Maori cannot depend on political whim alone, or reasonable settlements reached with a gross inequality of bargaining power. I do not think it has been or is appreciated by most New Zealanders that Maori have been denied recourse to the courts for their particular grievances, and have thus been denied rights that other New Zealanders take for granted.

The sad irony is that now legal rules are insufficient to deal adequately with the variables that time and changed circumstance have imposed, so that political solutions are still necessary. Large-scale land returns are impracticable in New Zealand, and the economy does not permit of the full monetary amends the law would require. There must be a compromise, a negotiated settlement that is in fact a second best. It then becomes nonsense to talk of compensation or full and final settlements if full legal recompense cannot be given. Long term strategies for a better future are rather to be sought, and claims must be resolved not so much to end the past, even assuming that can be done, but to create a new beginning.

Recent government policy has given cause for optimism. For the first time, following a century of Maori pleas, Government has provided a statutory base for tribal self-management,[29] which, though primarily intended for the devolution of government services through tribal bodies, dovetails well with the claims-settlement process, offering the structure for compensation to provide

[27] Recent intervention by the courts is reviewed by Sir Kenneth Keith in *The Treaty of Waitangi in the Courts* and by E. Taihakurei Durie and Gordon S. Orr in *'The Role of the Waitangi Tribunal and the Development of a Bicultural Jurisprudence'*, 14 *NZULR* (1990) 1, pp. 62–81.

[28] This is apparent, for example, in two Court of Appeal decisions, *NZ Maori Council v. Attorney-General* [1987] 1 NZLR 641, and *Tainui Maori Trust Board v. Attorney-General* [1989] 2 NZLR 513.

[29] See Runanga Iwi Act 1990, No. 125.

the independent economic base for tribal development programmes. Those programmes may benefit the nation as much the Maori in the future, and represent a cost-saving in the longer term.

The catch is that the will to promote reasonable settlements remains dependent on political motivation. Through its recommendations the Tribunal provides pressure, and serves the essential role of removing the determination of facts and the proof of a claim from the political or bureaucratic arena. In reality, however, the Tribunal itself is reliant on government policy for its own continuance. It currently exists in an environment where limitations on its role, and the termination of the recent provisions for tribal self-management, have been proposed by members of the new Government elected in October 1990. While those opinions may or may not be effectuated by the new Government, they serve nonetheless to show the uncertain status of the New Zealand native claim process.

Should it be part of our modern world ethic that indigenous minorities' claim to justice should so depend on domestic political circumstance? I do not think so. In the absence of constitutional safeguards, or satisfactory conventions on indigenous peoples' rights in domestic law, Maori must seek a role in developing the common law of humankind. It is that which promises the greater influence on local political action.

It does not follow, that their reliance on the Treaty of Waitangi is misplaced. Its new found status in domestic law could prove tenuous, but its existence cannot be denied and as such it proclaims standards the international community has yet to aspire to. Those who see a contest, however, miss the point. The Treaty provides concrete evidence for Maori of the value of the norm setting process to condition national governance. The international criteria provide in addition the force of persuasion the Treaty may be seen to lack. Both may work in concert to provide for the more equitable participation of Maori in the national life.

CHIEF OVIDE MERCREDI*

First Nations and Self-Determination

1. Introduction

When I agreed to write this paper I was not convinced that it would lead to anything useful. To discuss human rights with people that are themselves, to varying degrees, already advocates of human rights is perhaps redundant. The message about human rights really should be heard in the House of Commons and in the Legislative Assemblies across this country, because that is where it is needed the most. The fact is that it is in our collective interest to work together to advance the rights of all people in Canada and elsewhere whose rights are being violated by nation states.

2. Cultural Perceptions About Human Rights

The perceptions that we have about human rights are influenced by our cultures and by the events that we experience in life either individually or collectively as a culture or a race of people.

The topic of the relationship between individual rights and collective rights is discussed in more detail later in the paper but the following section provides a factual background within which the argument is framed.

In my case I grew up as a Cree in a community called Grand Rapids in northern Manitoba. I was not raised as "a Canadian". That imagery, that concept of Canadian was introduced later on in my life as part of the curriculum of the white educational system. But I grew up to consider myself as different, because we were taught, and I am sure this happens in all different cultures, that we are different. The white people too are different. Now these are powerful concepts. By themselves they are not enough but our culture is comprehensive, and holistic. We were also taught by our parents and our elders other lessons. One of them was to be different does not mean you are better. And just as important, to be different is not to be inferior. When you go through life with

* National Chief, Assembly of First Nations, Ottawa, Ontario, Canada.

K.E. Mahoney and P. Mahoney (eds.), Human Rights in the Twenty-first Century, 161–166.

those concepts in your mind you approach society with an identity that gives you strength to meet any challenges that come your way. But in the context of self-determination we also had lessons that we learned from our parents and our elders. I will say them to you. The white people do not own us, they do not control us. We are responsible for ourselves, or the other meaning, we have self rule. So if you can imagine me entering your society with those concepts, you are not looking at an empty shell. You are not looking a person without sense of self, or without identity. You are looking at an individual that is complete, having been taught to be complete within his own culture.

Let me tell you about some of the other events that shaped my life. I went to elementary school in Grand Rapids. I entered elementary school about age 6 or 7 years old, I don't quite remember the date. But what struck me was that my language was not allowed, not only in the school, but it was not allowed in the playground or for that matter at any time within the yards of the school at anytime during the week. If we did speak our language in the schools we would be punished for it either by staying after school or by getting strapped. So my first entry to a white institution was one of rejection of my culture and exclusion of my language. Now, that was not in and of itself a devastating blow because what it said to me was that equality of peoples that we were taught in our culture is not a concept that is understood or embraced by the dominant society. An important lesson it taught me was that I was going to stay in that white institution for a long time and if I wanted to survive, and obtain a public education, valued by my parents as well as the dominant society, I had no option of escape. Or for that matter even, the desire to escape.

A little later on I went to an urban setting for the first time in my life. Up until now I had been fairly sheltered in a Cree society, in a Cree community. My exposure to white society was very minimum, having seen the town of The Pas, having done high school there. It was not really a strong or a total emersion into a white society, so after completing high school, I was supposed to have all that it takes to find acceptance in the dominant society. But entering the world as an emerging adult presented a different reality. It was difficult to find an apartment because landlords refused to rent their premises to those they perceived as being different, those they judged on the basis of stereotypes about Indian people.

The message taught about success was that all I needed to do was to shed my cultural skin, my Indian cultural skin and adopt a new one and I would find acceptance and equality of opportunity. I learned very quickly that even if I wanted to assimilate completely, that even if I embraced the other culture's values entirely, it did not guarantee acceptance, and it did not translate into racial equality or equal treatment.

So I found even as I entered the adult world that I was faced with rejection and exclusion even on an individual basis.

Later on in my life after a few bumps here and there, I entered law school and I learned the law. I entered there with a silly idea that this is where I would learn about justice. This was where equality would mean something. I found out very quickly that there is no aboriginal law taught in the law schools. Not that it doesn't exist, but it is not embraced by those institutions. While I knew that my people had a different idea of property and that they could never own animals for example, and while I knew that I would deal with issues on child custody or child welfare in a different way, I was not taught these things in the law school. What I was taught in the law school was more and more of what the other society wanted me to embrace as the rule of law. And the rule of law as taught in the law schools did not include aboriginal law. Aboriginal law was something that was different, too different to be considered as equal and having a place in the law schools. Now I went through this in the 1970's. Since then there has been some changes. The law schools are beginning to recognize, at least individuals within the law schools, that there is something they call legal pluralism which allows our culture and our laws to be part of the system of legal education. In the end result, if this is what happens in the law schools, right across the country, it will be beneficial to all of us.

3. Canadian Constitutional Perceptions About Collective Rights and the Right to Self-Government

What happens to minority cultures during the constitutional processes reveals a lot about human rights culture. The first ministers of Canada consistently ask, what it is that the Indians, Metis or Inuit want? Yet when people talk about the right to self-government or a collective right to a culture, they do not understand. The message from them seems to say our society is so wonderful it needs no perfection, why don't you just fit into it, why do you want your own self-government? In 1988, the Meech Lake constitutional process in Canada failed because the first ministers could not accept that we have a right to remain different, a right to continue as distinct peoples and a right to self-government. Rather than resisting it, the Ministers ought to have protected and enhanced it. But that concept of Canada was foreign to them. The prevailing idea, that everybody has human rights, meaning individual rights, was the accepted view. What most Canadians forget is that human rights also entails collective rights, like the collective rights to a culture, to a language, to institutions of government like a parliament, or a court system, a law school, or a public educational system. These are collective rights of citizens within a nation state that everybody takes for granted in Canada.

When aboriginal peoples wish to exercise their collective rights as well, the response is "We already have a parliament. Why do you want self-government? We already have a court system. Why do you want your own court system? We already have universities and public schools. Why do you want your own separate schools? Why don't you just become one of us?" The answer of course is that when aboriginal people try to become part of the dominant collectivity, we are rejected and excluded. We cannot even enjoy individual human rights much less our collective human rights under the current thinking in this country.

The Prime Minister's comments with respect to the 1990 Mohawk crisis are illustrative. He made it very clear that there is only one law for all Canadians. He ignored the fact that the law of Canada was changed in 1982 and that the Treaty on Aboriginal Rights of the Aboriginal people of Canada are now recognized. It is very possible under the treaty that the Mohawk people had a legal right to defend their land as they did. The courts will determine that. But for political purposes, the politicians fooled the Canadian people into believing that their perfect society was under seige by the Mohawk warriors. It is not surprising that the response of the people was to rush to defend it. That is a normal response. That is what I would do. And I do not begrudge the Canadian people for telling their politicians after Oka that sending the army in was the correct thing to do. Because after all that is your society. The tendency of people is to protect the society and culture they love. That is what the Mohawks were trying to do, to protect their culture and their society. The problem with human rights in this country is the inability of the majority to accept or appreciate the human rights of those that are different. It is a problem that I personally have experienced throughout my life. While my parents might have taught me that the right to be different is not the same as being inferior, all my experiences in my society have told me that to try to be different is in effect to remain inferior. That is what I call schizophrenia in Canada in terms of human rights.

4. Canadian Responses to Internationally Recognized Collective Rights

Later on I went to Geneva along with indigenous peoples from all over the world to be involved in a process to develop the Declaration of Indigenous Rights to protect our distinct rights as Indigenous peoples. And what do you think the role of Canada is with respect to the Declaration of Indigenous Rights? Do you think that they have rushed in there to say to the United Nations yes, we will work with you, we will make sure that we produce a declaration of human rights that respects the rights of Indigenous people? For a country that advocates human rights for others, you would think that is what Canada would do for aboriginal people or indigenous peoples throughout the world. But it is not doing that. It is doing the reverse. It takes every opportunity to deny the aboriginal people of this country our collective rights domestically and it takes every opportunity to do likewise in the international fora. The role of Canada is to deny us our collective rights. And they even do it in what I consider areas totally silly. For example, the ILO Convention was amended about a year ago. One of the amendments that indigenous people wanted made in the Convention, was that we did not want to be referred to as populations. We wanted to be referred to as peoples. And what do you think Canada's position was? The position it took was that indigenous people are not peoples. If we were, it would put us within the meaning of the declarations that recognize the right of self-determination for peoples. That was the response. They fought our efforts to amend the ILO convention so that at least in the international arena there would be respect for the right to be different and the right of our people to self-identify.

This is not dissimilar to what the Canadian government did through the *Indian Act*. There, they tried to define who is and who is not an Indian. They made our right to our culture against the law and outlawed the Potlaches and the Sundance of the Indian people. If our people wanted to pursue their claims to their land, there was a provision in the *Indian Act* that made sure that they could not hire a lawyer. If they did, they would be convicted of a criminal offense.

It is not that long ago either that it was a criminal offense for Indians to defend their land rights. An understanding of aboriginal history requires a study of the *Indian Act* and all the amendments it has gone through since the 1800's. It is only then that the full extent of the violations of our collective rights can be appreciated.

Now, the attitude that created the *Indian Act* is being transferred into the international arena where government people are doing whatever they can to subvert our human rights, our collective human rights as distinct peoples.

5. The Potential of Power

Then, I saw what is possible if you have power. I went to another conference about a year and a half ago, where the convention on the Rights of the Child was being finalized in Geneva. I attended on behalf of the Assembly of First Nations. While there it became very apparent to me that the convention itself was not a document built on consensus of nation states. Rather it is a document built by the Western civilized nations, a document full of Western thought, wherein the drafters imposed their political will on the world stage just as they do in Canada domestically.

But what I saw was that if you have power you do not have to abide by other people's rules. One of the Arab countries gave up trying to convince the United States, Canada and other Western countries to a specific amendment they wanted regarding provisions on religion for children. When it became apparent that the amendments were not going to be successful, they gave notice that that part of the convention, the rights of the child, would not apply to their state because it violates their culture and religion.

Now that is the kind of power we need to have as aboriginal people in Canada. We need to be able to say to the government when you pass laws that violate our culture, they are not going to apply to us. You can have it in your books but it is not going to apply to us. If we had that kind of power then it might be possible for Canada to have a human rights policy that respects not only the dominant majority's collective and human rights but also the collective and human rights of the aboriginal people. Unless that development takes place there is not very much hope, in my view, that Canada will cure its own schizophrenia about human rights.

6. Conclusion

Canada recently joined the Organization of American States. What Canada did not appear to know is that there was already a movement within that organization for a development of a declaration of indigenous rights within the Americas. We are part of that movement now. The aboriginal leaders, the South and Central American Indian leaders will be meeting either in Mexico or in Canada in 1991 to begin working on a declaration for Indigenous Rights for Indigenous Peoples in the Americas. And that is going to be another opportunity for Canada to change its policy. It can either maintain what it does now which is to resist and reject our right to be different, or they can adopt a new policy based on respecting our right to be different. My prediction is we will be fighting the Canadian government in a Declaration of Indigenous Rights for the Indigenous Peoples in the Americas in a very short time.

SECTION II(c): EQUALITY RIGHTS OF DISABLED PERSONS

Introduction

The section on Equality Rights and the Disabled specifically addresses three groups: those who are disabled by being carriers of contagious diseases, the physically disabled and those disabled by mental handicaps.

David Lepofsky describes the circumstances of disadvantage which commonly confront persons with disabilities; the scope of equality rights protection for person with disabilities in Canada; equality rights concerns of persons with disabilities in other countries, particularly developing countries, and Canada's position on the international scene.

In her paper on Human Rights of People with Contagious Diseases, Katarina Tomasevski notes that trends in protection for human rights of those with AIDS or HIV virus are alarming. While legislation permitting forced quarantine or other restrictive measures is being enacted with some regularity, legislated protection for the human rights of those with the disease or thought to have the disease, is rare. Tomasevski points out that discrimination against people with contagious diseases has always existed, particularly when medicine could provide no cure. Harmful, ineffective, coercive and compulsory measures incompatible with human rights are often justified under the banner of public health. She argues that development of policies and practices to deal with the AIDS pandemic should take place with the participation of those affected. The problems of those with contagious diseases cannot be dealt with through efforts to legally control them. The author concludes that human rights safeguards against abuses of power must be applied to public health just as in other areas of State power and that the AIDS situation may provide a turning point in the relationship between human rights and public health policies.

Niall MacDermot addresses the rights of the mentally handicapped, using the example of the treatment and protection of the mentally ill in Japan since World War II. He argues that the World Health Organization should develop a massive program to promote reform in the treatment and protection of the mentally ill in all parts of the world. He suggests that this reform should prioritize the creation of modest but essential facilities at the local level, education to overcome ignorance and misguided attitudes toward the mentally ill and adequate training for care-givers.

K.E. Mahoney and P. Mahoney (eds.), Human Rights in the Twenty-first Century, 167.

DAVID LEPOFSKY*

Equality Rights of Persons with Disabilities – Canadian and International Perspectives

1. Introduction

In her article in this volume, Rosalie Abella, aptly noted that Canada is currently caught up in a frenzy of rights. Many are now advancing the most trivial of claims in the guise of human rights and civil liberties. Canada's experience with its new constitutional guarantee of equality rights in the Canadian Charter of Rights and Freedoms provides a most compelling example of this unfortunate trend. When first enacted, section 15(1) of the Charter of Rights[1] heralded great potential for the advancement of the status of traditionally disadvantaged groups in Canada, such as women, disabled persons, visible minorities and others. Yet a large bulk of section 15 litigation to date has consisted of corporate and commercial claims, aimed at attacking business and economic regulations which impede the pursuit of profit.

There is a serious risk that such trivial claims could eclipse important equality rights issues in this country. This ought not to happen. Canada must now confront a wide range of important human rights questions, which focus on the desire of disadvantaged persons and groups in Canada to have equality of opportunity to participate fully in society's benefits and burdens. This paper focuses on one such group, namely persons in Canada with physical or mental disabilities.

This topic is addressed in five parts. First, this paper describes the circumstances of disadvantage which commonly confront persons with disabilities.

* Counsel, Constitutional Law and Policy Division, Ministry of the Attorney General for Ontario, Canada. This article is written in the author's personal capacity. It does not purport to represent the views of Ontario's Attorney General or his Ministry.

[1] Charter s. 15 provides as follows:

"(1) Every individual is equal before and under the law and has the right to the equal protection and equal benefit of the law without discrimination and, in particular, without discrimination based on race, national or ethnic origin, colour, religion, sex, age or mental or physical disability.

(2) Subsection (1) does not preclude any law, program or activity that has as its object the amelioration of conditions of disadvantaged individuals or groups including those that are disadvantaged because of race, national or ethnic origin, colour religion, sex, age or mental or physical disability."

K.E. Mahoney and P. Mahoney (eds.), Human Rights in the Twenty-first Century, 169–190.

Second, the scope of equality rights protection for persons with disabilities in Canada is outlined. Third, the equality rights concerns of persons with disabilities in other countries, and particularly in developing countries, are considered. Thereafter, Canada's position on the international scene is examined, by focusing on legislative restrictions on the immigration to Canada of disabled persons. Finally, some concluding reflections are offered on equality rights for disabled persons in the specific context of this Conference.

2. Persons with Disabilities as a Disadvantaged Minority

In a crucial move aimed at bringing legal equality guarantees into step with the practical reality confronting disadvantaged groups in society, the Supreme Court of Canada has enunciated basic principles governing the application of the Charter's equality guarantee which recognize that the goal of this guarantee is to secure equality of opportunity for discrete and insular minorities – groups who have been traditionally victimized by social exclusion, disadvantage, stereotyping and prejudice on account of a personal characteristic.[2] Within the Charter's doctrinal framework, disabled persons in Canada are clearly a discrete and insular minority. This is not simply because section 15(2) of the Charter recognizes disability to be a cause of disadvantagement in society. It is also so as a matter of practical societal fact.

Disabled people number in the range of 10 to 15 per cent of Canada's population, a percentage likely to increase as Canada's population ages. It is reasonable to expect that this percentage will grow over the next few years. Persons with disabilities in Canada are a highly heterogeneous group. They come from all walks of life, from both sexes and from all races, nationalities, ethnic origins and religions. As individuals, they have a diversity of talents, interests, ambitions, expectations and abilities. Of Canada's population, disabled persons are disproportionately represented among the ranks of the unemployed, the impoverished, the welfare dependent and the institutionalized. They are commonly dependent upon public sector bureaucracies, and are the clients of private sector charitable social service organizations. They live in a society that is largely designed on the incorrect assumption that all of its members are able to mount stairs, to read printed signs, to hear announcements, and to process information and communicate at a rapid pace. Most compelling, disabled persons in Canada pervasively share in common the experience of discrimination. This discrimination does not necessarily take the form of hatred, scorn or antipathy, akin to that from which members of racial and religious minorities often suffer. Rather, it is frequently disguised in attitudes of pity, patronization, condescension or over-protectionism. It is often rooted in stereotypical expectations that disability is equivalent to inability. At its core, it is predicated on the assumption that one's ability and

[2] *Andrews v. Law Society of British Columbia*, [1989] 1 S.C.R. 143.

worth is commensurate with one's physical, sensorial and mental capacity.

This pervasive pattern of discrimination against persons with disabilities manifests itself in many ways. In a context of economic activity, persons with disabilities often confront substantial attitudinal barriers when they seek access to employment, housing, goods and services. Employers, landlords and service providers often operate on the false assumption or presumption that persons with disabilities could not effectively meet the standards or requirements expected of an employee, tenant or a consumer of goods and services. In the social context, persons with disabilities regularly find that pervasive social attitudes towards them often lead able-bodied persons to feel uncomfortable or awkward when they first meet a person with a disability. This is especially so if the disabled person is disfigured, or has a hearing or speech impediment.

At the institutional level, disabled persons often find that society expects and believes that their needs are fully met by specialized, charitable, non-profit service agencies, which raise money from donors on a promise of providing caring services to the disabled. Yet these agencies are often not directly accountable to those whom they are expected to serve. They are often unequipped to provide services as effectively as society believes them to provide. Moreover, the attitudes of staff working at these agencies or volunteers serving on their governing boards do not always reflect a sufficient sensitivity to the equality rights of disabled persons or to their capacity to function independently in society.

In the governmental context, legislators, policy makers and others involved in operating the machinery of government often design social policies on the assumption (be it explicit or implicit) that only able-bodied persons would participate in or benefit from them. This is evident from the physical layout of the buildings in which such services and policies are often put into effect. It is also revealed by the content of these policies and programs. When such conditions are discovered, the traditional governmental response has frequently been to create specialized and segregated programs for disabled persons in an effort to redress the ensuing inequality. It is only recently that governmental initiatives have focused increasingly on the provision to disabled persons of opportunities to participate in an integrated setting in some of the programs and benefits which government provides to the public generally.

The wall of discrimination that hems in many disabled persons is the product of a self-regenerating vicious circle. At the start of this cycle, society has entertained pervasive attitudes about disabled persons, by which it is assumed that they are incapable of participating in many if not most of life's opportunities. As a result of this, society's institutions, organizations and activities were designed to accommodate only able-bodied persons. This led disabled persons to be excluded from these institutions, programs and opportunities. Consequently, those able-bodied persons who grew up in society thereafter often tend to entertain the view that disabled persons are incapable of participating in the mainstream, since they have never been seen participating in the mainstream in the past. This in turn leads the next generation of able-bodied persons to entertain the same stereotypes about the incapacity of disabled persons that had pervaded a generation before. This next generation again designs institutions, organizations, policies, programs and activities based on the same exclusionary stereotypes as had the generation before. Disabled persons again confront massive attitudinal and physical barriers to their full participation in society. A legacy of exclusion is perpetuated.

Standing in marked contrast to this legacy of exclusion is the substantial and ever-expanding capacity of persons with disabilities to live full, productive and self-reliant lives. Many disabled persons have been able to prove that the inherent limitations imposed by physical or mental disabilities are substantially less than is commonly believed. By modifying the way in which one tackles life's daily chores, employment responsibilities and the like, many disabled persons have been able to develop those skills and techniques needed to secure for themselves a full and equal place in society's mainstream.

The capacity of persons with disabilities to minimize or eliminate the barriers inherent in their physical or mental conditions has been increasing geometrically in recent years. This is in part because of the rapid development of new technology to assist persons with disabilities. The advent of computers has been critical to this. Minor adaptations to computers enable visually handicapped persons to use them, either through large print video displays, electronically synthesized voice outputs or Braille computer interfaces. Persons with severe muscle or communication impairments are increasingly able to use computers to control their environments, to operate devices within their homes and to communicate with others, where such activities were hitherto impossible or exceedingly difficult. In tandem with these technologies are increases in the capacity for disabling conditions to be reduced or prevented through medical intervention.

The rapid development of technology in the disability context parallels advancements in the computer field generally. New products are constantly invented. Existing products become more commonly available and less expensive at unprecedented rates. However, the simple existence of such technologies, in tandem with rehabilitation training and medical interventions, does not assure that disabled persons are able in practice to profit from them. This is so for three important reasons. First, disabled persons may not even have been made aware of the existence of such services and technologies. Second, even if aware of them, persons with disabilities may not have the financial resources to acquire them. Third, even where a disabled person has gained access to training and technical services which enable him or her to enter society's mainstream, he or she often encounters the massive physical and attitudinal discriminatory barriers described above.

In many respects, disabled persons' experience with discrimination is similar to the experience confronting women, visible minorities and other disadvantaged groups in society. However, there are certain features of the disadvantage confronting persons with disabilities which may be unique, at least to some extent. First, disabled persons may find themselves institutionalized, and hence at a disadvantage when attempting to assert their rights. In an institutional setting, one's freedom of action can be constrained, directly or subtly, by virtue of the relationship of dependency on the institution in which one lives, and by virtue of the scrutiny which necessarily is maintained on one's activities.

Second, more than most if not all other disadvantaged groups, disabled persons, including those who are not institutionalized, can find that their freedom of action may be consigned, at least in part, to the supervision of others, be they individuals or institutions. For example, persons with mental disabilities can be subjected to the discretionary power of doctors or legal guardians over their financial affairs and/or over their physical persons. People with mental or physical disabilities can also be highly dependent on non-profit, charitable service agencies for access to needed rehabilitation and support services. Hence, they can be subject to the whims of these organizations. These agencies' powers are often not statutory in character, and are therefore not subject to judicial supervision by way of judicial review proceedings. Additionally, more than virtually any other group, persons with disabilities may well find themselves in a subordinate or dependent relationship with government agencies, be they welfare departments, social service branches and/or others.

In sum, persons with disabilities can find themselves in an ironic situation. They will often have the capacity and the desire to participate fully in society's mainstream. Yet, at the same time, they will often confront self-regenerating attitudinal and physical barriers to their access to this mainstream. Society will twice suffer on account of this. First, society suffers because it loses out on the contributions which persons with disabilities could make if provided greater access to the mainstream. Second, society is often compelled to shoulder increased costs, such as those incurred through welfare support, because many disabled persons are unable to secure gainful employment. But for the barriers to access to employment confronting many disabled persons, numerous welfare-receiving disabled persons could become productive tax-paying members of society. These two situations, taken together, connote a substantial, unnecessary and unfortunate societal waste.

The conditions of serious disadvantage confronting persons with disabilities clearly conform to the "discrete and insular minority" status enunciated by the Supreme Court of Canada in its earliest rulings on Charter section 15, such as Andrews, *supra*. Disabled persons have often been unable to secure access to the levers of power, because of their minority status, and because of the very barriers which give rise to their disadvantaged status. Until recently, disability issues were not among those with which politicians felt themselves compelled to be concerned, with the exception of narrow "social service" administration questions. Moreover, persons in institutionalized settings, whose liberty of movement and activity is subject to the authority of the institution in which they are housed, are not in an effective position to be lobbyists in federal or provincial legislatures. Additionally it was not unheard of for legislation governing elections to exclude some persons with mental disabilities from the right to vote. This disenfranchised them from a crucial means of securing the attention of those in positions of power.

A lesser known but critically important condition that contributes to the status of disabled persons as a discrete and insular minority is the extent to which the legal profession is not meeting their legal needs. A key means by which a disadvantaged minority can seek equality is through the legal process. This is done by invoking anti-discrimination legislation, the Charter of Rights and/or any other legal process that is available to challenge barriers to access to society's mainstream. The legal process is of little use to a minority unless the legal profession is effectively available to assist them in invoking that process.

Several years ago, Ontario appointed a judicial inquiry into the extent to which the legal needs of disabled persons in that province were met by the legal profession. This study produced troubling conclusions. It determined that the legal needs of disabled persons were substantially unmet by Ontario's legal profession. The legal profession was not trained to effectively serve disabled clients, and was generally not equipped to do so in accessible facilities.[3] There is no reason to suspect that the legal professions of other jurisdictions in Canada have fared better in this regard than had Ontario's bar.

With this background in mind, attention can now turn to the legal protections available in Canada to foster and promote the equality rights of persons with disabilities.

3. Canada's Guarantee of Equality Rights to Persons with Disabilities

Twenty years ago, one would have found in Canada a legal system that increasingly recognized the importance of protecting individuals from discrimination in both the public and private sectors. However, one would have also found that this increasing recognition did not extend to persons with disabilities. In this regard, the legal situation in Canada has changed drastically between 1970 and 1990. As of 1990, every jurisdiction in Canada, federal and provincial, has in place an anti-discrimination statute (usually called a Human Rights Code) that bans discrimination in employment, housing and other economic activities, where such discrimination is based (among other things) on disability. Such legislative guarantees of equality must be construed liberally, with exceptions thereto being interpreted narrowly. Human rights legislation has primacy over all other legislation, being not quite constitutional in character, but more important than the ordinary statute.[4]

Operating in tandem with these statutory equality rights guarantees is

[3] See "Access to Legal Services by the Disabled: Report of a Study by Judge Rosalie S. Abella" (Toronto: Queen's Printer, 1983).

[4] See *Ontario Human Rights Commission v. Simpson Sears Ltd.*, [1985] 2 S.C.R. 536–547.

section 15 of the Canadian Charter of Rights and Freedoms. It guarantees that every individual is equal before and under the law, and has the right to the equal protection and equal benefit of the law without discrimination, and in particular without discrimination predicated upon one's mental or physical disability (among other grounds). As in the case of human rights statutes, this equality rights guarantee must be construed liberally. While it is subject to restrictions that are "reasonable limits [that] ...can be demonstrably justified in a free and democratic society" pursuant to Charter section 1, such limitations have generally been required to meet a very high test in order to be constitutionally permissible, according to early Supreme Court Charter pronouncements.[5] The core content of the guarantees to disabled persons in human rights legislation and in the Charter is comparable. However, the reach of each of these legal instruments is different.

Human rights codes apply to both the public and private sectors. However, they only prohibit discrimination in a finite range of activities, namely specified economic activities such as the provision of opportunities for employment, accommodation, the undertaking of contractual relations and the offering of goods, facilities and services to the public. In contrast, the Charter's equality rights guarantee to disabled persons applies only to the activities of legislatures and governments within the meaning of s.32(1) of the Charter. As well, the Charter's reach with respect to government goes far beyond the simple scope of the provision of employment opportunities, housing or the offering of goods, facilities and services to the public. The Charter's equality rights guarantee applies to all governmental activity and all legislation. Charter section 15 requires equality to be assured with respect to the protection and benefit of the law, thereby making the Charter apply to all government action, irrespective of its form or content.

Whether the guarantee be under the Charter of Rights or under a statutory human rights code, the purpose of the guarantee of equality to persons with disabilities is the same. It is to assure to every disabled person equality of opportunity to participate fully in the rights, benefits, burdens and obligations available in society, to the extent of their individual abilities. The goal is to have people judged on their individual ability, based on what they can do and not based on what they cannot do. The aim is to have a society which accommodates a wide spectrum of individual abilities, and not a society which simply expects all to conform to one hypothetical and, often unachieved, standard of "normalcy".

Under statutory and constitutional guarantees against discrimination because of disability, the law embodies the following core protections:

1. protection against being singled out for worse or adverse treatment because of one's disability;
2. protection against having society treat all as if they were able-bodied, and against having society or groups within society providing opportunities on

[5] See *R. v. Oakes*, [1986] 1 S.C.R. 103.

the assumption that all who would participate in them are able-bodied;
3. providing a legal assurance that in the rights, benefits, burdens and obligations in society, the needs of persons with disabilities will be accommodated, except where adequate accommodation is wholly unfeasible without fundamentally disrupting the nature of the benefit, opportunity, burden or obligation in question;
4. providing a strong legal assurance that individuals will be assessed on the basis of their true abilities, and not on the basis of group assumptions, stereotypes, or prejudices about their abilities or disabilities.

In legal parlance, these protections traditionally are translated into two overlapping requirements.

The first is a requirement that disabled persons not be subjected to "direct discrimination" or "intentional discrimination". Direct or intentional discrimination occurs when a disabled person is denied a job, accommodation, service or other opportunity, where one of the reasons for this denial is his or her disability. In such cases, it is open to a defendant to attempt to establish that the disabled individual was incapable of performing or fulfilling the essential duties attending the opportunity sought, even with appropriate accommodations to their disability. Absent persuasive proof of such, direct or intentional disability-based discrimination is simply illegal.

By the second requirement, disabled persons have the right to be free from "adverse affects discrimination", "constructive discrimination", systemic discrimination or "unintentional discrimination". These somewhat synonymous terms generally refer to a situation where a disabled person is required to comply with a requirement, qualification, or condition which is equally applied to everyone (regardless of disability), but which has the *effect* of precluding full participation in the opportunity sought by the disabled person. Where a neutral requirement has the effect of discriminating against disabled persons, there is an obligation on the part of the defendant to either remove this requirement, if it is not needed, or to take sufficient steps to accommodate the needs of disabled persons with respect to that requirement. This obligation applies regardless of the fact that there was no intention[6] to exclude disabled persons from the opportunity, or diminish their access to it.

The duties to refrain from direct and indirect discrimination each entail a requirement to take appropriate steps to accommodate persons with disabilities. Such accommodations ordinarily can take several forms. They can involve the provision to persons with disabilities of adaptive equipment or services to enable them to participate fully in the opportunity in question. They can include modification of the non-essential requirements of the opportunity. They can involve changes to the physical premises in which the opportunity

[6] There has evolved a degree of confusion surrounding the term "intent" in the discrimination context. Properly understood, "intent to discriminate" exists where a reason for denying a disabled person a job, apartment or other opportunity is their disability. It does not need to involve any ill will or animus against disabled persons. From time to time, however, discriminatory intent or purpose have incorrectly been doctrinally confused with prejudicial antipathy.

takes place, so as to ensure that these premises are physically accessible to persons with disabilities.

Whenever a question of affirmative accommodations for persons with disabilities is raised, a virtually automatic reaction is that such accommodations entail excessive costs. In the context of Canadian anti-discrimination law, a defendant can avoid a particular accommodation only if the defendant can establish affirmatively that the making of such accommodations would be so costly that the financial burden would constitute an "undue hardship".[7] In ascertaining whether the cost of accommodating disabled persons constitutes "undue hardship", several factors should be considered.

First, the scope of the cost burden that any defendant shall be required to undertake will vary with the size of the defendant. Where the defendant is a large company, it will be expected to bear a larger burden of cost to accommodate disabled persons than where the defendant is a small sole proprietorship.[8] The cost of accommodation should be measured against the defendant's total assets and, where possible, its total revenues.

Where the defendant is the government, and the claim is based either under statutory human rights law or under The Charter of Rights, this "size" consideration should be applied to the government as a whole. In other words, the question, that is properly posed is whether accommodating the disabled individual or group would involve a cost which would impose undue hardship on the government in its entirety. It would be wrong simply to ask whether the cost would constitute an undue hardship to the particular department, division or branch of the government which is asked to provide the accommodation. This is because the indivisible Crown ought not to be able to evade its responsibilities under The Charter of Rights or under anti-discrimination statutes by creating internal budgetary systems which would lead to the impression that individual departments are impoverished and incapable of providing accommodations to disabled persons, when the overall government is in fact one of the largest employers and service providers in the marketplace.

Second, the burden of proof is on the defendant in a disability equality rights claim (whether under The Charter of Rights or under human rights legislation[9]) to establish what the actual cost of accommodation would be, and that this cost would constitute an undue hardship to the defendant. Such cost assertions cannot simply be speculative or based on impressionistic evidence.[10] They must be the specific and inevitable incremental costs which are directly and exclusively attributable to the accommodation of the disabled person.

Third, in assessing the merits of a "cost" defence, it is important to have regard to the spending priorities of the defendant in question. If the defendant is allocating resources to other, less important budgetary needs than com-

[7] See *Simpson-Sears, supra* and *Alberta Human Rights Commission v. Central Alberta Dairy Pool* (1990), 72 D.L.R. (4th) 417 S.C.R.

[8] See *Central Alberta Dairy Pool, supra.*

[9] See *Ontario Human Rights Commission v. Borough of Etobicoke* [1982] 1 S.C.R. 202.

[10] See Borough of Etobicoke, *supra.*

pliance with their human rights obligations, then it can be argued that their complaints about costs are a mere disguised assertion that human rights for disabled persons are simply of insufficient importance to them. Put simply, one should measure the costs of accommodating disabled persons against the defendant's existing wine and cheese budget, in order to ascertain whether the problem is in reality one of excessively harsh costs or of a defendant's attitude.

The duty to accommodate persons with disabilities is a critical, core component of any guarantee of equality rights. During the 1960's, the conventionally accepted concept of equality held that persons were treated as equals when they were treated as being identical. By the 1990's, this conception of equality is recognized as insufficient to meet the anti-discrimination requirements of most, and is entirely destructive of the equality rights of persons with disabilities. The old maxim that equality requires that persons who are similarly situated must be treated similarly, if applied under the Charter or under human rights legislation, would ensure that disabled persons retain their subordinate status as a disadvantaged, discrete and insular minority. While some of the earliest judicial attempts to interpret equality rights under the Charter held that the core purpose of Charter section 15 is to ensure that persons be treated similarly when they are similarly situated,[11] this approach to equality was strongly criticized and is now rejected as inappropriate by the Supreme Court of Canada.[12]

Despite the important strides made in guaranteeing equality, there are several practical barriers or obstacles that lie in the path over which disabled Canadians must travel to secure full protection of their legal equality rights in Canada.

The first barrier was referred to above, namely the limited access of disabled persons to effective legal services. It is reasonable to expect that defendants in disability equality rights claims, under the Charter or under human rights legislation, will have access to effective legal talent to defend against such challenges. However, disabled persons will often be left to the services of legal aid clinics and *pro bono* services from law firms for representation as Charter plaintiffs in such cases.[13]

[11] See e.g., *R. v. Ertel* (1987), 20 O.A.C. 257 (Ont.C.A.), leave to appeal to the Supreme Court of Canada denied, December 3, 1987.

[12] See *Andrews*, *supra* at 143 per MacIntyre J.

[13] There have been two important strides in this context in recent years. In 1980 Ontario's first legal aid clinic was established which is specifically dedicated to providing legal services in the disability rights context. Toronto's "Advocacy Resource Centre for the Handicapped" has an excellent team of experts, equipped to skillfully spearhead litigation and lobbying efforts in this context, and to train legal professionals in the provision of legal services to disabled persons. In addition, in recent years the national Canadian Disability Rights Council was established as a nationwide organization to advocate for the legal rights of disabled persons, in the Charter context and otherwise. While these advances are of critical importance, it cannot reasonably be expected that such groups would be able to shoulder all the legal requirements of the 10 to 15 per cent of Canada's population who have a physical or mental disability. For measures which can be taken to improve the access to legal services for disabled persons in Canada, see "Access to Legal Services by the Disabled: Report of a Study by Judge Rosalie S. Abella", *supra*; see also M. David

The second important barrier to access to equality rights pertains particularly to the context of the Charter of Rights. Charter litigation is fought primarily in the courts, and often must be fought up several levels of courts before a final and authoritative ruling can be secured. The cost of litigating such claims can be extraordinary, especially where, as is often the case, litigants must develop an extensive evidentiary record, replete with expert testimony and complex cross-examinations. Where multiple appeals are involved, this cost barrier is exacerbated.

The third barrier pertains to both the Charter and human rights code contexts. The prosecution of a claim of discrimination, based on disability or other grounds, can take a great deal of time, amounting to numbers of years, whether such claims are under the Charter of Rights or under human rights legislation. Complaints brought under human rights legislation ordinarily must undergo a process of investigation, conciliation and human rights commission deliberations before the matter can proceed to a full hearing at an administrative tribunal. Results of such hearings can be taken on appeal or on review to courts. In the case of Charter litigation, court backlogs, combined with the time allocations provided in civil procedure rules, can make it difficult to secure an expeditious court hearing to have a matter resolved on the merits. Thereafter, such matters can be taken on appeal through several judicial levels.

This is not to suggest that there is any calculated antagonism on the part of human rights commissions or courts in dealing with disability equality claims, or in dealing with any other human rights claims. Similarly, this is not to suggest that the processes of investigation, conciliation and mediation under human rights legislation are unimportant or unnecessary. However, delays caused by backlogs in courts or in human rights commissions nevertheless must be identified as an important barrier to the full and effective implementation of equality rights for disabled persons, as well as for others seeking protection of their equality rights.

In the face of these barriers, there are increasing calls for additional initiatives to be undertaken to foster and promote the equality rights of disabled persons in Canada. Within the employment context, these include claims for the enactment of mandatory employment equity legislation. Such laws which would require the achievement of increased representation of disabled persons in the workforce. Additionally, there have been increasing claims for the enactment of omnibus legislation which would impose specific and substantial requirements to ensure that disabled persons have full access to the mainstream of society. Such a measure was recently enacted into law in the United States. The Americans With Disabilities Act[14] which was recently enacted imposes detailed, nationwide standards of access and accommodation for disabled

---

Lepofsky, *Disabled Persons and Canadian Law Schools – The Right to the Equal Benefit of the Law School*, 36 McGill Law Journal, 636 (1991).

[14] Americans With Disabilities Act of 1990, 104 Stat. 327, Leg. Hist. 267 U.S. Code Congressional and Administrative News.

persons in the workplace, in transit facilities, in buildings and elsewhere. There is now a move in Canada to call for the enactment of comparable "Canadians With Disabilities" legislation, and provincial counterparts, to ensure that within the full scope of legislative jurisdiction in Canada full legal protections are available.

The advantage of such omnibus legislation is that it can provide far greater legislative detail than is now incorporated into The Charter of Rights and statutory human rights codes. Both the Charter and human rights legislation tend to speak in broad-brush terms. They leave it to the courts and to human rights boards of inquiries to articulate detailed standards which these legislative equality guarantees impose. Hence, before one can have any legal specificity in the equality rights context, it is now often necessary to undergo years of litigation, replete with appeals, to establish clear legal principles and to rectify conflicts in the case-law. In contrast, a Canadian counterpart to the Americans With Disabilities Act could include exhaustive, detailed and precise standards as to the scope of accommodations which must be provided, and the time within which they must be provided.

4. International Perspective on Equality Rights for Disabled Persons

As this volume focuses on international perspectives on human rights issues, it is appropriate to turn our attention to international perspectives on equality rights for persons with disabilities. Canada itself owes much to the international community in this context. Canadians can now be proud that their Constitution is perhaps one of the only western democratic constitutions, if not the only such constitution, which explicitly enshrines equality rights for persons with disabilities.

However, when the Charter was first proposed in Parliament in 1980, the inclusion of disability in Charter section 15 was not a foregone conclusion. To the contrary, the initial draft of Charter section 15 was formulated in a fashion which would only have guaranteed equality rights to some persons, and not to all. Disabled persons were clearly and deliberately excluded from it. During Canada's national debate over The Charter of Rights in 1980 and 1981, intensive lobbying efforts in the face of substantial government resistance were required to persuade Parliament to amend Charter section 15 before it was enacted into law, so as to include persons with disabilities within its protection.[15] It was necessary to marshall all available arguments to persuade Parliament to make this desired amendment. One of the important arguments which unquestionably contributed to Parliament's decision to include disability in section 15 was international in character.

The Charter was to be passed by Parliament in 1981. The United Nations

[15] See Lepofsky and Bickenbach in A.F. Bayefsky and M. Eberts (eds.) "Equality Rights and the Canadian Charter of Rights and Freedoms" (1985).

had declared 1981 to be the "International Year of the Disabled Person". The theme of this year was "Equality and Full Participation". Parliamentarians were told that it would be grossly inappropriate for Canada to intentionally omit disabled persons from the protection of Charter section 15's equality rights guarantee during the very year that the U.N. had dedicated for disabled persons, with the avowed aim of promoting their equality. The new outlook on equality rights for persons with disabilities heralded by the United Nations in 1981 consequently contributed positively towards the enactment of constitutional equality rights protections for persons with disabilities in Canada, by assisting Canadians with disabilities to convince Parliament to pass the disability amendment early in 1981, and hence to make protection against disability-based discrimination in Canada a fundamental constitutional right.

If attention turns from the developed world to the developing nations, one quickly discovers that issues concerning persons with disabilities can change drastically. The following does not purport to be an exhaustive or comprehensive survey of equality issues concerning disabled persons in developing countries. Rather, it is simply an effort to identify the extent to which a developed country's core focus in the disability equality context can apply to countries lacking a high gross national product and powerful industrial sector.

In a country such as Canada that has a far-reaching system of socialized health insurance, it is reasonable to expect that the population of persons with disabilities is made up largely, if not almost entirely, of those whose disabilities are not medically curable. If a person has a major visual impairment due to near-sightedness or far-sightedness, refractive glasses are readily available to correct this condition. If the visual impairment is due to a cataracting of their eyes' lenses, quick and efficient cataract surgery is available to eradicate the cause of the sight loss. If a person has a life-threatening diabetic condition, this condition can be effectively diagnosed, and insulin treatment prescribed to ensure that the individual's life can be drastically extended. The list is almost endless. Hence, if one meets a Canadian who has a disability, it is generally correct to presume that the physiological cause of their disability is likely not medically reversible at the present time. The focus for disabled persons in Canada is largely upon the process of securing adjustment training and accommodations to their disability in schools, housing, employment and other social situations, as well as massive reform of public attitudes towards disabled persons.[16]

In contrast, the disabled population of many developing countries includes a large component of persons whose disabilities are medically curable, preventable or substantially reducible. This is so because in these countries, the population, disabled as well as able-bodied, generally does not have available to

[16] This generalized presumption is, however, not universal. It is less likely to be appropriate in those regions of Canada which are severely medically-underserved, such as is the case in the remote communities of the northern territories.

it important primary health care services. These societies often suffer from severely limited overall resources, the limited availability of trained health care providers, equipment and medications, and the frequent inability of members of the public to afford needed health care services. This situation can also be linked to the existence of major environmental causes of preventable disability, such as water supply impurities, which have not been eradicated. As well, in those developing nations which are rapidly industrializing, additional causes of preventable disability are created through rapid urbanization, insufficiently regulated industrial pollution and avoidable industrial accidents.

In these societies, the most pressing focus for health care reform concerns the creation of a medical and health infrastructure which can effectively deliver primary health care to the public. Standing ahead of the need to treat and cure large numbers of preventable disabilities may well be the need to first get enough rudimentary health care to the public to prevent the occurrence of fatal diseases such as measles, and to treat preventable causes of death such as diarrhoeal diseases, pneumonia and malaria. This is not to denigrate in any way the importance of the provision of needed health care to those in developing countries who have preventable disabilities. Rather, it is to highlight the fact that in such countries, the pressing need to provide such health care must be juxtaposed with the pressing need to eradicate preventable causes of mortality.

In such settings, some of the considerations described in the preceding part of this presentation would appear to be of questionable immediacy. Demands that employers provide disabled employees with the latest technological breakthroughs are of less relevance in societies whose overall unemployment rates for the public parallel those which have been reserved in Canada for persons with disabilities. These demands are also of less relevance in societies which do not have a technological and industrial infrastructure to make them work. Put simply, a blind person in a developing country would likely give little priority to acquiring a relatively low-cost talking computer which provides him or her efficient access to the blossoming worlds of word processing and data processing, if he or she lives in a small rural village which has no electricity and no businesses which could gainfully employ this computer technology.

To date, the international community has yet to enshrine equality rights for persons with disabilities in any of the existing international human rights covenants. The subject of disabled persons' rights has been the focus of a broadly-worded, if not somewhat nebulous United Nations Resolution. The U.N. General Assembly's "Declaration of the Rights of Disabled Persons"[17] enunciates broad principles regarding the entitlement of disabled persons throughout the world to equality and to full participation in society. However, it provides no enforcement machinery to ensure its effective implementation. It can certainly serve as an important and informative guide to the interpretation

[17] See Declaration of the Rights of Disabled Persons, 9 December 1975, U.N. G.A. Resolution 3447 (XXX).

of domestic laws guaranteeing equality rights to disabled persons, such as Canada's Charter of Rights. However, this is not sufficient.

It is important for the international community to take the next critical step, that is, to formulate and enact amendments to existing international human rights covenants, so that they provide forceful international guarantees of equality rights for people with disabilities. It is preferable to enshrine such guarantees into existing, mainstream human rights instruments, rather than segregating such guarantees in a new, special covenant dedicated only to the rights of disabled persons. This would be a small but vital step away from a global history of segregating and ghettoizing disabled people. Of course, an international guarantee of the rights of disabled persons, even one replete with sophisticated enforcement machinery, will be of questionable utility beyond the realm of the rhetorician, unless it is wedded to improved, constructive means for advancing the economic development of the world's poorer countries.

5. Canada on the International Scene – The Immigration to Canada of Disabled Persons

No discussion in Canada of the international dimensions of equality rights for disabled persons would be adequate unless it reflected back on Canada's own approach to the international movement of persons with disabilities. International mobility is an important aspect of human rights.

Canada's own immigration legislation imposes a serious and unwarranted barrier to the free and equal movement of disabled persons from other countries to Canada. Clause 19 (1) (a) of the Immigration Act[18] prohibits entry into Canada, generally, of anyone who suffers from disease, disorder or disability, which in the opinion of two medical officers is a danger to public health or whose entry might reasonably be expected to cause excessive demands on health or social services.

An examination of s. 19(1)(a)(ii) of the Immigration Act, and its impact on the equality rights of disabled persons, provides a highly instructive example of how to analyze a case of alleged discrimination based on disability. This provision seriously violates both the letter and the spirit of section 15 of the Charter of Rights, by discriminating with respect to immigration on the ground of disability. While all potential immigrants to Canada must meet a range of legislated selection criteria, disabled applicants have an added hurdle placed in their path by this provision. They must persuade two government-appointed physicians that their disability will not pose an "excessive demand on health and social services". No other immigration applicant is subjected to this standard. Others can be admitted to Canada, despite the fact that they may pose an "excessive demand on health and social services". Only disabled applicants are subjected to this specific requirement. This disadvantageous treatment

[18] *Immigration Act*, 1976–77, c.52, s. 1.

amounts to direct, and purposeful discrimination against disabled persons because of their handicap. It is not justifiable under Charter section 1's reasonable limits clause, for several reasons. First, in assessing the reasonableness of this limit on equality rights, it is necessary to determine how significant an infringement on equality is imposed by this provision. The burden on the Government to justify an infringement of a Charter right increases with the severity of the infringement itself.[19]

Section 19(1)(a)(ii) of the Immigration Act imposes the most severe abridgement of disability equality rights. It reflects an unfounded stereotype that disabled persons presumptively constitute an excessive demand on health and social services. The eradication of such adverse stereotyping of disabled persons is a core objective of section 15 of the Charter. Additionally, this provision involves discrimination against disabled persons vis à vis a right which the Charter itself considers fundamental. The right of a prospective immigrant to remain in Canada has been found to be included in Charter section 7's liberty guarantee, at least in so far as refugee claims are concerned.[20] It is appropriate to view the right to remain in Canada as fundamental, whether it is exercised by a refugee, a Canadian citizen[21] or an immigration applicant. Where discrimination bears on the exercise of a right which is itself fundamental, it is all the more serious a case of inequality. Accordingly, the burden on government under Charter section 1 to justify section 19(1)(a)(ii) of the Immigration Act is an exceedingly exacting one.

To meet this onerous burden, the Government must, as a first step, show that the denial of disability equality rights in section 19(1)(a)(ii) of the Immigration Act serves a pressing and substantial social objective. This test cannot be met in the case of this federal provision. Section 19(1)(a)(ii) appears to have as its core goal a purely discriminatory objective, namely the substantial exclusion from permanent admission to Canada of disabled immigrants. Its goal is not simply the avoidance of excessive demands on Canadian health and social services, since it does not apply this test across the board to all immigration applicants. Such a legislative objective cannot be sustained under Charter section 1. Under section 1, a law's objective can only be sustained if it is sufficiently pressing and substantial to warrant the overriding of the equality rights of disabled persons. Section 1 will not tolerate legislative objectives which are inimical to or discordant with the goals of a free and democratic society.[22]

The legislative objective of section 19(1)(a)(ii) of the Immigration Act seems to be clearly discordant with and inimical to the Charter values of freedom and democracy. The Supreme Court has recognized that among the values which are fundamental to a free and democratic society, and hence pivotal to the

[19] See Reference re Criminal Code ss. 193 and 195.1(1)(c) (Prostitution Reference) [1990] 1 S.C.R. at 1190.

[20] See *Singh v. Minister of Employment and Immigration*, [1985] 1 S.C.R. 177 per Wilson, J.

[21] See Charter s. 6(1).

[22] See *Oakes*, *supra*, at 138.

Charter itself, are equality, diversity and social justice.[23] Such an overtly discriminatory legislative aim as is rooted in section 19(1)(a)(ii) of the Immigration Act cuts to the core of these constitutional goals. It would be constitutionally intolerable to add to the Immigration Act a provision which stipulated that a person could not immigrate to Canada where, in the opinion of a government medical officer, his or her race, sex or ethnic origin was likely to make them an excessive demand on government services. A comparable enactment which ties such an assessment to disability is similarly unwarranted. It bespeaks a pejorative attitude that the bulk of the world's disabled population should be simply cast aside as "someone else's problem".

In the defence of section 19(1)(a)(ii) of the Immigration Act, it might be suggested that the true goal of this provision is simply to save the Canadian public from the excessive costs of certain disabled immigrants. For the reasons set forth above, this would not be a correct characterization of the federal law's objective. However, even if it were the provision's actual goal, it would nevertheless fail to withstand scrutiny under Charter section 1.

The question presented in this context is not simply whether it is a pressing and substantial objective in Canada to avoid excessive drains on health and social services. Rather, the constitutional question demanding a juridical response is whether the asserted goal of avoiding the alleged demand on health and social services is so compelling that its achievement warrants the sacrifice of the equality rights of disabled persons. This goal is not sufficiently important to meet section 1's requirements. The cost-saving rationale pales in significance when measured against the societal importance of disability equality, as outlined earlier in this article. As well, the marginal increment of health and social services costs which is provably attributable to some increase in the immigration of disabled persons to Canada would be trivial when measured against Canada's current total health and social service budget.

Even if, despite the foregoing, it were assumed that the purpose of section 19(1)(a)(ii) of the Immigration Act was sufficiently important to warrant the imposition of limits on the section 15 rights of disabled persons, the means employed by the Immigration Act to achieve this objective is not rationally connected to this goal. Section 1 of the Charter requires that a law burdening Charter rights be carefully tailored to avoid the unnecessary trenching on constitutional rights.[24] It is unnecessary and irrational, short of impermissible prejudice or stereotype, to single out disabled persons alone for screening under section 19(1)(a)(ii) of the Immigration Act. In order to address itself to demands on its health and social services system, Parliament could have passed a provision which excludes any immigration applicant if they pose an excessive demand on health and social services, including those whose need for such services is due to other personal needs or requirements apart from disability. There is no need to single out disabled persons for this standard, short of

[23] See *Oakes*, *supra*, at 136.

[24] See *Oakes*, *supra*, at 139.

adherence to a traditional stereotype which is historically tied to the disadvantaged treatment of persons with disabilities.

Furthermore, the immigration legislation employs an unduly vague and unfair standard. It provides that an applicant's demands on health and social services be "excessive". The "excessive" standard is not defined in the Act. The legislation itself provides no insight whatsoever into the level of demand on the part of an immigration applicant which is acceptable. Is it a level of demand for health and social services which exceeds that which able-bodied Canadians present on average? Is it the level of demand which disabled Canadians present on average? Is it tied to the applicant's age in any way? After all, more elderly Canadians likely present on average a higher demand on health and social services than do younger Canadians.

The statutory provision does not stipulate the period of time over which the immigration applicant's health and social service needs are to be assessed. Is the demand to be judged over the individual's entire lifetime? Is it only to be assessed for a period of the first few years after the immigrant settles in Canada? Is the demand to be measured against an immigration applicant's financial capacity to finance their own health and social services? Must it be assumed that each immigration applicant will turn exclusively to government for all of their health and social service needs? Section 19(1)(a)(ii) of the Immigration Act is fundamentally flawed because it delegates the critical policy decision with respect to these core issues entirely to public officials at the first instance.

A federal regulation was enacted under the Immigration Act, which set out criteria to assist a medical officer in deciding whether an applicant for admission to Canada meets the "excessive demand" critera.[25] However, the regulation does not cure the Act's defects on its face for several reasons. Indeed, in some ways, the regulation compounds the Act's discriminatory character.[26] First, the regulation does not answer any of the critical questions enumerated above regarding the application of section 19(1)(a)(ii)'s inherently ambiguous standard. Second, the regulation's criteria pertaining to the excessive demand standard are themselves extremely ambiguous. Third, two of

[25] (a) any reports made by a medical practitioner with respect to the person;

(e) whether the supply of health or social services that the person may require in Canada is limited to such an extent that
  a) the use of such services by the person might reasonably be expected to prevent or delay provision of those services to Canadian citizens or permanent residents, or
  b) the use of such services may not be available or accessible to the person;

(f) whether medical care or hospitalization is required;

(g) whether potential employability or productivity is affected; and

(h) whether prompt and effective medical treatment can be provided."

[26] It is certainly arguable that when a statute is itself excessively vague and discriminatory, it cannot be saved by enacting regulations such as is the case here. Regulations, unlike statutes, can be enacted and revoked by Cabinet, and are thus more tenuous in nature than a statute passed by a legislature. While regulations have the force of law, they are not juridically as durable as a statute.

the regulation's criteria can have the practical effect of directing a medical officer to exclude a disabled applicant from admission to Canada on account of pre-existing discrimination against disabled persons which now pervades in Canada.

For example, section 22(g) of the regulation requires a medical officer to consider whether the applicant would be employable in Canada. Given the extremely high unemployment rate in Canada for disabled persons living here already, caused in large part by attitudinal barriers and discriminatory employment practices, a medical officer could readily conclude that most disabled applicants are not likely to meet this requirement, no matter how valuable are their work skills and talents. In addition, section 22(e)(ii) of the regulation requires a medical officer to consider whether health and social services required by the applicant are "accessible". It is likely that the greatest barrier to their accessibility will often be physical. That Canada's health and social services system may itself discriminate against disabled Canadians by permitting such physical barriers to remain in place should not justify exclusion from Canada of additional disabled immigrants.

The statute's and regulation's unduly vague and discretionary "excessive demand" standard is rendered all the more arbitrary and capricious when regard is had to the procedure by which it is implemented in individual immigration cases. An immigration applicant's compliance with the section 19(1)(a)(ii) standard is not determined on its merits at first instance either by a court or a quasi-judicial administrative tribunal. Rather it is determined by a government medical officer, whose opinion is vetted by a second government medical officer. There is no requirement under section 9 of the Immigration Act or Clause 19(1)(a)(ii) that both of these physicians ever personally examine the applicant or that an examination, if undertaken, be sufficient to yield useful information on the basis of which a judgment can be attempted. At most, section 9 requires one medical officer to perform a medical examination.

Moreover, it is manifestly unwarranted to delegate this judgment to doctors. Physicians are trained to practise medicine. They are not trained to assess an individual's potential demand for social services. They are unqualified to make the social policy judgment of what health and social service demands are "excessive" in Canadian society. A medical officer may have no expertise in the disability field generally, or in the specific field of disability and employment. It is generally doubtful that a doctor could effectively determine whether a disabled applicant in another country could secure gainful employment in Canada, especially if that doctor himself or herself resides in the applicant's home country and not in Canada.

These administrative determinations under section 19(1)(a)(ii) of the Immigration Act are not appealable either to court or to the Immigration Appeal Board, with only one exception. Where the applicant seeks admission to Canada as a sponsored dependent, the sponsor, and not the applicant himself or herself, can appeal an adverse finding to the Immigration Appeal Board. In any case, the applicant himself or herself can only challenge adverse findings under section 19(1)(a)(ii) of the Immigration Act by way of judicial review proceedings in the Federal Court. Such proceedings provide a very limited safeguard. They do not constitute an appeal. The Federal Court's power to review adverse findings is extremely narrow. Moreover, in administrative law, judicial review is constrained by a strong tendency towards judicial deference to the decisions of regulatory agencies and tribunals.

When the open-ended and ambiguous "excessive" standard in section 19(1)(a)(ii) of the Immigration Act and the related regulation is combined with the absence of due process protections, the consequence is a strong risk of inaccurate decisions, administrative unfairness and inconsistent determinations. The same applicant could be admitted to Canada by one immigration official, while he or she would be excluded from Canada pursuant to section 19(1)(a)(ii) of the Immigration Act had their case been reviewed by a different immigration official. Such an arrangement is the antithesis of Charter section 1's standards of reasonableness, rationality and narrow legislative tailoring. Furthermore, the absence of adequate procedural safeguards increases the risk that section 19(1)(a)(ii) of the Immigration Act, which is discriminatory on its face, will be open to discriminatory application in individual cases. Because medical officers do not make their assessments of individual immigration applicants "on the record", their decisions could well reflect stereotypical and inaccurate presuppositions about the alleged costly demands on health and social services that will be posed by various kinds of disabilities. Such discriminatory actions would be difficult to detect and to judicially review, because the Act imposes no procedural safeguards which would force such official attitudes to the surface.

These fundamental legislative deficiencies cannot be cured by the adoption of governmental administrative guidelines addressed to medical officers. This legislation must be tested for its constitutionality on its face. Moreover, because of the absence of adequate procedural safeguards, it would not be feasible to detect whether administrative policy has been followed in specific cases.

There are ample adequate legislative alternatives to section 19(1)(a)(ii), which would not involve such unconstitutional discrimination against immigration applicants on the ground of disability. As but one example, section 19(1)(a)(ii) of the Immigration Act could simply be repealed, with all applicants, disabled or otherwise, being effectively screened for admission to Canada under the myriad of other mechanisms in place in the Immigration Act for filtering out the least appropriate immigrants to Canada. In other words, all applicants for admission to Canada, disabled or not, could be assessed on the basis of what they can contribute to Canada, and why they need access to Canada, and not by a speculative assessment of what social or health needs they may hypothetically experience in future. It is exceedingly doubtful that the consequence of a repeal of the offending portions of section 19(1)(a)(ii) of the Immigration Act would be the sudden onslaught of immigrants to Canada who threaten to bankrupt or fundamentally disrupt Canada's large health and social service infrastructure.

Alternatively, the "excessive demand" standard could be carefully and narrowly defined in the statute with legislative criteria which are fair, meaningful and capable of consistent application by the bureaucracy. Instead of singling out disabled applicants alone for subjection to this standard, it could be applied to all immigration applicants, with appropriate safeguards built in to ensure that it does not have adverse discriminatory effect on disabled applicants. Due process protections could be enacted, including on-the-record decision-making and full appeal rights, to ensure that applicants are assessed in a fair and accurate way.[27]

In sum, Canada can stand prominently among the developing and developed nations of the world as a country which has formally recognized the fundamental importance of the equality rights and full participation of disabled persons in society. Canada has an incredible potential for the full and productive integration of disabled persons into the mainstream of society. Unlike many of the world's developing societies, Canada has an enormous economic potential to equip persons with disabilities to be independent, productive and self-fulfilled, and to benefit from their productivity. It would constitute a bizarre state of affairs for Canada to recognize equality rights for disabled persons domestically, for Canada to promote the recognition of this right internationally, and yet, for Canada to place a deliberate, substantial and arbitrary barrier in the way of disabled persons in other countries from immigrating to this land.

6. Conclusion – Equality Rights for Persons with Disabilities and This Confernce

This International Human Rights Conference constitutes an important step in Canada's effort to contribute constructively to the recognition and enforcement of human rights around the world. By including in its agenda a presentation on equality rights and persons with disabilities, this Conference has acknowledged, at least tacitly, that international human rights can no longer be adequately examined and discussed unless the discussion includes as an agenda item the equality rights of persons with disabilities.

It is a matter of most profound regret that the location chosen for this Conference was the Banff Springs Hotel. While this hotel's facilities are quite plush, its food is superb and its stunning mountain views are unparalleled, the Banff Springs Hotel is not designed to be adequately accessible to disabled persons, and particularly to those who use wheelchairs and cannot climb stairs. While it is possible to gain physical access to the building itself, a number of

[27] See *Anvari v. Canada (Employment and Immigration Comm.)* (1988), 10 C.H.R.R. D/5816, where the Canadian Human Rights Tribunal found that s. 19(1) of the Immigration Act contravened the guarantee against disability-based discrimination in the Canadian Human Rights Act, S.C. 1976–77, c. 33, as amended. This case is currently under appeal.

meeting rooms, used at this Conference, were accessible by way of a series of steps. Those who came to Banff to attend this conference witnessed the spectacle of a conference attendee who uses a wheelchair, sitting in a hotel corridor and watching an important conference session on a television monitor, because it was convened in an inaccessible room. This cruel irony was amplified by the fact that the wheelchair-using attendee is the chief commissioner of Canada's largest provincial human rights commission – the agency responsible for enforcing anti-discrimination laws. Exacerbating this situation further was the fact that the very room in which this Conference's presentation on disability equality was convened was also only accessible by way of a flight of stairs.

This constitutes a serious stain on the complexion of this Conference. Applying the approach to equality rights and disability set out in this presentation, it is abundantly clear that this serious barrier to disabled persons' full and equal participation in this Conference's proceedings was discriminatory and unnecessary. Other conference facilities in Alberta and elsewhere in Canada are equipped to ensure that disabled persons can secure admittance to all meeting rooms, and can readily accommodate a conference of this size. In light of the fact that this conference brought to Canada speakers from around the world and was intended to be international in dimension, the selection of an accessible venue somewhere else in Alberta, or indeed somewhere else in Canada, would not have posed an economic or administrative hardship. Indeed, other venues may well have been cheaper and easier for conference attendees to reach. The only sacrifice which may have occurred if another venue had been chosen would be the loss of Banff's spectacular mountain views. However, in light of the fact that this Conference's focus is on international human rights, and protection of the disadvantaged around the world, this loss would be marginal if not entirely irrelevant.

On any list of those places where one would expect and indeed strongly presume that accommodations and accessibility for disabled persons would be assured as a matter of obvious priority, a conference on human rights would rank rather near the top. It would be unthinkable to locate an international human rights conference in a facility which only permitted men, but not women, to actually sit in the rooms where some of the sessions were held. It would be unthinkable to select a venue which had certain rooms that were open only to white persons to sit in, leaving blacks to watch the proceedings in a corridor on a video monitor. It should have been equally unthinkable for such a situation to confront disabled attendees.

There can be no hierarchy among equality seekers or equality rights, whether intentional or unintentional. If disabled persons cannot be assured access to conferences at which their own equality rights will be discussed, they cannot be optimistic about the chances for securing broader recognition for their full participation in society. Put simply, the experience with inaccessibility at this Conference should never have happened.

KATARINA TOMASEVSKI*

Before AIDS, Beyond AIDS: Human Rights of People with Contagious Diseases

1. Introduction

Before AIDS, epidemics were thought to be part of history, and so was fear of epidemics. Safe water and good sanitation coupled with vaccines and drugs, seemed to have freed the developed part of the world from epidemics. Inability of medicine to provide a cure for AIDS or a vaccine against HIV infection, shattered our "unrealistic optimism about medical capabilities"[1]. When technology proved unable to provide means of control, social control was applied instead. Our response to AIDS is a historical reminder: whenever humanity could not cope with a disease, its response was to change the target and undertake measures against the people affected by this disease. None of the repressive measures that today are applied against people affected by HIV/AIDS are new – all were used in similar circumstances when medicine had no cure, when fear of epidemics demanded action.

2. HIV/AIDS as a Human Rights Issue

If measures against people affected by HIV/AIDS have not contributed much in terms of novelty, response to them did. Challenging coercive and compulsory public health measures, was virtually non existent before AIDS even when it could be shown they were harmful and ineffective. The pattern was broken by the international community. The Secretary-General of the United Nations said that our fight against AIDS "is also a fight against fear, against prejudice and against irrational action born of ignorance",[2] and added

* Senior Research Associate at the McGill Centre for Medicine, Ethics and Law.

[1] Congress of the United States, Office of Technology Assessment – Biology, Medicine, and the Bill of Rights. Special Report, OTA-CIT-371, Washington, September 1988, at p. 61.

[2] Statement by the Secretary-General of the United Nations before the General Assembly, Press release SG/SM/816/GA/334, 20 October 1987, at p. 3.

K.E. Mahoney and P. Mahoney (eds.), Human Rights in the Twenty-first Century, 191–207.

later "that the world should make war *against AIDS*, and *not* against *people* with AIDS."[3]

Arguing human rights in the context of HIV/AIDS has not been easy. Responses to AIDS are created, first and foremost, within public health: "since AIDS is a disease, it is handled within a medical model, not one of civil liberties."[4] Paradoxically, this "medical model" does *not* include human rights considerations, even though virtually any measure of disease control has human rights implications. All public health measures are intrusive: surveillance may be confined to population-based data or it may include personal identity; notification may be anonymous or nominal; the same disease may be classified differently. The choice as to how public health surveillance will be carried out, whether a disease will be subject to compulsory notification and, if so, what data will be required, how a disease will be classified, is never "technical".

A pandemic of the severity of AIDS triggered off the whole gamut of public health measures for coping with epidemics, many of which are incompatible with human rights. This part of public health heritage has been, however, challenged within public health itself, nationally and internationally. The World Health Organization has affirmed that human rights apply in AIDS prevention and control, thus nullifying claims that denial or violation of human rights is necessary from the public health viewpoint.[5]

Epidemiological studies of HIV/AIDS within the "medical model" have revealed that AIDS has disproportionately affected those already stigmatized and disprivileged, and this might have been a "cause of people becoming infected with HIV".[6] The Panos Institute called AIDS a "misery-seeking missile".[7] Those identified as most seriously affected by HIV/AIDS had been named "high-risk groups" early in the pandemic. These "high-risk groups" encompassed those already stigmatized and disprivileged: homosexuals, prostitutes, prisoners, drug-dependent persons, racial and ethnic minorities.

[3] Statement of Javier Perez de Cuellar, the Secretary-General of the United Nations, on the occasion of the World AIDS Day, 1 December 1988, [mimeographed], at p. 5.

[4] C.A. Tauer, "AIDS and Human Rights: An Intercontinental Perspective", in C. Pierce, and D. Van De Veer, (eds.) *AIDS, Ethics and Public Policy*, Wadsworth Publishing Company: Belmont, California, pp. 154–169, at p. 155.

[5] In its statement on the social aspects of AIDS prevention and control, WHO's Global Programme on AIDS (called "Special Programme on AIDS" at the time) said that "AIDS prevention and control strategies can be implemented effectively and efficiently ... in a manner that respects and protects human rights", and added that "there is no public health rationale to justify isolation, quarantine, or any discriminatory measures based solely on the fact that a person is suspected or known to be HIV infected". Moreover, "failure to prevent discrimination may endanger public health". Social Aspects of AIDS Prevention and Control, WHO/SPA/GLO/87.2, Geneva, December 1, 1987.

[6] M. A. Somerville, and A. J. Orkin, "Human Rights, Discrimination and AIDS: Concepts and Issues", *AIDS* (1990), vol. 3, Suppl. 1, pp. S283–S287, at S285.

[7] R. Sabatier, *Blaming Others. Prejudice, Race and Worldwide AIDS*. The Panos Institute, London, 1988, at p. 145 et seq.

Stigmatization was reinforced by treating them collectively as "source of infection" and individually as "carriers", rather than affected people. Much research has been carried out into HIV incidence and prevalence in "high-risk groups", and data on high infection rates linked AIDS further to these "groups". Results of epidemiological studies were often used to justify coercive and compulsory measures to protect the "general population" from "sources of infection".

Human rights organizations recognized human rights violations in many compulsory, coercive or discriminatory measures applied in the context of HIV/AIDS. The fact that targets of such measures coincide with most frequent victims of human rights violations in other areas prompted the use of the "civil liberties model" to challenge HIV/AIDS-related policies, laws and practices. This challenge received endorsement by international bodies. The fact that international health rather than human rights bodies started first merits emphasis.[8] The Global Commission on AIDS, established by WHO, emphasized that no "blanket exemption from observance of human rights obligations" may be accepted in combatting AIDS,[9] and the International Consultation on AIDS and Human Rights concluded that exemptions from observance of human rights could not be justified simply by claiming that they were required for public health reasons.[10]

(1) Public Health Heritage

The language of AIDS provides ample evidence for the assertion that human rights are alien to the public health heritage. This language, developed through the history of epidemic control, borrows heavily from military terminology, using terms such as defence, agent, sentinel surveillance, fight, combat, battle. Moreover, it embodies linguistic barriers that divide humanity into "us" and "them": the infected people are referred to as "carriers" of the disease, they are not "us" any more. As public health deals with protecting the community against disease, these linguistic barriers signify the process of ex-communication, whereby "they" are identified with the disease and become legitimate targets of measures to "fight" the disease.

These linguistic barriers are reminders of the physical barriers used earlier in

[8] The Council of Europe was the first international organization to link respect of human rights to AIDS prevention and control in a series of recommendations developed by and addressed to health authorities. Cf. Recommendation No. R (83) 8 of the Committee of Ministers to Member States on preventing the possible transmission of Acquired Immune Deficiency Syndrome (AIDS) from affected blood donors to patients receiving blood or blood products, June 23, 1983, and Resolution 812 (1983) of the Standing Committee on behalf of the Parliamentary Assembly on the Acquired Immune Deficiency Syndrome, November 23, 1983.

[9] Report of the Global Commission on AIDS, Geneva, March 29–31, 1989, WHO Doc. GPA/GCA(1)/89.1, para. 19.6.

[10] International Consultation on AIDS and Human Rights, Geneva, July 26–28, 1989, Final Document, U.N. Doc. HR/AIDS/1989/3, paras. 18(d) and p. 13.

history to prevent passage to all except those carrying a certificate of good health. This practice has been revived in the AIDS pandemic through "AIDS-free certificates" in international migration and travel. Erecting barriers between the healthy and the infected is a typical (in)human response to epidemics. It continues despite knowledge that expulsion or isolation victimizes those already affected by a disease, while failing to prevent its spread:

> "... isolation of the sick did not stop the spread of infection; this was so even in the days when travel was slow and along well-known routes, and when the threat of death penalty was used to persuade the sick to obey instructions to remain apart from their fellows."[11]

Treatment of people with communicable diseases has steadily progressed from less to more humane, but we have not yet reached the stage where the human rights of the ill are fully recognized, let alone respected and protected. The societal treatment of the ill has progressed historically according to the growing recognition of the worth of human beings. As long as people were treated as means and not an end, the notion of inherent rights pertaining to everybody could not have been accepted. Suffice it to recall the dominant view of the sixteenth century, when measures to protect the health of the population started: "it was recognized... everywhere that effective use of population within a country required attention to problems of health."[12] The historical evolution of societal responses to epidemics can be outlined in a nutshell as follows:

- The earliest response to an epidemic was to eliminate people affected by it. Physical extermination of those affected was a brutal but understandable reaction to fear of disease in ignorance of how it is caused and transmitted, and the consequent lack of possibilities of self-protection. People with the disease were eliminated because humanity was not able to identify and eliminate the cause of disease in people.
- The second stage in the development of societal responses to epidemics was to isolate the infected people, thus advancing to a more humane measure, whereby physical barriers were erected between the ill and the healthy to prevent further spread of epidemics.
- The third stage was marked by the emergence of concern for the ill. Still kept isolated, the ill were cared for and attempts were made to cure them, so that they would stop being a danger to the healthy and, also, not constitute a burden to society, having to be fed, clothed and cared for while kept in isolation.
- In the fourth stage humanity advanced from merely responding to epidemics to disease prevention. This has not yet changed the treatment of

[11] "Disease Control and International Travel: A Review of International Sanitary Regulations", *Chronicle of the World Health Organization*, vol. 10, 1956, No. 9–10, Special Issue, at p. 275.

[12] G. Rosen, *A History of Public Health* (1958), MD Publications, New York, at p. 110.

the ill once there is an outbreak of an epidemic: in the name of protecting the healthy, human rights of the ill are denied or – at best – disregarded.

These evolving societal responses to epidemics resulted in the recognition of individual obligations rather than rights in public health. WHO confirmed this in its submission on limitations on human rights in 1975, stating the following:

> "The individual is obliged to notify the health authorities when he is suffering from communicable diseases (including venereal diseases) or has been exposed to infection, and must undergo examination, treatment, surveillance, isolation or hospitalization. In particular, obligatory isolation or hospitalization in such cases constitutes a limitation on freedom of movement and the right to liberty and security of person."[13]

Whether denying or limiting human rights is indeed necessary to cope with an epidemic is determined by those designing the "medical model", and thereby gives much power to public health authorities. The exercise of their police powers is seldom subject to public oversight or judicial review as in the conventional areas of policing. Safeguards against abuses of power – representing the cornerstone of human rights – have yet to be applied to public health. Despite the recognition that public health officials indeed exercise police powers,[14] courts have been reluctant to challenge them. In a typical example, an American court declared that public health measures are beyond the rule of law: "[H]ealth regulations enacted by the state under its police power and providing even drastic measures for the elimination of disease ... are not affected by constitutional provisions."[15]

Recognizing this historical heritage, international human rights law has accepted that individual rights may be limited on public health grounds, but the imposition of any limitations ought to respect due process of law. Limitations may affect some, not all human rights and fundamental freedoms,[16] and are legitimate only when required for the protection of public health and compatible with the general human rights principles.[17] One of the main human rights principles is that full application of fundamental rights and freedoms is

[13] E.-I. Daes, The Individual's Duties to the Community and the Limitations on Human Rights and Freedoms under Article 29 of the Universal Declaration of Human Rights, United Nations Publication, Sales No.E.82.XIV.1, New York, 1983, at p. 100.

[14] Cf., M. Turshen, "The Police Power and the Public Health", in *The Politics of Public Health* (1986), Zed Books, London, at pp. 41–57.

[15] D. J. Merrit, "Communicable Disease and Constitutional Law: Controlling AIDS", 61 *New York University Law Review* (1986), pp. 739–799, at p. 754.

[16] The International Covenant on Civil and Political Rights envisages limitations on public health grounds specifically in regard to freedom of movement (Article 12, para. 3), freedom to manifest religion or belief (Article 18, para. 3), freedom of expression (Article 19, para. 3(b)), freedom of assembly (Article 21), and freedom of association (Article 22). International Covenant on Civil and Political Rights, Annex to General Assembly Resolution 2200A (XXI) of December 16, 1966.

[17] Cf., P. Sieghart, "AIDS & Human Rights: A UK Perspective", British Medical Association Foundation for AIDS, London, 1989, at pp. 25–28.

always presumed; limitations are exceptional and the public authority wishing to avail itself of "the right to limit rights" has the burden of proof that this is necessary, legitimate and proportionate. This entails the duty of public health authorities to prove that limitations upon human rights are indeed required, that is, necessary to protect public health. Thus it would be fairly easy to argue in favour of isolating persons affected by diseases that are transmitted through casual contact, but difficult, if not impossible, to extend this argument if a disease can be transmitted through specific behaviour, that is furthermore subject to human control. The latter applies to HIV/AIDS and it provided grounds for arguing human rights. This has also been facilitated by disunity amongst public health professionals: while some exercised their police powers by introducing coercive, compulsory or discriminatory measures, others argued that none of these are necessary in AIDS prevention and, moreover, detrimental to it. Opposition to limiting human rights has thereby emerged in public health and created an opportunity for introducing human rights into public health.

Only the first steps towards reconciling human rights and public health have been made within the AIDS pandemic. There is a long way to a systematic inclusion of human rights in public health. The widespread opposition to denial of human rights in public health in the context of the AIDS pandemic may well trigger off a change within public health to recognize that people with communicable diseases are "us" rather than "them", and advance to a fifth stage in the development of societal responses to epidemics, where the protection of human rights of the ill will become recognized as the corollary to the protection of the rights of the healthy.

(2) Enter Human Rights

Viruses and diseases can neither respect nor negate human rights. Human rights problems are man-made. Societal responses to HIV/AIDS challenged the core of human rights, the postulate that all human beings have equal rights. Human rights of those ill with AIDS, those who are HIV-infected, those suspected of being HIV-infected, and those living with, working with or working for people who are HIV-infected or ill have been denied, violated, limited.

Reasons have often been irrational, fear of "catching AIDS" and disapproval of lifestyles mentally associated with HIV infection and AIDS. The mental image of HIV/AIDS that caused such responses through reinforcing fear and strengthening moral crusades is man-made. Hence denial of human rights has been provoked, or at least facilitated, by societal response to HIV/AIDS rather than the disease itself. Some of the reasons have been rational, such as high cost of HIV/AIDS for society, and the cost of medical treatment for those ill with AIDS. Most often, however, the explicit reason for denying or limiting human rights has been the necessity of coping with the pandemic. It has been argued that the protection of public health necessitates denying human rights to those affected by HIV/AIDS. While denial of inherent human rights to anybody, on any grounds, jeopardizes the 'human' in human rights, public health has developed this assumption known in human rights as a trade-off, that rights of some can be protected at the expense of rights of others. Public health has historically developed this assumption that individual rights have to be denied to protect society, and that the rights of the affected minority have to be sacrificed for the sake of the unaffected (or uninfected) majority. Therefore the main aim of traditional public health, is to identify those affected by an epidemic, who thereby loose their identity, privacy and dignity, their individuality, and become "carriers" of a disease, the minority sacrificed to protect society.

Since public health follows this line of reasoning, it is hardly surprising that human rights of people with communicable diseases are denied more often than recognized and respected. Discrimination against people with impaired health is part of public health heritage. It is important to recall that an explicit international policy to prohibit discrimination against mentally ill persons was not adopted until 1971,[18] and against disabled persons until 1975,[19] and there are still no specific provisions regarding discrimination against persons with communicable diseases. The international protection of human rights has broadened to encompass the rights of those with impaired health the last and the least. Conceptually, this development can be linked to the fairly recent recognition of solidarity in human rights discourse. If "the degree of solidarity of a society can be measured by its attitude towards the vulnerable and the marginalized",[20] the treatment accorded to people who are ill and may infect others is probably the ultimate measure of solidarity. The vulnerability and marginalization of such people as a result of their impaired health is further exacerbated by fear of contagion.

Many human rights problems that emerged in the context of the AIDS pandemic are thus not AIDS-specific, but a reflection of the inherited denial of human rights to persons with communicable diseases. It is sometimes suggested that "anti-discriminatory legislation or regulations specific for HIV infection and AIDS may be counterproductive",[21] by singling out people with HIV/AIDS further. The United Nations policy has been to reaffirm the universal application of the prohibition of discrimination on the grounds of health. In its resolution on non-discrimination in the field of health the Commission on Human Rights emphasized that all are "equal before the law and entitled to equal protection of the law from all discrimination and from all incitement to

[18] Cf. Declaration on the Rights of Mentally Retarded Persons, General Assembly Resolution 2856 (XXVI) of December, 20, 1971.

[19] Cf. Declaration on the Rights of Disabled Persons, General Assembly Resolution 3447 (XXX) of December 9, 1975.

[20] T. van Boven, "The Future of Human Rights in Europe", *The Netherlands Quarterly on Human Rights* (1989), No. 1, at p. 8.

[21] Final activity report of the Committee of Experts on the Ethical and Social Implications of AIDS, Council of Europe, European Health Committee, Doc. CDSP89.11A, Strasbourg, August 17, 1989, para. 190.

discrimination relating to their state of health".[22] Nevertheless, a Special Rapporteur was appointed for HIV/AIDS-related discrimination,[23] because AIDS has become a test case for applying human rights in responding to a disease, by demonstrating pertinent problems in their extreme, but also offering solutions applicable beyond HIV/AIDS.

3. The Pandemic of AIDS Legislation

Few people outside the circle of public health officials are familiar with their police powers or the ways whereby these are exercised, even fewer with the wide-ranging provisions of public health laws, those concerning communicable and/or sexually transmitted diseases, for example. Publicity for all aspects of the AIDS pandemic, and opposition to coercive and compulsory measures by those affected, brought public health to the public agenda. The fact that many compulsory, coercive and discriminatory measures have been cloaked in legislation made them more transparent and – as they entered the domain of law – subject to challenge within national and international legal systems. As public health embodies neither due process nor remedies, public health laws made such measures subject to challenge.

HIV/AIDS-related laws are illustrative of the prevailing global response to AIDS. Never before has there been so much legislation relating to a disease. This over-reaction to the AIDS pandemic is illustrated by the diagram *Cumulative number of countries with AIDS legislation* (Appendix I below). It shows that in less than ten years 104 countries, two-thirds of the world community, have adopted some HIV/AIDS-related law.[24] As Carol Levine concluded in 1985, "where technology is still unable to provide a solution to the spread of disease, people look to the law,"[25] despite helplessness of law in preventing the spread of a virus or the development of a disease. Laws are conventional means of regulating the conduct of people rather than transmission of viruses or natural history of diseases, therefore the best example of measures affecting people with HIV/AIDS rather than HIV/AIDS itself.

[22] Commission on Human Rights, Non-discrimination in the Field of Health, Resolution 1989/11 of 2 March 1989, preamble.

[23] Cf. Sub-Commission on Prevention of Discrimination and Protection of Minorities, Decision 1988/111 of 1 September 1988, and Resolution 1989/19 of August 31, 1989; and Commission on Human Rights, Decision 1990/65 of March 7, 1990.

[24] Tabulations and general conclusions presented here are part of an exhaustive study of comparative AIDS legislation. Providing commentaries of and references for the legislation in individual countries would have exceeded the scope of this text, so minimum background information has been included. Readers who wish to obtain any further information are welcome to contact the author.

[25] C. Levine, AIDS: Public Health and Civil Liberties, Introduction, Hastings Center Report, Special Supplement, December 1986, at p. 2.

AIDS legislation emerged as early as 1983, less than two years after AIDS had become known and more than two years before HIV was identified as its cause. The first regulations on the prevention of AIDS were adopted in 1983, both in individual European countries[26] and by the Council of Europe. The first legislative enactments were adopted in 1983 also in Canada, Israel and the USA,[27] and in five more countries in 1984.[28] In this early period, up to 1985, no country adopted a comprehensive law on AIDS; legislative enactments most often laid down safeguards for national blood safety and introduced compulsory notification of cases of AIDS.

As the diagram entitled *Number of countries adopting AIDS legislation by year* (Appendix II below) shows, the next period, 1985–87, marked the peak of the pandemic of AIDS legislation: the cumulative number of laws on AIDS almost doubled, from thirty-nine by the end of 1985, to seventy-eight in 1988. The number of countries which adopted AIDS laws each year is indicative of this intense legislative activity: twenty-one countries adopted HIV/AIDS-related laws in 1985,[29] sixteen in 1986.[30] The largest number, twenty-three, were adopted in 1987.[31] In the USA alone more than 180 laws relating to HIV/AIDS were enacted in the period 1985–87,[32] more than 840 were proposed to the States' legislatures during these two years, out of which 450 in 1987 alone.[33] After this peak of legislative activity in 1985–87, there has been a considerable slow-down in the adoption of HIV/AIDS-related laws.[34]

Analysis of the contents of laws shows that the discovery of HIV and of the possibility to identify HIV-positive persons, particularly the commercialization of HIV tests, was the strongest incentive for adopting laws: the largest number of countries orientated their AIDS control to HIV screening and testing, and

[26] Austria, Denmark, France, Greece, Italy, Norway, Sweden, Turkey.

[27] With respect to federal countries and others with decentralized systems of health policy and law, the date of the first legislative enactment by a federal unit or provincial authority has been recorded here.

[28] Australia, Chile, Luxembourg, Uruguay, and Venezuela.

[29] Bahamas, Barbados, Belgium, Bermuda, Brazil, Congo, Costa Rica, Ecuador, Finland, French Polynesia, Hungary, Malaysia, Panama, Paraguay, Peru, Romania, Singapore, Spain, Thailand, United Arab Emirates and United Kingdom,

[30] China, Cuba, Egypt, Grenada, Guatemala, Iceland, Kuwait, Malta, Mexico, Monaco, Mozambique, Philippines, Poland, Portugal, Switzerland and Yugoslavia.

[31] Belize, Brunei Darussalam, Bulgaria, Burundi, Cyprus, Dominican Republic, El Salvador, Iraq, Jordan, Kenya, Republic of Korea, Liberia, Libya, Liechtenstein, Mauritius, Netherlands, Niger, Papua New Guinea, South Africa, Sudan, Syria, Togo and USSR.

[32] C. Thomas, A Synopsis of State AIDS Laws Enacted During 1983–1987 Legislative Sessions, Intergovernmental Health Policy Project, George Washington University, Washington, October 1988, preface.

[33] H. E. Lewis, "Acquired Immunodeficiency Syndrome: State Legislative Activity", *Journal of American Medical Association* vol. 258, No. 17 (1987) pp. 2410–2414 at p. 2410.

[34] In 1988 twelve countries adopted HIV/AIDS-related laws (Bulgaria, Chad, Colombia, Comores, Czech and Slovak Republic, Equatorial Guinea, Guinea, Hong Kong, Japan, Mali, Sri Lanka and Suriname), ten in 1989 (Algeria, Bolivia, Guinea-Bissau, India, Mongolia, Nicaragua, Rwanda, Tunisia, Viet Nam and Yemen), and four in 1990 (Argentina, Bahrain, Madagascar and Senegal).

notification of AIDS and HIV infection. The content of HIV/AIDS-related legislation is illustrative of the role attributed to law in AIDS prevention and control. Obligatory notification and testing have been legalized in most countries, while legislative provisions on national blood safety have been adopted in fewer (forty-four countries).[35] The traditional public health measure of notifying cases of AIDS was introduced in the largest number of countries: sixty-eight.

The diagram *Contents of national AIDS control measures* (Appendix III below) singles out those adopted by the largest number of countries. Not all these countries have adopted laws authorizing public health authorities to carry out compulsory HIV testing or to impose restrictions on HIV-infected people. Compulsory HIV testing – without any legislative authority in quite a few cases – was introduced in at least forty-seven countries.[36]

Once identified, HIV-infected people could be subject to various restrictions, and legal authorization of their isolation, detention or compulsory hospitalization emerged as well. Only one country has made hospitalization of all HIV-infected people mandatory and automatic (Cuba), but many adopted laws giving powers to public health authorities to resort to restrictive measures. Thus in China, Czech and Slovak Republic, Hungary, Japan, Myanmar, Norway, Mexico, Republic of Korea, Peru and USSR, HIV-infected people may be placed under surveillance. Mandatory hospitalization has been explicitly envisaged for HIV-infected people in Chile, China, Republic of Korea, Panama, Poland, Romania and Viet Nam. In quite a few countries restrictions upon HIV-positive persons were not contained in AIDS-specific new enactments, but already authorized by the existing public health laws, which were made applicable to HIV/AIDS by classifying it as contagious, communicable or sexually transmitted. The publicity for the exercise of such powers in the AIDS pandemic inspired increased interest in general public health laws and practices.

Disease classification is one of many public health measures that has a direct impact on the respect of human rights. Classification of a disease as contagious, communicable, transmissible, infectious or sexually transmitted entails the application of corresponding law that may include compulsory medical examin-

[35] Countries that enacted legislative safeguards against transmission of HIV infection through blood transfusions and blood products are: Argentina, Australia, Austria, Belgium, Brazil, Chile, China, Colombia, Costa Rica, Czech and Slovak Republic, Denmark, Dominican Republic, France, French Polynesia, Finland, Greece, Guatemala, Hungary, Italy, Republic of Korea, Kuwait, Luxembourg, Malta, Mexico, Norway, Oman, Panama, Portugal, Spain, St. Vincent and Grenadines, Suriname, Sweden, Switzerland, Syria, Thailand, Trinidad and Tobago, Tunisia, Turkey, Uruguay, United Arab Emirates, United Kingdom, USSR, Venezuela and Zimbabwe.

[36] Argentina, Australia, Austria, Bahamas, Bulgaria, Chile, China, Costa Rica, Cuba, Czech and Slovak Republic, Guatemala, Hungary, Indonesia, Iraq, Israel, Italy, Japan, Jordan, D.P.R. Korea, Republic of Korea, Kuwait, Mali, Mongolia, Myanmar, Nepal, Niger, Nigeria, Oman, Pakistan, Panama, Philippines, Poland, South Africa, Spain, Sri Lanka, St. Vincent and Grenadines, Sudan, Syria, Thailand, Tunisia, Turks and Caicos Islands, United Arab Emirates, Uruguay, USA, USSR, Viet Nam and Yugoslavia.

ation or hospitalization, restrictions upon travel or immigration, or quarantine. A recent case, where the New York State Public Health Council refused to classify HIV infection as sexually transmissible "because such declaration would trigger certain statutory requirements permitting isolation and quarantine, reporting, testing and contact tracing"[37], illustrates the importance of such apparently "technical" public health decisions. Likewise the suggestion within Proposition 64 to classify HIV/AIDS as an "infectious, contagious and communicable disease"[38], thus showing the weight attributed to disease classification.

Notification of communicable diseases is another traditional public health measure and, like any other, apparently "technical". By requiring physicians to report a case (anonymously) or a patient, that is, by including personal identity or protecting anonymity, public health officials create or avoid human rights problems. Such problems are rarely anticipated when disease notification is legislated. They can be avoided if public health officials are sensitive to the ramifications of their seemingly "technical" reporting procedure. It is necessary to determine how many people are ill with AIDS and HIV-infected in order to develop AIDS prevention programmes, but it is not necessary to disclose personal identity of these people. Many countries aimed nevertheless to ascertain who the ill and the infected are by making personal identity part of the obligatory notification of cases of AIDS and of results of HIV tests. Thus two different public health measures have been merged: epidemiological surveillance and case finding, with detrimental consequences for both, and for protection of human rights as well. If compulsory notification is nominal, protection of confidentiality is essential to prevent stigmatization and discrimination. Consequently, drafting notification regulations and reporting forms represents a choice that is inherently political but seldom subjected to due process of making political choice:

> "Controversies about disease reporting in the present as in the past must be understood as political conflicts; that is, conflicts about power and about values. The critical issues have never been scientific or technological."[39]

Human rights problems raised by the prevailing response to HIV/AIDS are illustrated in the diagram *Notification and data protection* (Appendix IV below). It is indicative that out of sixty-eight countries that prescribed compulsory notification of AIDS and/or HIV infection, only six determined that such notification should be anonymous (Chile, Denmark, France,

[37] Refusal to designate AIDS communicable upheld by New York State Appellate Court, *AIDS Policy & Law* (May 16, 1990), vol. 5, No. 9, at pp. 1–2.

[38] Proposition 64, led by Lyndon LaRouche, aimed to increase the power of public health authorities in combatting AIDS (in the narrowest sense of the term). R. Bayer, Private Acts, Social Consequences. *AIDS and the Politics of Public Health* (1989), The Free Press: New York, at pp. 148–153.

[39] D. M. Fox, "From TB to AIDS: Value conflicts in reporting disease", *Hastings Center Report* vol. 16, No. 6 (1989) Special Supplement, p. 15.

Germany, Greece, Iceland) and thirteen added special safeguards for confidentiality in the required notification of AIDS and HIV infection (Australia, Austria, China, Costa Rica, Italy, Liechtenstein, Malta, New Zealand, Norway, Panama, Sweden, Switzerland and USA). In many cases routine disclosure of personal identity of HIV-infected people brought about the loss of employment, housing, insurance, residence and work permits, and, often, social ostracism and increased rates of suicide.

This legislative pandemic was much criticized in both legal and public health literature and the press reports did not fail to add its voice. Thus, the *South* magazine entitled its survey "How paranoia fuels the AIDS epidemic",[40] and the *New Internationalist* "AIDS witch-hunts: Legislative hysteria".[41] It is significant that in the period of 1982–1989 by far the smallest number of countries, only twelve, adopted laws on non-discrimination (Argentina, Victoria (Australia), China, Costa Rica, Denmark, France, Italy, Japan, Republic of Korea, Kuwait, USSR, USA and Yugoslavia).

4. Targets of Compulsory Measures

History of compulsory and coercive public health measures reveals that they were regularly applied in a discriminatory manner.[42] This is particularly transparent when the burden of an epidemic is not spread evenly but concentrated in specific populations, where the identification of "carriers" is accompanied by the stigmatization of whole categories as "sources of infection". The idea that some people have a predisposition to become affected by an epidemic, originating in the Middle Ages, has undoubtedly influenced the contemporary responses to AIDS, as evidenced in the term "high-risk groups".

Whenever an epidemic is transmitted sexually, stigmatization accompanying the process of attributing an epidemic to a specific human "source of infection" is regularly followed by the attribution of blame and scapegoating. As no country could have screened its whole population, because of prohibitive cost rather than human rights considerations, HIV testing has been selective. In most cases, the choice of categories to be screened reflected the ongoing epidemic of scapegoating. The listing of the most frequent targets of HIV testing is presented in the table *Categories tested for antibodies to HIV* (Appendix V below).[43] The list of categories subjected to compulsory HIV

[40] M. E. Hurtado, "How paranoia fuels the AIDS epidemic", *South* (June 1988), at p. 95–96.

[41] AIDS witch-hunts: Legislative hysteria, *New Internationalist* (May 1988), at p. 27.

[42] Institute of Medicine and National Academy of Sciences – Confronting AIDS, National Academy Press: Washington, 1986, at p. 96.

[43] Information on countries that introduced compulsory testing has been derived from their legislative enactments, that in many cases prescribed compulsory testing of specific categories or gave public health authorities powers to determine which categories ought to be screened, and also from national AIDS programmes, as many countries carried out compulsory testing without any legislative authority. Country-specific information is not included due to space limitations, but readers who wish to know details are welcome to contact the author.

testing in the largest number of countries does not conform to the rationale of AIDS prevention. The modes of HIV transmission make some categories understandable, such as blood donors for example. Financial rather than public health considerations appear to be the dominant factor in the screening of immigrants, applicants for scholarships and applicants for insurance. There are also categories for which the reason for HIV testing appears to be institutionalized discrimination, a process of screening out undesirable members of specified professions (such as applicants for foreign or civil service).

Blood donors have been tested in the largest number of countries for obvious and justified reasons. The second most frequent category, "high-risk groups" (homosexuals, prostitutes and drug users) has obviously been subject to HIV testing because of – however unjustified – association with HIV/AIDS. As HIV infection is transmitted through individual behaviour, seroprevalence studies among "high-risk groups" shows that they are neither "high-risk" nor indeed "groups": HIV infection is widespread amongst some, while virtually non-existent amongst others.

"Captive populations" (prisoners, refugees in closed camps, pregnant women attending antenatal clinics, STD patients, military recruits) have been subjected to compulsory HIV testing to such an extent that the only possible explanation is a cynical one – they are an easy target. They are within the reach of public health authorities, and often unable to refuse HIV test, as safeguards against compulsory and/or coercive measures are unavailable or ineffective. In many cases, HIV testing can be carried out without the knowledge of the persons concerned.

Aliens have been a particularly frequent target of compulsory HIV screening. As usual in the case of epidemics, every country blamed another, scientific proof that AIDS originated somewhere else mushroomed, and many countries carried out epidemiological surveys to show that the first cases of AIDS came from abroad. Haiti was the first victim through terming all "immigrants from Haiti" a "high-risk group" in the USA.[44] Africa and Africans were often attributed blame for the origin of AIDS and compulsory measures victimizing their populations used such theories as support. Africans living in other regions, or travelling to them, have borne a heavy burden of discrimination, leading the former Director-General of WHO, Dr. Halfdan Mahler, to note "the ugly head of racism" in such practices.[45]

This quick review of targets of compulsory screening shows that other criteria, not always the necessity of protecting public health, prompted

[44] In March 1983, the American Red Cross included "Haitian immigrants" among categories excluded from blood donation because of "high risk of carrying AIDS". Two years later, in March 1985, CDC deleted "recent Haitian immigrants" from the list of categories at greatest risk. H. R. Malinowsky, et al., *AIDS Information Sourcebook 1989–90* (1989), Oryx Press: Annex 1, Chronology, at pp. 1–2.

[45] "WHO can help to fight AIDS: Interview with Halfdan Mahler", *Newsweek* (July 13, 1987), at p. 48.

compulsory HIV testing. The pattern of targeting by compulsory HIV testing fits the general pattern of discrimination in the world of today. It cannot be a coincidence that prisoners, aliens, prostitutes, drug-dependent persons, find themselves on the list of most frequent of human rights violations, and most frequent targets of compulsory and coercive HIV/AIDS-related measures.

5. Aren't They Us?

The presence of antibodies to HIV in one's blood became the dividing line between "us" and "them", the "general population" and "AIDS-carriers". Thus it became dangerous to know one's infection and avoidance of HIV testing developed as a means to avoid crossing this dividing line and losing one's rights. Moreover, the paucity of complaints against HIV/AIDS-related human rights violations is a result of fear of being publicly recognized as "them". Thereby exposure of HIV/AIDS-related human rights violations has been pre-empted by the stigmatization of its victims.

It has been documented in a number of countries that the lack of safeguards for confidentiality in HIV testing, and for the avoidance of discrimination against persons who test positive, caused decreased participation in voluntary testing for HIV. Suffice it here to mention few examples. A study of patients consenting to and declining HIV testing at an STD clinic in New Mexico, carried out in 1986–88, revealed that those declining to be tested were five to eight times more likely to be HIV-infected.[46] Reasons were, unfortunately, not inquired into nor systematically recorded, but researchers subsequently determined that the main reason was concern about confidentiality and fear of potential reprisals if knowledge of involvement in high risk activities, which is regularly mentally associated with HIV infection, became known. A study in New York City showed that 22% of patients of an STD clinic would not take HIV test if their identity was to be disclosed.[47] In a survey carried out in March 1989 in San Francisco, "the vast majority of men said they would consent to required testing if anti-discrimination laws were in place".[48] In 1987 the publicity for the then-forthcoming legislation in Japan on HIV/AIDS, which included provisions for disclosure of personal identity for those testing positive, caused a decreased attendance at STD clinics.[49] Attitudes towards HIV testing were further examined in 1988 to determine whether notification of personal

[46] H. F. Hull, et al. "Comparison of HIV-Antibody Prevalence in Patients Consenting to and Declining HIV-Antibody Testing in an STD Clinic", *Journal of American Medical Association* vol. 258, No. 17 (1988), pp. 935–938.

[47] E. J. Fordyce, "Mandatory reporting of Human Immunodeficiency Virus testing would deter blacks and hispanics from being tested", *Journal of American Medical Association* vol. 262, No. 3 (1989) at p. 349.

[48] "Mandatory HIV reporting testing deterrent?", *CDC AIDS Weekly* (March 27, 1989), Centers for Disease Control: Atlanta, Georgia, at p. 8.

[49] G. Ohi, et al. "Notification of HIV carriers: Possible effect on uptake of HIV testing", *The Lancet* (October 22, 1988), London, at pp. 947–949.

identity to the authorities would deter people from HIV testing. More than 30% of homosexuals and female prostitutes indicated their preference for HIV testing without such notification.[50] In Bavaria (Germany) decrease of participation in educational programmes, even cases of persons leaving Bavaria to avoid compulsory HIV testing, were caused by the announcement of forthcoming restrictive measures in 1987.[51] Empirical evidence has thereby confirmed the link between participation in voluntary testing and the existence or the lack of protection of HIV-positive people against stigmatization and discrimination.

Dr. Everett Koop, the then U.S. Surgeon General, said that to make HIV testing effective "individuals must have confidence that they will be protected fully from HIV-related discrimination."[52] This link between the promotion of HIV-testing and protection against discrimination has become the policy of the Council of Europe: "Society ... has an obligation to alleviate the possible negative consequences of such detection by preventing discrimination which may act as a disincentive to the detection of infection... [Therefore an explicit policy] should state unequivocally that HIV-infected individuals have the right to enjoy the same civil and social rights as the non-infected, while bearing ethical, civil and legal responsibilities to contain transmission."[53]

6. AIDS Prevention: Everyone's Responsibility

Epidemiological studies have shown that the vast majority of HIV infections worldwide result from sexual intercourse. Sexual practices are the least known and the most difficult to influence and change by public policies. No country in the world has the capacity to police sex lives of its entire population. Therefore AIDS prevention is necessarily based on the need for every individual to accept responsibility for his or her own conduct.

Responsibilities are the counterpart of individual freedoms. Freedom involves choice and this entails responsibility. Respect of human rights and individual responsibility are two sides of the same coin. Persons who could infect others ought to behave responsibly because there is no such thing as freedom to transmit infection. This emanates from the basic human rights principle whereby rights of any person are limited by equal rights of all others. Irresponsible behaviour on the part of those who might transmit infection jeopardizes the right of others to protect themselves from contracting infection.

[50] Ibid.

[51] K. Gorgens, "Address before the Parliamentary Committee on AIDS", in *The Third Epidemic* (May 1989), Special Report, WorldAIDS, Panos Institute: London, at p. 11.

[52] Letter to the Office of the Legal Counsel, Department of Justice, Daily Lab. Rep. (BNA), October 7, 1988.

[53] Explanatory memorandum to Recommendation (89)14 on the ethical issues of HIV infection in the health care and social settings, Council of Europe, Strasbourg, October 24, 1989, paras. 154 and 163(iv).

The importance of balancing individual rights and duties, freedoms and responsibilities, is evidenced by unacceptable results which are achieved by arguing either side of the coin in isolation. Thus the line of reasoning which discusses only rights ends up suggesting that "potential [HIV] carriers are free not to submit to testing or not to change their behaviour after identification as carrier".[54]

In some countries discussion of individual responsibility has been avoided by the assumption that persons who are HIV-infected should not be expected to behave responsibly, hence they ought to be isolated. This approach assumes that because they may infect others they will invariably do so, and is the underlying reason for adopting measures for their segregation, isolation or deportation. This assumption links two unrelated issues: the presence of antibodies to HIV in somebody's blood and the human capacity of behaving responsibly. Such reasoning negates the essence of human rights. By analogy, one could argue against recognizing the right to vote, assuming that people cannot be trusted to cast their votes responsibly.

Once individual responsibility is accepted as the key to AIDS prevention, little, if any, difference can be made between persons who are HIV-infected and thereby liable to infect others (unless they behave responsibly), and those who are not infected but might contract HIV infection (also unless they behave responsibly). On this basis the whole edifice of ascertaining HIV-status and restricting the rights of those identified as seropositive loses its foundations.

When the global strategy for the prevention and control of AIDS (the Global AIDS Strategy) was first outlined, it stressed that transmission of HIV is preventable, every individual has a responsibility to prevent contracting or transmitting HIV infection.[55] The London Declaration on AIDS Prevention reaffirmed this approach by saying that "HIV transmission can be prevented through informed and responsible behaviour".[56] The World Health Assembly Resolution on the avoidance of discrimination in relation to HIV-infected people and people with AIDS emphasized in its preamble "the responsibility of individuals not to put themselves or others at risk of infection with HIV".[57]

Detailed provisions on individual responsibilities, as a corollary to human rights guarantees, have been elaborated by the Council of Europe. Its recommendation on the common European health policy on AIDS stated that health education should emphasize that "the individual is responsible for the outcome of his behaviour towards himself, others and the society", and that sex education "should encourage individuals to assume responsibility for their

[54] J. K. M. Gevers, "AIDS: Screening of possible carriers and human rights", *Health Policy* vol. 7, No. 1 (1987) pp. 13–19, at p. 17.

[55] World Health Assembly – Global strategy for the prevention and control of AIDS, Resolution WHA40.26 of May 15, 1987, preamble.

[56] World Summit of Ministers of Health on Programmes for AIDS Prevention – London Declaration on AIDS Prevention of January 28, 1988.

[57] World Health Assembly – Avoidance of discrimination against HIV-infected persons and persons with AIDS, Resolution WHA41.24 of May 13, 1988, preamble.

health by becoming aware of risks and benefits inherent in various lifestyles".[58] Restrictive or repressive measures have not been endorsed by WHO, and explicitly rejected by the Council of Europe, because of the "impossibility of imposing behaviour modification".[59] The Council of Europe recommendation on AIDS in prison, for example, stated that "unless future scientific findings should indicate otherwise, HIV-infected prisoners [should] not [be] isolated or segregated, provided they do not act irresponsibly".[60]

The International Consultation on AIDS and Human Rights developed a link between informed and responsible behaviour and protection against discrimination in the notion of empowerment. It emphasized the need "for protection of the human rights of those specially at risk to exposure to HIV so that they will be empowered to protect themselves. By so doing, they are enabled to fulfil their responsibility to protect others".[61]

[58] Council of Europe – Guidelines for the drawing up of a public health policy to fight AIDS, Annex to Recommendation No. R (87)25 of November 26, 1987, paras. 2.1.2 and 2.1.3.

[59] Explanatory memorandum to Recommendation No. 1116 (1989) of the Parliamentary Assembly on AIDS and Human Rights, Doc. 6104, at pp. 13–14.

[60] Council of Europe, Parliamentary Assembly – Recommendation 1080 (1988) on a coordinated European health policy to prevent the spread of AIDS in prisons of 30 June 1988, para. 14(iv).

[61] International Consultation on AIDS and Human Rights, Final Document, Geneva, July 26–28, 1989, U.N. Doc. HR/AIDS/1989/3, para. 18(D).

NIALL MacDERMOT*

The Rights of Mentally Handicapped Persons in Japan

1. Introduction

As in many other countries, there used to be, and indeed still is, a popular but mistaken belief in Japan that mental illness is hereditary. This had a tragic effect for the mentally ill. They were locked away in the basements of their homes and no-one outside the family was aware of their existence. The reason for this was that it was feared that if it became known that there was a mentally ill person in the family, the other sons and daughters would be unable to marry.

After the second world war the Government agreed to finance mental hospitals throughout the country. Consequently, the families of the mentally ill were only too glad to bring them to these hospitals. Any medical doctor could be in charge of a mental hospital. He did not need to have any training in psychiatry. Indeed there were no faculties teaching the subject. Any medical doctor was assumed to have the necessary knowledge to run a mental hospital. The creation of mental hospitals then became a growth industry.

Since successive Liberal Party Governments were opposed to developing public medicine, the main growth was in the private sector. The Medical Service Law of 1948 allowed any registered medical practitioner to establish a private clinic for mental patients.

In 1983 Japan's population was 120 million. Japanese mental hospitals had over 333,000 inpatients. 93.6% of these patients (totalling 310,000) were being detained involuntarily. They were called euphemistically "consent patients", but the consent came from the patient's family, not from the patient. Over 80% of the private mental hospitals were located in rural areas because land prices were much lower. Consequently, many patients were and still are hospitalized at long distances from their homes, with the result that they get few visits from their families.

There was no such thing as voluntary hospitalization, that is to say admission with the consent of the patient, and treatment of mental patients in

* C.B.E., Q.C., Secretary-General of the International Commission of Jurists, 1970–1990.

K.E. Mahoney and P. Mahoney (eds.), Human Rights in the Twenty-first Century, 209–217.

ordinary hospitals was prohibited. There were two ways by which a patient could be admitted to a mental hospital.

Under section 29 of the Mental Hygiene Act of 1950, patients who were certified by two or more doctors as dangerous to themselves or others were made subject to indefinite detention in a mental hospital. 13.5% of inpatients were in this category.

Section 33 of the Act allowed a mental hospital superintendent to detain a patient if he considered that the patient was suffering from a mental disorder and needed treatment or care in a mental hospital, and if a family member gave consent to the hospitalization. This category represented 80% of all inpatients.

For this vast number of patients there was no legal protection. There was no possibility to appeal against the detention, no court procedure, no independent tribunal, no lawyer, no advocate, no hearing, no access to any report or documents, no free and independent expert witness, no notification of the reasons for detention and no freedom to communicate with anyone or have visitors. The patients had no say in the matter, had no access to a lawyer or anyone else to object to their admission. There was no outside control and no possibility of appeal by the patient.

The lack of legal protection, understaffing and insufficient rehabilitation services encouraged custodial care and lengthy admissions. In 1983 over half the inpatients had been hospitalized for more than 5 years, whereas in western countries, the great majority of hospital patients are discharged after a few months. 69% were kept in wards locked 24 hours a day, and one fifth of the private mental hospitals had no open wards. Custodial mental health care, unintegrated with general health services and lacking in community-based care, became the norm and was hardly questioned until 1984. There was no centrally organized system of standard setting, quality control or inspection.

Professional and public opinion was not widely alerted until in 1984 two patients in the Hotukai Hospital in Usunomya City were beaten to death by the staff, one for complaining about the food and the other for trying to escape from the hospital. Serious financial irregularities were also uncovered and the medical director was sentenced to one year in prison and fined. Examination of the hospital patients revealed that one third of them did not require any treatment in a hospital. The investigation also revealed that 222 unexplained deaths had occurred within three years among some 1,000 patients. Although the circumstances surrounding these deaths were very suspicious only 8 of the 222 cases were examined by the authorities. As the bodies had been cremated and inquests had not been held, there was no way to make thorough investigations of the 222 cases. Police investigations revealed similar abuses in ten other hospitals.

At that stage a Japanese lawyer, Etsuro Totsuka, approached the International Commission of Jurists (ICJ) and other international NGO's. Mental patients in Japan owe a great debt to this lawyer who has devoted himself untiringly to bringing about reform in the law and practice governing mental patients. At first he worked solely in Japan, getting the support of fellow lawyers in the Daini Tokyo Bar Association and members of the Japan Civil Liberties Union, one of the best non-governmental organizations in Japan. In March 1984 it submitted a report on mental patients to the Prime Minister, Mr. Nakasone, who ignored it. The report was also sent to the International Commission of Jurists and to the New York based International League for Human Rights, another international human rights organization which played an important part in helping to bring about reforms in Japan.

Totsuka had realized that he had to enlist the support of leading international non-governmental organizations in the world, in order to influence the Japanese Government. He had been working for several years in Japan trying to arouse public opinion about the abuses and their illegality in international law.

These scandals occurred because of the complete lack of any supervisory body to make regular inspections of treatment and conditions in the hospitals. Hospital doctors had discretionary powers to restrict all patient freedoms and were able to exercise any kind of compulsory individual treatment, including psycho-surgery. As a result not even a Government Minister could interfere in the so-called medical practice that prohibited patients from seeing a lawyer. Any interference was considered to invade the hallowed territory of medical discretionary powers and clinical judgment.

It was widely stated that the hospital doctors often wrote false certificates in order to cover up unnatural deaths, but these practices could not be proved as the deaths were diagnosed by the doctors as natural deaths. The bodies were cremated immediately after the death certificates were produced. In the Usunomya case, one of the dead bodies was not cremated, and the police were able to confirm the brutal violence which caused the death. The staff involved were arrested and confessed.

When the International Commission of Jurists learned about these matters from Totsuka, the Secretary General wrote to the Japanese Prime Minister in May 1984 suggesting that his Government should consider appointing an independent commission to enquire into the treatment of mental patients and the legislation relating to it. As there was no answer to this letter, the Commission decided to appoint its own mission and invited the International Commission of Health Professionals (ICHP) to co-sponsor it.

2. The Independent Commission

The mission visited Japan in May 1985.[1] They were able to visit several mental hospitals, and had discussions with the Ministry of Health, psychiatrists, social workers, nurses, occupational therapists, and representatives of many

[1] The mission was composed of two internationally known psychiatrists, Dr. Tim Harding, Head of the Division of Legal Psychiatry at the Geneva University (Institute of Legal Medicine),

organizations and individuals concerned with mental patients. They received the active cooperation of the Ministries of Justice and Health and Welfare.

The conclusions and recommendations of their 94 page report included the following:

- the Japanese mental health system must be regarded as being seriously inadequate in terms of the human rights of mentally disordered persons and of their treatment;
- the major sources of concern were:
  - a lack of legal protection for patients during admission procedures and during hospitalization, and
  - a system of care characterized by a preponderance of long-term institutional treatment and a relative lack of community treatment and rehabilitation;
- there was a steadily rising number of hospital inpatients despite ministerial policy statements since 1965 calling for a reversal of this trend;
- over 80% of psychiatric beds were in private mental hospitals not under direct ministerial control; two thirds of the beds were in closed locked wards, and patients tended to stay very long periods;
- the mission did not investigate any cases of abuse, but they commented that the existing structure and function of the Japanese mental health services created conditions conducive to serious human rights violations on a significant scale, including overcrowding, poor nutrition which might lead to physical deterioration and high mortality, physical abuse of patients, exploitation of patient labour, unjustifiable detention, inability of patients to communicate with friends and family members and receive visits under reasonable conditions;
- the rights of patients under the Japanese Constitution and the International Covenant on Civil and Political Rights, of which Japan is a State Party, were not fully guaranteed to the mentally handicapped;
- reform of the Japanese Mental Health Law was overdue.[2]

The report of the mission stated that the *minimal* response to the serious problems in the Japanese mental health system would be:

- an independent review of all cases of involuntary hospitalization within a month of admission and thereafter at least twice yearly,

---

Dr. Harold M. Visotsky, Professor and Chairman of the Department of Psychiatry (at the Northwestern Memorial) Hospital in Chicago, and a Chicago Judge, The Honourable Judge Schneider, a legal expert on mental health law in the United States who presided over a special court in Chicago which controlled mental health institutions and their patients. Dr. Charles Graves, Executive Secretary of the International Commission of Health Professionals acted as Secretary of the mission.

[2] On this last point it is significant that it appears to have been the Japanese Foreign Ministry that brought pressure upon the Ministries of Health and Welfare and of Justice for the reform of the mental health law. The Foreign Ministry were aware that without it Japan would continue to be harassed by non-governmental organizations in the United Nations Human Rights Commission and Sub-Commission.

- the creation of an independent tribunal system with adequate resources to respond to all appeals, and composed of members of the health and legal professions,
- regular inspection of all mental hospitals to check on staffing and treatment standards,
- informing patients of their rights as fully as possible, with free access by letter or telephone to the tribunal and to a representative of their choice,
- assistance and advice to patients from an independent qualified person, and
- recording any incidents leading to personal injury and reporting them to an independent body which could investigate when appropriate,
- the Ministry of Health and prefectorial authorities should provide a stimulus, and the necessary resources, for the development of community care and rehabilitation, together with greater incentives for brief periods of hospitalization with intensive forms of treatment leading to early discharge, and significantly higher levels of reimbursement for all forms of outpatients and community care,
- health authorities should closely monitor the activities of mental hospitals with the aim of encouraging the rehabilitation of existing "long-term" patients, preventing unnecessarily long periods of hospital care, and
- recognizing that some patients, particularly the elderly, will not live independently in the foreseeable future, decent levels of care and conditions should be provided for them, for example in group homes or hostels.

The mission also recommended improved education and training:

- for psychiatrists, with a formal scheme of certification;
- for other mental health workers more oriented towards rehabilitation and out-patient care;
- for all health workers, in medical ethics and legal aspects of medicine;
- for the legal profession, to improve their understanding of mental health issues; and
- for community leaders and the general public, aimed at changing public attitudes towards the mentally ill.

This report was translated and published in Japanese. It was widely read in legal, medical, governmental and parliamentary circles, and made a considerable impact.

3. The Results of the Commission

In June 1984 the ICJ published an article in its Review on violations of the rights of mental patients in Japan based on information received from Totsuka. The Review reaches lawyers and lawyers organizations in 107 different countries in English, French and Spanish languages. In August 1984 the International League for Human Rights raised the issue of these violations at the UN Sub-Commission. The Japanese Government responded saying that serious abuses constituted no more than a few exceptional isolated cases, and that the compulsory hospitalization cases were only 12% of all admissions, and not the 80% claimed by Totsuka and others. It transpired that the Government had not included involuntary admission with family consent in their figures.

The International League wrote to the Prime Minister raising other examples of mental hospital scandals which occurred even after the Usunomya scandal, but the Government still refused to admit any need for reform.

At the meeting of the UN Sub-Commission in August 1985 there was a combined assault by three international organizations, – the ICJ, with the report of its mission to Japan, the International League for Human Rights with its unanswered letter to the Prime Minister and the Disabled Peoples International based on its mission to Japan in April 1985.

Responding to these NGO statements, the Director of Japan's Department of Mental Health at the Ministry of Health and Welfare, Dr. Kobayashi, officially declared that Japan had decided to take the necessary steps to amend the Mental Hygiene Act for the further protection of mental patients' human rights.

The Government then acted with remarkable speed. Eighteen months later they submitted a Bill to the Parliament after complicated procedures which included obtaining the approval of the governing Liberal Democratic Party, in face of opposition from the influential Association of Private Mental Hospitals. Finally the Liberal Party admitted that the changes were necessary because of international criticism.

The new Bill was approved by the Parliament on September 18, 1987 and came into force on 1 July 1988. Under the new law the Minister of Health was empowered to make regulations on standards for the treatment of hospital patients. These prohibited such matters as the ban on sending and receiving correspondence, and on meetings between inpatients and lawyers.

For the first time specific provision was made for voluntary hospitalization by a patient. This means that the patient will be able to leave the hospital at will, unless it is established that to do so would be dangerous to the patient or to others.

Perhaps the most important matter was the right of patients to make complaints to the new Psychiatric Review Boards (PRB's) which are created in each prefecture. These boards are usually comprised of three doctors, one lawyer and one lay person. Criticisms have been made that the number of doctors on the boards is excessive and weakens rather than strengthens the boards.

The PRB's are required to consider and report to the Governor of the prefecture on two matters. The first is whether continued hospitalization is necessary. This may arise from the periodic report on involuntary patients made by every mental hospital, or as an appeal procedure arising on a request for discharge by an involuntary patient, or on such a request made by an experienced psychiatrist. The second matter is whether the patient requires better treatment. This arises on a request made by or on behalf of the patient for discharge or for better treatment. This is an innovative and important measure of protection.

As described above, the great majority of mental patients were involuntary patients. It is hoped and believed that a large number of these patients will be persuaded to become voluntary patients, which would enhance their dignity and self-respect, and as a rule result in transfer to an open ward.

Some critics have referred to Article 9 (4) of the International Covenant on Civil and Political Rights to which Japan is a State Party. This provides that a person deprived of his or her liberty shall be entitled to take proceedings before a court which can order release if the detention is not lawful. Such a court need not be one of the ordinary courts, but may be a specialized tribunal comparable to the PRBs and operate with more informal procedures. However, it should be independent, and should allow the parties to be heard and to be represented by a lawyer or other person chosen to represent them. The representative of the patient should be entitled to attend the proceedings, and see and comment upon all documents considered by the PRB even if these are not disclosed to the patient in his own interest.

In its report the members of the ICJ mission recommended the creation of an independent tribunal system. They stated that the "proceedings [of the tribunal] should correspond to fundamental concepts of due process".

In April 1988, at the request of a committee in Japan, the ICJ sent the same three experts to undertake a second mission to examine the preparations which were being made for reform based on the revised Mental Health Act.

One of their main concerns was to study the plans for the Psychiatric Review Boards. In their first visit they recommended the creation of a system of independent tribunals whose "proceedings should correspond to fundamental concepts of due process". In their second report they spelt out what was needed to comply with due process. This included recommendations that:

- the members of the PRB panel should be chosen from an area other than that of the hospital concerned;
- the hospital should provide information to the panel on the patient's condition, and the plan for treatment and rehabilitation;
- the patient should be allowed to attend the hearing unless there is reason to think that this would be harmful;
- the patient should be entitled to address the full panel, to pose questions and to request a second opinion by a psychiatrist of his or her choice;
- the patient should be represented throughout the hearing by a lawyer or other representative of his or her choice, who should have access to all the documents before the PRB and be allowed to address the panel;
- the decision of the PRB and the reason for the decision should be explained in a sympathetic way to the patient.

Reports received by the ICJ indicate that the present practice of the PRBs falls short of these recommendations, which were designed to enable the Review Boards to be accepted as "courts" for the purpose of Article 9 (4) of the Covenant on Civil and Political Rights. In the view of Mr. Totsuka, only one of these recommendations is adhered to, namely that the hospital should provide information to the PRB panel on the patient's condition and the plan for treatment and rehabilitation. If he is right, this means that Japan is not meeting its obligation under Article 9 (4) of the Covenant to enable an involuntary patient to challenge the lawfulness of his or her detention before a court.

The Government has stated that it will consider whether any further legislation is required when the Act has been in force for five years, that is by June 1993. With this in mind, the same committee in Japan has asked the ICJ to send its mission once more to make any further recommendations which appear to be required after the 1988 Act has been in force for some years.

4. Conclusion

The most recent information from Japan is encouraging. There is at last a movement towards providing local facilities where patients can get treatment without going to a mental hospital. The central Government will support the running of these facilities – but not their construction. The Association of the Families of Mental Patients has raised money to start some of these facilities.

All this is made possible by a change of attitude of the public who have at last understood that the vast majority of mental patients offer no threat to them.

So much for the development of the treatment and protection of the mentally ill in Japan since World War II. But we are supposed to be discussing the treatment and protection of the mentally ill in the twenty-first Century. I can only hazard a guess as to how this will develop. My own hope is that the World Health Organization will be persuaded to develop a massive programme to promote reform. I understand that the percentage of the population who are mentally ill is much the same in all parts of the world.

I do not think that the experience of Japan offers a desirable example for others to follow, but it does point to the way in which a programme should be developed.

First and foremost priority should be given to the creation or development of facilities at the local level. Every effort should be made to overcome ignorance and misguided attitudes towards the mentally ill. The number of patients who are dangerous to themselves or to others is only a small proportion of the total number of patients. Japan is now recognizing that in its post-war programmes far too many patients have been locked away quite unnecessarily, and is taking steps to rectify this.

In the Third World, instead of using the available funds for building prestigious hospitals in the capitals, priority should be given to more modest but essential facilities in the rural areas. Above all, to make this possible training will have to be given to the doctors and nurses who are to give treatment. An adequate training programme will be a first necessity.

The skills and contribution of traditional healers are not to be spurned. One of the experts on ICJ missions to Japan relates an interesting example of this. For some years he was a practising doctor in Nigeria. One of his patients was a traditional healer, whom he had treated for a serious illness by western methods. He then asked if he could examine a number of the healer's patients and diagnose them by western methods. It was agreed that after a period of three years he would return to see what results the healer had achieved. He found that the results of the healer were at least as good as those he would have expected by western treatment. He was also very impressed by this healer's methods of treatment. One of his patients had been brought to him in a state of raving madness, and had to be chained up to bring him under control. The healer spent 48 hours in calming the patient, by caressing him and talking gently to him. This example indicates the importance of a sympathetic method of treatment as one form of therapy.

SECTION III

Violence: The Need to Respect Human Life and Dignity

Introduction*

The violence discussed in this Section ranges from one-to-one brutality in a domestic context, through exploitation and oppression of dominated groups such as women and children, to overt and covert use of force by the State to maintain power and, at the other extreme, mass destruction in the form of war and nuclear destruction.

The thematic overview of the Section is given by John Ladd. His aim, as a philosopher, is to clarify the conceptional framework of ideas within which the practical issues of violence, human rights and solidarity are situated. His basic premise is that attitudes to these issues are necessarily controversial, partisan and relative, since they are grounded in complex, shared systems of ideas, beliefs and values that he calls ideologies. He therefore stresses the need to adopt an "ideological analysis" in order to be able to understand these essentially contested concepts.

For example, the Western democratic model of violence, when reconstructed, can be seen to equate collective violence and private violence. Hence the notion of a "just war" and other justifications of collective violence on the model of private criminal law. This kind of reasoning entirely disregards, in his view, the disanalogies between individuals and collective entities like nations. He therefore urges a more sophisticated analysis of violence than is found in the Western "privatisation" model.

Similarly, any analysis of human rights and solidarity must take account of the ideological background of such concepts and of how and in what ways they are ethnocentric. Only when stripped of their ethnocentricity and reconstructed can their full relevance to the dangers facing us be appreciated.

* Summary prepared by the editors.

K.E. Mahoney and P. Mahoney (eds.), Human Rights in the Twenty-first Century, 221.

JOHN LADD*

Ideological Components of the Concepts of Collective Violence, Human Rights, and Solidarity

1. Introduction

I shall approach the subject of violence, human rights and solidarity as a philosopher, that is, as a questioner, a Socratic gadfly. I have no special expertise that would qualify me to set forth authoritative answers to some of the pressing practical and political problems involving violence, human rights and solidarity. Rather, I shall simply try to examine some facets of the basic ideas themselves and to raise some questions about them. In doing so, I hope to make clear some of the complexities of the ideas and some of the theoretical and conceptual problems that make the practical issues of violence, rights and solidarity much more complicated than they are frequently taken to be.

Following the classic tradition of philosophy, it is assumed that the principal contribution that philosophy can make is the clarification and critique of ideas, which is taken to comprise all sorts of concepts, theoretical and practical, as well as general beliefs, values and ideologies. By this is meant not simply looking for definitions of concepts without regard to context, but analyzing and placing them in context and examining their logical interconnections with other concepts. A perspicuous grasp of the connections and relationships between different kinds of concepts is a *sine qua non* of understanding ideas in depth, especially highly charged ideas such as the ideas of violence, of human rights and of solidarity that are the subject-matter of this essay. Although all three of these ideas are dealt with in a general way, the final part of the paper will concentrate on violence.

The value and use of the kind of ideological analysis employed in this paper is first to help us to see how these ideas are linked to the presuppositions, implications and consequences of our own beliefs and practices. This in turn will help us to understand the ideological commitments (both of others and of ourselves) that form the background for the application and use of concepts like violence, human rights and solidarity.

Second, ideological analysis also has a special use in ethical argumentation

* Brown University, Providence RI, USA.

K.E. Mahoney and P. Mahoney (eds.), Human Rights in the Twenty-first Century, 223–232.

concerning controversial issues, especially in developing counter-arguments. There are two kinds of arguments for rejecting an unacceptable position: negative and positive. A negative argument reasons that the position in question is unacceptable because its allegations are unproved, inasmuch as key premises in the arguments for them are questionable, false, invalid or incoherent, etc. A negative counter-argument of this kind may be called refutation. A positive counter-argument, on the other hand, argues against the other position on the grounds that it violates some valid moral principle. It starts with the speaker's own premises, which are assumed to reflect the 'correct', 'valid' or 'true' position, perhaps a consensus. This kind of positive argument may be called a confutation.

The different directions these two forms of counter-argument take can be illustrated by a dispute over whether or not a particular war (X v. Y) is just. X's claim that the war is just, might be refuted by showing that none of X's claims for the justness of the war (X v. Y) can be established; in other words, the conclusion is that the war in question is simply not proven to be a just war. On the other hand, X's position that the war is just can be confuted by showing that, regardless of what X believes about it, the war is indeed unjust, because it violates an accepted principle of justice.

Much more might be said about the differences between these two kinds of argument. It is enough to point out that in a refutation the burden of proof rests on the person making the claim, whereas in a confutation the burden of proof rests with the challenger. Thus, a refutation is more secure and solid than a confutation, which depends on the assumption that one's own premises are acceptable. It is obviously easier to show that the other side is mistaken, than that one's own side is right!

It should be clear now that ideological analysis can play a useful role in refuting an ethical position, for it can provide materials ("ammunition") for use in the refutation, by displaying unacceptable presuppositions, questionable premises, fallacious arguments and false analogies. Thus, although an ideological analysis may not give us a positive theory, it can help to protect us against false and mischievous theories. In the discussion that follows, the reader must keep this particular use of ideological analysis in mind, remembering that the purpose of a good deal of the analysis is not to defend the position being analyzed. Rather, it is negative and critical by providing the "tools" for refuting an unacceptable position.

Returning to the original subject, the ideas of violence, rights and solidarity, it is obvious that one of the challenges that we face with regard to them is that, if we wish to apply them globally, we must find some kind of cross-cultural meaning for them. But finding common meanings in this area is not an easy task. Clearly, the search for common meanings is beset with conceptual and philosophical pitfalls, in addition to well known practical and political obstacles. Must we conclude that the ideas in question are ethnocentric Western ideas?

Questions such as these, however they are answered, at once bring us face to face with familiar tensions between absolutism and relativism in ethics and political philosophy. As I have argued elsewhere, however, this is no simple dichotomy, but one that must be approached with some sophistication. I hope that what follows will shed some light on the subject.[1]

2. The Essentially Contested Character of These Concepts

The first thing to note in connection with the relativism-absolutism question is that the ideas of violence, rights and solidarity are controversial. Like many basic concepts of political discourse, the three ideas belong to the category of what Ian Gallie has called "essentially contested concepts."[2] They are the kind of concepts with regard to which "different persons or parties adhere to different views of the correct use of the concept."[3] Disputes of a substantive nature take the form of disputes over the use of a concept. Hence, "to use an essentially contested concept means to use it aggressively and defensively."[4]

In a word, concepts like those we are concerned with are not only controversial, but their use is partisan. They serve as rallying points for political differences and political disputes. Although Gallie assumes that one party "recognizes the fact that its own use is contested by other parties"[5], I want to stress the fact that each party claims that its own use (or interpretation) is the correct one and that other uses are mistaken or even wicked.

If it may be called such, the inherent "relativity" (partisanship?) of concepts like violence is evident in the fact that what is held by one party to be violence is held by another party to be a strike for freedom or justice. Furthermore, dissensus exists not simply with respect to particular cases but with respect to general underlying principles concerning, for example, what is to be construed as violence and even with respect to the models and ideological basis of the concepts. Being appraisive and controversial, the other two concepts, the concepts of human rights and solidarity, are relative in much the same sense.

There are, of course, stock defenses against the charge of relativity. For example, the adherents of a particular interpretation (e.g., 'definition' of violence), will charge their opponents with being uninformed, irrational or morally incompetent. Accordingly, Western democratic liberals tend to believe that people who disagree with them are primitive and backward. The parties so charged come back with the allegation that Western liberalism is inconsistent and hypocritical, both in theory and in practice. It is unnecessary to elaborate

[1] I have discussed relativism in a number of places. See J. Ladd, *Ethical Relativism* (1973). Also, J. Ladd "The Poverty of Absolutism" in T. Stroup (ed.) in *Edward Westermarck: Essays on his Life and Work*, Vol. 34 (1982).

[2] I. Gallie, *Philosophy and Historical Understanding* (1964), Chapter 8.

[3] Ibid., p. 158.

[4] Ibid., p. 161.

[5] Ibid.

on the issue, every daily newspaper is filled with illustrations of this kind of verbal contest.

The point that I wish to make and defend in this paper is that charges and countercharges of this kind are not mere rhetoric or mud-slinging, but are rational in the sense that they are grounded in complex systems of ideas that I call ideologies.

3. Ideologies

Moving now to a consideration of the ideological setting of essentially contested concepts like those that concern us, the argument of this paper is that only when placed in that setting can these concepts be properly understood, analyzed and, if need be, refuted.

To begin with, although the ideological underpinnings of other people's concepts of, say, violence, rights and solidarity differ markedly from our own, nonetheless these underpinnings provide conceptual strength and resilience to the positions taken with regard to them. The ideologies in question confer on the concepts and their use a certain robustness and power that must not be underrated. It is a mistake, and sometimes even a disastrous mistake, simply to take a cavalier attitude towards the positions with which we disagree and to dismiss them as beneath contempt, simply because we are unaware of or cannot understand and accept the ideology behind them.

Before continuing, it should be explained how I plan to use the term "ideology". Historically, the term "ideology" has had a number of meanings.[6] Owing to the influence of Marx and his followers, it is often used pejoratively and "ideology", as "false consciousness", is contrasted with science. However, the pejorative uses of "ideology" are overnarrow and limited in usefulness. For our purposes, it will be more useful to use the term "ideology" as a more general and neutral concept, that is, as a descriptive rather than an evaluative concept.

Accordingly, an ideology is defined here as a shared system of ideas, beliefs and values, held collectively by a specific group, which itself is often defined and identified by reference to the ideology. Their ideology provides members of the group with the means for rationalizing, defending, justifying and vindicating social actions, policies, programs, institutions and practices. "Ideology" in this sense has affinities with Durkheim's notion of collective representations and collective mind, although Durkheim's language may be considered quaint and unphilosophical.[7]

Accordingly, there are two sides to an ideology: first, it is a *coherent system* of ideas and, second, it is *collective* in the sense that it belongs to or

[6] For a useful survey, see D. McClellan, *Ideology* (1986).

[7] See E. Durkheim, *Sociology and Philosophy* (1953). Also S. Lukes, *Emile Durkheim: His Life and Works* (1985).

characterizes a particular group of people. As a system of ideas an ideology is a complex whole consisting of many interrelated parts, including general religious, quasi-religious or secular beliefs and mythologies. The interrelationships between the parts are quasi-logical and are not, as is sometimes thought, merely casual or adventitious.[8]

As far as the collective side is concerned, I am inclined to think that groups as collective entities, especially formal organizations, need to have an ideology of some sort or another in order to make their group actions viable and coherent. Social institutions and practices, insofar as they govern the behavior of a group, need some sort of ideological underpinning.

In saying that an ideology is a coherent system, I do not mean to imply that the basic structure of an ideology, as a whole or even in its essential parts, is perspicuous to believers or to observers. In order to acquire a complete understanding of an ideology as a whole, reconstruction of the premises and articulation of the arguments are necessary and this is a task that may be difficult to accomplish fully and satisfactorily. Yet, in lieu of more direct evidence, an effort at reconstruction is required, since, for the kinds of reasons already presented, it is absolutely necessary for political if not ethical purposes to find out as much as possible about the ideologies of other peoples, cultures and groups that we come into contact with. A great deal of the present attempts at ideological analysis involves some sort of reconstruction.[9]

The main point to be emphasized in connection with the claim that ideologies are coherent logical systems is the importance of recognizing that there are logical connections between the ideas that make up the different components of an ideology. These connections, in turn, make it a matter of logical necessity that given certain premises quite specific conclusions inevitably follow. Conversely, if particular conclusions are rejected, then at least one of the premises must be rejected. To state the matter logically, if in a particular ideological system *p entails q*, then in order for a person who accepts the system to give up *q*, he must necessarily give up *p*. This means logically, that in order for persons with different ideologies from ours to accept, say, an enlightened liberal position with regard to violence, rights or solidarity, they may need to relinquish some central and vital parts of their own ideology. A couple of illustrations should make this point clear.

First, if we consider the Nazi ideology as set forth in *Mein Kampf*, it is clear that given the premises of the doctrine (e.g., about the strength and purity of the German people (*Volk*), along with the attendant hygienic analogies) the necessity of the "Final Solution" is unavoidable. It has been a cause of wonder for many people why Hitler should have expended so many resources on liquidating the Jews when he could have spent them more cost-effectively on trying to win the war. But such questions ignore the underlying ideology for

[8] For an illustration of this type of system, see J. Ladd, *The Structure of a Moral Code* (1957).

[9] A method of reconstruction along these lines is described in Ladd, *The Structure of a Moral Code, ibid.*.

which, as Hitler himself made clear, that the Jewish question was not a side issue, but the central issue. If he had given up the "Final Solution", then he would have had to give up the basic premises of his ideology.[10]

This particular example of Nazism contains the lesson that it is a mistake to disregard a group's ideological commitments, i.e. premises. At the time, many people, both within and without Germany, regarded Hitler as a madman whose rantings were not worth listening to. They paid no attention to *Mein Kampf*, which contained the blueprint for his entire program; he was perfectly consistent. Because his ideology made no sense to us, we failed to take it seriously. We failed to see that, according to the Nazi ideology, what appeared to us as wanton violence was instead conceived of as a defensive, therapeutic operation. We did not understand what Hitler was all about because his ideas differed from ours.

Another example is the case of Salmon Rushdie. For Western democratic liberals it is inconceivable that a person, such as the Ayatollah Khomeini, should issue a death warrant for the author of the *Satanic Verses*. It goes against all of our principles, our ideology; for it violates the sacred principles of freedom of expression and of due process. But our dismay reflects an ignorance, perhaps deliberate, of what was behind Khomeini's decree, namely the religious ideology of Islam, Mahomet and the origin and authority of the Qu'ran. If the Muslims had remained silent, they would have had to repudiate the fundamental basis of their religion. What appears to the rest of the world as violence or the threat of violence is, according to Khomeini's ideology, a defense of the faith.[11]

Along the same lines, our repeated failure as Americans to take the ideologies of strangers or of our enemies seriously is a consequence of our own ideological preconceptions about "rationality". Thus, we become captives of our own ideology, an ideology according to which our world view is the only rational one and other world views are only "tales told by an idiot signifying nothing". More will be said about our own, that is American, ideology in the later discussion of concepts of violence.

4. Ideologies as Closed Systems

A typical feature of most ideologies is that they are closed systems in the sense that the basic premises as well as subsidiary premises, analogies and generalizations are not open to discussion. Their central tenets are absolutist and categorical; they are "self-evident".[12] To assure the closed character of the system, closed ideologies often create an authority of some kind or another,

[10] The importance of the ideology is emphasized by L. Yakil, *The Holocaust: The Fate of European Jewry* (1990).

[11] See D. Pipes, *The Rushdie Affair: The Novel, the Ayatollah and the West* (1990).

[12] For further discussion of this point, see John Ladd, "The Poverty of Absolutism", note 1, *supra*.

who (or which) dictates what is acceptable or unacceptable within the ideology. Having an authority protect the closed nature of the system, makes it impervious to outside input.

Several consequences of a closed ideological system may be noted. First, closed systems require some sort of differentiation between believers and non-believers. Accordingly, every closed system considers those who challenge or oppose the central tenets of the ideology to be *eo ipso* beyond the pale ethically, incompetent, irrational, impious or Satanic.

The social consequences of closed ideologies are also important. Since ideologies are associated with groups, acceptance of the ideology and of the authority speaking for it has a wider meaning; for it is a *sine qua non* of membership in the group. By the same token, dissent or disbelief is tantamount to disloyalty, heresy or apostasy. For that reason, in societies accepting closed systems, to question parts of the orthodox ideology is to risk ostracism, excommunication or execution. All these things come in one package.

Finally, closed ideologies have significant consequences for cross-ideological dialogue. It is obvious that for the outsider who does not subscribe to a particular alien ideology, there are questions of how to relate to those who do. Clashes of ideologies are common and perhaps inevitable. If the ideologies are closed systems, they become refractory and crucial ideological differences become intractable. Key tenets are unarguable, inasmuch as they are derived from premises that themselves are unarguable. Such systems are, as it were, hermetically sealed against interaction and feedback from other ideologies. That means not only that dialogue is impossible, but also that conflicts of ideologies are irresolvable. Thus, insofar as the ideas of violence, rights and solidarity are based on closed ideologies, they may present insuperable difficulties for the rest of us.

Nevertheless, the situation is not as hopeless as it may seem. For, although ideologies appear in the guise of Platonic realms of closed and timeless systems, in actuality, in a world of change, they come on the scene and fade away. Old ideologies are superseded by new ones, just as old religions and cultures give way to new ones. Believers may perceive their truths as self-evident and eternal, but in fact they are not so. Changing political, social, economic and intellectual conditions make for changes in ideologies. In addition, ideologies, as systems of ideas, are always subject to philosophical critique and evaluation.

5. Violence: The Western Model

In order to bring this abstract discussion down to earth, this essay ends by trying to show how the generalities previously mentioned apply to the concept of violence, in particular to what may be called the Western democratic model or, if you wish, the American model. Here an earlier warning must be repeated, namely that in describing, or more accurately reconstructing, this model, the present paper is not in any sense endorsing it. Perhaps it should be said that I describe it in order to condemn it.

The question before us is: what is violence? Here we can begin with the assumption that violence, however else it is defined, entails the intentional destruction or injury, primarily of persons and secondarily of their property. To that notion we should include the additional qualification that the destruction in question is excessive and wanton. Controversies concerning the definition of violence generally turn on the question of what is to be considered excessive and wanton. Was the bombing of Hiroshima excessive and wanton? Are terrorist bombings excessive and wanton? Is capital punishment excessive and wanton?

For present purposes, the discussion begins by distinguishing collective violence from private violence. Collective violence is violence inflicted by one group on another group, as in wars, massacres and pogroms. Both agents and victims of collective violence are identified, not as individuals, but as representatives of their respective groups, such as ethnic, religious or national groups.

Private violence, in contrast (e.g., family violence or street violence) is interpersonal, not intergroup. That is, it is violence that is inflicted for private purposes by individuals on other individuals on account of some personal characteristic that one or the other of them has as an individual, for instance being a woman (rape), a personal foe (revenge) or someone with money (robbery). In our society, private violence is generally considered a crime.

A basic axiom of Western thinking about violence is that violence is to be distinguished from force. Force comprises uses of coercion and destruction that, in contrast to violence, are legitimate or justified, perhaps simply legal. Accordingly, violence is sometimes defined as the illegal or illegitimate use of force (coercion). Kant, for example, goes so far as to define law and violence in terms of each other as opposites.[13] In terms of this distinction, killing is violence if it is illegitimate or unjustified. In that case, it is murder. On the other hand, if the killing is in self-defence, or by a public official for the purpose of enforcing the law, or by a soldier in war, then it is considered to be force rather than violence. There are, of course, disputes over which particular kinds of coercive acts belong to which category, violence or force.

On closer scrutiny, the distinction between violence and force, that is, between illegitimate and legitimate coercion or destruction, appears to be based on the model of private criminal violence. The assumption that the private model of violence is the correct model for all violence, including collective violence, will be called the *privatization of violence*.

The privatization model begs many questions about violence. It implies that violence is by its very nature deviant and abnormal and that those who practice it are criminal and pathological. Furthermore, in cases in which coercion and

[13] I. Kant, *The Metaphysical Elements of Justice, Part I of Metaphysik der Sitten*. Translated with an introduction and notes by John Ladd (1965).

destruction are legal (legitimate, justified?), they can no longer be considered violence. When pressed to the extreme, some authors take State violence to be a contradiction in terms!

Many morally objectionable views about violence can be traced to the privatization of violence. I have pointed out in greater detail elsewhere some of the consequences of using this model, arguing that it leads to misleading, and perhaps even mischievous conceptions of, say, collective violence.[14] To confuse collective violence with private violence in this way is a kind of categorical mistake. It is the kind of confusion that courts disaster.

Some of the significant and ostensibly disastrous consequence of the privatization of collective violence may be mentioned here:

First, by equating collective violence, such as terrorism, torture or military aggression, with private violence, collective violence is automatically converted into a kind of illegitimate and unjustified violence that is wanton and *ipso facto* irrational.

This line of thinking, when applied in the public sphere, leads to the conclusion that Hitler, Saddam Hussein, Khomeini and all the other leaders who have recourse to collective violence are criminal and pathological; that is, they are madmen and criminals comparable to ordinary criminals in the everyday world. Since they are like ordinary psychopaths and criminals, their behavior must be abnormal and irrational; consequently, there is no need to inquire into their motives or their ideology. As already pointed out above, this kind of denial is a dangerous self-delusion.

Second, if our opponents and their actions are criminal, then our political authorities (or we as a nation) are justified in using whatever force (destructive coercion) against them that is necessary to prevent, defend against or retaliate for their criminal use of violence. Hence, when our political authorities order the destruction of persons or groups, for example in war, it is not violence, but only the legal or legitimate use of force against "criminals" for the purpose of enforcing the law, human rights and justice. That is the thinking behind our unreflective commitment to the "just war doctrine", which, by the logic just outlined, makes war into a police action.[15]

A corollary of this doctrine and an essential component of the just war theory is that a legitimate, if not the chief purpose of a just war or of a just military action, is punishment, that is retaliation. It is held that in a just war the enemy nations and their leaders are at fault and guilty, and therefore it is a right and a duty for nations to punish them as nations, just as it is a right and a duty to punish individuals who have committed private violence in the private sector. Furthermore, our duty to punish evil-doers, whoever they are, holds even when our national interests are not at stake or even if we have to sacrifice them. Thus, by reducing collective violence to private violence, the American Government is

[14] See "The Idea of Collective Violence", in J. Brady and N. Garver (eds.) *Justice, Law and Violence*, (1991).

[15] For a straightforward defense of this point of view, see J.T. Johnson, *Can Modern War be Just?* (1984).

able to justify military intervention whenever it feels that it is necessary to carry out its role of international policeman.

In many typical versions of the just-war theory, the ethics of intervention on the international (collective) level, is explicitly based on an analogy to intervention on the individual level. Augustine is said to have compared a situation in which one person attacks another and the third person, an onlooker, is obliged "from love" to "seek to prevent the criminal from carrying out his evil intention by defensive measures designed to thwart whatever the criminal may try, etc".[16] Where the three persons involved are nations, the same principle pertains. Third nations, as onlookers, have the right and duty to intervene if one nation is attacking another.

This kind of argument entirely disregards the disanalogies between individuals and collective entities like nations. The latter are not the individual "writ large", as Plato would have it. When it is maintained that a nation is guilty or ought to be punished, who are we talking about? The rulers, the populace, some, most, everyone? Who is punished in a war? Are they the guilty ones? All sorts of answers are possible, but none of them are plausible. Such questions make no sense where large groups of individuals, associations and societies are involved. Concepts of guilt, fault and punishability in the individual sense cannot be applied unambiguously to collectivities without being entirely arbitrary. The conclusion is obvious. The privatization of group action, of collective violence and of collective victimization wreaks havoc with any plausible theory of group morality. That does not mean that we ought not to condemn collective violence. All it means is that we need to find a more sophisticated analysis than is found in the privatization model and the just war theory.

6. Conclusion

This has been just a sketch of a particular ideology about violence. No claim is made that the account offered here is more than speculative. Nonetheless, even if it is a caricature, it illustrates some of the contentions advanced earlier about the significance of the logical connections between various components in an ideology, in this case between violence, destruction, legality (or legitimacy), criminality, punishment and, of course, war.

If the notions set forth were to be applied to the concepts of human rights and of solidarity, an argument could be made along the same lines as that made here about violence. The analysis would try to show the ideological background of these concepts and how and in what ways, they are ethnocentric. Finally, it would attempt to show how one might escape the ethnocentricity of particular concepts like those we have been examining and to show how, when reconstructed, they still have relevance to particular kinds of issues that confront us and the dangerous situations in which we find ourselves.

[16] Ibid., at p. 4.

SECTION III(a): STATE VIOLENCE

DAVID MORRISON*

Introduction

In this section the role of the State in gender violence and exploitation, overt State violence, covert and indirect forms of State violence and accountability for State and interstate violence are discussed.

The frame of reference of the section is the underlying principle of human dignity. In its broadest sense, any act committed or omitted by the State which lessens the possibility for full human centred development is an act of violence against that person or group.

Ninotchka Rosca discusses the burgeoning global problem of trafficking in women in the Filipino context, particularly in relation to militarization. She argues that a continual existence of war conditions shifts economic responsibility from males to females, which in turn forces a quarter of a million women each year from their home base as exported and exploited labour. The huge migrations of Filipino women from their homeland are generated by social disruptions created by militarization which intrudes into traditional ethical codes and accepted behaviour patterns.[1] This situation, she argues, leads further to the suppression of women who are organizing women.

A whole conference could have been dedicated to the subject of State violence against women, only beginning to be more widely exposed. International human rights activists (and domestic lawyers/judiciary) will be required to challenge and change the legal framework that undergirds male violence (unequal inheritance, discriminatory family laws, the institutionalization of prostitution) and also challenge the social inequalities and cultural beliefs that leave women economically dependent. With damage to children growing up in an atmosphere of continual military rule, social upheaval and

* Chair, Department of Religious Studies at the University of Prince Edward Island.

[1] United States military bases within the Philippines create a situation in which Filipinos become prostituted to the American dollar, literally and figuratively. The only real industry in the "cities" which surround the bases is sex, so anyone who tries to protect or support the women and children prostitutes is accused of trying to undermine the economy and thus the government. The people face threats of State violence in various forms.

K.E. Mahoney and P. Mahoney (eds.), Human Rights in the Twenty-first Century, 233–235.

economic collapse which leads to apathy, alienation, disaffection, violence is already reaping its global results. Unfortunately, violence against women is not a priority item as long as States create the international agenda.

Jonathan Kuttab's paper is written in the context of the relationship of the State of Israel to the West Bank. He argues that overt forms of State violence are based on the opportunity of the State to legalize violence through its monopoly of the legal apparatus and administrative structure and a judiciary which can prevent (or enhance) human rights considerations as the State carries out its objectives. Deriving legitimacy from legality, the State has significant advantages as a perpetrator of violence. He points out that when following a path of violence against civilian populations, States engage in mass murder, torture, physical injuries, restrictions of liberty through imprisonment and/or extra-juridical means, destruction of property and forceful closing of universities, schools and other social outlets. More subtle forms of State violence may be travel restrictions, enforced deportation or prevention of family reunifications. Economic violence perpetrated by the State includes tactics such as the suspension of essential services and social, economic and cultural restrictions which can affect a whole population.

The establishment of accountability for State and inter-State violence is the subject of Michael McClintock's paper. He emphasizes the importance of establishing accountability for State violence that is in contravention of international standards based on human rights and humanitarian law. States often misrepresent either the nature of the violent acts which they perpetrate, or the extent of their involvement. Often, the State attempts to justify acts of violence by claiming that they are necessary. McClintock argues the only way to distinguish arbitrary and unlawful killings from those allowed by international standards is to ensure that the full facts of disputed deaths are brought to light. One particular problem is differentiating spontaneous civilian violence or independent terrorist acts from State violence of a similar appearance. As well, political alliances can work to shield offending States by moulding public opinion and suppressing human rights reporting. However, he points out that the means of establishing State accountability for violence have increased, not only through the growing power of non-governmental organizations but also through the new force of global human rights awareness.

Dinah Shelton discusses covert and indirect forms of violence by the State, underlining the gravity of State obligations and responsibility as State violence becomes increasingly concealed. As a result of international, widespread condemnation of overt State human rights violations there is increased covert, State support of violence perpetrated by private actors. This is done in a myriad of ways, either directly or indirectly through the failure to act to protect international human rights standards. She argues that not only are States required to respect and ensure human rights obligations, but they also have the responsibility to ensure that these rights are not violated covertly. The role of customary international law through the action of recognized tribunals could assist in combating State complicity.

The theme running through the paper of Brian Currin and Paula McBride[2] is the inherently political character of capital punishment in South Africa, in the congruence of racial domination and legalized murder. Whereas the legislators and judges who have drafted and applied the capital laws are exclusively white, the bulk of the death row population – apart from the significant number of political offenders – are criminal offenders who are black and impoverished. The manifestations of racial oppression within South Africa have conditioned not only the law and sentencing practice relating to capital punishment, but also the behaviour of those sentenced to death. Some welcome advances contained in legislation enacted in 1990, for example the introduction of the notion of mitigation, have been deprived of effectiveness because the State has failed to ensure their full and proper implementation. Currin and McBride see this limited foray of the South African Government into the arena of "enlightened" legislative change as a tinkering with the legislative and constitutional framework designed to stave off their inevitable downfall. At the outset of their paper Currin and McBride signal the remarkable fact that in 1991 South Africa, after having been one of the most energetic hanging nations, became *de facto* an abolitionist State with a moratorium on executions; and they end with the optimistic wish that the hangman in South Africa has joined the ranks of the unemployed. But their paper provides a chilling analysis of the way in which the death penalty can be used by the State as an instrument of political control and repression.

The five papers in this section bring to light some of the many faces of violence. The State's role as an active or passive player in its prevention, perpetration or perpetuation is paramount. Continued maintenance and upgrading of international human rights law, conscientization and moral suasion are called for by all those committed to the principle of human dignity as the foundation for our common existence, if State violence is not to be a behaviour of the first or last resort.

[2] The paper of Brian Currin and Paula McBride was not delivered at the Conference.

NINOTCHKA ROSCA*

Effects of Militarism and State Violence on Women and Children

The percentage of countries of the third world which have reverted to some form of military or military civilian hunta type governments has been increasing in the last three decades. About half of underdeveloped nations now spend over 50% of their incomes on two major items, on defense and foreign debt servicing. The connection between the two does not need further elaboration. We know that the most lucrative international business of the moment is the arms industry. The frightening fact about militarization is it occurs in countries where the majority of the alienated and disenfranchised are women and children. Considering that these women are already viewed largely in terms of their production and reproduction capabilities we can approach the subject at hand by studying how militarization enhances or warps these capabilities.

In the next decade the majority of the foreign born population of the world will be women. This indicates the establishment of a migratory pattern quite the reverse of that before the second world war when men dominated migration. It also indicates the establishment of pockets of population with high vulnerability to high exploitation based on foreignness, with its implied unfamiliarity with local customs and laws and the resulting alienation and further disenfranchisement; lack or absence of skills which reduce these pockets of migrants to a source of cheap labour; and gender related exploitation.

The significance of this migrant pattern is paradoxical. On the one hand it indicates a shift of economic responsibility from the male to the female. On the other hand it also indicates that familial non-economic responsibilities are shifted to the male. The question which arises is whether our current cultures can justify this shift or this role reversal. That is the first question. Can we maintain an environment conducive to the survival of the family with a healthy matrix for child rearing and development? All indicators are negative. This shift in migratory pattern has been accompanied by the increase in the number of street children and child deaths. UNESEF expects that 50 million children will die over the next 10 years from such curable disorders as measles, dehydration and pneumonia.

* Amnesty International, New York, NY.

K.E. Mahoney and P. Mahoney (eds.), Human Rights in the Twenty-first Century, 237–240.

The dislocation of large numbers of women and their funnelling into the international labour trade, breeds its own special set of problems. Because women are usually low skilled and untrained and for the most part culturally barred from assuming work at a certain level of production, the job situation leaves them highly vulnerable to abuse and exploitation. Consider the specific case of the Philippines which sends out annually around a quarter of a million women for work overseas. These are official figures and they are staggering. There are 50,000 Filipinos in Hong Kong, 10,000 in Singapore, 35,000 in Japan, 75,000 in Italy, 100,000 in the Middle East. The selling of bodies has become the top dollar earner of the country. Around 1.2 billion dollars were remitted through official channels last year with an equal amount remitted through unofficial channels. Most of these women work as domestics, which means they are incorporated as junior and disenfranchised members of the household, usually patriarchal and hierarchical in structure and nature. Abuses occur more as a rule than an exception. Rape is a constant. In some cases in the Middle East women who get pregnant from employer rape are remanded to insane asylums on the theory that only crazy women get pregnant when they are not married. Physical abuse is also rampant, as many of the cloistered females of the household vent their frustration on the most helpless and most disenfranchised member of the family structure.

Because female labour is undervalued the world over there are also problems relating to wages and contracts. Benefits, especially with regards to reproduction, are nonexistent. To be blunt about it, international labour market posters, a disguised form of slavery are designed for these women. Which brings us to the growth of the trafficking of women as sex workers. This is directly related to militarization and the erosion of ethos which militarization occasions.

First we have to keep in mind the propensity of the military outlook to reduce human beings to a statistic, accounts, cost of operation, and so on and so forth. Also the military ethos of war which bluntly stated, is that men are killed and women are raped. This dictum has been in operation since the first tribal war, it seems, and it will be most interesting to see how it will work out in the current integration of women in the military, particularly with the dangers of war in the Middle East.

The direct impact of militarization on women can be itemized as follows: First is the conscription and decimation of male members of the family resulting in the downloading of economic responsibilities on women. Second is the destruction of the community resulting in the creation of the phenomena called internal refugees, largely consisting of women and children. Third, is the destruction of the social, cultural matrix of both the family and the community resulting in the exacerbation of the view of women in terms solely of their production and reproduction capabilities. (In this case, we should replace "reproduction" with the word "sexual".) Fourth, the occurance of gender abuse as a specific human rights violation, including sexual torture, the use of women prisoners as sex slaves for the military, deprivation of health care specific to women and maternal instincts used as a means of psychological torture. Fifth and most importantly is the increasing suppression of women who are organizing women. The last point is very important as it is a direct attack on women's efforts to meet problems created by militarization itself, and it is a pattern developing on a world-wide scale.

Let us examine closely how the dynamics operate in a particular instance of the Philippines. The shift of economic responsibility to women generally occasioned by militarization and the death of men, or their running away, takes place in a social context where because of militarization, survival has become the sole ethos of the community. For men who have no marketable skills, the presence of the military, which is no more than a large concentration of men with political economic power, offers a particular means of survival, through sexual labour or prostitution. In the pervading chaotic ambience of war where all normal human interaction is suspended and where survival is the highest virtue, it is easy to make the decision to trade favours or cash for sex. The corruption goes both ways and in an amazingly short period this survival mode develops into a pervasive industry with the military firmly implicated in its operations.

The Philippines is the principal recruiting ground for prostitutes for the Japanese underworld. Around 35,000 Filipinos work as sex workers in Japan doing what they call a six month tour of duty, in rotating batches. Recruiting agencies are disguised as entertainment agencies looking for dancers and singers. They are protected and are sometimes owned and operated by military personnel. This is one reason why despite the global scandal surrounding the sex industry in the Philippines, the government has not been able to even limit its operations. There is both direct and spillover involvement of both the military and the civilian branches of government.

To meet the challenges created by the pressure of militarization, women take to organizing around their social and cultural interests. This response brings them into direct conflict with the military or with military intentions which have become inextricably linked with the flourishing of disguised forms and overt forms of white slavery. The consequence is the increase in the number of women who are suppressed in terms of arrests, detention, and disappearances for the reasons that they are organizing women around the issues.

Last year the Philippine military proposed the outlawing of among others, Gabriella, a coalition of 105 women's organizations and institutions in the country. This organization was and is at the forefront of the struggle to end prostitution around military bases, to unionize even the sex industry, the sex workers, to ban the mail order bride industry, to build self-reliance social economic projects for women, to build drop in centres for adult and child prostitutes, and so on. But, since 1986, around 50 of its organizers have been "salvaged", which is the military term for kidnapping and summary execution.

The situation at the moment is so bad that if you are a feminist, or declare yourself to be a feminist, you are automatically considered subversive, radical, communist, and a good target for the death squads.

In conclusion, and this is my main thesis, the time when we can look at militarization as a localized phenomenon is over. In its particular impact on women, there are both global involvement and global repercussions. I have been proposing an international conference involving human rights activists on the issue of trafficking in women, which is directly linked to militarization. This is not only a gender issue. Two years ago, Gabriella launched a major campaign around this and other issues of women in the Philippines, under the slogan women's rights are human rights. And I think that sums it up.

JONATHAN KUTTAB*

Overt Forms of State Violence

1. Introduction

The purpose of this paper is to address overt forms of state violence. I examine the nature of state-sanctioned violence from a global perspective, without focusing on any particular state or region. However, some of the examples draw upon experience in my region (the Israeli occupied West Bank and Gaza Strip), as it is these with which I am most familiar.

Forms of state violence not addressed include covert or indirect acts of violence by vigilantes, settlers, paramilitary groups, collaborators, and militia. Other forms of state violence such as acts of war, aggression, military raids on neighbouring or distant countries, mining of harbours (as the United States did in Nicaragua), and violations of territorial integrity (including the territorial waters, airspace and land of other countries) are discussed elsewhere in this chapter. My paper focuses on state violence in the form of misuse of police power, destruction of property, deliberate infliction of psychological harm and economic and social restrictions.

2. State Violence from a Human Rights Perspective

We, as people concerned with human rights must deal with the reality that since the beginning of nation–states, the State has claimed an almost virtual monopoly on the use of violence and on the possession of weapons. The State also enjoys an absolute monopoly on legality. It has legislative power. Within its borders, the State determines what the law is and what it should be. This is quite significant because the State always derives legitimacy from that legality. The State, through its laws, establishes certain norms of behaviour to which it and others adhere. Sometimes the laws themselves create or perpetuate violence upon citizens (and others), but they continue to be regarded as "the law of the

* Director, AL HAQ (Law in the Service of Man), Jerusalem, via Israel.

K.E. Mahoney and P. Mahoney (eds.), Human Rights in the Twenty-first Century, 241–245.

land" carrying with them the weight and authority of legitimacy. Whether law-making or legitimacy comes from religious theory, assertion of force, or from some kind of social contract theory (whereby the citizens grant the State the authority to set up the laws), the State ultimately exercises authority of law.

Furthermore, in carrying out acts of violence every State has at its disposal an administrative structure and a tremendous organization for executing and imposing its policies and practices upon those under its control. This makes the State a significantly different player than mere individuals or other subgroups in the game of violence and in the violation of human rights.

Finally, the state has a judiciary that promotes, prohibits, or prevents the proper investigation of human rights violations. When one considers the doctrine of a sovereign immunity which allows a State, by virtue of being a state, to claim a certain immunity from review, inspection, trial and prosecution, responsibility for violations of human rights is often difficult to establish.

3. Different Forms of Overt State Violence

(1) Violence Causing Death

There are different forms of overt state violence. Leading the list are those actions which take the lives of individuals. This category not only includes the death penalty but also murders that occur at the hands of State agents during disturbances, demonstrations, or states of emergency. Deaths may be random, as when shots are fired in a crowd. Or they may be highly selective, as when the State extrajudicially seeks and kills an individual it wishes to eliminate. This type of violence may be committed against individuals or may be directed against the masses, as in the case of massacres. There are many cases throughout the world of states engaged in mass murder. Usually it follows the form of excessive use of military forces, weapons, or tactics against the civilian population.

(2) Death in Detention

Many countries around the world, including Western countries, have experience with death in detention. It is always stated as having taken place under "mysterious circumstances". Suicide is an excuse which is often used. An extreme example of this form of state violence reportedly occurred in Syria where as many as 300 prison inmates were supposedly killed or massacred by authorities under the guise that they were killed while attempting to escape.

(3) Torture

A third form of overt state violence is torture. Despite the Convention on Elimination of Torture, countries continue to practice torture. Of particular concern are those countries where the use of torture is systematic and where the judicial structure, like the military court system in the Israeli occupied territories with which I am very familiar, is based entirely on coerced confessions taken under torture.

(4) Physical Injury

The State often causes non-fatal physical injury by using live ammunition in the form of plastic or rubber bullets on people and by permitting police brutality. Practically every country is guilty of using violence against individuals to cause physical injury, although there are few cases which compare to that of Israeli Defense Minister Yitzhak Rabin. During his reign, Rabin issued specific orders to Israeli forces to break the arms and legs of Palestinian demonstrators. Throughout this period, there were tens of thousands reported cases of broken bones resulting directly from army activities.

(5) Restrictions on Liberty

The fifth type of overt state violence includes restrictions of liberty in the form of imprisonment. Of particular note are administrative detention and extrajudicial imprisonments. This category involves hostage-takings where members of foreign nationalities or one's own nationality are kept against their will in order to achieve certain desired goals like "deliver to us members of your family we are seeking" or "encourage your government not to start a war against us". The State enjoys and practices use of its power, its jails, its detention centres and its authority to arrest and detain people against their will without due process of law.

(6) Destruction of Property

The State, through its police, army and civilian machinery, often destroys property without compensation or due process to its owners. In fact, property destruction is often used as a form of punishment which may transpire through the systematic demolition of a series of houses or the targeting of individual properties, through the blowing up or bulldozing of houses where suspects or undesirables are believed to live, or through the destruction of complete sections of neighbourhoods. One practice which has been experienced in the occupied West Bank and Gaza Strip has been the systematic up-rooting of trees by Israeli officials. A similar tactic used by States in other parts of the world is the destruction of farm property and other economic resources upon which citizens rely. A practise common throughout many areas of the globe is the destruction of household goods, supplies and productive equipment during army and police raids. Other disturbances which may be classified as property destruction include the closure of schools, universities, union halls, newspapers, societies and other places where people congregate and carry out activities.

(7) Invisible Forms of Violence

All the forms of state violence described above are direct and visible. (i.e. the blood, broken bones, damage and injury may be witnessed). However, other forms of violence by the State, with some bases in domestic law, can be just as violent and destructive yet not involve direct contact with the victim. For instance, easily verifiable travel restrictions, forcible deportations and prevention of family reunifications administered through structures of law are arguably instruments of state violence. I do not fully accept the violence/law dichotomy as put forward by some of my peers. Law itself, at least domestic internal law, is often an instrument of grave violence. If I may parenthetically offer a challenge to those who have worked for the right of Soviet Jews to immigrate from Russia under a human rights principle of "the right of any individual to leave any country including his own" to remember that the same human rights principle refer to the right of people to return to their homes (See Article 14 of the Universal Declaration of Human Rights). Those who are not willing, with equal fervour, to support the Palestinian right of return to their home must question themselves very closely as to whether in championing the rights of Soviet Jews they are following human rights principles or following their own ideological and political predispositions.

(a) Deprivation of Services

A further form of violence which indirectly impacts its victims is the suspension or total elimination of services by the State. Basic necessities which may be limited or restricted under this category include electricity, water, food supplies, and medical services. Other violent acts include interfering with ambulance service, or preventing medical care for injured persons.

(b) Economic and Social Restrictions

Last but not least, is a special category of deliberate economic and social restrictions which include planning processes that prohibit a population from meeting its normal economic, housing, development, and industrialization needs. This type of state violence is difficult to prove as most decisions of this kind are based on a balance of competing social considerations. However, it is often possible to demonstrate practices and policies which systematically deny housing or restrict citizens from exercising their normal functions. Such practices and policies deliberately invoked to injure should be regarded as a form of state violence.

4. Conclusion

As we look towards the next century of human rights, it is important to recognize the progress achieved during this century. We are beginning to see the imposition of serious restrictions on the ability of the State to carry out violence against its own citizens and others. Human rights of individuals and the obligation of the international community to see to the protection of those rights are now recognized. Treaties and conventions exist which impose clear duties on States to refrain from certain acts of violence and the violation of rights of others. Unfortunately, these contain insufficient mechanisms to ensure their enforcement.

As we approach this coming century, we must work for, hope for, and struggle for new mechanisms and theories, both nationally and internationally, to further restrict the ability of a State to exercise forms of violence against its citizens and others. Integrally, these restrictions can take the form of democratic safeguards, constitutions, and legal prohibitions. Internationally, conventions, enforcement mechanisms and bilateral or multilateral sanctions should be used to a greater effect. We must require governments, as a matter of their own laws, to provide mechanisms to safeguard human rights. Where no such laws exist or where the laws themselves violate human rights norms, they should be sanctioned. Externally, the community of nations must seriously address its collective obligation to enforce fundamental standards, whether through economic sanctions, universal prosecution of violators of human rights, or through other mechanisms which have yet to be established.

MICHAEL McCLINTOCK*

Establishing Accountability for State Violence

1. Introduction

The use of violence by States is subject to international standards applying to situations of peace and war. These standards, based on human rights law and humanitarian law, are in a continual process of refinement and elaboration – as are the mechanisms for their implementation. State violence in violation of these norms may affect an individual, a community, a people, or the population of another State. At its most extreme such violence takes the form of extrajudicial executions: deliberate and unlawful killings. Establishing accountability for such killings is a major problem in human rights protection.

States may accept responsibility for certain acts of violence without acknowledging that they are abuses in breach of international standards. They may deny any involvement. They may take extraordinary steps to conceal evidence, obstruct investigation or attribute criminal violence to others. A first step in establishing accountability is to determine that human rights abuse occurred.

The shootings of suspected terrorists, the use of lethal force in crowd control situations, and killings of noncombatants in military operations are frequently disputed as to cause and circumstances, necessity or proportionality, in the face of a threat. Allegations may be made of premeditation – or that the intent was other than that stated in an official version.

Disputed killings occur in vastly different circumstances. A series of six killings of suspected supporters of the Irish Republican Army (IRA) in Northern Ireland in the 1980s led to allegations of a "shoot to kill" policy, although it could never be shown incontrovertibly that agents of the State had committed murder. In Colombia, by contrast, the indisputable victims of murder by the State on political grounds have numbered in the thousands, as deliberate "death squad"-style killings of detainees and others have been a military and police practice for many years. In India, on a more limited scale,

* Office of the Head of Research, Amnesty International, International Secretariat, London, U.K.

K.E. Mahoney and P. Mahoney (eds.), Human Rights in the Twenty-first Century, 247–264.

suspects are seized and killed and the deaths attributed to the legitimate use of force in armed "encounters". In China, the killings in Beijing on 4 June 1989 well illustrated disputed killings of demonstrators. The killing by troops in May 1988 of 28 residents of the remote Peruvian village Cayara, in turn, illustrates that killings in armed conflict that are not always what they seem.

The killings of suspected gunmen in Northern Ireland, of purported subversives in Colombia and India, of demonstrators in China, and of suspect villagers in Peru's counterinsurgency offensive had a common denominator: the respective governments each obscured the facts while holding that the killings were justifiable under international standards.

2. International Standards

International standards provide the criteria by which to distinguish arbitrary and unlawful killings from others that occur in the course of law enforcement and armed conflict, and procedures for the investigation of disputed killings. A particular contribution to standard setting has been made through the initiatives of the United Nation's Committee on Crime Prevention and Control and through the five-yearly congresses called by the General Assembly on the Prevention of Crime and the Treatment of Offenders.[1] Early recognition of the problem of arbitrary and unlawful killings was made by the Sixth UN Congress in the series, held in Caracas, Venezuela in 1980. The congress adopted a resolution condemning what it termed "extralegal executions," and expressing alarm at the widespread killings "of political opponents or suspected offenders carried out by armed forces, law enforcement or other governmental agencies or by paramilitary or political groups often acting with the tacit or other support of such forces or agencies."[2]

The Sixth Congress cited international human rights law concerning the right to life, liberty and security of person in condemning unlawful killings, as well as the four Geneva Conventions of August 1949 as they concern wilful

[1] For a review of the role of the UN Congress on Prevention of Crime and Treatment of Offenders see Nigel S. Rodley, *The Treatment of Prisoners Under International Law* (1987), Oxford: Clarendon Press, in association with UNESCO, pp. 24–26. A trend toward a coming together of the UN's specialized crime prevention and control and human rights machinery in combating gross human rights abuse can be illustrated by General Assembly resolution 42/141, 7 December 1987. This condemns the large number of summary or arbitrary executions in the world, including "extra-legal executions", and recognizes the need for closer cooperation between the UN Centre for Human Rights, the Vienna-based Crime Prevention and Criminal Justice Branch of the Centre for Social Development and Humanitarian Affairs and the Committee on Crime Prevention and Control in efforts to bring to an end summary or arbitrary executions. (This aspect of the 1987 resolution is again stressed in Resolution 1989/65, adopted by the United Nations Economic and Social Council on 24 May 1989 ("Effective prevention and investigation of extra-legal, arbitrary and summary executions")).

[2] Sixth United Nations Congress on the Prevention of Crime and the Treatment of Offenders, 25 August – 5 September 1980, Resolution 5: Extra-legal executions. Reproduced in Rodley, Ibid., Annex 7.

killing. It cited in particular article 3, common to the four conventions, in respect of non-international armed conflict, which "further prohibits at any time and in any place whatsoever violence to life and person, in particular murder of all kinds."[3] It observed further, in calling for an end to the practice, "that murder committed or tolerated by Governments is condemned by all national legal systems and, thus, by general principles of law."[4]

The United Nation's standard setting with regard to crime prevention has also resulted in codes of conduct that provide useful measures through which to assess disputed killings. The Code of Conduct for Law Enforcement Officials, adopted by United Nations General Assembly resolution 34/169 of 17 December 1979, set out clear standards for the use of lethal force in law enforcement.[5] Article 3 of the code states that "Law enforcement officials may use force only when strictly necessary and to the extent required for the performance of their duty." The Code includes an official commentary which, in the text approved by the General Assembly, is said to have been provided "to facilitate the use of the Code within the framework of national legislation or practice." The Commentary sets out the basis for the use of lethal force and a foundation for human rights monitoring.

The refinement of international standards concerning extrajudicial executions has continued. The most comprehensive body of such standards is set out in the Principles on the Effective Prevention and Investigation of Extra-Legal, Arbitrary and Summary Executions, adopted by the UN Economic and Social Council on 24 May 1989 and endorsed by the UN General Assembly in December of that year. These principles obligate governments to "make every effort to prevent extra-legal, arbitrary and summary executions" and to conduct "a thorough, prompt and impartial investigation" of all such executions.

Governments are responsible for ensuring that effective procedures and safeguards are instituted to prevent unlawful killings by their agents. If such killings occur, governments must establish the facts, make them public and hold those responsible accountable before the law. The United Nations Special Rapporteur on summary or arbitrary executions noted in a 19 January 1988 report that the following should be considered *minimum* elements of the standards for proper investigations into all cases of suspicious death:

[3] Ibid.

[4] Ibid. Common Article 3 (1) of the Geneva Conventions stipulates that "Persons taking no active part in the hostilities, including members of armed forces who have laid down their arms and those placed *hors de combat* by sickness, wounds, detention, or any other cause, shall in all circumstances be treated humanely without any adverse distinction founded on race, colour, religion or faith, sex, birth or wealth, or any other similar criteria.

To this end, the following acts are and shall remain prohibited at any time and in any place whatsoever with respect to the above-mentioned persons:

(a) violence to life and person, in particular murder of all kinds, mutilation, cruel treatment and torture..."

[5] The full text is in Rodley, cited in note 1, Annex 5a.

a) Promptness: the investigation should be carried out immediately following the discovery of such a death;
b) Impartiality: the investigation should be carried out by a person or persons or an authority whose impartiality is guaranteed and protected;
c) Thoroughness: the investigation should include an adequate autopsy, collection and analysis of evidence, and statements from witnesses, hence the person(s) or authority investigating should be given the necessary powers, assistance and logistic support;
d) Protection: complainants, witnesses and persons investigating and their families should be given effective protection from violence or any form of threats;
e) Representation of the family of the victim: the family of the victim and its legal counsel should be able to participate in the investigatory proceedings and have access to substantive information at various stages of the investigation;
f) Publication of the findings: the methods and findings of the investigation should be made public;
g) Independent commission of inquiry: in cases in which the normal investigatory procedure is inadequate, an independent commission of inquiry or similar procedure should be secured. Such a commission should have the necessary authority and powers to carry out impartial and effective investigation.

By bringing the full facts of disputed killings to light, governments can show that their agents are fully accountable for their actions – and that those abuses that do occur are a consequence of indiscipline, accident or error, and not of government policy. The obstruction of inquiries, limiting or delaying of inquests or the blanket award of immunity from prosecution for actions in the line of duty are indicators, albeit not conclusive, to the contrary.

3. Establishing Accountability for Disputed Killings

(1) Targeting the Suspect

International standards provide a framework for analysis that applies to the full range of disputed killings, from selective assassinations by government "death squads", to mass killings of demonstrators, as well as to the deaths of criminal or political suspects at the hands of law enforcement officers. They apply both to the blatant cases of murder by agents of the State and to those grey areas in which the legitimate use of force in law enforcement shades into the arbitrary and the unacceptable.

Often governments routinely claim that deliberate and unlawful killings occurred when government forces confronted armed resistance or sought to halt an escaping prisoner. In India, extrajudicial executions are routinely characterized as deaths that occurred in armed clashes with the authorities. A term of art for such killings, in use throughout the country, is the "encounter killing". A recent example of the almost daily incidents of disputed killings in India's Punjab was widely reported in the press. According to New Delhi's *The Statesman* (29 June 1990), two students, 24 year old Harpal Singh and Baljit Singh, 20, both of them members of the All India Sikh Students Federation, were killed by the police in what they said was an "armed encounter" in Kotla Ajner village. But local accounts maintain the two had been prisoners at the time of their killing and that no encounter occurred. According to the press report: "The circumstantial evidence in the case collected by this correspondent after visiting the site and speaking to a number of villagers....clearly shows that it was a case of fake police encounter....According to the villagers, the victims were tortured by the police for a couple of hours and later killed".

The evidence of deliberate killings as a matter of policy in India includes an order issued on 30 August 1989 by the Director General of Police in the Punjab to all district superintendents of police in the state. The order included a list of 53 people, and specified "Rewards for the apprehension/liquidation of wanted terrorists/extremists." A year later, the new Attorney General told the Supreme Court in April 1990 that the order had now lapsed. Its specifying of bounties to be paid for "liquidation", however, when viewed in the context of frequent disputed killings in the Punjab, may be interpreted as having offered direct encouragement to the police to extrajudicially execute those listed in the order in killings to be attributed to "encounters". Acknowledging that such extrajudicial executions continued to occur, the new Governor of Punjab, on assuming office in June 1990, issued an appeal to police officers "to stop fake encounters". But the killings continue.

Not all unlawful killings by agents of the State are as clear cut as many of the cases reported in India – or so clearly representative of a policy of deliberate and unlawful killings at some level of government. Often suspect killings may be small in number and investigation of them ultimately inconclusive; but even incomplete evidence of government wrongdoing in a disputed killing, where combined with a failure to investigate a killing fully and publicly may serve to sap public confidence in government. An inquiry marred by evidence of deception, the suppression of evidence or intimidation will exacerbate any doubts outstanding on the killings in question while undermining confidence in the government's readiness to see that justice is done.

In Northern Ireland, public disquiet in this respect for a time centered on inquiries into six fatal shooting of unarmed suspects by security forces there in 1982. Procedures for the investigation of killings by the security forces in disputed circumstances were found to present a series of obstacles to a prompt, fair and public determination of the facts. The six killings, in three incidents, had given rise to allegations that the security forces had killed suspected members of the IRA with premeditation. Testimonies and forensic evidence subsequently emerged to show that in all three incidents official cover-ups had occurred.

Public disquiet over the killings resulted in the conduct of a police inquiry by a senior officer from the Manchester police, Deputy Chief Constable John Stalker. The inquiry, begun in 1984, was marred by the withholding of evidence from John Stalker and his removal immediately prior to its conclusion. The inquiry was completed in April 1987 by Chief Constable Colin Sampson. In January 1988 the government stated that the inquiry had revealed evidence that police officers had conspired to pervert the course of justice or had attempted to do so, but that a decision had been taken not to prosecute those allegedly responsible because of "national security" and "public interest" considerations. The report itself was also withheld from the public on grounds of national security. There was little room for confidence that the truth had come out.

The six Northern Ireland cases also illustrated the legal barriers to bringing out the facts in disputed killings through inquest procedures. The procedures relied upon by the government to investigate such incidents are police investigations, inquests and, rarely, criminal proceedings. Royal Ulster Constabulary (RUC) investigations into the 1982 incidents were found to have been obstructed by senior RUC officers who conspired to falsify and conceal crucial information. This, in turn, resulted in the presentation of hopelessly flawed cases in the criminal proceedings brought against police officers for murder in some of the cases. The Stalker/Sampson inquiry, in turn, was obstructed and its findings withheld; more than eight years after the events the government has yet to provide a full and public account of the circumstances of the six killings.

Inquests in the 1982 killings, postponed pending police investigations and criminal proceedings, have yet to be held. Inquest procedures, in any case, are subjected to restrictions that apply only to Northern Ireland in the United Kingdom which severely limit their potential for a thorough, independent and public investigation of disputed killings. The coroner's court cannot make the finding of an unlawful killing by an unnamed person, as is possible in England and Wales. Since 1980 they can not issue verdicts, but only "findings" regarding the cause of death. Security forces personnel involved in killings are not summoned to give evidence or to testify under cross-examination. The family or legal representatives of the deceased are further hampered in that forensic and eyewitness reports are not revealed until the beginning of the inquest. The years' long delay of the opening of a coroner's inquest may mean that autopsy reports that are critical to establishing the cause and circumstances of death may be indefinitely withheld from the parties to the complaint and from the public. Although autopsy reports can be released at the discretion of the coroner, this has rarely been the case in Northern Ireland.

The same procedural obstacles to investigation may be a feature of disputed killings where the rule of law is strained, but largely intact, and where the rule of law has been shattered by years' long state violence beyond the limits of the law. Special inquest procedures, government agencies' legal exemption from releasing certain documentary or other evidence to coroner's courts or criminal courts, and special provisions exempting military or police personnel from testifying or facing cross-examination are just some of the common obstacles to the full determination fo the facts in disputed killings.

In some systems, security personnel responsible for extrajudicial executions are commonly immune to full investigation by any civilian authority or prosecution by the ordinary courts. In Colombia, the exclusive jurisdiction of the military courts over matters concerning the military and the police has posed major obstructions for investigations by civilian legal authorities, as well as generally insuperable barriers to prosecutions of security personnel for unlawful killings. Autopsies of people who are victims of disputed killings may be carried out by forensic examiners of the Ministry of Justice's Legal Medicine division, but when the nature or circumstances of killings in the context of law enforcement is disputed, the military and police personnel are under military court jurisidiction. The military courts, in turn, have refused almost across the board to act against killers in uniform in Colombia (this is just one of the factors suggesting such killers are acting on orders at the highest level). Autopsy reports are declared *sub judice* pending resolution of military court enquiries; these enquiries, however, rarely come to a formal conclusion and the legal representatives of the dead may never gain access to them.

In a case from September 1985, 11 teenaged supporters of Colombia's M-19 group held up a milk-truck at gunpoint and attempted to distribute the load to the people of a Bogota slum. They were surrounded by some 200 heavily armed police and, according to witnesses, surrendered without shots being fired. Police subsequently said they had all been killed in a gun battle. Witnesses said they saw several youths shot in the head after being forced to lie prone in the street. A then Minister privately observed to Amnesty International (AI) that the autopsy reports indeed bore this out, showing that youths had been shot from a distance of less than one meter, while flat on the ground, but added that according to the law he should not even have seen the report or confided its findings. They were formally under wraps in the military courts (and are apparently still buried in the files of the military justice system).

(2) Targeting the Demonstrator

The government of the People's Republic of China's response to public outrage over the killings in and around Beijing's Tiananmen Square on 4 June 1989 has illustrated some of the obstacles to accountability posed when large numbers of people are killed in disputed circumstances in what could roughly be termed "crowd control" situations. To this day, the government maintains that some 200 civilians – and "several dozen" soldiers – were killed in the incidents. AI estimates – in part on the basis of reports of detailed counts of bodies in the morgues of area hospitals – that over 1,000 civilians were shot dead by troops or crushed by tanks. The detailed information available indicates that about 16 soldiers were killed. The government said no one was killed in the square, despite video and eyewitness testimony to the contrary. It said civilian casualties were a consequence of the self-defence of soldiers under attack by armed demonstrators.

AI acted *before* the armed forces moved to halt the demonstration in Beijing's principal square, to urge Chinese authorities to take steps to ensure that troops were instructed in international standards regarding the use of lethal force in law enforcement. AI's 24 May appeal to the authorities, prompted by the major troop movements already under way, was evidently unsuccessful. The aim was to call attention to international standards that restrict the use of firearms in accord with principles of proportionality and necessity.

In the aftermath of the massacres, the international human rights community sought to establish the facts in the face of systematic government obstruction of independent investigation. A sophisticated governmental campaign was conducted to present a view of the events tailor-made for the evasion of accountability. Although it included carefully edited video footage, it failed in large part because the world had already viewed uncensored broadcasts from the independent news media. The UN Sub-Commission on Prevention of Discrimination and Protection of Minorities, to which AI had submitted a report and made an oral statement, adopted a resolution expressing concern about the events in China. For the first time the Sub-Commission acted on China, asking the UN Secretary-General to transmit information about the situation there to the UN Commission on Human Rights. Super-power politics, however, subsequently shielded China from further effective attention by the UN human rights apparatus.

Mass killings of demonstrators and others gathered together in crowds or processions are regularly reported, to a greater or lesser extent, around the world. The basic questions to be asked are the same. Who was killed and wounded and under what circumstances? Did police or military need to resort to gunfire to protect themselves or others from serious injury or death? Were the killings disproportionate to the real or perceived threat? If the use of gunfire was disproportionate, was it the consequence of deliberation or of panic?

A police riot in which people are killed is quite distinct from a massacre in which troops or police set out at the beginning to slaughter a group of people. The former may be a crime of omission, a consequence of poor discipline, inadequate training, flawed regulations or general incompetence. The latter is a matter of policy; it can be traced to an order or orders, to standard operating procedures or to an explicit plan of action. Killings in a police riot, too, if tolerated and blindly defended by central authority, may represent a kind of policy. A pattern of such killings, of official impassivity and of generalized impunity could show that high authority wanted them to happen. This element of volition, when governments clearly want unlawful killings to occur, is at the heart of the distinction between arbitrary mayhem and what could be equated with premeditated murder.

Classic examples of killings of demonstrators as murder include the massacre of Kekchi Indians in the town square of Panzos, Alta Verapaz, Guatemala on 29 May 1978. Premeditation was indicated by the army's having previously set up machineguns on the perimeter of the square, the sealing of exits from the square so that dispersal was impossible (even had that been the aim of the operation), and the prolonged firing into the crowd. The incident was perhaps unique in that it was also confirmed that army bulldozers had prepared mass graves outside of the town *before* the demonstration, called over disputed land rights, had even taken place. Even so, had photographs of dump trucks heaped with the bodies of the dead en route to the graves not reached the outside world, the massacre might have gone unreported and unremarked.

Governments frequently claim that police or military gunfire in situations of crowds and demonstrations came only after they had themselves come under attack by gunmen hidden in a crowd. Often, even with sworn eyewitness testimony, the facts in such cases are elusive. On 21 May, dozens of unarmed civilians were killed near the Islamic College in Srinager, in the Indian State of Jammu and Kashmir, when forces of the Central Reserve Police Force (CRPF) opened fire on mourners accompanying the body of Maulana Mohammad Faroq, the head priest of Srinagar (who had been shot earlier that day by three unidentified gunmen).

The exact number of people killed is still unconfirmed. Official reports said 20 people died on the spot and 27 later died of gunshot wounds in hospital. However, some unofficial reports put the total number of people killed as high as 117. During a debate in parliament on 22 May, government ministers reportedly said that militants mingling in the crowd of mourners had opened fire first on the CRPF and that civilians had been killed in the "crossfire". Witnesses and journalists disputed this and said police had fired indiscriminantly and without provocation on unarmed people.

(3) Targeting the Insurgent – and the Sympathizer

Often, disputed killings occur on a large scale in situations of insurgency and armed conflict. Evasion of accountability may be the object of elaborate efforts to justify those killings which cannot be concealed, and to keep the details of the killings – and often their full extent – from investigators and the public.

Troops of the Peruvian army killed 28 civilian men, women and children near the high Andes village of Cayara on the morning of 28 May 1988. Troops hunted down and killed others, witnesses to the massacre, in the days and weeks afterwards. The truth of the events of that May morning emerged slowly, and contrasted vividly with army communiques that said only that several guerrillas had been killed in fire-fights. The raid on Cayara came a day after a nearby attack on an army convoy by guerrillas in which four soldiers were killed: the killings that followed appeared to have been straightforward reprisals on a community held to have sheltered the guerrillas.

A civilian public prosecutor pressed forward with an investigation, interviewed survivors, photographed the scene and collected a broad range of evidence to show that troops had carried out reprisals against the villagers, seizing dozens, torturing them, and shooting and hacking them to death. The prosecutor's efforts to bring the regional military commander to trial came up against the obstacle of military court jurisdiction and the political interference of his superiors; he subsequently fled Peru after threats to his own and his family's lives. Obstruction of his inquiry went rather beyond the suppression of autopsy reports. Troops secretly removed corpses from common graves in order to prevent forensic examinations; nine of the witnesses who testified to what had occurred were killed or detained and "disappeared"; and the investigators were threatened themselves by the military and in the name of a mysterious "death squad."

The documented evidence that troops of the Peruvian armed forces committed murder at Cayara is voluminous and largely public. That a gross violation of human rights occurred there has been established. But accountability has yet to be established before the law.

4. Establishing Accountability for "Authorless" State Killings

Different problems are posed by situations in which unlawful killings indisputably occur at the hands of State agents, often on an enormous scale, but governments systematically deny responsibility of any kind for them.

Mass killings may be partly concealed by restrictions of access to the scene and by measures to prevent independent investigation that could confirm that killings occurred and tie them to government forces. Independent observers and investigators, from the media, religious bodies or human rights organizations may be physically denied access or subjected to intimidation. Those who have dared to investigate murder by the State have themselves become victims of murder by the State.

Even the first stage of investigation, establishing the identity of the victims and the cause, manner and circumstances of their deaths may be obstructed. Measures may be taken by perpetrators to conceal the identity of the victims and, sometimes at the same time, obliterate the evidence that a crime occurred – or that a victim ever existed. In Sri Lanka, regulations allowed the police and military to immediately burn the bodies of those killed in the counterinsurgency campaigns of recent years; where there are no bodies, there can be no inquests. In Argentina, even the dental and medical records of secret prisoners slated for murder were taken and destroyed.

Evidence that bodies were deliberately mutilated or concealed in order to prevent their identification may in itself, particularly in situations of mass killings, be a part of a pattern that leads to government accountability. In many situations of mass extrajudicial execution, efforts have been made to conceal the victim's identity through the destruction of clothing and personal effects, the amputation of hands or mutilation of fingertips, the obliteration of facial and other features through fire, acid or other physical trauma.

In the Philippines, decapitation has frequently been reported as a medium of terror and a means to evade accountability. Although two headless bodies were found soon after the detention of Nestor Loberio and Diomedes Abawag, development workers on the island of Samar who were detained by a military intelligence squad on 29 January 1990, they have not been positively identified. The head of Diomedes Abaway, with a gunshot wound in the temple, was found awash in the sea some days later by fishermen. Nestor Loberio is still unaccounted for but presumed dead.

The bodies of victims may also be found many miles from the places at which they were seized, implying an access to transport and the perpetrators' freedom from concern that they could be stopped at military or police roadblocks. These practices are sometimes of a persistent and systematic nature and a sufficiently large scale to be clearly beyond the capacity of individuals or clandestine groups. The mutilation and display of bodies, in contrast to their clandestine disposal, may be intended to intimidate and terrorize a sector of the population, while evading accountability before the law.

Concealment of a victim's identity – or body – may aim to obscure government responsibility for the fate of a person last seen being picked up by police or soldiers, in a police cell, a prison or a military camp. If there is no body or a body which cannot be identified, the missing prisoner "disappears" for good. But bodies that were never intended to be found regularly do appear and provide evidence of extrajudicial executions. The experience of the exhumation of the mass graves of Argentina after the change of government there is now being repeated in Chile. But the concealed bodies of the dead also emerge in situations of ongoing state terror and mass extrajudicial execution. The dead of El Salvador and Guatemala have appeared in clandestine dumping grounds, sand pits, rivers and washed onto the shore of lakes and ocean beaches. The killing of three priests and a group of peasant organizers seized by troops of the Honduran army in 1974 were found in a deep well that had been dynamited and then covered over with a bulldozer.

In Peru, in August 1984, 50 bodies were discovered in five shallow graves outside Huanta, at a desolate site called Puccayacu. This was possible only because a civilian investigator was guided there by a shepherd. The guide had seen a group of Peruvian Navy Marines from the Huanta base go there with a truckload of prisoners and return without them. The evidence remained. The distinctive tracks of the military's vehicles, shell casings, and the bodies themselves were revealed: some of whom could be identified as people last seen held captive of the Marines in Huanta.

The role of forensic medicine and anthropology in investigating the cause and circumstances of death in suspected extrajudicial executions, as well as in identifying the dead, has grown significantly since the early 1980s. Forensic medical specialists played a major role in the investigation of the mass killings in Argentina after the coup there, and play an increasing role in both the government and non-governmental investigation of disputed killings.

Flat denials that authorities were even aware of killings have frequently alternated with formulas by which killings are blandly attributed to forces outside the government's purview or control. Killings may be attributed to spontaneous violence spurred by inter-communal conflicts of religion, caste, class, language or ethnicity, to anonymous 'vigilantes' taking the law into their own hands, or to ceaseless battles between "extremists of left and right" from which the government stands aloof.

Since 1981, Columbian authorities have attributed killings by the security forces to mysterious civilian "death squads" – groups they say cannot be controlled. Military courts which claim jurisdiction over such cases have refused to take action even when civilian legal authorities have identified police and military personnel as responsible. Governments are often the first to attribute killings of their critics to shadowy "death squads".

In many parts of the world, conventional security services operate jointly with part-time civilian auxiliary services organized in paramilitary formations. Paramilitary forces responsible for extrajudicial executions sometimes have both official status and an identity of their own. Some are built around religious sects, as in the Philippines; some reflect ethnic groupings, as with the forces raised by officials of South Africa's "homelands".

Civilian militias often provide the framework for part-time, irregular forces to be incorporated into government service. In the Philippines, Guatemala, El Salvador and Peru, official civil defence or civil self-defence militias participate in joint operations with conventional forces. The governments in question evade accountability for routine extrajudicial executions by blurring the official status of the forces involved. A task for human rights researchers is to examine the position of such organizations, in law and in practice, vis-à-vis the government and the regular security services.

The problem posed in such cases is not whether killings were within the limits of the permissible, but whether they can be attributed to government at any level. The "death squad" or "vigilante" group model serves as a tool of murder designed to evade accountability. Distanced from the regular security services by acting under a flamboyant name, its anonymous members sow terror by a mysterious ability to strike at will and with impunity – and give it resonance through publicity in the form of tracts and communiques and the grotesque display of bodies. Killings attributed to shadowy "death squads" with dramatic names – like Sri Lanka's 'Black Cats' – may in fact be carried out by members of the uniformed services, with the handbills in their names churned out in army print shops (as revealed in Colombia in 1988 and years before in Guatemala). "Disappearances", too, may be attributed to shadowy forces and so mask arbitrary arrests, secret imprisonment or extrajudicial executions by agents of governments.

5. Indicators for Establishing Accountability[6]

A checklist of indicators of government responsibility for actions attributed to mysterious "death squads" or spontaneous "vigilantism" can take into account the nature of the victims, potential motives for their elimination, what is known about the perpetrators and their *modus operandi*, changing patterns over time and territory, the public attitude or response by officials to individual killings (or the overall phenomenon of political killings), and the record of efforts to provide legal remedy to political killings and to bring to justice those responsible. The same criteria can find application to similar phenomena from Guatemala and El Salvador to South Africa's townships, from Sri Lanka's ruthless campaign of extermination against supporters of the Janatha Vimukthi Peramuna (JVP), to the paramilitary dimension of the Armed Forces of the Philippines' campaign against insurgency. Patterns of state-sponsored abuse from one part of the world have been repeated across the world.

As further progress is made in deciphering the workings of the secret side of government human rights abuses, new indicators by which to assess responsibility will emerge to collate with those already known through experience.

Identifying the structure, composition and doctrine of the military and security apparatus can sometimes provide a means to identify ostensible vigilantes and "death squads" as a formal part of a security system. A challenge to the researcher is to distinguish spontaneous, unsponsored 'vigilante' or 'death squad' action which authorities actively seek to halt, from a) officially tolerated and encouraged civilian violence, and b) violence by officially organized and accredited civilian auxiliaries or by regular units of the security forces that is merely cloaked in the language of vigilantism and "death squad" terror. States hold direct responsibility under international standards for such actions.

When responsibility for political killings is *displaced* by attributing threats and killings to private individuals and organizations, there is often a considerable body of literature published or broadcast in their names. The message may in itself suggest official responsibility for threats – or complacency at lesser links between the regular security services and "death squad" killings. In El Salvador, the Press Council of the Armed Forces (COPREFA) published a list of 138 people in May 1981 who it described as "bandits and terrorist criminals," "Cuban, pro-soviet extremists," and "psychopaths" in what was widely interpreted as a "death list." Most of those named were living openly in El Salvador and were active in public life. The same list had been published a year before in the name of a "death squad", with the same names in the same non-alphabetical order. The May 1980 broadsheet had identified the 138 as "traitor Communists" who would be physically "eliminated."

[6] The checklist is available by contacting the author at Amnesty International, International Secretariat, 1 Easton Street, London, WC1X 8DJ, U.K.

The conjunction of anonymous threats with direct threats and accusations from public officials may also be a factor in assessing official responsibility for extrajudicial executions. In the Philippines, people who receive anonymous death threats are also the object of what is known locally as "branding": labelled as sympathizers of insurgent groups by local military commanders and leaders of the officially sponsored paramilitary organizations.

In many cases, communiques issued in the name of "death squads" make explicit reference to the frustration of the armed forces in combating terrorism with due regard for the limits of the law. Revenge for colleagues murdered in terror attacks is another recurrent theme; sometimes killings are overtly attributed to "death squads" made up of "off-duty" officers acting without the knowledge or assent of superiors.

In Sri Lanka, a "death squad" formula has only recently been invoked to justify some of the mass killings by government forces. This followed the move by the JVP opposition group to terror tactics in which the families of police, military and government personnel were sought out and murdered. The posters in the name of the "Black Cats" in turn warned that the families of dozens of JVP sympathizers would die for every service family harmed.

The message taken to the public or to an individual target may frequently draw upon confidential intelligence files, or, where the killing of petty criminals, vagrants and others considered social outcasts forms part of the pattern of political murder, police mug-shots and details of criminal records. The latter information may figure in public information materials published *after* murders have been carried out, and so tend to provide justification.

The political activist and alleged subversive may appear slated for murder on a poster, with photographs and captions drawn directly from police or military intelligence files, but published in the name of a "death squad" or other nominally covert paramilitary organization. This tactic has been most dramatically used in those situations in which the security services have been shown from top to bottom to be engaged in programmatic murder, notably in Guatemala and El Salvador.

The use of confidential intelligence dossiers has also been observed in the context of political murder without blatant government sponsorship. It is equally disturbing in situations in which there is evidence that government action has been taken to halt and to punish security personnel engaged in political murder, but with imperfect success. The recent inquiries into the leaking of United Kingdom intelligence reports on suspected Catholic extremists in Northern Ireland to covert Protestant "death squads" like the "Ulster Freedom Fighters" have done little to increase the confidence of the minority Catholic population there.

The way threatening slogans, threats and communiques reach the public, communicated in the name of ostensibly autonomous groups, may also suggest complicity or direct responsibility by government forces. The communication of threatening material, its dissemination, promulgation, broadcast or display, may be undertaken by regular military or police personnel, using official vehicles or operating from government buildings and bases. The distribution of leaflets, the painting of "death squad" slogans and the use of 'propaganda bombs' may be undertaken by unidentified personnel, but take place in the presence of and with the apparent acquiescence of security personnel.

In Guatemala, as "death squad" killings were first reported in late 1966 and 1967, light aircraft distributed leaflets in the name of Mano Blanca, the White Hand. They were observed making frequent landings and takeoffs from the military base at La Aurora airport outside Guatemala City.

Under the government of General Romeo Lucas Garcia (1978–1982), Guatemalan security spokesmen neatly distinguished between victims of "death squads" who were killed for their politics and those eliminated because they were common criminals and the dregs of society. The murdered "criminals" were said to have been brought to justice by the Escuadron de la Muerte (EM), the Death Squad or, alternatively, the Ejercito Secreto Anticomunista, (ESA), the Secret Anticommunist Army. The press secretary of the Interior Ministry, after fleeing the country, later confirmed that the headed stationary used for periodic threats and communiques in the name of 'EM' and 'ESA' was stored in the office of the Minister.

In Peru's city of Ayacucho, over the past years, threatening letters have been sent to government critics from anonymous sources, sometimes accompanied by small explosive devices sufficient to blow in doors, delivered to prospective victims by personnel travelling openly in vehicles through roadblocks during strictly enforced curfew hours. Slogans in the name of ostensibly independent "death squads" have been painted on walls during curfews and on the closely guarded walls of military installations.

In the Philippines, threatening slogans in the name of Alsa Masa, a name applied to quite distinct military-sponsored paramilitary organizations in many parts of the country, have been liberally daubed on miles of masonry walls with the sponsorship and under the protection of local commanders.

In Colombia, uniformed troops working from army trucks were observed in recent years daubing the slogans of Muerte a Secuestradores (MAS), Death to Kidnappers, on walls around the country. At first, when it emerged in 1981, MAS was said to be a 'vigilante' group organized by the head of the Medellin drug cartel after the kidnapping of his daughter: as such, however, it seems to have ended its independent existence a few weeks after it was announced, upon the release of the girl. But within months, operations in the name of "MAS" were evidently an army endeavour, albeit with civilian components. It provided a cover for the army's campaign to hunt down and kill communists, activists and others targeted in a broad-spectrum counterinsurgency offensive. In several incidents in the Magdalena Medio region, investigation of mass killings attributed to MAS and other ostensibly private organizations were halted when identified gunmen were held to be subject only to the jurisdiction of the military courts on the grounds that they were part of the armed forces.

The masquerade with MAS was not the first time in which the Colombian army cloaked its actions in the colourful guise of an independent "death squad". In November 1978, leaflets were distributed in the name of the American Anti-communist Alliance (AAA or Triple A) that threatened to murder, among others, members of the Supreme Court who opposed a draconian security statute that gave new powers to the armed forces. Responsibility was claimed in the name of AAA for several political murders of leftwing trade unionists and suspected guerrilla sympathizers in 1978 and 1979. It faded from the scene after a group of officers formerly attached to the army's chief military intelligence group, the Intelligence and Counter-Intelligence Battalion "Charry Solano" (BINCI), described having been ordered with other battalion personnel to serve as "a terrorist group called the Triple A". They provided details of the battalion's role in the detention, torture and murder of several opposition leaders and the bombing of three leftwing Bogota periodicals.[7]

The "death squad" formula continued to be used in Colombia throughout the 1980s and into the 1990s. A massacre of 43 people and the wounding of over 50 others by plainclothes gunmen in November 1989 in the Magdalena Medio town of Segovia was officially attributed to an independent "death squad" directed by private landowners and drug traffickers. Investigations subsequently showed that the town's army battalion commander had arranged for the printing of a leaflet announcing the existence of the "death squad" in question and had made other preparations for the massacres because the town had voted overwhelmingly for leftwing candidates in the municipal elections. Civilian gunmen provided by drug interests were apparently employed in the operation, but under army and police protection: the regular army and police garrisons stood aside as gunmen shot up the town.

Colombia's drug traffickers provided a convenient manpower pool for gunmen, and the "death squad" formula of nomenclature a convenient lightning-rod to deflect attention away from the armed forces. The *quid pro quo* of this unusual partnership was a freedom to operate for increasingly large numbers of armed civilian gunmen whose loyalty to their civilian patrons was greater than their commitment to the army's anti-communist pogrom. Today's confrontation between the government and the drug barons, in which the army has only gradually been obliged to play a seemingly reluctant role, may in large part be a consequence of a counterinsurgency scheme of programmed murder which got out of hand.

6. The International Community and State Accountability

The role of the international community has not always been a positive one in bringing gross human rights abuse to light, and in holding governments to account for such abuse. Second governments providing security assistance or

[7] Amnesty International, *Amnesty International Report 1981* (1981), London: Amnesty International Publications, p. 130.

directly intervening in an armed conflict may play a major role in shielding allies from accountability for gross human rights abuse by defusing international opprobrium. Aggressive campaigns of misinformation play a role in deflecting criticism, molding public opinion and suppressing human rights reporting, while power diplomacy may hamstring efforts to bring a government to account through the United Nations' or regional organizations' human rights mechanisms. The role of second governments in shielding Iraq from criticism within the UN Commission on Human Rights in recent years is a contemporary example.

However daunting the obstacles, the means of establishing State accountability for arbitrary killings have in the aggregate increased. The UN's human rights machinery now directly addresses the matter of "summary and arbitrary executions" – and the full range of what Amnesty International calls "extrajudicial executions". In addition to the Commission on Human Rights' Special Rapporteur on Summary and Arbitrary Executions, Special Rapporteurs and Representatives on individual countries have dealt with extrajudicial executions in countries from a broad spectrum of political systems. Their work has been most forceful, and credible, on El Salvador, Afghanistan and Iran. (The Commission has not, however, subjected the mass killings in Colombia, pre-war Iraq and Peru to the attention of a Rapporteur, however, despite the voluminous documentation submitted to it by Amnesty International and other national and international organizations).

The Commission's Working Group on Enforced and Involuntary Disappearances, has also advanced this work, confirming, through its investigation of thousands of "disappearances", that most were unlawfully detained (and many secretly and unlawfully executed).

A recent resolution of the Commission, adopted on 7 March 1990, condemned acts of intimidation and reprisal against private individuals and groups which seek to avail themselves of UN human rights procedures. It called on all governments to allow access by private individuals and representatives of UN human rights bodies and to remove all legal and practical obstacles that could prevent or discourage such contacts. Freedom from fear of reprisal, of course, would remove a major barrier facing petitioners for remedy to human rights abuse. The resolution requested all UN human rights representatives to take urgent steps to help prevent the occurrence of intimidation or reprisal and to devote special attention to the issue in their respective reports to the Commission or the Sub-Commission.[8]

Regional IGOs, too, have developed more effective machinery for human rights protection. But although accountability must be founded on the tenets of international human rights and humanitarian law, it is not dependent solely on inter-governmental organizations. International human rights awareness has increased and is reflected in the media, through the growing movements of

[8] Commission on Human Rights, 54th meeting, 7 March 1990, Resolution 1990/76, "Co-operation with representatives of United Nations human rights bodies" (adopted without a vote).

national and international NGOs, and by the incorporation of international human rights concerns into parliamentary debate, foreign policy and international trade relations.

The international human rights community's capacity for research and reaching out to the public and to governments has both fueled and been boosted by the growth of global human rights awareness. Human rights researchers are now better equipped for fact finding and better prepared for the analysis of situations involving concealed state violence than in the past. Improved standards through which to assess the use of lethal force at the margins of the law – and codes of conduct for law enforcement officers – should help prevent arbitrary killings and establish routine procedures with which to assess disputed killings. At the other end of the spectrum of state violence, it is now less likely that situations of gross human rights abuse will go unnoticed, or that smokescreens of misinformation will allow governments to repeat the patterns of the past and wholly evade accountability for mass murder.

DINAH SHELTON*

State Responsibility for Covert and Indirect Forms of Violence

1. INTRODUCTION

One of the most significant achievements in international law since the Second World War has been the development and general acceptance of an international code of human rights. So widespread is the consensus on basic principles and standards, that States no longer freely admit to widespread acts of violence, such as torture and summary executions, against those within their control. No longer is it generally claimed that human rights violations are a matter of domestic jurisdiction. Where human rights violations occur, States increasingly attempt to conceal such acts or deny responsibility for them. Indeed, the "radical breach" of human rights norms involved in the practice of disappearances[1] may be seen in part as an effort to eliminate evidence of other human rights violations. Moreover, to insulate the government from accusations of illegality, such acts now are often committed by private or quasi-governmental bodies, allowed by governments to function with impunity.

Such developments may be a tragic compliment to the universal acceptance of human rights norms, but they also pose questions for the future effective implementation and enforcement of human rights protections. These questions concern both substance and procedure. First, under existing law, when is a government liable for human rights violations committed by private actors? From another perspective, when does government failure to act give rise to international responsibility? How extensive is the duty to act with regard to economic and social rights, particularly concerning basic needs? Procedurally, how can government involvement in death squad activities or disappearances be proved? What is the requisite degree of proof and how should the burden of proof be allocated?

Apart from violations which occur within the State, whether overt or covert, governments also may contribute indirectly or covertly to human rights

* Professor of Law, Santa Clara University.

[1] Inter-American Court of Human Rights, *Velasquez Rodriguez* case, Judgment of July 29, 1988, Ser. C. No. 4, p. 149, para. 158.

K.E. Mahoney and P. Mahoney (eds.), Human Rights in the Twenty-first Century, 265–276.

violations through assistance to other repressive governments. These actions, for example selling torture implements, training officials, providing foreign aid or participating in or encouraging acts of violence, demand consideration of the question whether a State violates its international human rights obligations when it participates in or furthers the commission of human rights violations within another State.

The scope of State responsibility for failing to prevent or remedy private human rights violations, and the extent to which a State may be liable for furthering human rights violations committed by another government, are issues likely to be of increasing importance in the future. Powerful non-governmental institutions as well as governmental bodies threaten human rights. The affirmative duties of the State both within and across boundaries thus must be considered.

Most generally, the question presented is how extensive are the duties of States to promote and protect human rights? Are there affirmative duties imposed by human rights law, as well as obligations to abstain from violating guaranteed rights? Do States have any responsibility outside their territorial boundaries or are human rights obligations only imposed in favor of those within the geographical limits of the State? A review of international human rights texts is the starting point for considering these issues.

2. A Review of Human Rights Instruments and Their Position on the Affirmative Duties of States

The Universal Declaration of Human Rights[2] contemplates international and national action by both governmental and private actors. Its proclamation calls upon "all peoples and all nations", "every individual and every organ of society" to promote respect of human rights and for "progressive measures, national and international, to secure their universal and effective recognition and observance, both among the peoples of member States themselves and among the peoples of territories under their jurisdiction". Article 2(1) of the United Nations Covenant on Civil and Political Rights[3] imposes a duty on each State Party to "respect and to ensure to all individuals within its territory and subject to its jurisdiction" the rights recognized in the Covenant. Specifically, the Covenant requires each State Party to take the necessary steps to adopt such legislative or other measures required to give effect to the rights recognized in the Covenant, to ensure an effective remedy to any person whose rights or freedoms are violated, whether or not by persons acting in an official capacity, and to ensure that the competent authorities enforce the remedies granted. This

[2] Universal Declaration of Human Rights, G.A. Res. 217 A (III), December 10, 1948, U.N. Doc. A/810, at 71 (1948).

[3] International Covenant on Civil and Political Rights, G.A. Res. 2200 (XXI), December 16, 1966, 21 U.N. GAOR Supp. (No. 16) at 52, U.N. Doc. A/6316 (1966), 999 U.N.T.S. 171, entered into force March 23, 1976.

language imposes affirmative duties and potential liability for inaction by a State, but only for conduct "within its territory and subject to its jurisdiction".

The Covenant on Economic, Social and Cultural Rights explicitly imposes a duty for each State to take steps, individually and through international assistance and cooperation, to achieve the realization of the rights recognized in that instrument,[4] thus indicating certain affirmative obligations both domestically and internationally.

Other United Nations Conventions are more explicit on the obligations of States to take affirmative action to prevent private violations. For example, States Parties to the United Nations Convention on the Elimination of All Forms of Racial Discrimination[5] not only undertake to engage in no act or practice of racial discrimination, but agree to prohibit and bring to an end, by all appropriate means, including legislation as required by circumstances, racial discrimination by any persons, group or organization (article 2). The Parties also are required to provide effective protection and remedies, including reparations or satisfaction for damage suffered, against any acts of racial discrimination (article 6). The recent United Nations Convention against Torture and Other Cruel, Inhuman or Degrading Treatment or Punishment[6] is also clear in imposing affirmative duties on the States Parties. It requires States to take effective steps to prevent any acts of torture or other acts of cruel, inhuman or degrading treatment, when such acts are committed by or at the instigation of or with the consent or acquiescence of a public official or other person acting in an official capacity. Thus, failure to act, amounting to acquiescence, is sufficient to constitute a breach of the treaty's obligations.

On the regional level, the European Convention of Human Rights[7] requires the States to "secure recognition to everyone within their jurisdiction" the guaranteed rights. Similarly, the American Convention on Human Rights[8] demands that "States Parties undertake to respect rights and freedoms recognized herein and to ensure to all persons subject to their jurisdiction the free and full exercise of those rights and freedoms" (article 1).

While the language of the various human rights instruments seems to make clear that States parties have affirmative duties to ensure as well as to respect human rights, it is important to take into account the practice of supervisory organizations in reviewing State compliance with these instruments. Other

[4] Article 2(1), International Covenant on Economic, Social and Cultural Rights, G.A. Res. 2200A (XXI), December 16, 1966, 21 U.N. GAOR Supp. (No. 16) at 49, U.N. Doc. A/6316 (1966), 993 U.N.T.S. 3, entered into force January 3, 1976.

[5] International Convention on the Elimination of All Forms of Racial Discrimination, 60 U.N.T.S. 195, entered into force January 4, 1969.

[6] Articles 1, 16, Convention Against Torture and Other Cruel, Inhuman or Degrading Treatment or Punishment, G.A. Res. 39/46, 30 U.N. GAOR Supp. (No. 51) at 197, U.N. Doc. A/39/51 (1985, entered into force June 26, 1987.

[7] Convention for the Protection of Human Rights and Fundamental Freedoms, November 4, 1950, 213 U.N.T.S. 221, entered into force September 3, 1953.

[8] American Convention on Human Rights, November 22, 1969, O.A.S.T.S. 36, at 1, OEA/Ser. L./V/II.23 doc. rev. 2, entered into force July 18, 1978.

international jurisprudence also may be relevant in determining the extent of obligations imposed on States in promoting and protecting human rights.

3. Transboundary Obligations Imposed on States

Taking first the issue of transboundary obligations, the language of the human rights instruments generally refers to States obligations toward those within its territory or subject to its jurisdiction, raising the issue of whether this precludes responsibility for furthering violations committed within another State. The issue was considered by the European Commission of Human Rights in the case of *Cyprus v. Turkey*.[9] The petition was filed by the government of Cyprus following invasion of the island by Turkey. Cyprus charged Turkey with human rights violations in that part of the island taken by Turkish troops. Turkey responded that its obligations under the Convention extended only to acts committed within its "national territory". The European Commission instead looked at liability from the perspective of "actual authority and responsibility", stating:

> "In Article 1 of the Convention, the High Contracting Parties undertake to secure the rights and freedoms defined in Section 1 to everyone 'within their jurisdiction' (in the French text: *relevant de leur juridiction*). The Commission finds that this term is not, as submitted by the respondent Government, equivalent to or limited to the national territory of the High Contracting Party concerned. It is clear from the language, in particular of the French text, and the object of this article, and from the purpose of the Convention as a whole, that the High Contracting Parties are bound to secure the said rights and freedoms to all persons under their actual authority and responsibility, whether that authority is exercised within their own territory or abroad."[10]

Thus, the Commission concluded, it may examine cases even where the State involved has not established either a civil or a military government or annexed any part of the territory under its effective control. Similarly, it has been said that the Covenant on Civil and Political Rights imposes an obligation on States which maintain civil or military control over a given territory to ensure the rights guaranteed by the Covenant, irrespective of whether there has been formal annexation or whether the occupation is legal.[11]

State practice at the United Nations offers some support for a duty not to assist States engaged in gross and systematic human rights violations. In particular, the United Nations has adopted resolutions condemning complicity in the maintenance of apartheid in South Africa. In Resolution 37/233C of December 20, 1982, the General Assembly called upon the Council for Namibia

[9] *Cyprus v. Turkey*, 18 Y.B. Eur. Conv. H.R. 1975, p. 83.
[10] Ibid., p. 118.
[11] Buergenthal, in *The International Bill of Rights* (Henkin, ed. 1981) p. 77.

to "notify the Governments of States whose corporations, whether public or private, operate in Namibia of the illegality of such operations". Similarly, in discussing the legal consequences for States of the continued South African presence in Namibia, the International Court of Justice specifically stated the obligation of States Members of the United Nations to recognize the illegality of South African actions and to "refrain from any acts and in particular any dealings . . . lending support or assistance to such presence and administration".[12]

In Resolution 37/35 of November 23, 1982, the General Assembly reaffirmed its view that the continuation of colonialism was incompatible with the Charter of the United Nations, the Universal Declaration of Human Rights and the Declaration on the Granting of Independence to Colonial Countries and Peoples. As such it requested all States to withhold assistance of any kind from the Government of South Africa until the inalienable right of the people to self-determination had been implemented.

Concerning Rhodesia, Security Council Resolution 216 (1965) of November 12, 1965 condemned the unilateral declaration of independence by the minority Smith regime and called upon all States "to refrain from rendering any assistance to it".

In 1974, the Economic and Social Council, in Resolution 1864 (LVI) condemned the activities of States which continue to give political, military, economic and other assistance to the racist and colonial regimes in southern Africa or which refrained from taking any steps to prevent natural or juridical persons within their jurisdiction from assisting those regimes and thus encouraging them to continue violating fundamental human rights. In sum, "all States are required to refrain from giving assistance of any kind to colonial and racist regimes".[13]

Other resolutions have addressed human rights concerns outside the colonial context. In 1982, the General Assembly considered the situation in Guatemala. In Resolution 37/184 of 17 December, it expressed deep concern at the serious violations of human rights reported to have taken place in Guatemala and, among other measures, called upon governments to refrain from supplying arms and other military assistance as long as serious human rights violations continued to be reported.

The case brought by Nicaragua against the United States at the International Court of Justice poses both the question of complicity in human rights violations committed in another State and the issue of responsibility for violations committed by private actors. In particular, Nicaragua sought to attribute responsibility to the United States for activities of the "contra" rebel military force, including the killing, wounding and kidnapping of Nicaraguan

[12] Legal Consequences for States of the Continued Presence of South Africa in Namibia (South West Africa) notwithstanding Security Council Resolution 276 (1970), Advisory Opinion, I.C.J. Rep. [1971], p. 58, para. 133.

[13] A. Christescu, *The Right to Self-Determination: Historical and Current Developments on the Basis of United Nations Instruments* (U.N. Pub. Sales No. E.80.XIV.3).

citizens.[14] The Court accepted the principle that a State could be liable for humanitarian violations committed outside its territory. The question was

> "whether or not the relationship of the Contras to the United States Government was so much one of dependence on the one side and control on the other that it would be right to equate the Contras, for legal purposes, with an organ of the United States Government, or as acting on behalf of the Government."[15]

The Court established a high standard for imposing responsibility for complicity in the wrongful acts of others. Finding "no clear evidence of the United States having actually exercised such a degree of control in all fields as to justify treating the Contras as acting on its behalf", the Court held:

> "United States participation, even if preponderant or decisive, in the financing, organizing, training, supplying and equipping of the Contras, the selection of its military or paramilitary targets, and the planning of the whole of its operation, is still insufficient in itself, on the basis of the evidence in the possession of the Court, for the purpose of attributing to the United States the acts committed by the Contras in the course of their military or paramilitary operations in Nicaragua. All the forms of United States participation mentioned above, and even the general control by the respondent State over a force with a high degree of dependency on it, would not in themselves mean, without further evidence, that the United States directed or enforced the perpetration of acts contrary to human rights and humanitarian law alleged by the applicant State. Such acts could well be committed by members of the Contras without the control of the United States. For this conduct to give rise to legal responsibility of the United States, it would in principle have to be proved that the State had effective control of the military or paramilitary operations in the course of which the alleged violations were committed."[16]

The Court's opinion is disappointing in its restrictive view of State responsibility. It appears to retreat from the imposition of liability for complicity in internationally wrongful acts, imposed at Nuremberg.[17] The International Law Commission draft Code of Offences against the Peace and Security of Mankind also includes conspiracy, incitement and complicity as well as direct perpetration of any of the offences, which include human rights violations, as offences.[18] General principles of law also would support imposition of liability for furthering human rights violations committed by others. Within the

[14] Military and Paramilitary Activities in and Against Nicaragua *(Nicaragua v. U.S.)*, Judgment of June 27, 1986, I.C.J. Rep. [1986] 4, 63–64, para. 113.

[15] Ibid., at 62, para. 109.

[16] Ibid., at 64–65, para. 115.

[17] Charter of the International Military Tribunal, 59 Stat. 1544, 1546.

[18] The Work of the International Law Commission, 3rd ed. (U.N. Pub. Sales No. E.80.V.11) pp. 116–17.

common law tradition, a person who aids, abets or encourages another to commit a wrongful act is considered a principal actor in the crime. Advice, encouragement and support are sufficient for liability; even knowledge of the act without more has sometimes sufficed for culpability.

The Nicaragua and Cyprus decisions, together with the general language of obligation imposed on States to protect and promote the human rights of those within their territory and subject to their jurisdiction, suggest that efforts to impose liability on States for providing assistance to other States engaged in systematic human rights violations will have limited results in the absence of the elaboration of new normative standards. The thrust of existing human rights instruments is to protect citizens and others within a State from the actions of that State. The responsibility of other States for furthering or assisting in the commission of the violations generally is not contemplated. The interdependence of modern States suggests that the more limited obligations are insufficient to ensure full implementation of human rights guarantees. Thus, amendment or extension of existing obligations to prohibit acts furthering the commission of human rights violations by another State needs to be considered.

4. State Responsibility for Violations by Private Actors

Apart from liability for transboundary violations, the scope of State responsibility also is raised where human rights violations are directly committed by private actors such as death squads or vigilante groups. Acts contrary to international law can involve either a breach or non-performance of an international obligation. Breach includes both acts and omissions according to the type of conduct required by the rule in question. In fact, one United Nations report found that "the cases in which the international responsibility of a State has been invoked on the basis of an omission are perhaps more numerous than those based on action taken by a State".[19] In the widely-cited *Corfu Channel* case, the International Court of Justice found Albania liable for failing to act because it knew or should have known of the illegal conduct involved.[20] Recently, section 207 of the Restatement (Third) of the Foreign Relations Law of the United States provided that a State is responsible for any violation of its obligations under international law whether these violations result from action or inaction.[21]

The International Law Commission's draft code of the law of State responsibility declares that the conduct of private individuals shall not be considered as acts of State.[22] However, the State is responsible if it fails to carry

[19] R. Ago, Second Report on State Responsibility [1970], 2 Y.B. Int'l L. Comm'n 177, 188, U.N. Doc. A/CN.4/233.

[20] *Corfu Channel (U.K. v. Albania)*, Judgment of April 9, 1949, I.C.J. Rep. [1949] p. 4, 23.

[21] Restatement (Third) of Foreign Relations, section 207.

[22] W. Riphagen, State Responsibility [1980] 2 Y.B. Int'l L. Comm'n 107, 111–13, para. 20, 24, 31, U.N. Doc. A/CN.4/330 (Part 2).

out an international obligation to act. As early as 1598, Gentili wrote that one who knows of a wrong is free from guilt only if he is not able to prevent it. Therefore, the State which knows because it has been warned, and which ought to prevent the misdeeds of its citizens and through its jurisdiction can prevent them, will be at fault and guilty of a crime if it does not do so.[23]

Traditionally, the duty of States has been formulated in terms of the obligation of due diligence in the protection of aliens. Failure to exercise due diligence to prevent or remedy an attack on an alien gives rise to State responsibility, as does failure to exercise due diligence to apprehend and hold any person committing such an act.[24] Due diligence is the reasonable measures of prevention that a well-administered government could be expected to exercise under similar circumstances. In tort law terms, "the [danger] reasonable to be perceived defines the duty to be obeyed".[25]

In the *Iranian Hostage* case,[26] the International Court of Justice held Iran responsible for the acts of the militants who seized the U.S. Embassy. While the acts were not initially "directly imputable to the Iranian State", the Iranian Government's subsequent approval of the militants' actions made them so. Moreover, Iran's failure to take appropriate steps to protect the Embassy constituted by itself a clear and serious violation of international law.[27]

The due diligence standard establishes that a State is not responsible for purely private harm. Although this standard developed in regard to the protection of aliens, it recently has been adopted and applied in regard to State responsibility for human rights violations.

Between mid-1988 and 1989, the Inter-American Court of Human Rights decided three contentious cases based on individual petitions filed by the families of disappeared persons against the government of Honduras. In two of the cases, *Velasquez Rodriguez* and *Gondinez Cruz*, the Court unanimously found that Honduras had violated the rights of personal liberty, humane treatment and life guaranteed by the American Convention on Human Rights.[28] The Court ordered compensation to be paid to the victims' next-of-kin. In the third case, the Court held there was insufficient evidence to establish Honduran responsibility for the disappearances.[29]

[23] A. Gentili, De Iure Belli Libri Tres 100 (J. Rolfe trans. 1933). See also Shelton, "Private Violation, Public Wrongs, and the Responsibility of States", 13 Fordham Int'l L. J. 1, 21 (1990).

[24] Draft Convention on the International Responsibility of States for Injuries to Aliens (L. Sohn & R. Baxter, reporters), reprinted in F.V. Garcia-Amador, *Recent Codification of the Law of State Responsibility for Injuries to Aliens* (1974).

[25] *Palsgraf v. Long Island R.R.* 248 N.Y. 339, 344, 162 N.E. 99, 100 (1928).

[26] *United States Diplomatic and Consular Staff in Teheran (U.S. v. Iran)*, Judgment of May 24, 1980, I.C.J. Rep. [1980] 3.

[27] Ibid.

[28] *Velasquez Rodrigues* case, Annual Report of the Inter-American Court of Human Rights, OAS/Ser.L/V/III.19, doc. 13 (1988); *Godinez Cruz*, Inter-American Court of Human Rights, Decisions and Judgments (ser. c) No. 5 (1989).

[29] *Fairen Garbi and Solis Corrales case*, Inter-American Court of Human Rights, Decisions and Judgments (ser. C) No. 6 (1989).

The Court's opinions detailed three distinct obligations of States Parties to the American Convention on Human Rights: (1) abstention from violating guaranteed human rights; (2) prevention of violations by State and non-state actors and (3) investigation and punishment of both State and private human rights infringements. These obligations were found in article 1 of the Convention, which obliges States Parties to respect and to ensure the rights guaranteed.

The disappearances alleged in the three cases were among the 100 to 150 disappearances under similar circumstances which the Court found proved to have occurred between 1981 and 1984. The Court found that "[i]t was public and notorious knowledge in Honduras that the kidnappings were carried out by military personnel or the police, or persons acting under their orders".[30] However, the State was responsible even if the disappearances were not carried out by agents who acted under cover of public authority, because the State's apparatus failed to act to prevent the disappearances or to punish those responsible. Therefore, Honduras was responsible either for carrying out the disappearances or for acquiescing in the kidnappings.

Every case in which a violation of the American Convention is alleged involves a claimed breach of article 1, which contains the general obligations of States Parties to respect and ensure human rights. As interpreted by the Court, article 2 contains several separate duties. First, a State shall respect the rights and freedoms recognized in the Convention. This must necessarily comprise the concept of the restriction of the exercise of State power. The existence of a legal system designed to permit exercise of human rights does not alone ensure compliance with a States obligations, because rights may be violated in spite of legal protections. Thus, the Court declared, whenever a State organ, official or public entity violates a protected right, this constitutes a failure of the duty to respect the rights and freedoms set forth in the Convention because public power is used to infringe the rights recognized. In general, then a State is responsible for the acts and omissions of its agents undertaken in their official capacity, even if they are acting outside the scope of their authority or in violation of internal law. Intent or motivation is irrelevant.

Second, States must ensure the free and full exercise of the rights recognized by the Convention. This obligation requires States to organize the governmental apparatus and, in general, all the structures through which public power is exercised, so that they are capable of juridically ensuring the free and full enjoyment of human rights. This implies, first, that States must prevent violations of the rights recognized by the Convention. In addition, the State must attempt to investigate and punish violations of human rights, restore the right violated and provide compensation as warranted for damages resulting from the violation.

The existence of affirmative duties to prevent and to remedy human rights violations implies that State responsibility extends to omissions by State actors.

[30] *Velasquez Rodriguez*, Inter-Am. Ct. H.R. at 64, para. 147 (c).

The Court cites the example of a State that is not directly responsible for a human rights violation because the act is that of a private person, but that becomes responsible because of the lack of due diligence to prevent the violation or to respond to it as required by the Convention. In addition, the Court declares that where human rights violations committed by private parties are not seriously investigated, those parties are aided in a sense by the government, thereby making the State responsible on the international plane. Thus, even if the State were not shown to have directly caused the disappearances, the failure of the State to act is a failure on the part of Honduras to fulfil the duties it assumed under the Convention to ensure the full and free exercise of human rights. In sum, the Convention imposes

> "a legal duty to take reasonable steps to prevent human rights violations and to use the means at its disposal to carry out a serious investigation of violations committed within its jurisdiction, to identify those responsible, to impose the appropriate punishment and to ensure the victim adequate compensation".[31]

Thus, any omission of a public authority may give rise to liability just as any act of a public authority violative of guaranteed human rights may result in State responsibility.

Imposition of international responsibility for failure to protect human rights is particularly important for individuals within States whose domestic laws impose no such liability. Such is the case in the United States, where the recent case of *DeShaney v. Winnebago County Department of Social Services*[32] enunciated a highly restrictive view of United States constitutional protections. Four-year old Joshua DeShaney was subjected to repeated brutal child abuse by his divorced, custodial father, finally resulting in a life-threatening coma. Joshua will spend the rest of his life institutionalized. His mother sued the county for failure to protect Joshua, based on the fact that county workers had intervened on behalf of Joshua several times and each time returned him to the custody of his father. The Supreme Court held that the county had no responsibility because its omissions did not amount to State action. The *DeShaney* Court concluded that State responsibility for omissions exists only when an individual is in actual physical custody of the government, because in such situations the individual is no longer able to provide for his own basic needs including physical safety.

The Supreme Court noted that "nothing in the language of the Due Process clause itself requires the State to protect the life, liberty, and property of its citizens against invasion by private actors".[33] The clause is written only to limit the State's power to act and "not as a guarantee of certain minimal levels of

[31] *Velasquez Rodriguez*, Inter-Am. Ct. H.R. at 71, para. 174; *Godinez Cruz*, Inter-Am. Ct. H.R. at 152, para. 184.

[32] 109 S.Ct. 998 (1989).

[33] Ibid., at 1003.

safety and security". Indeed, "its purpose was to protect the people from the State, not to ensure that the State protected them from each other". Because of this, "the Due Process Clauses generally confer no affirmative right to governmental aid, even where such aid may be necessary to secure life, liberty, or property interests of which the government itself may not deprive the individual". Therefore, "a State's failure to protect an individual against private violence simply does not constitute a violation of the Due Process Clause".

The *DeShaney* opinion is of dubious merit on constitutional terms, and incompatible with international human rights obligations enunciated by the Inter-American Court in the *Velasquez Rodriguez* case. Failure to control private violence, acquiescence in human rights violations committed by non-State actors, renders the State as culpable as if its officials had initially committed the violations.

5. Procedure and Proof

The third issue to be considered in regard to covert and indirect human rights violations concerns procedure and proof. By their very nature, these types of violations are more difficult to prove and to link to State action. How should international supervisory bodies address this problem? This issue also was addressed in *Velasquez Rodriguez* case. The Court stated that in principle the burden of proof should be on the victim to establish the facts supporting its allegations. This burden may be discharged by indirect or circumstantial evidence including inferences and presumptions. Indeed, proof of an official practice of disappearances carried out or tolerated by the government, plus evidence linking the disappearance of an individual to that practice, would be sufficient to prove the violation, provided the proof had sufficient weight to meet the standard established by the Court.

The Court also recognized the difficulties of meeting the burden of proof when the necessary evidence is in the control of the defending government and cannot be obtained without the government's cooperation. In such a case, the burden may be shifted to the government to produce evidence to refute the petitioner's allegations. Failure to come forward may cause the Court to presume from the government's silence that the allegations are true.

6. Conclusion

The evidentiary rulings and development of State responsibility for private violations enunciated in the *Velasquez Rodriguez* case represent a necessary evolution in the application of international human rights norms. While States generally have accepted that protection of human rights is a matter of international concern and have agreed upon basic human rights to be protected, there remain widespread violations which demand to be remedied. As States are under increasing pressure to adhere in practice to the norms accepted in theory, more covert violence appears as a means of coercion. Covert human rights violations may involve transboundary activities, aiding and abetting violations committed by other governmental or private bodies. A principal task for the next century will be to apply existing norms and develop new standards to ensure that individual rights remain protected and that States do not substitute one form of repression for another.

BRIAN CURRIN*
PAULA McBRIDE**

Hangings in South Africa – On the Trap Door to Oblivion

1. Introduction

November 14, 1991 marked a second year free of judicial executions in South Africa.[1] In a country which has witnessed 4,280 executions since 1910[2] at an average of 71 per year, this event is a remarkable one. In 1987 South Africa ranked with China, Nigeria, Iraq and Iran as the most energetic of the hanging nations. In that year alone 164 persons were hanged. Although today there are over 300 prisoners under sentence of death, there is now good reason to believe there may never be another hanging in South Africa.

On February 2, 1990, State President de Klerk outlined a change of direction in Nationalist Party policy. Amongst other things he announced the unbanning of various political parties and liberation movements (including the African National Congress (ANC) and the Pan Africanist Congress (PAC)); the release of political prisoners; a willingness to negotiate with representative black leaders and a moratorium on all executions pending a revision of the legislation governing capital offences. Commenting at the time, Etienne Mureinik Dean, Faculty of Law, University of Witswatersrand said:

> What is most significant is that they [announcements relating to changes in capital law] were included in the speech at all. By what right did changes to the detail of the penal system earn a place in a speech intended to herald a different South Africa? By what virtue did a temporary suspension of one

* National Director, Lawyers for Human Rights, South Africa
** Personal Assistant to the National Director, Co-ordinator, Capital Cases and Prisoner Abuse Moniter.

[1] For the purposes of this article, the term "South Africa" will exclude the areas known as Transkei, Bophuthatswana, Venda and the Ciskei. In these areas the following circumstances prevail: Ciskei – abolished the death penalty in 1990; Bophuthatswana – 12 persons on death row, the last execution took place in November 1990; Transkei, a moratorium on all executions since October 1989, 85 people on death row; Venda, 18 people on death row, the last execution took place in July 1991.

[2] "The Death Penalty in South Africa – Statistics" (1989) SACJ 2 SAS.

K.E. Mahoney and P. Mahoney (eds.), Human Rights in the Twenty-first Century, 277–292.

option in the sentencer's armoury merit mention in the proclamation of the new era?[3]

2. Political Inequities of Capital Punishment

By including the question of capital punishment in his speech, State President de Klerk recognized two very important elements of the death penalty and its application in South Africa: first, the extent to which this issue has become intensely politicised in the minds of many South Africans, and secondly, the congruence of racism, racial domination and legalized murder. As Mureinik stated, "systematic racial oppression and systematic execution are natural cousins ... Our race laws beget the kind of contempt for the personhood of people that has made it thinkable to hang 164 human beings in a single year".[4] In a society based on a relentless denial of the humanity of millions of people, it is easy to execute. When the law of the land defines the vast majority of its inhabitants as "non-persons", the moral anguish over the taking of a human life loses its edge.

The political character of the application of the death penalty in South Africa is obvious in both its creation and application.

The laws governing its imposition are created and administered by an unrepresentative and oppressive government whose illegitimacy makes it impossible for citizens to believe that such legislation could ever protect them. When the vast majority of the population understands that the underlying rationale driving most laws is to degrade and oppress them, to achieve mere adherance to the law is extremely problematic to say nothing of engendering trust or respect for it.

The judiciary too, lacks legitimacy in the minds of the majority of South Africans because of its unrepresentative nature. This is underscored by the fact that approximately 95 percent of the persons hanged since 1910 have been black[5] and 100 percent of the persons who have imposed the death sentence have been white.

In addition, a significant number of political offenders have been sentenced to death and hanged. Sporadic but very high profile political campaigns spearheaded by the ANC surrounded the executions, creating martyrs in the struggle to overthrow Apartheid.[6] These events increased the perception that the death penalty was used as an instrument of political control and repression. Further political inequities of the capital system were exemplified in the 1980's

[3] E. Mureinik, "From Moratorium to Reprieve", *Star* (March 5, 1990).

[4] Ibid.

[5] "Black" here will refer to all those persons who fall outside the classification of "white" in South Africa.

[6] Amongst the most well known of these persons were Solomon Malangu, Andrew Sibusiso Zondo, Benjamin Moloise and Marcus Motaung; *Umkhonto we Sizwe* guerrillas, whose names have become symbols of resistance in the African National Congress.

by the court's use of the controversial "common purpose" doctrine[7] in murder cases arising out of the political turmoil in the country. Several cases, in particular that of the "Sharpville 6" and the "Upington 14"[8] gained immense media coverage and focused world attention on the unfair and inhumane use of the death penalty.

Shortly following the announcement by President de Klerk of the moratorium on all executions, the Minister of Justice, H.J. Coetsee described the process which led to the proposed changes to the legislation.

> We were assisted in this investigation [into capital legislation] by the Chief Justice and Judges President, who in turn consulted with the Bench. I wish to explain that these investigations and considerations stretched over a period of approximately eighteen months. Attorneys General were also involved. We had on this case an extremely responsible group of professional people in posts which command respect.[9]

This speech contains alarming and strange admissions, made all the more extraordinary by the manner of their deliverance. The Minister apparently believed that the eighteen months deliberation over this issue by him and his respected colleagues was to be admired. He forgot to mention that during this period, one hundred and fifty persons had been hanged. These persons will never receive the benefit of the "wise deliberations" of the honourable Minister as they are now dead.

During the same period, respected human rights groups, representative political organizations, church groupings, lawyers organizations and others had been involved in a vociferous and active campaign against the death penalty. For example, in various submissions to the State President and the Minister of Justice, Lawyers for Human Rights called for a moratorium on executions to enable a thorough review of the provisions relating to the death penalty in the *Criminal Procedure Act*.[10] The Minister in his wisdom, however, chose only to consult persons responsible for the prosecution and conviction of

[7] This doctrine was introduced into South African law from English law in the 1880's and in the last century has undergone a number of interpretations. However, the doctrine when applied to murder trials, allows for a murder conviction based on association in the common design of the principal offender. Once this participation (through association) has been established, the court needs only to find intention to commit the crime. In the common purpose cases which gained notoriety in the nineteen eighties (namely the Upington 26 and Sharpeville 6 cases) the accused had all been participants in mob actions which had resulted in death. Although it was found that the conduct of the individuals had not necessarily caused or contributed causally to the deaths, they were convicted for murder. In some instances, the conviction (and subsequent death sentence) was based on evidence that threatening language had been used.

[8] See *S v. Safatsa and Others*, 1989 (1) SA 868 A, *S v. Khumalo and Others*, Case 110/86 (unreported).

[9] Minister of Justice, Mr. H.J. Coetsee, MP, "The Death Penatly" (Address during a joint meeting of Parliament, 7 February 1990).

[10] Memorandum submitted by Lawyers for Human Rights to the State President requesting an immediate declaration of a moratorium on all executions and the appointment of a Commission of Enquiry to investigate the high incidence of violent crime in South Africa and the appropriateness

capital offenders. He sought the opinions of those persons whose views confirmed and gave meaning to his own prejudices, and avoided those who questioned them. The question examined was not whether the death penalty was appropriate – it was merely to look at how to improve the image of its application in South Africa in light of local and international criticism.

The net effect of the belated moratorium and legislative change is to give persons now under sentence of death a fighting chance for life. It also opens up more space for abolitionists to make numerous legal and political challenges to any proposed executions. For these reasons, and for these reasons alone, we welcome the changes.

3. The New Legislation

The new legislation was introduced in July, 1990[11] after referral to a Parliamentary Sub Committee on Justice. The changes to the law and the manner of their implementation are discussed here only in the context of the crime of murder, as at any given time (both pre and post legislative change) approximately ninety percent of persons under sentence of death were convicted of murder.[12] Prior to the introduction of the 1990 amendment, section 277 of the Criminal Procedure Act of 1977 made the death penalty mandatory for murder[13] except when the accused was under eighteen years of age, or if the accused was a woman convicted of the murder of her newborn child or if the court was of the opinion that there were extenuating circumstances.

The most contentious legal principle surrounding capital sentencing practices was the whole question of extenuation. An inquiry into the existence of extenuating factors was an inquiry into facts associated with the crime which,

---

and effectiveness of capital punishment for our society, taking into account international trends towards abolition. (29 September 1988).

January 1989 – a delegation from Lawyers for Human Rights met with the Department of Justice with a view to initiating appropriate amendments to aspects of the law affecting capital punishment.

[11] Criminal Law Amendment Act, 1990.

[12] In terms of the 1977 Criminal Procedure Act there were 11 capital offences, including kidnapping, childstealing, treason, robbery, attempted robbery, housebreaking or attempted housebreaking if there are aggravating circumstances present such as, rape, murder, terrorism. The 1990 Criminal Law Amendment Act makes provision for ..... capital offences including murder, treason during a time of war, rape, robbery and attempted robbery with aggravating circumstances, kidnapping and child stealing.

[13] Murder is defined as the unlawful and intentional causing of the death of another human being, a broad definition by any standard. Because the actual physical act of killing is not an essential element of the crime, "causing the death" could be realised through assisting another to commit suicide. The definition is further widened by the interpretation of intention, where *dolus eventualis* (indirect intention where although the accused foresees the possibly fatal consequences of his or her actions, he or she pursues such action recklessly) suffices.

in the court's opinion, served to diminish the moral blameworthiness of the accused. This demanded of the court the exercise of a moral judgment. In our country, where the law of the land has very successfully enshrined the notion of "separateness", the exercise of this kind of moral judgment took on a very specific character. We were (and bar one exception and unfortunately remain) faced with an entirely white judiciary charged with passing moral judgment on people who were, in the most part, alien to them. Apartheid has divided our society in such a way that people of different racial classification who live in the same town have consummately different life experiences. Yet judges were asked to decide whether the accused's unknown and largely unexplained life experience served in any way to extenuate his actions. When you add to this the problems of interpretation and underpaid, uninspired *pro deo* counsel, it is not surprising that the doctrine of extenuating circumstances remained largely unchanged and unchallenged since its introduction in 1935.

While the law itself provided no precise definition of extenuating circumstances, its application was limited predominantly to provocation, youth, intoxication, a belief in witchcraft and an absence of premeditation. One of the more damaging developments in the interpretation of the concept and its applicability was a judgment in 1947 which established that the onus of proving extenuating factors lay on the accused[14]. This has had serious consequences for indigent accused who were normally represented through *pro deo* counsel. In a recent study Professor D.M. Davis found that in only 10% of all capital cases heard in the Cape Division of the Supreme Court was any evidence at all led in extenuation.[15] There is nothing to indicate that statistics were dissimilar in other provinces.

For many years defence lawyers argued (unsuccessfully) that political factors, in particular participation in the political, armed conflict, should be regarded as extenuation. In a landmark minority judgment in 1989, Justice de Klerk (overruled by his two assessors) in the "Delmas II" trial[16] found that training in an African National Congress (ANC) camp had influenced the minds of the accused in a way as to warrant the finding that extenuating circumstances existed. Although obliged to pass the death sentence by the majority judgment of the two Assessors, this judgment gave the first glimmer of hope to the oft expressed argument that members of *Umkhonto we Sizwe*[17] should be regarded as prisoners of war.

[14] *S.* v. *Lembete,* 1947 (2) SA 60 A.

[15] D.M. Davis "Extenuation – An Unnecessary Halfway House on the Road to a Rational Sentencing Policy", (1989) 2 SACJ 205 at 218.

[16] *S v. Masina and Others,* (16 June 1989) TPD (Unreported). Their appeal against the death sentence was successful on August 15, 1990, and the sentence was replaced by a prison term of twenty five years. On July 1st, 1991 all of the accused in the matter were released under the terms of agreements reached between the African National Congress and the Government.

[17] The armed wing of the African National Congress, formed in 1961 to pursue an armed struggle towards the overthrow of Apartheid. Up until 1961 the African National Congress had utilized peaceful methods of political struggle, including passive resistance.

The court exercised its discretion in its investigation into the existence of extenuating circumstances, but upon a negative finding it was compelled to pass the death penalty.[18] If however the court found that extenuating factors were present, it was given a further discretion to impose the death sentence if it saw fit. A positive finding was therefore no guarantee of escaping the noose. In terms of the Criminal Procedure Act there was no automatic right to appeal against either sentence or conviction, and often people were hanged without recourse to a higher court.

Prior to the establishment of the Lawyers for Human Rights Execution Monitoring programme[19] many condemned persons remained oblivious to their further right to petition the Chief Justice for leave to appeal. In the years before 1988, hundreds if not thousands of condemned prisoners died in ignorance of even those limited rights afforded them. The Monitoring Programme was initially regarded as somewhat of an impertinence by those in authority – an intrusion into the domain of total control enjoyed by a government for far too long.[20]

The 1990 amendments to the capital law were geared in part towards providing slightly more protection within the law for accused and condemned persons. The most significant amendments relate to the introduction of the concept of mitigating factors, which effectively abolished the old and more restrictive concept of extenuation[21]; the increased powers of the Appellate Division allowing it "to confirm the sentence or delete or amend the sentence and impose such punishment as ought to have been imposed at the trial"[22]; the introduction of an automatic right to an appeal and the creation of a Review Panel for the reconsideration of death sentences passed prior to the legislative amendment.

Persons sentenced under the old law now have a three stage review process: an investigation by the Review Panel into the "appropriateness of the death

[18] It has a further discretion upon finding the existence of extenuating factors as it could then impose the death penalty or any other appropriate sentence.

[19] This programme was established during 1988 and monitored amongst other things, the Notices of Executions handed out. In the majority of cases it was found that the condemned persons had either not exhausted their appeals procedure or had not petitioned the State President for clemency. During 1989 Lawyers for Human Rights was instrumental in staying 22 executions – all of these persons have now either had their sentences commuted or are awaiting further appeal.

[20] Initial monitoring was done through encoded messages brought out of the prison by family members after visits. One of the more interesting codes was the use of the acronym WCCS to alert as to an impending execution – Western Christian Civilized Standards!

[21] Criminal Law Amendment Act 107 of 1990 Substitution of s 277 (2) (a).

[22] Criminal Law Amendment Act 107 of 1990, Amendment of s. 322 of Act 5lb of 1977, 12 (a)(b). In broadening the powers of the AD, the law reduces in some measure the necessary arbitrariness of the imposition of the death penalty, and it is interesting to note that this proposed change was met with outrage by certain members of the bench in the Cape Division who felt that it emasculated their position. Prior to the amendment, the Appellate Division was very limited in the scope of its interference, and could only alter the sentence if it found that the court *a quo* had misdirected itself. The Appellate Divisions *opinion* on, for example, a finding on extenuation, could have no bearing on its decision.

sentence", a referral to the Appeal Court upon a negative finding in the Review Panel, and finally the right to petition the State President to exercise his prerogative of mercy.

4. Problems with the Review Panel

In this section, the serious problems encountered with the Review Panel are discussed, as this in many ways encapsulates the inadequacies of the other provisions within the Criminal Law Amendment Act 1990.

The Review Panel consists of six judges and retired judges and three academics appointed by the Department of Justice. It is empowered to investigate cases of persons sentenced under the old law and decide whether or not the death sentence is still an appropriate sentence in terms of the new law. For this purpose the Panel is provided with the trial record of the convicted person, written arguments drawn up by an appointed legal representative and written arguments submitted by the Attorney General's Office. The deliberations and conclusions of the Panel are not revealed other than to the Minister of Justice and the State President if a decision is reached in favour of the applicant. The Review Panel is restricted in its investigation to facts before the trial court, where the investigation during sentencing phase was restricted to the far narrower concept of extenuation.

The most important area of investigation for both the Review Panel and the Appellate Division is the question of *mitigation* as opposed to *extenuation*. The wider connotation given to mitigation includes factors unrelated to the crime, such as the accused's behaviour after the crime has been committed or the fact that he has a clean record.[23] It also involves far more than a listing of certain identifiable factors. If approached thoroughly and seriously, it requires a full investigation into the life history of the accused – from both a psychological and a social perspective. But the approach by the Review Panel to mitigation is impossible to assess when its deliberations and findings are not made public. If the Panel decides that the death sentence is in fact an appropriate sentence in a particular case, it gives no reasons in its referral to the Appeal Court.

What we are able to assess is that in light of the limitations on what can be placed before the Panel, it cannot do justice to the question of mitigation. All the matters examined by the Review Panel are pursuant to the old law and a finding on extenuation. No new evidence is submitted to the Review Panel. In the majority of cases, the trial record contains minimal evidence on extenuation. Attempts by the Panel to translate such evidence into a finding on mitigation become meaningless. It is not accident and certainly not surprising that out of the approximately 170 cases referred to involving 160 persons, the Review Panel's, sentences were commuted in the cases of only 34 applicants.

In April 1991, seventeen persons whose cases had been referred to the

[23] *S v. Masina and Others*, 1990 (4) SA 709, 714.

Review Panel had their sentences commuted to various terms of imprisonment. The most noteworthy fact about this particular group is that all but one were sentenced for politically motivated actions. Included in the group was Barend Hendrik Strydom, a self proclaimed right wing fanatic who had received a total of eight death sentences for gunning down black pedestrians in the streets of Pretoria. As he had become somewhat of a cause célèbre amongst the lunatic fringe, his presence on death row was not to the government's political advantage. Cloaking itself in a veneer of legal respectability, the government abused the review process to further its own political agenda by removing Strydom from death row, suggesting he was a political offender from the right.

In addition to the problems regarding mitigation described above, defence counsel preparing arguments for the Review Panel are denied access to the submissions made by the Attorney General. This in our view constitutes a fundamental breach of the *audi alteram partem* rule and renders the process entirely inadequate.

On July 24 1991, Lawyers for Human Rights submitted a lengthy memorandum to the Chief Justice, Minister of Justice and Chairman of the Review Panel, Justice Viljoen, requesting an urgent meeting to discuss the inadequacies of the Panel and the concomitant prejudice to those persons sentenced to death prior to the 1990 amendment. The request was turned down. The Review Panel has to date (December 1991) almost finalised its work. We believe that the exercise has to a large extent been a spurious and deficient one. It was created by the government to serve a political purpose, largely achieved in April this year with the reprieve of political offenders. Since then, it has laboured through its considerable workload with negligible results.

Many of the same inadequacies surface in cases where persons sentenced under the old law were taken on appeal since the introduction of the 1990 amendment. In a recent appeal in the matter of Almond Nofomela, counsel argued unsuccessfully for referral back to trial court for presentation of new evidence in mitigation. At trial, no evidence whatsoever was led in extenuation let alone in mitigation. The arguments presented for referral back to the trial court are particularly compelling in this case. Nofomela is a former security policeman who was sentenced to death on November 18, 1987 for the robbery and murder of a farmer. After the dismissal of his appeal (heard in terms of the Criminal Procedure Act 1977) he was scheduled for execution on October 20th, 1989. His execution was administratively stayed on the basis of a confession made by him regarding his involvement in Security Police Hit Squad activities. Such activities included the murder of Griffiths Mxenge, a prominent human rights lawyer and political activist. The evidence in the confession (later expanded upon in the Harms Commission appointed to investigate government sponsored death squads) was unknown and unavailable at the trial court. Defence counsel at the Appeal Court argued that evidence in mitigation relating to Nofomela's involvement in legitimated killings and his consequent desensitization to violence should be presented to a court with original jurisdiction. This submission, as well as the appeal against the death sentence, was rejected by the Appellate Division on November 28th, 1991. The rejection of this application bodes ill for others sentenced in terms of the old law and awaiting appeals under the present system.

There have been a number of successful appeals against the death penalty, despite the limitations placed on the Appellate Division disallowing the presentation of evidence outside of the trial record. Some of the successful appeals heard recently have involved accused persons who fall into the broad category of political offenders. At trial they were able to present substantial argument on extenuation, giving defence counsel material to work with in developing a case in mitigation. In some of these cases, offenders were represented by human rights lawyers whose strategy was to extend and stretch the narrow definition of extenuation. In political cases this was made possible by foreign funding enabling counsel to employ the services of expert witnesses. Most condemned persons however, cannot access such funding and the results are often very different. In the cases detailed below, we will attempt to examine the way in which the Appellate Division has been interpreting the concept of mitigation.

5. Judicial Interpretation of Mitigation

In *S v. Matshili and Others*[24] four offenders found guilty on four murder charges at trial, appealed their death sentences. They were sentenced and convicted under the Criminal Procedure Act 1977. The murders took place during a South African Transport Services strike organised by the South African Railway and Harbour Workers Union (SARHWU). The accused were all SARHWU members and the deceased were all persons identified as "scab" workers. The murders were carried out through a combination of stabbing and the dropping of a 31kg rock repeatedly on the deceaseds' heads. While the court found several aggravators to the crime, including the barbarity, brutality and premeditation it found that these factors were outweighed by the mitigators. Included in the mitigators were the sense of extreme frustration experienced by the strikers during the deadlocked talks, the lack of money to buy food and the influence of deindividuation and mob psychology. In other words, consideration was given to the subjective effect of the strike on the appellants.[25] This decision is highly significant in that it will permit accused persons in future capital trials to explain how various manifestations of oppression within our country have motivated or influenced their behaviour.

In other cases, youth and immaturity have been identified as mitigating factors. In *S v. Nkosi and Another*[26], the accused was nineteen years old and the

[24] (1991) (3) SA 264.

[25] One of the appellants said at the time, "I was still very much cross.. Personally I was cross because these people [the deceased] were working... Well it affected me because people at my home were suffering or dying of hunger and I did not have money."

[26] (1991) (2) SACR 194 (A).

court found that he acted "impulsively" as a result of his youth. In the case of *S v. Dlamini*,[27] the accused was a Zulu man who killed his employer and the employer's wife for withholding his wages. The court identified the Zulu manner of handling fiscal matters as a mitigator, stating that "we are well aware of the punctiliousness which the Zulus demand and observe in money matters and of the rage they experience when they believe they have been cheated". Recent judgments as in the case of *S v. Ngobeni*[28] have also identified extreme anger and the fact that murders are committed in the "heat of the moment" as a strong mitigator. In this particular case the accused had strangled an eleven year old boy whose actions had resulted in him losing his job.

The significance of all these cases is the fact that mitigating evidence was prepared and led which allowed the court to identify human reactions and reasons for actions. In cases where appeals have been dismissed, the accused is not presented as a human being with human frailties. As a result, greater attention is given to the victim. In *S v. Makie*[29] the appellant stabbed a woman sixteen times causing her death. He then had intercourse with her. The *only* evidence led in extenuation at the trial court was that he had no prior convictions. The court's attention then focused on the safety of elderly people and the "inherently abhorrent" nature of attacks on a defenceless old woman. In another appeal *S v. Malgas en andere*[30] the appellant had participated in a prison gang murder.[31] It was a particularly gruesome murder with ritual slaughter following the killing and the court's attention focused on these factors as aggravation. Mitigating evidence regarding gang culture in prisons and the dehumanising and brutalising effect of our prisons system is under-developed in our country and was not presented to the court.

For mitigation to have any meaning the State must provide resources for its proper implementation. It must also ensure that those sentenced under the old law have their cases given proper and thorough attention. The only way this can be done is to refer these cases back to trial court where new evidence relevant to mitigation must be led. For counsel to be able to present even the most cursory of arguments in mitigation, an extensive investigation into the developmental history of the accused is necessary as well as access to social workers, psychologists and other expert witnesses to assess and evaluate the accused through a series of tests and other mechanisms. The financial resources required for this type of preparation however, are far beyond the present

[27] 1991 (1) SACR 128.

[28] 1990 (2) SACR 458 (A).

[29] 1991 (2) SACR 139 (A).

[30] 1991 (1) SACR 284 (A).

[31] Prison gangs and prison violence are rife in our jails – with an extremely effective national network of gangs operating . It is interesting to note here that in the eighteen months leading up to the moratorium on executions, a large percentage of those persons hanged were persons convicted of prison murders. Common wisdom has it on death row that if you are sentenced for a prison murder, the only way you ever leave there is through the gallows.

allocation provided to *pro deo* counsel.[32] Today, contact between *pro deo* counsel and client remains extremely limited, with a first meeting occurring in many instances after an initial hearing before a magistrate in which the unrepresented accused often implicates him or herself.

In *S v. Banda*[33], Justice Friedman set out a list of mitigating factors including age and family circumstances. He stressed the importance of a "perceptive understanding of the accused's human frailties as effected by the circumstances surrounding the commission of the offence in question and a balancing of these frailties against the evil of the offender's deed". But it is difficult, if not impossible, for a judge to reach an understanding of the human frailties of the accused if the defence counsel is either unable or unwilling to present such evidence. In addition, if the relationship between the accused and his counsel is of a superficial and cursory nature, the counsel will be hard placed to present a sympathetic picture at all.

When the concept of mitigation was introduced into our capital law it was a welcome advancement to the restrictive application of extenuation, but we believe that it is nothing short of criminal for the State to introduce such a concept and then fail to ensure that it is fully and properly implemented.

Both the manner in which capital legislation was changed as well as the process through which it has been implemented are in fact evidence of a far deeper malaise in our society. It reflects a belief by the government of the day, that tinkering with the existing legislation and constitutional framework will stave off their inevitable downfall. Their recent forays into the arena of "enlightened" legislative change have proved to be singularly unimaginative and limited in scope. This is not surprising given that they are a government whose reign in power has been uninterrupted for forty years. This lends itself to complacency and rigidity of thought.

There are currently over forty people on death row who have exhausted all the legal avenues now open to them – they are dependent on the extension or otherwise of the mercy of the State President. Given his recent record (where this year, outside of those persons he directed to reprieve by the Review Panel he has commuted the sentences of possibly five persons) their prospects are not good. They were sentenced under a law which by the government's own admission was inadequate and outdated, had their cases reviewed in a half-hearted and post-dated manner and now await a decision on their lives to be made by a State President elected into office by possibly four percent of the population.

[32] *Pro deo* counsel are currently paid R300 per day (U.S. equivalent – $100), a rate far below standard fees. Although provision exists for the payment of expert witnesses, such provision involves extra effort on the part of the State-appointed counsel and the funds available for such witnesses are extremely limited.

[33] *S v. Banda and Others*, 1991 (2) SA 362.

6. Recent Developments

There have, however, been two recent developments with regard to the death penalty which, in spite of the government's "best" intentions, offer a ray of hope to condemned prisoners and abolitionists. In June this year, Justice Curlewis took the unusual step of publishing a response to an article on sentencing trends in the Transvaal Division which had identified "hanging judges".[34] While Justice Curlewis is regarded by some as a maverick on the bench, his remarks have serious implications for the application of the death penalty in our society. In the article he stated as follows:

> The object of the work ... is to show that "*judicial attitudes towards the death penalty play a material role*" in imposing or not imposing that sentence. Only an ignoramus or a person with little regard for the truth would deny this.[35]

He stated further that:

> Let me make my meaning plain. A person who deserves to hang was more likely to get the death sentence from me or my ilk than (at random) my brothers Roux MacArthur, Van Schalkwyk, Nestadt, Goldstone or Gordon. The reason is that these judges are at heart abolitionists for one reason or another. Nothing wrong with that, after all the present Chief Justice is one, and their beliefs are to be respected. Obviously, and for that reason, they cannot be sound on the imposition of the death penalty. The answer to this problem ... for the good of the community and for the peace of mind of such Judges, is they should not sit on capital cases.[36]

In response to the publication of this letter, Lawyers for Human Rights wrote to the State President submitting that on the basis of Justice Curlewis's admissions, all executions should be suspended immediately pending a public commission of enquiry into the attitudes of judges towards the death penalty. We also reiterated our position that no further executions should take place until a new constitution is in place. We sent this letter to the State President on August 28th, 1991 and four months later we anxiously await a response. We welcomed Judge Curlewis's honesty, though we are sure that many of his brothers on the bench rued the publication of his letter.

In November this year we saw the long awaited publication of the Law Commission's Interim Report on Group and Human Rights.[37] Article 1 in this

[34] Laurel Angus and Evadné Grant, "Sentencing in Capital Cases in the Transvaal Provincial Division and Witwatersrand Local Division: 1987–1989." (1991), 7. S. Afr. J. Hum. Rts., pp. 50–69.

[35] SAJHR (8) 1991, *Correspondence,* Mr. Justice Curlewis DJP.

[36] *Op cit.* – SAJHR.

[37] South African Law Commission Project 58 Group and Human Rights – Interim Report August 1991. The Report was commissioned by the Minister of Justice on April 23, 1986 to make

Interim Report deals with the right to life and the limitations on this right in terms of the imposition of the death penalty. The conclusions are very interesting. Lawyers for Human Rights summarised the conclusions as follows:

The Law Commission found the issue of the imposition of the death penalty a highly controversial one which they felt unable to resolve with finality. Their solution (which we believe reflects proper caution and sensitivity) was to refer the issue to a constitutional court – "a middle course between the retention of the death penalty and the abolition thereof.[38]

The Interim Report also highlighted the fact that the issue of the death penalty is inextricably linked in the minds of many South Africans to the political process. The recommendations contained in the Report have profound implications for the government should they elect to carry out any further executions. While the Commission did not go so far as to suggest a moratorium on executions, their recommendation that the issue be referred to the as yet non-existent constitutional court, speaks for itself.[39] The fact that these recommendations were made by a government-appointed commission cannot have pleased a Minister of Justice who is a self-avowed retentionist. For abolitionists, these recommendations served to open the door even wider. The Lawyers for Human Rights submission to the State President is that, on the basis of this Report and in the light of present negotiations, no further executions should take place until a new constitution has been written. We believe that on this basis they will be unable to proceed.

Several months prior to the publication of the Interim Report, the government announced with much pomp and ceremony that they were reactivating the gallows. In an extraordinary departure from custom, the Minister of Justice H.J. Coetsee utilised his parliamentary platform to make this announcement and in doing so he detailed in glorious colour the barbarity of the crime committed by the selected candidate, Paul Bezuidenhout.[40] The inappropriateness of the announcement and the vigour with which the government fought the ensuing opposition to the execution presented a graceless spectacle.

The condemned person, Paul Bezuidenhout presented a pathetic picture – an illiterate, uneducated, under-represented, poverty stricken youth. A person who did not even fully appreciate or even understand the import of his Notice of Execution. Facing him, with all flags flying, was the might of the South African Government through its Department of Justice.

Bezuidenhout has been sentenced to death for a particularly brutal murder.

---

recommendations regarding the definition and protection of group rights within the context of the South African constitutional dispensation and the possible extension of the existing protection of individual rights.

[38] Letter to the State President from the National Director of Lawyers for Human Rights, (19 November 1991).

[39] In South Africa we have, as yet, no constitutional court. If it comes into existence this will only be upon the completion of political negotiations for a new constitution and the introduction of a bill of rights.

[40] *S.* v. *Bezuidenhout*, 1991 (1) SACR 43 (A).

During the course of his trial he had been sent for psychiatric observation where State-appointed psychiatrists had pronounced him normal and competent to stand trial.[41] Upon receiving information that Bezuidenhout had been scheduled for execution, Lawyers for Human Rights appointed a psychologist and psychiatrist to evaluate and test him. The findings were startling – the tests showed that he was retarded and had the mental age of a seven year old. Further investigation showed that his childhood was one characterised by extreme brutality where he had seen his mother repeatedly stabbed by her boyfriend and following her death had seen his aunt undergo the same treatment. An application to stay the execution to allow for further investigation into these findings was refused by the Minister of Justice but later granted by a Supreme Court Judge one day prior to the scheduled execution. Bezuidenhout is currently awaiting a response to a petition lodged with the Minister of Justice for a reopening of the trial.

The proposed execution met with vociferous opposition from human rights bodies, church groups, political parties, international human rights groups and liberation movements on a scale which surprised a government used to doing things how and when they pleased. Since then, no further announcements of impending executions have been made, despite the fact that there are people on death row who have exhausted all the remedies available to them.

Where are we now? In December 1991 as the major political parties gear themselves up for constitutional talks, approximately 300 people await their fate on death row. All these people are being processed through the wringer of laws created by a parliament which continues to represent a tiny minority of the population. Apart from the people on death row whose actions were directly political (two years after the historic February 2nd speech of State President de Klerk, we still have political offenders on death row) the bulk of the death row population are criminal offenders who are black and impoverished. Our society and our system of government has for years denied people fundamental human rights and choices: it has forced them into selected group areas; denied them basic education; denied them a say in the political process; kept unemployment high and deprived people of their land. The people most battered and bruised by this system, the people at the very end of the victim scale, are to be found in the condemned cells of Pretoria Maximum Security Prison.

In a petition from common law prisoners on death row published earlier this year by Lawyers for Human Rights, the following is stated:

> "Today we are classified as common law prisoners, but who is not a victim of this system of government or the reign of the minority in this country ... we have been provoked and depressed by this system of our country ... we do not say our acts were right – they were wrong acts at the wrong time during the wrong system of Apartheid ... if the government wants to rectify its mistakes it should reprieve us, it should not just add more wrong laws onto the old wrong laws."

[41] This was despite the fact that when asked what year it was he had responded "June".

Their call is a lonely and desolate one to a system which has failed them. They have been processed (whether under the old law or the new "improved" law) by a system geared towards their oppression; a system designed to deny them their essential humanity – a system perfected by a small group of people who regard the bulk of the population in this country as sub-human. We cannot and will not isolate the use of the death penalty from the political system within which it was so comfortable.

It is the force of political change which has rendered the use of the death penalty less comfortable. Our task is to ensure that this continues. In the publication of its draft Bill of Rights, the position of the African National Congress is unequivocal. Article 2 reads as follows:

"1. Every person has the right to life
2. No one shall be arbitrarily deprived of his or her life
3. Capital punishment is abolished and no further executions shall take place."

The ANC enjoys majority support in this country and all indications point towards their holding a majority position in a democratically elected government – their abolitionist stance is therefore welcome. In newly independent Namibia the introduction of a constitution enshrining universal franchise was accompanied by the abolition of the death penalty, and we hope that the same will happen here.

We are currently in the middle of an extremely fragile but essentially irreversible political process and the carrying out of an execution now would indicate immeasurable bad faith on the part of the Government. In a recent demonstration of the increasing unwillingness on the part of the population to accept unilateral decisions, the country was paralysed by a national strike against the introduction of a new tax. The carrying out of an execution, given the position adopted by the major political party, would send a message of contempt to the people of South Africa.

In a climate of spiralling violent crime the Nationalist Government may well be tempted to bolster dwindling white support through a resumption of hangings. Their experience during the Paul Bezuidenhout attempt and the publication of the Law Commission's Report has, we believe, tempered their enthusiasm somewhat. However, nothing is certain.

Right now we are a *de facto* abolitionist State, a strange state of being in a country governed by people who support hanging with unseemly vigour. In 1987, 1988 and 1989 both the Executioner and the deputy Sheriff were busy men. Listed in the 1992 legal diary are the tariffs for the Deputy Sheriff:

In cases of prisoners sentenced to death

a) Where the prisoner is executed, arranging for and attending capital punishment an inclusive fee of R150.00;
b) Where the prisoner is not executed an inclusive fee of R75.00[42]

[42] Butterworths Law Diary and Directory 1991.

For the Sheriff who does the work – the fee is R200.00 for each neck he breaks. If there are multiple executions (and our gallows are designed to hang seven people simultaneously), his fee is multiplied. One shudders to think of his take-home pay in December 1987 when the Christmas rush affected the execution of twenty eight people over a seven day period.[43]

Today, when the thud of the trap door remains a distant memory on death row, the hangman has joined the ever swelling ranks of the unemployed. In Lawyers for Human Rights we welcome this particular infringement of the right to work – long may it continue.

[43] During that period, as the back combis carrying the dead bodies became a familiar sight to visitors, a family member expressed her horror to a wardress working at the prison. The wardress, a young Afrikaans girl, turned to her with a dreadful smile and said, "Yes, we are so *busy* right now."

SECTION III(b): NON-STATE ACTORS AND VIOLENCE

Introduction*

This section is devoted to violence committed by persons who are not directly or indirectly at the service of the governing powers. The State has traditionally been seen as the entity responsible for upholding human rights, both on the international level and, constitutionally, in the domestic sphere. In so far as the State is not the author of the violence committed, to what extent is the human rights approach relevant, to what extent can it help the victims or contribute to eliminating the violence? The three papers in this section, by looking at women and children as victims of violence committed by non-State actors and at insurgents as perpetrators of violence, provide insights into answering these questions.

Arguing from conceptual, political and legal perspectives, Nigel Rodley posits that it is appropriate to consider human rights rules as being applicable *only* to the relations between, on the one hand, governments or groups having power similar to that of governments and, on the other, those over whom the governments or groups exercise that power. Consequently, in respect of armed opposition groups not exercising effective power over a significant segment of the population, it would be inappropriate to treat their violent behaviour (for example torturing or kidnapping) as being capable of violating human rights. This does not mean, however, that on a human rights approach, we must simply turn a blind eye to the atrocities of armed opposition groups. Human rights reporting, for example, need not and should not be so narrowly focused as to be misleading: it should acknowledge the situation as a whole, including abuses or atrocities committed by insurgent groups.

Patricia Freeman Marshall opens her paper by signalling "a terrible commonality... shared by women throughout the world; their experience of violence, and the threat of victimization they constantly face". In contrast to the subject of Nigel Rodley's paper, this is an instance of violence committed by non-State actors which is in principle capable of giving rise to State liability under international human rights law; the responsibility of the State may be

* Summary prepared by the editors.

K.E. Mahoney and P. Mahoney (eds.), Human Rights in the Twenty-first Century, 293–295.

engaged through its passivity or through its having a legal system which fails to protect the victims of violence.[1] However, though this may be the position in principle, Marshall demonstrates in her case study of Canada that there is still an overwhelming need for international human rights instruments and agencies to recognize the extent to which sexual assault, wife abuse, pornography and prostitution deny women and children their basic human rights. For Marshall, the example of Canada shows that governments – and international human rights mechanisms – have not yet recognised the dimensions of this violence or developed any initiatives to address the problem. The reality is that the courts' and the legal system's response to, for example, sexual assault and wife assault does not effectively protect the human rights of the victims. In our societies, Marshall concludes, violent behaviour perpetrated against women by men is pervasive and widely tolerated. She closes her paper with a list of recommendations making up a comprehensive programme to reverse discriminatory policies and practices and to replace them with those that will support women's human rights.

Vitit Muntabhorn's paper outlines the manifold forms of the violence and abuses – such as exploitation for labour and sexual purposes – of which children are victims in various parts of the world. In order to understand better this complex reality of cruelty, he investigates the groups of children requiring urgent attention: rural, slum and street children; refugee and stateless children; child soldiers, child labourers, child prostitutes and female children in general; juvenile delinquents, handicapped children and medically abused children. Not surprisingly, he identifies rampant poverty and its destructive impact on children and their families as one of the root causes of the violence and abuses. Muntabhorn accepts implicitly that, because of their greater vulnerability, children need State-provided protection against violence committed by non-State actors if their basic human rights are not to be illusory. At the international level some action has started to be taken, notably the UN Convention on the Rights of the Child. However, in Muntabhorn's view, the key to overcoming the violation of children's rights is at national and local levels, with action in relation to laws, policies, practices and budgetary commitment. He advocates a comprehensive approach to eradicating the violence and abuses perpetuated against children, precisely because the reasons underlying the victimization process are many.

The conclusion to be drawn from the sombre picture painted by these three papers is that the human rights approach is engared notwith standing the identity of the author of the violence. Even talking in the purely legal terms of

[1] The general principles on State responsibility under international human rights law for violence committed by private, non-State actors is not dealt with as such in Marshall's paper – but see the paper by Mahoney and Sundberg, below in the following chapter on The Human Rights Response to Violence.

human rights law, the State is under a duty not only to abstain from perpetrating violence itself or through its agents, but also see to it that non-State actors do not perpetrate violence against innocent victims. We are, however, a long way from adequate recognition of this in practice.

NIGEL S. RODLEY*

Can Armed Opposition Groups Violate Human Rights?

1. Introduction

Human rights are violated every day in all parts of the world. Reports of human rights watchdogs, such as Amnesty International, the Anti-Slavery Society, Human Rights Watch, the International Commission of Jurists, the International Federation of Human Rights, the International League of Human Rights and the Minority Rights Group continually document this depressing reality. No group of states has a monopoly on respect for or the flouting of the traditional fundamental freedoms of conscience, expression, association or assembly. The same applies to the field of socio-economic rights.

However, even a cursory familiarity with human rights reporting leads to an awareness that one "group" of states is very much prone to the occurrence of the gravest human rights violations, often on a widespread scale, namely, states whose governments are confronted by organized armed opposition. Here, there is a real danger that such atrocities as torture, extra-legal execution and even enforced disappearance will occur. The less sophisticated in terms of the training, material and motivation of the security forces being challenged by such opposition, the greater will be their propensity to resort to practices of this sort. Indeed, the practices may well serve as the very basis for a ruthless counter-insurgency strategy, aimed at eliciting political or operational intelligence or deterring moral or practical support for the insurgents.

Typically, the governments being threatened, unable or unwilling to curb their security forces, will deny the practices or dismiss them as regrettable excesses. Sometimes they will move from rhetorical defence to attack, accusing the armed opposition not only of "terrorism", but also of "violating human rights".

The temptation of governments feeling under siege to resort to this "*tu quoque*" type of propaganda is understandable. It is the purpose of this paper, however, to suggest that it is misguided and that, when governmental or non-governmental human rights monitors acquiesce in it, they compound the error.

* Reader in Law, University of Essex.

K.E. Mahoney and P. Mahoney (eds.), Human Rights in the Twenty-first Century, 297–318.

Before embarking on the argument, it is necessary to distinguish between various types of "actors" in any conflict of the sort under discussion. There are four main types: 1. governments and their security forces; 2. unofficial "paramilitary groups", sometimes known as "death squads", acting in collusion with, or with the approval, consent or acquiescence of, the government or its security forces; 3. armed opposition groups exercising "effective power"[1] over a significant segment of population and conducting sustained, organized armed hostilities; and 4. armed opposition groups not exercising such effective power.

As regards to the first three types, the problem we are dealing with does not arise. There is no doubt that governments can be and are responsible for violating human rights. Similarly, to the extent that "paramilitary groups", the second type, act as *de facto* agents of government, it is the government in question that is to be considered as either directly or vicariously responsible.[2] The third type of actor, the group exercising effective power, may, for both conceptual and legal reasons be considered as capable of violating human rights. It is in respect of the fourth type, the armed opposition group not exercising effective power, that I contend it is inappropriate to characterize their behaviour as capable of violating human rights.

I shall approach the issue from conceptual, political and legal perspectives.

2. The Conceptual Perspective

A frequently posed question goes like this: What difference does it make to a victim of torture if the torture is inflicted by a policeman or someone else? The implicit point of the question is to suggest that if torture by a policeman is a violation of human rights, so must be torture inflicted by someone else. It follows further that, if persons other than officials can violate the human right not to be subjected to torture, so such persons can notionally violate other human rights: they can be human rights violators.

This approach, I suggest, misconceives the significance of the term "human rights", both as a historical construct and as a notion distinguishable from other notions such as "crime" or, simply, "rights".

It is no accident that the term "human rights" seems to appear contemporaneously with the rise of positivist doctrines of law and state sovereignty. In feudal times, the divine right of kings carried with it the notion of the sovereign himself (or, occasionally, herself), being subject to divine law. To use modern terminology, divinely authorized rights and privileges were balanced by divinely-ordained duties and responsibilities. The church was influential in maintaining the balance. As secularism grew, untrammelled sovereignty carried

[1] This term is borrowed from the UN Declaration against Torture: see below, note 49 and accompanying text.

[2] See remarks on collusion and complicity below, text accompanying notes 17, 37 and 40.

with it the seeds of arbitrary despotism. Furthermore, the development of industry, commerce, transport and increasingly rapid means of communication carried a certain centralizing dynamic. This could further enhance the uninhibited authority of the sovereign. Yet the same developments also produced a class, the so-called middle class, which could or would not function effectively in too authoritarian or arbitrary an environment. They needed a buffer against it. The claim for human rights was that buffer. *Human rights were, then, primarily the historical response to the rise of the modern nation state.* They were the limitations on the authority of the sovereign over his, her or, gradually, its subjects.

As the state became ever more powerful, so the demand for human rights became ever more insistent. Similarly, as the European-type nation state has spread across the globe, so the need for human rights has been correspondingly demanded by the citizens of these states.

It may be asserted that merely because a concept has a certain historical origin, that should not predetermine its evolution. Perhaps not. Yet, as long as a particular sense needs to be expressed, it may be argued that, in the absence of alternative terminology, the terminology already available is the most suitable. Arguably there is still a need to express the concept of rules applicable to the relations between governments and governed. "Human rights" remains the term best suited to express that concept.

This does not necessarily mean that the term has to remain static. In their inception, human rights could have been defined merely as limitations on the authority of governments over their subjects. Nowadays, we see human rights also being conceived of as imposing positive obligations on governments. Such obligations may range from the prevention of actions by private persons capable of harming other private persons,[3] to the provision of services and resources necessary for a decent life.[4] While some human rights philosophers may demur,[5] for the purposes of this paper, it is argued that there is no insuperable obstacle to amending our definition of human rights to become "rules that mediate the relationship between governments and their subjects".

Further, it is not necessary to insist on the use of the words "government"

[3] So the German constitutional law concept of *Drittwirkung* (or third-party effect) may be adopted by the organs of the European Convention on Human Rights: E.A. Alkema, "The Third-Party Applicability or 'Drittwirkung' of the European Convention on Human Rights", in F. Matscher and H. Petzold (eds.), *Protecting Human Rights: The European Dimension* (1988), p. 33. The notion is that if the state fails to take protective measures (to prevent murder, for example) it will be failing to guarantee human rights, in the case of the example: the right to life. Albeit still controversial, the concept is extendable to areas that international human rights law tends to have overlooked, such as man-made ecological disasters resulting in loss of life, where honest and competent government regulation might have avoided the disaster: see Dias, "Realizing the Human Rights of the Disadvantaged" (1990), 45 Review – International Commission of Jurists, 37.

[4] See, for example, the International Covenant on Economic, Social and Cultural Rights, below note 27.

[5] For example, see M. Cranston, *What Are Human Rights?* London: Bodley Head (1973), chapter VIII.

or "subjects". If we can identify an entity exercising powers analogous to those of governments, as, for example, in a civil war between two equally-matched contending parties, where the insurrectionary party exercises government-like authority over a portion of the population, there is no reason not to apply the notion of human rights to such an entity in its relations with those under its jurisdiction.[6]

So, still in terms of the historical conception of human rights as governing a particular type of relationship, we can further amend the definition to read as follows: "human rights are those rules that mediate the relationship between, on the one hand, governments or other entities exercising effective power analogous to that of governments and, on the other, those who are subject to that power".

The person who posed the earlier question about torture may perhaps still be heard to object that if torture is wrong and it is a violation of human rights when inflicted by or under official authority, why should we not allow the concept of human rights to evolve to cover torture inflicted outside the domain of official action? The sub-text may well be: "Why may we not bring the emotive power of the term human rights to bear on the same reprehensible activity by whomever committed?"

The answer may be framed in three ways. 1. We still need a term to cover the notion of rules mediating the relationship of those who govern with those who are governed and if we were to allow the term to describe only a particular kind of harm from the victim's perspective, we should have to find a new term to denote those rules. 2. There are various other appropriate terms to describe the harm when committed by others (with the necessary sense of opprobrium). 3. Each of those terms can and should be distinguished from human rights (and from each other), if they are not to become interchangeable and, ultimately, deprived of their own conceptually-specific meaning.

The first response speaks for itself. I am not aware of any contenders for alternative terms to denote human rights traditionally understood. The second and third responses require us to look at existing terms to describe torture (or other acts) which, if committed by governments or their ilk, would be categorized as human rights violations.

For example, in most, if not all, legal systems, torture is a *crime*. It may be called torture, aggravated assault, battery, infliction of grievous bodily harm, and so on. The perpetrator may be a family member, a habitual criminal, a member of the mafia, a terrorist, a policeman, a soldier, or, indeed, anyone. A crime is a very serious wrong, entitling the victim not only to claim a private right of redress, but to expect the repressive action of the state. The criminal law

[6] That in law human rights may belong both to citizens and foreigners within the jurisdiction of a given state is clear: see, e.g., the UN Declaration of the Human Rights of Individuals who are not Nationals of the Countries in which They Live, UN GA res. 40/144, 13 Dec. 1985; and General Comment 15(27) (The position of aliens under the Covenant), UN *Report of the Human Rights Committee*, Official Records of the General Assembly, 41st Session, Supplement No.40 (A/41/40)(1986).

expresses, in practical terms, society's abhorrence of the acts by and against whomsoever committed. Moreover, I suggest that it would not occur to many to suggest that torture inflicted in the home or by a common criminal, or a gang of common criminals, is a human rights violation. Why then should it become one when inflicted by a politically-motivated criminal? Perhaps a proponent of such a notion would respond to this question that the essence lies in the aspiration of the politically-motivated criminal to govern.[7]

This point will be revisited later, when the international law aspects of the problem are considered. At this stage a number of points must be noted. First, not all politically-motivated criminals aspire to govern; some aspire merely to impede government or draw attention to perceived injustice; so, we should have to distinguish between the politically-motivated torturer aspiring to govern (a human rights violator) and a politically-motivated torturer not aspiring to govern (a criminal). Second, since in practice we are concerned not with the isolated political criminal, but with the political criminal belonging to an organized group, we should probably further find ourselves having to distinguish between the latter (a human rights violator) and the former (a criminal). Third, the relevance of the aspiration to govern is not obvious. Probably, the idea is that those who aspire to govern should be held to the same standard as those they claim to replace. This may be so, as a proposition of abstract political ethics. Yet the realities of the different planes on which the two parties function – the government with all the institutional apparatus of effective power, the armed opposition group without that apparatus – makes the balance implausible. Moreover, there is no reason why moral balance requires the appropriation of language that would disguise the practical imbalance.

Just as torturers may be described as committing a crime, so they may be described as infringing or violating legal *rights*. A torture victim may well have various causes of action, for example, in tort against the perpetrator. As with crime, it matters not who is the perpetrator or the victim. It is not necessary to become embroiled in the various theories of rights in law.[8] It is sufficient to note that every time the law entitles a person to make a certain kind of demand on someone else, that person has a legal right to make that demand. It is evident that not every legal right is a human right. If we ask ourselves "why not?", we may well answer that human rights are special kinds of rights.[9] What then is special about them? Here are two possible alternative answers: 1. They are still

[7] The point is argued in Matas, *AI and NGES – Revised version of remarks prepared for delivery to Amnesty International, Moose Jaw, Saskatchewan – 27 October 1990*, [hereinafter "Matas"], on file with the author (by NGEs the author refers to "non-governmental entities", equivalent to the notion of "armed opposition groups" as used in the present paper).

[8] For a splendid survey of the literature on the concept of "rights", see J. Shestack, "The Jurisprudence of Human Rights", in T. Meron (ed.) *Human Rights in International Law: Legal and Policy Issues*, Oxford: Claredon Press (1984), Chapter 3.

[9] For the notion of rights as "trumps", see R. Dworkin, *Taking Rights Seriously*, London: Ducksworth (1977).

what history led us to understand them to be, that is, rules mediating the relations between governors and governed. 2. They are rights, the violation of which is seen as a particularly grave invasion a) of one's well-being or b) of one's "human dignity" or c) of some special quality that is inherent in the nature of human beings as such. It may be that b) and c) are respectively Kantian or Natural Law variants of a).

A problem with any of the formulations of the second alternative explanation of the specificity of human rights is the one we have already seen when talking about crime. We would have to conclude that any murder is a violation of the human right to life (any manslaughter, too?), that any kidnapping is a violation of the right to freedom from arbitrary arrest and detention (not to mention freedom of movement, expression, association and assembly), that any theft is a violation or the right to property, and so on. I shall not labour the notorious difficulties of identifying the content of "human dignity" or "human nature" that are posed by versions b) and c) of the second alternative. I do submit that what is special about human rights in the general field of rights is more adequately revealed by the first of the two alternative answers.[10]

3. The Perspective of International Law

It is the contention of this section that the international law of human rights is consistent with the concept of human rights discussed in the previous section; namely, that the law is addressed to the behaviour of states, as personified by their governments. The law deals with acts or omissions of government officials.

The very structure of international law tends towards this approach. Traditionally, international law was that body of law binding on states in their relations with each other.[11] There are, however, areas where international law is concerned with the behaviour of individuals or groups. One of these is the traditional crime of piracy. More modern analogues to piracy have come to be the subject of international legislation, including aircraft hijacking,[12]

[10] While I hope that the foregoing provides a convincing case for conceiving of human rights as being best explained by the modified traditional definition considered above, I also find myself wondering whether the original challenge we faced, that is, the argument that, from the perspective of the victim, torture is torture by whomsoever committed, is indeed as self-evident as at first appears. As soon as one is aware of one's own situation in the broader society, one also has a reasonable hope of protection by the institutions of that society, notably the police and the courts, against certain harms. Psychologically, therefore, there remains the prospect of redress of some sort for the harm sustained. May it not, then, follow that the torment is particularly aggravated when the agents of the pain or suffering are precisely those who are supposed to protect against or at least potentially provide relief from the acts causing the suffering?

[11] Oppenheim, L., *International Law* (1955), 8th ed., Lauterpacht, pp. 4–5.

[12] Hague Convention for the Suppression of Unlawful Seizure of Aircraft 1970 (1971), 10 ILM 133.

sabotage[13] and hostage-taking[14] and offences against diplomats and similar internationally-protected persons.[15] All of the offences contemplated by customary international law (in the case of piracy) or by the relevant treaties (in the case of other offences) are or can be committed by private individuals or groups. There is always a transnational component to the offence. Does that mean that, in respect of these crimes, international law now imposes duties directly on private persons or groups? A respectable theory holds that it does not.[16] What is common to the crimes in question is that international law either authorizes or requires *governments* to act to prevent or repress the crimes. The law may go as far as authorizing or requiring governments to institute criminal proceedings against suspected perpetrators of the crimes, even if the only connection between the suspected perpetrator and the government is the mere presence of the former within the jurisdiction of the latter. This is called "universal jurisdiction"; it applies even where the perpetrator is not a national of the state of jurisdiction, where the crime has been committed in another state, and regardless of the nationality of the victim. In so doing, the law may well be authorizing or requiring governments to exercise their criminal jurisdiction in circumstances that would not be justified in respect of ordinary criminal behaviour. But the law is still directing itself at governments, stipulating what governments should do in respect of the crimes. It is not imposing obligations directly on the perpetrators. In any event, the perpetrators have to be acting transnationally against inter-state interests.

Another area where international law concerns itself with the behaviour of individuals is that contained in what are now known as the Nuremberg Principles. Here international law seemed to articulate certain categories of crime that individuals could commit in direct violation of that law, namely, crimes against peace, war crimes and crimes against humanity, as well as conspiracy to commit any of the three. They all had to have been committed during or in connection with the recent international armed conflict.[17] Some might argue that even here the legal obligations in question were jurisdictional rather than substantive, that the International Military Tribunal was merely exercising a jurisdiction that international law authorized each and any state to exercise separately. This is a doctrinal point that cannot be pursued here, nor need it be. The crucial point about the post-World War II trials is that the accused were either state officials (the overwhelming majority) or private individuals acting in *collusion* with the state, in the context of a fundamental event involving interstate relations.

[13] ICAO Montreal Convention for the Suppression of Unlawful Acts against the Safety of Civil Aviation (1971), 10 ILM 1151.

[14] International Convention against the Taking of Hostages (1979), 18 ILM 1456.

[15] Convention on the Prevention and Punishment of Crimes against Internationally Protected Persons 1973 (1974), 13 ILM 41.

[16] See, e.g. Schwarzenberger, I *A Manual of International Law* (1960), 4th ed., pp. 73–74.

[17] Agreement for the Establishment of an International Military Tribunal (1945), 5 UNTS 251, Annex, Art.6.

So the first category of "crime under international law" deals with private individuals or groups acting against state interests in a transnational context. The law addresses itself to states, in the traditional way, requiring them to act, mainly on the jurisdictional plane, to prevent or repress the type of offence. There is nothing here to affect the traditional definition of international law as the law regulating interstate relations. The second category of such crime is that committed by or in collusion with state officials. This category was certainly novel at the time: it broke through the "corporate veil" of the state, casting aside the notion of sovereign immunity, the defence of "act of state" and the plea of *respondeat superior*.[18] But, the novelty lay in targeting those who were responsible for *state* misbehaviour. Taking the view that international law addressed these people directly, it did so in their capacity as the real authors of grievous wrongs committed by the state. And it did this much only in the context of international hostilities.

This is the basis from which we can now specifically address the attitude of the international law of human rights to individuals involved in violating such rights. What the foregoing suggests, first of all, is that we cannot easily presume that international law has invested certain private individuals or groups with sufficient status to become themselves violators of that law. Moreover, the very fact that international law concerns itself with a subject matter that generally has no transnational component is a radical development of relatively recent origin.[19] It would be a conceptual and structural evolution of considerable moment to compound one novelty with another, namely the imposition of duties on individuals (other than those acting on behalf of or in collusion with the state) not to violate human rights. The evidence for such an evolution would have to be incontrovertible. Existing evidence does not meet that test.

One argument that may be made pertains to the realm of legal theory. It is the common affirmation that one cannot have rights without duties.[20] Assuming this to be so, it does not mean that the right and duty inhere in the same person.[21] Rather, the conception is that I can only claim a legal right properly so-called if I can claim it as against someone else – that someone else has a duty to vouchsafe me that right. So conceived, human rights, traditionally understood, create no conceptual difficulty: if I have a right to free speech, the government has an obligation to permit me to speak freely.

[18] i.e. the defence that obedience to superior orders exculpates the person complying with such orders.

[19] Except for slavery, trade union rights and certain minorities, human rights were, at least until the UN Charter, considered a question falling within the "domestic jurisdiction" of states and thus not a matter of "international concern".

[20] See Daes, *Freedom of the Individual under Law – A Study on the Individual's Duties to the Community and the Limitations on Human Rights and Freedoms under Article 29 of the Universal Declaration of Human Rights* (UN Centre for Human Rights, Geneva, Study Series No. 3, 1990) [hereinafter "Daes"], p. 50.

[21] For example, if a relation of mine dies without leaving a will, the law may determine that I have a right to some portion of the deceased's estate. The only duty in question is that of the personal representative to distribute to me that to which I am entitled.

It might also be noted in passing that the argument is, at all events, dependent on an assumption that is itself contestable, namely, that international law directly invests individuals with rights.[22] While that assumption may well be gradually evolving into reality, it could be argued that it has not yet fully materialized. The view could be asserted that international law imposes an obligation on governments to respect human rights, rather than conferring on individuals rights against governments.[23] The resolution of this point is beyond the scope of this paper.

Let us now look at some of the major international human rights instruments to see what guidance they offer. According to the proclamatory paragraph of the Universal Declaration of Human Rights,[24] the United Nations General Assembly:

> *Proclaims* this Universal Declaration of Human Rights as a common standard of achievement for all peoples and all nations, to the end that every individual and every organ of society, keeping this Declaration constantly in mind, shall strive by teaching and education to promote respect for these rights and freedoms and by progressive measures, national and international, to secure their universal and effective recognition and observance, both among the peoples of Member States themselves and among the peoples of territories under their jurisdiction.

At first sight this landmark document seems addressed to "every individual and every organ of society". But what is the nature of the obligation? It is to "strive to promote respect" for human rights and "to strive...to secure their universal and effective recognition and observance". Even if we take the Declaration as laying down international legal obligations,[25] the obligation contained in the quoted language cannot be interpreted as being imposed either on individuals or on organs of society directly to respect or observe human rights. It is merely to engage in teaching and education to *promote* respect for them and to *secure* their observance.

[22] Daes, *supra* note 20, argues the case for duties in this area, but acknowledges that the issue is one of intense controversy (p.50, para. 196 and p. 51, para. 210). It is not clear how far Daes is insisting on reading legal, as opposed to moral, duties into the Declaration and other instruments (see pp. 52–3, paras. 224–29).

[23] Until the adoption in October 1990 of Protocol No. 9 to the European Convention on Human Rights, no international instrument permitted access by an individual to an intergovernmental body capable of awarding a legally-binding decision. Even this right is subject to the states' original acceptance of the compulsory jurisdiction of the European Court of Human Rights under Article 46 of the Convention (Protocol 9, Article 5, amending Convention Article 48), which in turn is subject to the possibility of a state's denouncing the Convention under Article 65.

[24] UN General Assembly res. 217A (III), 10 Dec. 1948.

[25] Technically, the Declaration, being a resolution of the General Assembly, is merely a recommendation. The better view nowadays is that some, if not all, of the rights and freedoms it proclaims are those referred to but not spelt out in Articles 55 and 56 of the UN Charter, by which UN member states are pledged to act "to promote universal respect for, and observance of, human rights and fundamental freedoms for all". The Charter does not, of course, mention duties.

The language coming closest to that of formal obligation may be found in the two preambular paragraphs preceding the above quoted proclamatory paragraph:

> *Whereas* Member States have pledged themselves to achieve, in cooperation with the United Nations, the promotion of universal respect for and observance of human rights and fundamental freedoms,
> *Whereas* a common understanding of these rights and freedoms is of the greatest importance for the full realization of this pledge,

It is states, then, that are *pledged* to promote respect for and observance of human rights, the contents of *their* pledge being spelled out in the articles of the Declaration.

Article 1 of the Declaration is partly addressed to individuals. It states: "All human beings are born free and equal in dignity and rights. They are endowed with reason and conscience *and should act towards one another in a spirit of brotherhood.*" All but the words I have emphasized are in the language of fact or, perhaps, of faith. The only normative words are the emphasized ones. The use of the word "should" makes them manifestly hortatory, not obligatory.

It is Article 29 that contains language most susceptible of interpretation as imposing duties on individuals. It reads:

1. Everyone has duties to the community in which alone the free and full development of his personality is possible.
2. In the exercise of his rights and freedoms, everyone shall be subject only to such limitations as are determined by law solely for the purpose of securing due recognition and respect for the rights and freedoms of others and of meeting the just requirements of morality, public order and the general welfare in a democratic society.
3. These rights and freedoms may in no case be exercised contrary to the purposes and principles of the United Nations.

The first paragraph speaks plainly of duties, but it is silent as to what these may be. The next two paragraphs indicate merely that the scope of the rights is not necessarily infinite, that they, or some of them, may not be absolute. The article must, of course, be read as a whole. That way the significance of the first paragraph emerges. It is not a free-standing assertion of a radically-new doctrine, whose content is perversely left unstated. It is language similar to that in Article 1 – language of fact or faith. It reflects the notion on which the next two paragraphs are based. It is, ultimately, simply the ideological basis for acknowledging that the scope of the enunciated rights is not absolute. Nothing more in the way of normative obligation can justifiably be read into the quoted words.[26]

The last article of the Declaration (Article 30) also contains language relevant to our discussion:

[26] Thus, the range of duties Daes hangs on to Article 29(1) [Daes, *supra* note 20, pp. 53–64] must generally be understood to refer to moral, rather than legal, duties: see above, note 22.

> Nothing in this Declaration may be interpreted as implying for any State, group or person any right to engage in any activity or to perform any act aimed at the destruction of any of the rights and freedoms set forth herein.

Here we have words touching the acts of groups and individuals. What is more, the context is one where, if the Declaration were to impose duties on groups or individuals, such duties might most be expected to be found. What more central duty might there be than that of refraining from acting to destroy the human rights of others? Yet Article 30 imposes no such duty. It limits itself to laying down a rule of interpretation, a rule similar to those contained in Article 29, paragraphs 2 and 3.

The Declaration seems, therefore, a most fragile basis on which to construct a doctrine of individual duties to respect human rights, in the sense that a failure to comply would make the individual a human rights violator. We shall see that the international human rights treaties offer even less support for such a doctrine.

Thus preambular paragraph 5 common to both International Human Rights Covenants[27] describes States Parties as:

> *Realizing* that the individual, having duties to other individuals and to the community to which he belongs, is under a responsibility to strive for the promotion and observance of the rights recognized in the present Covenant.

The language is a combination of that contained in the proclamatory paragraph and in Article 29(1) of the Universal Declaration. It has been argued that it should not be treated as being "without legal significance".[28] This may be so. But, even if it could be understood as being a basis of obligation, the content of that obligation is, as has already been seen, not far-reaching. It is one of *striving* for the promotion and observance of human rights only. It hardly supports an interpretation by which there would be imposed a direct obligation to refrain from committing acts which, if committed by government officials, would be considered human rights violations.

Article 5 of the International Covenant on Civil and Political Rights (ICCPR) virtually repeats the language of Article 30 of the Universal Declaration.[29] It too can therefore have no more significance than had the latter.

[27] International Covenant on Economic, Social and Cultural Rights and International Covenant on Civil and Political Rights, adopted by UN General Assembly res. 2200A(XXI), 16 Dec. 1966.

[28] Daes, *supra* note 20, p. 50, para. 190.

[29] According to Article 5, "1. Nothing in the present Covenant may be interpreted as implying for any State, group or person any right to engage in any activity or to perform any act aimed at the destruction of any of the rights or freedoms recognized herein, or at their limitation to a greater extent than is provided for in the present Covenant. 2. No restriction upon or derogation from any of the fundamental human rights recognized or existing in any country in virtue of law, conventions, regulations or custom shall be admitted on the pretext that the present Covenant does not recognize such rights or that it recognizes them to a lesser extent."

It is an interpretative article, not a duty-creating one.[30]

On the other hand, the structure of both Covenants makes clear that their whole thrust is towards establishing obligations on *states*. The second article of each Covenant develops at length the nature of the undertaking involved in adhering to the instruments. In the case of the ICCPR the obligations are those of respecting and ensuring the human rights laid down in the subsequent text.[31] In the case of the Covenant on Economic, Social and Cultural Rights, the obligation is one of taking steps towards the rights established.[32]

What are we to make, it may nevertheless be asked, of the fact that Article 20 of the ICCPR requires states parties to prohibit incitement to racial hatred and war propaganda?[33] Surely this is suggestive of the imposition of duties upon individuals? Certainly, this is the one article of the Covenant that goes so far. In so doing, it passes beyond language merely restricting the scope of the rights contained in the Covenant, in this case, freedom of expression spelt out

[30] This is certainly the approach of the organs of the European Convention on Human Rights in interpreting Article 17 of that Convention, which is framed in terms similar to those of Declaration Article 30 and Covenant Article 5(1). Moreover, it appears to apply only to those freedoms that would be destroyed as a result of their exercise by those seeking to invoke them, not to rights which would not be so effected; in other words, freedom of expression may not be invocable on behalf of expression advocating totalitarian government, but such persons would still have a right to a fair trial: see, e.g. A. and D. Spielmann, "La Notion de l'abus de droit à la lumi]ere de la Convention européenne de sauvegarde des droits de l'homme et des libertés fondamentales" in Council of Europe – Legal Affairs, *Abuse of Rights and Equivalent Concepts: The Principle and Its Present Day Application* (1990), p. 58.

[31] Article 2(1): "Each State party to the present Covenant undertakes to respect and to ensure to all individuals within its territory and subject to its jurisdiction the rights recognized in the present Covenant, without distinction of any kind, such as race, colour, sex, language, religion, political or other opinion, national or social origin, property, birth or other status." By paragraph 3 of the same article, states undertake to provide an "effective remedy" in the case of a violation of the rights, "nothwithstanding that the violation has been committed by persons acting in an official capacity". This latter formulation lured Matas (*supra* note 7, p. 23) into believing that the implication is that "persons who do not act in an official capacity can violate rights and freedoms recognized by the Covenant." This strained reading misses the obvious point of the clause, namely, that traditional doctrines of sovereign immunity at the national level (e.g. "the crown can do no wrong"), by which the state and its officials may not be sued or, in some cases, prosecuted, should not be invocable to prevent the appropriate remedy being claimed by the victim of the violation.

[32] Article 2(1): "Each State Party to the present Covenant undertakes to take steps, individually and through international assistance and co-operation, especially economic and technical, to the maximum of its available resources, with a view to achieving progressively the full realization of the rights recognized in the present Covenant by all appropriate means, including particularly the adoption of legislative measures." The vague nature of the legal obligations undertaken by States Parties to the Economic and Social Covenant stems from the dependence of the rights on the availability of the economic resources necessary to vouchsafe them.

[33] Article 20: "1. Any propaganda for war shall be prohibited by law. 2. Any advocacy of national, racial or religious hatred that constitutes incitement to discrimination, hostility or violence shall be prohibited by law."

in Article 19. Insofar as states have not made reservations to Article 20,[34] they are bound to ensure that they have legislation prohibiting the expression in question. But it is not the contention of this paper that international law in general, or international human rights law, in particular, may not impose obligations on states to constrain the behaviour of private individuals. On the contrary, a state may well fall foul of its human rights obligations by failing to create the conditions necessary for the enjoyment of human rights. A state which allows private individuals or groups to prevent others from exercising their rights to freedom of expression, association or assembly, for example, may well be failing in its duty to ensure those freedoms.[35] The point is that it is in this failure that human rights would be violated. In other words, the human rights violation would consist not in the actions of the private individuals or groups, but in the omission of the state in preventing their actions.

Similarly, the International Convention on the Elimination of All Forms of Racial Discrimination[36] requires extensive action against individuals and groups. For example, under Article 2(1)(d), States Parties are to "prohibit and bring to an end...racial discrimination by any persons, group or organization", while Article 4 expands on the Covenant Article 20 requirement of prohibiting incitement to racial hatred. Again it is state action that is required; no direct international legal obligation is imposed on private groups or individuals engaging in the activities that are to be repressed. The human rights violation again occurs when the state fails to discharge its obligations to prevent the undesired acts.

We saw earlier in this section that there is the notion of "crimes under international law", in respect of which states are expected to exercise criminal jurisdiction even if it has no direct connection with the crime, the victim or the perpetrator. We must now ask the question whether international human rights law envisages such crimes and, if so, whether it does so in respect of the activities of private individuals or groups other than those acting in some form of collusion with public authorities. Two treaties are especially pertinent to this inquiry: the Genocide Convention and the Convention against Torture.

The Genocide Convention[37] explicitly contemplates the possibility of private individuals being guilty of the crime of genocide. Having, in Article I, proclaimed genocide to be a "crime under international law", the Convention proceeds to define the crime, in Article II, as consisting in various measures, including killing, committed with the intent to destroy a national, ethnic, racial or religious group "as such". According to Article II, genocide is to be punished and, under Article III, the inchoate offences of conspiracy, incitement and attempt to commit genocide, as well as complicity in it, are also to be punished.

[34] Several countries, e.g. Australia, Denmark and the United Kingdom, have made reservations to Article 20.

[35] See, e.g., my remarks on *Drittwirkung*, *supra* note 3, and accompanying text.

[36] Adopted by UN General Assembly res. 2106A(XX), 21 Dec. 1965.

[37] Convention on the Prevention and Punishment of the Crime of Genocide, adopted by UN General Assembly res. 260A(III), 9 Dec. 1948.

Article IV stipulates that offenders are punishable "whether they are constitutionally responsible rulers, public officials or *private individuals*" (emphasis added). This would seem to suggest that we are faced with a departure from the normal pattern.

This is not necessarily so. Except for the fact that the Convention applies in peacetime as well as wartime (Article I), the definition is essentially that applied by the Nuremberg Tribunal to the most heinous of the crimes against humanity it was called upon to judge. Genocide had been a crime committed by Nazi Germany and the international trials indicted public officials and private individuals, acting *in collusion with* the state. It was probably not conceivable that genocide could occur without the framework of the state apparatus. So it could well be argued that the Convention should be interpreted in this context. In any event, the reference to private individuals in Article IV can easily be understood as being necessary to ensure proper scope for the inchoate offences referred to in Article III.

If we nevertheless take the view that genocide may be committed outside a programme of state-sponsored activity, it would still only be necessary to acknowledge it as an exception to the rule, applicable to a phenomenon that, far from being a simple violation of the rights of an individual, is an extreme, massive assault on a specific population as such. One could not think of a more appropriate exception.[38]

The Convention against Torture,[39] however, provides us with a manifest reaffirmation of the rule. Article 1 of that Convention defines torture. An integral part of the definition is that torture has to be "inflicted by or at the instigation of or with the consent or acquiescence of a public official or other person acting in an official capacity". Under Article 4, an attempt to commit torture or participation or complicity in torture are to be offences punishable by the state. The torturer does not have to be a public official for the purposes of committing an offence contemplated by the Convention, but does have to be acting at the instigation of one, with the consent or acquiescence of one, or together with, or in complicity with one. It is the official connection which makes the offence one of international concern.[40]

[38] The same could be said for the crime of *apartheid*, which is the subject of the International Convention on the Suppression and Punishment of the Crime of *Apartheid*, adopted by UN General Assembly res. 3068(XXVIII), 30 Nov. 1973. Of course, the essence of *apartheid* is that it is a state-imposed system.

[39] Convention against Torture and Other Cruel, Inhuman or Degrading Treatment or Punishment, adopted by UN General Assembly res. 39/46, 10 Dec. 1984.

[40] The Inter-American Convention to Prevent and Punish Torture confirms the approach. A most controversial issue in the drafting process – one that was left unresolved until the final adoption of the text by the General Assembly of the Organization of American States – was whether there should be the same sort of "public official" limitation on the regional instrument. The view that prevailed was in favour of the limitation. The majority clearly felt that international concern did not extend to private torture: see N. S. Rodley, *The Treatment of Prisoners under International Law*, Oxford: Clarendon Press (1987), p. 49.

It has been argued that "the more specific instruments should not be used to read down the

Furthermore, the international community has been called upon to consider recently the basic proposition under consideration here. In 1990, Peru, joined by Colombia and the Philippines – all constitutional democracies faced with violent armed oppositions[41] both political and, in the cases of Colombia and Peru, connected to organized drug traffic – brought the activities of "armed groups and drug dealers" to the attention of the UN Commission on Human Rights. Peru is understood informally to have sought a resolution, by which the Commission would establish a study group on "acts of violence committed by armed groups and drug dealers that infringe human rights". What emerged was a resolution expressing concern at the "adverse effect on the enjoyment of human rights" of such acts by such groups.[42] Commission rapporteurs and working groups were asked to give consideration to the matter. The debate made it clear that there was opposition to the notion of the acts of non-governmental groups being considered a proper subject for Commission consideration even in this reduced context.[43] Yet, it would seem obvious that the acts of the groups in question can have an adverse effect on the enjoyment of human rights, if only because of the difficulties they create for governments in pursuing counter-insurgency strategies without recourse to human rights violations. At all events, the Commission was patently unprepared to countenance the notion that the group in question could directly infringe human rights.[44]

This attitude seems entirely consistent with, and corroborative of, the general argument of this paper so far, that is, that international law imposes duties on governments to respect and ensure human rights; it imposes no such duties on private individuals and groups beyond, perhaps, expecting them to strive for the promotion of human rights. However, the area of law known as international humanitarian law contains elements leading us to some modification of this position. The UN has called this branch of the law that of "human rights in armed conflicts". The main instruments of international humanitarian law are the four Geneva Conventions of 1 August 1949 on the protection of victims of war and the two Additional Protocols of 1977 to the

---

more general instruments" (Matas, *supra* note 7, p. 24). The statement seems to assume that the public-official limitation is a down-reading, rather than a necessary clarification once precise and strict obligations are being assumed. And, as has been seen, the more general instruments cannot be easily "read up" to target individuals as human rights violators.

[41] See, e.g. *Amnesty International Report* 1990, pp. 69–72 (Colombia), 190–94 (Peru) and 194–97 (Philippines).

[42] UN Commission on Human Rights res. 1990/75, 7 March 1990.

[43] See UN doc. E/CN.4/1990/SR.54, paras. 1–15.

[44] Interestingly, two of the Commission's thematic bodies (the Working Group of Enforced or Involuntary Disappearances [UN doc. E/CN.4/1991/20 and Add.1] and Special Rapporteur on Torture [E/CN.4/1991/17] seem to have ignored the resolution. In the past, the Special Rapporteur on Summary or Arbitrary Executions has expressed concern about the "non-respect for the right to life by groups opposing the Government or not under its control" [e.g. E/CN.4/1988/22, paras. 182–87 and E/CN.4/1989/25, para. 23]. In his 1991 report he drops this classification addressing rather "situations of internal conflict" [E/CN.4/1991/36, paras. 583–96]. That this latter approach is consistent with the argument of this paper emerges from what appears below.

1949 Conventions.[45] Most of the 1949 Conventions and the First Additional Protocol of 1977 deal with international armed conflict and is not of concern to us here. While they do envisage state imposition of legal duties on individuals, including criminal prosecution of grave breaches, this concerns mainly state officials in a transnational context.

However, Article 3 common to the four Conventions and the Second Additional Protocol (Protocol II) relate to the conduct of armed conflicts not of an international character. Moreover, they apply to any party to such a conflict, not merely the governmental party. Many of their provisions cover subject matter analogous to human rights norms, in respect of non-combatants or persons *hors de combat*. For example, they prohibit torture, murder and execution of sentences imposed after unfair criminal trials.[46] There are good grounds, therefore, to consider a non-governmental party to non-international armed conflict as being capable of violating human rights in armed conflict. The problem is to determine when such a conflict exists and what body of persons can qualify as a non-governmental party to such a conflict.

Article 1 of Protocol II defines non-international armed conflicts as ones

> "which take place in the territory of a High Contracting Party between its armed forces and dissident armed forces which, under responsible command, exercise such control over a part of its territory as to enable them to carry out sustained and concerted military operations and to implement this Protocol."

[45] Geneva Convention for the Amelioration of the Condition of the Wounded and Sick in Armed Forces in the Field of August 12, 1949; Geneva Convention for the Amelioration of the Condition of the Wounded, Sick and Shipwrecked Members of Armed Forces at Sea of August 12, 1949; Geneva Convention relative to the Treatment of Prisoners of War of August 12, 1949; Geneva Convention relative to the Protection of Civilian Persons in Time of War of August 12, 1949; Protocol Additional to the Geneva Conventions of 12 August 1949, and relating to the Protection of Victims of International Armed Conflicts (Protocol I); and Protocol Additional to the Geneva Conventions of 12 August 1949, and relating to the Protection of Victims of Non-International Armed Conflicts (Protocol II).

[46] The normative part of Article 3 common to the four Geneva Conventions reads:

> "In the case of armed conflict not of an international character occurring in the territory of one of the High Contracting Parties, each Party to the conflict shall be bound to apply, as a minimum, the following provisions:
>
> (1) Persons taking no active part in the hostilities, including members of armed forces who have laid down their arms and those placed *hors de combat* by sickness, wounds, detention, or any other cause, shall in all circumstances be treated humanely, without any adverse distinction founded on race, colour, religion or faith, sex, birth or wealth, or any other similar criteria.
>
> To this end, the following acts are and shall remain prohibited at any time and in any place whatsoever with respect to the above-mentioned persons: (a) violence to life and person, in particular murder of all kinds, mutilation, cruel treatment and torture; (b) taking of hostages; (c) outrages upon personal dignity, in particular humiliating and degrading treatment; (d) the passing of sentences and the carrying out of executions without previous judgment pronounced by a regularly constituted court, affording all the judicial guarantees which are recognized as indispensable by civilized peoples. (2) The wounded and sick shall be collected and cared for."

Excluded from the scope of the Protocol are "situations of internal disturbances and tensions, such as riots, isolated and sporadic acts of violence and other acts of a similar nature, as not being armed conflicts." This language is generally considered as signifying that the conflict would have to be of virtual civil war proportions, with the non-governmental party able to deploy force on a scale barely distinguishable from the governmental party. This implies a very high threshold, possibly only attainable by a party about to be successful. It is rarely found. Common Article 3 to the four Conventions contains no threshold at all. It is generally believed that it should not be interpreted as implying a threshold as high as that contained in Protocol II. On the other hand, it is similarly understood that it does not apply whenever any group of people takes up arms against the state. The proper threshold of Common Article 3 is probably somewhere above "a mere act of banditry or an unorganized and short-lived insurrection"[47] but below hostilities of civil war dimensions. There would certainly be no reason not to include certain "national liberation movements" which, controversially, were considered by Additional Protocol I as taking part in international armed conflicts.[48]

Interestingly, the UN Declaration against Torture gives us language that can be said to summarize this test.[49] The paragraph of the resolution by which the General Assembly adopted the Declaration stipulated that the Declaration was a "guideline for all States and *other entities exercising effective power*". I suggest that the emphasized words capture precisely the spirit of both the conceptual scope of human rights and the rationale behind the international law approach to them. It conveys the reality of the human rights equation: the individual at the mercy of a government or of another power over whose actions the government is impotent. Of course, there may be difficulty in identifying whether a particular armed opposition group should be considered as falling above or below the threshold, as being required *directly* to respect basic rights or not. The concept, however, remains intact.

This notion also permits us to deal with a final argument that can be made to justify treating armed opposition groups as human rights violators. Accord-

[47] This is the language of the official International Committee of the Red Cross Commentary to common Article 3, taken from Pictet (ed.), *Geneva Conventions of 12 August 1949 – Commentary – I Geneva Convention* (1952), p. 50.

[48] Article 1(4) of Protocol I includes within its purview: "armed conflicts in which peoples are fighting against colonial domination and alien occupation and against racist regimes in the exercise of their right of self-determination, as enshrined in the Charter of the United Nations and the Declaration on Principles of International Law concerning Friendly Relations and Co-operation among States in accordance with the Charter of the United Nations." Parties to such conflicts would include the African National Congress and the Pan-Africanist Congress (South Africa; recognized by the UN and the Organization of African Unity); Polisario (Western Sahara/Morocco; recognized by the Organization of African Unity); and the Palestine Liberation Organization/Palestine (Israeli-occupied Territories; recognized by the UN and the League of Arab States).

[49] Declaration on the Protection of All Persons from Being Subjected to Torture and Other Cruel, Inhuman or Degrading Treatment or Punishment, adopted by UN General Assembly res. 3452(XXX), 9 Dec. 1975.

ing to this argument, principles of state responsibility recognize that insurgent groups, if they are successful, can engage the responsibility of the state for acts they committed during the insurgency.[50] This being so, it is suggested, such groups can be considered as human rights violators. The argument has to confront an obvious difficulty, namely that it is necessary to await the successful outcome before the state may be held responsible under international law for the insurgents' acts. This difficulty could be overcome, however, if we could treat the acts of a *potentially* successful insurgent group on the same plane as those of an *eventually* successful such group. The notion of a party to an armed conflict permits us to do just that. An insurgent group effectively becomes a party to an armed conflict when it has sufficient attributes to put the outcome of the conflict in doubt. That is the effect of the application of the criteria just discussed for identifying a party to an armed conflict. A non-governmental party to an armed conflict so understood is a potentially successful insurgent group. Such a group can and should be considered as capable of violating human rights. The argument simply does not apply to groups not qualifying for the title.

4. The Political Perspective

It does not necessarily follow that, because the law has a particular approach (in this case one consistent with the amended traditional version of human rights expounded in the section on the conceptual perspective), political discourse should be constrained by the same approach. The history of human rights as a political programme has been the history of attempts first to formulate concepts of their specific content and then to secure the legal recognition of those concepts. Their recent entry into the domain of international law was mainly an achievement of the post-World War II era. So the mere fact that they have succeeded this far is not of itself an argument for not going further, if such progress were perceived to be desirable.

I have heard this point made in terms suggesting that, by definition, going further is desirable, as though any legal approach were automatically suspect. Since the legal approach on the present topic is consistent with the sounder conceptual approach, the burden of advocating a different approach is arguably on those who propose that political doctrine demands the different approach. In fact there appears to be no coherent attempt to make the case (other than on the basis of the above discussed conceptual and legal issues). But the case that has generally been made during policy discussions of how to deal with the problem is as follows.[51]

(a) A government, particularly one facing activities of an armed opposition

[50] Matas, *supra* note 7, p.20.

[51] Amnesty International has long debated the issue internally. The paper by Matas, *supra,* note 7, is a contribution to that continuing debate.

group that commits acts which, if committed by a government, would be called human rights violations, will wish to discredit that group and may then wish to call its activities human rights violations. It will be especially inclined to do this if its own agents are committing human rights violations, with the aim of dissipating the discredit such violations bring on itself (the "*tu quoque*" argument referred to earlier). It may also wish to reproach those, such as human rights organizations, who draw attention to its human rights violations, for not being impartial in expression of concern if they have ignored the equivalent actions of the opposition. Sometimes such reproaches go as far as identifying such human rights reporters as collaborators with the opposition.[52] In this respect, it is understood to be in the *interests* of governments (or at least those governments confronted with the problem) to denote armed opposition groups as "human rights violators". 2. A human rights defence organization may see various reasons for taking the same line. First (and, I believe, foremost), it will not wish to be politically wrong-footed when confronted by the governmental reproach just referred to. Second, it will be sensitive to the suggestion that the moral integrity of its message needs to be unambiguous both to the outside world and to its own internal constituency. Conceptual and legal subtleties do not always ring out clear in the clash of political debate. I shall take the arguments attributed to these two key political actors in turn.

There are many examples of *governments* using the "*tu quoque*" retort, or otherwise complaining of a lack of even-handedness when their human rights violations are denounced. So they obviously see some merit in it, sometimes. It should be noted, however, that the retort is not always couched in "human rights" terms. Usually, the armed groups members are denounced as "terrorists" rather than human rights violators, and their acts as "acts of terrorism" rather than human rights violations.

Why should this be so? Presumably governments adopt that terminology because they see it as more calculated to elicit public support for themselves and condemnation of the opposition than other terminology, such as that of human rights. Indeed, a moment's reflection would reveal how ludicrously inapt human rights language would be. Another explanation might be that, precisely because the traditional concept of human rights is the one most readily understood in common parlance, governments do not wish to dignify the armed opposition groups as having government-like attributes.

A further explanation may be that not all governments speak in the language of extreme short-term interest (even if the occasional angry political official may be tempted to do so). After all, what is the legal position detailed earlier if not a formal description of the settled view which governments generally maintain of what is appropriate language from the perspective of their long-

[52] E.g. the Philippines, and "red-labelling", see UN Commission on Human Rights, *Report on the Visit to the Philippines by two members of the Working Group on Enforced or Involuntary Disappearances*, UN doc. E/CN.4/1991/20/Add.1, para. 163; *Amnesty International Report 1990*, p. 194.

term interests, established after protracted reflection? It is true that not all governments are confronted with armed opposition at any one time. Yet many are the states, possibly a majority, that have had to face the problem during the major period of drafting international human rights instruments. Indeed, insofar as the "Western group" has been the principal mover in initiating international human rights standard-setting, that group has known extensive problems of organized armed opposition.[53] They would have had to be profoundly neglectful of their own interests blindly to allow the standards to be framed as applying to their own behaviour and not to that of their opponents, if such were in fact against their interests. Indeed, their vigorous resistance to any idea of extending the scope of those standards suggests most strongly that the legal position is an accurate reflection of those interests.

A further reason why governments may, on reflection, consider the "*tu quoque*" strategy not in their long-term interests is that, since the strategy is a means of minimizing the negative public impact of human rights violations committed by their own agents, it may have the effect of encouraging those agents to pursue a counter-insurgency programme that relies on human rights violations, including the most extreme violations. Such a counter-insurgency programme may have the opposite of the effect intended: far from achieving pacification it may well engender hatred and deprive the government of the very legitimacy it seeks to defend. For example, it would be rash not to suggest that, as a result of the atrocities committed by governments in the "southern cone" of South America, there were fewer adherents of the "doctrine of national security" in the late 1980s than in the early 1970s.[54] Furthermore, a human-rights-violating counter-insurgency programme can severely delegitimize a government abroad. It is hard to imagine, for instance, that world reaction to the Argentinean invasion of the Falkland Islands (Islas Malvinas) or to the Iraqi invasion of Kuwait would have been as vigorous if the governments of the invading states had not already, by virtue of their notorious internal brutality, been deeply discredited. It is well-known that external relations, such as in the area of foreign economic assistance, can be undermined in a less extreme form when governments engage in systematic human rights violations. In a real sense, then, governments have an interest in not being held responsible for human rights violations and, therefore, an interest in discouraging resort to them by their security forces when the latter are called on to combat an armed opposition. The "*tu quoque*" argument may have the contrary effect, by implicitly cancelling out one set of violations (those of the security forces) by

[53] E.g. the Irish Republican Army in the United Kingdom (and operating in numerous other countries), the Red Army Faction in Germany (and also operating in numerous other countries) and the Red Brigades in Italy, not to mention the activities of various Palestinian and other Middle Eastern groups operating in Western Europe.

[54] According to this doctrine, the Latin American military conceived itself as having an extra-constitutional role, using extra-legal methods, to protect the state from communist "subversion": see Weschler, *A Miracle, A Universe Settling Accounts with Torturers* (1990), *passim*.

another set (the abuses of the armed opposition), thus encouraging that which is to be discouraged.

Non-governmental organizations (NGOs) monitoring human rights violations have certainly been stung by the taunt that in ignoring human-rights-like abuses by armed opposition groups they are failing to distribute moral disapproval impartially. We might first ask why they have exposed themselves to this charge. The historical answer probably lies in their unstated, and perhaps at first unconscious, acceptance of the notion of human rights as traditionally understood. Another reason might be found in a broader concept of impartiality: this is particularly the case for international human rights NGOs. Such organizations are expected to be impartial as between different governments.[55] The 170-odd governments of the world owe their positions to various factors, ranging from popular legitimation by pluralist, constitutional institutions to the threat or use of naked terror. Adherents of all political doctrines, except absolute pacifism, would encompass the legitimacy of internal resort to armed force to displace governments at the latter end of the range.[56] Yet they would not agree on which those governments are, nor could they do so without abandoning the principle of impartiality towards all governments. So a politically viable conception of human rights must avoid ruling out resort to armed opposition. And, until an armed opposition group has succeeded in becoming an entity exercising effective power as defined in the previous section, there are few traditional manifestations of armed resistance that could not also be described as human rights violations, were they to be undertaken by governments. Meanwhile, they have been able to demonstrate impartiality by holding all governments to the same standard. In the case of governments facing armed opposition, impartiality means applying the standard whatever the colour of the government or of the opposition it faces.

Finally, a factor that may also be in the minds of human rights NGOs is the very invocability of international standards. Such organizations may be expected to feel more comfortable in urging their concerns on governments when they can point to international standards relevant to those concerns that have been accepted, expressly or implicitly, by the governments. In essence, they can claim to be holding the governments to pledges the governments themselves have made, thereby avoiding the reproach that they are seeking to

[55] Thus, a ground for the withdrawal of consultative status from a non-governmental organization enjoying such status with UN-ECOSOC includes "systematically engaging in...politically motivated acts" against UN member states: ECOSOC res. 1296(XLIV), 23 May 1968, para. 36. It is generally understood that this implies an obligation to refrain from questioning the legitimacy of a government of a UN member state or otherwise asserting that resort to armed force against such a government may be justified.

[56] As, seemingly, would be the Universal Declaration of Human Rights which, in its third preambular paragraph, considers it essential that human rights be protected by the rule of law "if man is not to be compelled to have recourse, as a last resort, to rebellion against tyranny and repression".

impose unwanted or alien values on the governments and the societies they govern. The same cannot usually be said regarding armed opposition groups. Only rarely will they have reason to feel bound by international standards.[57]

5. Conclusion

Conceptually, legally and politically it is appropriate to consider human rights rules as being applicable only to the relations between, on the one hand, governments or groups having power similar to that of governments and, on the other, those over whom the governments or groups exercise that power. Does this mean we must simply turn a blind eye to the atrocities of armed opposition groups (not being parties to an armed conflict) or ignore the difficulties of official security forces called upon to confront such groups? I suggest not.

This is not the place to discuss the complexities of counter-insurgency warfare. There are, however, at least two avenues of constructive involvement that could enhance an approach based on the spirit of human rights.

First, human rights reporting need not and should not be so narrowly focused as to be misleading. The ethos of such reporting is that of shedding the light of truth on areas that human rights violators normally seek to conceal. Where human rights violations occur in the context of and in response to armed opposition, it is not in keeping with that ethos to fail to acknowledge the situation as a whole, including abuses or atrocities committed by the opposition.[58] Reporting of this nature, albeit refraining from categorizing such abuses or atrocities as human rights violations, would make it much harder for governments to legitimately reproach human rights reporters with moral selectiveness and would thus undermine their attempts implicitly to excuse the behaviour of their own agents. It would also make it that much more difficult for the opposition cynically to exploit the human rights issue without regard to their own behaviour.

Second, there are increasing possibilities of technical cooperation to assist governments in complying with international human rights and humanitarian law standards. The United Nations, the Commonwealth and the International Committee of the Red Cross all have programmes of assistance in this area. There are also bilateral programmes available. Governments genuinely seeking to avoid violating human rights while confronting armed opposition may well be able to seek material help and expertise from such sources. They should seriously consider doing so.

[57] E.g., where such a group formally accepts to be bound by all or part of the Geneva Conventions of 12 August 1949 and the Protocols. The PLO has done so (and it has also sought to do so on behalf of the "State of Palestine"): International Review of the Red Cross, No. 274 (Jan-Feb. 1990), pp. 64–65.

[58] An excellent example of such contextual reporting may be found in the report of the Working Group on Enforced or Involuntary Disappearances on its visit to the Philippines, *op. cit supra*, note 52.

PATRICIA FREEMAN MARSHALL*

Violence Against Women in Canada by Non-State Actors: The State and Women's Human Rights

1. Introduction

A terrible commonality is shared by women throughout the world: their experience of violence, and the threat of victimization they constantly face. Robin Morgan summed it up well when she wrote:

> Look closely at her. She crosses a city street juggling her briefcase and her sack of groceries or she walks down a dirt road balancing a basket on her head. Or she hurries toward her locked car pulling a small child along with her. Or she trudges home from the fields, the baby strapped to her back.
>
> Suddenly there are footsteps behind her. Heavy, rapid.
>
> A man's footsteps. She knows this immediately, just as she knows that she must not look around. She quickens her pace in time to the quickening of her pulse. She is afraid. He could be a rapist. He could be a soldier, a harasser, a robber, a killer. He could be none of these. He could be a man in a hurry. He could be a man merely walking at his normal pace. But she fears him. She fears him because he is a man. She has reason to fear.
>
> She does not feel the same way – on city street, on dirt road, in parking lot or field – if she hears a woman's footsteps behind her.
>
> It is a footstep of a man she fears. This moment she shares with every human being who is female.
>
> This is the democratization of fear.[1]

2. Sexual Assault and Human Rights

Women's right to security of the person and the right of women and children to equal benefit and protection of the law are basic human rights enshrined in the

* Co-Chair of the Federally appointed Canadian Panel on Violence Against Women.

[1] Robin Morgan, *The Demon Lover, Or The Sexuality of Terrorism* (1989), p. 23.

K.E. Mahoney and P. Mahoney (eds.), Human Rights in the Twenty-first Century, 319–334.

UN Declaration on Human Rights, articles 3 and 7, and also in Canada's own *Charter of Rights and Freedoms*, specifically in sections 7 and 15.

There is an overwhelming need for international human rights agencies and instruments to recognize the extent to which sexual assault, wife abuse, pornography and prostitution practised by non-state actors violate women's and children's human rights. Often the State supports these practices by its passivity or through legal systems where rights of victims are ignored or subverted.

This paper takes a first look at many of the ways in which Canada as a state, plays an active role in increasing the harm sexual violence does to women and thereby furthers the violation of their basic human rights.

3. Sexual Violence against Women in Canada

While we in Canada are quick to condemn overt violent practices against women in other parts of the world, the violent behaviour perpetrated against women by men in our society is pervasive and widely tolerated. In Canada the continuum of violent behaviour experienced by women includes sexual assault, wife assault, sexual harassment at home, at work and on the streets, the widespread celebration of violence in advertising and entertainment, attacks on prostitutes, and the violence and degradation of women in the production and consumption of pornography. It includes sexual abuse perpetrated in all kinds of institutions: in doctors' clinics, in lawyers' offices, in classrooms, and in churches.

Victimization research tells us that in Canada, at least one woman in four will be sexually assaulted at some time in her life.[2] The Canadian Governments have not acknowledged the dimensions of this violence, and no comprehensive initiatives have been developed to address the problem. As a society, we are reluctant to admit the existence of this unrelenting, constant, and ubiquitous violence perpetrated against women by men. We rarely acknowledge that it is, in reality, gender-based oppression and sexual terrorism – an assault against women's basic human rights.

Most women in Canada never report sexual assault. Estimates of reporting rates vary from 10 to 40 per cent of actual sexual assaults. Mistrust of the criminal justice system has been identified as the major reason women give for not reporting the crimes to which they have been subjected. The courts, which embody the official State response to sexual assault, are identified as adding to the injury women experience in a number of ways.[3]

In 1985, in an effort to identify some of the factors influencing reporting rates of crimes against women, Toronto-based METRAC (Metro Action

[2] Brickman and Brière, 'Incidence of Rape and Sexual Assault in an Urban Canadian Population' (1984), 7 *International Journal of Women's Studies*, pp. 195–206.

[3] Canada, Solicitor General, *Urban Victimization Survey: Reported and Unreported Crimes* (1984).

Committee on Public Violence Against Women and Children) began to develop a Canadian sexual assault sentencing database. This database records and analyzes the interpretation by judges of the facts in those sexual assault cases which have made it through the many filters of the criminal justice system and have proceeded to conviction and sentencing.

4. Women and the Criminal Justice System in Canada

For the victim of sexual assault there is often a life sentence; for many, the trauma has been such that they will never recover the degree of well-being or the sense of personal security they felt before the assault.

The State response to sexual assault has many components, a number of which result in infringements of women's security rights: the disproportionate frequency with which police decide not to press charges in sexual assault cases and the bias evident in the prosecution process. Myth, misogyny, bigotry and opinionated ignorance have contributed to a distrust and disbelief of the woman victim that are evinced at every stage and in every part of the criminal justice machinery.

Refusal to trust women's testimony was actually enshrined in our law until 1983, through the evidentiary requirements that a rape be reported at the earliest opportunity and that there be corroboration. Even as recently as 1988, according to a study commissioned by the province of Ontario, one in three people still generally disbelieved rape victims. Of those questioned, 35 per cent agreed that "women often agree to have sex but later complain that they were raped".[4]

Women's complaints of sexual assault are frequently met by a State response that has a clear impact on her security interests: acquittal of the offender. And women under threat – of death or the harm of their loved ones – sometimes retract their complaints. Their experience has taught them that the State will not protect them.

At times, the right of women to security of the person and to equal benefit and protection of the law is obliterated by concerns, albeit important ones, about the right of accused men to a fair trial. Late 1990 saw an extreme illustration of this imbalance in Canada. As a result of a Supreme Court decision,[5] judges in the province of Ontario dismissed prosecutions before them on the grounds that the accused could no longer be guaranteed a fair trial due to extreme delays caused by a backlog in the courts. Recently, many charges of sexual assault have been dropped, not because the accused men have been found innocent, but because a legal technicality has caused the inefficiency of the court system to work in their favour.

[4] Informa Inc., 'Sexual Assault: Measuring the Impact of the Launch Campaign', report prepared for the Ontario Women's Directorate, August 1988, 43.

[5] *Askov et al. v. R.*, [1990] S.C.R. 1199.

One woman who was raped saw the charges dropped by the Crown before the case even *entered* the court, thus shutting down any opportunity for redress. Shortly afterwards, as she left her night job, she was followed on the street by an unknown man. All she could think of, she said, was:

> He can do anything he wants to me and nothing will happen. I'm not safe. No woman in Canada is safe.[6]

5. Sentencing in Sexual Assault Cases

While the statements judges make while passing sentence reflect the content of the law, they also provide us with a significant means to assess the degree to which the State has, or has not, supported the Charter rights and human rights of victim-survivors.

METRAC studies Canadian judges' comments for two additional reasons. First, judges are products of our society and as such their thinking reflects society's thinking. Second, judges' remarks can give us a clear sense of the nature and degree of judicial misunderstanding of the crime of sexual assault.

Our review of over 600 full sentencing decisions from across Canada has made clear that in a significant number of cases judges have relied, for their definition of sexual assault, on the stereotypical notion of the rapist as a monstrous stranger disguised in a balaclava hiding behind a bush waiting for a victim. The review of sentencing decisions also demonstrates a remarkable misunderstanding of what is violent and what constitutes consent to sexual intercourse. It shows that many judges typically ignore gender bias and accept expert testimony at face value; they allow and use euphemistic language to disguise facts; and they allow mitigating factors to work for the accused and do not often consider aggravating factors such as victim impact.

(1) Sentencing: The Misunderstanding of "Violence"

In 1983 the law in Canada on sexual crimes was changed to redefine rape as "sexual assault". This was intended to better acknowledge the assaultive and violent aspect of the crime. For example, where a sexual assault is accompanied by physical violence, the courts now tend to focus on this aspect of the victim's experience. However, this construct of sexual crime contains no acknowledgment of the violation *inherent* in the sexual violation or the interference with a victim's bodily integrity. It fails to acknowledge situations where the assailant has emotional, physical or authority-based power over the victim (such as a father, employer or therapist) and has no need to overpower her physically or with the use/threat of a weapon.

The shortcomings of assessing the gravity of a sexual crime on the same basis

[6] Telephone conversation with the author.

as other forms of assault can easily be illustrated from judges' comments on sentencing.

In sentencing a man convicted of indecent assault and gross indecency against three young girls, including weekly sexual assault of his foster daughter, the judge noted that "none of the acts involved violence except for one child on one occasion who refused to submit and who was pushed down".[7]

In a case concerning a man who had raped his 14-year old daughter at least a dozen times, the judge pointed out that there had been "no allegation he had used physical force or violence."[8]

In one case, sentencing the perpetrator of sexual assaults on two four-year-old girls to one year's imprisonment plus two years probation, the judge deemed it noteworthy that the convicted man had not "threatened or used violence in the circumstance".[9]

In these examples, the judges fail to address the trauma of sexual violation, let alone the violation of trust relationships. Breach of trust, the abusive manipulation of an authority, power or trust relationship can cause damage that lasts a lifetime.[10] Most victims experience a general dislocation of their lives as well as symptoms ranging from impaired ability to trust, sleeplessness and anger, through to suicidal tendencies and other symptoms requiring hospitalization. Yet the courts often equate the absence of physical injuries with consent, finding cuts and bruises more impressive than any amount of emotional damage.

(2) Sentencing: The Misunderstanding of "Consent"

A fundamental problem, as shown repeatedly in METRAC's review, is posed by judicial confusion of consent with compliant behaviour, a confusion rarely evident in cases of robbery.

If a robber tells his victim that he is carrying a concealed gun, he does not need to make his threat explicit by displaying the weapon. His victim will appreciate the nature of the threat, and will probably comply with the robber's demands. A witness who could not hear the verbal exchanges between robber and victim might assume that money was simply being handed over freely. Yet a judge and jury will have no conceptual difficulty in apprehending the risk of harm. The victim felt at risk; he therefore complied with the robber's demands, even though there was no overt display of power. There is really no argument as to whether or not he consented to giving his money away. A past history of

[7] *R. v. C.*, Ont. Dist. Ct., February 5, 1981 (unreported).

[8] *R. v. C.* (1982), 69 C.C.C. (2d) 81 (Ont. C.A.).

[9] *R. v. DeGenova*, [1985] B.C.W.L.D. 3402 (C.A.).

[10] The harms of patient-therapist sexual abuse, for example, are now well documented. See Pope, 'How Clients Are Harmed by Sexual Contact with Mental Health Professionals: The Syndrome and its Prevalence' (December 1988), 67 *Journal of Counselling and Development*, pp. 222–26.

giving money away, or of being robbed, is never taken to detract from the non-voluntary nature of the present robbery.

Sexual assault is confused with consensual sex when compliant behaviour (that is, behaviour which has been exacted through the threat of further harm, the abuse of unequal power or the exercise of authority) is confused with consenting behaviour. There are countless situations where a man need not articulate a threat of harm for women to know that the threat exists, just as a thief who is known to carry a gun has no need to display the weapon. Yet judges and juries who see the coercion in the robbery do not see that in a situation where she experiences coercion or perceives a threat, the victim of a sexual assault is *forced* to comply. This is especially true in instances where there is a pre-existing relationship of trust between victim and assailant.

Quasi-judicial tribunals, like criminal and civil courts, have failed to recognize non-consensual, compliant behaviour exacted through the use of unequal power. One Canadian Human Rights Commission hearing officer described the "requested sex" from a probationary employee by a supervisor who threatened job retaliation as "voluntary participation".[11]

(3) Sentencing: Gender Bias in Expert Testimony

Expert evidence is central to judicial understanding of the severity of sexual assault, its impact on the victim and the prospects for rehabilitating the offender. Yet the courts frequently give uncritical weighting to expert testimony from psychiatrists, even though research indicates that psychiatrists often do not recognize risk of harm to the victim and that no one is able to predict with any accuracy the future dangerousness of an accused.

One expert assessment detailed the abuse of *one* girl for *two* years. According to the sentencing decision, the abuse involved *three* girls over a period of *nine* years. He describes "the girl in question", a pre-schooler, as "encouraging and enjoying" the sexual activity. In spite of the offender's long history of abusing, the expert maintained that "there is no evidence that he has any pedophilic or other deviant sexual compulsions". The abuse was described as a "sexual relationship" which is "of an opportunistic nature and not the result of deviant or compulsive behaviour" with "no coercion on his part".[12]

In the case of a man who had sexually abused his own daughter and a deaf child for a total of seven years, both the treating psychiatrist and the judge seem to have had great confidence in the doctor's pre-trial assessment that the accused was not "at risk for harming himself or others".[13]

Courts do not generally allow the introduction of expert testimony that describes and supports women's perception of the violence they experience. A

[11] *Bonnie Robichaud v. Dennis Brennan* (Treasury Board), January 13, 1992, Human Rights Tribunal, Canadian Human Rights Commission.

[12] Author would prefer to keep cite confidential.

[13] *R. v. D.P.*, May 24, 1985, SCC (unreported). Ont. H.C.?

recent Supreme Court of Canada decision,[14] in allowing the hearing of such testimony, has contributed to a new understanding of the nature of the forms of self-defence to which victims of wife assault may be forced to resort.

(4) Sentencing: Use of Euphemistic Language

Euphemistic language, used by defence counsel, expert witnesses and judges alike, helps minimize the offence, disguise the dangerousness of the offender and trivialize the victim impact.

Sexual abuse has been described by judges as "fondling", or an "exaggerated paramedical exam by the father". The abuser has been described as a "non-violent and non-aggressive pedophile"; even, after committing an assault at knifepoint, as having "a mild anti-social orientation".

(5) Sentencing: Aggravating and Mitigating Factors

In sentencing, traditionally recognized aggravating and mitigating factors are often used in such a way that they work to the advantage of the offender and do not uphold the equality or security rights of the victim.

In many sentencing decisions, mitigating factors are used to favour and excuse the accused.[15] They are named as: "victim provocation" (by employment or dress, for example); "offender under duress" at home or at work; "good character" (equated to public behaviour); "use of alcohol" (whether by the accused or victim, favours the accused).

Among aggravating factors are breach of trust where the perpetrator has used the unequal power of an authority or trust relationship to effect the abuse. These cases are among the least understood by the courts, presumably because they are farthest away from the stereotypical paradigm of a "real rape". Breach of trust should always be recognized as an aggravating factor, and in financial situations the courts do not find this a difficult concept. Yet, in METRAC's review of 460 sexual assault cases, judges failed to recognize breach of trust, or to cite it as an aggravating factor in 44 per cent of the approximately 200 cases in which it appeared.[16] The Charter implications for victims in these cases have not yet been pursued; they cannot be said to have received "equal benefit and protection of the law", let alone the "security of the person" guarantees the Charter professes to protect.

[14] *R. v. Lavallee*, [1990] 1 S.C.R. 852.

[15] For a more detailed explanation see P. Marshall, 'Sexual Assault, The Charter, and Sentencing Reform', (1988) 63 C.R. (3d) pp. 216–235.

[16] Symons and Marshall, 'Breach of Trust in Sexual Assault: Statement of the Problem, Part One: Sentencing', prepared by METRAC for the Ontario Women's Directorate, 1990.

(6) Sentencing: Class Bias

Middle-class sexual offenders are particularly well situated to benefit from a court's scrutiny of their public behaviour. The focus on "good citizenry", as well as education and employment achievements, can be used to obscure evidence of sexual abuse and breach of trust. Such offenders often target their victims carefully and choose those who will be physically or psychologically unlikely to offer much resistance and who will be reluctant to tell because they do not expect to be believed (perhaps because some past behaviour will make their credibility suspect).

(7) Sentencing: Victim Impact

In sentencing for other forms of assault, judges regularly consider the impact of the assault on the victim. When sexual assault is treated simply as another form of physical assault, it obliterates a whole dimension of the trauma experienced by women victims. Courts repeatedly find little or no evidence of victim impact when they are not presented with documentation of physical injuries.

One judge, sentencing a man for the buggery and oral rape of a 13-year-old girl, commented that "there was no evidence of any permanent injury inflicted upon the complainant".[17]

In another case, sentencing a rapist to nine months imprisonment, the judge pointed out that "there were no threats or use of force. The victim was not hurt in any way and has not suffered any psychological damage". In this incident the victim had passed out in the course of the rape and, when she became conscious, there was a blanket over her. The judge commented that "although [the rapist] once told her to shut up as she screamed, he never threatened her with harm or otherwise physically assaulted her and did not harm her physically in the act of intercourse".[18]

The courts' repeated findings of little or no victim impact in instances of sexual assault contrast starkly with women's experience, some of which is documented, although this area has not been a funding priority. In one study, 19 per cent of rape victims attempted suicide and 44 per cent seriously considered it.[19]

(8) Sentencing: Rehabilitation

Rehabilitation of the offender is a critical component of a violence reduction plan in any society. It is a cornerstone of our criminal justice system, central to the work of the parole boards, and an important factor in judicial sentencing

[17] *R. v. Barrera*, Ont. H.C., November 23, 1983 (unreported).

[18] *R. v. Guitard*, Ont. Dist. Ct., January 7, 1980 (unreported).

[19] D. Kilpatrick, 'Effects of Crime on Women', in *Journal of Consulting and Clinical Psychiatry*, Vol. 53, pp. 866–873.

deliberations. Because it is also perhaps the most humane and desirable method of dealing with offenders, it is a tempting notion for courts.

In METRAC's experience, judges have frequently equated *any treatment* whatsoever with rehabilitation programmes and have often revealed little knowledge of the effectiveness of various treatment programmes. Expert assessments of an offender's prospects for rehabilitation often seem unjustifiably optimistic, for they skip over the fact that in Canada and elsewhere rehabilitation programmes for sexual offenders – low-priority for the State and severely underfunded – are in a very early stage of development. They also lean to an alarming extent on the offender's previous public behaviour to aid their predictions of success. The inaccuracy in predicting recidivism is rarely recognized in research on rehabilitation.

The risk of harm to women and children resulting from unsuccessful rehabilitation of a sexual offender is not clearly recognized. Young sexual offenders are often given short sentences because of their youthfulness, when in fact their violent sexual nature at a young age should be of particular concern. A singular focus on human rights of perpetrators of sexual violence and the lack of understanding of rehabilitation by judges and parole board members has directly affected the safety of women in Canada. Women have died as a result.[20]

6. Wife Assault

Wife assault is not treated by the courts and legal system in a way that protects the human rights of the victims. Indeed, women around the world have expended enormous amounts of energy simply to secure a recognition that violence against wives is criminal behaviour.

In Canada, spousal immunity for rape was enshrined in the law until 1983. The hangover effects of that old law are still with us and are frequently highlighted by recent judgments which clearly demonstrate judicial resistance to the changes in the law.

One judge excused a husband's sexual assault on his wife as an "outburst" and questioned whether the courts should be involved "whenever transitory passion triumphs for a brief instant". He urged the "exercise [of] ordinary common sense" to achieve justice and went on to say, "In my view, a criminal intent, as opposed to an emotional intent, must be of superior concern to the court".[21]

In another case, the judge described the sexual assault as a husband's "drunken enthusiasm". The judge stated honestly that he felt "somewhat unprepared and incompetent to deal with it" and he suggested that he, like the

[20] Official Investigation Unlawfully At Large Inmate on Unescorted Temporary Absence Montgomery Centre, 1988 01 27, Addendum February, 1988, Follow-up May, 1990. Also known as the Pepino Inquiry.

[21] *R. v. E.W.*, Ontario Provincial Court, December 12, 1989.

State, had "no business in the bedrooms of the nation".[22]

The State court system of justice is in many ways an extension of the family and its system of justice. Protection from sexual terrorism within the home may be offered to the monogamous wife, the "blameless victim"; but for those women who do not meet a standard of wifely conduct imposed by the courts, the protection offered is severely curtailed, and their credibility as witnesses will be impugned.

The use of euphemisms results in an *ipso facto* decriminalization of wife abuse. Assault is referred to as "marital conflict", "family fights," and "domestic violence" – terms which also disguise the gender of abuser and victim.

On a State level, too, violence is decriminalized, as for example when the police refuse to press charges. Those entrusted with the responsibility "to serve and protect" can seriously undermine the equality rights promised to women in the Charter. State decisions "not to interfere" with a man's family home, his castle, reinforce the dichotomy between the treatment of assaults in public and assaults in private. Women's and children's vulnerability is increased when appropriate protection is not provided to them.

In promoting the image of the idealized family as a safe haven for its members, our society has failed to protect and promote the basic human rights of those family members most at risk: the women and children. The husband, safe at the top of the family hierarchy, usually older, stronger and wealthier than his wife, has often enjoyed immunity from the consequences of any violent behaviour he perpetrates against family members.

As in sexual assault cases, the victim of wife assault is often herself put on trial. This is illustrated by a recent Canadian trial of some notoriety.[23] A victim of wife assault (a new immigrant whose arrival and reunion with her Canadian husband had been much publicized) was put on the witness stand for an intense cross-examination by defence counsel over several days. There was little question of whether her husband had assaulted her; cross-examination focused on her behaviour prior to the marriage, apparently in an attempt to determine whether she deserved the assault.

At the appeal hearing, the defendant's counsel went to great lengths to employ research data to "prove" that this woman – who suffered extensive facial injury – was not a battered wife, because there was no evidence either that she had contemplated suicide or that she had been beaten the widely accepted average of 35 times before calling the police.

[22] *R.* v *L.B.*, Ontario Provincial Court, October 10, 1989.

[23] *R. v. Inwood*, Ont. C.A., (1989) 48 C.C.C. (3d) 173.

7. Prostitution

Prostitution, the trafficking in women and children, has been defined as "any industry in which women's or children's bodies are bought, sold or traded for sexual use and abuse".[24] In Canada, pornography, live sex shows, peepshows, sexual slavery, massage parlours, street prostitution, escort services, call girls and the sex provided for money in brothels are forms of prostitution that manifest the pervasive sexual exploitation of women by men in our culture.

Prostitution is seldom a career choice. The institution of prostitution takes advantage of the poverty and economic exigencies of many women to keep them trapped in sexually coercive, exploitative, relationships.[25]

In prostitution, the behaviour of clients poses a constant threat to security of the person. The euphemistic phrase "bad tricks" covers a range of abuse including knifings, rapes, beating, coercion into degrading acts, and all too frequent murders.

The permission to perpetrate violence against prostitutes is illustrated by a 1984 American survey, in which 19 per cent of rape victims tried to curtail the rapist's physical violence by telling them that they were prostitutes. In each case, the rapist increased the violence of the assault.[26]

Although it has not been a research priority in Canada, findings suggest that prostitutes are vulnerable to sexual victimization by police.

When a prostitute's rights are violated, the rights of all women are put at risk. And for women involved in prostitution in Canada, the right to equal benefit and protection of the law and to security of the person has been very elusive.

8. Pornography

When pornography models the abuse of women and children and sells it as entertainment, there is an impact on women and children. In her 1980 study on pornography and violence, Diana Russell found that 10 per cent of women were upset by pornography.[27] A mid-1980's Toronto survey conducted by Susan Cole,[28] confirmed what shelter workers and counsellors had been saying for some time: women are raped and beaten for not having bodies like the women in magazine pictures, for not smiling and being receptive like the women in the

[24] Giobbe, 'Confronting the Liberal Lies About Prostitution,' in Leidholdt and Raymond (eds.) *The Sexual Liberals and the Attack on Feminism* (1990).

[25] See the publication *Whisper: Women Hurt in Systems of Prostitution Engaged in Revolt*.

[26] Silbert and Pines, 'Pornography and Sexual Abuse of Women' (1984), 10 *Sex Roles*, pp. 857–68, at 864.

[27] Diana Russell, 'Sexual Exploitation: Rape, Child Sexual Abuse, and Workplace Harassment', *Sage Library of Social Research* (1984), volume 155, p. 124.

[28] Susan Cole, 'A View from Another Country,' in Leidholdt and Raymond (eds.) *The Sexual Liberals and the Attack on Feminism* (1990), pp. 191–97.

pictures, to anal sex, to bondage or indeed to whatever fantasy the pornographer conceives. In Cole's pilot study, 30 per cent of assaulted women described experiencing abuse directly related to the abuser's consumption of pornography.

The contribution of the State to the harm done by pornography consists primarily of glaring errors of omission. In Canada, as elsewhere, the State has not supported the research needed to provide systematic documentation of women's experience of pornography, and of the harm directly linked to pornography. American research, however, gives us some small glimpses into the reality.

A 1984 survey of 200 prostitutes established that 73 per cent of the women interviewed had been raped.[29] Of these women, 24 per cent mentioned that the rapist, during the rape, had alluded to pornographic material. Generally, the rapist referred to the pornography, then insisted that the victim enjoy the rape and the accompanying physical violence.

The study showed similar results in relation to the sexual exploitation of girls.[30] In 22 per cent of 178 cases of juvenile exploitation, women recalling earlier abuse mentioned the use of pornography by the adult prior to the act of sexual abuse; 10 per cent of the women respondents in this survey had also been used, as children, in pornographic films and magazines.

Recent descriptions by Peggy Reeves Sanday and Robin Warshaw of fraternity gang rape and male-bonding practices graphically illustrate the desensitizing effects of pornography.[31] Fraternity brothers who had watched a gang rape commented on their difficulties in distinguishing between a real gang rape and the pornography versions they had repeatedly seen on video.

Despite the implications of this research, the State in Canada has not funded further investigation of the impact of pornography on the incidence of sexual crimes, or the ramifications of the sexual targeting of women and children by pornographers. Moreover, since this type of data collection is not a priority, no police force in Canada has recorded the incidence of the use of pornography by sexual criminals, although police officers have reported finding pornographic materials at the scene of a sexual assault or homicide and identifying similarities in the *modus operandi* of the assailant and the acts depicted in the pornography.

Inappropriate State policies and practices continue to support the proliferation of pornography and harmful media material. In courts, much of the violence is excused as "fantasy". Outdated laws focusing on morality and decency do little to support the security rights of women.

When the State does intervene, inadequate understanding of the nature of

[29] *Supra*, note 26, pp. 857–68.

[30] *Ibid.* at p. 865.

[31] Sanday, *Fraternity Gang Rape: Sex, Brotherhood and Privilege on Campus* (1990), New York: New York University Press; Warshaw, *I Never Called It Rape* (1988), New York: Harper and Row.

pornography and its effects usually ensure that the intervention is not very effective. Customs officials and censor boards seem to look only for exposed genitals while leaving untouched the accompanying depictions of violence and degradation of women.

Pornography is found everywhere, with few restrictions: in our homes and workplaces, on billboards and on the street, at train stations, in airports, hotel rooms and subway stations, and where we buy our bread and milk. Violence against women and children is normalized when it is freely circulated everywhere.

Pornography is available to sexual offenders incarcerated in State-run correctional institutions in Canada, undermining what few, small rehabilitation programmes exist. Where pornography is listed in jails as "adult reading material", the State – where it should be most vigilant – has deflected the focus from the infringement of women's and children's security interests to a "freedom to read" and "freedom of expression" focus.

9. Crime Prevention Programs

Although the Canadian Federal Government has designated one week each fall to be National Crime Prevention Week, crime prevention in this context has little to do with the violence perpetrated against women and children. The police promote "Safety for People", a term that neatly avoids the gender specific nature of sexual and wife assault. Property crime is deemed the most important area in crime prevention.

In Canada, we cannot look at community violence perpetrated by non-State actors against women without making reference to the Montreal massacre of December 1989. Fourteen women were killed and others were seriously wounded by a man who said he was angry at feminists – women involved in equality-seeking work.

With tragic irony, the European and North American Conference on Urban Safety and Crime Prevention, held in Montreal a few weeks before the December massacre of students at Ecole Polytechnique, had reinforced the conspiracy of silence, the freedom to live in a state of ignorance about women's experience of victimization. More than 900 delegates, representing 31 countries stated in their final declaration that women's fear is out of proportion to crime rates.[32]

[32] Final Declaration of the European and North American Conference on Urban Safety and Crime Prevention, October 10–13, 1989, Montreal, Quebec.

10. Refugee Status for Women: The Need for an Expanded Understanding

Canada could play a vital leadership role in defining the refugee status of women whose lives and well-being have been threatened by violence . Women have come to Canada to escape from sexual slavery and other forms of violence. If they return home, they will be victims of violence as surely as will any refugee persecuted for their religious or political activities.

One woman in Toronto is claiming refugee status because, after suffering years of abuse, she left her husband and a violent marriage. If she is returned to Trinidad, she knows that, no matter where she goes and how she tries to hide, her husband, a police officer, will be able to find her. As an instrument of the State, he will be able to treat her as violently as before, with the impunity he has always enjoyed. Yet she has been told that she will probably be deported to Trinidad because she does not meet the traditional criteria for refugee status.

11. Conclusion

The traditional "minute of silence" is not an adequate response to Montreal and other tragic human rights violations caused by the known realities of violence. If human rights are to be supported, federal and provincial government agencies must initiate, support and continue work in naming the problem and developing a State response that will support women's basic human rights to dignity and to security of the person.

12. Appendix

Organizations representing many millions of women, professional bodies, mayors and others in Canada have asked for a Royal Commission – a massive, comprehensive federal initiative to reverse discriminatory policies and practices and to replace them with those that will support women's human rights. The following recommendations are made:

1. A mandatory violence prevention curriculum in school classes from kindergarten to college will be necessary.
2. Women's safety and security concerns must figure prominently on the public agenda of municipalities. Urban planners and designers must be required to give priority to these issues in all building and planning. In Toronto, METRAC has had some success in pioneering projects: conducting a sexual assault safety audit of the public transportation system;[33] developing, with the City of Toronto, an amended bylaw for lighting and

[33] METRAC and the Toronto Transit Commission, *Moving Forward: Making Transit Safer for Women* (1989).

security in underground parking garages;[34] and developing and producing a women's safety audit kit to direct the systematic safety auditing of public and semi-public spaces.[35]

3. Those professions and institutions, such as doctors, churches and hospitals, to whom we give special privilege, powers, moral authority and funding must develop a systematic response to sexual abuse within their own membership, including educational initiatives as well as review of the effectiveness of policies, procedures, and practices in dealing with instances of sexual abuse.
4. A review of all of the components involved in the State response to sexual assault is urgently needed.
5. The criminal justice system and its related agencies are in need of a drastic overhaul so that their activities can be brought up to equity standards.
6. It is essential that courts allow the introduction of expert testimony that describes and supports women's perception of the violence they experience.
7. A Charter-driven review of defence practices and the development of guidelines for counsel should be a first step toward correcting the imbalance between victims' and offenders' rights.
8. A "demonstrated understanding of equality issues" must be one of the key criteria for the appointment of judges, parole board members and other personnel of the criminal justice system.
9. In law schools and continuing legal education programs, judicial education on issues related to women's inequality and to sexual violence is urgently needed.
10. Resources must be made available for the adequate prosecution of cases involving sexual assault (and other forms of woman abuse) by designated prosecutors.
11. Amendments to the Criminal Code and the Canada Customs Act are needed to produce effective legal responses to pornography and thus support women's equality and security interests. Both federal and provincial work is needed for the introduction of civil remedies (modelled on those developed by Andrea Dworkin and Catherine Mackinnon in the United States) for women harmed by pornography. Film and video review boards must be disbanded or reconstructed to meet equality/security interests.
12. Policy directives, social programmes and statutory amendments that will recognize the sexual exploitation and coercion involved in much of the prostitution in Canada are long overdue.
13. To ensure that the definition of refugee conforms with equality standards, all women who would be returned to almost certain violence at the hands of

[34] City of Toronto Housing Standards By-law #73–68 with respect to April 5, 1988 amendments concerning Security Improvements to Underground Garages.

[35] *METRAC Women's Safety Audit Kit Guidebook*, METRAC, Toronto 1989.

non-State actors must also be considered for refugee status. The call for refugee status for women victims of violence made at the 1983 conference for victims of sexual slavery[36] is a minimal but important first step.

[36] Barry, 'International Politics of Female Sexual Slavery,'in Barry et al., (eds.) *International Feminism: Networking Against Female Sexual Slavery* (1984).

VITIT MUNTARBHORN*

Violence Against and Abuse of Children

1. Introduction

"I killed you because you didn't study and had no future... The government must not allow the streets of the city to be invaded by Kids."

This message was tied around the neck of a young boy in the streets of Rio de Janeiro in 1989. As reported by Amnesty International, the boy was probably killed by a death squad. His fate and many others like his attest to the shocking cruelties and abuses afflicting children in various parts of the world and in manifold forms. As recognized explicitly by the World Declaration on the Survival, Protection and Development of Children adopted by a record number of Heads of State who attended the World Summit for children in 1990:

> "Each day, countless children around the world are exposed to dangers that hamper their growth and development. They suffer immensely as casualties of war and violence; as victims of racial discrimination, apartheid, aggression, foreign occupation and annexation; as refugees and displaced children, forced to abandon their homes and their roots; as disabled; or as victims of neglect, cruelty and exploitation".

2. The Context of Violence and Abuse

The root causes of violence and abuses are multiple and complex. A key cause is rampant poverty and its destructive impact on children and their families; family disintegration often turns children out onto the streets and into the dangers beyond. Discrimination, underdevelopment, armed conflicts, neglect and abandonment add insult to injury. In particular contexts of child exploitation for labour and sexual purposes, there is a demand factor as well as availability of supply.

* Associate Professor of Law, Chulalongkorn University, Bangkok, Thailand.

K.E. Mahoney and P. Mahoney (eds.), Human Rights in the Twenty-first Century, 335–342.

This complicated reality is better understood by identifying and describing groups of children who increasingly require urgent attention and correlative action. These groups are summarized as follows.

(1) Rural Children

The majority of the world's population, including children, live in rural areas. In developing communities, children do not have sufficient access to basic services, resources and infrastructure to enable them to realize their fullest potential. Increasingly, they bear the brunt of the economic burden, whether it be working in the fields or drifting to urban areas in pursuit of work. The break-up or break-down of their families, compounded by environmental decline, constrains their normal development as children; the socio-economic deprivations prevent them from undertaking activities generally expected of children, such as proper education and recreation.

Their plight is not self-contained. The types of social subsidies already available to children in these areas tend to neglect the concomitant needs of their families. For instance, the mere fact that one gives a grant to help children go to school does not necessarily mean that they will be able to go there if the family expects them to till the fields during school hours. Unless there are some provisions to help the family too, the children will not be able to enjoy their own rights.

(2) Slum Children

Migrant families from rural areas often end up in urban slums near their newly found workplaces. If a family moves from a rural area and fails to inform the authorities of its change of residence, it will not have residential papers. Ultimately this could mean a lack of identification for the purpose of school enrollment or other official services. In effect, the children of the family may become "non-entities" for the purpose of schooling or other benefits.

The congested environment of the slums sometimes lead to family and neighbourhood conflicts. Gambling and drugs are widespread in some slums, while AIDS and inhalant abuse are only a step away. Sometimes desperate parents send their children out to work as street vendors late into the night to the detriment of their health. In other situations children are often left to their own devices unprotected from potential abuses surrounding them while the parents are at work.

(3) Street Children

These children are similar to those in the previous category, except that their plight is more extreme. Amnesty International, for example, has revealed that many children in Brazil and Guatemala have been killed because of the fact that they are street children. The tragedy is certainly not limited to South America.

The phenomenon is found in many parts of the developing world, including Asia and Africa. Even in countries which are generally seen as economically developed, there are street children who are seen as "runaways, walkaways or throwaways".

In developing countries the scenario is closely related to the displacement of children and their families when they move from rural to urban areas in search of employment. This is aggravated by the disintegration of the family system, sometimes leading to physical and mental violence committed by parents against children.

The activities of street children range from selling flowers to criminal practices. Evidently, these children find it difficult to go to formal schools and seek official services for lack of time, will and/or financial resources. Thus, there is a need to target alternative services to reach the streets, e.g. street-schooling.

(4) Female Children

Although a number of advances can be noted in the promotion of gender equality, there is still an imbalance which works against girls in relation to basic needs and respect for women's rights. Female illiteracy is higher than male illiteracy. Although in many settings there is little *de jure* discrimination, *de facto* discrimination against girls is pervasive. For example, in most parts of Asia, parents still prefer to send boys rather than girls to school. Gender stereotypes prevent girls from undertaking certain male dominated activities such as technical professions.

The situation is compounded by certain cultural stigmas and social taboos which relegate girls to passive and domesticated roles. This is particularly visible in some ethnic groups which do deny gender equality to women and girls. On another front, sexual abuses of children within the home and the sale of children into prostitution occur much more frequently to girls.

(5) Child Labourers

Although most countries have laws on the minimum age of employment (e.g. in some developing countries, it is 13 years of age), in many parts of the world the age criterion tends to be lower than the minimum age advocated by the International Labour Organizations (15 years of age). Moreover, many employers frequently violate the law, especially in small scale factories where children are kept against their will and in unsafe conditions.

The problem of child labourers is related to the sale of children sometimes wittingly, sometimes unwittingly, by parents. Job placement agencies and their intermediaries are often conduits for the flow of rural children to urban factories. Monitoring against such exploitation is difficult due to the limited number of government inspectors. Lax law enforcement by law enforcement authorities indicates the gap between law making and implementation. From another angle, it seems that while there are some strategies to help child labourers, there is a paucity of strategies to mobilize the private sector against those who indulge in such exploitation. The watchdogs, where they exist, tend to be non-governmental and community organizations interested in the protection of children. The magnitude of the problem however calls for national action of a broader nature.

(6) Child Prostitutes

Although child prostitution is generally illegal, it is commonplace. The issue of child prostitution has come to the fore increasingly in recent years partly because the number of young girls and boys in the trade seems to be on the rise. As noted by the recent report of the Special Rapporteur to the UN Human Rights Commission (on the Sale of Children):

> "In the case of girl prostitutes, there may be elements of gender discrimination leading them into this profession, compounded by certain cultural practices, such as elevating girls from a young age to the status of sex goddesses. The problem has been aggravated by sex tourism, and has led to a greater number of pedophiles and boy prostitutes. Prostitution is only one step away from other tragic enticements such as drugs and child pornography."

The worst transgressions are linked to the sale of young children by the parents, on the one hand, and the tricking of young children into the trade by various agents, on the other hand. The situation is particularly invisible in small scale operations. The current legal structure suffers from poor law enforcement as well as a failure to sanction customers. On another front, preventive measures, such as social development assistance for families, and rehabilitation of prostitutes with social subsidies for changes in livelihood, are neglected.

(7) Handicapped Children

In many communities, handicapped children are often marginalized. They have little or no access to basic services. At times they are abandoned by the families that are too poor to care for them. Sometimes they are used by gangs of profiteers to beg on the streets. Their enrollment rate at school is lower than that of able-bodied children. This is partly due to the fact that ordinary schools fail to provide special facilities which would allow handicapped children to be accommodated. There is discrimination against handicapped children not only in regard to access to facilities but also in regard to State commitment. This is reflected in the questionable State tendency of sending them to institutions. Logic would suggest that it is better to provide support to the families so they may look after the children at home, rather than place them in State institutions. This rationale may prevail except in such cases as the mentally handicapped.

(8) Refugee and Stateless Children

The presence of millions of refugee children in the world today raises the sensitive issue of how to deal with them. In national law and official policy in many countries, they are regarded as illegal immigrants entering in breach of the local immigration law, not refugees with vested rights. The official line implies that the services accorded to them should be bare minimum and that they can be pushed back across the border at any time. Because of their illegal status, they have no rights and their destiny is at the mercy of those who regard them as a security threat rather than as children with special needs.

The issue of statelessness often overlaps with refugee children, although the two may differ. There is, for instance, a category of children who are not of refugee parentage but who are discriminated against because their parents are aliens, even though the children are born on the territory where protection is sought. This is closely linked to the nationality issue and the fact that many countries do not confer nationality by reason of birth on their soil. It is also influenced by mistrust of those of alien parentage, with the consequence that those who do not have local lineage are treated as stateless. In this way they are deprived of the rights accorded to local nationals.

(9) Juvenile Delinquents

Generally, municipal systems have special provisions to deal with young offenders. The legal process is influenced by the various pronouncements of the United Nations on the administration of justice. For example, the Minimum Standards for the Treatment of Prisoners set by the UN has resulted in the practice that young offenders are segregated from adult offenders in the criminal process. However, there are shortcomings, including the tendency to send "problem cases" too quickly to reform schools without examining or determining underlying causes. Regrettably, corporal punishment is still permitted in some systems.

The notion of delinquency itself is open to debate. If an act of delinquency is due to the failure of the family system (remembering that often the abused becomes the abuser elsewhere), one may question the premise that young offenders should pay for the offenses attributed to them. A move away from institutionalization and a shift towards preventive and rehabilitative strategies within the home and the community should be pursued.

(10) Child Soldiers

In many parts of the world where there are armed conflicts, children are used directly or indirectly as soldiers. The traumas inflicted by war take their toll in terms of permanent psychological and physical harm, if not death itself. Internationally, there have been numerous pronouncements against the use of child soldiers, including the 1977 Red Cross Protocols and the 1990 Convention on the Rights of the Child. However, even with such standard-setting, arguments still occur over what the age threshold should be for draftees. Logic would indicate the need to raise the age threshold to as high as possible and to prevent young persons from becoming embroiled in armed conflicts.

(11) Medically Abused Children

The rise of AIDS as a world phenomenon has brought to light the plight of AIDS affected children and AIDS orphans. The services required to help affected families and children are still greatly lacking in many communities. This entails more extensive provision of longer term medical and other services to help alleviate the vast repercussions of AIDS in all communities. It also calls for protection of infected children and their families against discrimination, as well as stronger preventive measures such as education.

On another front, the horrendous tales of sale of human organs for commercial purposes is riddled with rumours and denials. As noted by the World Health Organization in 1990:

> "Rational argument can be made to the effect that shortage has led to the rise of commercial traffic in human organs, particularly from living donors who are unrelated to recipients. There is clear evidence of such traffic in recent years, and fears have arisen of the possibility of related traffic in human beings."

Prevention is again better than cure, especially as the latter is often too late and irremediable. This is linked with better education, community watch efforts, law enforcement, family development and respect for children's rights.

(12) Other Abused and Neglected Children

There is a broad array of abused and neglected children who do not necessarily fall under the headings listed above. Sometimes they are victims of violence within the home; sometimes outside the home. At times they are abandoned. Often the violations take place in a hidden manner bolstered by threats and intimidation of the children or their families. The structures that cause these injustices vary between political repression to socio-economic deprivations and cultural constraints.

3. The Need for Action

The categories of children identified above are not a sampling. There are many more. Strategies needed to cater to different groups must be multi-pronged because the settings and circumstances children find themselves in may differ so radically from one another. Internationally, two guiding lights appeared in 1990, The World Declaration on the Survival, Protection and Development of

Children and its Plan of Action for Implementing the World Declaration on the Survival, Protection and Development of Children in the 1990's; and the Convention on the Rights of the Child.

The former document (with its Plan of Action) is not a treaty and lacks binding force. However, it is persuasive. As a policy statement, it presses for various forms of action at the national and international levels to respond to many aspects of child survival, development and protection. Various goals to be realized by the year 2000 are stipulated such as the reduction of 1990 child mortality rates for children under five years by one third or to a level of 70 per 1,000 live births, whichever is the greater reduction; universal access to safe drinking water and to sanitary means of excreta disposal; and universal access to basic education and completion of primary education by at least 80% of primary school age children.

The second document, the Convention on the Rights of the Child is a legal instrument, binding upon States. It requires law and policy changes to comply with the provisions of the Convention. The rights enunciated cover a wide array of civil, political, economic, social and cultural concerns (e.g. the right to life, the right to a nationality, the right to freedom of expression, etc.)

More particularly on the question of violence against and abuse of children, there are a number of relevant provisions including those dealing with the protection of child prostitutes, child labourers, refugees, and child soldiers. As part of a preventive strategy social programmes for children and their families are advanced. In addition, an International Committee on the Rights of the Child has been set up to monitor implementation of the Convention by States Parties.

While these international yardsticks are important, it is submitted that the key to overcoming the violation of children's rights is at national and local levels. Action in relation to laws, policies, practises, programming, and budgetary commitment is required. The following points provide the foundation for future action plans in this regard.

(1) Prevention

More preventive measures are required including social development and subsidies to prevent the root causes of exploitation which are primarily poverty and family disintegration. Basic needs such as education, health services, nutrition and shelter must be served as well as occupational opportunities to enable families and their children to develop their fullest potential without becoming displaced from their home settings.

(2) Protection

Protection requires action beyond the provision of services. It requires an appraisal of laws, policies and practices which work against children. Where they are found, they should be replaced by alternatives aimed at protecting children. Once in place, new laws policies and practices must be more effectively enforced by means of sanctions against the violators and better incentives to enforcement officers. The private sector which was in the past contributed to child abuse should be more constructively brought into the dialogue to protect children. They must be pressured to influence their peers to respect the law.

(3) Remedies

Children must have access to formal institutions, the courts and non-formal entities, such as village councils and religious leaders which are in a position to provide remedies once abuses have occurred. Legal aid and assistance need to be complemented by social aid and assistance in order to promote the rehabilitation process. This implies accountability of abusers to compensate the victims as well as the need to strengthen community institutions and resources to rehabilitate children and support needy families.

(4) Intervention

Precisely because children do not often have access to institutions which can protect their rights, the role of intermediaries who may intervene on their behalf should be fostered. In particular, non-governmental and community organizations, including the mass media, must be encouraged to represent the best interests of the child and governmental and business institutions which may be called upon to act on behalf of the child must be identified. Needless to say, collaboration rather than inter-institutional rivalry should be encouraged.

(5) Participation

All too often, children are excluded from the development process. To overcome this, children should have more access to information and forums such as public inquiries, where their grievances could be heard. Children and youth groups should be organised and mobilized as community watchers and disseminators of information to their peers. In terms of protection, innovations such as hotlines enabling children to call in for help, and educational materials, such as cartoons, games and plays, to spread the message of children's rights can be linked more effectively with the children themselves to inculcate a cultural ethic favourable to childrens' interests.

The field of child protection is vast and insufficiently explored. Our approach to eradicating the violence and abuse of children must be more comprehensive than it is at present because the victimization process affecting many children arises from many reasons and many perpetrators. Indeed, comprehensiveness underscores the need for greater understanding of children in their environment both as potential victims and as potential catalysts for change.

SECTION III(c): THE HUMAN RIGHTS RESPONSE TO VIOLENCE

Introduction*

Just as there is a whole gamut of violence – ranging from violence in the home to violence writ large in wars between States – so there is a whole gamut of possible responses covering what one might call the human rights approach. The papers in this section examine those responses and their efficacy in a number of different spheres and from a number of different perspectives. The questions posed are many. What role can institutional human rights mechanisms of the classic international law variety play in repressing and preventing violence? The existing systems for the protection of human rights are not of universal application and their defects are patent. Where the existing institutions do not provide protection against oppression, in what circumstances, and to what extent, is violence itself a permissible response, whether by citizens of an oppressive State or by other States resorting to armed intervention in a "just war"? When subject to gender analysis, how "human-rights" oriented as opposed to "man-rights" oriented do the rules of international law on the peaceful settlement of international disputes and on armed conflict prove to be? What positive contribution can feminist analyses make to peace studies?

The contributions to Section I of this book emphasise the need that a violation of human rights should be the subject of an effective response. Two of the papers in this chapter are very much directed to this issue, focusing on human rights breaches that involve violence.

Christian Strohal, describes the working of the United Nations Commission on Human Rights. The Commission has a wide remit. The functions are both protection and promotion of human rights. It provides a political forum for governments and non-governmental organizations publicly to address human rights violations and protection against violations. Through its special rapporteurs and working groups it can look at the situation in particular countries.

* Summary based in large part on the introduction given at the Conference by Sir Basil Hall, British member of the European Commission of Human Rights, to the panel session entitled: "Response to Human Rights Violations: Violence or Non-Violence". The papers by Christine Chinkin and Judith Gardam were not delivered at the Conference.

K.E. Mahoney and P. Mahoney (eds.), Human Rights in the Twenty-first Century, 343–345.

There are also procedures for intervention in particular cases which demand urgent action. But there are weaknesses. In general the Commission operates after the event. It is political. It is necessarily selective, and it does not continually monitor human rights performance. No sanctions are available to it. These weaknesses could be eradicated, particularly by increased public awareness and by the development of a consultative diplomatic network for preventive action.

The topic of the study of Paul Mahoney and Fredrik Sundberg is likewise the response of international human rights law to violence. They examine State responsibility for violence under the European Convention on Human Rights. The Convention machinery provides a vehicle for response to violations of human rights to both Contracting States and private individuals, and in practice the sanctions imposed by the Convention organs are effective. Recent jurisprudence has extended to establishing the duty of States to prevent, as well as to remedy, human rights breaches involving violence. Certain rights impose on the State an obligation to create a legal framework protecting against acts of violence committed by anyone, and not only agents of the State. Mahoney and Sundberg use their analysis of the European system to offer a tentative assessment of the strengths and weaknesses of international human rights law as a means for combating violence.

The contribution of Francis Boyle relates principally to the right of private individuals to protest against the policies of their governments involving the use of force or violence. Much of what he describes as "ongoing criminal activity by members of the Reagan/Bush administrations under well recognized principles of international and US domestic law" cannot readily be regarded as violations of human rights. And many readers will not agree with the announced thesis of his paper that "for at least the last decade the Government of the United States of America has constituted an international criminal conspiracy under the Nuremberg Principles that is legally akin to that of the Nazi Government in pre-World War II Germany". But the non-violent civil resistance to which he refers was in relation to what the protesters saw as criminal resort to violence and as violations of human rights by the State, and the right to protest is itself a human right. Boyle comments, for example, that "there exists a basic human right under international law for all persons to resist the production and deployment of nuclear weapons and all their essential accoutrements by whatever peaceful means they can mount". He vigorously denounces the interference with this right by the arrest and prosecution of protesters. His paper ends with a plea for preventive action in favour of nuclear disarmament.

Anna Michalska discusses the question of humanitarian intervention by States. She questions the validity of the theory that there is a body of fundamental human rights which all States have an international obligation to guarantee and that a failure of a State to give effect to this obligation justifies forcible intervention by another State. Her conclusion is that international law has moved; that it is accepted that the right to intervene is now vested exclusively in international organizations in ways determined by international public law; and that the right must be exercisable whether or not the offending State is a party to human rights treaties.

The ultimate use of violence by public powers, namely war, is the subject of the final papers by Christine Chinkin and Judith Gardam. Writing as international lawyers but from a feminist perspective, they not surprisingly seek to expose the gender bias underlying this overtly male-dominated sphere. A sphere where, as they put it, the traditional invisibility and powerlessness of women in the patriarchal power structures of nation States are even more pronounced.

As Chinkin notes, the patriarchy of the nation State is seen by some as the fundamental cause of war and oppression, in that patriarchy breeds militarism. She points to the role that feminist analyses can play in dismantling the patriarchal values that engender militarism and its natural accompaniment, the use of force to maintain control. The objective to be sought is peace, in the sense not just of the absence of conflict but of a substantial modification of the inherent tendencies of the international system to conflict. The (hitherto patriarchal) terms in which the debate on war and peace is expressed need to be changed. She stresses the richness and diversity of feminist approaches in this debate: women as carers, as nurturers not killers, and therefore as natural antidotes to violence; women as peace activists demonstrating the existing lack of neutrality and objectivity of the law in the context of the citizen's response to official violence (a theme developed by Boyle from another angle in his paper); the ideal of women as equals in the decision-making process. The conclusions drawn are that feminism can contribute to reformulating national power structures – away from the prevailing patriarchal ideology to one where welfare is a central component – and to opening the paths for non-violent interaction between States.

In similar vein, Gardam's starting point is that the law of armed conflict – or international humanitarian law, as it is now frequently referred to – is law made by men in the interest of men to regulate an activity which is essentially decided on and carried out by men, but which impacts so enormously on the lives of women (and children). The results of this exclusion of women are the predominance of military necessity over humanitarian considerations, and a resultant preferential treatment and level of protection for (male) combatants over civilians (mainly women and children), who are the innocent victims of war. Her conclusion: for the development of a truly humanitarian system for the regulation of armed conflict, "human" needs to be defined as including women on a true basis of equality; otherwise the inherent oppression and victimization of women by the patriarchal State in the conduct of war will continue unabated. An insight – like those of Chinkin's paper – that could undoubtedly be applied to the "human rights" approach to violence in general.

CHRISTIAN STROHAL*

The United Nations Responses to Human Rights Violations

1. Introduction

This paper addresses responses of the United Nations to human rights violations, and describes the mechanisms which have been developed by the United Nations over the last decades. These responses can be seen as an excellent example of non-violent intervention, its possibilities and limitations.

First, a brief survey of the major steps towards the UN's human rights "machinery" as we see it today is provided; secondly, the main features of the system are examined; and thirdly, some attempt is made to guess where current developments in the UN's human rights debate might lead over the next few years.

It is exciting times we are living, not only for diplomats, but for all of us: times of rapid and fundamental change in international relations, providing new and unheard-of opportunities for international cooperation.

Since I will be focusing my discussion on the United Nations, I will not deal with other institutions which respond to human rights violations, such as agencies like the International Labour Office (ILO); regional arrangements of either a legal or political character – the Council of Europe or the inter-American human rights systems, or the Conference on Security and Cooper-

* U.N. Austrian Delegation, Geneva, Switzerland.

As this paper reflects an oral presentation to an international conference, I have added only the minimum of references, not claiming a complete overview of the wealth of literature on all aspects of the work of the UN in the protection and promotion of human rights. The most recent (and excellent) general overview is provided by the textbook by Frank Newman and David Weissbrodt, *International Human Rights: Law, Policy, and Process* (1990), Cincinnati: Anderson Publishing Co. For a – quickly available – summary on the results of the sessions of the Commission on Human Rights, both the "Human Rights Monitor", published by a Geneva based non-governmental organization particularly active in this field, the International Service for Human Rights, as well as the relevant articles in the Human Rights Quarterly, seem especially useful. For regular bibliographic updates, the Human Rights Internet Reporter, in particular its special bibliographic issue, is very useful.

Finally, it is obvious that the paper reflects my own opinion and not necessarily that of my government.

K.E. Mahoney and P. Mahoney (eds.), Human Rights in the Twenty-first Century, 347–360.

ation in Europe (CSCE); bilateral inter-governmental cooperation in human rights (a relatively new element in this field which has grown considerably over the last few years); and the International Committee of the Red Cross.

A fundamental underlying question concerns the relationship between the tools for human rights action – as represented by the UN's mechanisms – and the society which is called upon to make optimum use of these tools. The often used argument of non-interference in the internal affairs of states to reject any expression of international concern over specific human rights situations still exists, even though it has been discredited by numerous scholars and other experts.[1] Lately, however, this argument is being heard somewhat less often in the UN's conference rooms.

In this paper, the assumptions are made – following the UN Charter – that human rights are a legitimate global concern, and that the international community has a duty to deal with the protection and promotion of human rights in all parts of the world.

2. The Evolution of the UN's Intervention Machinery

Since 1945, one can discern a steady path from a *"no-powers"* situation (as ECOSOC called it in an early resolution), to standardization work, fact-finding and monitoring of the implementation of these standards (increasingly through specific country missions or "visits"), to interventions in individual cases of human rights violations.

The so-called human rights "machinery" includes both political and legal instruments or, as some prefer to call them, Charter-based and Convention-based mechanisms.[2]

The Convention or treaty-based mechanisms are all described in Section I, *infra*.[3]

They are the following:

- Committee for the Elimination of Racial Discrimination;
- Human Rights Committee;
- Committee on Economic, Social and Cultural Rights;
- Committee on the Elimination of all Forms of Discrimination Against Women,

[1] F. Ermacora, "Human Rights and Domestic Jurisdiction" (Article 2, para. 7 of the Charter), in 124: Recueil des cours (1968), II, p. 371.

[2] T. Opsahl, "Instruments of Implementation of Human Rights", in *Human Rights Law Journal* (1989), 10, p. 13.

[3] Section I, See M. Bossuyt, *infra*, at p. 48.

For an excellent overview on "effective implementation of international instruments on human rights", including a wealth of proposals from an insider (member of the Committee on Economic, Social and Cultural Rights) on improving all aspects of the work of the implementation organs, cf. the Note of the Secretary-General transmitting a study on these questions by Philipp Alston to the 44th session of the General Assembly (Doc. A/44/668 of 8 November 1989).

- Committee Against Torture, and the (forthcoming)
- Committee for the Rights of the Child.

In the UN Charter, the organization's function with regard to human rights is not very consistent.[4] In retrospect, this has its positive sides because it allowed the central human rights organ of the UN, the Commission on Human Rights, to develop flexibly its own structures and mechanisms on a step-by-step and issue-by-issue basis, laying the groundwork for a "multi-faceted practice"[5] of human rights protection.

Since its establishment in 1946, the Commission on Human Rights has developed into one of the most dynamic elements of the whole UN system. During its yearly six week sessions several hundred delegates debate, often far into the night, the whole spectrum of human rights questions, on which some 90 resolutions and decisions are adopted every year. Some of these are painstakingly negotiated word-by-word among the governmental representatives, all under the watchful eyes of representatives of nearly 200 non-governmental organizations.

This multi-faceted practice has developed over time from the major standardization work undertaken by the Commission in the 1950s and 1960s, in particular the elaboration of the two Covenants to the so-called *1503 procedure*,[6] (a confidential, and sometimes quite effective process which deals with individual allegations of gross human rights violations, where the government concerned is invited to respond), to specific public methods of dealing with human rights situations in individual countries.

Specific mechanisms for a sort of intervention in individual countries have continued to develop since 1967, when the *ad hoc* Working Group of Experts on Human Rights in Southern Africa was established. The further steps in this development are described in Section I, *infra*,[7] and can be summarized as follows:

1979 – the first nomination of a Special Rapporteur on an individual country situation (Equatorial Guinea);

1981 – the first Special Rapporteur nominated with a mandate for a fact-finding mission, including recommendations for assistance to the country in question (El Salvador);

[4] H. Kelsen, *The Law of the United Nations, A Critical Analysis of its Fundamental Problems* (1950), London: Stevens and Sons.

[5] K. Herndl, "Recent Developments Concerning United Nations Fact-Finding in the Field of Human Rights", in M. Nowak et al. (eds.) *Progress in the Spirit of Human Rights, Festschrift für Felix Ermacora* (1988), Kehl – Strasbourg – Arlington: N. P. Engel Verlag, p. 1 at p. 4.

[6] Named after ECOSOC-resolution 1503 (XLVIII) of 1970 which – on the basis of ECOSOC-resolutions 728 F (XXVIII) of 1959 on the treatment of communications (itself, in turn, starting the rescinding of the "no power" opinion) and 1235 (XLII) of 1967 authorizing the Commission and the Sub-Commission to examine information relevant to gross human rights violations established the first procedure of dealing systematically, albeit confidentially, with communications on human rights violations.

[7] See Section I, M. Bossuyt, *infra*, p. 50.

1982 – the first fact-finding mission entrusted by the Commission on Human Rights to the UN's Secretary-General (Poland);

1983 – the first time the Commission accepted a proposal from its main subsidiary organ, the Sub-Commission on Prevention of Discrimination and Protection of Minorities, to nominate a Special Rapporteur (Afghanistan);

1980–1990 – the first "thematic" approach to questions of human rights violations (which has developed into one of the most promising methods) was adopted when the Working Group on Disappearances was appointed. This was followed in quick steps by special rapporteurs on the subjects of:

- arbitrary or summary executions (1982);
- torture (1985);
- religious intolerance (1986);
- mercenaries (1987); and
- certain aspects of the rights of the child (1990).[8]

The creation of these numerous mechanisms also constitutes a reflection of a realistic assessment of the possibilities of intervention by the Secretary-General of the organization: as long as interventions in the field of human rights are seen as being unfriendly or hostile, the Secretary-General is bound by the need of maintaining relations of confidence to all member states in order to allow him the effective discharge of his many duties.

3. The Structure of the Mechanisms: From Fact-Finding to Direct Intervention and Dialogue

The methodology of the various UN mechanisms adopted a systematic pattern more or less as follows:

The first step is information gathering or fact-finding, followed by a reporting to the international community. Conclusions and recommendations of the Rapporteur on a specific situation are offered, which are followed by debate and action by the Commission. This mostly takes the form of adoption of resolutions, sometimes followed by similar action in ECOSOC and the General Assembly.

The "thematic" mechanisms, while also following this methodology, developed, in addition, so-called "*urgent action*" mandates. These constitute action with regard to information on human rights violations of individual human beings. In practice, telegrams or letters are sent to the government

[8] A brief summary of the mandates of all these mechanisms is given in a UN publication, United Nations Action in the Field of Human Rights, (New York, 1988), pp. 16 – 18. For a complete overview of the mandates, the relevant Commission resolutions – which are mentioned in this publication – should be consulted.

concerned, mostly without publicity, but reporting thereon annually to the Commission.

A recent intervention by the UN's Under Secretary-General for Human Rights, Jan Martenson, before the Third Committee of the General Assembly, provided a succinct summary of this development:

> "... we find that in the first nine months of 1990, 799 cases transmitted by urgent cable to Governments and many more cases were transmitted by letter. Several thousand communications were screened in connection with these cases, as were numerous replies from Governments ... 22 rounds of consultations of special rapporteurs were organized ... a total of 16 field missions to 29 countries were organized".[9]

The basis for most, if not all, of this work is these "*communications*", i.e. information provided by governments, non-governmental organizations or individuals, and collected and processed by the UN Centre for Human Rights in Geneva.

A steady growth of communication with governments has led to increasing possibilities for a real dialogue between the various elements of this system: most importantly, between the international mechanism and the governments concerned, but also between governments and non-governmental organizations, and at the national level, between governments and their own citizens.

The Commission on Human Rights is a forum for much, if not most, of this dialogue. This is particularly true for non-governmental organizations which play a crucial role in urging the Commission forward. They do this by collecting relevant information in the field, and then bringing it to an international audience by quite often providing a public conscience in the face of inter-governmental relations, and by offering expertise on monitoring and fact-finding.

The dialogue developed at the Commission's sessions has contributed, over the longer term, to an improvement in attitudes of a number of countries. Cooperation with the Commission's mechanisms at their beginning was rather the exception than the rule. Today, it is the other way around. There are, however, limitations to the Commission's effectiveness, not least of which is the fact that the Commission meets only once a year. All human rights issues of the last 12 months have to be discussed within this very short period of time.

Depending upon the relationship between the mechanism and the government of the country in question, the dialogue – if it exists – takes on diverse forms. One of the potentially and most rewarding dialogue is visits to the country in question. Such visits – which are essentially fact-finding missions – are undertaken not only by country-specific rapporteurs, but increasingly by representatives of "thematic" mechanisms. In the year 1989 alone, thematic

[9] Transcript of a declaration made to the Third Committee of the General Assembly on 8 October, 1990.

visits, in addition to visits by country-specific rapporteurs, took place in Guatemala, Honduras and Zaire on the subject of torture; in Columbia on summary or arbitrary executions; and El Salvador, the Philippines and Sri Lanka invited representatives of Working Group on Disappearances.

These visits normally result in a special report to the Commission. If the Commission finds the time for a comprehensive debate, the report contributes to an even higher degree of involvement of the government concerned in the human rights issues addressed in the report.

4. Shortcomings Remain

In spite of these impressive and effective methods of work, a number of shortcomings remain.[10] They fall into two main categories: the methods and effectiveness of the work, and the dependence of the work on decisions which have to be taken by the Commission , a political body, (which, in turn, must be endorsed by ECOSOC), which determines the mechanism's continued existence.

Some of the more striking shortcomings of the Commission on Human Rights include the lack of immediate and effective sanctions vis-à-vis violators of human rights, other than the weapon of international public opinion. Linked with this is the relative lack of immediately effective political incentives for governments who do cooperate with international mechanisms, as compared to those who dispute any legitimacy of international concern. Furthermore, all the mechanisms constitute essentially an *ex post* approach to human rights violations. They have little, if any, immediate preventive powers or effects apart from the general desire of governments not to be exposed as human rights violators.

An additional problem is that before mechanisms reach the point of becoming operative, the hurdle of the Commission on Human Rights must be overcome. Any proposal for the establishment of a new mechanism, as well as the annual reports of existing ones, are exposed to the political wheeling and dealing of Commission diplomats. These diplomats are often less concerned about achieving a balanced overall view and clear expression of opinion on effective protection and promotion of human rights in all parts of the world, and in individual countries with a record of human rights violations, than they are in reaching *consensus* or conducting bilateral feuds in multilateral surroundings.

This leads to the common reproach of "*selectivity*" with regard to international action on country-specific situations. The most prominent example of selectivity in recent years is the failure of the Commission to either adopt a resolution on the situation of human rights in Iraq, or to appoint a special rapporteur on this subject. It was left to the experts of the Sub-Commission at

[10] See note 3, *supra*.

its session in August 1990 to finally forward a request to the Commission to consider the appointment of a special rapporteur on Iraq.

The most important problem, however, is the difficulty of translating international action into national effect, of reaching from the international conference room to the individual human being whose rights are being violated. The gap between norm and reality remains much too often.

5. Detente and the Next Steps: Dangers and Opportunities

The current fundamental and dynamic developments and changes in the international arena[11] in Eastern Europe and elsewhere both benefit and endanger further development in the international system for the protection of human rights.

The most immediately recognizable benefits in international fora are the final recognition of human rights as a global concern, a "coming of age of human rights". This development is largely due to the end of the Cold War and the concomitant sterile East-West confrontation, which was particularly manifested in international human rights bodies. The new changes are expressed in a forceful and clear statement in the last Report of the UN's Secretary-General to the General Assembly on the work of the Organization. The Report states:

> "the past year has seen the conversion of human rights from a subsidiary theme of the international discourse to a dominant concern .... Resolution of conflicts, observance of human rights and the promotion of development together weave the fabric of peace; if one of these strands is removed, the tissue will unravel."[12]

This positive development will lead to new constellations and new coalitions which will affect the structures of international negotiations in human rights bodies, especially the Commission on Human Rights.

As the old confrontation of East and West over human rights has practically disappeared, delegations from East European countries, especially the Soviet Union, no longer spend their energies devising counter-proposals and counter-strategies to "western" ideas. They not only join "western" resolutions to which they were bitterly opposed for many years, but they also actually have their own constructive proposals to further strengthen and widen these mechanisms and seek support from other countries for them. Now, such resolutions can be adopted, more often than not, without a vote.

Even with this very beneficial new attitude to human rights issues, however, new problems emerge. Potential dangers of the recent upheavals in inter-

[11] See I. Cotler, *infra*, at p. 7.

[12] (Annual) Report on the Work of the Organization, Doc. A/45/1 (cited here after Press Release SG 139-GA/451 of 17 Sept. 1990, pp. 19–20).

national relations are widely recognized. In particular, there is the danger that the easing of East-West tensions could lead to a growing North-South configuration or, even worse, confrontation.

Until the recent past, developing countries, more often than not, have been able to take the relatively comfortable position of bystander to heated verbal battles between East European and western countries over human rights concepts and attitudes. Now, these developing countries have lost a powerful protector who shielded them from too fast a development of effective international mechanisms; they might, in addition, feel being left alone in confronting potential international scrutiny of their human rights record as the considerable improvements, which have taken place recently in this field, in most East European countries take away a group of prime "targets" for such international action. There are, however, quite a number of positive political developments outside Eastern Europe, indeed on all continents, to support an optimistic outlook on the attitudes of many developing countries towards human rights issues.

This new constellation of diplomatic, and political, realities and powers make the current moment particularly important for reconsidering the status quo, for reviewing old habits, and for revising attitudes in multilateral negotiations. The new developments in the general political arena, in other words, bring about not only new diplomatic constellations, but also a need to translate them into change. The moment for such opportunities is now, and should not be lost.

6. Old Proposals and New: Towards a Really Effective System?

Indeed, a number of new ideas and proposals, some new, some old but hitherto "unrealistic", is emerging; more and more attempts to use these developments for bringing about change are being undertaken. In the remainder of this paper, I shall briefly look at some of these ideas and undertakings.

(1) Improving the "Machinery"

First, with regard to the various UN mechanisms themselves, the proposals for increasing their effectiveness are practically endless. Every few years, working groups, both formal and informal, have been looking into this question. They have quite often come up with suggestions which were then taken on board by the Commission if they introduced only relatively marginal changes; more often, however, if they presented a danger of real reform, they were being carefully laid to rest. Such proposals centred around some of the following issues:

(a) finding possibilities for responding quickly to emergency situations, for example through extraordinary sessions of the Commission or by providing an inter-sessional, i.e., continuous, role for the Commission's Bureau (its chairperson, three vice-chairpersons and a rapporteur, one each from the five regional groups within the UN system); these ideas have, so far, not found much support outside western delegations;

(b) giving the Secretariat a greater substantial role, or – to mention the potentially most far-reaching proposal in this field – creating the post of a High Commissioner for Human Rights, modelled after the function of an "ombudsman" in a number of developed countries; this particular idea (which goes back to the director of the then UN Division for Human Rights in the early 60s, Professor J. Humphrey, if not further), however, has lost some of its attraction in direct proportionality to the increase in thematic mechanisms. In the mind of some delegations, it is feared that the functions of these mechanisms might be hampered or endangered by a High Commissioner without real intervention powers. If attributed with a clear mandate to function both within the UN system as well as outside, however, such a High Commissioner could still prove to be extremely valuable;

(c) creating an ongoing dialogue between the various elements of the system, in particular between the political and the treaty-based organs, and between the Commission and its main subsidiary body composed, at least in theory, of independent experts (as opposed to government representatives), the Sub-Commission on Prevention of Discrimination and the Protection of Minorities, a body for which, in turn, a number of proposals for reform are being made every year.

More recently, ideas for change within the UN system have become bolder, and seek, among other things, a "real" human rights role for the Secretary General, a framework for continuous preventive diplomacy together with an "early-warning system" within the UN Secretariat, the creation of stand-by intervention groups of experts for emergency situations, or, indeed, a Security Council for Human Rights.

Some of the ideas labelled "reform" or "strengthening of the UN", however, seem rather like thinly-disguised attempts at weakening the system. To mention only one example, recent proposals made by the movement of non-aligned states to a working group of the Commission included the following:

> "The practice in respect of the appointment of Special Rapporteurs on thematic issues should be re-examined ... Working Groups of five persons from different regions should be formed. (They) ... could also include members from various Permanent Missions in Geneva, which would result in reduction of expenditure ..."[13]

(To some, it might have been evident to see how a group of five Geneva-based diplomats – subject to constant profession-bound rotation – could be more efficient or forthcoming than an independent and expert Special Rapporteur or a Working Group composed of experts appointed in their personal capacity.)

[13] Doc. E/CD.4/WG.3/WP.10 (1 March 1990). (For proposals from five western countries on measures to improve the efficiency of the mechanisms, made to the same working group of the Commission, see document E/CN.4/WG.3/WP.8 of 23 February, 1990).

(2) "Positive Intervention": Human Rights Development Assistance

Secondly, turning to proposals which directly influence the situation in individual countries, (i.e., to improve specific human rights performances), there is one proposal in particular which is promising to make a difference: a vastly improved and enlarged programme for multilateral technical assistance in the field of human rights. Let me briefly sketch the current situation and give a brief outlook at likely developments.

The United Nations have had, since the 1950s, a relatively small programme called "advisory services in the field of human rights", which provided – and provides – the framework for international seminars and workshops; for fellowships and scholarships to participate in some of the United Nations's work in the field of human rights; and for the occasional expert advice to governments on questions such as the proper formulation of their reports to treaty organs. Undoubtedly, all these services were useful – and some still are. Increasingly, however, it was felt that what was really needed were more precise country-related development projects in specific human rights questions in order to reach the area where human rights efforts matter most, that is, at the national level. It was clear that the programme would have to undergo fundamental change and receive considerably larger funds than the U.S. $500,000, or so which the UN budget provided annually. The United Nations were unable or unwilling, however, to decide on such an expansion.

Therefore, some delegations active in this field looked for alternatives. It took until 1987 when the endeavours of the former Assistant Secretary-General for Human Rights, K. Herndl, succeeded in having the Commission on Human Rights adopt Resolution 1987/38, a resolution which created a Voluntary Fund for Advisory Services and Technical Assistance in the Field of Human Rights, and which was endorsed, in turn, by ECOSOC and the General Assembly that same year.

Voluntary contributions of a number of States, essentially from the industrialized world, to this fund have currently reached the total of some U.S. $2–3 million and allowed the first concrete projects to be realized. On the experience gained with these projects, the Centre for Human Rights is currently reviewing procedures and practices in order to establish a valid new programme taking into account the availability of more funds.

The sums involved so far, however, are comparatively minimal (The UN Development Programme, UNDP, has funds in the magnitude of approximately U.S. $1 billion and the human rights related development projects conducted by the ILO cover altogether a budget of nearly half of that amount again). Therefore, two further measures are currently being discussed:

- introducing more "human rights-relevance" into the development cooperation programmes of the big international agencies such as, in particular, the UNDP and the World Bank; and/or
- using some of the funds existing in other organizations for projects carried out under the auspices of the UN Centre for Human Rights.

With these aims, it is felt, one could make use of the specific expertise within the Centre for Human Rights in order to turn it into a "clearing house" within the overall UN system for human rights assistance. It is hoped that the current endeavours will quickly lead to results which would have to include the following:

- raise the international awareness – both within the United Nations system and outside, in particular also that of governments – for the need for development assistance in the field of human rights; and thus
- also raise the degree of acceptability of such assistance (as many governments still seem to fear that a request for assistance could be interpreted as an admission of guilt); as well as
- raise the degree of generosity of the governments of rich countries to provide the necessary funds.

At the same time, such an enlarged programme of technical assistance has to be seen as being complementary to the fact-finding, monitoring, and intervening of the various mechanisms which I have sketched. Advisory services and technical assistance, in other words, must not be seen as a possible loophole for escaping international scrutiny. If developed with circumspection, these programmes will become a necessary corollary to scrutiny and might thus, constitute an element of additional protection of the various fact-finding mechanisms *vis-à-vis* attempts at avoiding, or circumventing them, if not trying to diminish them in scope and effectiveness. In order to reach this stage, the mechanisms – both of the Commission as well as the treaty-based bodies – in turn, will have to be more forthcoming in suggesting concrete assistance measures.

(3) Reaching Directly All Individuals Concerned through Information and Education

A further element in using the current favourable international political climate for change in the international protection and promotion of human rights undoubtedly lies in the field of information and education. Only if the individual human beings in all parts of the world are actually aware of their rights, and the individual governments of their obligations, will international protection really become effective in all parts of the world. Under the inspiration of the current Under Secretary-General for Human Rights, J. Martenson, a World Information Campaign has been launched in order to make this happen. It is hoped that the first results of this Campaign will soon be tangible; for this, a continuous evaluation process seems highly desirable.

Taking these three elements together – improving the mechanisms; providing effective assistance at the national levels; and increasing awareness of the general public, as well as of authorities concerned and thus, increasing the general level of information about human rights – it should also be possible to reduce the degree of politicization of the international human rights debate and action. Thus, both elements in this framework for international action –

remedial as well as preventive – will benefit. On the basis of the existing framework, it should be possible to make the big step forward, which is necessary in order to render this action really effective.

7. A World Conference: Better Tools for Cure and Prevention?

The place to realize this step forward into real effectiveness might well be the World Conference for Human Rights which is proposed for 1993. Currently, it is much too early to appraise the likelihood of this conference attaining such an aim; it is safe to say, however, that it will present a unique opportunity which should not be lost.

Whereas the first – and, so far, last – such conference, the International Conference on Human Rights, which took place in Teheran in 1968, resulted in the adoption of a "*Proclamation of Teheran*",[14] as well as of a number of individual resolutions, it is generally felt today that its impact on the further development of the promotion and protection of human rights – seen with the hindsight of more than twenty years – has remained marginal. Without entering into a discussion of an evaluation of the Teheran Conference, it seems obvious that an international conference on human rights held 25 years after the conference in Tehran is likely to not only raise much more general interest, but can also have a more lasting impact, given the international political climate in which it probably will take place. The current session of the UN General Assembly is called upon to lay the ground for the preparatory process to start next year. At this moment, one can only speculate about its prospects; in general terms, as the gist of my intervention should have shown, these prospects are quite good.

It is to be expected that the World Conference will constitute the end of an elaborate preparatory process, involving various international instances: a Preparatory Committee proper, the General Assembly as final decision maker, and in between them, all existing human rights bodies, in particular the Commission and the treaty-based organs, as well as regional institutions. In addition, it is obvious that not only governments and the UN mechanisms themselves will have to be involved on a continuous and quite intensive level in these preparations; considerable input will be expected from the academic world, as well as from non-governmental organizations.

As a side-effect – given the challenge presented by the Conference – it is likely that a quasi continuous informal preparatory network will soon develop, in particular among Permanent Missions in Geneva where most of the preparatory work is likely to take place, if for no other reason than the location of the UN Centre for Human Rights which will provide the secretariat of the Conference. In view of the cordial atmosphere which generally reigns among

[14] See Human Rights – A Compilation of International Instruments, UN (New York: 1988).p. 43 sqq.

human rights diplomats from all regions, in Geneva as well as in New York, it is to be expected that such a network will not only constitute a quite effective focal point for the preparatory process, but that it might become quite an interesting general human rights framework *per se*, which could develop into an effective preventive mechanism.

On the assumption that this preparatory process will be successful, the World Conference – which will then be able to adopt the fruits of two years of intensive preparatory labour – should also constitute the starting point for turning change into action; it should not only lay the groundwork for, but also decide upon action in order to turn at least some of the proposals I mentioned earlier – and some of the doubtless innumerable proposals still to be made during the preparatory process – into reality.

On this rather promising conclusion, however, – and here I come back to the underlying question mentioned at the beginning – one must not forget that all these developments concern international structures and mechanisms, in other words tools, which prove their usefulness only in the use we make of them. And there is a role for all of us, individually, in groups, in national and international non-governmental organizations, and in international governmental cooperation. We all are practitioners of human rights.

8. Post-Script: The Speed of Change

Having reviewed this paper six months after the Conference, Human Rights in the Twenty-first Century, took place, I cannot resist adding a post-script on some of the developments resulting from the unprecedented acceleration of change within the UN's human rights framework.

First of all, the proposal of holding a World Conference on Human Rights in 1993 has not only been adopted by the General Assembly, but has led, during the 1991 session of the Commission on Human Rights, to very fruitful discussions paving the way for the first meeting of the Preparatory Committee later this year. So far, a North-South confrontation was not only avoided, but indeed the informal network among Permanent Missions in Geneva is already busy in working towards a very cooperative effort of preparations.

Human rights, democracy, and development appear to be key elements in these preparations for which both the General Assembly and the Commission have laid down the general objectives. Essentially, and on the basis of the universal character of human rights, the Conference shall take stock of the system, evaluate its effectiveness, examine the relationship between human rights and development, and propose measures to address obstacles and improve the system. All existing human rights bodies are called upon to contribute to the preparation for the Conference over the next two years; groups, in particular the academic world and non-governmental organizations, should be ready to formulate proposals. It will be exciting to see if the international community, in the preparatory process and at the Conference itself, will live up to the challenge.

There were other successes at the last session of the Commission which also merit being mentioned in the present context, specifically, appointing two new special rapporteurs on country situations, one on the situation of human rights in Iraq, and another on the situation in occupied Kuwait. Even if it finally took a war to make these decisions of the Commission successful (earlier attempts did not find enough positive votes), it undoubtedly constitutes a step towards a higher credibility of the whole country-related approach.

Furthermore, the Commission decided on a new thematic mechanism which has all the elements of turning into a most important new body. Upon suggestion from the Sub-Commission (and due to, in particular, long-time preparatory work of its expert from France, L. Joinet[15]), the Commission created a Working Group on Administrative Detention which will be able to close the largest remaining gap between the subject matters of the various thematic mechanisms.

In addition, the Centre for Human Rights laid the ground for an enlarged programme of technical assistance, in particular by elaborating guidelines on project formulation, execution and evaluation.[16]

These decisions, taken together and seen in the context of a new strength of, and confidence in the United Nations (which has developed over the last few months) create further opportunities which only a few months ago seemed still rather far away. Although this is not the place to speculate about the possibilities of the world organization, such recent developments appear perched to invoke a "droit d'ingérence" on humanitarian grounds, to bring about change in its member states, to bring, in particular, human rights closer to where they really matter – to the level of the individual human being.

The tools are there, old and new, fresh and shining all of them, and the craftsmen are called upon to make the best use of them.

[15] See in particular his report to the Sub-Commission on the practice of administrative detention (Docs. E/CN.4/Sub.2/1990/29 and Add. 1).

[16] See the Report of the Secretary-General to the 47th session of the Commission on Human Rights on Advisory Services in the Field of Human Rights, (Doc. E/CN.4/1991/55).

PAUL MAHONEY AND FREDRIK SUNDBERG*

The European Convention on Human Rights: A Case Study of the International Law Response to Violence

1. INTRODUCTION

One response of the international community to the existence of human rights violations has been to submit sovereign States to independent enforcement machinery allowing other States or (even) individual victims to lodge complaints and, if successful in proving their case, to obtain adequate redress. The 1950 European Convention on Human Rights ("ECHR") – with its two control bodies, the European Commission and European Court of Human Rights, which are based in Strasbourg, France, the seat of their parent Organisation, the Council of Europe – represents a functioning example of such international enforcement machinery, currently binding 23 European States.[1] The present paper endeavours to summarise the implications of the existing reach of the European Convention on Human Rights in terms of State responsibility for violence and, in the light of that analysis, to offer a tentative assessment of the present and future capability of international human rights law to prevent and remedy violence.[2]

* Officials of the Council of Europe. The views expressed are personal. The authors wish to thank Michael O'Boyle of the Registry of the European Court of Human Rights for his helpful comments.

[1] To present a necessarily simplified picture, the European Commission of Human Rights is vested with the vital preliminary role of filtering admissible complaints (1648 applications registered in 1991) and then of expressing a legal opinion on the 10% or so of cases declared admissible; the European Court of Human Rights is empowered to give a final and binding judgment in the cases referred to it after completion of the proceedings before the Commission (93 cases referred in 1991); admitted cases which are not settled or referred to the Court are decided by the Committee of Ministers of the Council of Europe (17 cases in 1991).

[2] There is of course much highly relevant case law (a) of the Inter-American Court of Human Rights under the American Convention on Human Rights, in particular concerning the State's obligation to prevent and investigate murders, disappearances, etc. perpetrated by armed groups, and (b) of the United Nations Human Rights Committee under the International Covenant on Civil and Political Rights. The present paper does not purport to take account of that material. For a discussion of the Inter-American jurisprudence, see the paper by Dinah Shelton, ..., [*infra/supra*], pp. 267-268.

K.E. Mahoney and P. Mahoney (eds.), Human Rights in the Twenty-first Century, 361–376.

2. Responsibility for What?

The protection of human life and human dignity is expressly secured in two Articles of the ECHR, one guaranteeing the right to life, and the other prohibiting torture and inhuman or degrading treatment or punishment.[3] These provisions, however, are directed against extreme manifestations of violence.

The right-to-life provision outlaws the taking of life, save in a limited number of exhaustively listed circumstances. Use of lethal force is permissible, for example, in cases of legitimate self-defence, in order to effect a lawful arrest, in action lawfully taken for the purpose of quelling a riot or (if an appropriate written derogation has been filed by the State) where death results from "lawful acts of war".[4] Capital punishment is another such expressly recognised exception, although under an optional protocol to the Convention, so far ratified by 17 States, the death penalty in time of peace is prohibited.[5] The European Court of Human Rights has no case-law on this Article, and the European Commission very little.

One of the major questions of interpretation so far unresolved is whether the right to life of an unborn child is guaranteed and, if so, to what extent. When rejecting the complaint of a husband that his wife had, without his consent, aborted their child under British legislation designed to protect the health of the mother, the Commission unambiguously excluded an interpretation recognising an *absolute* "right to life" of the foetus.[6] Beyond that, however, it left the issue open by holding that, even assuming that the right to life might extend to the foetus in the initial stages of pregnancy, the facts of the case would fall within an implied limitation protecting the life and health of the woman. To this extent, therefore, the mother's right to life was given priority over a possible right to life of the foetus. The position is further complicated because attempts, likewise inconclusive, have been made by women to argue that the right to respect for private (sexual) life, which is also safeguarded under the ECHR[7], allows a woman the liberty to control her own body as she reasonably chooses and so includes the right to have an abortion.[8] Such arguments raise complex issues, as the ECHR is to be read as a whole[9]: the right to life, even assuming that it applies in some degree to unborn children, cannot be construed

[3] Arts. 2 and 3 ECHR.

[4] Arts. 2(2) and 15(2) ECHR. See Michael O'Boyle, "*The Use of Lethal Force under Article 2 of the European Convention on Human Rights*", Council of Europe doc. DH-ED-COLL(90)9.

[5] Protocol No. 6 to the ECHR. Ratifications as at 1 July 1991.

[6] Application no. 8416/79, *X v. UK*, admissibility decision, 19 Decisions and Reports of the European Commission of Human Rights ("DR") 244(1980). See also Application no. 767/60, *X v. Norway*, admissibility decision, 4 Yearbook on the ECHR (YBECHR) 270 (1961), and Application no. 7045/75, *X v. Austria*, admissibility decision, 7 DR 87 (1976).

[7] Art. 8 ECHR.

[8] See, eg, *Bruggemann and Scheuten v. FRG*, European Commission of Human Rights ("ECmHR"), 10 DR 100 (1977).

[9] *Klass and Others v. FRG*, European Court of Human Rights ("ECtHR") 6 Sept. 1978, Series A Vol. 28, para. 68.

so as to nullify an aspect of women's right to respect for private life, and *vice versa*.

It was established by the Commission in *Stewart v. United Kingdom*, a Northern Ireland case, that the right-to-life guarantee is not directed exclusively against intentional killing: the State's duty to protect life covers the taking of life caused by negligent or reckless acts as well as premeditated acts.[10] The recourse to force which the right-to-life clause permits for certain exhaustively listed purposes must be "no more than absolutely necessary". If the use of force is judged to have been disproportionate in the circumstances to the legitimate aim pursued, any resultant loss of life will be contrary to the ECHR even if it was unintentionally caused. On the facts, the Commission found that the accidental killing of the applicant mother's son by a plastic baton fired by the British Army during a riot in Northern Ireland was the result of a justified use of force.[11]

The ECHR's prohibition of torture and of inhuman and degrading treatment or punishment, as the Court has made clear, is limited to what generally constitute extreme forms of violence:

> "[I]ll-treatment, including punishment, must attain a minimum level of severity if it is to fall within the scope of [the prohibition]. The assessment of this minimum is, in the nature of things, relative; it depends on all the circumstances of the case, such as the nature and context of the treatment or punishment, the manner and method of its execution, its duration, its physical or mental effects and, in some instances, the sex, age and state of health of the victim..."[12]

A few cases serve to illustrate the kind of ill-treatment caught by the relevant Article.[13]

In the case brought by the Netherlands and the Scandinavian countries against the regime of the Greek Colonels (the *Greek case*), the Commission concluded in its report that political detainees had been subjected by the security police to torture for the purpose of extracting confessions or information.[14] The main method of torture took the form of *falanga*, a beating of the feet which causes excruciating pain but which leaves no marks.

In the case of *Ireland v. United Kingdom*, which concerned the internment and ill-treatment of suspected terrorists in Northern Ireland in the early 1970's, the combined application of five "sensory-deprivation" techniques of inter-

[10] Application no. 10044/82, *Stewart v. UK*, admissibility decision, 39 DR 162 at 169–171 (1984).

[11] Ibid. at 173.

[12] *Soering v. UK*, ECtHR 7 July 1989, Series A Vol. 161, para. 100.

[13] Art. 3 ECHR.

[14] Applications nos. 3321/67, *Denmark v. Greece*, 3322/67 *Norway v. Greece*, 3323/67, *Sweden v. Greece*, and 3344/67, *Netherlands v. Greece* 12 YBECHR 1 at 504 (1969).

rogation was judged by the Court to constitute inhuman treatment but not torture.[15]

In its following judgment in *Tyrer v. United Kingdom*, the Court ruled that a judicial sentence of birching (whipping) imposed on a youth in the Isle of Man constituted "degrading punishment".[16]

In the recent case of *Soering v. United Kingdom*, the Court held that the extradition of a young German national to the United States of America to face a capital murder charge and the attendant risk of a death penalty would, if implemented, give rise to inhuman treatment, notably because of his exposure to the so-called "death-row" phenomenon".[17] It can reasonably be surmised that the European attitude to capital punishment influenced the Strasbourg Court's assessment of the suffering caused by the death-row phenomenon, that is whether that suffering went beyond the acceptable threshold set by the prohibition of inhuman treatment under the ECHR. *De facto* the death penalty no longer exists in time of peace in the ECHR countries. In the few Contracting States that retain the death penalty in law for some peace-time offences, death sentences, if ever imposed, are nowadays not carried out. The judgment quoted from Amnesty International's third-party brief which spoke of the "virtual consensus in Western European legal systems that the death penalty is no longer consistent with regional standards of justice".[18]

It was spelt out in these cases that not only physical assault but also mental suffering and anguish, if sufficiently serious, may involve torture and inhuman or degrading treatment.[19] Mental as well as physical violence is thus recognised as a deserving target of human rights law. In *Tyrer*, for example, the Court took account not only of the physical pain experienced but also, since there had been a considerable delay before execution of the punishment, of the sentenced person's mental anguish of anticipating the violence he was to have inflicted on him.

In sum, these two Articles of the ECHR provide a valuable but limited net of protection, in that they can be of little assistance to victims of less serious violence. Thus, in the *Northern Ireland* case the Court, although describing the harsh conditions of detention at a military camp as "discreditable and reprehensible", did not find them to be "inhuman" or "degrading" within the meaning of the ECHR.[20]

[15] ECtHR, 18 Jan. 1978, Series A vol. 25, paras. 165–68.

[16] ECtHR 25 April 1978, Series A Vol. 26.

[17] See note 8, *supra* paras. 105–11.

[18] Ibid., para. 102.

[19] See note 16 *supra* at para. 33. Cf. also *Campbell and Cosans v. UK*, ECtHR 25 Feb. 1982, Series A Vol. 48, para. 26, where the Court declared that the mere threat of prohibited ill-treatment may itself give rise to a violation; on the facts, the threat of corporal punishment as a disciplinary measure in Scottish schools was not found to involve inhuman or degrading treatment.

[20] See note 15 *supra* at paras. 179–81. See also *Guzzardi v. Italy*, ECtHR 6 Nov. 1980, Series A Vol. 39 (preventive detention of a Mafia suspect in dilapidated, insanitary buildings in a restricted part of an isolated island not held to constitute "inhuman treatment"), and Application no. 6870/75, *B v. UK* ECmHR report, 32 DR 5 at 29–30 (1983) ("deplorable overcrowding" and

Protection against violence, and in particular lesser forms of violence, has however been held to constitute an element of other fundamental rights and freedoms guaranteed by the ECHR.

Recourse by the police to violence not amounting to inhuman or degrading treatment – for example to extract a confession or an accusatory statement from a suspect or a witness – may undermine the overall fairness of criminal proceedings and thus give rise to a breach of the defendant's right to a fair trial.[21]

In *Campbell and Cosans v. United Kingdom* the use of corporal punishment in State-run schools in Scotland was held to violate parents' right to respect for their philosophical convictions in the public education given to their children.[22]

In the case of *X and Y v. Netherlands* the sexual assault of a 16 year old female patient in a Dutch psychiatric hospital was found to involve a denial of her right to respect for her private life.[23] A compulsory medical intervention, even of minor importance such as a blood test, will also constitute an interference with this right, although there will be no actionable violation if the interference is justified.[24] By extension, the right to respect for family life presumably also includes some safeguards for family members against violence. Similarly the Court accepted in an Austrian case *(Plattform Àrzte für das Leben ("Doctors for the right to life" Campaign) v. Austria)* that violence may destroy an individual's or a group's enjoyment of their freedom of peaceful assembly and freedom of association:[25]

> "A demonstration may annoy or give offence to persons opposed to the ideas or claims that it is seeking to promote. The participants must, however, be able to hold the demonstration without having to fear that they will be subjected to physical violence by their opponents; such fear would be liable to deter associations or other groups supporting common ideas or interests from openly expressing their opinions on highly controversial issues affecting the community."[26]

"less than satisfactory" sanitary arrangements in a psychiatric hospital not considered to amount to "inhuman treatment"). Contrast with two cases where the Commission did judge the conditions of detention to be appalling enough to give rise to inhuman treatment: *Greek case, supra* note 14, and Applications nos.6780/74 and 6950/75, *Cyprus v. Turkey*, ECmHR report, 4 European Human Rights Reports 482 at 560 (1982) (withholding of food, water and medical treatment – both cases).

[21] This follows from the general principle (which the ECHR bodies have recognised) that the way in which evidence is obtained may render criminal proceedings unfair. Art. 6 ECHR safeguards the right to a fair trial in civil and criminal proceedings.

[22] See note 19 *supra*. The parents' right in question is part of the right to education, safeguarded by Art. 2 of Protocol No. 1 to the ECHR.

[23] ECtHR 26 March 1985, Series A Vol. 91; having regard to its conclusion under Art. 8 ECHR (right to respect for private and family life), the Court did not find that it also had to examine the case under Art. 3 (prohibition of torture and inhuman treatment) – ibid. at para. 34.

[24] Application no. 8278, *X v. Austria*, admissibility decision, 18 DR 154 at 156 (1979).

[25] Freedoms safeguarded by Art. 11 ECHR.

[26] ECtHR 21 June 1988, Series A Vol. 139, para. 32.

A crucial question is just how far the other (largely civil and political) rights in the ECHR can be stretched to cover lesser forms of violence not prohibited by the right-to-life and torture articles.

The European Court and European Commission of Human Rights employ what is sometimes termed the technique of evolutive interpretation. In the 1978 *Tyrer* case the Court affirmed for the first time that "the Convention is a living instrument which ... must be interpreted in the light of present-day conditions".[27] In holding the sentence of birching to be "degrading punishment" outlawed by the ECHR, the Court "[could not] but be influenced by the developments and commonly accepted standards in penal policy of the member States of the Council of Europe in this field".[28] The unstated implication is that whether or not the drafters of the ECHR would have classified judicial corporal punishment as "degrading", the meaning of the adjective "degrading" in 1978, as shown by the contemporary penal policy of the Contracting States as a whole, prompted that conclusion.

As far as making the ECHR's net of protection cover the myriad forms that violence can take in our societies, there is thus *some* scope for extending the existing list of ECHR rights by interpretation into areas or directions not foreseen by the drafters. Nonetheless, the potential for the ECHR (and selective instruments like it) to catch all manifestations of violence, and in particular mental violence, is necessarily limited. One gap, we have seen, concerns ill-treatment of prisoners which is not severe enough to pass the threshold of inhuman or degrading treatment. Another is the absence of provisions guaranteeing the right to institute private criminal proceedings in respect of illegal acts of violence and the right to compensation for criminal injuries. Yet another is the protection of minorities, now a matter of major concern in Europe since the collapse of the communist regimes in Central and Eastern Europe. Non-discrimination and individual rights may not be sufficient to meet the collective needs of minorities: special rights and preferential treatment are doubtless necessary to afford minorities appropriate safeguards.[29] These, and other gaps will have to be filled by legislation, that is by adoption of new international standards. And there has been call within the Council of Europe for action along such lines.[30]

[27] See note 16 *supra*, para. 31.

[28] Ibid.

[29] Although the ECHR does not guarantee specific rights to minorities, the existing rights under the ECHR would appear capable of providing them some degree of protection. The Commission has for example ruled that a minority group in Northern Europe (Lapps making a living out of reindeer breeding, fishing and hunting) was as a matter of principle entitled to respect for the particular lifestyle it traditionally led, as part of the right to respect for "private life", "family life" and "home" under Art. 8 ECHR: Applications nos. 9278/81 and 9415/81, *G and E v. Norway*, admissibility decision, 35 DR 30 at 35 (1984).

[30] Notably at the Council's 7th International Colloquy on the ECHR (Scandinavia, 30 May – 2 June 1990). See the final report presented by Mr. Rolv Ryssdal, President ECtHR, doc. CDDH (90) 22, pp. 3, 4–6; to be published in the proceedings of the Colloquy.

3. Protection against Whom?

(1) Responsibility of a State for Its Own Agents

A State is evidently liable for acts of brutality of its own agents (police, soldiers, security forces, prison guards, etc).

In the *Northern Ireland case* the United Kingdom Government conceded that the use of the five "sensory-deprivation" techniques of interrogation had been authorised at "high level". The resultant liability under the Convention (for inhuman treatment) was the direct product of a governmental policy.[31] In the same case the Court said in another connection: "...under the Convention [the higher authorities of a State] are strictly liable for the conduct of their subordinates; they are under a duty to impose their will on subordinates and cannot shelter behind their inability to ensure that it is respected".[32] The Commission had stated a similar principle in its report: "[The State's] obligations can be violated also by a person exercising an official function vested in him at any, even the lowest, level, without express authorization and even outside or against instructions."[33]

If an administrative practice consisting of the use of prohibited violence is established, as in the *Greek case*, the case of *Cyprus v. Turkey* and to a lesser extent in the *Northern Ireland case*, this is treated as a more serious violation of the Convention.[34] Signs of an administrative practice are repetition and official tolerance of the incriminated acts as manifested through lack of serious investigation of complaints of ill-treatment or lack of remedial action once the recurrent character of the exercise of violence is known.[35]

In sum, the international law prohibition of illicit violence imposes both direct responsibility for high-level governmental policies and vicarious liability for the acts of low-level public officers even though those acts may be contrary to governmental policy and the national law.

(2) Responsibility of a State in Respect of Violence Committed by or in Another State

Under the terms of the ECHR the Contracting States are bound to secure the guaranteed rights to all individuals "within their jurisdiction"[36], which was interpreted by the Commission in the case of *Cyprus v. Turkey* (concerning the occupation of parts of Cyprus by Turkish troops in 1974) as meaning "all

[31] See note 15 *supra*, para. 97.

[32] ibid., para. 159.

[33] Report ECmHR, 19 YBECHR 513 at 78 (1976).

[34] See note 14 *supra* at pp. 501–05 for the *Greek* case; note 20 *in fine* at pp. 557–61 (cf also p. 588) for *Cyprus v. Turkey*; note 15 at ECtHR judgment paras. 168, 174, and note 33 at ECmHR report pp. 762–64 for *Ireland v. UK*.

[35] *Greek case*, ibid., pp. 194–96.

[36] Art. 1 ECHR.

persons under their actual authority and responsibility".[37] The duty therefore extends beyond the frontiers of the national territory and, in particular, to acts of violence committed abroad by its duly authorised servants and agents, such as members of the armed forces, police and national security officers, diplomatic staff and so on.[38] What counts is the exercise of "jurisdiction" in the sense of "actual" authority and control. Thus, the Commission decided that the United Kingdom could not be held responsible for the killing, presumably by IRA terrorists, of a person on the territory of the State of Ireland. It is noteworthy that the Commission nevertheless also examined whether "any active measures by the United Kingdom authorities could have contributed to the murder".[39]

The *Soering case* goes a step further: confirming the Commission's already well established case-law, the Court in its judgment recognised a degree of responsibility on the part of a Contracting State in respect of serious ill-treatment administered abroad by another State.[40] Although the primary purpose of the prohibition of torture and inhuman treatment under the ECHR is to prohibit serious violence by the Contracting State's own agents, whether by overt or covert action, the obligation imposed is such a fundamental one in a democratic society, the Court held, that it also embraces not deporting or extraditing an individual to a destination where he runs a foreseeable risk of torture or inhuman treatment. The same reasoning would evidently apply to cases where an extradition or deportation measure to a third country would expose the individual to a foreseeable risk of violation of his right to life as protected by the ECHR.[41]

(3) Responsibility of a State in Respect of Violence Committed by Non-State Actors

The ECHR, like other classic international law human rights instruments, is mainly concerned with imposing on States the *negative* obligation not to

[37] See note 20 *supra in fine*, p. 587.

[38] See, eg. Application no. 1611/62, *X v. FRG*, admissibility decision, 8 YBECHR 158 at 168 (1965) (diplomatic or consular representatives); Application no. 6231/73, *Hess v. UK*, admissibility decision, 2 DR 72 at 73 (1975) (joint allied supervision of Spandau prison: no "jurisdiction"); Application nos. 7289/75 and 7349/76, *X and Y v. Switzerland*, admissibility decision, 9 DR 57 at 71 (1977) (Swiss immigration measures producing effects in Liechtenstein: "jurisdiction"); Application no. 8916/80, *Freda v. Italy*, admissibility decision, 24 YBECHR 354 at 358 (1980) and Application no. 10689/83, *Altmann (Barbie) v. France*, admissibility decision, 37 DR 225 at 233 (1984) (placement in custody of police abroad). Conversely a State cannot be held liable for acts committed on its soil but solely attributable to another State or an international body not subject to its control – see, eg, Application no. 182/56, *X v. FRG*, admissibility decision, 1 YBECHR 167 at 169 (1955–57) (US Court of Restitution Appeal sitting in FRG).

[39] Application no. 9348/81, *W v. UK*, admissibility decision, 32 DR 190 (1983).

[40] See note 12 *supra*, paras. 81–91.

[41] Cf. Application no. 5961/72, *Amekrane v. UK*, friendly settlement, published in Petzold. *The European Convention on Human Rights: Cases and Materials*, 5th ed., pp. 170 et seq. (1984) – see note 61 *infra*.

interfere through their own agents with the exercise by the individual of his or her fundamental rights and freedoms.

However, certain of the human rights guaranteed by the ECHR also imply for the State a *positive* duty, which varies according to the context, to put in place a legal, judicial and administrative framework effectively protecting against violence, including violence committed by non-State actors. The State's responsibility will be engaged, not by the commission of the act of violence itself (which may well not be directly imputable to the State), but because of the failure to prevent or respond to the act.[42] The ECHR expressly provides that "everyone's right to life shall be protected by law".[43] This implies that the taking of life should be made illegal under national law and also, so the Commission has ruled, that the relevant law should be properly enforced.[44] As reiterated by the Commission in the *Stewart* case, the State is obliged to take appropriate steps to safeguard life.[45] As other commentators have put it, the State is required "to undertake not only not to kill but also to see to it that others do not kill".[46] The ECHR control bodies would evidently have no difficulty in adopting the same approach as the Inter-American Court of Human Rights in the *Velásquez Rodríguez* case in holding the State responsible for a breach of the right to life in circumstances where enforced disappearances have been carried out with impunity by private or unidentified groups.[47]

This positive obligation to secure the right to life is not absolute or unlimited. It does not, as the Commission has stated, involve a positive duty to "exclude any possible violence".[48] No violation was found in the case of a man who, following an attempt on his life, had for several years been under police protection in Ireland but who had lost the benefit of a personal bodyguard. His claim was declared inadmissible by the Commission on the grounds that the right-to-life article "cannot be interpreted as imposing a duty on a State to give protection of this nature, at least not for an indefinite period of time".[49] In another case relating to Northern Ireland, the applicant claimed that, as a result of the murder of her brother and of threats to her own life, the United Kingdom had failed in its duty "to protect the right to life not only by criminal prosecution of offenders but also by such preventive control, through deployment of its armed forces, as appeared necessary to protect persons ...

[42] Cf also *Velásquez Rodríguez v. Honduras*, Inter-American Court of Human Rights, 29 July 1988, Series C No. 4, paras. 159 et seq. especially at para. 172 (also reported in 9 Human Rights Law Journal 212 at 239–44 (1988)), where such a principle is explicitly spelt out as regards the American Convention on Human Rights. Cf. also *Godinez Cruz v. Honduras*, Inter-American Court of Human Rights, 20 Jan. 1989, Series C No. 5, paras. 181 et seq. For a discussion of these cases, see *Shelton*, *supra* note 2.

[43] Art. 2 ECHR, first sentence.

[44] See note 39 *supra*, pp. 199–200.

[45] See note 10 *supra*.

[46] *O'Boyle*, see note 4 *supra*, quoting the Nobel Peace Prize Winner, René Cassin.

[47] See note 42 *supra*.

[48] Ibid.

[49] Application no. 6040/73, *X v. Ireland*, admissibility decision, 16 YBECHR 388 (1973).

exposed to the threat of terrorist attacks".[50] The Commission found that the United Kingdom could not be required to take measures going beyond those actually taken by the authorities. It noted that the peace-time army strength in Northern Ireland had been increased from 4,000 to 10,500 men and that between August 1969 and December 1981 several hundred members of the security forces had lost their lives there combating terrorism.

Other questions not yet resolved include whether and to what extent the State's duty to take adequate measures to protect life requires it to take active steps to ensure for "everyone" adequate life-saving services such as medical care and road safety or to take measures to protect individuals against the harmful effects of hazardous wastes.[51]

As regards the prohibition of torture and inhuman treatment, it is possible to extrapolate from the Court's reasoning in *Soering* an inherent obligation in the ECHR to make illegal under domestic law, and to take all active measures in practice to repress, such violence, whether administered by the State's own agents, by parallel para-military organisations or by private individual against private individual.[52]

The Court has read a similar positive duty on the State to legislate and protect against violence into the ECHR article which secures to everyone the right to respect for his or her private and family life and home. In the case of *X and Y v. Netherlands*, the Court states that the positive obligations inherent in the State's undertaking under this article "may involve the adoption of measures designed to secure respect for private life even in the sphere of the relations of individuals between themselves".[53] Because of a procedural gap in Dutch law no criminal prosecution could be brought in respect of the sexual assault of which Miss Y had been the victim, although civil-law proceedings were possible. The Court considered that only criminal-law provisions could provide the deterrence which was indispensable. A violation of the right-to-privacy guarantee was accordingly found since Netherlands law did not afford Miss Y practical and effective protection of her right to sexual privacy.

In determining the State's responsibility to take positive action to ensure respect for the individual's private life, the Court has also taken account of what one might call mental violence, such as the mental anguish suffered by

[50] See note 39 *supra*, p.200.

[51] See, eg, Application no. 6839/74, *X v. Ireland*, admissibility decision, 7 DR 78 (1976) (claim that non-availability of free medical treatment by the State jeopardised a disabled child's right to life – point not pursued); Application no. 7154/75, *Association X v. UK*, admissibility decision, 14 DR 31 (1978) (having regard to precautions taken to reduce risks of death from "adverse reactions", a programme of voluntary vaccination against infectious diseases not found to give rise to violation of State's positive duty); Application no. 715/60, *Dr. S. v. FRG*, admissibility decision, unpublished (claim concerning the tipping of nuclear waste into the North Sea, held to be "manifestly ill-founded").

[52] Similar obligations, limited to torture, are explicitly imposed by the United Nations Convention against Torture and Other Cruel, Inhuman and Degrading Treatment or Punishment, Arts. 4 and 5.

[53] See note 23 *supra*, para. 23.

transsexuals as a result of non-recognition, for various legal and practical purposes, of completed sex-reassignment treatment. On the facts, the Court found no violation of the ECHR in the two cases concerned.[54]

Likewise, as noted above, freedom of peaceful assembly and freedom of association under the ECHR include protection against physical violence committed by other individuals. As the *Plattform* judgment put it, "like [the right to privacy, freedom of peaceful assembly] sometimes requires positive measures to be taken, even in the sphere of relations between individuals if need be".[55] In the particular circumstances, however, it was found that the police protection provided for the applicant Association's demonstration was such as not to raise even an arguable claim of a violation of this positive obligation.

The frontiers of this additional "positive" head of State responsibility for violence committed by non-State actors remain to be fixed by future case-law. As yet, there are too few precedents to be able to discern other than a few sketchy principles.

4. Relevance of the European Experience

The remedy provided by international law enforcement systems such as the ECHR will, in practice, only have any bite in respect of States which have already taken the initial, crucial step of submitting themselves to international control. States which resort to or tolerate violence usually do not fall into this category. The European system is even more selective in that it binds only the member States of the Council of Europe, that is European States which have already accepted political democracy and the rule of law, the latest members of this club being Hungary and Czechoslovakia. Furthermore, although securing universal rights and freedoms, the ECHR is a regional instrument. As far as the present area of inquiry is concerned, the net of protection it offers will reflect European conceptions of culture, civilisation and violence, so that, taking the *Tyrer* and *Soering* cases as examples, what is now regarded as inhuman and unacceptable judicial punishment in Europe would not necessarily be so in other parts of the world, and *vice versa*. The relatively disappointing results of some inter-State cases where violations involving large-scale violence have been found (for example the *Cyprus*[56] and *Turkey*[57] cases) raise the question whether the ECHR control bodies have been invested with the resources necessary to handle this type of complaint.

[54] *Rees v. UK*, ECtHR 17 Oct. 1986, Series A Vol. 106; *Cossey v. UK*, ECtHR 27 Sept. 1990 Series A Vol. 184; see also Application no. 13343/87, *B. v. France*, case currently pending before the ECtHR.

[55] See note 26 *supra*, para. 32.

[56] See note 20 *supra in fine*.

[57] Applications nos. 9940–9944/82 (joined), *France, Norway, Denmark, Sweden and Netherlands v. Turkey*, admissibility decision, 35 DR 143 (1984), and friendly settlement report, 44 DR 31 (1985).

Subject to those provisos, international law instruments like the ECHR instituting mechanisms for enforcement of human rights do have their place, in our opinion, in the arsenal of weapons for combating violence. This is not to suggest that they represent the only or even one of the best means available. The wholly general merit they have is an ethical one: they contain a solemn recognition by the international community of the need to eliminate many, if not all, forms of violence. In addition, complaint-based systems which generate case-law provide a laboratory for the ongoing development of human rights protection to keep pace with changes in society. The ECHR system of protection in particular, because it has been in existence longer and on a larger scale than other comparable international systems, can provide an indicator as to the strengths and weaknesses of international human rights law as an instrument for combating violence in the world of the twenty-first century.

5. Prevention As Well As Redress

The principal subject of enquiry of this paper is State responsibility for human rights violations involving violence. A related question is the capability of an international human rights instrument such as the ECHR, in its impact on the conduct of States, to prevent as well as remedy violence.

The machinery of protection under the ECHR we have been discussing is a complaints procedure. Individuals may only lodge a petition if they can claim themselves to be or to have been the victim of a violation of one of the guaranteed rights by a Contracting State.[58] The relief the ECHR thereby offers is essentially an *ex post facto* remedy for the individual directly concerned. In simple terms the Commission's and the Court's task is to redress wrongs already committed, not to pronounce on potential violations.

The *Soering* case illustrates when there may be a departure from this principle: where there is a foreseeable risk of "serious and irreparable" suffering, the Strasbourg institutions may intervene before implementation of the threatened measure to the detriment of the individual, in order to ensure the utility of the safeguard provided.[59] Indeed *Soering* exemplifies what can be achieved under the international system of protection of human rights set up by the ECHR. Pending examination of the case in Strasbourg, the United Kingdom Government stayed Soering's surrender to the United States authorities in accord with the interim measures indicated by the Commission and by the Court.[60] The United Kingdom Government then bowed before the Court's judgment: they withdrew their previous consent to extradition on the capital murder charge. Soering faced trial in the United States for the violent crimes of

[58] Art. 25 para. 1 ECHR.
[59] See note 12 *supra*, para. 90.
[60] *Ibid.*, paras. 4, 24, 77 and 111 *in fine*.

which he was accused but he was no longer exposed to the risk of the death penalty and, thus, of the death-row phenomenon.[61]

Judgments of the Court can also have a preventive effect for the future in the respondent State concerned: the execution of a judgment has on a number of occasions involved not only affording redress to the individual victim of a human rights violation,[62] but also the adoption by the respondent State of general remedial measures such as the enactment of legislative reforms.[63]

Generally speaking as well, the Court's judgments, although binding only on the State(s) party to the particular case, furnish guidance to the other Contracting States. It is not unusual for the legislative, executive or even judicial authorities of an uninvolved State to introduce changes as a result of a judgment, so as to bring the national legal system into line with the ECHR before the finding of a violation in Strasbourg.[64]

A number of fundamental democratic values have been identified as underlying and giving the concrete meaning to the loosely-defined rights enumerated in the ECHR. When interpreting the ECHR and faced with decisional choices, the Commission and the Court have taken notice of these values, which include pluralism, equality of treatment, tolerance, and protection of minorities from abuse of power by the majority. The fostering of such values, which is an implicit obligation for States that have ratified the ECHR, is in itself likely to reduce the incidence of violence in society.[65] Consequently, quite apart from the substantive content of given safeguards directed against violence, the ECHR (and other international instruments like it) are in general likely to encourage a climate inimical to violence.

One possibility for initiating preventive action under the ECHR which has not yet been exploited is perhaps to be found in the article which empowers the Secretary General of the Council of Europe to request any Contracting State to "furnish an explanation of the manner in which its internal law ensures the

[61] This can be compared to the much earlier *Amekrane* case, see note 41 *supra*, where, in the absence of any interim measure from the Commission, a Moroccan Air Force Colonel (who had taken part in an unsuccessful putsch and fled to Gibraltar) was returned to his country by the United Kingdom authorities and later executed.

[62] By virtue of Art. 50 ECHR, the Court may afford "just satisfaction" to the victim of a violation. Responsibility for supervising execution of the Court's judgments is vested not in the Court itself but in the Committee of Ministers of the Council of Europe (Art. 54 ECHR).

[63] See eg. recent Committee of Ministers Resolutions adopted pursuant to Art. 54 ECHR: Resolution DH (90)1 (concerning the *Tre Traktörer v. Sweden* judgment, ECtHR 7 July 1989, Series A Vol. 159) and Resolution DH (90)3 (concerning the judgments in *O v. UK*, ECtHR 8 July 1987 and 7 June 1988, Series A Vols. 120 and 130).

[64] See eg. Marc-André Eissen, "L'interaction des jurisprudences constitutionnelles nationales et de la jurisprudence de la Cour européenne des Droits de l'Homme", in Dominique Rousseau and Frédéric Sudre, ed., *Conseil constitutionel et Cour européenne des Droits de l'Homme*, 137 (1990).

[65] See, *inter alia*, Resolution (78)41 of the Committee of Ministers of the Council of Europe "On the teaching of human rights".

effective implementation of any of the provisions of [the] Convention".[66] International reporting mechanisms such as this and international fact-finding missions, if backed up by adequate resources and constructively used, are not only capable of providing a response to existing human rights violations but may also have some potential as a preventive means of control.

A further avenue of progress in terms of preventive control on the international level is illustrated by the recent European Convention for the Prevention of Torture and Inhuman or Degrading Treatment or Punishment, concluded in 1987. This Convention establishes a supervisory committee which does not have to rely on reports from the Contracting States. Rather, it has the power to conduct visits, regular and *ad hoc*, to any place within the jurisdiction of the Contracting States where persons are deprived of their liberty by a public authority and to address confidential reports and nonbinding recommendations to the States visited, with a view to protecting such persons from torture and inhuman or degrading treatment or punishment.[67] This preventive technique of a supervisory body having independent investigatory powers is evidently well suited to dealing with risks of serious ill-treatment by State actors in State institutions, but it may well prove capable of being applied to other domains.[68]

Another possible means of reducing human rights violations is the establishment (and funding) by the international community of nonregulatory mechanisms such as advisory and educative agencies, "observatories" to monitor and warn against worrying developments ("early warning systems"), machinery for pacific settlement of disputes, and transfrontier agencies for coordinating national initiatives.[69] International instruments setting up such assistance-giving bodies represent another tool at the disposal of international law for eradicating violence, rooting it out before it has had a chance to become the source of a human rights violation.

[66] Art. 57 ECHR. See Paul Mahoney, "*Does Article 57 of the European Convention on Human Rights Serve Any Useful Purpose?*", in Franz Matscher and Herbert Petzold, eds., *Protecting Human Rights: The European Dimension – Studies in Honour of Gerard Wiarda*, pp. 373–93 (1988).

[67] See The Torture Committee's first General Report, Council of Europe doc. CPT (91)3.

[68] See the proposal made at the Council of Europe's 7th International Colloquy on the ECHR to draw up a convention for the prevention of discrimination, with an *ad hoc* committee empowered to visit places and identify situations where risks may occur (Ryssdal final report, note 30 *supra*, p. 15).

[69] The provision of advisory services relating to the protection and promotion of human rights is a role that has recently been advocated for the Council of Europe by its Secretary General, Catherine La Lumière (doc. CIM-DH (90)3, p.8 Secretary General's contribution to the Informal Ministerial Conference on Human Rights, Rome 5 Nov. 1990). At the Council of Europe's 7th International Colloquy on the ECHR, recommendations were made to set up a European "observatory" to monitor discrimination and some forum for bringing together national advisory committees on human rights (*Ryssdal* final report, *supra* note 30, pp. 10 and 15).

6. Conclusion

Pulling these various strands together, we can see that on the whole, subject to unresolved areas of doubt, the ECHR adequately legislates against serious violence – illicit killing, torture, inhuman treatment – committed by State actors. A State will be liable both for high-level government policies generating violence and vicariously for the acts of its low-level agents. A State will also be responsible for lesser forms of violence which amount to a denial of one of the other fundamental rights guaranteed under the Convention, for example, the right to respect for one's private and family life, the right to a fair trial, or freedom of association and assembly. Violence is recognised as being mental as well as physical. In addition to its responsibility for its own agents, the State has a broader (positive) duty, the extent of which will vary according to the context, to protect individuals against violence committed by non-State actors and even, in some exceptional circumstances, by agents of other States.

The strength of the ECHR, and other international law instruments like it, is not so much in being standard-setting but in backing up the enunciated rights with enforcement machinery and in empowering the control bodies to push forward, through evolutive interpretative case law, the frontiers of the protection afforded so as to keep pace with the needs of contemporary democratic society. This *collective* system of enforcement set up by like-minded sovereign States is a worthwhile, albeit perfectible, example of international solidarity: States ceding their sovereignty to independent international control bodies in favour of the individual human being.

The weaknesses are that, the ECHR being a classic instrument of international human rights law safeguarding a selective list of rights and freedoms, the net of protection against violence has substantive gaps in it; the inter-State complaint (where large-scale violence has been involved) has too often proved to be of only very limited effectiveness, at least in the short term; and the enforcement machinery, being complaint-based, can provide after-the-event redress for human rights violations, but necessarily play only a limited role of prevention and education.

Looking to the future, the question to be asked is: how can international human rights law be developed so as to reduce – or rather contribute, with initiatives at a national level, to reducing – the incidence of violence in the world? Some of the practical lessons that can be learnt from the experience of the system of protection under the ECHR are, in brief, that further standards protecting against violence could be incorporated within the existing framework of regulatory mechanisms (for example minority rights, prisoners' rights and right to criminal compensation); that, if international human rights instruments are not to remain idealistic declarations of intent, the accompanying control bodies must be allocated adequate means and resources to enable them effectively to perform their mandate, in particular by being accessible to the most likely victims of violence, namely the poorer, less privileged and vulnerable members of society; that reporting systems and fact-finding missions, by NGO's as well as international organisations, can also help to remedy continuing human rights violations; and that parallel to complaint-based and other after-the-event responses to human rights violations, avowedly preventive means of control, perhaps linked and adapted to specific problem spheres, could be developed further to play a useful role in eliminating violence.

Contemporary international human rights law is the product of its history and its governmental context, and by its very nature can only have a "diluted" impact on the day-to-day life of the disadvantaged people who make up the vast majority of the victims of violence. In addition, international human rights law has a long way to go before it adequately reflects the needs of all the groups making up the diverse societies of our world. The constraints that poverty, for example, places on access to actual enjoyment of theoretically guaranteed human rights have up till now largely gone ignored.[70] Nevertheless, the conclusion of this paper is that international human rights law, even in its present state, can serve as one brick in the wall that must be built against oppression and the violence engendered by oppression.

[70] The case of *Airey v. Ireland*, ECtHR 6 Feb. 1981, Series A Vol. 41 (which held that the absence of legal aid in the circumstances amounted to a denial of equal access to the courts) perhaps marks the first recognition of such constraints by the ECHR interpretative bodies.

FRANCIS BOYLE*

The Right of Citizen Resistance to State Crimes

1. Introduction

The thesis of this paper is that for at least the past decade the government of the United States of America has constituted an international criminal conspiracy under the Nuremberg Principles that is legally akin to that of the Nazi government in pre-World War II Germany. Consequently, American citizens possess the basic right under international law and United States domestic law, including their own constitution, to engage in acts of nonviolent civil resistance in order to prevent, impede or terminate ongoing criminal activities by U.S. government officials in their conduct of foreign affairs and so-called defense policies. Although this paper was written and delivered before the United States waged war against Iraq starting in January of 1991, the U.S. government's wanton extermination of a quarter of a million people in Iraq – of whom only 100,000 or so were soldiers – provides definitive proof of the validity of this Nuremberg proposition for the entire world to see.

This paper explains why citizen resistance to such crimes of state is not "civil disobedience" as logically defined by the American Establishment (i.e., the C.I.A. and the Military-Industrial Complex) that effectively controls the government, the economy, and the mass media in the United States. The analysis describes in necessarily general terms how American civil resisters and their lawyers have been successful in convincing American juries to acquit them from a variety of criminal charges on the grounds that it is high-level U.S. government officials, not the citizen resisters, who are the real criminals under international law and United States domestic law. The paper concludes by providing a more detailed analysis of the legal principles used by American lawyers to defend anti-nuclear civil resisters from governmental prosecution and persecution.

The spectre of nuclear extinction that has been created by the nuclear weapons states, and especially by the two nuclear "superpowers", hovers over

* Professor of International Law at the University of Illinois College of Law in Champaign, Illinois, U.S.A. 61820.

K.E. Mahoney and P. Mahoney (eds.), Human Rights in the Twenty-first Century, 377–392.

the heads of all the peoples in the world. Nuclear weapons and all their essential accoutrements are criminal under well recognized principles of international law. Consequently, all citizens of the world community have both the right and the duty under international law to resist nuclear weapons by all nonviolent means possible. Universal nuclear disarmament is the only legally defensible, morally acceptable and logically consistent position that can be taken. And anti-nuclear civil resistance becomes one of the very few but effective strategies open to the peoples of the world – and especially the citizens living in the nuclear weapons states – to accomplish this objective.

2. International Criminality

Since January of 1981, the government in the United States of America has demonstrated little if any observable respect for fundamental considerations of international law and organizations or appreciation of the requirements for maintaining international peace and security. Instead, a comprehensive assault upon the integrity of the international legal order has been perpetuated by a group of men and women Machiavellian in their perception and conduct of international relations, foreign policy and domestic affairs. The Reagan/Bush administrations' foreign policy represents a gross deviation from even basic rules of international deportment and civilized behavior which governments pioneered and promoted for the entire world community. Moreover, in several instances, specific components of the Reagan/Bush administrations' foreign policy has amounted to criminal activity according to well-recognized principles of both international law and U.S. domestic law.

These international crimes include but are not limited to the Nuremberg Offenses of crimes against peace, crimes against humanity and war crimes, as well as grave breaches of the Geneva Conventions and the Hague Regulations, genocide, torture and assassination. In addition, various members of the Reagan/Bush administrations have committed numerous inchoate crimes incidental to these substantive offenses (viz., planning, preparation, solicitation, incitement, conspiracy, complicity, attempt, aiding and abetting, etc.) that under the Nuremberg Principles are international crimes in their own right. Of course the great irony of today's situation is that forty-five years ago at Nuremberg, representatives of the U.S. government participated in the prosecution, punishment and execution of Nazi government officials for committing some of the same types of heinous international crimes that members of the Reagan/Bush administrations have inflicted upon innocent people around the world.

Furthermore, according to basic principles of international law, all high-level civilian officials and military officers in the Reagan/Bush administrations who either knew or should have known that civilians or soldiers under their control committed or were about to commit international crimes, and failed to take the measures necessary to stop them, or to punish them, or both, were likewise personally responsible for the commission of these international crimes. This category of officialdom who actually knew or at least should have known of the commission of such substantive or inchoate international crimes under their jurisdiction and failed to do anything about them typically included the Secretary of State, Secretary of Defense, Director of Central Intelligence, the National Security Adviser, the Attorney General, and presumably the President and Vice President. These Reagan/Bush administration officials, among others, are minimally responsible for commission or at least complicity in the commission of crimes against peace, crimes against humanity and war crimes as specified by the Nuremberg Principles.

3. Domestic Civil Resistance

In direct reaction to the Reagan/Bush administrations' attack upon the international and domestic legal orders, large numbers of American citizens have engaged in various forms of nonviolent civil resistance activities to protest against distinct elements of the Reagan/Bush administrations' foreign affairs and defense policies. These citizen protests have led to numerous arrests and prosecutions by federal, state, and local government authorities around the United States. Most regrettably for all concerned, many individuals involved in these nonviolent protests have been prosecuted, convicted and sentenced in a particularly harsh and vindictive manner.

For example, the Reagan/Bush administrations' offensive nuclear weapons buildup generated enormous protests by numerous groups and individuals against U.S. nuclear weapons installations, facilities, programs and personalities around this country and abroad. In this regard, the Plowshares, the Greenham Common Women, Greenpeace, and the Catholic nonviolent civil resistance group known as Pax Christi were four of the most prominent movements. In addition, much outstanding work in the anti-nuclear arena was likewise performed by the numerous groups of individuals who protested the production of plutonium triggers for U.S. hydrogen bombs at the PUREX facility before the Hanford Site in the state of Washington, as well as protesting at the U.S. government's nuclear weapons test facility in Nevada and at the Rocky Flats Nuclear Arsenal in Colorado, etc.

Similarly, the Reagan administration's policy of so-called "constructive engagement" toward the criminal apartheid regime in South Africa spawned a nationwide campaign directed against apartheid and U.S. governmental complicity therein. Protests were mounted before the South African Embassy and consulates, business establishments that sell krugerrands, IBM for selling computers to the South African police, and other economic targets. On American college campuses, students vigorously demanded that their administrators divest university portfolios of all stock held in American companies that do business in South Africa. These citizen protests led to numerous arrests and prosecutions for several types of nonviolent civil resistance activities designed to produce official and unofficial condemnation and sanction of apartheid. To a great extent, the American anti-apartheid protest movement has been quite successful at producing a marked change in U.S. government policy toward the adoption of more aggressive practices against South African apartheid at the national, state, local and university levels.

The Reagan/Bush administrations' illegal military interventions into Grenada, Nicaragua, El Salvador and Panama were probably responsible for the greatest number and degree of nonviolent civil resistance activities in America during the 1980s. First came the so-called Sanctuary Movement, which consists of approximately 400 American church and synagogue communities that provide sanctuary to refugees fleeing from the conflicts of Central America in dire fear for their lives. In explicit violation of the requirements of both the 1967 Protocol to the U.N. Convention Relating to the Status of Refugees and the U.S. Refugee Act of 1980, the Reagan/Bush administrations refused to give these refugees political asylum so as not to undercut the pseudo-legitimacy of the military dictatorships that actually rule El Salvador and Guatemala with the active political, economic and military support of the United States government. To sustain this policy the Reagan/Bush administration launched a vendetta against the church people who had organized the Sanctuary Movement as an expression of their deeply-held religious convictions. The latter were prosecuted to the absolute limit of the law, if not beyond, despite the protections afforded their activities by the First and Fourth Amendments to the United States Constitution.

Next came the self-styled Pledge of Resistance Movement, whose 100,000 members took a vow that in the event the Reagan/Bush administration decided to launch an invasion of Nicaragua, its membership will engage in a nationwide campaign of nonviolent civil resistance activities. The Pledge of Resistance Movement called out its members on several occasions to demonstrate against repeated votes by the U.S. Congress to provide military and so-called humanitarian assistance to the contra mercenary bands which, at the Reagan/Bush administrations' behest, had been illegally attacking both the people and the government of Nicaragua in violation of the U.N. Charter, the O.A.S. Charter, the Geneva Conventions of 1949, and two World Court Orders of 1984 and 1986, *inter alia*. These civil resistance activities consisted of sit-ins and other forms of nonviolent protest conducted at federal military installations and the offices of U.S. congressional representatives and senators who voted in favor of such aid. In significant part these individuals were motivated to protest by the conviction that the Reagan/Bush administrations' foreign policy toward Nicaragua violated fundamental principles of both international law and U.S. domestic law.

U.S. military intervention into the affairs of Latin American states has only been exacerbated during the tenure of the Bush administration. First came the blatantly illegal invasion of Panama during December of 1989, where large numbers of innocent Panamanian civilians were brutally killed by American troops in violation of the United Nations Charter, the O.A.S. Charter, and international humanitarian law. The Bush administration continued and expanded U.S. military assistance to the military dictatorships that actually rule El Salvador and Guatemala by means of a naked reign of terror. And the Bush administration is now threatening a new round of U.S. military intervention into large numbers of Latin American states on the alleged grounds of some need to fight its self-proclaimed "war" against drugs. Arguably, the Bush administration should be instituting a crop-eradication program and military intervention into the American state of North Carolina where the drug-traffickers of the U.S. tobacco industry produce cigarettes for the rest of the country as well as for export to the developing world. On a daily basis, the U.S. tobacco industry addicts and then kills far more people around the entire world than the drug-traffickers of Latin America ever could.

Finally, the Reagan/Bush administrations have continued to supply enormous quantities of weapons, equipment, supplies, loans and grants to the Israeli government, which has used this assistance to inflict atrocities against the Palestinian people. These violations of international humanitarian law constitute "war crimes" that create personal criminal responsibility for the perpetrators under international law. Thus, those Israeli soldiers and political leaders who have committed, ordered, condoned, or aided and abetted these war crimes against the Palestinian people can be criminally prosecuted by any state in the world that obtains control over them.

Common article 1 of the Four Geneva Conventions of 1949 requires every state of the world community to bring to bear whatever pressure it can upon the Israeli government to terminate its violation of these Conventions: "The High Contracting Parties undertake to respect and to ensure respect for the present Convention in all circumstances." By contrast, the Israeli government has refused to apply the Four Geneva Conventions of 1949 and the 1907 Hague Regulations on Land Warfare to their illegal occupation of Palestine and to their conduct of hostilities against the Palestinian people. In direct reaction thereto, large numbers of American people have been arrested and prosecuted for mounting peaceful non-violent protests against the United States government because it continues to support and finance the perpetration of Israeli war crimes against the Palestinian people.

4. The Separation of Powers?

Throughout this decade of opposition to the Reagan/Bush administrations' international lawlessness, there have occurred many disappointments, setbacks, and failures in the defense of those who have engaged in such nonviolent civil resistance. People have been sent to jail or otherwise vindictively prosecuted and punished simply for opposing the ongoing commission of international and domestic crimes by the Reagan/Bush administrations in their daily conduct of foreign affairs. Many have been treated as if they were common criminals, and sometimes prosecuted and punished more severely than murderers, robbers, and rapists. As former U.S. Attorney General Ramsey Clark has aptly put it: "Our jails are filling up with saints!"

Nevertheless, despite governmental repression, it is probably the case that on a daily basis there are thousands of people in the United States of America who are either planning, preparing, committed to, or actively participating in some form of nonviolent civil resistance activities directed against some aspect of the Reagan/Bush administrations' foreign affairs and defense policies. In the opinion of this author, these activities represent a positive development for the future role of democratic government in the United States of America with its historical commitment to the rule of law both at home and abroad.

Due to the personal popularity of Presidents Reagan and Bush, Congress proved to be pusillanimous when it came to the enforcement of respect for its own laws on the part of the executive branch of the federal government. And the federal courts were essentially unwilling to prevent or impede the international lawlessness of the Reagan/Bush administrations. Even when given a rare opportunity to exercise some small degree of restraint on executive branch excesses in foreign affairs, federal judges generally decided to defer or abstain under the so-called doctrines of "political question" or "judicial restraint." For the most part, the members of the federal judiciary completely, and in my opinion quite inappropriately, abnegated any constructive role they might have played in support of the widespread public demand that American foreign policy be conducted in a manner consistent with the requirements of both international law and U.S. domestic law.

Furthermore, a "conspiracy of silence" occurred within the mainstream news media not to report on the amount and extent of nonviolent civil resistance activities in America during the 1980s, which by comparison dwarfed the occasionally violent anti-Viet Nam War demonstrations of the 1960s. Until the outbreak of the Iran-contra scandal toward the end of 1986, the American news media basically served as uncritical transmission belts for the conveyance of whatever propaganda line the Reagan/Bush administration chose to justify its attacks on the international and domestic legal orders.

Thus in America we witnessed a total breakdown of the constitutional doctrine of separation of powers when it came to the illegal and oftentimes criminal conduct of foreign policy by the Reagan/Bush administrations. In light of this breakdown, large numbers of American citizens decided to act on their own to demand that the Reagan/Bush administrations adhere to basic principles of international law, of U.S. domestic law, and of our own Constitution in its conduct of foreign affairs. Predictably, however, such actions have been defined by the American Establishment to constitute classic instances of nonviolent "civil disobedience" as historically practised in the United States, the traditional admonition for which is punishment for *prima facie* breach of the positive law. It is this writer's view that this definition fails to accurately describe these 1980s and 1990s form of civil protest.

5. Civil Resistance versus Civil Disobedience

Here I would like to suggest a different way of thinking about nonviolent civil resistance activities that were specifically designed to prevent or impede ongoing criminal activity by members of the Reagan/Bush administrations under well-recognized principles of international and domestic law. Such civil resistance activities represent the last constitutional avenue open to the American people to preserve their democratic form of government with its historical commitment to the rule of law. Civil resistance is the last hope this country has to prevent the Reagan/Bush administrations from moving even further down the path of lawless violence in Latin America, military intervention into the Middle East, and nuclear confrontation around the world.

Such measures of "civil resistance" must not be confused with, and indeed must be carefully distinguished from, acts of "civil disobedience" as traditionally defined. In such civil resistance cases, what we witness are individuals attempting to prevent the ongoing commission of international crimes under well-recognized principles of international and U.S. domestic law. This is a phenomenon very different from the classic civil disobedience case of the 1960s where individuals said they were purposely violating a domestic law for the express purpose of changing it.

These civil resisters are constitutionally presumed to be innocent until proven guilty beyond a reasonable doubt to the satisfaction of a jury in accordance with all the substantive and procedural requirements of due process of law. Furthermore, people who engage in nonviolent civil resistance have a constitutional right to rely upon whatever statutory and common law defenses are generally made available to every other criminal defendant in the jurisdiction concerned: e.g., defense of self, defense of others, necessity, choice of evils, prevention of crime, prevention of a public catastrophe, measures otherwise authorized by law, absence of general or specific criminal intent, etc. They are also entitled to receive the most vigorous defense that can be mounted on their behalf. After all, alleged murderers, robbers and rapists are entitled to the presumption of innocence, a vigorous defense, and all the protections of due process of law. Society's standards and expectations should be no less for those who have engaged in nonviolent civil resistance activities designed to prevent the ongoing commission of international and domestic crimes.

Finally, under the First Amendment to the United States Constitution, civil resistance protesters are exercising their rights "peaceably to assemble", and "to petition the Government for a redress of grievances." Note that the First Amendment does not require their assembly to be "lawful" in a positivist technical sense, but only that it be peaceable. Similarly, ongoing criminal activity committed by officials of the government itself is certainly the type of grievance the people should have a right to petition for redress against by means of nonviolent civil resistance. Therefore, we must recognize that the First Amendment includes within its scope the right for the American people to engage in acts of nonviolent civil resistance specifically intended for the purpose of preventing or impeding ongoing criminal activity in the conduct of foreign policy on the part of this or any other government in the United States.

6. The American Criminal Jury System

Ultimately, therefore, the final arbiter of the constitutionality, technical legality and overall legitimacy of such acts of nonviolent civil resistance will become the American people themselves. In particular, under the Sixth and Fourteenth Amendments to the United States Constitution, those individuals who have been charged with alleged *prima facie* breaches of positive law by engaging in acts of nonviolent civil resistance are generally entitled to a trial by a jury of their own peers. Thus it is the American criminal jury system that has proven to be the last bastion of democracy and law against the Reagan/Bush administrations' assault on both. I would submit that under the currently existing political conditions in the United States of America, our criminal jury system has become a long-overlooked but vitally independent institution within the separation-of-powers arrangement created by the Founding Fathers of the U.S. Constitution.

Fortunately, the American jury system consists of common, everyday, ordinary citizens. Most Americans consider themselves to be law-abiding and peaceful, and strongly believe that their government should be law-abiding and peaceful as well. The fate of those prosecuted for nonviolent civil resistance has therefore been committed by the Constitution to the common sense of decency, justice, fair play, and peaceableness, so characteristic of the American people and thus of the typical members of an American jury.

During the past decade, it has been my personal experience that whenever the members of American juries have been made aware of the Reagan/Bush administrations' gross international lawlessness, they have usually refused to convict those who have engaged in acts of nonviolent civil resistance for the express purpose of stopping it. Invariably the jurors have compared the minor nature of the crime for which the defendants were charged (typically trespass) against the terrible nature of the international crimes committed, supported, condoned, or threatened by U.S. government officials. The jurors usually concluded that the defendants were privileged to act as they did under basic principles of international and U.S. domestic law in order to prevent the ongoing commission of international criminal activity by members of the United States government on an everyday basis.

Because the juries refused to convict these protesters, then it was obvious that the latter had never committed any crimes. In other words, these civil resisters were completely innocent of any wrongdoing at all. In essence, the jurors had *sub silentio* ratified the argument that such protesters were merely engaged in the exercise of their First Amendment rights to peaceably assemble, to petition their government for a redress of grievances, or to freely exercise their religion.

It is in this fashion, then, that I believe we must distinguish acts of nonviolent "civil resistance" from acts of "civil disobedience." The former are not crimes, and the people who engage in them are not "criminals" – at least until they have been proven to be guilty of an offense beyond a reasonable doubt to the satisfaction of the men and women sitting on a jury in accordance with all the substantive protections and procedural requirements of due process of law. Thus we must not expect those who have performed acts of nonviolent civil resistance to accept any punishment for having committed an alleged *prima facie* breach of a positive law. Rather, we must actively work to obtain their acquittal at trial by a jury of their peers precisely because they were exercising their constitutional rights for the express purpose of restoring to the United States of America a democratic government with a commitment to the rule of law both at home and abroad. These civil resisters have become the real American heroes for the 1980s and 1990s.

7. The Future of International Law and American Foreign Policy

I believe that most of the American people are basically unaware of the gross violations of international law being perpetrated in their name by their own government on a daily basis. Once they have been informed, however, they are often outraged and usually decide to do something to stop the elementally lawless behaviour. For example, during many of the civil resistance cases I have worked on during the past decade, the jury would acquit defendants of all or some of the charges and then afterwards several members of the jury would publicly state that they were "shocked" to discover that the United States government was committing such gross violations of international law, and that this factor had led them to acquit the defendants. Moreover, some of the jurors would state that they had been so "radicalized" by the trial that they thought they themselves should go out and start to protest in order to do something about the situation!

In any event, most jurors who are permitted to hear and consider our international law arguments in defense of civil resistance protesters reach the conclusion that in light of the international criminal activities by the Reagan/Bush administrations with respect to nuclear weapons, Central America, South Africa, the Middle East, etc. the defendants did what they had to do in order to stop them. I submit that most American people would have the same reaction. The thesis propounded by so-called political "realists" of the Reagan/Bush administrations that a democracy is inherently incapable of developing a coherent and consistent foreign policy without Machiavellianism simply reflects their obstinate refusal to accept the well-established primacy of law over power in the American constitutional system of government, and most importantly, in the hearts and minds of the common people of America. The future of international law and American foreign policy lies in the hands of the American people – not the bureaucrats, legislators, judges, lobbyists, think-tankers, professors, and self-styled experts who inhabit Washington, D.C. and New York City.

8. Defending Anti-Nuclear Resistance under International Law

In this brief paper there is no way to discuss in general terms precisely how we defend civil resistance protesters on all of those various substantive issues mentioned above. Some of these matters have been discussed by me at greater length in my book *Defending Civil Resistance Under International Law* (Transnational Publishers: 1987). Here, however, I would like to briefly describe the general theory behind our defense of anti-nuclear protesters around the world. In addition, I would also like to develop my thesis that there exists a basic human right under international law for all persons to resist the production and deployment of nuclear weapons and all their essential accouterments by whatever peaceful means they can mount.

The human race stands on the verge of self-extinction as a species, and with it will die most if not all forms of intelligent life on the planet earth. In the hope of preventing a nuclear Armageddon, the lawyers and human rights activists of the world must come together to proclaim certain fundamental principles concerning the requirements of international law with respect to nuclear weapons. It is my hope that the following analysis will serve to define in legal terms the stark dilemma of nuclear extinction that confronts the human race today.

We must also seek to establish an anti-nuclear agenda for our fellow lawyers and human rights activists around the world to pursue by applying their unique training, skills, and expertise in a productive and meaningful way toward the progressive yet complete elimination of nuclear weapons from the face of the earth. Realistically speaking, we can not expect this to happen in the immediate future. Nevertheless, as lawyers and human rights activists we owe a duty to our fellow men and women around the world to struggle toward this goal with all the powers of our professions.

(1) Hiroshima and Nagasaki

Any attempt to dispel the ideology of nuclearism and its attendant myth propounding the legality of nuclear weapons must directly come to grips with the fact that the nuclear age was conceived in the original sins of Hiroshima and Nagasaki on August 6 and 9, 1945. The atomic bombings of Hiroshima and Nagasaki were clearly and egregiously violative of basic principles of international criminal law that were fully subscribed to by the United States government at that time. In particular, the atomic bombings of Hiroshima and Nagasaki constituted crimes against humanity and war crimes as defined by the Nuremberg Charter of August 8, 1945, and violated several basic provisions of the Regulations annexed to Hague Convention No. IV Respecting the Laws and

Customs of War on Land (1907), the rules of customary international law set forth in the Draft Hague Rules of Air Warfare (1923), and the United States War Department Field Manual 27–10, *Rules of Land Warfare* (1940). According to this Field Manual and the Nuremberg Principles, all civilian government officials and military officers who ordered or knowingly participated in the atomic bombings of Hiroshima and Nagasaki could have been (and still can be) lawfully punished as war criminals.

Hence, the use of nuclear weapons in combat was and still is today absolutely prohibited under all circumstances by both conventional and customary international law. Under the Nuremberg Principles, soldiers would be obliged to disobey egregiously illegal orders with respect to launching and waging a nuclear war. Furthermore, all civilian government officials and military officers who might nevertheless launch or wage a nuclear war would be personally responsible for the commission of international crimes. All such individuals could be quite legitimately and most severely punished as war criminals, up to and including the imposition of the death penalty, without limitation of time.

(2) The Criminality of Nuclear Weapons

Today, article 2(4) of the United Nations Charter of 1945 prohibits both the threat and the use of force except in cases of legitimate self-defense as recognized by article 51 thereof. But although the requirement of legitimate self-defense is a necessary precondition for the legality of any threat or use of force, it is certainly not sufficient. For the legality of any threat or use of force must also take into account the customary and conventional international laws of humanitarian armed conflict.

Thereunder, the threat to use nuclear weapons (i.e., nuclear deterrence/-terrorism) constitutes ongoing international criminal activity: namely, planning, preparation, conspiracy and solicitation to commit crimes against peace, crimes against humanity, war crimes, as well as grave breaches of the Four Geneva Conventions of 1949, their Additional Protocol One of 1977, the Hague Regulations of 1907, and the International Convention on the Prevention and Punishment of the Crime of Genocide of 1948, *inter alia*. These are the so-called inchoate crimes that under the Nuremberg Principles constitute international crimes in their own right. The conclusion is inexorable, therefore, that the possession, design, testing, development, manufacture, deployment, and the threat to use nuclear weapons together with all their essential accouterments are criminal under well-recognized principles of international law.

The start of any progress toward resolving humankind's nuclear predicament must come from the realization that nuclear weapons have never been legitimate instruments of state policy, but rather have always constituted illegitimate instrumentalities of internationally lawless and criminal behaviour. Thus, those government decision-makers in the nuclear weapons states with command responsibility for their nuclear weapons establishments are today subject to personal criminal responsibility under the Nuremberg Principles for this criminal practice of nuclear deterrence/terrorism that they have daily inflicted upon all states and peoples of the international community.

(3) The Human Right to Anti-Nuclear Civil Resistance

Nuclear weapons establishments as well as the entire system of nuclear deterrence/terrorism currently practised by today's nuclear weapon states are criminal – not simply illegal, not simply immoral, but criminal under well-recognized principles of international law. This simple idea of the criminality of nuclear weapons can be utilized to pierce through the ideology of nuclearism to which many citizens in the nuclear weapons states have succumbed. It is with this simple idea of the criminality of nuclear weapons that such people can proceed to comprehend the inherent illegitimacy and fundamental lawlessness of the policies that their governments pursue in their names with respect to the further development of nuclear weapons systems.

The idea of the criminality of nuclear weapons is quite simple. And yet simple ideas are oftentimes the most powerful. For example, at one point in historical time, people saw no moral or legal problem with the institution of slavery. But as a result of the Abolitionist Movement in England and the United States, the entire international community eventually came around to the point of view that slavery and the slave trade were immoral, illegal, and criminal and therefore must be abolished and repressed, which they were and still are today. The same type of moral and perceptual transformation must occur now with respect to nuclear weapons among the citizenry of those states that possess them.

In all fairness, however, I should point out that there are tens of thousands of people in the United States of America who truly believe that nuclear weapons are criminal under well-recognized principles of international law that have been fully subscribed to by the United States government and incorporated into United States domestic law. That number is increasing every day. Furthermore, there are hundreds of thousands of people in Canada, Europe, and the Western Pacific who believe that nuclear weapons systems are criminal, and that number is increasing every day. Finally, there are tens of millions of people around the world who believe that nuclear weapons systems are criminal. It therefore becomes necessary to further propagate the idea of the criminality of nuclear weapons in order to increase the number of people who hold that opinion in the United States as well as in the other nuclear weapons states for the purpose of compelling them to consider developing constructive strategies for the abolition of nuclear weapons from the face of the earth.

In this regard, every person around the world possesses a basic human right under international law to be free from this criminal practice of nuclear deterrence/terrorism and its concomitant spectre of nuclear extinction. In light of the fact that nuclear weapons systems are prohibited, illegal and criminal under all circumstances and for any reason, all human beings possess the basic human right under international law to engage in non-violent civil resistance activities for the express purpose of preventing or terminating the ongoing commission of these international crimes. Every citizen of the world community has both the right and the duty to oppose the existence of nuclear weapons systems by whatever non-violent means are at his or her disposal.

(4) The Criminal Conspiracy of Nuclear Deterrence/Terrorism

Humankind must abolish nuclear weapons before nuclear weapons abolish humankind. Nonetheless, a small number of governments in the world community continue to maintain nuclear weapons systems despite the rules of international criminal law to the contrary. This has led some international lawyers to argue quite tautologically that since there exist a few nuclear weapons states in the world community, therefore nuclear weapons must somehow not be criminal because otherwise these few states would not possess nuclear weapons systems. In other words, to use international lawyers' parlance, this minority state practice of nuclear deterrence/terrorism by the great powers somehow negates the existence of a world *opinio juris* (i.e., sense of legal obligation) as to the criminality of nuclear weapons.

There is a very simple response to that specious argument: Since when has a small gang of criminals – in this case, the nuclear weapons states – been able to determine what is legal or illegal for the rest of the community by means of their own criminal behaviour? By what right do these nuclear weapons states have to argue that by means of their own criminal behaviour they have ipso facto made criminal acts legitimate? No civilized nation state would permit a small gang of criminal conspirators to pervert its domestic legal order in this manner. Moreover, both the Nuremberg Tribunal and the Tokyo Tribunal made it quite clear that a conspiratorial band of criminal states likewise have no right to opt out of the international legal order by means of invoking their own criminal behaviour as the least common denominator of international deportment.

To the contrary, the entire human race has been victimized by an international conspiracy of ongoing criminal activity carried out by the nuclear weapons states under the doctrine known as "nuclear deterrence," which is really a euphemism for "nuclear terrorism." This international conspiracy of nuclear deterrence/terrorism currently practised by the nuclear weapons states is no different from any other conspiracy by a criminal gang or band. They are the outlaws. So it is up to the rest of the international community to repress and dissolve this international criminal conspiracy as soon as possible and by whatever non-violent means are available.

(5) The Nuclear Perversion of Constitutional Democracy and the Rule of Law

In the United States of America, there are several ramifications that follow ineluctably from the conspiratorial doctrine and practice known as nuclear deterrence/terrorism. First, criminality is said to be legitimacy. When nuclear weapons were first developed and used, there was absolutely no consideration given to the rule of law. Thus, nuclear weapons represent the absolute negation of the rule of law both at home and abroad. The very existence of nuclear weapons requires that the rule of law be subverted both at home and abroad.

Furthermore, nuclear weapons are anti-democratic. There has never been any form of meaningful democratic accountability applied to the U.S. nuclear weapons establishment. The American people as individuals or as a whole have never had any significant input into the process of developing nuclear weapons systems except to the extent that the U.S. Congress has voted blank checks. The existence of nuclear weapons systems and their requisite degrees of super-secrecy require that our system of nuclear government be stealthily anti-democratic.

Finally, the same is true for the U.S. Constitution. Constitutional protections became meaningless when nuclear weapons were integrated into the U.S. foreign affairs and defense establishment. Indeed, the U.S. Constitution has become a farce and a facade in the name of national security as a direct result of nuclear weapons. Nuclearism has perverted America's constitutional democracy with its commitment to the rule of law both at home and abroad.

Nuclear deterrence/terrorism as currently practised by today's nuclear weapons states cannot succeed over the long run (which it must) because it is premised upon assumptions and practices that are immoral, illegal, unconstitutional, criminal, and irrational in the estimation of the respective public opinions in the various nuclear weapons states as well as around the world. Unless it is destroyed, nuclear deterrence/terrorism will ultimately fail and destroy all of humankind because of its own inherent contradictions.

In particular, the assumptions, policies and practices underlying the U.S. nuclear weapons establishment are irrational and insane from any meaningful perspective. Nevertheless, this conspiratorial doctrine of nuclear deterrence/-terrorism has required that what is inherently irrational and insane somehow be made to appear to be completely rational and sane. America has quite simply had to invert and pervert its entire system of democratic values, legal ethos, and constitutional practices in order to account for and accommodate the existence of nuclear weapons.

(6) The Irrationality of Irrationality

For example, a good deal of the U.S. nuclear weapons establishment and its deterrence/terrorist practices are premised upon the Harvard political scientist Thomas Schelling's theory known as the "rationality of irrationality" that was expounded in his classic book *The Strategy of Conflict* (1960). According to this pernicious doctrine, in theory it could sometimes prove to be a rational strategy for government decision-makers to pretend to be completely irrational in their dealings with other states in order to get their own way. Adolph Hitler was said to be the paradigmatic example of this phenomenon during the 1930s. The outbreak of the Second World War in 1939, however, demonstrated the severe limitations of Schelling's theory.

Applying Schelling's concept to nuclear weapons, an analyst could mistakenly come to the conclusion that it might prove to be useful for a government to threaten to commit the completely irrational and insane act of starting a nuclear war in order to avoid a conventional or nuclear war, or more cynically and realistically, to achieve certain geopolitical objectives. Furthermore, in order to make this insane threat credible, the threatening state must then proceed to develop the capability to launch and wage a nuclear war so that in the eyes of its intended adversary the completely irrational threat begins to look somewhat more rational. When the adversary inevitably responds in kind, these psychological and bureaucratic dynamics produce the momentum for generating the self-fulfilling prophecy of nuclear Armageddon.

I will not bother here to analyze at any length the logical contradictions and psychological fallacies of U.S. nuclear deterrence/terrorist doctrine since that task has already been performed quite admirably by Robert Jervis in his definitive book *The Illogic of American Nuclear Strategy* (1984). But I simply wish to point out that the entire theory of nuclear deterrence/terrorism as currently practised by the world's nuclear weapons states represents a working-out of Schelling's hypothesis propounding the so-called "rationality of irrationality." All of the world's nuclear weapons states, and especially the two nuclear superpowers, have spent the past 45 years trying to make a completely irrational threat appear to be rational and in the process have had to pervert and destroy all elements of rationality, legality, constitutionality, morality and sanity that stood in their way. The task itself is ultimately doomed to failure unless and until the citizens of the world's nuclear weapons states can figure out some practical means to eliminate nuclear weapons before nuclear weapons eliminate them.

(7) The Illegal Status of Nuclear Arms Control Agreements

These observations then logically bring us to the question of the international legal status of nuclear arms control agreements. From the perspective developed above, nuclear arms control agreements are simply part of an international criminal conspiracy between a small gang of criminal states designed to further perpetuate the conspiracy. Nuclear arms control agreements attempt to rationalize, regularize, modernize and perfect these instrumentalities of international criminal activity. Hence, they are entitled to no validity at all as a matter of positive international law.

That being said, until humankind can get rid of those instrumentalities of crime, it is probably preferable to try to control nuclear weapons than not to try to control them. On the other hand, a compelling argument can be made that nuclear arms control negotiations and agreements have never constituted more than soporifics designed by the nuclear weapons states, and especially by the two superpowers, to lull world public opinion into a false sense of trust in the process while, under their deceptive guise, such governments have pursued an unrelenting nuclear arms buildup and modernization. The recently concluded START Treaty is yet another confirmation of the validity of this critique. Nevertheless, whatever position one ultimately takes on this latter issue, we must never forget that all forms of nuclear arms control and reduction treaties concluded between the United States and the Soviet Union and among the nuclear weapons states themselves still deal with instrumentalities of internationally criminal and lawless behaviour.

Thus, nuclear arms control and reduction agreements can only constitute a temporary expedient. Their overall objective must always remain that prescribed by article 6 of the 1968 Treaty on the Non-Proliferation of Nuclear Weapons, which the United States, the Soviet Union and the United Kingdom are strictly bound to obey as parties: "Each of the Parties to the Treaty undertakes to pursue negotiations in good faith on effective measures relating to cessation of the nuclear arms race at an early date and to nuclear disarmament, and on a treaty on general and complete disarmament under strict and effective international control." Universal nuclear disarmament is the only legally defensible, constitutionally valid, morally acceptable and logically consistent position that can be taken.

(9) Conclusion

We must call upon all lawyers and human rights activists around the world, as well as all men and women of good faith everywhere, to join us in this crusade for universal nuclear disarmament. Otherwise, the human race will suffer the same fate as the dinosaurs, and the planet earth will become a radioactive wasteland. The time for preventive action is now! *And civil resistance is the way to go.*

ANNA MICHALSKA*

Humanitarian Intervention

1. Introduction

Customary international law, in the pre-Charter period, recognized two grounds on which a State or group of States could intervene in another State to put an end to human rights violation that appeared to reach intolerable proportions.

The first doctrine allowed a State to intervene, eventually with the use of armed forces, to protect the lives and the material interests of its national abroad. This theory was closely related to the principle of State responsibility for injury to aliens, the international standard of minimum treatment of foreigners and the identification of the security of the State with that of its citizens.

The second doctrine, that of humanitarian intervention, permitted a State to intervene in situations where another State mistreated its own citizens in a way failing the "general standards recognized by civilized peoples" as to "shock the conscience of mankind."[1]

The doctrine of humanitarian intervention was elaborated in the seventeenth century by Hugo Grotius and other early international lawyers. This doctrine is based on the assumption that States in their relations with their own nationals have the international obligation to guarantee to them certain fundamental rights which are considered to be necessary for their existence and for the maintenance of friendly relations among nations. The violation of these rights by any State cannot be ignored by other States. This assumption would authorize international intervention in case of flagrant denial of these rights by any State to its own citizens.

The theory of humanitarian intervention came into being toward the end of the last century and the beginning of the twentieth century. At that time, and in

* Professor of International Law, Faculty of Law, The Adam Michiewicz University, Poznan, Poland.

[1] Jean-Pierre L. Fonteyne, "Forcible Self-Help by States to Protect Human Rights: Recent Views from the United Nations, in R. Lillich, (ed.) *Humanitarian Intervention and the United Nations* (1973), p. 198.

K.E. Mahoney and P. Mahoney (eds.), Human Rights in the Twenty-first Century, 393–404.

the years immediately after, a good number of scholars recognized the lawfulness of this kind of intervention. But at the same time numerous other authors explicitly denied the legality of humanitarian intervention.

It is necessary for us to stress the fact that authors and followers of the humanitarian intervention theory differed from one another in some questions of particular character. Above all, three problems have then constituted the object of analysis and controversy: 1) the grounds for intervention, 2) the character of intervention, 3) who is permitted to intervene.

In recent years we have witnessed growing interest in the problems of humanitarian intervention – especially since the United States intervention in Panama. But the method of discussion is quite different from methods used at the beginning of the century. In recent times, notwithstanding the lack of a coherent doctrine of humanitarian intervention, the validity and legality, in international law, of every particular case of intervention is considered and evaluated. This is done with very little reference to previously elaborated and adopted doctrine. However, this does not necessarily mean that one should ignore this historical theory. While it is true that the system of international law itself has undergone an essential evolution, nevertheless, some questions put many years ago have only recently been answered and many doubts continue to persist.

(1) The Grounds for Intervention

According to Professor Antoine Rougier, one of the main proponents of the theory of humanitarian intervention, intervention is legitimate only when: a) *le fait qui la motive soit un fait de la puissance publique, et non le fait de particuliers; b) ce fait constitue une violation du droit humain, et non une simple violation du droit national positif; c) l'intervention reunisse certaines conditions d'opportunite.*[2]

The fundamental human rights criteria for purposes of humanitarian intervention merits our attention here. For instance, Rougier mentions *a propos:* the right to life, the right to liberty, the principle of legality. It is an attempt to isolate and put together all these human rights which are today ranked among the norms of the *jus cogens* type, i.e., obligatory norms which must be observed by all members of the international community.

In the book "*International Protection of Human Rights*"[3] by M. Ganji, we can find the opinions of several well-known authorities who support the theory of humanitarian intervention. It should be noted that these authors agree in general that humanitarian intervention, at times, is not only permissible but also necessary. They are all silent however when it comes to the question of giving a precise definition to the word "humanitarian". Their general con-

[2] A. Rougier, "La théorie d'intervention d'Humanité", *Revue Générale de Droit International Public* (1910), pp. 468–525.

[3] Geneve-Paris 1962, pp. 11–13.

sensus is that, when a government's conduct toward its citizens is such that it leads to massacres, brutality, religious or racial persecutions, and when these acts are of such nature that they shock the conscience of mankind, then the right of intervention is legally justified.

(2) The Character of Intervention

Intervention, as it is generally understood in international law, implies a peremptory demand from outside of the State for positive conduct or abstention. Most international jurists distinguish between intervention which can be defined as dictatorial interference in the internal affairs of a State, and diplomatic action which may involve the use of good offices, request for information, discussion in international forums, etc. Juridically speaking, intervention must always take "an imperative form". It implies an action undertaken by one or more States in regard to another State.

In practice, however, armed interventions had been far from the above theoretical bases and only very rarely were undertaken for humanitarian purposes. The cases better known as "Cases of Humanitarian Intervention" were, for example, the intervention of France, Great Britain and Russia against the Turkish massacres and suppression of the Greeks which resulted in the independence of Greece in 1830; the 1860 intervention by Austria, France, Great Britain, Russia and Prussia in Syria; Russian intervention against Turkey in 1877–1878; the intervention of Austria, Russia, Great Britain, Italy and France in Turkey as a result of insurrections in Macedonia during 1903–1908. All these interventions involved the protection of persecuted religious minorities. The intervening States were, in every case, those which had the same religious beliefs and institutions as the persecuted minorities.

In almost all cases, while the actions of intervening powers were motivated by humanitarian considerations, they were justified on the basis of treaty stipulations. This leads to the question of whether the doctrine of humanitarian intervention was necessary to justify an intervention of States. It seems that the violation of an international treaty was sufficient justification for action by States; whether armed action was really necessary remains open to question.

(3) Who Is Permitted to Intervene

In determining who should be permitted to intervene, the following possibilities should be considered: a) whether a State is competent to intervene unilaterally; b) whether a group of powers may intervene in concert; and c) whether intervention should be based on the decision of an international organization of a universal nature.

Intervention by one State is usually suspected of being undertaken with a view to its own interests. It has been used by some States for achieving certain political objectives which had little direct relation with the proclaimed humanitarian motives. Thus, the theory of humanitarian intervention does not allow for intervention by an individual State.

Intervention by a group of powers is based on a collective decision. An essential condition of such an intervention is that it be of "disinterested character" on political or economic grounds.

That is characteristic of M. Ganji who does not mention intervention by international organization in his writings. All we read is that ". . . in absence of an international organization of universal nature, intervention by a group of powers is permitted." Yet, as far as can be remembered, an international organization of universal character was well-known and functioning at least during the period when L. Oppenheim, P. Guggenheim, and H. Lauterpacht were formulating their opinions. Nevertheless, a function which could be fulfilled within such a framework by an international organization has never been subjected to an analysis in the doctrine of humanitarian intervention and this point is still fully neglected there. Thus, we can see doubts arising – namely, whether the doctrine of humanitarian intervention does serve a cause of universal protection of human rights or whether it provides different States with a justification for their real politics. In my opinion, the act of intervention must be the result of a decision of the Organization, in an organized international community.

This doctrine was greatly misused in the past and often served as a pretext for the occupation or invasion of weaker countries.[4] Nevertheless, the doctrine of humanitarian intervention was the first to give an expression to the principle that there were some limits to the freedom of States in dealing with their own nationals.

(4) The Weakness of This Doctrine

The doctrine of humanitarian intervention was a very important step towards elaboration of a *conception* of international protection of human rights, and no one is licensed to disregard this function of the doctrine. Nevertheless, it cannot be recognized as being a basis – moral or legal – of the contemporary system of human rights protection on a universal scale. It simply has too many weak points.

First, there is no precise definition of "intervention". The lawfulness of the use of force – as a principal form of such an intervention – for the protection of human rights may be called into question as being contradictory to fundamental norms of international law. In almost all cases when interventions were motivated by humanitarian considerations, the States to whom they had been addressed invoked the principle of national sovereignty and domestic jurisdiction.

Secondly, the lack of a precise definition of the notion of "fundamental

[4] I. Brownlie, "Humanitarian Intervention", in J.N. Moore (ed.) *Law and Civil War in the Modern World* (1974) Baltimore: John Hopkins University Press, p. 217–228.

human rights". The practice of humanitarian intervention was limited to cases based on the conventions such as: peace treaties, and minority treaties.

Thirdly, the lack of a general consensus on who is permitted to intervene. Even as we recognize that an intervention by a State or group of States is lawful, its limits can always be called into question.

An examination of the practices which were prevalent in the late nineteenth and early twentieth centuries shows how the legality of humanitarian intervention was based more on theoretical arguments than on a rigorous analysis of the diplomatic papers of the day. Many cases must be seen in the light of the considerable freedom States enjoyed in resorting to armed intervention. Sometimes it was a matter of enforcing one's own right; on other occasions, military operations took the form of real war. After the Covenant of the League of Nations and of the Kellog-Briandt Pact entered into force, States almost never resorted again to the theory of humanitarian intervention to justify the use of force.

2. Contemporary Approach

(1) The Lawfulness of the Humanitarian Intervention under the U.N. Charter

A. Opinions Expressed by States during the Drafting of Certain Resolutions
The doctrinal debate on the validity of humanitarian intervention continued after the adoption of the U.N. Charter. The normative ambiguities inherent in the concept and the very strongly differing positions on question of law and policy, make slim prospects for a consensus on the definition and scope of humanitarian intervention. Moreover, the position of States is not at all uniform. The divergence of opinion is very visible during debates in different organs of the United Nations, largely due to the lack of agreement on a proper interpretation of Article 2, paragraph 4 of the U.N. Charter in connection with the Article 51 of the Charter.

The prohibition of the use of force and the principle of non-intervention were discussed during the debates of the Special Committee on Principles of International Law Concerning Friendly Relations and Co-operation Among States, the Special Committee on the Question of Defining Aggression and the Sixth Committee. The claims which were advanced have been analyzed by Jean-Pierre Fonteyne. Some of the more interesting discussions on humanitarian intervention are as follows:

a) Most delegations stressed that the only cases of permissible use of force in contemporary international law are individual and collective self-defence under Article 51 and U.N. enforcement action in cases of threats to the peace, breaches of the peace and acts of aggression as specified in Chapter VII. Consequently, all unilateral use of force other than in the exercise of the right to self-defence is unlawful ab initio.

b) Article 51 of the Charter restricts the right of individual and collective self-defence to the cases where an armed attack has occurred. The majority of States favored the view that Article 51 of the Charter should be interpreted literally.
c) A great many delegations insisted that the rendering of armed assistance to colonial peoples engaged in a struggle for independence is a particular modality of self-defence. But only a small number of representatives extended this point of view to all cases involving gross human rights violations of large parts of a population.
d) The large majority of the delegations argued that Article 2.4 of the Charter contains an absolute and unconditional prohibition of the use of force; regardless of motive or purpose, the use of force constitutes a violation of the Charter.

During the drafting of the Resolutions on Non-Intervention, Friendly Relations and Definition of Aggression, very few opinions were expressed by States concerning humanitarian intervention. Only Jamaica and Mexico made reference to humanitarian intervention. Jamaica had pronounced in favour of the lawfulness of humanitarian intervention, whereas Mexico stated that humanitarian intervention is forbidden as being contrary to the U.N. Charter.

During the drafting history of the Definition of Aggression, certain opinions categorically opposed humanitarian intervention. For example, the representative of China stated:

> "The accomplishment of atrocities by a State against its own nationals would be a case of an offense against the peace and security of mankind . . . and armed intervention in that connection would be justified only if taken in pursuance of a United Nations decision under Chapter VII of the Charter."

The Israeli representative stated:

> ". . . neither the realities of modern life nor the accepted concept of legal and illegal use of force nor the teaching of history could justify the use of force in favour of co-national minority. Humanitarian intervention had frequently been invoked to justify intervention, although the true motives had been very different."

These statements against the theory of the legality of humanitarian intervention were unequivocal and gave rise to no problems of interpretation.

B. Doctrine

Where the interventions have occurred, intervening States have usually denounced large-scale violation of human rights in the territory where the intervention occurred. But, in intervening, all these States rather than invoking the doctrine of humanitarian intervention, preferred to ground the lawfulness of their actions on other arguments.[5]

[5] N. Ronzitti, *Rescuing Nationals Abroad Through Military Coercion and Intervention on Grounds of Humanity* (1985), Netherlands: Martinus Nijhoff Publishers, p. 108 et passim.

A good example is the United States intervention in Panama. It has been argued that the intervention in Panama disregarded pertinent norms and principles of international law. Yet, others considered that the invasion of Panama was a lawful response to a tyranny.[6]

The following four grounds were given for the United States intervention in Panama: safeguarding the lives of American citizens, restoration of democracy, integrity of the Panama Canal treaties, and bringing General Manuel Noriega to justice. In the context of the United States response to human rights violations, only the second argument is of some interest. Ved P. Nanda does not deny that Noriega's regime was of autocratic character. However, he argues that no international legal instrument permits an intervention to maintain or impose a democratic form of government in another State.[7] Even though the United States argued that the people of Panama were being deprived of the right to political independence, Oscar Schachter takes the position that the principle of self-determination, while an important principle of international law, has no priority over well-established and important international legal principles – such as noninterference in internal affairs.[8] Nanda concludes that the intervention was dictated by political considerations in disregard of the existing norms of the use of force.[9] Tom Farer adds that if sovereignty means anything, it means that one State cannot compromise another State's territorial integrity or dictate the character of the occupants of its governing institutions, the U.N. Charter gives the Security Council the authority to use or authorize members to use force against other members only to maintain or restore peace.[10]

In light of the clarity of international law norms, the kind of arguments D'Amato uses to justify the lawfulness of the intervention are questionable.[11] He proposes to adopt a new approach towards the international law and reproaches the above cited authors for their "static" conception of international law. In his opinion, they are unable to see the reality of human beings struggling to achieve basic freedoms. D'Amato rejects the conception that international law regulates the relations between the States only – instead, he favours the view that only peoples are subject to this law.

He says that the U.S. interventions in Panama and in Granada are milestones along the path to a new non-statical conception of international law,

[6] V. Nader, T. Farer, and A. D'Amato, "U.S. Forces in Panama: Defenders, Aggressors or Human Rights Activists?" in *American Journal of International Law*, Vol. 84 No. 2 (1990) pp. 494–525.

[7] *Ibid.*, p.498 V. Nanda, *The Validity of United States Intervention in Panama under International Law.*

[8] O. Schachter, "The Legality of Pro-Democratic Invasion", in *American Journal of International Law*, vol. 78 (1984) pp. 645–650.

[9] See note 6, *supra* at p.503.

[10] *Supra*, see note 6 Tom J. Farer, Panama, "Beyond the Charter Paradigm", at p. 514.

[11] *Supra*, see note 6 Anthony D'Amato, "The Invasion of Panama was a Lawful Response to Tyranny", at pp. 519–522.

and that they change previous nonintervention formulas. He argues that human rights law demands intervention against tyranny. This kind of intervention he says is not only legally justified, but morally required.[12]

In my opinion, D'Amato's views are unacceptable. They shake the still limited effectiveness of international law norms – norms elaborated by the whole international community. Moreover, the dangers they present are self-evident.

D'Amato rejects the positivist conception of international law and he is not alone nor exceptional in his views. Many others nowadays are occupied with the search of moral arguments for humanitarian intervention. For example, the book entitled, "*Humanitarian Intervention: An Inquiry Into Law and Morality*" by Fernando R. Teson,[13] asks the question: is it legal and moral for States to use military force to stop serious violations of human rights? The author advocates the need for a new philosophy of international law which would throw off the paradigm of States' sovereignty in favour of the protection of human rights. He contends that international legal discourse suffers from a congenital tension between the concern for human rights and the notion of State sovereignty. One of the most pressing challenges of our time is – in his opinion – to solve this tension. He clearly gives priority to human rights.

Teson says that when forcible action is taken to stop serious human rights deprivations, it is permitted by international law, *properly constructed*. The author tries to show that the *best* interpretation of relevant treaty materials and State practice is that humanitarian intervention is consistent with the present international legal order.

In my opinion, Teson proposes creating new international legal order, yet he fails to formulate a new interpretation of international law. His presumptions relating to an "international law properly constructed" as well as to "the best interpretation of international treaties" lead us to an interpretation of *extra legem* type and even – *contra legem*, as far as the international norms being actually in force are concerned. Moral postulates aimed at putting the system of international law into new shape are worthy of approving, but they are postulates *de lege ferenda*. On the other hand, when justifying the legal character of humanitarian intervention in terms of *de lege lata* – the argument is not convincing.

C. Conclusion

Upon analysis, international law norms suggest that humanitarian intervention is not lawful. In my opinion, the doctrine does not permit sufficiently convincing arguments to lead to the conclusion that humanitarian intervention can be lawful. No case of humanitarian intervention to date has been evaluated unanimously as such.

When asking the questions is humanitarian intervention lawful, and is it

[12] Ibid., at p. 519.

[13] Dobbs Ferry, New York: Transnational Publishers (1988).

efficacious as a means of international protection of human rights, the followers of humanitarian intervention seem to forget that the intervention itself is a real threat to fundamental human rights, in particular, to the right to life. This is all the more important when a tyrant is strong and decides to undertake an armed resistance.

An acceptance of humanitarian intervention by the international society would mean a recognition of a division of wars into just ones and the unjust ones. The latter would be a substantial menace for peace which is the main value in international relations. As long as sovereignty of States and territorial integrity belong to fundamental principles of international law, the principle of humanitarian intervention cannot be introduced into the international legal order because it is contradictory to both above quoted principles.

Recognizing the legality of humanitarian intervention requires a simultaneous creation of mechanisms to prevent it from being exploited for political reasons. In my opinion, all such attempts are bound to be abortive. To institute a democratic regime and human rights by means of foreign armies arouses both legal and moral objections.

The conception of humanitarian intervention understood as an armed intervention has, of course, a non-political character. However, the practice of humanitarian intervention has always had – in my opinion – a political context. The reasons for humanitarian intervention and its consequences have necessarily been of a political character.

Human rights have been too often exploited as an element of political confrontation between States. The time has now come for human rights to be one of the basic elements for international co-operation.

(2) A New Conception of Intervention for Human Rights Protection

A. Legal Grounds

International implementation of human rights has some inherent limitations. These flow from the existing structure of the international community whose basic principle is the sovereign equality of States. In principle, States themselves determine the ways and means for giving effect to human rights. International institutions as well as third States may have *limited* powers to deal with violations of human rights in a given country. But they may not intervene directly by force to remedy a situation contrary to fundamental human rights.[14]

Nevertheless, the field of domestic jurisdiction is in constant change and, in general, it suffers more and more restrictions. The protection of human rights is no longer exclusively within the domestic jurisdiction of States. This does not mean that all human rights fall outside the area of domestic jurisdiction. In my opinion, two categories of human rights exist outside the sphere of domestic jurisdiction. First, there are human rights which have been formulated in

[14] Ch. Tomuschat, "Human Rights in a World-Wide Framework, Some Current Issues", *Zeitschrift für öffentliches Recht und Völkerrecht*, Vol. 43, No. 3, 1985, p. 572.

international treaties. Secondly, there are human rights which are considered by the international community as creating obligations *erga omnes*.

The international obligations of States to ensure the observance of human rights derives from many international treaties. The ratification of these treaties takes the element of "domestic affairs" away from the rights proclaimed in these treaties. At the universal as well as the regional level, human rights treaties provide for the creation of certain organs entrusted with the task of investigating alleged human rights violations or, more generally, the conformity of national legislation and practice with the obligations contained in the relevant human rights treaties. The protection of human rights by treaties and the agreed competence of the human rights organs goes outside the field of domestic jurisdiction. The extent of the competence of international bodies is determined by the treaty, and no State can unilaterally withdraw from or deny this competence.

Fundamental human rights create obligations *erga omnes*. For example, in contemporary international law, such obligations derive from the outlawing of acts of aggression and genocide and also from the principles and rules concerning the basic rights of the human persons – including protection from slavery and racial discrimination.[15] International crime may result from a serious breach on a wide scale of an international obligation for safeguarding the human being, such as those prohibiting slavery, genocide and apartheid.[16]

In discussing derogations from human rights, a United Nations document speaks of the "intangibility" of certain fundamental rights.[17] International doctrine has recognized that a number of international obligations in the field of human rights – by reason of their importance for the international community – are obligations in whose fulfilment all States have a legal interest. Practice shows that the international community has accepted this position and the practice is supported by a widespread *opinio iuris*.

B. Methods of interventions

There is no longer any doubt that human rights extend beyond the domestic jurisdiction of States. Consequently, it is important to more precisely define the conditions and limitations imposed by international law on measures that may be taken by States and international organizations in response to violations of human rights.

The methods and forms of intervention determined in human rights treaties are defined quite precisely. What is of greater interest are those forms of intervention which are not regulated in the human rights treaties.

One of the questions that can be asked is to what extent are international organizations in general entitled to criticize the human rights situation in other countries? I fully share the opinion expressed by R. Bernhardt, that the dis-

[15] The dictum of the International Court of Justice in the Barcelona Traction Case.
[16] The draft treaty on State responsibility.
[17] U.N. Doc. E/CN.4/Sub.2/1985.

cussion of the human rights situation in one State by an international organization and the adoption of a resolution is never a violation of international law nor an unlawful intervention in domestic affairs.[18] This is true regardless of whether or not the State being criticized is a member of the organization or a party to a relevant human rights treaty.[19] This view is confirmed by the Helsinki Final Act and follow-up documents which all confirm the necessity and the common intentions to protect human rights.

International organizations resort to different forms of intervention in situations where human rights are violated. Such enforcement measures as proclamation of embargoes and reprisals, may also be utilized. It seems, however, that enforcement measures of any kind may only be undertaken if an international legal obligation is violated.

International organs resort only to peaceful methods of intervention for purposes of human rights protection. Neither treaty law nor customary international law provides or admits an armed form of humanitarian intervention.

A third State is severely limited in its possibilities to intervene in favour of the protection of human rights in another country. What it can do is initiate instituting international legal procedures provided for in human rights treaties or resort to classical diplomatic measures which are generally of confidential character. More recently, there has been some general tendency towards enlarging States' powers in the framework of the Helsinki process.

What is clear is that the international community does not confer on any State a right to intervene in an armed way in favour of human rights protection in another country. A response to human rights violations cannot be made through violence. In a recent resolution entitled, "The Protection of Human Rights and the Principle of Non-Intervention in Internal Affairs of States", this thesis was adopted by the Institute of International Law.[20] This resolution clearly mentions diplomatic, economic and other measures that could be undertaken by a State when acting individually or collectively. At the same time, the resolution qualifies this with the proviso that ... "such measures are permitted under international law and do not involve the use of force." (Article 2)[21]

3. Conclusion

In conclusion I would like to call more attention to two problems which are not directly linked to the question of humanitarian intervention but should take an important place in all discussions on efficacious protection of human rights.

[18] R. Bernhardt, "Domestic Jurisdiction of States and International Human Rights Organs", vol. 7 (1986) *Human Rights Law Journal*, pp.205–216 at p. 208.

[19] Annual Report 1989, p. 625 et passim.

[20] Council of Europe. Human Rights. Information Sheet No. 25, 1989.

[21] T. van Boven, "Strengthening the U.N. Human Rights Capacity", *Nordic Journal of Human Rights* (1986), No. 4, p. 30.

All acts of humanitarian intervention up until now have been undertaken in order to protect individual freedom as well as public rights and liberties. Almost all mechanisms of international control aim at protecting these rights. However, violations of social and economic rights very seldom become objects of interest to international organs and third States notwithstanding the fact that thousands of human beings, including children, die of hunger and malnutrition every day. There is a tendency to disregard certain social phenomena such as poverty. I believe problems such as these must be approached not only from economic, social or assistance angles, but also from the point of view of human rights.

After an initial phase of standard-setting U.N. activities in the field of human rights have moved progressively toward implementation. There is a growing awareness that the work for human rights is not only a question of coping with symptoms but also a matter of *creating conditions*. The State's function in the implementation of international human rights standards is of double character: A State is the main actor in the violation of human rights but, at the same time, it is also the main actor in the protection of these rights. Therefore, efforts of the international community must be focused not only on punishment of a State for having violated human rights but also on the *prevention* of human rights violations. It is a matter of urgent concern that States be encouraged to take whatever *positive measures* are necessary to ensure – for each human being – satisfaction of the needs and values recognized in the human rights instruments.

CHRISTINE M. CHINKIN*

Women and Peace: Militarism and Oppression

1. Introduction

This paper considers the contribution of feminist analysis in examining the causes of international disputes, and the use of their findings in preventing and resolving international disputes. It attempts to address the contradictions presented by the concept of women as carers in the context of the significant role played by women in peace studies, peace research, and peace activism.[1] There have been a number of applications of feminist theory to these topics and it has been argued that "women's peace organising is strengthened and transformed through confrontation with feminist questions of gender".[2] The reverse is equally true: looking at feminist theory in the context of peace studies highlights a number of complexities. The paper discusses some of the reasons for the contradictions that arise and their implications, both for peace research and for feminist theory, rather than attempting to answer them.

The paper is written from the perspective of an international lawyer, not that of a political scientist, anthropologist, psychologist, or peace researcher. As an international lawyer it concerns me that international law remains largely immune from the lessons to be learnt from these other disciplines, and has remained unaffected by an gender analysis.[3] The fundamental norms of modern international law are laid down in the United Nations Charter, Article 2 which prohibits nation States to use force against the territorial integrity and political independence of any other State,[4] and requires States to settle their

* Associate Professor, University of Sydney. The author thanks Graeme Coss for his research assistance in the preparation of this article.

[1] An earlier version of this paper was presented as part of a Panel on Women and Caring, at Conference on Women and the Law, Women's Studies Centre, Sydney University, November 1990.

[2] A. Harris & Y. King (eds), *Rocking the Ship of State, Toward a Feminist Peace Politics*, Introduction, 1 (Westview Press 1989).

[3] However see H. Charlesworth, C. Chinkin & S. Wright, "Feminist Approaches to International Law", 85 AJIL 613–645 (1991).

[4] United Nations Charter, Article 2(4).

K.E. Mahoney and P. Mahoney (eds.), Human Rights in the Twenty-first Century, 405–418.

disputes through peaceful means.[5] These obligations are essential to promoting the primary purpose of the United Nations as laid down in Article 1 of the Charter:

> To maintain international peace and security, and to that end: to take effective collective measures for the prevention and removal of threats to the peace, and for the suppression of acts of aggression or other breaches of the peace, and to bring about by peaceful means, and in conformity with the principles of justice and international law, adjustment or settlement of international disputes or situations which might lead to a breach of the peace.

Members of the organised international community have spent considerable time since 1945 working on expanding these general principles and attempting to formulate more precisely the legal obligations imposed upon States in a way that is workable and effective. Thus the General Assembly has defined what constitutes aggression[6] and reasserted the principles relating to the use of force;[7] the International Court of Justice has specified the preconditions for a claim of collective self-defence;[8] and the International Law Commission has drafted provisions spelling out the consequences of an illegal act of aggression.[9] There is a great deal of discussion in many international law texts about what behaviour constitutes an illegal use of force and what exceptions to its prohibition are established in State practice and treaty.

However, there seems to have been less energy directed by international lawyers at seeking ways to achieve this primary objective, and in seeking how to determine and contain threats to international peace. One of the reasons is the Statist orientation of an international legal system founded upon the sovereign equality and inviolability of States.[10] This places the interests of States higher than those of individuals within a State, and frequently denies the legitimate interests of individuals or groups of individuals in dispute resolution processes.[11] Thus the international community, acting through the Security Council, had no difficulty in condemning the invasion and annexation of one sovereign State by another in August 1990 when Iraq invaded Kuwait.[12] It also

[5] United Nations Charter, Article 2(3).

[6] General Assembly Resolution 3314 (XXIX), GAOR, 29th Session, Supp. 21 (1974).

[7] General Assembly Declaration on Principles of Friendly Relations and Co-operation Among States in accordance with the Charter of the United Nations, General Assembly Resolution 2625 (XXV), 24 October 1970.

[8] *Military and Paramilitary Activities in and against Nicaragua*, (Nicaragua v. United States), Merits, 1986 ICJ Rep. 14.

[9] International Law Commission, Draft Articles on States Responsibility, Article 19, [1979] 2 YBILC Pt II, 90.

[10] United Nations Charter, Article 2(1).

[11] See C. Chinkin and R. Sadurska, "The Anatomy of International Disputes", forthcoming 6 Ohio State Journal on Dispute Resolution, No. 3 1991.

[12] Security Council Resolution 660, 2 August 1991; Security Council Resolution 661, 6 August 1991.

authorised the use of force to ensure the withdrawal of Iraq from Kuwait.[13] However those same members of the Security Council found it more problematic to authorise the intrusion of foreign troops or humanitarian organisations into Iraq for the protection of the Kurds.[14] The international community has not persistently rejected the annexation of East Timor with the same vigour as it did the annexation of Kuwait,[15] and indeed condemned the Vietnamese invasion of Kampuchea although that had the effect of stopping the mass murder of the Pol Pot Khmer Rouge regime. These apparent inconsistencies are explicable to an international lawyer focusing attention on the promotion of the rights of sovereign States rather than upon the values of human life and freedom.

However even a very cursory examination of the United Nations Charter demonstrates that there is a recognised link between the maintenance of international peace and security between States and the other purposes of the United Nations, notably the protection and promotion of human rights. Article 1(3) states the purpose of achieving international co-operation through "promoting and encouraging respect for human rights and for fundamental freedoms without distinction as to sex, language or religion." The General Assembly Declaration on the Granting of Independence to Colonial Territories and Peoples states:

> The subjection of peoples to alien subjugation, domination and exploitation constitutes a denial of fundamental human rights ... and is an impediment to the promotion of world peace and co-operation.

This is an assertion that oppression and denial of rights to groups within a State's domestic jurisdiction of itself poses a threat to the maintenance of international peace and security. The first Resolutions in the General Assembly and Security Council after the invasion of East Timor by Indonesia relied upon this right. However they were not made effective as were those condemning the invasion of Kuwait. While other factors explain the concerted international response to the invasion of Kuwait,[16] there is little doubt that the violation of the rights of Statehood was viewed more seriously than violation of the rights of claimants to Statehood. While there have been moves in international law towards according higher priority to the protection of human rights, States remain the primary subjects and objects of international law, and will be so even in a new world order.

[13] Security Council Resolution 678, 29 November 1991.

[14] It did eventually insist that Iraq allow access by international humanitarian bodies to those in need of assistance; Security Council Resolution, 688, 5 April 1991.

[15] Although Resolutions of the Security Council and General Assembly at first condemned the invasion and reasserted the right of self-determination of the East Timorese the matter has not been voted upon within the United Nations since 1982.

[16] Notably the unanimity in the Security Council which allowed Resolutions to be passed without exercise of the veto contained in United Nations Charter, Article 29(3), and the threat to the continued flow of oil from the Gulf area.

2. The Patriarchy of the Nation State and Oppression of Women

A number of feminist writers have concentrated upon the primacy accorded to nation States in the international legal structure to examine the relationship between the patriarchal structure of most, if not all, nation States and the systematic and structural oppression of women therein. From this starting point some have moved on to look at the symbiotic relationship between the military and sexism. Many of these writings have been developed in the particular context of the arms race and movements for disarmament. Although the fears of a nuclear holocaust have somewhat receded with the apparent end of the Cold War, the underlying issues remain of vital importance. First, although the threat of a super-power confrontation has lessened there remains the fear of the use of nuclear or, as was made apparent during the Gulf conflict in 1990–91, of chemical weapons by lesser powers. Second, the threat of outbreak of conventional warfare has not diminished, as was also illustrated by the Iraq/Kuwait conflict, and many of the conclusions are equally applicable in that context.

(1) Patriarchy and Militarism

First, States are patriarchal structures not solely in the sense of the exclusion of women from elite positions and decision-making roles, but also in the assumptions as to the concentration of power and control in an elite and the domestic legitimation of the use of force to maintain that control. Militarism is the belief system that upholds the legitimacy of the military control that the State exercises and the assumption that military values and policies are conducive to creating an orderly and secure society.[17] "Indeed some see patriarchy itself as the fundamental cause of war and oppression. ... The authority structures that pervade the military also pervade the entire society."[18] It is not just that the patriarchy of the nation State fosters militarism but that the two – patriarchy and militarism are interdependent and mutually supportive.

These aspects of patriarchy at home are replicated on the international arena by the principles of sovereign equality of States, territorial integrity and political independence. Further, the same forces that operate to maintain marginalisation and oppression of women at home operate internationally in actions by stronger States against weaker States. The methods used are also identical – rape,[19] battering, aggression, economic exploitation, rendering invisible and humiliation.[20] Thus peace, in the sense of not just an absence of

[17] B. Reardon, *Sexism and the War System* 14 (Teachers College Press 1985).

[18] Ibid., at 38.

[19] On the connection between rape and war see P. Strange, "It'll Make a Man Out of You" in D. Russell (ed.), *Exposing Nuclear Phallacies* 104, 114 (Pergamon Press 1989).

[20] A. Scales, "Militarism, Male Dominance and Law: Feminist Jurisprudence As Oxymoron?" 12 Harv. Women's LJ 25, 26 (1989). These words could well be used to describe the Iraqi invasion of Kuwait in August 1990.

conflict but as a substantial modification in the inherent tendencies of the international system to conflict,[21] is not fostered by the prevailing patriarchal ideology of most nation States, the prevailing emphasis on statism within the international legal order, nor the militarism that sustains them.

(2) The Masculinisation of the Military

Second, the overwhelming connection between men and the military is well recognised. At the instrumental level men hold the leading positions in command, in policy making, in the invention, construction and sale of weapons. "The world's generals and negotiators, bombardiers and captains, chiefs of staff, and defense secretaries have been and still are mostly men. More men than women shoot the pistol and work the missiles; certainly more men than women command them."[22] The images and language of conflict are masculinised. There are numerous examples: war makes "men" out of boys; weapons are judged by their depth of "penetration"; countries are "raped"; rape is used as an instrument of war.[23] An article in the Sydney Morning Herald during the Gulf war described the "rape" of Kuwait. This concentrated upon the pillaging and removal from Kuwait by Iraq of essential transport, industrial machinery, luxury goods and food rather than on the physical rape of Kuwaiti and foreign women. Rape is not merely an image or metaphor of war, but a reality to women as victims of war.[24] It is both an instrument of war and a response to it:

> Rape ... is to male-female relations what the behaviour of conquering troops is to occupied territories, what the trappings of imperial authority are to colonialism. Rape in various forms has been a traditional war system device used for symbolic or deterrent purposes as well as the basic intimidating mechanism to maintain submission."[25]

Since "women-hating is a fundamental part of military training and militarism"[26] the prevalence of rape and images of rape in war should come as no real surprise. "Rape in war is never random violence."[27]

[21] J. Crawford, "The Rights of Peoples: Some Conclusions", in J. Crawford (ed.), *The Rights of Peoples* 163 (Oxford 1988).

[22] S. Ruddick, "Mothers and Men's Wars", in A. Harris & Y. King (eds.), *Rocking the Ship of State, Toward a Feminist Peace Politics* 77 (Westview Press 1989).

[23] There is a wide literature on this see eg., A. Scales, "Militarism, Male Dominance and Law: Feminist Jurisprudence as Oxymoron?" 12 Harv. Women's LJ 25 (1989); R. Morgan, *The Demon Lover: On the Sexuality of Terrorism* 139 (Methuen 1989); P. Strange, "It'll Make a Man Out of You" in D. Russell (ed.), *Exposing Nuclear Phallacies* 104 (Pergamon Press 1989).

[24] But when Australian women attempted to commemorate that fact on ANZAC Day the full weight of the patriarchal State was brought to bear upon them. See S. Erika, "Patriarchy and the State", 3 Aust J. Law & Soc. 53, 59–62 (1986).

[25] B. Reardon, *Sexism and the War System* 39 (Teachers College Press, 1985).

[26] B. Roberts, "Reclaiming the Discourse: Feminist Perspectives in Peace Research", in D. Russell (ed.), *Exposing Nuclear Phallacies* 278, 279 (Pergamon Press 1989).

[27] C. Enloe, "The Gulf Crisis, Making Feminist Sense of It", Pacific Research 1990 4.

Where the language of war is not sexual it acts to dehumanise the victims or to neutralise the atrocity and horror of the actions described.[28] For example Carol Cohn describes graphically how military talk relies on abstractions and euphemisms which prevent the speaker or listener from dwelling on the realities of nuclear war. Another example is the doctrine of the "just war" which disguises that any war, just or unjust, still causes suffering and deprivation. "The analytic fictions of just war theory require a closure of moral issues final enough to justify killing and 'enemies' abstract enough to be killable."[29] Simone Weil described how victims and targets are reduced to things through force, which is defined as "that x that turns anybody who is subjected to it into a *thing*".[30] The driving force of militarism has been described as this "thingification: of women, of less powerful peoples, of nature itself."[31]

Women are victims of war in other ways than physical injury, although with the growing numbers of civilian casualties in war those numbers are increasing. Equally, of course, there need not be a war for women to be victims of force and violence; "the most common form of violence in our society is violence against women by men."[32] Women play a minimal role in the decision making with respect to commencing or continuing hostilities or in the build up and supply of weapons but "increasing military spending at the cost of social expenditures impacts most negatively on women. It contributes significantly to the feminization of poverty."[33] Another consequence of war for many women is the deprivation of home and food thereby forcing them to become refugees. An example was the creation of a vast refugee flow into Pakistan out of the fighting in Afghanistan; 30% of these refugees are women, 40% children under 13.[34] Yet another role imposed upon women is to produce the fighters of the next generation. Robin Morgan describes graphically the position of refugee women in the Palestine camps where, under appalling conditions, they are expected to have children who will become the next generation of freedom fighters to continue the fight for Palestinian self-determination against Israeli occupation.[35] Any attempt by the women to resist this role and to assert control

[28] C. Cohn, "Sex and Death in the Rational World of Defense Intellectuals" 12 Signs No. 4, 687, (1987).

[29] S. Ruddick, "Mothers and Mens Wars", in A. Harris & Y. King (eds.), *Rocking the Ship of State, Toward a Feminist Peace Politics* 77 (Westview Press 1989).

[30] Cited A. Scales, "Militarism, Male Dominance and Law: Feminist Jurisprudence as Oxymoron?", 12 Harv. Women's LJ 25, 26 (1989).

[31] Ibid.

[32] B. Roberts, "Reclaiming the Discourse: Feminist Perspectives in Peace Research", in D. Russell (ed.), *Exposing Nuclear Phallacies* 278 (Pergamon Press 1989).

[33] B. Reardon, *Sexism and the War System* 14 (Teachers College Press 1985).

[34] New York Times 27 March 1988, sec. 1 p.16. The majority of the world's refugees are women and children. The refugee flow from Kuwait was unusual in that so many of the refugees were male guest workers but there were still thousands of Asian women working as domestic house servants who were trapped in Kuwait.

[35] R. Morgan, *The Demon Lover: On the Sexuality of Terrorism* (Methuen 1989) especially Chapter 8 "What Do Men Know About Life?: the Middle East."

over their own reproductive capacity is seen as undermining the Palestinian cause.

Where there are claims (by men or women) that there have been violations of the laws of war or appears to the illegality of war itself justifying some act of resistance or civil disobedience, men are typically the judges, the law enforcers and the interpreters of what constitutes legitimate military action.[36] Where they consider it appropriate, one group of men in positions of authority (the judiciary) will even abdicate the responsibility of determining the legitimacy of what another group of men (the government or the military) have done under the abstract, supposedly neutral, legal doctrines of "political question" or "military necessity".

3. Feminist Responses to Patriarchy and Militarism

If one accepts that the patriarchal power structures of the nation State are oppressive for women and lead to their marginalisation and silencing, even where they are not actually abused by the military structures of society, and that militarism is of itself conducive to violence within or between States, it seems inevitable that women would be active in movements challenging the military authority of the State. Such challenges go to the very structure of the international legal order with its statist orientation and are thus typically resisted by the national elites. Women have been active in a number of ways in peace research and peace activism, but there have been many opposing views expressed to the role and position they should play that have caused friction, divisiveness and tension. Some of these divisions which have occurred both at the theoretical level and the practical level will be outlined.

(1) Women as Carers: "To Accept the Male and Female Stereotypes, But ... Subvert Them to a Feminist Purpose"[37]

First, there has been the approach based on the theory of "difference".[38] This approach rests upon the premise that women are different from men, and that

[36] Eg., the use of domestic courts by citizens to challenge government (military) policy in the war/peace area, as in the cases brought arising out of the peace camps at Greenham Common and Seneca: see A. Scales, "Militarism, Male Dominance and Law: Feminist Jurisprudence as Oxymoron?", 12 Harv. Women's LJ 25 (1989); B. Harford and S. Hopkins, Greenham Common: Women at the Wire (The Women's Press 1984); D. Russell (ed.), *Exposing Nuclear Phallacies* 104, 114 (Pergamon Press 1989).

[37] M. Burguieres, "Feminist Approaches to Peace: Another Step for Peace Studies", 19 Millenium 1, 3 (1990). The classifications that follow draw heavily on the analysis in this paper.

[38] This approach is most frequently associated with Carol Gilligan. See C. Gilligan, *In a Different Voice, Psychological Theory and Women's Development*, (Cambridge Harvard UP 1982); C. Gilligan, P. Lyons and T. Hanmer (eds.), *Making Connections, The Relational Worlds of Adolescent Girls at Emma Willard School*, (Harvard UP 1990).

the difference should be exploited to use the role typically played by women as people who care, who are concerned about relationships and contact, and who reject prevailing hierarchies to present their views with respect to reducing conflict. Practically, this view sees women as antithetical to everything that the military stands for, as nurturers not killers, as people who care about the effect of their actions on people not on abstract military targets which may or may not be human. The relevance of this view for international relations is evident. "There is a sober basis for this rhetoric. All of women's work – sheltering, nursing, feeding, kin work, teaching of the very young, tending the frail elderly – is threatened by violence".[39] The underlying assumption is that if women moved their traditional private role of caring into the public sphere so that their voice was heard in the public arena and became influential in running public activities, there would be a greater likelihood of achieving peace.

> Throughout this century, women have worked for peace on the basis of traditional and idealized visions of womanhood and femininity ... Consigned to the relative powerlessness of the private sphere, women moved into public political life while maintaining the protective cover of their traditional role.[40]

Theoretically this concept is supported by the idea that women have been trained and conditioned to respond differently to men to moral issues, and that it is desirable to incorporate this different voice into national and international decision-making. There is no greater moral issue than the legitimacy of the use of force to kill and subjugate other peoples.[41]

But this view of women in peace studies which has been influential throughout the twentieth century is problematic for a number of reasons. First this stereotyping places women firmly and restrictively in their traditional role of carers. Secondly, accepting women as the other, "the outsider, the person at the margins of power" can too readily lead to their being accepted by others and themselves as victims. This is especially destructive when combined with the dehumanising notion of "thingification".

Thirdly, it is just not true that all, or even many women, fit this mould or that all women always speak with the same voice. It is true that women are typically nurturers and carers, but this does not mean they are necessarily opposed to use of force and conflict in certain circumstances. Similarly not all men speak with a militaristic voice. As Sarah Ruddick points out in her deconstruction of the myth that masculinity is always equated with the military and that women are invariably opposed to it: "men are not so warlike and

[39] S. Ruddick, "Mothers and Mens Wars", in A. Harris & Y. King (eds.), *Rocking the Ship of State, Toward a Feminist Peace Politics* 77 (Westview Press 1989).

[40] A. Harris & Y. King (eds.), *Rocking the Ship of State, Toward a Feminist Peace Politics*, Introduction, 1 (Westview Press 1989).

[41] D. Dinnerstein, "What Does Feminism Mean?", in A. Harris & Y. King (eds.), *Rocking the Ship of State, Toward a Feminist Peace Politics*, 13 (Westview Press 1989).

women are certainly not peaceful". The very concern with relations and connectedness of many women can lead to their advocating or committing acts of violence. It has been argued that the masculinity of war is largely a myth that is sustained or at least tacitly connived in by both men and women; "Women as a sex cannot shrug off their complicity in militarism."[42] Cynthia Enloe describes how women support the military on bases, on the battlefield, on rest and recreation. Sarah Ruddick suggests a number of reasons for the continuance of the myth; these include excitement, personal adventure and economic advantage. Women as well as men are susceptible to the claims of nationalism and patriotism fostered by national elites. The myth is sustained to perpetuate the difference, and to reinforce the power structures of the patriarchal State.

Another perspective on the notion of women's caring is that of Catherine McKinnon who asserts that women's morality is not "morality in a different voice" but "morality in a higher register". "Women value care because men have valued us according to the care we have given them", an observation which has considerable validity in the context of armed conflict where women offer care and succour to the wounded.[43] This in turn is praised as a nationalist response to the war effort. Thus the role of women as carers can be viewed as a male construct that can in fact be perpetuated by women in the very context of attempting to reduce the destructive effects of male power and domination within the nation State.

Women can of course benefit from participation in conflict. Enloe describes how while "militarization is providing Palestinian men with new opportunities to prove their manhood", Palestinian women are bearing the brunt of the *Intifadah*.[44] The imposition of a strict curfew and the arrest and detention of numerous Palestinian males have raised women's household and other chores to the position of "national imperatives" essential to the continuing struggle.[45] As ever, the issue of whether the importance of their role will be recognised and women's issues remain on the agenda when and if self-determination is achieved remains the crucial question. Indeed the role of women in National Liberation Movements raises another whole host of difficult questions as women from third world countries support the use of armed force to fight other forms of oppression – colonialism, racism and foreign occupation. Their feminist agenda may well have been closely entwined with what they regard as legitimate uses of violence and they may see western feminists as self-indulgent

[42] D. Thompson, "Women, Peace and History: Notes for an Historical Overview", in R. Roach Pierson, *Women and Peace* 29, 41 (Croom Helm 1987). Dorothy Thompson shows that historically many women simply have not behaved according to the feminine virtues of caring.

[43] C. McKinnon, *Feminism Unmodified: Discourse on Life and Law* 39 (Harvard UP 1987).

[44] C. Enloe, *Bananas, Beaches and Bases, Making Feminist Sense out of International Politics* 58 (Pandora 1989).

[45] Cf., C. Enloe, "The Gulf Crisis, Making Feminist Sense of It", Pacific Research 1990 4; "Many observers are portraying wartime mobilisation as good for women. Saddam Hussein ... has made wide use of women in his wartime build up."

in placing an emphasis on peace. However the role of third world feminists is often also problematic as women within nationalist movements have frequently had to align their priorities in support of nationalist goals rather than with their feminist objectives.[46] Further the achievement of the goals of Nationalist movements – Statehood – means only too often the replication of the western patriarchal model of a nation State.

(2) Women as Peace Activists

Another response is that symbolised through the women's peace camps of the 1980's. Women's activism in the peace movement was vividly highlighted for example at Seneca and Greenham Common. These peace camps raised a number of different approaches that appeared far removed from the traditionalist female response to militarism, and were accordingly subject to criticism from many sources. The women involved were denigrated and abused by the members of the media and public (both male and female) for rejecting their traditional private and caring roles, neglecting their families and domestic responsibilities to live very publicly in the camps. On the other hand some feminists were concerned that "the camps were advancing an anti-feminist, biological determinist rationale of women as natural moms, nurturers and peacemakers."[47] Still other feminists were concerned that the peace campers had weakened feminist goals by giving priority to nuclear issues, or by reinforcing the image of women as pacifists and victims. They were also accused of splitting the peace movement by taking a separatist line in the camps.

Those who supported the camps and what they stood for argued that they dramatically and symbolically presented a number of feminist themes and objectives. First, the women most emphatically were not silenced in the face of the full range of patriarchal authority. They made their case in the most public and dramatic of arenas. Secondly, they used the symbolism of the web and weaving to demonstrate concepts of women's interconnectedness and relational thinking, and brought these symbols right out into the public arena. Thirdly, they abdicated their private lives and voiced their concerns in the most public of settings. Fourthly, their activities exposed the myth of national security and emphasised that the power and symbolism of the military bases rested solely upon public acquiescence. A few unarmed individuals trespassing into a military camp and dancing on the silos makes mockery of the much vaunted security, as well as undermining the authority and mystique of the military. In the words of the women who walked into the Boeing factory complex to talk to missile workers:

[46] C. Chinkin, "A Gendered Analysis of the Use of Force", paper given at Conference on Gender and International Law, Canberra August 1990, to be published in Australian Yearbook of International Law.

[47] R. Lederman, "Looking Back: The Women's Peace Camps in Perspective", in D. Russell (ed.), *Exposing Nuclear Phallacies* 244 (Pergamon Press 1989).

> ... the five of us women broke through the illusion of Boeing Company's authority, of its promise to provide security for these bombs. Boeing's lack of security for 'outside visitors' reveals that we cannot protect or be protected by nuclear weapons ... Nuclear weapons are protected by use – through our acceptance, our complicity and our inaction.[48]

Fifthly, these cases graphically demonstrated that it is men who define "peace" and bestow it with a very particular meaning. A number of women (in the United Kingdom and the United States) were charged *inter alia* with breach of the peace on the domestic level, a versatile charge which is always available to bring against any dissenters to the established social fabric. Various defences were presented on behalf of the demonstrators, including the one that the actions were justified under principles of international law such as had been enunciated at Nuremburg and adopted by the General Assembly. The argument was made that all actions had been performed with the objectives of ensuring peace for the wider global community. Although these arguments were rejected they had at least been articulated in public fora. The outcomes were conspicuous for reliance upon legalism (defences of necessity, concepts of remoteness and causation) and masculinist definitions of law and order, but the proceedings were notable for the inclusion of life experiences of the women defendants, their beliefs and emotions.[49] These however were not determination of the legal outcome. Anne Scales brilliantly demonstrates how these cases expose the inappropriateness of the law and legal system as avenues to be used by women to raise issues of policy. The parameters of those policies and the relevant legal principles have been set, defined, and are applied by men. She argues that women should not trust the supposedly neutral legal system as it is, or regard it as speaking for them. Even these acts of civil disobedience do not fit into the accepted paradigm of civil disobedience, as defined for example by Thoreau. She calls for feminist lawyering to overcome the insularity of law "to tear down the fences which in law school we were trained to revere ... to explore the supposedly necessary dichotomies and ... respond to alternative, context-governed social structures".[50]

[48] S. James, "Close Encounters with the Criminal Justice System: The Trial of the Boeing Five", in D. Russell (ed.), *Exposing Nuclear Phallacies* 236, 237 (Pergamon Press 1989).

[49] Ibid., at 239; 'Documents we had read, life experiences that led us to join the peace movement, and people with whom we had discussed our concerns made up what most media representatives, progressive lawyers and seasoned activists agreed was a most unusual trial of conscience.'

[50] A. Scales, "Militarism, Male Dominance and Law: Feminist Jurisprudence as Oxymoron?", 12 Harv. Women's LJ 25 (1989); cf., "Civil disobedience, the practice of militant non-violence by women in peace actions, can be seen as a form of *ecriture feminine*, or a new 'feminine text'." A. Harris & Y. King (eds.), *Rocking the Ship of State, Toward a Feminist Peace Politics*, Introduction, 2 (Westview Press 1989).

(3) Women as Equal: Reject the Female Stereotype

Another approach towards peace study that has been favoured by other feminists is "that to emphasise gender differences is merely a way of camouflaging and reinforcing men's attempts throughout time to disempower, oppress and violate women."[51] The response is the liberal, democratic approach which asserts equality and sameness for men and women. But that response ignores the reality that equality is as defined by men and men's expectation. This approach aims at providing women with an equal say and an equal role in decision-making and military activity. It is an attempt to resolve the problem of what has been called "female non-autonomy". How non-personhood renders women more vulnerable and likely to be treated as victims has already been considered. Their traditional invisibility to and within military hierarchies has been based on a number of myths, and has even denied them the rights to voice their challenge to decision-makers and law makers. Anne Scales describes how women were disenfranchised from protesting in the courts against the Vietnam war by their exclusion from the draft; they were not even given the standing to make their voice heard, but were removed from the public arenas of both the courts and the combat zone. As she says: "I wanted to be part of it. I wanted to be a history maker on the terms I understood history-making to involve. I wanted at least to have standing to resist."

The virtual exclusion of women from combat is frequently raised in debates about equality.[52] Women who favour demanding equality argue that while women do not participate in all aspects of citizenship, including military duty, they are easily relegated to the position of second class citizens, the protected, subject to the whim of the protectors. However, the reasons why women are excluded have also been considered. It has been argued that the debate is not in fact about the needs or interests of national security or the military but about the mystique of militarism. This is especially true with many aspects of modern combat where strength and willingness to use physical force seem less important than an ability to endure long periods of boredom and inaction. But without this exclusion, militarism would lose its distinct position within the nation State. "For militarism to work its morbid magic, it has to draw a radical distinction between the authority of men and women."[53] McKinnon expresses it vividly: "Somehow it takes the glory out of the foxhole, the buddiness out of the trenches, to imagine us out there. You get the feeling they might rather end the draft, they might even rather not fight wars at all than have to do it with

[51] M. Burguieres, "Feminist Approaches to Peace: Another Step for Peace Studies", 19 Millenium 1, 5 (1990).

[52] See *Rostker v. Goldberg* 453 US 57 (1982) where the exclusion of women from the registration was challenged on the grounds of sex discrimination, that is inequality; cited in A. Scales, "Militarism, Male Dominance and Law: Feminist Jurisprudence as Oxymoron?" 12 Harv. Women's LJ 38 (1989). See for a very full discussion L. Kornblum, "Women Warriors in a Men's World: The Combat Exclusion", 2 Law and Inequality 351 (1984).

[53] Ibid., at 39.

us."[54] This assumes that women will not achieve equality within the military, but even if they were to do so there is another problem: it assumes that women should accept militaristic values rather than that those values themselves should be changed. It apparently justifies the use of instruments of coercion by men and women rather than removing them. It does not include any blueprint for any change which might be effective in promoting domestic peace and consequently international peace. Enloe points out the propaganda consequence of including women in the military in the Gulf War:

> By constrasting the allegedly liberated American tank mechanic with the Saudi woman deprived of a driver's license, American reporters are implying that the United States is the advanced civilised country whose duty it is to take the lead in resolving the Persian Gulf crisis.[55]

4. Conclusions

In examining those theoretical and activist feminist perspectives[56] on the contribution women can make to peace studies, it becomes apparent that the notion of women as carers is problematic in that it perpetuates their traditional role, and is unlikely to result in their voice being effectively heeded. However rejection of that role through promotion of sameness and equality seems inimical to the very objectives sought, the development of non-patriarchal, national values. A number of other approaches have been suggested. For feminist lawyers the task might be to do further work to expose the myth of the appropriateness of the legal system, either domestic or international, as a neutral system for dealing with the dichotomies of war and peace, conflict and conflict management, perpetrator of offence and victim, aggression and self-defence, legal and illegal, just and unjust war and try to rethink the substance and role of the law itself. The illustration of the lack of neutrality and objectivity of the law in the context of citizen's response to official action is striking for feminist lawyers, and it is an area very much in need of further work and research. Lawyers have been too content to leave the implications of militarism to other disciplines without themselves exploring the role of law in this area. Feminist analysis of legal concepts or defences such as military necessity, political question, national security, incorporation of international law into domestic law, civil disobedience, standing before domestic courts, standing before international tribunals, the maintenance of international peace and security and the purpose and principles of the United Nations Charter could add significantly to the understanding of the debate, as could feminist deconstruction of the dichotomies mentioned.

[54] C. McKinnon, *Feminism Unmodified: Discourse on Life and Law* 38 (Harvard UP 1987).

[55] Cf., C. Enloe, "The Gulf Crisis, Making Feminist Sense of It", Pacific Research 1990 5.

[56] This is only a very limited indication of the wealth of work that has been done and the views expressed.

Another suggestion is that feminists should act to "reclaim the discourse", that is respond to the adverse characteristics of militarism, for example of dehumanisation and euphemism. Thus women should act to personalise the targets and victims of war by talking publicly and openly about the realities of war, and the suffering caused to victims of war without hiding behind the euphemisms of distorting language. Carol Cohn has demonstrated both the force of military language and how difficult it might be in fact to lead to any change. "But when we allow 'machothink' and 'nukespeak' to define the rules of discourse for us, we are complicitous by our silence. We must name what's going on and who is doing it."[57] This is another way of building upon the notion of women as different, as carers but by attempting to alter the terms in which the debate is expressed, rather than by emphasising that traditional role. This too is an area where lawyers could take a lead through their use of language in the courtroom and in nongovernmental organisations working in human rights, development, environmental, and aid matters.

Yet another aspect of this approach is to assert that values traditionally associated with women need to be reclaimed for society at large, but as defined by women.[58] Going further, other feminists have argued that what is required is a deconstruction of the traditional "conceptual pairs such as women and peace, men and war."[59] This approach has been tagged "feminism versus militarism" and argues for "the role of feminism in dismantling the imagery which underlines patriarchy and militarism." This makes reformulating national State structures "in which warfare is a central component and opening the pathers for nonviolent interaction" between States the responsibility of men and women.[60]

What is apparent is the richness of feminist debate in this field; it seems that diversity of theory, different feminist experiences and approaches can and should all be used and developed in context of peace studies. There is a dual effect: attempting to determine appropriate feminist responses to the oppression and militarism of the patriarchal State system enriches peace studies, while the experience of such events as the women's peace camps themselves contribute richly to feminist theory. Feminist theory has always been able to support different perspectives and theories without demanding uniformity. Approaching the issue of women and peace on a number of different fronts may be instrumental in developing thinking relevant to the emergence of a genuinely new world legal order, based on a workable peace system.

[57] B. Roberts, "Reclaiming the Discourse: Feminist Perspectives in Peace Research", in D. Russell (ed.), *Exposing Nuclear Phallacies* 281–285 (Pergamon Press 1989).

[58] R. Lederman, "Looking Back: The Women's Peace Camps in Perspective", in D. Russell (ed.), *Exposing Nuclear Phallacies* 248 (Pergamon Press 1989).

[59] M. Burguieres, "Feminist Approaches to Peace: Another Step for Peace Studies", 19 Millenium 1, 8 (1990).

[60] Ibid.

JUDITH G. GARDAM*

The Law of Armed Conflict: A Feminist Perspective

1. Introduction

The issue of gender and the law of armed conflict[1] is an area of the law that has largely been bypassed by feminist scholars. The system of international law itself, moreover, until relatively recently, has not been part of the feminist project in law.[2] It has been suggested that the explanation for this silence may lie in the perception that international law, regulating as it does relations between States not individuals, is gender neutral in its operation.[3] It is only in the area of human rights, which has as its focus individuals, that some analysis has been undertaken of the gender issues inherent in the system.[4] This phenomenon of apparent neutrality or abstraction, however, is the hallmark of law itself. It is the alleged "point of viewlessness" of legal rules that feminists

* Barrister and Solicitor of the Supreme Court of Victoria and the High Court of Australia; Senior Lecturer, Faculty of Law, University of Adelaide. I thank Margaret Davies for her valuable comments on this paper.

[1] "Armed conflict" is a term which has come to replace such terms as "state of war". Article 2(4) of the United Nations Charter 1949 outlaws the use of force, except in restricted circumstances, such as self-defence (Article 51). See generally D. Schindler, "State of War, Belligerency, Armed Conflict", in A. Cassese (ed.) *The New Humanitarian Law of Armed Conflict* (1979), p. 310–348 and J. Pictet, *Commentary On The IV Geneva Convention (1958)*, pp. 17–18. The law of armed conflict is also nowadays frequently referred to as international humanitarian law, a term favoured by the International Committee of the Red Cross.

[2] See however, C. Bunch, "Women's Rights as Human Rights: Towards a Re-Vision of Human Rights", 12 *Hum. Rights Q.* (1990); C. Chinkin, "A Gendered Perspective to the International Use of Force", *Aust. Yrb. I.L.* (1992 forthcoming); J. Gardam, "A Feminist Analysis of Certain Aspects of International Humanitarian Law", *Aust. Yrb. I.L.* (1992 forthcoming); H. Charlesworth, "The Public/Private Distinction and the Right to Development in International Law", *Aust. Yrb. I.L.* (1992 forthcoming); S. Wright, "Economic Rights and Social Justice: A Feminist Analysis of Some International Human Rights Conventions", *Aust Yrb. I.L.* (1992 forthcoming); and H. Charlesworth, C. Chinkin and S. Wright, "Feminist Approaches to International Law", *Am.J.I.L.*, Vol. 85 pg. 613 (1991).

[3] *Ibid.*

[4] See the sources cited in note 2.

K.E. Mahoney and P. Mahoney (eds.), Human Rights in the Twenty-first Century, 419–436.

have challenged.[5] The law of armed conflict, in common with human rights law, is designed for the benefit of individuals.[6] Moreover, the activity it regulates raises acutely the invisibility and powerlessness of women when faced with the most overtly destructive expression of the power of the State, the use of force. Possibly there are other factors which explain the silence of the feminist voice in this area. Cynthia Enloe writes of the seeming imperviousness of international politics to the impact of feminism.[7] Perhaps, she argues, it is because the conduct of international relations is perceived as such an inherently male activity.[8] If this is true for international politics how much more so is it true for the rules that govern the end result of the failure of international policy, armed conflict.[9] Any feminist analysis of these rules must confront the institution of the military and the nature of militarism which determine to a large extent the content and application of the rules. It is not a task for the faint hearted. The military has been described as constituting a "masculinity cult": a means of reinforcement of gender identification for men.[10] Michelle Benecke and Kirsten Dodge, in their equality analysis of the participation of women in the military, use the incidence of lesbian baiting in the armed forces to demonstrate the high level of hostility to women in the military establishment.[11] If merely seeking equality of access on men's terms to the military is perceived as such a threat to this institution, how much more so would a feminist analysis which reveals the assumptions underlying the rules governing military activities. These rules assume the silence and suffering of women and children and this suffering has been endless.[12] One looks in vain at the numerous war memorials listing the military dead of these conflicts, for any recognition of the thousands of women and children victims of these battles.

[5] See, M. Thornton, "Feminist Jurisprudence: Illusion or Reality?", *Aust J. L. & Soc.* (1986), p. 5, at p. 6; C. MacKinnon, *Towards a Feminist Theory of the State* (1989), p. 162; A. Scales, "The Emergence of Feminist Jurisprudence: An Essay", 95 *Yale L.J.* (1986), p. 1373 and F. Olsen, "Feminism and Critical Legal Theory: An American Perspective", 18 *Int. J. Soc. L.* (1990), p. 199.

[6] See Q. Wright, "The Outlawry of War and the Law of War", 47 A.J.I.L. (1953), p. 356 at p. 373; M. McDougal and F. Feliciano, *Law and Minimum World Order* p. 530 ff. and O. Schachter, "United Nations Law in the Gulf Conflict", 85 *A.J.I.L.*, (1991), p. 452 at p. 466.

[7] C. Enloe, *Bananas, Beaches and Bases*, (1989), p. 3.

[8] *Ibid.*, p. 4. See also H. Charlesworth et al., "Feminist Approaches to International Law", note 2, *supra*, where the authors analyse the masculine nature of international law.

[9] See K. Von Clausewitz, *On War*, Bk.1 (1968) p. 101, who wrote last century that "[w]ar is a mere continuation of policy by other means". This view, however, is probably not accepted in the era of the United Nations Charter prohibition on the use of force.

[10] M.A. Tetreault, *Gender Belief Systems and the Integration of Women in the U.S. Military*, *Minerva* (Spring 1988), p. 44, at pp. 55–56 cited in M. Beneke & K. Dodge, "Military Women in Non-Traditional Job Fields, Casualties of the Armed Forces War on Homosexuals", 13 *Harv. Women's L.J.* (1990), p. 215, at p. 234. Ann Scales regards militarism as a prime item on the feminist agenda and in "fundamental symbiosis with gender oppression". "Militarism, Male Dominance and Law: Feminist Jurisprudence as Oxymoron?", 12 *Harv. Women's L.J.* (1989), p. 25, at p. 26.

[11] *Ibid.*

[12] One only needs to consider certain practices during armed conflict in this century and their impact on civilians: the fire bombing of such civilian targets as Dresden and Cologne, the targeting of such objects as dams in the Ruhr Valley, the nuclear targeting of Hiroshima and Nagasaki and the total devastation of the infrastructure of Iraq in the recent Gulf conflict. Robin Morgan, *The*

It is not intended in this paper to examine the rules of armed conflict that relate specifically to the protection of women and children.[13] To do so would be to accept the existing framework and limit the task to attempting to improve these rules.[14] Neither will the concerted resistance by the military to the participation of women in the armed forces, particularly in combat situations, be considered.[15] Although this exclusion from the military is an important issue for feminists[16] the emphasis of this paper is on exposing some of the underlying assumptions on which the law is based. Feminists have referred to this approach as asking "the woman question". "In law, asking the woman question means examining how the law fails to take into account the experiences and values that seem more typical of women than of men, for whatever reason, or how existing legal standards and concepts might disadvantage women."[17] The dismantling of the myth of gender neutrality of the law of armed conflict, as with other areas of the law, is a considerable undertaking. After a brief discussion of the ways in which feminists have engaged with the law and of the way in which this paper attempts to continue this process, I will consider the development of the law of armed conflict and the divisions in its structure that have evolved over the years. The gender bias inherent in the arrangement will become apparent. From the perspective of women, the most important general principle of the law of armed conflict is that which requires parties to an armed conflict to distinguish at all times between civilians and combatants and between civilian and military objects, and to direct their operations only against the latter: the principle of non-combatant immunity as it is usually referred to.[18] Although in practice it is the rule most relevant to the protection of women, as generally speaking they

---

Demon Lover: On the Sexuality of Terrorism (1989), p. 132, writes that part of the rationale for the bombing of Hiroshima was that this action would save soldier's lives that would otherwise have been lost in a prolonged war: "[s]oldiers were saved. Women and children were expendable".

[13] For a description of these rules see M. Tabory, "The Status of Women in Humanitarian Law", in S. Rosenne, Y. Dinstein and M. Tabory (eds.), *International Law at a Time of Perplexity* (1989), p. 941.

[14] See M.J. Mossman, "Feminism and Legal Method: The Difference it Makes", 3 *Aust. J.L. & Soc.* (1986), p. 30, for a discussion of the dilemma posed for feminists lawyers in engaging with legal rules at all.

[15] See the sources cited note 10.

[16] As C. MacKinnon writes, "[d]on't they want us to learn to kill?", *Feminism Unmodified* (1987) p. 27.

[17] K. Bartlett, "Feminist Legal Methods", 103 *Harv. L. Rev.* (1990), p. 829, at 837.

[18] Non-combatant immunity, or the principle of distinction or discrimination, is variously defined. For example F. Kalshoven, *The Law of Warfare* (1973), p. 27, writes that the fundamental general principle of the whole of humanitarian law is that "belligerents shall not inflict on their adversaries harm out of proportion to the legitimate goals of warfare". From this general rule Kalshoven, at p.28, derives four more principles relating, *inter alia*, to the distinction which must be drawn between belligerents and the civilian population and civilian and military targets. See also John Bassett Moore, *International Law and Some Current Illusions and Other Essays* (1924), p. 5; E. Rosenblad, *International Humanitarian Law of Armed Conflict Some Aspects of the Principle of Distinction and Related Problems*, (1979), p. 53 and R. Baxter, "The Duties of Combatants and the Conduct of Hostilities", in Institut Henry-Dunant, UNESCO *International Dimensions of International Humanitarian Law*, (1988), p. 93, at p. 103.

and children make up the vast majority of civilians,[19] it would be a mistake to assume that the origins of the rule and its theorectical underpinnings are consistent with feminist concerns.[20] Recent developments, moreover, in the law of armed conflict have undermined this norm. Secondly, therefore, this paper will consider this principle of the law of armed conflict and the impact of these changes in the law of armed conflict, to demonstrate the factors relating to women's lives and experiences which remain unaccounted for.

2. The Feminist Project in Law

Feminists do not speak with a single voice. Neither do they readily fit within "schools" or categories of feminist theory. Within feminist theory itself there are many varied and often overlapping strands of thought. The avoidance of categorization is in fact vital to the feminist critique of law.[21] Law is traditionally constructed as a number of discrete categories of rules which are represented as forming a cohesive whole capable of or regulating all aspects of life. It is this very aspect of law that makes it so impenetrable to feminist analysis, the so called neutrality or objectivity of the law. Much of the feminist project in law has been to demonstrate the fallacy of the objectivity of the law, to reveal its underlying assumptions and value judgements as made by, and in the interests of men. Catharine MacKinnon writes: "The separation of form from substance, process from policy, adjudication from legislation, judicial role from theory and practice, echoes and re-echoes at each level of the [legal] regime its basic norm: objectivity."[22]

Feminists have differed as to strategies to achieve change in the law.[23] Moreover, divergent explanations are offered to account for the absence of women's voices in the formulation of the principles of the law, a system

[19] The relationship inherent in the rules of armed conflict between male and female civilians on the one hand, and combatants on the other, is discussed *infra*.

[20] An analysis of this point is beyond the scope of this paper, suffice to point out that the distinction was based largely on economic grounds. See J.B. Russell, *A History of Medieval Christianity, Prophecy and Order* (1968), p. 25 and R. Hartigan, *The Forgotten Civilian* (1982), p. 65 ff.

[21] On an analogous point C. Smart, *Feminism and the Power of Law* (1989), p. 66 ff., warns of the dangers for legal feminists in indulging in "grand theorizing" and attempting to develop a comprehensive feminist jurisprudence. She questions whether the result may be to merely "replace the abstraction with another".

[22] C. Mackinnon, note 5, *supra*, p. 162. See also A. Scales, note 5, *supra* and F. Olsen, note 5, *supra*.

[23] Much of feminist work has focused on the sameness/difference debate. Are women the same as men and thus to be treated equally before the law or are they different and entitled to special treatment by the legal system? In the view of many feminists, this debate has occupied too much time and energy and, in practical terms, has not achieved a great deal for women. See for example, L. Finley, "Transcending Equality Theory: A Way out of the Maternity and the Workplace Debate", 86 *Col. L. Rev.* (1986) p. 1118. Carol Smart, although conceding that these two approaches provide a concrete structure for changing the law, regards an exclusive focus on this

predicated on the silence and invisibility of women. The insight of feminism that is brought into stark relief by the law of armed conflict, however, is the public/private distinction, a common thread running throughout feminist dialogue.[24] This distinction, as feminists have demonstrated, is drawn on gender lines. The distinction between these two realms, a fundamental component of Western liberal theory, apparently neutral in its operation, has allowed the dominance of men over women to assume a guise of the natural order of things. In liberal theory a distinction is drawn between the public field of politics, economics, law and intellectual life and the private world of home, hearth and the family. Women's child bearing role places them naturally in the private world. The two spheres are not equal in importance in the eyes of the law. The realm of the public, the world of men, is where all the power and authority lie. The world of women, on the other hand, is subordinate and of less significance.[25] The law builds on this distinction, reinforcing the gender differential by choosing, in a seemingly neutral fashion, activities it regulates and those it leaves unregulated. Most of the feminist analysis of the public/private distinction in law has focused on domestic legal systems and the role of the law in perpetuating the dominance of men by leaving the private realm unregulated, thus perpetuating the invisibility of women and maintaining the dominance of the public realm.[26] Feminist scholars have only recently turned their attention to the operation of this division in international law.[27] They have demonstrated that the marginalization of women by domestic legal systems is exacerbated by the structure of international law with its emphasis on the abstract entity of the State and by the almost total exclusion of women from

---

debate as foreclosing a more fundamental assessment of the structure of law itself, of buying into law or, as she puts it, of incorporating "law's own paradigm". C. Smart, note 21, *supra*, p. 82 ff. It is the work of Catharine Mackinnon, however, that has been most fundamental to breaking out of this somewhat sterile debate. C. MacKinnon, "Feminism, Marxism, Method, and the State: An Agenda for Theory", 7 *Signs: Journal of Women in Law and Society* (1982), p. 515; C. MacKinnon, "Feminism, Marxism, Method, and the State: Towards Feminist Jurisprudence" 8 *Signs: Journal of Women in Society* (1983), p. 625 and C. MacKinnon, note 5, *supra*.

[24] See C. Pateman, "Feminist Critiques of the Public/Private Dichotomy", in S. Benn and G. Gaus (eds.) *Public and Private in Social Life*, (1983), p. 281; Taub and Schneider, "Perspectives on Women's Subordination and the Role of Law", in D. Kairys (ed.) *The Politics of Law: A Progressive Critique*, (1982), p. 117; K. O'Donovan, *Sexual Divisions in Law* (1985); J. Morgan, "Feminist Theory as Legal Theory", 16 *M.U.L.Rev.* (1988), p. 743 and H. Charlesworth, "The Public/Private Distinction and the Right to Development in International Law", note 2, *supra*. See also C. Mackinnon, "Feminism, Marxism, Method, and the State: An Agenda for Theory", *ibid.*, p. 536.

[25] See for example H. Charlesworth, "The Public/Private Distinction and the Right to Development in International Law", note 2, *supra*.

[26] As feminists have demonstrated, the choice to leave the private unregulated is not value free. One example is the failure of the law to recognize the value of work women do in the home, thus continuing the financial dominance of men. See for example M. Thornton, note 5, *supra*.

[27] See H. Charlesworth, "The Public/Private Distinction and the Right to Development in International Law", note 2, *supra*, and H. Charlesworth, et.al. "Feminist Approaches to International Law", note 2, *supra*.

participation in its processes.[28] The gendered public/private distinction that feminists have articulated has several aspects in the law of armed conflict. First, it is in the public world of men in which decisions are made that impact so enormously on the lives of women: in the present context, the resort to the use of force and the rules to regulate the conduct of force. Women's voices are absent from these processes. Secondly, the law prioritizes in its choice of areas to regulate. As we will see, the difference between the rules protecting combatants and those protecting civilians is based on this distinction. Moreover, the predominance of military necessity over humanitarian considerations in the development of the legal regime of armed conflict once again reflects the public/private split, perpetuating and reinforcing the legitimacy of these priorities. Thirdly, the law of armed conflict distinguishes between non-international and international armed conflicts on the basis that the former involves the private or domestic jurisdiction of States. This is a distinction, I will argue, that is meaningless for women and impacts on them unevenly.[29]

3. The Development and Structure of the Law of Armed Conflict

The legal system for the regulation of armed hostilities between States has traditionally comprised two main branches.[30] First, the *ius ad bellum*, which is concerned with the justness of the resort to force, and secondly, the *ius in bello*, the rules applicable in armed conflict.[31] This paper is primarily concerned with the latter. The sources of the law of armed conflict are both codified and customary.[32] With the movement in the latter part of last century and in this

[28] *Ibid.*

[29] For example, it has been reported (*The Australian*, 6 Dec. 1991) that women and children were prevented from leaving the besieged city of Dubrovnik in Yugoslavia in order to shield the city from further bombardment. If this were an international armed conflict such action would breach both customary and conventional rules of armed conflict. As it is not, such an activity is not proscribed by international law.

[30] There is no unanimity amongst commentators as to the definitions and divisions in the law of armed conflict, just as there are disagreements as to the relationship between the law of human rights and humanitarian law. For a comprehensive analysis of the scope and content of humanitarian law see Jean Pictet, *The Principles of International Humanitarian Law* (1966) and J. Pictet, *Humanitarian Law and the Protection of War Victims* (1975). For a discussion of the relationship between the principles of human rights and humanitarian law see A. Rosas, *The Legal Status of Prisoners of War* (1976), p. 39 and T. Meron, *Human Rights and Humanitarian Norms as Customary Law* (1989).

[31] Today there is a clear distinction between the *ius in bello* and the *ius ad bellum* and the application of the former is not dependent on the latter. This is, however, a relatively new development. See Lothar Kotsch, *The Concept of War in Contemporary History and International Law* (1956), p. 83.

[32] Although nearly all civilizations throughout history have placed some restraints on behaviour in war, the attempt to establish a system of binding international law did not begin until the codification of the law of armed conflict in the latter half of the ninetheenth century. Up to this stage the laws of war were of a customary nature only. For a comprehensive collection of the

century for the codification of the law of armed conflict, the *ius in bello* has been further divided into the Law of the Hague and the Law of Geneva.[33] The Law of the Hague is the term often used to describe the law of warfare proper, that is the means and methods of warfare. The Law of Geneva refers to humanitarian law whose purpose is to ensure respect for human life in armed conflict as far as is compatible with military necessity and public order.[34] The Law of Geneva imposes no restrictions on the means and methods of warfare but provides for such matters as the treatment of prisoners of war, civilians in occupied territories and persons *hors-de-combat*. There has been discussion amongst commentators as to whether the Law of Geneva and the Law of the Hague remain separate bodies of rules and the true content and sources of humanitarian law.[35] The Protocol of 8 June 1977 Additional to the Geneva Conventions of 12 August 1949, and relating to the Protection of Victims of International Armed Conflicts (Protocol I), deals with both the means and methods of warfare and the principles of the Law of Geneva, contributing to the gradual decline in the demarcation between the Law of the Hague and the Law of Geneva.[36] Such discussions may seem somewhat academic. The distinction, however, is significant from a gender perspective. Whether or not a particular rule is part of the law of warfare or restricted to the traditional definition of humanitarian law assumes importance when it comes to discussing changes to the rules. States are less willing to countenance changes to "combat rules" to protect civilians, such as non-combatant immunity, than to rules which operate outside that area.[37] This is illustrated by the comparative ease of the negotiation of the four Geneva Conventions of 1949,[38] a primary source of humanitarian law, as contrasted with the difficulties experienced in the

---

conventional rules of the Law of Geneva see, *The International Red Cross Handbook* (1983). See also A. Roberts & R. Guelff (eds.), *Documents on the Laws of War* (2nd ed. 1989).

[33] See J. Pictet, *International Dimensions of Humanitarian Law* (1988), pp. xi-xx.

[34] On the initiative of the International Committee of the Red Cross, as stated above, the totality of the law of armed conflict is often referred to nowadays as the humanitarian law of armed conflict.

[35] See note 30, *supra*.

[36] At the same time Protocols Additional to the Geneva Conventions of 12 August 1949, and relating to the Protection of Victims of Non-International Armed Conflicts (Protocol II), of 8 June 1977 was adopted by states. As at 30 July 1991, 103 states have ratified or acceded to Protocol I and 93 states have ratified or acceded to Protocol II. See also the sources cited in note 39 below.

[37] This is true on a more general level. It is more difficult to achieve agreement on the development of so called "games rules" for the protection of combatants than rules that do not interfere with the general conduct of hostilities. The negotiation of the Hague Conventions of 1899 and 1907, a primary source of the law of warfare proper, was a complex and exacting process. (Convention (II) with Respect to the Laws and Customs of War on Land. Signed at the Hague, 29 July 1899 and Convention (IV) with Respect to the Laws and Customs of War on Land. Signed at the Hague, 18 October 1907).

[38] Geneva Convention for the Amelioration of the Condition of the Wounded and Sick in Armed Forces in the Field of August 12, 1949; Geneva Convention for the Amelioration of the Condition of Wounded, Sick and Shipwrecked Members of Armed Forces at Sea of August 12, 1949; Geneva Convention relative to the Treatment of Prisoners of War of August 12, 1949 and Geneva Convention relative to the Protection of Civilian Persons in Time of War of August 12,

negotiation of Protocol I which interferes significantly with the means and methods of combat.[39] Moreover, the rules protecting civilians in the Protocol have attracted concerted opposition, in particular from the United States and its military establishment, and are one of the reasons underlying that State's decision not to ratify the Protocol.[40] A gender bias in the development and content of the rules of armed conflict thus becomes apparent. An analysis of the doctrine of military necessity as the underlying basis of this preference warrants closer analysis.

(1) Military Necessity

The military has been a constant barrier to the development of rules designed to protect individuals, particularly civilians.[41] This has been achieved primarily through the predominance of the doctrine of military necessity against which all attempts to delimit the conduct of warfare have to be measured.[42] The underlying assumption of this doctrine is that the paramount consideration in armed conflict is military victory by the State. Humanitarian considerations are always subordinated to this aim. As a consequence the emphasis of the law of

---

1949 (hereafter referred to as the Geneva Conventions of 1949). For the negotiating history of the Geneva Conventions of 1949 see the Commentary on each Convention published by the I.C.R.C. under the general editorship of Jean Pictet.

[39] For a comprehensive analysis of the proceedings of the Diplomatic Conference and the provisions of Protocols I and II see M. Bothe et.al., *New Rules for Victims of Armed Conflicts* (1982) and Y. Sandoz et. al. (eds.) *Commentary on the Additional Protocols of 8 June 1977 to the Geneva Conventions of 12 August 1949* (1987). For a description of the work of the Conference see Richard Baxter, "Humanitarian Law or Humanitarian Politics? The 1974 Diplomatic Conference on Humanitarian Law", 16 *Harv. I.L.J.* (1975), p. 1: D. Forsythe, "The 1974 Diplomatic Conference on Humanitarian Law: Some Observations", 69 A.J.I.L. (1975), p. 77; C. Cantrell, "Humanitarian Law in Armed Conflict: The Third Diplomatic Conference", 61 Marquette L.R. (1977), p. 253 and L. Green, "The Geneva Humanitarian Law Conference, 1975", 13 Can. Yrb. I.L. p. 96.

[40] See the remarks of President Reagan in Letter of Transmittal for the consent of the Senate to the ratification, Protocol II Additional to the Geneva Conventions of 12 August 1949, concluded at Geneva on June 10 1977. The White House, January 29, 1987. See also the detailed military criticism of the provisions of Protocol I, including those relating to the protection of civilians, by W. Hays Parks, the Head of the International Law Team of the Office of the Judge Advocate-General of the Army in, "Air War and the Law of War", 32 Air Force L.Rev. (1990), p.1.

[41] As Cynthia Enloe argues in *Does Khaki Become You?* (1983), p. 212, the military needs women but they need them to "behave as *gender women*. Military officials and allies in civilian elites have wielded their power to perpetuate these gendered processes that guarantee the military its manpower...". In other words, the military has been dependent on patriarchy. A. Scales, note 10, *supra*, at p.26, refers to the "symbiotic relationship between militarism and gender oppression". Militarism impacts on women in many ways. For example, it consumes State resources that would otherwise be available to improve the economic position of women and children.

[42] A. Roberts and R. Guelff, note 32, *supra*, at p. 5, define military necessity as permitting the use of [o]nly that degree and kind of force, not otherwise prohibited by the law of armed conflict, required for the partial or total submission of the enemy with a minimum expenditure of time, life and physical resources...".

armed conflict has always been on the protection of combatants, those engaged in the public activity of fighting for the State.[43]

To see how these considerations operate in practice, one has only to consider the military's approach to the new rules for civilians in Protocol I, although, as I argue later, these are illusory in the protections they offer civilians. The suggestion, for example, that the provisions of the Protocol may prevent the military from using a burnt earth policy as a tactic in order to ensure the survival of the civilian population, has been greeted with great indignation by certain sections of the military.[44] The idea that combatants may have to face additional dangers merely to protect the civilian population is regarded as an outrage. Why? Because a judgment is made about the relative value of lives. The judgment is made by men and it favours men, the combatants not the civilians. An added gender dimension can be discerned here. The distinction drawn in the law of armed conflict between combatant and civilian is not a biological one. "Male" signifies those who fight for the State and "female" signifies those who do not, the latter including male civilians.

The rationale for the judgment preferring combatants appears straightforward. It is in the interests of all soldiers that are protected in order to carry on the fight and protect civilians from the consequences of military defeat. It is argued that it is unreasonable for women to complain when they have to pay a price as well. This analysis, however, is based on a number of assumptions which, from a feminist perspective, can be challenged. The question needs to be asked as to whose conflict in reality it is. It is not those who are told their sacrifice is necessary, without any involvement in the decision that led to the conflict or in the way it is conducted. The assumption is made by men that women's interests mirror their own: "[r]epresentation of the world, like the world itself, is the work of men, they describe it from their own point of view, which they confuse with the absolute truth".[45] This perception of women as a reflection of men, as other, or as Catharine Mackinnon puts it as "object" not "subject",[46] runs throughout much of feminist discourse.[47] The presumption as to the autonomy or equality of women in society has been demonstrated as a fallacy by succeeding generations of feminists.[48] As we have seen, women, as society is presently constructed, exist and function only in the private domain. They are absent and silenced from the public realm inhabited by men. Relegated to the private sphere, women take no part in the decision-making in that most public and powerful function of the State: the making of foreign policy and

[43] See G. Best, *Humanity in Warfare* (1983), p. 147.

[44] See for example the comments by B. Greville, "Protocols that Spell Disaster" *The Australian* 11 July 1988. and W. Hays Parks, note 40, *supra*.

[45] S. de Beauvoir, *The Second Sex* (1970), p. 175.

[46] C. Mackinnon, note 16, *supra*, at p. 54ff.

[47] See for example S. de Beauvoir, note 45, *supra*, and L. Irigaray, *Speculum of the Other Woman*, Eng. trans. by Gilliam Gill (1985).

[48] See S. de Beauvoir, *ibid*; C. Mackinnon, "Feminism, Marxism, Method, and the State: An Agenda for Theory", note 23, *supra*; C. MacKinnon, "Feminism, Marxism, Method and the State: Towards Feminist Jurisprudence", note 23, *supra*, at p. 644, and C. MacKinnon, note 5, *supra*.

decisions as to the use of force in international relations.[49] The "non-personhood" or objectification of women takes on a particular perspective in conjunction with militarism. Ann Scales refers to "militarism" as "objectification perfected".[50] She argues that "[m]ilitarism requires of the participants an expertise in objectification".[51] The enemy must be regarded as a thing or the "other" in order for soldiers to kill in battle. This objectificaiton is already learned in gender terms: women are the "other" and the lesson is transferred onto the battlefield.[52] This phenomenon can be discerned in the language of armed conflict: women and children killed or wounded in hostilities are referred to as "collateral casualties" or even more remotely as "collateral damage". The choice of the word "collateral", although intended to distinguish these casualties from damage to military objectives, suggests that they are of secondary or peripheral concern. In contrast, combatant casualties are referred to in terms that acknowledge their humanity: killed, wounded or prisoners of war.[53] Once the alleged neutrality of the rationale for the priorities inherent in the law of armed conflict is revealed as fallacious, then the full impact of the inequity of the dominant role of the doctrine of military necessity becomes apparent.

(2) Priorities in Conventional Rules

As I have argued, the emphasis on the doctrine of military necessity and the perceived need to protect combatants have led to resistance from States and their military establishments to an improvement in the rules for the protection of civilians. This opposition has occurred against the background of increasing vulnerability of civilians in this century to the effects of armed conflict.[54]

[49] Every feminist is used to the argument that points to such powerful political leaders as Margaret Thatcher and Indira Ghandi and the fact that they have not hesitated to use armed force to resolve situations. Cynthia Enloe isolates the weakness in this argument: "when a woman is let in by the men who control the political elite it usually is precisely because that woman has learned the lessons of masculinized political behavior well enough not to threaten male political privilege". *Bananas, Beaches and Bases*, note 7, *supra*, pp. 6–7.

[50] See Scales, note 5, at p. 40.

[51] *Ibid.*, at p. 44.

[52] *Ibid.*

[53] The recent Gulf conflict exemplifies this pattern of objectivity of language. See for example the *Guardian Weekly*, February 10, 1991, p. 1. Even more significant is the absence of figures for civilians from published casualty tolls of that conflict. See Letter to the Editor from Alan McLean, Secretary General, Australian Red Cross Society, *Guardian Weekly*, March 24, 1991.

[54] Civilians have always suffered in armed conflict but until the advent of aerial bombardment in the First World War they were to a large extent isolated from the battlefield itself. They were most vulnerable after the battle had ceased and during occupation. See Higgins, *Non-Combatants and the War* (1914), p. 15. All this changed with the development of air warfare and other methods of warfare of mass destruction. For a description of aerial bombardment during the First World War see Cuneo, *Winged Mars*, Vol. 11 (The Air Weapon 1914–1916) (1947); Higham, *Air Power: A Concise History* (3rd ed.), (1988) and Cooper, *The Birth of Independent Air Power* (1986).

Despite the appalling loss of civilian life in the Second World War[55] as a result of the aerial bombardment of civilian targets such as Dresden and Leipzig, the only treaty rules for civilians to come out of this conflict were those contained in the Fourth Geneva Convention[56] for the protection of civilian persons which, despite its name,[57] only protects a strictly defined category of civilians from arbitrary actions by the enemy, not against the dangers of military operations themselves. Any provision in the draft of the Convention designed to protect the civilian population from the dangers of military operations was carefully removed.[58] Aerial bombardment, which was the major cause of civilian casualties during armed conflict remained unregulated.[59] Thus, the rules for civilians did not interfere with the means and methods by which military men get on with the task of winning wars. On the other hand, the international community at the same time adopted three Conventions dealing with the protection of combatants[60]. The protections offered to these groups of persons by these conventional rules are extremely detailed and the standard that States must meet in relation to the treatment of prisoners of war, for example, are considerably higher than the new treaty rules in Protocol I in relation to civilians.

The content of the Geneva Conventions illustrate the gender bias built into the rules, with civilian protection taking second place to the protection of combatants. Moreover, it was possible to protect cultural property by the Hague Convention for the Protection of Cultural Property of 1954, some twenty-three years before significant attempts were made to regulate the means and methods of warfare to protect civilians. It was not until 1977 that the principle of non-combatant immunity, which is alleged to be a foundation of the law of armed conflict, was finally codified.[61]

[55] For details of the loss of civilian lives during World War II, to a large extent attributable to the saturation aerial bombardment of civilian targets such as Leipzig, Dresden and Cologne, see W. Hays Parks, note 40, *supra*. See also H. Levie, *When Battle Rages, How Can Law Protect?* (1971), p. 24 ff.

[56] Geneva Convention relative to the Protection of Civilian Persons in Time of War of August 12, 1949.

[57] J. Pictet (ed.), *Commentary on the IV Geneva Convention Relative to the Protection of Civilian Persons in Time of War* (1958), p. 10.

[58] *Ibid.*

[59] In 1922–1923 an international conference of six States was held at The Hague to formulate a code of rules for the regulation of aircraft and radio in time of war. In 1923 the Commission of Jurists established by the conference produced the Hague Rules of Air Warfare. The Rules were never ratified by States.

[60] Geneva Convention for the Amelioration of the Condition of the Wounded and Sick in Armed Forces in the Field of August 12, 1949; Geneva Convention for the Amelioration of the Condition of the Wounded, Sick and Shipwrecked Members of Armed Forces at Sea of August 12, 1949; and Geneva Convention relative to the Treatment of Prisoners of War of August 12, 1949.

[61] See *infra*.

(c) Non-nternational and International Armed Conflicts

A further fundamental division within the law of armed conflict, and one that impacts unevenly on women, is the arbitrary distinction drawn between non-international and international armed conflicts.[62] This appears to be a neutral and appropriate division, given that international law deals primarily with relations between States. In gender terms, the institution of the State, however, is far from neutral in its impact. The patriarchal State is regarded by feminists as both creating and perpetuating the oppression of women:

> The State is male in the feminist sense. The law sees and treats women the way men see and treat women. The liberal State coercively and authoritatively constitutes the legal order in the interests of men as a gender, through its legitimizing norms, forms, relation to society and substantive policies.[63]

So a division of the application of the law of armed conflict on rigid distinctions that in no way reflect the reality of these disputes, is meaningless to women. It is not only of concern to feminists that a solution be found to the horrors of internal disputes and that the breakdown of the monolith of State sovereignty is achieved.[64] The extent, however, to which inroads have been made into this theory in the law of armed conflict only serves to illustrate that the voice of women is never heard while these life and death decisions are being made. Article 1(4) of Protocol I to the Geneva Conventions, relating to the protection of victims of international armed conflicts, recognizes the international status of certain wars of self-determination. That is, wars fought by people against

[62] International law has traditionally regarded civil conflicts as beyond its scope and the established state has treated the insurgents under its domestic laws, frequently with great harshness. See E. Castren, *Civil War* (1956), p. 19. Prior to the adoption of Protocol II to the Geneva Conventions, the only conventional regulation of civil disputes was Article 3, common to the four Geneva Conventions of 1949. Article 3 contains minimum standards for victims of civil conflicts. Protocol II expands these protections but only in relation to a more limited category of disputes. Overall, this Protocol is widely regarded as disappointing in its achievements. The issue as to whether there are customary rules in civil conflicts, which could supplement the inadequate treaty rules is an extremely controversial issue. See F. Kalshoven, "Applicability of Customary International Law in Non-International Armed Conflicts", in A. Cassese (ed.) *Current Problems in International Law* (1975), p. 267, at p. 269.

[63] C. Mackinnon, "Feminism, Marxism, Method, and the State: Towards Feminist Jurisprudence", note 23, *supra*, at p. 644. See also C. Mackinnon, note 5, *supra*.

[64] The International Committee of the Red Cross had, for some years, supported the elimination of the distinction between non-international and international conflict for the purposes of the application of the humanitarian law of armed conflict. The move to apply all these humanitarian rules to civil conflicts, irrespective of the legal status of the parties to the conflict, commenced as long ago as 1949 during the negotiation of the Fourth Geneva Convention. See Y. Sandoz et.al. (eds.), note 39, *supra*, at p. 1322. This approach is also reflected in the attitude of many of the delegations to the 1974–1977 Diplomatic Conference that adopted Protocol I and II. See for example the delegates of Finland, *Official Records of the Diplomatic Conference on the Reaffirmation and Development of International Humanitarian Law Applicable in Armed Conflicts, Geneva (1974–1977)*, (1978), CDDH/SR. 18 para.15, Sweden, *ibid.*, CDDH/SR.14, para.7 and Norway, *ibid.*, CDDH/SR.10, para.3.

colonial domination, alien occupation and against racist regimes, in the exercise of their right of self-determination, are international conflicts and the international law of armed conflict is applicable in these struggles.[65] At first sight this achievement by those States that supported the move seems to be an advance for the victims of such disputes, in particular women and children. Surely international regulation of these conflicts must be preferable for those involved to treating them as purely domestic disputes? This first impression is reinforced when one looks further at the detailed provisions of the Protocol in relation to civilian protection. For example, Article 48 codifies the customary norm of non-combatant immunity. Articles 51 to 54 and 57 to 58 provide complex practical rules to ensure the achievement of this immunity as far as possible in light of military considerations.[66] But is this the reality? The selection of these disputes is based on a political doctrine and one that perpetuates the subordinate position of women. The concept of self-determination of people has as its aim the achievement of the Western patriarchal State.[67] On this analysis the right of self-determination is just part of the existing power structure and has nothing to offer women.[68] Liberation movements, moreover, are no less patriarchal in their structure and operations than established States.[69]

There are other gender implications in the developments of humanitarian law which flow from the recogntion of the legal right of self-determination. In my view, the effect of Protocol I is to sacrifice the interests of the helpless

[65] Article 1(4) of Protocol I reads: "The situations referred to in the preceding paragraph [international armed conflicts within common Article 2 to the Geneva Conventions of 1949] include armed conflicts in which people are fighting against colonial domination and alien occupation and against racist regimes in the exercise of their right of self-determination, as enshrined in the Charter of the United Nations and the Declaration on Principles of International Law concerning Friendly Relations and Co-operation among States in accordance with the Charter of the United Nations."

[66] These Articles, *inter alia*, prohibit indiscriminate attacks (for the first time given a concrete definition); codify the rule of proportionality in relation to civilians; specify precautions to be taken in the event of attack and provide protection for civilian objects indispensable to the survival of the civilian population.

[67] The concept of patriarchy, as Carol Smart writes in, *The Ties That Bind* (1984), pp. 6-23, is a controversial one for feminists. Rifkin's "Toward a Theory of Law and Patriarchy", 3 *Harv. Women's L.J.* (1980), p. 83, describes patriarchy as "any kind of group organization in which males hold dominant power and determine which part females shall and shall not play, and in which capabilities assigned to women are relegated generally to the mystical and aesthetic and excluded from the practical and political realms, these realms being regarded as separate and mutually exclusive". See also Thornton, "Hegemonic Masculinity and the Academy", *J. of the Sociology of Law* (1989), p. 115.

[68] As Catharine MacKinnon argues in "Feminism, Marxism, Method, and the State: Towards Feminist Jurisprudence", note 23, *supra*, p. 635, "[feminism] has no theory of the State. It has a theory of power: sexuality is gendered as gender is sexualized".

[69] See R. Morgan, note 12, *supra*, p. 155 ff, and R. Maart, "Feminism and National Liberation Struggles", paper delivered at the Conference on Human Rights in the 21st Century, Banff, Canada 1990. Rozena Maart argues that when issues of gender oppression are raised by women in national liberation movements they are accused of "bourgeois" tendencies. In her view women's reality has nothing to do with liberation struggles.

victims of these conflicts in order to gain a political advantage for the patriarchal liberation movements involved in these struggles and the States that support them.[70] This impact of the Protocol has two aspects, both of which involve the principle of non-combatant immunity: the revival of just war theory and the new definition of combatant.

4. Protocol I and Non-Combatant Immunity

Non-combatant immunity is a fundamental component of the Law of the Hague and has the potential to impose considerable restrictions on the means and methods of warfare.[71] The principle has had a long and checkered history evolving against the background of the development over many centuries of Christian theories of the "just war".[72] As we saw earlier, it has been a constant struggle to develop and maintain the principle of non-combatant immunity in the light of considerable opposition from the military, for whom it serves no purpose other than to interfere with their decision as to the appropriate choice of the means and methods of warfare. Moreover, a review of armed conflict over the years reveals that there is no principle of the law of armed conflict that has been more universally disregarded, in contrast to the rules protecting combatants.[73] It is argued by States and the military that it is too difficult to draft rules to protect civilians from modern warfare without endangering

[70] States who opposed the elevation of these conflicts to the status of international were not motivated by considerations which necessarily involved an appreciation of the consequences for civilians. The majority of opposition was primarily political, a reflection of the continued opposition by Western states to the legal status of the right to self-determination and fears of interference with territorial sovereignty. There were some states, however, who objected to the expansion of the coverage of the Protocol on the basis that to do so would undermine the protection of civilians in these struggles. See note 76, *infra*.

[71] For an excellent account of the evolution of non-combatant immunity, from its earliest foundations in primitive and ancient warfare to modern times, see Hartigan, *The Forgotten Victim* (1982).

[72] There are a number of excellent works on the historical development of the Christian theory of the just war and on the modern form of this theory. The following is a selection: R. Bainton, *Christian Attitudes Toward War and Peace* (1960); J. Johnson, *Ideology, Reason and the Limitation of War* (1975); J. Johnson, *Just War Tradition and the Restraint of War* (1981); F. Russell, *The Just War in the Middle Ages* (1975); T. Taylor, *Nuremburg and Vietnam: An American Tragedy* (1970) and M. Walzer, *Just and Unjust Wars* (1977). The just war and international law has also received attention from legal scholars: W. O'Brien, *The Conduct of the Just and Limited War* (1981); J. Von Elbe, "The Evolution of the Concept of the Just War in International Law", 33 *Amer J.I.L.* (1939), p. 66 and A. Nussbaum, "Just War a Legal Concept?", 26 *Va.J.I.L.* (1942), p. 107.

[73] I am not suggesting that there have not been serious breaches over the years of the rules protecting combatants. Comparatively speaking, however, the rules protecting combatants have been largely adhered to. To illustrate the imbalance one can contrast the enormous public outcry over the public parading of a handful of coalition prisoners of war during the Gulf conflict while, at the same time, hundreds of Iraqi civilian women and children were wounded and dying with the Coalition forces insisting that they were complying with the rules of armed conflict.

military victory of the State.[74] Given that the resort to force is now outlawed by international law that argument seems a little inconsistent. Once again there is an underlying question of priorities in this allegation. Warfare is an extremely hazardous activity, the law is familiar with the regulation of hazardous activities. Moreover, the rules regulating the treatment of prisoners of war are complex and require a high level of organization and facilities for States to meet their obligations. Such compliance impacts detrimentally on the military efficiency of the armed forces, but States have willingly embraced the development and adoption of these rules: they protect men, or rather the male position in the combatant/civilian hierarchy.

Although non-combatant immunity is codified in Protocol I,[75] other changes in that document impact adversely on the fundamental distinction between combatants and non-combatants, and highlight the gender issues underlying this body of rules.

(1) The Just War Aspect of Protocol I

One of the arguments supporting[76] the elevation of some previously civil conflicts to international status was that these were "just" or legal wars.[77] The theory of the just war has brought untold suffering to innocent victims over the centuries, but from both a humanitarian law and a feminist perspective, its most alarming aspect is in relation to the unequal treatment of victims. One of the central principles of the modern law of armed conflict is the independence of the *ius in bello* from the *ius ad bellum* and the reciprocal application of the rules of the *ius in bello*. Although just war theory did not entirely dispense with just means,[78] the justness of the resort to force, however, determined to a large extent the application of the *ius in bello*.[79] The interdependence of the *ius ad bellum* and the *ius in bello* made it difficult to ensure compliance with the *ius in bello*.[80] This interdependence disappeared with the advent of nation States and the emergence of the *ius belli ac pacis*, the right to wage war.[81] Although the unequal application of the law of armed conflict is contrary to the current rules of international law, it is impossible to overlook the impact that the elevation

[74] See for example the views expressed by the French delegation to the 1977 Diplomatic Conference at CDDH/SR.41, para.111.

[75] See *ibid.*

[76] For details of State positions on Article 1(4) of the Protocol see CDDH/I/SR.2–5 and in the Plenary of the Conference and CDDH/SR.56.

[77] See note 72, *supra*.

[78] See Roland Bainton, note 72, *supra*, at p. 97; citing, *Le Doctrine Politique de Saint Augustine* (1927) and J. Johnson, note 72, *supra*, at p. 100, note 19.

[79] *Ibid.*

[80] See G. Draper, "The Development of International Humanitarian Law", in J. Pictel (ed.) *International Dimensions of Humanitarian Law* (1988), pp. 65, 67. See also Y. Dinstein, *War Aggression and Self-Defence* (1988) 145, note 13 and G. Draper, "The Christian and War" Vol. II No. 6 *International Affairs* (1982), p. 13.

[81] See L. Kotsch, note 31, *supra*, at p. 3.

of these struggles to the international level may have in practice. Protocol I, in its recognition of certain categories of non-international armed conflicts as international for the application of the law of armed conflict, lends support to the argument that these are legal or "just" struggles. The attainment of the just end of self-determination warrants any means and, moreover, those in opposition to this just cause are not entitled to the application of the law of armed conflict. Thus, on this analysis, the fundamental distinction between combatants and non-combantants which constrains the choice of means and methods of combat can be dispensed with in a just war.[82]

The preferable approach, which maintains the independence of the *ius ad bellum* from issues as to the "justness" of the war, is to do away with the arbitrary distinction between international and non-international armed conflicts. When it is recalled that the goal of self-determination will impose on women a system that is demonstrably contrary to their interests, the fact that its achievement may involve methods that exacerbate their suffering and death, highlights the illusory advantages of Protocol I other than for the liberation leaders and fighters. Morever, in providing further protections for the liberation fighters involved in these struggles, the Protocol legitimizes the exposure of women and children as targets, rendering deceptive the new provisions in Protocol I for the protection of civilians. How did this occur?

(2) The New Definition of Combatant

One of the fundamental rules of the law of armed conflict is that which provides for the acquisition by persons participating in the hostilities of the status of prisoner of war in the event of capture.[83] In addition to seeking the acknowledgement by the international community that wars of self-determination were international wars, the liberation organizations wanted their fighters to be afforded the sought-after status of prisoner of war. It was argued that if the scope of the law of armed conflict were expanded to include some categories of wars of self-determination as international in status, then in order to make the rules workable in relation to these conflicts it was necessary to take into account their particular characteristics.[84] To expect guerilla forces to meet the same requirements as the organized forces against which they are engaged in conflict was unrealistic. Thus, persons engaged in armed struggles for self-

[82] For example, in the view of the delegate of the Democratic Republic of Vietnam to the Diplomatic Conference, the distinction drawn by Protocol I between the *ius ad bellum* and the *ius in bello* and the equality of both parties in an illegal war was "condemned not only by modern positive law but also by logic, intelligence and morality". CDDH/III/Sr.16, para.21.

[83] For a comprehensive account of the development of the legal rules relating to prisoners of war see A. Rosas, note 12, *supra*, at pp. 43–81.

[84] See for example the reported statements of the Socialist Republic of Vietnam in its explanation of vote at the Committee stage on Article 42– New Category of prisoners of war, CCDII/IIISr.56 para.2; the Libyan Arab Jamahiriya *ibid.*, para.33; Nigeria, *ibid.*, para.61 and the Peoples Republic of Korea, *ibid.*, para.77.

determination should be entitled to the protection of the rules of privileged combatancy without meeting the same standards in distinguishing themselves from the civilian population as regular combatants.

The content of the new rules for the acquisition of this status for guerilla fighters was one of the most controversial issues in the negotiations of Protocol I.[85] Any lowering of standards required a careful balance to be drawn between protecting such irregular combatants and protecting civilians.[86] Civilians were already extremely vulnerable in such conflicts, and it was highly undesirable that their protection should be sacrificed to the cause of the combatant. The move to change the rules of privileged combatancy appears to have been motivated as much by the political gain to be achieved by a victory over opposing States as from any true desire to protect these fighters.[87] As Robin Morgan writes, death is the ultimate goal of the guerilla fighters.[88] Whatever the motivation, to accommodate the style of warfare used by these fighters, the standards that combatants must meet in distinguishing themselves from the civilian population are lowered by Protocol I. The armed forces of a party are defined in Article 43 of the Protocol and the changes to the standards designed to accommodate guerilla fighters are contained in Article 44(3) of Protocol I. Article 44(3) sets out the requirements for combatants in visually distinguishing themselves from the civilian population. This Article provides that where, owing to the nature of the hostilities, armed combatants cannot distinguish themselves from the civilian population, such combatants do not lose their right to be treated as prisoners of war provided that they comply with the lesser requirements set out in Article 44(3)(a) and (b) whilst engaged in a military operation preparatory to an attack. These provisions require such combatants to carry arms openly during

(a) each military engagement, and
(b) such time as he is visible to the adversary while he is engaged in a military deployment preceding the launching of an attack in which he is to participate.

There were considerable differences as to the meaning to be applied to the phrase in Article 44(3)(b), "engaged in a military deployment preparatory to an attack". Two possible interpretations are put forward.[89] Whatever the inter-

[85] See H. Wilson, *International Law and the Use of Force by National Liberation Movements* (1988), 178, G. Abi-Saab, "Wars of National Liberation in the Geneva Conventions and Protocols" 165 *Recueil des Cours* (1979), p. 353, at p. 422 and W. Solf, "A Response to Douglas J. Feith's Law in the Service of Terror: The Strange Case of the Additional Protocol", 20 *Akron L. Rev* (1986), p. 261, at pp. 277–278.

[86] See A. Rosas, note 30, *supra*, at p. 315.

[87] Keith Suter, *An International Law of Guerilla Warfare* (1984), p. 165, argues that in fact this status is not particularly important for guerilla fighters. In his view, the threat of loss of prisoner-of-war status is an empty one.

[88] See note 12, *supra*.

[89] One interpretation was that the necessity to carry arms only arose at the last moment before attack. See the discussion at CDDII/III/SR.55–56 and W. Solf, note 85, *supra*, at p. 277. The other

pretation of this phrase, this move has catastrophic implications for civilians. It legitimizes the use of women and children as shields for the guerilla fighter until the very last moment before an attack is launched. The result is that no commander in the field, when choosing a target, is realistically capable of complying with the other rules of the Protocol that require a distinction to be drawn between civilians and combatants.

5. Conclusion

If genuine humanitarian considerations are to be the basis of humanitarian law, in other words "human" defined to include the female sex, the obvious solution to the improvement of the protection of civilians in armed conflicts is not to focus on the justness of the dispute. For over half the world's population that approach is meaningless, it overlooks the fact that women play no role in the decision as to what is just or not. Moreover, women played no part in the development of that fundamental concept of existing international law, State sovereignty. This way of viewing the world and its peoples as a number of separate, non-connected autonomous units prevents the law of armed conflict being applied on the basis of the magnitude of the dispute rather than on whether the conflict is international or deemed to be international. The false barriers of State sovereignty should be lowered to facilitate the development of a genuinely humanitarian system for the regulation of armed conflict.

Moreover, once the fallacy is exposed that the goal of armed conflict is universal to men and women, all the arguments supporting military necessity as the primary consideration in the determination as to the rules governing such conflict lose their force. A recognition of the absence of women's voices in the decision-making as to the use of force and at least an acknowledgement of the price they pay in armed conflict would be a starting point towards a more equitable approach. True humanitarian considerations must prevail and the doctrine of military necessity must be revealed for what it is: a further aspect of the male State which oppresses and victimizes women.

---

explanation was that the phrase referred to "any movement towards a place from which an attack is to be launched", *id*. For a full explanation of the position taken by States on this issue, see M. Bothe, note 39, *supra*, paras 2.7.2.2 and 2.7.2.3, 254.

SECTION IV

Evolution of Human Rights Into New Areas*

* Summary prepared by the editors.

Introduction

The common thread running through this Section is the evolution of the concept of human rights from its civil and political homeground of "liberty" into new economic, social and cultural areas: food, health, environment, refugeeship, development.

The theme of the general introductory paper by Nani Palkhivala is that, despite ours still being a world of repression, atrocities and brutality, the concept of human rights has become one of the driving forces of our time – "the new gospel", as he calls it. He stresses the truism that human rights cannot exist in a cultural and economic vacuum. And in speaking of the inevitability of gradualness and the painfully slow progress of a perfecting world, he implicitly accepts the inevitable if gradual extension of human rights beyond their classic sphere of application. However, although recognising that the categories of human rights are never closed, he argues against confusing human rights with human needs. In his view, there is a danger of devaluating human rights by inappropriate proliferation. Although unstated, his conclusion is presumably one of advocating caution.

K.E. Mahoney and P. Mahoney (eds.), Human Rights in the Twenty-first Century, 439.

NANI PALKHIVALA*

Economic, Social and Cultural Rights

1. Introduction

The theme of this paper is the reassertion of the greatest single idea offered by humans to humanity – the idea of individual human rights.

Freedom is fragile and evanescent. Humankind has known so little of it in his entire history. The American Civil War was born of the conviction that a nation cannot remain half slave and half free. But the world continues to remain more than half slave and less than half free. Nearly four-fifths of the 160 members of the United Nations do not permit freedom of the press for example. In half of the countries of the world people are incarcerated for speaking their minds, often after trials that are no more than a sham. Torture – mental, physical and emotional – is regularly practised by a third of the world's governments, notwithstanding the Declaration Against Torture and Degrading Treatment issued by the United Nations in 1975. In several States, dissenters who are inconvenient to the authorities suddenly disappear and are never seen again. This vanishing act continues to remain widely popular. More millions have died at the hands of their own governments than in war. Human rights violations have created more deaths and more human misery than have all the weapons of mass destruction.

With our incredible scientific progress, we have reached a stage when the only threat to man left to be met is man himself. In the zoo at Lusaka, there is a cage where the notice reads, "The world's most dangerous animal". Inside the cage there is no animal but a mirror where you see yourself.

It is difficult to measure whether repression worldwide is increasing or decreasing. But awareness of that repression has undoubtedly increased since the human rights movement started as a world movement with the launching of Amnesty International in May 1961. The shifting benchmarks of international atrocities are faithfully recorded in the annual reports of that body.

The oldest human rights organization – the Anti-Slavery Society – was founded in 1839. It is still in business, because slavery is still in business. The

* Senior Advocate, Supreme Court, Bombay, India.

K.E. Mahoney and P. Mahoney (eds.), Human Rights in the Twenty-first Century, 441–445.

Anti-Slavery Society's latest publication, "A Pattern of Slavery: India's Carpet Boys", shows how millions of small children are pressed into bonded labour in India under conditions so abject as to make the distinction between their lot and conventional slavery a matter of semantics.

No doubt it is still a world of brutalities. But the historical perspective would make us realize that ours is a perfecting world, though its progress is painfully slow, sometimes by the millimetre.

There are two gleams of hope. The concept of human rights – the new gospel – has worked its way through the subsoil of human consciousness with speed and strength, and has become one of the great driving forces of our time. But we must be reconciled to the inevitability of gradualness. The slow drip of Amnesty International has begun to work. More and more people the world over realize, and realize more clearly, that there should be increased human rights inspections and publicizing of abuses because, as President Mitterrand said, "silence nourishes oppression". Secondly, there is a growing solidarity among the nations of the world who believe in freedom. The human rights record of a State has become the legitimate concern of the international community. Today the human rights movement is genuinely worldwide. There is, as Jerome Shestack observed, "a moral inevitability to human rights".

To attempt to define human rights definitively, would be merely to illustrate how the human mind tries, and tries in vain, to give a more precise definition than the subject-matter warrants. Human rights may be summed up in one word – Liberty. But Isaiah Berlin noted that there are more than 200 definitions of liberty; and, as Abraham Lincoln observed, the world has never had a good definition of liberty.

2. Economic and Social Rights

In the Third World today, governments that are the most successful economically are authoritarian ones and veneration for human rights promises to be a cult of slow growth. That is because human rights cannot exist in a cultural and economic vacuum. Their chances of being understood – and respected – improve as the economic and educational level of society rises. It is a noble maxim that it is better for a person to go wrong in freedom rather than go right in chains; but it sounds like empty rhetoric to people who live in economic chains below the minimum subsistence level.

The categories of human rights are never closed. But we must guard against the devaluation of human rights by proliferation. It is good to increase the currency, but not at the cost of depreciating it. In the verbal haze in which we live today, secondary concepts have taken the place of primary ones; relative terms have pushed over absolute ones; and the peripheral has been given the same status as the crucial. Let me illustrate.

The primary idea of human rights involves rights against the government. Modern liberalism has expanded the idea to include rights to be satisfied by the government. "Human rights" should be distinguished from "human needs". Clarity of thought and a sense of priorities would suggest that the essence of liberty which comprises rights *against* the State should not be confused with claims or entitlements which fall to be satisfied *by* State. Various resolutions and declarations of the United Nations list – as human rights – benefits like full employment, vacations with pay, maternity leave and free medical care. Such broad-banding enables leftist ideologues to make a specious claim that even totalitarian States respect human rights. They contend that while free democracies have a better record in certain areas of human rights, totalitarian States have a superior record in other areas. It was such depreciation of the currency of human rights which emboldened Lenin to proclaim that the Soviets represent a "higher form of democracy" and Hitler to claim to be an "arch democrat"; and which enables States that practise torture and ruthless repression at home to pay pious lip service to human rights at international forums.

However, this is not to say that economic and social rights evolved by present-day liberalism are irrelevant or unimportant. Rights of men and women are not only against the government but against the people collectively. Humanity is one enormous extended family, with all the obligations of family membership. One of the basic rights is the right to decent living embodied in Article 25 of the Universal Declaration of Human Rights, 1948. Paul Sieghart, pointed out that the test of rights is not whether the prosperous, with access to the law courts, are well protected, or whether living standards for the majority are improving, but whether the weak are helped by the strong. "The ultimate measure of whether a society can properly be called civilized", he concluded, "is how it treats those who are near the bottom of its human heap."

Violations of economic needs occur from negligence, such as the failure to save large numbers of people from famine or floods. But mostly they occur when governments – wedded to the eighth deadly sin, ideology – pursue economic policies which deprive the poor of employment and education, nutrition and health care.

3. Bill of Rights

Democracy and freedom are not synonymous. Adult franchise may merely amount to the right to choose your tyrants. In Lord Hailsham's words, you may have "Elective Dictatorship". Hence the conviction shared by several countries about the sovereign virtue of having a Bill of Rights in the Constitution – which would guarantee basic human freedoms including economic, social and cultural rights. Even in England where freedom is bred in the bones of the people, eminent judges like Lord Devlin, Lord Gardiner, Lord Hailsham, Lord Salmon and Lord Scarman have advocated the incorporation of a Bill of Rights in British law.

The very purpose of a Bill of Rights is to withdraw certain subjects from the vicissitudes of political controversy, to place them beyond the reach of majorities and officials, and to establish them as legal principles to be applied by the courts. One's right to life, liberty and property, to free speech, a free press, freedom of worship and assembly, and other fundamental rights may not be submitted to vote; they depend on the outcome of no elections.[1]

It is interesting to note that in the States of India which have been governed by the communist party, human rights have continued to be fully respected only because the Bill of Rights is firmly entrenched in the Indian Constitution. Incidentally, the right to equality of the sexes, which the United States has recently been attempting – so far unsuccessfully – to incorporate in its Constitution, has been provided for in the Indian Constitution right from its inception in 1950.

Since freedom cannot be passed on in the bloodstream, and is never more than one generation away from extinction, it is essential that the power to amend the Constitution should not extend to abrogating the Bill of Rights. The permanence of the core of human rights has been ensured in India by our Supreme Court which held in *Kesavananda v. State of Kerala*[2] that Parliament, in exercise of its power to amend the Constitution, cannot destroy or alter its basic structure. A constitution is not a jellyfish; it is a highly evolved organism. It has an identity and integrity of its own, the evocative Preamble to the Indian Constitution being its identity card. It cannot be made to lose its identity in the process of amendment. The fundamental rights are the very heart of our Constitution: taking them away would deprive the Constitution not only of its identity but of its life itself. Parliament, when it claims the right to amend the constitutional law, cannot set itself up as the Official Liquidator of the Constitution.

4. Legal Responsibilities

The human being has been called a rational animal, but this definition was given to humans by humans themselves in a characteristic moment of self-adulation. In the words of Lord Keynes, "Man will do the rational thing, but only after exploring all other alternatives". Dr. Konrad Adenauer, the former Chancellor of West Germany, remarked that in creating humans, God had hit upon a very poor compromise. If God had made humans more intelligent, they would have known how to behave; if God had made humans less intelligent, they would have been easier to govern. This remark neatly sums up the dilemma of democracy. Till humans rise higher in the process of evolution, the world situation will continue to remain fouled up.

Since humans do not know how to behave, the necessity arises of legal responsibilities to prevent liberty from degenerating into licence. No virtue is

[1] Per Jackson, *West Virginia State Board of Education v. Barnette*, 319 U.S. 624 at 638.
[2] A.I.R. 1973 S.C. 1461.

absolute – not even freedom. One person's freedom fighter is another person's terrorist.

It is true that eternal vigilance is the price of liberty. But it is true, in even a deeper sense, that eternal responsibility is also part of the price of liberty. Excessive authority, without liberty, is intolerable; but excessive liberty, without authority and without responsibility, soon becomes equally intolerable. De Tocqueville made the profound observation that liberty cannot stand alone but must be paired with a companion virtue: liberty and morality; liberty and law; liberty and justice; liberty and the common good; liberty and civic responsibility.

While we are commendably concerned with the issue of human rights, we may ask ourselves: are we equally mindful of the paramount need of legal responsibilities? Have we reduced the inalienable rights of man to – life, liberty and the pursuit of litigation?

Liberty has a hypnotizing sound; while, unfortunately, responsibility has less appeal. Freedom is like alcohol: it must be taken in moderation. Perhaps we are making life too easy for criminals and too difficult for law-abiding citizens. In free societies, too many crooks break the law, blight young lives, traffic in drugs, and claim the fundamental right to exploit commercially sex and violence. Our values today are drastically eroded, because too many people – with no more moral backbone than a chocolate éclair – claim the freedom of expression and action which results inevitably in increasing the numbers of violent criminals. American, British and Indian societies lit up the moral imagination of the world in the past; why are they crime-ridden today? Is not alienation – alienation of the individual from society, of the child from the family – too high a price to pay for the freedom to be a permissive society? Are we right in thinking that hard evidence, if collected illegally, cannot be used against a criminal in a trial even when there is no other way of securing a conviction? We have to strike an acceptable balance between the proper interests of society which wants criminals to be put out of harm's way and the equally proper instincts of libertarians anxious that nothing should imperil the rights of the citizen.

These questions have been debated over decades, but admit of no easy solution. The sun never sets on these debates. In the present state of human consciousness – when humankind continues to be merely a caricature of humankind to be – there is a certainty of freedom being abused unless legal responsibilities are given the same prime importance as human rights. Since the continuous intellectual enjoyment of the debate must depend to a large extent upon its inconclusiveness, it would be boorish as well as presumptuous to suggest a final conclusion.

SECTION IV(a): THE RIGHT TO FOOD

D. MARTIN LOW*

Introduction

World hunger is attributable to a mind-staggering group of factors, and it has come to be typified by heart-rendering imagery. Thousands of people die daily throughout the world from starvation and other causes related to hunger. Some of the great crimes of human history have turned on a strategy of deprivation of food – one has only to think of the Ukraine in the 1930's. But in many of the most economically advanced countries, during one of the richest stages of their history, large numbers of people do not have sufficient food to meet minimum nutritional requirements. The phenomenon of food banks and soup kitchens in the United States or Canada is not a case of *withholding* food for political or other motives but rather a matter of social, economic and organizational inadequacy, as a result of which food is *unavailable* to those in need.

It appears clear that public opinion in developed countries will not tolerate a policy of deprivation of food from people in need for strategic or tactical political reasons. Demonstrably, legal obligation and recognized morality coincide. Incidents where food relief is interfered with in the midst of civil unrest or military strife (as in Ethiopia and Somalia) are equally intolerable, but more complex and difficult to resolve on legal and practical grounds. Still more complicated is the phenomenon of hunger amid plenty, in our modern social democracies with effective systems of administration and organization, where law and policy become clouded by competing theories of public welfare, social organization and individual responsibility.

In all these cases, the human right to food is not fulfilled. The existence of that right, and its full and effective realization, is one of the major challenges of human history. Its expression as a legal right may be uncontroversial, in major international human rights instruments including the Universal Declaration of Human Rights and the International Covenant on Economic, Social and Cultural Rights. But the implementation of the right, however it may be articulated in legal instruments, has not been accomplished at the tangible level of delivering food in accordance with human needs. And definitional

* Senior Human Rights Officer, United Nations, Geneva, Switzerland.

K.E. Mahoney and P. Mahoney (eds.), Human Rights in the Twenty-first Century, 447–449.

issues, as well as technical and economic realities, may have much to do with that failure.

There is no doubt that considerations of law alone will have limited influence on the pace of agricultural reform, limited effect on the economic constraints on food production – and more significantly, distribution, and limited capacity to reorganize administrative systems that have a negative impact on the availability to food. But the legal obligations exist, and have been widely accepted by States throughout the world. They can be used as a lever to shift public opinion, and therefore political priorities, to re-order the status quo, and to find durable solutions to food production and distribution problems that are only apparently endemic. In order to produce such results, the law must operate in a context which is technologically, economically, socially and culturally integrated, and success will not come easily. The papers presented by the panelists demonstrate that hunger is never trivial, that law exists to promote adjustment in world society, and that effective change is not beyond human capacity.

The development of the right to food has been ineffective in feeding the hungry but Robert Robertson makes the point that progress in the establishment and definition of the right to food has been impressive. The most challenging part of his article is the section on "Ideas for Change". He suggests an education campaign to demystify the right, a preferential option for the poor and international standards on the quality and quantity of food the right would guarantee. He further suggests the need for appropriate mechanisms to hear complaints and monitor compliance as well as the legal resources to make them accessible. He stresses in his conclusion that the Right to Food is a human rights issue, not just a political or moral one.

Asbjorn Eide discusses some of the barriers that exist to the realization of economic social and cultural rights and demonstrates how they are unfounded and misperceived. He argues that the popular idea that social rights must be provided by the state, are costly and will lead to an overgrown state apparatus is a gross oversimplification. In relation to the right to food, a distinction must be made at the primary level between the state as provider and the state as protector. He maintains that the protective role in regard to civil and political rights is similar to the state obligation to protect the freedom of individuals or groups to use resources, exercise permanent sovereignty over them and to protect them from exploitation. This will assist greatly in assuring a right to food. He further believes that in order to realize the right to food, a minimum threshold applicable to rich and poor countries alike should be adopted. Variations in implementation will vary, depending on localized economic and social history. "Freedom from want", he argues, is a cornerstone of the entire human rights edifice and unless it is realized, respect for civil and political rights will diminish.

David MacDonald's perspective is a government one. He maintains that much of the inequities and inefficiencies in relation to the world hunger problem are caused by the failure of states to give the right to food the credibility and importance it requires. Implementation efforts have failed because the nature of food distribution systems are not questioned in any kind of sustained fashion and food is primarily seen as an instrument of economic activity rather than an instrument of human self-fulfilment. He concludes their crisis management is not a good way to deal with global hunger. Food problems must be resolved outside of periods of crisis taking into account larger issues of economic rights, self-determination, participation and equality.

ROBERT ROBERTSON*

The Right to Food in International Law

1. Introduction

The development of the right to food has meant little to the hungry. It shields neither the famine victim nor the welfare mother from the calamity of food shortage. Useful, but unused, the international law lies dormant in unimplemented treaties and seldom read scholarship. But the progress of human rights is measured in generations and centuries, and remarkable progress has been made in the last generation in at least articulating the right.

This paper will first look at the present international law on the right to food, and then suggest changes in it which would make the right to food a more effective instrument in the next century than it has been in this one.

2. The Current Law

The idea of food entitlement is an ancient one. Confucius stated that feeding the people was a primary obligation of the State.[1] The Old Testament prescribed detailed laws which Jews were bound to follow, which provided for the poor and hungry to have access to productive land or the food growing on the lands of others.[2] Revolutionary France gave birth to numerous declarations emphasizing the rights of the poor to basic sustenance.[3] And of course aboriginal societies have long followed norms which require sharing the bounty of the hunt.[4]

* Deputy Secretary and Associate General Counsel, International Development Research Centre, Ottawa, Ontario.

[1] P. Spitz, "Right to Food for Peoples and for the People: A Historical Perspective", in P. Alston and K. Tomasevski (eds.) *The Right to Food* (1984), Utrecht: Martinus Nijhoff Publishers, pp. 169–186 at pp. 171–173.

[2] Exodus 23, Deuteronomy 14 and Leviticus 19, 23 and 25.

[3] See note 1, *supra*, at pp. 174–175.

[4] For example see Michael Asch, *Home and Native Land – Aboriginal Rights and the Canadian Constitution* (1984), Toronto: Methuen, at p. 21, for a desription of the practices of the Shuswaps of British Columbia.

K.E. Mahoney and P. Mahoney (eds.), Human Rights in the Twenty-first Century, 451–457.

Some modern legal systems have food-related provisions in their constitutions, and countries as diverse as India and Ireland, Nicaragua and the Netherlands have constitutional references to various economic rights. However, they usually are framed as principles to guide policy rather than as clearly justiciable individual human rights.

The twentieth century has seen the development of the international human rights system. By one compilation, there are now over one hundred instruments which are relevant to the establishment and definition of the right to food.[5] These include treaties which require the provision of food to prisoners and refugees, those dealing with international food aid and food security, and treaties relevant to the control and preservation of agricultural resources.

The most frequently cited expression of the right to food is contained in the International Covenant on Economic, Social and Cultural rights, which entered into force in 1976. Article 11 says in part: "the States parties to the present Covenant recognize the right of everyone to an adequate standard of living for himself and his family, including adequate food..." This echoes article 25 of the Universal Declaration of Human Rights, proclaimed by the U.N. General Assembly in 1948.

In his 1987 report, the Special Rapporteur to the Economic and Social Council of the U.N. on the right to food gave the following formulation: "Everyone requires food which is (a) sufficient, balanced and safe to satisfy nutritional requirements, (b) culturally acceptable, and (c) accessible in a manner which does not destroy one's dignity as a human being."[6] As well, food which is adequate qualitatively, quantitatively and culturally, should be accessible in a sustained way. For the Special Rapporteur, this implies that "the physical and institutional environment in which food is procured must be optimally utilized [and] protected from erosion or distortion".[7]

This expansive definition of the content of the right to food widens its relevance to a variety of circumstances. For example, giving peasant farmers the chance to provide themselves with adequate food in a dignified and sustained manner is clearly an argument for those in developing countries who advocate land reform.[8] The right to food has also been invoked for the same reasons on behalf of African pastoral communities who see their grazing lands being encroached upon by expanding populations and the conversion of

[5] *The Right to Food: Guide Through Applicable International Law* in K. Tomasevski (ed.) Dordrecht: Martinus Nijhoff Publishers.

[6] "Report on the Right to Adequate Food as a Human Right" submitted by Asbjorn Eide, Special Rapporteur, E/CN.4/Sub.2/1987/23 para. 52.

[7] Ibid., at para. 135.

[8] For numerous specific cases where the right is asserted, see the Newsletter of the Foodfirst International Action Network, of Heidelberg, Germany. For example, there was alleged repression of sugar workers on the Philippine Island of Negros, where the collapse of the suger market led to widespread hunger among workers. The Philippine Government was criticized for not acting to implement a land reform program which would allow the workers to provide for themselves. (Newsletter No. 24 Dec. 87/Jan. 88).

grazing land to agriculture.[9] In a developed and urbanized country, the right to food is more readily applicable to issues touching the inadequate resources available to purchase food, as opposed to an individual's self-sufficiency in producing it.

What duty does the State have to establish the right to food? As with the question of the content of the right, the scope and nature of State duties are largely lacking in the international instruments which establish the right to food. Article 2(1) of the Covenant provides some guidance on how State obligations with respect to all of the rights in the Covenant are to be fulfilled. In essence, it obliges a State to participate in the universal implementation of the rights. Internationally, there is a duty to participate in co-operation and assistance to implement them. Domestically, legislative measures are an important, but not the sole, method through which the rights are to be implemented. The ultimate obligation is to achieve "full realization". However, this result is not necessarily to be achieved immediately. Circumstances may dictate a process of implementation which will be carried out progressively. This process must bring to bear a State's maximum available resources.

The article 2 formulation of duties, applicable for all rights in the Covenant, receives some elaboration in article 11 for a component of the right to food, namely "freedom from hunger". States are to take measures to improve the production, conservation and distribution of food; to disseminate information about nutrition; and to structure agrarian systems to make best use of natural resources. At the international level, States are expected to ensure the distribution of food according to need.

Although provisions of such brevity could hardly provide a formula for solving the complex question of world hunger, their intention is clear in one respect. States must devote their resources to the fullest extent possible to implementing the right to food. In some cases its implementation may not be immediate, but rather progressive. However, only the absence of resources justifies not fully implementing it.

Taking the above imperatives as a starting point, there have been various scholarly formulations of the types of duties which a State is required to undertake. For present purposes, the three levels of State responsibility set out by the Special Rapporteur are adopted. They are: (i) the obligation to respect the right to food, (ii) the obligation to protect the right to food, and (iii) the obligation to fulfil the right to food.

The first obligation, to respect the right to food, "calls for non-interference by the State in all cases where the individuals or groups can take care of their own needs without weakening the possibility for others to do the same".[10] This obligation is cited as being of particular importance to groups, such as aboriginal peoples, who wish to retain collective rights to the use of their food-

[9] Kaj Arhem, "Cultural Identity and the Right to Food: The Case of the Maasai" in A. Eide et al. (eds.) *Food as a Human Right* (1984), New York: The United Nations University, at p. 89.

[10] See note 6, *supra*, p. 170.

yielding resources. Governments are not to encroach upon these. Another example of the obligation to respect would be that States are to not interfere with the right of individuals to obtain work so that they can feed themselves.

The second obligation, to protect the right to food, "implies the responsibility of States to counteract or prevent activities and processes which negatively affect food security, particularly for the most vulnerable in society".[11] This obligation can be seen as the activist side of the obligation to respect. For example, the State is obliged to take actions to prevent the environmental destruction of food-yielding lands or waters by industrial polluters. As well, it could oblige the State to construct an appropriate legislative framework to control the marketing of food products which are inherently harmful or the use of which may lead to harm, such as breastmilk substitutes.

The third obligation, to fulfil the right to food, requires the State to give "assistance or direct provision".[12] Examples of this are giving food to prisoners, or the establishment of an effective social security and social assistance system.

These three types of duty – respect, protect and fulfil – each seem applicable to all States, although the emphasis on each in a given State will vary with factors such as the fiscal resources available to the State, the extent of urbanization, and the food-related practices of the various cultural groups constituting the population of the State. This fluidity of obligation has led to great difficulty in measuring State compliance. However, that does not make less real the fundamental nature of the right to food, or a State's obligation to fully implement it, if it has the resources to do so.

The monitoring of State compliance with the right to food is done by the U.N. Committee on Economic, Social and Cultural Rights, a committee of experts which meets once a year in Geneva. Its principal function is to consider periodic national reports on State implementation of the Covenant. It also makes what it calls "general comments" with the intention of building up jurisprudence in a given area. As well, it also has general discussions on the nature of various rights contained in the Covenant.

The future of the development of the right to food internationally appears to rest largely on this committee, which has now had five sessions. But the committee membership is of uneven experience and knowledge. There is very little NGO input into its deliberations, and the public is largely unaware of its existence, thanks in part to poor press coverage. It may be that the real fight to establish the right to food will be fought at the national level, as groups working for the poor begin to inject the concept into their political rhetoric, and into court actions. A solid base in national legal systems would fuel discussion of the right internationally, and encourage States to construct dynamic international mechanisms to promote its universal implementation.

[11] Ibid., para. 175.
[12] Ibid., para. 180.

3. Ideas for Change

In projecting what the right to food should look like in international law in the twenty-first century, the following analysis will ignore only one small thing – political reality. Writing once in a law review about economic rights, Pierre Trudeau said, "Governments must contend with questions of how, when and where. But in a law journal, it is possible to reach for the ultimate goal."[13] And so for present purposes, that same latitude may be accorded.

What the following projection will do is to look at international law in the way that a liberation theologian would look at national laws, that is with what is called "the preferential option for the poor", in this case to see the international right to food through the eyes of those for whom it is designed – the hungry and those threatened with hunger.

In that situation, the first thing one would want to know is whether there is a right to food in international law. Those claiming such a right may very well be among the less educated and sophisticated members of the population. But with the all-pervasive communication media of the twenty-first century available, international law should require governments to inform their populations of the existence of the right, in a popular form – television, radio, posters – and they should be obliged to teach every school child about it too.

As a hungry person, the next thing you would want to know is whether the right to food applied to you and to your situation. Hungry people should not be obliged to analyze and synthesize endless international instruments and scholarly studies trying to figure out what the right to food is and what they can do about it if their rights are being violated. The essence of the law should be in one place, written simply, and with enough concreteness for most people to know whether it fits their situation. Abstract principles are fine for lawyers, but they are not fine for the majority of people for whom the international law is being written.

The next thing you would want to know is how much food you were entitled to. In other words, the international law should set minimum standards by which everyone could be told what they need to eat in order to be healthy and productive. The medical community of the twenty-first century will surely be in a position to set some reasonable quantitative and qualitative standards of nutrition so that everyone can know how much food they deserve. Why not make those standards a part of international law? Domestic laws dealing with social assistance frequently lack minimum standards of adequacy, with the result that in Canada, for example, social assistance rates vary wildly from province to province and even city to city. Why repeat that mistake at the international level? Surely some standard can be developed which in effect says that what is good for an Englishman is good for an Ethiopian.

If hungry, the next thing you would want international law to do for you would be to let you complain to somebody. In other words, the civil guarantee

[13] P.E. Trudeau, "Economic Rights" McGill L.J. (1962), pp. 121–125 at p. 125.

of freedom of expression is just as necessary to the hungry people as the economic right to food. Countries accepting that people have the right to food must accept that it is of little value if they do not have the freedom to express their outrage at deprivation of the right. This interdependence of economic rights and civil and political rights could be reflected in nations guaranteeing, as part of their right to food obligations, popular access to the same media as the governments used initially to inform people of the existence of the right. But that right to complain should not be confined within national borders. Appropriate mechanisms should be set up to ensure that the international body responsible for monitoring compliance with the right to food can hear the hungry, not just every four or five years when their particular country reports to it on the implementation of the right, but when in fact they are hungry. This implies an individual complaint mechanism, and the allocation of sufficient resources to allow the complaints to be considered properly. Can you imagine the number of complaints and the amount of resources that would be needed? Fortunately, the analysis began by saying that it would be exempt from political realities. But if the world cares about anything, it should care about food. And if it cares about food, the nations of the world must invest in the means by which they can hear the cry of the hungry.

If you were hungry, the next thing you would want is a lawyer to help you enforce your rights. Unlike most lawyers in the twentieth century, this lawyer would know that the right to food existed, because he would have been forced to learn about it in law school. International law would require countries to publicly fund legal aid systems, so that adequate legal resources would be available to individuals or groups who wanted to assert their right to food. And naturally the international law on the right to food, set out in clear and simple terms, would have been transformed into the domestic law of your country exactly as it is written internationally, because international law would have required that. Poor people around the world would welcome the chance to go to court on these issues. One might cite the words of one poor person heard speaking recently in Canada who said, "We have tried politics and we have failed; now we must try law."

However it must be recognized that even if a person's right to food is being violated and they have the benefit of a perfect legal system, and of a national government truly struggling to meet its obligations to its citizens, they still may be hungry. To what extent should a person or a group be able to look outside their borders for relief? States are also holders of the right to food, not just individuals. If you were hungry, I would want your country to declare your hunger before the world, and not attempt to hide it out of political embarrassment. International law would require nations to follow certain procedures to attract emergency assistance to ensure the food security of their citizens.

What if a real threat were being posed to the right to food by international development agencies supporting projects inimical to the right. By this is meant the kinds of projects which might be ecologically disruptive, or which convert to other purposes land upon which people depend for their food. International agencies are moving toward an appreciation that they have a responsibility for an internal review of their activities to ensure that they are ethically supportable and consonant with human rights standards. If your food sources were threatened then you would want international law to articulate the obligations of international agencies to conduct such reviews in a transparent way, using as standards those principles comprising the right to food.

And what does a hungry person in the twenty-first century do if all else fails? Can he/she steal food? Can he/she engage in welfare fraud to get the resources he needs to purchase it? In Canada, our Supreme Court seems to be moving toward the view that people who believe that their security of the person is at risk can act to preserve themselves, with immunity from the criminal law. It struck down our abortion law on that basis.[14] A hungry person is quite likely to want international law to recognize that where a person or their family or group are in an extreme circumstance, the weight of the country's criminal law should not descend upon them. It is not lightly that one would counsel actions which might otherwise be called lawless and tumultuous, but the widespread insufficiency of food already constitutes a situation of turmoil and which is lawless in the sense that the basic right to food is being violated.

4. Conclusion

We have tried to put ourselves in the shoes of the hungry, assuming they are blessed with shoes, and in so doing we have tried to place the role of law in the forefront as an answer to the problem. There is good ground to believe that a human rights approach holds immense potential for advancing the economic and social well-being of people. The food question cannot be dealt with as simply a matter of politics or even morality. It must also be thought of as a matter of justice. Legal human rights must come to form the context for political and moral decision-making. If the twenty-first century sees that happen, then there is hope that the new century will be a better one for the hungry than the chaotic and desperate one in which we have been living.

[14] *R. v Morgentaler* (1988) 1 S.C.R. 30.

ASBJORN EIDE*

Strategies for the Realization of the Right to Food

1. Universalization of Human Rights: Three Stages

As we look towards the twenty-first century we should recognize that we are in the initial phases of the third stage in the universalization of human rights. The first stage was to agree on the catalogue of rights which were to be considered "universal"; the second was to give those rights a legal content, and the third is to bring reality into conformity with those rights. These may be termed the stages of idealization, positivization and realization, respectively.

The challenge we now face is to transform the rhetoric of universal human rights to universal reality. This paper will examine the challenges of that stage in regard to the right to food.

The first stage was to make human rights an international concern and to agree on the set of ideal rights to be collectively pursued. This stage was set in motion by the so-called "Four Freedoms" address, by the then United States President, Franklin D. Roosevelt, in January 1941. Until World War II human rights had essentially been a national concern, mainly left to national preferences, whatever they were. While some States had incorporated some human rights and freedoms, and included legal safeguards into their constitutions and laws, others had not. There were States which had experienced brief periods of human rights incorporation (the Weimar Republic), but had since completely rejected the whole human rights concern (the Nazi period in the 1930s).

The Four Freedoms address of 1941 is crucial in several respects, and it is appropriate to recall it now, in 1991, fifty years after it was made. Two aspects

* Norwegian Institute of Human Rights, Oslo, Norway. This paper draws heavily on my study for the United Nations Sub-Commission on Prevention of Discrimination and Protection of Minorities, entitled "The Right to Adequate Food as a Human Right", published by the United Nations Centre for Human Rights as Study Series No. 1, 1989. It also draws on my article "Realization of Social and Economic Rights and the Minimum Threshold Approach", *Human Rights Law Journal* (1989), vol. 10, No. 1–2. Several aspects are further developed in Asbjorn Eide, Arne Oshaug and Wenche Barth Eide, "Food Security and the Right to Food", *Transnational Law and Contemporary Problems* (1991), vol. 1, No. 2.

K.E. Mahoney and P. Mahoney (eds.), Human Rights in the Twenty-first Century, 459–472.

will be examined here: the universalizing ambition, and the scope of the freedoms mentioned.

Franklin Roosevelt looked forward to a future world in which the freedoms would be enjoyed "everywhere in the world". Thus, it was not only a proposition for the United States, or for the West, but for the whole world. Secondly, he included not only the well-established rights in American thinking (freedom of faith and freedom of speech), but also – startlingly – some new freedoms: freedom from want and freedom from fear. The freedom from want is the focus of this paper.

He claimed that his vision of that future world was not a blueprint for a distant millennium. He hoped, undoubtedly, that as soon as the world war was over, resolute steps would be taken to create a new humane world order. In a way it was. Immediately following his address, steps were taken to create a new world organization, which was to pursue the aims contained in the Four Freedoms address. The fruit of these endeavours was the creation in 1945 of the United Nations. Unfortunately, Franklin Roosevelt did not live to see its birth.

Undoubtedly, the United Nations has made great achievements in the promotion of a new international legal order where the four freedoms – and others – could be enjoyed. Freedom from want for everyone in the world, however, is very far from being realized.

What was, to Franklin Roosevelt in 1941, a somewhat distant millennium is now less than a decade away from us. Will we now be able to use these last few years of the present millennium to lay the foundation for an effective enjoyment of freedom from want in the next millennium?

The formation of the United Nations, and the adoption of the Universal Declaration of Human Rights, has given us the normative framework on which to build. The Universal Declaration is sufficiently broad to cover civil, political, economic, social and cultural rights. Thus, the package of rights envisaged in the Four Freedoms address is in place, but the follow-up in regard to economic and social rights has been less than impressive.

Following the adoption of the Universal Declaration in 1948, the United Nations set about adopting legally binding instruments, and decided in the process to make a distinction between two sets of rights: the civil and political which were incorporated into CCPR, and the economic, social and cultural rights which were incorporated into CESCR. It was understood and repeatedly reaffirmed by the United Nations that all of these rights would be seen as a totality. They should be interdependent and indivisible.

Two major reasons were used in favour of their separation. One was the claim that the two sets of rights needed different kinds of implementation approaches at the national level. It has frequently been argued that the civil and political rights can be implemented immediately and without cost, whereas the economic and social rights can be implemented only gradually, and with cost. The argument is grossly simplified, but not entirely without merit. Some aspects of civil and political rights will require for their realization considerable costs; many Third World countries have difficulties in funding a satisfactory, impartial judiciary and a disciplined corps of law enforcement officials. Some aspects of economic and social rights can best be realized if the State abstains from interfering; the right to join and to form trade unions does not in itself cost anything for the State. As we shall later see, one of the reasons for the widely held claim that social and economic rights by necessity are costly is because it is assumed that the State has to "provide" such rights out of the State budget. In many cases that is not so.

The second claim, relating more to political considerations, was that many States might be willing to ratify the CCPR but not the ESCR. By separating them into two documents, States which had problems in implementing economic and social rights could nevertheless undertake binding obligations in regard to civil and political rights by ratifying the CCPR. Empirical reality has shown this to be wrong. In practically all cases, States have ratified both Covenants. In those very few cases where States have ratified only one covenant,[1] it has been the CESCR, not the CCPR. As of March 1990, there is no case in which a State has ratified the CCPR but not the CESCR.

The only candidate likely to ratify the CCPR but not the CESCR would be the United States, which stands out as a very special case. If (under the present Administration) the United States decides to ratify the Covenant on Civil and Political Rights, it is very unlikely that it would also ratify the Covenant on Economic, Social and Cultural Rights. The factors (and possibly the misperceptions) making the United States so wary about the CESCR has been thoroughly analyzed by Philip Alston.[2]

During most of the post-war years the ideological confrontation made it difficult to universalize either category of rights. The "command economy" systems which had been erected in the Soviet Union and imposed also on several countries in Central and Eastern Europe could not be operative if civil and political rights were taken seriously (which they were not). It was claimed by those States, however, that they were particularly effective in realizing economic and social rights. An ideologically nurtured misperception arose, according to which the economic and social rights were "socialist" in the sense attached to the command economy system, and therefore dangerous to civil and political rights. Admittedly, the claim of better performance in regard to economic and social rights was exploited by the leaders of the pro-Soviet governments, as a justification for their centralized rule. It was, however, a justification, not a reality. Even in terms of economic and social rights those systems were failures. They were failures in that many aspects of economic and social rights were not in fact enjoyed. There was discrimination in the application of, for example, the right to education: those who did not follow

[1] By March 1990, 97 States had ratified the CESCR and 92 States the CCPR. The five countries which had ratified the CESCR but not the CCPR were Greece, Guatemala, Honduras, Solomon Islands and Uganda.

[2] Philip Alston, "U.S. Ratification of the Covenant on Economic, Social and Cultural Rights: The Need for an Entirely New Strategy", *American Journal of International Law* (1990), vol. 84, pp.365–393.

the Party line very often were barred from access to higher and tertiary education. There was violation of the right to free choice of employment: many workers had to accept the work given to them by State authorities. It is therefore a mistake to assume that economic and social rights in their different aspects were fully realized in the centralized socialist States of Eastern Europe in the past.

The rhetorical use of economic and social rights as justification for those regimes was also exploited by groups in the West who were reluctant to embrace economic and social rights. Liberal ideology, so it was said, could not absorb economic and social rights. Again, empirically, this was wrong: all Western States which have ratified the civil and political rights have also ratified the Covenant on Economic, Social and Cultural Rights. In fact, all "Western" industrialized States, including Australia, Canada, Japan and New Zealand as well as all members of the Council of Europe, have ratified the CESCR.[3] Not only that: the drafting of economic, social and cultural rights was based very much on the experience of the Western evolution of the Welfare State, an evolution which had set in from the end of the previous century in Western Europe, culminating in the years prior to and the first three decades after World War II. It was also deeply affected by the evolution in the United States itself, from 1933 onwards, and indeed the inclusion of economic and social rights was strongly endorsed by the United States delegation in 1947–1948, the crucial years when the modern framework for universal human rights was adopted. It was no coincidence that "freedom from want" was one among the four freedoms on which the whole human rights edifice was built.

The revolution which took place in the late 1980s has transformed the conditions under which this discussion is pursued. There is now in the East/West relation practically a full consensus on the importance of the civil and political rights. Let us hope that now, when the ideological confrontation over civil and political rights has disappeared, we shall also be able to do away with the ideological confrontation over economic, social and cultural rights, and thereby be able to move forward to a joint implementation and realization of the whole range of rights adopted in 1948.

Indeed, realization of economic and social rights is also essential for the consolidation of respect for civil and political rights. Neglect of economic and social rights is a cause of violence and social conflicts and therefore also of the violation of civil and political rights. "The general and apparently well-founded belief is that in some countries the extreme poverty of the masses – the result in part of less-equitable distribution of the resources of production – has been the fundamental cause of the terror that afflicted and continues to afflict those countries. ...The essence of the legal obligation incurred by any government in this area is to attain the economic and social aspirations of its people, by

[3] The only two "Western" exceptions are the U.S. (see below in the text) and South Africa, the latter country obviously due to its racial policy which flies in the face of the principle of non-discrimination, one of the most basic foundations of the human rights system.

following an order that assigns priority to the basic needs of health, nutrition and education".[4]

Freedom from want is only a distant dream for large groups of people. Hunger and malnutrition is widespread, and yet there is food enough in the world to satisfy the needs of all, provided produce was equally distributed. Hunger and inadequate access to food are a poverty problem, not a problem of insufficient food production. This fact, and strategies by which international food agencies deal with it, is examined in detail in *Transnational Law and Contemporary Problems*.[5]

2. The Nature of Obligations Regarding Economic and Social Rights

Traditional wisdom will have it that economic and social rights have to be provided by the State, out of its budget, and for this reason they are costly and lead to an overgrown State apparatus. This view results from a very narrow understanding of the nature of these rights and of the corresponding State obligations.

Fundamental to a realistic understanding of State obligations is that the individual is the subject of all economic and social development. This is stated in the following terms in the Declaration on the Right to Development, article 2:[6]

> "1. The human being is the central subject of development and should be the active participant and beneficiary of the right to development.
>
> 2. All human beings have a responsibility for development, individually and collectively, taking into account the need for full respect of their human rights and fundamental freedoms as well as their duties to the community, which alone can ensure the free and complete fulfilment of the human being..."

The individual is expected, whenever possible through own efforts and by use of own resources, to find ways to ensure the satisfaction of his or her own needs[7], individually or in association with others. Use of own resources,

[4] Annual Report of the Inter-American Commission on Human Rights, 1979–80. OEA/Ser.L/V/II.50, pp. 151–152.

[5] A. Eide, A. Oshaug and W.B. Eide, "Food Security and the Right to Food, in *Transnational Law and Contemporary Problems* (1991), Iowa University College of Law, vol. 1, No. 2.

[6] Adopted by the General Assembly on December 4, 1986, res. 41/128.

[7] A note on the historical origins of the contemporary international human rights system is revealing here. One of the very first drafts of an international declaration on human rights was prepared in 1942-1944 by an international group of experts, representing several cultures and world regions, under the auspices of the American Law Institute. The draft contained an article on the right to food (art. 41), which in its commentary stated: "The State is not required to provide food and housing unless the individual under existing conditions cannot obtain them through his own effort." The draft was subsequently presented to the San Francisco founding conference of the

however, requires that the person has resources that can be used – typically land or other capital, or labour. It could include the shared right to use communal land, and the land rights held by indigenous peoples. Furthermore, the realization of an individual's economic, social and cultural rights will usually take place within the context of a household as the smallest economic unit, although aspects of female and male division of labour and control over the produce, as well as various forms of wider kinship arrangements may present alternative alliances.

State obligations must be seen in the light of the above. States must, at the primary level, *respect* the freedom of the individuals to take necessary actions and use necessary resources – alone or in association with others. It is in regard to the latter that *collective* or group rights become important: the resources belonging to a collectivity of persons, such as indigenous populations, must be respected for them to be able to satisfy their needs by those resources.

Similarly, the rights of peoples to exercise permanent sovereignty over their natural resources may be essential for them to be able, through their own collective efforts, to satisfy the needs of the members of that collectivity.

State obligations consist, at a secondary level, in the protection of the freedom of action and the use of resources against other, more assertive or aggressive subjects (more powerful economic interests; protection against fraud, against unethical behaviour in trade and contractual relations, against the marketing and dumping of hazardous or dangerous products – to mention some examples from different fields).

Probably this is the most important aspect of the right to food and other survival rights: the State not as provider, but as protector. This is a function similar to the role of the State as protector in regard to civil and political rights: protecting the right to life, to freedom from slavery and servitude, from violence and mistreatment by third parties.

Significant components of the obligation to *protect* are spelled out in existing law. Much more could be elaborated, however. When further developed, such legislation becomes manageable for judicial review, and therefore belies the argument that economic and social rights are inherently non-justiciable. Legislation of this kind must, of course, be contextual – that is, it must be based on the specific situational requirements in the country concerned. To take one example: legislation requiring that land can be owned only by the tiller of the land is essential where agriculture is the major basis of income, but may be much less relevant in highly industrialized technological societies where only a small percentage live off the land. For groups of people whose culture requires a close link to the use of land, protection of that land is even more important as an obligation to realize the right to food. Again, the indigenous peoples serve as the clearest example.

United Nations in 1945 by Panama, and played a major inspirational role in drafting the Universal Declaration of Human Rights.

At the tertiary level, the State has – as a last resource – the obligation to *fulfil* the expectations of all for the enjoyment of the right to food, to be the provider.[8] This may take two forms:

- assistance in order to provide *opportunities* for those who have not;
- direct *provisions* of food or resources which can be used for food (direct food aid, or social security) when no other possibility exists, for example (1) when unemployment sets in (such as under a recession); (2) for the disadvantaged, and the elderly; (3) during sudden situations of crisis or disaster (see further below); and (4) for those who are marginalized (for example, as a consequence of structural transformations in the economy and production).[9]

It may now have become clearer why the allegation that economic and social rights differ from the civil and political in that the former require the use of resources by the State while the latter do not, is such a gross oversimplification. The argument is tenable only in situations where the focus for economic and social rights is on the tertiary level (the obligation to fulfil) while civil and political rights are observed on the primary level (the obligation to respect). This scenario is however arbitrary. Some civil rights require State obligations at all levels – also the obligation to provide direct assistance when there is a need for it.[10] Economic and social rights, on the other hand, can in many cases best be safeguarded through non-interference by the State with the freedom and use of resources possessed by the individuals.

In the light of the complexity of the issue, and the need for flexibility to respond to different situations, it now becomes understandable that the basic provisions (articles 2 and 11 of the Covenant on Economic, Social and Cultural Rights) were drafted more in the form of *obligations of result* rather than *obligation of conduct*. It is also understandable that these obligations, taken at their highest and most general level, cannot easily be made justiciable (manageable by third party judicial settlement). Nevertheless, the obligations exist and can in no way be neglected.

State obligations for economic and social rights were elaborated by a group

[8] Interestingly, this corresponds to the approach taken in the very first draft for the right to food, the one presented by Panama in 1945. See in particular the comment to article 14 in the Panama draft, A/148.

[9] It will be seen that most of these situations were already envisaged in the Universal Declaration, Art. 25 para. 1 *in fine*: "... and the right to security in the event of unemployment, sickness, disability, widowhood, old age or other lack of livelihood in circumstances beyond his control".

[10] The General Comment of the Human Rights Committee in regard to the right to life, art. 6 of the Covenant on Civil and Political Rights (GAOR, Supplement No. 40, A/37/40, 1982, p. 93), refers, among other matters, to widespread and serious malnutrition leading to extensive child mortality, as a non-fulfilment of the right to life. Remedies to counteract child malnutrition often require government-organized provision of food. In a field more well-known to lawyers, equal access to justice (which is essential for the protection of civil and political rights) requires legal aid to those in the lowest income brackets, another illustration that the State may have to be a provider in order to complete its range of obligations also in regard to civil and political rights.

of experts, convened by the International Commission of Jurists, in Limburg (Netherlands) in June 1986. The outcome is the so-called Limburg principles.[11] Among them we find the following:

> "6. The achievement of economic, social and cultural rights may be realized in a variety of political settings. There is no single road to their full realization. Successes and failures have been registered in both market and non-market economies, in both centralized and decentralized political structures.
> 7. States parties must at all times act in good faith to fulfil the obligations they have accepted under the Covenant.
> 8. Although the full realization of the rights recognized in the Covenant is to be attained progressively, the application of some rights can be made justiciable immediately while other rights can become justiciable over time."

Development essentially means realization of human rights in all their aspects, as implicitly stated in the Declaration on the Right to Development, article 1:

> "The individual is by virtue of the right to development entitled to participate in, contribute to and enjoy economic, social, cultural and political development in which all human rights and fundamental freedoms can be fully realized.[12]

3. Not Ideal Justice, But a Minimum Threshold Approach?

It is important to keep a certain realism in the quest for economic and social rights. Approaches to human rights, we know, are profoundly influenced by political and ideological controversies concerning the economic system and the role of the State. Economic liberalism and the "command economy" version of Leninism-Marxism have formed the two poles of this controversy, the former favouring maximum individual freedom of action and a minimal role to be played by the State; the other favouring – at least during the so-called socialist transition stage – a maximum role by the State, with central planning and a directive political system.

Economic liberalists give top priority to the right to property and to "the freedom to choose."[13] Civil and political rights are supported, but with some hesitation when the use of these leads to the emergence and consolidation of social reform movements calling for a stronger role of the State.[14] Marxist-

[11] The Limburg principles can be found in UN Doc. E/CN.4/1987/17, annex, and are reprinted in *Human Rights Quarterly* (1987), vol. 9, No. 2.

[12] Included is also the full realization of the rights of peoples to self-determination and their sovereignty over natural wealth and resources, art. 1 para. 2.

[13] See Milton and Rose Friedman *Free to Choose: A Personal Statement* (1980), Harcourt Brace Jovanovich, New York.

[14] The civil rights concept of the 19th century did not emphasize political rights for all – on the contrary, women were excluded, and so were non-propertied men in most States which considered

Leninists have claimed to have given priority to economic, social and cultural rights, and refused to accept pluralist political systems.

Between these two extremes are multiple variations, among which are the Welfare States of Western and Northern Europe, also sought to be developed in some of the Latin American countries prior to the military coups and the subsequent catastrophic debt crisis.

Internationally recognized human rights might seem to call for distributive justice. According to the Universal Declaration, article 25, "Everyone has the right to a standard of living adequate for the health and well-being of himself and of his family ...". This and other provisions, taken at their face value, might indicate that everyone shall be in equal control over resources. If this were so, two possible avenues might be pursued: one, that the State ensures an equitable redistribution of productive resources (land, capital, etc.) to every person under its jurisdiction; or that the State directs and controls the economic system and then becomes the provider for everyone of their material needs on a basis of equality.

There would, however, be serious problems with the application of the notion of ideal justice in practice. At the national level, it would require a powerful State. This would be so because, as a product of historical evolution, substantial differences have emerged in the control over productive resources. Without a powerful State it is difficult to envisage how this can be undone, and how new differences should be prevented in the future. A powerful State, however, has serious negative consequences for other human rights, such as individual freedoms and for political pluralism, and it is also inefficient in creating a base for general welfare.

It is also difficult to establish a powerful, distributive State in the first place. It will be resisted by the privileged, and in the process serious conflicts will emerge which will lead to extensive additional violations. Today, there is general awareness that the application of ideal principles of distributive justice is counterproductive to the evolution of welfare, partly because it creates disincentives to production and attendant dislocations to the point where the position of the least advantaged might in fact be lowered instead of raised towards the full-scale implementation of social-economic rights; secondly, because it is negative to capital accumulation by making it difficult to save for reinvestment, required in order to create the conditions for better future realization of economic and social rights.

There is now abundant evidence that when the economic system is centrally

---

themselves democratic at that time. Some contemporary authoritarian regimes – particularly the military regimes in Latin America of the 1970s and early 1980s – respected the civil rights of those who did not interfere with economic liberalism, but violated not only political rights and social and economic rights, but also the civil rights of persons involved in a quest for social justice. For a detailed study of the ideology and legal approach of these military regimes, see Jorge A. Tapio Valdes, *National Security, the Dual State and the Rule of Exception: A Study on the Strategocratic Political System* (1989), Rotterdam: Universiteitsdrukkerij.

planned and directed by the State (the "command economy") it leads to a decrease in creativity by individuals with an entrepreneurial spirit, reducing innovation and cluttering the processes of economic activity.

We also have to take into account that in a conflicting world, other national priorities, in particular security with its consequences for the arms race and militarization, will make it difficult to give sole attention to the organization of distributive justice.

At the *global* level, there are further difficulties. Global solidarity is at present very weak. National priorities are given much higher attention than global solidarity. Most, if not all, political systems are geared to respond to national demands and to national pressure groups, rather than to the needs by foreign groups of people, however poor they might be.

While the search for ideal distributive justice poses almost unsurmountable problems, and entails substantial threats to other human rights, this must not lead to the conclusion that economic and social rights can be neglected.

The Universal Declaration imposes at least a moral obligation, if not more, on all States to seek to realize social and economic rights included in it. Under Article 2 of the Covenant on Economic, Social and Cultural Rights, States have undertaken to take steps to the maximum of their available resources to achieve progressively the full realization of the economic and social rights in that Covenant.

Rich, industrialized countries have of course no justification to claim that they do not have the resources to ensure immediately economic and social rights for all, at least in the sense of ensuring the minimum subsistence rights.

But there are also steps which can be taken immediately even by poor countries. An interesting approach has been proposed by B'rd-Anders Andreassen, et al.[15] According to them, it is possible to operationalize a *minimum threshold for human rights realization* by means of country-specific thresholds measured by indicators tracking nutrition, infant mortality, disease frequency, life expectancy, income, unemployment and underemployment, and indicators relating to adequate food consumption.

The ways in which economic and social rights can be realized will vary with the nature of the national situation and the conditions applying there. There are great differences between industrial and post-industrial societies on the one hand, and subsistence cultures in rural settings on the other. Variations depend also on the economic and social history of the society concerned, with its habits and its stratification. In each State, different approaches are called for to realize in the most appropriate way economic and social rights.

As a minimum, all governments should establish a nation-wide system of identifying local needs and opportunities for the enjoyment of economic and

[15] B'rd-Anders Andreassen, Tor Sk'lnes, Alan Smith and Hugo Stokke, "Human Rights Performance in Developing Countries: The Case for a Minimum Threshold Approach", in Andreassen and Eide, *Human Rights in Developing Countries* (1988), Copenhagen: Akademisk Forlag, pp. 333–356.

social rights, and, in doing so, they should identify in particular the needs of groups which have the greatest difficulties in the enjoyment of these rights. Having done so, different governments may find different approaches most suitable to deal with the vulnerability thus identified. No blueprint, no general model will be applicable in all settings. We are much less in need of ideological proclamations, whether they stem from marxist, liberalist of other traditions, than in need of wise and well-informed mobilization of creativity in order to deal with the problems where they are greatest.

A well-developed, sophisticated application of economic and social rights should lay to rest some of the most profound ideological cleavages which have undermined international progress towards a comprehensive realization of human rights in their wide scope.

Industrial and post-industrial societies have developed their own particular solutions. In the Welfare States found in Western and Northern Europe, and to some extent in other parts of the world, there is at the basis a free market economy, but combined with the transfer of some part of the product, through direct and indirect taxation, in order to ensure equal opportunities for all. There are also some constraints on over-aggressive processes of private capital accumulation. These constraints result from social reform movements which have been made possible through wide and pluralistic political participation. The operation of free trade unions have also been essential in this connection. The outcome has therefore been a focus on equal opportunity combined with a social safety net for those who, for some reason or another, fail to secure their needs through their own endeavours.

This does not mean, however, that poverty does not exist in Welfare States. As pointed out, the social safety net often fails, in part because of a neglect to make serious efforts to mobilize for active creativity those who are presently among the destitute within the rich countries.

Nevertheless, the situation is much more difficult in many Third World countries, as pointed out by Andreassen, et al.: although many households achieve assurance of minimal well-being by autonomous activity or governmental provision, high percentages of various groups do not. Furthermore, the lack of assurance tends to fall disproportionately on certain deprived groups of which very low percentages of the group achieve minimal well-being levels, while very high percentages of other social categories are assured minimal basic needs.

The minimum threshold approach calls for the identification of the most deprived groups, not only according to conventional definitions of distinctions such as ethnic-cultural, racial, regional, and gender, but also distinctions defined by control over assets, for example the distinction between land-owners on the one hand and landless labourers or small-holding share-croppers on the other.

Distribution by sector is also needed in this approach. One aspect concerns the difference between rural and urban sectors. In development studies it has been pointed out that there is in many Third World countries a systematic pattern of urban bias in national development, to the detriment of the rural population. Most of the victims of non-fulfilment of economic and social rights are rural poor in Third World countries.

The minimum threshold approach can be developed in a much more detailed way. It is not the objective of this article to do so. It is necessary, however, to accept a pragmatic compromise between the ideal and the realistic. The ideal might call for equality for all, but realists point out that the powerful and the aggressive would continue to fight for their privileges. A pragmatic realization of human rights requires consistent vigilance to improve the conditions for the most vulnerable, without expecting dramatic and abrupt transformations of comprehensive and interlocking economic and social systems.

Strategies for the poor must seek to ensure for them an opportunity to take charge of their own destiny. This is often blocked by the more powerful and assertive members of society. Similarly, poverty in the Third World can be eradicated only through a combination of internal restructuring and an elimination of the obstacles imposed by the wealthy countries.

In particular, it is important to grasp the part played by military expenditure in international relations as well as national policies. Sophisticated arms are mainly produced in high-tech countries and sold at great cost to Third World countries, whose main possibility in exchange is to export agricultural products (not necessarily food, but also coffee, tea, flowers, etc.) at very low prices compared to the armaments they import. The exchange is profoundly destructive to the development of these countries. Wealthy countries nevertheless actively market armaments, and they are imported by Third World governments for prestige or for reasons of self-preservation. The "expenditure of death" should be turned into "expenditure on life" (public action to combat poverty), which could solve many of the problems now said to be insoluble owing to lack of resources (at the international as well as the national level).

4. International Responsibility and the Weakness of Supervision

The Universal Declaration, article 28 states that everyone is entitled to a social and international order in which all the rights contained in the Declaration can be fully realized. In accordance with the International Covenant on Economic, Social and Cultural Rights, article 2, the States Parties have undertaken to take steps, individually and through international assistance and cooperation, especially economic and technical, to achieve progressively the full realization of the rights contained in the Covenant. According to the same Covenant article 11 para 1, the States Parties shall take appropriate steps to ensure the realization of this right, recognizing to this effect the essential importance of international cooperation based on free consent.

In article 11 para 2, dealing with the fundamental right to be free from hunger, States again oblige themselves to take the steps, individually and through international collaboration, needed to achieve the aims set forth in that paragraph. They also undertake to ensure an equitable distribution of world food supplies in relation to need. In doing so, they shall take into account the problems of both food-importing and food-exporting countries.

To supervise the implementation of the obligations under the International Covenant, the Committee on Economic, Social and Cultural Rights reviews reports by States Parties to the Covenant and pursues a dialogue with them on more effective realization of these rights. Its work, however, is constrained by several factors: (i) the vagueness of the obligations flowing from economic and social rights; (ii) the unsatisfactory guidance to State Parties on how to report; (iii) the non-involvement of non-governmental organizations in monitoring economic, social and cultural rights; (iv) the inadequate cooperation with the specialized agencies; (v) the limited time and capacity available to the Committee. While improvement has been made over the last few years in seeking to make the obligations more precise, and in giving better guidance, the other issues still constitute serious constraints.

5. In Search of Strategies: Some Recommendations

Action by governments depends on the nature and strength of influences prevailing upon them. The relative neglect of economic and social rights, compared with civil and political, is not attributable to the special nature of the former set of rights but to the lack of attention to them by groups and organizations which consider themselves part of the human rights community. In part it is due to widespread misunderstanding about these rights, reinforced by past ideological confrontations. These misunderstandings and misrepresentations should not be allowed to be carried forward to the twenty-first century.

The most pressing task is to make more people understand what the issues are, and to encourage those who are negatively affected by developments to make use of these rights, which have been adopted at the international level and accepted through ratification by most States, including nearly all industrialized States, West and East. For the advancement of such understanding and encouragement, national non-governmental organizations, universities and research institutions dealing with development and human rights issues should now push for the adoption, and participate in the elaboration and implementation, of national plans for the realization of social and economic rights.

They should also disseminate information about international human rights standards and stimulate local and national debate in particular contexts on the implementation of these rights.

The specialized agencies (FAO, IFAD, WHO, the World Bank, UNESCO) and others should examine their mandates for their relevance and relationship to the economic and social rights and establish inter-divisional working groups or task forces for this purpose. They should intensify their presently very modest cooperation through special mechanisms for inter-agency cooperation in this field under the Administrative Committee on Coordination or existing coordinating mechanisms, and they should pay closer attention to the work of the human rights organs and be prepared to cooperate with them to develop and to operationalize the frameworks for promoting these rights.

International non-governmental organizations should support the efforts to realize the economic and social rights world-wide, through information, awareness-formation and action as appropriate, and base their efforts on the rights rather than on policy statements which are often vague and contentious. They should develop or strengthen their cooperation, on the basis of the right to food and other subsistence needs, with the specialized agencies, the Economic and Social Council and the Committee on Economic, Social and Cultural Rights.

States should draw up a framework for the realization of economic and social rights at the national level, built on local needs and opportunities, on lines suggested above, and take care to identify within such frameworks the needs of groups which have the greatest difficulties in their access to basic needs, and set specific goals to ensure sustainable satisfaction of such needs. It is essential to ensure popular participation in periodically assessing and analyzing local needs and opportunities, and facilitate input by the least privileged groups in society into the action plans that should follow from such assessment and analysis.

For purposes of international cooperation, they should specifically indicate the areas in which international assistance is required and spell out details of the assistance needed. States Parties to the Covenant should provide in their reports details of the national plans and of progress made and obstacles encountered in the implementation of them.

DAVID MacDONALD*

International Responsibility To Implement The Right to Food

1. Introduction

Today, we live in a world where if the total amount of world food production were divided by the world population, absolutely everybody, from pole to pole, would be quite well fed. But the reality is that everyday the numbers of those slipping into the condition of severe malnutrition and famine increase. In other words, we are looking at a deteriorating situation. That has to be an overlying motif of what we are trying to grapple with today.

2. The Right to Food

In 1941, in the context of the Second World War, President Roosevelt announced his four freedoms, one of them being freedom from want. There was at least the notion of a fundamental right to food. In the Universal Declaration the right to food was implicitly accepted as some kind of a normative right even though it was not spelled out. The International Covenants subsequently made it very clear that there was an absolute right to food. In article 11 of the 1966 International Covenant on Economic, Social and Cultural Rights, the state parties recognize the right of everyone to an adequate standard of living including adequate food, clothing and housing and for the continuous improvement of living conditions. In the meantime, over eighty countries have ratified the Covenant (and have as a consequence reported on a regular basis), thereby agreeing that they would in some measure live up to that right as a fundamental responsibility.

* P.C., Federal Government Member of Parliament, Toronto-Rosedale, Ontario, Canada.

K.E. Mahoney and P. Mahoney (eds.), Human Rights in the Twenty-first Century, 473–477.

3. Implementation Efforts

All of this is background to the landmark World Food Conference which took place in Rome in 1974. At that time I was, as I am today, a Member of the Canadian Parliament and, as such, took part in the conference in collaboration with non-governmental organizations. The NGO's monitored the behaviour of the Canadian Delegation at that Food Conference, were in daily contact with Canadian Members of Parliament, and from time to time during the course of several weeks questioned the Government about its behaviour, its activity and its statements at that Conference. This process worked extremely well. We were able to exert some influence at least in ensuring that Canada played an active and progressive role at the Conference. The establishment of a new declaration created some landmark principles. For example, the first principle said: "Every man, woman and child has the inalienable right to be free of hunger and malnutrition in order to develop fully and maintain his physical and mental facilities." And then it goes on to give greater detail as to how that is to occur.

When considering subsequent developments or the lack of them, it is important to remember the context in which the World Food Conference took place. From the early 1970's through to 1973, there was a growing international alarm about the shortage of food on a worldwide basis. Several books were published predicting the likelihood of global famine. In 1973, a kind of atmosphere had been created, especially as a result of some regional harvest failures, which triggered the call for the International Conference and the subsequent international agreement to the twelve fundamental principles as well as the establishment of two new international food agencies, International Fund for Agricultural Development, (IFAD), and the World Food Council.

In parts of Africa, IFAD has made some very important and fundamental differences for people because of its indigenous grassroots approach. This is especially true in some of the least developed countries. On the other hand, IFAD was really established without very much thought except that it would be an additional element within the general ambit of the food and agricultural organization of the World Food Program.

The other institution that was to be the central driving agency and that was to create a difference for the right to food and people's access to food, was the World Food Council. Unfortunately, however, we have seen nothing much more than a damp script from this institution. The World Food Council was proposed to be a regular meeting of Ministers at the most senior level of government to take into account the food situation in the global community. But the World Food Council has achieved precious little. It has not been given the kind of importance or credibility by members of governments and countries, including our own, that it required.

4. The Failure of Implementation Efforts

In 1984 the United States Congress decided that, ten years on, it would review the findings and the results of the World Food Conference. In its conclusions, it stated:

> "From the prospective of a decade later, two facts stand out. First, the availability of food in the world in comparison to demand is much greater than in 1984 than many analysts feared in 1974 that it might be. And second, the relative abundance of food has not reduced levels of malnutrition and hunger to the extent that many had assumed it would."

The Conference goals of ensuring within the decade, that no child should go to bed hungry, no family should fear for its next day's bread and no human being's future and capacity should be stunted by malnutrition, are goals which are as remote today as they were when they were enunciated in 1974. This is despite significant improvements in world food availability. It is essential to clarify particularly for people from developed, high-income countries that at this point in time we have no fundamental global food shortage. Rather, we have increased food production even more rapidly than the population of the world has increased. Another noteworthy fact is that the hunger situation is increasingly not only in Ethiopia or Sudan or Mozambique, but in countries like Canada. The dramatic increase in the number of food banks and the shortages they are confronted with are an awesome reminder that the phenomenon of hunger knows no borders.

It seems that in the mid 1970's, with the focus of the World Food Conference, with the debates at the United Nations on the new international economic order, and with the accessions to the International Covenant on Economic Rights, a high water mark was reached with respect to our governments understanding and awareness of the right-to-food issue. In Canada we witnessed an enormous amount of non-governmental activity directed towards the very same problems. Interesting organizations were established, including "Ten Days for World Development". This group, established by the five major churches spent three years looking at the food issue. The depth of analysis – which was not just confined to Canada extended as well to the United States and Europe – was extremely far-reaching. Major works were put forward under its auspices such as "Your Diet for a Small Planet" and "Food First" by Francis Moulapaîx and "How the Other Half Dies" by Susan George. These and other works formed the basis of a very powerful analysis. One might well ask, what has happened to all that? Where have all those people gone? What happened to the understanding that we seemed to be gaining a very large measure of fifteen years ago? I fear it was swept away by other interests, other pressures, other forces. Some we are readily aware of and perhaps others we need to go back and examine closely to fully understand.

In November of 1985, the Food & Agricultural Organization adopted what it described as a World Food Security Compact. While it was not legally binding, it set out moral criteria and fixed lines of action in order to help governments achieve the common objective of improving world security and eliminating hunger and malnutrition. My understanding and observation of what has occurred over the last fifteen to twenty years is that only in times of international crisis do countries even attempt to come to grips with issues of food rights and responsibility. By and large, countries of the world have not questioned the nature of food distribution systems or how they operate on a sustained basis. Over the last decade or so, individual analysis and conferences have examined large international distribution systems but not in any kind of sustained fashion.

We do know that much of the international food economy today is the product of a very elaborate transnational economic system. In many instances, the economic reality of food trading is fundamental for the economic situations of countries, Canada and the United States included. At best social issues and human rights responsibilities become peripheral in that context. If the question, is there a human rights aspect about food? is asked, the answer may be, of course there is. But when the questions as to operational reality are asked, there will be a very long pause in the conversation.

5. The Need for Information and Education

The reality faced by an increasing number of people totally vulnerable to food shortages must be much more closely examined. For example, if the world had been better informed about the situation in Saharan Africa in the late 1960's, through the 1970's and 1980's, it would not have been surprised by the announcement in 1984 of an African famine threatening some thirty countries, a dozen in a perilous way.

When I was asked to be Canadian Emergency Co-ordinator/African Famine (84–86), in the fall 1984, the figures were very stark indeed. We were told about the 150 million people in Africa who were at risk, 30 million people in perilous risk. But if anyone had been following the situation from the late 1960's they would have been able to predict with absolute accuracy what was to occur. In fact there were many warnings issued by various agencies and individuals. But it was only when the sophisticated "western media" decided to "discover" the African famine in 1984 that an outpouring of response and emotional fervour, the like of which has rarely been seen in this country, took place.

There is a certain irony to all of this because now we are able to look in hindsight at what was going on with respect to the economic situation for all of the afflicted African countries. Beginning at exactly the same time as we were in theory responding to the African famine by sending aid for the development of these newly independent countries we were increasingly asking African countries to repay debts and export capital over the amount that they were actually receiving. On one hand, by the end of the 1980's developing countries were receiving some eight to ten million dollars overall in external aid but on the other, close to fifty billion dollars was being sent back to large development organizations, banks and institutions to repay earlier disbursements. That was the upside down, unbelievable, inhumane way in which we responded to the economic rights that were enunciated, ratified and incorporated in the mid 1970's. The result is not easy to explain in rational or human terms. But one indisputable explanation is that those who believe that food rights are inalienable are no more than a small group; and, what is more, an unequal lobby pitted against a myriad of self interests and reinforcements within economic systems in both developed and developing countries which see food essentially as a main instrument of economic activity as opposed to an instrument of human self fulfilment. To those like myself who come from the developed societies of Europe or North America, a simple half hour in front of our television screens looking at the reaffirmation of those notions of food will make this reality absolutely clear.

How then do we break out of this reality? What must we do? To simply go on reinforcing in some kind of abstract way the basic integrity of food rights is not the answer. First, food rights must be contemplated within the much larger issues of economic rights, self-determination, participation and equality. Secondly, people must be able to actualize food rights. This can be achieved in a variety of ways, one of which is recognizing the fundamental importance of literacy and its relationship to access to information, access to power and access to communications. Rights of participation and accountability can only be fully realized with some fundamental norms of literacy.

6. Conclusion

Crisis management is not a very good way of dealing with global hunger. What happens during a crisis is management of damage limitation. The victims benefit the least. A better approach is to plan and work towards a resolution of food problems between periods of crisis. Those who are prepared to move the issue of food rights forward must form larger coalitions. It is the larger coalitions that are crucial. New coalitions are possible today. Those concerned with the basic rights of humanity be they environmentalists, equality seekers or food rights activists share a vision of rights to the global commons that is compatible with human life, of water that is safe to drink, of a land that is still arable, not resistant to national borders or municipal city states. This could be among the most important opportunities to ensure that the right to food is finally met and realized. Dr. Lesley Cook once said,

> "People have an inalienable right to food. They must, they need, they want food but they want bread and they want bread with dignity."[1]

Bread with dignity is a fundamental issue.

[1] Presented during a speech by Dr. Leslie Cook, at the General Council of the United Church, 1964, Newfoundland. United Church Archives.

SECTION IV(b): THE RIGHT TO HEALTH

LYNN SMITH*

Introduction

In Canada, there is a universal State-paid health care system which has led to a popular belief in the existence of a "right" to health care. The enforceability of such a right is beginning to be tested in various ways. Under-financing in the health care system has led to claims that inaccessibility of care to individuals has endangered life or health, and consequently to attempts to sue governments for failing to provide adequate health care. As well, governments have acted in various ways that have the effect of limiting women's access to a particular form of health care – safe medical abortion. Legal challenges have been brought against some of those actions and against some actions in the private sphere that limit access to health care, such as the exclusion of pregnant women from employment disability plans.

Virginia Leary discusses what a right to health would mean in the context of human rights; whether it can be translated into legal, operational terms; whether it is a legal right or a mere moral one and how the right to health care can be enforced and implemented.

Social rights, including the right to health care, have been afforded secondary status in international law in many respects. Therefore, attempts to spell out the implications of generalized guarantees of a right to health are worthwhile. Not merely health care, but health status should be considered.

Leary contrasts the Canadian and American health care systems, saying the Canadian health care system illustrates a "rights" perspective, while that of the United States illustrates a perspective which views health as a "good" to be distributed on a market basis. She points out that a "rights" perspective does not necessarily lead to the conclusion that everyone will be provided optimum medical care in all circumstances. However, a right to health care does imply that there will not be discrimination in the distribution of available health care facilities. It also implies that States have an obligation to regulate actions which injure their populations, such as permitting the merchandising of infant formula in developing countries.

* Dean, Faculty of Law, University of British Columbia, Vancouver, British Columbia, Canada.

K.E. Mahoney and P. Mahoney (eds.), Human Rights in the Twenty-first Century, 479–480.

The complexity of the issues (such as possible conflicts of rights where desires of health care personnel conflict with the needs of the population) and the traditional human rights focus on political and legal rights should not deter attempts to develop a meaningful right to health care in international law.

Daniel Wikler's paper puts the right to health care in the United States at the level of a moral ideal. The delivery of health care in the United States emphasizes privatization and the market place as its basic concepts. He describes a system "awash" in money which denies many of the sickest patients access to doctors or underutilized hospitals. Wikler cautions any nation moving towards health care financing against adopting the American model. His position is that health care systems should cater to human need, not profit and argues for community planning and health policy based on human rights.

The last paper in the section discusses the right to health care in quite a different way than the preceding two papers. Rhoda Howard sees the protection of the right to health including not only a socially acceptable minimum level of health care, but also state protection of women against the degradation and violence that many "cultural" customs require. She explains the connections between women's self-mutilation, the social degradation of women as a group and detrimental health consequences.

Social degradation is defined as the treatment of categories of people as inferiors, deserving of lesser respect than others or of no respect at all. The process of social degradation involves domination of the category of people who are dishonoured. One of the most effective methods of domination is persuading degraded categories of people that they are inferior, dirty and polluting, and deserving of a degraded status. This process has been applied to many categories of people including women, Jews, blacks, and homosexual men or women.

Subordination of women is universal in all existing societies, and female self-mutilation is commonly observed. The mutilating "beauty" practices of women in North American society include wearing restrictive clothing and shoes, use of cosmetics, undergoing cosmetic surgery and liposuction, and habitual dieting. Some of these practices can seem trivial or absurd, but the phenomenon of degradation they stem from is real. Further, the practices are often dangerous to life or health and show the health costs of the social degradation of women as a dishonoured group.

However, the consequences of the subordination of women and other dishonoured groups escape an analysis that focuses on the formal aspects of inequality in the economic or political sphere. The degradation of women must be recognized in order to counteract simplistic arguments for "group" rights that would leave intact that system of degradation. Internally entrenched social injustice must be replaced by new types of communities in which there are no ritually degraded categories of people.

VIRGINIA A. LEARY*

Implications of a Right to Health

1. Introduction

The term "right to health" suggests many questions. This panel is entitled "The Right to Health Care"; why have I chosen then to use the phrase "The Right to Health" in my presentation, dropping the term "care"? Is there a difference between the two expressions? If so, what do we mean when we refer to the "right to health" in the context of human rights? Is it just a slogan or is it a concept that can be translated into legal, operational terms? Does it refer to a moral right only or is it a legal right? Can it be made operational at the international level? How can the "right to health" be enforced or implemented? Is it unrealistic to speak of the right to health since no person and no government can guarantee good health to an individual? Does it mean that everyone has the right to unlimited health care?

Despite the complexity of such questions, claims of a right to health are increasingly heard. They are enunciated both as moral demands and as legal claims based on national constitutions and laws or on international human rights treaties; they give voice to the perception that issues of health are not solely technical issues but concern issues of human dignity and that a "rights approach" to health issues has practical consequences. But the questions remain. The phrase "right to health", perhaps more than other concepts in human rights, is "replete with ambiguities".[1] As Tom Campbell, the Scottish legal philosopher, has pointed out, "working out the specific implications of general statements of human rights is a necessary move if the rhetoric of human rights is to have a major impact on the resolution of social problems".[2]

This paper is a preliminary effort to examine some of the implications of the general statement of the right to health contained in international human rights instruments. Since the right has been proclaimed in international treaties, it is

* Professor, Faculty of Law, State University of New York at Buffalo, New York, USA.

[1] Fein, "Economic Aspects of the Right to Health Care", in R. Dupuy (ed.) *The Right to Health as a Human Right* (1979), Workshop, Hague Academy of International Law, p. 215.

[2] Campbell, "Introduction: Realizing Human Rights", in Campbell, Goldberg, McLean and Mullen (eds.) *Human Rights From Rhetoric to Reality* (1986), p. 3.

K.E. Mahoney and P. Mahoney (eds.), Human Rights in the Twenty-first Century, 481–493.

a legal right under international law, but if we are concerned that it becomes a right in action and not just a right "on the books", the content of the right must be elaborated, the duties and obligations implicit in the right must be clarified and means of implementing it must be developed. These tasks await human rights scholars if the rhetoric of the right to health is to have an impact on the resolution of contemporary issues concerned with health. This paper examines some of the issues concerning the right to health and suggests issues that warrant more extended consideration. It represents preliminary work in an ongoing effort by the author to grapple with the concepts of "rights" and "health"

The focus of the paper is on *international* aspects of the right to health. Much of the literature on the right to health or the right to health care in developed countries focuses on *national* issues of concern in rich countries, such as the right to the most advanced and expensive treatment and equipment or complex bio-ethical issues. Important as these issues are, they are not dealt with in this paper. In the international context, the most important issues centre on the fundamental problems such as freedom of a population from common communicable diseases, access to a minimum degree of medical care, and inequities and inequalities in health status. It is these issues in the international context with which this paper is primarily concerned.

2. The "Rights" Approach to Health Issues

Does approaching issues of health from the perspective of health as a human right make a difference in the manner in which these issues are resolved? In a presentation under the auspices of the Columbia University Center for Human Rights, Professor Louis Henkin clarified why it is important to look at health issues from a rights perspective.[3] According to Henkin, the "rights" approach begins with the individual and focuses on his or her welfare. It sees the welfare of the individual as an object of morality and as a legitimate purpose of a just society. It includes the concept of individual entitlement. Other approaches, such as the utilitarian or paternalistic or market approach have frequently been used in considering issues of health. The utilitarian approach would organize health care on the basis that brings the greatest good for the greatest number; the emphasis is on society and not on the individual and rights. The paternalistic or professional perspective regards the individual as a beneficiary, receiving advice and assistance from medical professionals who are regarded as the most competent to make health care decisions for individuals. The market perspective regards health care as a commodity to be sold as any other good and not as a public good to be distributed equitably to all.

Human rights are defined as justified claims to freedoms, immunities and

[3] Henkin, "Health and Medical Care in a 'Rights' Society", Center for the Study of Human Rights, Columbia University, 1982, pp. 1–23.

benefits that the individual has upon his or her society and which society must respect and ensure. Legal and philosophical writings contain technical discussions of the concept of rights, but the language of human rights in normal use is not confined to technical definitions. It is used to express, in a powerful form, the fundamental importance of a particular claim. Tom Campbell again has expressed this well. He writes that the rhetoric of human rights draws on the moral resources of our belief in the significance of our underlying common humanity; human rights discourse then serves both as a potent source of radical critiques of actual social arrangements and also as a powerful basis for working out and presenting alternative institutional practices.[4]

The rights perspective has many implications for health issues, but one aspect is particularly important: the principle of equality. A fundamental premise of all human rights, in the language of the Universal Declaration of Human Rights, is the "dignity and worth of the human person and the equal rights of men and women". Bills of rights and international human rights treaties speak of "all human beings" and refer to "everyone" as possessing rights. All human rights catalogues include non-discrimination as an essential element of rights. Equal treatment of every human person is the most basic principle of the concept of human rights.

If the right to health is considered as a fundamental human right, significant differences in access to health care and the health status of individuals must be seen as violations of the principle of equality. But what is the reality regarding access to health care and the health status of various populations? We hardly need to be reminded of it. Not long ago, the *Wall Street Journal* reported that of all the grim statistics from the Third World, the most telling surely is this: one child in nine dies during the first year after birth. The 1990 World Development Report stated that each year in developing countries ten million young adults die and that in most developing countries the chances at age 15 of surviving to 60 is between 50 and 75 percent as against 85 percent in developed countries. Within developed countries there are frequently enormous differences between the health status of various groups of individuals. A report prepared by the Congressional Budget Office in the United States some ten years ago revealed shocking statistics on differences in the health status between white and non white Americans, specifically blacks, native Americans and orientals. It reported that non whites were more than three times as likely to die of hypertension than white Americans in the same age group, were twice as likely to die from diabetes and nearly four times as likely to die of chronic kidney diseases. In the United States, one of the richest countries in the world, 37 million Americans are without medical insurance, while many others enjoy the very best medical care that can be bought. The market approach to health issues prevails over a rights approach. In the language of Tom Campbell, the human rights approach should lead us to make a radical critique of the social arrangements which perpetuate such injustices.

[4] See note 2, *supra*.

3. "Right to Health" or "Right to Health Care"?

In the literature on rights and health issues, the terms "right to health", "right to health care" and "right to health protection" are all employed. The choice of one or the other of these terms is not a mere issue of terminology; each term implies a specific meaning; consideration of the distinctions assists in clarifying what is meant by the "right to health" in international human rights law. While the three phrases can be, and sometimes are, used to convey the same meaning, more frequently they convey distinct meanings. The "right to health care" is the most commonly used term in national literature on human rights. It normally designates the right to medical services and is not usually considered as encompassing issues related to health protection and economic and social conditions. The "right to health protection" is the term favoured by the editors of a Pan-American Health Organization Study, referred to below, and is also a term used in national constitutions and legislation.[5]

In international human rights literature, the term "right to health" is more common than either of the other two terms. Despite the apparently greater specificity and clarity conveyed by the right to health care or the right to health protection, I have chosen to use the term "right to health" since it is increasingly used in the context of international human rights.

In 1978, a workshop on "The Right to Health as a Human Right" was organized by the Hague Academy of International Law (henceforth "Hague Workshop").[6] A recent scholarly publication of the Pan-American Health Organization is entitled "The Right to Health in the Americas" (henceforth "PAHO Study")[7] and, in an article in that volume on international human rights, Judge Thomas Buergenthal of the Inter-American Court of Human Rights, refers frequently to the "right to health".[8] The Additional Protocol of the American Convention of Human Rights in the Area of Economic, Social and Cultural Rights (Protocol of San Salvador) entitles Article 10, "Right to Health".[9] Article 5(e) of the Convention on the Elimination of All Forms of Racial Discrimination refers to "the right to health".

Yet use of the phraseology "right to health" is criticized by some scholars as imprecise and even absurd on the grounds that good health cannot be guaranteed by human means. It has also been pointed out that more extensive phraseology is used in the International Covenant on Economic, Social and

[5] See paragraph 11 of the Preamble to the 1946 French Constitution, which guarantees "health protection" to all citizens.

[6] See note 1, *supra*.

[7] H.L. Fuenzalida-Puelma/S. Connor (eds.) *The Right to Health in the Americas: A Comparative Constitutional Study*, (1989), Scientific Publication No. 509, Pan-American Health Organization, Washington, D.C.

[8] T. Buergenthal, "International Human Rights Law and Institutions", in PAHO Study, ibid., pp. 3–16.

[9] Done at San Salvador, November 14, 1988, 28 International Legal Materials (1989), p.156.

Cultural Rights.[10] Article 12(1) of that Covenant reads:

> "The States Parties to the present Covenant recognize the right of everyone to the enjoyment of the highest attainable standard of physical and mental health."

The addition of the word "attainable" makes clear that States Parties are not required to guarantee that all citizens be healthy – an absurd proposition. The Constitution of the World Health Organization (WHO) contains similar language:

> "The enjoyment of the highest attainable standard of health is one of the fundamental rights of every human being without distinction of race, religion, political belief, economic or social conditions."

In international human rights literature and in recent human rights instruments this lengthy phraseology is shortened to the "right to health"; that expression should be interpreted in the sense of the Economic Covenant and the WHO Constitution as signifying "the highest attainable standard of health" and should not be given the absurd connotation of guaranteeing health to each individual.

Professor Ruth Roemer entitles an essay in the PAHO Study "The Right to Health Care" rather than the Right to Health, stating that "everyone cannot be assured perfect health, nor could a right to health be an enforceable right". She defines the "right to health care" extensively to include a comprehensive range of services such as "protective environmental services, prevention and health promotion and therapeutic services as well as related actions in sanitation, environmental engineering, housing and social welfare".[11] Given such a broad definition, the specificity implied in the concept of the "right to health care" is lost. In addition, the problem of creating enforceable rights in all these domains suggests the same problems that appear to be involved in making the more general term "right to health" an enforceable right. Other writers use the term "right to health care" more specifically to relate solely to the provision of medical services.[12]

Professor Roemer's fundamental objection appears to be that the term "right to health" suggests an absurd proposition to most persons. Increasing use of the term and an understanding that it is a short-hand expression for the right to the highest attainable standard of health may dispel this objection in time. We have become accustomed to other short-hand expressions in the field of human rights, such as the "right of association", the "right to work" and the "right to a fair trial". The full meaning of these phrases is not clear from the short-hand expressions, yet these phrases have become consecrated and acquired a generally accepted meaning through frequent use and elaboration.

[10] See J. Marie, "Droits de l'homme et abus de langage", *La Croix* (November 20, 1981), p. 2.

[11] Roemer, "The Right to Health Care", in PAHO Study, note 7, *supra*.

[12] See for example, Dougherty, *American Health Care. Realities, Rights, and Reforms* (1988).

Despite its increasing use, the term "right to health" is not yet as commonplace as the terms immediately referred to, but intrinsically there is no reason why, like these other expressions, it may not acquire meaning and elaboration through use.

The editors of the PAHO Study, in turn, express doubts about the scope and accuracy of the phrase "right to health care" used by Professor Roemer and many others, finding it too restrictive. They prefer the phraseology the "right to health protection", which they consider the more inclusive term, encompassing not only the right to some minimum medical care but the right to healthy conditions, defined as "the purity and cleanliness of water, air, waste disposal.., foods, drugs, cosmetics, etc.". Ultimately, however, they opt, as I have, for the "right to health" for "the sake of convenience and to conform to standard usage in human rights texts...[b]ut the meaning is... a right to health protection, to health care and healthy conditions".[13] The term "right to health" rather than "right to health care" can, however, be interpreted as *excluding* a right to health care. States have long recognized an obligation to protect their population from obvious risks and hazards to their health. Governmental acts to protect against communicable diseases, immunization measures and fluoridation of water are examples of such protective health measures. The right to health interpreted in this manner can be considered a negative right; the government prevents certain actions which cause harm to citizens. The more controversial issue is whether the right to health, as is the case with other social rights, requires positive action by the government, namely the provision of medical care to citizens, particularly those who cannot afford to pay for such care.[14] During the drafting of the right to health article in the Convention on the Rights of the Child, which was recently entered into force,[15] the United States delegate was willing to accept the concept of the "right to health" but not the right to "health care", thus suggesting that the "right to health" did not encompass a right to health care.[16]

4. Right to Health in Human Rights Instruments

(1) Implicit in Concept of "Right to Life"

The Universal Declaration of Human Rights and the general treaties on human rights, such as the International Covenant on Civil and Political Rights, the European, African and Inter-American human rights conventions, all include

[13] See note 7, *supra*, p. 599.

[14] For a discussion of the use of the concept of the right to health as not encompassing a right to health care, see Beaucham and Faden, "The Right to Health and the Right to Health Care", *The Journal of Medicine and Philosophy* (1979), vol. 4, no. 2, p. 124.

[15] Convention on the Rights of the Child, Adopted by the UN General Assembly on 20 November 1989, entered into force 2 September, 1990.

[16] 1985 Report of the Working Group on the Convention on the Rights of the Child, p. 4.

the "right to life" as one of the fundamental rights of the human person. It does not strain imagination to consider the "right to health" as implicit in the right to life. While it is frequently contended that the right to life forbids only arbitrary deprivation of life, this restrictive interpretation has not met with general acceptance. The Human Rights Committee has interpreted the right to life provision in Article 6 of the International Covenant on Civil and Political Rights more broadly:

> "Moreover, the Committee has noted that the right to life has been too often narrowly interpreted. The expression "inherent right to life" cannot properly be understood in a restrictive manner, and the protection of this right requires that States adopt positive measures. In this connexion, the Committee considers that it would be desirable for States to take all possible measures to reduce infant mortality and to increase life expectancy, especially in adopting measures to eliminate malnutrition and epidemics."[17]

This interpretation by the Human Rights Committee, charged with monitoring the Civil and Political Covenant, may be considered an elaboration and development of the right to life provision in human rights instruments, including Article 3 of the Universal Declaration which provides that "Everyone has the right to life...". Thus, even in the absence of an explicit recognition of the "right to health" as such, as contained for example in the International Covenant on Economic, Social and Cultural Rights, it may reasonably be argued that the right to health, at least as it concerns efforts to reduce infant mortality and increase life expectancy, is implicit in the "right-to-life" provision of the Universal Declaration. Thus, States which have not yet ratified a treaty specifying an explicit right to health would be considered as bound to certain obligations of the right to health by the "right-to-life" provisions of the Universal Declaration, many of the provisions of which have become customary international law. The right to life is clearly a provision that may currently be considered binding on all States by virtue of customary international law. The obligations resulting from the concept of the right to health implicit in the right-to-life provisions require, of course, further elaboration and clarification, just as the concept of the right to life itself.

(2) Related Provisions

Other provisions relating to the right to health in the Universal Declaration and the International Covenant on Civil and Political Rights are the prohibition of torture or cruel, inhuman or degrading treatment, and the subjection of persons to medical or scientific experimentation without their free consent. Also,

[17] General Comments of the Human Rights Committee under Article 40, paragraph 4 of the International Covenant on Civil and Political Rights, General Comment on Article 6, Report of the Human Rights Committee to the Thirty-Seventh Session of the General Assembly, A/37/40, pp. 93–94. For a discussion of the need for a broad interpretation of the right to life, see B.G. Ramcharan, *The Right to Life in International Law* (1985), p. 6.

Article 25 of the Universal Declaration provides that "everyone has the right to a standard of living adequate for the health and well-being of himself and his family, including... medical care", and Article 24 provides that "everyone has the right to rest and leisure, including reasonable limitations of working hours and periodic holidays with pay". Article 10 of the International Covenant on Economic, Social and Cultural Rights (ESC Covenant) states that "special protection should be accorded to mothers during a reasonable period before and after childbirth" and that the employment of children and young persons "in work harmful to their morals or health or dangerous to life or likely to hamper their normal development" should be punishable by law.

Other international conventions, not strictly human rights instruments, contain obligations relating to health, including a number of international labour conventions on health and working conditions, as well as the Geneva Conventions on humanitarian law relating to health aspects of the treatment of prisoners and the civilian population during armed conflict.

Issues concerning health are also being increasingly considered in relation to environmental issues.[18]

(3) Explicit Recognition in International Instruments

While the provisions previously mentioned refer to various aspects of the right to health, they stop short of an explicit recognition of the "right to health". Nevertheless, they assist in interpreting the content of the right explicitly mentioned in other international instruments. The most important recognition of the right to health in an international convention is contained in Article 12 of the ESC Covenant. The Article not only refers to the right generally, but refers to steps to be taken to implement the right. It warrants citation in full:

> "1. The States Parties to the present Covenant recognize the right of everyone to the enjoyment of the highest attainable standard of physical and mental health.
>
> 2. The steps to be taken by the States Parties to the present Covenant to achieve the full realization of this right shall include those necessary for:
>
> a) The provision for the reduction of the stillbirth-rate and of infant mortality and for the healthy development of the child;
> b) The improvement of all aspects of environmental and industrial hygiene;
> c) The prevention, treatment and control of epidemic, endemic, occupational and other diseases;
> d) The creation of conditions which would assure to all medical service and medical attention in the event of sickness.

[18] See P.M. Dupuy, "Le droit à la santé et la protection de l'environnement", in *The Right to Health as a Human Right*, note 1, *supra*, pp. 340–389.

Two other recent conventions contain not only explicit recognition of the right to health, but also list in more detail than the Covenant the steps to be taken to implement the right. Article 24 of the Convention on the Rights of the Child provides that States Parties "recognize the right of the child to the enjoyment of the highest attainable standard of health" and lists a number of measures to be taken by States to implement the right, including diminishing infant and child mortality, the provision of necessary medical assistance and health care, with an emphasis on the development of primary health care, combating disease and malnutrition, ensuring pre- and post-natal health care for mothers, provision of information on child health and nutrition and the advantages of breast-feeding, developing preventive health care, and measures to abolish traditional practices prejudicial to the health of children.

The Children's Convention has been widely praised as one of the better drafted human rights instruments and the provision on the right to health is far superior to that in the International Covenant. The influence of the work of the World Health Organization is demonstrated by the emphasis on primary health care, preventive care and the provision of information concerning breast-feeding, although the failure of the WHO to participate actively in the drafting of the Convention has been criticized.[19]

In 1988, the Organization of American States adopted an Additional Protocol to the American Convention on Human Rights in the Area of Economic, Social and Cultural Rights (Protocol of San Salvador). As of June, 1991, the Protocol was not yet in force. Article 10 on the Right to Health is well drafted, apparently thanks to the influence of the Pan-American Health Organization. It states more directly than the ESC Covenant or the Children's Convention that "everyone shall have the right to health, understood to mean the enjoyment of the highest level of physical, mental and social well-being". It provides that the States Parties agree to recognize health as a public good and to take such measures as the provision of primary health care, extension of the benefits of health services to all individuals subject to the State's jurisdiction, education on health problems and adds a new and significant measure not expressed in other instruments, namely "[s]atisfaction of the health needs of the highest risk groups and of those whose poverty makes them the most vulnerable".

Other instruments such as the Convention on the Elimination of All Forms of Racial Discrimination and the African Charter on Human and Peoples' Rights include provisions on the right to health. The European Social Charter refers to the protection of health.

The detailed measures referred to in the ESC Covenant, the Children's Convention and the Protocol of San Salvador provide considerable guidance as to the content to be given to the concept of the right to health. Further clarification will be provided in the future through the reporting systems set up by all three instruments. Although the reporting systems for the Children's

[19] See Section on the WHO and the Right to Health below.

Convention and the Protocol of San Salvador are not yet functioning, we presently have the benefit of the experience of the Committee on Economic, Social and Cultural Rights to which States Parties to the ESC Covenant must report on the implementation of its provisions. In 1990, the Committee adopted Guidelines regarding information which should be included in reports by States Parties.[20] The Guidelines request States to provide information on health statistics and health measures relating to the infant mortality rate, life expectancy and measures taken to improve the health of vulnerable and disadvantaged groups. The Guidelines also request information on the proportion of the national budget attributed to health and whether the State has adopted a health policy. States are requested to furnish copies of recent reports made to WHO. The WHO indicators of health status have been used in the drafting of the Guidelines.

5. World Health Organization and the Right to Health

The attitude of the WHO to the concept of the right to health has been ambivalent. On the one hand, a number of WHO documents refer to the right to health; on the other hand, no consistent or serious effort appears to have been made by the WHO to emphasize the concept of health as a right. This attitude is in contrast to that of the Pan-American Health Organization, the Regional Office of the WHO for the Americas, which has contributed in a substantial manner to the conceptualization of the right, particularly with the recent publication of the excellent PAHO study, referred to earlier, on *The Right to Health in the Americas*. Although Article 12 of the ESC Covenant is based on a proposal of the WHO, the participation of the WHO in the drafting of the provisions on health in the international instruments has not been outstanding. A recent exception has been the participation of a representative of the WHO at meetings of the Committee on Economic, Social and Cultural Rights and the useful contributions made by that representative to the drafting of the Guidelines for government reports relating to Article 12 on the right to health.[21]

The unfortunate absence of the WHO during the discussion of the proposed article on handicapped children in the recent Convention on the Rights of the Child has been remarked, as well as the failure of the Organization to take an active part in discussions concerning the drafting of the article on the right to health.[22] The excellent article on the right to health in the Protocol of San Salvador can be credited to the Pan-American Health Organization and the

[20] See Guidelines, ECOSOE Official Documents, Supplement No. 3, Annex IV, 1991.

[21] See Summary Records, Committee on Economic, Social and Cultural Rights, E/C.12/1990/SR.48, 17 December, 1990.

[22] International Children's Rights Monitor, 1984, vol. 1, No. 4, p. 13. See also the following quote from the International Children's Rights Monitor, 1985, vol. 5, No. 4, p. 4, relating to the participation of the WHO in the Technical Review of the Convention, late in the drafting process:

similarly excellent article in the Children's Convention can be attributed to the States participating in the drafting and the non-governmental organizations who made important contributions to the final content of the Convention. Since the entry into force of the Children's Convention, however, the Maternal and Child Health and Family Planning Division of the WHO has taken an active role in plans for monitoring of the Convention.[23]

The WHO has employed the phraseology "right to health" in a number of WHO documents. F. Gutteridge has written,

> "The Technical Preparatory Committee for a World Health Organization established by ECOSOC and which drew up the text of the draft WHO Constitution had proposed that "health" as such should be stated to be the subject of a human right, in a statement that "The right to health is one of the fundamental rights to which every human being is entitled". This proposal was not retained by the International Health Conference in 1946, but since that time the WHO definition has often been spoken of as the right to health, both in the United Nations and in WHO itself. Thus, on two occasions, in 1979 and 1977 the World Health Assembly proclaimed that health (without qualification) is a human right. The same assertion was also made by the International Conference on Primary Health Care held at Alma-Ata in 1978 (Alma-Ata 1978: Primary Health Care, Geneva, 1978).[24]

The reality remains that the WHO, with the exception of the recent work concerning the monitoring of the Children's Convention, has shown little interest in defining the content of a right to health as an international human right. The Organization undertakes little normative activity and has not been greatly interested in the normative activity of other organizations with regard to health issues. It has also given little attention to human rights issues, apparently regarding them as unduly political and not within the technical mandate of the Organization. It is only recently with the development of the WHO Global Program for AIDS and the close relationship between non-discrimination and the eradication of AIDS that officials of the Organization have developed contacts with non-governmental human rights organizations and shown concern for human rights issues. Given this history of apparent lack of concern with human rights issues, it was a pleasant surprise to note the frequent references to human rights and to social justice and equity in the recent

---

"[The Technical Review] contained irrelevant notes from the World Health Organization which essentially confined itself to proclaiming – in a slightly paranoid manner and for reasons best known to itself – that such and such an article dealt with matters of concern to it. The WHO, of course, had until then been noticeably absent from the Working Group meetings, including the one that discussed what used to be Article 12b as relating, precisely, to health."

[23] See Convention on the Rights of the Child, A Framework for Monitoring of Implementation Using Data Reported to the World Health Organization, WHO, Maternal and Child Health and Family Planning, Geneva, May, 1991.

[24] Unpublished manuscript, F. Gutteridge, "Implementation of the International Covenant on Economic, Social and Cultural Rights by the World Health Organization."

Statement of Hiroshi Nakajima, WHO Director-General, to the WHO Executive Board at its Eighty Seventh Session in January, 1991.[25]

The work of the WHO, however, has not been without substantial influence on the efforts of others to define the right to health. The emphasis on primary health care and on preventive health measures as aspects of the right to health, included in several of the international instruments mentioned previously, owes much to the development of the WHO program of Health for All by the Year 2000 and its outstanding work in the promotion of infant and maternal health, particularly its work on the promotion of breast-feeding. The concept of Primary Health Care is of major importance for the implementation of the right to health internationally.

The WHO has not limited its work in this area to general exhortations, but has formulated specific strategies for the attainment of health for all with reference to guiding principles and essential issues and has developed indicators for monitoring progress towards the accomplishment of Health for All by the Year 2000. The guiding principles and indicators developed by the WHO should be used by the monitoring organizations of the various human rights conventions and by non-governmental organizations as references for evaluating national implementation of the right to health.[26]

6. Conclusion: Unresolved Issues

This paper has referred to some of the implications of the right to health, but space and time has permitted only a few of the implications to be raised here. Many issues remain to be considered by scholars and activists. The relationship of the right to health to other human rights, for example, is an important concern. Will doctors and nurses be required to work in remote or rural regions in order to provide health care to populations who would otherwise be without such care? Does this constitute forced labour?

The subject of limitations in the name of protection of health calls for additional analysis. The protection of public health is listed in most human rights conventions as permitting limitations on other human rights. In the case of AIDS, the WHO has been concerned with the unwarranted discrimination and limitations on the rights of persons infected with the HIV virus.

Lack of financial resources is too frequently invoked as a reason for the failure to implement social rights, including the right to health. The provision of medical care, just as the creation of a functioning judiciary system, does require the expenditure of funds. But much can be done to promote the right to

[25] WHO, EB87/INF. DOC./9, 14 January 1991.

[26] See WHO, "Health for All" Series: Primary Health Care, 1978; Formulating Strategies for Health for All by the Year 2000, 1979; Global Strategy for Health for All by the Year 2000, 1981; Development of Indicators for Monitoring Progress Towards Health for all by the Year 2000, 1981; Health Programme Evaluation, Guiding Principles, 1981; Plan of Action for Implementing the Global Strategy for Health for All, 1982.

health by preventing certain practices. The WHO International Code of Marketing Practices for Breastmilk Substitutes is an interesting case-study of an effort to forbid practices which are detrimental to infant health. Education in the requirements of good health and governmental and private actions to promote healthy personal habits could make substantial contributions to health in all countries. Financial problems involved in providing widespread health care, even in industrialized countries, have surfaced with special acuity recently, making it all the more essential that emphasis be placed on prevention rather than solely on cure.

The most significant implication of the "right to health", and the aspect that should be emphasized in conclusion, is that health care and health status have now been repeatedly recognized by the international community as important human rights issues. It is no longer possible to view health care and health status as only financial or market issues. It remains for those of us in the field of international human rights to continue to work out the many practical implications.

DANIEL WIKLER*

Privatization and Human Rights in Health Care: Notes from the American Experience

1. Introduction

Health care is not officially recognized as a human right in the United States, which alone among the major industrialized nations has no comprehensive system of health care delivery and insurance. Moreover, the vast majority of Americans, other than present and former soldiers, receive their health care from private hospitals, clinics, and physicians. In the strict sense of the term, therefore, the American health care system has not been "privatized", since it has been private from its beginnings.

Nevertheless, something akin to privatization has indeed occurred in the United States in the past decade. Since other nations seem to be interested in adopting some of the American model for their own health care systems, the implications of this process for human rights should be taken into account. The present paper relates both scholarly and informal observations of the American "privatization" strategy in health care, in light of the conception of health care as a human right.

2. Health Care as a Human Right

A growing philosophical literature in the United States examines the issue of whether health care is a human right.[1] That this body of work has emerged from American bioethicists is not surprising, for only in the U.S. is this taken seriously as an open question. Indeed, a consensus existed even in the U.S. until the Reagan era, supporting the right to health care as a moral ideal, even if not yet, a legal one. In the wake of the rightist trend in American politics, heralded

* Ph.D., University of Wisconsin, Madison, Wisconsin, U.S.A.

[1] President's Commission for the Study of Ethical Problems in Medicine and Biomedical and Behavioral Research, *Securing Access to Health Care* Vol. 1, *Report*; Vols. 2 and 3, *Appendices* (1983). N. Daniels, *Just Health Care* (1985), C.J. Dougherty, *American Health Care: Realities, Rights and Reforms* (1988).

K.E. Mahoney and P. Mahoney (eds.), Human Rights in the Twenty-first Century, 495–501.

in philosophy by the publication of Robert Nozick's libertarian work[2], philosophers for the first time published works focusing on the property rights of investors and liberties of physicians as fundamental, even if entitlements to care on the part of the sick were ruled out as a result.[3] In this social vision, the just society need not attempt to determine the health needs of the population, nor ought it organize health services in the manner most propitious for meeting these needs. It simply guarantees rights of property and liberty and permits individuals to make the best deals they can.

This libertarian outlook, however, remained a marginal view in health policy. In mainstream academic writing, in government documents, and in the public statement of officials, the ultimate criterion for success in health care delivery continues to be whether the system meets the public's health care needs. Interests of investors and providers, while politically and administratively impossible to ignore, have been viewed as having secondary moral importance. It is not clear, however, that the prevailing humane philosophy can coexist indefinitely with an increasingly harsh reality. The changes which have been imposed on the system in the spirit of privatization may yet undermine the nation's basic commitment to the right to health care as a moral ideal. Those nations which are looking to the American experience of the last decade as a model for health care financing must be alerted to the possibility that the organizational initiatives carry a moral and philosophical virus, the effect of which will not become apparent until after the model has been adopted.

3. What Is "Privatization" in the American Health Care Context?

The recent history of American health policy has been marked by fairly well-delineated eras. Before the late 1960's, government involvement, aside from the military, was small; this era ended with the passage of Medicare and Medicaid, government health insurance for the elderly and the poor, respectively. These steps in the direction of national health insurance, however, were partly responsible for a rocketing medical inflation rate which has never abated. An era of regulation, intended to curb over-building and other inflationary excesses, soon followed, only to be defeated politically by the providers. As conservative, Republican rule came to Washington in the early 1980's, the search for cost controls led to a reemphasis on the market as a basic concept in health care delivery.

Despite the important differences noted above, public and private initiatives in the era of competition have enough in common with classical privatization, understood as transferring public functions to private hands, to warrant the use of the term. It is true that very few publicly-owned hospitals went private; and

[2] R. Nozick, *Anarchy, State, and Utopia* (1974).

[3] L. Lomasky, "Medical Progress and National Health Care", 10 *Philosophy and Public Affairs* (1981), pp. 65–88.

government health care expenditures increased rather than decreased during this period. What has been privatized is not so much the actual delivery of care, but the mission of care for the deliverers. For the first time, investor-owned hospital chains became important players in American health care, fuelled by capital in search of margins rather than by communities in search of health care or charitable and religious orders in pursuit of good works.[4] In response to the market challenges of these for-profit institutions, and more generally in competition with each other, the long-dominant non-profit hospitals abandoned community planning for institutional strategy. Before long, they ceased to apologize for raiding their competitors market base. They signed exclusive contracts with referring physicians, paying bounties for patients, and exhibited other market behaviour, once considered unseemly. Some public hospitals, including even some military ones (in the Veterans' system), began to recruit well-insured patients to fill beds that were otherwise being denied to uninsured patients in their traditional constituencies.

The "private", or institutional, mission of each of these organizations was, of course, to prosper through selling services (fee-for-service providers), insurance (health insurance companies), or both (Health Maintenance Organizations and other hybrids). The optimistic expectation was that these units would have to offer greater customer satisfaction, lower prices, and more efficient operation to attract the patients needed for revenue and the capital needed for expansion and modernization. Thus, the best would be rewarded, care would improve, costs would moderate, and the need for regulation – a blunt instrument at best – would be minimized.

The competition strategy now earns less praise. It has utterly failed to restrain prices; physicians' morale is lower; access has deteriorated; and one important element in patient satisfaction, the ability to choose one's physician, is threatened with extinction. Americans now voice greater dissatisfaction with their health care system than do the citizens of any comparable country.

The reasons for the failure of the competition/privatization strategy to accomplish its primary mission of cost control are complex and need not concern us here. The source of the threat to health care as a human right, however, is plain: it is the mainspring, the central mechanism of the strategy itself. In what follows, I briefly survey some of the symptoms of this destructive tendency, proceeding afterwards to some philosophical conclusions.

4. Skim and Dump: Privatization as National Health Care Policy

Once individual health care providers are released from their community mission and encouraged to pursue private ends, some will prosper by improving services, lowering prices, and becoming more efficient, as the theory promises. These gains may be ephemeral; some clinics have allocated revenues to hiring

[4] B.H. Gray, (ed.) *For-Profit Enterprise in Health Care* (1989).

"smile" consultants from the airline industry to teach flight attendants' manners to gruff surgeons; but even this source of patient satisfaction counts as an improvement in service.

It took no time at all, however, for providers and payers to learn that a quicker, surer road to profit detoured entirely around efficiency and quality, leading instead to selection among patients. Insurers did well by identifying patients likely to need care, especially expensive care, and barring them from risk pools (and employers and other payers achieved lower insurance costs by refusing to hire these people). Clinics and physicians who were not in the insurance business, on the other hand, found it important to identify those who had insurance. The hybrid insurer-provider organizations had to manage both winnowing tasks, a feat made more difficult when the interests of the parts (doctors versus investors) were in tension.

Which patients then represented the "cream" depended on one's position in the health care game. But throughout the system, the profit-maximizing strategy was the same: skim off the cream (before your competitors did), dump the rest (onto your competitors if possible, to reduce their ability to compete; or onto the street, if no one else would take them).

The United States has lagged behind comparable countries in its reluctance to erect a substantial social safety net, but the health care system has been an island of relative security. Though access to care was far from assured, a tradition of cross-subsidization has permitted providers to offer some care to the uninsured at the expense of the better-off. During the privatization era, however, this tradition faded. A hospital which provided charity care, funded by its general revenues, had to charge higher prices, or else spend less than competitors who turned these patients away. This alienated the very patients who were funding the charity care, and dissuaded bankers from loaning the money for modernization needed to lure the wealthier patients back.

Just as American's heart toward the poorest was hardening in other sectors, with middle-class townsmen literally stepping over the bodies of homeless families living on city sidewalks, so too reports of heartlessness in health care began to appear and then they became routine. In one celebrated instance, a man was refused care in a St. Louis emergency room for want of insurance even though he had a knife in his back up to the handle; and religious hospitals in Texas turned away rural women minutes away from childbirth. This "economic patient dumping"[5] has become pandemic, doubling annually in many cities.[6] On one estimate, a million patients are denied care for economic reasons annually[7], and up to a quarter million in need of emergency care are transferred each year for economic reasons.[8]

[5] L.M. Beitsch, "Economic Patient Dumping: Whose Life is it Anyway?", 10 *The Journal of Legal Medicine* (1989), pp. 433–478.

[6] L. Uzych, "Patient Dumping", 77 *Journal of the Florida Medical Association* (1990), pp. 97–100.

[7] R.J. Blendon, "What should be done about the uninsured poor?", 260 *JAMA* (1988), pp. 3176–7.

[8] L. Uzych, note 6, *supra*.

These practices have made the "wallet biopsy" (pre-admission financial screening) as familiar a part of health care as the doctor's stethoscope. Ironically, the same competitive health policy which motivates this behaviour also creates needless duplication of services, as each clinic and hospital strives to offer the most and the best services to attract the cream of patients. The hospitals turning away patients are often half-empty.

Refusing care to emergency patients presenting themselves at the hospital door is offensive to the community, and statutes have been enacted in many states to prevent it. However well intended these laws may be, they treat a symptom rather than the underlying source of distress. The institutional self-preservation and self-enhancement mission now deemed suitable in health care dictates a host of practices which deny care just as effectively, but far less visibly. In skimming, as with medical care, an ounce of prevention is worth many pounds of cure; the trick is to ensure that wrong patients never come to the door in the first place.

Hospitals can change their patient mix and compete more effectively even before they physically exist. For-profit hospital chains often choose a site which is located near affluent neighbourhoods, as one might expect. But since the poor in America tend to congregate in the center of cities, the profit-maximizing hospital will be located on the outer edge of these neighbourhoods. This not only makes them inaccessible to the urban poor, but it also draws the well-insured patients away from inner-city hospitals which had cross-subsidized in the past, thus reducing their ability to modernize and consequently, driving still more of the richer patients to the new suburban facility. The ultimate financial woes, or even bankruptcy, of the older hospital do not show up on the new hospital's balance sheet.

A managed-care plan can offer services which appeal to healthy young families, such as excellent obstetrical care, including champagne breakfasts following childbirth, and sports medicine clinics, which advise enrollees on choosing running shoes; and it can permit its reputation in chronic care and mental health to sag. In this way it draws enrollees who are less likely to get sick, or to have long, expensive illnesses, and visits these unprofitable patients on competitors, who do try to provide first-rate care for these patients. The latter, once again, take a financial beating, and must offer less to the desirable patients, who abandon them in even greater numbers.

Hospitals can also prosper by carefully choosing the doctors to whom admitting privileges will be granted. For example, an applicant's patient list can be given an instantaneous analysis by computer to determine whether a large number of patients live in postal code areas marked by poverty and uninsurance. These doctors can be (and have been) denied privileges. One hospital found their wards swamped with illegal aliens who had no money or insurance; by spreading the word that the hospital was co-operating with immigration authorities to permit daily sweeps, the problem was handled at the source. Another hospital was unfortunately placed near a main traffic artery which passed through the center of the city; cars carrying poor emergency patients filled beds with nonpaying patients. The solution was to physically remove the hospital's sign so that the hospital could not be found by passers-by.

The American Hospital Association, which promulgates ethical guidelines to maintain high moral standards among its member institutions, assembled a working group to address the problem of emergency rooms which draw the wrong kind of sick people. Among the group's recommendations are:

- Provide little or no parking for emergency department patients
- Provide an unlisted number for the emergency department
- Segregate waiting areas for paying and nonpaying patients; in the area for nonpaying patients provide few seats, poor lighting, few signs, and no food or drink;
- Segregate treatment areas, providing fewer staff and less equipment in areas for nonpaying patients.[9]

Though these suggestions have not been officially endorsed by the AHA, they are indicative of a frame of mind which undermines the right of health care at a point of entry into the system. In the United States, with one seventh of the population uninsured, many patients have no doctor and wait until symptoms are unbearable before seeking help. Twelve-hour waits, which drive many of the sickest patients back home in pain and despair, are satisfactory neither to the patients or to the hospitals.

5. Rescuing the Right to Health Care

While readers from many countries, especially poorer ones, may recognize some of these same practices from their own health care experiences, it must be kept in mind that these incidents occurred in a nation which spends over $600,000,000,000 per year on health care. The system is awash in money. No other nation spends so lavishly on health care. Yet, each provider who engages in demarketing or who dumps or skims will say, in all sincerity, that they would like to offer the care needed by the patients but lack the funds to do so.

The picture of care denied by underutilized facilities points to a basic, even trite, moral truth in health care: the system should cater to human need, not to provider profit. To be sure, many backers of privatizing the health care mission viewed the strategy as a means to the higher end. Through the efficiencies and consumer sovereignty of the market, health care would be provided with greater sensitivity to patients at a lower cost. In practice, however, too few patients have realized these benefits. The regulations, which would have required providers to compete on the basis of price and service, rather than on ability to skim and dump, were never enacted, though the architects of the strategy urged their passage.[10] The providers and payers who opposed them have succeeded in

[9] L.A. Burns, "Hospital initiatives in response to ambulatory care programs". Working paper. American Hospital Association (1981).

[10] A. Enthoven, *Health Plan* (1980).

staving off their subsequent imposition, and would likely do so in any revived, more humane, plan. To be sure, the face of privatization in the United States would have been less ugly than it has been had it occurred in the context of a Government voucher system, which would have enabled all patients to buy into the system, as Enthoven suggested. Even so, the examples described here indicate the many ways in which the absence of community planning and health policy based on human rights provokes abandonment of the sick.

As denying care comes to be seen as normal, how long can the residual moral commitment to a right to health care persist? The hospitals and clinics which have heeded the nation's call to follow Adam Smith will someday forget, if they ever knew, that privatization in health care was intended to serve the interests of the community as a whole. All the while, doctors and nurses who work in these organizations have been instructed to keep their organization's interest foremost in mind; these allegiances cannot forever co-exist with professional commitment to health care as a human right. Finally, the patients themselves will have to adjust their expectations: having been denied care while in obvious need, having found responsibility for their care fragmented and dumped from one provider to the next, and sometimes back again ("reverse dumping"), how long can one maintain a sense of entitlement?

Readers of this essay will be aware that policy makers, who opt for privatization as health policy, expect certain benefits to follow: easier capitalization, less bureaucracy, and more responsiveness. This essay has not addressed these virtues of the strategy, which in some contexts may be important ones.[11] But those who urge privatization must ask their constituents, and themselves, whether the system once privatized, can possibly maintain its respect for human rights.

[11] B.H. Gray, note 4, *supra*.

RHODA E. HOWARD*

Health Costs of Social Degradation and Female Self-Mutilation in North America

1. Introduction

This paper discusses women's self-mutilation as an example of the health costs of the social degradation of dishonoured groups. After an explanation of the centrality of notions of dishonour and degradation to most societies' ideals of justice, I examine specific mutilatory "beauty" practices in North American society, comparing them briefly with genital mutilations in Africa. I conclude with a criticism of the core human rights literature, especially the new focus on group rights, for failing to acknowledge the cultural practices of social degradation and their adverse effects on subordinate social groups.

2. Social Degradation

In many societies timocracy – power based on differences in honour (from the Greek *time* [honour]) – is still an important political fact.[1] Yet in liberal Western societies and in much of the learned commentary on human rights abuses, we disregard this social phenomenon. Although the international human rights documents connect human rights with human dignity, analysts of actual human rights practices forget that dignity in the modern liberal sense, implying equal respect and concern regardless of social status,[2] is often not attainable for large categories of people because of the dishonour connected with social degradation.

I define social degradation as the treatment of categories of people as inferiors, deserving of lesser respect than others or indeed of no respect at all.

* Professor of Sociology, McMaster University, Hamilton, Ontario, Canada. For their comments on an earlier draft of this paper, I am most grateful to Ed Ezergailis, Lisa Kowalchuk, and Vivienne Walters.

[1] I have taken this term from Orlando Patterson *Slavery and Social Death: A Comparative Study* (1982), Cambridge, Mass: Harvard University Press, p. 386 n.14.

[2] Rhoda E. Howard and Jack Donnelly, "Human Dignity, Human Rights and Political Regimes", 80 *American Political Science Review* (1986), no. 3, p. 803.

K.E. Mahoney and P. Mahoney (eds.), Human Rights in the Twenty-first Century, 503–516.

Degradation reflects fundamental ascriptive categories in society. Ascribed characteristics are unchanging. One acquires them biologically at birth, as in sex or "race", or they are socially decreed at birth and permanently unchanging, as in caste or slave/free membership. In many societies, ascribed characteristics, including set roles for males and females of each relevant age group, are more important than achieved characteristics, or those that can vary throughout one's lifetime according to one's success in the marketplaces of prestige or wealth. The stratification of individuals in modern industrial societies often appears to be based more on achievement than on ascription, yet race and gender interact with stratification by achievement so that people of degraded social statuses find their ability to compete equally in the marketplace severely limited.

Three processes are necessary to degrade a category of people. The first is categorization itself, the social act of ordering. The ordering of society reflects the ordering of the natural world, especially the basic dichotomies of nature such as day and night, sun and moon. To impose order on the human world is, by primitive analogy, to impose order on the unpredictable forces of nature; to guard against flood, earthquakes, eclipses and other such frightening phenomena. The us-them, human-non-human ordering implied is basic to human hierarchies and caste/status distinctions.

The second process is to dishonour one of the groups that the categorization has created. The dishonoured group is considered to be dirty and polluting, while the honoured group is pure. Dirt is the most important symbol of inferiority. As Mary Douglas notes, "reflection on dirt involves reflection on the relation of order to disorder, being to non-being, form to formlessness, life to death... [C]ertain moral values are upheld and certain social rules defined by beliefs in dangerous contagion...".[3] "Cleanliness is next to Godliness" is a saying of the modern Western world. But certain groups are held to be inherently dirty, incapable of cleanliness. Women's cyclical bodily excretions, symbolic of the flood feared in Christian mythology[4], render them incapable of the purity of the dominant male group. Blacks' very skin is frequently viewed as dirt; witness those whites who are tempted to touch black skin just to discover if it will "rub off".

The third process involved in degradation is domination. Status distinctions both breed and justify inequalities of power. Max Weber defines power as the "chance of a man or of a number of men to realize their own will in a communal action even against the resistance of others who are participating in the action".[5] Dominance more broadly takes several forms, some of which overlap with each other. As Michael Walzer puts it, although "[p]olitics is always the

[3] Mary Douglas, *Purity and Danger: An Analysis of the Concepts of Pollution and Taboo* (1966), New York: Frederick A.Praeger, pp. 5 and 3.

[4] Klaus Theweleit *Male Fantasies: Volume 1: Women, Floods, Bodies, History* [(1987), 1st {German} Ed. 1977], Minneapolis, University of Minnesota Press.

[5] Max Weber "Class, Status and Party", in H.H. Gerth and C. Wright Mills (Eds.) *From Max Weber: Essays in Sociology* [(1958), 1st ed. 1946], New York: Oxford University Press, p. 180.

most direct path to dominance, and political power ... is probably the most important ... good in human history", there are many other modes of dominance. "[T]he means of domination are differently constituted in different societies. Birth and blood, landed wealth, capital, education, divine grace, state power..."[6] Gender and racially-based dominance, forms of dominance by birth, are frequently so ideologically powerful that Weber's definition becomes incorrect: dominated groups do not resist communal actions in others' interests because they are not able to articulate their own subordination.

Physical coercion is the ultimate and most immediately efficacious method of domination. But other, subtler methods are more useful in the long haul. Among these is the ideological capacity to persuade degraded categories of people that they are genuinely inferior, dirty and polluting; hence that they deserve the fate they endure.

In timocratic societies, some peoples' honour depends on others' subordination. Those who do not accept their own lower status are subjected by domination of a physically coercive nature. But the domination is actually more firmly rooted in the political and ideological spheres. Ideological domination is particularly important because it not only teaches those in power that they deserve their status, but it attempts to persuade – sometimes successfully – those who are despised that they deserve to be.

In state societies, that is, in the societies in which all human beings now live, however remote they may be from the centres of power, the subordination of women is universal. Patriarchal control over the reproductive and productive activities of the females of the family (wives, sisters, daughters and female slaves) was encoded by law as one of the earliest forms of property.[7] Whatever other statuses women may have in society, noblewoman or commoner, abbess or laywoman, rich or poor, they are always confined by their socially-created, reinforced and restricted gender. Although women in many modern societies now have formal rights equal to those of men, state societies and the communities and families within them are still influenced by ideologies of timocratic domination which decree that women should acknowledge their inferiority to men in symbolic ways, even if they no longer do so in formal legal, political or economic ways.

Women, says the sociologist Edwin Schur, are a deviant, stigmatized group, routinely objectified and degraded.

> "[I]n our society being treated as deviant has been a standard feature of life as a female... [S]ocial stigmatization must be recognized as a key mechanism that backs up and 'enforces' many of the restrictions and limitations placed on women... [The devaluation of women results in] induced female

[6] Michael Walzer *Spheres of Justice: A Defense of Pluralism and Equality* (1983), New York: Basic Books, pp. 15 and xiii.

[7] This analysis is based on Gerda Lerner, *The Creation of Patriarchy* (1986), New York: Oxford University Press, pp. 8–10.

preoccupation with physical appearance; concern about ascribed deficiencies and continuous efforts to conform to 'appearance norms'.[8] "

Socially degraded categories of people, such as women, blacks and (formerly) Jews in Western society, are taught to reproduce their own degradation. They absorb beliefs in their own social, psychological and physical inferiority, especially, as regards their physique, notions of ugliness, dirt and shame. Acting on these beliefs, degraded people then adopt measures to ameliorate their physical "deformities" and dirtiness, by, for example, attempting to lighten their skin colour, change the shape of their noses or alter bodily weight and shape.[9] These practices have severe personal and social health costs.

3. Female Self-Mutilation in North America

I define mutilation as a change in one's physical makeup or a way of adorning or clothing one's body that has detrimental health consequences. Female self-mutilation has three aspects. It includes mutilations that women perform directly upon themselves, voluntary submission to others for mutilatory purposes, and socialization practices by which older women either mutilate young girls directly or train them to mutilate themselves.

(1) Comparison with Self-Mutilation in Africa

Many North American women are extremely shocked when they first encounter the practice of female genital mutilations or circumcision.[10] In contemporary Africa and elsewhere in parts of Asia and the Arab world, female genital operations are a common practice. These operations vary from a simple clitoridectomy to the cutting off of the labia majora and minora (excision), to the internal "smoothing" of the vaginal walls by scraping out the protective vaginal flesh. Sometimes the vaginal opening is also sewn up (infibulation).

There are many reasons posed for this practice, which is not Islamic in origin although some Islamic societies practice it. Its origins may be connected to beliefs that uncircumcised women threaten the world's order by having "male" parts; female circumcision thus is evidence of Douglas' contention that ordering is a fundamental psychosocial imperative in all societies. Some societies believe that without such operations, female fertility will be inhibited.

[8] Edwin M. Schur, *Labelling Women Deviant* (1983), Philadelphia: Temple University Press, pp. 3, 11 and 33.

[9] On self-hatred among Jews and blacks, see Sander L. Gilman, *Jewish Self-Hatred: Anti-Semitism and the Hidden Language of the Jews* (1986), Baltimore: Johns Hopkins University Press, Chapter 1.

[10] This was my own reaction on first reading about female genital mutilations in Africa, and I have observed it in other women in my classrooms, in private conversations and when I give public lectures on the subject.

In others, it is believed that a woman who does not undergo such operations will be sexually insatiable. In still others, there is the belief that female circumcision renders the woman clean, that without this physical "smoothing" she will be polluted. While a cursory study of the practice might incline one to think that it is the women who independently "choose" to "cleanse" their and their female children's genitalia in such a fashion, what the practice actually reflects is an internalization of the ideology that whole women are unclean; that the smoothing of the external genitalia and scraping of the vaginal wall cleanses the inherently foul bodily processes of menstruation and childbirth.[11]

While many medical campaigns have been directed against these practices in Africa since 1979, the similarity between them and self-mutilatory practices in North America appears to have gone largely unnoticed. One possible reason for this is that mutilatory practices in Africa confirm the image that many white North Americans still hold of blacks/Africans as brutal "primitives".[12] But another reason is that North American women are so socialized to accept their own self-mutilatory practices as normal, indeed pleasurable activities that they do not recognize the similarities.

Part of what North American women find shocking is undoubtedly that in Africa, it is the sensitive genital area that is mutilated. This particular type of mutilation does not presently occur in the Western world. But clitoridectomies were performed in the United States from the 1860's to at least 1904 and possibly as late as 1925. Circumcision of women (removal of the hood over the clitoris) was practised from the 1890's to 1937, and removal of healthy ovaries ("female castration") was also a common operation from the 1870's to 1921. The purpose of all three practices was to control women who demonstrated untoward sexual appetites (for example by masturbating), or who were generally considered troublesome or unmanageable.[13] As in some African explanations for genital mutilations, there was an extreme fear of female sexual insatiability.

Another reason for the shocked reaction of North American women is that genital operations in Africa are performed without anaesthetic, in conditions that do not meet the standards of Western medical practice, whereas analogous operations in North America – cosmetic surgery – are performed, presumably, in medically safe surroundings.

Finally, female genital operations in Africa are frequently performed on young girls or infants. Our self-mutilatory practices so far are confined to adult women or teenagers, although such practices as dieting for non-medical reasons are becoming increasingly common among pre-pubescent girls. A doctor concerned with this problem in Hamilton, Ontario, the city where I live, reports

[11] The above two paragraphs are based on Rhoda E. Howard *Human Rights in Commonwealth Africa* (1986), Totowa, N.J.: Rowman and Littlefield, pp. 202–206.

[12] Marianna Torgovnick, *Gone Primitive: Savage Intellects, Modern Lives* (1990), Chicago: University of Chicago Press, Chapter 1.

[13] Ben Barker-Benfield, "The Spermatic Economy: A Nineteenth-Century View of Sexuality", in Michael Gordon (Ed.) *The American Family in Social-Historical Perspective* (1973), New York: St Martin's Press, pp. 353–356.

that she has treated several little girls of four or five who are very preoccupied with their weight. They are usually the daughters of very slender mothers, implying that the mothers are socializing their children into this obsession.[14]

The mutilation of women in Africa is thus only one instance of the global ubiquity of mutilatory practices among women. It is not unique to Africa, nor is it a sign of African primitiveness. It is a sign of the shame women feel because of their polluting qualities, and because of the inferiority of which their feminine physique is an omnipresent reminder. As Edwin Schur has argued, women are stigmatized defectives. There is something wrong with and unclean about the natural way they are born. Ashamed of their own bodies, in different societies women have absorbed different means of effacing themselves by acknowledging their physical inadequacies.

(2) Self-Mutilatory Practices in North America

In North American society, even as women have become more economically and politically liberated during the past century and particularly during the past two decades, they have become more firmly victims of the ideology of their own physical unworthiness. Women in this society despise their own bodies. They invest enormous amounts of time, energy and money in attempts to reshape themselves, cleanse themselves and diminish their bodily size.

In making this assertion I do not mean to discount trends in Western society other than the social degradation of women which cause both men and women to be preoccupied with their bodies. One such trend is the fear of death in a society that, ironically, has one of the highest longevity rates in the world but in which the "pursuit of happiness" is interpreted partly as the pursuit of eternal youth. Another more important trend in the last fifteen years has been what Christopher Lasch calls the culture of narcissism. The general stress on "human potential", self-fulfilment and attaining "growth experiences" in the 1970's and 80's has also increased individuals' preoccupations with their own bodies.[15] In this chapter, I am merely focusing on one of several important factors that explains female preoccupation with looks and physique in Western society.

Women are subject to extra pressures above those exerted on men in contemporary North America. Like men, they must strive to improve themselves. They must continue to fulfil their traditional roles as wives and mothers. They must also compete on unequal terms with men in the capitalist marketplace. Yet simultaneously they must deride their very accomplishments and demonstrate their continued acceptance of their degraded social status by diminishing themselves, both physically and symbolically, in the eyes of men. A difficult balancing act is called for; the more formally equal women become the more they must engage in personally degrading social rituals that assure the

[14] Personal communication from Dr. Peggy Barringer, 29 October 1990.

[15] Christopher Lasch, *The Culture of Narcissism: American Life in an Age of Diminishing Expectations* (1979), New York: W.W. Norton, chapter II.

men with whom they interact that they really know their place. In the business place, for example, they must engage in soft-spoken, manipulative verbal negotiations that do not challenge the men's sense that they are still in control.[16] Most women are victims of the pervasive ideology of degradation of their gender: they "know" that despite their new formal equality they are still actually inferior people. One way that they indicate this to themselves and to others is through continuous mutilatory activities that have severe personal and social health costs.

A very influential social myth in Western society is the Cinderella story, in which a prince finds a bride by trying a glass shoe on hundreds of young woman until the girl with the tiniest foot is found. In some versions of the story Cinderella's ugly big-footed step-sisters cut off their toes or their heels in order to fit into the slipper, but their subterfuge (not really being tiny, modest, quiet, good) is discovered.

The Cinderella myth is believed to have originated in Asia and its earliest known version is from China.[17] Pre-revolutionary Chinese practised footbinding. The feet of infant females were very tightly bound together, toes to heels, to prevent their growth. This process was extremely painful and dangerous, resulting in infections, swellings and deformed bones. Once an adult, the process continued to be painful; to unbind the feet for bathing was sheer torture, and walking was almost impossible. But a tiny foot was a sign of high status. A woman with bound feet could not walk and could not work; her tiny feet were thus a living and suffering embodiment of the wealth of the man whose daughter, wife or concubine she was.

This Cinderella myth is so ubiquitous and influential in North America that millions of women still routinely stuff their feet into shoes too narrow for them. Susan Brownmiller believes that tight, high-heeled shoes are a sexual fetish among many men.

> "[T]he impractical shoe ... induces helplessness and dependence. ... [T]he extra wiggle in the hips ... is seen as sexually flirtatious, while the smaller steps and tentative, insecure tread suggest daintiness, modesty and refinement. ... [T]he overall hobbling effect with its sadomasochistic tinge is suggestive of the restraining leg irons and ankle chains endured by captive animals, prisoners and slaves who were also festooned with decorative symbols of their bondage."[18]

Brownmiller's interpretation suggests that small feet are a symbol not only of the prestige of the man who has a wife who does not need to work (like the Muslim woman in purdah, the nineteenth century decorative bourgeois wife in Britain, or the wife/mother confined to suburban isolation in contemporary

[16] Rosabeth Moss Kantor, *Men and Women of the Corporation* (1977), New York: Basic Books, p. 234.

[17] Maria Leach, (Ed.) *Funk and Wagnells' Standard Dictionary of Folklore, Mythology and Legend* (1949), volume 1., New York: Funk and Wagnell, p. 233.

[18] Susan Brownmiller, *Femininity* (1984), Linden Press / Simon & Schuster, pp. 184–185.

North America) but also of the bondage of the woman. In contemporary North America, this particular form of bondage is declining as a result of the fitness movement and, perhaps, of the women's liberation movement. One frequently sees women walking to work in sensible running shoes. But they discard these sensible shoes for confining high heels when they arrive at the office. Symbolically then, high heels, like the tight skirts that are part of much business apparel, continue to confine the very women whose elevated occupations are supposed to be a sign of their liberation in the modern world.

Women engage in many directly self-mutilatory practices other than foot-squeezing. They take risks by applying cosmetics whose contents are unknown and potentially dangerous. They use so-called feminine hygiene products in their genital areas that can upset their natural chemical balance. And they voluntarily submit themselves to cosmetic surgery that, while unnecessary for reasons of physical health, nevertheless carries the risks that accompany any surgery.

Among the risks of surgery is death. In July 1989 a Toronto, Ontario woman died after liposuction on her thighs.[19] Liposuction is a procedure designed to suck out fat cells; there are estimated to be about 150,000 liposuction operations per year in North America.[20] Many women endure liposuction in order to eradicate the natural accumulation of fat on their thighs that childbearing and age bring. It would seem to a reasonable person that the risk of death, however minuscule, would be enough to deter voluntary submission to such surgical bodily mutilation. Quite the contrary in modern North America. As Brownmiller puts it regarding facelifts, another popular form of cosmetic surgery:

> "[T]he deep furrows that signify concentration, sensitivity and interesting experience in a man of middle years are the subject of massive emergency measures at their first sign of appearance in a woman, who embarks on her desperate maintenance program of moisturizers, facial masks, wrinkle creams, and perhaps some subcutaneous injections of silicone or collagen and a facelift."[21]

Aging women, accepting the ideology that even when young and slim their bodies are at best tolerable, react with despair and health-threatening measures to the signs of middle age considered dignifying in a male.

The ethics of doctors who commit such mutilations upon women are somewhat troublesome. Should "consumer sovereignty"[22] in the realm of cosmetic surgery be allowed to reign when such sovereignty derives from the severe self-hatred typical of degraded social categories? Is it appropriate to make money by

[19] "Ontario Probes Plastic Surgery Death", *The Globe and Mail* (July 7, 1989), Toronto, p. A4.

[20] "Jury Wants Tight Rules for Liposuction Work", *Calgary Herald* (February 1, 1990), p. D5.

[21] See note 18, *supra*, p. 132.

[22] Paul J. Schacht and Alec Pemberton "What is Unnecessary Surgery? Who shall Decide? Issues of Consumer Sovereignty, Conflict and Self-Regulation", 20 *Social Science and Medicine* (1985), no. 3, pp. 199–206.

agreeing to put a person's health at risk in order to change her bodily appearance when she is, in fact, normal, not defaced by genetics or accident? One must also wonder about the role of the state as a regulator of medical practice. The province of Ontario in Canada refuses to permit free-standing abortion clinics (not affiliated with hospitals) but does permit free-standing liposuction clinics. Women who attempt to control their roles as biological reproducers are subject to far more regulation by the state than are women, and their doctors, who attempt to enhance or alter their looks by degrading practices that are dangerous to their health. Women's control of their reproductive functions threatens the social ideology of women as child-bearers, whereas women's self-mutilatory practices reinforce the social ideology of feminine physical ugliness and pollution.

The final category of self-mutilatory practice is the socialization by which older women either mutilate young girls directly or train them to mutilate themselves. In Africa, older women perform genital operations on their daughters; in North America, mothers teach their daughters the overriding importance of being slim. Incessant cyclical dieting is a danger to health that is accepted as a normal female activity in North America. In the changing-rooms of the swimming pools that I frequent, for example, I hear constant, interminable conversations among women of all ages and sizes about their weight. Young girls of twelve or thirteen stand on scales, lamenting to each other that they are gaining, and pregnant women confide to complete strangers that they are worried about getting fat.

Enormous industries exist in North America by which women assist each other to alter their shape or weight or looks. These include tanning clinics, clinics to remove excess hair and weight-loss clinics, as well as the more traditional means of female beautification such as hair-dressing salons. The medical analogy here is interesting. A clinic is a place for medical treatment. The self-mutilatory clinics are successful in their use of medicalized analogy because smoothing, reshaping and reducing their bodies is considered to be a health measure, essential to women's psychological well-being. Women are so convinced that their bodies as they exist are shameful, dirty and degrading that mutilation for purposes of self-esteem is considered to be mutilation for health purposes.

The diseases anorexia nervosa (self-starvation) and bulimia (periodic binging on food followed by purging, or self-induced vomiting, that damages the stomach lining, etc.) increased dramatically in prevalence during the last decade. In the mid-1980's about one per cent of the female population of the United States was anorexic; the mortality rate of anorexia was between 5 and 18 per cent.[23] In numerical terms, a 1986 estimate was that there were at least a

[23] Figures are from Kathleen Winters Plehn, "Anorexia Nervosa and Bulimia: Incidence and Diagnosis", 15 *The Nurse Practitioner* (April 1990), no. 4, p. 22; and American Psychiatric Association *Diagnostic and Statistical Manual of Mental Disorders* (1987), (Third Edition – Revised), Washington, D.C.: American Psychiatric Association, p. 66. See also Catherine M. Shisslak and Marjorie Crago, "Primary Prevention of Eating Disorders", 55 *Journal of Consulting and Clinical Psychology* (1987), no. 5, p. 661.

million anorectics in the U.S., of whom 60,000 to 150,000 would die.[24]

Anorexia nervosa and bulimia are recognized in popular discourse as medical problems. But the incessant cyclical dieting in which a majority of North American women engage is not recognized as a less extreme form of the same behaviour. Dieting and anorexia are not discrete patterns; they are part of the same continuum. Dieting is a "normal" eating pattern that some women with particular psychiatric problems take to the extremes of anorexia and bulimia. By the mid-1980's, dieting was more prevalent among young American women and adolescent girls than not dieting.[25] Yet while health warnings are now included on all cigarette packages and truth-in-advertising laws affect a wide range of industries, the diet industry goes untouched. Weight-loss clinics are not obliged to advertise their recidivism rates (rates at which clients regain weight), nor are they obliged to warn that dieting is bad for the health. For example, a weight loss of over two pounds a week is associated with gall bladder illness.[26] Women's dieting behaviour, a ritualized, stressful and physically dangerous form of self-diminution, is merely seen as a rather silly custom in which women engage.

Why do North American women wish to make themselves small? What is the cause of the "implicit rejection of oneself that is involved in the decision to diet (i.e., to seek to become someone other than who one is)"[27] and why does this desire coincide with a general loosening of their social roles and a widening of their opportunities? Fat signals the female; it signals fertility with its ambiguous uncleanliness and messiness; it is a marker of low social status.[28] The fat that remains on her body even when she has become "male" in the public world reminds the liberated woman of her continued status as a subordinate entity; by trying to eliminate it, she tries to eliminate the last vestige of her polluting, unaesthetic self. Moreover, presenting a tiny, childlike and non-threatening image to males compensates for women's increased independence. Smallness is a physical symbol of women's acceptance of their lesser status in society.

But these women are not responsible on their own for imposing thinness on themselves. The mass media, reflecting wider social norms, encourage women to accept the ideal of thinness. The idealized woman portrayed in the mass media has become progressively more slender since the early 1950's and is now extremely thin, almost malnourished. Uneasy with the changing sex roles of modern society, the media unconsciously challenge that change with an ideal impossible for women to emulate. In the 1950's, women wishing to present a

[24] Hillel Schwartz, *Never Satisfied: A Cultural History of Diets, Fantasies and Fat* (1986), New York: Doubleday, p. 332.

[25] Janet Polivy and C. Peter Herman, "Diagnosis and Treatment of Normal Eating", 55 *Journal of Consulting and Clinical Psychology* (1987), no. 5, pp. 636 and 640.

[26] CBLT Television (Toronto), *Market Place* (8 January 1991).

[27] See note 25, *supra*, p. 641.

[28] Noelle Caskey, "Interpreting Anorexia Nervosa", in Susan Rubin Suleiman (Ed.) *The Female Body in Western Culture: Contemporary Perspectives* (1986), Cambridge: Harvard University Press, pp. 178 and 188.

slim silhouette squeezed themselves into confining girdles. In the 1980's and 90's, "liberated" from such underclothes, women starve themselves in order to present a pencil-thin profile.

The small woman is also a quiet woman. She speaks with a soft voice, almost with a whisper. Psychological self-assertion is still not permitted women in North American society. Alongside the popular "assertiveness training" seminars for women (and men) in the business and professional worlds is a powerful counteracting cultural stereotype of the passive woman serving men with downcast eyes, pitching her voice to the comforting coo used to quiet infants. Women with loud voices, women whose natural demeanour is not self-effacing and retiring, are stereotyped as bossy, harsh, strident or pushy. Such women are no longer physically punished by being fitted with "the branks" – "an iron muzzle with a triangular bit that fitted the mouth ... a punishment ... for raucous, troublesome women"[29] – but they are still subject to common social opprobrium.

Self-mutilation, then, is a violent process imposed by women upon themselves. Women who find themselves at odds with social norms compensate by inflicting pain upon their own bodies. If one cannot be quiet or passive, one can at least be thin, thus visually indicating one's acceptance of subordination to men. Women are willing to diminish themselves, both physically and psychologically, to fit the subordinate role imposed upon them, as they are also willing to undergo costly and repetitive cleansing rituals that are meant to control their polluting qualities. In an inversion of what dignity ought to mean in a liberal society, women's social honour demands acceptance of their subordination. This is not a material matter; it is not a consequence of women's role in production nor even, to complete the popular Marxist-feminist phrase, in reproduction. It is a matter that is fundamentally lodged in the ideological realm of values and social worth. The timocratic stratification of the two sexes is deeply rooted in the cultural psyche in North America, as it is almost everywhere else. The recently implemented political and legal equality of the two sexes threatens the social honour of males and impels women to reassure them by intensifying their own symbolic acceptance of their proper, degraded social status.

4. The Group, the Community and Social Degradation[30]

Why discuss self-mutilation in a volume that will presumably be read by people already committed to all human rights, including the right to health? I chose this topic because the cultural subordination of women and other degraded categories of people is routinely disregarded in much of the current

[29] See note 18, *supra*, pp. 112–113.

[30] This section is based on my *Human Rights and the Search for Community*, Part I (in progress).

international human rights debates, especially the debates on cultural relativism and on group or collective rights.[31]

The existence of self-mutilation makes clear that a human rights-oriented analysis of relations between the sexes that considers only the formal aspects of inequality such as economic opportunity or political participation cannot grasp the depths of subordination of women. Inequalities between the two sexes are not simply a matter of anachronistic customs surviving into the modern era. They are deeply rooted in women's symbolic meaning and in the almost universal societal tendency to degrade them, even in the liberal Western world. Like other degraded social categories such as homosexuals, blacks and Jews (in past Western society), women experience inferiorization in everyday life.[32]

One good reason for human rights scholars to take seriously this symbolic realm of degradation is to counter the mythology of the holistic, unitary and egalitarian group or community that many traditionalist advocates of group rights, and many communitarian critics of individual rights, believe to be typical of non-Western societies, and which they hold up as a social ideal for which Westerners, including those interested in human rights, ought to strive. These traditionalists stress their societies' organic wholeness and the individual's willing subservience to the society in the interests of social oneness, but they often fail to acknowledge the hierarchical basis of social order. This social oneness is then romanticized as facilitating in the individual a core of psychosocial integrity not only missing but impossible to realize in the competitive, alienated world of modern industrial capitalism. Traditionalist advocates of group rights tend in particular either to ignore the question of subordination of women completely, or to deal with it in an unscholarly fashion.[33]

As a sociologist I recognize the alienating aspects of modern Western society, and I recognize that to be human is to be social, to be part of a community. But I am also aware of the internally entrenched social injustice (in human rights terms) that characterizes many of the traditional close-knit communities that are so idealized in the group rights literature. Not only women, but also outsider ethnic groups, slaves and the descendants of slaves, homosexuals and other deviant categories suffer from such injustice. This injustice must be recognized and new types of communities must be created in which there are no ritually degraded categories of people; in which no social category is deprived of equal respect and concern because of its particular status.

[31] See e.g. Jan Berting *et al.*, (Eds.) *Human Rights in a Pluralist World: Individuals and Collectivities* (1990), Westport, Conn. and London: Meckler.

[32] Barry D. Adam, *The Survival of Domination: Inferiorization in Everyday Life* (1978), New York: Elsevier.

[33] For example, Josiah A.M. Cobbah, "African Values and the Human Rights Debate: An African Perspective", 9 *Human Rights Quarterly* (August 1987), no. 3, pp. 309–31, who dismisses feminist concerns out of hand without any serious analysis of the social conditions of women and children.

International human rights activists would like to see a world in which everyone is treated equally and with respect. Yet this is hardly likely to occur unless almost all indigenous cultures and ideologies, both traditional and modern, change. Degradation is a "natural" social phenomenon that we find in many societies. While some are honoured, others are shamed. In a well-ordered social system, as the communitarian and traditionalist critics of individual human rights have observed, those who are degraded (in human rights terms) accept their status; they do not strive for their individual rights. In the international documents, human rights are connected with human dignity. Yet the obverse side of dignity is the dishonour of those whose dignity must be in their submission to others and in their willing acquiescence in their own degradation.

In communitarian societies, shame, the willing acceptance of stigma, is the lot of many people. The society's culture frequently depends on preservation of hierarchies of honour and shame, and when such hierarchies seem threatened, coercive measures to preserve them are frequently taken. Gender hierarchies in particular are so entrenched that male commentators frequently do not notice them. In an important article on human dignity, for example, the distinguished human rights jurist Oscar Schachter does not mention discrimination against women, more than half the people in the world, in his list of examples of the way in which dignity can be denied, except perhaps by implication in his mention of discrimination according to status.[34]

Communitarianism from above, as it were, often defended by elite males whose very status as male means accumulated prestige as they acquire families and become heads of households, disregards the effects of community on those below. Communitarianism, as a philosophy, as a critique of modernized society and as a basis for the entrenchment of new international laws favouring the rights of groups over those of individuals, ignores intra-community violence perpetrated against particular degraded status categories, including socialization practices that cause degraded individuals to commit violence – self-mutilation – against themselves.

The international human rights debate on cultural relativism, like the debate on group rights, also disregards the existence of socially degrading categories and practices. All of the self-mutilatory practices described in this essay are cultural. They are practices voluntarily undertaken by women and customs that women unthinkingly pass on to their daughters. Women perform these mutilations on themselves and each other within ritualized friendship relationships. Their constant repetition furthers social solidarity among women and provides an approved social space into which they can withdraw from men. Nevertheless, they are objectively engaged in customs and rituals that threaten their health and reinforce a psychology of self-degradation. Cultural practices are often practices of social categorization and dishonour.

[34] Oscar Schachter, "Editorial Comment: Human Dignity as a Normative Concept", 77 *American Journal of International Law* (October 1983), p. 852.

The legal discourse on human rights must be supplemented by sociological understanding of the human social roots of categorized inequality and degradation. The immense amount of empirical and theoretical scholarship about women of the last 20 years appears to have made barely a dent in the international human rights literature: rather, women's rights, like women themselves, have been marginalized, kept out of the core human rights debates. "[F]or many human rights leaders, women's issues are still at best secondary. ... [T]hey are regarded as regrettable aspects of the situation of women in places where different customs prevail."[35]

But in fact, these "different" customs prevail even in the liberal Western world which is presumed to have solved most of its problems of discrimination by status. Women everywhere mutilate themselves as a form of self-effacement, an expression of their shame in being female. The African practice of female genital mutilations may seem primitive in Western eyes because it is practised on infants, and on genitalia, without benefit of anaesthesia. But our own medical practices not only during the nineteenth century but also in the immediate present are closely analogous to the African operations in their social meaning if not in the severity of their physiological consequences.

Protection of the right to health, then, is not only a matter of the state's being able to generate enough revenues and distribute them equitably to provide all its citizens with a socially acceptable minimum level of health care. Protection of the right to health also demands attitudinal, that is "cultural", change, not only within community groups but also within that most intimate of social realms, the family. And it requires state protection of women against the degradation and violence of which many social groups or communities still approve.

Non-discrimination, a key human right, must encompass recognition of cultural patterns of social degradation and attempts to overcome, indeed eradicate, these practices. This cannot occur as long as analyses such as those embodied in academic feminism continue to be ignored in the core human rights discourses. As long as comparative volumes and international conferences continue to marginalize feminist criticisms by categorizing them into "other" human rights debates, social degradation will remain an accepted and acceptable part of social organization even in supposedly rights-protective societies.

[35] Riane Eisler "Human Rights: Toward an Integrated Theory for Action", 9 *Human Rights Quarterly* (August 1987), no. 3, pp. 301 and 307.

SECTION IV(c): THE RIGHT TO ENVIRONMENT

SUSAN TANNER*

Introduction

Environmental law is a relatively new area of international law and one which is undergoing rapid change. This accelerated legal development is due to our current ecological crisis.

Humankind is being challenged to re-examine its social and legal structures in the light of potential extinction as a species. In response, the idea of a human right to a healthy environment has recently emerged.

In this section a group of experts was asked to bring together two areas of law – human rights and environmental law – to discuss the new "human right to environment". The authors, an Inuit leader, three lawyers, and a scientist from industrialized Europe, developing Brazil and Canada, describe the many similarities between human rights and environmental law and their joint evolution towards globalization. They identify a concern for future generations and a range of mechanisms which could be used to implement a right to environment. They offer constructive suggestions – both practical and philosophical. At the same time, there is a recognition in each paper that the new right to environment takes us into uncharted territory. The definitions, the jurisprudence, the international instruments and the mechanisms are still evolving. There is a notable consensus among the experts as to the links between human rights and environmental law. The question is whether the human rights framework is adequate to realize a right to environment for the world's population.

Mary Simon makes the point that the protection of the environment requires a new way of thinking. The environment cannot be protected within the current paradigm of dominance of the white culture. The adversarial process cannot be relied upon to protect the environment, native culture and the common heritage of mankind. Survival of the species requires social and legal structures which emphasize cooperation and social consensus. Linkages between environmental protection and indigenous societies or cultures must be recognized. The

* LL.B., M.E.S., Ottawa, Ontario, Canada; Executive Director, Friends of the Earth. Author's summary has been substantially shortened by editors.

K.E. Mahoney and P. Mahoney (eds.), Human Rights in the Twenty-first Century, 517–519.

Stockholm Declaration on the Human Environment[1] recognizes the links between different forms of oppression: the twin sins of exploitation of human beings and exploitation of the environment.

Dr. Roots, the scientist, asks the legal scholars to broaden the framework of their analysis beyond the human-to-human dimension, where one group or individual exercises power over another. The provision of a right to environment is, in a fundamental way, a humans-to-nature affair.

Dr. Trindade describes a conceptual shift in international thought. Traditionally, nation States have been concerned primarily with self-interest and the achievement of reciprocity in international agreements. With the emergence of the "common-concern-of-humankind" approach, States are required to act in accordance with global standards irrespective of reciprocity. This is an erosion of State sovereignty in the interest of global concerns.

The impossibility of separating environmental rights from social and economic rights was noted by all the experts. Dr. Roots points out that the belief in exponential economic growth through the exploitation of natural resources is not obsolete. Due to the finite carrying capacity of the earth, the issue is no longer only the unequal distribution of limitless wealth. The issue is now the allocation of dwindling world resources among increasing populations with raised expectations, in a manner that does not destroy Mother Nature in the process. All five authors agree that environmental law introduces an important new aspect into human rights law: the temporal dimension, that is the concern with providing for future generations.

The three legal scholars base their definitions of a human right to environment on the fundamental right to life and the right to health. Health is defined in broad terms including both physical and mental well-being. As the law develops, both the definition of human rights and that of environmental rights evolve.

The authors agree that there must be a wide spectrum of mechanisms used to provide a right to environment. The lawyers see the existing human rights mechanisms as transferable, in whole or in part, to the area of environmental rights. Dr. Roots advises however, that relevant scientific information is often missed in the existing processes.

The experts also agree that traditional human rights mechanisms are not sufficient on their own. These mechanisms deal primarily with redress once a problem has occurred. As the environment cannot be conserved except through preventive measures, there must be a procedure offered to individuals and groups who perceive that their environment is threatened before the event occurs. The preventive procedure described by Dr. Kiss and adopted by Drs. Trindade and Dejeant-Pons has three main components: right to information, right to participation in decision-making and right to compensation for damages. This participatory approach requires State support in providing the

[1] "Stockholm Declaration on the Human Environment" (1972), New York: United Nations Environment Programme.

opportunity for shared decision-making. Active State intervention is essential to implement a right to environment.

Where the authors disagree is with respect to potential conflicts between the right to environment and "pre-existing" human rights. Dr. Trindade sees no antagonism, environmental law helping to codify the social framework within which all human rights are inserted. In contrast, Dr. Roots decries the anthropomorphic nature of our laws, society and spirituality. He shares the view that ignoring Nature's rights will lead sooner or later to the relinquishing of mankind's own rights" and that consequently, "in reality the rights of Nature take precedence over the rights of humans". Dr. Roots also identifies a number of potential conflicts between competing human rights. For example, the strain that increased population places on the carrying capacity of the Earth might engender conflict between the right to natural resources and the right of humans to reproduce.

One positive sign is that concern for the protection of vulnerable groups such as indigenous populations, minorities and the handicapped can now be found in international instruments and initiatives pertaining to both human rights and environmental protection. "Protection" is not, however, the same as "involvement" of these groups in the setting of the framework in which environmental issues are considered: the rules of the game by which the globe is governed.

There is work to be done in the international community to honour the Stockholm Declaration and the report of The World Commission on the Environment by including women, aboriginal and other oppressed groups in the organizational structures and implementation mechanisms of a right to environment. Not only all peoples of the world but all modes of thought will be needed in the search for new ways to care for our planet. The five experts writing in this chapter present us with a challenge. The challenge is to make these international declarations into a tangible reality. The challenge is to protect the global environment – and to do so in a co-operative and participatory manner.

The ultimate challenge is to provide a right to environment in a context of scarcity. Even now, when we have a world surplus of food and idealistic human rights declarations, we are unable to provide food to vast numbers of people. What will happen when there is a shortage? We know that human rights abuses – the abuse of power over others – intensifies in a context of dominance and fear. Scarcity creates fear. As we enter this new era of limitation – limits to growth, limited carrying capacity of the Earth – we face a social, legal and spiritual challenge of unprecedented dimension. It is up to each of us to start now in ensuring that we will be ready to meet it.

MARY SIMON*

The Integration and Interdependence of Culture and the Environment

1. Introduction

Inuit culture is closely integrated with the environment and the living resources. As an Inuk from Northern Quebec and President of the Inuit Circumpolar Conference, my *argument* is from an Inuit perspective.

The term "culture" can have different significance for different people.

Culture illustrates the richness and diversity found in entertainment and the arts. It is also vividly portrayed by archaeological artifacts, monuments and ancient sites, which capture a particular history and way of life. For some people culture is the distinct Native content that is too often missing from curricula in education and broadcasting. Culture is also measured by the existence of aboriginal languages and dialects and their continued use and development.

All of these vital aspects of culture continue to be very important to Inuit in the circumpolar regions. Each of these areas require appropriate protection and support. At the same time, it is essential to recognize that our culture and heritage as aboriginal people must be described and valued in even broader dimensions.

In view of our profound relationship with and continuing dependence upon the land and its resources, the distinct identity and culture of Inuit cannot be separated from the Arctic environment and its land and marine areas. It is the natural Arctic environment that shapes Inuit spirituality, our linguistic and artistic expression, and our way of life. If we are to adequately protect our people and our culture, the environmental integrity of our vast circumpolar homeland and its living resources must be safeguarded.

As far as indigenous peoples are concerned, the destruction of the environment serves to accelerate our assimilation and undermine our most fundamental rights. The resulting deterioration of our culture is not only a tragedy

* President, Inuit Circumpolar Conference, Lachine, Quebec, Canada. The Inuit Circumpolar Conference (ICC) is an international organization whose members are made up of Inuit from Alaska, Canada and Greenland. Presently, two Soviet Inuit participate in ICC's Executive Council as *ex officio* members. The ICC has non-governmental organization status at the United Nations.

K.E. Mahoney and P. Mahoney (eds.), Human Rights in the Twenty-first Century, 521–527.

for indigenous peoples, but also a severe loss to the common heritage of humankind.

Yet, in most instances international and national laws and policies do not clearly establish the link between environmental protection and indigenous societies or cultures. For example, the 1982 United Nations Convention on the Law of the Sea (not yet in force) explicitly provides that coastal states have the authority to prevent and control marine pollution from ice-covered areas. However, no mention is made of the crucial significance of the northern marine environment to Inuit and other aboriginal peoples.

Also, the World Conservation Strategy represents a concerted international effort to provide for sustainable development in a manner that is consistent with environmental principles. Yet this comprehensive strategy does not contain any express and appropriate reference to aboriginal subsistence practices. This serious omission only serves to help those in the anti-harvesting movement, who seek to eliminate our food source and subsistence way of life.

It is, however, encouraging that draft revisions to the World Conservation Strategy are being prepared, in order to effectively incorporate indigenous values, perspectives and rights. We urge all countries to actively support these very important revisions.

There is a growing list of environment-related matters of great concern in circumpolar regions that have serious and far-reaching consequences for aboriginal peoples and the future of the Arctic. Many of these problems if left unresolved pose a mounting threat to the security and way of life of aboriginal peoples. Examples include, transboundary pollution by PCB's and other persistent chemicals, depletion of the ozone layer, arctic haze, militarization, inadequate regulation of resource development in the marine areas, oil spills, the impacts of hydroelectric projects and ocean dumping. Depending on the severity, environmental damage can irreversibly affect our way of life.

For Inuit people, there continues to exist a deep-rooted interrelationship between Inuit culture and our northern environment. The Governments never dispute that fact. But the problem is that they do not take our interdependence into account in their policies, regulations and actions.

The ensuing discussion will focus on how the key elements of culture and environment are being or may be integrated. The areas discussed are:

a) the inadequacies of the existing human rights framework;
b) some positive developments that are taking place in regard to indigenous peoples' rights; and
c) recommendations for a balanced and equitable approach.

2. Inadequacies of the Existing International Human Rights Framework

It is worth noting that the UNESCO Declaration of the Principles of International Cultural Co-operation (1966) makes no link between culture and the environment. In addition, the United Nations General Assembly Resolution[1] on the Declaration on the Right to Development includes cultural development as an integral part of the human right to development, but omits any reference to the natural environment.

In the International Bill of Rights, there are references to the "right freely to participate in the cultural life of the community"[2]. In our opinion, these provisions are not comprehensive. Nor are they explicitly related to environmental concerns.

For the most part, existing human rights instruments are drafted from an "individual rights" perspective. They fail to accommodate properly the collective rights of indigenous peoples. Generally, they do not serve to ensure our survival as distinct peoples.

During the past few years in Geneva, the Inuit Circumpolar Conference (ICC) has, with much effort, striven for international recognition of indigenous peoples' right to peace, right to development, and right to a safe and healthy environment. These are the fundamental rights that we seek to be affirmed and implemented. To date, countries who consider themselves progressive, both in the field of human rights and the environment, have been silent in their response to indigenous peoples on these key matters.

Indigenous peoples have always asserted that environmental protection and cultural survival must be addressed in terms of both present and future generations. Within the international community, a theory of "Intergenerational Equity" is emerging that appears to embrace an indigenous perspective. The central point of this theory has been described as follows:

> "... the right of each generation to benefit from and develop this natural and cultural heritage is inseparably coupled with the obligation to use this heritage in such a manner that it can be passed on to future generations in no worse condition than it was received from past generations."

Hopefully, suitable action will be taken to reflect this key notion in the international legal system.

3. Positive Developments in Regard to Indigenous Peoples' Rights

Despite ongoing resistance from many countries, some positive initiatives are beginning to take place at the international level in relation to human rights

[1] U.N.G.A. Resolution 41/128 of December 4, 1986.

[2] Universal Declaration of Human Rights, Article 27. See also International Covenant on Economic, Social and Cultural Rights, Article 15 ("the right of everyone ... to take part in cultural life"); and the International Covenant on Civil and Political Rights, Article 27 ("persons belonging to ... minorities shall not be denied the right, in community with other members of their own group, to enjoy their own culture"). Of course, indigenous peoples do not consider themselves to be "minorities", but are distinct "peoples" with all the status and rights that flow from such a term.

standards and indigenous peoples. In regard to indigenous cultures and the environment, these include the following:

(1) Indigenous and Tribal Peoples' Convention (No. 169)

This International Labour Convention which was revised over two years (but which is not yet in force) was adopted in 1989. Although inadequate in certain key areas, it obliges governments to respect the special importance for the cultures and spiritual values of peoples, and of their relationship with the lands and territories that they occupy or otherwise use. It also requires that studies be carried out, in cooperation with indigenous peoples, to assess the social, spiritual, cultural and environmental impact of planned development activities.

(2) Draft Universal Declaration on Indigenous Rights

This draft Declaration is being prepared by the United Nations Working Group on Indigenous Peoples in Geneva. A July 1990 report[3] of one of the drafting groups recommends recognition of the right to a safe and healthy environment. It also proposes that governments have a duty to respect in all relevant policies and actions the profound relationships indigenous peoples have with their traditional territories, lands and resources.

Presently, the ICC is working with other indigenous peoples to try and secure direct participation in all stages of the process, leading up to and including the 1992 United Nations Conference on Environment and Development (to be held in Brazil). It is critical that we participate in this conference which is seeking to advance environmental solutions. We must make certain that environmental actions are devised within appropriate cultural contexts.

In discussing the environment and its inseparable link to indigenous peoples' culture, spirituality and human rights, I believe it is important to refer to the recent Mohawk crisis in Quebec. After all, the land and pine forest that the Mohawks sought to protect from becoming a golf course involved all of these issues.

Indigenous peoples worldwide face, in one form or another, violence to their rights and dignity and a multitude of threats to their survival. The ICC believes that the Mohawk conflict tragically underscores the urgent need for adequate standards and equitable processes to resolve disputes concerning indigenous peoples in a peaceful and impartial manner. In the absence of appropriate international and national attention to indigenous rights and concerns, governments will continue to threaten our security.

Our territorial and other basic rights will continue to be denied, diminished or otherwise eroded. In regard to indigenous cultures and the environment, it is

[3] See Report of the informal drafting groups established to consider the first revised text of the draft Universal Declaration on Indigenous Rights, E/CN.4/Sub.2/AC.4/1990/7, July 30, 1990.

also worth noting that the proposed Canadian Environmental Assessment Act (Bill C-78)[4], if adopted in its present form, would fail to meet the minimum standards set out in International Labour Organization Convention 169. Instead of requiring a broad assessment of social, spiritual and cultural impacts on indigenous peoples, Bill C-78 only explicitly includes the effects of any (environmental) change on health and socio-economic condition.[5] The Bill seeks to authorize an excessive use of discretionary powers[6] for government officials (rather than mandatory requirements) at all stages of the assessment process.

It contains inadequate provisions for public input and provides far-reaching government powers for "varying or excluding" requirements for assessment. Low-level flight testing and training for military purposes could be exempted from assessment in the future.

4. Recommendations for a Balanced and Equitable Approach

When development decisions are taken that affect our territories, our cultures must be made an essential focal point. The strong and continuing bond between indigenous cultures and the environment calls for cooperative government policies and actions that would favour a more balanced and equitable approach.

Brief mention should also be made of the following recommendations that would favour such a balanced and equitable approach:

(1) Limits on State Sovereignty

For the purpose of environmental protection, it is increasingly urgent that governments appropriately limit their sovereignty by accepting mandatory standards through international agreements or conventions. However, these measures alone will not be sufficient since they are likely to cover only certain specific environmental issues and have limited or minimal goals.

(2) Expanded Human Rights Framework

What is also required is a broadening of the human rights framework to include fundamental environmental rights and remedies. The empowerment of indigenous peoples and others in relation to the environment would provide an essential balance to the wide-ranging powers of state governments. In this context, ways of recognizing and implementing the emerging right to a safe and

[4] First reading of Bill C-78 took place on June 18, 1990.

[5] Ibid., see definition of "environmental effect" in section 2 of the proposed Act.

[6] Requests by indigenous peoples and others for judicial review of government action or inaction would be enormously difficult, in view of the 60 or more provisions permitting government discretion.

healthy environment should be seriously considered. This basic right should become an integral part of a comprehensive Environmental Bill of Rights. For present and future generations, both environmental and cultural diversity must be ensured.

(3) Sustainable and Equitable Development

Planned development in or affecting indigenous territories must not only be "sustainable" in terms of the physical environment, but must also be equitable from the viewpoint of the indigenous people affected. Development activities must not undermine, but rather enhance, the social and cultural environment of indigenous peoples. In addition, development must not be imposed on us. It should only take place with our free and informed consent and must fully accommodate our rights, values and concerns.

(4) Indigenous Peoples Involvement

Consistent with the principles of self-government, indigenous people must have adequate powers to manage and control environmental and development matters affecting their traditional territories.

At the national and international levels, our full and direct participation in policy and decision-making must also be ensured. It is only in this way that we can begin to deal with the transboundary pollution problems that are jeopardizing our health, wildlife and future as distinct peoples.

At this time, the eight Arctic countries are in the process of formulating a "sustainable development strategy" for the circumpolar North. This process is referred to as the "Finnish Initiative". However, the extent of our participation in this crucial process is far from certain.

(5) Enforcement

Adequate enforcement opportunities are needed for indigenous peoples, in order to protect the environment and prevent harmful impacts on our societies. For proper enforcement, there must be suitable mandatory standards, recognition of indigenous rights, and timely access to effective remedies.

5. Conclusions

Indigenous peoples continue to be extremely vulnerable to the consequences of environmental change. Problems such as global warming, depletion of the ozone layer, and transboundary pollution by persistent chemicals may irreversibly alter life on this planet for all species and cultures if these issues remain unresolved.

It is clear to us as Inuit that we must work towards the security and future of our Arctic communities and circumpolar territories in environmental, social, cultural, as well as economic terms.

The history of deterioration of the Inuit people, in the face of mounting environmental and cultural assaults, is sufficient evidence that government representation and action alone "on behalf of" Inuit simply has not worked. Low national and international environmental standards and a chronic lack of political will are a fatal combination, contributing to the earth's degradation and the loss of cultural heritage.

It can be expected that governments will reluctantly agree to higher standards, as environmental conditions worsen. This is simply not enough. Ecological balance, the integrity of indigenous cultures, and social justice can only be secured through the empowerment and involvement of the peoples affected.

The existing human rights framework must be significantly altered to reflect new realities and threats to our collective security. In particular, the basic human right to a safe and healthy environment deserves appropriate recognition. In addition, indigenous peoples must be assured the right to participate directly in national and international matters that affect their interests. In this way, the trend to exclude us can be permanently reversed.

As human rights evolve into the twenty-first century, we must elaborate and build upon the fundamental rights of peoples and the corresponding duties of governments. In regard to indigenous peoples, we must begin now to develop a more responsive and socially just orientation – an approach that emphasizes genuine stewardship of the environment for both present and future generations.

E. F. ROOTS*

Population, "Carrying Capacity", and Environmental Processes

Most discussions and declarations of human rights focus on the relationships between humans as individuals or in groups, and take for granted that humans have a right to use natural resources and environmental amenities for human purposes. A fundamental aspect of human rights is also a stated or implied right of every human individual to food, clean water, and a healthy environment – all of which must be provided through natural processes. The concept of carrying capacity, referring to the number of people that a given land can support, is an imprecise and scientifically shaky idea, but it can serve in a general way to express limitations that finite natural resources and processes impose on expanding human needs and on the tolerance for environmental impacts. Expanding human populations and the use of energy and materials have not only caused local disruption of the environment and depletion of resources, but have begun to disturb planetary environmental processes and distort major ecosystems, leading to conflicts between the right to use resources and the right to clean environment. Changes in physical and biological characteristics on a global scale, more rapid and severe than any experienced in human history, appear to be imminent. These changes, which are in part the result of humans expressing their rights to exploit nature, portend inescapable constraints on the ability of all humans, now or in the future, to realize their "right" to food, clean water, a healthy environment and the resources necessary to achieve a satisfactory social and economic living. Major problems that cannot be escaped as the human race enters the twenty-first century include: adjustment to the reality that for the first time in history, humans must look upon themselves not as consumers but as exchangers of resources and energy, and that exercise of the right to use a resource or natural amenity henceforth may deny that action to someone else who has equal right to it; that individual and collective rights to natural resources and a healthy environment are, inevitably, incompatible with the unfettered right of individuals to reproduce; that deteriorating environmental conditions in many parts of the world are creating a new class of distressed human – the environmental refugees – whose rights, and the rights of

* Science Advisor Emeritus, Department of the Environment, Ottawa, Ontario.

K.E. Mahoney and P. Mahoney (eds.), Human Rights in the Twenty-first Century, 529–549.

those who must support them or make room for them, raise many ethical, political, and economic questions; issues of the rights of persons or societies with distinct cultures that have been displaced or which can no longer be sustained because of environmental, economic or technological changes; questions of the "rights" of future generations in light of the prospect of accelerating global environmental change; and of the rights of humans compared to the "rights" of non-human species. Achievement of human rights within an ecosystem perspective will require fundamental changes in legal, business, and religious concepts and practices. Despite the enormity of these problems, necessity and recent experience, and increasing scientific understanding and public awareness of our world and ourselves are leading to a rapidly deepening conviction and acceptance in many societies, at both political and individual levels, that the rights of humans must be based on the "rights" of Nature. Understanding of the rights of Nature, and of the constraints inherent in the workings of the natural environment, is an essential part of the achievement of human rights.

1. Introduction

The theme indicated by the conference organizers for this paper is human population and the carrying capacity of the natural environment, as it pertains to issues of human rights. The idea of carrying capacity, while it has been a useful concept in developing early, simplified ideas about ecological relations but does not make much sense as a principle applied to human behaviour in the modern world. However, the concept can serve as a starting point for considerations of the relationship of the scale of human activities to the characteristics and dynamics of the planet of which we are a part.

In so doing, we want to look a little farther than the year 2000 – which seems to be a hypnotic date. The twenty-first century will, we hope, be about 100 years long, like all the other centuries. What happens in the middle of the twenty-first century, when most of today's children will still be alive and will have had their own children, when the only trees that will be available for cutting are ones that are already saplings today, when garbage dumps we are filling today will be leaking most actively, and when changes in water supplies and climate will, for better or worse, have affected large parts of the world – that is the time when, from all our evidence, human rights will be most severely tested. Staying in the twenty-first century will probably be more onerous than getting into it.

Nearly all discussions on human rights, in the United Nations, in international humanitarian organizations, and even at this conference, deal with the actions of humans among humans – where one group of humans exercises power over other humans, or undertakes activities that constrain the ability of another group of humans, or of an individual, to act, or think, or live in a way that is fair or just. Most of these discussions, recognize implicitly the dependence of all humans upon the Earth's resources and upon an environment conducive to life and human activities. And thus, many declarations of human rights contain references to the basic right to food, to clean water, to earn a living, to a healthy environment.[1] But in these declarations, and in the sincere intentions that there should be food, clean water and a safe or healthy environment for each and for all, there is rarely a serious examination as to whether such life support systems can be sustained or the amenities can be attainable, even if all humans and all human societies co-operated harmoniously to make them available. There seems to be often an implicit assumption that these gifts and services from Mother Nature, the natural resources – are there for the taking, and will be adequate for all humans; and that human rights issues are primarily about problems of who gets how much, or who prevents others from getting their share or being treated fairly.

However, planet Earth, as we all know, is a finite and limited piece of rock, water and gas, on which there are some complex chemical and electro-chemical reactions that we recognize as biological life, nervous energy, and human or animal spirit. Natural processes within and on this planet operate at their own scale and speed, undoubtedly in some aspects affected by human activities and desires, but in no basic way, as far as anyone has evidence, controlled by them. It may be of interest to consider the extent to which the necessary gifts of Nature – the life-sustaining gifts and what we have come to think of as basic resources and amenities – to which all humans should have a right, are in fact likely to be available, now or in the future.

It has been said many times by scholars and politicians and at this Conference that the basic human right is the right to live, and close behind that the right to make a living. The survival of any human, or other organism, depends upon the integration of that individual within a productive biological ecosystem that can maintain its living members in a tolerable habitat; and the ability of humans to have actions, freedoms and association beyond bare biological existence depends upon the capacity of the Earth to provide energy, materials and space for all the activities that we associate with societies and civilizations. There are many indications that the demands that humans, in some groups or in total, are putting on the Earth and its environment may be exceeding the capacity of the Earth to provide these things, and moreover that the capacity of the Earth itself is being diminished or damaged by human activities.[2] Thus, the realization of basic human rights for all humans is more than a humans-to-humans affair. It is in a fundamental way a humans-to-Nature affair. The realization of human rights may be constrained as much by humankind's inhumanity to Nature as by the inhumanity of some humans to other humans.

[1] United Nations General Assembly (1948), *Universal Declaration of Human Rights*, expanded and up-dated into: United Nations (1978), *The International Bill of Human Rights*, including the Universal Declaration of Human Rights, the International Covenant on Economic, Social and Cultural Rights, and the Optional Protocol to the International Covenant on Civil and Political Rights, Office of Public Information, United Nations, New York.

[2] C. Mungall, and D. McLaren (eds.) *Planet Under Stress* (1990), Oxford University Press, Toronto and Oxford.

2. The Concept of Carrying Capacity

From the earliest hunting and gathering societies, people have been aware that a certain patch of territory could hold only so many food animals or so many berry bushes, and if all the animals were killed or all the berries were picked there would be no more. Families, or tribes, learned the hard way how many people could live in any particular area. And from the earliest days of cultivation of crops or domestication of animals, there was knowledge of a practical limit to biological productivity, and thus a limit to how many people could be supported. As knowledge became more systematically organized, the obvious and sensible notion of a limit to the amount that could be produced or supported within any semi-closed system became known as the *carrying capacity*.[3]

Taken in a simplistic manner, the idea is common-sense, and has value in drawing attention to the fact that, in any place or under any set of conditions, there is some sort of limit to productivity or to the population that can be supported from within that place. But when used for planning or analysis of issues involving humans, the concept of carrying capacity meets some real difficulties. One has to ask:

- at what level of activity, productivity, or "comfort" is the population to be maintained? Is the answer to be given in numbers of persons only, or should the degree of health, activity, etc. be included?
- where are the boundaries, in space or potential resources, or in time (borrowing from the past or mortgaging the future) that will be used to estimate the base of support?
- are humans to be considered separately from any other creatures on Earth?

It does not take much examination of these questions to conclude that:

- as all living or biological or environmental relationships are dynamic and continually shifting, the idea of a "capacity limit" for the human species in any area can have little validity or meaning except for a particular moment under a particular set of circumstances; and
- as the sustained or immediate life support depend greatly upon the technology used, the resources available, and the energy applied (all of which generally come from somewhere else), the idea of carrying capacity of a region makes little sense – unless one extends it to the whole planet (some would say the solar system).

In the modern human context, carrying capacity is a matter of technology and those particular components valued by humans. But because we are still dealing with natural systems and processes, the carrying capacity is also subject to natural interventions and surprises introduced by Nature but triggered by human actions. The history of mankind is replete with attempts to increase carrying capacity for human ends by deliberate planned actions, which have then been frustrated by complications which were unforeseen, or which, even if

[3] P. Ehrlich, and A. Ehrlich, *Population, Resources, Environment: Issues in Human Ecology* (1972), (2nd ed.) W.H. Freeman, San Francisco.

known about beforehand, became much more important than expected. A good current example is the river Nile. No river on earth is better known. For 5,000 years, clever people have been studying the Nile, using its vagaries and seasonal eccentricities to support, through most of human history, a vigorous society whose successive technologies were put to use as civilization advanced. The carrying capacity of the river system to support people was developed to its then practical limit in the Stone Age, increased again in the Bronze Age, once again in the Iron Age up to nearly modern times. But in the Electric Age, the Aswan High Dam was built to expand the carrying capacity to a still higher level, to provide power for the industrialization of Egypt, to control flooding, to irrigate new "reclaimed" desert lands, and, it was hoped, to support a population that had more than doubled in a century. Technically, the dam has worked, just as it was planned. But, in Egypt's most fertile area, the Nile delta, the cessation of annual flooding has led to alarming increase of the parasitic diseases schistosomiasis and bilharzia; farther upstream the salt content of irrigated desert soils has run wild; a centuries-old sardine fishery in the eastern Mediterranean has disappeared and the number of fish species in the river reduced from more than 130 to about 10.[4] Egypt, long an exporter of food to the surrounding region, now is dependent on imported fertilizer and has become a net food importer. There is little doubt that the vulnerability of the entire socio-economic complex in the lower Nile valley to a change in climate or to mismanagement is now greater than before the dam was built. The production of food has increased, for a few years, but at what cost? Has the net carrying capacity increased? Has the industrial development, designed to increase regional economic capacity, maintained the vigour of the nation and improved the "rights" of all its citizens? One could also ask, what might have been the situation in Egypt today had the Aswan High Dam not been built? Such questions are at the heart of the issues of carrying capacity and the rights of people or nations to use or manipulate natural resources. There are similar examples, on every continent, where the manipulation of carrying capacity has led to new or larger problems.

A difficulty with the concept of carrying capacity as a planning or assessment tool is that it tends to focus on meeting basic biological needs or physical needs, and to produce results expressed in numbers (of people, tonnes of grain, or GNP). The carrying capacity for quality of life remains subjective and elusive and all too often ignored. Carrying capacity, as usually understood, deals with materials, energy, and productivity in physical terms and is not suitable for describing the capacity to maintain values or express culture. And yet to have the capacity to express one's culture is, as Mary Simon has said,[5] one

[4] F. El-Gohary, (in press) "Water Quality of the Nile River and Development Projects". Paper presented at the International Conference on Statistical Methods for the Environmental Sciences, Cairo, Egypt, April 1989. Proceedings in press.

[5] Mary Simon, president of the Inuit Circumpolar Conference, in a speech to the International Conference on "Human Rights in the 21st Century", Banff, Alberta, November 1990.

of the most important rights of all.

On the whole, "carrying capacity" is not a term that has much meaning when examined closely or used for comparison or assessment. But it has value in a simple way to remind us all that resources and habitat are not limitless or indefinitely flexible, and that therefore the population or activities that depend upon them have limits. The concept reminds us that, in the game of life, Nature provides the playing field and sets the rules.

3. The Environmental and Resource Setting for Human Activities

What are the factors that set limits on the numbers and activities of people, regardless of their "rights"? The basic elements of the "life support systems" are obvious: Solar energy, fresh water and oceans, fertile soils. How precarious or how stable is the planetary life support system built on these basic elements?

- *Solar energy*. The natural ecosystems appear to use available sunlight (that part of the solar spectrum that has major biological significance) almost to the full for photosynthesis wherever there is adequate liquid water of pure enough quality for biological processes. Where there is insufficient water (as in deserts) or where water is not liquid (as in polar regions), sunlight "goes to waste", from a biological viewpoint (one of the objectives of the Aswan High Dam was to capture the productivity of "unused" sunlight on the desert). The Sun is a nuclear fusion reactor, not so far affected by humans. The only way we can likely change its capacity to support life on Earth is to shut out some of the incoming energy by opaque cloud, (this is a major basis for the "Nuclear Winter" concern), or by changing the spectrum of energy received, such as for example by destroying the ozone filter in the stratosphere. There have been instances when incoming sunlight was modified. Tamboro volcano erupted in Indonesia in 1815 and spewed out so much dust into the atmosphere over the northern hemisphere that radiation received at the surface was reduced, and 1816 became known as "the year without a summer".[6] Crops failed completely in some areas (New England, Gaspé, Sweden); parasites spread disease; social unrest and migration followed. Extensive forest fires (a possible consequence of drought from climate warming) could have a similar effect. The right to sunlight in all wavelengths to which our biology is accustomed, is taken to be universal; this right was a powerful factor in achieving political consensus on the Montreal Protocol on protection of the ozone layer.
- *Water*. Vulnerable to local and regional variations, by small change in weather patterns and climates, and physical changes in soils and topography. Changes or threatened changes in available water supply, due to variations in natural processes, or the effects of human activities, are

[6] Stommel, H. and E. Stommel, *Volcano Weather: The Story of 1816. The Year Without a Summer* (1983), Seven Seas Press, Newport, R.I. p. 280.

important human rights issues in many parts of the world because:[7]

(i) Most major food-producing areas of the world are characterized by marginal, not copious water supply;

(ii) Many areas of greatest population growth are areas where quantity of water is marginal or unreliable, and the quality is poor or in jeopardy.

- *Soils.* Soils suitable to support plants and all terrestrial ecosystems at optimun productivity form slowly but may be destroyed quickly. They are becoming impoverished or are eroding over large areas – (Africa, India, China, Eastern Europe, USSR are hardest hit, but there are areas of danger in the North American prairies, the U.S. southwest, and South America.)[8] Additions of chemical fertilizers or high-energy tillage practices to increase short-term productivity for selected plants usually initiates a vicious spiral that further reduces natural fertility.
- *Air.* Regional problems are persistent, and largely due to industrial activity, e.g., acid rain, but the short cycling time of air molecules in the lower atmosphere generally leads to rapid recovery when sources of contamination are cleaned up. Chemical change in the upper atmosphere (e.g., chemical precursors to ozone depletion) occurs more slowly and may persist for decades or centuries regardless of what is now done on the surface of the Earth.[9]
- *Oceans.* Not much affected in a physical sense by human activities, but pollution of surface layers over the world ocean may be having an effect on surface gas exchange and organic reactions; pollution near coastlines and hunting/fishing has severely affected major parts of the marine ecosystems by interfering with the top of the food chain (whales, salmon, tuna, herring) and the bottom (micro-organisms, diatoms, plankton, which appear to be most vulnerable to pollution).[10]

Of these essential elements of life-support, fresh water is probably the most critical and sensitive in the short term for the greatest number of people on Earth. Soils are more vulnerable than most societies have until now been concerned about, for they often do not show much visible change until their productive capacity is nearly all used up or the soils themselves have disappeared, after which recovery is very slow or impossible in time periods of

[7] S. Postel, "Water: Re-Thinking Management in an Age of Scarcity", *Worldwatch Paper 62* (1984), Worldwatch Institute, Washington.

[8] L. Brown, "The Worldwide Loss of Cropland", *Worldwatch Paper 24* (1978), Worldwatch Institute, Washington; and L. Brown, and C. Flavin, "The Earth's Vital Signs", in *State of the World 1988* (1988), W.W. Norton, New York.

[9] B. Schmidbauer, (Chair), *Protecting the Earth's Atmosphere: An International Challenge* (1989). Report to the German Bundestag by the Study Commission on Preventative Measures to Protect the Earth's Atmosphere, Bundestag Publishers, Bonn.

[10] GESAMP (IMO/FAO/UNESCO/WMO/WHO/IAEA/UN/UNEP Joint Group of Experts on the Scientific Aspects of Marine Pollution) (1990), *The State of the Marine Environment*. Reports and Studies GESAMP 39, United Nations Environment Programme, Nairobi.

concern to humans.[11] Atmospheric environmental problems can vary from severe and local, to chronic and insidious, and be temporary or long-lasting. Oceans, like the soil, may be slow to be affected by human actions, but when they do change, the effects may be major and long-lasting.

Beyond basic life support, natural resources provide second-level societal support to humans, without which societies and human populations as we know them could not develop. These resources include energy materials and sources; minerals; forests; pastures, and the hydrological waste dispersal network in groundwaters, streams and the ocean. While all of these have limits, either in total quantity at any grade or degree of natural productivity, from present evidence it does not appear that absolute limitation of the available quantities of the energy and mineral resources (the "non-renewable" resources) will be as constraining on future human activities as the effects of getting them, converting them, and using them. In other words, the damage that we may do to the environment or ourselves in using fossil fuels or minerals may be more critical to our future than the prospect of running out of them.[12] On the other hand, forests, pastures, fisheries and other "renewable" resources and the natural hydrological network are subject to definite limits of harvesting rates or utilization, and, as successive societies have learned to their despair in various parts of the world, can be destroyed or impaired permanently.

All these are the common heritage of all creatures on Earth. Humans have asserted or assumed that humans have a basic "right" to appropriate these resources for their own use. Leaving aside the question of the arrogance of this assumption, it is legitimate to ask: Are there enough to go around? Enough for all? For all time? To answer this question, we should look at environmental processes and limitations in a planetary and historical perspective.

4. Environmental Processes and Limitations

As far as is known, the physical, chemical and biological processes on Earth and throughout the Universe are not changed and cannot be changed by humans. And humans have not been able, so far, to invent new physical, chemical or biological processes. All humans can do is re-arrange some natural processes that are happening anyway. We need to look at these processes from a planetary perspective, to assess the present situation and the evidence for impending change, to consider what our "rights" may be.

[11] L. Brown, and E. Wolf, "Soil Erosion: Quiet Crisis in the World Economy", *Worldwatch Paper 60* (1984), Worldwatch Institute, Washington.

[12] G. Brundtland, (Chair) *Our Common Future* (1987). Report of the World Commission on Environment and Development, Oxford University Press, Oxford, New York, Toronto.

(1)The Planetary Perspective

Out of the enormous complexity of biological life on this planet, four features may be selected to show some perspectives in which it may be useful to view human rights:

(a) For the past 2 billion years, biological systems have executed a marvellously delicate control on the temperature and moisture conditions of the planet. From present knowledge, it appears not that the natural environment just happens to be suitable for biological life, or that biological life has by trial and error evolved to survive in the environment in which it found itself. Biological life processes are seen to be major factors in maintaining a natural environment suitable for biological life. [13] Change in the overall character or vigour of the biosphere will undoubtedly change the Earth environment. The reverse is also true, changes in the environment result in changes in biological life.

(b) At least 5 times in the past 600 million years, the entire planet has undergone severe and apparently sudden environmental changes, during which the biosphere was drastically altered.[14] The causes of these sudden changes are not always clear, and need not concern us here, but most seem to be the result of a sudden "outside" event – like impact of a meteorite, or a great volcanic eruption. In each case, it was the largest and most complex animals and plants that were most affected. At the end of the Cretaceous Period, for example, about 70 million years ago, there was a rapid world-wide extinction. No animal species with body weight greater than 35 Kg is known to have survived.[15] In each past example of these extinctions, there seems to have been a re-arrangement of environmental energy flow – a change of atmospheric transparency, or a rapid change of ocean surface temperature or currents. A conclusion from studies of these episodes of geological history is that the Earth's environment and the biosphere can be vulnerable to sudden change.[16]

(c) *Homo sapiens* is now the most abundant large animal on Earth. It is a fecund species, omniverous, with strong but erratic predatory, territorial and herd instincts. The numbers of individuals of this species are increasing rapidly, almost exponentially, and the species behaviour and habitat are changing in many fundamental ways. In geological history, species that have expanded rapidly in numbers typically have "crashed", apparently not because of simple

[13] J. Lovelock, *The Ages of Gaia: A Biography of Our Living Earth* (1988), W.W. Norton & Company, New York.

[14] D. Raup, "Biological Extinction in Earth History", *Science* (1986), Vol. 249, March 28, p. 286–294.

[15] D. McLaren, and W. Goodfellow, "Geological and Biological Consequences of Giant Impacts", *Annual Review, Earth and Planetary Sciences* (1990), Vol. 18, pp. 123–171.

[16] D.A. Hamburg, "Science and Technology in a World Transformed", *Science* (1984), Vol. 224, No. 4652, pp. 943–946. See also: W.C. Clark, "The Human Dimensions of Global Environmental Change", in H. Mooney, et. al. (eds.) *Toward an Understanding of Global Change* (1988), U.S. National Academy Press, Washington, pp. 134–200.

food shortage but because their habits and habitat changed; and often the first sign was change in intra-species behaviour and increased vulnerability to new parasites. By these usual biological criteria, *homo sapiens* is ready for a "crash".

(d) Intelligence, or a position on the top of the food chain, does not seem to be obvious attributes for biological survival. Leaving aside the touchy question of whether, within any one species, including humans, the biologically most successful members of groups are the ones that are the most intellegent, zoology in general gives us some lessons. The next most intelligent animals after humans, as far as we can apply human-like criteria such as reasoning ability and communicable memory, are the other great apes (gorillas, chimpanzees, orangutangs), the elephants and the whales. These groups of animals are also high on their respective food chains; but none is prospering in the human-dominated and environmentally changing world of today, and many seem to be on their way to extinction. The lessons from zoology are not reassuring to humankind.

(2) The Present Situation?

Human population is now more than 4 billion, and doubling every 35 years. Eighty-five percent of the increase is in countries where more than one-quarter of the people live on the margins of malnutrition or starvation. It is estimated that at present, about 35,000 people per year die of food shortage. In the next two decades, about eighty percent of the further increase of human population is expected to be in the 25 largest cities of the world, most of which have overloaded or inadequate water and sanitary facilities, and the danger of epidemic outbreak of new diseases is great; and their food and energy supply systems are increasingly precarious.[17]

Food Production, on a world basis, after spectacular gains three decades ago, appears to be on a plateau, and it is very hard to see where future great increases can come from.[18] At present, as has been pointed out many times, there is no absolute shortage of food on a world basis, and the greatest problem in feeding the humans of the world is distribution. However, full production and development of unused productive capacity of the temperate and tropical regions, if it could be sustained and if the products could be equitably distributed, would still appear to fall far short of meeting the inevitable demands of the increased world population expected in the next three decades. New technologies – biotechnology, multiple cropping, new usage of edible perennials in addition to annuals – can all help; but the sober lesson of the Green Revolution is that it is not possible to squeeze more out of Nature than she gives naturally without hurting her and paying perhaps a larger price, later

[17] L. Brown, et. al. *State of the World 1989* (1989), W.W. Norton, Washington, D.C.

[18] L. Brown, "The Changing World Food Prospect: The Nineties and Beyond", *Worldwatch Paper 85* (1988), Worldwatch Institute, Washington.

or somewhere else. Almost all areas available for new or restored food production are climatically or chemically marginal, susceptible to periods of crop failure, leading to the possibility of even greater human tragedy if society comes to depend upon such sources.[19]

Forests are the lungs of the world and the main governor in maintaining the stability of the terrestrial ecosystem. They are the principal global converter of solar energy into biomass (a mature forest is about 10 times as effective at this as an average cultivated farm or the sea) and incidentally the source of wood, paper, fuel for twenty-five percent of humankind, a vital element in the hydrological cycle, home to wildlife, etc. Throughout the world, forests are in serious trouble. The large-tree tropical forests have been reduced to less than half of what they were in 1920, and the rest are going fast.[20] The mixed forests and savannah of the sub-tropics are becoming open plains, often with bare windblown soil, almost everywhere they occur;[21] and the temperate hardwood and boreal coniferous forests, which 200 years ago together with their wetlands constituted the largest stocks of unoxided carbon on the surface of the planet, are shrinking rapidly under the attack of chain saw, acid rain, and agricultural or urban development. The ability of the world's forests to balance and regulate the world environment is very seriously declining.

Aquatic systems, estuaries, and coastlines are among the biologically most diverse and productive parts of the planet. But they are easily disturbed, and among the most affected by industrial activities.[22]

The list could go on. The *oceans* are the heavyweight player in the planetary game; slow to react, dominant when they change. What such a cursory review shows is that almost all parts of the planet upon which humans depend for sustenance have been impaired in their productivity by the activities of increasing numbers of people who each use, on the average, more energy and resources per capita with each succeeding year.[23]

(3) Global Change

Superimposed on the present situation with respect to the direct effect of human activities on the planet, there is the prospect of accelerating indirect effects –

[19] P. Blaikie, and H. Brookfield (eds.) *Land Degradation and Society* (1987), Methuen and Co., New York.

[20] FAO Forestry Department (1988). *An Interim Report on the State of Forest Resources in the Developing Countries*, Food and Agriculture Organization of the United Nations, Rome.

[21] UNEP (1988), "Sands of Change: Why Land becomes Desert and What Can Be Done About It", UNEP Environmental Brief No. 2, Nairobi.

[22] IUCN, *Wetland Conservation and Sustainable Development* (1989). International Union for Conservation of Nature and Natural Resources, Gland, Switzerland.

[23] L. Brown, et al (1980), "A World at Risk" in L. Brown et al (eds.). See note 21, *supra*, pp. 3–20. See also B. Turner, et. al. (eds.) *The Earth as Transformed by Human Action* (1988), MIT Press, Cambridge, Mass.

more subtle, insidious and world-wide in nature. The popular name for these, at least at the moment, is *global change*.

Much has been written about global change, and there is some controversy about whether changes are evidence and how rapidly they will occur; but there is strong, irrefutable scientific evidence for the main elements and consensus about the processes.

The basic idea of the global change concern is that, in a planetary system which appears at this stage of geological history to be rather more stressed and unstable than has been the usual case in the past few million years, the rapid increase in energy transformations and redistribution of chemical products together with alterations in landscape resulting from human activities is likely to cause, in the next half century or so, environmental and biological changes over the entire planet more severe and rapid than any experienced in the history of the human race.[24]

What have humans done to bring about this situation? And how does it impact on human rights?

What we have done is to go about our daily lives, to exercise our rights as individuals and as nations, and to use our ingenuity to compete with one another and wrest a temporary living from the rest of Nature. On a local scale, the results usually seem innocuous, or even a cause for pride and satisfaction. But as human numbers increase and technology advances, the effects become cumulative, global in scale, and threaten to upset natural processes and biological balances. There are many examples:

- We apply energy directly to disturb the earth. More soil is moved by diesel bulldozer each year than is carried by all the rivers of the world.[25]
- On a winter's day, it has been estimated that more energy is lost to the atmosphere from the chimneys of Montreal than is received from the sun in the same area.
- Carbon dioxide in the upper atmosphere has increased markedly since the beginning of the Industrial Revolution, from about 285 parts per million in 1880 to 350 ppm in 1980 and the increase is accelerating rapidly. Methane (CH_4) is increasing even more rapidly. Both of these gases are contributors to the "greenhouse effect" in the atmosphere and have the capacity to control, or change the surface heat balance of the planet.[26]
- We develop new chemicals, such as chlorofluorocarbons (CFC's) which do not exist in nature, and which, because of their "un-natural" stability, we find very useful as spray propellants and electrical cooling media. However when released into the environment, even in tiny quantities, these have a long-term effect on the chemical composition of the upper atmosphere,

[24] See Footnotes 2 and 16, *supra*.

[25] W. Fyfe, "The Environmental Crisis: Quantifying Geosphere Interactions", *Science* (1981), 213, pp. 105–110. See also Footnote 23, *supra*.

[26] See note 9, *supra*. Also J. Weiner, "The Next One Hundred Years", (1990), Bantam Books, New York.

destroying the ozone molecules which filter out some wavelengths of sunlight that otherwise will damage germination of plant seeds, kill ocean plankton, and cause skin cancers in animals.[27]

These are but examples, which seem to be increasing yearly, where the normal exercise of the rights and abilities of humans to develop technologies and improve their lot on a local basis has inadvertently or collectively led to unwanted damaging effect on the world environment and on biological processes or human health on a large scale.

The manifestations of these processes are likely to be several, all inter-linked and interactive. Important changes in the natural environment are likely to include:

- increased land erosion and reduction of land fertility.
- warming of the average annual temperature surface of the whole planet, greatest in the northern hemisphere. It is not likely that the change in temperature itself will be noticeable, except statistically. What is likely to be more obvious is a change in precipitation patterns and a change in the variability of the weather.[28] In general, the dry areas of the world will likely become drier, and the wet regions will become wetter.
- changed ocean currents and sea ice conditions.
- possibly, a rapid worldwide rise of sea level.
- changes in vegetation patterns, and in plant and animal communities on continents and in the oceans

How important, in human or environmental terms, are these changes which humans have helped to bring about? Some examples, not predictions but plausible consequences, that have had careful study by international teams include:[29]

- In the major present grain-producing areas, increased evapotranspiration will likely offset lengthened growing season, so productivity may drop.
- Temperate forest belts will reduce in size and productivity as climatically favourable belts shift northward; in North America the shifting will be to areas where the soil is less suitable for forests. Because of increased dryness in areas presently forested, the propensity for forest fires will increase.
- Coral atolls in the sub-tropics may be damaged or destroyed. Hundreds of small inhabited islands may be devastated.
- Extensive tropical coastlines now protected by mangrove swamps may be

[27] See notes 2, 9 and 24, *supra*.

[28] World Meteorological Organization/International Council of Scientific Unions, *Global Climate Change – A Scientific Review* (1990), WMO Secretariat, Geneva.

[29] There is an enormous literature on this subject. Useful summary compendi are: J. Topping, (ed.) *Coping with Climate Change* (1989), Climate Institute, Washington; M. Oppenheimer, (ed.) "Greenhouse Gas Emissions: Environmental Consequences and Policy Responses", *Climatic Change* (1989), Vol. 15, Nos. 1/2, pp. 1–335; and World Meteorological Organization, *The Changing Atmosphere: Implications for Global Security* (1989), proceedings of a conference in Toronto, Canada, June 1988, WMO Publication No. 710, Geneva. See also note 2, *supra*.

destroyed, leading not only to coastal erosion but likely loss of much lowland rice production.
- Warming of arctic and north Atlantic waters could cause the Gulf Stream to dissipate, leading paradoxically to a cooling of northwest Europe, and possible triggering of long-term instabilities in the Atlantic and World Ocean.
- The hydrological dynamics of the lower reaches and estuaries or deltas of major rivers may be altered, affecting pollution dispersal, aquatic and marine resources, with serious consequences for some of the world's most populous regions (e.g. Bangladesh, Netherlands).
- Stressed ecosystems will likely lead to loss of larger species of plants and animals, but favour development of parasites, viruses, and pests.

These aspects of the present situation, and of our possible or likely global near future, add up to an uncomfortable demonstration of the inescapable relationship between people and the planet on which we live.

This relationship is determined by the total numbers of people and their individual and collective use of natural resources and energy, compared to the planetary stock of resources and the ability of natural processes to renew or replace these resources, modified by the effects of technology that can increase or decrease the availability of the resources, decrease the stock, or disturb the natural processes.

As long as the numbers of people, their demands on resources, and use of energy were small compared to the planetary stock of resources and the workings of natural processes, such a relationship was not very important to the human race. So it has been throughout most of human history. But in the past few decades, human populations and energy use have grown enormously; technology has had an increasing and generally destructive effective on natural resources and environmental processes. The relationship has become an equation that can no longer be balanced. The degree of imbalance is increasing alarmingly. Some aspects of that imbalance, on a local scale, are factors in the loss of human rights. On a world scale, the imbalance becomes a matter of human survival.[30]

The only areas where humans can do anything to restore the balance are to change the numbers of people, to use less energy, or to refrain from using environmentally-damaging technologies. However, serious action on any of these, in a collective sense, infringes on the rights of individuals to pursue their own immediate short-term or culturally-determined interests and desires. Such action is contrary to rights that have been taken for granted or assumed to be natural in most human civilizations until now.[31]

Even though, at the present time, the equation no longer appears to be balanced, physical, chemical and biological laws still apply. So, before long a

[30] L. Brown, *In the Human Interest* (1974), W.W. Norton, New York.

[31] F. Mayor, (ed.) *Scientific Research and Social Goals: Toward a New Development Model* (1982), Pergamon Press, Oxford.

balance will be reached, by natural processes. A study of the factors and processes involved shows that if a balance is reached by natural processes alone, the result will most likely not be one that humans themselves would have preferred.

5. Carrying Capacity, Economic Enterprise, and the Global Environment

A community, a city, or a region often initially prospers because, although its individual inhabitants do not each provide for all of their personal needs in a self-sufficient way, collectively the activities and services of the inhabitants make possible the drawing in of wealth from the surrounding region, so that each supports the other. An expanding economy or an expanding population can no longer be said to be operating within a particular carrying capacity; however, if the sum of the disturbances by human activities does not distort the natural flow of chemical or biological energy in the region, the whole process seems to be a win-win situation from the human point of view, at small cost to Nature. This was the situation, for example throughout most of Europe until about the sixteenth century. But as the forest cover of Europe began to disappear, the character of the economic game began to change, although the importance of the change probably could be seen only in hindsight.[32] To keep an expanding economic system running, human enterprise must incorporate activities and resources farther and further from the centre of power – examples can be found in the European colonial enterprises of the 19th century – and to turn to use of concentrated forms of energy and "value added" materials that, by their very concentration, are distortions of natural energy processes and materials.[33]

When the effects of human energy and disturbance over a large region of the planet approximate the scale and exceed the rate of planetary processes, what had been a win-win process for humankind quickly, as far as the evidence goes, becomes a zero-sum game.

In a zero-sum game, you do not win in one area without causing a loss somewhere else. On planet Earth today, we can no longer move materials, food, or other things from where they are now to where somebody else wants them, without impoverishing the place and people they came from.

This is a new situation in the economic development of the world. For decades, planners, economists, and resource geographers have worried about the adequacy or sufficiency of natural resources. Agricola, in the 16th century, worried about whether there would be enough gold and silver to meet the needs

[32] J. Richards, "World Environmental History and Economic Development" in W. Clark, and R. Munn (eds.) *Sustainable Development of the Biosphere* (1986), IIASA – Cambridge University Press, pp. 53–74.

[33] L. White, "The Historical Roots of our Ecological Crises", *Science* (1967), 161, pp. 840–864.

of future emperors. But now, it seems, the shoe is on the other foot. The question is not: are there enough resources? – but rather: what will be the effect of taking them and using them? In the field of energy resources in particular, national and international concerns about the adequacy of energy supplies are in many respects being overtaken by concerns about the environmental effects of continued profligate energy use.[34] In such issues, "the right to ample energy" appears to conflict, at the present stage of technology, with "the right to a clean environment".

6. Environmental Processes and Human Rights

How does this overall situation affect the ideas and the attainability of human rights?

Human rights must have a basis in the right of each individual person to stay alive as a physically healthy animal. Human rights concerns, as expressed, usually go beyond the basic animal concerns and at the same time often ignore them. But there is an inescapable linkage between *human biology, human socioeconomic systems*, and *natural non-human processes and resources.* This linkage affects the nature of the environment or the quantity or quality of the resources to which the individual has access. Human biology needs, in their most fundamental, are needs for food, water for a degree of satisfaction of reproductive instincts, and for some exercise of predatory and social habits. Thus, in any society, fundamental issues of human rights are a function of the biology of the human animal, the maintenance of a socioeconomic system, the available natural resources and the characteristics of the environment.

The principles behind the "right to adequate food" or the "right to a healthy and safe environment", which are often stated as basic human rights, raise difficult questions if there is not a surplus of food or if the environment is progressively degrading. Do we settle, collectively and individually, for "adequate for as many as feasible?" or for the "right to at least as much as the next person"? That is, do we assume that some people are more equal than others, or do we all go downhill together? These problems not only mix together "the tragedy of the commons"[35] and "the lifeboat dilemma"[36], but call into question the basis of welfare and the responsibility of one group of humans toward their fellow humans.[37]

[34] E.F. Roots, "Environmental Aspects of Canada's Energy Problems", Proceedings of the X11 Canadian National Energy Forum, *CANWEC*, Ottawa, pp. 13–26.

[35] G. Hardin, "The Tragedy of the Commons", *Science* (1968), 162, pp. 1243–1250. See also F. Berkes, et. al. "The Benefits of the Commons", *Nature* (1989), 340, pp. 91–93.

[36] K. Boulding, "The Economics of the Coming Spaceship Earth" in H. Jarrett, (ed.) *Environmental Quality in a Growing Economy* (1966), Johns Hopkins Press, Baltimore.

[37] I. Sachs, "Environment and Styles of Development, in W. Mathews, (ed.) *Outer Limits and Human Needs* (1976), Dag Hammarskjold Foundation Uppsala.

The problems are not only those of inadequate supply or general deterioration. Most general deterioration, while it affects everybody, is primarily due to the actions of a small segment of humankind. The thinning of the ozone layer in the upper atmosphere is an example: all people and much of life on earth may be affected, but the chlorofluorocarbons that are a principal cause have until now been released to the environment almost exclusively by the wealthier ten per cent of humanity. Has each person on earth a "right" to a thicker ozone layer? And what about regional environments that have been specifically degraded by the actions of others? Take, for example, the present-day issue of toxic chemicals in the diet of Inuit in northern Canada, which come, at least partly, from pesticides and herbicides used in south-east Asia and in the Caribbean.[38] How is the Inuit right to non-contaminated food to be ensured? Does it conflict with the right of a farmer in Thailand to protect his crop? Should there be a "right" of citizens to be protected not only from the direct impacts but also from the environmental deterioration caused by industrial accidents, such as the long-range but unevenly distributed fallout of radioactivity from a malfunction of a nuclear reactor?

These are examples of a wide range of problems, conceptual and practical, that relate human rights concerns to the natural realities of the planet on which we live and to the changes in the global and regional environment being brought about by human activities. I will mention six types of issues that cannot be ignored or dismissed in considerations of human rights in the twenty-first century.

(1) If humans are now truly in a zero-sum game in living on this planet, whatever we win in one place will mean a loss in another. The resources used by any part of society in any region will mean, henceforth, not only that there will be fewer resources left for someone else, but that their use will often result in a direct loss for someone else. Thus the right to use some natural resource or amenity, exercised by one individual or a group, reduces the availability to someone else who, in theory, has equal rights. In short, in living on the planet, in the twenty-first century, *people must acknowledge that they are no longer consumers, but exchangers.* The right to exchange resources and energy will have to be defended as a collective right, as well as an individual right.[39]

(2) The dominant "forcing function" in the equation of humans living on the planet, and in the activities causing global change, is the near-exponential growth of human population. This poses a serious, but soon-to-be-inevitable dilemma, in which two sets of human rights are incompatible, given the present situation, on a world scale:

– *the individual and collective rights to natural resources and a healthy environment* versus

[38] J. Jensen, "Report on Organochlorines" in *State of the Arctic Environment; Reports*, Arctic Centre Publication No. 2, (1991), Rovaniemi, Finland, p. 335–384.

[39] H. Daly, and J. Cobb, *For the Common Good* (1989), Beacon Press, Boston.

– *the right of humans as individuals to reproduce.*

This dilemma strikes deep into all human values and practices. The sobering, even frightening aspect of this dilemma is that if it is not solved by voluntary and collective human behaviour, both sets of rights, and others, are likely to be extinguished by environmental and resource realities, with severe human tragedy.

(3) The deteriorating environmental condition of parts of the planet, plus the social and political stresses and injustices that are not likely soon to be eradicated, is creating a new class of distressed human – *the environmental refugees.*[40] Their numbers are growing even now, and we would be short-sighted not to expect, realistically, a great increase in the next few decades. This problem has not only a human dimension, but also an environmental dimension. What are the individual rights of such people, wherever they arrive, compared to the rights of people into whose region they come and whose resources they will want a part of? Whose responsibility will it be to ensure that these competing or displaced rights are balanced, protected, or enforced? Is it an issue of human rights to deal with whatever or whoever caused the global environmental degradation from which the refugees are fleeing, because their environmental rights at home were destroyed?

(4) No less disturbing on moral or ethical grounds is the problem of the rights to their own life style of *those who are forced to lose their cultural and economic identity* because their traditional activities, often helped by well-meaning modern technology, have so impaired the local productive capacity that, with populations increased because of medical aid and welfare, they have irrevocably lost their livelihood and means of expressing their culture. There are also refugees displaced by foreign-aid and nationally-sanctioned development programmes, as for example country folk displaced by large hydroelectric schemes that primarily serve cities and industries. These are real-life dimensions of the problem of the rights of minorities and indigenous people around the world.[41] A clear statement on the political aspects of this issue emerged from the international Northern Regional Conference in 1990: "If indigenous peoples are to survive as members of the family of nations, then the right to be different, the recognition of our status as distinct societies, and the fundamental political rights that flow from such identity must be guaranteed internationally, nationally, and locally."[42]

(5) If the present and immediate past generation has set in train the events that

[40] J. Jacobsen, "Environmental Refugees: A Yardstick of Habitability", *Worldwatch Paper 86* (1988), Worldwatch Institute, Washington.

[41] See for example, P. Adams, and L. Solomon, *In the Name of Progress* (1985), Energy Probe Research Foundation, Toronto.

[42] D. Sambo, "Report of the Political Rights of Indigenous Peoples Panel", in *Cooperation in a Changing World* (1990), Summary Proceedings of the Thirds Northern Regions Conference, Anchorage, Alaska, p. 63.

are reducing, inevitably, the quality of the environment for the next generation, *how do we identify and defend the rights of generations yet to come?* Does the Brundtland definition of sustainable development "to preserve the ability of future generations to meet their own needs" carry with it a "right" of future generations in terms we would accept today?[43] Should such "rights" be defined, perhaps in the manner of the "self-evident truths" of the American Constitution, as a guide to our present behaviour? But, are such rights valid, or can they have any meaning, in the light of impending global change?[44]

(6) Any consideration of the rights of humans to take unto themselves natural resources which are at the same time being affected by humans raises, seriously and inescapably, the question of *the rights of humans compared to the rights of non-human species.* This is not simply a case of "animal rights" in the popular confrontational sense,[45] or "whether trees have legal standing"[46]; but is rather a need to consider *whether it is possible, or logically defensible, for humans, who are integral parts of an ecosystem, to have activities, options and rights independently from other components of the ecosystem.*[47] It calls into question the principle, stated in Judeo-Christian theology and some other but not all religions, that Man shall have dominion over all the Earth; and the assumption, in most Western and Oriental legal systems, that humans can appropriate the whole Earth for their use, if they can get it.[48]

However, an important part of the broader awareness of environmental issues, in many societies, in the past few decades has been an increasing understanding that humans are part of the ecosystem, and that human beings, individually and collectively, must look at their "rights" in a broader natural perspective. Two recent examples show this trend and acceptance: Astro-physicist Carl Sagan, in a popular television series on the cosmos, was quoted with approval by many reviewers when he said, *"Mars belongs to the Martians, even if they be only microbes."* And in the humourous adventure-romance film, "Crocodile Dundee", the hero, when asked his opinion about the rights of the aborigines of Australia, replied that whites and aborigines quarreling about who owns the

[43] K. Lorenz, "The Enmity Between Generations and Its Probable Ethological Causes" in A. Tiselius & S. Nilsson (eds.) *The Place of Value in a World of Facts* (1970), Nobel Symposium 14, Almqvist and Wiksell, Stockholm, p. 385–418.

[44] E. Weiss, "Climate Change, Intergenerational Equity and International Law: An Introductory Note", *Climatic Change 15* (1989), p. 327–335.

[45] A. Herscovici, *Second Nature: The Animal Rights Controversy* (1985), CBC Enterprises, Montreal, pp. 1–254.

[46] C. Stone, "Should Trees Have Legal Standing? Toward Legal Rights for Natural Objects", *Southern California Law Review* (1972), Vol. 45, pp. 450–501.

[47] C. Frankel, "The Rights of Nature", in L. Tribe, et. al (eds.) *When Values Conflict* (1976), Ballinger, Cambridge Mass, pp. 93–113.

[48] M. Heidegger, *Discourse on Thinking* (1966), translated by J. Anderson and E. Freund, Harper and Row, New York.

land and resources of Australia reminded him of two fleas quarreling about which one of them owned the dog whose back they were biting.

These are trivial examples, perhaps, but telling ones. Both are indicative of a new widely shared perspective on human rights. Neither would likely have been stated, or accepted by the public, fifteen years ago. Both state viewpoints which will have to be more strongly expressed, and acted upon, if human society is to operate successfully in the twenty-first century.

7. Conclusion

The procedure of putting humans, and human institutions, legally and in practice within an ecosystem is a challenging one. It reverses most legal tradition, business practice, educational training, and religious teaching. It places new dimensions on the problem of achieving, and maintaining, human rights.

Advancing scientific knowledge and day-to-day events throughout the world show with increasing clarity the handicaps and contradictions, indeed the inevitable eventual failure, of attempts to maintain the illusion that the human race is distinct and separate from, and can by its own decision act independently of, other forms of life and the inorganic processes that constitute the planet of which we are a part.

How to develop an understanding of the social and human behavioural aspects of global environmental change is a difficult area of research in itself.[49] The way in which individuals and groups of humans define their rights and respond to environmental constraints is based on the myths and world-view of different societies as much as on practical aspects of economics and safety.[50]

There are many shifts of values needed for most people and societies to accept the inter-relatedness of the human and non-human aspects of the world system. To many, such a shift is a challenge to the human rights they hold dear. Kenneth Boulding has put the problem neatly:

> "The most worrying thing about the earth is that there seems to be no way of preventing it from becoming one world. If there is only one world, then if anything goes wrong, everything goes wrong. It follows that, if the earth is one world, then if anyone has rights, everyone has rights, and all living things also have rights."[51]

[49] H. Jacobsen, and M. Price, *A Framework for Research on the Human Dimensions of Global Environmental Change* (1990), International Social Science Council and United Nations Educational, Scientific and Cultural Organization, ISSC/UNESCO Series, Report No. 3, Paris.

[50] P. Timmerman, "Mythology and Surprise in the Sustainable Development of the Biosphere", in W. Clark, and R. Munn (eds.) *Sustainable Development of the Biosphere* (1986), Cambridge University Press, pp. 435–454.

[51] K. Boulding, "Spaceship Earth Revisited" in H. Daly, (ed.) *Economy, Ecology, Ethics: Essays Toward a Steady-State Economy* (1980), W. H. Freeman, San Francisco.

Despite these problems, as we enter the twenty-first century, the philosophical idea that the rights of humans in their dealings with one another must be based on an awareness of the characteristics and constraints of non-human components of the planet, is growing. In its "Green Plan for a Healthy Environment", released in 1990, the Government of Canada stated:

> "We must think, plan and act in terms of ecosystems. We live in a complex and integrated environment. All creatures, including humans, interact with and depend upon each other. They all draw on the materials and energy of the physical environment to obtain food and recycle wastes. They all affect each other's behaviour.
>
> In the past, responses to environmental problems paid very little attention to these important inter-relationships. Today the increasing number and complexity of environmental issues demand that we adopt a more integrated approach."[52]

The United Nations has adopted a World Charter for Nature,[53] and numerous national and international activities, in particular those undertaken in preparation for the 1992 United Nations Conference on Environment and Development, are recognizing that "human rights" cannot be separated from the "rights" of other components of the world ecosystem.[54]

As Dr. Erkki Pulliainen, Member of the Finnish Parliament and Vice-President of the International Parliamentary Union, said in The Hague in October 1990:

> "New economic policy must be based on the recognition and acknowledgement of ecological realities. The rights of Nature must take place alongside human rights. We have learned that ignoring nature's rights will lead sooner or later to the relinquishing of mankind's own rights. Hence, in reality the rights of nature take precedence over the rights of humans.
>
> The central message of the rights of Nature is that Nature's tolerance must not be exceeded if we are to live in a sustainable economy. Globally, the constitution of all countries should include a chapter delineating the rights of Nature in all areas. This should be a guideline for all other legislation.[55]

It is thoughts like these that must guide our concept of rights as we enter the twenty-first century.

[52] Environment Canada, *Canada's-Green Plan* (1990), Government of Canada, Ottawa, p. 18.

[53] United Nations *The World Charter for Nature* (1982). Also, *World Charter for Nature: A Commentary* (1984). IUCN Environmental Law Centre, 1984, Bonn.

[54] IUCN/UNEP/WWF (1991) *Caring for the World: A Strategy for Sustainability Living* (1991) (D.A. Munro, and R. Prescott-Allen, eds.), Gland, Switzerland, p. 228.

[55] E. Pulliainen, "Environmental Challenges to Canadian Society", in *Canada on the Threshold of the 21st Century*, John Benjamin, Amsterdam (1991), p. 89–94.

ALEXANDRE KISS*

Concept and Possible Implications of the Right to Environment

1. Introduction

The ecological era, which started in the late 1960's with the awareness of the depletion of natural resources and the destruction of the natural environment, has generated an important corpus of legal rules. The creation and the rapid development of environmental law has naturally raised the question of the guarantees which individuals and groups of individuals could be granted for assuring the legal protection of the environment and thus, the recognition of a "right to environment". On the other hand, since human rights and environment are emerging as the basic values of the twenty-first century, it is normal to establish a link between them. In fact, such a link already exists even in positive law, both national and international.[1]

Before trying to define the concept and the possible implications of the right to environment, it is useful to recall some general characteristics of human

* Director of Research, Centre National de la Recherche Scientifique, Strasbourg, France; Vice-President of the International Institute of Human Rights.

[1] Clauses concerning the protection of environment can be found in the Constitutions of 44 sovereign States, in those of 11 member States of the U.S., in those of all German Lander, as well as in laws having a basic character in several countries. For a complete list see: 2 Revue Universelle des droits de l'homme, (1990), p.445, footnotes 1 and 2 and also E. Brown-Weiss *In Fairness to Future Generations*, (1988), p. 297 s, and P. Kromarek (ed.) *UNESCO, Environment et droit de l'homme*, (1987), p. 152 s.

At the international level, apart from the Stockholm Declaration, quoted above, two important conventions proclaim the "right to environment". The African Charter on Human and Peoples Rights (Banjul, June 20, 1981) declares, in Article 24, that "[a]11 peoples shall have the right to a general satisfactory environment favourable to their development" (21 I.L.M. (1982), p.58. Article 11 of the Additional Protocol to the American Convention on Human Rights in the Area of Economic, Social and Cultural Rights (San Salvador, November 18, 1988), entitled "the right to a healthy environment", provides:

'1. Everyone shall have the right to live in a healthy environment and to have access to basic public services.
2. The States parties shall promote the protection, preservation and improvement of the environment". (28 I.L.M. (1989), p.698).

K.E. Mahoney and P. Mahoney (eds.), Human Rights in the Twenty-first Century, 551–559.

rights as embodied in the main international instruments, both universal and regional.

From the early days of the proclamation of human rights at an international level, the central issue has been the recognition of the "inherent dignity and of the equal and inalienable rights of all members of the human family" as the "foundation of freedom, justice and peace in the world".[2] In developing these concepts, despite the detail they might be able to provide on concrete points, international instruments protecting human rights essentially comprise principles which, in most cases, cannot be implemented as they stand: they need further legislative definition and regulation. A distinction is often drawn between "classic" rights and liberties (which require only the non-interference or the part of the State) and economic, social and cultural rights (for which a positive action is necessary). In reality, such a distinction is rarely justified: in the present economic, social and political context even the guarantee of the most "traditional" rights may necessitate the intervention of the State to ensure their full observance. The effective implementation of freedom of opinion and expression calls for action by public authorities aimed at the safeguard of the plurality of the press or mass communication media. Even the right to a fair public hearing presupposes the existence of independent and impartial courts, and, consequently, an adequately functioning machinery of justice. More often than not, the rights guaranteed to human beings in international instruments require not only legislative flashing out of the principle, but also appropriate procedures and institutions to ensure their effective enforcement.

These considerations – the very foundations of human rights and the importance of implementing procedures – are essential for understanding the possible implications of the recognition of the "right to environment" as one of the human rights guaranteed to everyone.

2. The Objectives of the Right to Environment

Whether environmental protection is considered as aiming at the preservation of the environment as the "*cadre de vie*" of human beings – which is an anthropocentric approach – or whether humans are to be protected indirectly as components of the environment from which they cannot be isolated, the right to environment is closely related to the basic concept of human rights, namely

---

Other international instruments also contain provisions which may be considered as corresponding to the concept of the "right to environment": Conference on Security and Cooperation in Europe, Conclusions of the Meeting held in Sofia, November 3, 1989 (CSCE/SEM.36/Rev. 1). Convention of the International Labor Organization concerning Indigenous and Tribal Peoples in Independent Countries, June 27, 1989, Articles 4(1) and 7(3) and (4), 28 I.L.M. (1989), p. 1384 etc.

[2] Universal Declaration of Human Rights, Preamble and also see Article 22, which proclaims economic, social and cultural rights, adding as second objective the free development of the personality of everyone.

the "dignity inherent to all the members of the human family". Indeed, an environment degraded by pollution and defaced by the destruction of all beauty and variety is as contrary to satisfactory living conditions and the development of personality as the breakdown of the fundamental ecologic equilibria is harmful to physical and moral health. The very first principle of the 1972 Stockholm Declaration on the Human Environment clearly expresses this connection:

> "Man has a fundamental right to freedom, to equality, to satisfactory living conditions, in an environment the quality of which enables him to live in dignity and in well-being".

The right to environment also completes the other rights guaranteed to each human being in another way: it contributes to equality among citizens, or at least to the reduction of inequalities in their material conditions. Indeed, environmental deterioration aggravates the differences between the richest, who will be able to escape degraded conditions of life such as polluted air, noisy or unhealthy areas, while the most disfavoured group must accept to live in inhuman agglomerations, slums or other heavily polluted areas. Similarly, the depletion of other natural resources, which increase prices, will hit more heavily poor, than well-to-do people. The requirement of a healthy and balanced environment and of the environmentally sound management of natural resources then become conditions for implementing other fundamental rights guaranteed to everyone.

The right to environment also adds a new dimension to human rights: a temporal one. The Stockholm Declaration adds to the previously quoted passage that "man has the solemn duty to protect environment for present and future generations".[3]

Here again, the link between human rights and environment conservation is clear: human rights must be guaranteed also for the future, to the coming generations, and this implies the management of natural resources with the aim of not exhausting them. This applies, in particular, to economic and social rights. No State is entitled to behave in such a way that its actions deprive future generations of economic and social rights or annihilate all hope for future generations to achieve the objectives which, unfortunately, are all that these rights represent at the moment for a large part of mankind.

3. Definition of the Right to Environment

The first difficulty to be solved in this connection is that the term "environment" itself is difficult to define. In its broadest sense, environment can be

[3] Such reference to future generations can already be found in the preamble of the UN Charter: "We the peoples of the United Nations determined to save succeeding generations from the scourge of war..., to reaffirm faith in fundamental human rights, in the dignity and worth of the human person, in the equal rights of men and women...".

assimilated to the whole biosphere, while in its more restricted sense "environment" may represent simply the immediate physical milieu of the individual, that is, his or her habitat and neighbourhood. In addition, the term "environment" is neutral in itself: any living creature, even any object, has its environment, good or bad. Usually, therefore, positive-law texts dealing with this issue qualify the term "environment". The Stockholm Declaration speaks of an environment as "the quality of which enables [man] to live in dignity and well-being" (Principle no. 1). National constitutional provisions employ qualifying terms which are more or less detailed and centre around humans and their needs. The Spanish Constitution of December 29, 1978 speaks (in Article 45, para 1) of an "environment suitable for the development of the person", while the Peruvian Constitution of July 12, 1978 recognizes (in Article 123) the right to everyone "to live in a healthy environment, ecologically balanced and adequate for the development of life and the preservation of the countryside and nature".

Even this last formulation, which is the most complete one, calls for further elucidation. One might think that it implies proper prior scientific studies in order to determine what is "ecologically balanced". But, in reality the situation is not so different from that confronting the implementation of human rights in everyday life. Indeed, even when it comes to the question of fixing the content of "conventional" rights and liberties, it may be necessary to utilize concepts which are incapable of being defined in a rigorous way. As an example, one might cite the freedom to express one's religious and other convictions or the condition that permissible restrictions to certain guaranteed rights be "necessary in a democratic society". It nonetheless remains that in the public conscience of a given geographic milieu, these notions are echoes in concepts precise enough to guide the lawyer, judge or administrator responsible for their application. Human rights are, of course, inherent and inalienable but, not unlike religious principles, their interpretation at a given moment and in a specific case can only be arrived at by reference to the collective conscience of the society and to its predominant system of values. It would appear more than probable that judicial institutions accustomed to adjudicating on human rights issues – such as the European Court of Human Rights or certain national courts – would not balk at the task of giving a concrete content to the notion of the right to environment.

4. Rights and Duties

In any legal system the recognition of a right in favour of a person (legal or natural) automatically creates duties towards other persons. This general rule certainly applies in the field of human rights, but appreciable differences may exist between guaranteed rights as far as their formulation is concerned. Rules may either proclaim a subjective right conferred as such on individuals – right to the liberty and security of person, right to hold opinions, etc. – or formulate the individual right as a duty of the State. In this connection one might cite Article 10 of the International Covenant on Economic, Social and Cultural Rights:

"The States Parties to the present Covenant recognize that:

1. A protection and assistance as large as possible should be granted to the family.
2. A special protection must be afforded to mothers during a reasonable period of time before and after the birth of children. Remunerated mothers must benefit, during this period, of paid leave and of leave accompanied by adequate social security benefits.
3. Special measures of protection and assistance must be adopted in favour of children and youth... Children and youth must be protected against economic and social exploitation. The fact of employing them in works likely to compromise their morality or their health, to put their life in danger or to harm their normal development must be sanctioned by law. The States must also fix age limits below which paid employment of child labour will be forbidden and sanctioned by law."

The two approaches, recognition of an individual right and proclamation of a duty for the State, may even be combined in one formula, which then shows very clearly that the two formulations express the same principle. This is the case of the most fundamental of all human rights, the right to life as enunciated in Article 6 para. 1 of the Covenant on Civil and Political Rights: "Every human being has the inherent right to life. This right shall be protected by law..."

The same combination also appears in several national constitutions.[4]

Whatever formulation may be employed, it seems permissible to conclude that the positive-law texts which proclaim only the State's obligation to protect the environment establish, in fact, a right to environment.

However, it becomes apparent from examination of the various texts, constitutional and other, setting forth the right to environment that States are not the only parties made responsible for implementing the obligations which are created. Quite a few of the texts provide that individuals themselves have obligations in relation to conservation of the environment.[5]

[4] The Constitution of Peru of July 12, 1979, Article 123, provides:

"Everyone has the right to live in a healthy environment; ecologically balanced and adequate for the development of life and the preservation of the countryside and nature. Everyone has the duty to conserve said environment. It is the obligation of the State to prevent and control environmental pollution."

The Portuguese Constitution of April 2, 1976, as amended on September 30, 1982, declares that all have the right to a healthy and ecologically balanced human environment, whilst at the same time affirming the duty of the State to protect the environment (Article 66). See also Article 11 of the San Salvador Protocol to the American Convention on Human Rights, note 1, *supra*.

[5] The model for such provisions may be considered to be Principle 1 of the Stockholm Declaration on the Human Environment, 1972: "Man ... [bears] a solemn responsibility to protect and improve the environment for present and future generations."

The principle that citizens have duties in this regard appeared in the Constitutions of the

In the field of human rights protection this constitutes an innovation. Everyone benefits from the right to environment, but at the same time everyone thereby assumes obligations: the States as well as individuals and associations of individuals. Economic, social and cultural rights have been styled "solidarity rights" since the solidarity of the whole collectivity is necessary for them to be effectively guaranteed. In the present sphere such solidarity is even more indispensable, and in this regard it is worth recalling Article 45 paras. 1 and 2 of the Spanish Constitution of December 29, 1978:

> "Everyone has the right to enjoy an environment suitable for the development of the person as well as the duty to preserve it.
>
> The public authorities shall concern themselves with the rational use of all natural resources for the purpose of protecting and improving the quality of life and protecting and restoring the environment, supporting themselves on an indispensable collective solidarity".

5. Implementation of the Right to Environment

One of the objections raised against the right to environment is that it is difficult if not impossible to implement it. Like other new rights – wrongly called "third generation rights" – such as the right to development or the right to peace, its enforcement, it is said, could not be claimed before a court. Who could vindicate such rights and before which judicial body?

Such criticism would not appear to be justified, for two reasons referred to earlier. In the first place, even if the environment cannot be defined "*in abstracto*", in concrete cases the economic, social and cultural context will indicate to the judge the path to follow, as in a number of situations where human rights and restrictions to them are at issue. Secondly, procedure plays an important role in the protection of human rights: in practice human rights are generally guaranteed by the existence and proper functioning of procedures protecting against arbitrariness. On the basis of these two elements, it is submitted that the right to environment must be interpreted not as a theoretical right to an ideal environment, but as a right protecting the present environment

---

communist countries. It has also been inserted in the Constitutions of Western and developing countries: "Everyone has the right to enjoy an environment suitable for the development of the person as well as the duty to preserve it": Spanish Constitution, December 29, 1978, Article 45(1); "The exercise and enjoyment of rights and freedoms is inseparable from the performance of duties and obligations, and accordingly it is the duty of every person in Sri Lanka ... (f) to protect nature and conserve its riches": Constitution of Sri Lanka, May 22, 1974, as amended on Aug. 24, 1984, Article 28. Reference can also be made in this connection to Principle 24 of the World Charter for Nature, adopted and solemnly proclaimed by the U.N. General Assembly on October 28, 1982 (Res. 37/7), which, implicitly recognizing the right to environment, declares: "Each person has a duty to act in accordance with the provisions of the present Charter; acting individually, in association with others or through participation in the political process, each person shall strive to ensure that the objectives and requirements of the present Charter are met."

from degradation by adequate procedures. In sum, the practical meaning of the right to environment is the right of everybody to the conservation of his or her environment.

Consequently, as with recognition of a number of other internationally guaranteed rights, recognition of the right to conservation of environment should entail the right to an effective appeal before a competent court and therefore include, as a minimum, the right to a "due process".

However, a supplementary element must be added to the equation. "Due process" generally comprises a remedy in respect of a violation of a given right. This would not be sufficient to ensure protection of the environment, which calls for preventive measures. Too often ecological damage cannot be repaired: it suffices to recall the sterilization of lakes by pollution which has killed all animal and vegetal life, or soil which has became unusable as a result of erosion or desertification. The necessity for prevention is the adjunct of the duty of everybody, States, collectivities and individuals – analyzed earlier – to protect the environment. It is an element that must be incorporated in the procedure guaranteeing the "right to the protection of the environment". The individual right becomes a "*competence*" in the sense of French law, that is concurrently a right and a duty to exercise the right, an example being the right of parents to secure the education of their children. The practical means of exercising this right "*competence*" will require that citizens be informed of the state of the environment in general and in particular of projects or events which threaten their environment. They must also be able to participate in the decision-making process and dispose of means of redress for non-observance of due process as well as, if necessary, for obtaining compensation for any damage their environment may have suffered.

Of the principal elements in this triad, including information, participation, and means of redress, the central one is participation in the decision-making process. It presupposes the information of the citizens, not only of specific instances where decisions have to be taken but also at a general level as regards the state of the environment and the dangers threatening it. Given the priority which must be accorded to prevention, means of redress are really helpful only in so far as they have a deterrent effect. Unfortunately, this is far from being the case in many situations: there may be too many obstacles in the way of establishing the causative link and assessing the damage, even if it be accepted that the courts are committed to imposing severe sanctions on those who harm the environment.

In common with quite a number of other fundamental rights, the exercise of the right to environment thus implies a co-operation between the State and its citizens. Participation in the decision-making process presupposes that adequate procedures and even structures are made available in order to facilitate the task of the citizens. Here, "task" is to be understood in the sense of a right/duty as in the case of participation in the governance of one's country.[6] Indeed, the right

[6] According to Article 21, paragraph 1 of the Universal Declaration of Human Rights, "Everybody has the right to take part in the government of his country, directly or through freely

to take part in the conduct of public affairs has no meaning if it does not incorporate at least a moral obligation to use it. The State must do everything in its power to facilitate its exercise, including ensuring the necessary previous education. As far as the right to conservation of the environment is concerned, this requirement is particularly well expressed in the Portuguese Constitution of April 2, 1976, Article 66:

> "(2) The State is obliged, through its agencies and by appeal and support of popular initiatives:
> a) to prevent and control pollution and its effects and harmful forms of erosion;
> b) to organize territorial space so as to establish biologically balanced landscapes;
> c) to create and develop natural and recreational parks..;
> d) to promote the rational enjoyment of natural resources, while safeguarding their responsibility and ecological stability.
> (3) It is granted to all the right to promote, in accordance with law, the prevention or cessation of factors of environmental deterioration, as well as the right to corresponding compensation in the case of direct damage."

This brings out fully the interweaving of public and private tasks in this realm. Moreover, public authorities must encourage citizens to take part in the performance of such tasks and must organize such participation. Consequently, the vocation of government will be less to command than to guide and assist citizens in the accomplishment of their duties. The whole concept of the State could thereby be modified in favour of greater democracy with better communication between administrators and at the same time improving human relations at a general level.

At present, the right to conservation of the environment is proclaimed in most cases, in one form or another, by the national Constitution. There are at least three good reasons for this. In the first place, constitutional recognition of a fundamental right confers upon the right the highest legal standing which exists in a country, since constitutional acts express and consecrate the most important social values of the State concerned. It will therefore be possible to measure environmental protection against other national interests, economic, military or other, so that when there is a conflict it can be placed at the same level and even be treated as having priority.

Another advantage of constitutional recognition of the right to protection of the environment is that it provides guidance for administrative and judicial authorities vested with responsibility for resolving concrete problem issues.

---

chosen representatives." The Article adds that the will of the people shall be the basis of the authority of government; it shall be expressed by universal and equal suffrage. The same principle is found in binding instruments: International Covenant on Civil and Political Rights, Article 25 b; Protocol No. 1 to the European Convention on Human Rights, Article 3; American Convention on Human Rights, Article 23.

Such authorities will, in the normal course, have to interpret and apply detailed legal rules. However, in the field of environment there may exist at least temporary lacunae in positive law: our knowledge is constantly developing, the more so since new threats or new elements may suddenly appear, with the result that existing law is often outdated or contains no response to a newly emergent problem. A constitutional principle may furnish a basis, permitting agencies entrusted with implementation of the law to find legal solutions for concrete cases.

Lastly, every Constitution also has an educational value. Constitutionalization of fundamental rights and freedoms has undoubtedly contributed to securing for them general acceptance and observance. Environmental values have now joined human rights and every year there is a better understanding that these two categories of rights are not parallel, but converging and even merging.

The foregoing analysis brings out clearly the place and role of the right to protection of the environment among the rights guaranteed to the individual. By reason of its objectives and content, as well as its implementation, this new right, consecrated as it is by the positive law of a large number of States and also increasingly at international level, comes within the category of fundamental rights whose enjoyment must be guaranteed to each individual. It is an integral part of this category of rights, on the same grounds as economic, social and cultural rights – it is in a way an economic right, a social right and a cultural right at the same time. It is also closely related to civil and political rights, by reason of the procedures which guarantee its implementation: information, participation, and due process. On the other hand, it brings with it new perspectives to human rights by introducing the interest of future generations, that is to say, the "time" dimension which is too often ignored in law. Through these characteristics the right to conservation of the environment not only enlarges the realm of human rights but may also modify, to a certain degree, its very nature and the general perspective of human rights in the twenty-first century.

A.A. CANÇADO TRINDADE*

Environmental Protection and the Absence of Restrictions on Human Rights

1. Introduction

The general theme chosen for the 1990 Banff Conference is a particularly suitable and most timely one: "Human Rights in the XXI Century: A Global Challenge". Not only does it allow the examination of a wide variety of aspects and concerns pertaining to the present state of the international protection of human rights, but it also facilitates the projection into the future of insights and ideas which may lead to the enhancement of the international protection of human rights in the next century. Within this general outlook, the topic which has been entrusted to use for presentation is a specific and so far virtually unexplored one: the parallelisms in the evolution of two domains of protection – human rights protection and environmental protection – and the impact of their expansion upon the exercise of previously recognized human rights.

For the purpose of examining this novel topic, we shall explore four lines of thought: first, the identification of affinities in the parallel evolution of human rights protection and of environmental protection; second, the identification of the wide dimension of the fundamental right to life, taken together with the right to health, at the basis of the *ratio legis* of international human rights law and of environmental law; third, the implementation (*mise en oeuvre*) of the right to a healthy environment; and fourth, the related effects witnessed in relation to the expansion of human rights and environmental protection and a critique of the so-called "restrictions" upon the exercise of previously recognized human rights.

* Ph.D. (Cambridge), Professor of International Law at the University of Brasilia and at the Brazilian Rio-Branco Diplomatic Academy, Member of the Board of Directors of the Inter-American Institute of Human Rights, Judge Ad Hoc of the Inter-American Court of Human Rights.

K.E. Mahoney and P. Mahoney (eds.), Human Rights in the Twenty-first Century, 561–593.

2. The Growth of Human Rights Protection and of Environmental Protection: From Internationalization to Globalization

(1) The Internationalization of Human Rights Protection and of Environmental Protection

The parallel evolutions of human rights protection and environmental protection disclose evident affinities. They both witness, and precipitate, the gradual erosion of so-called domestic jurisdiction. The treatment by the State of its own nationals becomes a matter of international concern. Conservation of the environment and control of pollution likewise become a matter of international concern. There has occurred a process of *internationalization* of both human rights protection and environmental protection. The former as from the 1948 Universal Declaration on Human Rights, the latter, years later, as from the 1972 Stockholm Declaration on the Human Environment.

With regard to human rights protection, eighteen years after the adoption of the 1948 Universal Declaration the International Bill of Human Rights was completed with the adoption of the two U.N. Covenants on Civil and Political (and Optional Protocol), and on Economic, Social and Cultural Rights (1966). Today, the normative corpus of international human rights law is a vast one. It comprises a multiplicity of treaties and instruments, at both global and regional levels, with varying ambits of application and covers the protection of human rights of various kinds and in distinct domains of human activity.

Similarly, the years following the internationalization of environmental protection (through the Stockholm Declaration) produced an increased range of relevant international instruments. These emerged equally at both the global and regional levels. It is estimated that there are presently more than 300 multilateral treaties and approximately 900 bilateral treaties providing for the protection and conservation of the biosphere. To which, over 200 texts from international organizations may be added.[1] This considerable growth of international regulation has, by and large, followed a "sectorial" approach, involving the adoption of conventions devoted to specific sectors or areas, or concrete situations (such as oceans, continental waters, atmosphere, wild life). In sum, international regulation in the domain of environmental protection has taken place in the form of *responses* to specific challenges.

The field of human rights protection has witnessed a similar process: parallel to general human rights treaties (such as the two U.N. Covenants on Human Rights and the three regional – European, American and African – Conventions), there are conventions aimed at concrete situations (e.g., prevention of discrimination, prevention and punishment of torture and ill-treatment), those which apply to specific human conditions (e.g., refugee status, national-

[1] Reference could also be made to the existence of domestic legislation on the matter in virtually all States: it is estimated that domestic legislative instruments currently total some 30,000. A.C. Kiss, *Droit international de l'environnement*, Paris, Pédone, 1989, p.46.

ity and statelessness) and at certain groups in special need of protection (e.g., workers, women, children, the elderly, the disadvantaged). Overall, human rights instruments have likewise developed, at normative and procedural levels, as *responses* to violations of human rights of various kinds.

This being so, it is not surprising that gaps become apparent, as awareness grows of the increasing need of protection. With regard to human rights, the lack of protection extended to certain vulnerable groups, in particular indigenous populations, represents such a gap. A corresponding example in relation to the environment may be seen in the need to enhance international regulation on climate change and protection of the atmosphere.

A significant task for the near future (if not for the present) will be ensuring the proper *co-ordination* of multiple instruments which have emerged during the past decades, pursuant to the "sectorial" approach (*supra*), in the domains of human rights protection[2] and environmental protection. During the course of the internationalization process pattern referred to above, it was soon realized that, in each domain there exists an inter-relatedness among the distinct sectors which have been the object of regulation.

(2) The Globalization of Human Rights Protection and of Environmental Protection

The awareness of this inter-relatedness has, in recent years, contributed in a decisive fashion to the evolution of both human rights protection and environmental protection from a state of internationalization to a state of globalization. As far as human rights are concerned, two decades after the adoption of the 1948 Universal Declaration of Human Rights, the 1968 Teheran Conference on Human Rights, in a global reassessment of the matter, proclaimed the *indivisibility* of all human rights (civil and political as well as economic, social and cultural rights). This was followed by the landmark Resolution 32/130, adopted by the U.N. General Assembly in 1977, where it was stated that human rights issues are to be examined globally.

That Resolution endorsed, from a globalist perspective the assertion of the 1968 Teheran Proclamation of the indivisibility and interdependence of all human rights. It also drew attention to the priority to be given to the search for solutions to massive and flagrant violations of human rights.[3] Thirty years after the adoption of the 1948 Universal Declaration, the U.N. General Assembly endeavoured, through Resolution 32/130, to overcome the old categorizations of rights and to proceed to a needed global analysis of existing problems in the field of human rights. This change of approach was doubtless conditioned by

[2] Cf. A.A. Cançado Trindade, "Co-existence and Co-ordination of Mechanisms of International Protection of Human Rights (At Global and Regional Levels)", 202 *Recueil des Cours de l'Académie de Droit International* (1987) pp. 21–435.

[3] Th. C. Van Boven, "United Nations Policies and Strategies: Global Perspectives?", in B.G. Ramcharan (ed.), *Human Rights: Thirty Years after the Universal Declaration*, The Hague, Martinus Nijhoff, 1979, pp. 88–89, and cf. pp. 89–91.

the fundamental changes undergone by so-called international society – including decolonization, capacity of massive destruction, population growth, environmental conditions and energy consumption.

The matter was taken up again by G.A. Resolutions 39/145 of 1984 and 41/117 of 1986, which reiterated the inter-relatedness of all human rights, whereby the protection of one category of rights should not exempt States from safeguarding the other rights. Thus, human rights instruments aimed at securing certain categories of rights, or at dealing with given situations, or at certain groups in special need of protection, are to be properly understood as being complementary to general human rights treaties. Multiple human rights instruments reinforce each other, enhance the degree of the protection due, and disclose an overwhelming identity of purpose.

As regards environmental protection, the presence, despite the "sector-by-sector" regulation, of "transversal" issues and rules contributed to the globalist approach. It was concluded that certain activities and products may increasingly cause harmful effects in any environment (e.g., toxic or dangerous substances, toxic or dangerous wastes, ionizing radiations, and radioactive wastes). In fact, the problem of dangerous substances permeates the whole of "sectorial" regulation, thus pointing to globalization and generating a "*réglementation se superposant aux différents secteurs*"[4].

As early as 1974, two years after the adoption of the Stockholm Declaration, the U.N. Charter on Economic Rights and Duties of States warned that the protection and preservation of the environment for present and future generations was the responsibility of *all* States (Article 30). In 1980, the U.N. General Assembly made its historical proclamation of the responsibility of States for the preservation of nature on behalf of present and future generations.[5] While, in the past, States regarded the regulation of pollution by sectors as a national or local issue, more recently they have realized that some environmental problems and concerns are essentially global in scope.[6] In its Resolution 44/228, of 22 December 1989, whereby it decided to convene a U.N. Conference on Environment and Development in 1992, the U.N. General Assembly recognized that the global character of environmental problems required action at all levels (global, regional and national), involving the commitment and participation of all countries. The Resolution further affirmed that the protection and enhancement of the environment are major issues affecting the well-being of peoples, and singled out, as one of the environmental issues of major concern, the "protection of human health conditions and improvement of the quality of life" (§ 12 (i)).

The global character of environmental issues is reflected in the question of

[4] A.C. Kiss, *op. cit. supra* n. (1), pp. 275–276 and 46, and cf. pp. 93, 106 and 204.

[5] Cit. in ibid., pp. 38–39.

[6] "Formal and informal linkages" across nations and States have contributed to this new perception; R.W. Hahn and K.R. Richards, "The Internationalization of Environmental Regulation" , 30 *Harvard International Law Journal* (1989) pp. 421, 423 and 444–445.

conservation of biological diversity. It is further illustrated, in particular, by the problems linked to atmospheric pollution (such as depletion of the ozone layer and global climate change). Those problems, initially thought of as being essentially local or even transboundary, were to disclose "*une portée pratiquement illimitée dans l'espace*".[7] For example, while global warming may threaten to damage many nations, it is a problem which cannot be traced to a single state or group of States. Accepting this position stimulated a need for a new approach to strategies of prevention and adoption as well as for considerable international cooperation.[8] Thus, the U.N. General Assembly, by Resolution 43/53, of 6 December 1988, recognized that climate change is a common concern of mankind, and determined that action should be promptly taken to deal with it within a global framework.

Likewise, the Intergovernment Panel on Climate Change (IPCC) has recognized that climate change is a common concern of mankind, affecting humanity as a whole, and should therefore be approached within a global framework.[9] The Panel has pointed to the need for a global approach to climate change as one of the possible elements to be included in a future framework convention on climate change.[10] The 1989 Hague Declaration on the Atmosphere insists on the search for urgent and global solutions to the problems of the warming of the atmosphere and the deterioration of the ozone layer. In the same vein, the 1989 International Meeting of Legal and Policy Experts, held in Ottawa, reported *inter alia* that the atmosphere constitutes a "common resource of vital interest to mankind".[11]

In November 1989, 67 countries participated in a Ministerial Conference on Atmospheric Pollution and Climatic Change held in Noordwijk, The Netherlands, at which components to be included in the future Convention on Climate Change were considered. The principle of shared responsibility by all States was reasserted. The 1989 Noordwijk Declaration on Climate Change pursued a globalist approach and expressly stated that "climate change is a common concern of mankind".[12] In conclusion, recent trends in environmental protection as well as in human rights protection (*supra*) disclose a clear and progressive tendency from internationalization towards globalization.

[7] A.C. Kiss, *op.cit. supra* n. (1), p.212.

[8] V.P. Nanda, "Global Warming and International Environmental Law – A Preliminary Inquiry", 30 *Harvard International Law Journal* (1989) pp. 380–385.

[9] WMO/UNEP, *IPCC Working Group III (Response Strategies) – Legal Measures: Report of Topic Co-ordinators*, Geneva/Nairobi, [1989] p.III (mimeographed, internal circulation).

[10] Cf. UNEP Governing Council decision 15/36, of 25 May 1989.

[11] Cf. *Statement of the International Meeting of Legal and Policy Experts*, Ottawa, 1989, p.2.

[12] Cf. Ministerial Conference on Pollution and Climatic Change, *The Noordwijk Declaration on Climate Change*, Noordwijk, Nov. 1989, p.4, and cf. pp. 1–13 (mimeographed, restricted circulation).

(3) The Globalization of Protection and Erga Omnes Obligations

The globalization of human rights protection and of environmental protection can also be identified in the emergence of *erga omnes* obligations and the consequent decline and end of reciprocity. As far as human rights are concerned, reciprocity has progressively given way to the notion of collective guarantee and considerations of *ordre public*. This constitutes a revolution in the postulates of traditional international law. Human rights treaties incorporate obligations of an objective character, aimed at the safeguard of the rights of human beings and not the reciprocal rights of States on behalf of their respective citizens, on the basis of a superior general public interest (of *ordre public*). Hence, the specificity of human rights treaties.

Likewise, the evolution of environmental protection bears witness of the emergence of obligations of an objective character without reciprocal advantages for States. The 1972 Stockholm Declaration on the Human Environment refers expressly to the "common good of mankind" (Principle 18). Rules on the protection of the environment are adopted, and obligations to that effect are undertaken, in the common superior interest of mankind. This has been expressly acknowledged in some treaties in the field of the environment.[13] It is further implicit in references to "human health" in some environmental law treaties.[14]

The evolution, from internationalization to globalization, of environmental protection, can also be detected in its spatial dimension. Initially, attention was turned to environmental protection in territorial zones under the competence of States. One thus spoke of control of *transboundary* or *transfrontier* pollution (a terminology reminiscent of that employed in the OECD), with an underlying emphasis on the relations between neighbouring countries or on contacts or conflicts between State sovereignties. It soon became evident that, to deal with wider threats to the environment (e.g., marine pollution and atmospheric pollution such as acid rain, depletion of the ozone layer, and global warming), it was necessary to also consider principles applicable on a global scale. Global in the sense of affecting zones where State interests were immediately affected (transboundary pollution), but also other areas where State interests appeared

[13] For example, preambles of the 1971 Treaty on the Prohibition of the Emplacement of Nuclear Weapons and Other Weapons of Mass Destruction on the Sea-bed and the Ocean Floor and in the Subsoil Thereof; the 1972 Convention on the Prohibition of the Development, Production and Stockpiling of Bacteriological (Biological) and Toxin Weapons and on Their Destruction; the 1977 Convention on the Prohibition of Military or Any Other Hostile Use of Environmental Modification Techniques; the 1972 Convention on the Prevention of Marine Pollution by Dumping of Wastes and Other Matter; the 1974 Convention for the Prevention of Marine Pollution from Land-Based Sources; the 1972 Convention for the Prevention of Marine Pollution by Dumping from Ships and Aircraft; the 1972 UNESCO Convention for the Protection of the World Cultural and Natural Heritage.

[14] E.g., the 1985 Vienna Convention for the Protection of the Ozone Layer, preamble and Article 2; the 1987 Montreal Protocol on Substances that Deplete the Ozone Layer, preamble; Article 1 of the three marine pollution Conventions above quoted.

not so visibly affected (e.g., protection of the atmosphere and of the marine environment). In this common international law of the environment, principles of a global character are to apply on the territory of States irrespective of any transboundary or transfrontier effect, and are to govern zones which are not under any national territorial competence.[15]

In this connection, the Brundtland Commission, reporting to the U.N. General Assembly in 1987, dedicated a whole chapter to the management, in the "common interest" of the so-called "global commons" (e.g., those zones falling outside or beyond national jurisdictions).[16] Similarly, the Centre for Studies and Research in International Law in 1985 singled out the gradual evolution from a transboundary or "transterritorial" perspective to a global perspective of the preservation of the environment (and action in favour of resources of the common heritage of mankind).[17]

That international law is no longer exclusively State-oriented can be seen from repeated references to "mankind" not only in academic writings[18] but significantly, also in various international instruments. This may possibly be pointing towards an international law of mankind which pursues preservation of the environment and sustainable development on behalf of present and future generations. As such, the notion of cultural heritage of mankind may be found.[19] The legal principle of the common heritage of mankind has found expression in the law of the sea and in the law of outer space.[20] The reconsideration of the basic postulates of international law to take account of the superior

[15] A.C. Kiss, *Droit international de l'environnement*, Paris, Pédone, 1989, pp. 93, 67–68, 70–72 and 8; L.A. Teclaff, "The Impact of Environmental Concern on the Development of International Law", *International Environmental Law* (ed. L.A. Teclaff and A.E. Utton), N.Y., Praeger, 1974, p.251; and cf. Ian Brownlie, "A Survey of International Customary Rules of Environmental Protection", in ibid., p.5.

[16] World Commission on Environment and Development, *Our Common Future*, Oxford, Oxford University Press, 1987, chapter 10 ("Managing the Commons"), pp. 261–289.

[17] P.M. Dupuy, "Bilan de recherches de la section de langue française du Centre d'Étude et de Recherche de l'Académie", *La pollution transfrontière et le droit international – 1985*, Dordrecht: Martinus Nijhoff/Académie de Droit International de la Haye, (1986), pp. 68–70, 65–66 and 81.

[18] Cf., e.g., C.W. Jenks, *The Common Law of Mankind*, London, Stevens, 1958, pp. 1–442; R.J. Dupuy, *La communauté internationale entre le mythe et l'histoire*, Paris, Economica/ UNESCO, 1986, pp. 11–182; among others.

[19] E.g., in the UNESCO Conventions for the Protection of Cultural Property in the Event of Armed Conflict (1954) and for the Protection of the World Cultural and Natural Heritage (1974)).

[20] E.g., the 1982 U.N. Convention on the Law of the Sea, Part XI, particularly Articles 136–145 and 311(6); the 1970 U.N. Declaration of Principles Governing the Sea-Bed and the Ocean Floor, and the Subsoil Thereof, Beyond the Limits of National Jurisdiction; and the 1979 Treaty Governing the Activities of States on the Moon and Other Celestial Bodies, Article 11; and cf. the 1967 Treaty on Principles Governing the Activities of States in the Exploration and Use of Outer Space, Including the Moon and Other Celestial Bodies, Article I. Cf. N.J. Schrijver, "Permanent Sovereignty over Natural Resources versus the Common Heritage of Mankind: Complementary or Contradictory Principles of International Economic Law?", *International Law and Development* (ed. P. De Waart, P. Peters and E. Denters), Dordrecht, Nijhoff/Kluwer, 1988, pp. 95–96, 98 and 101.

common interests of mankind has been the subject of general academic works on the subject.[21]

More recently an evolution can be discerned from the notion of common heritage of mankind (as found in the contexts of the law of the sea and space law) to that of common concern of mankind. Thus, U.N. General Assembly Resolution 43/53 of December 1988, recognized that climate change was a "common concern" of mankind, the wording of its first operative paragraph describing climate as "an essential condition which sustains life on earth".[22]

Such an essential or fundamental condition is inextricably linked to the new idea of "commonness". This recently proposed notion is inspired by considerations of international *ordre public*. It appears as a derivate of the earlier "common heritage" approach. Its evident intent is to shift emphasis from the sharing of benefits obtained from exploitation of environmental wealths to fair or equitable sharing of burdens in environmental protection, along with the needed concerted actions towards that goal within social and temporal dimensions.[23] It can hardly be doubted, as UNEP itself has acknowledged, that environmental protection is "decisively linked" to the "human rights issue".[24] That is, to the very fulfilment of the fundamental right to life in its wide dimension (right to life – cf. section 3, *infra*).

Resorting to the very notion of mankind, human kind, immediately places the whole discussion within the human rights framework. And it must be emphasized that this reference should not be left implicit or neglected as allegedly redundant. Just as law, or the rule of law itself, does not operate in a vacuum, mankind, the human kind, is neither a social nor a legal abstraction. It is composed of human collectivities, of all human beings of flesh and bone, living in human societies.

In the case that the concept of common concern for mankind becomes widely and unequivocally accepted, the introduction of certain rights and obligations are bound to follow. From this, one may consider the concept's materialization as the right to a healthy environment. Within the ambit of the *droit de l'humanité*, the common concern of human kind finds expression in the exercise of the recognized right to a healthy environment, in all its dimensions (individual, group, social or collective, and inter-generational – cf. section 5 – *infra*); precisely because mankind is not a social or legal abstraction and is formed by a multitude of human beings living in societies and extended in time.

[21] E.g., Jenks, Dupuy – references in *supra*, note 18.

[22] Cf. also the Report of the UNEP Group of Legal Experts Meeting convened in Malta in December 1990 in order to examine the implications of the concept of "common concern to mankind" on global environmental issues (co-*rapporteurs*, A.A. Cançado Trindade and D. Attard), published by UNEP.

[23] On this last point, cf. UNEP/Executive Director and Secretariat, *Note to the Group of Legal Experts to Examine the Implications of the "Common Concern of Mankind" Concept on Global Environmental Issues*, Malta Meeting, 13–15 December 1990, document UNEP/ELIU/WG.1/1/2, pp. 1–2, ? 4, and cf. pp. 4–5, ? 8–9 (mimeographed, internal circulation).

[24] Ibid., p. 14 & 22.

The human rights framework is ineluctably present in the consideration of the regime of protection of the human environment in all its aspects; we are ultimately confronted with the crucial question of *survival* of human kind, with the assertion – in face of the threats to the human environment – of the fundamental human right to live.

Just as a couple of decades ago there were questions which were "withdrawn" from the domestic jurisdiction of States to become matters of *international* concern (essentially, in cases pertaining to human rights protection and self-determination of peoples)[25], there are nowadays global issues, such as climate change, which are being erected as the *common* concern of mankind. Here, again, the contribution of human rights protection in piercing the so-called reserved domain of States can be perceived in historical perspective. The globalization of the regimes of human rights protection and environmental protection heralds the end of reciprocity and the emergence of *erga omnes* obligations.

Prohibiting the invocation of reciprocity as an excuse for non-compliance of *erga omnes* obligations is confirmed in unequivocal terms by the 1969 Vienna Convention on the Law of Treaties: in providing for the conditions in which a breach of a treaty may bring about its suspension or termination, the Vienna Convention (Article 60 (5)) expressly excepts "provisions relating to the protection of the human person contained in treaties of a humanitarian character". This provision makes an inroad into a domain of international law – the law of treaties – traditionally marked by the voluntarism of States, and constitutes a clause of safeguard for human beings. Thus, the contemporary law of treaties itself discards the principle of reciprocity in the implementation of treaties of a humanitarian character. The obligations enshrined therein generate effects *erga omnes*. The overcoming of reciprocity in human rights protection and in environmental protection has come about in the context of the constant search for an expansion of the ambit of protection (for the safeguard of an increasingly wider circle of beneficiaries, human beings and ultimately mankind), for a higher degree of the protection afforded and for the gradual strengthening of the mechanisms of supervision, in the defense of common superior interests.

Yet another affinity in the recent developments of human rights protection and environmental protection, which has not been sufficiently examined so far and to which we shall now turn, lies in the incidence of the temporal dimension.

[25] A.A. Cançado Trindade, "The Domestic Jurisdiction of States in the Practice of the United Nations and Regional Organizations", 25 *International and Comparative Law Quarterly* (1976) pp. 723, 731, 737, 742, 761–762 and 765.

3. Further Affinities in the Evolution of Human Rights Protection and of Environmental Protection

(1) Protection of the Human Person and Environmental Protection: Mutual Concerns

Just as concern for human rights protection can be found in the realm of international environmental law[26], concern for environmental protection can also be found in the express recognition of the right to a healthy environment in two recent human rights instruments, namely, the 1988 Additional Protocol to the American Convention on Human Rights in the Area of Economic, Social, and Cultural Rights (Article 11) and the 1981 African Charter on Human and Peoples' Rights (Article 24). In the former, it is recognized as a right of "everyone" (§ 1) to be protected by the States Parties (§ 2), whereas in the latter it is acknowledged as a peoples' right.

Presently, concern for the protection of the environment can also be found in the realm of international humanitarian law.[27] Likewise, recent developments in international refugee law are worthy of attention, such as the possible assimilation of victims of environmental disasters to protected [displaced] persons under refugee law.[28]

Furthermore, the protection of vulnerable groups (e.g., indigenous populations; ethnic, religious and linguistic minorities; mentally and physically handicapped persons) appears today at the confluence of international human rights law and international environmental law. As we have indicated in another study, concern for the protection of vulnerable groups can nowadays be found in international instruments and initiatives pertaining to both human rights protection and environmental protection, where the issue has been approached on the basis of both human and environmental considerations.[29]

[26] Preamble and Principle 1 of the 1972 Stockholm Declaration on the Human Environment; Preamble and Principles 6 and 23 of the 1982 World Charter for Nature; Principles 1 and 20 proposed by the World Commission on the Environment and Development in its 1987 report. Cf. A.A. Cançado Trindade, "The Contribution of International Human Rights Law to Environmental Protection, with Special Reference to Global Environmental Change", *in International Law and Global Environmental Change: New Dimensions* (ed. E. Brown Weiss), United Nations University (UNU) Project, 1992, 93 pp. (in print).

[27] Cf. Articles 35(3) and 55 of the 1977 Additional Protocol I to the 1949 Geneva Conventions (prohibition of methods or means of warfare severely damaging the environment); the 1977 U.N. Convention on the Prohibition of Military or Any Other Hostile Use of Environmental Modification Techniques; and the 1982 World Charter for Nature (paragraphs 5 and 20).

[28] E.g., the 1984 Cartagena Declaration on Refugees, recommending an expanded concept of refugee for use in Central America.

[29] Cf. references and sources in A.A. Cançado Trindade, "The Contribution ...", *supra* note 26.

(2) Incidence of the Temporal Dimension in Environmental Protection and in Human Rights Protection

The notion of time, the element of foreseeability, inhere in legal science as such. The predominantly *preventive* character of the normative *corpus* on environmental protection, stressed time and time again[30] and reiterated in clear and emphatic terms in the reference to the temporal dimension in the 1990 Ministerial Declaration of the II World Climate Conference (paragraph 7), is also present in the field of human rights protection.

Its incidence can be detected at distinct stages or levels, starting with the *travaux préparatoires* (e.g., of the U.N. Covenant on Civil and Political Rights, and Optional Protocol), the underlying conceptions and the adopted texts of human rights instruments.[31] The temporal dimension is further present in international refugee law.[32] Second, the incidence of the temporal dimension can also be found in the "evolutionary" *interpretation* of human rights treaties, which has ensured that they remain living instruments. There has been occurring a dynamic process of evolution of international human rights law through interpretation.[33]

Thirdly, in respect to the *application* of human rights treaties, the practice of international supervisory organs affords illustrations of the temporal dimension in human rights protection. Thus, the *jurisprudence constante* of the European Commission and Court of Human Rights under the European Convention on Human Rights has in recent years upheld, in numerous cases, the notion of *potential* or *prospective* victims (that is, victims claiming a valid potential personal interest under the Convention), thus enhancing the condition of individual applicants.[34] Likewise, in 1988 the Inter-American Court of Human Rights, in the *Velasquez Rodriguez* and *Godinez Cruz* cases against Honduras (1988), stressed the States' duty of due diligence to prevent violations of protected human rights.[35]

In fact, the incidence of the temporal dimension can be detected not only in the interpretation and application of norms pertaining to guaranteed rights but also in the conditions of their exercise, as in public emergencies. It can be further detected in the protection not only of civil and political rights but also – and perhaps even more pronouncedly – of economic, social and cultural

[30] Cf. ibid.

[31] E.g., the three recent Conventions – the Inter-American, the U.N. and the European – against Torture, of an essentially preventive character; the 1948 Convention against Genocide; the 1973 Convention against *Apartheid*, along with other international instruments attuned to the prevention of discrimination of distinct kinds.

[32] E.g., the definition of "refugee" under the 1951 Convention (Article 1(a)(2)) and the 1967 Protocol on the Status of Refugees (Artile 1(2)), with the element of the "well-founded fear" of persecution, the threats or risks of persecutions; reference can also be made to the recent U.N. "early warning" efforts of prevention or forecasting of refugee flows.

[33] A.A. Cançado Trindade, "Co-existence and Co-ordination ...", *supra* note (2), pp. 91–112.

[34] Ibid., pp. 243–299.

[35] Cf. A.A. Cançado Trindade, "The Contribution ...", *supra* note 26.

rights (e.g., right to education, right to cultural integrity). This may be carried through to include the right to development and the right to a healthy environment, – extending into time.[36] Manifestations of the temporal dimension become quite concrete, particularly in the field of human rights protection, where they do not appear as soft law. Here, more clearly than in other areas of international law, the evolving jurisprudence (e.g., on the notion of potential victims, on the duty of prevention of violations of human rights) may also serve as inspiration for environmental protection.

4. The Rights to Life and to Health at the Basis of the *Ratio Legis* of International Human Rights Law and of Environmental Law

(1) The Fundamental Right to Life in Its Wide Dimension

The right to life is basic or fundamental because "the enjoyment of the right to life is a necessary condition of the enjoyment of all other human rights".[37] As indicated by the Inter-American Court of Human Rights in its Advisory Opinion on *Restrictions to the Death Penalty* (1983), the human right to life encompasses a "substantive principle" whereby every human being has an inalienable right to have his life respected, and a "procedural principle" whereby no human being shall be arbitrarily deprived of his life.[38]

The Human Rights Committee, qualifying the human right to life as the "supreme right of the human being", has declared that this fundamental human rights *"ne peut pas être entendu de façon restrictive"* and its protection *"exige que les Etats adoptent des mesures positives"*.[39] The Inter-American Commission of Human Rights has also drawn attention to the binding character of the right to life.[40] In its recent Resolution No. 3/87, on case No. 9647, concerning the United States, the Inter-American Commission, after identifying a norm of *jus cogens* which "prohibits the State execution of children", warned against "the arbitrary deprivation of life" on the basis of a patchwork scheme of legislation which subjects the severity of the punishment to the "fortuitous element of where the crime took place".[41]

Under international human rights instruments, the assertion of the inherent right to life of every human being is accompanied by an assertion of the legal

[36] Ibid.

[37] F. Przetacznik, "The Right to Life as a Basic Human Right", 9 *Revue des droits de l'homme/Human Rights Journal* (1976) pp. 589 and 603.

[38] I.-A. Court H.R., Advisory Opinion OC-3/83, of 08 September 1983, Series A, No. 3, p.59.

[39] Cited in J.G.C. Van Aggelen, *Le rôle des organisations internationales dans la protection du droit à la vie*, Bruxelles, Story-Scientia, 1986, p.23.

[40] Cited in ibid., p.38.

[41] OAS, *Annual Report of the Inter-American Commission on Human Rights – 1986–1987*, pp. 170 and 172–173.

protection of that basic human right and of the *negative* obligation not to deprive arbitrarily of life.[42] However, this negative obligation is accompanied by the *positive* obligation to take all appropriate measures to protect and preserve human life. This has been acknowledged by the European Commission of Human Rights. The Commission's case-law has evolved to the point of holding (*Association X v. United Kingdom*, 1978) that Article 2 of the European Convention on Human Rights also imposed on States a wider and positive obligation *"de prendre des mesures adéquates pour protéger la vie"*.[43]

Taken in its wide and proper dimension, the fundamental right to life comprises the right of every human being not to be deprived of his or her life (*right to life*) and the right of every human being to have the appropriate means of subsistence and a decent standard of life (preservation of life, *right of living*). As identified by Przetacznik, "the former belongs to the area of civil and political rights, the latter to that of economic, social and cultural rights".[44] The fundamental right to life, properly understood, affords an eloquent illustration of the indivisibility and inter-relatedness of all human rights.[45]

In fact, some members of the Human Rights Committee have expressed the view that Article 6 of the U.N. Covenant on Civil and Political Rights requires the State

> to take *positive measures* to ensure the right to life, including steps to reduce infant mortality rates, prevent industrial accidents, and protect the environment".[46]

Taking the essential requirements of the right of living (*supra*) as a corollary of the right to life, Desch argued that inequitable distribution of food or medication by public authorities, or even the toleration of malnutrition or failure to reduce infant mortality, would constitute violations of Article 6 of the Covenant if they result in an arbitrary deprivation of life.[47]

During the drafting of the 1948 Universal Declaration of Human Rights, attempts were made to make its Article 3, which proclaims the right to life, more precise.[48] A number of issues were the object of discussion in the drafting

[42] E.g., U.N. Covenant on Civil and Political Rights, Article 6(1); European Convention on Human Rights, Article 2; American Convention on Human Rights, Article 4(1); African Charter on Human and Peoples' Rights, Article 4. Th. Desch, "The Concept and Dimensions of the Right to Life (As Defined in International Standards and in International and Comparative Jurisprudence)", 36 *Osterreichische Zeitschrift fur Offentliches Recht und Volkerrecht* (1985) pp. 86 and 99.

[43] Cited in J.G.C. Van Aggelen, *supra* note (36), p.32.

[44] F. Przetacznik, *supra* note (34), p.603, e cf., p.586.

[45] On the right to life bearing witness of the indivisibility of all human rights, cf. W.P. Gormley, "The Right to a Safe and Decent Environment", 20 *Indian Journal of International Law* (1988) pp. 23–24.

[46] Cited in Desch, *supra* note (42), p.101.

[47] Ibid., p. 101.

[48] Cf. H. Kanger, *Human Rights in the U.N. Declaration*, Uppsala/Stockholm, Almqvist & Wiksell, 1984, pp. 81–82.

of corresponding provisions on the right to life in subsequent human rights treaties.[49] However, it is the opinions and decisions more recently rendered by international supervisory bodies that have gradually given more precision to the right to life as enshrined in the respective human rights treaties (cf. *supra*). Even those who insist on regarding the right to life strictly as a civil right[50] cannot fail to admit that, ultimately, without an adequate standard of living (as for example recognized in Articles 11–12 of the U.N. Covenant on Economic, Social and Cultural Rights, following Article 25(1) of the 1948 Universal Declaration) the right to life could not possibly be realized in its full sense[51] (for example, in its close links with the right to health and medical care, the right to food, and the right to housing[52]). Thus, both the U.N. General Assembly (Resolution 37/189A of 1982) and the U.N. Commission on Human Rights (Resolution 1982/7 and 1983/43) have unequivocally taken the firm view that *all individuals and all peoples* have an *inherent* right to life. And furthermore that the safeguarding of this *foremost right* is an essential condition for the enjoyment of the entire range of civil and political, as well as economic, social and cultural rights.[53]

Two points are deserving of particular emphasis here. First, it has not passed unnoticed that the provision of the U.N. Covenant on Civil and Political Rights on the fundamental and inherent right to life (Article 6(1)) is "the only Article of the Covenant where the inherency of a right is expressly referred to".[54] Secondly, the United Nations has formed its conviction that not only all individuals but also all *peoples* have an inherent right to life (*supra*). This brings to the fore the safeguard of the right to life of all persons as well as of human collectivities, with special attention to the requirements of survival (as a component of the right to life) of vulnerable groups (for example, the dispossessed and deprived, disabled or handicapped persons, children and the

[49] On the legislative history of Article 6 of the U.N. Covenant on Civil and Political Rights, cf. [B.G. Ramcharan], "The Drafting History of Article 6 of the International Covenant on Civil and Political Rights", in *The Right to Life in International Law* (ed. B.G. Ramcharan), Dordrecht, Martinus Nijhoff, 1985, pp. 42–56; on the legislative history of Article 2 of the European Convention on Human Rights, cf. B.G. Ramcharan, "The Drafting History of Article 2 of the European Convention on Human Rights", in ibid., pp. 57–61; and on the legislative history of Article 4 (and antecedents) of the American Convention on Human Rights, cf. J. Colon-Collazo, "The Legislative History of the Right to Life in the Inter-American Legal System", in ibid., pp. 33–41.

[50] Cf., to this effect, the analysis by Y. Dinstein, "The Right to Life, Physical Integrity, and Liberty", in L. Henkin (ed.) *The International Bill of Rights*, New York: Columbia University Press, (1981), pp. 114–137.

[51] Th. Van Boven, *People Matter – Views on International Human Rights Policy*, Amsterdam, Meulenhoff, 1982, p.77.

[52] On this latter, cf. S. Leckie, "The U.N. Committee on Economic, Social and Cultural Rights and the Right to Adequate Housing: Towards An Appropriate Approach", 11 *Human Rights Quarterly* (1989) pp. 522–560.

[53] Cited in B.G. Ramcharan, "The Right to Life", 30 *Netherlands International Law Review* (1983) p. 301.

[54] Ibid., p. 316.

elderly, ethnic minorities, indigenous populations, and migrant workers – cf. section 3, *supra*).[55]

From this perspective, the right to a healthy environment and the right to peace appear as extensions or corollaries of the right to life.[56] The fundamental character of the right to life renders inadequate any narrow approach in current times; under the right to life, in its modern and proper sense, not only is the prohibition against any arbitrary deprivation of life to be upheld, but furthermore States are under the duty "to pursue policies which are designed to ensure access to the means of survival"[57] for all individuals and all peoples. To this effect, States are under the obligation to avoid serious environmental hazards or risks to life, and to set into motion "monitoring and early warning systems" to detect serious environmental hazards or risks and "urgent action systems" to deal with such threats.[58]

In the same vein, in the First European Conference on the Environment and Human Rights (Strasbourg, 1979), the point was made that mankind needed to protect itself against its own threats to the environment. Particularly when those threats had negative repercussions on the conditions of existence – life itself, physical and mental health, and the well-being of present and future generations.[59] In a way, it was the right to life itself, in its wide dimension, which entailed the needed recognition of the right to a healthy environment; this latter point appears as *"le droit à des conditions de vie qui assurent la santé physique, morale, mentale et sociale, la vie elle-même, ainsi que le bien-être des générations présentes et futures"*.[60] In other words, the right to a healthy environment safeguards human life itself under two aspects. The first is physical existence and health of human beings. Second is the dignity of that existence, as in the quality of life which makes it worth living.[61] The right to a healthy environment thus encompasses and enlarges the right to health and the right to an adequate or sufficient standard of living. Furthermore, it has a wide *temporal* dimension as, *"en matière d'environnement, certaines atteintes à l'environnement ne produisent d'effets sur la vie et la santé de l'homme qu'à long terme, (...) la reconnaissance d'un droit à l'environnement (...) devrait donc admettre une notion large des atteintes"*.[62]

Thus, the widening of the dimension of the right to life and the right to a

[55] Ibid., p. 305, and cf. p. 306; and Th. Van Boven, *supra* note 51, pp. 179 and 181–183.

[56] B.G. Ramcharan, *supra* note 53, pp. 303 and 308–310.

[57] Ibid., p. 302.

[58] Ibid., pp. 304 and 329. – Views reproduced in B.G. Ramcharan, "The Concept and Dimensions of the Right to Life", in B.G. Ramcharan (ed.) *The Right to Life in International Law*, Dordrecht, Martinus Nijhoff, (1985), pp. 1–32.

[59] P. Kromarek, "Le droit à un environnement équilibré et sain, considéré comme un droit de l'homme: sa mise-en-oeuvre nationale, européenne et internationale", *I Conférence européenne sur l'environnement et les droits de l'homme*, Strasbourg, Institute for European Environmental Policy, 1979, pp. 2–3, 31 and 34 (mimeographed, restricted circulation).

[60] Ibid., pp. 13 and 5 (emphasis added).

[61] Ibid., p. 12.

[62] Ibid., pp. 43 and 21.

healthy environment entails the consequent wider characterization of possible threats against those rights, which in turn calls for a higher degree of protection. An example of such threats is provided by the effects of global warming on human health such as skin cancer, retinal eye damage, cataracts and eventual blindness, neurological damage, lowered resistance to infections, and alteration of the immunological system (through damaged immune cells). As a result, depletion of the ozone layer may result in substantial injury to human health as well as the environment (harm to terrestrial plants, destruction of the zooplankton, a key link in the food chain)[63], thus disclosing the needed convergence of human health protection and environmental protection.

For example, in the realm of international environmental law, the 1989 Hague Declaration on the Atmosphere states that "the right *to live* is the right from which all other rights stem". It adds that "the right *to live* in dignity in a viable global environment" entails the duty of the "community of nations" vis-à-vis "present and future generations" to do "all that can be done to preserve the quality of the atmosphere". The use of the expression "the right *to live*" (rather than right *to life*) seems well in keeping with the understanding that the right to life entails negative as well as positive obligations as to preservation of human life (cf. *supra*). The *Institut de Droit International*, while drafting its Resolution on Transboundary Air Pollution (Session of Cairo, 1987), made sure to include provisions referring to the protection of life and human health.[64]

Together with the right to a healthy environment, the right to peace also appears as a necessary prolongation or corollary of the right to life. In fact, both the Inter-American Commission on Human Rights[65] and the U.N. General Assembly[66] have addressed the requirements of *survival* as a component of the right to life. In its general comment 6(16) of 1982 on Article 6(1) of the Civil and Political Covenant, the Human Rights Committee observed that the right to life is "the supreme right from which no derogation is permitted even in time of public emergency." Recalling the earlier comment, in 1985, in its general comment 14(23) on Article 6, the Human Rights Committee went on to relate the current proliferation of weapons of mass destruction to "the supreme duty of States to prevent wars". The Committee associated itself with the growing concern, expressed during successive sessions of the U.N. General Assembly, by representatives of all geographical regions, at what was considered to be "the greatest threat to the right to live which confronts mankind today". In the words of the Committee, "the very existence and gravity of this threat generates a

[63] J.T.B. Tripp, "The UNEP Montreal Protocol: Industrialized and Developing Countries Sharing the Responsibility for Protecting the Stratospheric Ozone Layer", 20 *New York University Journal of International Law and Politics* (1988) p. 734; Ch. B. Davidson, "The Montreal Protocol: The First Step toward Protecting the Global Ozone Layer", in ibid., pp. 807–809.

[64] Cf. preamble and Article 10(2) and 11; text in : 62 *Annuaire de l'Institut de Droit International* (1987)–II, pp. 204, 207–208 and 211.

[65] Cf. Comisión Interamericana de Derechos Humanos, *Diez A_nos de Actividades – 1971–1981*, Washington, Secretaría General de la OEA, 1982, pp. 338–339, 321 and 329–330.

[66] B.G. Ramcharan, *supra* note 53, p. 303.

climate of suspicion and fear between States, which is in itself antagonistic to the promotion of universal respect for an observance of human rights" in accordance with the U.N. Charter and the U.N. Covenants on Human Rights.[67] The Committee, accordingly, "in the interest of mankind", called upon "all States, whether Parties to the Covenant or not, to take urgent steps, unilaterally and by agreement, to rid the world of this menace".[68]

The maintenance of peace is an imperative for the preservation of human life. The Final Act of the 1968 Teheran Conference on Human Rights contains several references to the relationship between the observance of human rights and maintenance of peace.[69] In this light, further reference may be made to the preambles of the two 1966 U.N. Covenants on Human Rights. More recently the "right to peace" has been the subject of a number of U.N. resolutions, which relate peace to disarmament and détente, thus disclosing the temporal dimension of the underlying duty of *prevention* of conflicts[70] (e.g., *inter alia*, G.A. Resolutions 33/73 of 1978, and 34/88 of 1979). The States' duty to co-exist in peace and to achieve disarmament is acknowledged in the 1974 Charter on Economic Rights and Duties of States (Articles 26 and 15, respectively).

The right to peace includes as a corollary the "right to disarmament".[71] In this regard attention has been drawn to the fact that limitations or violations of human rights are often associated with the outbreak of conflicts, the process of militarization and the expenditure on arms[72] – especially nuclear weapons and other weapons of mass-destruction.[73] These have led, and may unfortunately still lead, to arbitrary deprivation of human life. The conception of "sustainable development", as propounded by the Brundtland Commission, points to the ineluctable relationship between the rights to a healthy environment, to peace and to development.[74]

The relationship between the right to life and the right to development as a human right becomes clearer as one moves from the traditional, narrow approach to the right to life (seen as strictly a civil right) into the wider and

[67] U.N. *Report of the Human Rights Committee, G.A.O.R.* – 40th Session (1985), suppl. n. 40 (A/40/40), p. 162.

[68] Ibid., p. 162.

[69] Cf. U.N., *Final Act of the International Conference on Human Rights* (Teheran, 1968), U.N. doc. A/CONF.32/41, N.Y., U.N., 1968, pp. 4, 6, 9, 14 and 36.

[70] Cf. J.-M. Becet and D. Colard, *Les droits de l'homme*, Paris, Economica, 1982, pp. 128–131.

[71] To this effect, cf. ibid., pp. 129–131; Ph. Alston, *infra* note 72, pp. 324–325 and 329–330.

[72] Ph. Alston, "Peace, Disarmament and Human Rights", *Armement, Développement, Droits de l'homme, Désarmement* (Colloque à l'UNESCO, 1982) (ed. G. Fischer), Paris/Bruxelles, Bruylant, 1985, pp. 325–330.

[73] Cf. discussion in, e.g., A.A. Tikhonov, "The Inter-Relationship between the Right to Life and the Right to Peace; Nuclear Weapons and Other Weapons of Mass-Destruction and the Right to Life", in B.G. Ramcharan (ed.) *The Right to Life in International Law*, Dordrecht, Martinus Nijhoff, (1985), pp.97–113.

[74] Cf. World Commission on Environment and Development, *Our Common Future*, Oxford, Oxford University Press, 1987, pp. 19 and 290–307, and cf. in particular pp. 294–300 on conflicts as a "cause of unsustainable development".

modern approach, which encompasses the minimum conditions for an adequate and dignified standard of living (cf. *supra*). Then the inter-relatedness of the right to life and the right to development as a human right becomes self-evident, as the latter element purports to demand all possible endeavours to overcome obstacles (of destitution and under-development) preventing the fulfilment of basic human needs.[75] Not surprisingly, the U.N. Working Group of Governmental Experts on the Right to Development recommended in 1984 *inter alia* that particular attention should be paid to the basic needs and aspirations of vulnerable or disadvantaged and discriminated groups.[76]

In sum, the basic right to life, which includes the right of living, entails negative as well as positive obligations in favour of preservation of human life. Its enjoyment is a precondition of the enjoyment of other human rights. It belongs concurrently to the realm of civil and political rights, and to that of economic, social and cultural rights, thus illustrating the indivisibility of all human rights. It establishes a "link" between the domains of international human rights law and environmental law. It inheres in all individuals and all peoples, with special attention to the requirements of survival. It has as extensions or corollaries the right to a healthy environment and the right to peace (and disarmament). It is closely related, in its wide dimension, to the right to development as a human right (right to live with fulfilment of basic human needs). And it lies at the basis of the ultimate *ratio legis* of the domains of international human rights law and environmental law – focusing on the protection and survival of the human person and mankind.

(2) The Right to Health as the Starting-Point towards the Right to a Healthy Environment

Like the right to life (right of living, *supra*), the right to health entails *negative* as well as *positive* obligations. In fact, the right to health is inextricably interwoven with the right to life itself, and is a precondition for the exercise of freedom. The right to health implies the *negative* obligation not to practise any act which can endanger one's health. Thus, this basic right is linked to the right to physical and mental integrity and to the prohibition of torture and of cruel, inhuman or degrading treatment.[77] But this duty of abstention (so crucial, for example, in the treatment of detainees and prisoners) is accompanied by the *positive* obligation to take all appropriate measures to protect and preserve human health (including measures of prevention of diseases).

[75] P.J.I.M. De Waart, "The Inter-Relationship between the Right to Life and the Right to Development", in B.G. Ramcharan (ed.) *The Right to Life in International Law*, Dordrecht, Martinus Nijhoff, (1985), pp. 84–96, at pp. 89 and 91–92.

[76] Cited in ibid., p.91.

[77] As recognized and provided for in the U.N. Covenant on Civil and Political Rights, Article 7; the European Convention on Human Rights, Article 3; the American Convention on Human Rights, Articles 4 and 5.

Such positive obligation,[78] linking the right to life to the right to an adequate standard of life[79], discloses the fact that the right to health, in its proper and wide dimension, concurrently has the character of an individual and a social right. Belonging, like the right to life, to the realm of basic or fundamental rights, the right to health is an individual right in that it requires the protection of the physical and mental integrity of the individual and his dignity. It is also a social right in that it imposes on the State and society collective responsibility for the protection of the health of the citizenry and the prevention and treatment of diseases.[80] Like the right to life, the right to health, properly understood, affords a vivid illustration of the indivisibility and interrelatedness of all human rights.

(3) The Right to a Healthy Environment as an Extension of the Right to Health

The right to health in its "positive" aspect (*supra*) found expression at a global level, in Article 12 of the U.N. Covenant on Economic, Social and Cultural Rights. That provision, in detailing the guidelines for the implementation of the right to health, singled out, *inter alia*, "the improvement of all aspects of environmental and industrial hygiene". The way appeared paved for the future recognition of the right to a healthy environment (*infra*).

This point was the object of attention at the 1978 Colloquy of the Hague Academy of International Law on "The Right to Health as a Human Right", where the issue of the human right to environmental salubrity was raised. On this occasion, after warning that the degradation of the environment nowadays constituted a *"menace collective à la santé des hommes"*[81], P.M. Dupuy advocated that the human right to environmental salubrity be recognized as the "supreme guarantee of the right to health".[82] In proposing that the environment ought to be protected *"en fonction de l'ensemble des intérêts de la collectivitié"*, he argued:

> "Il nous paraît que la chance fournie par l'affirmation d'un droit à la salubrité du milieu est justement de donner l'occasion à l'environnement de

[78] As recognized and provided for in the U.N. Covenant on Economic, Social and Cultural Rights, Article 12; in the European Social Charter, Article 11; and also in WHO and ILO Resolutions on specific aspects.

[79] As proclaimed by the 1948 Universal Declaration of Human Rights, Article 25(1). – On the "negative" and "positive" aspects of the right to health, cf. M. Bothe, "Les concepts fondamentaux du droit à la santé: le point de vue juridique", *Le droit à la santé en tant que droit de l'homme – Colloque 1978* (Académie de Droit International de la Haye), Netherlands: Sijthoff & Noordhoff, 1979, pp. 14–29; Scalabrino-Spadea, "Le droit à la santé – Inventaire de normes et principes de droit international", *in Le Médecin face aux droits de l'homme*, Padova, Cedam, 1990, pp.97–98.

[80] R. Roemer, "El Derecho a la Atención de la Salud", in OMS, *El Derecho a la Salud en las Americas* (ed. H.L. Fuenzalida-Puelma and S.S. Connor), Washington, OPAS, publ. n.509, p.16.

[81] P.M. Dupuy, *infra* n. 83, p.406, and cf. p.351.

[82] Ibid., p. 412, and cf. p.409.

cesser d'être d'abord perçu en termes économiques, ainsi qu'un bien susceptible d'exploitation, afin d'apparaître au moins autant comme un patrimoine de l'individu, necessaire à l'épanouissement de son droit fondamental à la vie, et donc à la santé.[83]

The protection of the whole of the biosphere as such entails "indirectly but necessarily" the protection of human beings, in so far as the object of environmental law and hence of the right to a healthy environment is *"protéger les humains en leur assurant un milieu de vie adéquate"*.[84] The right to a healthy environment, in the perspicacious observation by Kiss, supplements other recognized human rights from another point of view, namely,

> *"il contribue à établir une égalité entre citoyens ou, du moins, à attenuer les inégalités dans leurs conditions materielles. On sait que les inégalités entre humains de conditions sociales différentes sont accentuées par la degradation de l'environnement: les moyens materiels dont disposent les mieux nantis leur permettent d'échapper à l'air pollué, aux milieux degradés et de se créer un cadre de vie sain et équilibré, alors que les plus démunis n'ont guJere de telles possibilités et doivent accepter de vivre dans des agglomerations devenues inhumaines, voire des bidonvilles, et de supporter les pollutions.*
>
> *L'exigence d'un environnement sain et équilibré devient ainsi en même temps un moyen de mettre en oeuvre d'autres droits reconnus à la personne humaine.*
>
> *Mais, par ses objectifs mêmes, le droit à l'environnement apporte aussi une dimension supplémentaire aux droits de l'homme dans leur ensemble"*.[85]

The interrelatedness between environmental protection and the safeguard of the right to health is clearly evidenced in the implementation of Article 11 (on the right to protection of health) of the 1961 European Social Charter. The Committee of Independent Experts operating under the Charter, has recently been attentive to national reports which outline measures taken at domestic levels to prevent, limit or control pollution.[86] With regard to the removal of causes of ill-health (Article 11(1)), the Committee has concentrated on measures taken to prevent or reduce pollution of the atmosphere.[87] Thus, in the consideration of a French report, the Committee took note of "the intention of the public authorities to achieve a 50% reduction in sulphur dioxide emissions

[83] P.M. Dupuy, "Le droit à la santé et la protection de l'environnement", *Le droit à la santé ... – Colloque ...*, *supra* note 79, p.410.

[84] A.C. Kiss, "Le droit à la qualité de l'environnement: un droit de l'homme?", in *Le droit à la qualité de l'environnement: un droit en devenir, un droit à définir* (ed. N. Duplé), Vieux-Montreal (Quebec), ed. Quebec/Amerique, 1988, pp.69–70.

[85] Ibid., p.71.

[86] Cf., e.g., Council of Europe/European Social Charter, *Committee of Independent Experts – Conclusions IX–2*, Strasbourg, C.E., 1986, p.71 (Austrian and Cypriot reports); ibid., *Conclusions XI–1*, Strasbourg, C.E., 1989, p.119 (Swedish and British reports).

[87] E.g., German and Italian reports, in ibid., *Conclusions IX–2*, cited *supra* note 86, pp. 71–72.

into the atmosphere during the period 1980–1990".[88] Reviewing the air pollution measures outlined in the latest Danish report, the Committee noted that "emissions of nitrogen oxide into the atmosphere was to be reduced by 50% before 2005 and of sulphur dioxide by 40% before 1995".[89]

The collection *Case Law on the European Social Charter* refers to other pertinent indications of the connection between environmental protection and the right to health. The Committee of Independent Experts has manifested its wish to find information in forthcoming national reports (under Article 11 of the Charter) on "the measures taken to reduce the release of sulphur dioxide and other acid pollutants in the atmosphere".[90] The Committee has called for amplified measures for control of environmental pollution.[91] The Committee has further expressed the opinion that States bound by Article 11 of the Charter should be considered as fulfilling their obligations if they provide evidence of the existence of a medical and health system comprising *inter alia* "general measures aimed in particular at the prevention of air and water pollution, protection from radio-active substances, noise abatement, the food control environmental hygiene, and the control of alcoholism and drugs".[92]

In fact, an attempt has been made under the European Convention on Human Rights itself to extend the protection of the rights to life and health to include well-being. Prior to the convening of the 1973 European Ministerial Conference on the Environment, a Draft Protocol to the European Convention on Human Rights was prepared by H. Steiger. The Draft Protocol, containing two articles, provides for the protection of life and health as encompassing well-being and admits limitations on the right to a healthy environment. It further provides for the protection of individuals against the acts of other private persons. This point (*Drittwirkung*), though giving rise to much debate and controversy, has been touched upon by the European Commission of Human Rights, which, in its 1979 report in the *Young, James and Webster* cases, admitted that the European Convention contained provisions that "non seulement protégent l'individu contre l'Etat, mais aussi obligent l'Etat à

[88] In ibid., p.71–72.

[89] In ibid., *Conclusions XI–1*, cited *supra* note 86, p.118.

[90] Council of Europe/European Social Charter, *Case Law on the European Social Charter-Supplement*, Strasbourg, C.E., 1986, p.37.

[91] Council of Europe/European Social Charter, *Case Law on the European Social Charter*, Strasbourg, C.E., 1982, p.105.

[92] Ibid., p.104 – On the protection of health vis-à-vis the environment under Article 11 of the European Social Charter, cf. further: Council of Europe doc. 6030, of 22.03.1989, p.9; C.E.; *Comité Gouvernemental de la Charte Sociale Européenne – 10e rapport* (1989), p.28 (control of atmospheric pollution); Conseil de l'Europe/Charte Sociale Européenne, *Comité d'Experts Indépendants-Conclusions X–2*, Strasbourg, C.E., 1988, pp. 111–112 (reduction of atmospheric pollution); Council of Europe/European Social Charter, *Committee of Independent Experts – Conclusions X–1*, Strasbourg, C.E., 1987, 108 (reduction of atmospheric pollution, air and water pollution control).

protéger l'individu contre les agissements d'autrui".[93] Although Steiger's proposed Draft Protocol was not accepted at the time by member States, it remains the sole existing proposal on the matter (in so far as the European Convention system is concerned) and its underlying ideas deserve further and deeper consideration[94] (cf. *infra*). Though the question remains an open one, there has however been express recognition of the right to a healthy environment in more recent human rights instruments, as we have already seen (cf. section 3, *supra*).

5. The Question of the Implementation ('Mise en Oeuvre') of the Right to a Healthy Environment

(1) The Issue of Justiciability

It can hardly be doubted that the appropriate formulation of a right may facilitate its implementation. But given that certain concepts escape any scientific definition, it becomes necessary to relate them to a given context for the sake of normative precision and effective implementation. Thus, the term "environment" may be understood as the immediate physical *milieu* surrounding the individual concerned to the whole of the biosphere. It may therefore be necessary to add qualifications to the term.[95] In the implementation of any right, one can not ignore the context in which it is invoked and applies. That is, relating it to the context becomes necessary for its vindication in the particular circumstances.[96]

This applies not only to the right to a healthy environment, but also to any other "category" of rights. But such "new" rights as the right to a healthy environment and the right to development present a greater challenge when one comes to implementation. Whereas many of the previously crystallized civil and political, and economic, social and cultural rights had found expression in domestic law at a much earlier stage and had been formally recognized in national constitutions and other legislation, the above-mentioned "new"

[93] See J.P. Jacqué, "La protection du droit à l'environnement au niveau européen ou regional", *Environnement et droits de l'homme* (ed. P. Kromarek), Paris, UNESCO, 1987, pp. 74–75, and cf. pp. 72–73. And, on Steiger's proposed Draft Protocol, cf. W.P. Gormley, *Human Rights and Environment: The Need for International Co-operation*, Leyden, Sijthoff, 1976, pp. 90–95, P.M. Dupuy, *op. cit. supra* note 83, pp. 408–413.

[94] W.P. Gormley, *supra* note 93, pp.112–113; J.P. Jacqué, *supra* note 93, pp.73 and 75–76; P.M. Dupuy *supra* note 83, pp.412–413. For the complete text of Steiger's 1973 proposed Draft Protocol, cf. Working Group for Environmental Law (Bonn – *rapporteur*, H. Steiger), "The Right to a Humane Environment / Das Recht auf eine menschenwürdige Umwelt", in *Beiträge zur Umweltgestaltung* (Heft A13), Berlin, Erich Schmidt Verlag, 1973, pp. 27–54.

[95] A. Ch. Kiss, "La mise-en-oeuvre du droit à l'environnement: problematique et moyens", *II Conférence européenne sur l'environnement et les droits de l'homme*, Salzburg, Institute for European Environmental Policy, 1980, p.4 (mimeographed, restricted circulation).

[96] Ibid., p.5.

rights, for their part, were still "maturing" in their process of transformation into law. They were "conceived directly in international forums" (such as the United Nations system), and had "not had the benefit of careful prior scrutiny at the national level".[97] Many rights, whether classified as civil and political, or else as economic, social and cultural rights, "can only be defined with specificity when located in a given context".[98]

While the element of *formal justiciability* is taken as an "indispensable attribute" of a right in positivist thinking,[99] international human rights law has distinctly considered that "an international system for the 'supervision' of States' compliance with international human rights obligations is sufficient to satisfy the requirement of 'enforceability'".[100] In short, international human rights law has "clearly adopted the notions of 'implementation' and 'supervision' as its touchstones, rather than those of justiciability or enforceability".[101] International human rights law depends largely on means of implementation other than the purely judicial one.[102] Besides recourse to such judicial organs as the European and the Inter-American Courts of Human Rights, various other (non-judicial) means of implementation are often resorted to ensure guaranteed human rights (e.g., friendly settlement, conciliation, fact-finding).[103]

Formal justiciability or enforceability is by no means a definitive criterion to ascertain the existence of a right under international human rights law. The fact that many recognized human rights have not yet achieved a level of elaboration so as to render them justiciable does not mean that those rights simply do not exist; enforceability is not to be confounded with the existence itself of a right.[104] Attention is to be focused on the *nature* of obligations. For example, it is certain that obligations under the U.N. Covenant on Economic, Social and Cultural Rights were drafted in such a way (e.g., the basic provisions of Articles 2 and 11) that they "cannot easily be made justiciable (manageable by third-

[97] Ph. Alston, "Conjuring up New Human Rights: A Proposal for Quality Control", 78 *American Journal of International Law* (1984) p.614.

[98] For example, "it would not seem inherently more difficult for a particular society to define a 'right to primary education' (an economic right) than a 'right to take part in the conduct of public affairs' (a political right)". Ph. Alston, "Making Space for New Human Rights: The Case of the Right to Development", 1 *Harvard Human Rights Yearbook* (1988) p.35.

[99] Ibid., p.33.

[100] Ibid., p.38.

[101] Ibid., p.35.

[102] K. Vasak, "Pour les droits de l'homme de la troisi]eme génération: les droits de solidarité", *Résumés des Cours de l'Institut International des Droits de l'Homme* (X Session d'Enseignement, 1979), Strasbourg, IIDH, 1979, p.6 (mimeographed).

[103] For a recent study of the operation of international mechanisms of human rights protection, cf. A.A. Cançado Trindade, "Co-existence and Co-ordination of Mechanisms of International Protection of Human Rights (At Global and Regional Levels)", 202 *Recueil des Cours de l'Académie de Droit International* (1987) pp.21–435.

[104] A. Eide, "Realization of Social and Economic Rights and the Minimum Threshold Approach", 10 *Human Rights Law Journal* (1989) pp. 36 and 38.

party judicial settlement). Nevertheless, the obligations exist and can in no way be neglected".[105]

In sum, as far as the issue of justiciability is concerned, one may deduce that there are rights which simply cannot be properly vindicated before a tribunal by their active subjects. However, in the specific case of the right to a healthy environment, if, as pertinently pointed out by Kiss, this is interpreted not as the (virtually impossible) right to an ideal environment but rather as the right to the conservation – that is, protection and improvement – of the environment, it can then be implemented like any other *individual* right. That being so, it is taken as a "procedural" right, the right to a due process before a competent organ, and thus assimilated to any other right guaranteed to individuals and groups of individuals. This right entails, as corollaries, the right of the individual concerned *to be informed* of projects and decisions which could threaten the environment (the protection of which aims at preventive measures), and the right of the individual concerned *to participate* in the taking of decisions which may affect the environment (active sharing of responsibilities in the management of the interests of the whole collectivity).[106] In addition to such rights to information and of participation one can refer to the *right to available and effective domestic remedies*. In this connection, it should not be overlooked that some economic and social rights were made enforceable in domestic law once their component parts were "formulated in a sufficiently precise and detailed manner".[107]

Focusing on the *subjects* of the right to a healthy environment, we see first that it has an individual dimension, as it can be implemented, as just indicated, like other human rights. But the beneficiaries of the right to a healthy environment are not only individuals but also groups, associations, human collectivities and, indeed, the whole of mankind. Hence, it has a collective dimension as well. The right to a healthy environment, like to the right to

[105] Ibid., p.41.

[106] A.C. Kiss, "Le droit à la qualité de l'environnement: un droit de l'homme?", *Le droit à la qualité de l'environnement: un droit en devenir, un droit à définir* (ed. N. Duplé), Vieux-Montreal/Quebec, ed., Quebec/Amerique, 1988, pp. 69–87. As the environment is a common good ("le bien de tous"), "l'ensemble du corps social aussi bien que les groupes ou que les individus qui le composent sont appelés à participer à sa gestion et à sa protection"; P. Kromarek, "Le droit à un environnement équilibré et sain, considéré comme un droit de l'homme: sa mise-en-oeuvre nationale, européenne et internationale", *I Conférence européenne sur l'environnement et les droits de l'homme*, Strasbourg, Institute for European Environmental Policy, 1979, p.15 (mimeographed, restricted circulation). On the remedies (in domestic comparative law) for the exercise of the right to information and the right of participation, cf. L.P. Suetens, "La protection du droit à l'information et du droit de participation: les recours", *II Conférence européenne sur l'environnement et les droits de l'homme*, Salzburg, Institute for European Environmental Policy, 1980, pp.1–13 (mimeographed, restricted circulation); and, on private recourses for environmental harm (in domestic comparative law), cf. S.C. McCaffrey and R.E. Lutz (eds.), *Environmental Pollution and Individual Rights: An International Symposium*, Deventer, Kluwer, 1978, pp. XVII–XXIII and 3–162. On the "procedural" conception of the right to the conservation of the environment, cf. A.C. Kiss, "Peut-on parler d'un droit à l'environnement?", *Le droit et l'environnement – Actes des Journées de l'Environnement du C.N.R.S.* (1988) pp.309–317.

[107] A. Eide, *supra* note 104, p.36.

development, discloses an individual and a collective dimension at the same time. Whether the subject is an individual or a private group, the legal relationship is exhausted in the relation between the individual (or group of individuals) and the State. But if we consider mankind as a whole, the legal relationship is not exhausted in that context. This is probably the reason for making the distinction between individual and collective dimensions.

If we focus on *implementation*, it is conceded that all rights, whether "individual" or "collective", are exercised in a societal context. As such, they all have a "social" dimension in that sense, since their vindication requires the intervention, in varying degrees, of public authority for them to be exercised. There is, however, yet another approach which may shed some light on the problem at issue. This entails focusing on the *object* of protection. If we take a common good such as the human environment as the object of protection, not only are we thereby provided with objective criteria to approach the matter, but also we can better grasp the proper meaning of "collective" rights.

These rights pertain equally to each member, as well as to all members, of a given human collectivity. Since the object of protection is the same (a common good, such as the human environment), the observance of such rights benefits both individual members and all members of the human collectivity. Correspondingly, their violation equally affects or harms each member and all members of the human collectivity at issue. This reflects the essence of "collective" rights, such as the right to a healthy environment, in so far as the *object* of protection is concerned.

The multi-faceted nature of the right to a healthy environment thus becomes clearer. That is, the right to a healthy environment has an individual and a collective dimension – being both an "individual" and a "collective" right – in so far as its *subjects or beneficiaries* are concerned. Its "social" dimension becomes manifest in so far as its *implementation* is concerned (given the complexity of the legal relations involved). And it clearly appears in its "collective" dimension in so far as the *object* of protection is concerned (a common good, the human environment).

This matter has not been sufficiently studied to date, and considerable in-depth reflection and research are required to clarify the issues surrounding the implementation of the right to a healthy environment and the conceptual universe in which it rests. In terms of the subjects of the relationships involved, one has moved from the individuals and groups to the whole of mankind, and in this wide range of right-holders one has also spoken of *generational* rights (rights of future generations – cf. *supra*). In terms of the methods of protection careful exploration is required to determine the extent to which protection mechanisms which have evolved under international human rights law (essentially the petitioning, the reporting, and the fact-finding systems)[108] may

[108] On their functioning and co-ordination, cf. A.A. Cançado Trindade, "Co-existence and Co-ordination of Mechanisms of International Protection of Human Rights (At Global and Regional Levels)", 202 *Recueil des Cours de l'Académie de Droit International* (1987) pp.13–435.

also be utilized in the realm of environmental protection.

It seems that the experience accumulated over the last decades of human rights protection can, if properly assessed, be of assistance to the development of methods of environmental protection. Some inspiration can indeed be derived from the application of mechanisms of international implementation of human rights. In this context, it is reassuring to note that the conclusions of a recent Forum on International Law of the Environment, held in Siena, Italy, in April 1990, recognize *inter alia* that "certain procedures used for the protection of human rights could serve as models in the field of the protection of the environment".[109] Likewise, expert writing on international environmental law has suggested that U.N. international environmental bodies could be given "powers similar to those" of the U.N. Committee on Economic, Social and Cultural Rights. Such a move would vest the appropriate bodies with the authority "to study and comment on reports submitted by States since the right to a good environment is similar to and partakes of all the difficulties and drawbacks of social and economic rights".[110] These types of acknowledgements are quite understanding and beneficial to environmental protection, given the fact that human rights protection antedates it in time. In sum, the experience gained through the implementation of human rights protection can be of significant value to the implementation of environmental protection.

(2) The Issue of Protection Erga Omnes: "Drittwirkung"

In the fields of both human rights protection and environmental protection there occur variations in the obligations, in that some norms are susceptible of direct applicability, while others are rather programmatic in nature. Thus, attention ought to be turned to the *nature* of the obligations. An important point from this perspective is the *erga omnes* protection of certain guaranteed rights, which raises the issue of third-party applicability of conventional provisions. This issue, called *"Drittwirkung"* in German legal literature, can be examined from the standpoint of both human rights protection and environmental protection.

In the former, *Drittwirkung* is still evolving in the case-law under the European Convention on Human Rights[111] (*infra*). Bearing in mind the considerable variety of rights guaranteed under human rights treaties, there are provisions which seem to indicate that at least some of the rights are susceptible to third-party applicability. Thus, Article 2(1)(d) of the U.N. Convention on

[109] *Conclusions of the Siena Forum on International Law of the Environment* (April 1990), p.8, 23 *in fine* (mimeographed, restricted circulation).

[110] L.A. Teclaff, "The Impact of Environmental Concern on the Development of International Law", in L.A. Teclaff and A.E. Utton (eds.) *International Environmental Law*, N.Y., Praeger, 1975, p.252.

[111] Cf. A.Z. Drzemczewski, *European Human Rights Convention in Domestic Law – A Comparative Study*, Oxford: Oxford University Press, 1983, ch. 8, pp. 199–228; and cf. J. Rivero, "La protection des droits de l'homme dans les rapports entre personnes privées", *René Cassin Amicorum Discipulorumque Liber*, vol. III, Paris, Pédone, 1971, pp. 311ss.

the Elimination of All Forms of Racial Discrimination prohibits racial discrimination "by any persons, group or organization". Under Article 2(1) of the U.N. Covenant on Civil and Political Rights, States Parties undertake not only "to respect" but also "to ensure" to all individuals subject to their jurisdictions the rights guaranteed under the Covenant – which may be interpreted as at least the States Parties' duty of due diligence to prevent deprivation or violation of the rights of one individual by others. And it has been argued that Article 17 of the Covenant (right to privacy) would cover protection of the individual against interference by private organizations or individuals as well as public authorities.[112] In addition, Article 29 of the Universal Declaration of Human Rights refers to "everyone's duties to the community".

The European Convention on Human Rights states in Article 17 that nothing in the Convention may be interpreted as implying "for any State, group or person" any right to engage in any activity or perform any act aimed at the destruction of the guaranteed rights. Articles 8 to 11 indicate that account is to be taken of the protection of other people's rights. And from Article 2, whereby "everyone's right to life is protected by law", may be inferred the State's duty of due diligence of prevention and of making violation of the right a punishable offence.[113] The supreme values underlying fundamental human rights are such that they deserve and require protection *erga omnes*, against any encroachment, by public or private bodies or by any individual.[114]

Even though the issue of *Drittwirkung* was not considered when the European Convention was drafted, the subject matter of the Convention lends itself to *Drittwirkung*. This is apparent in that some of the recognized rights deserve protection against private individuals as well as public authorities, and States have to safeguard everyone – in relations between individuals – against violations of guaranteed rights by other individuals.[115] For instance, with regard to the right to privacy (Article 8), there is also need to protect this right in the sphere of relations *between* individuals (persons, groups, institutions, besides States). In practice, situations have occurred where the State may be involved in the relations *between* individuals (e.g., custody of a child, clandestine recording of a conversation by a private individual with the help of the police).[116] Certain human rights have validity *erga omnes*, in that they are

[112] *Supra*, note 50 at p.119; Jan De Meyer, *op. cit. infra* n.116, p.263.

[113] E.A. Alkema, "The Third-Party Applicability or 'Drittwirkung' of the European Convention on Human Rights", in *Protecting Human Rights: The European Dimension – Studies in Honour of G.J. Wiarda* (ed. F. Matscher and H. Petzold), Koln, C. Heymanns, 1988, pp. 35–37.

[114] E.A. Alkema, *supra* note 113, pp. 33–34.

[115] This has led one to speak of a sort of "indirect *Drittwirkung*", since "it is realized *via* an obligation of the State". P. van Dijk and G.J.H. van Hoof, *Theory and Practice of the European Convention on Human Rights*, Deventer: Kluwer Law & Taxation Publishers, (1984), pp. 14–18.

[116] Jan De Meyer, "The Right to Respect for Private and Family Life, Home and Communications in Relations between Individuals, and the Resulting Obligations for States Parties to the Convention", in A.H. Robertson (ed.), *Privacy and Human Rights*, Manchester, University Press, 1973, pp. 267–269.

recognized in relation to the State but also and necessarily "in relation to other persons, groups or institutions which might prevent the exercise thereof".[117]

Therefore, a human rights violation by individuals or private groups can be sanctioned indirectly when the State fails, in "its duty to provide due protection", to take the necessary steps to prevent or punish the offence.[118] Article 8 of the European Convention effectively illustrates the "absolute effect" of that right to privacy, as well as the need for its protection *erga omnes* against frequent interferences or violations not only by public authorities but also by private persons or the mass media.[119]

In the same vein, it has been forcefully argued that the right to a healthy environment should be *"opposable aux tiers, avoir un effet direct à leur égard"*, and should also be *"opposable directement aux particuliers de façon à assurer la protection des intérêts des individus et des groupes en matière d'environnement"*.[120] *Drittwirkung* focuses on a situation whereby everyone is a beneficiary of the right and everyone has duties *vis-à-vis* the other citizens and *vis-à-vis* the whole community: *"tout le monde est bénéficiaire de ce droit, mais en même temps tout le monde assume aussi des obligations de son fait: État, collectivitiés, individus"*.[121]

6. The Right to a Healthy Environment and the Absence of Restrictions in the Expansion of Human Rights Protection and of Environmental Protection

(1) No Restrictions Ensuing from the Co-Existence of International Instruments on Human Rights Protection

In the field of the international protection of human rights, restrictions are not to be inferred from the possible effects of multiple co-existing instruments of human rights protection upon each other. On the contrary, in the present context, international law has been made use of in order to improve and

[117] Ibid., p. 271, and cf. p.272.

[118] Ibid., p. 273.

[119] Ibid., pp. 274–275.

[120] P. Kromarek, "Le droit à un environnement équilibré et sain, considéré comme un droit de l'homme: sa mise-en-oeuvre nationale, européenne et internationale", in *I Conférence européenne sur l'environnement et les droits de l'homme*, Strasbourg, Institute for European Environmental Policy, 1979, p.38 (mimeographed, restricted circulation).

[121] A.C. Kiss, "Le droit à la qualité de l'environnement: un droit de l'homme?", in *Le droit à la qualité de l'environnement: un droit en devenir, un droit à définir* (ed. N. Duplé), Vieux-Montreal/Quebec, ed. Quebec/Amerique, 1988, p.80, and cf. p.83. "En ce qui concerne le droit à l'environnement, tout le monde est 'créancier' et 'débiteur' en même temps: État, collectivitiés, individus". A.C. Kiss, "La mise en oeuvre du droit à l'environnement: problematique et moyens", in *II Conférence européenne sur "Environnement et droits de l'homme"*, Salzburg, Institut pour une Politique Européenne de l'Environnement, 1980, p.8, and cf. pp.6–9 (mimeographed, restricted circulation).

strengthen the degree of protection of recognized rights. In fact, the interpretation and application of certain provisions of one human rights instrument have at times been relied on as guidance for the interpretation of corresponding provisions of other – usually newer – human rights instruments.[122]

Normative advances in one human rights treaty may indeed have a direct impact upon the application of other human rights treaties, with the effect of enlarging or strengthening the States Parties' obligations of protection and restricting the possible invocation or application of restrictions to the exercise of recognized rights. Multiple human rights instruments appear complementary to one another; and their complementarity reflects the specificity of the international protection of human rights, a domain of international law characterized as being essentially a *droit de protection*. Where States have pursued obligations under multiple co-existing instruments of human rights protection, it may be taken to have been their intention to accord individuals a more extended and effective protection. In sum, there exists a clear trend towards the expansion and enhancement of the degree and extent of protection of rights recognized under co-existing human rights instruments.[123]

(2) No Restrictions Ensuing from the Co-Existence of International Instruments on Environmental Protection

Likewise, in the field of international environmental law, restrictions are not to be implied from the possible effects upon each other of multiple co-existing instruments on environmental protection. To this effect, in propounding the elaboration of a Universal Declaration and a Convention on Environmental Protection and Sustainable Development in its well-known 1987 report, the World Commission on Environment and Development stressed the need "to consolidate and extend relevant legal principles" on the matter in order "to guide State behaviour in the transition to sustainable development". It also stressed that multiple co-existing as well as new international conventions and agreements in the area were to *strengthen and extend* environmental protection.[124] As in human rights protection (*supra*), there is no room for [implied] restrictions in the domain of environmental protection.

Having thus considered the point from the perspective, on the one hand, of the effects of human rights instruments upon each other and, on the other hand, of the effects of environmental instruments upon each other, we have found no room for the incidence of restrictions. These instruments, in both domains, were meant to reinforce each other and strengthen the degree of

[122] A.A. Cançado Trindade, "Co-existence and Co-ordination of Mechanisms of International Protection of Human Rights (At Global and Regional Levels)", 202 *Recueil des Cours de l'Académie de Droit International* (1987) pp. 401 and 101, and cf. p.104.

[123] Ibid., pp. 110, 121–122 and 125.

[124] World Commission on Environment and Development, *Our Common Future*, Oxford, Oxford University Press, 1987, pp. 332–333.

protection afforded. What remains is to examine the effects of norms or instruments of human rights protection and of environmental protection *inter se*, or, more precisely, the effects of the recognition of the right to a healthy environment upon the corpus of human rights already recognized.

(3) No Restrictions Ensuing from the Expansion of Systems of Protection (As Evidenced by the Recognition of the Right to a Healthy Environment) in Their Effects upon Each Other

A fairly recent trend of thought has perceived in the development of environmental policies of States the incidence of *restrictions* upon the exercise of certain recognized human rights. Such restrictions are seen as justified on the ground that they protect the environment. It has been suggested that, while some of the more classic civil and political rights are not apparently affected, certain economic and social rights are susceptible of suffering restrictions. By way of example, reference has been made to the rights of free circulation, of choice of residence, and to property, in face of protected areas or zones; the right to work, in face of anti-pollution measures; the right to equality, in face of disparities in administrative measures as to the environment; the freedom of association, in face of measures against noise pollution; the right to family, in face of birth-control measures; and the rights to development and to leisure, in face of measures for conservation of nature.[125]

This approach, it is submitted, is inadequate and short-sighted, even though it is forced to admit that the right to a healthy environment comes ultimately to guarantee and reinforce such basic rights as the right to life and the right to health.[126] In historical perspective, the emergence of new rights has generated the need for their "adaptation" to the corpus of rights already recognized. Thus, economic, social and cultural rights had an impact on classic civil and political rights, and what appeared to be restrictions on the exercise of these latter amounted rather to conditions for the effective exercise of the former.[127] This helped to enlarge the scope of protection of human rights. In the same way, it became clear that the exercise of recognized rights was to take place

[125] Cf. F. Doré, "Conséquences des exigences d'un environnement équilibré et sain sur la définition, la portée et les limitations des différents droits de l'homme – Rapport introductif", *I Conférence européenne sur l'environnement et les droits de l'homme*, Strasbourg, Institute for European Environmental Policy, 1979, pp. 3–5, 7–12 and 14 (mimeographed, restricted circulation); and cf. F. Doré, [Interventions] in ibid., pp.25–27 and 37–38 (mimeographed, restricted circulation).

[126] Cf. F. Doré, "Conséquences des exigences...", *supra* note 125, pp.16–19; F. Doré, [Intervention] *supra* note 125, p.27.

[127] Cf., to this effect, A.C. Kiss, [Interventions] in *I Conférence européenne sur l'environnement et les droits de l'homme*, Strasbourg, Institute for European Environmental Policy, 1979, pp. 43–45; and in *Résumé des débats*, ibid., p. 20 (mimeographed, restricted circulation).

having regard to the exigencies of *ordre public* or the general welfare.[128] The apparent restrictions amounted rather to adjustments to render effective new rights[129] and thereby strengthen the degree of the protection due. From this perspective, it becomes clearer that the right to a healthy environment, once asserted as a *human right*, rather than entailing restrictions to the exercise of other rights, comes to enrich the corpus of recognized human rights.[130]

Hence, the appropriateness of the anthropocentric outlook and the need to place the theme of the environment within a human rights framework. There is no antagonism between international human rights law and environmental law, and the latter helps to clarify the social framework within which all human rights are inserted.[131] The recognition of the right to a healthy environment enriches and reinforces existing human rights and discloses other rights in new dimensions (for instance, the much-needed right of citizen participation, which, in turn, requires the effectiveness of the rights to information and to education in environmental matters).[132]

(4) The Recognition of the Right to a Healthy Environment and the Consequent Enhancement, rather than Restriction, of Pre-Existing Rights

International human rights law, in short, is unequivocal in indicating that limitations or restrictions on the exercise of guaranteed rights are to be narrowly interpreted. This ensues, to begin with, from interpretative principles enshrined in human rights treaties themselves.[133] As maintained elsewhere, the narrow interpretation of restrictions to the exercise of recognized rights is sanctioned by the application of the test of primacy of the most favourable norm to the alleged victims in respect of the same rights guaranteed by two or more human rights treaties to which the State concerned is a Party. This test therefore discards undue limitations or restrictions to the exercise of a given right (recognized in another treaty to a lesser extent).[134]

The international supervisory bodies themselves have made statements to that effect. For instance, the European Court of Human Rights held in its

[128] P. Kromarek, "Le droit à un environnement équilibré et sain, considéré comme un droit de l'homme: sa mise-en-oeuvre nationale, européenne et internationale", in *I Conférence européenne ...*, *supra* note 127, p.26.

[129] M. Ali Mekouar, "Le droit à l'environnement dans ses rapports avec les autres droits de l'homme", *Environnement et droits de l'homme* (ed. P. Kromarek), Paris, UNESCO, 1987, pp. 95–96.

[130] Cf., to this effect, K. Vasak, [Interventions] in *I Conférence européenne...*, *supra* note 127, pp. 68–69; and in *Résumé des débats*, ibid., p.22.

[131] *I Conférence européenne...*, *cit supra* note 127, *Conclusions*, pp. 72–73 (mimeographed, restricted circulation).

[132] Ibid., p.73; and cf. F. Doré, "Conséquences des exigences...", *op. cit. supra* note 125, pp.21–22 (mimeographed, restricted circulation).

[133] E.g., U.N. Covenant on Civil and Political Rights, Article 5(1); American Convention on Human Rights, Article 29.

[134] A.A. Cançado Trindade, "Co-existence and Co-ordination...", *supra* note 2, p.104, and cf. pp., 104–108.

judgment in the *Golder v. United Kingdom* case (1975) that there was no room for implied limitations under the European Convention on Human Rights. The same was upheld by the Inter-American Court of Human Rights in its Advisory Opinions on *Compulsory Membership in an Association of Journalists* (1985) and on the *Word "Laws" in Article 30 of the American Convention on Human Rights* (1986). Likewise, in its Report of 1987 on a recent case concerning the observance by the Federal Republic of Germany of the 1958 ILO Discrimination (Employment and Occupation) Convention (n.111), the Commission of Inquiry (appointed under Article 26 of the ILO Constitution) made clear that no implied exceptions were admissible under ILO Convention n.111.[135]

The gradual recognition of "new" human rights cannot possibly have the effect of lowering the degree of protection accorded to existing rights. That would simply go against the course of historical evolution of the process of expansion of international human rights law, which has consistently pointed towards the enlargement, improvement and strengthening of the degree and extent of protection of recognized rights. In conclusion, the only permissible limits to the exercise of recognized rights are those expressly provided for under human rights treaties themselves (namely, as limitations or restrictions; as exceptions; as derogations; or as reservations). Such limits are to be restrictively interpreted, always having regard to the achievement of the object and purpose of the treaty.

It is regrettable that the recognition of the right to a healthy environment has led some to the misunderstanding that it might clash with other rights or the object of other rights. This can only result from an inadequately fragmented or atomized conception of the corpus of international human rights law. Instead, human rights are indivisible and the mechanisms devoted to their protection complement each other, so as to expand and strengthen the degree of the protection due. Rights belonging to distinct "categories" have more in common than one may *prima facie* assume, quite apart from the fact of their being interrelated.

The emergence of "new" rights is followed by their "adaptation" to the corpus of existing rights and their means of implementation. No restrictions on existing rights can be justified by the recognition of "new" rights, as these cannot possibly have been articulated to lower the prevailing degree of protection. Rights belonging to such distinct domains as the civil and political, or the economic, social and cultural, have found their way to co-existence. Likewise, as regards newly-emerged rights, what may at first sight appear as restrictions on pre-existing rights are in reality no more than needed adjustments entailed by the "new" rights.[136]

[135] Cases cited in ibid., pp. 106–107 and 116.

[136] M. Ali Mekouar, "Le droit à l'environnement dans ses rapports avec les autres droits de l'homme", *Environnement et droits de l'homme* (ed. P. Kromarek), Paris, UNESCO, 1987, p.96, and cf. pp.94–95.

Given the continuing expansion of international human rights law and the multiplicity of co-existing rights, in some circumstances it may be necessary for "priorities ... to be set and limited resources devoted to fulfilling one right which is at more risk or more significant in the circumstances than another".[137] This does not mean that the other rights are restricted, contradicted or ignored; a balance between the various recognized rights is set by the human rights treaties themselves, which indicate the considerations relevant to restrictions or limitations on the recognized rights, including in times of public emergency.[138] Restrictions, as already pointed out, are to be restrictively interpreted.

Here, a key role is reserved to the international supervisory bodies themselves. This issue of the balancing between rights may arise not only with regard to such "new" rights as the right to a healthy environment, but also between any other rights (e.g., reconciling the right to freedom of expression and the right to privacy, the freedoms of association and of movement, the right to property and certain social rights, and so on).[139] Furthermore, the recognition of such "new" rights as the right to a healthy environment cannot have the effect of restricting, but only of complementing, enriching and enhancing pre-existing rights (e.g., the right to work, the freedom of movement, the right to education, the right of participation, the right to information, etc.).[140]

One last remark: it should not pass unnoticed that rights that are at the basis of the *ratio legis* of both environmental protection and human rights protection – such as the right to life and the right not to be subjected to inhuman or degrading treatment – are asserted by human rights treaties[141] as non-derogable. They admit of no restrictions whatsoever; they are truly fundamental rights. As for the other recognized rights, in the "balancing" between them dictated by circumstances, "new" rights such as the right to a healthy environment have emerged ultimately to enhance rather than to restrict, in the same way as they enhance the fundamental non-derogable rights.

[137] J. Crawford, "The Rights of Peoples: Some Conclusions", in J. Crawford (ed.) *The Rights of Peoples*, Oxford, Clarendon Press, 1988, p.167.

[138] Ibid., pp. 167–168.

[139] Cf. ibid., p.168.

[140] M. Ali Mekouar, *op. cit. supra* note 136, pp. 96–100 and 103–104.

[141] E.g., U.N. Covenant on Civil and Political Rights, Article 4(2); European Convention on Human Rights, Article 15(2); American Convention on Human Rights, Article 27.

MAGUELONNE DÉJEANT-PONS*

The Right to Environment in Regional Human Rights Systems

The right to the environment will unquestionably be one of the major human rights of the twenty-first century, since the most fundamental human right of all, the right of existence, is under threat.

In any hierarchy of human rights, if such a thing were possible, it would have to be placed among the most important of all. For many years now scientific experts have been pointing out that it is not just the quality of life but life itself which is in danger.[1] The growing number of dangerous substances allowed to find their way into water, the soil and the atmosphere is leading to an increase in pollution. Together with over-exploitation of resources and destruction of landscapes, these factors are transforming what were once nuisances into serious dangers for the human race and the whole biosphere. These risks extend not just beyond State frontiers but also beyond the frontiers of the Earth.

The human race has a special responsibility towards the environment, and even "a solemn responsibility to protect and improve [it] for present and future generations".[2] Humans must, as the World Conservation Strategy adopted in 1980 points out, maintain essential ecological processes and life-supporting systems, preserve genetic diversity and ensure the long-term use of species and ecosystems. However, they can only do this if their rights in certain areas are recognised.[3]

On 16 June 1972 the United Nations Conference on the Environment adopted the Stockholm Declaration, whose first principle proclaims:

* Doctor of Law, Administrative Officer at the Council of Europe (writing in her personal capacity only).

[1] UNEP, 'Development and Environment: The Founex Report (Founex, 4–12 June 1971)', *In Defence of the Earth, The Basic Texts on Environment* (Founex, Stockholm, Cocoyoc, 1981), UNEP, Nairobi.

[2] Stockholm Declaration of 16 June 1972 on the environment.

[3] Progress is being made in this area in national legislation. Clauses relating to environmental protection are included in the constitutions of 44 States and those of 11 States in the USA, as well as in the general legislation of a number of countries. See Alexandre-Charles Kiss, 'Le droit à la conservation de l'environnement', *Revue Universelle des Droits de l'Homme* (1990), Vol. 2, No. 12, pp. 445–448; W. Paul Gormley, *Human Rights and Environment: The Need for International Co-operation*, (Leyden: A.W. Sijthoff, 1976), p. 247.

K.E. Mahoney and P. Mahoney (eds.), Human Rights in the Twenty-first Century, 595–614.

"Man has the fundamental right to freedom, equality and adequate conditions of life, in an environment of a quality that permits a life of dignity and well-being...."

The international community thus affirmed for the first time the importance of the human right to the environment. The twentieth anniversary of that conference will be celebrated in Rio de Janeiro in June 1992. What progress will have been made by then to implement this principle? While the human right to the environment no longer seems to be disputed, it is now time to guarantee enjoyment of that right.

1. Affirmation of the Human Right to the Environment

(1) Universal Recognition

The international human rights protection system is based on the United Nations Charter of 26 June 1945, which proclaims the promotion of respect for human rights as one of the fundamental aims of the United Nations.[4] However, the term "human rights" itself is not defined therein, since the concept must be interpreted in an evolutive way taking account of constant extensions in scope brought about by environmental, political, social and cultural changes, together with technical and scientific progress.

The Charter requires members to pledge themselves to co-operate in solving international economic, social, health and related problems and in promoting universal respect for, and observance of, human rights. However, a link between health – the primary element of the human right to the environment – and environment only appears through the concept "well-being".[5]

The Universal Declaration of Human Rights, adopted by the General Assembly of the United Nations on 10 December 1948, does not explicitly set forth a human right to the environment, but its preamble recognises the "inherent dignity" and the "equal and inalienable rights of all members of the human family". It affirms the right to life and states that "Everyone ... is entitled to realization ... of the economic, social, and cultural rights indispensable for his dignity and the free development of his personality" and that "Everyone has the right to a standard of living adequate for [his] health and well-being ...".[6] Health is not regarded as determined by one's surroundings but by "clothing, housing and medical care and ... social services".

Further progress was made with the International Covenant on Civil and

[4] Karel Vasak, 'Le droit international des droits de l'homme', *Collected Courses of the Hague Academy of International Law*, 1974, Vol. IV (Leyden: A.W. Sijthoff, 1976), pp. 333–413, at p. 404.

[5] United Nations Charter, Articles 55 and 56.

[6] UNGA, UN Doc. A/811 (1948), Articles 3, 22 and 25.

Political Rights and the International Covenant on Economic, Social and Cultural Rights concluded under the aegis of the United Nations in 1966. The first of these states that every human being has the "inherent right to life",[7] while the second recognises "the right of everyone to the enjoyment of the highest attainable standard of physical and mental health" notably through "the improvement of all aspects of environmental and industrial hygiene".[8] A direct link was thus established, even though the terminology used was still imperfect, between health and environmental hygiene, and the right to health was inscribed in a legal system whereby States' actions could be scrutinised by the United Nations Commission on Human Rights.[9] Article 11 of the Covenant proclaims in more general terms that "The States Parties ... recognize the right of everyone to an adequate standard of living for himself and his family, including ... the continuous improvement of living conditions".

The international texts adopted subsequently no longer concentrate on the health aspect, but have gradually introduced the concept of a human right to the environment as such. Following the International Conference on Human Rights in Teheran in 1968, held to promote the establishment of a balance between scientific and technical progress and the intellectual, spiritual, cultural and moral development of mankind,[10] the General Assembly of the United Nations adopted the Declaration on Social Progress and Development, drawing attention to the interdependence between environmental protection and human rights.[11] In 1971 the Secretary-General of the United Nations stated that the forthcoming United Nations Conference on the Environment would draw its inspiration from the "philosophy of action of the United Nations as formulated in the Preamble to the Charter and in the Universal Declaration of Human Rights" the struggle for a decent environment being no more than "a demand that man should be able to develop more fully".[12]

The Stockholm Declaration on the environment, adopted on 16 June 1972, is based on the common convictions which strengthen the principles and objectives of the United Nations Charter.[13] Its preamble states that an environment of satisfactory quality is indispensable for man's well-being and full enjoyment of his fundamental rights, including the right to life itself. Principle 1, quoted above, affirms the indissoluble link between the environment and fundamental human rights.

It makes all governments responsible for preserving and improving the

[7] Article 6.

[8] Article 12. Mention should also be made of Article 25, which states: "Nothing in the present Covenant shall be interpreted as impairing the inherent right of all peoples to enjoy and utilize fully and freely their natural wealth and resources."

[9] Pierre-Marie Dupuy, 'Le droit à la santé et la protection de l'environnement', *Hague Academy of International Law, Workshop on 'The Right to Health as a human right'*, 1978 (Leyden: A.W. Sijthoff & Noordhoff, 1979), pp. 340–427, at p.350–351.

[10] United Nations document A/Conf.32/41, p. 13.

[11] United Nations General Assembly Resolution 2542 (XXIV), 11 December 1969.

[12] United Nations document A/Conf.48/9, of 21 December 1971.

[13] Document of the United Nations General Assembly A/Conf.2/SR.1469, p. 163.

environment and emphasizes that the human race has a considerable measure of responsibility for the protection and improvement of the natural environment. Admittedly, it does not have binding legal force, but its scope is considerable in so far as it constitutes a generally accepted interpretation of the concept "human rights" referred to in the United Nations Charter. It also provides a philosophical and legal foundation for the effort to define the human right to the environment.[14]

Another solemn declaration, the World Charter for Nature, adopted by the General Assembly of the United Nations on 28 October 1982, places certain obligations on States and individuals as regards application of the principles it lays down.[15] It states, in particular, that "All persons, in accordance with their national legislation, shall have the opportunity to participate, individually or with others, in the formulation of decisions of direct concern to their environment, and shall have access to means of redress when their environment has suffered damage or degradation".[16]

The question of "human rights and the environment" will be discussed again in 1992 at the United Nations Conference on Environment and Development in Rio de Janeiro. The United Nations Sub-Commission on Prevention of Discrimination and Protection of Minorities, which affirms in its Resolution 1990/7 of 30 August 1990 the inextricable relationship between human rights and the environment, will make a contribution to this process.[17]

(2) Regional Recognition

(a) Europe

Of the two European legal instruments for the protection of human rights prepared within the Council of Europe,[18] neither the 1950 Convention for the Protection of Human Rights and Fundamental Freedoms – with its protocols – nor the 1961 European Social Charter refers to the concept of environment. However, environmental protection can be taken into consideration indirectly through the limitation of certain guaranteed rights or through a "knock-on effect", that is when damage to the environment simultaneously infringes a guaranteed right.[19]

The provisions limiting exercise of the rights set out in Articles 8 (respect for private and family life), 9 (freedom of thought and conscience), 10 (freedom of expression) and 11 (freedom of assembly and association) of the Convention

[14] Andrzej Makarewicz, 'La protection internationale du droit à l'environnement', *Environnement et Droits de l'Homme* (1987), UNESCO, pp. 80–81.

[15] United Nations General Assembly Resolution 37/7, 28 October 1982.

[16] Ibid., Paragraph 23.

[17] See also Document E/CN.4/Sub.2/1990/12.

[18] A distinction must be drawn between these two texts in so far as the European Social Charter, unlike the European Convention on Human Rights, does not permit petitions by individuals against States but is based on a system of reports submitted by Contracting Parties to the Secretary General of the Council of Europe and examined by a Committee of Independent Experts.

[19] Series A Vol. 192, p. 16, para. 48.

are worded in similar terms. They give States the possibility of limiting or interfering in the right, where the law so prescribes, using measures necessary in a democratic society for the protection of certain values, including health.

The first article of Protocol No. 1 to the Convention, which sets forth the right of property, permits a State to "enforce such laws as it deems necessary to control the use of property in accordance with the general interest ...".

Thus the right of property does not stand in the way of the adoption of legislation designed to protect the environment. The European Court of Human Rights confirmed this interpretation in the Fredin judgment of February 1991 by declaring in a preliminary observation that "in today's society the protection of the environment is an increasingly important consideration".[20] The applicants had alleged that revocation by the Swedish authorities of their permit to extract gravel from their gravel pit amounted to a deprivation of property, contrary to Article 1 of Protocol No. 1. After noting the lawfulness of the revocation decision and the legitimate aim of the legislation on which it was based, the Court referred to its case-law laying down the need for a reasonable relationship of proportionality between the means employed and the aim pursued. In determining whether that requirement had been met, the Court recognized that the State enjoyed a wide margin of discretion with regard both to choosing the means of enforcement and to ascertaining whether their consequences were justified in the general interest for the purpose of achieving the object of the law in question. The Court unanimously held that on the facts there had been no violation of the right of property.

The European Social Charter also states that the rights and principles it sets forth must not be subject to any restrictions or limitations not specified therein "except such as are prescribed by law and are necessary in a democratic society for the protection of ... public health ...".[21]

The environment can be protected indirectly when environmental damage can be shown to constitute a violation of a right guaranteed by the Convention, its protocols or the European Social Charter (life, private and family life, property, health etc).[22] The case of *Arrondelle v. United Kingdom*, brought before the European Commission of Human Rights in 1976, provides one example of this.[23] The applicant, who owned a house situated between an airport runway and a motorway, lived in particularly distressing conditions on account of the noise; several attempts to sell the house had come to nothing. The Commission took the view that, while the government had not caused the

[20] Article 31.

[21] Jean-Paul Jacqué, see note 19, *supra*, p. 68; Michele de Salvia, "Tutela dell'ambiente e Convenzione europea dei Diritti dell'Uomo: verso una ecologia del diritto?", *Rivista internazionale dei diritti dell'Uomo* (September-December 1989), No. 3, pp. 432–438.

[22] *Arrondelle v. United Kingdom*, (No. 7889/77) (June 1982), 26 Eur. Comm. H.R.D.R., pp. 5–12.

[23] See in particular Conclusions I, adopted in 1968 and 1969, p. 59, Conclusions IV, adopted in 1975, p. 75, and Conclusions V, adopted in 1977, p. xvii.

nuisances, it was not exonerated from all responsibility, since the airport and the motorway had been constructed and were still managed by public authorities. It pointed out that the applicant had suffered intolerable stress and declared the application admissible, particularly with regard to the articles protecting private and family life and the right of property. The case ended in a friendly settlement.

Article 11 of the European Social Charter deals with "the right to protection of health" and requires Contracting Parties, with a view to ensuring the effective exercise of that right, to take appropriate measures designed *inter alia* "to remove as far as possible the causes of ill-health". Damage to the environment likely to affect the health of persons protected by the Charter is therefore taken into consideration. The bodies responsible for monitoring implementation of the Charter have confirmed this interpretation. The Committee of Independent Experts, set up to scrutinize the biennial reports by Contracting Parties, has declared on several occasions that its supervisory role required it to consider environmental protection problems.[24]

In other texts adopted subsequently by organisations covering geographical areas of varying size there has been an increasing tendency to recognize a human right to the environment, or at least certain aspects thereof.

The recommendations adopted by the Council of the OECD on transfrontier pollution contain essential principles intended to promote implementation of a regime of equal right of access and non-discrimination.[25] Moreover, as early as 1979 the OECD member countries undertook, in a Ministerial declaration, to give the public information about major risks. The adoption in 1988 by the Council of the OECD of the Decision-Recommendation concerning provision of information to the public and public participation in decision-making processes related to the prevention of, and response to, accidents involving hazardous substances, and the Decision on the exchange of information concerning accidents capable of causing transfrontier damage represented an important step in the same direction.

The European Charter on Environment and Health, adopted on 8 December 1989 in Frankfurt-am-Main by the Ministers of the Environment and of Health of the member States of the European Region of the World Health Organisation, and by the Commission of the European Communities, contains the following, more general, provisions:

"Every individual is entitled to:

- an environment conducive to the highest attainable level of health and well-being;

[24] Recommendation of 14 November 1974 on principles concerning transfrontier pollution [C (74) 224]; Recommendation of 11 May 1976 on equal right of access in relation to transfrontier pollution [C (76) 55 (Final)]; Recommendation of 17 May 1977 on implementation of a regime of equal right of access and non-discrimination in relation to transfrontier pollution [C (77) 28 (Final)]; Recommendation of 21 September 1978 on strengthening international co-operation on environmental protection in transfrontier regions [C (78) 77 (Final)].

[25] *Dr. S. v. Federal Republic of Germany* (715/60) (1960) Eur. Comm. H.R.

- information and consultation on ... plans, decisions and activities likely to affect both the environment and health;
- participation in the decision-making process."

(b) Africa

The African Charter on Human and Peoples' Rights, adopted in Nairobi on 28 June 1981, is particularly important because its preamble refers to "the values of African civilization", while Article 24 states that "All peoples shall have the right to a general satisfactory environment favourable to their development".

The right to the environment thus recognized is not individual but collective, since it belongs to peoples. However, it should be noted that for the first time this right was included in a treaty drawn up by developing countries, for which it is particularly difficult in the short term to reconcile environmental protection with development.

When seen against the background of the right to the environment, other articles of the Charter are of capital importance. This applies to Article 9, which states that "Every individual shall have the right to receive information"; to Article 13, which mentions the right of every citizen to "participate freely in the government of his country"; and to Article 16, which states that "Every individual shall have the right to enjoy the best attainable state of physical and mental health".

The Charter entrusts the task of protecting the above rights to the African Commission on Human and Peoples' Rights.

(c) America

The Additional Protocol to the American Convention on Human Rights in the area of economic, social and cultural rights, adopted in San Salvador on 17 November, 1988, devotes one article (Article 10) to the "right to health" and another (Article 11) to the "right to a healthy environment".

The first of these states that "Everyone shall have the right to health, understood to mean the enjoyment of the highest level of physical, mental and social well-being", while the second states that "Everyone shall have the right to live in a healthy environment and to have access to basic public services".

Thus, for the first time in an international agreement, the right of every individual to the environment was recognized. However, this right does not concern the aesthetic quality of the environment, only its healthiness.

These rights are protected through periodic reports by States Parties on measures adopted, since it is not possible to petition the Inter-American Commission or Court of Human Rights in respect of Articles 10 and 11 of the Protocol. However, the Inter-American Commission on Human Rights may make appropriate observations and recommendations as to their application and include these in its annual report to the General Assembly or in a special report.

Although a reading of the international texts and case-law mentioned above tends to give an overall impression that the human right to the environment is recognized, in reality such recognition is far from perfect. Under the African Charter on Human and Peoples' Rights, for example, this right is held not by human beings, as individuals or groups of individuals, but by the people. The way this right is actually asserted in practice therefore depends on the way the concept "people" is defined. The environment, which is the subject of the right proposed, is usually not mentioned and is only indirectly perceived through other guaranteed rights (European Convention on Human Rights) or through the concept of "health". The European Social Charter, for example, covers damage to the environment only when such damage affects the health of the persons it protects.

All this means that the substance of the right to the environment, whether explicitly recognized or subsumed in the right to health, is not precisely defined in any of the binding texts. In particular, there is no procedural right whereby individuals can put their point of view when operations likely to damage their environment are being carried out.

But the importance of environmental problems and the urgency of finding solutions to them justify the adoption of appropriate and carefully defined counter-measures. It is no longer possible for the solution to certain crucial problems to depend on the interpretation of this or that provision of texts drawn up for other purposes. A 1960 decision of the European Commission of Human Rights is revealing in several respects.[26] The applicant, who had complained of the dangers to humanity of nuclear tests, the installation of missile launching sites for tactical nuclear weapons and the dumping of nuclear waste at sea, was protesting against the dumping of nuclear waste in the North Sea by the Federal Republic of Germany, the storage of nuclear material in the territory of that State and the installation of rocket launching sites near his home. He alleged violations of the right to life and the right to liberty and

[26] Heinhard Steiger and the Working Group for Environmental Law, *The right to a humane environment. Proposal for an additional protocol to the European Human Rights Convention*, Beiträge zur Umweltgestaltung, Erich Schmidt Verlag, Heft A 13, Berlin, 1973, pp. 58. The two main articles of this draft protocol are worded as follows:

Article 1

(Right to health)

"1. No one should be exposed to intolerable damage or threats to his health or to intolerable impairment of his well-being as a result of adverse changes in the natural conditions of life.

2. An impairment of well-being may, however, be deemed to be tolerable if it is necessary for the maintenance and development of the economic conditions of the community and if there is no alternative way of making it possible to avoid this impairment."

Article 2

(Protection against private persons)

"1. If adverse changes in the natural conditions of life are likely to occur in his vital sphere as a result of the action of other parties, any individual is entitled to demand that the competent agencies examine the situation, and that they remedy such situation in all cases where Article 1 applies.

2. Any individual acting under paragraph 1 shall, within reasonable time, receive detailed information stating what measures – if any – have been taken to prevent those adverse changes."

security of person of the European Convention on Human Rights. The Commission declared the application inadmissible as being manifestly ill-founded. Consequently, it seems impossible for an applicant to claim a right to environmental protection directly under the Convention. This application identifies a second difficulty. The applicant, who was also protesting against nuclear tests carried out by France, the United Kingdom, the United States and the USSR, directed his application against the Federal Republic of Germany alone, pointing out that it was impossible for him to refer to the Commission complaints against the other States concerned. This case illustrates the general problem of ensuring equal access and non-discrimination when endeavouring to deal with transfrontier pollution within the framework of regional legal instruments for the protection of human rights.

2. Guaranteeing the Human Right to the Environment

Effective recognition of the human right to the environment requires the definition of that right to be sufficiently precise for it to be enforced by machinery providing an adequate judicial guarantee. Several initiatives along these lines have already been taken, and it is now time to put these suggestions into practice.

(1) Proposals

Various proposals have been made for incorporation of the human right to the environment into the international-law texts, namely the Universal Declaration of Human Rights and the International Covenant on Economic, Social and Cultural rights, and the regional, particularly European, texts.

As early as 1970 the European Conservation Conference, organized by the Council of Europe, suggested that a protocol to the European Convention on Human Rights be drawn up "guaranteeing the right of every individual to enjoy a healthy and unspoiled environment". The intention was for this protocol to guarantee the right to breathe air and drink water reasonably free from pollution, the right to protection against excessive noise and other nuisances, and lastly the right of reasonable access to the seashore, the countryside and mountain areas. This idea was discussed in Vienna in 1971 at the Parliamentary Conference on Human Rights, convened on the initiative of the Consultative Assembly of the Council of Europe. In its Resolution 683 (1972) the Parliamentary Assembly of the Council of Europe invited the responsible inter-governmental committee to consider "whether the right to an adequate environment should be raised to the level of a human right" and to devise "an appropriate legal instrument to protect this new right".

The 1973 European Ministerial Conference on the Environment repeated this proposal in similar terms, and the German Federal Minister of the Interior presented a draft protocol to the European Convention on Human Rights guaranteeing the right to a healthy and balanced environment.[27]

Other suggestions, with a view to complementing the European Social Charter, have been made by the Charter's Committee of Independent Experts. These would involve adding to the Charter – a provision to the effect that "Everyone has the right to satisfactory conditions of existence in an environment which does not endanger his health".

The theme of a European Conference held in 1980 on "The environment and human rights" was "Implementation of the right to environmental protection: information and participation".[28] The Declaration, adopted at the end of the conference, states that "Everyone has the right to a healthy environment, conducive to his personal development and ecologically balanced" and that "implementation of the right to conservation of the environment requires individuals, alone or in association with others, to be informed about possible decisions which might affect their environment, to have the opportunity to participate in the decision-making process and, where necessary, to be able to avail themselves of suitable remedies".

Subsequently, these initiatives seem[29] to have been forgotten, but they are re-emerging because of the scale of the problems and the urgency of solving them.

In its report "Our common future" published in 1987, the World Commission on Environment and Development (WCED)[30] adopted a list of "Proposed legal principles for the protection of the environment and sustainable development", chief among which is the "fundamental human right" to "an environment adequate for ... health and well-being".[31] Principle 6 concerns in particular the right to information, equal access to administrative and judicial bodies and guarantees of due process.

A Ministerial conference held in Bergen in May 1990 on the follow-up to this report in the region covered by the United Nations Economic Commission for Europe led to the drafting of a "Charter on environmental rights and

[27] Proceedings of the European Conference on the environment and human rights (Salzburg, 2–3 December 1980), Institute for European Environmental Policy, Bonn, 1980. See also An individual right or an obligation of the State? International Colloquium on the right to a humane environment (Bonn, 23–25 June 1975), Beiträge zur Umweltgestaltung, Heft A 41, Erich Schmidt Verlag, Berlin, (1976), p. 242; Alexandre-Charles Kiss, "Peut-on définir le droit de l'homme à l'environnement?", *Revue juridique de l'environnement* (1976), No. 1, pp. 15–18. And Proceedings of the European Conference on the environment and human rights (Strasbourg, 19–20 January 1979), Institute for European Environmental Policy, Bonn, 1979.

[28] But see Proceedings of the UNESCO international Colloquy on new human rights: the right to a healthy environment (1980), *Environnement et droits de l'homme*, UNESCO, (1987), pp. 178; Actes de la V]eme Conférence internationale de droit constitutionnel, Nicole Duplé, *Le droit à la qualité de l'environnement: un droit en devenir, un droit à définir*, (1988), pp. 507; Proceedings of the International Conference on "Guaranteeing the right to the environment", Portuguese Environment Association, Lisbon, 4–6 February 1988.

[29] Independent working party set up in 1983 following a proposal by the United Nations General Assembly.

[30] World Commission on Environment and Development, *Our Common Future* (Oxford: Oxford University Press, 1987), p. 86, Appendix I.

[31] Ministerial Declaration, paragraph 16g, and Action programme, paragraph 5e.

obligations of individuals, groups and organizations", which was adopted by non-governmental organisations. The text has six sections (general principles; access to information; obligation to make information available; participation; legal protection and compensation; implementation), but at the intergovernmental level it has remained no more than a preliminary draft.

In accordance with the final recommendations of the Bergen conference, which called for the drafting of a document on "the environmental rights and obligations of individuals, groups and organizations",[32] an informal meeting of experts on environmental law was convened in Oslo by the Ministers of the Environment of the Netherlands and Norway in October 1990.[33] A draft, "Charter on environmental rights and obligations in the ECE region", was drawn up and is currently under discussion with a view to its adoption by United Nations member States in this region. It is planned to extend the scope of the Charter to cover the whole world by means of its formal adoption at the 1992 World Conference on Environment and Development. The Oslo draft is different from the Bergen document and contains a preamble and six sections (fundamental principles; environmental information, education and training; decision-making; legal protection and compensation; transboundary impacts; implementation).

This idea has also been taken up by the Conference on Security and Co-operation in Europe. On the basis of the report of the CSCE meeting in Sofia in 1989 on environmental protection, in which the participating States reaffirmed their respect for the right of individuals, groups and organisations concerned with environmental issues to information and participation, the Charter of Paris for a New Europe, adopted in November 1990, contains the following statement:

We emphasize the significant role of a well-informed society in enabling the public and individuals to take initiatives to improve the environment. To this end, we commit ourselves to promoting ... public reporting of the environmental impact of policies, projects and programmes.

Recommendation 1130 (1990) on the formulation of a European Charter and a European convention on environmental protection and sustainable development, adopted by the Parliamentary Assembly of the Council of Europe on 28 September, 1990, suggests that the Committee of Ministers include the preparation of such a Charter and convention in the Council of Europe's intergovernmental work programme. The preamble of the draft charter and convention states that "Every person has the fundamental right to an environment and living conditions conducive to his good health, well-being and full development of the human personality".

[32] The meeting was attended by experts from Czechoslovakia, France, Hungary, the Netherlands, Norway and the United Kingdom. The UNEP and the United Nations Economic Commission for Europe also participated in the discussions.

[33] Robert Pelloux, 'Vrais et faux droits de l'homme – problèmes de définition et de classification', *Revue de droit public*, (1981), p. 60; Frédéric Sudre, *Droit international et européen des droits de l'homme*, (1989), pp. 126–127.

The Final Declaration of the Pan-European Parliamentary Conference on the Protection of East-West Environment, adopted in Vienna on 26 October, 1990, refers to the concept of a human right to the environment: governments are invited "to work progressively towards the recognition of a real individual right to a healthy and protected environment as a corollary to the already recognized right to health".

(2) Prospects

If there is to be effective implementation of the human right to the environment through appropriate international monitoring machinery, this right must first be precisely defined, since the holder of any right must be specified, it must have a definite and achievable object and it must be binding on one or more specific persons.

The human right to the environment, like environmental law, upsets traditional legal patterns and is based on new concepts. If the latter cannot be made to fit into existing moulds, it is perfectly possible – since law is not immutable – to create new moulds. Having been identified, the right to the environment must be detached from the so-called "third generation"[34] rights and given its own place in the "catalogue of human rights".

(a) The Basis of the Right Concerned

Must the human right to the environment be interpreted strictly as the right to health, or should it be regarded more generally as a right to well-being or even a right to aesthetic sensitivity?

Several successive levels or "layers" of protection can be envisaged. When one attempts to place the human person as a living being in the context of his or her environment, one realizes that it is very difficult to disentangle the different elements mentioned above, since the quality of the environment is a determining factor of health. In this connection one can refer to a definition formulated by the World Health Organisation, according to which health is not just the absence of disease but "a state of complete physical and mental well-being". Physiological and psychological states are closely dependent on the environment. There is a transitive causal relationship between damage to the environment and the subsequent appearance of a physical or mental disorder or disease. Any damage to the environment can be regarded as deleterious to health in the long term.[35]

Although it is primarily the protection of health which justifies recognition of a human right to the environment, the economic aspect cannot be neglected. The environment is our heritage, a rich reservoir of resources which only sound management can preserve from spoliation, for the benefit of present and future generations. Recommendation 1131 (1990) on environment policy in Europe,

[34] See note 9, *supra*, pp. 347–348.

[35] See John Laird, 'Environmental Accounting: Putting a Value on Natural Resources', *Our Planet*, (1991), Vol. 3, No. 1, pp. 16–18.

adopted by the Parliamentary Assembly of the Council of Europe, recognizes that natural habitats and the environment are production factors which have their own price and must be taken into consideration urgently in the market economy.[36] In general, it seems that a number of guaranteed rights, particularly economic, social and cultural rights, cannot be effectively secured without protection of the environment and natural resources.

However, should not the main basis of the human right to the environment be, paradoxically, a much more cosmic and less human-centred perception of the world? We now know enough about the biosphere to recognize that "if we do not conserve its resources and respect its principal balances, human beings will not have any more hope of survival than many other living creatures".[37] The General Assembly of the United Nations has recognized that "Mankind is a part of nature and life depends on the uninterrupted functioning of natural systems which ensure the supply of energy and nutrients".[38]

(b) The Substance of the Right Concerned

Whereas observance of traditional rights is generally guaranteed when the State refrains from taking action, positive action by the State authorities is indispensable for effective protection of the right to the environment. The holder of this right must be able to secure the adoption by the State of legislation or regulations designed to prevent environmental damage which it would be difficult to reverse, and must be protected not only against damage caused by States but also against damage caused by private persons. Consequently, the true guarantee of this right lies in organisation by the State of procedures whereby private persons, whether individuals or corporate bodies, can make known their opposition when there is a risk of environmental damage.[39] The substantive right must be complemented by this procedural right.

(i) Where the substantive right is concerned, the "human right to the environment" should be recognized as such, with or without reference to "health" or "well-being". Nor does it seem necessary to introduce the concept of "conservation" of the environment, since, on the contrary, the human population must sometimes seek to reverse certain tendencies which show signs of becoming dangerously irreversible.

In any event, whatever uncertainties surround the definition of the environment, "it seems very probable that, in specific cases, a judicial body accustomed to dealing with human rights questions, such as the European Commission or European Court of Human Rights ..., would not find it any

[36] Alexandre-Charles Kiss, "Définition et nature juridique d'un droit de l'homme à l'environnement", Environnement et droits de l'homme, *supra*, pp. 16–17; Alexandre-Charles Kiss, "Droit international de l'environnement", *Revue juridique de l'environnement* (1990), No. 1, pp. 73 and 78.

[37] Preamble to the World Charter for Nature of 28 October 1982.

[38] See note 19, *supra*, pp. 65–66.

[39] See note 37, *supra*, pp. 20–21.

more difficult to interpret the substance of the right to the environment than it now does to apply some of the concepts enshrined in international texts protecting human rights, such as 'public order', 'public health' or 'a democratic society'".[40]

If interpretation did prove difficult, it would be possible to seek the opinion of a committee of eminent scientific experts.[41] In certain cases, such an expert opinion would even be necessary.

There should also be a provision similar to the one contained in Article 3 of Protocol No. 1 to the European Convention on Human Rights, under which "High Contracting Parties undertake to hold free elections at reasonable intervals by secret ballot, under conditions which will ensure the free expression of the opinion of the people in the choice of the legislature". States could undertake to develop and codify their legislation on the environment, while ratifying and incorporating into domestic law, wherever necessary, international agreements concerning the environment to which they were parties.

In this connection it should be noted that international conventions adopted on the question of environmental conservation tend to define thresholds of salubrity to be respected or types of species to be protected in particularly precise, technical and even numerical terms. The addition of detailed technical annexes to preventive conventions diminishes the scope for discretion left to the contracting parties. It would therefore be useful if individuals alleging a violation of their right to the environment could complain to international supervisory bodies of the failure or partial failure to apply these international environmental texts or standards.

(ii) With regard to the procedural aspect, this would involve the right to information, to participation and to suitable remedies.

Admittedly, universal and regional legal instruments for the protection of human rights generally guarantee the right to information,[42] the right to

[40] See Hans Jonas, *Le Principe responsabilité. Une éthique pour la civilisation technologique* (Paris, Cerf Coll. Passages, 1991), p. 336.

[41] Universal Declaration of Human Rights, Article 19; International Covenant on Civil and Political Rights, Article 19; European Convention on Human Rights, Article 10; African Charter on Human and Peoples' Rights, Article 9; American Convention on Human Rights, adopted in San José on 22 November 1969, Article 13. See also the Helsinki Final Act of 1 August 1975, Part 3, Section 2 – "Information"; Recommendation 854 of the Parliamentary Assembly of the Council of Europe of 1 February 1979 on access by the public to government records and freedom of information; Recommendation No. R (81) 19 of the Committee of Ministers of the Council of Europe on access to information held by public authorities, adopted on 25 November 1981, and the Declaration on the freedom of expression and information, adopted by the Committee of Ministers of the Council of Europe on 29 April 1982.

[42] Universal Declaration of Human Rights, Article 21; International Covenant on Civil and Political Rights, Article 25; Protocol No. 1 to the European Convention on Human Rights, adopted in Paris on 20 March 1952, Article 3; African Charter on Human and Peoples' Rights, Article 13; American Convention on Human Rights, Article 23.

participation[43] and the right to judicial remedies.[44] However, the scope of these rights is not always very clear.

Moreover, in the interests of conservation of the environment, the basic objective of environmental law, it must be possible to exercise procedural rights not just after an action or event which has already caused damage to the environment, but also before that action or event. Prevention is in fact one of the main pillars of environmental law, compensation being regarded as a mere stopgap. The *Arrondelle* case previously cited provides an example of this. The "compensation" the applicant received following the friendly settlement did nothing to end the nuisances of which she had complained.[45]

Thus a precise formulation of the procedural rights to be included in legal instruments for the protection of human rights is seen to be indispensable.[46]

(A) The right to information[47]

The right to information means that States have to distribute data and information relating to facts, activities, practices or projects with a considerable impact or potential impact on the environment, and to provide access to data and information concerning or potentially concerning the environment. This information should cover not just cases of pollution but all the factors likely to cause environmental damage, such as over-exploitation of resources, erosion, floods, earthquakes etc.

Whereas States should urgently inform individuals likely to be affected by any situation or event which could suddenly produce effects deleterious to their environment, they should also give them due notice of an intention to undertake or authorize activities which might make a considerable impact on their environment.

Decision-Recommendation C (88) 85 (Final) concerning provision of

[43] Universal Declaration of Human Rights, Article 8; International Covenant on Civil and Political Rights, Article 14; European Convention on Human Rights, Article 13; African Charter on Human and Peoples' Rights, Article 7; American Convention on Human Rights, Article 25.

[44] Pierre-Marie Dupuy, 'Le Droit à la Santé et la protection de l'environnement', See note 9, *supra*, pp. 401–402; Pierre-Marie Dupuy, 'La réparation des dommages catastrophiques', *Travaux des XIIIes Journées d'études juridiques Jean Dabin*, (Brussels: Biblioth]eque de la Faculté de droit de l'Université de Louvain, 1990), XIX, pp. 220–245.

[45] See Alexandre-Charles Kiss, 'La mise en oeuvre du droit à l'environnement: problématique et moyens', Proceedings of the Salzburg Conference (1980), see note 28, *supra*, p. 16; Benoît Jadot, 'Les procédures garantissant le droit à l'environnement', ibid., pp. 51–63; Pascale Kromarek, 'Quel droit à l'environnement? Historique et développements', Environnement et droits de l'homme, ibid., p. 148.

[46] See Christa Vogt, 'La mise en oeuvre du droit à la protection de l'environnement par l'information', Proceedings of the Salzburg Conference (1980), p. 6.

[47] There has been a gradual change of attitudes on this question which has been reflected in European legal systems. The operators of potentially dangerous installations, having been obliged from the beginning of the 20th century to inform certain "competent" authorities – such as the factories inspectorate – of their activities, gradually came to be obliged to communicate information to all public authorities, national and local, and to the workforce concerned. They are now bound to inform the local population and even certain foreign authorities. See Henri Smets, 'Risques industriels et droit à l'information', *L'Observateur de l'OCDE* (June-July 1989), No. 158, pp. 16–19.

information to the public and public participation in decision-making processes related to the prevention of, and response to, accidents involving hazardous substances, adopted by the Council of the OECD in July 1988, is of significance because it recognizes that "the potentially affected public has a right to be informed".[48] The 24 OECD member countries undertook to ensure that the potentially affected public "is provided with general information on the nature, extent and potential off-site effects on human health or the environment, including property, of possible major accidents at a planned or existing hazardous installation". The decision does not specifically state who should inform the public but does call for information "comprehensible to the general public" to be provided in a timely fashion, updated if necessary and reissued periodically.[49]

Similarly, the "Seveso" Directive, adopted by the Council of the European Communities in November 1988, requires member States to ensure that information is supplied, without their having to request it, to all persons liable to be affected by a major accident originating in a classified storage installation. This information must also be made publicly available. An annex to the Directive lists the items of information to be communicated.[50]

The chapter on information of the Oslo draft of the ECE Charter on environmental rights and obligations distinguishes between the general principle of the right to both general and specific information about the environment, the right to information in the event of an emergency, the right to appeal for administrative or judicial review when the requested information is not provided or is withheld, the right to environmental education and the obligation of States to provide regular reports on the environment.

(B) The right to participation

The right to participate in hearings and preliminary inquiries includes the possibility of raising objections to proposed decisions by public authorities likely to have a deleterious effect on the environment.

The chapter of the Oslo draft Charter on "decision-making" covers arrangements for public participation in decisions likely to have a harmful effect on the environment. It sets out the principle of the right to participate, the obligation of States to carry out impact studies and to implement a prior authorization system, the arrangements for public participation and the

[48] Henri Smets, 'The right to information on the risks created by hazardous installations at national and international level', Proceedings of the Conference on International Responsibility for Environmental Harm Resulting from Industrial Activities (Sienna, 23 and 24 March 1990).

[49] *OJCE* L 336 of 7 December 1988.

[50] See Pascale Kromarek and Konrad von Moltke, 'La mise en oeuvre du droit à la protection de l'environnement par la participation', Proceedings of the Salzburg Conference (1980), p. 27; Gerrit Vonkeman, 'Participation du public et rôle des associations', See note 19, *supra*, p. 15; Dorothy Nelkin, 'Participation du public à la mise en oeuvre d'un droit à l'environnement', see note 14, *supra*, pp. 39–50; Michel Prieur, Le droit de l'homme et les citoyens: la participation', *Revue juridique de l'environnement* (1988), No. 4, pp. 397–417.

obligation to give reasons for decisions.[51]

(C) The right to suitable remedies[52]

Recognition of a right under domestic law to suitable procedures for requesting an administrative or judicial review – including emergency procedures such as requests for a stay of execution – whereby individuals, alone or in association with others, could lodge a complaint with a view to preventing environmental damage, enforcing the abatement of such damage or securing compensation therefore would be of vital importance.

The Oslo draft Charter contains a chapter on "legal protection and compensation" which provides for "full and prompt" compensation for damage and the right to "restoration or reinstatement of the environment".

(c) The Holder of the Right

It seems that the greatest difficulty concerns the concept of "victim" and therefore of *"locus standi"*, since it throws doubt on the legitimacy of "collective" rights, or even putative "biosphere" rights.

Human rights to the environment are frequently collective – more so than in any other field – since they concern moving natural elements or shifting resources, to which the concepts of ownership or even sovereignty cannot be applied except through a legal fiction.

That being the case, could human beings, either acting as individuals or in groups, take on responsibility for protection of an environment exposed to or already subject to damage without being directly affected by that damage? As the proxy of present or future generations of their fellows, or of other living species, human beings would in a sense assert the right to the environment of the biosphere itself. Concern for the fate of future generations and the emphasis on timescale which can be perceived in all the environmental texts are not without importance; did the General Assembly of the United Nations not declare its conviction that "Every form of life is unique, warranting respect regardless of its worth to man"?[53]

Although the human right, or peoples' right, or even right of humanity, as defined above, may not be an individual right, it could be accorded appropriate international recognition. There seems to be a movement in this direction, at least as regards major disasters. In 1976 the International Law Commission adopted Article 19 of the draft articles on codification of the law of international liability, which describes as "crimes" unlawful acts of such gravity that they endanger the interests of the international community, one of these being "pollution of the sea, air or water".[54] Introduction of an *actio*

[51] See Louis-Paul Suetens, 'La protection du droit à l'information et du droit de participation. Les recours', Proceedings of the Salzburg Conference (1980), p. 17.

[52] Preamble to the World Charter for Nature of 28 October 1982.

[53] See note 9, *supra*, pp. 405–406.

[54] Alexandre-Charles Kiss considers that it would perhaps be desirable to look into how in the longer term an *actio popularis* could be lodged with a world intergovernmental organisation, following the pattern laid down for questions of international security in Article 35 of the United Nations Charter. Alexandre-Charles Kiss, *Survey of current developments in international environmental law* (Morges: I.U.C.N.N.R., 1976), No. 10, p. 48.

popularis procedure, to which individuals could have recourse when damage to the environment extended beyond national borders, has also been suggested.[55] It seems that the European Environment Agency could play a role in this field.[56]

However, recognition of a human right to the environment in existing legal instruments for the protection of human rights implies the existence of a sufficiently direct link between the applicant as such and the injury he believes he has suffered as a result of the alleged violation.[57] Nevertheless, when transposed to the field of the human right to the environment, the concept of "potential" or "possible" victim used as a criterion by the bodies of the European Convention on Human Rights could justify a considerable relaxation of the conditions governing the submission of petitions, especially in the case of applications from groups of private persons, such as nature conservation associations. For example, the European Court of Human Rights has held that in certain exceptional circumstance the victim of a violation may be any person who runs a real risk of being affected by application of a law alleged to be incompatible with the Convention.[58] The status of victim is thus conceivable even in the absence of detriment.[59]

Although the Court has made it clear that Article 25 of the Convention – by virtue of which applicants must claim to be "the victim of a violation ... of the rights set forth in [the] Convention" – "does not institute for individuals a kind of *actio popularis* for the interpretation of the Convention" and "does not permit individuals to complain against a law *in abstracto* simply because they feel that it contravenes the Convention",[60] some commentators consider that the possibility of being able to claim to be a victim is sometimes interpreted so broadly that the procedure begins to resemble an *actio popularis*.[61]

(d) The Respondent State

It would be desirable to define the precise extent of the liability of States in respect of legal instruments for the protection of human rights to which they are party in such a way as to take into consideration the case of the "transfrontier victims" of disputed measures. The Oslo draft charter contains a chapter on transboundary impacts.

[55] Ida J. Koppen, 'Environmental rights', *Proceedings of the Conference on 'Human Rights and the European Community: Towards 1992 and Beyond'* (November 1989), pp. 52–72.

[56] The European Court of Human Rights considers that the term "victim" denotes "the person directly affected by the act or omission which is in issue" (Adolf judgment of 26 March 1982, Series A Vol. 49, p. 17, para. 37).

[57] Klass and others judgment of 6 September 1978, *Series A* Vol. 28, pp. 16–20, para. 30–38; Marckx judgment of 13 June 1979, *Series A* Vol. 31, p. 13, para. 27; Dudgeon judgment of 22 October 1981, *Series A* Vol. 45, pp. 18–19, para. 41.

[58] Eckle judgment of 15 July 1982, *Series A* Vol. 51, pp. 30–31, para. 66–67; Inze judgment of 28 October 1987, *Series A* Vol. 126, p. 16, para. 32.

[59] Klass and others judgment of 6 September 1978, Series A Vol. 28, p. 17–18, para. 33.

[60] Henri Delvaux, "La notion de victime au sens de l'article 25 de la Convention", Proceedings of the Fifth International Colloquium on the European Convention on Human Rights (Frankfurt, 9–12 April 1980), Paris, Pedone, 1981, p. 73. See also the discussion, pp. 78–96.

[61] Recommendation C (77) 28 (Final), Annex, Section B, "Legal protection of persons", paragraph 4.

Implementation of the principles of "non-discrimination" and "equality of access" advocated in the previously mentioned OECD recommendations on transfrontier pollution is of vital importance. In particular, the Recommendation of May 1977 states that "countries of origin should ensure that any person who has suffered transfrontier pollution damage or is exposed to a significant risk of transfrontier pollution shall at least receive equivalent treatment to that afforded in the country of origin in cases of domestic pollution and in comparable circumstances to persons of equivalent condition or status". From the procedural standpoint, "this treatment includes the right to take part in, or have resort to, all administrative and judicial procedures existing within the country of origin in order to prevent domestic pollution, to have it abated and/or to obtain compensation for the damage caused".[62]

Decision C (88) 84 (Final) on the exchange of information concerning accidents capable of causing transfrontier damage, adopted by the Council of the OECD in July 1988, contains recommendations on informing the public in neighbouring countries.

It seems that incorporation of similar provisions relating to the right to the environment would not raise particularly difficult problems as far as the European Convention on Human Rights is concerned, since the case-law of its organs shows that the Convention binds States in respect of all the functions they exercise, irrespective of the place where their actions take effect.[63]

Ideally, there is absolutely no doubt that universal establishment of the human right to the environment is desirable, because environmental problems can be tackled only on a worldwide basis, but this right can be established in practice only by the kind of regional approach which the United Nations Environment Programme has already begun to try out.

However, such an approach presupposes the existence of effective regional judicial machinery capable of protecting the human right to the environment in different continents.

Although systems to monitor the application of human rights which rely on reports are useful, they simply cannot be compared with the right of individual petition approach, which is the only one that enables private persons, whether individuals or corporate bodies, to secure a full hearing of their case. Relying on any environmental rights which might be recognized, individuals should mainly aim at prevention, in order to ensure that States comply with national and international regulations.

The Council of Europe member States, which include some of the most highly industrialised countries in the world, could lead the way in this area by adopting a protocol to the European Convention on Human Rights.

The need to preserve the world environment is of such vital importance,

[62] See *X and Y v. Switzerland*, (7289/75 and 7349/76), 9 Eur. Comm. H.R.D.R. pp. 57, 89 and 91; Groppera Radio AG and others judgment of 28 March 1990, *Series A* No. 173, pp. 20–21, para. 46–48.

[63] Jean-Paul Jacqué, 'La protection du droit à l'environnement au niveau européen ou régional', *Environnement et droits de l'homme* (1987), UNESCO, pp. 67–70.

since it now concerns every human being, that the question of human rights to the environment can no longer be ignored, tackled indirectly or treated as a marginal issue. These rights must be precisely defined in appropriate instruments. Progress in this direction seems inevitable, because of its absolute necessity.

SECTION IV(d): A NEW FRAMEWORK FOR REFUGEES AND DISPLACED PERSONS

DEBORAH E. ANKER*

Introduction

The title of this section, "A New Framework for Refugees and Displaced Persons", implies a critique of the current framework for refugee protection: some aspect of that critique is developed in each of the papers presented. The current international framework for the protection of refugees is contained in the 1951 United Nations Convention Relating to the Status of Refugees[1] and the 1967 Protocol Relating to the Status of Refugees.[2] These instruments were very much a part of the development of the institutional and legal framework for the protection of human rights of the post World War II period.

The Refugee Convention and Protocol define a refugee as a person outside his or her country of origin who is unwilling or unable to return, owing to a "well-founded fear of persecution on account of race, religion, nationality, membership in a particular social group or political opinion".[3] Recent interpretations of the refugee definition, and in particular expanded notions of the concepts of "persecution" and "political opinion", have accommodated newer forms of oppression, and have, at least to some degree, extended protection to victims of civil and political violence in the third world.[4]

However, the immediate object of the Refugee Convention was the resettlement of European World War II refugees and many critics have argued that, in the concept of persecution and in the emphasis on violations of political and social rights, the refugee definition is limited and Eurocentric. This is certainly part of the critique developed forcefully by Jim Hathaway in his

* Coordinator, Immigration and Refugee Programs, Harvard Law School, Lecturer on Law, Clinical Instructor, Boston, Mass., U.S.A.

[1] Convention relating to the Status of Refugees, July 28, 1951, 189 U.N.T.S. 137.

[2] Protocol relating to the Status of Refugees, done Jan. 31, 1967, 19 U.S.T. 6223, T.I.A.S. No., 6577, 606 U.N.T.S. 267. The Protocol contains the same substantive provisions as the Convention, but eliminates certain date limitations and creates the option of removal of geographical limitations for signatory States.

[3] *Id.*, art.1.

[4] For a discussion of some of these interpretations in the U.S. context, see Anker, *The Law of Asylum in the United States* (1989), at 56–77.

K.E. Mahoney and P. Mahoney (eds.), Human Rights in the Twenty-first Century, 615–617.

paper.[5] These critics have argued that the current scheme for international refugee protection, including the creation and operation of the Office of the United Nations High Commissioner for Refugees, has proven inadequate to address the problems of third world refugees. This is because most of these refugees cannot establish individual claims of persecution, but rather flee generalized conditions of civil war and foreign aggression. Furthermore, the Refugee Convention, Hathaway and others argue, promoted third-country resettlement as a major solution and that solution has become increasingly problematic. Beginning in the 1970's and intensifying in the 1980's, more of the refugees arriving in the West were not from Europe, but from the third world.

The North/South character of the refugee flow has meant that the West has limited its commitment towards resettlement and has placed numerous restrictions on asylum-seekers arriving at or appearing within its borders. This problem underscores another fundamental limitation in the Refugee Convention and Protocol: these instruments leave the determination process for refugee status to the discretion of acceding States. Thus, salient foreign cold-war policies and domestic policies of immigration control have resulted in unfair application of an admittedly very malleable definitional concept.[6]

As already noted, the papers which follow all acknowledge some of the most important aspects of this critique. Where they may differ is in the author's view of its implications.

David Matas' paper presents an historical view of the political use by Western States of the Refugee Convention. He argues, however, for more procedural regularity and control of discretion, rather than for a rejection of the current scheme.

Marshall Conley's paper provides an excellent overview of various approaches to refugee law and protection since the Refugee Convention. He, like Hathaway, urges a closer linkage between refugee law and human rights.

The theme of Nirmala Chandrahasan's paper on refugee law and families is that refugee law is not responsive to the vast majority of refugees from Asia and Africa. She proposes an expanded definitional framework that borrows from human rights law (in particular in its recognition of social and economic rights) as a "source and inspiration" for interpretation. She, however, like Conley, does not propose a radical abandonment of the current scheme of international refugee law, but rather views human rights law as filling the lacunae of the existing refugee law framework.

For Jim Hathaway, the implications of the critique are profound and irredeemable: refugee law, as currently conceived, is a failure. He proposes a new scheme which acknowledges the sovereignty of States and proposes a

[5] See also Coles, "Approaching the Refugee Problem Today" in Loescher and Monahan (Eds.) *Refugees and International Relations* (1989), at 373.

[6] For an analysis and critique of the foreign policy bias in U.S. asylum determinations, see, e.g., *Reasonable Fear: Human Rights and the United States Refugee Policy* (1990), Amnesty International.

system of meaningful protection and assistance to third world refugees which, he argues, will be viable because it is consistent with the self-interest of nation States.

Indeed, the question raised in this section may be the critical one for refugee law in the years ahead: whether, despite its limitations, refugee law has created a powerful moral rhetoric and to some extent legal structure for protection and assistance that is worth building upon and defending,[7] from seriously addressing the most pressing problems and from considering more viable solutions.

[7] For example, the political and legal battles in the United States over the past ten years concerning discriminatory treatment of Salvadoran, and to some extent Guatemalan asylum claimants have resulted in legislation and court settlements granting temporary protection and new hearings to potentially over 500,000 persons. For a discussion of these developments, see generally *Immigration Newsletter*, vol. 19, no. 2 (1990).

DAVID MATAS*

A History of the Politics of Refugee Protection

1. Introduction

Refugees no matter where they are in the world, have always faced inordinate difficulty in receiving protection. The reason is not, in the end, a legal failure, although the law is insufficient. Neither is the reason a failure of human rights or humanitarian standards, although there is room for improvement in these standards. The reason is politics.

The politics of refugee protection have evolved over the years around certain constants that have created problems. Because of these constants, historical changes have been limited to varying adaptations of political realities.

2. Constant Political Realities

Historically constant underlying realities in the politics of refugee protection are racism, ideology, economics, concern over numbers, and assertion of sovereignty.

(1) Racism

The forms and viciousness of racism vary historically, but racism, as a constant has always been present. Refugees come from far away places. They are culturally disparate from the people of the country of protection. They often do not speak the local language. They may have no ties whatsoever before their arrival. And they did not even want to be there. They have fled unwillingly.

Before and during World War II, racism opposing refugee protection was blatant, universal and overt. The history of the failure of the world community to protect Jews fleeing the Nazi perpetrated Holocaust of World War II is a history of racism of the most crude and obvious sort.

* Refugee Lawyer, Winnipeg, Manitoba and the author of *Closing the Doors: The Failure of Refugee Protection* with Ilana Simon, published by Summerhill Press.

K.E. Mahoney and P. Mahoney (eds.), Human Rights in the Twenty-first Century, 619–628.

Today racism is more subtle. It is more impact discrimination than overt discrimination. Refugees, even though their lives may be at stake, are denied basic procedural protections in the determination of their claims which are granted by the determining country to their own nationals for the most trivial legal disputes. Refugees are denied elements of social support – denied the right to work, the right to go to school, freedom of movement, reunification with family – rights and privileges granted as a matter of course to others in society. Refugees today are not told they cannot be resettled because of their race. But the pattern of resettlement of refugees has shown that resettlement countries resettle more eagerly those of the same race as the predominant one than those of different races.

(2) Ideology

Another constant is ideology. Refugees have a relatively easy time receiving protection in a country whose government is ideologically opposed to the government of the country fled. Refugees find it difficult or impossible to seek and receive protection in a country whose government is ideologically in harmony with the government of the country fled. Refugees vote with their feet. Enemies welcome the vote. Allies reject it. A refugee outflow discredits the government of the country fled. Those opposed to the government welcome the implied criticism, and the weakening of the enemy government through loss of manpower. Those supporting the government of the country fled try to shut their eyes and ears to this implied criticism of a refugee outflow. They try to pretend the outflow does not exist, by denying protection.

(3) Economics

A third constant is economics. Refugee protection and resettlement is expensive. Even though refugees benefit the economy, on balance, over time, there are initial outlays, for support, language retraining and refugee determination, which create hesitation over protection.

Even more important is the economic suspicion surrounding refugees. Peaceful resettlement countries are invariably better off economically than countries in turmoil from which refugees flee. Even a refugee going from a rich country to a poor country will improve his/her lot economically if the refugee can work, and earn without persecution in the host country. Where the refugee movement is from a poor country to a rich country, as it often is, suspicions are multiplied. A refugee is seen as a person with a hand out, trying to seize an economic prize through the refugee protection system to which the person otherwise would not be entitled.

At the last session of the Executive Committee of United Nations High Commission for Refugees, held in Geneva in October, 1990, the head of the Canadian Mission to the U.N. in Geneva, Gerald Shannon, identified this suspicion in a speech to the Committee. His main theme was the pressure on refugee systems from people seeking the economic prize that comes with recognition. He said, "The perceived prize (from recognition) in fact is considerable enough to encourage refugee claims from many people who know that they are not generally in need of protection."

(4) Concern over Numbers

The fourth constant is concern over numbers. The total refugee population has fluctuated considerably over time. Currently the figure is high, around 17 million. Historically the figure has been a good deal lower than that. What is constant is the notion that there are too many refugees. No matter how few there have been, there are always more than resettlement countries are willing to absorb. In 1945, a Canadian senior official, when asked how many Jews should be allowed into Canada after the war, said, "None is too many". That remark became the title of a book by Irving Abella and Harold Troper about Canada and Jews of Europe from 1933 to 1948. While we cannot say today that Canadian officials believe none is too many, they certainly believe 17 million is too many. Whatever the level of the figures, the world community has never been able to absorb and resettle all refugees in a satisfactory fashion.

(5) Assertion of Sovereignty

The last constant is an assertion of sovereignty. The very notion of refugee protection flies in the face of State sovereignty. Refugees are not people foreign States choose to allow to enter. Refugees are people who decide, themselves, to flee. States continue to assert, in the face of refugee outflows, their entitlement to decide whom they should allow to enter. In the refugee context, this assertion plays itself out not so much in the denial of the concept of refugee protection as in an attempt to halt spontaneous movements of refugees from countries of first arrival. In Canada, this assertion of sovereignty has manifested itself in the safe third country rule, fines on airlines for bringing undocumented foreigners to Canada, criminalization of volunteer assistance to help undocumented foreigners come to Canada, and imposition of visa requirements on refugee producing countries.

Given the fact of these constants one might ask how any historical evolution could occur at all? Of the five constants mentioned, four are negative, without mitigation. Only one, ideology, has a practical tendency to generate protection for refugees, but only for those refugees who flee a country whose government is ideologically opposed to the government of the country in which protection is sought. Since these constants are negative, how has the world community been able to generate any protection for refugees at all?

3. Positive Trends

There have been four positive trends that have been locked in combat with the five negative factors. It is the combat of these positive trends with the negative constants that have led to historical evolution. The positive trends are developments in the humanitarian, human rights, administrative law and communications domains.

The development of protection for refugees has not been so much a political evolution as a legal evolution. Refugee protection increases where refugee protection is depoliticized. The battle over refugee protection is a battle of law against politics.

(1) Administrative Law

Administrative law and the protection of those caught up in administrative and quasi-judicial procedures, has developed tremendously in recent years in Canada and around the world to the benefit of refugee claimants. It has not occurred as part of refugee politics however. Administrative law is a new element in refugee politics for the reason that refugee protection has been impossible hermetically to seal off from general developments in administrative law. The notion of a fair hearing, the right to hear the case against you, the right to an oral hearing, the right to an independent and impartial decision maker, the right to reason, the right to access of counsel of choice, the right to an appeal are by no means all accepted universally, or in Canada in particular, as part and parcel of the refugee determination procedure. But there has been a filtering of these concepts into the field of refugee determination, to the benefit of refugees.

(2) Human Rights

In a sense it is absurd to talk of human rights as depoliticized. The apportionment of human rights blame has been blighted continuously by politics.

However, hand in hand with politicized condemnation, there has been a development of standards and mechanisms of an unpolitical nature. The Refugee Convention of 1951 and the UN High Commission for Refugees themselves were part of the first wave of human rights instruments and mechanisms that came out of a reaction to the atrocities of World War II.

Human rights standards and mechanisms have been penetrating the refugee domain, to the benefit of refugees, but only fitfully and intermittently. Regrettably, the human rights world and the refugee world, on a day-to-day basis, function separately and apart from one another. But the penetration of the human rights world into the refugee world is probably the most important countervailing factor to negative constants working against refugees.

(3) Humanitarian Considerations

The Geneva Conventions on the laws of war of 1949 and the two Protocols of 1977, the source of humanitarian law, have been invoked from time to time in courts of law to assert protection of refugees. So far, these efforts have not succeeded. It seems the use of humanitarian law to benefit refugees is more a hope than a reality.

The customary international law norm of temporary refugee is also more of a future hope than a present reality of refugee protection, although it has met with some legal success. In the humanitarian field it is more appropriate to talk of humanitarian discretion rather than humanitarian law. Governments for reasons of humanity and compassion intervene to prevent a refugee being returned to danger.

The assertion of humanitarian discretion represents a delegalization of refugee protection much like developments in human rights law and administrative law represent a depoliticization of refugee protection. While people who seek protection are denied a right of protection as refugees, in many cases, they are not sent back to danger. Instead, they are given temporary refuge. In Canada this reality manifests itself in a list of countries to which the government does not deport and refugees may be given compassionate permanent residence. In the U.S., it is called, "extended voluntary departure"; in Europe it is often referred to as "B" status. What is distinctive about all these forms is that refugees are extracted from the system of legal entitlements, the right to be refugees.

Although humanitarian discretion has been a negative in the development of refugee law, it has not been a totally negative development for refugees. A refugee's concern is whether or not he or she gets protection, not how it comes about. Whether it comes through entitlement or through an exercise of discretion to an individual refugee is not particularly relevant.

Overall, however, humanitarian discretion does not offer the protection refugee law does. Humanitarian discretion is neither as long lasting nor as broad in its benefits as refugee protection is.

(4) Communications

The communications revolution which made the world into a global village, impacts on refugee protection. It becomes harder and harder to deny the reality of the dangers a refugee faces when they are documented in newspapers, broadcast on radios or seen on T.V. screens. The work of non-governmental organizations may be even more important. Non-governmental organizations collect detailed information about persecution in the most remote corners of the world and make it available everywhere. This flow of information about the horrors refugees have fled helps to dispel the skepticism and disbelief many refugees face particularly the perception that they are mere economic migrants.

4. Historical Events and Today's Refugee Crisis

There are two historical events of major significance to the present international refugee structure. One is the Holocaust, the other is the Cold War.

(1) The Holocaust

The Holocaust demonstrated the failure of voluntary, humanitarian resettlement refugee policies before and during World War II and the need for refugee norms or obligations.

The failure of the voluntary system was manifested at an international conference at Evian, France, in 1938. The governments of 32 nations formed an inter-governmental committee to assist refugees leaving Germany and Austria.[1] Notwithstanding these efforts the Evian system failed because although everyone was in favour of resettlement, no one was prepared to offer it[2] and no one was obliged to offer it.

Without legal recourse, refugee claimants were unable to confront anti-Semitic or anti-alien immigration officials who prevented the good will of Evian from having concrete results. In Canada for example, the Immigration Department under Fred Blair, was motivated by anti-Semitism into attempting to prevent every Jewish refugee from entering Canada. Yet nothing could be done.[3] The U.S. State Department under Breckenridge Lodge, who was Assistant Secretary for Special Problems was also motivated by an anti-alien attitude. It did everything it could be block entry of Jewish refugees to the U.S., including suppressing news of the Holocaust.[4] On another front, in order to appease Arab leaders, Britain was determined to maintain quotas for Jews entering Palestine, (which was under British mandate) at a minuscule figure.[5] The British turned ship after ship of Jews away from Palestine.[6]

If the Holocaust showed the need for obligations, the Cold War led to a desire for condemnation. Prior to the Nazi phenomenon, refugees had been described as people who no longer enjoyed the protection of their governments.[7] Nazism led to attempts to define refugees in terms that judged the government of the countries from which the refugees were fleeing. For example, the 1938 Geneva conference excluded as refugees, people who left for "purely personal convenience". In other words, refugees were only people

[1] B. Nichols, "Religion, Refugees and the U.S. Government During World War II", a paper presented to the Oxford Symposium on Refugees, August, 1985 at p. 11.

[2] Ibid., at p. 19.

[3] I. Abella and H. Troper, *None is Too Many: Canada and the Jews of Europe, 1933–1948* (1982), p. 158.

[4] D. Wyman, *The Abandonment of the Jews: America and the Holocaust, 1941–1945* (1984).

[5] B. Nichols, See note 1, *supra*, at p. 11.

[6] See note 4, *supra*, at p. 158.

[7] G. Melander, "The Concept of the Term 'Refugee'", Oxford Symposium on Refugees, August, 1985, at p. 2.

forced to leave by their government.[8] The 1943 Bermuda conference defined refugees as people who had to leave because of "danger to their lives or liberties".[9]

With the collapse of Nazism, these judgmental definitions disappeared. In 1943, the United Nations Relief and Rehabilitation Administration (UNRRA) was established to assist displaced persons or victims of war. Its object was securing their repatriation or return.[10]

(2) The Cold War

The emphasis on repatriation quickly ran up against the problem of Ukrainians and Baltics who did not wish to return to Soviet rule. Humanitarianism mitigated this forced repatriation.[11]

One notable aspect of the International Refugee Organization (IRO), which replaced the United Nations Relief and Rehabilitation Administration (UNRRA) in 1947, is that it allowed a person to refuse repatriation if he or she had been persecuted or feared persecution. This shift to resettlement was not just for the purpose of accommodating humanitarian demands; it was motivated by anti-Communism. It said and meant to say that the Communist regimes persecuted their peoples.

Eighteen States ratified the I.R.O. Convention between May 1947 and March 1949. Needless to say, the Eastern Europeans did not join in the I.R.O. because they did not wish to share in their own condemnation. Several Western countries did not join because they were not ready to condemn the Eastern European bloc openly.

The United Nations Convention on Refugees, signed in 1951, saw greater participation. The definition of refugee was more restrictive. To be a refugee, a person had to have a "well founded fear" of persecution. A simple fear of persecution was not enough. But the implied condemnation remained. Eastern Europe countries still did not sign. The West, by and large, did. One ironic exception was the United States: ironic because the U.S. had played a key role in drafting the refugee definition and pushing it through the U.N. General Assembly.[12] But the U.S. did not sign because it displayed no interest in distinguishing between refugees and those fleeing Eastern Europe for economic reasons. The latter were excluded from the U.N. definition.[13]

This system of resettlement and condemnation was meant to discredit the

[8] Quoted in A. G. Madsen, *The Status of Refugees in International Law* (1966), Vol. 1, at pp. 31–32.

[9] G. Melander, See note 7, *supra*, at p. 3.

[10] Ibid., at pp. 3–4.

[11] Y. Boshyk, "Between East and West", paper presented to the Oxford Symposium on Refugees, August, 1985.

[12] G.D. Loescher and J.A. Scanlan, "The Politics of Escape", paper presented to the Oxford Symposium on Refugees, August, 1985, at p. 24.

[13] Ibid.

Eastern bloc by showing that its people were prepared to flee Communism.[14] Those who fled became tools for psychological warfare, conveying a message to those remaining.[15] They could also be used to conduct sabotage, to engage in guerilla warfare, and to establish governments in exile.[16] Defections removed people valuable to the Communist regimes.[17]

The continuation of the Cold War and the Soviet invasion of Hungary of 1956 showed that the problem of refugees from Eastern Europe was not just a World War II phenomenon, but a continuing issue. The 1951 Convention had been restricted to refugees forced to flee because of events before 1951. In response to the realization that the refugee problem was a continuing one, a 1967 Protocol was signed that deleted the 1951 dateline. As of January 1988, 104 countries have signed the Convention or Protocol,[18] including the U.S. However, none of the Eastern European countries except Yugoslavia and Hungary, have signed. Hungary did not sign until after the end of the Cold War, in 1989.

(3) Decolonization

The post-war period was a period of decolonization. Turbulence and civil war became part of the independence process of colonial peoples. The West had little desire to condemn newly independent governments for their political behaviour because these Third World governments were military allies, trading partners and ideological colleagues.

The problem of condemnation could be solved by changing the refugee definition. That is what the Organization of African Unity has done. Its Convention of 1969 includes as refugees everyone who is compelled to leave by reason of external aggression, occupation, foreign domination or events seriously disturbing public order.[19] The notion of persecution is thereby side-stepped.

However, the West has not wanted to change the refugee definition if its effect is to increase admissions. On the contrary, the larger than expected number of people who meet the current restrictive refugee definition has more than exhausted the Western willingness to absorb refugees. Nor is the West prepared to abandon the concept of obligation; the spectre of the Holocaust prevents it from doing that.

[14] K. Salomon, "Refugees in the Cold War", paper presented to the Oxford Symposium on Refugees, August, 1985, at p. 15.

[15] G.D. Loescher and J.A. Scanlan, See note 12, *supra*, at p. 5.

[16] Ibid., at p. 6.

[17] Ibid., at p. 21.

[18] U.N.H.C.R. Handbook on Procedures and Criteria for Determining Refugee Status.

[19] Ibid., at p. 280.

(4) The Refugee Flow through Berlin

The Refugee Convention, as said earlier, was originally designed by the West to provide refuge to anti-Communists fleeing Eastern Europe after the Second World War. Ironically, today's refugee crisis can itself be traced to Eastern Europe, which turned the tables and applied the Convention against the West.

In recent years, East Germany began to allow the entry of large numbers of Third World refugees. Visa requirements were waived and travel made cheap. East Germany intended not only to earn foreign currency, but also to force West Germany into closing off Berlin. West Germany viewed Berlin as a unified city and allowed free travel in and out of the non-Communist zone. East Germany on the other hand, viewed Berlin as a divided city and built a wall around the Communist zone. Refugees were brought to East Berlin, but directed to West Berlin and the West German refugee protection system. East Germany's flood of Third World refugees was used to try to coerce the West Germans to retreat from their commitment to Berlin as an open city, and to close off access from East Berlin to West Berlin.

West Germany maintained its commitment to Berlin as a united city in spite of the refugee influx. Instead, it tried to cut off the flow of refugees by setting up disincentive schemes. Claimants were denied work, education, freedom of religion and their native diet. They were exposed to extreme crowding and restricted in mobility. The refugee definition was restrictively applied in the courts. Claimants were forced to lead lives of idleness and despair, waiting for positive determinations which never come.

The disincentive schemes worked, not to send the refugees back to their homes, where they feared civil war or persecution, but to drive them elsewhere in Europe and North America. The Tamils that came to Canada by ship in the summer of 1986 and the Sikhs that came by ship in the summer of 1987 were part of this group.

As refugees fanned out from West Germany throughout Europe and North America, or simply skipped West Germany to go to other countries with less harsh systems, other countries in turn reacted to the overflow by setting up disincentive schemes and removing procedural protections.

West Germany eventually talked East Germany into imposing visa restrictions on the Third World by using economic leverage. The refugee flow through Berlin decreased, but the damage had been done. Once the West got caught up in this game of competitive destruction of safeguards, the contest could not be stopped.

Of course, the refugee problem is not just a Berlin problem. Even without Berlin as a political pawn, the world refugee problem was testing the West's generosity. But Berlin led to the fall of its first domino, West Germany, and all other dominoes fell in sequence.

5. Conclusion

Where are these historical forces taking us? The current dominant approach to refugees is thwarting spontaneous arrivals, or what governments call "irregular movements". Governments do not want refugees to choose their country of protection. Governments themselves want to decide the country of protection for refugees. If we look at what is happening on the world stage now and for the foreseeable future, the frustration of so-called irregular movements appears to be at the top of the agenda.

Yet thwarting spontaneous arrivals amounts to denying refugee protection in another form. In Europe, the battle over forced return to the country of first entry is all but lost. In Canada, prosecution of volunteers who help refugees arrive and the safe third country rule-hang like a Damocles sword over the refugee country.[20] Visa impositions and airline fines continue with unmitigated regularity.

It is impossible to say with confidence that refugee protection in the future will be strengthened. We witness the past, but we make the future. The fate of refugee protection in the future depends on what we individually and collectively decide to do.

[20] The safe third country rule is a rule that a person passing through a country designated by the Government of Canada as safe on his/her way to Canada is ineligible to make a refugee claim in Canada. To date no country has been put on the safe third country list.

MARSHALL CONLEY*

The Institutional Framework of Refugee Law and Political Forces

1. Introduction

James Hathaway wrote a few years ago that refugee law does not derive from a commitment to either humanitarianism or human rights.[1] He suggested that Western national interest determined the refugee law system. Although he presents a relatively strong argument for this position, the strenuous efforts of the Office of the United Nations High Commissioner for Refugees, the U.N. General Assembly, various non-governmental organizations and some conscientious nations during the 1980's, have begun to surmount this self-interested approach.

In this paper, the various aspects of international refugee law, beginning with the *1951 Convention Relating to the Status of Refugees* and ending with an examination of the *Comprehensive Plan of Action* which was adopted by the Prepatory Meeting for the International Conference on Indo-Chinese Refugees in March 1989, are outlined.[2] It concludes with the establishment of linkages between refugee law, humanitarian law and human rights.

2. The Beginnings of Refugee Law

It has been suggested that refugee movements since the end of the nineteenth century have been substantially different than in other periods of history for

* Professor, Department of Political Science, Acadia University, Wolfville, Nova Scotia, Canada.

[1] J. Hathaway, "International Refugee Law: Humanitarian Standard or Protectionist Ploy?", in A. Nash (ed.) *Human Rights and the Protection of Refugees Under International Law*, Halifax, N.S.: Institute for Research on Public Policy, 1988, pp. 183–188 at p. 184.

[2] I am indebted to the generosity and kindness of Gervase Coles, senior legal advisor, Division of Refugee Law and Doctrine, United Nations High Commission for Refugees, Geneva, who gave of his time and provided me with copies of his numerous writings on the subject of refugees. His assistance made a major task manageable. Other unnamed officials at UNHCR were kind to provide interviews which assisted this research during June, 1990.

K.E. Mahoney and P. Mahoney (eds.), Human Rights in the Twenty-first Century, 629–643.

three reasons. The size of those forcibly displaced was far greater than seen before. Secondly, as nation-States evolved they took over the policy roles previously occupied by the church and other local institutions. Finally, the duration of refugee displacements surpassed those of other periods.[3] The result was new initiatives in dealing with what came to be massive problems.

World War I rendered millions of people homeless as States' boundaries and identities were changed. Poles, Russians, Armenians, Hungarians, Jews and former prisoners of war all found themselves dispossessed and in need of assistance. The initial voluntary work of Fridtjof Nansen in assisting repatriation of prisoners of war and internees to their countries of origin was the impetus for the League of Nations to establish a High Commissioner of Refugees in Europe in 1921. Nansen was asked to serve as its first Head. The League did not include provisions for repatriation against one's will, and as more and more people were forcibly returned to the Soviet Union criticism was leveled against Nansen. This period was the beginning of the recognition that the principle of voluntary return must be upheld. In order to deal with those stateless persons who did not wish to return home and who were prevented from any movement because of lack of proper documents, the "Nansen passport" was introduced and became an early concrete symbol of the international community's responsibility for the legal protection of refugees.

During World War Two, the United Nations Relief and Rehabilitation Agency (UNRRA) was created by the Allied powers to deal with disaster-relief caused by the "total" war. Forty nations were signatories to the agreement establishing UNRRA. It ultimately spent vast sums of money (estimated at U.S. $4.25 billion) on food and medical supplies, industrial and agricultural reconstruction, and aid to refugees in most of eastern Europe, Italy, Ethiopia, China, Korea and the Philippines.[4]

UNRRA's mandate finished in 1947 leaving more than a million refugees in Europe for which no durable solutions had been found. Taking up the challenge was the International Refugee Organization (IRO) which was established in July 1947. Its primary orientation was not toward relief, rehabilitation and repatriation but toward resettlement.[5]

There was heated, and at times acrimonious debate in the United Nations before the IRO was established. However, The U.N. General Assembly did recognize the importance of dealing with the refugee problem and on February 12, 1946, approved a resolution which included two declarations which have been recognized as the cornerstone of international refugee protection. It declared that the refugee problem was "international in scope and nature" and

[3] Michael R. Marrus, *The Unwanted: European Refugees in the Twentieth Century*. (New York: Oxford University Press, 1985), pp. 3–5.

[4] See William Shawcross, *The Quality of Mercy: Cambodia, Holocaust and Modern Conscience*. (New York: Simon and Schuster, 1984), pp. 80–81, for observations on the role of UNRRA.

[5] Dennis Gallagher, *The Era of Refugees: The Evolution on the International Refugee System*, (Washington, D.C.: Refugee Policy Group, February, 1989), p. 24.

that no refugee or displaced person should be forced to return to their country of origin if they had produced satisfactory reasons for not returning.[6] However only 18 of the then 54 members of the United Nations actually supported its existence until the end of 1951.

In 1949, after the debate over the IRO was over, discussion on a new international framework for assisting and resettling refugees was taking place. The result was the creation of the United Nations High Commissioner for Refugees (UNHCR), which was created in 1950. In 1951 the *Convention Relating to the Status of Refugees* was approved.

The 1951 Convention had four important features: the main characteristic of a refugee was to be that of persecution; individuals and not groups were to be the primary focus; resettlement outside of one's original territory of residence would be the norm; and, that the refugee definition referred specifically to persons outside their country of origin.

It is fair to say that in most instances, the solution to the refugee problem in 1951 was seen in terms of external settlement and not voluntary repatriation. Gervase Coles argues that "the aspect of the country of origin, its role and responsibility and the rights of its nationals had now disappeared almost entirely from the view of the issue".[7] This resulted in some considerable hostility on the part of East European nations which were unhappy to see their citizens in exile about to receive long-term international aid.

Those countries supporting the creating of the new Office of the United Nations High Commissioner for Refugees and the subsequent *Convention* were generally of the opinion that the major function of the new body would be that of international protection which is a euphemism for the phrase "legal and political protection". The *Convention* was to define the standards of treatment accorded to refugees by those States ratifying the international instrument. Thus responsibility for the refugees was transferred from the countries of origin to the ratifying States. There were no specific provisions as to how the High Commissioner could, or should, promote voluntary repatriation, but there were detailed provisions about how external settlement should be promoted.[8] The *Convention* was even more restrictive than the *Statute* in that the operative parts concerned local settlement only, with no provision for either voluntary repatriation or resettlement through international co-operation or burden-sharing.

A major problem from the outset was that those countries outside of Europe saw the refugee problem as a temporary European one caused by the Second World War. They saw that the majority of the European refugees had been, or

[6] Zarjevski comments on this extensively. See Yéfime Zarjevski, *A Future Preserved: International Assistance to Refugees*. (Oxford: Pergamon Press, 1988), pp. 8–10.

[7] Gervase Coles, *Placing the Refugee Issue on the New International Agenda*. (Geneva: United Nations High Commissioner for Refugees, March, 1990), p. 7.

[8] For an examination of the development of the Office of UNHCR see, Gervase Coles, *Solutions to the Problem of Refugees and the Protection of Refugees: A Background Study* (Geneva: UNHCR, 1989), pp. 74–85.

would be resettled overseas and therefore there was need only for a temporary organization. Gordenker observes that the "drafting of the Convention on Refugees and the establishment of UNHCR reaffirmed the principle, already adopted in the creation of IRO, that the international responsibilities for general relief and protection of refugees would be limited in both time and place".[9] The signatories to the Convention, after all, accepted a definition of a refugee as a person affected by "events occurring in Europe (or elsewhere) before 1 January 1951".

The Statute creating UNHCR which emerged from the debates with the United Nations was a compromise between varying Western positions. Some wished that the Office would be limited and temporary, whereas others had strived for one which was broad in scope and permanent. From the humanitarian law perspective we are fortunate that the Statute creating UNHCR turned out to be an adaptable one. UNHCR was not created as a Specialized Agency like the ILO or WHO but as a subsidiary body under the direction of the General Assembly and the Economic and Social Council (ECOSOC). In addition, some have argued that the definition of *refugee* finally adopted has added to the authority of the High Commissioner to deal with refugee problems.[10]

The definition of a refugee allows the UNHCR to intervene at any time on behalf of a person because of their "well-founded fear of persecution". This has provided a great deal of adaptability for the High Commissioner. The *Statute* of the UNHCR states that, "The work of the High Commissioner shall be of an entirely non-political character; it shall be humanitarian and social and shall relate, as a rule, to groups and categories of refugees". This suggests the right of the High Commissioner to intervene on behalf of refugees without having to become involved in the debate on the causes of, or responsibility for, the actual refugee movement. Zarjevski suggests that it also shields the High Commissioner from pressures of governments attempting to challenge this right when used on behalf of refugees escaping from its territory.[11]

The *Statute* indicates that the High Commissioner shall follow instructions from the General Assembly or the Economic and Social Council (ECOSOC) and shall seek the advice of the [Executive Committee of the High Commissioner's Programme].[12] Through these procedures and the maintenance of contacts with governments and intergovernmental and non-governmental organizations, international refugee law is promoted.

By 1967 two new instruments relating to refugees were adopted by the United Nations – the *Protocol* and the *United Nations Declaration on Territorial Asylum*. The 1967 Protocol omitted the reference to events occurring before January 1, 1951, which is part of Article I of the *Convention*. The importance

[9] Leon Gordenker, *Refugees in International Politics* (London: Croom Helm, 1987), p. 29.
[10] See note 6, *supra*, p.11.
[11] Ibid., p. 13.
[12] Statute of UNHCR.

of the *Protocol of 1967 Relating to the Status of Refugees* was that it became a universal legal instrument as a result of the number of States which ratified it.

Coles suggests that there were serious flaws in the *UN Declaration on Territorial Asylum*, however.[13] For reasons of national security or in order to safeguard a population from a mass influx of persons, a State might refuse asylum. This was possible because Article I of the *Declaration* stated that the granting of asylum was an act of State sovereignty and therefore it could withhold the granting of asylum if it so desired. Coles states that "the instrument was essentially a watered down version of the traditional 'Western' approach" and did not recognize "the quite different approach of the African region where the major refugee problem now existed".[14] This position only exacerbated the problem created the year before when the adoption of the *International Covenant on Civil and Political Rights* specifically excluded the right to asylum from its articles because there was no support for including it as a human right. This was the result of the Member States of the United Nations failing to realize the scope of the problem of mass influxes and its relation to the question of asylum.

3. Regional Arrangements for the Protection of Refugees

During the latter part of the 1960's, two regional instruments came into force for dealing with refugees. The 1966 "Bangkok" *Principles Concerning Treatment of Refugees* was adopted by the Asian-African Legal Consultative Committee. This included a qualification on the duty of States to admit at the frontier and on *non-refoulement* (not to return or expel to the country of origin). Asylum was linked to the position of sovereign discretion. From the positive aspect, however, the *Principles* asserted for the first time in an international agreement relating to refugees, the individual right of return and the right to compensation.

The *Organization of African Unity Convention Governing the Specific Aspects of Refugee Problems in Africa (1969)*, which came into force in 1974, built some new elements into the structure of refugee protection and international law. There were no exceptions to the principle of asylum claimed by mass influxes of people. Rejection at the frontier was not acceptable. And it included the rights and duties of countries of origin as well as those of receiving countries in terms of subversive activities and voluntary repatriation. The definition of refugee was enlarged to comprise all those who fled "owing to external aggression, occupation, foreign domination or events seriously disturbing public order".[15] It also called for international solidarity in dealing with refugees ... "Where a Member State finds difficulty in continuing to grant

[13] See note 7, *supra*, pp. 152–157.
[14] Ibid., p. 153.
[15] See note 6, *supra*, p. 67.

asylum to refugees, such Member States may appeal directly to other Member States and through the OAU, and such other Member States shall in the spirit of African solidarity and international co-operation take appropriate measures to lighten the burden of the Member State granting asylum."[16]

Bierzanek points out, that Article III seems to suggest that the Contracting Parties were much more interested in safeguarding the interests of the States granting asylum against some political activity of the refugees.[17] Article III is a special provision laying down the principle that "every refugee ... shall abstain from any subversive activities against" any member of the Organization of African Unity.

The Conference on the Situation of Refugees in Africa was held in Arusha, Tanzania in May 1979. Striking of the recommendations emanating from the Conference was, once again, the concept of burden sharing and African solidarity. These recommendations were adopted by the Heads of State and Government of the Organization of African Unity in Monrovia in July 1979, and subsequently by the United Nations General Assembly as an *ad hoc* resolution on the "Situation of African Refugees" in that same year.[18]

However, as Ricca states, "the ratification of an international convention by a country is not enough to guarantee its application. The status and rights of refugees are recognized only if the provisions of international instruments are taken up in national legislation".[19] Legislation varies widely in quality and content in African countries and much work must be done to further codify these national laws.

The OAU position seems relatively mild when one examines the *Caracas Convention on Territorial Asylum (1954)*. According to the Caracas Convention, "at the request of the interested State, the State that has granted refuge shall take steps to watch over, or to intern at a reasonable distance from its borders, those political refugees who are notorious leaders of a subversive movement as well as those against whom there is evidence that they are disposed to join it" (Article IX). Articles VII and VIII limit freedom of expression and freedom of assembly or association respectively. Héctor Gros Espiell in examining the *American Convention on Human Rights*, states that it parallels the *International Covenant on Civil and Political Rights* but that the *American Convention* recognizes the right to seek and be granted asylum (Article 22,7). However, he indicates that the *Caracas Convention* still governs territorial asylum.[20]

[16] *OAU Convention Governing the Specific Aspects of Refugee Problems in Africa*, 10 September 1969, U.N.T.S. No. 14,691, art. II(4).

[17] Remigiusz Bierzanek, "International Solidarity and the Protection of Refugees", in *Congress on International Solidarity and Humanitarian Actions* (San Remo: International Institute of Humanitarian Law, September, 1980), p. 249.

[18] UNGA, Resolution 34/61, Thirty-fourth Session, 1979.

[19] Sergio Ricca, "Refugees in Africa: legal and administrative aspects," *The Courier*, no. 121, May-June 1990, p. 75.

[20] See, Héctor Gros Espiell, "The Organization of American States", in K. Vasak (ed.), *The International Dimensions of Human Rights*. Vol 2. (Westport, Connecticut: Greenwood Press, 1982), fn. 44.

The Cartegena Declaration, resulting from a colloquium organized by UNHCR in 1984, adapts the concepts written in international refugee instruments to the situation of Central American refugees by enlarging the definition of refugee, in response to the extensive nature of the problem of conflict, rather than persecution, which has affected persons in the region. A comprehensive formula for *non-refoulement*, the humanitarian aspect of asylum and minimum standards of treatment to those in camps and settlements provides the Declaration with the basic terms of reference to deal with refugee questions in the area.[21] However, it is unfortunate that the Cartegena Declaration is not binding on States, although a number do subscribe to its principles.

Another positive action in Latin America in recent years has been *Contadora Act on Peace and Co-operation in Central America* which was signed in 1986 by the Governments of Costa Rica, El Salvador, Guatemala, Honduras and Nicaragua. The Act dealt with voluntary repatriation in the region, co-operation to facilitate third country resettlement and a promise by the Governments of the area to undertake efforts to eliminate the causes of the refugee problem.

4. The European Communities and Refugee Policy

Refugee policy has been inextricably linked to the Community's mandate with regard to the protection of human rights. In their Joint Declaration of April 5, 1977, the European Parliament, the European Commission and the Council stressed the importance they attached to the protection of fundamental rights, as derived from the constitutions of the Member States and the European Convention on Human Rights. They declared their intention to respect those rights in the exercise of their powers.[22]

In 1984 the European Parliament began work on a full catalogue of human rights, which ultimately was presented as a draft Declaration of Fundamental Rights and Freedoms and adopted in April 1989. The result of the Declaration and a growing body of case-law of the European Court is the protection of the fundamental rights of individuals under Community law. As Zwamborn has written, "the development of such a policy has to be seen in relation to powers that have been vested in the institutions by the EC treaties, and include the powers with regard to the external relations of the Community in the areas of

[21] See "Report to the Conference by the Office of the United Nations High Commissioner for Refugees," International Conference on Central American Refugees (CIREFCA), 29–31 May, 1989, document CIREFCA/89/10.

[22] See P. Pescatore, "The Context and Significance of Fundamental Rights in the Law of the European Communities", 2 *Human Rights Law Journal*, (1981), p. 295–308, for a fuller exploration of this topic.

trade, aid and association agreements".[23] This was reflected in the inclusion of references to human rights in Lomé III and in the co-operation agreement with the countries which are party to the General Treaty on Central American Economic Integration.[24] Respect for human rights is an important ingredient in the relations between the European Community and third countries. To bolster this position, the European Parliament has requested in its *Annual Report on the Human Rights in the World* that the Community's mandate concerning human rights should be provided with a stricter legal basis.

To link this position with the question of refugees, the European Commission presented a proposal for a directive on the co-ordination of rules on the right to asylum and refugee status. A resolution was presented to the European Parliament in March 1987 and adopted. The resolution stipulated that ... "all measures adopted in regard to the right of asylum must take as their starting point respect for human dignity, the Convention on Human Rights of the Council of Europe, the United Nations Declaration of Human Rights and guidelines adopted by the European Parliament on the drawing up of a European policy on human rights".[25] The main principles in the European Parliament's resolution were: (1) strict respect of the principle of *non-refoulement* and non-discrimination of those asylum seekers who appeared at frontiers without visas; (2) visa requirements should not make it impossible for people to seek refuge from their own countries; (3) applications for asylum should be dealt with thoroughly and rapidly with procedural safeguards and with legal assistance and under strict observance of the relevant international instruments; (4) the applicant must be free to choose the country of asylum in the EC and the chosen country will have sole responsibility for granting asylum; (5) a refusal to grant asylum should be duly motivated in writing and must be ultimately the subject of independent judicial review and appeal, with suspensive effect; and, (6) recognized refugees in the EC should have the same rights and obligations as Community citizens from other Member States.

The head of the European Commission indicated that given the nature of the Community the concept of "country of first asylum" probably would have to be adjusted so that a balance could be attained between the applicant's right of choice of the country of asylum and the prevention of the emergence of systematic flows within the Community in a single direction in order "to take advantage of greater benefits, particularly in the social field".[26] When the Commission circulated a draft proposal amongst representatives of Member States on harmonization of asylum policy in the framework of the EC it did not receive endorsement. As a consequence the Commission has delayed a decision to submit a formal proposal for a directive.

[23] M. Zwamborn, "The Scope For a Refugee Policy of the European Communities as Part of an Overall Human Rights Policy", p. 5, a paper presented at the International Conference on Refugees in the World: The European Community's Response, The Hague, 7–8 December, 1989.

[24] Ibid., p. 5.

[25] OJ C99/170 (par. L), Ibid., p. 16.

[26] Ibid., p. 18.

Of all the European institutions it is only the European Parliament that has utilized the human rights approach for dealing with the right of asylum and the rights of refugees. It has taken as a starting point the international human rights instruments and pointed out what is needed to effectively institute the right to seek and enjoy asylum. However, "the lack of a policy with regard to the promotion and protection of human rights within the Community legal order has important consequences for the development of the refugee policy for the EC. In view of the lack of a human rights mandate for the Community legal order, the Community institutions (with the exception of the Parliament) seem not to be concerned with the right to seek and enjoy asylum as such. The only concern is the harmonization of the asylum policy of the EC Member States in view of the abolition of internal frontiers."[27] At this date it is problematic whether or not intergovernmental co-operation will result in a viable protection for the rights of asylum seekers and refugees. Bossuyt seems to reflect the general European preference of keeping refugees closer to their country of origin. "It is to a great extent preferable to encourage as far as possible that refugees find hospitality in neighbouring countries rather than to have to provide shelter in far away countries. Therefore, it should be encouraged to assist in the relief for refugees in countries close to the country from which the refugee is fleeing, as well for reasons of international solidarity as in the interest of the refugees themselves."[28]

5. UNHCR and the Comprehensive Plan of Action

The Comprehensive Plan of Action (CPA) was drawn up and approved at the Prepatory Meeting for the International Conference on Indo-Chinese Refugees at Kuala Lumpur, Malaysia from March 7–9, 1989. It was presented to the International Conference in Geneva in April of that year. It is an agreement to undertake action to resolve the on-going problem of Indo-Chinese asylum-seekers. It was developed in recognition that since 1975, over two million persons have left their countries of origin in Indo-China and that the flow of asylum-seekers remains unabated. It also recognized that this flow of asylum-seekers across frontiers in the South-East Asian region is a subject of intense humanitarian concern to the international community. The fear of UNHCR and others of the current arrangements designed to find solutions for asylum-seekers and to resolve problems stemming from the outflow may no longer be responsive to the size, tenacity and complexity of the problems in the region. This prompted them to develop the CPA.

The CPA addressed the majority of the central problems concerning Indo-Chinese asylum-seekers. There was a recognition that clandestine departures

[27] Ibid., p. 24–25.

[28] Marc J. Bossuyt, "For an Integrated Refugee Policy Better Adapted to Present Circumstances," *Refugees in the World: The European Community's Response, SIM (Netherlands Institute of Human Rights) Special no. 10*, The Hague, 7–8 December 1989.

contributed to extreme human suffering and hardship, often resulting in loss of lives. It is the desire of the CPA to implement humane measures to deter them. This would include official measures directed against those organizing clandestine departures and the creation of a mass media activity. The mass media publicity would identify the dangers inherent in this type of departure; the creation of a status-determination instrument under which those determined not to be refugees would have no opportunity for resettlement; the absence of any real or perceived advantage in relation to third-country resettlement of clandestine or unsafe departures; and the encouragement of the use of regular departure and other migration programmes.

In order to address unsafe or clandestine departures, emphasis would have to be placed on the Orderly Departure Programme(ODP). This programme has never been recognized as fulfilling its original objectives. The CPA indicated that the ODP should be fully encouraged and promoted. It also stated that, "Emigration through regular departure procedures and migration programmes should be accelerated and expanded with a view to making such programmes the primary and eventually the sole modes of departure".[29] To achieve this objective, the CPA proposes a media campaign to increase awareness of regular departure procedures, the inclusion of Amerasians and former re-education centre detainees and the fact that all persons eligible under regular third-country migration programmes would have full access to regular departure and migration programmes.

Viet-Nam agreed to fully co-operate with UNHCR and the Intergovernmental Committee for Migration (ICM) in expediting and improving processing. The CPA also envisioned that Viet-Nam would also co-operate with UNHCR and ICM to ensure that air transportation and logistics were sufficient to deal with all those accepted under the regular departure and migration programmes.

The CPA recognized the need for the early establishment of a consistent region-wide refugee status-determination process and that it would take place in the context of national legislation and internationally accepted principles. This, of course, also required that continued permanent resettlement was part of the overall CPA strategy.

Resettlement has always been the major sticking problem for dealing with the asylum seekers. The CPA calls upon a total of twenty countries active, or potentially active, in resettlement to deal with those who are described as long-stayers (i.e., those who have resided in asylum camps for a long period of time), and for a speedier resettlement of newly-determined refugees.

Finally, the CPA deals with the thorny question of repatriation. UNHCR has agreed with the statement in the Declaration that, "Persons determined not to be refugees should return to their country of origin in accordance with international practices reflecting the responsibilities of States towards their own citizens. In the first instance, every effort will be made to encourage the

[29] A/CONF.148/2, 26 April 1989, p. 3.

voluntary return of such persons".[30] This provision recognizes the ever-increasing problem of the so-called "economic" migrants, so forcefully brought to the world's attention by the plight of asylum-seekers in Hong Kong.

6. Human Rights and Refugee Law

Although not always made explicit, there are direct links between human rights and refugee law. The adoption of the Universal Declaration of Human Rights in December, 1948 set out basic principles with respect to the individual and therefore can be directly linked to all facets of the refugee problem, from causes to solutions. Articles 9 (the prohibition of arbitrary exile), 13 (the right to leave and return) and 15 (the right to a nationality and the prohibition of the arbitrary deprivation of nationality), are all principles of immediate relevance to the refugee problem. However, it is only Article 14.1 which is specifically directed towards refugees: "Everyone has the right to seek and to enjoy in other countries asylum from persecution".

In spite of this seeming linkage, Gervase Coles has suggested that humanitarian concerns came to be contrasted with human rights concerns which were considered to apply only partially to the refugee problem.[31] The consequence was that it was not until the 1980s that there was a reassertion by the international community of the linkage between human rights and the refugee problem.

Beginning in 1980, a series of initiatives began the establishing of linkages between human rights questions and the refugee problem. In 1980 a Canadian initiative was brought forward to the United Nations Human Rights Commission. At its thirty-sixth session the Commission adopted a resolution dealing with human rights and mass exoduses. The resolution[32] asked the Secretary-General to consider establishing direct contacts with involved governments to assess the relationship between the current situation and full enjoyment of human rights, in those cases where large-scale exoduses became a matter of international concern and solidarity. It also called upon the Secretary-General to make concrete recommendations for dealing with such situations. Canada was concerned about three aspects of the growing phenomenon of mass exoduses. It wanted to guarantee protection and assistance to those in need. It wished to promote the sharing of the immense burden placed on countries of initial refuge. And most importantly of all, Canada desired to deal with the question of mass exoduses in a proactive way by contributing to the elimination of the causes of exoduses.

New ground in humanitarian law was broken by the Canadian initiative

[30] Ibid., p. 7.

[31] Gervase Coles, *Solutions to the Problem of Refugees and the Protection of Refugees: A Background Study*. (Geneva: UNHCR, 1989), p. 99.

[32] Adopted at the 1576th meeting of the Human Rights Commission on 11 March 1980, by 34 votes to 4, with 3 abstentions.

requesting that the Secretary-General play a role in building international solidarity on the refugee issue. Canada saw the mass exodus coming out of Viet-Nam as the result of human rights violations and was of the opinion that many exoduses were the result of human rights violations in the country of origin. Consequently, emphasis had to be placed on this problem if mass exoduses were to be ameliorated.

In 1981 the United Nations Commission on Human Rights adopted another Canadian supported resolution to appoint a Special Rapporteur to study the question of human rights and massive exoduses. Sadruddin Aga Khan, a former High Commissioner of Refugees was commissioned to prepare a *Study on Human Rights and Massive Exoduses*.[33] In addition to a number of case studies, the report made a number of recommendations which were ground-breaking for the United Nations. A call for a New International Humanitarian Order was put forward to include the updating of refugee, nationality and labour law. He also proposed a standardization of international aid criteria, as well as a reappraisal of developing countries' economic needs in relation to possible causes of exoduses. Most importantly he proposed the introduction of an early-warning system based on impartial information gathering and data collection concerning potential mass exodus situations which would lead to timely reporting to the U.N. Secretary-General in order for him to take appropriate action in concert with the competent intergovernmental organs.

Whilst the Special Rapporteur's study was an important one, it was compromised by the successful attempt by a number of states to have the Annexes of the report deleted. Of the twenty-two countries identified in the first annex, no less than twelve had mass exoduses because of human rights violations. The remaining mass exoduses were caused by either civil war or economic hardship. Nine years later, the enduring value of the Special Rapporteur's study on human rights and massive exoduses is that it correctly identified the fact that without economic and social development respect for human rights would be very difficult.

The same year that Canada introduced its resolution in the Commission on Human Rights, the Federal Republic of Germany proposed an item on the agenda of the General Assembly. The item, *International Co-operation to Avert New Flows of Refugees*[34] , stated that massive flows of refugees not only affect the domestic order and stability of states of first refuge but can jeopardize the stability of entire regions and therefore can add a threat to international peace and security. In fact, what the Federal Republic of Germany(FRG) wished to do was to go beyond humanitarian measures concerning new flows of refugees and to have the United Nations consider

[33] Initially issued as E/CN.4/1503 on 31 December 1981, and subsequently reissued as E/CN.4/1503* (*reissued for technical reasons: i.e., all three of the Annexes identifying countries and providing case studies were dropped because of opposition from the countries named in the report).

[34] UNGA Resolution 35/124 was adopted by an affirmative vote of 105 States.

measures to avert such flows. Like Canada, the FRG initiative dealt with causes.

Causes, of course, are usually considered to be political in nature. The role of UNHCR has been to deal with humanitarian questions and as Coles rightly points out, the UNHCR felt that since causes were a political issue, they were outside their concern.[35] "As long as external settlement was the general solution...the issue of causes became almost marginal. ...the moment that the question of solution was posed in its variety and complexity because of the inadequacy of external settlement as the sole, or main, solution of the refugee issue, the aspect of causes became critical in determining the entire response.[36]

A group of experts was set up by the General Assembly to deal with the German resolution and submitted its report in 1986. The report clearly suggests that States must assume responsibility for mass flows of refugees and should therefore refrain from creating or contributing to policies which would contribute to massive flow of refugees. The international law here is quite clear. If a State's actions generated massive refugee flows which endangered international peace and security, this could be seen as a violation of the Charter of the United Nations.

The latest aspect of this concern is that in March 1987 the Secretary-General created the Office for Research and Collection of Information, within his Office, to undertake early warning activities. This office is charged with co-ordinating information gathering and analysis so that it can provide early warning on situations which might require a response by the Secretary-General.

The Director of the Division of Refugee Law and Doctrine at UNHCR, Dr. G. Arnaout, has identified one of the problems of refugee law. He explains that the term humanitarian law has been used to describe the law applicable to armed conflicts, whilst others feel that it includes human rights law. His own position is that refugee law should be added to this list to add a complementarity encompassing all three, "since refugees are mostly victims of the violations of the laws of armed conflicts and human rights". "The difference between humanitarian law understood in this wider sense and the other branches of traditional international law would be that the former would have as its main distinguishing criteria the protection of the human being and the safeguarding of [his] basic needs, while the latter would relate, as it traditionally has, to regulating inter-State relations."[37]

It has been suggested by the High Commissioner for Refugees in February 1990 that, "It is of imperative importance to ensure that the refugee issue appears on this new international agenda".[38] One way that this can be

[35] Gervase Coles, *Placing the Refugee Issue on the New International Agenda*. (Geneva: UNHCR, March, 1990), p. 17.

[36] Ibid., p. 18.

[37] G. Arnaout, "Respect of Fundamental Human Rights of Refugees and Displaced Persons", in *Yearbook 1986–87 of the International Institute of Humanitarian Law*. (San Remo, 1989), p. 42.

[38] Thorvald Stoltenberg, United Nations High Commissioner for Refugees, "Our Common Future", 72 *Refugees*, (February 1990), p. 5–6, at p.5.

accomplished is a reconceptualization of humanitarian law. In a recent interview, the High Commissioner indicated that he would try to bring the refugee issue on to the political agenda in the international context, "because it's not on the political agenda. It's really to a large extent considered as a technical issue and to a certain extent as a charity but not as something affecting the whole international community."[39]

This reflects the concern of the Refugee Policy Group in a recently published article by Roberta Cohen: "Too often it has been assumed that refugees are the subject only of refugee and humanitarian law, notwithstanding the growing body of human rights law relevant to them."[40] Cohen points out that in addition to the *Universal Declaration of Human Rights* and the *International Covenant on Civil and Political Rights* other human rights treaties have provisions for refugee protection. The Convention Against Torture prohibits *refoulement* when there is a possibility of torture. The *Convention on the Rights of the Child* and the *Convention on the Elimination of All Forms of Discrimination against Women* apply protection for children and refugee women respectively.[41]

7. Conclusion

If links between refugee law and human rights law already exist, then what must be done to overcome the political forces affecting their useful implementation? Over the years we have seen how much easier it is for governments and humanitarian institutions to address actual refugee situations than it is for them to deal with impending crises. The early warning process as is currently located in the Office for Research and the Collection of Information (ORCI) within the office of the Secretary-General could provide the strengthening of linkages between human rights law and refugee law. This unit could be the catalyst for a more effective early warning system for human rights and refugee crises. It could build on the prestige of the office of the Secretary-General to encourage closer co-operation between the U.N. Centre for Human Rights and UNHCR. Both the Centre and UNHCR suffer from inadequate resources. Through co-operative efforts, rather than concern for jurisdictional authority, these three would have the resources to co-ordinate efforts to deal with the objects of their existence – people. If Hathaway is correct when he writes that, "...one has to understand clearly that the [refugee] protection system was and is the promotion of the national interest of States, not refugees"[42], then it is incumbent on all involved to follow the admonition of Gervase Coles that ... "it

[39] "Refugee work is not charity ... but part of our own future security," interview of Thorvald Stoltenberg, U.N. High Commissioner for Refugees, 121 *The Courier*, (May-June, 1990), p. 81.

[40] Roberta Cohen, *Introducing Refugee Issues into the United Nations Human Rights Agenda*. (Washington, D.C.: Refugee Policy Group, 1990), p. 5.

[41] Ibid., p. 5.

[42] Ibid., p. 188.

is only by ensuring respect for human rights generally that an adequate general notion of solution ... can be obtained".[43]

[43] Gervase Coles, "The Human Rights Approach to the Solution of the Refugee Problem: A Theoretical and Practical Enquiry," in Alan E. Nash (ed.) *Human Rights and the Protection of Refugees Under International Law*. (Halifax, N.S.: Institute for Research on Public Policy, 1988), p. 195–222 at p. 221.

NIRMALA CHANDRAHASAN*

The Effects of Refugee Law on Families

When we speak of refugee law we are referring to that body of rules which international law has developed to give some measure of protection to persons fleeing from persecution and seeking asylum in third States. Such persons do not have the protection of their own States and governments, and hence international law has developed rules to protect them.[1]

The protection of individuals and groups necessarily has to encompass the family too. The family is the fundamental group unit of society recognized as such in the human rights instruments and as being entitled to protection by society and the State.[2] However, the Convention on the Status of Refugees, which is the principal instrument dealing with refugee law, makes no direct mention of the "family" or "dependants". The definition of a refugee is in fact framed in terms of individuals rather than groups. But in "The Final Act of the United Nations Conference of Plenipotentiaries on the Status of Refugees and Stateless Persons" in 1951[3] the family was given recognition. The Conference in its recommendations stated that the unity of the family was "an essential right of the refugee", and it urged governments to "take the necessary measures for the protection of the refugee's family especially with a view to ensuring that the unity of the refugee's family is maintained particularly in cases where the head of the family has fulfilled the necessary conditions for admission to a particular country, and the protection of refugees who are minors, in particular

* LL.B. (Ceylon), LL.M., (Cantab), Ph.D. (Colombo), Attorney-at-Law, Madras, India.

[1] "[The] characteristics [of a refugee] may be summed up as being abroad, fearing persecution and lacking protection. But the crux of the matter is that the relationship between the State and the refugee has turned sour for political reasons. Instead of trust and allegiance we find fear and alienation." A. Grahl-Madsen, "The Emergent Law Relating to Refugees", in 13 *The Refugee Problem* (1987), p. 192.

[2] Universal Declaration of Human Rights Article, Article 16(3): "The family is the natural and fundamental group unit of society and is entitled to protection by society and the State." G. A. Res. 217. A(III), 3(1) U.N. GAOR. Res 71, U.N. Doc. A/810. (1948).

See also Article 23(1), International Covenant on Civil and Political Rights (1966), and Article 10, International Covenant on Economic, Social and Cultural Rights (1966).

[3] See Collection of International Instruments Concerning Refugees, 2nd ed., Office of the UNHCR, Geneva (1979).

K.E. Mahoney and P. Mahoney (eds.), Human Rights in the Twenty-first Century, 645–657.

unaccompanied children and girls, with special reference to guardianship and adoption".[4]

Although the principle of the protection of the refugee families, and especially of minors and unaccompanied children and girls, has been spelled out here, the definition of the term "refugee" in the Convention has resulted in a restrictive approach which excludes the application of this principle to a large category of persons whom I shall refer to as *de facto* refugees, to distinguish them from the *de jure* refugees under the Convention. The Convention defines a refugee as "a person who owing to a well-founded fear of being persecuted for reasons of race, religion, nationality, membership of a particular social group, or political opinion is outside the country of his nationality, and is unable or owing to such fear is unwilling to avail himself of the protection of that country".[5] This definition sets out both a subjective as well as an objective standard, as the fear must be actually present and have an objective basis. Moreover, it requires a case-by-case determination.

In today's world the vast majority of refugees are composed of large groups of people fleeing from conditions of civil war, violence, starvation, etc. They do not therefore, fall within the grounds set out in the Convention. However, they do not have the protection of their governments, and may be either displaced within their own country or have crossed an international boundary to safety. As they do not satisfy the Convention criteria, they are not eligible to be given refugee status under the refugee determination processes of those countries which are parties to the Convention, and which generally apply this definition. Hence, we have two categories of refugees, and when we deal with the effects of refugee law on families we have to make this distinction.

The United Nations High Commissioner for Refugees (UNHCR),[6] which is the chief U.N. agency entrusted with the protection of refugees has, on the other hand, extended its mandate to take account of the new type of refugee flows. It exercises its protection and assistance functions not only with respect to persons falling within the 1951 Convention definition, but also to persons crossing international boundaries as a result of conflicts or radical social or economic changes in the country of origin, who are or may be presumed to be unable to avail themselves of the protection of their governments.[7] The Executive Committee of the UNHCR programme on the International

[4] Section IV.B (principle of unity of the family). In making this recommendation the conference noted with satisfaction the official commentary of the Ad-Hoc Committee on Statelessness and Related Problems (E/1618 p. 40), which states that the rights granted to a refugee are extended to members of his or her family.

[5] Article 1A(2) of the Convention on the Status of Refugees, (1951) 189 UNTS. 137 ("the 1951 Convention"), together with Article 1 of the Protocol Relating to the Status of Refugees (1967) 606 UNTS 268. The Protocol extends the scope of the Convention definition of a "refugee" to apply more broadly than the 1951 definition, so as to take account of the post-World War II European context, but does not change the material definition of a "refugee" found in the 1951 Convention.

[6] Statute of the Office of the United Nations High Commissioner for Refugees, G. A. Res 428, 5 UN GAOR supp (no. 20) at p. 46. UN. DOC A/1775 (1950) ("the UNHCR statute").

[7] G. Goodwin-Gill, *The Refugee in International Law*, pp. 6–12.

Protection of Refugees has also reiterated the principle of family unity in its "Conclusions". For example, the Conclusion on "Refugees Without an Asylum Country"[8] states that countries should "facilitate the admission to their territory of at least the spouse and minor or dependent children of any person to whom temporary refuge or durable asylum has been granted". Those granted "temporary refuge" covers the case of *de facto* refugees allowed to remain on humanitarian grounds, and hence seeks to extend the principle of family unity to this category too. It is submitted that as the principle of family unity flows from the human rights principle of protection of the family as the basic unit of society, it should apply equally to all categories of refugees as a basic human right.

The practice of States reveals that, in general, the Western countries have not applied the principle of family re-unification to non-Convention refugees.[9] However, in some Western countries, for example Canada, a more liberal approach has been followed. Under special programmes, persons affected by civil disturbances and racial riots and still within their own countries have been admitted to Canada on the basis of family re-unification when they had family members in the country.[10] In Asian and African countries, on the other hand, there has been on the whole a practice of accepting and giving temporary refuge to large scale influxes across State boundaries, caused by civil wars, political strife, famine, etc."[11] The nature of the refugee flows in such cases of mass influxes makes it difficult to distinguish between refugees, family members, and dependents. Moreover, in cases of group persecution, family members themselves have an independent claim to refugee status. Recent examples of such influxes in 1990 are the estimated 150,000 refugees fleeing the civil war in Liberia into the neighbouring countries of the Cote d'Ivoire and Guinea and approximately 120,000 Sri Lankan Tamils crossing into India. The majority of these people are fleeing from danger to life and limb, caught as they are in the crossfire of fighting and faced with starvation and deprivation brought about by the war situation. In the course of a civil war many people are also displaced.[12] These persons, driven from their home by aerial bombing or

[8] Conclusions adopted in 1979 by the Executive Committee, 30th Session, No. 15, para (e), "Conclusions on the International Protection of Refugees", Office of the UNHCR, Geneva, 1980.

[9] For example, many Tamil men who fled to the West in 1983–87 had family members left behind in Sri Lanka. Such persons were often refused visas or turned back at borders. See N. Chandrahasan, "A Precarious Refuge: A Study of the Reception of Tamil Asylum Seekers into Europe, North America and India", *Harvard Human Rights Yearbook* Vol. 2, (1989).

[10] "Special Protection for Sri Lankan Tamils", *Refugees* (Feb. 1987), p. 28.

[11] For example, in Africa, Ethiopian refugees were given shelter in Somalia and Sudan; Angolans were given shelter in the Central African Republic; Mozambique refugees in Malawi, Tanzania and Zimbabwe. In Asia, Thailand has granted refuge to persons fleeing Vietnam, Laos and Kampuchea; India has accommodated refugees from East Pakistan and Sri Lanka; and Iran and Pakistan refugees from Afghanistan.

[12] In Sri Lanka, for example, approximately 800,000 persons were displaced within the country during the civil war; in Mozambique, around 2 million people. See "Uprooted Mozambicans: An Appeal for Support", *Refugees* (June, 1990), p. 32.

attacks by the rival forces, are no less refugees, although they may not have had the good fortune to cross an international boundary.

In countries of Asia and Africa which have accepted refugee influxes, the refugees are being dealt with within the boundary of humanitarian considerations rather than refugee law. Many of the countries concerned, for example India, are not parties to the Refugee Convention and have no official refugee determination processes. Hence, there has been no differentiation between *de jure* and *de facto* refugees. In India, Tamil asylum seekers coming over from Sri Lanka are registered on arrival as a family and then sent to refugee camps in different parts of the State. They are provided with certain basic items such as clothes, mats for sleeping and cooking utensils.[13] Although family members are sometimes divided and sent to different camps as a result of arriving at different times by boat, and separation caused while fleeing, in general camp authorities attempt to rectify this and re-unite families where it is brought to their attention.[14] This is done on humanitarian grounds but shows a recognition of the principle of family unity.

The UNHCR has consistently been attempting actively to implement the principle of family unity.[15] Activities which it undertakes to meet this end include helping to trace missing family members; co-ordinating training and re-unification efforts among governments; endeavouring to see that unaccompanied minors are not re-settled or adopted before efforts have been made to trace family members; and assisting family members to receive the same status as the refugees with whom they are re-uniting. The UNHCR also takes action to ensure that refugee marriages are legally recognized and arranges for official recognition of new marriages and divorces. This recognizes the fundamental human right of adults to marry and establish a family.

The UNHCR, in providing assistance to refugees, follows an integrated approach. (This aspect of its work is set out in the "UNHCR Handbook for Social Services".[16]) In order to prevent social problems among refugees, the Handbook advocates the promotion of family unity as a preventive measure. It states:

> "When refugees leave their country of origin, family members are often separated. Pressures may develop after arrival in a country of asylum and cause further separation. For humanitarian and social reasons, as well as to improve the ability of refugees to achieve self support it is imperative that efforts are made to prevent family separation and to assist separated families to re-unite. It is envisaged that preventing separation and helping families

[13] Hindu (Madras), "Dole Raised for Sri Lankan Repatriates, Refugees" (June 29, 1990).

[14] Hindu (Madras) "Refugee Families to be Re-united", (September 9, 1990).

[15] The guidelines for UNHCR policy in regard to its protective function are set out in the "Conclusions" adopted by the Executive Committee of the UNHCR on International Protection of Refugees. These conclusions have frequently re-iterated the principle of protection of families and the unity of the family. See particularly Conclusions 9, 22 and 24.

[16] UNHCR Handbook for Social Services, Provisional Edition, (Feb. 1984), Geneva.

re-unite can reduce the number of refugees needing special assistance, and that the following groups in particular would benefit from re-unification; i.e. unaccompanied minors, the elderly, the disabled, and families headed by single parents."

In its definition of "family" the UNHCR Handbook states, "Outside the nuclear family, others who are socially or economically dependent on a family unit can in certain circumstances be considered for re-unification."[17] The Executive Committee of the High Commissioner's Programme has also encouraged countries of asylum to apply liberal criteria in identifying family members who can be admitted with a view to promoting comprehensive re-unification of the family.[18] The work of the UNHCR in this field can be regarded as a pragmatic application of refugee law.

The term "family" can be used to denote the "nuclear family" consisting of the father, mother and minor or dependent children who are living in the household. This is the modern concept which is followed in the Western countries and in many parts of the world today. In such a context, it is in all probability this concept of the family which is referred to in the Final Act of the 1951 U.N. Conference on the Status of Refugees and Stateless Persons, which recommended that the principle of family unity be applied by governments, and particularly where the head of the family has fulfilled the necessary conditions for admission to a particular country.

However, it must be pointed out that there are variations to this pattern, and cultural diversity. For example, in India we have the joint family system which is recognized under Hindu law.[19] Under this system the male children, even after they have established their own families, continue to live together in a common parental home, and the ancestral property is held in common by the male members of the household. In these cases, the family unit would consist of the spouses, the sons and their families, and the unmarried daughters if any. In such families, the question arises whether all the members of such an extended family could claim refugee status on a derivative basis where the head of the family has fulfilled the necessary conditions for admission to a particular country. In African tribal societies we also find extended family systems, and this may be the case in some Islamic societies where monogamy is not the rule.

The term "head of the family", although used in the Recommendations of the Final Act of the UN conference, has no significance today. There are no rules which lay down who is the head of the family. In earlier times, the father was so considered mainly because he was the breadwinner. Today, when working wives are the rule, this classification does not hold. War and situations of conflict can also change family relationships and social values. For example, in the war-torn society of Jaffna in Sri Lanka, commentators[20] have pointed to

[17] Ibid., Chapter 2, S:2.1, p. 6.
[18] Conclusion 24, para 5.
[19] S. Venkataraman, "A Treatise on Hindu Law", Part II, Chapter IV.
[20] "Jaffna-Peace Amidst War", *Tamil Times* Vol. VII, No. 12, (November, 1988).

the changed role of women, who have increasingly taken over the role of running businesses and earning and providing for the family, in a context where many of the men have fled and others are afraid to carry out these duties in the face of attacks by the armed forces. This is also the case in many of the war-ravaged States in Africa[21], where the women work the fields and are in many instances the breadwinners of the family.

It has now become a customarily established rule of a legal character that members of the immediate family of a refugee are entitled to refugee status.[22] In such cases the refugee status conferred on members of the family would be derivative. However, in order to qualify as a family, the marriage would have to be a going concern.[23] Spouses who are divorced cannot claim derivative status from the other. In regard to children, minor children could claim such status. Dependent children living in the household may claim derivative status, but once they have left the household, and particularly where they have established their own households, they can no longer claim to be assimilated to the status of the parents. As one commentator points out, the terms "household" or "living together" should not be understood literally. The decisive factor in determining the term "household" is that the family's sense of belonging and unity should not have been lost.[24] In all these instances where one member has a claim to refugee status qualifying under article 1(A) of the Refugee Convention, the other members of the family also can claim a derivative status.

The dependency of the family members on such a member need not be pecuniary, but could also be emotional or psychological dependency or interdependency. Thus, for example, an aged mother or father dependent on their children, or even a younger brother or sister of one of the spouses, might still be regarded as a member of the household. In Asian families it is often the case that elder brothers or sisters who have been educated by the parents are in turn expected to educate and look after the younger members of the family even after they themselves have married. Thus, a household could constitute such people as well, who would be dependants. The Executive Committee of the High Commissioner's Programme probably had such categories in mind when it recommended to countries of asylum that "they apply liberal criteria in identifying family members who can be admitted with a view to promoting comprehensive re-unification of the family".[25]

Apart from derivative status, members of a family may also be able to claim a presumption of equal status, along with the individual who initially makes the claim. Where an individual has a reasonable fear of persecution on any of the first four grounds mentioned in the Convention, namely nationality, race, religion or membership of a group, the members of the family of the persecuted

[21] *Refugees*, June 1990; See under African States.
[22] A. Grahl-Madsen, "The Status of Refugees in International Law", Vol. I. (1966) at p. 416.
[23] Ibid., S:152.
[24] Ibid., principle of family unity, pp. 412–432.
[25] See note 18, *supra*.

individual would also be presumed to have a reasonable fear of persecution as they would fall into the same category. Even where the husband or wife belongs to a different group, the very fact of marriage could become a reason for persecution, and even children of such unions could be subjected to persecutions. In the instance of group-specific persecutions and genocide, as in the case of Jews in Nazi Germany, all members of that group, irrespective of age or sex, have an equal claim to recognition as refugees. It must be pointed out that although civil wars and internal strife are not a ground under the Convention, such conflicts, particularly in the post-colonial African and Asian States, are often the outcome of inter-tribal and inter-ethnic tensions. In such situations, although there may be no explicit persecution of the tribe or ethnic group *per se*, all members belonging to a tribe or ethnic group could be potential victims of persecution. The refugee determination processes of many Western countries do not sufficiently consider this aspect, and the general situation of civil strife is treated as precluding a finding of persecution under the 1951 Convention.[26] Family members could also be subjected to indirect persecution, for instance, where, the breadwinner of the family is killed or held in a detention camp or deprived of his or her possibility of earning a living. This could seriously harm the members of a family. Families of militants or persons fighting against the State may themselves be denied employment or prevented from earning their livelihood.[27]

The fifth ground set out in Article 1A(2), namely "well-founded fear of persecution for reasons of political opinion", does not necessarily give rise to the presumption of persecution of family members, unless of course they too profess the same political opinion. Persecution on grounds of political opinion could cover all kinds of opposition or non-conformity to the regime and could involve persons of both sexes as well as different age groups. Examples of this include college students in the agitation for democracy in China and Nepal, as well as members of mother fronts protesting against disappearances in Chile and Argentina. Family members of those involved in political opposition to a regime could be potential victims of persecution in repressive regimes where political conformity is imposed by the taking hostage of family members, or where death squads are used to eliminate family members in revenge, or as a deterrent, by both government and anti-government forces.[28] In such situations the family members also would have a claim to refugee status in their own right on grounds of direct or indirect persecution. In Asian and African societies, where the "family" is a more broadly based institution, a wider category of persons having relationship to the targeted individual could find themselves threatened and hence eligible to be recognized as refugees in their own right.

[26] Chandrahasan, see note 9, *supra*, pp. 63–67.

[27] For example, in Sri Lanka in the period 1983–1987 the Government set up surveillance zones and prohibited zones in the seas bordering the Indo-Sri Lankan frontiers. Large numbers of Tamil fisher folk could not make a livelihood because of these restrictions and fled to India as refugees. Many of the militants fighting the Government forces were from these families.

[28] For example, during the J.V.P. insurgency in Sri Lanka in 1989.

In these ways, refugee law has been extended to provide protection to family members too, and is the source of the norms which guide States in admitting and giving protection to the family. A person who at a relevant time has been a refugee by reason of well-founded fear of direct or indirect persecution continues to be a refugee until he or she falls under one of the cessation clauses enumerated in the Convention.[29] But a person who has only been recognized as a refugee by application of the principle of family unity and who never has had any well-founded fear of being persecuted directly or indirectly, may lose refugee status when the family unit to which he or she has belonged is dissolved. For example, by the death of parents, or when he or she breaks away from the family unit. His or her own spouse and children with fall outside the scope of the Ad-Hoc Committee's statement and will have no legal claim to derivative refugee status. Grahl-Madsen points out that this prevents the danger of refugee status being perpetuated in certain families, except where there continues to exist a well-founded fear of being persecuted upon one's eventual return to the country of origin.

The Refugee Convention also provides protection to the refugee in the country of refuge by setting out a standard of treatment to be accorded to refugees which is largely based on human rights norms and standards. It spells out the refugee's rights with respect to employment, primary and higher education, public relief, labour legislation, social security, freedom of movement and the issue of travel documents. It also imposes upon State Parties an obligation not to return a refugee to a country where he or she may be subjected to persecution, that is the principle of *non-refoulement*.[30] However, it should be kept in mind that these provisions apply only to those persons who can bring themselves within the Convention definition of a refugee, therefore excluding the category of *de facto* refugees. The Convention also facilitates the process of naturalization for those persons accepted as Convention refugees.

The right to work, which is essential for the support and well-being of the family, is set out in the human rights instruments.[31] The Convention refugee has the right to engage in wage-earning employment and to be accorded the most favourable treatment accorded to foreign nationals in the same circumstances. The Contracting States are also enjoined to give sympathetic consideration to assimilate the rights of refugees in this respect to that of nationals. However, asylum seekers and other *de facto* refugees are not accorded this right. In some countries, for example Canada, work permits are given to asylum seekers while their claims are being processed. In other countries, West Germany for example, asylum seekers are not permitted to work, although they are given social security. But this too is sometimes linked to the performance of certain types of work, or may be provided in kind, that is to say, food and accommodation arranged by the Government.

[29] Article 1.C(1)–(6) of the 1951 Convention.

[30] Ibid., Articles, 17, 18, 22, 23, 24, 26, 28 and 33.

[31] Article 23, Universal Declaration of Human Rights, Articles 6 and 7, International Covenant on Economic, Social and Cultural Rights.

Refugees in camps in African and Asian countries are generally sustained by cash doles and provisions provided by the government, the UNHCR and other voluntary organizations such as the Red Cross. But in many of those countries, refugees living outside the camps sustain themselves by self-employment. For instance, Tamils in India and Afghans in Pakistan have opened small businesses whereas Liberian refugees in the Ivory Coast and Mozambique refugees in Malawi and other neighbouring states have taken plots of land for cultivation or worked on the land of the villages.[32] Even refugees in the camps may sometimes be permitted to do wage-earning work in the vicinity of the camps.

Employment activity helps families to sustain themselves, and it is also psychologically beneficial to the individual family members. Commentators have pointed out that life in refugee camps can bring about many psychological problems which affect the male more than the female members of families. While the women can still perform traditional roles within the home, the men have no major activity to occupy them. The situation makes them idle and redundant. The consequent breakdown of the male role may lead to such problems as violence within families, alcohol and drug abuse, and men abandoning their families. This analysis is borne out by accounts of emotional depression and outbreaks of violence among Tamil asylum seekers in the West.[33] Bearing in mind the human right to work, some provision should be made to allow refugees who are awaiting the processing of their application, and those given temporary refuge, the opportunity to work, within the constraints placed by economic conditions in the host countries.

The provisions in the Convention dealing with education are those which affect family members, namely the children, of refugees most of all. Article 22 states that the Contracting States shall accord to refugees the same treatment as is accorded to nationals with respect to elementary education. It should be recalled that the Universal Declaration of Human Rights provides that everyone has a right to education, and International Covenants on Economic, Social and Cultural Rights also reiterate that primary education shall be compulsory and freely available. It has been held that even children of illegal immigrants have a right to such education. Hence, children of refugees, without distinction according to whether they be *de jure* or *de facto* refugees, should be accorded this right of elementary education. However, in most Third World countries, with a few exceptions,[34] most refugee children go without education.[35] In some parts of the world, refugee girls are particularly deprived. In many of the African countries it is the shortage of trained teachers and the

[32] See note 21, *supra*.

[33] Greenberg, "Tamil Refugees", *The Nation* (Sept. 13, 1986); and *Hindu* (Madras) (July 2, 1987, and *L.A. Times*, (April 9, 1989).

[34] In Tamil Nadu India, for example, refugee Sri Lankan Tamil children were enroled in schools in the vicinity of the refugee camps.

[35] According to UNHCR Statistics, in 1987 less than 1 in 10 of the children receiving assistance from UNHCR were enroled in schools. In Eastern Ethiopia, for example, only 5% of the young Sudanese refugees attend primary school. Among Chadian refugees in Western Sahara, the

lack of appropriate educational material and other facilities which have brought about this situation, and not a discriminatory policy as such. In 1987, the UNHCR Executive Committee called upon all States individually and collectively to intensify their efforts to ensure that all refugee children benefit from primary education. Most recently, the 1990 World Conference on "Education for All", declared that an active commitment must be made to removing educational disparities, especially for under-served groups such as refugees and displaced people.

In respect to higher education, the Convention enjoins the Contracting States to accord to refugees treatment as favourable as possible, and, in any event, not less favourable than that accorded to aliens generally in the same circumstances. It is generally in the context of this provision that a distinction is made between the *de facto* and the *de jure* refugees. In the allotment of places in universities and technical colleges and recognition of foreign degrees and certificates, it is only those refugees who have been officially recognized, who are given the benefit of these provisions. However, in some countries like India, where there is no refugee determination process, there is no distinction made between *de jure* and *de facto* refugees and *de facto* refugees have been given the same treatment.[36]

The Convention also makes provision for public relief, labour legislation and social security to be applied to refugees. It enjoins the same treatment as that accorded to nationals, so that laws and regulations relating to remuneration including family allowances, hours of work, over-time arrangements, holidays with pay, restrictions on home work, minimum age of employment, apprenticeship and training, women's work, etc., are to be made applicable to Convention refugees.[37] These provisions are beneficial to the families too. Similarly, social security, that is legal rules in respect of employment, injury, occupational diseases, maternity sickness, disability, old age, death, unemployment, etc., should be made applicable. These provisions do not, however, cover *de facto* refugees. Many such persons are illegally employed by employers, who are therefore able to exploit them.

Freedom of movement is also accorded to Convention refugees, who have under the Convention the right to choose their place of residence and to move freely within the territory of the refuge State. This allows families to live together in a place of their own choice. In the case of *de facto* refugees and asylum seekers, restrictions are often placed on their freedom of movement. It has become the practice in most Western European countries, such as

---

proportion of refugee children receiving education is less than 1%. Similarly, in the Liberian crisis, thousands of refugee children who received education in their own country are now deprived of education. See *Refugees*, September 1990.

[36] The Sri Lanka Tamil refugees were given treatment as favourable as possible, and special allocations made for them in the higher educational institutions over and above the quota allocated for foreign students.

[37] Article 24, 1951 Convention.

Germany, the Netherlands and Switzerland, to put asylum seekers into what are called reception centres or collective accommodation. In the Federal Republic of Germany the law prescribes that they must be accommodated in collective housing. Apart from this, detention of asylum seekers has also become common.[38] Detention is generally mandated by administrative orders, under which persons are committed to prisons or remand centres. Such detention affects family members and in these instances refugee law has not been able to offer any protection to the refugee. It should not be forgotten that freedom of movement as well as the right not to be subjected to arbitrary arrest or detention are basic human rights and should apply to all categories of persons, without any differentiation.

Convention refugees are entitled to travel documents.[39] The Convention makes it mandatory for the Contracting States to issue such documents to refugees staying in their territory. *De facto* refugees are not entitled to such documents and this often creates problems for them in their search for durable asylum. Travel documents are necessary for family members wishing to relocate from the country of first flight to a third country where there are family members or greater chances of obtaining durable asylum. The inability to obtain travel documents has led to the practice among some refugees of using forged passports and visas, which in turn is treated by immigration authorities as a ground for refusing refugee claims and barring admission.[40]

Refugee law also provides protection for the refugee and his or her family by way of the principle of *non-refoulement*, which prevents a Contracting State from expelling or returning a refugee to a country where his life or freedom would be threatened on account of one of the grounds set out in Article 1A(2) of the Convention. Although *de facto* refugees do not come within the scope of the Convention provisions, in practice, States have tended to give a liberal interpretation to this provision. Even in Western countries, those *de facto* refugees who have managed to gain admission have not in general been forced to go back and have been allowed to remain on humanitarian grounds. In countries not parties to the Convention, the granting of temporary asylum may be regarded as a tacit acceptance of this principle. To some extent it has also protected *de facto* refugees. However, in some countries, notably those in South-East Asia, the forcible turning away of refugees may in fact result in their being forced to return to the country where their life is endangered.

Apart from the right of non-return to a country where one's life is endangered, the right to leave and to return to one's country of origin are also important and are recognized as human rights. The Executive Committee of the UNHCR in its Conclusions on family re-unification refers to this. It has stated that "given the recognized right of everyone to leave any country including his

[38] See note 9, *supra*.

[39] Article 28, 1951 Convention.

[40] For example, the case of the 52 Tamils at Heathrow Airport, in Feb. 1987. See "Tamil Asylum Seekers – Implications for British Asylum Policy and Carriers Liability. *Report of British Refugee Council* (April, 1987).

own, countries of origin should facilitate re-unification by granting exit permission to family members of refugees to enable them to join the refugee abroad."[41]

CONCLUSION

The foregoing examination of the effects of refugee law on the family shows that human rights principles and norms have helped the progressive development of refugee law in this field. It is submitted that new developments and remedies for the restructuring of refugee law could also constructively borrow from and develop human rights principles and norms.

One of the major defects in the present law is, as we have seen, the restricted definition of "refugee" in the Refugee Convention, which has the effect of denying to a large number of Third World refugees the protection developed in refugee law, and thereby to the family also. The UNHCR has sought to enlarge its mandate and to give protection to all categories of refugees and even displaced persons. However, ultimately it is the States that have to apply refugee law. As matters stand, it lies in the discretion of states to give a strict or more liberal application to the provisions of the Convention, which in a climate of political reluctance is not a desirable situation. This calls for a revision of refugee instruments.

The evolution of new rights and remedies must take into account the problems faced by refugee families in their flight to third countries, as well as in the country of origin. Human rights law has enunciated two rights that have a bearing on the problems of refugees and it is submitted that we can build on these rights. One is the right to seek asylum and the other is the right not to be exiled.

As we have seen, the greatest number of refugees, particularly in the Third World, are fleeing from conditions of civil war and generalized violence. What is threatened is their very lives. The only means of saving themselves is to obtain at least temporary refuge in a third country, together with a guarantee that they will not be returned to the place where their lives are endangered. In such situations, it could be argued, the grant of asylum becomes in fact a corollary to the right to life, which is a basic human right. Refugee law has not been able to formulate a right of asylum mainly because asylum is still regarded as a prerogative of the receiving State, although the mandatory requirement of *non-refoulement* contained in the Convention gives the refugee some guarantee of security. However, a right to asylum as a corollary to the human right to life could be developed within the framework of human rights law, which would in turn buttress provisions of the Convention.

The outflow of vast groups of people from regions or localities within a State consequent upon civil wars and generalized violence also raises the question of

[41] Conclusions 24, on Family Re-unification, para. 4.

providing preventive strategies focusing on the responsibilities of the State of origin to safeguard its own people. The movements of refugees often belonging to specific tribal, ethnic or religious groups from particular localities or regions could be viewed as forced migrations, and this includes displaced persons. The Universal Declaration states that "no one shall be subjected to arbitrary arrest, detention or exile."[42] The reference to "exile" here, although framed in terms of individuals, could be extended to include groups and hence act as a prohibition against forced migrations. However, the positive aspect is not sufficiently emphasized. Consequently, it would no doubt be preferable to develop a separate human right to a secure habitat or domicile, and thus protect the right of people in general to live in their own land and the people of a region, whether they be tribal or ethnic, to security of domicile within their own region.

Such a right is beneficial to family units as it seeks to protect the family within its own environment. The integration of the family with its geographical and social surroundings is important for the well-being of the family. Furthermore, the exercise of rights has not only a material or ideological content but also a local or regional aspect. Men and women can best enjoy the rights and protections accorded to them within the socio-geographical surroundings forming part of their personal and family tradition.[43] The driving away of people from their own localities or regions is in fact an invasion of their basic liberties. This notion takes into consideration environmental concerns as well, and the human being's interaction with his or her own environment.

It is arguable that new rights are not necessary and serve no purpose. However, it cannot be denied that the assertion of a new right does have an impact in that it focuses attention on a particular matter and, by internationalizing an issue, builds up solidarity. Furthermore, in this instance, the objective would be to pinpoint the responsibility of governments to provide their people with a secure habitat. In the case of those governments who are themselves responsible for such forced migrations, the onus is placed on them as the violators of a human right. It would also serve to emphasize the notion that the state of refugeehood itself is a denial of a human right.

[42] Article 9.

[43] Kurt Rabl, *Indian Year Book of International Affairs* (1966), p. 45.

JAMES C. HATHAWAY*

Reconceiving Refugee Law as Human Rights Protection

International human rights law is fundamentally a means of delimiting State sovereignty. Human rights – including respect by States for a sphere of freedom, a commitment to meeting basic needs, and the sharing of resources to effect these purposes – establish a benchmark for a government's right to claim sovereign authority over a people. A State which does not respect these essential constraints on its autonomous authority fails the test of minimum international legitimacy.

Yet because international human rights law is designed and implemented by States which see themselves as fundamentally self-governing, and which admit only reluctantly to a limited range of shared values and interests, the type of collective consensus needed to drive a meaningful body of law is largely absent. In particular, its implementation structures are generally sluggish and only occasionally effective. The divergence between the theory and the reality of international human rights law is strikingly apparent.

This paper examines the potential for a closer relationship between the international law of refugee protection and the regulation of authentic State sovereignty through international human rights law. Larger questions of the moral legitimacy and continuing political viability of the nation State system are not addressed here, the assumption being that international lawmaking in at least the medium term is likely to remain very much within the province of a disparate group of governments. The strategic challenge to reformers is thus to frame the human rights vision of refugee protection in a way which takes reasonable account of the perceived self-interest of States, and hence stands a chance of adoption and meaningful implementation.

* Associate Dean, Osgoode Hall Law School of York University, Toronto. The helpful comments on an earlier draft by Deborah Anker, Lisa Gilad, Andrew Shacknove and the participants at the 1991 meeting of the International Research and Advisory Panel of the Refugee Studies Programme, Oxford, are gratefully acknowledged.

K.E. Mahoney and P. Mahoney (eds.), Human Rights in the Twenty-first Century, 659–678.

1. The Dilemma of International Refugee Law

Its rhetoric of humanitarianism aside, refugee law as it exists today is fundamentally concerned with the protection of powerful States.[1] It is also increasingly perceived by powerful States to perform that role inadequately.[2]

From its inception, refugee law has been a means of reconciling the commitment of States to discretionary control over immigration to the reality of coerced international movements of persons between States. It has long been understood that failure to define and regulate involuntary migrations would leave States vulnerable to a multiplicity of needs-driven claims to entry, not all of which would be reconcilable to their perceived self-interest. By establishing a regime which purports objectively to define those with a preferred right to admission, refugee law legitimizes the protectionist norm. Because self-interest is taken into account in the definition both of refugee status and of the form of protection, a reasonable accommodation between the inevitability of special claims and the sovereignty of the States to which those claims are addressed is established.

The formal universalization of a refugee law initially designed and administered by European States for European refugees was accompanied by a substantive and procedural narrowing of the underlying commitment to protection.[3] Refugee law as codified in the 1951 Convention and 1967 Protocol relating to the Status of Refugees not only continues the original rejection of the notion of comprehensive assistance for all involuntarily displaced persons, but it allies international law with a series of strategic limitations determined by Western political objectives. It is premised on a Eurocentric notion of burden-sharing, and defines need in terms which exclude most refugees from the less developed world. It is both substantively and procedurally malleable at the instance of State Parties, with no effective form of international supervision. In the result, contemporary international refugee law is marginal to the protection of most persons coerced to migrate, who must rather accept whatever emergency assistance or limited resettlement opportunities are voluntarily made available to them through various official and nongovernmental initiatives. The notion of refugee law as a rights-based regime is largely illusory.

Regional initiatives in Africa[4] and Latin America[5] have, at least in theory,

[1] This critique is elaborated in my earlier essay, "A Reconsideration of the Underlying Premise of Refugee Law" (1990), 31(1) *Harvard International Law Journal*, 129.

[2] "... [M]any States, some of whom were among the architects of the international refugee protection structures, are adopting responses to asylum-seekers attempting to enter their territories which result in denial of admission and hindering of access to procedures for determination of status": Executive Committee of the High Commissioner's (United Nations High Commissioner for Refugees – "UNHCR") Programme, "Note on International Protection", U.N. Doc. A/AC.96/750, August 27, 1990, at 5–6 ("EXCOM 1990").

[3] J. Hathaway, note 1, *supra*, at 143 ff.

[4] Convention Governing the Specific Aspects of Refugee Problems in Africa, concluded September 10, 1969, 1001 U.N.T.S. 14691, entered into force June 20, 1974 ("OAU Convention").

[5] Declaracion de Cartagena, approved by the 1985 General Assembly of the Organization of

expanded the range of protection available to refugees in those regions,[6] but the response of industrialized States of the northern hemisphere has been to constrain what few duties currently are owed to refugees. The inhumane charade of protection currently underway in Hong Kong[7] is only a more poignant manifestation of the general trend to restrictionism evident in, for example, American practices of carrier sanctions and interdiction at sea;[8] Canadian incorporation of "safe third country" screening in its legislation;[9] Australian denials of due process to refugee claimants;[10] and, perhaps most appalling, European efforts systematically to constrain access to asylum through so-called harmonization of immigration policies.[11] In the face of all of

---

American States: reproduced in "Annual Report of Inter-American Commission on Human Rights 1984–1985", OEA/Ser.L/II.66, doc. 10, rev. 1, at 190–193 ("Cartagena Declaration"). See generally H. Gros Espiell et al., "Principles and Criteria for the Protection of and Assistance to Central American Refugees, Returness and Displaced Persons in Latin America", (1990) 2(1) *International Journal of Refugee Law*, p. 83.

[6] But see C. Gasarasi, "Durable Solutions to the Refugee Problem in Africa: An Elusive Subject", unpublished, 1991.

[7] Regarding policies of inhumane detention and forced repatriation of Vietnamese asylum-seekers in Hong Kong, see R. Mushkat, "Refuge in Hong Kong", (1989) 1(4) *International Journal of Refugee Law*, p. 449; and Amnesty International, "Memorandum to the Governments of Hong Kong and the United Kingdom Regarding the Protection of Vietnamese Asylum Seekers in Hong Kong" (1990).

[8] See E. Feller, "Carrier Sanctions and International Law", (1989) 1(1) *International Journal of Refugee Law*, p. 48. The U.S. Department of State has rationalized its interdiction of Haitian asylum-seekers by a narrow reading of Article 33 of the Convention, arguing that the duty of *non-refoulement* applies only to refugees already within the territory of an asylum State: M. Nash Leich, "Contemporary Practice of the United States Relating to International Law", (1989) 83(4) A.J.I.L. 905, at p. 906.

[9] See J. Hathaway, "Selective Concern: An Overview of Refugee Law in Canada", (1988) 33(4) McGill L.J. 676, at p. 705. This power has not yet been operationalized by regulation. Resort to a "country-of-first-asylum" principle has been criticized by UNHCR: "Not only is this principle not a consideration necessarily to be taken into account under the definition, it is itself too ill-defined while concepts such as 'safe country' or 'transit country' lack satisfactory definition": EXCOM 1990, See note 2, *supra*, at pp. 6–7.

[10] See P. Hyndman, "Australian Immigration Law and Procedures Pertaining to the Admission of Refugees", (1988) 33(4) *McGill Law Journal*, p. 716.

[11] Of particular importance are the "Schengen Agreement" and "Dublin Convention." The Schengen process was commenced by a treaty among France, the Federal Republic of Germany, the Netherlands, Belgium and Luxembourg (*Tractatenblad*, 1985, 102) pursuant to which these States agreed gradually to remove border controls on joint frontiers. As part of this process, an Agreement on asylum controls was entered into on June 19, 1990: See H. Meijers, "Refugees in Western Europe: 'Schengen' affects the entire Refugee Law", (1990) 2(3) *International Journal of Refugee Law*, p. 428. The more far-reaching Convention Determining the State Responsible for Examining Applications for Asylum lodged in one of the Member States of the European Communities ("Dublin Convention") was signed by all members States of the E.E.C. except Denmark in June, 1990, and effectively limits asylum-seekers to adjudication of their refugee claim in a single E.E.C. country, the same to be identified under the rubric of the Convention. The text of the "Dublin Convention" is reproduced at (1990) 9(3) Refugee Abstracts 66. For a succinct critique of the European harmonization process, See Amnesty International, Harmonization of Asylum Policy in Europe (1990).

these efforts to minimize international refugee protection, the Office of the United Nations High Commissioner for Refugees has been either silent or a tacit co-conspirator,[12] since its negligible funding base makes it virtually entirely dependent on the continuing goodwill of the very industrialized States it ought to be attempting to influence.[13]

Ironically, the reform of refugee law is now on the international agenda,[14] not because the exacerbation of its protectionist tendencies has made it nearly irrelevant to meeting the needs of refugees, but rather because it is viewed by many powerful States as insufficiently attentive to their sovereign right to exclude aliens. Refugee law, as a system intended to contain and channel demands for protection, has proved vulnerable to the challenge of a small but visible minority of desperate humanity. Limited as the protections of international law are, developed States have increasingly sought to undercut even the duty to consider claims to asylum in an age of inter-continental – and inter-cultural – movement of persons.[15]

The only cause for optimism in this scenario is the fact that we are now at a point when fundamental questions about refugee protection can be asked in a receptive political context. While the impulse of powerful States has thus far been to push for a narrowing of current obligations, it may be possible to re-orient the discussion towards a fundamental re-definition of the international response. Insofar as that reformulation can be shown to be consonant with the

[12] Note, for example, UNHCR's response to European efforts dramatically to curtail access to asylum: "While UNHCR has some concerns about the content of certain of these rules, which it has already shared with the concerned countries, it nevertheless welcomes the fact that these agreements could help to resolve the serious, humanitarian problem of orbit cases": EXCOM 1990, note 2, *supra*, at p. 7. As Gervase Coles writes, perhaps with UNHCR's role in the repatriation of refugee claimants from Hong Kong in mind, "a mixed mandate for the Office to protect the individual and, at the same time, to assist States to exclude the individual is bound, in the difficult conditions of today, to lead the Office, as a United Nations body, into a perilous and, even ultimately, fatal situation where its impartiality and universality will be increasingly impugned": G. Coles, "Placing the Refugee Issue on the New International Agenda", unpublished, March 1990, at p. 63.

[13] The actual operating budget of UNHCR is nearly completely derived from the voluntary contributions of 15 developed States, all with Western political and economic structures: J. Hathaway, note 1, *supra*, at p. 161.

[14] Among the fora where the appropriate international legal response to involuntary migration is presently under discussion are the United Nations General Assembly, the Executive Committee of the UNHCR, the United Nations Commission on Human Rights, the United Nations Sub-Commission on the Prevention of Discrimination and Protection of Minorities, and the International Organization for Migration: G. Coles, note 12, *supra*, at 79 ff. See generally Refugee Policy Group, "Introducing Refugee Issues into the United Nations Human Rights Agenda" (1990).

[15] "The reaction among the receiving nations of the North, many of which were among the pioneers of refugee protection, has been, at first unilaterally but now with increasing co-ordination, to attempt to contain or 'regionalize' refugee problems; that is, to keep those in need of protection and solutions within their regions of origin": G. Goodwin-Gill, "Refugees: The Functions and Limits of the Existing Protection System", in A. Nash (ed.) *Human Rights and the Protection of Refugees under International Law* (1988), p. 152.

self-interest of the States which control the evolution of international law, it may even be possible to reconsider refugee law in the context of human rights obligations.[16]

(1) The Failure to Focus on the Right to Community

Gervase Coles takes up the challenge of re-thinking the human rights dimension of refugee protection by issuing a forceful challenge to the "exilic bias" of contemporary refugee law.[17] He argues that a human rights vision of refugee law requires a reformation to focus squarely on the effectuation of the refugee's right to re-join her community of origin, since the essence of the refugee problem "is the denial of individual freedom of movement in relation to the country of nationality by virtue of the compulsion to leave or stay abroad, i.e., the state of involuntary separation or exile".[18] Coles criticizes the persecution-based standard of refugee status on the ground that it is not logically the distinguishing feature of refugeehood, as persecution may also be feared by those still inside their home State.[19] Rather, it is the generally coercive nature of the refugee's separation from her home community which demarcates refugee status; and it is accordingly to the restoration of the ordinary bonds between citizen and State that refugee law should direct its energies.[20]

Coles attributes the marginalization of refugee law to an incomplete, anachronistic conceptualization of the problem which focuses on residence abroad as an acceptable answer to coerced migration. He contends that legal and institutional efforts which focus on the facilitation of opportunities for asylum are inconsistent with the refugee's right to return home,[21] and result in

[16] See e.g. Refugee Policy Group, "Refugees and Human Rights: A Research and Policy Agenda" (1989).

[17] "An assumption of external settlement as the correct durable solution to the refugee situation in structuring law and policy could not be justified on either humanitarian or political grounds. It would effectively relieve the country of origin of its serious responsibility to take whatever measures were possible and necessary to enable people who had fled its territory to return... and it would institutionalize exile at the expense of the fundamental rights of the individual to return to his country and to enjoy his basic human rights": G. Coles, See note 12, *supra*, at p. 10. See also Coles' earlier work on this theme, including "The Human Rights Approach to the Solution of the Refugee Problem: A Theoretical and Practical Enquiry", in A. Nash (ed.) *Human Rights and the Protection of Refugees Under International Law* (1988), 195; "Approaching the Refugee Problem Today", in G. Loescher and L. Monahan (eds.) *Refugees and International Relations* (1989), p. 373; and "Solutions to the Problem of Refugees and the Protection of Refugees: A Background Study", unpublished, 1989.

[18] G. Coles, note 12, *supra*, at p. 37.

[19] G. Coles, note 12, *supra*, at p. 38.

[20] "The refugee issue should be presented, therefore, as basically *not* one of admission to a receiving country, or of eligibility criteria or of migration controls, but as essentially that of the adverse conditions within the country of origin which are producing the transfrontier movement. If the refugee problem is ever to be solved, the solution must be basically that of those adverse conditions": G. Coles, note 12, *supra*, at p. 64.

[21] "Exile is generally an evil... since it is, by definition, an involuntary separation from the homeland": G. Coles, note 12, *supra*, at p. 31.

a skewed approach to protection which is not politically tenable in a world characterized by situations of mass exodus. While acknowledging that the protection of refugees while abroad remains of importance,[22] Coles calls for the re-orientation of efforts towards solution by voluntary repatriation in the context of "a comprehensive and coherent approach which is linked integrally to human rights generally".[23]

Coles is undoubtedly right that there will be no true solution to refugeehood in the absence of the restoration of the individual's right to re-join her community. If interpreted as an admonition to States to commit themselves simultaneously to the interim protection of involuntary migrants *and* to the promotion of human rights in countries of origin through a process of democratic development, his proposal is of tremendous value. There is, however, a very real risk that governments will seize on the Coles framework in order to divert attention from their failure to provide meaningful protection to refugees. The discussion and elaboration of long-term solutions to human rights abuse are perceived as less threatening to States because they have few immediate consequences. Agreements in principle and statements of intention are a small price to pay for a deflection of focus from the failure of the international community to come to grips with the protection needs of today's involuntary migrants.

The risk, then, of a merger of refugee law with international human rights law is that such a re-orientation may lead to the neglect of the needs of individuals and communities forced to migrate. Refugee law, intended to serve a strictly remedial or palliative function, has its own claim to legitimacy, distinct from the interventionist or facilitative mandate of international human rights law. There seems to be little to be gained in humanitarian or human rights terms from the collapsing of the interim protection function into the broader human rights struggle. Coles' call for enhanced coordination between the two bodies of law should therefore not be misconstrued to suggest a downgrading of the protection of involuntary migrants while abroad.

It is argued here that we must not accept the propriety of reconceptualizing refugee law as no more than a system to regulate or reform State behaviour. If refugee law is genuinely to reflect a commitment to international human rights, it is not enough that refugees be the intended beneficiaries of a system in which they have no voice. The human dignity of today's coerced migrants demands that refugee law reform guarantee refugees themselves the opportunity to leave situations in which their basic human rights are at risk, and that this goal not be sacrificed to the pursuit of long-term solutions. A new vision of the interim protection system must therefore be seen as a necessary adjunct to the systemically focused initiative proposed by Coles.

[22] "... [T]he interim protection of the refugee receives its full and necessary validation from the broad context of human rights which extends to every facet of the human situation and which must be oriented towards solution, including prevention and return as well as external settlement": G. Coles, note 12, *supra*, at p. 65.

[23] G. Coles, note 12, *supra*, at p. 70.

(2) The Absence of Inter-State Obligation

Jack Garvey has argued that the problem with refugee law is that it fails to pursue a human rights goal through politically pragmatic means.[24] Because refugee law is currently defined in terms of the relationship between individual refugee claimants and an asylum State (see Figure C, *infra*), it incorporates no mechanism to ensure the continuing viability of the protection system as a whole. This approach may have been workable in the post-War era when the States of origin and of asylum were Cold War ideological opponents, as a result of which the latter States welcomed refugees for political and economic reasons.[25] The countries from which refugees come today, however, are as likely to be strategic or trading partners as foes, and the value of the refugees themselves to States of asylum is questioned.[26] The assumptions upon which the current refugee law system is premised, therefore, are no longer accurate.[27]

Garvey's solution addresses the practical sustainability of a protection system. Specifically, he argues for a new approach to inter-State obligation which holds States legally accountable for the refugee flows they produce.[28] This would provide a source of compensation to States of asylum, thus making the reception of refugees a more palatable prospect. More important, the duty to compensate would deter States from allowing refugee-producing situations to emerge.

Garvey thus defines the appropriate role of refugee law to be akin to a system of tort law in which the parties are the States of origin and the States of asylum. However, the compensatory scheme may prove more illusory than real, since, as Garvey acknowledges, so many refugee-producing States lack the means to make restitution.[29] Moreover, viewed from the perspective of deterrence, there is no guarantee that the system will actually result in the improvement of human rights conditions. Rather, it may lead only to enhanced efforts by States to prevent the escape of their victims, lest the State be saddled with the cost of providing asylum.

Fundamentally, it must be recognized that Garvey intended his proposal to

[24] "It is in fact obvious – undeniable – that refugee flow imposes severe social and economic burdens on receiving States. Failing to pursue the legal implications of this, while insisting, as we must, on the principle of *non-refoulement*, ultimately undermines *non-refoulement*. Potential receiving States see themselves being asked for one-sided sacrifices, while a State that allows or actually induces the flow remains wholly unburdened": J. Garvey, "The New Asylum Seekers: Addressing Their Origin", in D. Martin (ed.) *The New Asylum Seekers: Refugee Law in the 1980s* (1988), 181, at p. 188. This essay draws in part on analysis earlier published by Professor Garvey in "Toward a Reformulation of International Refugee Law", (1985) 26 *Harvard International Law Journal*, p. 483.

[25] J. Hathaway, note 1, *supra*, at p. 169.

[26] See e.g. J. Crisp, "The high price of hospitality" (1990), 80 *Refugees Magazine*, p. 20.

[27] "It is evident that the refugee situation has fundamentally altered in character and that this necessitates changes in the asylum policies of States": EXCOM 1990, note 2, *supra*, at p. 8.

[28] J. Garvey, note 24, *supra*, at pp. 188–191.

[29] J. Garvey, note 24, *supra*, at p. 191, fn. 30.

address only one aspect of the refugee protection paradigm: it speaks to the necessity of creating a system of interrelated States, in which there is an incentive for protection to be offered.[30] To the inter-State dimension, then, a human rights derived system of refugee law would necessarily add some means to take account of the rights of refugees themselves. The value of Garvey's critique is his holistic sense of refugee protection, in which some form of international mechanism is established to ensure the continuing viability of asylum in a world governed by fiercely self-interested sovereign States.[31] Equally important is his insistence that pious admonitions to focus efforts solely on the causes of refugee movements may be little more than attempts to avoid dealing with the hard, immediate realities of coerced migration.[32]

2. Reconceiving Refugee Law as Human Rights Protection

The reform of refugee law should be premised, first, on the alignment of the interim protection function with Coles' vision of refugeehood. Fear of persecution by reason of one's civil or political status[33] is simply not an adequate definitional standard to embrace all those who require protection because they have been coerced to migrate. If the new systemic human rights focus of refugee law is to strive for solutions to the causes of all forms of coercive migration, it follows that all those forced to migrate should similarly be entitled to interim protection.

Second, any new system must take account of the unwillingness of States simply to open their doors to all who seek their protection. It is thus logical to endorse Garvey's call that inter-State obligation be squarely addressed as part of a new refugee protection system. In view of the serious risks to refugees of direct accountability between States of origin and asylum, the better approach

[30] "In today's context of growing reluctance on the part of receiving States, addressing the State of origin has become necessary not only to secure the latter's involvement and responsibility, but also to secure essential cooperation of the former towards constructive resolution of refugee crises": J. Garvey, note 24, *supra*, at p. 185. See also D. Ayling and S. Blay, "Australia and International Refugee Law: An Appraisal" (1989), 9(3) U. Tasmania L.R. 245, at 268 ff.

[31] "We begin with a cliched but unassailable verity about this world of sovereign States – that international law is respected where it represents mutual political interests or fear of political sanction. Our objective, therefore, must be to design the legal regime that best capitalizes on the political interests which cluster around refugee crises": J. Garvey, note 24, *supra*, at p. 182.

[32] "The natural tendency when we concentrate on 'root causes' is to perceive the refugee problem as a mere symptom, to be treated superficially pending fundamental political change. The policy conclusion that follows is this: real cure must wait": J. Garvey, note 24, *supra*, at p. 186.

[33] The term "civil or political status" signifies the five enumerated grounds in the Refugee Convention (race, religion, nationality, membership of a particular social group or political opinion), to which a fear of persecution must be related. See generally J. Hathaway, *The Law of Refugee Status* (1991), at Ch. 5.

to realization of this principle is through a binding regime of international burden-sharing.[34]

The critical third element of a new refugee protection system should be the reservation of a sphere of autonomy for the victims of human rights violations: any person whose basic human dignity is at risk in their home State must be empowered to leave the abusive situation. Refugee law should be an effective means of enabling persons to disengage from States which have forfeited their claim to international legitimacy by failure to adhere to core norms of human rights law.[35] Conceived in this way, refugee law would allow people to become directly and immediately involved in the process of calling attention to affronts to human dignity in their home State. By "voting with their feet", refugees deny a State's abuse of sovereignty to oppress.

One of the inherent weaknesses of international human rights law is the fact that it is largely constrained to the encouragement or facilitation of solutions to problems of a systemic nature. This approach may be a necessary accommodation to a world of sovereign States unwilling to renounce meaningful authority to a super-national authority, but it means that few of the millions of people currently denied basic human rights will themselves benefit from short or even medium term solutions to their own predicaments. As the wheels of international scrutiny of human rights slowly turn, people continue to suffer. Refugee law can be a means of beginning to address this inadequacy of international human rights law. Its essential premise would be the affirmation of an autonomous right of individuals and communities to access an interim remedy when continued residence in their own State ceases to be viable. Refugee law would therefore facilitate and complement the implementation of international human rights law, but would retain a distinctly palliative orientation.

(1) A New Conceptual Standard

While the conceptual narrowness of the Convention refugee definition is often ascribed to the inapplicability of the "fear of persecution" standard to the predicament of most contemporary involuntary migrants,[36] it is suggested here

[34] For example, an idea recently proposed would see the internationally funded purchase of easements in developing countries in which refugees could receive first asylum. UNHCR would have unobstructed access to the easement territory in order to supervise the quality of asylum: E. Burton, "Leasing Rights: A New International Instrument for Protecting Refugees and Compensating Host Countries", (1987) 19(1) *Columbia Human Rights Law Review*, p. 307.

[35] In view of its acceptance by the majority of the community of states, the International Bill of Rights (including the Universal Declaration of Human Rights and the two Human Rights Covenants) is suggested as an appropriate standard of core, internationally recognized human rights norms. The application of this approach to interpretation of the refugee definition is set out in detail in J. Hathaway, note 33, *supra* at Ch. 4.2 ff.

[36] See e.g. P. Hyndman, "Refugees Under International Law with a Reference to the Concept of Asylum", (1986) 60 *Australian Law Journal*, 148, at 149; and G. Melander, "The Protection of Refugees", (1974) 18 *Scandinavian Studies in Law*, 153, at p. 159.

that it is rather the Convention's insistence that fear of persecution be linked to the refugee's civil or political status which is most limiting. This privileging of the norm of non-discrimination[37] in relation to other essential attributes of human dignity accounts for the inapplicability of the Convention to most refugees today (see Figure A).

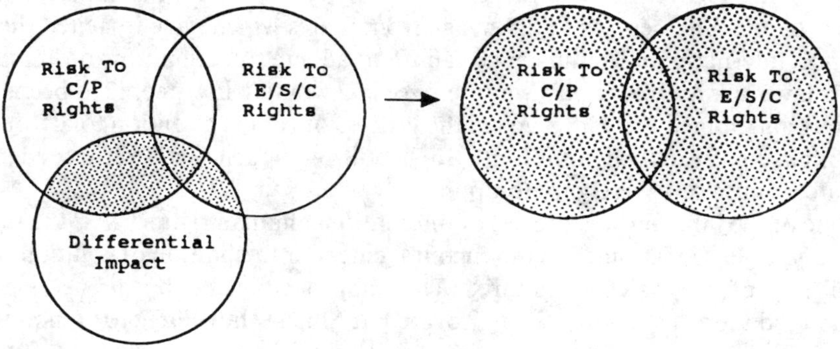

Fig. A Fig. B

Under current interpretations, refugee status requires a risk to basic human rights (predominantly to civil or political rights, though a risk to economic, social, or cultural rights is increasingly seen as sufficient), *in addition to* some differential impact based on civil or political status: Figure A. The proposal here is that refugee status become the entitlement of all persons whose basic human rights are at risk: Figure B.

The drafters of the Convention intentionally left the meaning of "persecution" undefined because they realized the impossibility of enumerating in advance all of the forms of maltreatment which might legitimately entitle persons to benefit from the protection of a foreign state.[38] Two basic tenets of the concept of persecution are nonetheless clear. First, the drafters viewed persecution as a broadly inclusive concept, premised on the risk of serious harm but not necessarily of consequences of life or death proportions. In addition to the Convention's acceptance of deprivation of basic civil and political freedoms as sufficient cause for international concern, serious social and economic consequences were also acknowledged to be within the purview of persecution. Second, the intention of the drafters was not to protect persons against any and all forms of even serious harm, but was rather to restrict refugee recognition to situations in which there was a risk of a type of injury that would be inconsistent with the basic duty of protection owed by a State to its own population.

These basic understandings of the notion of persecution – a liberal sense of the types of past or anticipated harm which might warrant protection abroad,

[37] Risk to basic human rights is not sufficient to establish a claim to Convention refugee status; *but for* some differential risk grounded in civil or political status, the claim to refugee status is not made out.

[38] See generally note 33, *supra*, at Ch. 4.0.

and a fundamental preoccupation to identify forms of harm demonstrative of a breach by a State of its basic obligations of protection – are of continuing relevance today. Fear of persecution can therefore remain a meaningful concept if interpreted in the light of these principles as they apply in modern context. Specifically, as advocated by the Committee on Population and Refugees of the Council of Europe,

> "... [T]he concept of persecution should be interpreted and applied liberally and also adapted to the changed circumstances which may differ considerably from those existing when the Convention was originally adopted... [A]ccount should be taken of the relation between refugee status and denial of human rights as laid down in different international instruments."[39]

This conceptualization of persecution as the failure of basic State protection demonstrated through the denial of core, internationally recognized human rights is a helpful means of breathing new life into refugee law. Because international human rights law is conceived as the means of defining the basic duties of States to their citizens, including both freedoms from interference and entitlements to resources, individuals ought not to be required to endure life in societies which fail to meet its standards. As argued and accepted in the decision of the French *Conseil d'Etat* in *Esshak Dankha*,[40]

> "the existence and authority of the State are conceived and justified on the grounds that it is the means by which members of the national community are protected from aggression, whether at the hands of fellow citizens, or from forces external to the State" (unofficial translation).[41]

Thus, the State which ignores or is unable to respond to legitimate expectations as defined in international human rights law fails to comply with its most basic duty, thereby giving rise to the prospect of legitimate disengagement from that community in favour of surrogate protection elsewhere.

Viewed from this perspective, the conceptual weakness of the Convention definition is its requirement that a refugee's fear of persecution derive from her race, religion, nationality, membership of a particular social group, or political opinion. In other words, under the Convention it is not enough that basic liberties or entitlements are in jeopardy. If the peril faced cannot in some sense be linked to civil or political status, the claim to refugee status fails (see Figure A, *supra*).

The theoretical rationale for this requirement derives from the deference of

[39] Resolution of January 1976 cited in remarks by J. Thomas in A. Woods (ed.) *Refugees: A New Dimension in International Human Rights* (1976), 70 A.S.I.L.P. 58, at p. 69.

[40] Decision No. 42.074, May 27, 1983.

[41] Conclusions of M. Genevois, Commisaire du Gouvernement, in *Esshak Dankha*, id., Reported in F. Julien-Laferriere, "Bulletin de jurisprudence francaise", (1984) 3 Clunet 119, at p. 122.

international law to national protection.[42] Refugee law has traditionally embraced only those persons who are fundamentally excluded from the national community, in the sense that it is unlikely that they will be in a position to vindicate their claim to protection from within their own country. Those whose human dignity has been infringed in a manner which is internally remediable by working within or to restructure the national community of which they are nominally a part have not been treated as refugees.

Given the primacy of the civil and political rights paradigm at the time of the Convention's drafting, it was contextually logical that this notion of fundamental marginalization should be defined by reference to norms of non-discrimination: a refugee was defined as a person at risk of serious harm *for reasons of* race, religion, nationality, membership of a particular social group, or political opinion. The rationale for this limitation was not that other persons were less at risk, but was rather that, at least in the context of the historical moment, persons affected by these forms of fundamental socio-political disfranchisement were less likely to be in a position to seek effective redress from within their State.

The formulation of the membership principle in terms of civil or political status, however, may be unhelpfully anchored in a particular era. In addition to the traditional Convention grounds, delegates to the abortive 1977 Conference on Territorial Asylum had agreed to extend status to persons at risk of "foreign occupation or domination".[43] The regional accord of the Organization of African Unity now recognizes "external aggression, occupation, foreign domination or events seriously disturbing public order"[44] as additional grounds of claim, while the Latin American Cartagena Declaration also embraces persons in flight from "generalized violence, foreign aggression, internal conflicts, massive violations of human rights or other events which have seriously disturbed public order".[45] These extensions are logical in human rights terms, and result in a refugee definition more in keeping with modern political reality.

The common bond among the various formulations is a need to demonstrate circumstances in which there is no reasonable prospect that meaningful protection will be forthcoming in the State of origin. Taken together with the essential meaning of persecution, refugee status should be the entitlement of any person or community for whom there is no reasonable likelihood of meaningful protection of basic human rights – whether civil, political, economic, social, or cultural – in their own State (see Figure B, *supra*). The role of refugee law should be to provide a source of interim protection for all such persons, until and unless the risk to human dignity in the country of origin ceases to exist. In this sense, refugeehood becomes an autonomous response

[42] See generally note 33, *supra*, at Ch. 5.0.
[43] A. Grahl-Madsen, *Territorial Asylum* (1980) p. 208.
[44] OAU Convention, note 4, *supra*, at Art. I(2).
[45] Cartagena Declaration, note 5, *supra*, at Conclusion 3.

to human rights abuse, and gives people some amount of direct control over their own lives. While not resolving the underlying human rights problems, refugee law would at least facilitate self-determination in situations where a State fails to meet minimum standards of legitimacy.

(2) Creating Political Sustainability

As Garvey makes clear, it is unrealistic simply to advocate a broadened notion of refugeehood without addressing simultaneously the structure of the protection regime (see Figure C). Indeed, since many States honour current obligations in only a half-hearted way, any attempt to impose more generous conceptual standards on the existing system would undoubtedly fail to attract State support. If governments are to undertake a duty to a more expansive class of refugees, there must be some structural inducement which will appeal to their sense of self-interest.

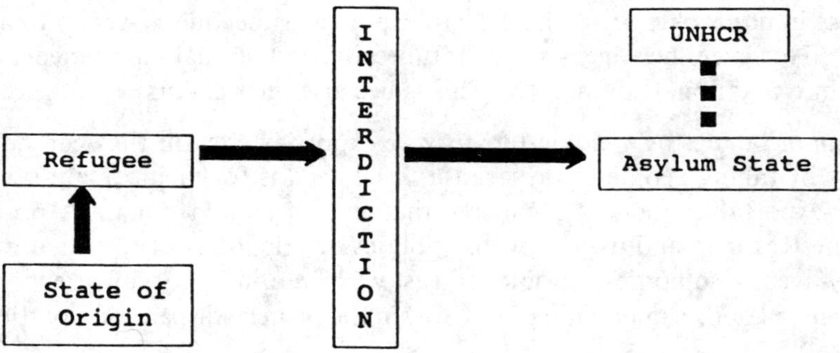

Fig. C

The current international protection system requires refuges successfully to navigate the interdiction schemes of states and then to satisfy an asylum state acting only loosely in concert with UNHCR that protection is warranted. Protection is ordinarily in the form of permission to remain in the asylum state.

Michael Walzer offers an eloquent analysis of the concept of membership in national communities.[46] While his theory does not explicitly address the international context,[47] it suggests a plausible construction of the *status quo* framework within which particular States consider issues of immigration policy.[48] It is therefore a helpful point of reference in designing a protection structure for refugees which is reconcilable to national self-interest.

[46] M. Walzer, *Spheres of Justice* (1983).

[47] *Id.* at p. 30.

[48] Reference is made to Walzer's theory not as an endorsement of his position, but rather because it appears accurately to reflect the dominant view of States. Walzer's theory has been attacked in particular for its implied equation of the nation with the State. See e.g. J. Carens, "Aliens and Citizens: The Case for Open Borders", (1987) 49 *Review of Politics*.

Walzer defends the general right of States to exclude non-citizens from membership in their community:

> "The distinctiveness of cultures and groups depends upon closure and, without it, cannot be conceived as a stable feature of human life. If this distinctiveness is a value, as most people (though some of them are global pluralists, and others only local loyalists) seem to believe, then closure must be permitted somewhere. At some level of political organization, something like the sovereign state must take shape and claim the authority to make its own admissions policy, to control and sometimes restrain the flow of immigrants."[49]

This position legitimizes the political decision of States to grant preference in admission to national or ethnic "relatives", as well as to those whose ideology conforms to the norms of the community. Walzer argues that this right of communal exclusion can be defended even in the face of claims by necessitous strangers, so long as the State is prepared either to alienate part of its territory to those in need, or more commonly to export its superfluous wealth to assist them.[50] However, he suggests that refugees have a special entitlement to be taken into a national community. This is because their claims

> "cannot be met by yielding territory or exporting wealth; they can be met only by taking people in... [because their] need is for membership itself, a non-exportable good. The liberty that makes certain countries possible homes for men and women whose politics or religion isn't tolerated where they live is also non-exportable: at least we have found no way of exporting it. These goods can be shared only within the protected space of a particular State.[51]

This assumption, however, warrants reconsideration in the light of Coles' position that refugee law should direct its energies toward the *restoration* of the refugee's right to membership in her home community.[52] Under the Coles paradigm,[53] the refugee has no need for a new form of membership as Walzer suggests, but only for meaningful protection pending the resumption of her

[49] M. Walzer, note 46, *supra*, at p. 39.

[50] "... [T]he collective version of mutual aid might require a limited and complex redistribution of membership and/or territory... The same difficulty arises with regard to wealth and resources. These, too, can be superfluous, far beyond what the inhabitants of a particular State require for a decent life... [In these circumstances members of the State] could share their wealth with necessitous strangers outside their country or with necessitous strangers inside their country": M. Walzer, note 46, *supra*, at pp. 47–48.

[51] M. Walzer, note 46, *supra*, at pp. 48–49.

[52] "... [A] refugee movement is a grave human rights issue... It is as destructive of the individual as of social well-being... [I]t is essential that countries of origin assume a significant responsibility in realizing solutions to today's refugee problems, including addressing root causes and facilitating return. Logic, equity and the current international climate towards receiving refugees in third countries all argue strongly for this position": EXCOM 1990, note 2, *supra*, at pp. 8–9.

[53] See text at note 16, *supra*, 16 ff.

rightful entitlement to membership in the State of origin. Except in the case of intractable situations of human rights abuse,[54] the special moral claim of refugees to integration in a new community is therefore suspect, and may indeed constitute an infringement of the refugee's right to be restored to full membership in her own society. This position opens the door to renewed analysis of the morally acceptable options to address the claims of refugees.

Specifically, it may be more appropriate to view most refugees simply as "necessitous strangers"[55] with no place to go, rather than as persons with a special entitlement to membership in a new community. Walzer's analysis suggests that two conclusions would flow from this characterization. First, refugees would have a legitimate claim based on principles of mutual aid to surplus territory or wealth to the extent necessary to meet their needs.[56] Second, account should be taken of the preference of States to admit "national or ethnic relatives", or those who are otherwise affiliated to the asylum state, and whose admission may therefore be seen to be less of an intrusion of a state's right to communal closure.[57] Taken together, these two principles offer the foundation for a new system of conceptually broadened refugee protection which is consonant with the claims of sovereign States to exclude most aliens, rather than existing as a theoretical exception to the general rule (see Figure D).

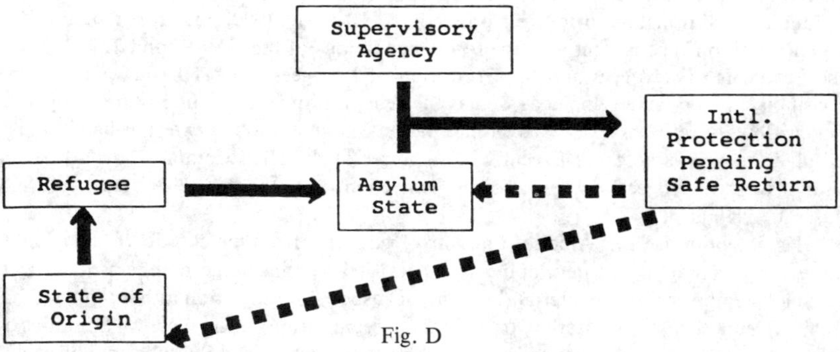

Fig. D

The proposed international protection system removes national interdiction schemes, and involves the international supervisory agency directly in the provision of first asylum, status determination, and the designation of appropriate protection (in the state of first asylum or elsewhere) pending the viability of safe return to the state of origin: Figure D.

[54] Law must, however, take account of the social reality of settlement and integration of refugees following a period of *de facto* residency. Thus, the norm of temporary refuge must at some stage be converted to permanent residency where there is no reasonable prospect of safe repatriation to the state of origin.

[55] M. Walzer, note 46, *supra*, at p. 47.

[56] M. Walzer, note 46, *supra*, at pp. 46–48.

[57] "Clearly, citizens often believe themselves morally bound to open the doors of their country – not to anyone who wants to come in, perhaps, but to a particular group of outsiders, recognized as national or ethnic 'relatives.' In this sense, States are like families rather than clubs, for it is a feature of families that their members are morally connected to people they have not chosen, who live outside the household. In times of trouble, the household is also a refuge": M. Walzer, note 46, *supra*, at p. 41.

First, the cornerstone of the system suggested here is that States must agree unequivocally to grant first asylum to persons arriving in their territory and identified as refugees by the responsible international authorities. No person who meets the conceptual threshold of refugee status should be turned away. This basic guarantee of access is essential for any system of international protection to function effectively.[58] As discussed below, however, refugees would not be guaranteed protection beyond the first asylum stage in the country of initial reception.

Second, there must be a legally binding, internationally administered system of resource sharing to meet the needs of refugee populations,[59] drawing broadly on the 1979 initiative to establish a Durable Solutions Fund.[60] To move the system in this direction, the current practice of forcing the international supervisory agency to rely on voluntary funding,[61] with oversight of programs by a politically and economically skewed Executive Committee, must come to an end.[62] The responsible international agency – whether a fundamentally re-tooled UNHCR or another organization[63] – must be allowed to respond to protection and material assistance needs at a moment's notice, and with fully

[58] "Both international conventions and customary international law reaffirm the prohibition against return or *refoulement* of a refugee to situations endangering life or freedom as one of the most fundamental principles of refugee protection": EXCOM 1990, note 2, *supra*, at p. 5.

[59] This position is consistent with the recommendations of the 1989 Round Table on Solution to the Problems of Refugees and the Protection of Refugees: "... [T]he law relating to State responsibility should be developed as well as the general principles of inter-State co-operation to avert new flows of refugees so as to cover international co-operation *after* a flow had begun or had taken place as well as before": Executive Committee of the High Commissioner's Programme, "Solution to the Refugee Problem and the Protection of Refugees", U.N. Doc. EC/SCP/55, August 23, 1989, at p. 9.

[60] "The intention [of this American initiative] was clear from the context of the proposal: to enhance the acceptability to developing countries of accepting large numbers of refugees for settlement by emphasizing the interim (i.e. durable) aspects of protection rather than its final (i.e. permanent) end (i.e. naturalization or voluntary repatriation)": G. Coles, "Solutions to the Problem of Refugees and the Protection of Refugees: A Background Study", unpublished, 1989, at 192. A subsequent Australian initiative on temporary refuge was discussed by the UNHCR Executive Committee in 1980, leading to the adoption of Conclusion 19 (XXXI) in which the study of temporary refuge, particularly in the context of mass influxes, was recommended: U.N. Doc. HCR/IP/2/Eng/REV.1986.

[61] "We have the authority to go out and look for a certain sum of money – just under US$ 350 million for General Programmes in 1991. But we have no guarantee of actually collecting that sum. There is no predictability about how much money will be pledged, when it will arrive, and what programme it will be earmarked for. It's a financial manager's nightmare, and something has to be done to ensure that we have a certain amount of core funding which we can rely upon every year": Deputy High Commissioner for Refugees Douglas Stafford, quoted in J. Crisp, "Managing the crisis", (1990) 80 *Refugees Magazine*, p. 41.

[62] See generally J. Hathaway, note 1, *supra*, at pp. 160–161.

[63] Research in the sphere of international organizations is clearly called for on the question of the relative merits of a reconstruction of UNHCR versus the establishment of a new agency to assume responsibility for international oversight of refugee protection. See e.g. J. Dacyl, "A Time for Perestroika (Restructuring) in the International Refugee Regime?", (1990) 3(1), *Journal of Refugee Studies*, p. 26.

adequate resources.[64] It must moreover be the effective representative of the international community as a whole, with the authority to intervene in relation to any instance of coerced international migration stemming from threats to basic human rights, and to make binding determinations of refugee status.[65] Most important, the international supervisory organization must be in a position to rely on firm assurances from State Parties that they will accept their fair share of those refugees who cannot readily be received in the country of first asylum.

Drawing on Walzer's notion of a moral duty to meet the claims of necessitous strangers, a system for sharing out the duty of refugee protection should be formulated on the basis of each State Party's resources and absorptive capacity. This framework would determine each State Party's *prima facie* responsibility for the admission of internationally identified refugees. Within the context of these allotments, the international authority would identify culturally appropriate sites of asylum for particular groups of refugees, organize the process of relocation, and supervise the quality of asylum provided to ensure compliance with international standards.[66]

For the most part, the result would be that poorer States would have a minimal duty to provide for refugees beyond the first asylum stage. Governments might be permitted, however, to assume part of another State's asylum quota in return for cash or development assistance on such terms as might be mutually agreeable, subject to approval by the supervisory agency. Less developed States might be willing to admit refugees beyond their quotas if the additional resources received would enable them to enhance the standard of living of their nation as a whole. Conversely, wealthier countries may feel that it is in their best interests to fund the transfer of part of their quota, rather than admit large numbers of refugees to their territory.[67] Through a consensual dynamic, however, no State would be compelled to enter into any arrangement not reconcilable to its own sense of self-interest.

Critical to the vision of refugee law as a system of interim protection of human rights, the international supervisory agency should not be a creature of States alone. Rather, it should draw on the expertise of human rights agencies

[64] "... [T]he economic and environmental consequences of providing asylum can be of such proportions that international material assistance is vital at an early stage. In some recent instances, government officials have suggested that the continued granting of asylum might be dependent on adequate resources being made available by UNHCR for those admitted to the territory": EXCOM 1990, note 2, *supra*, at p. 7.

[65] The predecessors to UNHCR engaged in refugee status determination of behalf of state parties. See generally J. Hathaway, note 1, *supra*, at pp. 166–167.

[66] The quality of asylum must meet the standards elaborated in Arts. 3–33 of the Refugee Convention, including respect for basic civil, political, social, economic, and cultural rights.

[67] This view is consonant with evolving policy in the United States "to promote mutually beneficial economic development so as – over time – to diminish the need for unilateral enforcement measures to control unauthorized immigration": Commission for the Study of International Migration and Cooperative Economic Development, *Unauthorized Migration: An Economic Development Response* xvi (1990).

and refugees themselves in determining refugee status, supervising the sufficiency of protection, and in monitoring the potential for the secure return of refugees to their home society. While there is no need for this agency to replicate the systemically focused, interventionist role of other international human rights organizations, it must come to see its role as fundamentally concerned with the facilitation of a refugee's right to be restored to her own community. It would thus be important that the supervisory organization assist in the communication of current human rights information to refugees, and provide them with the resources to repatriate when conditions are secure.

3. The Viability of Refugee Law Reform

The major "cost" of this new system would be the notion of an unrestricted right of a refugee to access enduring asylum in the State of his or her choice. This loss is, however, more apparent than real, since all but a very small minority of refugees – predominantly young, male and mobile[68] – either find protection in States adjoining their own or are unable to escape at all. In any event, it is increasingly clear that little remains of the institution of territorial asylum. Since the collapse of the effort to codify a right to claim asylum,[69] many States have successfully curtailed claims to refugee status by resort to visa, transportation and other access controls,[70] as well as through narrow interpretations of existing legal duties.[71] We are truly at a point where the existing regime of international refugee law offers protection to a small minority of involuntary migrants.[72] The proposal outlined here, in contrast,

[68] D. Indra, "Gender: A Key Dimension of the Refugee Experience", (1987) 6(3) Refuge pp. 3–4.

[69] For an account of the failure of the 1977 Conference on Territorial Asylum, A. Grahl-Madsen, note 43, *supra*.

[70] "Visa regimes and stricter passport requirements have proliferated, with nationals of countries from which refugees regularly come often being specific targets of such measures. Entry and access to full procedures has as a result become very much a function of prior authorization, with discretion to allow entry on the basis of need considerably curtailed by visa enforcement mechanisms such as indiscriminate sanctioning of airlines for carrying improperly documented passengers... [T]he concern is the inflexibility of the measures where asylum-seekers with valid refugee claims are involved and the fact that, in individual cases, persons in need may be denied protection": EXCOM 1990, note 2, *supra*, at p. 6.

[71] "... [A] number of States are increasingly adopting a narrow view of the scope of their Convention responsibilities. This is reflected in part in any interpretation of Article 1 of the Convention, containing the refugee definition, so that it is held to apply to only a very limited group of people": EXCOM 1990, note 2, *supra*, at p. 6.

[72] "Today, there is a gap between what is expected of international organizations and what States are prepared to concede as a matter of law; between the refugee and refuge; between *non-refoulement* and asylum; between protection and solutions; and often between the individual and the ideal of fundamental human rights regardless of nationality or status. Politics and prejudice in selection and asylum programmes often put ethnic origin, capacity for assimilation, history or advantage, above status and the human dimension of necessity": G. Goodwin-Gill, "The future of international refugee law", (1988) 57 *Refugees Magazine* 27, at pp. 28–29.

would guarantee meaningful protection to all victims of coerced migration until and unless they are able to rejoin their own communities.

Would a reform of the type suggested here be viable from the perspective of potential States of asylum? While empirical evaluation is clearly called for, several forms of inducement may be posited.

Less developed States, which currently host the substantial majority of the world's refugee population,[73] would benefit from a guarantee of international financial and logistical support in meeting the needs of persons seeking first asylum. Since any duty of reception beyond the first asylum stage would be a function of the State's available resources and absorptive capacity, most less developed countries would ultimately host only those refugees deemed to provide a net benefit to their society because, for example, they are culturally or otherwise "related" or because industrialized States prove willing to negotiate the transfer of reception quotas on terms acceptable to the less developed nations. In this way, the new refugee protection system would give poorer countries access to meaningful development assistance, and support the underlying philosophy of a new international economic order. Furthermore, since in all but the most intractable cases protection would be conceived as an interim form of relief pending return, community membership would not ordinarily need to be re-shaped.

For industrialized States, the primary benefits of the proposed protection regime are in terms of politics, predictability and the possibility effectively to control the entry of refugees. Politically awkward, expensive and only partially effective interdiction schemes could be abandoned, since no long-term consequences would follow from the arrival of refugees on their territory. The removal of authority for status determination to the international agency would minimize the scope for conflict between refugee protection and the pursuit of more general foreign policy goals, and could free-up the resources needed to support protection abroad.[74] Developed states would be afforded greater policy latitude, since they could elect to negotiate the transfer of portions of their admissions quota to other countries, rather than granting the right to remain beyond the first asylum stage to all refugees. The proposed restructuring of asylum policy also provides an answer to concerns about "irregular movements" of refugees, since the site of asylum would be determined by the supervisory agency. Most fundamentally, the ending of the assumption that the country of first asylum is ordinarily looked to as the source of enduring protection, together with the re-casting of protection as an interim duty pending return home, may fundamentally undermine the logic of many south-north refugee migrations.

All States would moreover benefit from the furthering of order in migration,

[73] EXCOM 1990, note 2, *supra*, at p. 7.

[74] Presently, industrialized States spend US$ 5–8 billion per annum on refugee determination schemes, more than ten times the total budget of UNHCR: See Refugee Policy Group, "The Ramifications of Soviet Emigration", unpublished, December 1990, at 4; and M. Moussalli, "Refugees – The Challenge of the Nineties", unpublished, December 1990, at p. 8.

with the concomitant enhancement of international security and stability. The shared preference of all governments for the regularization of potentially disruptive refugee flows simply cannot be unilaterally achieved:[75] the current decentralized protection regime has proved unable to respond to such concerns as the fair allocation of asylum seekers among the various State Parties to the Convention, and the need to take account of threats to national self-determination which may occur in the context of a large influx of refugees.[76] By working to establish a protection regime based on cooperative arrangements, however, some degree of administrative routinization can be achieved without jeopardizing the ability of refugees to access protection. The proposal advanced here attempts to address structural concerns of this kind, in the hope that in so doing it may be possible to convince States simultaneously to move toward a more holistic conceptual standard of refugeehood as human rights protection.

[75] "All of the above-mentioned challenges to the institution of asylum have had the combined effect in many regions of the world of making asylum less accessible. This is a major problem in itself. As important, however, is the spin-off effect on asylum policies of other countries. Unilateral measures limiting the availability of asylum in any country will inevitably have the effect of shifting the burden to other States": EXCOM 1990, note 2, *supra*, at p. 7.

[76] "Clearly, the arrival of large numbers of asylum-seekers and the absorption of some or all of them as refugees, even on a temporary basis, can create serious strains for host countries. This is particularly the case for the poorer communities where the ability and readiness of the host population and the government to shoulder the resulting burden may be severely affected by socio-economic problems": EXCOM 1990, note 2, *supra*, at p. 5.

SECTION IV(e): DEVELOPMENT AND HUMAN RIGHTS

PETRONELLA MARAMBA*

Introduction

The Right Honourable Joe Clark's paper serves as the lead paper for the section on Development and Human Rights.[1] Titled, "Human Rights and Democratic Development", his paper outlines Canadian foreign policy in this area. Mr. Clark stresses that human rights and democracy must be seen as key components of "functional, stable and prosperous societies."

In his view, the tools of democracy are the same as the tools of development. Education, the advancement of women, the rule of law, an independent press, freedom of expression and assembly are fundamental concepts underlying development assistance along with the recognition that societies which are more prosperous than others have a duty to assist the less prosperous in the spirit of partnership, practicality and friendship, not condescension or impatience.

Canada's position on conditional aid is flexible yet a principled one. This means that trends of improvement are respected as well as levels of development. Democracy is not the central criterion for development assistance because if it was, "we could end up rewarding the wealthy and punishing the poor". He says the end of the cold war may be the beginning of freedom and justice for all, not just a frill for the few.

The other papers in the chapter deal with the philosophical and political dimensions of development and human rights from both Western and Third World perspectives.

To adequately understand the relationship between development and human rights, it is first of all important to define the two terms. Although all three papers by Denis Goulet, Edward Broadbent and Clarence Dias deal with the definition of these terms, it is primarily Goulet who traces the different ways in which theorists have conceptualized development. Clarence Dias on the other hand, looks at what constitutes human rights.

Traditionally, development has always been inextricably linked with economic growth and hence a better life. According to Denis Goulet,

* Enda, Harare, Zimbabwe, Africa.

[1] Mr. Clark was a keynote speaker at the conference. He did not give his paper on the Development and Human Rights panel.

K.E. Mahoney and P. Mahoney (eds.), Human Rights in the Twenty-first Century, 679–681.

"development has been seen as simultaneously the vision of a better life, a life materially richer, institutionally more modern and technologically more efficient and an array of means to achieve that vision". He goes on to argue that when closely analyzed, however, development has tended to be nothing more than either mimetic Westernization or its antithesis. What has been termed "development" and therefore positive for a target group, particularly in the Third World has in fact tended to destroy old institutions, practices and solidarity networks and replaced these with Western institutions or practices. This factor has led to an outcry against present day "development" by Third World theorists who feel that economic growth does not always mean that such growth is positive and therefore benefits all. Recent formulations have however tried to include this component of equitable distribution of wealth but still leave the question of development's effects on cultural practices and institutions unanswered.

It is obvious that the definition of development cannot be exclusively economic, technological, organizational or managerial but must encompass all these aspects. One cannot take a monolithic viewpoint in defining or conceptualizing development. However, although Professor Goulet's paper tries to expose all various perceptions of development, it does not come up with an all encompassing definition of the term. (This may be proof of the ambiguity of the term that he talks of in the introductory part of his paper).

Using an essentially materialist approach, Clarence Dias looks at some of the myths surrounding Western thinking about human rights. In doing this, he identifies those at the grassroots level as the most affected by most forms of violation of human rights (that is at the political, civil, cultural, social and economic levels). He also identifies the state and multinational corporations as the main perpetrators of such violation. The paper combines both a theoretical analysis of the shortcomings of Western perceptions of human rights and a discussion of one practical example of how grassroots people are being mobilized to "develop a countervailing power in demanding redress or asserting their rights" in Asia. In fact, Mr. Dias calls for the empowerment of those who are most affected by violation of human rights to enable them to articulate their own concerns and form their own strategies. This method is meant to ensure that all their grievances are addressed at all levels of their lives, that is at the political, civil, social, cultural and economic levels. It is also meant to ultimately lead to a society within which all economic, religious, cultural and other groups get a fair representation in all matters that affect them.

While Clarence Dias analyses the debate from a Third World perspective, Ed Broadbent tackles it from a First World point of view. He looks at the role that the richest and most powerful nations could play in the proper implementation of human rights. Central to his argument is that aid to Third World countries fails to take into account human rights in their totality (that is political, civil, economic, social and cultural) and their violations.

In his opinion, there is a broad spectrum of fundamental values that humanity shares in common and which are enshrined in international documents such as the 1986 United Nations Declaration on the Right to Development. He argues that it is these which all countries, both developing and developed should try to enforce. He calls for international aid, bilateral aid and agreements that contain human rights conditions. The danger, however, is the criteria that will be used to ascertain violation. This may run the risk of being too ethnocentric. Ed Broadbent bases his definition of human rights on the United Nations Declaration and presupposes that because of these, there is a consensus among all nations on what constitutes development and human rights, an assumption which is strongly challenged by Dias and Goulet. Broadbent's paper does not analyze why a lot of these resolutions have remained valid only on the paper on which they are written and have rarely been adhered to by the contracting members both in the developed and developing world.

Thomas Axworthy looks at development from the perspective of a "new world order". The principal inquiry of his paper is the question of how much importance should be placed on human rights and democratic advance. His argument has four parts: that the end of the cold war reduces constraints on placing human rights at the top of the world agenda; that real devotion to human rights and popular participation in government is essential for individual development, a civil society and ultimately peace and security; that to date, democracy and human rights have not been taken seriously in development policy and that economic and political development must move in concert; that human rights must become a pre-condition for aid. His arguments are not dissimilar to those of Broadbent but they put more emphasis on democracy as an essential pre-condition to economic advance which in turn will break the traditional acceptance of poverty and its companion human rights abuses.

On balance the issues covered are important in that they are all presented from differing perspectives and bring out the fact that all parties, that is Third World grassroots people, the state, and First World development agencies who provide aid to Third World countries can all have a role to play in the shaping and determination of human rights. The question remains how to determine what role each actor will play.

JOE CLARK*

Human Rights and Democratic Development

One year ago today, the polls were closing in Namibia. Democracy had just been tried there for the first time. And it worked. The Constituent Assembly chosen in that election went on to draft one of the most progressive constitutions in the world. And independence came to the last colony in Africa. That experiment in democracy was a victory for Namibia, a success for the United Nations, and a signal to Southern Africa that democracy could be secured peacefully, through partnership.

That same day Berliners from East and West were celebrating in their streets and climbing over the barrier which had once divided them. What was once a wall had become a gate. People had proven stronger than barbed wire, more powerful than dictators and secret police.

In November, 1990, the leaders of 34 countries will gather in Paris at a CSCE Summit which is the consequence of that wall coming down. That Summit will signal a Europe whole, prosperous and free, where democracy and human rights are no longer concepts which divide, but a reality which unites.

Those events frame a year of extraordinary accomplishment. Never have there been such grounds for optimism that the observance of human rights around the world will become more the rule and less the exception. And never have so many societies embraced democracy – in Europe, in Latin America, in Asia and Africa – some for the first time and some once again.

But this is not a time to be complacent. The process is just beginning. In some countries, walls have been torn down – real walls and walls of the mind. But new structures remain to be built. It is easier to tear down than to build up. And there is the danger that if new systems fail to improve lives quickly, democracy will be blamed and human rights could be threatened again.

And in so many other parts of the world, walls remain. Walls of power and poverty. Walls which deprive people of their most basic rights, walls which divide societies between those who rule and those who suffer. Walls which consign whole sectors of society to an existence barely worth the name. The fact

* Constitutional Affairs Minister, Government of Canada, Ottawa, Ontario, Canada.

K.E. Mahoney and P. Mahoney (eds.), Human Rights in the Twenty-first Century, 683–688.

that some battles have been won tells us that there are many battles yet to fight, many victories yet to declare.

What has happened in Eastern Europe – and in Latin America and in Asia – is the realization that human rights and democracy are not luxuries, nor are they the result of being developed or wealthy. They are conditions which make wealth develop.

It has been tempting for some to claim that peoples and governments have come to embrace democracy and human rights because they believe their old systems were immoral or illogical. I believe that perspective is wrong. Those societies have rejected other systems and other approaches because they did not work; they did not deliver. They denied people food for the body or for the spirit. The challenge is to ensure that the new systems work better.

Governments in the new democracies may recognize that societies which suppress are systems which self-destruct. They may accept that systems which deny prosperity are systems which will always be poor. They may know that societies which deprive human rights in the interest of social peace are societies where that peace is only a truce. But their citizens will draw other conclusions if these new experiments do not work either. If people become frustrated, if prosperity remains a promise, if democracy does not deliver, there is a real danger of a return to the old ways, to the old regimes.

What is critical here is that human rights and democracy must be seen, not as a change in style, but as key components of societies which work, societies which are stable and prosperous. Otherwise, human rights and democracy could fall away as quickly as they have arisen.

Those of us who come from societies where prosperity has come with freedom and stability has come with democracy have an obligation. It is an obligation to prove that what we have said is universal in theory can be made universal in practice. It is an obligation to assist – not as preachers but as partners.

That effort will come from attitudes and from action. That effort will also come from knowing both what to do and what not to do.

First, we must avoid the easy error of declaring that we have models to mimic. Our societies have developed the way they have for particular reasons which lie in history, in tradition and in culture. Our democracies were not delivered to us like prefabricated housing. They were home-grown. And because they were home-grown, they grew firm roots.

And our democracies themselves vary considerably. From the social democracy of Sweden to the traditions of Westminster to the unfettered capitalism of the United States, we ourselves are not uniform. We cannot expect others to be.

Second, we must avoid impatience and the search for instant perfection. Democracies which are developing will not be perfect from day one. Human rights which are new will not be adhered to at the outset with the rigour we would all like. That does not mean we develop excuses or ignore abuses. It simply means we must be sensible in our expectations, and realistic in our demands.

Our own achievements were secured over centuries. We cannot ask others to do in days what we have done over decades. And we must always bear in mind that democracy is developing here too, that none of us is perfect and that all of us are prey to poverty, intolerance, propaganda and prejudice.

Third, we must move beyond rhetoric. It is easy to be a cheerleader or a critic. It is more difficult to be a companion or a friend. When countries choose to move towards options we have championed, we must offer them practical, potent help in practising what we have so long preached.

But there is another issue too, and that is the question of what assistance we should offer. I think it is now recognized that societies which are not democratic are unlikely to become developed. But the opposite is also true. Societies which are underdeveloped are unlikely to become democratic. We must act accordingly.

That means we cannot demand democracy and deny development. It means we cannot expect people to cherish ballots when their stomachs are empty. Effective development assistance is far more valuable in promoting democracy and human rights than any admonition from the West. Democracy is not secured by building parliament buildings or observing polling booths. Democracy and human rights require a foundation of belief and a foundation of development.

So the tools of development are also the tools of democracy and human rights. Teaching people to read helps them develop but it is also a step towards democracy. Making people productive fights poverty, but it is also a step towards other human rights. Helping women in development helps families become more prosperous and makes societies more just, but it also deflects prejudice and inequality.

Fourth, we must recognize the wide variety of factors required to make democratic systems work. Democracies are based on the rule of law – fairly and justly applied. The establishment of legal institutions and processes is crucial to democratic development and the West can assist.

Equally, democracies require freedom of the press. They require an impartial and professional civil service. And they require freedom of speech and assembly. Helping build the institutions and the expertise to support those fundamentals is a task for development assistance which also builds democracy.

Fifth, we must face squarely the issue of the conditions we put on development assistance. This is not an easy question. It often poses the difficult choice between supporting human rights and fighting poverty. I believe people should not be punished for regimes they do not support, regimes which are punishing them already. We may abhor governments and detest regimes but that distaste should not become a prejudice against people.

That does not mean there are no limits. There must be fundamental standards which cannot be discarded. Regimes must know that tolerance is not total and that if they insist on inhumanity as a systematic tool of governance, there will be consequences from the world which watches.

Canada's development assistance effort reflects that approach. We look at human rights records in deciding on the level of aid we give and on what type of aid that should be. But we do not expect societies which have been prisons to become perfect overnight. So we look for trends of improvement and we review those trends annually.

In addition, as an alternative to the severance of aid, we will often alter the type of assistance given. If a regime becomes a systematic, gross and continuous abuser of human rights, we will cease to deal with that regime. But we will not cease to deal with the people as long as they can be reached. We will not add to their suffering. So what we do is work through local organizations – churches and NGOs – to allow help to get through without helping those governments. I admit that this does not always work perfectly. But I believe it is morally correct.

Sixth, I think we must avoid delivering development assistance as if we were rewarding horses in a race. There are real reasons why some societies are able to develop their democracies and human rights practices more quickly than others. And one of those reasons can be their level of development. If democracy becomes the central criterion for development assistance, we could end up rewarding the wealthy and punishing the poor.

Seventh, we must recognize that there can be a contradiction between our demand for democracy and our insistence on structural adjustment. Structural adjustment, if crudely designed and bluntly applied, can itself erode the roots of democracy and human rights. Structural adjustment is necessary if societies are to develop seriously and if they are to grow without destructive inflation. But our financial institutions should act in partnership with developing countries to ensure that structural adjustment preserves the social foundations for future growth.

Eighth, we must recognize the crucial importance of partnership in building democracy and strengthening human rights. Just as democracies do not work if they are imposed, so too democracy is only maintained if all elements of society are involved. Equally, governments do not have all the answers. Resources, expertise and experience are present throughout society and should be drawn on.

Partnerships within societies can be encouraged by partners abroad.

That is why the Canadian government established the independent International Centre for Democratic Development and Human Rights in Montreal.

That is also why we emphasize democracy and human rights in regional organizations of which we are a part. Last June, we proposed a Unit for Democratic Development within the Organization of American States to provide expertise and assistance to countries which are on the democratic path. That proposal was accepted. Through the Commonwealth High Level Appraisal Group we are working to establish a similar capacity within the Commonwealth Secretariat. We are exploring similar ideas for La Francophonie and are encouraging the Group of Experts on Judicial and

Judiciary Co-operation to take an active role in promoting both human rights and democratic development.

Those regional units can provide a wide range of potential assistance and support including:

- facilitating the exchange of information and expertise;
- developing an inventory of experts on democratic systems and institutions;
- developing regional standards and procedures for elections;
- organizing electoral observer missions;
- co-operating with other regional and multilateral organizations; and
- fostering dialogue within those regions on democratic principles and values.

In Europe, Canada took the lead in Copenhagen at the CSCE Conference on the Human Dimension in proposing strengthened commitments and the rights of minorities. We are currently discussing an office for free elections and democratic institutions as part of the new CSCE structure. And we have encouraged NATO to adopt programs – including scholarships – which will allow it to share its democratic experiences with its old adversaries.

In addition, we have established a Political Co-operation Fund as part of our Program of Assistance for Central and Eastern Europe. That fund will provide grants and contributions to foster dialogue and co-operation with those countries so as to encourage democratic institutions, political pluralism, the rule of law and the respect of human rights.

In the past year alone, Canada has assisted in elections in Romania, Bulgaria and Czechoslovakia. We sent election observers to Namibia and provided 100 RCMP officers to help ensure stability as that society moves towards democracy. We are currently helping Benin as it moves away from totalitarianism. We have agreed in principle to participate in a Commonwealth observer mission for Guyana and have sent election observers last month to Malaysia through the Commonwealth. We participated in the OAS and UN efforts in Nicaragua, are working with both these organizations in the upcoming elections in Haiti, and are prepared to assist the UN in constructing democracy in the Western Sahara and Cambodia.

Those activities relate to elections. But we are providing other types of assistance beyond the mechanics. In South Africa, we are assisting that country move towards a multiracial democracy. Canadian expertise is being offered to all parties. But in order to level the playing field, we are providing financial support to the black majority to conduct constitutional research, consultations and development. In addition, we are supporting a two-year research project on constitutional development in a post-apartheid South Africa, a project being led by a Canadian professor in criminology.

There are other areas where human rights and democratic development can be furthered.

Literacy is one. Increasing literacy provides a better ability to participate in political and economic life. Canada is already involved in this area and will continue to be, particularly for women and children who are the major victims of illiteracy.

A free media is a second area for action. An independent press is an important element in combating corruption and the abuse of human rights and in promoting and preserving freedom of speech and association. Canada has hosted journalists from many developing countries in the past. I believe there may be avenues for new initiatives in this area including assistance and dialogue on such matters as media ethics, the organization of a free press and media law.

A third area may be the institution of ombudsmen. Ombudsmen provide people with redress against legal abuse. The Canadian experience with this institution may be an area of interest to other countries.

A fourth area is public administration. A civil service which is excellent and impartial and well trained is key to ensuring the implementation of, and respect for the rule of law which lies at the heart of democracy.

A fifth area is police training. Canada has established a unique program in Namibia, where we are following up our contribution to the UN effort with an initiative which involves training the Namibian police force to train themselves. Professional police, well trained in the law, reinforce a commitment to democracy and human rights.

These are not grand designs and they do not in and of themselves convert despotism into democracy. They are small steps. But that is how democracy is built and that is how we can move forward. Such steps educate, they build institutions and trust – and in so doing they make democracy strong and human rights more secure.

Democracies are not inherently peaceful. But societies which are free and developed are less likely to choose war as a common course of action. In the global village we have become, it is in the interest of everyone that incentives to conflict be reduced and that the stakes in peace be strengthened.

The Cold War distorted our priorities and led us to neglect global problems. With the Cold War over, the world may at long last see freedom and justice for all as a factor for security, not just a frill for the few.

The pursuit of human rights and democracy is central to Canadian foreign policy. It is a commitment which comes from what Canada is. Canadians sometimes denigrate their own accomplishments. But what we have built here is unique. It is worth preserving and it is worth sharing. We have built a community by inviting the world to come and share our luck. We have built a democracy with millions who have fled tyranny for freedom. We have built a nation which Barbara Ward once called "the first international country". We have done that through tolerance, through compromise and through understanding. And we have built a democracy and a structure of human rights which, while not perfect, are things others dream to share.

The world outside recognizes the Canadian commitment to justice and human rights, the Canadian achievement. Nelson Mandela does. The Soviet refuseniks do. The governments of China, of Sri Lanka, of Nicaragua, of Kenya and of Haiti have. That commitment will continue and strengthen. It is central to our values and sustains our spirit. Our goal is a world where justice knows no borders and human rights no caveat.

DENIS GOULET*

Development: Creator and Destroyer of Values

1. Introduction

The French novelist Léon Bloy (1846–1917) lamented that "when those who love God try to talk about Him, their words are blind lions looking for springs in the desert."[1] Those who would speak about "development" are not reduced to such total blindness but are, nonetheless, saddled with a heavy linguistic burden.

Development is both an ambiguous term and an ambiguous practice. The term is used *descriptively* or *normatively*: to depict a present condition or to project a desirable alternative. Descriptive usage prevails in the growing body of testimonial writings on development[2], in statistical and policy reports issued by such international financing agencies as the World Bank and the International Monetary Fund, and in the voluminous academic literature now appearing in a myriad of disciplines. Normative usage of the term is found in works of criticism and alternative advocacy[3] whose authors employ value-laden language to criticize development as now conducted or to advocate a different vision deemed ethically or politically superior. Moreover, the identical word "development" refers either to the ends or to the means of social change. Development is simultaneously the vision of a better life – a life materially

* Professor, University of Notre Dame, Notre Dame, Indiana, U.S.A.

[1] L. Bloy cited in "Frontispiece" of T. Merton, *The Tears of the Blind Lions* (1949), New York: New Directions.

[2] C. M. De Jesus, *Child of the Dark* (1962), New York: E. P. Dutton & Co., Inc. D. B. de Chungara with M. Viezzer, *Let Me Speak!* (1978), New York: Monthly Review Press. H. Johnson and H. Bernstein with R. H. Ampuero and B. Crow, *Third World Lives of Struggle* (1982), Ibadan: Heinemann Educational Books Ltd. J. D. Sexton (ed.) *Campesino, The Diary of A Guatemalan Indian* (1985), Arizona: The University of Arizona Press.

[3] L. J. Lebret, *Développement = Révolution Solidaire* (1962), Paris: Les Editions Ouvrières. E. Fromm, *To Have or To Be?* (1976), New York: Harper & Row, Publishers, World Perspectives, Vol 50. N. Dower, *World Poverty, Challenge and Response* (1983), York, England: William Sessions Limited, The Ebor Press. D. H. Pollock and A. R. M. Ritter (eds.) *What Kinds of Development?* (1980), 3 Vols., Ottawa, Canada: Norman Paterson School of International Affairs, Carleton University.

K.E. Mahoney and P. Mahoney (eds.), Human Rights in the Twenty-first Century, 689–700.

richer, institutionally more "modern", and technologically more efficient – and an array of means to achieve that vision. These means range from economic planning to propaganda campaigns, from comprehensive social engineering to sectoral interventions of all sorts with a view to altering values, behaviors, and social structures.

It is not only the terminology of development which is fraught with ambivalence, but its practice as well. A bewildering assortment of policy prescriptions parade under the single banner of development, among them:

- a "big push" into self-sustained economic growth;
- the Westernization of social institutions and practices;
- the repudiation of Westernization in pursuit of an "endogenous" model of change;
- the mobilization of national resources and energies around "giant projects" or, conversely,
- the glorification of the slogan "small is beautiful" for a strategy based on small, locally controlled projects.

At times what is sought is mimetic Westernization, at other times its antithesis – the activation of latent dynamisms present in traditional values and capable of serving as the engine of new indigenous forms of development. Many alternative development prescriptions set out to combat the ethnocentrism of dominant paradigms, whereas others view the elitism of ideologues, technocrats, or politicians as the evil to be countered. Here the main component of development is taken to be participation or people's control over the goals, the direction, and the pace of change processes. Although many planners still equate development with efficient economic growth, others repudiate this reductionist view and plead for the multi-dimensional advance of society in all realms – economic, social, political, cultural, environmental, and spiritual.

Development strategists in growing numbers subscribe to a dictum attributed to Senegal's former President Leopold Senghor "that we Africans do not wish to be mere consumers of civilization." Senghor argued:

- that no people wishes to commit cultural suicide, by repudiating its history and identity, on the grounds that this sacrifice is the only road to modernity; and
- that the "global culture" now in gestation worldwide needs the contribution of African civilizations to counter the economic reductionism still in force in dominant paradigms of modernity.

In 1945, the year before his death, John Maynard Keynes, father of neo-classical economics and chief architect of the post-WW II financial institutions created at Bretton Woods, proposed a toast "to economics and to economists, who are not the trustees of civilization, but of the possibility of civilization."[4] Keynes thereby acknowledged the purely instrumental value of the economic sphere. Translated to contemporary idiom, "economic development" is

[4] Cited in Benjamin Higgins, *Economic Development, Problems, Principles, and Policies* (1968), New York, N.W. Norton & Company, Inc., p. 3.

valuable only to the degree that it creates possibilities for "human development." Indeed, in 1990 a group of notable economists issued the first annual report on Human Development in the World.[5] Its authors strive to transcend the narrow economic vision of development implicit in the World Bank's annual development report, which ranks nations around aggregate economic growth performance as measured by GNP (Gross National Product). The burgeoning movement to construct new development indicators is further testimony to the growing disaffection with prevailing conceptions and measures of that fugitive, complex reality known as "development."[6]

Given the present crisis of definition and of measurement, it may prove illuminating to briefly review the evolution of the concept of development – its nature, goals, and processes. How, in a few decades, specialists have moved from adhering to the myth of development as progress to denouncing it as regression.

2. From the Myth of Progress to Anti-Development

After World War II, the spectacular success of the Marshall Plan made development a shibboleth for progress. It was assumed that rapid industrialization and generalized improvement in material conditions of life could be won quickly by following the formula that had worked in reconstructing war-damaged Europe, namely injecting massive foreign aid for investment in infrastructure in order to restore or create a modern productive economy. Investment priorities were planned and technology was harnessed to boost productivity. It was simply assumed that development was a good thing. Sociologist Daniel Lerner, writing in 1958 on *The Passing of Traditional Society*,[7] noted in his research throughout six countries of the Middle East (Lebanon, Egypt, Syria, Jordan, Iran, Turkey) that people viewed development as an unalloyed good. For them the term "development" evoked images of a better life and hope for improvement. Twenty years later[8] Lerner returned to the site of his earlier studies and discovered that the same people he had interviewed earlier – merchants, peasants, goat-herders, and village homemakers had now come to view development as a mixed blessing rather than as an unalloyed good. People still wanted development but saw it as a mixed good about which they were ambivalent. Likewise, a growing body of fiction coming from the Third World highlights the ambiguous nature of development as a mixture of goods and evils. For the Senegalese writer, Cheikh Hamidou Kane, development is an *Ambiguous Adventure* undertaken at great risk and

[5] *Human Development Report 1990* (1990), New York: Oxford University Press.

[6] *Redefining Wealth and Progress, New Ways to Measure Economic, Social and Environmental Change* (1990), New York: The Bootstrap Press.

[7] D. Lerner, *The Passing of Traditional Society* (1958), Glencoe, Illinois: The Free Press.

[8] "An Interview with Daniel Lerner," in *Communications and Development Review* (Summer/Autumn 1977), Teheran, Iran, Vol. I, Nos. 2–3, p. 5.

uncertainty. The Nigerian novelist, Chinua Achebe, describes development around the title, *Things Fall Apart*. The experience which villagers in traditional societies have of what Westerners call "technical or economic progress", is that the values which matter most to them – religious institutions, local practices, and extended family solidarity networks – fall apart under the impact of technology, the monetization of the economy, and the specialization of tasks. V.S. Naipaul, an expatriate writer of Indian origin now living in England, returned after many years to the land of his ancestors. He found there *India: A Wounded Civilization*, a nation many of whose values had been destroyed by its quest for yet unachieved development.

Nowadays, development is increasingly denounced as an evil thing. The noted French agronomist René Dumont considers the performance of the last forty years to be a dangerous epidemic of misdevelopment.[9] In Africa, he states, development has simply not occurred. Latin America, on the other hand, has witnessed the creation of great wealth, ranging from sophisticated nuclear and electronic industries to great skyscraper cities. But this growth, Dumont laments, has been won at the price of massive pollution, urban congestion, and a monumental waste of resources. Moreover, the majority of the continent's population has not benefited. For Dumont,[10] misdevelopment is the mismanagement of resources; it is the main cause of world hunger and afflicts "developed" countries as severely as it does Third World nations.

Other development writers strike the same theme: growth is often irresponsible, inequitable, destructive, and worsens the lot of poor people. The late Swiss anthropologist Roy Preiswerk and his colleagues conclude that change processes have led to maldevelopment in rich and poor countries alike.[11] In an earlier work I labelled much of what was called progress, "antidevelopment," because it is the antithesis of authentic development, which is qualitative improvement in any society's provision of life-sustaining goods, esteem, and freedom to all its citizens.[12]

The most absolute attack, however, comes from those who totally repudiate development, both as concept and as project. The French economist Serge Latouche urges us to discard development because it is a tool used by advanced Western countries to destroy the cultures and the autonomy of nations throughout Africa, Asia, and Latin America.[13] Similarly, the Intercultural Institute of Montreal, through its review *Interculture*, tirelessly promotes the thesis that development must be rejected as the instrument which destroys the political, juridical, economic, and symbolic meaning systems of native cultures.

[9] R. Dumont and M. F. Mottin, *Le mal-développement en Amérique latine* (1981), Paris: les Editions de Seuil.

[10] See Bob Bergmann, "René Dumont on Misdevelopment in the Third World: A 42 Year Perspective," in *Camel Breeders News* (Spring, 1987), Ithaca, New York: Cornell University, p. 7.

[11] See CETIM (Centre Europe-Tiers Monde), *Mal-Développement Suisse-Monde* (1975), Geneve: CETIM, p. 11.

[12] D. Goulet, *The Cruel Choice* (1969), New York: Atheneum Press, pp. 215–235.

[13] S. Latouche, *Faut-il refuser le développement?* (1986), Paris: Presses Universitaires de France.

The Cultural Survival Movement, headquartered at Harvard University, has likewise struggled, since its creation in 1972, to prevent "development" from destroying native cultures. Its founder, anthropologist David Maybury-Lewis, writes that "violence done to indigenous peoples is largely based on prejudices and discrimination that must be exposed and combated. These prejudices are backed up by widely held misconceptions, which presume that traditional societies are inherent obstacles to development or that the recognition of their rights would subvert the nation state. Our research shows that this is untrue."[14]

In policy arenas of national governments and international financing agencies, however, development is still operationally defined as maximum economic growth and a drive toward industrialization and mass consumption. The national success stories lauded worldwide are South Korea and Taiwan, twin paragons of high-capital and high-tech economic growth, allied to success in international trade.[15] Development reports remain discreetly silent, however, about the costs in political repression attendant upon these economic successes.[16] Many national planning ministries not only follow the old model of development, but ignore those sound elements of policy contained in that old model – investments in infrastructure, job creation, and market expansion. A single imperative guides most national strategists: to achieve "structural adjustment." Structural adjustment is but a euphemism for survival, to avoid sinking in a sea of debt, recession, and inflation. The policy recommendations promoted under the banner of adjustment range from tightened credit to budget discipline, wage freezes, and export expansion. Some observers, it is true, are concerned over the impact of macroeconomic policy on the lives of poor people and champion adjustment with a human face.[17] But in most cases even the "developmental" objectives of the earlier growth model (improved standards of living, job creation, better social services, and a diversified basket of available consumer goods) are forgotten. The rhetoric of development is still invoked, but in reality debt-servicing and crisis management now occupy center stage in arenas of development policy setting.

Nevertheless, a new development paradigm is now in gestation, and one sign of its growing legitimacy is that lip-service is now paid to its values even by those who pursue traditional growth strategies. These alternative values include the

[14] D. Maybury-Lewis, editorial letter "Dear Reader" in *Cultural Survival Quarterly* (1987), Vol. 11, No. 1, p. 1.

[15] Cf., e.g., L. J. Lau (ed.) *Models of Development, A Comparative Study of Economic Growth in South Korea and Taiwan* (1986), San Francisco: Institute for Contemporary Studies; A. C. Harberger (ed.) *World Economic Growth* (1984), San Francisco; Institute for Contemporary Studies.

[16] S. S. Harrison, "Dateline South Korea: A Divided Seoul," *Foreign Policy* (Summer, 1987), No. 67, pp. 154–175. Y. Shaw and G. Huan, "The Future of Taiwan," *Foreign Affairs* (Summer 1985), Vol. 63, No. 5, pp. 1050–1080.

[17] See R. E. Feinberg and V. Kallab (eds.) *Adjustment Crisis in the Third World* (1984), New Brunswick, NJ: Transaction Books; and J. P. Lewis and V. Kallab (eds.) *Development Strategies Reconsidered* (1986), New Brunswick, NJ: Transaction Books. Also Giovanni Cornia et al. (eds.) *Adjustment with a Human Face Volume 2* (1988), New York: Oxford University Press.

primacy of basic needs satisfaction and the elimination of absolute poverty over mere economic growth, the creation of jobs, the reduction of dependency, protection of the environment, and respect for local cultures. Although it is often perfunctory, such lip-service at least implicitly admits that development is essentially an ethical concern.

Two recent formulations of this alternative paradigm reveal how thoroughly value-laden any serious talk is about development. In September 1986, the Marga Institute held a week-long seminar in Colombo, Sri Lanka, on Ethical Issues in Development.[18] Theorists and practitioners who gathered at Marga reached a consensus that any adequate definition of development must include five dimensions:

- an economic component dealing with the creation of wealth and improved conditions of material life, equitably distributed;
- a social ingredient measured as well-being in health, education, housing, and employment;
- a political dimension including such values as human rights, political freedom, enfranchisement, and some form of democracy;
- a cultural dimension in recognition of the fact that cultures confer identity and self-worth to people; and
- a fifth dimension called the full-life paradigm, which refers to meaning systems, symbols, and beliefs concerning the ultimate meaning of life and history.

Integral human development encompasses all of these things.

Some years earlier, a seminar on Latin American chose four pairs of words as essential components of development. These include economic growth, distributional equity, participation/vulnerability, and transcendental values.[19] The two final sets of words require explanation. Participation is a decisive voice exercised by people directly affected by policy decisions. Vulnerability is the obverse side of the participation coin: poor people, regions, and nations must be rendered less vulnerable to decisions which produce external shocks upon them. The words "transcendental values" raise a vital question – "Do people live by GNP alone?" As David Pollock writes:

> "Let us assume that a country's economic pie increases. Let us further assume that there is a heightened degree of equity in the way the fruits of that economic pie are distributed. Let us, finally assume that decisions affecting production and consumption of the economic pie – nationally and internationally– involve the full participation of all affected parties. Is that

[18] No documents have issued from the seminar. The author participated in it and here reports from notes taken at the time.

[19] D. H. Pollock, "A Latin American Strategy to the Year 2000", in A. Ritter and D. Pollock (eds.) *Latin American Prospects for the 80's: Equity, Democratization and Development* (November 1980), Ottawa: Norman Patterson School of International Affairs, Carleton University, Conference Proceedings, Vol. I, pp. 3–21.

the end of the matter? Does man live by GNP alone? Perhaps the latter has been the prevailing line of thought throughout the postwar period since, in the short-run, policy makers must focus primarily upon the pressing issue of increased incomes for the masses; particularly for those below the poverty line. But, despite the obvious importance of such short-run objectives, we should also be asking ourselves other, more uplifting questions. Should we not take advantage of our longer-term vision and ask what kind of person Latin America may wish to evolve by the end of this century. What are the transcendental values – cultural, ethical, artistic, religious, moral – that extend beyond the current workings of the purely economic and social system? How to appeal to youth, who so often seek nourishment in dreams, as well as in bread? What, in short, should be the new face of the Latin American Society in the future, and what human values should lie behind the new countenance?"[20]

Contemporary development trends reveal three facets:

1. There is economic growth and progress in equitable distribution of the fruits of that growth for a small number of countries – the four Asian tigers and a few others.
2. There is regression for a large number of losers, especially in sub-Saharan Africa, Latin America, Eastern Europe and the Soviet Union. Countries with heavy foreign debts are particularly hard hit.
3. Contemporary development co-exists with micro successes and macro failures. In such countries as Bangladesh and Brazil numerous small-scale, local micro activities may succeed economically, socially, culturally, and institutionally alongside a generalized macro or nationwide failure of development strategies leading to uncontrolled inflation, massive recession, and increasing dependency on outside economic forces.

3. Development, a Two-Edged Sword

Development is best conceptualized as a two-edged sword which cuts two ways. It brings benefits, but also produces losses and generates value conflicts.

(1) Gains

Among the major gains achieved by development are clear improvements in material well-being, standards of living, levels of comfort, of consumption, and of amenities for large numbers of people. The latest annual Development report of the World Bank stresses these accomplishments in the last thirty years: large numbers of people have more food, more comfortable lodgings, a greater

[20] Ibid., p. 9.

variety of clothing, access to books, and numerous other material goods than ever before.

A second gain attendant upon development is technological progress. Machines, equipment, and processes of all kinds have freed millions of people from burdensome physical tasks. One finds radar in every airport, supermarkets in the Amazon, and long-distance telephones in Papua-New Guinea.

The third benefit traceable to development is institutional specialization. It is now possible to find statistical offices even in the smallest and poorest countries. One may also find specialized organizations dealing with education, transportation and banking.

A fourth gain is increased freedom of choice, especially for women and children. Pre-modern societies assign fixed roles to practically all their members. Modernity and development have brought an expanded range of possible roles, along with an increased social tolerance for freedom of choice by individuals in these roles and definitions of their personal destinies. The sociologist Peter Berger[21], judges that the main result of development is to make people free to choose what they will believe, which values they will adopt, and how they will live.

A fifth gain associated with development is greater worldwide interdependence. Whatever takes place even in small and remote areas is communicated everywhere. Conversely, events occurring in large and powerful countries are also passed along to remote places everywhere. The world is linked together in a chain of interdependence.

Still another benefit of development is a higher degree of tolerance than ever before for diversity in religion, laws, customs, ideologies, clothing, and taste in foods. All societies are learning that they must accept other societies different from their own, that they cannot simply brand others as less human or civilized on the strength of some parochial standard.

(2) Losses

These positive gains constitute one blade of the two-edged sword. But what of the destructive, other edge of the development sword? Among the losses traceable to development is the shattering of the dynamism of desire which kept all societies in cultural equilibrium. Before development held out the promise of unlimited gains in material goods for millions of people within their lifetime, all societies imposed brakes or limits upon the desire for possessions entertained by their members. It was assumed that only limited possibilities existed for augmenting the overall stock of goods available to any society. Therefore, if cultural communities were to preserve a social cement or a bond of solidarity among their members, personal desires had to be curtailed and acquisitive aspirations had to be subordinated to the requirements of the common good,

[21] P. L. Berger, *The Heretical Imperative* (1979), Garden City, New York: Anchor Press/Doubleday.

the meeting of the needs of all. Thanks to its multiple demonstration effects, development has wrought an explosion in these cultural limits on individual desires for goods.

A second negative effect of development is an increase in vertical dependence among nations. Even relatively rich developing countries such as Mexico, Brazil or Nigeria have seen their dependency increase because of their financial debt. The policy of import substitution promoted in the sixties by Raul Prebisch and ECLA (the UN's Economic Commission for Latin America) was intended to reduce Latin American nations' dependence on external imports. Instead, the policy efforts merely shifted the locus of dependency away from finished products to intermediate goods, technology, access to finance capital, and markets.

A third negative feature of development is the increase in *anomie* or social alienation and role ambiguity among members of all societies. In the past, every person knew his or her place in life. Now, that place is neither fixed once and for all, nor is it defined for specific actors in society. Small, closely-knit communities or extended families within which people knew their place, their role, and their assigned vocation in life, have yielded ground to large impersonal institutions.

Another negative effect of development is the destruction or dilution of cultures. Especially affected are nomadic or semi-sedentary cultures which depend on extended families, local networks, and the possibility of ranging over wide territory for food. One of development's greatest achievements has been to reduce infant deaths and to multiply populations. As a result, there are more people than ever before, and frequently more people with access to the same limited stock of resources. The limits on resources themselves have doubtless been expanded by technology, but until technology is adopted – and it is expensive to adopt technology – large populations grown larger because of rapid and inexpensive medical interventions now see their way of life destroyed.[22] They are obliged to enter circuits of hired labor in order to earn money. This fragments their patterns of living, their ways of being, and destroys their culture.

More significantly, the meaning systems of numerous cultural communities are evacuated. Meaning systems are the religious, philosophical, and cosmic symbols and codes providing explanations as to the significance of life and death. The *Weltanschauung* of modernity simply treats questions about the ultimate meaning of tragedy, of suffering, of the fleetingness of human experience as insignificant. People are caught up in the pursuit of goods, in the rat race to gain upward mobility for jobs or social status. The more profound meaning systems are largely abandoned, to say nothing of damage wrought to the biological natural systems, all in the name of development.

Most significantly, however, development generates value conflicts over the meaning of "the good life". Competing models of "the good life" are presented

[22] R. E. Gamer, *The Developing Nations* (1976), Boston: Allyn and Bacon, Inc., *Passim*.

in such works as psychologist Eric Fromm's book *To Have Or To Be?*, the French novelist George Perenc's work called *Les Choses, (Things)*, or Ursula K. LeGuin's science fiction novel *The "Dispossessed"*[23]. In the latter book, two models of communities vie for the loyalties of people. One is a community which prizes collaboration, friendship, health and a high degree of equality achievable only in an austere regime of resource use. The other model prizes comfortable selfishness and competition and depends on abundant material resources. Clearly Karl Marx's postulate that the material infrastructure powerfully conditions the possibilities for spiritual or cultural superstructure are operative here. A further question poses itself: Does "the good life", whose possibility is assured by laws and institutions, consist of equality of opportunity or equality of results? In most developed nations this ancient argument has never been resolved.[24] Another facet of the value debate over "the good life" is whether societies should rely more dominantly on material or on moral incentives.[25]

A second contradiction bears on what is the foundation or the basis of a just society. Does justice reside in inherited authority, in opinion polls, in the rule of the majority or in some social contract? Are civil and political rights assuring individual freedoms enjoy primacy over collective social and economic rights having to do with needs being met and the collective good of society being pursued? To what extent are institutions and social structures a function of the ideological preference for either individual democratic ideologies which stress political and civil rights or socialist and communitarian ideologies which stress economic and social rights in the community? Are human rights to be treated in instrumental fashion, or are they ends in themselves worthy for their own sake?

A third set of value conflicts centers on the criteria to adopt towards nature. Is nature to be viewed simply as raw material for Promethean exploitation by humans, or is nature to be viewed as the larger womb of life in which humans live, move, and have their being, and whose rhythms and laws they must respect? The title words of a book published in Sri Lanka some years ago, *Man in Nature, Guest or Engineer?*[26], ask a critical question. Is the dominant human stance toward nature to be extractive and manipulative or harmony-seeking?

[23] U. K. LeGuin, *The Dispossessed* (1975), New York: Avon Book, p. 20. G. Perenc, *Les Choses* (1965), Paris, Les Lettres Nouvelles. E. Fromm, *To Have OR To Be?* (1976), New York: Harper & Row.

[24] E. Z. Friedenberg, *The Disposal of Liberty and Other Industrial Wastes* (1975), Garden City, New York: Doubleday.

[25] D. Goulet, *Incentives for Development: The Key to Equity* (1989), New York: New Horizons Press.

[26] S. J. Samartha and L. de Silva (eds.) *Man in Nature, Guest or Engineer?* (1979), Columbo: The Ecumenical Institute for Study and Dialogue.

4. Conclusion: A Wisdom to Match Our Sciences

Because numerous contradictions surround discourse and the practice of development, we need a wisdom to match our sciences. Wisdom offers a larger view of the purposes of human life and of human efforts to guide the formulation of development paradigms. If development deals essentially with the nature of "the good life" and the relationship between having goods and being good; if, moreover, development is concerned essentially with the foundations of life together in society – what Aristotle called political friendship and Ivan Illich conviviality – it is clear that no definition of development which is exclusively economic, technical, organizational or managerial can be adequate. In addition, if development concerns the criteria which govern the stance human societies adopt toward the forces of nature, toward that second nature they have created with their technological artifacts, and toward that third nature which they have created with their social institutions, something like wisdom, or the capacity to make sense of the whole and to see the relative importance and position of parts in the whole, is no less necessary than science. In his study of history, Arnold Toynbee concluded that an inverse relationship exists between the levels of technical achievement obtained by different societies and their degrees of spiritual wisdom.[27] Wisdom here is defined as the unity of meaning achieved after facing complexity, contradiction, and struggle, perhaps even tragedy or defeat. This distinguishes it from naivete or oversimplification which also achieves unity of meaning but only at the cost of turning away from contradiction, complexity, suffering, and tragedy.

Is wisdom achievable and, if so, can wisdom be taught? Human genius exists. Wisdom is a form of genius and, just as artistic genius can be displayed by exhibiting models of human creativity, so too can the example of people who have sought wisdom or of societies which have prized wisdom be displayed. This effort calls for new models of learning[28] and even new models of decision-making in which competing rationalities founded on ethical, political, or technical logic, vie for influence in decision-making arenas[29].

The pathway to wisdom necessarily takes us to a dialogue among cultures, for no wisdom is obtainable simply by assuming that it already exists, in adequate or finished fashion, within the confines of a single cultural meaning system.

Wisdom will be needed to teach human beings how to link micro and macro practices in the social policies. Wisdom will likewise be needed to determine how national societies are to integrate the demands of global interdependence

[27] A. J. Toynbee, *A Study of History*. Abridgement by D. C. Somervell (1965), New York: Dell, Vol. I, pp. 59, 379, 382.

[28] D. Goulet, "Interdisciplinary Knowledge and the Quest for Wisdom", (Spring, 1991) vol. 7, number 2, pp. 131–132.

[29] D. Goulet, "Three Rationalities in Developing Decision-making." *World Development* (1986), Vol. 14, No. 2, pp. 301–317.

with the no-less urgent demands for decentralization. New functional and institutional arrangements in world governance clearly are required.

In no domain is wisdom more necessary than in the redefinition of personal and social identities. Modern men and women must come to recognize that they are the bearers of multiple, partial overlapping identities and loyalty systems, no single one of which can claim their total allegiance. Several years ago I interviewed an elderly Guarani Indian chief in eastern Paraguay, whose forest habitat had been destroyed in the construction of the Icaray Dam. He bemoaned the disappearance of the forest, the destruction of familiar Indian rituals, and the loss of interest in younger members of his tribe in the values, language, and culture, of his people. This leader then declared that more important than the destruction of the forest and the destruction of his people was the disappearance of the sacred dance. I asked him why the sacred dance was so important and he replied, "It is what holds the cosmos together." Twenty years ago, this was a declaration of cultural faith, today it is a statement of ecological fact!

The world needs many sacred dances, many wisdoms coming from non-developed societies in creative and critical and constructive dialogue with the powerful scientific, technological, political, and managerial rationalities of "developed" societies. Only through such dialogues can we humans generate a wisdom to match our sciences and can we stop behaving as "one-eyed giants"[30]. The term is from the poet Laurens Van Der Post who speaks of the white man coming into Africa as a one-eyed giant who had science without wisdom. Thomas Merton, in commenting on Van Der Post, explains that the one-eyed giants broke in upon ancient civilizations which had wisdom without science. He adds that it is "wisdom which transcends and unites ... opens the door to a life in which the individual is not lost in the cosmos and in society but found in them. Wisdom which made all life sacred and meaningful – even that which later ages come to call secular and profane."[31]

[30] L. Van Der Post, in *The Dark Eye in Africa* (1955), New York: William Morrow and Co., p. 123.

[31] T. Merton, *Gandhi on Non-Violence* (1965), New York: New Directions, p. 1.

CLARENCE DIAS*

Rural Development, Grassroots Education and Human Rights: Some Asian Perspectives

1. THE WESTERN LIBERAL APPROACH TO HUMAN RIGHTS: IS IT ENOUGH?

Human rights activism in the U.S. and Europe today is not the same as human rights activism in Asia today. Indeed, human rights paradigms and practices evolved in the West might well prove to be inadequate to the task of redressing the *inhuman wrongs* that result from human rights violations currently taking place in Asia with frequency and on a widespread scale. But human misery and suffering, like human rights violations in the abstract, can tend to lose their power to generate outrage and indignation when they are so frequent as to be endemic and so pervasive as to become commonplace. The printed word documents horror story after horror story and yet the international community seems unmoved and unmoveable. Three examples of human rights problems, typical of Asia, underscore the point.

(1) A few years ago an infant was used by drug carriers to smuggle narcotics from Thailand into Malaysia. The drug carriers killed the child, stuffed it with heroin, then wrapped it up and carried the "sleeping" child across the border. Though the gruesome incident has been denied by the authorities, the fact remains that, for the last decade, children have been smuggled from Thailand to Malaysia for crime, prostitution, cheap labour and especially for illegal adoption. The reason behind this active trade is the great demand for babies in Malaysia. The gangs involved in the trade abduct the children or else buy them from prostitutes, unwed mothers and others desperate enough to sell their child for a pittance. In 1984 the Malaysian Marine Police rescued four babies who had been stuffed in suitcases and were being smuggled from Thailand into Malaysia. They had almost suffocated to death. In December 1987 a one-year-old baby girl was thrown into the river by her captors when police raided the house in Southern Thailand where she was being hidden. The child was in

* President, International Center for Law and Development, New York, N.Y.

K.E. Mahoney and P. Mahoney (eds.), Human Rights in the Twenty-first Century, 701–714.

serious condition when she was found by the police and died later.[1]

(2) In February 1988 nine deaths, all suicides by small cotton farmers (including three women), were reported within a two-month period in the Prakasam district of Andhra Pradesh in India. All the victims were young, below 30 years of age. They had borrowed heavily to meet the costs of raising the crop. But the returns were poor. Two factors were responsible. One was the "white fly" menace. The other, even more dangerous, was the sale of spurious pesticides, supplied by "human vultures" out to exploit them. The heavy debt burden and consequent humiliation prompted some of the suicides. In the case of the three women, there were pressures from their in-laws. The District Collector of the area stated that arrangements were being made to provide compensation of Rs 3000 to each victim's family under the social security insurance scheme. He assured that no criminal action would be taken against the victim's families on humanitarian grounds.[2]

(3) Residents in a northeastern province in China are fighting against serious and unabated ecological degradation occurring as a result of the Government's developmental activities. They claim that their livelihood and their very survival are threatened. They are faced with leaving their homes and lands or else with slow death.[3]

These and countless other "case studies" are not generally viewed by the international community as involving human rights problems. Therein lies the key to the dismal record, over the last 40 years, in the realization of the rights of the disadvantaged. Crucial but disturbing questions need to be asked. Who are the disadvantaged and how did they become victims of denial of human rights? Why does such victimization take place predominantly at a grass roots level? Who are the victimizers and why have they not been held accountable to human rights standards? What gaps in existing international human rights machinery and what flaws in existing international human rights conceptualization have led to a frustrating impotence, not only in realizing the human rights of the disadvantaged but also in preventing utterly inhuman wrongs?

Any effort to address these questions requires an understanding of why the Third World has rejected Western liberal paradigms of human rights, and of the emerging Third World human rights empowerment approach.

2. The Baby and the Bathwater

In the decades after decolonization, several serious Third World scholars began to voice a trenchant criticism of the Western liberal human rights paradigm. They were accused of having "thrown out the baby with the bathwater". But

[1] Source: *Newsletter* of the Union of Civil Liberties, Thailand.
[2] Sources: *Indian Express*.
[3] Source: *The New York Times*.

the fact remains that their critique was essential to exploding four myths that dominate Western thinking about human rights.

(1) The Myth of Harmony

The myth of harmony would have us believe that it is truly possible to increasingly realize the rights of all without there being any losers. This is wishful thinking. Both between countries and within countries, the rights of the have-nots can only be successfully realized by restricting the rights of the haves. This was quite candidly and blatantly admitted as far back as 1948 by George Kennan (then Head of the U.S. State Department Planning Staff) who stated:

> "We have about 50% of the worlds wealth, but only 6.3% of its population... In this situation we cannot fail to be the object of envy and resentment... Our real task... is to maintain this position of disparity without positive detriment to our national security... To do so we will have to dispense with all sentimentality and day-dreaming... We should cease talk about vague and unreal objectives such as human rights, the raising of living standards and democratization. The less we are then hampered by idealistic slogans, the better."[4]

Indeed, many of the human rights violations occurring in Asia today can be traced to the causal relationship that exists between need in the Third World and greed in the First World.

(2) The Myth of Universality

While the values enshrined in human rights might be truly universal, it is a myth to believe that universal consensus exists about living up to such values. While human rights may be of a universal nature, their protection strongly relies on regional systems which can better take into account regional particularities with regard to the implementation of human rights. All too often, universality has been invoked as an excuse by the West to justify cultural imperialism and certainly U.S. State Department practice has tended to use human rights to impose economic ideologies of capitalism and the free market system.

(3) The Myth of Equality

While theoretically all persons are equal, in practice some are clearly more equal than others. In the words of a Philippine NGO, "all that there is, is all for the strong and none for the weak". Recognizing this fact of life, the Philippine national hero, Jose Rizal, urged that "those who have less in life should have more in law". But this is all too rare in practice.

[4] As quoted by Noam Chomsky, *The Managua Lectures*, p. 15, Boston, 1989.

(4) The Myth of Governmental Lawfulness

Human rights in the West developed in societies where governments were essentially law-abiding. Human rights then came into play to correct the occasional aberrations of the State machinery. However, in much of the Third World, we face large-scale governmental lawlessness. The chief lawmakers are also the chief lawbreakers. In such a context, human rights assume even greater significance but call for different strategies of enforcement.

There are many reasons for Third World rejection of Western liberal paradigms of human rights. Some of these stem from some of the values embodied in the Western articulation of rights. They are individual-oriented and rely on adversarial procedures for their implementation. There is an emphasis on vindication of right rather than conciliation and consensual give and take. Their emphasis on individual property and the individuals' right of privacy are culturally alien to societies which are organized around social groupings such as the clan or the extended family. Moreover, the process for international enforcement of human rights has tended to reek of hypocrisy with powerful countries adopting holier-than-thou attitudes in declaring, "Do as I say and not as I do". Many Third World countries have tended to feel that Western concepts of human rights emphasize stability rather than social change. Hence, while they may be appropriate in countries with an egalitarian distribution of wealth, resources and power, they can be invoked as an obstacle to the process of redistributive justice in countries marked by highly-skewed patterns of distribution of resources and power. It is also felt that certain Western articulations of human rights might be appropriate in monocultural societies but fail to address the problems and needs of plural societies. Hence, the inadequacies in the protections of minorities in the current international human rights system.

But, most of all, Western liberal paradigms of human rights have three major flaws. The first of these relates to basic human needs and to economic, social and cultural rights. Both classical and contemporary Western liberal thought – from John Stuart Mills to John Rawls – has tended to ignore the problem of basic human needs. This problem often gets translated, both in human rights thought and in action, as a conflict between "bread" and "freedom". Freedom usually wins with the liberal conceptions of rights. Despite the awareness that, as the Indian Jurist Upendra Baxi reminds us, "without bread, freedom of speech and assembly, of association, of conscience and religion, of political participation (even through symbolic universal adult suffrage) may be existentially meaningless for its victims". The issues are not really "bread" and/or freedom" in the abstract. But rather *who* has how *much* of each, for how *long*, at what *cost* to others, and *why*. Some have both bread and freedom; others have freedom and little bread or none at all; yet others have half-a-loaf with or without freedom; and still others have a precarious mix where bread is assured if certain (and possibly all) freedoms are bartered away. We witness this cruel formula for exploitation at work throughout the developing world, both between the disadvantaged and their governments as well as between the disadvantaged and powerful private actors.

The problem of human rights, in situations of mass poverty, is one of redistribution, of access and of needs. It is one of taking economic, social and cultural rights seriously and, in this regard, the experience of the last 40 years has been disappointing. There has been repeated reaffirmation that all human rights are of equal importance and repeated reaffirmation of the interdependence of the two sets of rights (civil and political on the one hand and economic, social and cultural on the other). Nevertheless, civil and political rights have tended to become the focus of international human rights advocacy while economic, social and cultural rights have tended to become the focus of international development assistance. Somehow in the process, economic, social and cultural rights have suffered a downgrading. They have become something to be realized gradually within the resource constraints of States and governments. They have, moreover, been used as a justification for curbing civil and political rights. Thus, certain developing country governments have been advocating a "trade-off" whereby certain curbs on civil and political rights are justified in order to attain the economic development necessary to meet economic, social and cultural rights. Yet history has shown that such a trade-off has produced neither development nor human rights. The dichotomy between the two sets of rights has been greatly exaggerated and the symbiotic nature of their relationship often ignored. Failure to realize the economic, social and cultural rights of the disadvantaged has meant that their ability to effectively exercise civil and political rights has been considerably curtailed.

A second flaw in conventional and modern human rights thinking results from its being excessively State-centred, thereby neglecting the problems of human rights in the domain of civil society. The liberal discourse on rights is focused primarily on the rights of citizens against the State. Rights may not be transgressed by State power and authority. But from the point of view of a victim of human rights violations, it makes little difference whether the violator is the State; or a powerful landowner or employer; or a multinational corporation; or a bilateral or multilateral development assistance agency. The human harm and human suffering remains as acute and indeed problems of securing relief and redress may be greater in pursuing non-State actors than the State.[5]

Thus, a capitalist farmer in a "green revolution" area has the right to hire migrant labour at low wages. He has the right to use any amount of chemical fertilizers, herbicides and defoliants, all affecting, sooner or later, both the quality of the soil and genetic diversity. In exercising this right, he may generate microtoxicity in foods and vegetables, often with a carcinogenic effect on consumers. He may also exploit groundwater with a rapacity which eventually causes drought in the region. Since the State and law does not treat these actions

[5] Upendra Baxi, "From Human Rights to the Right to Be Human: Some Heresies", in S. Kothari and H. Sethi (eds.) *Rethinking Human Rights* (Delhi, 1989), pp. 151 at 160.

as causing "harms", the farmer is at liberty to do all this. Thus, rights become the resources for powerful persons to cause lawful harms to others, with the power and legitimacy of the State standing as a sentinel of their freedom. Hence, it is essential that the reach of human rights be extended to sanction non-State actors so that rights can become a resource for the disadvantaged in their struggle for amelioration.

A third flaw in the liberal paradigm of human rights stems from its unwillingness to address issues relating to the use of violence in the claimed assertion of human rights. Violence by the State, resulting in violation of human rights, is clearly proscribed. But what about violence by non-State actors purporting to be exercising their rights? This is an issue that has tended to be swept under the rug of inadequately defined concepts of self-defence and self-determination. It is a historical truth that violence can create rights. Certainly, both the violence of the oppressed and the violence of the oppressor play a crucial role in the creation, promotion and protection of human rights. Violation of the elites' rights is usually labelled as violence. But violation of the rights of the impoverished to remain human is not labelled as violence. This is a perplexing issue which must be addressed. The use of violence of any person must be brought under a regime of human rights law. Otherwise, as the experience in Sri Lanka and the Punjab shows, the grossest violations of human rights can be justified in the very name of human rights. Violence spawns violence and force begets force in a vicious, ever-escalating spiral towards self-destruction. Terrorism provokes and promotes State terrorism in response. State terrorism incites and inflames terrorist responses. Internal armed conflict is a fact of life in many modern States. If the weak and disadvantaged are to be protected, the violence of both State and non-State actors must be denounced as giving rise to human rights violations. In this respect, the growing gap between international human rights law and international humanitarian law must be closed.

Given these flaws, it is hardly surprising that those in the Third World who take human rights and human suffering seriously have rejected Western liberal approaches to human rights and pose the rhetorical question, "Is it enough?"

3. The Participatory Human Rights-Empowerment Approach

Instead, Third World human rights activists have been working to develop an alternative approach to human rights activism. This approach places fundamental importance on the organizing of victim groups. Individually, victims are powerless. But collectively, the strength of their numbers enables them to develop a countervailing power in demanding redress or in asserting other rights. Thus, enabling victims to assert effectively their rights to organize is the first task of Third World human rights activists. Through organization, the approach seeks to have victim groups assert human rights in an instrumental fashion as a means to secure empowerment, accountability and participation.

Only then can the victims of human rights violations fight back effectively against the structural causes and processes of victimization, since the key to such processes of victimization are marginalization, governmental lawlessness and exclusion. Thus, human rights are a means for empowerment of victims through resisting exploitation, debt bondage, pauperization and marginalization. Human rights are also an important means of disempowerment of the violators by holding them accountable for their acts and by exposing governmental lawlessness.

If human rights are to prove meaningful to those who most need them (namely the victims of human rights deprivations), it is vital to adopt a "participatory approach" to the development of human rights and their enforcement. Thus, for example, in the development of a human right to food, it is vital that groups of the rural poor presently confronted with hunger and malnutrition (and other support and action groups working with them) articulate their concerns and needs in regard to deteriorating food situations and formulate their strategies to effectively address such situations. Such a participatory, human rights-empowerment approach stresses victim group and grass roots participation in all aspects of human rights activism, from standard setting and promotion to monitoring and enforcement.

The essence of any human right is the power to command the protections promised by the right. The participatory human rights-empowerment approach is designed to help victims of human rights deprivation gain that power. The participatory human rights-empowerment approach is based on four underlying propositions.

1) Law is a resource which can be used both defensively and assertively by the rural poor in their struggles against conditions which produce impoverishment, deprivation and oppression.
2) Human rights are very important "legal resources" because they empower the rural poor to participate in these struggles and demand protection of their basic interests.
3) Non-governmental organizations (NGO's) of various kinds (from grass roots to international groups) have vital roles to play in these struggles.
4) Human rights must help bring about the structural changes needed to ensure the dignity and worth of all human persons, especially the "have nots". In the words of Theo Van Boven, the "have nots" "regard human rights as a means of change, as tools in a process towards emancipation and liberation. Human rights are arms in their struggle for liberation".

4. Addressing Asian Realities: Disempowering Violators

The impoverishment of a majority of the peoples of Asia has largely resulted from the feeding of several transnational/international (usually developed country) hungers.

1) Hunger for developing country *natural resources*. Historically, this hunger

was for the primary commodities and primary products of developing countries. Today the hunger is also for developing country lands on which transnational agri-business plantations are producing, cheaply (for global markets), bananas and pineapples in the Philippines, strawberries in Mexico, horticultural products in Kenya and oil palm in Malaysia. More recently, there is a new hunger for developing country lands as pollution havens for ultrahazardous industry and even as dump sites for toxic wastes! Ruling elites in developing countries are willing accomplices in the feeding of such international hungers bargaining away long-term pauperization of the human and natural environment for short-term profits and wealth.

2) Hunger for developing country *labour*. This hunger is both for cheap unskilled labour (in export processing zones or as "guest workers") and for skilled labour (creating perpetual brain drain). All this takes place in the name of a so-called international division of labour. But the link between feeding international hungers for developing country labour and the pauperization of the human environment and degradation of the physical environment in developing countries is rarely made.
3) Hunger for developing country *markets* stems from their use as a dumping ground for surplus production as well as to sustain levels of economic growth in industrialized countries. The feeding of this international hunger also takes a heavy toll on the human and natural environment of developing countries.
4) Hunger for ways (including development projects) to *recycle* developed country *capital surpluses* can result in the export of debt and inflation to the developing countries with very real costs in terms of human suffering.
5) Hunger for superpower *spheres of influence* has led to the unfortunate militarization of the developing world with, once again, heavy costs to the human and natural environment.

These international hungers are not without their national counterparts, of course. For example, the growing incidence of bonded labour and slavery-like practices are the product of models of development which are primarily oriented to serving the needs of minorities of urban-industrial population. There is thus a vested interest in keeping a large sector of the population disorganized and depoliticized, so that the poor can be availed of as a source of perennial, cheap and docile labour. Similarly, policies of rural development have tended to make only such inputs into the rural economy as are necessary to insure outputs needed by the urban-industrial sector. Development, for most countries, has been geared towards perpetuating a colonial-type exploitation by a small urban-industrial elite (and its client class of dependent rural elite) of the primary producers who comprise the vast majority of the population of landless labourers, small and marginal farmers, rural artisans and tribals in the forest economy.

It is important to identify the violators who are responsible for ruthlessly denying the basic human rights of the masses in order to feed such transnational hungers and perpetuate their own self-interest. These violators comprise local elites (e.g., landowners and moneylenders) and national elites (government bureaucrats and political parties) who are willing and eager accomplices in colluding with international elites comprising transnational corporations, developed country governments and international development agencies.

The task then is to fashion a strategy to disempower these violators and to hold them accountable. Three such strategies being employed are empowerment of the victims through organizing counter-vailing people power; imposition of legal and social accountability through the generation of outrage, indignation, and shame regarding gross human rights violations; articulating and living the vision and values of a new humane society founded on the most basic and fundamental of human rights, namely the right to be human.

The role of human rights education and human rights activism in the above three strategies needs to be carefully determined and addressed.

5. Development and Human Rights in Asia

At first blush there appears to be no contradiction between the values and goals embodied in the concept of development and the concept of human rights. Indeed, development is often viewed as a vehicle for achieving economic growth and this is an important goal where the absence (or inadequacy) of growth acts as a constraint on realizing the human rights of all. Development is also seen as a vehicle for redistribution. At the very least, it is claimed, there will be the growth-trickle-down effect. Moreover, consciously redistributive policies can be adopted allocating a differentially large proportion of the benefits of development to the poor, thus correcting historically skewed patterns of distribution of resources, wealth and power. But all too often development policies equate development with economic growth at any cost and all too often human rights are traded off in the pursuit of such economic growth.

Human rights in turn can help provide the value framework for development. Human rights can, and should, provide the evaluative criteria for holding developmental actors responsible. Human rights can also provide the means for ensuring that development will be "sustainable", ecologically sound, and will not create "ecological deficits". Development today should not be allowed to mortgage (or, worse still, destroy) the future of generations yet to be born. Human rights can provide a very strong basis for the concept of inter-generational justice. There is indeed a close interrelatedness between development, growth, poverty and the environment. Human rights have a crucial role to play in ensuring that development addresses all three GNP's: the gross national product, the gross nature product and, most importantly, the gross national poverty.

But the gap between the rhetoric of development and development practice appears to be ever-widening in Asia despite slogans such as "growth with distribution", "basic needs", "people first", and "sustainable development". A review of development practice in Asia reveals this clearly. In most Asian countries, examples abound of government development policies and projects which bring benefits to a privileged few but displacement, starvation and exploitation to the many. Such projects include: industrialization projects which unquestioningly embrace arduous (so-called "high") technologies and sacrifice or imperil the life of workers and communities; agricultural development projects which are intended to achieve "food self-sufficiency" or export earnings but which end up financing unequal urban development while causing rural hunger, exploitation and impoverishment; and large-scale infrastructure or dam building projects which displace thousands and ruin ecology for survival, to provide energy and water for a privileged few.

Thus, development has often produced and reproduced conditions of impoverishment and powerlessness which have fostered systemic disregard for and violations of human rights of the vast majority of the poor.

More often than not in Asia, development has meant for the grass roots: impoverishment, exploitation, debt bondage and slavery; ethnocide; forced resettlement; being made into ecological refugees; violation of all basic human rights; and repression of organized self-help.

The challenge for human rights activists in Asia lies in fashioning a rights-oriented strategy to address the above practices. Such a strategy would demonstrate that the inhuman wrongs resulting from the above practices also constitute violation of human rights such as the rights to life and livelihood, the right to food, the right to habitat, the right to health, and also of important group rights such as rights of association and the right to cultural identity. Moreover, current international efforts to articulate and enforce a right to development as a human right are clearly steps in a most welcome direction, especially if the victims of development are to have a major say in such efforts.

6. Ecology and Human Rights in Asia

In many Asian countries certain environmental trends have become evident:

1) expropriation of the survival resources (e.g., fuel, fodder, ancestral lands) of grass roots communities in the rural areas is taking place at an accelerated pace;
2) patterns of resource exploitation and use are at such a scale as to bring about huge "ecological deficits", mortgaging and threatening future generations;
3) environmental refugees are being created at an ever-increasing scale.

These trends reveal a close complementarity between environmental degradation and human degradation leading to massive human rights violations at the grassroots level. Accordingly, there is an urgent need for closer cooperation between environmental activists and human rights activists to fight to reverse these harmful trends. Sustainable development is often a misnomer for desperate survival struggles at the grassroots. The challenge for both human rights and environmental activists is to help achieve participatory environmental protection in which affected communities and groups have the key role in efforts aimed at: damage limitation (e.g., obtaining injunctive relief and resources for undertaking clean-up); ecology restoration (e.g., reforestation or watershed reconstruction); prevention/conservation (e.g., safeguarding community sources of fuelwood and grazing through ecologically sound practices).

7. Peace and Human Rights in Asia

There is little peace in Asia. The struggles of superpowers to maintain spheres of influence and military bases in the region has led to massive militarization through both arms aid and arms sales. The manipulation of ethnic tensions by ruling governments and neighbouring countries (with tacit encouragement by super-powers) has led to savage ethnic conflict in Sri Lanka, India and Pakistan and, on a lesser scale, Bangladesh and the Philippines. Malaysia appears to be an ethnic time bomb. Internal armed conflict is everywhere and the U.S. has exported the tactics of low-intensity conflict into the region. The results, in terms of human suffering are tragic: ever-increasing military expenditures are incurred at the expense of meeting basic human needs and providing essential basic services; restrictive laws are being rapidly enacted and invoked to deal with alleged threats to national security, often against legitimate opposition to the ruling elites; and governments are increasingly using these weapons against their own citizens; civilian casualties are mounting while international humanitarian law is being flouted.

The situation is especially difficult for villages and grassroots communities who are caught in the crossfire between the protagonists of internal armed conflict.

The need for human rights activism is crucial, to impose human rights standards and international humanitarian law upon both State and non-State parties to conflict; to challenge and resist abuse and over-use of restrictive laws in the alleged defense of national security; and to restore human needs priorities in government expenditures and to press for demilitarization.

8. Implenting the Human Rights-Empowerment Approach at Grassroots Level in Asia

Grassroots problems in Asia cannot be adequately addressed through conventional human rights activism on the part of sympathetic (if paternalistic) legal and other professional elites alone. The participatory human rights-empowerment approach is essential. Grassroots participation is essential at every stage of human rights activism.

Human rights organizations in Asia have demonstrated the feasibility of such an approach in their work with indigenous peoples. By starting first with the problems faced by indigenous peoples (namely ethnocide, forced integration, exploitation, paternalistic development which erodes self-reliance), they have helped indigenous people to articulate and struggle for recognition and enforcement of a number of vital *group rights*:

1. *The right to land*: not any land but traditional and ancestral homeland. Not land just as an economic resource or factor of production but land as territory, as habitat which has economic as well as cultural, social and historical significance. Land which is the *sine qua non* of the groups' survival as a group.
2. *The right of internal self-determination*: which includes the right to customary laws and the rights to devolution, sharing of powers and resources, and the right of local self-government.
3. *Rights to institutional structures of separateness*: social and political institutions including institutions of dispute resolution.
4. *Rights of cultural continuity*: including rights to language, education, culture and religion.
5. *Rights of identity*: including the right of indigenous peoples to determine who is and who is not an indigenous person.
6. *The right of ethnodevelopment*: which refers to the human right to development as applied to indigenous peoples. Classical development models have failed to solve the problems of humankind such as poverty, unemployment and environment. People are taking a second look at so-called traditional cultures which provide answers regarding agricultural food production, traditional medicine, resource and environment management in rural areas, construction and irrigation techniques, social security and solidarity in times of crises. Ethnodevelopment means control over land, resources, social organization and culture *and* freedom to negotiate with the State what kind of relationship the group wishes to have. In the words of Rudolfo Stavenhagen, "ethnodevelopment means looking inwards and finding in the group's own culture the resources and creative force necessary to confront the challenges of the modern changing world. It does not mean autarchy or retreat into a museum of tradition".[6] The basic human right of isolation (rather than integration) must be recognized as the group-right counterpart of the individual right of privacy.

The experience with indigenous peoples must be replicated in respect of all other grassroots and exploited communities. Human rights activists must work closely with and in grassroots communities, starting with grassroots problems, realities and priorities, then moving to holistic analyses which trace linkages between local, national and global actors and forces. Only then can effective mechanisms be devised for solidarity and support. There is also a crucial need to devise, working with grassroots communities, alert and early warning systems regarding a variety of transnational influences and macro forces such as: aid dependency and technological dependency; the spread of conspicuous consumerism; "perverse" development projects and the role of transnational

[6] Speech delivered at the 1988 Nobel Symposium in Oslo, Norway.

corporations and international development assistance agencies therein; the incurring of ecological deficits; debt and structural adjustment leading to food and job riots and massive human deprivation and suffering; and militarization.

9. Towards Human Rights Education at the Grassroots Level

Human rights lawyers will need to rethink their basic assumptions if they are to be of any help in work aimed at human rights education at the grassroots. They will need to start with an unlearning process: discovering how irrelevant is much of what they know and realizing how little in fact they know. They will then need to undergo a relearning process: learning from the victims and realizing that education is not a process of "putting in" but rather one of "drawing out". They will need to devise a people-based and not a law-based approach to human rights education.

This will, of course, necessitate a search for new methodologies which are participatory and not passive; accessible and not alien; relevant and not redundant. There will need to be collective rethinking with the grassroots about the content, values, format, objectives, use and evaluation of human rights education programs. In doing this, human rights NGO's will have to face and overcome formidable problems and constraints, both external and internal. From external actors (be they government or private sector) they will have to contend with efforts aimed at cooptation, control and repression. At an internal level, NGO's will have to face problems of fragmentation, distrust, and lack of solidarity among fellow NGO's. But these problems can and must be overcome. After all, what the mind can conceive, we can achieve! Moreover, not only can we achieve, we must achieve. Only then can we realize that most precious of human rights, the right to be human. Noting that it would be impossible to realize the right to be human in any serious sense without full and ungrudging recognition of the right to be a woman as a crucial component of the right to be human.

Bibliographical Note

Since Asian legal scholars find it difficult to secure access to Asian writings on law, human rights, and grassroots development, this brief bibliographical note lists a few of the important recent publications in the Asian region.

1. Asian Coalition of Human Rights Organizations, *Human Rights Activism in Asia: Some Perspectives, Problems and Approaches*. New York: Council on International and Public Affairs, 1984.
2. Asian Exchange, *Law, Rights and Participation*. Hong Kong, 1988.
3. S. Kothari and H. Sethi, *Rethinking Human Rights*. Delhi, 1989.
4. SALAG, *Understanding Human Rights*. Manila, 1989.
5. C. Espiritu, *Law and Human Rights in the Development of ASEAN*.

Singapore, 1986.
6. R. Kanniah and M. Raman, *People's Access to the Legal System: A Grassroots Perspective*. Singapore, 1986.
7. Chee Yoke Ling, *Legal Education in Asean Universities: A Critical Appraisal*. Singapore, 1986.
8. A. Nusantara, M. Kusumah, and T. M. Lubis, *Non-Formal Legal Education: Reflections on the Experience of the Legal Aid Institute*. Singapore, 1986.

EDWARD BROADBENT*

Human Rights and Democratic Development: Foreign Policy Concerns in the Western World

1. Introduction

The topic of this paper concerns the critical linkages between development and human rights and the roles that our governments must increasingly play in securing both. Alexander Solzhenitsyn said that the most enduring achievement of the United Nations was the creation of the Universal Declaration of Human Rights in 1948. He might well have been right. Clearly its assertion about the inherent dignity and the equal and inalienable rights of all members of the human family has a universal appeal. It *does* transcend all cultural and historical differences.

Immediately following World War II, a strong pro-democracy, pro-human rights atmosphere prevailed in the Western world. The creation of the United Nations itself and the Universal Declaration were greeted with enthusiasm. Shortly after the adoption of the Universal Declaration, however, the Cold War began in earnest and lasted for four decades. A consequence of this unfortunate turn of political events in the international arena was to marginalize policy interest in pursuing international human rights standards and applications. Not only were hundreds of billions of dollars used up in armaments which could have contributed significantly to economic rights, but the super-powers, more concerned about the requirement to gain geo-political advantage over their adversary, either ignored or actively supported violations of human rights and the absence of indigenous democratization in developing countries. The Cold War, therefore, contributed to the inherently ambivalent attitude of Western democratic states about making human rights and democratic institutions a central concern in foreign relations.

The ambivalence of Western attitudes existed because of how they set their priorities. Any democratic state has at least three potentially competing matters to be concerned about in foreign relations: trade, security (defence) and human

* President, International Centre for Human Rights and Democratic Development, Montreal, Quebec, Canada.

K.E. Mahoney and P. Mahoney (eds.), Human Rights in the Twenty-first Century, 715–719.

rights. During the past four decades, human rights concerns have been given very low priority compared to trade and security in the crafting of foreign policy. It is now time for a committed citizenry to insist that their governments install human rights concerns as a major concern of foreign policy.

The death of the Cold War, symbolized by the fact that Presidents Gorbachev and Bush now meet to consult not confront, provides greater latitude in which to elevate human rights concerns as a key component of foreign relations. Not only in Eastern Europe, but also in Kenya, the Philippines, Guatemala and Cuba, and dozens of other countries, there is now an actively expressed demand for human rights and democratic institutions to be fully realized. The world is now at one of those crucial moments in history when a major change in international power relations will enable human values to play a greater role in shaping the future.

This also comes at a time when international human rights law has evolved in the direction of having precedence over domestic law. Established democracies must seize the occasion. Without denying any injustices at home they can and must play an active role in placing human rights and democratic practices as a top priority of external relations. This means changing a number of Western practices and taking a more outspoken position about the consistent and systematic violations of human rights in other states. The latter work cannot be left to the courageous activists in non-government organizations who work so steadfastly in the face of imprisonment or death.

2. Development and Trade Policy

Charting the course for a more activist role by governments in developing coherence in foreign policy is neither the utopian project nor the minefield that some would suggest. This can be done effectively by putting the whole family of human rights (political, civil, economic, social and cultural) in their rightful place in all our developmental thinking *and* by integrating human rights with our international aid, trade and commercial policies.

This approach has already been advocated by Members of Canada's Parliament. A number of parliamentary committees have called upon the federal government to establish coherence in Canadian foreign policy *vis-à-vis* our official Development Assistance, Trade and Commercial policies. The most recent of these initiatives, the Interim Report of the Sub-Committee on International Human Rights, stated that, "There appears to be a serious lack of coherence and consistency between many of Canada's aid, trade and financial assistance relationships with other countries, on the one hand, and our human rights commitments on the other. Canada, like most other human rights supporting nations, seems often to be in the position of piously condemning human rights abuses 'on Sundays' and then carrying on business as usual – including mutually lucrative business – with human rights abusing countries, during the rest of the week." Surely it is time to develop and apply a coherent policy in aid, trade and human rights. We must stop condemning the brutality of Tiananmen Square on Monday and carrying on trade on Tuesday.

Just as we are coming to understand that no major development project should be undertaken without considering its impact on the environment, we must also consider an internationally funded project's impact on human rights: a dam may be a source of energy but it may also obliterate the housing rights of people or destroy an indigenous people's mode of existence. Economics, the environment and human rights are common links in what should be an indivisible human chain. In development, the human family deserves both clean air and individual and cultural freedom. Any economic policy that ignores either element is not worthy of the name.

At the official opening of the International Centre for Human Rights and Democratic Development, Canada's Secretary of State for External Affairs, Joe Clark, (as he then was), emphasized that the Government of Canada will make this connection in its bilateral relations. He suggested that the Canadian government would be prepared to "cease to deal through the regime" in cases of the extreme abuse of human rights, although it would attempt by other means to get aid directly to those who need it. Earlier in 1990, the President of France, a U.S. Under-Secretary and the British Foreign Minister, indicated that their respective governments intended to make a similar link between aid policy and human rights. Surely it's time these assertions were followed by action.

3. What Should Be Done?

A starting point is the 1986 U.N. Declaration on the Right to Development. The essence of this Declaration is that, notwithstanding real differences in cultures, religions and economies, "development" means there is a broad spectrum of fundamental values that humanity shares in common and this family of human rights, as established by the U.N., must be taken seriously. How can we do this?

At the bilateral level, in our international aid practices, and in pursuit of our trade and commercial objectives, treaties and agreements must contain human rights conditionality which goes beyond a simplistic pro-forma consideration of a country's human rights record. The Government of Canada has committed itself to terminating bilateral aid agreements to ODA-recipient countries whose governments violate the human rights of its citizenry in a gross, continuous and systematic fashion and re-directing that aid to the same population through local non-government organizations.

At the multilateral level, concrete measures should be taken to ensure that, as a matter of routine, all aid, trade and commercial policies include human rights and democratic practices considerations. Already agreed upon U.N. resolutions and covenants should be taken into account. By extension, it is also time that national governments who participate in the decision-making of the World Bank and the other international and regional financing institutions consider as a matter of control, the human rights impact of a proposed project and, as importantly, the impact of debt burden decisions on the economic and social rights of citizens in developing countries. Third World countries are now paying millions more in interest payments to the industrialized countries than they are receiving in aid.

It is time also that the General Agreement on Tariffs and Trade (GATT) included a clause whose purpose would be to help prevent the exploitation of the world's poor either by multinational corporations or by governments. Such a clause would take into account existing differences in development but would obligate contracting parties to observe certain minimum labour standards based on ILO agreements. Such standards could be worked out by an advisory committee to be established by the GATT and the ILO. When it comes to work conditions we must insist that in international commerce, freedom of association, the protection of children, abolition of forced labour and the rights of trade unionists be regarded as important as the right to make a profit. What we demand for ourselves as basic human rights, we must also support for others.

At home, established democracies should also demonstrate their commitment to human rights and democracy by ensuring an annual debate in their Parliaments and Congresses comparable in principle to the yearly budget debates. This debate would include the participation of senior members of the government. The Ministers would be expected to give a full accounting, including a record of votes at the United Nations, the World Bank, the IMF and the GATT. During the same debate, the whole range of human rights issues which had arisen domestically during the previous year would also receive a full discussion.

A week-long debate on human rights and democratic practices, at home and abroad, would be a significant contribution to ensuring human rights would receive the priority they deserve by governments. Such a debate would also contribute significantly to the human rights education of people throughout the country. These and other fora of debate are essential elements to the involvement of citizens in the critical need to make human rights an integral part of all our policies.

4. Western Experience versus Third World Experience

There is a danger in the solutions listed above of the Western countries being seen to impose their own particular experience on developing nations. It is essential that no one model of democracy be seen as the standard. We Canadians do not have the right – nor does anyone else – to suggest our model as the standard for the world. However, there are certain key elements that any democratic society must have if it is to be regarded as democratic. It is, therefore, essential for humanity that those principles of democracy and human rights that the developing nations themselves have accepted at the United Nations be applied to all. And it is equally essential that the full range of human rights, economic and cultural and not just the political and civil, be taken into account.

In the final analysis we must take our stand with those citizens and governments in developing countries who are struggling for liberty in all its dimensions. A citizen of the Philippines said, authoritarianism is not essential for development, but it *is* essential to perpetuate the status quo. A Canadian Inuit once said in a similar context, it is time that we do constructive damage to the status-quo.

5. Conclusion

Whatever we do it will remain in the future as it has been in the past: a more humane and just order in any country will ultimately be created by those living within that country. What we can do is aid or hinder the process. By our action or inaction we will take sides one way or the other. Surely we must be on the side of those favouring human rights and democracy.

THOMAS AXWORTHY*

Democracy and Development: Luxury or Necessity?

1. Introduction

There are certain years which define the age in which they fall – the Glorious Revolution of England in 1688, America in 1776, France in 1789 and now, in our time, that sequence of events in that *annus mirabilis,* 1989. The Berlin Wall no longer divides. The Soviet Union no longer threatens. The Cold War is over. A new world order beckons.

Debate on why the Cold War ended in a complete Western victory is only beginning.[1] Conservatives argue that containment worked, that the line drawn in Europe in 1948–1949 by George Kennan, Dean Acheson and Harry Truman prevented immediate Soviet adventurism and, over time, the intrinsic economic weakness of the Soviets lessened their ability to compete. In short, the arms race bankrupted the Russians into moderation.

Liberals argue that détente worked: increased contact and trade with the West gradually reduced traditional Russian fears about attack so that in time a new leadership could take a chance on reform at home and retrenchment abroad. Both analyses ring true. Sweeping historical change is due to many causes. The important point is that our generation too can be present at the creation – the creation of a post-Cold War world order. What should be the components of that new world and in particular, how much importance should be placed on human rights and democratic advance?

This paper makes a four-part argument:

1. The end of the Cold War reduces most of the *realpolitik* constraints on placing human rights at the top of the world agenda. We are presently witnessing one of greatest democratic explosions in world history: our task

* Adjunct Lecturer at the John F. Kennedy School of Government, Harvard University.

[1] For a spirited discussion of why Soviet Communism failed see Ralf Dahrendorf, *Reflections on the Revolution in Europe* (1990), New York: Random House. An excellent eye-witness account of the 1989 revolution in Europe is contained in Timothy Garton Ash, *The Magic Lantern* (1990), New York: Random House. See also Timothy Garton Ash, *The Uses of Adversity: Essays on the Fate of Central Europe* (1989), New York: Vintage Books.

K.E. Mahoney and P. Mahoney (eds.), Human Rights in the Twenty-first Century, 721–727.

is to consolidate the gains, fix the root of liberty solidly into the fabric of societies like the Philippines, the Soviet Union or Brazil, and promote democracy in other areas like Africa and the Middle East which have not yet made the democratic breakthrough.

2. The nature of regimes matters. Real devotion to human rights and popular participation in government are not only essential for individual development; they also form the basis of civil society. Civil societies in turn are usually peaceful societies. The spread of democracy and human rights across the globe will not only improve the lives of millions, but it will ensure the safety of the rest of us.
3. Despite their importance, democracy and human rights have only received lip service in development policy. The World Bank, the International Monetary Fund and the bilateral aid programmes of the West virtually ignore the nature of the recipient country's regime. Pinochet's Chile, for example, was lauded by many in the West because of its monetarism, despite the human rights atrocities. This paper argues that ignoring the democratic dimension is not only bad politics but leads to bad economics. The new global economy demands intelligence, entrepreneurship and information exchange – precisely the qualities promoted by democracy and stifled by autocracy. It is time to end the divide between economic and political development. The two must move in concert.
4. Therefore, it is time that countries like Canada put the criteria of democracy and human rights at the centre of our foreign policy. Human rights must become a pre-condition for aid. This will require massive changes to existing policy. Promoting freedom rather than mouthing the rhetoric of freedom must become a compelling priority. The new world order must be a democratic world order.

2. A Golden Opportunity to Promote Democracy

Citizens who enjoy the benefit of democracy probably underestimate how difficult a system it is to create and sustain. Ancient Athens, the inventor of popular participation in government, practised democracy for two hundred years. After Phillip of Macedon conquered the city, the rule of the many vanished until the creation of the United States in 1789. American democracy has now lasted as long as the Athenian model – two hundred years. Throughout world history democratic practice has always been a minority faith.

The 1990's may finally close the chapter on this sad story. Democracy is on the march: Boris Yeltsin in Russia, Corazon C. Aquino in the Philippines, Lech Walesa in Poland and Raul Alfonsin in Argentina are examples of leaders who are transforming world politics. And the end of the Cold War can only hasten this process. In the era of Cold War rivalry, autocrats could play one superpower off against another: "He may be a son of a bitch", Franklin Roosevelt said about Somoza of Nicaragua, "but he is *our* son of a bitch."

Human rights were seen as a luxury that unfortunately had to be sacrificed on the altar of *realpolitik*.

Jimmy Carter was generally derided by the foreign policy establishment because he had the temerity to advocate human rights as a basic principle of American foreign policy. But democratic nations now hold the cards. It is the West that possesses the technology and wealth that the rest of the world needs. If the West does not make human rights and democratic rule a pre-condition of its aid and trade, it is because western policy makers choose not to do so. Arms exporters like France or the United States may want to continue to flog their wares amongst the military regimes of the Third World, but they can no longer plead the Cold War as an excuse. For the first time since 1945, we have a real choice: will we promote liberty or not?

3. Link between Democracy and Security

Morality should dictate that the West finally lives up to its ideals. But self interest also should propel the West to promote a democratic agenda. In 1795, Immanuel Kant in *Perpetual Peace* made the elementary point that regimes matter. Kant reasoned that if "the consent of the citizenry is recognized in order to determine whether or not there will be war, it is natural that they will consider all its calamities before committing themselves to so risky a game"; but where "the ruler is not a fellow citizen, but the nation's owner, and war does not affect his table, his hunt, his places of pleasure, his court festivities..., he can decide to go to war for the most meaningless of reasons, as if it were a kind of pleasure party, and he can blithely leave its justification (which decency requires) to his diplomatic corps, who are always prepared for such exercises".[2]

Since Kant wrote in 1795, no democracy has ever fought another democracy in a war. Democracies have fought authoritarian regimes. Democratic citizens have sometimes even seemed eager for war as many appeared to be in the heady days of 1914, but no democracy has ever attacked another. Rather than spending billions or even trillions on the instruments of war, to prevent attack from the Soviet Union, it would be prudent, cost effective and morally more correct to spend millions on helping democracy to flourish in the old Soviet empire. The best guarantee of a peaceful world is a democratic world. As Kant wrote, citizens know that in war they are the losers, not their rulers. Therefore, if they have meaningful participation in their government they will never wilfully subject themselves to war's horrors.

[2] Immanuel Kant, *Perpetual Peace and Other Essays*, trans. Ted Humphrey, (1983), Indianapolis: Hackett Publishing Co., p. 113.

4. Link between Democracy and Economics

Kant's wisdom, however, has not been reflected in current Western statecraft. Canada spends a billion dollars a year to contribute to NATO, to defend Western Europe from attack from the East, but when Lech Walesa comes to call to see what assistance we could offer to help Poland's transition to democracy, he left with a paltry $4 million. Mrs. Aquino ends the autocracy of Marcos, but then she is on her own. Democracy emerges in Latin America at precisely the same time that the World Bank and the International Monetary Fund decree austerity to be the way to pay back old loans. It would be laughable if it were not so tragic.

Ralf Dahrendorf captures this conundrum very well in what he calls the Martinez Paradox, named after the Nicaraguan Minister of Foreign Trade. Under Somoza, the Sandanista minister explained the super markets were full, but no one could afford the goods inside. Now after the revolution, the shop windows were empty but everyone could afford what was there.[3] The revolution had transformed a world of plenty for the few into one of little for all. Nicaragua had gone from growth without redistribution to redistribution without growth.

Dahrendorf's point, which we must heed if we want the democratic revolution in Eastern Europe, the Soviet Union and Latin America to endure, is that citizens require both liberties and goods. Growth of provisions gives citizens choices. Entitlements or rights give people a claim to things. To create civil democratic societies, the Martinez paradox must be solved – there must be access for all and plenty of goods.

This inter-relationship between provisions and entitlements, between goods and rights, has been neglected in most development policies. This single-minded devotion to growth, while ignoring internal structures of power and the mechanisms of distribution, has meant that where growth has occurred it has not contributed to the creation of civil societies. Individuals have gotten rich (usually through corruption) but the society has continued to be impoverished.

Even the most cursory look at statistics tells a depressing tale. It has been fifty years since the United States in Point IV and Canada in the Colombo Plan initiated large-scale development plans. Yet of the 5.5 billion humans on the globe, one billion according to the World Bank are absolutely poor or live at the margin, one billion have increasing life chances (those who live in OECD countries) and the majority in between – three billion – live in their traditional circle of poverty. John Kenneth Galbraith, for example, who helped President Truman develop Point IV and was later ambassador to India, concludes that despite all the effort of Western aid since 1950 "in the countries of mass poverty – India, Pakistan, Bangladesh, Indonesia, large parts of Africa and Latin

[3] Ralf Dahrendorf, *The Modern Social Conflict* (1988), New York: Weidenfeld & Nicolson, pp. 7–8.

America – the deprivation remains extensively unabated and unchanged".[4] Indeed, a recent report by Helmut Schmidt, the former Chancellor of West Germany, demonstrates that in recent years the developing world has very much fallen behind.[5] It points out that for the past five years the net transfer of funds to the developing countries has been negative; the level of external indebtedness in a number of developing countries has skyrocketed; gross national product (GNP) per capita in many developing countries has fallen; and over the last twenty years the gap between industrialized and developing countries has widened enormously (from 1965 to 1987, real per capita GNP increased from $140 to $270 for low income countries, from $980 to $1,680 for middle income countries, and from $8,820 to $14,550 for industrialized market economies.

Economically the developing world is in a worsening state at the precise moment that the democratic spark has finally burst into flame. This is no time for the West to lose interest or to lose heart.

5. Human Rights as a Pre-Condition for Aid

But why so little progress? The West has provided capital and technical assistance to the Third World, while ignoring the nature of the regimes. The elites and the oligarchies have spent much of the money on the military or themselves. The trickle down theory has not worked. Unless the traditional authoritarian structures are broken, "macro-economic growth means little for the mass, however satisfactory the International Monetary Fund may find the statistics".[6]

This is certainly the lesson of our own history. William Beveridge and John Maynard Keynes were wise enough to advance both rights and provisions at the same time. Wealth increased but was also distributed. It was distributed, not because of altruism, but because democracy allowed working men and women a measure of power.

The pre-condition to solving mass poverty, according to Galbraith, is to break the equilibrium of poverty – the passivity or acceptance of fate which many traditional societies exhibit.[7] At a minimum, democracy is a means to stir people up. It requires participation. By giving responsibility it demands involvement. The first principle of development, said Martin Luther King, is "to teach people to believe in themselves". Democracy does not assure economic advance; countries with a tradition of freedom like Senegal still have a myriad of problems to solve. But without democracy there will never be fair

[4] John Kenneth Galbraith, *The Nature of Mass Poverty* (1979), Cambridge, Mass.: Harvard University Press, pp. 42–43.

[5] Helmut Schmidt, *Facing One World* (1989), Hamburg: Report by an Independent Group on Financial Flows to Developing Countries, pp. 3–5.

[6] R. Dahrendorf, see note 3, *supra*, p. 14.

[7] J. Galbraith, see note 4, *supra*.

distribution, and without a minimum level of distribution, there will never be a civil society.

So democracy is a pre-condition to distribution. But it has an added economic dimension that will become even more important as the world economy evolves. Peter Drucker has written most convincingly about the new realities of economic growth: information exchange, computer link-ups and individual entrepreneurship. This transformation of the economy has, according to Drucker, as large an impact on government as it does on profits.[8]

Authoritarian societies, for example, have no way of coping with new technologies. How can you control information in the era of the personal computer, fax machine and satellite television? The attempt to control information and to keep a closed society will inevitably have a negative impact on technological development and hence growth. By enhancing individual capacities to create and to communicate, technology strikes a blow at autocracy. In this dimension, at least, economic progress and democratic progress run in tandem.

Analysts like Dahrendorf, Galbraith and Drucker, then, make a strong theoretical argument for the inter-relationship between freedom and development. A recent study published for the United Nations Development Programme, *Human Development Report 1991*, begins to make the case empirically.[9] The report develops a human freedom index for 88 countries and concludes "overall, there seems to be a high correlation between human development and human freedom".[10] Countries that rank high on the freedom index also rank more highly on the development scale. Political freedom unleashes the creative energies of people which leads to higher levels of income and progress. "If a society is free," the report concludes, "influence does not always require affluence. Democracy is a valuable ally of *all*."[11]

The release of this report, and especially the finding that the world's poorest nations are generally also the least free, has provoked a storm of controversy among Third World countries. Kenya's deputy, Robert Ramau Gathungu, for example, strongly questioned the right of the United Nations to publish the index[12] and several Third World countries drafted a resolution to ban further publication of the human freedom index. This attempt at censorship has to be resisted at all costs. If the Third World desires Western assistance, donor nations have the right to insist that aid be well spent. If freedom and a commitment to human rights are essential components of development, then the donor country should insist upon incorporating these criteria into their aid policies. This may discomfit nations like Zaire, China, Tanzania or Kenya, but so be it. Such dictatorships should not be able to have it both ways: if they wish

[8] Peter F. Drucker, *The New Realities* (1989), New York: Harper and Row, pp. 173–187.

[9] United Nations Development Program, *Human Development Report 1991* (1991), New York: Oxford University Press.

[10] Ibid., p. 21.

[11] Ibid., p. 9.

[12] "UN Index on Freedom Enrages Third World", *New York Times*, June 23, 1991. p. 11.

to suppress freedom, they should, at a minimum, pay the price of doing so without international assistance.

6. Conclusion

The argument can now be summarized – the world is in a democratic upsurge unprecedented in history. This upsurge not only conforms to the highest ideals of Western philosophy, it is also our best guarantee of a peaceful world. But this democratic moment will be fleeting unless the West helps newly emergent democracies to provide both provisions and rights; and those parts of the Third World which have not yet adopted democracy must come to understand that democracy is an essential pre-condition to economic advance since it is necessary above all to break the traditional equilibrium or acceptance of poverty. To thrive, democracy requires growth; and to grow, economies need democracy.

The policy implications are clear. Acceptance of human rights and democratic practice must become a condition of Western aid and development. The World Bank and the International Monetary Fund must include political criteria in their granting policies and rich countries like Canada must become more generous toward newly emerging democracies like Poland or the Philippines. The world needs more development and more liberty. We must accept the wisdom of John F. Kennedy that "if a free country cannot help the many who are poor, it cannot save the few who are rich". And we best help the many who are poor by insisting upon respect for human rights and ensuring popular participation. Our way is clear – we must put democracy first.

SECTION V

New Threats to Human Rights Through Science and Technology – The Need for Standards*

* Summary prepared by the editors.

Introduction

The overview to the Section on New Threats to Human Rights Through Science and Technology is provided by Ursula Franklin. She argues that the advances in science and technology have increased the machinery of dominance and oppression; and they have done this by changing the context and environment in which human rights are placed and must be defended.

Defining technology as the practice or application of science, she first explores some of the more threatening implications of technology for human rights; it allows invisible control of people; it trivialises the fundamental principles involved; it enables automatic exclusion or compulsory inclusion of groups; it separates human rights issues into macro- and micro- situations, the latter being much more difficult for the human rights movement to handle. The new human rights standards needed must be derived from a recognition of how technology has changed the context and environment. From the nature of the threat posed by technology, she infers the need to shift the point of human rights intervention from the incident of infringement to the moment of planning, from the action to the potential: in short, mechanisms for identifying and preventing threats before technologies become unmanageable.

K.E. Mahoney and P. Mahoney (eds.), Human Rights in the Twenty-first Century, 731.

URSULA FRANKLIN*

New Threats to Human Rights Through Science and Technology – The Need For Standards

1. Introduction

Disadvantaged groups who have spoken earlier, articulated their disadvantage very well. We have heard about *how* they are disadvantaged. But we have heard less about *why* they are disadvantaged. The work for human rights needs to know those reasons. We have to concern ourselves with why it is that dominance and oppression seem to be growing. One of the reasons is doubtless that the maintenance of privilege in fact requires continued dominance and oppression. Another reason – and that is the thesis of this short paper – is that recent advances in science and technology have increased the machinery of dominance and oppression. The tools of that machinery that are now available and the ways in which human rights can be infringed in manners not foreseen or foreseeable in the liberal, democratic pseudo tradition that we assume must be understood. In particular, the advancements of science and technology have changed the context in which human rights are placed and must be defended. The ensuring discussion attempts to show, on the basis of some examples, what the change in context is and, with it, what the new tasks as well as the new standards needed in the work of protecting human rights are.

2. Significance of Science and Technology for Human Rights

Science is an endeavour that separates knowledge from experience. That is both the glory of science and its greatest drawback because in many ways science finds it impossible to bring experience back into the newly acquired knowledge. As a consequence we have now to struggle with the application of non-contextual, scientific knowledge to the very context-bound problems of human rights.

* University Professor Emeritus, Massey College, University of Toronto, Toronto, Ontario, Canada.

K.E. Mahoney and P. Mahoney (eds.), Human Rights in the Twenty-first Century, 733–737.

It is the application of scientific knowledge, not the knowledge itself, that impacts on human rights. What this overview is primarily concerned with therefore is applied science and technology, "technology" being defined, as in my book on *The Real World of Technology*[1], as practice. "Technology" is defined not just as devices, machinery or electronics, but as socially sanctioned practice. Technology for present purposes is to be understood as the way we do things, because we have the advances of science translated into a host of infrastructures and mechanisms that can incorporate new threats to human rights.

Technology then, is as Jacques Ellul[2] called it, a milieu. And the technological order is distinctly different from the liberal, democratic order that we consider the basis of human rights.

3. Implications of Technology for Human Rights

(1) Invisible Control

One of the important aspects of modern technological practice is that it allows the control of people in ways that make the control invisible. No longer does Big Brother blare out of loud speakers. Big brother barely beeps today. The invisibility of control ought to concern us very profoundly. Even the most undramatic, trivial examples show how this control, this headless tyranny, has permeated "normal" life and become invisible. One of my pleas for new standards is to make these occurrences visible, to name them and to make the process open and transparent.

For instance, the bar code on the magnetic strip of any plastic card is very much a part of life, as is the single bar code on the card that lets car owners into the parking lot. The latter is an electronic key, not really different from the old lock and key; it is just easier. Now think of the combination of two bar codes: the one on your library card and the one on the book you borrow. Suddenly you see the possibility that somebody can track what you read. Even a decade ago in Germany, when the question of the Berufsverlot (the check of political loyalty of teachers) formed part of the attack on human rights of our German colleagues, dossiers of the books they had taken out of the library were used as evidence showing their divergent political views and their potential disloyalty to the Constitution. Consequently, even a simple library card can become a pervasive control mechanism, activated by purely technological means without consent and knowledge of the user.

Another familiar example concerns security of "smart" buildings. Here a card allows those who occupy the building entry to certain floors; if they want to go somewhere else, they may come to realise that their card does not work to

[1] Ursula Franklin, *The Real World of Technology*, CBC Enterprises, Toronto, Canada, 1990.
[2] Jacques Ellul, *The Technological System*, New York, Continuum, 1980.

provide access. The exclusion of people from particular parts of the building is automatic and mechanical, for it is not possible to knock on some responsible person's door to ask, "Why can I not enter there?" A couple of months ago, I went with an employee into the building that houses the Canadian International Development Agency in Ottawa. We wanted to see someone else in a different part of the building but we found that my colleague's card could not let us in.

'Trivial' it might be replied. But imagine that instead of the card, access was controlled by an armed guard who demanded identification and refused entry. Blood pressure would rise. People would say to the guard, "Who has given you the right to exclude me?" In the "technological" example there is only a mere bar code, a little bit of magnetic tape. Replacing the armed guard, or even the traditional concierge, by a bar code means that the control potential is much greater. People can be tracked all around the building. A real surveillance can be made without any human face. It institutes a headless tyranny.

(2) Trivialisation of Principles

Replacing the armed guard by a mere bar code also has another consequence: it trivialises arguments of principle. What was previously a human rights argument, namely as to who has the right to exclude categories of citizens, suddenly becomes the sum of small and trivial steps. It is characteristic of the impact of technology that principled decisions, and the locus for principled decisions, become hidden in a multitude of small trivial steps.

(3) Exclusion and Inclusion of Groups

Another very blatant, and quite old, example of technological exclusion is found in the New York State Parkways designed by Robert Moses.[3] The bridges are very low. They were deliberately designed so that they are too low for buses to pass. The effect is racial bias technically packaged, because the consequence is that those who own a car are able to enjoy the amenities of the park. Those who are black, poor and take the bus, cannot. Nobody has to say, "I don't want them Niggers around here." The bridges are simply made low enough not to allow it.

This example is also cited to make the point that those who defend human rights in a technological order must shift their intervention from the point of infringement to the point of planning. Once the bridges are built, it is too late to protest to the New York authorities saying, "You should have put in higher bridges. This is an affront to civil rights." These arguments must be made before the contract for constructing the bridge is given. This shift of locus from the infringement to the planning and the intent, from the action to the potential, is one of the important impacts of technology.

Even more serious than technological ways to exclude groups is the

[3] Robert A. Caro, *The Power Broker*, New York: Alfred A. Knopf, 1974.

compulsory inclusion of groups in situations that may infringe their human rights and from which they cannot escape. The technology of war first showed us the extent to which the range of violence can be extended. The radius increases – through planes, through bombs, through nuclear weapons – both in space and in time. The notion of the innocent bystander, the difference between combatant and non-combatant, totally disappears. Today the world is faced with many variations of compulsory inclusion into life-threatening attacks. There is no way to be a refugee from pollution, from global warming, from the threat of nuclear war. The very basis of the right to have in one's own hands the destiny of one's life, and have control over the time and the mode of one's death, is taken out of the hands of all people. The right to live in peace and health, to associate with those with whom one wishes to associate and not with those with whom one does not, all have been limited by technology.

(4) Separation of Human Rights Issues Into Macro- and Micro-Situations

We must realise that technology and the technological order have separated human rights issues into macro- and micro-situations. Human rights organisations may prevent the torture of individuals in specific micro-situations. But the human rights movement has no handle on the macro-torture of those subjected to gas warfare or the effects of nuclear radiation. The linkages have not been made.

(5) Shifting of the Point of Human Rights Intervention

It is this author's view, however, that it is possible to begin to link the micro- and the macro-level. An understanding of technology would underscore the need to move from the incident of infringement to the intent of a particular technological situation. This would allow intervention to be made on behalf of human rights at the point of planning instead of the point of execution.

An illustration that makes the point is the position of the conscientious objector in a technological world. To a certain extent, conscientious objectors have successfully convinced civilised nations that those who, on grounds of conscience, object to war should be allowed alternate service. In the past that possibility included alternate service not only in war but also where military conscription in peace time existed. The situation today is different. No longer can conscientious objections begin if and when war is declared. War is fought primarily by machines and devices, by bombers, missiles, not in hand-to-hand combat. The bombers and the missiles are built in peace time. They are prerequisites for war. What does a pacifist do now when her taxes are taken to provide the instruments necessary for war? She is told: when war breaks out, we will take account of your pacifism; we have some laws. The point is, however, that people are not needed anymore for war; devices are needed. So instead of the conscription of bodies in war time, there is a conscription of money in peace time. That therefore is the basis on which one now has to test the right to conscientious objection. The right to conscientious objection has been tested in Canada by those who chose to put part of their income tax into a peace trust fund so as not to deprive the public revenue of that portion that they, like all citizens, owe the State. The object is to keep that money out of preparations for war. That is a matter of conscience. As yet, Canadians do not have the option to exercise conscientious objections at the new technologically determined focus.

We need discussion and debate on these dilemmas. If we cannot devise instruments to accommodate the new reality of the technological milieu, our assurance of human rights to our own citizens is compromised and the larger question of the compulsory inclusion into a threatening non-human rights environment will not be addressed.

4. Conclusion

The new standards that we need must first of all derive from the recognition of how technology changes the context and the environment of human rights. Attention must shift from the occurrence to the potential of an occurrence. Then, as Professor Cotler points out in his paper,[4] we need fact-finding mechanisms. We need to make clear at a sufficiently early stage the relationships between specific technologies and their potential for the abuse of human rights. We cannot allow States to hide evidence of techno-infringements as some have hidden evidence of murders or disappearances. We have to begin to develop the apparatus which will enable us to realize if and when we are faced with the risk of technologies becoming intrinsically unmanageable in terms of their human rights impacts. These are technological threats to which the international community will have to respond, because humanity cannot afford to allow them to materialize.

[4] Professor Cotler's paper titled *Human Rights as the Modern Tool of Revolution*.

SECTION V(a): MASS COMMUNICATIONS AND HUMAN RIGHTS

JOHN McLAREN*

Introduction

The topic, Mass Communications and Human Rights explores the ways in which mass communications both help and hinder the cause of international human rights. To what extent are the media and those who work within it the victims of human rights abuses and what protection has the law afforded? Conversely, how far do the media or other modes of communication go in infringing human rights by the material or commentary published or broadcast and is the law effective in dealing with this form of conduct? What is the contribution of the media by biased and insensitive reporting to the misrepresentation of the experience of minority cultural communities? How can the media of the Western world be induced to report in an understanding and responsible way news from Third World countries? These are the questions posed and addressed in the four papers in the chapter on Mass Communications and Human Rights.

Hans Christian Krüger traces the treatment of the right to freedom of expression and speech by both the European Commission and Court of Human Rights, as rooted in Article 10 of the European Convention of Human Rights. He does so in the context of a series of cases in which the media have both been seeking to challenge state action designed to limit its promotion of human rights and by contrast, where they have been under attack for providing a vehicle for parties intent on infringing the human rights of others (i.e., by spreading totalitarian or racist views). The jurisprudence, he suggests, illustrates the challenge which the European human rights institutions have faced in establishing a balance between the desire to give a broad scope to freedom of speech and expression and the state's legitimate interest to impose necessary restrictions on certain forms of communication in the public interest. The challenge continues, but is becoming less daunting as the Commission and Court have in their decisions developed both well-defined principles of interpretation and a discernible normative order. The body of law which has evolved represents supranational law in the member states. It is also having a

* Lansdowne Professor of Law, University of Victoria, Victoria, B.C., Canada.

K.E. Mahoney and P. Mahoney (eds.), Human Rights in the Twenty-first Century, 739–741.

persuasive impact outside the European Community in countries with similar constitutional provisions, for example in Canada.

Kathleen Mahoney focuses on the use of the media of communication to infringe the rights of women and children to equality and bodily security. She argues forcefully that these rights are constantly being infringed by the purveyors of pornographic images which present sexual violence against women and children as legitimate and pleasurable entertainment for men. This "right" of the pornography industry to publish what it wishes, she notes, is generally supported by civil libertarians relying heavily on traditional liberal ideology. Mahoney challenges this mode of thinking as abstract, hierarchical and unduly individualistic. It ignores, she suggests, the unequal distribution of speech rights and the social meaning of pornography as womens' oppression. Her analysis leads her to assert that the liberal view of free speech has lost its credibility when applied to this form of material. She advocates that the freedom of expression guarantees in the Convention on Civil and Political Rights should not be extended to pornography because it amounts to discrimination against women. Rather, she says, freedom of speech guarantees should be understood and interpreted in the context of the Convention on the Elimination of All Forms of Discrimination Against Women so that the equality protections afforded to women therein are respected and given full weight. She argues that recent jurisprudence of the Supreme Court of Canada which recognizes the gender-specific harms of pornography and rejects the liberal view is a major breakthrough towards supporting the regulation of pornography as a practice of inequality and should be used as a basis for establishing international standards.

The destruction of the black community as a vital cultural element in the life of contemporary America is the focus of the paper by Carl Ginsburg. His starting point is that the economic and social position of many blacks in the United States has deteriorated in the past decade. He argues that the mass media rather than attributing this decline in living conditions to the diversion of resources from the black community has employed a notion of "behavioural affliction" to explain the demise of the community. Ginsburg asserts that in addition to suffering the privations and indignities created by decreases in social and educational programs and economic opportunity, blacks increasingly face "blame the victim" campaigns which both the print and broadcast media have mounted to explain problems of drug addiction, broken homes and urban blight. In the 1980's the media, he suggests, have been ready with advice about "self-help" to America's black population and explanations of how the economic dislocation caused by corporate policies and practices have increasingly impacted on local black communities. At the same time there has been no recognition of the adverse human rights implications of this form of corporatism.

The ignorance of and insensitivity to the realities of life and labour in the Third World by the mass media of the Western world provides the focus for Kevin Hamilton's paper. He points to the fact that the Western world media treats the Third World as a "giant disaster zone", reporting almost exclusively on natural and human tragedies. In the process, evidence of advances in economic and social development which is related to the needs of Third World societies rarely sees the light of day. Hamilton attributes this skewed reporting of life in the Third World in part to narrow editorial vision and the assumed insignificance of events outside the Western world. However, he also believes that some Third World countries share the blame because of their governments' penchant for victimizing journalists and suppressing any independent reporting and commentary. The solution, he suggests, is the establishment of trust between the Western world media and Third World communities. The Western media needs to take the problems and achievements of the Third World seriously and the latter to provide the facilities and guarantees of access and non-interference to allow for realistic reporting by First World media representatives.

HANS CHRISTIAN KRÜGER*

Use of the Media to Promote and Infringe Human Rights

1. Introduction

A topic linking the media with human rights necessarily relates to the general subject of freedom of speech and freedom of the press. The promotion and infringement of human rights, in the context of the media, concerns the purpose to which the freedom of speech is put.

In the European Convention on Human Rights, Article 10 protects freedom of speech. This Article provides in para. 1:

> 1. Everyone has the right to freedom of expression. This right shall include the right to hold opinions and to receive and impart information and ideas without interference by public authority and regardless of frontiers. This Article shall not prevent States from requiring the licensing of broadcasting, television or cinema enterprises.

One finds similar guarantees in Article 19 of the UN Covenant on Civil and Political Rights and in Article 13 of the American Convention on Human Rights.

The freedom is subject to limitations. The European Convention on Human Rights provides in para. 2 as follows:

> 2. The exercise of these freedoms, since it carries with it duties and responsibilities, may be subject to such formalities, conditions, restrictions or penalties as are prescribed by law and are necessary in a democratic society, in the interests of national security, territorial integrity or public safety, for the prevention of disorder or crime, for the protection of health or morals, for the protection of the reputation or rights of others, for preventing the disclosure of information received in confidence, or for maintaining the authority and impartiality of the judiciary.

* Hans Christian Krüger is the Secretary to the European Commission of Human Rights. Any views expressed in this article are his own and in no way involve the responsibility of any of the Convention institutions or the Council of Europe.

K.E. Mahoney and P. Mahoney (eds.), Human Rights in the Twenty-first Century, 743–756.

Important case law interpreting Article 10 of the Convention is being developed by the European Commission and Court of Human Rights, two bodies set up to ensure the observance of the engagements undertaken by States under the Convention. Case law interpreting the first paragraph shows that the right has a very wide application with the result that practically all State legislation which interferes with freedom of speech can be challenged. The limitation in the second paragraph is actually the "corrigendum" to the wide recognition of the freedom. Through this mechanism, States are granted a margin of appreciation in assessing the need within their local context to restrict the freedom concerned. The important feature is therefore the way in which the margin of appreciation is interpreted or applied.

Landmark cases, such as the *Sunday Times Case*[1] or the *Handyside Case*[2] laid down principles concerning freedom of speech and freedom of expression that continue to govern the law in Europe. Today, not only are political and social expression protected in the case law of the Court and Commission of Human Rights, the protection of commercial and economic speech is sought to an increasing degree.

In this paper, the manner in which the media are used today to either promote or infringe human rights is discussed. The paper will mainly try to show this by means of examples taken from the European experience.

2. Access to the Media

Access to the media can either promote or infringe human rights.

As early as 1967, a case was brought against the United Kingdom[3] claiming access to the media. The applicant claimed that access to the BBC was necessary in order to defend himself against allegedly defamatory statements made against him on the BBC network. The Commission rejected the case when it was discovered that contrary to his claim, the applicant was given access.

The question of access to the media arose again in 1970 in *X. and the Association of Z.*, an application brought against the United Kingdom.[4] X had founded the Association of Z. in 1968 in order to, as he described it, "gather together in a single organisation all British people who wish to determine the destiny of Britain" and "to demand that in all matters affecting the British way of life and the British Constitution the issue shall be determined directly by the people of Britain". He complained that the BBC and other broadcasting companies refused him broadcasting time to put forward the Association's

[1] Eur. Court H.R., judgment of 26.4.79, Series A, N.30. The case concerned an injunction imposed by the English courts under the law of contempt of court on reporting the fate of children having been marked by the thalidomide tragedy in the 1970s.

[2] Eur. Court H.R., judgment of 7.12.76, Series A, N.24. This case concerned the prohibition of the publication of the "Little Red Schoolbook", a book intended for schoolchildren.

[3] Application N. 3059/67, Decision of 4.10.68.

[4] Application N. 4515/70, Collection of Decisions 38, p. 86.

point of view and claimed that this interfered with his right to impart information under Article 10 of the Convention. The Commission declared the application inadmissible stating that it was evident that the freedom to "impart information and ideas" could not be taken to include a general and unfettered right for any private citizen or organisation to have access to broadcasting time on radio and television in order to forward its opinion. On the other hand, the denial of broadcasting time to one or more specific groups or persons may raise an issue under Article 10 alone or in conjunction with Article 14 (prohibiting discrimination) where, for instance, one political party was excluded from broadcasting facilities at election time while other parties were given broadcasting time. However, such circumstances did not prevail in that case.

The question of access to the media arose again in two recent cases involving prisoners.[5] The applicants complained that the prison authorities interfered with their rights under Article 10 because they did not allow television interviews to be filmed with them in prison. In both cases the Commission found that the claims were manifestly ill-founded and therefore inadmissible for the reason that there was ample opportunity for the prisoners to tell their story to the journalist by means of correspondence. In addition, any interference with their freedom of expression caused by the refusal to allow filmed documentaries and interviews in prison, was justified as being necessary in a democratic society for the prevention of disorder in prison.

It is clear from the case law that it is difficult for an individual to obtain access to the media as of right. There is no general and unfettered right of access but an obligation not to discriminate in providing access exists.

3. Use of the Media to Promote Human Rights

Examples of how the media is used to promote human rights raises different legal issues. In the first place the media themselves assert their right to express themselves freely in the context of political debate. There are also cases concerning restrictions on the intention to inform the public or to provide information in the media on matters of general interest.

An important case in the first category was that of *Lingens against Austria*.[6] The applicant Lingens, was the editor of the magazine "Profil" in Austria. He published articles criticising certain television interviews wherein the late Chancellor of Austria, Mr. Bruno Kreisky, supported the then President of the Austrian Liberal Party, one Mr. Peter. Mr. Peter had been denounced earlier by Simon Wiesenthal, President of the Jewish Documentation Centre, for his SS activities during the Second World War. Mr. Kreisky's comments included a reference to Mr. Wiesenthal's organisation and activities as being a "political

[5] Application No. 12656/87 v. United Kingdom, decided on 13.5.88, and Application No. 14869/89 v. Netherlands, decided on 8.6.90.

[6] Eur. Court H.R., judgment of 8.7.86, Series A, N.103.

mafia" and using "mafia methods". These comments were described by Mr. Lingens as being "immoral" and "undignified" and he described Mr. Kreisky as a "basest opportunist".

On the basis of these articles, Mr. Kreisky brought a private prosecution against Lingens resulting in criminal proceedings against him that lasted a total of six years. In the end, Mr. Lingens stood convicted for having made defamatory remarks against Chancellor Kreisky. He was fined 15,000 Austrian Schillings. Lingens then appealed to Strasbourg claiming a violation of Article 10 of the Convention. He succeeded before both the Commission and the Court. The Court recalled that freedom of expression constitutes one of the essential foundations of a democratic society as well as one of the basic conditions for individual self-fulfilment. These principles were of particular importance as far as the press was concerned because of its duty to impart information and ideas on political issues as well as on other areas of public interest. The Court recognized the correlative public's right to receive information and ideas. Freedom of the press affords the public one of the best means of discovering and forming an opinion of the ideas and attitudes of political leaders. More generally, freedom of political debate was recognized to be at the very core of the concept of a democratic society which prevailed throughout the Convention.

In the Lingens case, both the Commission and the Court considered that the limits of acceptable criticism were wider when applied to a politician than when applied to a private individual. The background against which the critical remarks were made was also considered, namely a post-election controversy. They found that the interference with Mr. Lingens' exercise of the freedom of expression was not necessary in a democratic society for the protection of the reputation of others, as had been argued by the Austrian Government, and there had consequently been a breach of Article 10 of the Convention. Mr. Lingens was also awarded over 280.000 Schillings as "just satisfaction" under Article 50 of the Convention.

Several cases of a similar kind have been declared admissible and are pending at present before the Commission or the Court of Human Rights. One case before the Court is that of *Gerhard Oberschlick against Austria.*[7] Mr. Oberschlick is a journalist working for the periodical "Forum". He published information in "Forum" regarding a television interview given by the Secretary General of the Austrian Liberal Party who suggested that family allowances for Austrian women should be raised by 50% in order to prevent abortions based on financial reasons, but that family allowances paid to immigrant mothers should be cut by 50%. The applicant and others alleged that the statements constituted crimes under the penal code as they incited hatred, instigated and approved criminal offences and constituted activities contrary to the *Austrian National Socialism Prohibition Act*.

The Secretary General of the Liberal Party then brought defamation

[7] Application N. 11662, Commission Report of 14.12.89.

proceedings against the applicant journalist which ended with a conviction and a fine of 4.000 Schillings as well as compensation to be paid to the injured party. Subsequently, the applicant complained to the European Commission of Human Rights claiming a breach of Article 10 of the Convention.

The Commission admitted the application in May 1989 and found that Article 10 had been violated, reasoning that the applicant made his statements in response to a proposal in a political context. In the same way as the Secretary General of the Liberal Party was free to make his statements, the applicant in a political discussion must have the freedom in a democratic system to react strongly to it. The Court confirmed this finding in its judgment of 23 May, 1991.

Two cases before the Commission have been declared admissible recently. They concern Spain and Iceland. The case against Spain[8] related to an article published by a Basque senator in a Basque periodical, wherein the applicant author drew attention to physical attacks allegedly suffered by Basque citizens at the hands of armed groups which, he alleged, could act with impunity and for which the Government was responsible. He was prosecuted and convicted for the publication. The Commission found a violation of Article 10 and sent the case to the Court where it is still pending.

The Icelandic case[9] concerned an article published in the Icelandic press about police brutality in Reykjavik against a journalist. The responsible policemen were later prosecuted and convicted, but the applicant author referred to other cases of police brutality and to the practice of letting policemen examine complaints against other policemen. The Association of Policemen in Reykjavik then requested the public prosecutor to investigate the matter from the point of view of whether there was a violation by the applicant of the offences against state officials' provisions of the Icelandic penal code. On the basis of this investigation the applicant was charged with having made various defamatory remarks against policemen. In June 1986 he was convicted and fined 10.000 Icelandic Crowns and costs. In October 1987 the Supreme Court confirmed this conviction and sentence, with one judge dissenting. The European Commission of Human Rights found, however, that the conviction violated Article 10 of the Convention and sent the case to the Court for decision.

These cases have been mentioned because they concern the use of the media by journalists and other authors in order to inform the public on matters of general interest and thus to promote human rights. But, it cannot be denied that the paths on which such writers walk when asserting their rights is a narrow one. Numerous decisions of the Commission show that the margin of appreciation of the State to impose sanctions is a wide one where it is considered that the use of the freedom of expression has gone beyond permissible limits. Here are a few interesting examples from this rich, but negative jurisprudence of the Commission.

[8] Application N.11798/85, Decision of 7.9.89, not yet published.
[9] Application N. 13778/88, Decision of 14.3.90, not yet published.

In Application N. 10343/83 against Switzerland[10], the applicant, an accredited parliamentary journalist, was convicted and sentenced in 1981 to a fine of 750 Swiss Francs for having published secret documents. The background of the case was that a commission under the Swiss National Council was asked to investigate a matter relating to an affair between Switzerland and Austria concerning espionage. In the course of this investigation a confidential report, drawn up by the Federal Ministry of Defence, was distributed among the members of the commission. The applicant had received a copy of the report from a member of the commission and had published parts of it in his daily newspaper. In his application to the Strasbourg Commission he complained that his freedom of expression was unduly restricted in that it was not for the State to exclude the protection of Article 10 by declaring that the information in question was not generally accessible. Also the law proscribing the interference was not formulated with sufficient precision to enable him to regulate his conduct.

The Commission declared the application inadmissible as being manifestly ill-founded. It observed that the applicant was assigned to work with political matters in the editorial office of the "Bundeshaus" and he could therefore be expected to pay particular attention to the documents he received. The purpose of the restriction in the present case was clearly to prevent "the disclosure of information received in confidence". The report in question was marked confidential and the applicant was obliged to be aware of the fact. In this situation the European Commission found that the obligation not to make public the secret discussions concerned did not go beyond what may be reasonably considered necessary in a democratic society.

Another interesting case is that of *B. v. The United Kingdom.*[11] The applicant was a senior scientist employed as a civil servant by the Ministry of Defence at Aldermaston Atomic Weapons Research Establishment. His responsibilities at Aldermaston included safety management for the plant's radioactive work. In 1971 he was elected first Borough, and later County, Councillor by the Civil Service Administration. In 1976 he was approached by constituents who were concerned with the question of the adequacy of the safety precautions. In August 1978 all the radioactive plants at Aldermaston were closed temporarily as being health hazards. In the same year, the applicant was given a formal warning following his contacts with the press in relation to official material.

In January 1980, the BBC approached the applicant asking whether he would agree to be interviewed in a programme entitled: "Is Aldermaston safe?". The BBC assured the applicant that the interview would only concern matters of public record. In February 1980, the applicant sought permission from his superiors to appear on the programme. Before he had received a reply he agreed to grant an interview on the understanding that if the Ministry of

[10] Decisions and Reports 35, p. 224.
[11] Application N. 10293/83, Decisions and Reports 45, (DR) (1986) p. 41.

Defence raised significant objections, appropriate omissions would be made from recording. The reply to his request for permission to give the interview was given in March 1980 and permission was refused. The reason given was that the Ministry might be held in contempt of court because of cases under consideration regarding persons who had contracted cancer while working at Aldermaston. However, no case had been set down for hearing and the County Solicitor whom the applicant had contacted for advice in the matter advised that in these circumstances there appeared no risk of the applicant being in contempt of court. A week later, the programme was transmitted unamended with no further reaction having been received from the Ministry. The following month, the applicant was charged with a disciplinary offence of taking part in a television programme contrary to the regulations and without permission from the Ministry. He subsequently received a severe reprimand which was entered on his record. An appeal to the Permanent Under Secretary of State was rejected.

The applicant then complained to the European Commission of Human Rights that his freedom of expression had been interfered with contrary to Article 10 of the Convention. The Commission rejected the application as being manifestly ill-founded, saying that the interference with his freedom of expression, which had no doubt taken place, was prescribed by a law sufficiently clear and accessible to the applicant for him to know that he could not give the interview without authorisation from the Ministry. The Commission found that the restriction was necessary in a democratic society for the protection of the rights of the employer and was not disproportionate to the aim to be realised. In coming to that conclusion the Commission stressed two points: 1) that the programme was concerned with the safety conditions at Aldermaston about which the applicant had first-hand knowledge and experience which he had gained in his official capacity as an employee of the Ministry of Defence; and 2) that the programme was broadcast at a time when inquests into deaths from cancer, suspected to have been caused by radioactivity at Aldermaston, were in progress. Regulations concerning the use of information obtained by Government employees in Government service and its dissemination to the public are *prima facie* reasonable. In these circumstances, the applicant could also not rely on the fact that he was an elected representative which imposed on him special duties towards his constituents. It could not be assumed that an individual may opt to respect only one set of responsibilities at the expense of the other.

The conclusion that can be drawn from the case-law is that whilst the Convention grants a right to use the media in order to impart information and ideas without interference, the exercise of that right is hazardous for the individual as it is measured against the margin of appreciation of the State authorities. Where the controversy is a political one it is safe to say that this margin is very narrow. However, it becomes wider in the areas of public safety, environment and commerce. The law in Europe is presently in a state of development and it will be important to observe it.

4. Use of the Media to Infringe Human Rights

In cases where the media is used to infringe human rights it is interesting to note at the outset that the negative is the positive. That is to say the fact that the applicant's claim was declared inadmissible constitutes the actual protection of the human rights which he or she sought to infringe. The cases remain very topical and can be situated mainly in the area where the use of the media was intended to incite or to propagate racist or terrorist ideas.

An early case under this topic was decided by the Commission in October 1979.[12] The two applicants, Messrs. Glimmerveen and Hagenbeck, are of Dutch nationality. In 1974, Mr. Glimmerveen became president of a political party called "Nederlandse Volks Unie" whose basic principles were described by the applicant to be, "a world conception which grants each nation a proper State, as well as the belief that the general interest of a State is best served by an ethnically homogeneous population and not by racial mixing". He was convicted for possessing leaflets inciting racial discrimination.

The leaflets addressed "white Dutch people" and contained statements such as:

> "the major part of our population since a long time has had enough of the presence in our country of hundreds of thousands of Surinamers, Turks and other so-called guest workers, who moreover are not at all needed here, and ... the authorities merely have to see to it that these undesired aliens leave our country as soon as possible". The leaflet further announced "that the N.V.U. will continue its battle for the white people of the Netherlands until political power of [certain political parties] ... will have definitely been broken. As soon as the Netherlandse Volks Unie will have gained political power in our country, it will put order into business and to begin with: 1) remove Surinamers, Turks and other so-called guest workers from the Netherlands ..."

The applicants then sought to participate in the municipal elections in Amsterdam and The Hague but they were refused as their party was proscribed. They complained to the Commission under Article 10 of the Convention guaranteeing freedom of expression, and Article 3 of the First Protocol guaranteeing the right to free elections.

The Commission declared the applications inadmissible. It referred to Article 17 of the Convention which provides that "Nothing in this Convention may be interpreted as implying for any State, group or person any right to engage in any activity or perform any act aimed at the destruction of any of the rights and freedoms set forth herein or at their limitation to a greater extent than is provided for in the Convention". The Commission considered that the policy advocated by the applicants was inspired by the overall aim to remove all

[12] Joined Applications Nos. 8348/78 and 8406/78 v. the Netherlands, Decisions and Reports 18, p. 187.

non-white people from the Netherlands' territory in complete disregard of other factors. It clearly contained elements of racial discrimination prohibited under the Convention and other international agreements. The Commission concluded that the applicants were trying to use Article 10 to establish a basis under the Convention for a right to engage in activities which are contrary to the text and spirit of the Convention. The Commission recognized that if granted, such a right would contribute to the destruction of rights and freedoms in the Convention. The applicants could not therefore, by reason of the provisions of Article 17, rely on Article 10 of the Convention.

Another case arose in Belgium in 1981.[13] The applicant was a Belgian national who occupied a senior editorial post with the publishing house "Europe Reelle". In 1978 she agreed to have her name appear as "responsible author-editor" in connection with a text by Mr. Leon Degrelle, former head of the Belgian "Rexisme" Movement during World War II. The text contained a commentary which cast doubt on the reality of the extermination of six million Jews, particularly at Auschwitz, and put the Nazi atrocities into relative terms vis-à-vis other wartime activities.

The applicant was charged with an offence under Article 123(1) series 6 of the Belgian Penal Code. She was convicted as charged and sentenced to one year's imprisonment and a fine. Her appeals were unsuccessful and she finally complained to the Commission under Article 10 of the Convention.

The Commission rejected the application as being manifestly ill-founded considering that the interference complained of was justified as being necessary in a democratic society for the prevention of disorder as well as for the maintenance of the authority of the judiciary. The Commission emphasised that the applicant had agreed to participate in the publication of a work despite the fact that its author, Degrelle, had previously been deprived of his right to publish for life under Belgian legislation. This legislation would be rendered meaningless if the courts were unable to convict a person who aided the commission of an offence which otherwise could not have occurred. The Commission rejected the contention that the Auschwitz atrocities were a matter of mere historical interest and that there were few survivors. It said the families of those survivors continue to be entitled to the protection of their relatives' memory. It also observed that there were events which demonstrated that anti-democratic ideologies, resembling those which inspired the Auschwitz atrocities, had not disappeared from Europe.

Two similar cases arose in the Federal Republic of Germany, one in 1981 and one in 1986. In the first case[14], the applicant displayed pamphlets alleging that the assassination of millions of Jews during the period of the Third Reich was a Zionistic swindle or a lie. A Jewish neighbour whose grandfather had been killed at Auschwitz, felt defamed by these pamphlets and brought a civil action against the applicant seeking the discontinuance of his behaviour. The

[13] *T. v. Belgium*, D.R. 34 (1983), p. 158.
[14] Application No. 9235/81, D.R. 29 (1982), p. 19.4.

complainant won in the court of first instance but lost on appeal, the appellate court finding that he had no *locus standi* as he was not personally involved. However, on a further appeal to the Federal Court of Justice the first judgment was restored, the court leaving no doubt that the publication of the pamphlets violated the plaintiff's rights.

The applicant's subsequent application to the Commission under Article 10 of the Convention was declared manifestly ill-founded. The Commission found that it was neither arbitrary nor unreasonable to consider the pamphlets as a defamatory attack against the Jewish community and against each individual member of this community. The restrictions on the applicant's freedom of expression was a necessary restriction for the protection of the reputation of others.

The second German case[15] was brought by a journalist who was a leader in an organisation allegedly attempting to reinstitute the National Socialist Party in Germany. In one pamphlet he wrote *inter alia*: "We are called 'Neo Nazis'! So What? We are *against*: big-wigs, bolshevists, Zionists, crooks, cheats and parasites. We are *against* capitalism, communism, Zionism, estrangement by means of masses of foreign workers, destruction of the environment. We are *for*: German unity, social justice, racial pride, community of the people, camaraderie". For these and similar writings, the Frankfurt Regional Court convicted the applicant for preparing and disseminating propaganda material appertaining to an unconstitutional organisation. He was sentenced to 3 years' and 4 months' imprisonment. His appeal and a constitutional complaint were dismissed and the applicant then filed an application with the Commission invoking Article 10 of the Convention. Once again, the Commission rejected the claim as being manifestly ill-founded. It referred to Article 17, the Glimmerveen/Hagenbeck case (see above) and the detailed reasons given by the German courts finding that the applicant was seeking to use freedom of information enshrined in Article 10 as a basis for activities which are contrary to the text and spirit of the Convention and which, if admitted, would contribute to the destruction of the rights and freedoms set forth in the Convention.

The Commission seems to alternate in its reasoning between the application of Article 17 and the application of paragraph 2 of Article 10. Perhaps the position is that both provisions are applicable. The most recent case, *H., W., P. and V. against Austria*[16] was rejected by the Commission as being manifestly ill-founded in October, 1989. Again, judicial proceedings had been taken against the applicants leading to their conviction and sentence under the relevant Austrian legislation for having performed various Nazi inspired acts in connection with their membership and leading functions in certain right-wing political organisations. The Commission stated that the "prohibition against activities involving the expression of National Socialist ideas is both lawful in

[15] Application N. 12194/86, not yet published.
[16] Application N. 12774/87, not yet published.

Austria and, in view of the historical past forming the immediate background of the Convention itself, can be justified in the interests of national security and territorial integrity as well as for the prevention of crime. It is therefore covered by Article 10 para. 2 of the Convention." The Commission then referred to Article 17 and noted "that National Socialism is a totalitarian doctrine incompatible with democracy and human rights and that its adherents undoubtedly pursue aims of the kind referred to in Article 17."

5. Present Problems Pending before the Commission

At present, there are a number of cases concerning the use of the media pending before the Commission or Court. For example, cases have been brought by Times Newspapers Ltd.,[17] The Observer and The Guardian Newspapers and journalists[18] concerning temporary injunctions imposed upon them preventing the publication of excerpts from the book, "Spycatcher". The Commission concluded that Article 10 of the Convention had been violated by the injunctions. While accepting that the interferences were prescribed by the law of interim injunctions in England and that they had a legitimate purpose of protecting interests of national security (although the United Kingdom Government had not directly relied on this aspect of justification for the purposes of the proceedings before the Commission), the Commission found that the interferences were not necessary in a democratic society. It noted that, by the time the book was published in the United States the confidentiality of the information would be destroyed. The Government had taken no steps to prevent earlier disclosure of information by the author nor had they made any attempt to prevent the importation of "Spycatcher" into the United Kingdom. The Commission stated that it "failed to see a pressing social need to prevent the British public from reading about something which the rest of the world were free to read by then and which concerned a matter of major interest to them". In October 1990, the case was referred to the European Court of Human Rights for judgment which was given on 26 November, 1991. The Court held that Article 10 had been violated for reasons similar to those stated in the Commission's Report.

Another pending case is that of several journalists and two trade unions against Ireland[19]. The applicants complain of restrictions on them by a ministerial order ("Section 31 Order") prohibiting them from broadcasting interviews with members of certain listed organisations, such as Sinn Fein and the IRA. They claim that the effect of this prohibition is that journalists are deterred from covering social and political events in Northern Ireland. The Commission has referred this case to the Government of Ireland for obser-

[17] Application N. 13166/87, not yet published.
[18] Application N. 13585/88, not yet published.
[19] Application N. 15404/89, not yet published.

vations on its admissibility and merits. Following an oral hearing on 16 April, 1991, the Commission declared the application inadmissible finding that the restrictions imposed were justified for the protection of national security and the prevention of disorder and crime.

The same procedural approach has been taken in two cases against the Federal Republic of Germany which concern the use of the media in a commercial context. The leading case here is *Markt Intern and Beermann v. the Federal Republic*[20]. The applicant company was enjoined by an injunction from repeating statements which it had published in its bulletin on the commercial behaviour of a certain firm on the grounds that it constituted an unlawful interference with its competition with others. The Federal Constitutional Court had held in essence that freedom of expression did not prevail over other legally protected interests such as the promotion of economic interests in the context of competition. The Commission, in its Report of 18 December 1987, concluded that there had been breaches of Article 10 of the Convention because the interference with the applicants' right to impart information, to impart ideas and to receive information were not necessary to protect the rights of others. However, the European Court of Human Rights[21] came to the conclusion that there was no violation. This result was reached by nine judges against nine with the President's casting vote.

The Court agreed that it was essential for the specialised press to be able to disclose facts which could be of interest to its readers and thereby contributed to the openness of business activities. However, it held that under certain circumstances the publication of items describing real events may be prohibited, particularly if isolated incidents deserve closer scrutiny before being made public. Thus, the prohibition of an article, written in a commercial context and expressing doubts about the reliability of a commercial undertaking, was not contrary to the Convention.

In a case now pending before the Commission and communicated to the Federal Republic of Germany[22], the prohibition to publish critical statements about a firm's products under unfair competition law was again in issue but declared inadmissible by the Commission on 27 May, 1991. Another[23] concerns a restriction, under unfair competition law, on the dissemination among journalists of articles criticising the applicant's employer, a news agency, which had dismissed the applicant after first having attacked him in the press. This later case was declared admissible on 3 December, 1991.

[20] Application N. 10572/83, Report of 18.12.87.

[21] Eur. Court H.R., judgment of 20.11.89, Series A, N. 165.

[22] Application N. 12278/86, not yet published.

[23] Application N. 15088/89, not yet published.

6. Conclusion and Outlook

A review of the Commission's and the Court's case law shows that the media are used both to promote and to infringe human rights. In the context of concrete cases under the European Convention, the first step is to determine whether or not there has been an interference with the freedom of expression guaranteed in Article 10 of the Convention. If there was interference it is then necessary to determine whether or not the interference was justified.

Both the Commission and the Court have had relatively little difficulty in identifying interferences which often take the form of refusing access to the media, applying censorship to the expression sought, or imposing sanctions for written or published work. It is always more difficult to determine the justification issue and decide whether the infringement was prescribed by law and necessary in a democratic society for one of the purposes limitatively listed in paragraph 2 or Article 10. In doing so the Convention organs are called upon to balance, on the one hand, the interest of the individual to assert his right under the Convention to speak freely and without having to fear censorship or sanctions and, on the other hand, the interest of society and the State to protect the rights of others and its own institutions against unreasonable and unjustified attack in the media. This balance is a continuing process and it requires a constant awareness of the developments in the changing world around us. Full knowledge of the social and political needs of countries before the Commission and Court will lead to a just assessment of the limitations which may be imposed on the basic principle that all expression must be free and unfettered.

The world in which we live is changing. New challenges are ahead. Everyone is aware of the recent new technologies that have been developed which enable us to receive information via satellite from all corners of the world right into our homes. That is in principle a welcome development, but it also creates problems in the field of programme selection, advertisement, frequency allocation and so forth. In Europe, the Council of Europe Convention on Transfrontier Television and the EEC Council Directive of October 1989 on the co-ordination of certain provisions laid down by law, regulation or administrative action in Member States concerning the pursuit of broadcasting activities attempt to cope with many of the problems arising out of the transfrontier transmission and retransmission of television programme services. Both instruments seek to set up certain minimum rules relating to the content of programming, advertisement and sponsorship, and the protection of the individual viewer, whose principal objective is "to ensure a reasonable equality of opportunity between the different services transmitted, thereby seeking to avoid a 'law of the jungle' which would be detrimental to pluralism, diversity and choice"[24].

[24] J. Dinsdale, "New Trends Emerging at the Legislative Level in the Council of Europe", in A. Cassesse, A. Clapham (eds.) *Transfrontier Television in Europe: The Human Rights Dimension* (1990), European University Institute Florence, Nomis Valey, Baden-Baden, pp. 215–220.

Examples of the rules are regulations on the content of programmes including the prohibition of indecent or pornographic programmes and those which give undue prominence to violence or are likely to incite racial hatred. The frequency, duration and the content of advertisements, including the prohibition of advertising particular products such as alcohol and tobacco are regulated in these legal instruments as well.

For the press, the main threat to freedom of expression is censorship of the type used to suppress ideas and information in an arbitrary and unjustified way. The impressive study, "Information, Freedom and Censorship" in the Article 19 World Report 1988[25] gives a very good picture of the problems involved. Professor Michael Scammell presents what he calls: Censorship and its History – A Personal View. He concludes with the following words:

> There will always be debate and disagreement where the balance is to be struck, and there will always be pressures and forces pushing and pulling in different directions. These skirmishes, in my view, are but the usual expressions of competing forces and opinions within a healthy society ... They are tokens of energy and life, rather than of sickness and decline. We should bear in mind that a society that is totally safe and tranquil, in which there are no controversies over freedom of expression, is a society that is dying or dead.

These words are borne out by the increasing number of important cases with which the European Commission and Court are faced and through which they contribute to the setting of standards in an area where one finds the traditional threats to human rights together with new threats to human rights through modern science and technology.

[25] Prepared by the staff of Article 19 and published by Longman Group UK Limited 1988.

KATHLEEN E. MAHONEY*

Destruction of Women's Rights through Mass Media
Proliferation of Pornography

1. Introduction

Gross human rights violations in the form of sexual violence practiced against women and children transcend cultures and national boundaries. Sexual assault, sexual harassment, wife battery, incest, marital rape and forced prostitution exist as serious social problems in all member states of the United Nations – states which, by virtue of their membership, agree to principles of inviolability of the person and gender equality.[1]

At the same time, the mass media in virtually all its forms displays and distributes pornography with impunity. Pornographic movies, videos, films, magazines, posters and television present sexual degradation, sadism and violence against women as legitimate and pleasurable "entertainment" for men.

One of the reasons the mass media is able to promote such violations against women without state interference is because only international law can effectively control it and there are no international instruments that deal with pornography and violence against women in any clear, meaningful or comprehensive way. A number of international instruments address "obscene" expression but none offer any guidelines as to the content or definition of pornography.[2] Even the 1983 U.N. Resolution based on the Special Report on

* Professor, Faculty of Law, The University of Calgary and Conference Director, "Human Rights in the Twenty-First Century: A Global Challenge."

[1] See Article 6, the right to life in the International Covenant in Civil and Political Rights which the United Nations Human Rights Committee has described as the supreme human right (General Comment No. 6, [1982] Rep. H.R.C. 93, (para. 1), as well as the right not to be subjected to cruel, inhuman or degrading treatment (Article 7) and the right to security of the person (Article 9). Violence against women also impairs their enjoyment of rights contained in the International Covenant on Economic, Social and Cultural Rights including the right to an adequate standard of living in Article 11 and the right to the highest attainable standard of physical and mental health in Article 12.

[2] For example, the Agreement for the Suppression of the Circulation of Obscene Publications, May 4, 1910, as amended by the Protocol of May 4, 1949, Can. T.S. 1951 No. 34; Convention for the Suppression of the Circulation of and Traffic in Obscene Publications, September 12, 1923, as amended by the Protocol of November 12, 1947, Can. T.S. 1951, No. 33.

K.E. Mahoney and P. Mahoney (eds.), Human Rights in the Twenty-first Century, 757–775.

the Suppression of the Traffic in Persons and the Exploitation of the Prostitution of Others, stopped short of providing a definition. It merely recommended that member states draw up policies aimed at "curbing the pornography industry and the trade in pornography".

By leaving the decision of the definition of pornography to individual member states, incoherency in international and national policies is guaranteed. Without a precise definition, effective strategies cannot possibly be developed to curb this expanding industry. The mass media's instantaneous global access requires international regulation and co-ordination. National laws on their own cannot effectively deal with mass media technology, particularly satellite communication which is becoming an increasingly popular method of pornography distribution. The absence of action by the international community creates a void which western liberal countries, particularly those in which pornography is a multi-million dollar industry, are only too happy to fill with an approach which characterizes pornography as a freedom of expression issue and ignores the gender specific, discriminatory nature of its content.[3]

When deciding whether or not pornographic speech should be protected, liberals invoke abstract values of freedom of expression which are devoid of context, devoid of any requirement of reasonableness, premised on a notion of universal equality. Traditionally, liberal theorists emphasize the value of free speech as the preeminent value in a democratic society. Attaining the truth, achieving and maintaining the democratic values of self-government, and achieving personal growth through self-expression are identified as the critically important reasons we protect speech from government interference. Liberal theory has not, however, been equally effective in confronting the reality of protecting pornography. Its real value as expression is not assessed as against the real harms it inflicts. Rather, traditional abstract values are invoked, such as the value of seeking "the truth." Reliance on this value begins to break down when these forms of "speech" strike at the heart of other values deeply cherished in a free and democratic society, particularly the values of equality and bodily security. As a result, disjunction is created between the protection of pornography on the one hand, and protection of the vilified group it attacks, on the other.

It is argued here that a principled approach which would protect legitimate speech but also protect women's bodily security and equality rights requires a harms-based equality analysis. When this approach is adopted, it becomes obvious that protection of pornography results in a loss of rights for women as a class. For men as a class, it results in a gain. This is because pornography subordinates and harms women in order to "entertain" men by sexually stimulating them. Because the portrayal of and actual subordination of women

[3] This was certainly the case in the United States until the decision in *American Booksellers v. Hudnut* 771F. 2d 323 (7th Cir. 1985), aff'd 475 U.S. 1001 (1986), when Easterbrook, J. found that pornography injures women yet he and the rest of the Court of Appeal for the Seventh Circuit proceeded to find that harm to women could not outweigh the interest in protecting freedom of expression.

in pornography contributes to and exacerbates subordination of women generally,[4] pornography has a disparate, disadvantaging impact on all women. If women are to be recognized as full bearers of rights and if any progress toward protecting women's human rights and the elimination of violence against them is to be achieved, limits on the exploitation of women in pornography are required.[5]

In the first section of this article, liberal values which affect their analysis of freedom of expression are discussed in detail. In the second section, a critique of the liberal approach is provided; in the third section, an alternative approach recently adopted in Canada is suggested which is more consistent with the protection of women's human rights.

A. Liberal Values

Some of the liberal values that influence the free speech principle are abstract individualism, individual liberty, political freedom, the public/private distinction, and the preference liberals have for theoretical definitions and principles rather than social reality. They see individuals, no matter how social their development might be, in complete abstraction and isolation from each other – as separate competitive units. As such, human beings are or appear to be "naturally" free and equal to each other. Each human being is regarded as an agent with a capacity for free choice and self-development. All judgments and actions are based on an individual's own subjective viewpoint. In other words, each individual's reasoning is entirely self-interested[6] and any social order has to begin by respecting his or her wants, preferences, needs abilities,

[4] E. Donnerstein, "Pornography: Its Effect on Violence Against Women", N. Malamuth and E. Donnerstein, eds., (1984), *Pornography and Sexual Aggression* 53; E. Donnerstein and L. Berkovitz, "Victim Reaction in Aggressive Erotic Films as a Factor in Violence Against Women", (1981) 41 Journal of Personality and Social Psychology 710; N. Malamuth, "Factors Associated with Rape as Predators of Laboratory Aggression Against Women", (1983) 45 Journal of Personality and Social Psychology 432; N. Malamuth, "Predictions of Naturalistic Sexual Aggression", (1986) 50 Journal of Personality and Social Psychoology 953; N. Malamuth and J.V.P. Check, "Aggressive-Pornography and Beliefs in Rape Myths: Individual Differences", (1985) 19 Journal of Research in Personality 299; J.V.P. Check and T.H. Guloien, "Reported Proclivity for Coercive Sex Following Repeated Exposure to Sexually Violent Pornography, Nonviolent Dehumanizing Pornography, and Erotica", (1989) in D. Zillmann and J. Bryant (eds), *Pornography: Research Advanced and Policy Considerations* (New Jersey: Erlbaum, 1989); M. McManus, Introduction to Report of Attorney General's Commission on Pornography, (Nashville: Rutledge Hill Press, 1986) at xviii (consensus of all researchers as released by Surgeon General Koop).

[5] *Monitoring the Implementation of the Nairobi Forward-Looking Strategies for the Advancement of Women – Examining Existing Mechanisms for Communications on the Status of Women*, Report of the Secretary-General to the thirty-fifth session of the Commission on the Status of Women, 1991 (E/CN.6/1991/10).

[6] Carole Pateman, *The Problem of Political Obligation* (New York: John Wiley and Sons, 1979), 25.

pleasures and pains as a matter of respect.[7] Because liberals think all human beings are equal, there is no justification for any one person or class of persons to exercise self-realization more than any other. There are, for example, no grounds for making gender differences the basis for differential rights to self-realization. The equal rights of women and men are thus grounded in the nature of human agency itself.[8] Liberals believe that even though human individuals comprise the basic constituents that form social groups, human individuals could exist outside a social context. They say essential human characteristics, needs, interests, capacities, and desires are neither created nor altered by context.[9]

Individual liberty is the arrangement that maximizes freedom for all, limited only by the requirement that one does not harm others or interfere with their similar liberty. Liberals say it is wrong for the state to interfere with the conduct of the lives of adults as long as they are not harming others.[10] The "harm principle" is interpreted as direct physical harm or some forms of psychic harm.[11] Direct harm in the liberal sense has a very narrow meaning. It means definable harm of the kind that would be caused by shouting "fire" in a crowded theatre.[12] Unless a "clear and present danger" exists as a result of the expression, restrictions cannot be justified.[13] In other words, liberals view speech harm as something which involves a risk of immediate unlawful acts or an element of public offensiveness. These harms are further minimized when they take for granted that any unlawful "action" induced by speech will be punished by other laws and any "offence" it creates can be avoided by the victim. Liberals acknowledge that social harm related to speech can occur, but it is only considered on a case by case basis and the burden of explaining and proving the harm is placed on the victims.

[7] Naomi Schemman, "Individualism and the Objects of Psychology," in Sandra Harding and Merrill B. Kintikka, eds., *Discovering Reality* (Boston: D. Reidel, 1983), 225–44.

[8] Alison Jagger, *Feminist Politics and Human Nature* (Totowa, N.J.: Rowman and Allanheld, 1983).

[9] Carol C. Gould, "Private Rights and Public Virtues: Women, the Family and Democracy," in Carol C. Gould, ed., *Beyond Domination* (Totowa, N.J.: Rowman and Allanheld, 1983), 3–18.

[10] John Stuart Mill, *On Liberty* (1859), A. Castell, ed., (1949).

[11] "Psychic" harm is recognized as that type of harm individuals experience when they are involuntarily exposed to offensive conduct or depictions of offensive conduct in public. See A. Alan Borovoy, *When Freedoms Collide: A Case for Our Civil Liberties* (Toronto: Lester and Orpen Dennys, 1988), at p.40–41.

[12] *Schenck v. United States* 249 U.S. 47 (1919).

[13] Liberals often incorrectly apply this test to obscene speech. In *Commonwealth v. Gordon*, 66 Pa. D. and C. 101 (1949), Judge Bok sought to establish the principle that no book should be suppressed unless it could be shown that there was a clear and present danger of the commission of a crime as a result of its publication. This reasoning was not upheld in the Appeal Court. In *Miller v. California*, 413 U.S. 15, at 34 (1973), Mr. Justice Burger held that "to equate the full and robust exchange of ideas and political debate with commercial exploitation of obscene material demeans the grand conception of the First Amendment and its high purposes in the historic struggle for freedom. It is a misuse of the great guarantees of free speech and free press". But see A. Alan Borovoy *supra*, note 11 at p. 63.

Even when social harm is shown, the liberals say the clear and present danger requirement disallows state interference.[14] The only way to legitimate censorship of pornography in these terms, would be to turn to social scientific studies for proof that there is a clear, causal link between pornographic material and physical harm such as sexual assault or some other crime. Liberals agree that material which depicts real abuse, such as sexual expression involving children and sexual expression including real sexual assault, torture or murder should be censored.[15] This limitation is rationalized as a variant of the direct harm principle because if a legal market exists for this type of expression, an incentive is provided for the commission of crimes and a causal relationship is created between distribution of the material and direct harm to individuals.

The liberal tradition values the capacity to reason and consequently prioritizes the rational ahead of the emotional and the mind over the body. This is reflected in law in the distinction that is made between protected and unprotected expression based upon whether expression is an appeal to reason or an appeal to passion.[16] It also provides an explanation for the liberal penchant for universalist descriptions and neutral, symmetrical principles that do not permit contextualized approaches reflecting the experiences of real people.

Traditional liberal theory also draws a line between the public and private spheres of life equating them to legitimate and illegitimate interference by the state. Much of the privacy doctrine relies on the premise that "so long as the public does not interfere [with private life], autonomous individuals interact freely and equally."[17] In relation to pornography, liberals distinguish between publicly displayed sex depictions (which can be regulated) and private possession in the home (which cannot).

Other than the exceptions noted above, liberals see pornography as a moral issue of competing values rather than one involving harm to women. Viewed this way, they conclude the state has no role to play in limiting speech for the purpose of furthering a specific civil or sexual morality. To impose a certain standard of public and sexual morality, solely because it reflects the conventions of a given community, is inimical to the exercise and enjoyment of

[14] An illustration of this principle is provided in *Report of the Special Committee on Pornography and Prostitution* (Can. 1985, Vol. 1) 16:

> "Thus, for example, it is legitimate to proscribe driving while under the influence of drink because it has been proven to cause accidents. It is not, however, legitimate to proscribe drinking for that reason."

[15] Borovoy, *supra*, note 11 at p. 64.

[16] J. Finnis, "Reason v. Passion: The Constitutional Dialectic of Free Speech" (1967), 116 *U. Penn. L.R.* 222, at p. 223–30.

[17] Catharine MacKinnon, *Feminism Unmodified* (1989), at p. 99. See also Martha Minow, "Rights for the Next Generation: A Feminist Approach to Children's Rights" (1989), 9 Harv. Women's L.J.; Francis Olson, "The Family and the Market" (1985), 96 Harv. L. Rev. 1497; and Wendy Williams, "The Obliging Shell, An Informal Essay on Foreign Equal Opportunity" (1989), 87 Mich. L.Rev. 2128.

individual freedoms, which form the basis of our social contract.[18] Furthermore, moral disapprobation is a subjective concept, impossible to define and incapable of consistent interpretation and application.

John Locke, described as the father of American liberalism because of his influence on the framers of the American Constitution[19] and the development of liberal thought in western democracies,[20] said that there are no binding, moral ends for human activity and that each person possesses the right to pursue happiness, however understood. He rejected the notion that duties or responsibility to others can override the pursuit of selfish interests as a fundamental orientation point for justice.[21] In moral terms, Locke's views lead to the claim that because each person has the right to pursue his or her own version of happiness, and that no one has a prior claim on any other person's activities, it is immoral for the state or anyone else to interfere with the exercise of these rights.

Political freedom is another essential liberal value because it operationalizes abstract individualism and individual liberty by allowing individuals to decide best for themselves their own development and self-determination by choosing who will govern them.[22] Each person must have the right to consent to a government or reject it if it threatens individual rights because freedom from arbitrary authority is essential to the individual pursuit of happiness.[23] The purpose of democratic government is not to lead humanity to a higher moral purpose, but rather to preserve life, liberty and property.[24] In other words, the social order is not seen as a valued end in itself but rather a means to maximize individual freedom.

Of all the fundamental freedoms, liberals see freedom of speech as the most crucial in preserving these values. Consent to be governed would be impossible without the free exchange of ideas and criticism; intellectual and scientific projects leading to the acquisition of private property require freedom of expression; and the pursuit of happiness makes speech an end in itself. These vital interests that prevent tyranny and the smothering of creative and intellectual pursuits require unimpeded access to speech.

The paradigm that liberals use for thinking about the functions of free speech is the "marketplace of ideas."[25] It is a utilitarian marketplace, where citizens meet as equals and no idea is suppressed. The purpose of the get-together is to come to wise decisions for the general good based on a hearing of

[18] David Dyzenhaus, "Obscenity and the Charter: Autonomy and Equality", (1991), 1 C.R. (4th) 367, at p. 370.

[19] J. Rawls, *A Theory of Justice* (Cambridge: Harvard University Press, 1971), 11.

[20] N. Tarcov, *Locke's Education for Liberty* (Chicago: University of Chicago Press, 1984), 1.

[21] J. Locke, *Essay Concerning Understanding* (Oxford: Clarendon Press, 1984), at p. 351.

[22] *Cohen v. California*, 403 U.S. 15 at 24 (1971), per Harlan J.

[23] Locke, *supra*, note 18 at p. 351.

[24] J. Locke, *Two Treaties of Government* (New York: New American Library, 1965), at p. 378–84.

[25] Mill, *supra*, note 8 at p. 15–54. See also *Abrams v. United States*, 250 U.S. 616, at p. 630 (1919), Holmes J., (diss.).

all viewpoints. If relevant information in the form of opinion, doubt, disbelief or criticism is not heard, the result of the deliberations will be ill-considered or unbalanced.[26]

The objective of free speech is thus result-oriented. Practical, concrete benefits are said to flow to the community from this process and, as a result, almost all forms of speech should be protected. When it comes to extremist speech on the periphery of the freedom, liberals believe that it, too, must be protected. If it is not, the important, highly valued speech at the core of the freedom is threatened.

In summary, liberals see the law as an inappropriate vehicle to deal with most expression, including pornographic expression. Exceptions to the rule are recognized when some measurable, recognized harm can be causally linked to the expression.

B. Criticisms of the Liberal Approach

Many of the liberal values and principles that inform legal responses to pornography issues are outdated, irrelevant, unrealistic concepts that ignore other fundamental values and consequences. The neutral, universalist application of the individual rights principle; the blinkered characterization of "harm"; the reliance on the "marketplace of ideas" theory and the rhetoric of free speech and its role in democracies neither contemplate modern technology of the mass media, which has facilitated the growth of a multi-million dollar pornography industry, nor the fact that pornography subordinates and harms women.[27] The criticisms are discussed in detail below.

(1) The False Assumption of Equality and Universality

The liberal concept of freedom of expression assumes equality. This assumption has given rise to the view that every time speech is strengthened in one place, it is strengthened in another. In real terms, liberals would necessarily say strengthening the speech of the Klan strengthens the speech of blacks; strengthening the speech of Nazis strengthens the speech of Jews; or strengthening the speech of pornographers strengthens the speech of women and children.[28] Historical fact as well as present day reality suggest this view is

[26] T. Emerson, "Towards a General Theory of the First Amendment" 72 *Yale L.J.* 877, at p. 882–83.

[27] See comments of Easterbrook J. in *American Booksellers v. Hudnut*, 771 F. 2d 323 at p. 328–29 (7th Cir. 1985), aff'd 475 U.S. 1001 (1986) where he makes the point that pornography is more than representational material depicting the subordination of women. He recognized that pornography actually subordinates women, yet under American law, free speech principle constitutionally outweighs harm to women and their equality rights. On the other hand, the Supreme Court of Canada found unanimously in *R. v. Butler* Feb. 27, 1991 (as yet unreported) that harm to women outweighed Charter protected expression rights.

[28] For a discussion of the jurisprudential dimension of liberalism and the definition of justice as neutrality between abstract categories, see Catherine MacKinnon, "Pornography, Civil Rights and Speech" (1985), 20 *Harv. CR– CL. LR.* 1.

fundamentally wrong. Symmetry of expression is not possible where unequal distribution of rights is a fact of life. The substantive, systemic inequality of women throughout the world is obvious, acknowledged and proven. When neutral principles are applied to highly prejudicial speech which undermines an already unequal group, their inequality is not only perpetuated, it is exacerbated. The liberal view that "however pernicious an opinion may seem, we depend for its correction not on the conscience of judges and juries but on the competition of other ideas"[29] requires the state to treat pornography in the same way it treats other forms of speech. It is widely acknowledged that neutral application of law is legitimate and desirable unless it results in further disadvantagement of those systemically disadvantaged historically, economically and culturally. It is also widely recognized as a fundamental principle, that government intervention, rather than impeding the enjoyment of fundamental freedoms such as freedom of expression, may in some instances protect and enhance their enjoyment.[30] This is certainly the case if one considers women's freedom of expression, their bodily security and equality rights in relation to pornography. Laws prohibiting pornography enhance and promote women's rights. Insistence on procedural sameness in the constitutional treatment of pornography laws compared to other laws limiting expression is a methodology of inequality.

The assumption of equality also skews the marketplace of ideas concept. The metaphor loses any connection to reality in a world of vastly disparate economic and social power. The mass media are major corporations right at the core of the highest level of the corporate system. They share its aims of profit and increasing market share. The media must frame its messages in terms of the interests and concerns of those who dominate the system. The picture of the world they present is shaped from the perspectives and in the interests of the sellers, the product and the buyers. Allowing such a marketplace of ideas to determine the truth results only in the ideas of the powerful, the rich, those with access to mass media production, becoming the "truth". In the pornography context, that truth dictates that women and children are legitimate targets for male exploitation, abuse, violence and even death and that they have no value as individual human beings.

The line liberals draw between the public and private spheres of life relating them to legitimate and illegitimate interference by the State again rely on the assumptions of autonomy and equality which ultimately disadvantage women. Liberals do not consider that, unlike men, most women spend most of their lives in the "private" sphere. In many aspects of their private lives, including in their sexual lives, women are not autonomous individuals on an equal footing with men. The distinction liberals make between "public" and "private" allows pornography to be inflicted on them and their children in the private sphere

[29] *Collin v. Smith* 587 F. 2d. 1197 (1978) at p. 1204–1205.

[30] See for example the comment of Chief Justice Dickson in *Reference Re Public Service Employee Relations Act* (Alta), [1987] 1 S.C.R. 313 at 367.

without protection or acknowledgement of competing rights.[31]

In order to avoid freedom of expression becoming a gender-biased value favoring men, the whole relationship between "freedom" and the social role of pornography must be evaluated. Questions to contemplate are: how does pornography make men "free" and does it "free" women in the same way? Do women have the same freedom of speech that men have? How would the regulation of pornography affect that allocation? How can something be experienced by one person as "freedom" at the same time it is experienced by another as violence, oppression, containment or some other variant of non-freedom?[32] It is only by asking questions such as this that a true balancing of interest can take place.

(2) The Blinkered Characterization of Harm

By characterizing harm as they do, liberals neatly avoid any analysis of the social meaning of pornography or the public context of freedom of expression.

Describing pornography as merely morally, visually or otherwise "offensive" for example, obscures the harm it causes. No recognition of the impact of pornography on the status and treatment of women is possible when the only harms are thought to be infractions of moral rules or are avoidable irritants. The offensiveness categorization, moreover, is a form of victim-blaming which wrongly places pornography within women's control. It suggests that if women are harmed, it is their own fault because they could or should have avoided it – by averting their eyes or not listening. This approach ignores the essence of discrimination, which is not how members of disadvantaged groups feel about themselves, but rather how they are viewed by members of the dominant group.

On the other side of the coin, the liberal use of the clear and present danger test as the test for harm precludes consideration of harms which do not entail such an identifiable danger point. An examination of the scientific data makes it clear that pornography's effects are much more subtle. It promotes an ideology that fosters and supports sexual agression, disrespect and callousness

[31] Many women report that men abuse them through pornography. See for example, Susan Cole, *Pornography and the Sex Crisis* (Toronto: Amanita Press, 1989) at 44; Charlene Y. Senn, "Women's Reactions to Violent Pornography, Nonviolent Pornography and Erotica," (1985) Unpublished Master's Thesis, University of Calgary, Alberta; E. Sommers and James V.P. Check, "An Empirical Investigation of the Role of Pornography in the Verbal and Physical Abuse of Women," (1987) 2 *Violence and Victims* 189; M.H. Silbert and A.M. Pines, "Pornography and Sexual Abuse of Women," (1984) 10 *Sex Roles* 857. For further critical comment and analysis of the public/private distinction discussing its political implications, see Martha Minow, "Rights For the Next Generation: A Feminist Approach to Children's Rights" (1989), 9 *Harv. Women's L.J.*; Francis Olsen, "The Family and the Market" (1983), 96 *Harv. L. Rev.* 1497; and Wendy Williams, "The Obliging Shell: An Informal Essay on Formal Equal Opportunity" (1984), 87 *Mich. L. Rev.* 2128.

[32] Kathleen Lahey, "The Charter and Pornography: Towards a Restricted Theory of Constitutionally Protected Expression", in Weiler and Elliot, eds., *Litigating the Values of a Nation: The Canadian Charter of Rights and Freedom* (Toronto: Carswell, 1986) at p. 265.

towards women. It helps to create and maintain a climate that is more likely to tolerate the actual physical abuse of women and in which opportunities for women are limited.[33] Trying to prove that direct harm results from pornography is like trying to prove alcohol causes traffic deaths or smoking causes cancer. The links are suggestive, but none of them are dispositive.[34] The liberal requirement to prove "clear and present danger" ignores these realities and analytically predetermines the issue in favor of pornographers.

To privatize the concept of harm as liberals do erects yet another barrier to the achievement of equality for women. A more open-minded posture and willingness to give genuine consideration to important countervailing interests in society is required in order to respond to the true nature of pornography. The highly complicated, analytical and empirical questions underlying the issue of harm cannot be answered by such a rigid and narrow approach. For example, if pornographic speech is viewed as a practice of discrimination the analysis changes. It makes sense to limit pornography when its real harms include group-based enmity, ill-will, degradation and prejudice which produce exclusion and subordination of the target group.[35] These are legally recognized harms which deserve sanction because they shape the social image and reputation of group members, often controlling their opportunities more powerfully than their individual abilities do.[36]

(3) Reliance on the "Truth" Rationale

The third criticism is the degree to which liberals rely upon the truth-seeking rationale to defend all forms of speech, including pornography. In the case of highly emotive speech where the speech seeks to subvert the truth-seeking process itself, a forceful argument can be made that the interest in seeking truth cuts against, rather than in favour of speech and the values relied upon to support freedom of speech lose their force. While the general proposition that open discussion advances the pursuit of truth cannot be questioned, the way liberals use the truth rationale pushes the claim too far. For example, opinions advocating the sexual torture or degradation of women in pornography cannot be said to contribute to the benefit of truth-seeking. The content of the opinion fundamentally contradicts the basic principles and values of a free society. In terms of any individual rights-bearing constitutions or international human rights instruments, such propositions are false ideas. The more societies believe in the falseness of the speech, the weaker the "truth" justification becomes. Unlike the American courts which continue to insist that freedom of expression must predominate regardless of competing interests or rights,[37] other courts,

[33] *Supra*, note 4.

[34] *R. v. Fringe Product Inc.* (1990), 53 C.C.C. (3d) 422.

[35] *R. v. Butler*, *supra*, note 27.

[36] This reasoning was adopted by the Canadian Supreme Court in *Butler* Ibid., and also in *R. v. Keegstra* [1990] 2 S.C.R. 697, an analogous case involving a constitutional challenge to hate propaganda laws.

[37] *Hudnut v. American Booksellers*, *supra*, note 27.

particularly the Supreme Court of Canada, have inextricably linked rights such as equality with the concept of a free society, and held that where there is a collision between freedom of speech and other important rights, freedom of speech may be cut back.[38]

Furthermore, while it can be argued that pornography may have some educational value through its exposure of misogyny, it is far from clear that an open confrontation with pornography in the marketplace of ideas leads to a richer belief in the truth. It is more likely that the opposite is true. The marketplace theory states that if ideas are false or bad, they will die out and be replaced by true or good ones. Applied to pornography, one would think the idea that women are equal to men and that children have dignity and deserve to be treated with respect, would prevail over the message in pornography that women and children are sex objects, available to be violated, subjugated and coerced at the will of men. Yet the debasement of women and children in the mass media is an ever increasing phenomenon.[39] In Canada for example, the presence of pornography increased by 326.7 percent between 1965 and 1980. This represents an increase of at least fourteen times the growth of the Canadian population during the same period. Furthermore, pornographic ideas are replicated in real life in statistics which are also increasing at a very rapid rate. Widespread sexual assault,[40] wife battery,[41] sexual harassment and sexual abuse of children[42] indicate that competing ideas about equality, dignity and respect are not emerging from the marketplace of ideas in any significant way. The "value" of pornography as a truth-seeking device in these terms ranges from remote to none. It makes no sense to suggest that the uninhibited activity of pornographers is important to maintaining a belief that what they have to say is wrong. Rather than serving as a means to discover truth, pornography conceals the truth about women and takes away or chills their speech through a system of sexism.

If one looks at other areas of social life where the primary objective is the pursuit of truth, the marketplace of ideas is not the model used. In the criminal justice system, for example, speech is recognized as being important to the goal of learning the truth, but at the same time its potential to undermine the truth is clearly recognized. Parties may present their arguments as they wish, but

[38] *Slaight Communications Inc. v. Davidson*, [1989] 1 S.C.R. 1038 at p. 1056.

[39] It is widely reported that revenues from pornography in the United States alone exceed 8 billion dollars annually. (See C. MacKinnon [1985] *Harv. L.R. FW.* 54).

[40] See L. Clark and D. Lewis, *Rape: The Price of Coercive Sexuality*, Toronto: Women's Educational Press, 1977, at p. 61. They state that the incidences of rape increased by 174% between 1961 and 1971. In the period 1969–1973, it increased 76%.

[41] Armstrong, "Wife Beating: Let's Stop it Now" (July 1983), *Canadian Living* 89, states that one woman in every ten is beaten by her husband or common-law mate. This has been replicated in a number of studies.

[42] *Report of the Committee on Sexual Offences Against Children and Youths*, Badgley ed., 1984; Supply and Services Canada (Ottawa), at 180–83 states, among other staggering statistics of abuse, that 50% of women and 30% of men have been victims of unwanted sexual acts, the majority of these occurring before they were legal adults.

speech that is "inflammatory", or highly emotive, may be excluded because of its potential prejudicial effects on the judgment of the judge or jury. In other words, it is recognized that certain forms of speech can undermine the truth.

A more realistic assessment would say Gresham's Law, that bad money drives out good, is a more sensible rule of thumb in the commercial world of pornography. It has also been persuasively argued that Mill, if he were living today, would interpret his words as including the requirements of social justice.[43]

(4) The Fallacy That Pornography Cannot Be Defined

Liberal arguments regarding definition must be addressed. They maintain that it is impossible to draw the distinctions between pornography and art, or valuable sexual expression. They question the law's ability to formulate a standard that will prohibit pornography without supressing other valuable expression.

Liberals correctly point out that words capable of more than one precise meaning may create opportunities for unintended distinctions to be drawn. If imprecise words are used to describe a criminal offence, the law can be misused or misinterpreted to cause an unjust result. However, they are not correct when they suggest that unless we have absolute certainty in words, we cannot have laws. This is a false suggestion because in any legal system, uncertainty is inevitable. The choice does not exist between a legal system without uncertainty and one with it. Open-ended words such as "reasonable" or "dangerous" create opportunities for abuse, but they are the starting point for principled approaches to legal issues. The word "pornography" should be similarly viewed. Although exact precision in language is the optimum, imperfection cannot be used to foreclose action. To merely ask how much uncertainty any given law or definition carries with it, is an incomplete inquiry. The companion question, how much uncertainly are we prepared to live with given the interests the law is trying to protect, must also be asked. It is a question of balance in every case. In all the world's legal systems, contours and content have been given to seemingly undefinable words like "reasonable" and "dangerous" and there is no reason why the same cannot occur with respect to the word "pornography".

Canadian Courts define pornography by distinguishing between depictions harmful to women and children and those that are not.[44] Sexual depictions which are labelled as "pornography" are linked to the context within which they are presented. In the landmark decision of *R. v. Butler*[45], the Canadian Supreme Court unanimoulsy held that anti-pornography laws are justifiable limits on freedom of expression when their purpose is to avoid harm to society

[43] J. Humphrey, "The Just Requirements of Morality, Public Order and General Welfare in a Democratic Society" in *The Practice of Freedom*, eds. R.St. J. Macdonald and John P. Humphrey, Toronto: Butterworths, 1979.

[44] *R. v. Butler*, *supra*, note 27.

[45] Ibid.

– specifically to women and children. Based on the definition that pornography is "any publication or dominant characteristic of which is the undue exploitation of sex, or of sex and any one or more of the following subjects, namely, crime, horror, cruelty and violence,..."[46] the Court ruled that pornography depicting child sex and violent, degrading or dehumanizing sex is illegal in Canada. Explicit sex that is neither degrading nor dehumanizing is not. The Court used the tolerance of the community as the arbiter in determining the limits on pornographic expression saying the Canadian community does not tolerate portrayal of sex where harm or the risk of harm is substantial. This contextually sensitive method of defining pornography is responsive to progress in the knowledge and understanding of pornography and its harms. To demand a precise, content-specific definition of an inherently elusive notion is yet another liberal methodology which pre-determines the issue.

(5) Liberal Free Speech Rhetoric Is Out-Dated and Irrelevant

More often than not, traditional liberal rhetoric has a distinct eighteenth century tone. Its characterization of government as a constant threat to the freedom of its citizens, as perpetually hostile and aggressive towards individuals and society, has promoted the fear that once in possession of power, governments will revert back to the autocratic powers of their predecessors. Faced with such a threat, any attempt to limit or make exceptions to the free speech principle becomes almost subversive. In setting up the freedom of expression/democracy equation, liberals create a rigid and unbending "either/or" proposition which acts as a form of closure for further discussion and makes a contextualized analysis of the experience of women as disadvantaged members of society impossible.

While some threat of tyrannical tendencies of governments to turn against democracy may exist, the speech issues raised by pornography are much different than those facing fledgling democracies. Transposing the rhetoric and platitudes designed to protect discussion of public issues and free elections to deal with subordinating and discriminatory forms of speech, misses the mark.

Moreover, the assumption that a commitment to the democratic system of government requires an unqualified commitment to free speech is not necessarily accurate. While it is true that a democratic society cannot tolerate unilateral denial of the freedom of its citizens to express their views, it is surely consistent with democracy to limit certain forms of speech. Many constitutional documents embody this concept. Certainly the Canadian Charter of Rights and Freedoms does when it permits limitations on rights if they can be justified as reasonable, prescribed by law in the context of a free and democratic society.[47] How the unhindered promotion of pornography facilitates an exchange of views necessary for good government or can be

[46] Criminal Code of Canada, R.S.C., 1985, c. C-46 s. 163(8).

[47] *The Canadian Charter of Rights and Freedoms*, Part 1 of the *Constitution Act*, 1982, being Schedule B of the *Canada Act* 1982 (U.I.C.), 1982, c.11, s.1.

characterized as either elemental to the structure of democracy or an advancement in the protection of freedoms is very difficult to imagine. The liberal conviction that the original meanings and purposes underlying the free speech principle continue to have contemporary relevancy, may explain why newer purposes are overlooked in their analyses. By not examining speech in its context and in relation to other rights, liberals divert the legal analysis away from the social meaning of what is being done by pornography, and force a defence of it on neutral ground. This in turn reduces society's responsibility for the result being reached, and protects freedom of expression as a process without a public context or egalitarian dimension. It does not allow for any consideration as to whether or not free speech might have the result of diminishing, eradicating or colliding with the freedoms of others.

Related to the liberal emphasis on political freedoms, is the assumption that laws limiting certain forms of expression necessarily put the government in the position of being the singular antagonist infringing individuals' rights. Arguably, a more accurate characterization would be that pornographers who promote hatred, violence or degradation of women as a class, are aggressors in a social conflict between unequal groups. By prohibiting the undue exploitation of women in sex depictions, the government advances the interests of a disadvantaged group (women) in relation to the interests of the group discriminating against them (men). A fundamental principle of government responsibility is that where groups conflict, governments must draw a line between their claims, marking where one set of claims legitimately begin and the other fades away. This line drawing exercise is routinely done by states when they pass laws relating to hate propaganda. Pornography is analogous to hate propaganda in that its express or implied intent is to distort the image of a group or class of people, to deny their humanity, to make them such objects of ridicule and humiliation that acts of aggression against them are viewed less seriously.[48] The major difference between hate propaganda and pornography is the method used to achieve the desired results and the harm it causes. Pornography is much more commonplace, socially accepted and widely distributed across class, race, and geographical boundaries. It follows that its harms must be deeper, wider and more damaging to social life than the harm of hate propaganda. When states fail to regulate pornography and draw lines between the permissible and prohibited, they fail in their responsibility of maintaining social harmony in the society.

In conclusion, it is apparent that liberal views are not as liberating and fair as some theorists would have us believe. When tested against the theories and analyses of those who seek social equality with the dominant male elite, liberalism reveals itself as very limited in scope. The centrality of the autonomous and undifferentiated individual to liberal thought shows how its abstract principles fail to address the historically specific oppression actually experienced by dominated groups.

[48] Susan Brownmiller, "The Place of Pornography", *Harpers*, November, 1984, at p. 34.

C. Balancing Rights and Freedoms Using a Harms-Based Equality Approach

A harms-based equality approach starts from the position that any interpretation of competing rights and freedoms must balance tensions between harms. In the case of pornography, harms that flow from regulating it must be balanced against the harms it actualizes. Ultimately, the decision will rest on how seriously decision-makers view the importance women's equality and bodily security rights compared to the importance of freedom of expression in pornography. In deciding on the proper balance, values and principles enunciated in documents such as the Universal Declaration of Human Rights and the Convention to Eliminate All Forms of Discrimination Against Women provide guidance. Respect for the inherent dignity of the human person, commitment to social justice and equality for women, accomodation of a wide variety of beliefs, respect for cultural and group identity, and faith in social and political institutions which enhance the participation of individuals and groups in society should be the context in which the balance is assessed. Additionally, the broader societal, political and legal context of sex inequality – the fact of rape, battery, prostitution, incest and sexual harrassment as part of daily life for women – must be considered. When this type of contextual assessment is made, it becomes clear that compared to men, women are profoundly unequal socially, politically and individually. The encouragement and promotion of subordination in pornography, particularly the depictions of violence and sexual exploitation of women at the hands of men, reinforces the systemic violence and social harm they suffer. The vast proliferation and sheer volume of pornography makes the harm even more serious and generalized. Equality-seekers see pornography as particularly damaging because it reinforces the discriminatory idea that women are inferior and entitled to only a limited role within society. When women are set up as objects of male sexual pleasure, frustration and violence, efforts to improve the rights of women to equality and dignity and freedom from violence are directly undermined.

The social harm of pornography was discussed in Canada in the Report on Pornography by the Standing Committee on Justice and Legal Affairs as follows:

> The clear and unquestionable danger of this type of material is that it reinforces some unhealthy tendencies in Canadian society. The effect of this type of material is to reinforce male-female stereotypes to the detriment of both sexes. It attempts to make degradation, humiliation, victimization, and violence in human relationships appear normal and acceptable. A society which holds that egalitarianism, non-violence, consensualism, and mutuality are basic to any human interaction, whether sexual or other, is clearly justified in controlling and prohibiting any medium of depiction, description or advocacy which violates these principles.[49]

[49] Canada. House of Commons. Standing Committee on Justice and Legal Affairs. *Report on Pornography* Issue No. 18 (March 22, 1978) at p. 18:4.

The Canadian Report of the Task Force on Sex-role stereotyping addresses the harm inherent in sex-role stereotyping in the broadcast media:

> Male dominance and female submissiveness are at the very heart of the stereotypes of men and women. Pornography reflects the extreme portrayal of dominance and the exploitation of women's sexuality. Pornography or any portrayal of violence against women, is the ultimate expression of dominance/submissiveness, the objectification of women. As such pornography or the portrayal of violence against women has no place in the broadcast media.[50]

Social scientific research over the last twenty years clearly supports the view that pornography is harmful to equality and bodily security rights. It has been demonstrated in content analytic research that violent and degrading pornography can have a number of effects. Subjects exposed to pornography demonstrate an increased acceptance of rape myths, increased acceptance of violence against women, increased rape fantasies, increased aggressive behaviour toward women in a laboratory setting, decreased future perceptions of rape victim suffering, a future desensitization to sexual violence and an increased reported willingness to rape.[51]

In their book, *Sex, Violence and the Media*, Eysenck and Nias undertook an extensive review of the literature on violence and pornography and concluded that:

> [W]here the context is hostile to women, as most pornographic films are, we felt that such films should fall under the category of "incitement to violence towards minority groups" – even though women are not a minority group. Nevertheless such films do constitute a clear case of incitement to maltreat women, downgrade them to a lower status, regard them as mere sex objects, and elevate male *machismo* to a superior position on the scale of values. Evaluative conditioning, modelling, and desensitization all point to the same conclusion, namely that such presentations have effects on men's attitudes which are detrimental to women; in fairness to more than one half of the population, such incitements should be proscribed.[52]

Unlike rape, wife battering and incest aggression where the victims are individuals, pornography and sex-role stereotypes in the media make all women victims. The harm it causes is public, generalized harm resulting in the degradation of women as a class which in turn results in reduced credibility and opportunity for women. Many women's goals, such as greater participation in public life, equal pay for work of equal value, quality daycare and greater

[50] *Report of the Task Force on Sex-Role Stereotyping in the Broadcast Media (Images of Women)* (Can. 1982) at p. 35.

[51] Check and Malamuth, "Pornography and Sexual Aggression: A Social Learning Theory Analysis" (1985), *Communication Yearbook* 9. *See also* N. Malamuth & E. Donnerstein eds., *Pornography and Sexual Aggression*, 1984.

[52] H. Eysenck and D. Nias, *Sex, Violence and the Media*, 1978, at p. 259.

physical security are that much more difficult to achieve when female credibility is assaulted on such a massive scale. The British Columbia Court of Appeal recognized this when it found in *R. v. Red Hot Video Ltd.* that the exploitation of women and children depicted in publications and films can, in certain circumstances, lead to "abject and servile victimization,"[53] and that if true equality between male and female persons is to be achieved, we cannot ignore the threat to equality resulting from exposure to audiences of certain types of violent and degrading material.[54]

On the other side of the equation, the values which underlie the protection of freedom of expression relate to the search for truth, participation in the political process and individual self-fulfilment. Liberals argue that pornography forces the questioning of conventional notions of sexuality and by doing so, provokes an inherently political discourse. Further, they say materials which have scientific, artistic or literary merit may be "chilled" or captured by regulations on pornography. They suggest that rather than prohibition, restrictions on time, manner and place where pornography is sold would be preferable. The further suggestion is made that these are more effective techniques than regulating pornography to discourage violence against women. Techniques such as counselling rape victims to charge their assailant, provision of shelter and assistance for battered women, lobbying for anti-discrimination laws and the creation of educational programs to increase the public's sensitivity to violence against women issues (are further suggested by liberals).[55]

All of these arguments lose their force if it is clear that the objective of regulating pornography is the avoidance of harm to women. It becomes untenable to argue that time, place and manner restrictions are a better form of regulation than prohibition. Imposing heavy taxes on pornography for example, or requiring special licences for its distribution rather than condemning it, sends the message that harm to women will be tolerated as long as the user pays. By virtue of collecting the tax, the state would legitimize the pornography trade and even become a participant in it. As Sopinka J. states in the *Butler* case, it is inconsistent and hypocritical to argue that once the State has reasonably concluded that certain acts are harmful to certain groups in society such acts could be permitted as long as conditions are more restrictive. The harm sought to be avoided remains the same in either case.[56]

Reactive solutions suggested by liberals such as the provision of counselling for rape victims, imply that women must absorb the harm caused by the very behaviour encouraged by pornography as part of the cost of protecting freedom of expression. It is hard to believe such a requirement could have any credibility in any society which is free and democratic and aspires to the most basic human rights norms. Certainly these and other strategies should be offered to protect

[53] *R. v. Red Hot Video Ltd.* (1985), 45 C.R. (3d) 36 (BCCA) at p. 43–44.
[54] Ibid., per Anderson J at p. 59.
[55] Borovoy, *supra*, note 11 at p. 65–66.
[56] *R. v. Butler*, *supra* note 27 at p.62.

women from violent men, but to say they are preferable to controlling the dissemination of the very image that contribute to such behaviors diminishes the harm and consequently diminishes women and children as full citizens. A serious social problem as violence against women and children requires a multi-faceted approach.[57]

The argument that pornography provokes an inherently political discourse, is a critique of the *status quo* or presents a dissenting but repressed voice, is difficult to accept within an equality, harms based analysis. Once the harm to women is recognized, it is obvious that pornography is nothing more than an economically motivated social practice of discrimination which entrenches and embodies society's most repressive and anti-egalitarian norms. As such, it is not a form of political speech as traditionally protected and thus lies far from the core of the guarantee of freedom of expression.

The recognition by the Canadian Supreme Court that the social harm of discrimination can outweigh the free speech interest, marks a major new development in freedom of expression jurisprudence. It is inclusive rather than exclusive, more communitarian than individualistic and more aware of the actual impacts of speech on the disadvantaged members of society than have ever before been articulated in a freedom of expression case. It is an approach that re-distributes speech rights between unequal groups which other countries and the international human rights community should contemplate if they are genuinely serious about women's human rights.

D. Conclusions

Human rights start where civil liberties end. Human rights go beyond the relationship of the individual to the state and emphasize the relationship of individuals to one another. They invoke the state's intervention and assistance because individuals in their capacity as members of groups are disadvantaged for arbitrary reasons. Human rights principles allow for different treatment because not all individuals have suffered historic, generic exclusion because of their group membership. Where barriers impede fairness for some individuals they should be removed, even if this means treating some people differently. Intellectual pluralism does not and cannot mean that racism or sexism will be given the same deference as tolerance.[58]

Where we can make common cause with civil liberties we should. But when the debate involves the clash of interests presented by pornography, eighteenth and nineteenth century theories that served a need modern democracies have outgrown, does not seem to be the best way to solve the problem. I do not see why any democracy should be embarrassed or uncomfortable prioritizing the

[57] Ibid., at p.61.

[58] R. Abella, Keynote Address, National Symposium on Women, Law and the Administration of Justice, June 10, 1991. Paper available from the Department of Justice, Canada.

needs of the impoverished, disempowered and disadvantaged over those who are more privileged.

Equality is an emerging right. Establishing it requires reciprocity of respect and parity of regard for physical dignity and personal integrity. Legal interpretation must be guided by these values and goals if the constitutional mandate of equality is to be met. Problems of the future cannot always be solved using the intellectual frameworks of the past. The goal of a more humane and egalitarian society requires new ways of talking about the problems of free expression; otherwise we will find the progressive tools of an earlier era turned against progress. I hope that the international community will follow the path that has been mapped by the Canadian judiciary in deciding what is and is not pornographic and what limits can be set on it based on a context driven, harm-based equality analysis. If they do, rights and duties will be allocated equitably, not simply on the basis of abstract, doctrinally stagnant grand principles of formal equality which thwart rather than achieve substantive liberty and substantive equality.

CARL GINSBURG*

Destruction of Local Cultures Through Mass Communications

1. Introduction

In addressing the topic – The Destruction of Local Cultures Through Mass Communications – I shall focus specifically on blacks in the United States and the treatment they receive from the American press, of which I am a working member in the broadcast faction. To focus on local culture in the U.S. means looking at its components, many of which are minority groups. Their existence brings into question the role of human rights in American society. If the minority, even in part, is denied these rights – as indeed is the case today for many of America's blacks – the legitimacy of the majority should be challenged.

2. Stigmatizing Black Culture through the Media

There is no question that the Universal Declaration's social and economic entitlements, including the right to work, to an education, the right to food, clothing, housing, and an adequate standard of living, are denied most blacks in the United States. Mass communications can either expose these violations and point the spotlight on the injustice done to a significant cultural entity of the community or it can pointedly ignore any notion of human rights violations, passing off social inequities as inborn ineptitude, and in the process stigmatize that culture. The American mass media favours the latter.

It is noteworthy that on the occasion of the Universal Declaration's 40th anniversary – celebrated worldwide – scarcely a mention was carried in the United States press. One network's television program that did examine the Declaration failed to fully cite the social, economic and cultural rights embodied in it. It is no surprise that the press watchdog group "Fairness and Accuracy in Reporting" characterized that program as "in keeping with the

* Producer, CBS Evening News, New York, New York.

K.E. Mahoney and P. Mahoney (eds.), Human Rights in the Twenty-first Century, 777–781.

dominant tendency in the U.S. to define human rights primarily in civil-political terms".

For the press to ignore the Universal Declaration (it is, after all, a threat to the interests and practices of U.S. corporatism), poses no dilemma. But, the anger and frustration blacks in America feel at being denied equal access to the country's resources requires interpretation. That interpretation can ultimately sustain or destroy a culture because it defines it and determines its value to society. Two recent excerpts from press reports on the plight of blacks in the United States are illustrative:

> "The black underclass seems incapable of progress. After all the work done by blacks and whites to destroy the stereotype of the shiftless, irresponsible black man, here come these characters."[1]

> "Why, after 25 years of equal rights – indeed of special remedial treatment under the law – do so many blacks remain outside the bounds of middle class society?"[2]

The negative messages in the two examples demonstrate clearly how the interpretation undercuts the culture. The assessments suggest that blacks not only cannot, but do not want to better their fate. This can only be destructive to their culture.

3. Destruction of the Black Community

Indicators by which government agencies measure a culture's survival show that blacks are being destroyed. For example, infant mortality for blacks is 18 per 1,000, approximately twice that of whites. Cancer mortality rates show that 30 years ago blacks and whites were equally stricken by the disease. But while white rates increased incrementally over those 30 years, the cancer mortality rate for blacks jumped by 50%. Yet, as blacks continue to die from cancer, civil libertarians in the U.S. argue in public debate about the "rights" of tobacco companies to blanket poor black communities with their advertisements. One leading first amendment scholar has argued that blacks, like everyone else, constitute a "legitimate market".

One of the most revealing indicators of cultural destruction is life expectancy rates. In the 1980's, for two years in a row, blacks suffered a DECLINE in the expectancy while life expectancy for whites rose.

In terms of access to education, opportunities for blacks are in decline. Today, there are more black men in jail than there are attending college in the United States. The numbers of blacks in professional and graduate schools are

[1] P. Hamill, "Breaking the Silence: A Letter to a Black Friend", *Esquire* (March, 1988), pp. 93–94.

[2] *New York* (May 29, 1989), p. 34.

falling and black unemployment is twice the national average. For blacks who work, real earnings are falling. Median earnings of full-time black male workers fell ten percent from 1979–87. Other measures of living standards, such as ownership and quality of housing show a marked deterioration for blacks over the past 20 years.

The rate of poverty for blacks is over 30%. By official standards, one of every three black people is poor – a rate unchanged since 1970. And yet a recent report from the Joint Economic Committee of the U.S. Congress revealed that the official poverty line – its methodology unadjusted since the mid-1960s – seriously underestimates the nation's poor. The report states that for black Americans, the poverty rate is actually 49.4% – or nearly one out of every two.

4. The Media's Recurrent Theme: Blame the Victim

The press, whose task is to formulate and disseminate the final message, attributes black deprivation to behavioral affliction. Phrases, such as an "absence of role models", "lifestyles" or "culture of poverty" are recurrently used in press reports as explanations of blacks' conditions. We continue to read that black "character flaws" are eliminated by correcting black "behavioural problems". In other words, "blame the victim" is the popular message that has been and continues to be propagated by the American press. Their problems, according to the mass media, are not society's, not indications of the growing inequity in the distribution of the country's wealth, not an ingredient of the free market, but rather a matter of "a flawed family structure".

This ideological rationale – the "family problem" – was first popularized in the mid-1960's. That it continues to be the dominant theme today is an indication of the press's uniformity for more than a generation.

The "black family problem" is a message carried by news reports inundating readers and viewers. TIME magazine attributed, without qualification, the problem of inner city blacks to "the breakdown of the family structure".[3] To TIME, "unemployed and undereducated, [blacks] seem unable, and in some cases unwilling, to fit into the broader society."[4] The *Baltimore Evening Sun* put it in these terms: "The crisis in black families is the biggest problem facing American blacks. All other problems, transportation snarls, deterioration of the infrastructure, the sunset of smokestack industries, are dwarfed by the disintegration of the black family in our society."[5] The same message underpinned the CBS-TV documentary entitled "The Vanishing Family: Crisis in Black America," which was handed countless journalism prizes and heralded in the print press.[6] One popular columnist wrote that the "problem in the inner

[3] *Time* (December 1, 1986), p. 28.
[4] Ibid., p. 27.
[5] *Baltimore Evening Sun* (December 5, 1983), p. 3.
[6] See e.g., *Boston Globe* (January 24, 1986), pp. 24–30.

city is that millions of blacks are victims of many irresponsible blacks."[7] "New Black Theme: Save Yourselves" was the front-page feature of the *Los Angeles Times*, reporting "a bold attempt ... to seize the initiative in the renewed debate over how to deal with the deep-rooted problems accompanying black poverty."[8] The *Times* went on to call for "more personal responsibility" in the inner cities and to encourage "individual initiative" with such programs as sub-minimum wages for teenagers and enterprise zones to attract businesses to poor neighbourhoods.[9] A situation caused by exploitation is thus solved by further exploitation – the not-so-subtle agenda of the free market.

Some newspapers simply called for "self-help" on the part of poor blacks – a different approach to blaming the victim. "Blacks Debating a Greater Stress on Self-Reliance Instead of Aid", was the way the daily, *USA Today*, put it, claiming that "blacks had to bear some of the blame."[10] The *Wall Street Journal* provided in an editorial that "the black underclass is at least partly responsible for its continuing impoverishment and self-help must be a large part of any strategy to improve its situation... There is little disagreement that vast income transfers really have not moved many blacks out of the inner cities and up the economic ladder."[11] (One wonders just what "vast income transfers" The Wall Street Journal is referring to.) In *Esquire* magazine, an article dubbed a plea to middle-class blacks, who it called "too proud to depend upon the kindness of strangers. [To them] a true man was someone who housed, clothed and fed his family... There is very little now," the article states, "that whites can do in a direct way for the maimed and hurting citizens of the [black] Underclass."[12] On WNET-TV, the Public Broadcasting System's New York – area station, a program commentator suggested that "black kids be sent to camps to be trained."[13] And on the cover of *The New Republic* magazine, ran the headline: "The two Black Americas: A Regress Report" – "It is now universally accepted", the article instructed, "that black poverty is heavily *THE RESULT OF* family breakdown."[14]

These press attacks on black people defy the very existence of a culture. At a minimum they redefine that culture in terms of deprivation, atrophy, and destruction.

[7] *Boston Globe* (January 24, 1986), p. 36.
[8] *Los Angeles Times* (March 8, 1986), p. 16.
[9] Ibid.
[10] *USA Today* (April 20, 1989), p. 14.
[11] *Wall Street Journal* (July 9, 1987), p. 28.
[12] *Esquire*, See note 1, *supra*.
[13] "The Eleventh Hour", (April 25, 1989), WNET-TV.
[14] *The New Republic* (February 6, 1989), p. 18. (emphasis added).

5. Conclusion

The ongoing destruction of black culture is a frightening reality. The United States prison population, now over one million and galloping forward, is disproportionately black. Entire black inner cities, such as Philadelphia, St. Louis, Newark, Detroit, Hartford, Gary, New York's Harlem and South Bronx, once thriving (or at least surviving) are now boarded up. AIDS and drug addiction among the abandoned black populations are at epidemic proportions.

For the mass media to cast this state of affairs as a matter of black irresponsibility is an act of cultural destruction which serves as a grand obfuscation of the system's design. It is an indicator, too, of the treatment other cultures have received or may expect down the road from the faceless masters of the free market.

An effective human rights strategy must include concrete plans, such as stopping the on-going centralization of the mass media, teaching our students to be organizers against exploitation, and creating, supporting and participating in popular movements committed to protecting communities against the onslaught of the culture of the free marketeers. A GLOBAL human rights strategy must ultimately address the GLOBAL strategy of corporate capitalism in which local cultures are destroyed because they are considered to be nothing more than part of the market equation.

KEVIN HAMILTON*

Control of and Access to the Media in the Third World

To most people in Canada, most people in the west, Africa probably means a place where people die of famine in the north, where blacks are killed by white policemen in the south, and in the middle not a lot happens except an occasional elephant or rhino being poached. But in fact, in a curious way probably the most endangered species in Africa for the moment is the reporter.

In the 1960s there were dozens of British correspondents based in newly independent Africa, living there, specializing in its affairs, and travelling widely throughout the continent. Now there are effectively none. Not CBS, not NBC, not ABC, not a single American television network other than CNN has a staff correspondent based anywhere in Africa between Johannesburg and Cairo. The reporter is dying out in Africa. Why? There are probably two reasons. He is being killed off by cutbacks in the foreign budgets of news organizations, which are appalled by the rocketing expense and the sometimes sheer impossibility of sending somebody around the continent, where the roads, the railways, the airways, the telephones and the telexes are just crumbling away. They are reluctant to do so unless there is a story like the famine in Ethiopia in 1984 that even journalists cannot miss.

But they are also being killed off by the governments of Africa, most of whom do not tolerate opposition or criticism of any kind and many of whom have reduced their own press and radio and television to little more than sycophancy. To them foreign reporters are at best mischievous, malicious agents of a patronizing white developed world. So foreign reporters, and I am one of them, are routinely banned from many African countries.

Not surprisingly this leads many people working in the media to declare that they are not interested in what is happening in the third world. That is possibly a justification for the easy, cheap route of insular self-interest, for an unrelieved diet of home news, sprinkled, if you are in Europe, with news from America; if you are in America, with news from Europe.

It should be noted that there is a bonus in that as well. Both America and

* Editor-in-Chief, News Vision International, London.

K.E. Mahoney and P. Mahoney (eds.), Human Rights in the Twenty-first Century, 783–787.

Europe are so stitched up electronically that one correspondent can cover the whole of America just by sitting in an office in Washington, reporting predigested news three or four times a day via the cheap satellites to Europe. It is filling air time and it is value for money. We, in Europe, have a rather dismissive attitude on some occasions to American television news. The saying is that on American network television there are two kinds of news: domestic American news and domestic American news that happens abroad. The Gulf War is probably an interesting example of the latter.

But, make no mistake, we, in Britain, are probably just as bad. Some years ago an editor at the BBC called Derek Maude invented a principle he called Maude's Law, which was all about making values about news judgments. And Maude's Law was this, that one person killed in an elevator accident inside the BBC was to be equated to 5 people killed in a car crash on the other side of London, 35 people in a coach crash in Wales, 250 in a train accident in France, 500 in a ferry disaster in Turkey, until the entire population of Bangladesh had to be wiped out before it got on the news agenda. The ripple effect.

So, who is left in Africa to report knowledgeably on events rather than just jetting in, looking at the latest disaster with a pocket full of clippings and then merely reinforcing the existing preconceptions of Toronto or Manhattan or London? Who is now left to report on the whole of Africa, which has to be the most fascinating continent on earth, and the most cruel, and most contradictory?

This is a continent where the President of a sovereign country can personally with his own hands murder hundreds of his own opponents, have tens of thousands of others, including his Anglican Archbishop killed, yet get a standing ovation when he walks into an African summit conference wearing a stetson hat and a pair of revolvers. Another country's most respected leader for many years was Julius Nyerere, a mesmerizing man, such a delightful man to meet personally. A man whose arguments and style are absolutely captivating. He is widely regarded as gentle, austere, idealistic. And yet at one time Mr. Nyerere kept 10,000 political prisoners in jail. That is many more than in South Africa. More importantly, he argued gently and reasonably, through an idealistic system that has made his country one of the most lethargic and inefficient on earth. Yet, we have not reported it. We, the media, have not properly reported it in a reasonable rather than a sensational way. We have not examined what this great and good man has done and why it has not been appropriate for Africa.

Let me try to address why this should be so. I come back to the two fundamental points, two problems that face journalists operating in Africa. Let me give one brief example. CNN, unlike the other networks, does maintain a correspondent based in Nairobi. His name is Gary Striker. Gary is an extremely fine reporter and not too long ago he did two rather remarkable things. Firstly, he managed to convince his foreign desk back in Atlanta, Georgia to make available funds for him to go and do a story in Uganda – not about civil war or Idi Amin but about the reconstruction, the very real reconstruction that is going on in that country in the wake of things that have happened in the past. Secondly, he managed to persuade the Ugandan Embassy in Nairobi to get him a media permit within three weeks, which is probably a record. He flew to Entebe. The following day he went to State House, an integral part of his story about the reconstruction of Uganda being an interview with the President of the country, President Museveni. He arrived only to be told that Museveni was not available. The interview had been cancelled. No explanation, no warning, no reason.

Now Gary had a problem. He did not want to write a negative story about the country he was visiting. On the other hand, if he returned to Nairobi and announced to CNN that he had been unable to get the story he had promised, he might have found himself in some trouble. It so happened that he did what most journalists do when they are in that kind of situation: he propped up the bar at the local hotel for a while until he met some aid workers who were doing some research in Uganda on AIDS. Gary had deliberately gone into that country to try and do a routine interview. He had no alternative: he was there, his organization had spent several thousands of dollars getting him there, he had to go back with a story. He regrets that the story he went back with was negative, but it got on air, and his trip was vindicated. He will not now be allowed back in Uganda, but he has still got a job with CNN.

The other brief example I wanted to talk about concerns Ethiopia in 1984, the famine. It is very interesting to consider how that story got told. A lot of false trails have been laid. The reality was that Mohamed Amin, a cameraman based in Nairobi, had for many months been following the growing plight of the people in Ethiopia. Finally he managed to convince his boss (who was me at the time) to send him in and at the last moment the BBC was persuaded to send Michael Buerk in with Mohamed. When they arrived, they discovered that although the Ethiopian Government had given them entry permits and permits to travel inside Ethiopia – because in Ethiopia you need a permit not only to get in but also to move around internally – they were not authorized to go to the north. However, they managed to overcome that difficulty. They found an organization that had an airplane, travelled up to the north and got the stories which everyone must be familiar with, and those reports were then broadcast on the BBC a couple of days later. They were very nearly not broadcast in North America. When NBC was told about these reports, the response from the news desk was: "frankly we are not interested, we have had enough of people dying in Africa". It was only when the European manager of NBC news in London disobeyed an order from New York and satellited the pictures to New York, where they were then seen by the executive producer of nightly news, that they got on air. We all know what happened after that.

Whether that outcome was negative or positive is possibly subject for another debate. In any event, the media image of Africa for the next few years was firmly established as the starving Ethiopian child. Many reporters swarmed in from Fleet Street and New York and Toronto and elsewhere. One cannot decry what they did because they did help to sensitize the world to the distress of Africa. What they did not do, of course, was to focus on the cause of that distress.

We must not merely challenge the stereotypes that we have created over the last few years. Why do we not tell people that it is not true that all Africans are totally uncivilized or were totally uncivilized before the white man came? Where do we tell people that Nigerians, for example, were smelting iron 500 years before Christ, or that the 16th century empire in West Africa was considered then to be the equal to anything in Europe? Anybody who has climbed over the ruins of great Zimbabwe would know that Africans, as well as Europeans, were building stone castles in the 11th century. The point – and it is an important point – is that none of Africa's great civilizations left much trace. Because crucially, with the solitary exception of Ethiopia, none of them had developed a written language. Without a means to store and transfer information, a lasting civilization proved impossible.

Where have reporters also truly examined the poisoned chalice that was the legacy of colonialism? Five centuries of varying degrees of exploitation. The way tribal rivalries were used to divide and rule. The way African colonies were used to provide raw materials for the mother country and a market for its goods, so that subsistent agriculture was replaced by cash crops. African countries were not allowed to have a broad self-sufficiency or an industrial base. Until the 1950s Europeans acted as if their colonies would last forever. African advancement was not a high priority or a priority at all. Yet between 1956 and 1980, 43 new countries were born, taking over the government structures, the economies, and sophisticated jobs designed by Europeans for Europeans.

I suppose that the Portuguese are my particular pet hate. After 300 years of colonial rule in Mozambique, thousands of Portuguese just fled leaving only one in twenty of the population able to read; half the children dying before the age of five; only 24,000 jobs in the entire country, nearly all of them in the civil service; only 14 black African graduates, not a single doctor, not a single accountant, not a single engineer; only 300 miles of road and one factory – and guess what that factory produced: beer, for the Portuguese troops that had been stationed there. That was the legacy of 300 years of colonialism in one African country. Journalists do not report it. I do not know why.

I wonder if reporters might seek help from human rights activists or people who work for aid and development agencies. However, the interests of a reporter, who is in the news business are not parallel with those of people in human rights business or the aid business. Too close a relationship with any pressure or interest group, even one as worthwhile as human rights or international aid, is a little worrying for a reporter. So let us not complain about shallow and superficial pictures painted by the media. Let us see how we can perhaps capitalize on them. Human rights, aid and development people can help the media by prolonging general interest in what is going on in their spheres: the more extensive the coverage, the more likelihood of escaping from the stereotypes. For example, a reporter detailed to cover a story can go to the news library, get the cuttings from the last colleague who had been to the place in question, drop out of the airplane and do the same report all over again. But the longer a reporter stays in a country, the more often he or she goes there, the less stereotypical the coverage will be.

So instead of complaining about the media, the thing to do is to attempt to enhance and prolong the interest the media can create. In my opinion, not many aid, development or human rights agencies do that very well at the moment. Such agencies benefit from so much public sympathy, and yet I quite often think they waste it. It drains away for a number of reasons. One is that a number of people, particularly in the aid industry, just take themselves too seriously. It is perhaps an awful thing to say but they are so fastidious about their personal, moral and ethical high ground and they are so esoteric in their concerns and their languages that they do not make their concerns accessible to simple journalists and, through them, to the public that journalists serve.

Why do not human rights, and aid development people, instead of complaining about the media as they do very often, treat the media as a necessary evil? It strikes me as astonishing that the agencies which are so adaptable to necessary evils in the countries in which they operate, and which they manage to adapt to all sorts of government regimes and still carry on working, are, once back in the developed world, so reluctant to get their feet into the sometimes murky waters of the media world. Why the ambivalence?

I suggest in conclusion that human rights, and aid development activists should play the media world at its own game. That does not necessarily mean that they have to compromise their high standards. It means that they have to be effective, rather than lofty about things. The first realization they have to make is that the media does not feel that they owe them anything. Just because what human rights, and aid development agencies are doing is basically more worthwhile than somebody who manufactures widgets, this does not mean that they do not have to use the same techniques to get the media to print their story. They need to use the same techniques because the end result of not getting their story across, whether they are in the human rights business, the aid business or the development business, is that they are dead as organizations. They will not get the money, they will not get the workers, and they will not get supporters where they need them. Much more importantly, the people they are trying to help might literally be dead as a result.

SECTION V(b): INFORMATION TECHNOLOGY AND CONFIDENTIALITY

KNUT O. H. A. HAMMARSKJÖLD*

Introduction

Privacy of the individual is the topic of this chapter. Privacy raises issues at both national and international levels, and is high on both agendas. Internationally, it is well handled by the OECD and the Council of Europe. But, despite this widespread involvement with the concept, there remains a fundamental issue as to the nature of privacy. What is privacy? This problem was addressed by the Hon. Justice Michael Kirby, President of the Court of Appeal of New South Wales, Australia, in a speech at the University of Guelph about a year ago:

> "In Australia, we cannot even agree on how to pronounce 'privacy', let alone how to define it. The concept is illusive. None of the definitions offered is entirely satisfactory. Most individuals and agencies charged with the task of dealing with privacy related to information technology try to avoid hard and fast definitions. And attitudes to privacy very much vary from one culture to another."

The reasons for the difficulties and, to some extent, confusion in defining privacy are complex and of multiple origins. First, concepts which have a difficult-to-define content are often found to be performing functions outside their established and recognized areas of operation. This may well be true of the rapidly evolving concept of privacy. Second, apart from the cultural differences referred to earlier, there is the speed with which the evolution of computerization – and also telecommunications and transport – has transformed our world to what is often called the Global Village. Everybody – from the individual to national governments and international organizations – has been taken by surprise by this speed, and by the scope and seriousness of the issues raised. As a matter of "self-defence" against the invasion of rights made possible by computerization, rules and principles to protect privacy were adopted on a national basis – initially without much international co-ordination or common purpose. There is now, however, an increasing

* Chairman, Atwater Institute, The World Information Economy Centre, Montreal, Quebec, Canada.

K.E. Mahoney and P. Mahoney (eds.), Human Rights in the Twenty-first Century, 789–792.

awareness of the forces of integration, and where they are leading us. In this respect, industry and business have pre-empted the slower pace of national States. Many industries are already globally organized as transnational entities or through networks of alliances. States are following in creating customs unions, free trade areas or aiming even further, such as in the example of the European Community. There are, of course, also, counter-trends of disintegration – such as in the USSR, Yugoslavia and Canada.

The papers in this section help us understand how in this rapidly changing world, privacy is being perceived and dealt with in different fora and from different perspectives.

Heather Menzies looks at data bases, monopolies of knowledge and the right to be informed on one's own terms. She explores the concept of solidarity in the context of electronic information systems, from the perspective of these systems' capacity to inform difference. Questions, beyond those of access to information, are opened up when one considers the power of individuals and groups to be informed and their immensely increased ability, through the use of modern technology, to articulate a position on the basis of how they are different. The issues go beyond the right to obtain access to information contained in various data bases, into the more difficult area of the choice of "information" determined to be relevant for documentation and indexing in the first place. With the support of examples, the critical question is raised as to whether there are certain trends which bear the markings of monopolies of knowledge.

Alan Rodger deals with the subject of surveillance and intrusion taking the "local" experience of the United Kingdom as indicative of the kind of problems posed by new developments in those spheres. He believes that the problems themselves are essentially old and that their resolution will depend, not so much on some great new principle, but on a proper appreciation of how existing general principles of human rights law are to be applied in new circumstances. He concludes: "Working out the necessary distinctions and adjustments in the use of those great principles may not perhaps be the most heroic task for human rights lawyers in the twenty-first century, but one may rather suspect that it will be one of the most important."

He stresses the impact that the European Convention on Human Rights has had on surveillance and intrusion in the United Kingdom, one judgement by the European Court of Human Rights (or the right to respect for private life and correspondence) leading directly to the passing of new legislation on the interception of communications by public authorities and by the police and the security services. He also deals with intrusion into privacy by non-state actors such as the press, and discusses the content of the State's duty to protect individuals as part of such intrusions.

Lawrence Early, from his vantage point at the Council of Europe, penetrates what is beyond the "right to private life", that is the new problems that have been thrown up in relations to privacy by an increasingly complex society. He examines data protection from this perspective, exploring the threats to human identity, dignity and, above all, privacy which have accompanied the exponential increase in data processing, and notably in the possibilities for exploitation of pastoral information that its technology allows.

He succinctly states that "these new threats have both individual and collective dimensions and may be provoked through the use of data processing technology by both public and private powers". The inference he draws reflects the theme underlying this book as a whole: "if human rights protection is to be neither a museum nor a mausoleum, it must be capable of evolving so as to respond to the new challenges brought about by the introduction and use of new technologies". The objective to be achieved in the particular context is "to ensure that the autonomy of the individual is secured in the technological age, by ensuring that the right people (and only the right people) receive the right information (and only the right information) for the right purposes (and only the right purposes)". Like Rodger, he acknowledges the remarkable resilience of the classic right to private life in the new automated environment. However, unlike Rodger, he is also convinced of the need to develop new fundamental principles to take privacy protection into the technological age.

The three presentations are linked by a recognition that the new information technologies have enormous potential both for good and harm, and that delicate balances must be struck in order to use them in a manner that allows the benefits they can deliver to be maximized and the harms to which they can give rise to be minimized. Ms. Menzies recognizes that control, not only of the technology itself but also of matters beyond the technology, for example data input, are necessary to achieve certain goods, for example to "maintain difference" as defined by oneself. Mr. Rodger recognizes privacy as a relative good, which must be protected but also balanced against the State's need to prevent crime and to apprehend criminals – a competing good. And Mr. Early recognizes that maintenance of human identity and dignity, a fundamental good, may depend on sophisticated, nuanced and concurrent use of a variety of data protection mechanisms.

In conclusion to these remarks, it may be appropriate to remind ourselves of some current "realities". First, we are in the run up to the twenty-first century with new dimensions not only geographically – spacewise – but also in time. Both space and time have been diminished by our new technologies. In short, we are in the prelude to a one-world reality. Second, as we come closer to each other, in terms of time and distance, daily living in our society is also gaining considerably in complexity. This increases the need for privacy at the same time as it renders it more threatened. Third, many societal activities and disciplines, all of considerable weight, for instance technology, ethics and law, need to be concurrently at the centre in addressing this new complexity. This means, as in many other areas, that in order to solve our problems in relation to privacy, an increased transdisciplinary openness is required – we know from experience that this is a large order; it is, however, a necessity. Finally, our societal structures, themselves, are also changing – look at the evolution in Eastern Europe; look at the steady increase of involvement of non-governmental entities in world affairs – and this again adds layers of complexity to addressing privacy issues.

The role of lawyers is not only to "mend fences" once the damage is done, but also to be the shapers of the new ideas needed to carry evolution in all rapidly evolving areas of society; to scout the path through unexplored terrain, to give some of the guidance needed to move in the least traumatic and least destructive way towards the new society. Providing protection for the individual in the highly technological and, perhaps, depersonalized society of the twenty-first century is certainly a worthy objective. Development of the concept of privacy is fundamental and essential to ensuring this protection.

HEATHER MENZIES*

Information Gathering and Confidentiality: Data Bases, Monopolies of Knowledge and the Right to Be Informed

1. Introduction

Wanting to anchor my paper in the theme of the overall collection, I looked up "solidarity" in the Oxford dictionary, and found it fascinatingly described as "a community of (or between) interests". That definition is apt because it catches the different interpretations one can take from the concept of global solidarity: solidarity grounded in the homogenization of difference between individuals, or grounded in respect for and preservation of difference among peoples and groups. In one, the tendency of policy would be toward global synchronization and inter-connectivity – specifically for present purposes, through integrated information systems for everything from news and entertainment to education and expertise. In the other, the policy emphasis would be on offsetting the well-established dominance of Western, and particularly American, commercial information industries– by finding material ways to ensure that different groups can effectively inform themselves on their own terms however they define these along lines of gender, nationality, race, class and so on.

In purely global terms, it is the choice between free-flood flows of information or some of the original ideas behind the New World Information Order.

The second term needed to be defined is the one that is the subject of this paper: confidentiality. There is a great deal to be said about confidentiality as non-disclosure of personally identifying information. However, the following discussion focuses on a more active, and even inter-active sense of the word. It examines confidentiality in the context of social relations between individuals and between cultural groups. It emphasizes the importance of the fiduciary relationship – the trust relationship – between the person giving information that goes into data bases and the person receiving information from data bases. On the giving end of information, can individuals and groups ensure that they

* Ottawa-based writer and adjunct professor, Canadian Studies and Women's Studies, Carleton University, Ottawa, Ontario, Canada.

K.E. Mahoney and P. Mahoney (eds.), Human Rights in the Twenty-first Century, 793–800.

do not inform against themselves; or that information which is abstracted from their lives and extruded through increasingly standardized frames of reference to become part of global data sets will not misinterpret them, especially in ways which could then foreclose on choices in their personal and collective lives? (This question is reverted to later with a concrete Canadian example.) Viewing the problem from the receiving end of information, can individuals and groups ensure that the information they obtain through the global information systems is complete and – most important – relevant? Relevant in terms of their own conception of what is relevant, defined out of their own cultural values and reality – not simply relevant to the global experts selecting, indexing and organizing information in data bases. How can each set of people – on the giving and the receiving end – check this out?

And if they cannot, does not that imply a no-choice scenario of blind distrust or blind trust? The first can lead to balkanized apartheids and anti-science absolutism both at the local level of protest groups and at the global level of countries such as Cambodia under Pol Pot and Iran under the Ayatollah. Conversely, the second option – blind trust – will almost invariably produce solidarity only of the homogenized variety – through dependence on the monopolies of knowledge associated with global information systems.

2. Three Aspects Inherent to the Monopoly of Knowledge

The reference to monopolies of knowledge draws on the work of Canadian economic historian Harold Innis and especially as his analysis has been interpreted by the American communications theorist James Carey.[1] There are three aspects of monopoly of knowledge, all of which are pertinent to current trends in global information industries, particularly the data base industry.

The first is the physical dimension: a monopoly is conferred on whoever can transmit information faster and farther and at less cost than a competitor. To a certain extent, you could say that electronic information services as a whole have this monopoly compared to the traditional print media of communications which are slower. Examples of the former include: (1) the business-oriented data bases like Dow Jones and Reuters; (2) the news data bases like Reuters, InfoGlobe, New York Times and Knight Ridder; (3) the expert knowledge bases such as Dialog, founded by the aerospace giant Lockheed, and Mead Data General, owned by the pulp and paper giant Mead (Mead alone offers access to 75 million documents).

Then consider the context of information in today's world. Decision-making rates have been pushed up by a thousand percent and more.[2] More information

[1] See in particular J. Carey, "Canadian Communications Theory: Extensions and Interpretations of Harold Innis", in G.J. Robinson and D.F. Theall (eds.) *Studies in Canadian Communications* (1975), at pp. 27–60.

[2] In a study of intellectual work conducted by an engineers' organization, it was found that computerized working environments have increased decision-making rates by approximately 1900

is being produced faster and faster,[3] and is becoming obsolete faster and faster as well,[4] requiring new decisions, requiring new information, and so on. Accordingly, the monopoly centres around those who can deliver the most up-to-the-minute information and quickly guide users through the burgeoning info-glut to information most pertinent to their needs – which tends to mean the biggest data-base suppliers like Dialog, selling access to 400 data bases worldwide. It is also significant that the world's biggest health-care data base, Medline out of the U.S., not only has sophisticated expert-level software to guide users through its structured references to retrieve its digitized abstracts, but also that these references only go back as far as 1966. From 1966 on back, you have to use the slower print-based references.

The second dimension of monopolies of knowledge pertains to the structuring of the data bases themselves. What is important here is where the information is stored or more generally who controls it. A 1987 British study found that the United States dominates the world data base industry. It produces two-thirds of the world's data bases[5] – in virtually all the categories listed earlier, from financial data to news and bibliographic and expert knowledge. While on the one hand new companies are entering the market by the minute, on the other corporate takeovers, producing vertical and horizontal integration and on a global operating scale, are occurring just as fast. For example, the expert-knowledge data base company, BRS, has been bought up by Maxwell Communication Corp., which runs an on-line search service called Orbit and also owns the book publisher Macmillan. The New York Times recently sold its data base operations to Mead Data General. While Mead is a data-base publisher, its own data base, Lexis, dominates the business. In a similar mega-firm example, Dialog, is now owned by Knight-Ridder, a major data base publisher in the news-information area and also a major producer of information through its own chain of newspapers and television stations in the U.S. An article in the U.S.-based *Library Journal* reported that two data-base vendors, Mead Data General and Dialog, accounted for 82 percent of the revenue and 69 percent of the usage in the on-line searching business.[6]

This aspect of monopolies of knowledge has generated the most public

---

percent. See Mike Cooley, *Architect or Bee: The Human/Technology Relationship* (1980), John Goodman & Sons at p. 32.

[3] In an analysis of publishing history of *The Psychological Abstracts*, which by 1987 listed 36,327 references published in about 1,470 sources, a colleague at Carleton University, Warren Thorngate, estimated that "psychologists are now collectively publishing articles at the rate of about 100 per day, about one every 15 minutes". See "The Economy of Attention and the Development of Psychology" in *Canadian Psychology/Psychologie Canadienne* (1990), 31:3 at p. 262.

[4] "It is now the case in many fields of endeavour that simply to stand still you have to spend 15 percent of your time updating your knowledge". See Cooley, note 2, *supra*, at p. 10.

[5] Jill Hartley, Amanda Noonan, Stan Metcalfe, *New Electronic Services: An Overview of the U.K. Database Industry in an International Context* (1987), London: Gower Publishing, at p. 120.

[6] News report in *The Library Journal*, Feb. 1, 1984.

discussion so far. Questions have ranged from access to information across barriers of cost (as access and retrieval fees) and across barriers of geography (where information vital to national security and sovereignty is stored outside the country, in IBM mainframes in the U.S. for instance), to questions of privacy and security of information.

But there is another aspect of monopolies of knowledge which deserves perhaps more urgent attention: the cultural aspect or cultural monopolies of knowledge. This monopoly lies inside the data bases themselves. It resides with the people who are hired to select information for input into the data base, who index it and write expert-level software to structure relative speed of access to it according to their mental maps of reality. And that is the key: *their* mental maps, their paradigms, their world view; *their* cultural assumptions of what is relevant and what is not, what is rational and sensible, and what is frivolous or marginal and "controversial". For Innis, this power to pre-define what people will look for and pay attention to – in a nutshell, the power to define what reality is – represents "the fundamental form of social power in society".[7] It is this aspect which opens most clearly onto the questions raised at the outset about global solidarity based on diversity depending on social relations of confidentiality and trust being built into the global information systems.

The ability to trust that the information you give and the information you receive is consonant with your terms of reference – with your own understandings of what is real, what is relevant – is not built into the current data base industry. On the contrary, the structures are instead inclined toward blind trust and global homogenization.

First, in reference to the receiving end, we already see evidence of the kind of blind-trust, blind distrust scenario referred to earlier. An article in the journal *On-line* quoted a clinical psychologist using an on-line data base as saying: "I also don't know where my inadequacies end and (those of) the data bases begin. In other words, I'm not sure every article is indexed to its fullest potential."[8] The truth of the matter is that not every article is indexed. There tend to be tiers. With Medline, a core set of journals is coded for input and indexed fairly thoroughly, an outer tier is indexed selectively and in a third tier of journals some article abstracts are sometimes coded and indexed. A 1983 Australian study found that "only about a third of the approximately 20,000 scholarly articles published in or about Australia are indexed in the international data bases. Coverage of the humanities and social sciences is particularly poor".[9] In order to increase their chances of inclusion, journals in many non-English-speaking countries which used to publish an English translation are now publishing in English only. *Tumori* out of Italy is one example of the trend.

[7] See note 1, *supra*, at p. 44.

[8] Natalie Kupferberg, "A Librarian Interviews Six Do-it-yourself Searchers", *On-Line* (March, 1986), at p. 25.

[9] Alex Byrne, "How to Lose a Nation's Literature: Database Coverage of Australian Research", *Database* (August, 1984), at p. 3.

Then there is the homogenization as participants in the global information society depend on these sources of information, and in doing so, adjust themselves to their frames and terms of reference.

Traces of this socializing influence can usefully be looked for in the health-care field in Canada because this is a clear-cut area of public activity and policy where Canadians have a distinctly different approach from their vast neighbour to the south. In Canada, where health is considered a public good and health care is provided as a universal public service, there is a strong theme of prevention, whereas in the U.S., where medicine is a private industry, the theme of treatment pushes prevention into the margins.

The orientation comes through when using Medline. In an Ottawa hospital, the librarian browsed through the listings for "hormone-dependent" cancer in the latest (Fall, 1990) version of Medline on compact disc and found that by far the greatest number of entries were under the sub-heading "drug therapy". There were 183 references listed, compared to a scant three entries for "prevention and control". At a major Toronto hospital, the librarian explained that the de-emphasis on prevention is reflected by a de-emphasis on anything understood in the social context. "It's bio-medical, and that's it. Nutrition is just terrible. There's no sensitivity to malnutrition, nor nutrition in pregnancy; nor nutrition in any disease state." As she points out, it is not that the information is not accessible at all. It is just not "readily accessible... It takes more time, it's harder because the controlled vocabulary isn't as sensitive as it should be".

The librarian in the Ottawa hospital herself detected the greatest differences in the field of health-care administration. When using Medline, not only do Canadian doctors and administrators have to forget the specifically Canadian terminology such as Medicare. They have to piggyback onto American terms – such as health insurance instead of Medicare – as a way of routing themselves to the information they need. And this has consequences. "Canadian terms tend to be subsumed by American terms," she said. "Over time," she added, "the Canadian term may eventually sort of move off to the sidelines if there is another term used by Americans that means approximately the same thing." As an example, she noted that many health-care administrators are now using the American term "HMO's" or Health Maintenance Organizations (which are private health-care insurance companies) because that is the reference they use when using Medline to search for something to do with community-based health care. She said, "Now Canadians are talking about HMO's as comprehensive community-based care, but which wouldn't work in Canada in a socially-based health care environment."

What is in a word? Nothing greater or less than the power to shape mental pictures: the power to put HMO's in the centre as the norm, against which the Canadian model might subtly begin to look awkward and inefficient.

Let us turn from the right to be informed on one's own terms of reference, according to one's own cultural relevancies, to the right to provide information in terms that are true to one's own meanings and relevancies. Here, the discussion will focus on the Commission of Inquiry into the MacKenzie Valley Pipeline in the mid-1970's, otherwise known as the Berger Inquiry, after its chief commissioner, Judge Thomas Berger. The inquiry was set up to investigate whether opening up the Northwest Territories to major oil and gas development was beneficial, not just for the consortium of multi-national and Canadian petroleum companies who wanted to do so, but for the native peoples, the fish and the animals, the trees and the rivers that had existed there since the dawn of history. As can be imagined, much of the ensuing discussion centred around the viability of the local native economy. Research presented to the Commission by the oil and gas interests, as well as by federal government departments (such as the Department of Indian Affairs and Northern Development), argued that the local native economy was not viable. Man-made growth and development projects such as the MacKenzie Valley pipeline were necessary to provide jobs and income for the burgeoning native population.

One of the characterizing features of the Berger inquiry, however, is that it was consciously designed as a participatory research instrument, with funds made available to ensure that marginal groups such as those associated with the native population could both do their own research and appear at the hearings.

Consequently, while the Arctic Gas Consortium economists maintained that there were only 96 native trappers in the MacKenzie Valley, the Indian Brotherhood of the Northwest Territories said that there were at least 1,075. It was not that the Arctic Gas people were lying. Rather the problem was that in applying traditional economic frames and terms of reference, they left out important pieces of data and presented a false view of reality as a result.[10]

At the time, the most readily available data were (1) tax returns from sales of furs in the cash fur market and (2) hunting licence data. However, as the economists for the native people pointed out, counting one hunter per licence misses the fact that several members of a family will hunt under that one licence; this is consistent with the fact that in the native economy, the household is the basic unit of production, not the individual wage earner as in the man-made market economy. But perhaps the most significant omission was in assuming away all the other economic returns associated with hunting and trapping which were not strictly measurable in cash-market terms: the meat from the animals whose pelts were sold; the inferior pelts which were kept back for domestic clothing and handicrafts – plus of course the meat associated with those additional pelts – as well as the meat and fish harvested just for food. Berger estimated that "as little as a tenth of the real gross value of fur, fish and game production" had been acknowledged as real using the economic calculating terms of reference of traditional market economics.[11]

Dr. Peter Usher has subsequently extended the research he did for native

[10] Thomas Berger, *Northern Frontier, Northern Homeland: The Report of the MacKenzie Valley Pipeline Inquiry; Vol. II* (1977), Ottawa: Minister of Supply and Services Canada, at p. 8.

[11] Ibid., at p. 7.

people during the Berger Inquiry. In a 1990 study prepared for the Northwest Territories Government, he estimated that while the production of fish and fur as saleable commodities only amounts to about $5 million a year in the Northwest Territories, the value of the roughly 5 million kilograms of meat and fish harvested by natives for their own consumption is conservatively estimated at $50 million. The lumber and firewood harvested is valued at another $5 million, and the wild berries and plants harvested adds another $5 million in kind to the gross domestic product. In short, the "domestic" economy, the self-sustaining economy centred in the land of the North is viable, and deserves government support as part of the diverse mixed economy of the North.[12]

But that economy would have been bulldozed under 15 years ago if the monopoly of knowledge associated with traditional economic measures as well as with traditional research methodologies – where research subjects are reduced to inert data spoken for by experts, and the real people behind the data sets do not get a chance to speak for themselves – had not been broken. If the information which had been bulldozed under or made to disappear had not been retrieved, and the subjects of the research not given a chance to speak for themselves, the mega-project pipeline would most certainly have gone ahead. And instead of having this example of difference to inform a pluralistic vision of economics centred both on "developing sustainability" and not just "sustainable development", the data available would have locked us within the homogenized mindset of market-centred growth and development.

3. Conclusion

Visualize a global information world as a sheet of paper laid down over all the world's experience, with a magnet underneath. The magnet pulls at all the world's experience, and it becomes a zillion iron filings which are drawn together by the magnet under the surface of the global page: they are no longer scattered and anchored in their own gravitational ground, but all organized around this one point where the magnet is, where the data bases are.

The Berger inquiry was cited to dramatize the urgency of being able to provide information on one's own terms. The experience of Canadian doctors depending on American data bases in the health care field was used to dramatize the dangers of homogenization of world views and cultural synchronization when one cannot inform one's self on one's own terms. In turn, these examples were set within the context of monopolies of knowledge to demonstrate that the concerns raised are not just minor oversights to be corrected through personal goodwill and superficial tinkering. They go right to the heart of the structuring of (and the division of power within) global and local information systems.

[12] Peter Usher, *Towards a Strategy for Supporting the Domestic Economy of the Northwest Territories* (1989), Yellowknife, NWT. Clerk of the Legislative Assembly, pp. 8–13.

We need standards and concrete measures to promote open-ended information systems locally and globally. By this is meant not only participatory research structures with built-in accountability measures. At the receiving end, it would be simplest to say that we need to renew the original agenda for discussion about the New World Information Order. The issue cannot be reduced to transferring technology and money so that marginal groups and countries can have access to information systems. The issue is equitable participation in the control of these information systems: pluralistic participatory control in the design and structuring of the systems themselves as well as in the organization of the information content so that difference can be reflected at both the input and output end, on its own terms. Without such affirmative public policies, locally as well as globally, the trends toward global monopolies of knowledge will reach a point of rigidity and closure, and blind trust and global homogenization or blind mistrust and balkanization will be inevitable.

LAWRENCE EARLY*

Science, Technology and Human Rights: The Role of Data Protection

1. Introduction: New Challenges

The ingenuity of policy-makers and judges is being increasingly taxed in the light of an increasingly complex society. New demands are being made on them and new legal and policy responses are required to meet new challenges. We are far removed from a concept of the State as a "night watchman". Regardless of economic policies designed to reinstate free market economies freed from State intervention, on the eve of the 21st century the State still finds itself as a regulator, a provider, a manager, a controller and an entrepreneur. These roles spawn a vast network of relationships between the individual and the various agencies of government. The emergence of the bureaucratic administrative model of government has engendered new concepts of control and accountability of decision-makers. Administrative law has emerged out of the inability of the private law techniques in the common law world to deal effectively with the activities of public powers. New public law institutions have been created to compensate for the increasing inability of parliaments to control the activities of governments. At the same time, the inability of private law areas such as contract and tort to regulate the phenomenon of mass production and the consumer society has required the legislator to intervene so as to establish charters of consumer rights and product liability schemes. New branches of law are emerging as subsets of the well-established legal institutions. Consumer law is now regarded as a legal discipline in its own right, a recognition of the inability of the general law of contract to hold the ring between parties of unequal bargaining power. Environmental law shares a similar tendency, namely the impossibility of consigning all legal problems concerning the environment to the law of tort, in particular the law of nuisance. Similarly, the emergence of the mass media has created a separate legal

* Head of Media Section, Directorate of Human Rights, Council of Europe, Strasbourg, France. The ideas and observations contained in this report are expressed in the author's personal capacity.

K.E. Mahoney and P. Mahoney (eds.), Human Rights in the Twenty-first Century, 801–815.

discipline – media law. Other examples abound: social security law; housing law; anti-trust law; and so on.[1]

At the level of human rights protection, new claims are being made on the traditional freedoms set out in international charters and national constitutions. Scientific progress is a motivating factor. For example, advances in the biomedical sciences have considerably enlarged individual choice. This in turn has encouraged individuals to defend their new options in terms of human rights protection. For example, the new artificial procreation techniques have resulted in demands to found a family outside the traditional matrimonial bond and outside sexuality. It is argued that the right to family life needs to evolve so as to meet the new demands of individuals now living in the "New Republic of Choice". Again, advances in genetic engineering have prompted new claims on the traditional right to private life. Discussions in the field of genetic science are now taking on human rights' considerations expressed in a new currency: the right to be different, the right not to be discriminated against on the grounds of genetic pre-disposition, and the right to a genetic identity. If the biomedical sciences have called into question the established consensus on the precise moment of birth, advances in medical technology and pharmaceuticals have similarly rendered the moment of death increasingly problematic. The choice of the individual has been expanded through the development of new medical techniques for prolonging life. In turn, courts have been faced with new claims argued on the basis of human rights protection, in particular the right to private life, the right to die in dignity, and the right to self-determination.[2]

2. Information Technology

The need for new legislative responses, the need for the evolution of legal institutions in the face of scientific and technological development are also signally illustrated by the emergence of computer science and telecommunications which, when coupled, produce information technology or data processing technology.

Information technology is a new science which brings in its wake inestimable advantages for mankind. It improves the quality of life by freeing man from mundane and routine chores in the office, in the factory and in the home. It improves the quality and rapidity of decision-making within the public and private sectors. It allows for a greater access to, and hence circulation of, information within society through the creation of on-line data bases. It has spawned a new commodity – information – which can be bought, sold and exchanged in bulk form. It has made the world a smaller place by allowing

[1] See, generally, Friedmann, *Law in a Changing Society* (1972), Penguin Education, Second Edition.

[2] Rodota, "Law and Moral Dilemmas Affecting Life and Death – a General Presentation of the Issues", in the *Proceedings of the XXth Colloquy on European Law* (September, 1990).

information to be shifted across continents and seas at the press of a keyboard button.

Nevertheless, there is a deficit side which needs to be evaluated in the introduction and application of data processing technology. From the point of view of human rights protection, a careful assessment must be made of the extent to which the technology produces adverse consequences for the individual, in particular his right to private life, his human identity, his dignity and his autonomy. The risks to these values must be evaluated against the following characteristics of the technology.[3]

(1) Pervasiveness

The marriage of computer science and telecommunications has meant the move away from large centralized mainframe computers with dedicated applications to an environment linked by networks, powered by small computing units and in which personal data may transit freely around the network at the will of the user. Data processing technology is not confined to those who can afford it. It is now cheap, powerful and at the disposal of all aspects of the public and private sectors as well as in the home.

(2) Processing Power

The consignment of manual storage techniques to the distant past has been made possible by the ability of data processing technology to collect, store and process personal data on a scale which was never possible in the age of manual files. Voice, image, data and text can now be processed electronically and carried through the same network as a result of the introduction of integrated services digital networks (ISDN). Personal data can be now collected remotely through telemetric means without the intervention of the individual. File interlinkage produces the same informational result.

(3) New Concerns

The combination of the pervasiveness of information technology and its processing power gives rise to concerns as to the increased possibilities which it offers:

1. for surveillance of the individual;
2. for cutting the individual out of the information circuit;
3. for unlimited collection and storage of personal information without the knowledge of the data subject;
4. for the exploitation of personal information for different purposes; and

[3] This analysis of the risks accompanying the introduction and use of new technologies borrows on the Report of the Committee of Experts on Data Protection of the Council of Europe, *New Technologies: A Challenge to Privacy Protection* (1989). See also the Report of the U.S. Congress Office of Technology Assessment, *Electronic Surveillance and Civil Liberties* (1985).

5. for increasing the powers of public and private bodies in the absence of democratic or regulatory controls.

(4) Sectoral Analysis of Individual and Group Vulnerability in the New Automated Environment

The risks outlined above may be illustrated by the following sectors.

(a) Interactive Media

The installation in homes of videotex, including two-way cable television, is illustrative of the popularization of information technology. Equipped with a specially adapted television set or a home computer, the individual may have access to a whole range of interactive services. He can engage in a transactional dialogue with a service provider offering him goods for sale, airline reservations, theatre reservations, home banking facilities, electronic games or simply the weather forecast over the next few days. The minitel system is now part of the home furniture in France. The Netherlands has introduced the Viditel system of interactive videotex. Germany has introduced Bildschirmtext allowing users with specially adapted television sets or home terminals to avail of a wide array of transactional services or simple consultation of thousands of pages of retrievable information. The United Kingdom offers the Prestel system, a videotex system using specially adapted television sets or computer terminals linked via a telephone to a data base which can provide home banking services, travel reservations, theatre reservations, teleshopping as well as access to specialist data bases. Two-way cable television as a form of interactive media has also been popularized in various Canadian provinces, allowing users access to a range of services.[4]

This is the acceptable face of technology referred to in the introduction. Quite simply, it makes life easier for the consumer. Additionally, it provides them with quicker and easier access to information. However, at the same time, the individual is becoming what Professor Flaherty of the University of Western Ontario has described as "the unwitting generator of the single largest repository of personal data in the history of the world". In initiating a transactional dialogue with a service provider via interactive media, the individual is unconsciously releasing to the system various bits and pieces of his personality, various details concerning his tastes in literature or general consumer behaviour, his intelligence when playing electronic games, his movements when making travel arrangements, even his personal politics when replying to electronic opinion polls. These data are being stored somewhere in the system. But where and for what purposes may they be used, and by what people? May the data be exploited for purposes unrelated to the transaction in question? These issues become more urgent when there is a risk of the individual's information being used for purposes of automatic profiling of his

[4] For a detailed analysis of the North American experience, see Faherty, "Privacy Protection in Two Way Electronic Services", Mansell, London.

lifestyle. A computerized image can be drawn of the individual, building on his disclosure to the system of his tastes in literature, consumer products, films, intelligence quota, and so on.

(b) New Developments in Telephony

As noted previously, the digitalization of networks and their integration has allowed text, image, voice and data to transit through the same telecommunications line. At the same time, it has allowed for an increased sophistication in telephony. It is now possible to offer subscribers detailed telephone bills, setting out details of the station called, the station from which the call was made, the time of the call, the length of the call. This presents enormous consumer advantages. The individual is given the possibility to check the accuracy of his bill and to challenge errors made by the telecommunications companies. At the same time, the new technology employed in telephone networks has given rise to a marked increase in personal data storage by the telecommunications companies. As with interactive media, certain basic questions must be raised. Must the individual be empowered to prevent the drawing up of itemized bills? Should they only be given to him on request? And what of the co-users of his terminal – what are their rights in regard to the itemization of their calls made from the subscribers terminal? How long may the data be stored by the telecommunications company, and to whom may they be communicated and under what circumstances?

Moreover, integrated services digital networks now allows for the display of the telephone numbers of incoming calls. Of course, this is no doubt an advantage for combating abusive or malicious telephone calls. But the technology must also enable individuals who do not want their telephone numbers to be released to called third parties to block them. The privacy of the individual (as well as his freedom of communication) is considerably infringed in circumstances where he is obliged to forego his anonymity. In this regard, we should recall the relationship of anonymity which must exist between caller and called party in the context of helpline services such as: Alcoholics Anonymous, drug treatment centres, AIDS helplines, battered women's hostels as well as Samaritans' organizations.[5]

(c) The Medical Sector

The medical sector has enthusiastically embraced data processing technology. Hospitals as well as general practitioners' surgeries have become increasingly automated. Medical files are seldom stored manually. Within the hospital, networks have allowed patient data to be accessed directly by physicians and other authorized medical staff. Expert systems are increasingly being introduced as an aid to clinical diagnosis. Outside the hospital walls, the patient may carry his medical record on a automated medical dossier in the form of a "smart card".

[5] See Katz, "Caller – ID, privacy and social processes" (October, 1990), Telecommunications Policy, Volume 14, p. 372 et seq.

We are far removed from the discrete patient/physician relationship suggested by the Hippocratic oath. Data processing technology has allowed more and more actors to access medical data, including computer staff working within hospitals and firms responsible for the remote maintenance of the computers and the networks. At the same time, the needs of the medical research community to have access to health data for the purposes of epidemiological research projects have grown. Medical researchers require access to the data stored on automated medical data bases.

Medical data are sensitive *per se*. Their collection, storage and use requires strict safeguards in the new automated environment over and above those prescribed for personal data in general: free and informed consent of the individual in writing before his medical data may be collected and used for purposes outside the strict confines of the therapeutic context, for example medical research purposes. In addition, the fact that medical data transits through networks requires strict security measures to prevent unauthorized interception or manipulation of the data. Moreover, the incorporation of the individual's medical history into an intelligent/smart medical card requires additional security reflections, given that the individual will henceforth carry around with him a significant quantity of sensitive data which could expose him to third party pressure to reveal what is stored on the micro-chip for the purposes of employment or insurance.[6]

(d) The Police Sector

Data processing technology considerably facilitates the classic functions of police forces: the prevention, investigation and suppression of criminal offences. Common law, statute or penal procedure codes determine the range of powers at the disposal of the police to discharge these tasks. Nevertheless, data processing technology has considerably increased the powers of the police in the absence of corresponding safeguards for the individual. Technology now allows the police to collect and store personal information on a scale never possible in the days of manual processing. It allows for file interlinkage, making it possible to match up different sets of information collected for disparate purposes, not always of a police nature. It opens up the possibility for data base surveillance so as to allow it to track down a suspect or locate an individual or a vehicle through linking up the various "electronic traces" which have been left behind in different contexts. In Germany, the technique has been called *Rasterfahndung*. Professor Jon Bing has illustrated the operation of the technique with the following real-life example:

> "The most famous instance is probably the efforts exercised to locate a known terrorist, Rudolf Clemens Wagner. The Hamburg police, in co-operation with the Federal police, approached the Hamburg Electricity

[6] For a general overview of the risks in this sector, see the proceedings of AIM (Advanced Informatics in Medicine) Conference, organized by the Commission of the European Communities in Brussels (March, 1990).

Board. Using data on electricity consumption, the purpose was to locate an apartment with a certain pattern in its consumption, including breaks in certain periods. Authorized by a court decision, the police obtained tapes from the Electricity Board. The data was processed and correlated in Wiesbaden until only a small set of subscribers was left. These were visited by the police."[7]

While recognizing the important societal interests at stake in crime control and prevention, and while recognizing the enormous advantages which data processing technology offers for the protection of these interests, we must also seek to ensure that other values are preserved. In particular, there is a need to place the use of data processing on a principled basis so as to ensure that it does not gravitate towards an electronic surveillance of individuals and groups, that it does not adversely affect the balance between rights and police powers. The circumstances in which personal data may be collected, stored and processed by the police must be clearly defined, as must the circumstances justifying data file interlinkage.[8]

(e) The Financial Services Sector

The coupling of computer science and telecommunications in the financial services sector has produced a whole range of telematic banking operations. With the necessary hardware, as well as a data transmission link, the individual can interrogate from his domicile the state of his account, order cheque books or give instructions to his bank to make a standing order in favour of a beneficiary. Automatic cash dispensers allow him similar facilities, including the withdrawal of cash. Point of sale terminals located in the premises of retailers, traders and service providers allow the individual to debit electronically his account and instruct the bank to credit the account of the beneficiary of the transaction.

Data processing technology has placed us at the dawn of the cashless society. New forms of electronic money are replacing cash, cheques and plastic cards for the purposes of settlement operations. The smart or intelligent banking card, equipped with a micro chip, integrates the qualities of the credit card, the debit card and the cheque guarantee card and provides at the same time an entry into the automatic teller machine or point of sale terminal. Undoubted advantages for the consumer, the financial institution and the retailer. But concerns for the way in which personal data will henceforth be collected, stored and processed by third parties. While to all intents and purposes the informational value of a cash transaction is zero, since it is characterized by the absence of documentation, the use of electronic money gives rise to electronic traces. The

[7] J. Bing, "Data protection and social policy", reproduced in the Proceedings of the XIVth Colloquy on European Law, organized by the Council of Europe, Lisbon (1984).

[8] The Council of Europe's Committee of Experts on Data Protection has endeavoured to provide a legal framework for this sector: Committee of Ministers of the Council of Europe, Recommendation No. R (87)(15), (1988).

individual may no longer maintain his anonymity. As a result of the new payment media, the individual is obliged to reveal a considerable quantity of personal data at the time of their use: time and location of the transaction, identity of the beneficiary, possibly the nature of the transaction, and name of the user. The release of this personal information to third parties, principally the body issuing the means of payment, entails privacy risks. Once the data are stored by the third party, it is possible to link up isolated and fragmented uses of the means of payment in the form of a profile which can allow the individual's economic and consumer behaviour, and even his movements, to be monitored.

Once again, basic questions have to be raised: what use may be made of the data by third parties; to whom may the data be communicated; and what are the rights of the data subject at the stages of collection, storage and processing of the personal data? These issues are not given an adequate response in the law relating to banking secrecy. In the first place, banking secrecy only refers to the stage of information disclosure by the bank and does not regulate the stages of collection and processing. Secondly, banks *stricto sensu* no longer have a monopoly over the issue of means of payment. Other financial bodies, not covered by principles of banking secrecy, are now involved in the provision of financial services.[9]

(5) Beyond Privacy

The need for legal institutions to evolve so as to take account of new problems created by an increasingly complex society holds true for the concept of "private life". The right to private life is an old and venerable value. Brandeis and Warren, in their seminal article published in the 1890s, sought to interpret the right to private life in terms of "the right to be let alone".[10] This rather negative view of private life was inspired by the perceived need to protect the upper echelons of Bostonian society from the worst excesses of the American yellow press. However, the sacred sphere or the intimate zone into which unauthorized third parties may not trespass, which has underpinned the subsequent reflections on the value of privacy, may not be a sufficient counter-weight to the risks created for the individual through the introduction and application of information technology. There is a perceived need to render the legal institution more dynamic, more in keeping with the new problems which information technology has created: surveillance; profiling of individual and group behaviour; the undermining of autonomy through the processing of personal data unknown to the data subject; the taking of decisions based on automated profiles which offend human dignity and identity; and vulnerability.

[9] As with the police sector, (see note 8, *supra*), the Committee of Experts on Data Protection has elaborated guidelines for the financial services sector: Council of Ministers of the Council of Europe, Recommendation No. R (90) 19, (1991).

[10] Warren and Brandeis, "The Right to Privacy", *Harvard Law Review* (1890–1891), pp. 193–220.

(6) Constitutional Trends

The preceding analysis of data protection in terms of constitutionalism and human rights protection finds concrete expression in the approach which a number of countries have taken in regard to the need to protect the individual against the possible abuses attendant on the use of data processing technology. It is interesting to observe that this approach treats data protection as a value independent of the right to private life by devoting separate constitutional recognition to it.

By way of illustration, Article 10 of the 1984 Constitution of *the Netherlands* enshrines the right to respect for individual privacy. However, Article 10, paragraphs 2 and 3, provide:

> "2. Rules to protect privacy shall be laid down by Act of Parliament in connection with the recording and dissemination of personal data.
> 3. Rules concerning the rights of persons to be informed of data recorded concerning them and of the use that is made thereof, and to have such data corrected, shall be laid down by Act of Parliament."

A similar programmic right is set out in the recently revised (July, 1989) *Portuguese Constitution*. Article 35 proclaims:

> "1. Without prejudice to the provisions of the law on State secrecy and judicial secrecy, all citizens shall have the right of access to the data contained in automated data records and files concerning them as well as the right to be informed of the use for which they are intended; they shall be entitled to request that the contents thereof be corrected and brought up to date.
> 2. Access to personal data records or files shall be forbidden for purposes of getting information relating to third parties as well as for the interconnection of these files, save in exceptional cases as provided for in the law and in Article 18.
> 3. Data processing shall not be used in regard to information concerning a person's philosophical or political convictions, party or trade union affiliations, religious beliefs or private life, except in the case of non-identifiable data for statistical purposes.
> 4. The law shall define the concept of personal data for the purposes of data storage as well as the conditions for establishing data banks and data base by public or private entities and the conditions of use and access.
> 5. The law shall define the provisions applicable to transborder data flows establishing adequate norms of protection of personal data and of any other data in which the national interest is justified."

The constitutional recognition of a right to data protection in the Portuguese Constitution is symptomatic of the constitutional retreat away from the authoritarian political environment which characterized the State prior to the emergence of the new order in 1974. Article 35 can be seen as a deliberate attempt to impose constitutional restraints on information handling by public powers with the aim of minimizing the surveillance possibilities offered by information technology. A similar rationale can be seen in the approach taken by the drafters of the *Spanish Constitution* in their attachment to the need to protect the rights of the citizen against the possible abuses of information technology. Article 18, paragraph 4, of the Spanish Constitution proclaims (programmically):

> "The law shall limit the use of data processing so as to guarantee honour and personal and family intimacy for the citizen, and the full exercise of his rights."

Even more significant is the approach followed by the constitutional draftsmen in *Hungary*. Emerging from a prolonged period of authoritarianism and centralized control, it is not surprising that the tableau of fundamental rights and freedoms laid down in the new constitutional document prescribes a constitutional right to data protection.

For the sake of completeness, reference can also be made to the decision taken by *Sweden* to incorporate data protection into the Fundamental Instrument of Government in 1987. *Austria* has also elevated data protection to the status of a fundamental freedom.

The approach taken in these constitutions is significant. Data protection, while having its genesis in the right to private life, is emerging as a new fundamental value in its own right. It is being viewed in terms of constitutionalism, human rights protection as well as a mechanism of control over the exercise of public powers.

(7) Existing Human Rights Guarantees – Neither a Museum Nor a Mausoleum

Even in the absence of specific constitutional guarantees of data protection, courts working within the framework of the right to private life have shown their preparedness to regulate problems raised by data processing technology. For example, the European Court of Human Rights in a series of decisions beginning with its judgment in the *Klass* case[11] has shown how the use of new technological means of surveillance by the police must be accommodated with the need to respect private life. The case law of the Court of Human Rights in the area of wire-tapping technology notes the intrusive and dangerous nature of the technology for the private life of individuals. The judgments of the Court in this area are not expressed in the language of data protection. Nevertheless, the reasoning of the Court has come close to it. It is interesting to note the concurring opinion of Judge Pettiti in the Malone case:

> "The danger threatening democratic societies in the years 1980–1990 stems

[11] Case of Klass and Others. Eur. Court H.R. Series A. No. 28, 1978.

from the temptation facing public authorities to 'see into' the life of the citizen. In order to answer the needs of planning and of social and tax policy, the State is obliged to amplify the scale of its interferences. In its administrative systems, the State is being led to proliferate and then to computerize its personal data-files. Already in several of the member States of the Council of Europe each citizen is entered on 200 to 400 data-files."[12]

Judge Pettiti analyzes the telephone tapping technique as part and parcel of the general data processing phenomenon which can lead to the automated construction of profiles or mosaics on individuals, or groups, and hence increased surveillance possibilities.

In addition, the Court in the *Malone* case was also called upon to address the privacy problems raised by the process known as "metering", a device which records the numbers dialled on a particular telephone and the time and duration of each call (c.f., the earlier discussion on itemized call bills). Could the passing on of such information to third parties (the police) without consent of the subscriber amount to an interference with the right to private life guaranteed by Article 8 of the European Convention on Human Rights? The Court replied in the affirmative. Although the reasoning of the Court is not dressed up in the language of data protection, there is nevertheless a clear indication of the Court's willingness to ensure that personal information must be collected, stored and used by public powers in accordance with clearly defined conditions.

These early indications of the Court's willingness to embrace data protection as a right falling within Article 8 of the European Convention on Human Rights have received confirmation in the later case law. Most recently, in the *Leander* case,[13] the Court has shown its readiness to recognize data protection as a value inherent in the protection afforded by Article 8.

The German Constitutional Court has also illustrated this tendency to read data protection into existing constitutional guarantees. In the *Census* decision of 1983,[14] the *Bundesverfassungsgericht* derived a right of informational self-determination out of the classic right to the development of personality laid down in the 1949 Basic Law. In analyzing the impact of the collection, storage and processing of personal information by government, the Court emphasized the need to ensure the protection of the individual. In particular, the individual has a fundamental right based on Article 2 in combination with Article 1 of the *Grundgesetz* to decide for himself who shall collect and store his personal information and for what purposes. For the German Constitutional Court, the institution of a system which would allow an indiscriminate and unprincipled collection and storage of personal data on individuals would have a chilling effect on the exercise of other fundamental rights, in particular freedom of

[12] *Malone* judgment, *supra* note 11.

[13] *Leander* judgment of 26 March 1967, Series A No. 116.

[14] For an analysis of the decision, see Schwartz, "The Computer in German and American Constitutional Law: Towards an American Right of Informational Self-Determination", *American Journal of Comparative Law* (1989) p. 675.

association, freedom of movement and freedom of expression. The Court in the *Census* case, by positing the principle of informational self-determination has located data protection firmly within the constitutional dialogue between the State and the citizen and the functioning of a community founded on principles of liberty and democracy and individual and collective participation in that system.

3. Conclusion

Exercises in futurology are always beset with difficulties. We can only speculate on the characteristics of the new order. Nevertheless, the exponential increase in information technology which appeared in the last two decades make it possible to affirm the continuing ingenuity of computer scientists and telecommunications engineers. While not speculating on concrete technologies, we may nevertheless state that data processing will become even more pervasive in both the public and private sectors. The possibilities for remote collection and storage of personal information will be increased. Expert systems will characterize decision-making in many walks of life. The amount of electronic traces left behind by the individual in his dealings with public and private bodies will increase.

Into the Twenty-First Century: The Constitutional and Legislative Framework for Individual and Group Protection

The following points provide a constitutional and legislative framework for individual and group protection which may lead us into the next century.

1. Information technology must be seen in terms of its impact on human dignity, human identity and privacy. The need for a principle-based approach to the application of information technology in society must be informed by respect for these fundamental values.

2. The possible abuses which may be engendered by information technology must be discussed at the constitutional level. At the very most, constitutional draftsmen should show their preparedness to include data protection as a specific fundamental freedom within the general tableau of basic liberties.

3. In the absence of a specific right to data protection, judges should show their willingness to bring the right to private life into the technological age by interpreting it as a right to informational self-determination.

4. Over and above the affirmation of data protection as a separate fundamental value or as a value inherent in the right to private life, a legislative framework is an additional *sine qua non* of individual protection in an automated environment. This legislative framework should lay down broad protective principles regulating the collection, storage, processing, use and conservation of personal data. It should confer rights on data subjects and impose obligations on data users. Borrowing on the principles laid down in the

Data Protection Convention of the Council of Europe of 28 January 1981,[15] the general legislative framework should ensure that:

"1) Personal data shall be obtained and processed fairly and lawfully;
2) they shall be held only for a specified and legitimate purpose or purposes;
3) they shall not be used or disclosed in a way incompatible with those purposes;
4) they shall be adequate, relevant, and not excessive in relation to those purposes;
5) they shall be accurate and, where necessary, kept up-to-date;
6) they shall be preserved in a form which permits identification of the data subjects for no longer than is required for those purposes and what is done with the data;
7) everyone shall be entitled to know of the existence and main purposes of applications handling personal data, as well as the identity and location of the person who determines those purposes and what is done with the data;
8) the data subject shall have an enforceable right to discover who holds personal data about him, to access to those data, and to their correction or erasure where the provisions reflecting these principles have not been complied with;
9) appropriate security measures shall be taken against unauthorized access, alteration or dissemination, accidental loss, and accidental or unauthorized destruction of such data."

5. The data protection norms laid down in the legislative framework should embrace data processing in the public as well as the private sector. Moreover, the principles should be applicable to both manual processing techniques as well as automated processing techniques.

6. The legislative framework should avoid rigid approaches to the control of information technology. Rather, the draftsman should remain at the level of broad principles so as to ensure that the approach does not become technologically specific and frozen at a particular stage of technological development.

7. The approach followed by the legislator should not be seen as Luddite. It should unfold in full recognition of the enormous benefits to be gained from advances in technology and have as its avowed aim the need to allow technology to develop in full respect for human dignity, human identity and privacy.

8. The broad normative framework should be completed by conflict resolution rules for particular sectors. The principles should be concretized in the form of binding rules so as to make them meaningful to the application of information technology in various sectors. For example, sectors such as employment, police, health, insurance, credit and so on should be placed under their own specific data protection regime which is constructed on the basis of a detailed analysis of the informational needs and requirements of the sector in

[15] European Treaty Series No. 108.

question, and, against the background of the general normative framework and the individual privacy requirements in that sector.

9. Independent control machinery should be set up within the framework of the legislative structure. The functions of the data protection authority should extend to the auditing of processing in the public and private sectors, the investigation of complaints, the power to sanction in the event of breach, the power to develop awareness among users and data subjects of data protection principles, and finally the competence to alert decision-makers to the possible threats attendant on the introduction of new technologies.

10. Information technology should develop in full respect for human dignity, human identity and privacy. What is technologically possible is not necessarily socially acceptable. There will be increasingly a need to evaluate the ethical implications of new technological applications. As noted previously, data protection authorities should have a vital watchdog role to play in the scheme of things.

11. Manufacturers of information technology hardware and software should be encouraged to exploit technology so as to minimize the possible abusive consequences accompanying its use. If information technology has given users the potential for unlimited collection and storage of personal data, it may equally integrate, technically, mechanisms which avoid unnecessary processing operations.

12. The rights of the data subject in the technological age should be discussed in an international framework. The increasing ease with which vast quantities of personal data may be shifted across national borders and continents makes it necessary to engage reflection at the level of the need for international principles of data protection. Data protection is not country-specific. It must be seen as part and parcel of the universal principles which should bind all nations. The activities of international organizations such as the Council of Europe, the Organization for Economic Co-operation and Development (OECD) and the United Nations should be actively encouraged to pursue and promote further the need for international consensus on the need to protect the individual in the technological age.

13. Data protection cannot be divorced from the need for a general information policy. Significantly, Canada (at the Federal level) and the provinces of Ontario and Quebec (at the provincial level) have sought to rationalize data protection and freedom of information within the same legislative approach. It cannot be overlooked that data protection norms determine the conditions under which personal information may circulate within a given society, including the circumstances which justify its disclosure to third parties. Freedom of information legislation, for its part, inevitably restricts the release of personal data to requesting third parties for privacy reasons. If freedom of information laws are seen as a form of control over decision-makers by ensuring transparency for their activities, data protection

norms, in particular the right of subject access, perform a similar role in regard to personal data handling by public powers. The interrelationship between both sets of norms argue in favour of a rational integrated approach to information circulation policy, rather than a policy which treats data protection and sunshine laws as mutually exclusive.

ALAN RODGER*

Human Rights: Surveillance and Intrusion

1. Introduction

The subject of surveillance and intrusion can be seen as very modern, brought into prominence by developments in information technology. But though such developments may have focused attention on these problems, the problems themselves are essentially old.

Spying on others and listening in to their conversations have occurred in all ages. Legal systems have been called upon to respond. In the nineteenth century, for example, the Scottish criminal courts wrestled with the question of what to do about admissions made by a prisoner and overheard by a prison warden who had deliberately stationed himself in a place where he could listen to what was being said.[1] Legal systems of all ages have dealt with intrusions on others' property and have discussed problems relating to intrusions on others' privacy. For instance, the early third-century jurist Ulpian deals with the case of an owner who finds that someone is sitting fishing in the sea just in front of his seaside villa, thus obviously disturbing his privacy.[2] Ulpian says that the owner is not entitled to stop the man fishing and can be sued if he does. This is plainly because Ulpian will not qualify the public right to use the sea for fishing by any private right to peace and quiet.

Whether one agrees or disagrees with the decisions reached in such old texts does not really matter. Doubtless there were other jurists at the time who would have reached the opposite conclusion – otherwise such decisions would scarcely have merited recording. The point is rather that the matters were being discussed. This suggests that what modern technological developments have done is not so much to create brand new legal problems in this field, as to increase the opportunities for, and the effectiveness of, surveillance and intrusion. This means that the legal issues involved are now more prominent than in the past.

* The Lord Advocate, Attorney General of Scotland, London, U.K.

[1] *H.M.A. v. Johnston* (1845) 2 Broun 401, 411 et seq. (High Court of Justiciary) See the authorities listed in *The Laws of Scotland Stair Memorial Encyclopedia*, vol. 10, par. 730.

[2] D.47.10.13.7, Ulpian 57 *ad edictum*.

K.E. Mahoney and P. Mahoney (eds.), Human Rights in the Twenty-first Century, 817–828.

That having been said, it is obvious that even the legal world changes, at least in its emphasis. One significant change in emphasis in the United Kingdom is that the European Convention for Human Rights has come to form the background of any discussion of what should be permitted by way of surveillance or intrusion. The change is fairly recent. In 1970, technological and other innovations led to the setting-up of a committee under Mr. Kenneth Younger to study the law of privacy in the United Kingdom. That committee reported in 1972.[3] In 1989, concern about the activities of certain sections of the press led to a committee being set up under Mr. David Calcutt Q.C. Its remit was to consider the need for the protection of individual privacy from the activities of the press. The committee, which dealt with certain related matters, reported in June 1990.[4] It is fair to say that, when the Younger Committee reported in 1972, the impact of the relatively new right of British residents to present individual applications to Strasbourg had yet to be felt. Only the Scottish member of the Committee – Mr. Donald Ross, Q.C. – laid any stress at all on Article 8 of the European Convention for Human Rights, and that was in a dissenting note.[5] By contrast, by 1990 the Calcutt Committee were plainly very conscious of the existence and influence of the Strasbourg convention, Articles 8 and 10 of which were reproduced in an appendix to their report.[6] This was doubtless because judges and lawyers, not to mention many members of the general public and criminals, are now well aware that there is a body somewhere on the Continent which interests itself in such matters, though many tend to confuse the human rights court in Strasbourg with the European Court of Justice in Luxembourg.

2. Impact of the European Convention for Human Rights on Surveillance and Intrusion in the United Kingdom

Two general points are worth making. First, this change in outlook in the United Kingdom has taken place despite the fact that the Convention forms no part of the domestic law of the United Kingdom. The Convention is simply a treaty to which the United Kingdom is a party. As such it does not form part of the domestic legal order and British courts are strictly limited in the purposes for which they can have regard to its provisions.[7] Individuals must seek their

[3] Report of the Committee on Privacy (Chairman, the Rt. Hon. Kenneth Younger) (Cmnd 5012).

[4] Report of the Committee on Privacy and Related Matters (Chairman: David Calcutt Q.C.) (Cm 1102).

[5] Younger Report, see note 3, *supra*, pp. 213 *et seq.* As a judge, Lord Ross gave the leading Scottish decision that the Convention forms no part of Scottish domestic law: *Kaur v. Lord Advocate* 1980 S.C. 319 (Ct. of Sess.).

[6] Appendix C. See note 4, *supra*.

[7] *Brind* v. *Secretary of State for the Home Department* [1991] 1 All E.R. 720 H.L; cf. *Garland v. British Rail Engineering Ltd.* [1982] 2 All E.R. 402, 415 b-e, per Lord Diplock, H.L.; *Kaur v. Lord Advocate* 1980 S.C. 319 (Ct. of Sess).

remedies under the Convention in proceedings before the Commission and Court in Strasbourg. Nonetheless, the impact of the Convention on many aspects of life in the United Kingdom has been significant.

Secondly, since the right of individual petition to the Commission was introduced in 1966,[8] both the public and the legal profession have come to think that, even though they are time-consuming, the Strasbourg remedies are worthwhile, and they have been found worthwhile even though there is no direct means of enforcing any judgment against the Government. In practice this has not proved a significant weakness because the judgments of the Human Rights Court are treated with great respect by most member States. Certainly, wherever possible,[9] the necessary amendments in our domestic law are introduced to give effect to the judgments. Equally, the United Kingdom has regard to decisions in cases involving other countries. Indeed all proposals for legislation are scrutinized nowadays to ensure that they are consistent with the principles enshrined in the growing jurisprudence of the Commission and Court, and process known colloquially as "Strasbourg-proofing".

Returning to the particular topic of surveillance and intrusion, we find that in the European Convention these matters have tended to be dealt with principally in connection with Article 8, which provides *inter alia* that "everyone has the right to respect for his private and family life" and for his home and correspondence. Now that right is not set down in absolute terms. Rather, the Article provides that "there shall be no interference by a public authority with the exercise of this right except such as is in accordance with the law and is necessary in a democratic society" in the interests of certain matters including national security, public safety, the prevention of disorder or crime, and the protection of the rights and freedoms of others.

It is perfectly clear, therefore, that those who framed the Convention recognized that public authorities could infringe this right of privacy if the circumstances merited it. The Commission and the Court have, of course, accepted this. For instance, in the 1978 *Klass* case[10] the Court held that telephone tapping was an interference with "private life" and "correspondence", but they accepted that legislation granting powers of secret surveillance over the mail, post and telecommunications is, under exceptional conditions, necessary in a democratic society "in the interests of national security and/or for the prevention of disorder or crime". This has been reaffirmed several times.[11] The Court has also accepted that a certain margin of appreciation must be left to the national authorities and that it will not readily substitute its own

[8] For the text of the Declarations made at Strasbourg, January 14, 1966, see Treaty Series No. 8, 1966 (Cmnd. 2984). The declarations have been renewed from time to time.

[9] Following the decision in *Brogan*, Judgment of November 29, 1988, Series A Vol. 145, the United Kingdom derogated from certain of its obligations under Article 5. This step was taken in terms of Article 15.

[10] Judgment of September 6, 1978, Series A No. 28.

[11] See, for instance, the *Malone* case, *infra*, note 14.

assessment for that of the authorities whose responsibility it is to weigh the competing interests.[12]

Nonetheless, the Court has stressed in such cases as *Klass* that such permissible interference is to be regarded as an exception to the general rule affording protection to a person's private life and, as an exception, its scope is to be interpreted narrowly. In particular, there can be no interference by a public authority "except such as is in accordance with the law".

The United Kingdom came up against the force of these few words in the well-known case of *Malone*[13] in which the Human Rights Court gave judgment in 1984. Mr. Malone, who was an antiques dealer, became suspicious that his telephone had been tapped. It was admitted that there had been telephone interception under a warrant from the Home Secretary, who had authorized it for the prevention and detection of crime. Mr. Malone sought a declaration from the English Chancery Division that such telephone tapping was unlawful even when done under a warrant from the Home Secretary. In a characteristically learned judgment[14] the then Vice-Chancellor, Sir Robert Megarry, dismissed the application and held that there was nothing in domestic law which made such tapping unlawful.

When the matter eventually reached the Court of Human Rights, the Vice-Chancellor's decision that the tapping was lawful according to English law was not challenged. Rather, attention was focused on the requirement in Article 8 that any interference should be "in accordance with the law". In earlier cases,[15] the Court had had occasion to rule as to what was meant by the words "prescribed by law" in Article 10. The Court had held that, in order to count as law, a norm must be "formulated with sufficient precision to enable the citizen to regulate his conduct: he must be able – if need be with appropriate advice – to foresee, to a degree that is reasonable in the circumstances, the consequences which a given action may entail".[16] This is the so-called "foreseeability test". In Mr. Malone's case it was argued that, if a similar approach were adopted in interpreting Article 8, then the rules governing telephone tapping in English law were too obscure and uncertain to meet the requirements of the foreseeability test. The Court upheld this contention, ruling that "the law of England and Wales does not indicate with reasonable clarity the scope and manner of exercise of the relevant discretion conferred on the public authorities".[17]

[12] See, for instance, the *Leander* case, Judgment of March 26, 1987, Series A No. 116. There is a useful discussion of the authorities in P. van Dijk and G.J.H. van Hoof, *Theory and Practice of the European Convention on Human Rights* (2nd edition, 1990), pp. 595–602.

[13] Judgment of August 2, 1984, Series A Vol. 82.

[14] *Malone v. Commissioner of Police of the Metropolis No. 2* [1979] 2 All E.R. 620, Ch. Div.

[15] *Silver* case, Judgment of March 25, 1983, Series A No. 61; *Sunday Times* case, Judgment of April 26, 1979, Series A No. 30.

[16] *The Sunday Times* case, Judgment of April 26, 1979, Series A No. 30, para. 49; *Silver* case, Series A No. 61, para. 88.

[17] Series A No. 82, para. 79.

Following this decision, the British Government introduced what became the Interception of Communications Act 1985.[18] The effect of that Act was not to alter the practice which had been followed by successive Secretaries of State of Governments of both parties. Rather, its purpose and effect were to place the established procedure on a statutory basis and so to meet the criticism of a lack of clarity in the relevant law and practice which had been made in the *Malone* judgment. The decision of the Human Rights Court can therefore be seen as playing a major role in bringing about this change in United Kingdom law.

Some critics have argued that not much in practical terms is achieved by such a change to more formal procedures. Under the previous system one knew that the relevant Secretary of State could authorize telephone tapping and the sorts of cases in which this might be done, but one did not, and at no stage would one know that one's telephone was tapped. Likewise today, because telephone tapping must remain secret if it is to have any effect, an individual cannot know precisely when his or her telephone is likely to be tapped. To that extent the citizen is no more able to regulate his conduct or to foresee its consequences than he was before. What can, on the other hand, be said is that there now remains no doubt, if there was ever any doubt before, that telephone tapping will not be authorized except under a warrant from the Secretary of State.[19] That may well be regarded as a sufficiently important advance in principle to be worthwhile in itself. In addition, the aggrieved citizen can complain to a Tribunal which has full powers to examine the whole process of authorization of any warrant which may exist.[20] The authorization of tapping and the circumstances in which it takes place are also subject to review by an independent Commissioner.[21] Again, this is something of a formalization of pre-existing practice, since before the 1985 Act two senior judges, Lord Diplock and then Lord Bridge, had carried out precisely that function.

A similar kind of change to a more formal approach in matters of surveillance and intrusion on to private property can be seen in the Security Service Act 1989.[22] This Act recognized the previous existence of the security service ("There shall continue to be a Security Service")[23] and gave it formal statutory recognition with defined objects.[24] Again, this was essentially a matter of giving precise legal definition to something which had existed on an informal, administrative basis before. For what it is worth, it appears that the Service itself welcomed this development as giving everyone a clear idea of what they do and what they stand for.

Section 3 of the Act in particular deals with "entry on or interference with

[18] c. 56.

[19] 1985 Act. s. 1. The power to issue a warrant is contained in section 2. The test to be satisfied is found in section 2(2).

[20] 1985 Act, s. 7(2) and (3).

[21] 1985 Act. s. 8(1)(a).

[22] c. 5.

[23] 1989 Act, s. 1(1).

[24] 1989 Act, s. 1(2) and (3).

property" by members of the Security Service. This is permitted only by a warrant under the hand of the Secretary of State himself.[25] That is to say, he or she must deal with the matter personally, not through an official or even through a junior minister in the department.[26] Without going into the detail, it is worth noting that no warrant is to be issued unless the information "cannot reasonably be obtained by other means".[27] Again, this apparently constitutes no real change in practice, but it is surely a significant advance to have the criteria set out in a statute, rather than endorsed in administrative practice, however well settled.[28] Looking at it from the point of view of Article 8 of the Human Rights Convention with its requirement that any interference with privacy should be "in accordance with the law", the new statute means that the relevant requirements for issuing a warrant to intrude on property are now stated on the face of the statute and are accessible to all with an interest to know about such matters.

Not only that, but under the statute a Security Service Commissioner must be appointed.[29] He or she is a judge of the High Court or of a court of similar level, and among the duties which he must carry out is that of reviewing the exercise by the Secretary of State of his powers to issue warrants under the Act.[30] In addition, the 1989 Act introduced a new protection for any person who is aggrieved by anything done by the Service in relation to him or to his property. He may complain to a Tribunal comprising at least three lawyers.[31] The Tribunal must investigate whether the complainer has been the subject of inquiries by the Service.[32] If they find that he has been, then, if they also find that there was no proper basis for such inquiries, they may make a determination in his favour and may, in some cases, order the Service to stop their inquiries and to destroy any relevant records.[33] If the Commissioner finds that any warrant was improperly granted,[34] then the Tribunal may quash the warrant and again award compensation. Provision is made for the payment of compensation in appropriate cases.[35]

All these represent new rights which are available to citizens affected by the operations of the Security Service. Insofar as issues of privacy arise it is considered that the Act satisfies the requirements of Article 8, while the new remedies should fulfil the United Kingdom's obligation under Article 13 to

[25] 1989 Act, s. 3(a).

[26] In the absence of such a specific statutory rule, delegation would usually be possible. See most recently *Oladehinde v. Secretary of State for the Home Department* [1990] 3 All E.R. 393, H.L.

[27] 1989 Act, s. 3(2)(a)(ii).

[28] For a critical account of the legislation with some comparative references see I. Leigh and L. Lustgarten, "The Security Service Act 1989" (1989) 52 M.L.R. 801.

[29] 1989 Act, s. 4(1).

[30] 1989 Act, s. 4(3).

[31] 1989 Act, s. 5(1) and (2) and Schedules 1 and 2.

[32] 1989 Act, Schedule 1, para. 2(1).

[33] 1989 Act, Schedule 1, paras. 5(1) and 6(1)(a).

[34] 1989 Act, Schedule 1, para. 4(1) and para. 6(2).

[35] 1989 Act, Schedule 1, paras. 6(1)(b) and 6(2)(b).

provide an effective remedy for any breach of those requirements.

As said earlier, the increased formality of approach seems to be a change brought about at least in part by the jurisprudence of the Strasbourg Court. It is easy for us in the United Kingdom – and for our critics also perhaps – to feel that our previous rather informal approach was something peculiarly British. Its critics could represent it as the product of a system relying on an old-boy network and a spurious public school ethos. On the other hand, its supporters could see it as enshrining the idea that we have no separate system of *droit administratif* as found on the Continent and that instead everything is controlled by the common law. In truth, however, we were neither in such absolute, nor in such splendid, isolation as some may have thought.

This is made clear, for instance, by the decision of the Human Rights Court in the *Huvig* case in 1990.[36] This was a case involving France, but it had similarities with *Malone*. The applicants claimed that there had been a breach of Article 8 by virtue of certain telephone tapping directed against them. The Government argued that there was an elaborate series of safeguards under French law. Nonetheless, the Court held that "French law, written and unwritten, does not indicate with reasonable clarity the scope and manner of exercise of the relevant discretion conferred on the public authorities".[37] In other words, France was found to be in breach of Article 8 for precisely the same reason as the United Kingdom in the *Malone* case – which was indeed cited by the Court in reaching its decision.[38] It therefore seems that the jurisprudence of the Court will lead to a greater degree of formality in the law of the civil law countries as well as the common law countries.

3. Invasion of Privacy by Non-State Actors as Well as by Public Authorities

The discussion up to this point has been principally concerned with surveillance or intrusion by public authorities. There is no doubt that it is this kind of intrusion which is highlighted in Article 8 and that is not surprising, given the background of the drafting of the Convention in the years following the Second World War. Whether the authors of the Convention looked to the immediate past in Germany and Italy or to the situation which then prevailed in Eastern Europe, they saw all too clearly the lengths to which totalitarian governments could go to interfere with such basic liberties as the right to a private life and a family life. The circumstances in which we find ourselves are now rather different. Of course, one can never for a moment forget that what has changed for the better can change again for the worse if we are not duly vigilant.

[36] Judgment of 24 April 1990, Series A No. 176-B; also the *Kruslin* case, Judgment of 24 April 1990, Series A No. 176.

[37] *Huvig* case, *supra*, note 36, para. 35; *Kruslin* case, *supra*, note 36, para. 36.

[38] *Huvig* case, *supra,* note 36.

Nonetheless, it is fair to say that for most people in a modern democracy, interference with their private life is more likely to come from the press or television than from, say, government or police telephone tapping or electronic eavesdropping by the government or police. Mention can therefore usefully be made of some of the issues which we in the United Kingdom are confronting in relation to the activities of press and television reporters.

It will be recalled that Article 8 provides *inter alia* that "everyone has the right to respect for his private and family life" and for his home. Wise men that they were, the draftsmen did not stoop to define these matters more closely, leaving it instead to those who have to grapple with the Convention to gloss their text and so to fill out its meaning. What is important, however, is that the Article confers a right which, subject to permitted limitations, is to be upheld by the contracting states.[39] So far as the media are concerned, another important article is Article 10 which proclaims "the right to freedom of expression". This right is also qualified, however, and particular regard is to be had to the need for "the protection of the reputation or rights of others". It therefore seems to follow that the right of freedom of expression enjoyed by the media must be qualified to some extent by the need to protect the right of privacy conferred by Article 8. In the *Sunday Times*[40] case the Court held that exceptions to freedom of expression are to be admitted where, but only where, they can be justified by "a pressing social need" and that the contracting states have a margin of appreciation in assessing what constitutes a pressing social need in their country at any given time.[41]

Undoubtedly there is at present in the United Kingdom a considerable unease among the public about some of the material printed by the popular press about the private lives of individuals. For instance, the Calcutt Committee quote an opinion poll carried out in November 1989 which showed that 73% of those questioned thought that there was too much intrusion into the lives of public figures.[42] One has perhaps to treat such surveys with a degree of caution: people may profess to deplore such revelations, but there is no sign that they boycott the newspapers which publish them. Quite the opposite. However, in so far as the preparation of such stories does not involve any degree of surveillance or intrusion, they are not directly relevant to the present topic. Scandalous revelations have been the fare of many publications over the years and the source of such revelations is, more often than not, a lover who has been superseded in the affections of the public figure concerned. Such stories can be produced without any degree of surveillance or intrusion by third parties. Nonetheless, it is fair to say that Article 10 and the scope of any exception designed to protect "the reputation or rights of others" are of relevance to the

[39] *X and Y v. The Netherlands*, Judgment of 26 March 1985, Series A No. 91.

[40] *Sunday Times* case, Judgment of 26 April 1979, Series A No. 30, para. 59 under reference to the decision in *Handyside* Judgment of 7 December 1976, Series A No. 24, para. 49.

[41] Ibid.

[42] Calcutt Report, *supra*, note 4, para. 4.6.

extent that they may inhibit the kinds of revelations which can be published. In other words, if certain revelations about a person's private life *ipso facto* infringe his right to respect for his private life, irrespective of the method used to obtain them, then the temptation to obtain information about such matters by surveillance or intrusion by third parties will be correspondingly reduced.

It is well known that, although they belong to the same legal family, English and American law have diverged sharply on the matter of privacy.[43] American law had developed a tort of interference with privacy. English law has not done so and the judgments of the Court of Appeal in *Kaye v. Robertson and Sport Newspapers*[44] indicate that it will not do so, unless the House of Lords should take a particularly bold and decisive line. It is sometimes said that Scots law could develop a delict of infringement of privacy by developing the Roman *actio iniuriarum*[45] However, there is little or nothing in the Roman law which could be readily moulded to suit today's conditions. Moreover, if the Scottish courts have not seen fit to begin the process hitherto, then it may be doubted whether they would enter such a delicate field now. The matter is really one for the legislature.

There is another important point which is made by the Calcutt Committee. In practice, even the most sophisticated law of tort is not likely to give the kind of protection required. If the *paparazzi* are besieging you with sound bugs and telephoto lenses, then any damage is likely to be done long before the speediest civil law remedy can be obtained.

It is for this kind of reason that the Calcutt Committee recommended[46] that three new offences should be established in the criminal law of England and Wales: first, entering private property without the consent of the lawful occupant, with intent to obtain personal information with a view to its publication; secondly, placing a surveillance device on private property under the same conditions; and thirdly, taking a photograph, or recording the voice of an individual who is on private property, without his consent, with a view to its publication and with intent that the individual shall be identifiable.

It will be noticed that the proposed offences are carefully limited to circumstances where the conduct is "with a view to . . . publication". This is doubtless because the Committee were careful not to go beyond the scope of their remit which was limited, as noted earlier, to protection of individuals from the activities of the press.[47] But it may well be thought that an offence with a wider scope, covering for instance the actions of inquisitive neighbours, would risk catching conduct which, while socially undesirable, would not merit the sanction of the criminal law.

The Committee also recommended that an individual should be able to seek

[43] See, for instance, R. Wacks "The Poverty of Privacy" (1980) 96 L.Q.R. 73.

[44] The texts of the judgments of the Court of Appeal are reproduced in Appendix I of the Calcutt Report.

[45] See, for instance, T.B. Smith, *A Short Commentary on the Law of Scotland*, p. 655.

[46] Calcutt Report, *supra*, note 4, paras. 6.30–6.37.

[47] Calcutt Report, *supra*, note 4, paras. 2.5.

an injunction to restrain publication of material obtained by committing one of these offences, or damages if it is published.[48]

It is apparent that offences in these absolute terms could limit what is seen as the legitimate investigatory role of the press. If an injunction could be obtained to restrain publication of material obtained in these ways, then in the absence of some qualification, there would be a risk that English law would fall foul of Article 10 of the Convention guaranteeing freedom of publication.

The Committee are, of course, very much aware of these points and they recommended[49] that the proper balance should be maintained by making a certain defence available to anyone accused of an offence. The defence is that the act was done:

a. for the purpose of preventing, detecting or exposing the commission of any crime, or other seriously anti-social conduct; or
b. for the protection of public health or safety; or
c. under any lawful authority

The Government gave a general welcome to the proposal that these offences should be introduced for England and Wales.[50] Since the criminal law of Scotland is very different, being for the most part still a common law system, the Government has indicated simply that it will consider whether similar offences should be introduced in Scots law.[51] In a response to the Calcutt proposals, the Scottish newspaper editors have urged that the offences should not be introduced into Scots law since, they argue, that has already a perfectly adequate method of dealing with offensive conduct.[52] To some extent this is true. Scots common law system is very flexible. So, for instance, fraud is defined widely as dishonestly making a false representation which achieves a practical effect.[53] Using this definition, the Crown were able to obtain a conviction of a newspaper reporter who had obtained entry to a particular patient's hospital room by pretending to be his sister.[54] In this way, the criminal law was able to provide a sanction against a particularly nasty kind of invasion of the privacy of a person who was ill and vulnerable.

That said, and despite the urgings of the Scottish editors, the matter will require the most careful consideration for the very reason already mentioned in connection with the English law. If in Scotland we simply used the ordinary loosely defined criminal law of breach of the peace, say, where reporters laid siege to private premises, the reporters would not have available to them the

[48] Calcutt Report, *supra*, note 4, para. 6.38.

[49] Calcutt Report, *supra*, note 4, para. 6.35.

[50] Statement of the Home Secretary to the House of Commons, 21 June 1990, Official Report, Sixth Series, Commons, vol. 174, col. 1125.

[51] Answer by Lord James Douglas-Hamilton to Mr. A. Darling M.P., 26 June 1990, Official Report, Sixth Series, Commons, vol. 175, Written Answers, col. 144.

[52] Letter dated 1 November 1990 from the Scottish Daily Newspaper Society to the Secretary of State for Scotland.

[53] Cf. J.H.A. Macdonald, *A Practical Treatise on the Criminal Law of Scotland* (5th edition, 1948), p. 52.

[54] See Calcutt Report, *supra*, note 4, para. 6.6.

kind of public interest defence which it is intended to write into the Calcutt offences. If that happened, there would doubtless soon be pressure from various quarters to bring the Scottish law into line with the English law.

It will be apparent that it is in the formulation of any defence to the offences that much of the difficulty will lie. The provision will require the most careful drafting. For instance, the defence as formulated by the Calcutt Committee would apply where the conduct was for the purpose of detecting "any crime".[55] On the face of it, this would seem to apply even if the "crime" was just a minor traffic offence, but should that really be a defence to all such surveillance and intrusion offences? More importantly, there is likely to be considerable discussion about what would be embraced under the heading of "*seriously* anti-social conduct". Is getting drunk in a restaurant seriously anti-social, or just anti-social? Is it seriously anti-social to be promiscuous in these days of AIDS? Can it ever be seriously anti-social for an unmarried man to have an affair with an unmarried woman who is in a long-term relationship with someone else? Or might that apply only where there were children involved? Is adultery always, or alternatively never, seriously anti-social? The room for discussion is great. So there may be a temptation to say that the scope of the exception should be more tightly drawn. But then Parliament would run the risk of enacting a statute enshrining the moral judgments of today and giving insufficient scope for development to meet the changed circumstances of tomorrow.

4. Conclusion

The discussion in this paper may be regarded as somewhat parochial. The focus has been on an issue which appears narrow by comparison with some of the grander themes which are nowadays addressed in looking at human rights. No apology, however, for this. The British are uncomfortable with lofty themes and prefer to examine concrete matters. In any event, while the United Kingdom's experience is local even within Europe, our impression is that we are tackling exactly the same kinds of problems as many countries at a similar stage of development elsewhere. So an account of the developments in Britain may prove of interest to a wider audience.

Moreover, if, as is to be hoped, the grosser forms of tyranny pass away in more and more countries, then the practical importance of human rights provisions in those countries will not be for dealing with things like State torture or murder. The human rights provisions will be applied to less dramatic, but still very significant questions. One such question would indeed concern the legitimate scope of properly authorized surveillance methods as a tool for furthering the common good by catching criminals, such as fraudsters, terrorists or drug traffickers, who are out to wreak havoc and misery in the lives of their fellow citizens. In such cases the decision may well depend, not only

[55] Calcutt Report, *supra*, note 4, para. 6.35.

on some great new principle, but on a proper appreciation of how existing general principles are to be applied in particular circumstances. Working out the necessary distinctions and adjustments in the use of those great principles may not perhaps be the most heroic task for human rights lawyers in the twenty-first century, but one may rather suspect that it will be one of the most important.

SECTION V (c): MEDICAL ETHICS AND HUMAN RIGHTS

PAULA KOKKONEN*

Introduction

In this section three well known commentators enlighten the topic of medical ethics and human rights from different angles.

Alan Scheflin witnesses what kind of obscure, irresponsible experiments to control the human mind can and have been carried out in "our society" with official government funds by leading scientists – and this without any harmful consequences for those involved despite the serious breaches of human rights committed. He makes us aware of the essential question: "As we approach the twenty-first century, will freedom of mind remain a fundamental human right?". His paper gives a warning to the international human rights community to awaken to the threat of mind control before it becomes too late.

Dr. Glenn Randall surveys the medical technologies currently available for diagnosing and documenting human rights for abuses involving torture and ill-treatment, for identifying their perpetrators and for treating the victims. No effective redress for the survivors of torture or ill-treatment is conceivable in the absence of documentation supplying objective evidence. The contribution of the medical scientific community – as described in Dr. Randall's paper – makes that possible.

The topic considered in Ian Kennedy's paper is biomedical research. He dismisses the "Luddite" view that all biomedical research involves an abuse of human rights by a conspiratorial pharmaceutical industry seeking material gain through exploitation of the vulnerable. But he recognises the clear dangers of abuse of human rights. Taking up a point made by Ursula Franklin in her overview paper, he advocates visibility of control at the planning rather than the infringement stage. He urges the utility of developing norms at an international level to ensure observance of human rights in this sphere, norms which can then be translated into national law for effective implementation; the aim being to devise appropriate procedures for solving concrete problems rather than to elaborate general exhortations. In his view, there may be new threats and a need for new standards, but any call for the development of new international

* LLM., Director of the Department of Administration, National Board of Health, Finland.

K.E. Mahoney and P. Mahoney (eds.), Human Rights in the Twenty-first Century, 829–830.

declarations is far less strong than the need for structures to operate and enforce the current standards and such new standards as may emerge.

Sheila McLean addresses issues involving the impact of medical technology raised by withdrawal of treatment and euthanasia, in particular, in relation to rapidly aging populations. She presents a complex picture which challenges the reader to consider many difficult and sensitive questions. She stresses, in her concluding remarks that the individual right to die should be kept separate and distinct from resource problems since the ultimate values are human and not clinical.

The material presented in this section brings out once more, very clearly, that the human being is driven by many conflicting motives. It is therefore important that we should all be constantly alert to the risk of human rights abuses, in our own acts as well as in our surroundings and our societies. We are all responsible.

ALAN W. SCHEFLIN*

The Use of Medicine and Psychiatry to Commit Human Rights Violations: The Mind Control Experiments

1. Introduction

In September 1955 America's premier atomic scientist, J. Robert Oppenheimer, addressed the American Psychological Association. He spoke of the awesome responsibilities facing the physicists whose pursuit of knowledge placed in their hands power that could imperil the very existence of the human species.

Psychologists, too, have an equally great responsibility, because for them, he said, "the acquisition of knowledge opens up the most terrifying prospects of controlling what people do and how they think and how they behave and how they feel".

It is this terrifying prospect this paper addresses. The thesis is simple: As we approach the twenty-first century, freedom of the mind may no longer remain a fundamental human right.

At a time when the human rights agenda is already overcrowded with injustices crying out for relief, I humbly request that another item be added to the docket.

The complicity of physicians, psychologists and psychiatrists in torture of the body has been well-documented.[1] Less well known, and ultimately more horrifying, is the complicity of healers in control of the mind. For the first time in history, mind and behavior control is becoming scientifically feasible.

In this brief paper it is not possible to prove the point. A modest goal, therefore, is to frighten readers in the hope that the international human rights community will awaken to a threat that is only now beginning to surface from secret laboratories and hidden facilities. This report is not mere speculation. After reading thousands of pages of U.S. military and intelligence agency documents on secret mind control research, and after studying and in-

* Professor of Law, Santa Clara University Law School, Santa Clara, California, U.S.A.

[1] E. Stover & E. Nightingale (eds.) *The Breaking of Minds and Bodies: Torture, Psychiatric Abuses & the Health Professions* (1985), W. H. Freeman, N.Y.; Eric Stover, "The Open Secret: Torture and the Medical Profession" (July,1987), Committee on Scientific Freedom and Responsibility, American Association for the Advancement of Science.

K.E. Mahoney and P. Mahoney (eds.), Human Rights in the Twenty-first Century, 831–843.

vestigating mind manipulation in many of its forms,[2] let me assure you that the threat to human rights is quite real. A 1951 Central Intelligence Agency (CIA) memo states bluntly: "CIA interest [is] in the specific subject of devising scientific methods for controlling the minds of individuals." Other branches of the U.S. government, and other governments,[3] have had and continue to have similar goals.

As we entered the 20th Century, science fiction writers warned that the day might come when freedom of the mind was an historical relic. As we close the 20th Century, scientists themselves are now sounding the alarm.[4] Indeed, the evolving science of mind and behavior control has itself now become the subject of science fiction.[5]

Brain research, and a rudimentary understanding of the mechanics of the mind, began as the last century closed. In one hundred years we have progressed from knowing very little to knowing perhaps too much.[6]

2. State Sponsored Mind Control

The real possibility that mind control was within the grasp of science first surfaced in the Soviet Union with the infamous Moscow Show Trials in the 1930's. Staunch revolutionaries were reduced to marionettes when put on trial for alleged crimes against the State. Torture did not provide the explanation; something more sinister was afoot.

It was not until the next decade, however, with the trial of Cardinal Mindszenty and others in eastern Europe, that State support of mind control research began in earnest. By the 1950's, when American prisoners of war in Korean prison camps began "confessing" to germ warfare, the concept of "brainwashing" became an international human rights nightmare.

To Western political leaders, it appeared that communist scientists had an

[2] A.W. Scheflin & E.M. Opton, Jr., *The Mind Manipulators* (1978), Paddington Press, London.

[3] Peter Watson, *War on the Mind: The Military Uses and Abuses of Psychology* (1978), Basic Books, Inc., N.Y.

[4] Chorover, *From Genesis to Genocide: The Meaning of Human Nature and the Power of Behavior Control* (1979), MIT Press: Cambridge, Mass.

[5] Three novels inspired by government sponsored mind control research are James Mills, *The Power* (1990), Warner Books, N.Y.; Larry Collins, *The Maze* (1989), Simon & Schuster Inc., N.Y.; and Tom Seligson, *Stalking* (1979) Signet Books, N.Y.

[6] For general reference see Maya Pines, *The Brain Changers: Scientists and the New Mind Control* (1973), Harcourt Brace Jovanovich, Inc., N.Y.; T. H. Pear, *The Moulding of Modern Man* (1961), George Allen & Unwin, London; Erwin Lausch, *Manipulation* (1974), Aidan Ellis, London; Peter Schrag, *Mind Control* (1978), Pantheon Books, N.Y.; and Vance Packard, *The People Shapers* (1977), Little, Brown and Company: Boston. Packard had sounded a warning decades earlier in his international bestseller *The Hidden Persuaders* (1957), David McKay Company, Inc., N.Y.

ability to manipulate minds that posed grave danger unless countermeasures were taken.

The blueprint for one of these countermeasures was laid out by CIA Director Allen Dulles in a public speech in 1953.[7] The United States and the Soviet Union, he told his audience, were locked in what he called a "battle for men's minds". The Soviets possessed the power to "wash the brain clean of the thoughts and mental processes of the past and ... create new brain processes and new thoughts which the victim, parrotlike, repeats". "In effect," Dulles continued, "the brain under these circumstances becomes a phonograph playing a disc put on its spindle by an outside genius over which it has no control."[8]

Subversion of the personality and the creation of human automatons had now become the finish line in a most dangerous race run by Eastern and Western governments.

The goal, as described in a secret 1952 CIA document, was succintly stated: "Can we get control of an individual to the point where he will do our bidding against his will and even against such fundamental laws of nature...as self-preservation?"[9]

If there were to be any hope that the United States would win the "brain warfare" struggle, Dulles opined, at least one serious obstacle must be overcome: "we have no human guinea pigs... on which to try out these extraordinary techniques."[10]

That problem was quickly solved. A CIA document from 1963 noted that in reference to certain mind control techniques, "the effectiveness ... on

[7] For a full treatment of the CIA experiments, as well as Army experiments, see A.W. Scheflin & E.M. Opton, Jr., see note 2, *supra;* A.W. Scheflin, "Freedom of the Mind As An International Human Rights Issue", 3 *Human Rights Law Journal* (1982), pp. 1–64. See also John Marks, *The Search for the "Manchurian Candidate:" The CIA and Mind Control* (1979), Times Books, N.Y., [reissued by Dell Books in 1988 with a new Introduction by Thomas Powers] and W. H Bowart, *Operation Mind Control* (1978) Dell, N.Y. The following three sets of hearings directly involve CIA and U.S. military mind control programs: (1) *Biomedical and Behavioral Research*, 1975, Joint Hearing Before the Subcommittee on Health of the Committee on Labor and Public Welfare and the Subcommittee on Administrative Practice and Procedure of the Committee on the Judiciary, United States Senate (Government Printing Office 1975); (2) *Project MKULTRA, The CIA's Program of Research in Behavioral Modification*, Joint Hearing Before the Select Committee on Intelligence and the Subcommittee on Health and Scientific Research of the Committee on Human Resources, United States Senate (Government Printing Office, 1977); (3) *Human Drug Testing by The CIA*, 1977, Hearings Before the Subcommittee on Health and Scientific Research of the Committee on Human Resources, United States Senate (Government Printing Office, 1977).

Additional material on governmental mind and behavioral control programs may be found in: *Individual Rights and The Federal Role in Behavior Modification*, A Study Prepared by the Staff of the Subcommittee on Constitutional Rights of the Committee on the Judiciary, United States Senate (Government Printing Office, 1974).

[8] Allen Dulles, Address to Princeton Alumni, at Hot Springs, Virginia, April 10, 1953. See "Brain Warfare – Russia's Secret Weapon", U.S. News & World Report, (May 8, 1953), p. 54.

[9] Memorandum for Chief, Medical Staff, "Project Artichoke, Evaluation of I & S Role" (January 25, 1952).

[10] A. Dulles, see note 8, *supra*.

individuals at all social levels, high and low, native American and foreign, is of great significance and testing has been performed on a variety of individuals within these categories".[11] The document concluded that the testing phase of the mind control experiments "places the rights and interests of U.S. citizens in jeopardy".[12] As outlined below, the rights of citizens of other nations were placed in jeopardy as well.

Immediately after his speech, Dulles authorized what was called MKULTRA, a massive program that included 149 subprojects. In its effort to conquer the mind and control behavior, the CIA funded, studied, experimented with and tested a breath-taking array of techniques which can be partially listed as:

- lobotomy, psychosurgery and electrodes in the brain,
- devices to deliver concussions by remote control,
- electrical and chemical shock,
- electrosleep,
- torture and stress,
- deception, duress and fear,
- hunger and fatigue,
- sensory deprivation and subconscious isolation,
- brainwashing and thought control,
- personality assessment and alteration,
- hypnosis (verbal and narco-induced),
- interrogation tactics,
- ultrasonics, subsonics and vibrations,
- drugs, chemicals and biologicals,
- amnesia-inducing agents,
- brainwave reading.

And the list goes on.

One set of experiments involved the employment of prostitutes who secretly administered narcotics and psychoactive drugs to their unwitting clients while CIA personnel watched from behind one-way mirrors.[13] In another set of tests a psychologist volunteered his services for free when told that sensory deprivation experiments could be arranged which would put the lives of the experimental subjects at terminal risk.[14]

One of the more ghoulish research projects was conducted for the military in the 1950's at Tulane University. Psychiatrists placed electrodes into the brains of mental patients and then gave those poor souls mescaline, LSD and other psychoactive drugs. When these victims later complained about having their

[11] [CIA] Inspector General's Report on MKULTRA,1963, pp. 1–2.

[12] Some types of experimentation have now been forbidden by Executive Order. Exec. Order No. 12333, s. 2.10, 3 C.F.R. 213 (1982).

[13] Scheflin & Opton, Jr., see note 2, *supra*, at pp. 134–141.

[14] John Marks, see note 7, *supra*.

minds invaded, the psychiatrists wrote on their charts that the patients suffered from paranoid delusions.[15]

As the following discussion outlines, one of the boldest leaps into conquering the mind involved the complicity of two Governments, the United States and Canada. It is a story of the marriage between psychiatric hubris and man's inhumanity to man. It is also a story about how the nightmares of science fiction tragically turn out to be the reality of science fact.

(1) Dr. Ewen Cameron and the Canadian Connection[16]

Dr. Ewen Cameron was a great man in psychiatry. He was, at various times, the president of the Quebec, Canadian, American and World Psychiatric Associations. He led Canadian psychiatry out of the dark ages and into world prominence. The fact that his theories were outrageous and that his patients have lived an agonizing hell has only recently come to light.

Cameron believed that personality was as capable of being "unformed" as it was of being "formed." With substantial funding from the Canadian Government and the CIA, Cameron labored to erase the personalities of his patients and then give them a psychological rebirth. The two-step process began with a technique he called "depatterning".

(a) Depatterning

Cameron took his patients through a procedure that we would be likely to call torture. Massive electroshock, three to four times daily, and amounting to 100 times the normal therapeutic regimen, was coupled with heavy doses of LSD and other psychoactive substances to break up existing personality patterns. This, however, was not the real horror. The real horror was that for most of the process, patients were conscious that their minds and memories were slowly but steadily slipping away.

[15] Details of this experiment have not yet been fully revealed. After obtaining essential documentation, I gave the information to ABC-TV producer Paul Altman who used it in a television documentary entitled "Mission: Mind Control" (1979).

[16] The story of Dr. Cameron's experiments was first revealed in J. Marks, see note 7, *supra;* Fuller accounts are now available in Don Gillmor, *I Swear By Apollo: Dr. Ewen Cameron and the CIA-Brainwashing Experiments* (1987), Eden Press, Montreal; Anne Collins, *In the Sleep Room: The Story of the CIA Brainwashing Experiments in Canada* (1988), Lester & Orpen Dennys, Toronto; and Gordon Thomas, *Journey Into Madness: Medical Torture and the Mind Controllers* (1988), Bantam Press, Toronto. Numerous articles and television news reports have also shed light on this episode. I want to thank Dr. Harvey Weinstein, of Stanford University, for many discussions about these events. His eloquent recitation of the human tragedy befalling his father, one of Cameron's victims, may be found in Harvey Weinstein, *A Father, A Son and the CIA* (1988), James Lorimer & Company, Toronto. The American edition was renamed *Psychiatry and the CIA: Victims of Mind Control* (1990), American Psychiatric Press, Inc., Washington: D.C.. It contains additional valuable information.
I also want to thank the late Val Orlikow, another victim of Dr. Cameron, who further informed me about her personal experiences. Discussions with John Marks and Don Gillmor have also been of great assistance to me.

To quiet the unbearable agony and anxiety that such realizations brought to his patients, Cameron induced what he called "differential amnesia". Patients were put in a state of prolonged sleep lasting for weeks. In its final stages, depatterning made patients incontinent, unable to feed or care for themselves, and devoid of any memories of their lives. They had, in fact, been regressed to infancy with their minds now a clean slate.

Of these victims Cameron later wrote that "sensory deprivation could be borne indefinitely". When this point had been reached, phase two began.

(b) Psychic Driving

Phase two was called "psychic driving". Its goal was to rebuild a new personality, often in the image of its creator. Psychic driving sought to bypass the slow and tedious method of psychoanalysis by automating the process, and making it completely unconscious. Patients were once again placed in a chemically induced prolonged sleep where they listened to thousands of hours of programmed messages recorded on electronic tape loops. As the sleep went on for weeks or months, positive and negative messages would be heard over half a million times.

Cameron's work attracted the attention, and the financing, of the Canadian and American Governments, but not because of any therapeutic value it might have. The interest and the money were focused on potential new discoveries for brainwashing. Cameron was able to comfortably continue his erasure of souls. He left in his wake shattered and worsened lives, the remnants of those who came to him for cure. Some of his patients filed suit against the CIA in 1980. After unconscionable governmental cover-ups, denials and delays, the case was settled just before trial in November 1988.

Alfred Bester, in a 1953 science fiction novel entitled *The Demolished Man*, could have been describing Cameron's work. Writing about how criminals will be treated in the future, Bester observed:

> "When a man is demolished at Kingston Hospital, his entire psyche is destroyed. The series of osmotic injections begins with the topmost strata of cortical synapses and slowly works down, switching off every circuit, extinguishing every memory, destroying every particle of the pattern that has been built up since birth....
>
> But this is not the pain; this is not the dread of Demolition. The horror lies in the fact that the consciousness is never lost; that as the psyche is wiped out, the mind is aware of its slow, backward death until at last it too disappears and awaits the rebirth. The mind bids an eternity of farewells; it mourns at an endless funeral."[17]

In the case of Dr. Cameron, the speculative horrors of science fiction became acts of medical immorality.

This same Dr. Cameron, the man who subjected his patients to

[17] Alfred Bester, *The Demolished Man* (1953), Sidgwick & Jackson, London, p. 174.

unimaginable psychological terrors, had been sent by the Allies as one of ten psychiatrists to participate at the Nuremberg Trials. After this experience, he wrote an impassioned paper against the moral decay which occurred under the Nazi regime. Less than a decade later, and for the rest of his life, he performed his own psychiatric atrocities.

The brief stories I have recounted are not isolated incidents. The quest of States to master the secrets of the mind has been a multi-million dollar venture and has required the aid of scores of the world's best and brightest physicians, psychiatrists and psychologists, as well as researchers at universities, pharmaceutical houses, mental institutions, prisons, private offices and laboratories. For nearly 50 years, every conceivable avenue of mind and behavior control research has been covertly funded by governments. This research will become far more dangerous in the 21st Century.

3. Private Sector Mind Control

States are not the only entities interested in controlling the way people think and act. In the last few decades the private sector has made its own contribution to mind control.

There are, generally speaking, two types of mind control – coercive or conversational. *Coercive* mind control techniques are recognized by their intensity and by their physical components. Thought reform programs,[18] religious cult mind control programs,[19] brainwashing,[20] menticide[21] – whatever the name, the salient aspects include domination over the body to obtain mastery of the mind.

Is it truly possible to manipulate the human mind into a personality alteration? Can unflinching obedience, without guilt, remorse or conscious knowledge, secretly be programmed into an innocent person? In theory, the answer is yes.

One particularly pernicious avenue of cult mind control experimentation has not yet been given public attention. The technique involves creating multiple personalities within a person and then separately programming each of these

[18] See Robert Jay Lifton, *Thought Reform and the Psychology of Totalism* (1961), W. W. Norton & Company, Inc., N.Y.

[19] See generally Lowell D. Streiker, *Mind-Bending: Brainwashing, Cults, and Deprogramming in the '80s* (1984), Doubleday & Co., Inc., Garden City: N.Y.; Steve Hassan, *Combatting Cult Mind Control* (1988), Park Street Press, Rochester: Vermont; Thomas W. Keiser & Jacqueline L. Keiser, *The Anatomy of Illusion: Religious Cults and Destructive Persuasion* (1987), Charles C. Thomas, Springfield: Illinois.

[20] See Albert D. Biderman, *March to Calumny: The Story of American POWs in the Korean War* (1963), The MacMillan Company, N.Y.; Eugene Kinkead, *In Every War But One* (1959), W. W. Norton & Company, Inc., N.Y.; and Edgar H. Schein, *Coercive Persuasion* (1961) W. W. Norton & Company, Inc., N.Y.

[21] See Joost A. M. Meerloo, *The Rape of the Mind* (1956), Grosset & Dunlap, N.Y.

personalities. Some personalities are programmed to be unconscious assassins.[22]

These things are possible; we are not back in the realm of science fiction. Hypnotists have known for over a century that false ideas, beliefs and memories can be instilled in a subject in trance with subsequent amnesia for the process.[23] A highly respected psychiatrist has written about erasing a patient's memory of her past and replacing it with a new one that he, for therapeutic reasons, created for her.[24] More than one well-respected psychologist has claimed credit for creating multiple personalities for the military.[25]

The California Supreme Court, after an extensive evaluation of the use of brainwashing and mind control techniques by some religious cults, has permitted former members to sue the cults for fraud and for the exercise of coercive persuasion tactics upon them.[26] Such a suit, of course, requires the cult member to later become aware that such methods were used, and to be angry about it. Once these methods are perfected, however, victims would never know they had been abused, and certainly would not care.

Conversational mind control techniques, by contrast, work on free populations. Advertisers, merchants, preachers and political campaigners are mastering the art of manipulating mass public opinion.[27]

We are living in an age filled with media consultants, speech writers, pollsters, public relations executives, image makers, propaganda specialists and influence peddlers. Their cumulative efforts are directed toward a single goal: to persuade us to buy a product, an idea or a political candidate. In most cases they know more about what we think and feel and believe than we do.

The hallmark of freedom of thought is the ability to make informed, intelligent decisions. Too often, the manner in which a point is made will carry more meaning than the substance of the point itself.[28] People are just as inclined

[22] See D. Corydon Hammond, "The Manchurian Candidate: Antisocial Uses of Brainwashing and Hypnosis in Satanic Cults," a talk presented to the American Society of Clinical Hypnosis, 1989. I would like to thank Dr. Hammond, who is President of ASCH, for his kindness in sending me a videotape of his presentation, and for many hours of enlightening and entertaining conversations.

[23] See Alan W. Scheflin & Jerrold Lee Shapiro, *Trance on Trial 81–82* (1989), The Guilford Press, N.Y.

[24] See Milton H. Erickson & Ernest Lawrence Rossi, *The February Man: Evolving Consciousness and Identity in Hypnotherapy* (1989), Brunner/Mazel, N.Y.

[25] For descriptions of the work of Dr. George H. Estabrooks, see the first three references note 7, *supra*. For the remarks of Dr. Milton V. Kline, see J. Marks, note 7, *supra* at p. 191. One person who claims to have been a CIA-created multiple personality is former model Candy Jones. See Donald Bain, *The Control of Candy Jones* (1976), A Playboy Press Book, Chicago: Illinois.

[26] *Molko v. Holy Spirit Ass'n for The Unification of World Christianity*, 46 Cal.3d 1092, 252 Cal. Rptr, 122, 762 P.2d 46 (1988), cert. denied, 109 S.Ct. 2110, 104 L. Ed.2d 670 (1989).

[27] See Shearon Lowery & Melvin L. DeFleur, *Milestones in Mass Communication Research* (1983), Longman, N.Y. and London.

[28] See Mark Hertsgaard, *On Bended Knee: The Press and the Reagan Presidency* (1988), Farrar Straus Giroux, N.Y.

to discount the truth because it is poorly expressed as they are to accept falsehood because it is well expressed.

Those who do not know the techniques of conversational mind control are condemned to be manipulated by them. As individuals our responsibility is to pierce the pretty packaging to see what we are really being sold.

4. The Human Rights Response

What actions should the human rights community take to protect the fundamental right of freedom of thought? Here are four proposals.

(1) Education

Many techniques to control the way people think and act are capable of being rebuffed, provided people have been given enough information about them. Schools and other educational institutions should be encouraged to present courses on the human influence process. In these courses students would learn about the principles of persuasion used by advertisers, politicians and others to sway our views. They would also learn about logic, and about the use of logical fallacies and emotional appeals to create persuasive illusions. Television commercials would be examined, as would the talks given by politicians. Critical thinking skills also would be taught.

The human rights community could help prepare relevant materials, help design courses, and help prepare instructional materials (including videos).

These materials would also be of interest to the general public. A television documentary, for example, would attract wide public appeal and would serve to reinforce respect for human rights.

In addition to the goal of educating the public, the human rights community might profitably turn its attention to deterring mind and behavior control experiments. The following proposals are directed to this purpose.

(2) Censure by Professional Associations

One of the sad aftermaths of the revelations of mind control experimentation has been the lack of response by professional organizations. No national association has censured its members nor even had the moral courage to speak up against its members participating in this type of unethical and illegal work.

After the legal case involving Dr. Cameron's experiments was settled in 1988, Stanford University psychiatrist Harvey Weinstein, whose father was one of Cameron's victims, attempted to obtain a statement of regret from the American and Canadian Psychiatric Associations.[29] Neither organization was willing to provide regrets, assistance or even a forum to air the issues.

[29] H. Weinstein, see note 16, *supra*.

Dr. Weinstein did receive a statement of regret from the Northern California Psychiatric Society, the only professional group to rise to its moral obligation. In a statement released on December 6, 1989, the Society declared Cameron's experiments to be unethical, expressed its regret to his patients, and urged that "a physician who becomes aware of such deviation from standard practice has the obligation to ensure that an external review be undertaken."[30]

Human rights organizations should lobby professional associations to follow the lead of the Northern California Psychiatric Association. Healers who harm should be censured, and professional groups should assist victims in need. When other members have knowledge of human rights violations, they should be under an ethical mandate to make their information public or be censured themselves.

Continued failure of professional associations to address the wrongs committed by members will breed more medical immorality. Dr. Weinstein's conclusion is most surely correct:

> "And so, forty years later, by avoiding the past, the medical establishment continues to condone the goals and policies of Cameron. By the silence of his colleagues and by the inability of medicine's professional bodies to confront a transgression, the leader stands unchallenged....If we have learned nothing from the experiments in Montreal, if we have learned nothing from the deaths of those who died in MKULTRA or related experiments, then we are all at risk and, despite the work of human subjects committees and institutional review boards, we will all be vulnerable."[31]

(3) Criminal Charges

In the summer of 1968, the Court of Assize of Rome sentenced Aldo Braibanti to nine years in prison for the crime of *plagio*. According to the court, Braibanti "with physical and psychological means, in execution of [a] criminal purpose, ...brought [two young men] under his power, in such a way as to reduce them to a total state of subjection".[32]

Never before had the Italian courts applied this little used section of the Penal Code to a case of mind control. Only twice this century had the section been applied at all. In both of those cases, physical, not mental, enslavement was involved.[33]

The basic charge against Braibanti was that he had befriended two young men, both above the age of consent, and through the force of his personality deliberately subjugated their wills to his own. No force was involved.

[30] Quoted in Weinstein, ibid., at p. 277.

[31] Ibid., at p. 286.

[32] Albert Borowitz, *Innocence and Arsenic* (1977), Harper & Row, N.Y.

[33] Edith Schloss, "Can You Plagiarize Another Man's Soul?", *The Village Voice* (Jan. 23– Jan. 29, 1970), vol. xv, #4, p.1.

The Court's 180-page opinion covered centuries of psychiatric and psychological theories. Everything relevant was discussed, including the trial of Socrates for suppression of his ideas, the "hidden persuaders" of advertising, political brainwashing, religious mind control, and the suggestive power of love.

Of special importance was hypnosis and the power of suggestion. By careful use of suggestion, according to the judges, Braibanti had undermined the men's powers of critical judgment to the point where they could no longer be self-determining. According to Albert Borowitz, an attorney who has studied the case, "much of the evidence in the case suggests that witnesses as well as [the] court had hypnosis on their minds".

The Court considered Braibanti's conduct to be serious. It consisted

> "of a plan coldly prearranged to result in the annulment of the freedom of will of others, a plan pursued with such suggestive means as would not be noticed by the victims".[34]

One year later the Appeal Court affirmed the conviction but reduced the charge to "attempted" *plagio* and lowered the sentence.[35] This decision was upheld by Italy's highest court in 1971.[36]

New criminal laws to punish those who tamper with the minds of others might be difficult to draft, but they would serve as fair warning that freedom of the mind is a fundamental human right protected by the penal code.

(4) Civil Liability

Victims of State sponsored mind control have had a difficult time holding governments responsible, accountable and civilly liable. The first impediment has been the refusal of goverments to release the information necessary to identify appropriate victims. The United States Supreme Court has protected governmental non-disclosure in certain circumstances.[37]

On the assumption that a person discovers that he or she has been a victim of government mind control experimentation, other barriers prevent financial compensation for the physical, emotional and economic losses suffered. If the victim happens to be in the military, recovery is precluded by a harsh doctrine[38] which immunizes the government from tort liability for injuries "incident to service".

In *United States v. Stanley*,[39] a serviceman sued for compensation for emotional and physical injuries caused by his involuntary contact with a mind altering drug known as LSD. Stanley, a master sergeant in the Army,

[34] Borowitz, see note 32, *supra*.

[35] Ibid.

[36] Ibid.

[37] *Central Intelligence Agency v. Sims*, 471 U.S. 159, 105 S.Ct. 1881, 85 L. Ed.2d 173 (1985).

[38] It is known as the *Feres* doctrine. See *Feres v. United States*, 340 U.S. 135 (1950).

[39] 483 U.S. 669, 107 S.Ct. 3054, 97 L. Ed.2d 550 (1987).

volunteered in February 1958 for an experiment to test protective clothing against chemical weapons. He was not told that he was secretly being given doses of LSD as part of an Army program to test the effect of the drug on unwitting human subjects. As a consequence of the LSD, Stanley underwent hallucinations, memory loss, impaired military performance, bouts of physical violence against his wife and children (which he would forget immediately afterwards) and other personality changes that forced his military discharge and led to the end of his marriage.

Stanley had no idea what was happening to him until he received a letter from the Army in December 1975 which informed him of the experiments. He filed suit for compensation and his case went to the United States Supreme Court in 1987 where a divided court slammed the door in his face.[40] His only remaining recourse is the arduous task of shepherding a private bill through Congress.[41]

New laws need to be written making it easier for victims of mind and behavior control to receive compensation for their suffering. Access to relevant information is only one dimension that must be pursued. New causes of action are needed to hold private perpetrators liable to their victims. Intentional tort theory, for example, could be shaped to support such liability. Legislation specifically directed towards deterring unethical mind control research, however, would be more desirable.

5. Conclusion

Unlike torture of the body, control of the mind leaves no marks and no evidence of its occurrence. Even the victim is unaware of what has happened. Though mind control is the ultimate threat to human rights, it is, because of its aura of unreality, unfortunately the one threat likely to be ignored, disbelieved or discounted.[42]

Yet, there is an undeniable paradox about medical and psychiatric know-

[40] *United States v. Stanley*, 483 U.S. 669, 107 S.Ct. 3054, 97 L. Ed.2d 550 (1987).

[41] See Mary Hladky, "Surviving the Acid Test", *Broward Review* (February 24, 1989), vol. 29, no. 57, p. 4.

Another military victim of Army mind control experimentation was James R. Thornwell. He too was denied judicial relief. See *Thornwell v. United States*, 471 F.Supp. 344 (D.C. 1979). Thornwell was, however, successful in 1980 in receiving $625,000 compensation by way of a private bill through Congress. In June of 1984, he was found dead under unusual circumstances. The fullest version of his Army LSD ordeal may be found in A.W. Scheflin & E.M. Opton, Jr., see note 2, *supra*, at pp. 183–193. The popular CBS TV show "60 Minutes" examined this story in "The Thornwell File", a show which aired March 25, 1979. An excellent movie about these these tragic events is *Thornwell* (1981). I want to thank the late Jim Thornwell for generously spending many hours with me concerning his case.

[42] Mind control is not as immediate as homelessness nor as life-threatening as starvation. It is not as visible as torture nor as concrete as imprisonment. Mind control, appears, at best, as a "theoretical" or future threat and this fact, of course, makes it all the more dangerous.

ledge. The more we learn how to cure physical and mental illness, the more we learn how to cause it. As medicine and psychiatry discover techniques to help people, governments and private sector entities may use that knowledge to control people. Without some safeguards on abuse of this knowledge, mind control is as historically inevitable as is scientific progress. The international human rights community has not yet responded to the threat of mind control.[43] It is already becoming too late. As brain researcher Stephan L. Chorover has noted, "to deny the power and political appeal of repressive psychotechnology is to expedite its encroachment, and to refrain from combatting it is to surrender not only our constitutional freedom, but also our human dignity."[44]

This paper began by quoting a physicist. It ends by quoting a visionary, Aldous Huxley:

> "We have had religious revolutions. We have had political, industrial, economic, and nationalistic revolutions. All of them, as our descendants will discover, were but ripples in an ocean of conservatism, trivial by comparison with the psychological revolution toward which we are so rapidly moving. That will really be a revolution. When it is over, the human race will give no further trouble."

[43] See generally George J. Alexander, "International Human Rights Protection Against Political Abuses of Psychiatry". This paper is based on two lectures delivered on July 11 and 12, 1988, at the Session of the International Institute of Human Rights in Strasbourg, France.

[44] Stephan L. Chorover, "Psychosurgery: A Neuropsychological Perspective" (1974), 54 Boston U. L. Rev. 231, p. 248.

GLENN R. RANDALL*

Use of Medical Science in Protecting and Promoting Human Rights

1. Introduction

This paper focuses on currently available technologies that are in use or have the potential for use in documenting human rights abuses or identifying the perpetrators of abuses. The need for documentation to supply objective evidence to substantiate allegations of torture or mistreatment occurs often. Documentation may be required to (i) support a claim for political asylum, (ii) as a basis for civil damages, or for reparations or restitution, (iii) as a part of an international investigation, or (iv) as a basis for evaluation or treatment. The technologies introduced here are imaging techniques to support documentation, body fluid markers of trauma, methods of using DNA for identification such as "genetic fingerprinting" and polymerase chain reaction for amplification of DNA sequences. Justification, goals, techniques and assessment of treatment methods are also briefly discussed.[1]

Evaluation for documentation of human rights abuses now consists of a physical examination and psychological evaluation.

(1) Medical Evaluation

The physical evaluation focuses on the history of the trauma and its relationship to the physical signs and symptoms.[2] The psychological evaluation often reveals

* Medical Doctor, specialist in treating survivors of torture for over ten years. Medical Group of Encino, Encino, California, USA.

[1] The original presentation used slides to clarify some of the points of the presentation. This text briefly describes some of the slides that were shown.

[2] Slides: winged scapula (scapula sticking out from the thorax with application of pressure against the palm of the hand on the affected side) indicating damage to the long thoracic nerve in a person who had been suspended from the wrists; a recent cigarette burn; remote cigarette burn with keloid (increased scar) formation; multiple ecchymoses (bruises) involving areas of the body where unintentional bruising would be unlikely to occur; postmortem photograph of Joelito Filartiga showing whip marks, burns, and lacerations; photograph of typical electric shock scars; and a photograph of a healed dislocated fracture of the fifth metacarpal of the right hand.

K.E. Mahoney and P. Mahoney (eds.), Human Rights in the Twenty-first Century, 845–852.

a characteristic picture of decreased affect and mistrust often accompanied by depression, psychosomatic symptoms or concerns, reexperiencing or reliving the trauma, feelings of panic, or at times numbing.

The psychological symptoms brought about by torture and related to human rights abuses are long lasting and may extend for several decades or a lifetime. Survivors often suffer from Post-traumatic Stress Disorder (PTSD).[3] PTSD is an anxiety disorder characterized by periods of intrusion and denial. Survivors also may develop symptoms when exposed to objects that were not used during their torture but, in their minds, are similar. Several areas of the brain believed to be involved in this disorder are the limbic system, which is in part concerned with memory, recollection of events and fear; and the locus ceruleus located in the hindbrain which, when stimulated, causes fear and alarm. A phenomenon called "kindling" explains how repetitive stimuli such as threats and torture that do not elicit any noticeable neurological signs may eventually produce major behavioral changes much larger than expected, based on the intensity and size of the area being stimulated.[4] Other data suggests that a synaptic (nerve connection) reorganization of the brain or alteration of neural proteins allow these thoughts and symptoms to be persistent.[5]

(2) Imaging Techniques

Specialized tests may be performed to document trauma. These tests may give information about structure or function. Plain x-ray radiographs show differences in density such as those between bone, air and water.[6] Computerized Axial Tomography, (CAT) scanning, another test that uses beams of x-rays, also detects differences in density. Through computerized algorithms it is also able to generate cross-sectional images with high resolution. Magnetic Resonance Imaging (MRI) uses radio waves in the presence of a strong magnet to produce photons that are detected and transformed into

[3] American Psychiatric Association, *Diagnostic and Statistical Manual of Mental Disorders* (1987), Third Edition (Revised), Washington, D.C.: APA.

[4] J. O. McNamera, D. W. Bonhaus, Cheolsu Shin, B. J. Crain, R. L. Gellman, J. L. Giacchino, "The Kindling Model of Epilepsy: A Critical Review", in *CRC Critical Reviews in Clinical Neurobiology* (1985), 1, pp. 341–391.

R. M. Post, R. Kopanda, "Cocaine, Kindling and Psychosis", *American Journal of Psychiatry* (1976), 133, pp. 627–634.

[5] E. R. Kandel, "Environmental Determinants of Brain Architecture and of Behavior: Early Experience and Learning", in E. R. Kandel, and J. H. Schwartz (eds.) *Principles of Neural Science* (1982), Eisevier, New York, pp. 620–632.

T. J. Nelson, C. Collin, D. L. Alkon, "Isolation of a G Protein That Is Modified by Learning and Reduces Potassium Currents" in *Hermissenda, Science* (1990), 247, pp. 1479–1483.

[6] Slide shows evidence of a healed lumbar vertebral fracture brought about by beating. The survivor had been beaten severely upon the back. He suffered a paraparesis (inability to move both legs) with subsequent diminution of his symptoms and restoration of function over several months. His history of the cause of the injury, the clinical course, and the radiographic findings were consistent with his alleged mistreatment.

computerized images displayed along any two axes, in any orientation. This technology is useful in showing anatomical or pathological differences in tissues of similar density.[7]

The imaging techniques that have been discussed so far can be used to identify anatomic or structural changes. The next two techniques, single photon emission tomography (SPECT) and positron emission tomography (PET)[8], focus on detection of alterations in function. SPECT scanning, in which the patient is injected with a radioisotope, is able to measure in cross-sectional fashion blood flow in the brain or other areas and to detect some tumours. It may show abnormalities even when CAT and MRI scans are normal. It also can detect decreased blood flow following a cerebrovascular accident or a concussion. SPECT scanning thus may corroborate a history where damage cannot otherwise be documented.[9] Positron emission tomography also involves injecting the patient with a radioisotope. This technique allows investigators to monitor how and where the brain is working. Because positrons are of higher energy and are released in pairs that are separated by 180 degrees, PET scanning has a resolution on the order of 3–5 millimetres, a higher resolution than SPECT scanning. In addition radioisotopes can be bound to different molecules to investigate oxygen consumption, glucose utilization, or to see where different receptors in the brain are located or how they function.[10]

(3) Biochemical Assays

Analysis of blood and urine may also be used to corroborate a history of acute trauma or deprivation. Blood tests measuring creatinine phosphokinase, aidolase or myoglobin can support allegations of physical abuse, such as beating. These substances, which are released from injured muscle, are present in blood for hours. To be detected a blood sample must be collected very soon after the abuse. This was done in one South African case in which beatings were alleged.[11] The authorities stated that the elevations in muscle enzymes were the result of therapeutic injections. However, an experiment in which the same person was given injections of the alleged therapeutic substance according to

[7] Slides were shown illustrating comparisons and contrasts between CAT and MRI in demonstrating a subdural hematoma (a collection of blood under the dural covering of the brain often caused by trauma) containing blood of various ages. An additional series of MRI scans was shown showing blood in the thigh as well as anatomy of the normal surrounding structures secondary to trauma.

[8] National Cancer Institute Workshop Statement, "Advances in Clinical Imaging Using Positron Emission Tomography", 1988, *Archives of Internal Medicine* (1990), 150, pp. 735–739.

[9] Slide of abnormal SPECT image after trauma with normal CAT scan of the same patient; slide of cerebrovascular accident (stroke) as shown on CAT scan and SPECT.

[10] M. E. Phelps, J. C. Mazziotta, "Positron Emission Tomography: Human Brain Function and Biochemistry", *Science* (1985), 228, p. 799, Table 34–1.

[11] Dr. Michael A. Simpson, "A World View of Traumatic Stress, The South Africa Experience" (1987), Society for Traumatic Stress Studies Annual Meeting: A World View of Traumatic Stress, Baltimore, (1987).

the purported schedule failed to show the same elevated enzyme levels.

An elevated alkaline phosphatase may occur in the presence of fractured or healing bone, but plain x-rays or a bone scan would have higher specificity and sensitivity.[12] In malnutrition, albumin and lymphocytes decrease in number. Drug screens and toxicological screens may be used to detect drugs administered during a torture or interrogation session. The use of antipsychotics (for their unfavourable side effects) and sedative/hypnotics have been reported and could be detected in blood or urine within days after their use.

Chemical tests and psychophysiological measurements are able to distinguish between normal controls, individuals with PTSD, and other psychiatric disorders. For example, measurements of urinary free cortisol and urinary epinephrine/cortisol ratios have been used to distinguish different psychiatric illnesses.[13]

Unfortunately, these biochemical tests are not as specific as an in-depth clinical interview. Blood pressure, skin resistance and pulse responses to sensory stimuli such as combat sounds are able to distinguish between individuals with PTSD and other psychiatric illnesses.[14] In addition, peripheral receptors on blood platelets (cells involved in coagulation), which reflect activity of less accessible receptors in the brain, indicate changes in receptor number and affinity after traumatic stress.[15] Studies evaluating the endocrinological effects of controlled and uncontrolled stress indicate that neurochemical and neuroendocrine changes last long after the termination of an uncontrolled stress.[16]

[12] Veli Lök, Mehmet Tunca, Kamil Kumanlioglu, Emre Kapkin, Güurkan Dirik, "Bone Scintigraphy as Clue to Previous Torture", *The Lancet* (1991), 337, pp. 846–847.

[13] T. R. Kosten, J. W. Mason, E. L. Giller, R. B. Ostroff, L. Harkness, "Sustained Urinary Norepinephrine and Epinephrine Elevation in Post-traumatic Stress Disorder", *Psychoneuroendocrinology* (1987), 12, p. 13–20. J. W. Mason, E. L. Giller, T. R. Kosten, L. Harkness, "Elevation of Urinary Norepinephrine/Cortisol Ratio in Post-traumatic Stress Disorder" (1987), Department of Psychiatry, Yale University School of Medicine, West Haven V.A. Medical Center (1987) (unpublished).

[14] E. B. Blanchard, L. C. Kolb, T. P. Pallmeyer, R. J. Gerardi, "A Psychophysiologic Study of Post Traumatic Stress Disorder in Vietnam Veterans", *Psychiatric Quarterly* (1983), 54, pp. 220–229.

P. D. Malloy, J. A. Fairbank, T. M. Keane, "Validation of a Multi-method Assessment of Posttraumatic Stress Disorders in Vietnam Veterans", *Journal of Consulting and Clinical Psychology* (1983), 51, pp. 488–494.

[15] E. L. Giller, S. M. Southwick, B. D. Perry, "Blood Element Adrenergic Receptors in Post Traumatic Stress Disorder and Other Affective Disorders", (Abstract no. 285) *Proceedings of the Society of Biological Psychiatry* (1987).

[16] A. Breier, M. Albus, D. Pickar, T. P. Zahn, O. M. Wolkowitz, S. M. Paul, "Controllable and Uncontrollable Stress in Humans: Alterations in Mood and Neuroendocrine and Psychophysiological Function", *American Journal of Psychiatry* (1987), 144, pp. 1419–1425.

(4) Genetic Techniques

Genetic techniques use various types and amounts of tissue samples to identify an individual. Human leukocyte antigen (HLA) typing can determine the probability of a relationship between two individuals based on extensive published gene frequencies in populations. HLA typing is being used to determine whether or not a particular child is related biologically to a particular family. HLA typing has been used in Argentina to help identify kidnapped and subsequently "adopted" children whose parents disappeared in the "Dirty War" in Argentina between 1975 and 1983. It is also used to establish the probability that the child is related to another person such as a presumptive grandparent.[17]

The basic technique of "genetic fingerprinting" or restriction fragment length polymorphism (RFLP) can be used to establish that a sample of DNA is from a certain individual. This technique uses endonucleases (a type of enzyme) to cut DNA wherever specific nucleotide sequences occur. Thus, DNA can be cut up into many reproducibly identical fragments of different lengths. The fragments are then separated from each other on the basis of size and electrical charge by using a technique called a Southern Blot. DNA from different samples may then be compared to see how closely the fragments correspond. Probabilities may be calculated to determine the closeness or identity of the relationship. An identical match indicates that the identity of the specimen is that of the suspect. If enough DNA is available the technique may be used to identify a victim from postmortem tissues or to identify a perpetrator.

DNA often is not present in sufficient amounts to perform RFLP. Fortunately a technique to rapidly replicate pieces of DNA is available. This powerful amplification technique is called polymerase chain reaction (PCR).[18] Small amounts of DNA such as a single cell, hair, sperm, skin scrapings, saliva, blood, urine or mouth washings can provide enough DNA for this technique. Theoretically, a torture survivor could obtain some skin cells under their fingernails by scratching a torturer, save some dried blood from a torturer's scrape or injury, or some semen or sperm from a rape or attempted rape and smear this material somewhere in a cell. Because DNA is very stable in the environment upon a wide variety of materials the genetic material later could be retrieved for processing and examination and analysis by RFLP or for sequencing the DNA of the fragment(s) after the survivor is released or when a government changes. The material then could be compared with DNA from

[17] A. M. Di Lonardo, P. Darlu, C. Orrego, M. Baur, M-C. King, "Human Genetics and Human Rights:Identifying the Families of Kidnapped Children", *American Journal of Forensic Medicine and Pathology* (1984), v. 5., pp. 339–347.

[18] Polymerase chain reaction uses pieces of DNA called "primers" to identify specific sequences of DNA and to allow replication at these sites. A quadrillion copies of a DNA sequence may be produced in hours. Primers of 17 nucleotide base length have a specificity of approximately 1 in 17,000,000 and a primer of 20 base pairs has a specificity of approximately 1 in 1,099,500,000,000, thus enabling them to pick out a piece of DNA with great specificity.

suspects. To my knowledge PCR has not yet been used in this type of a situation.

A drawback with PCR is that results can be used fraudulently or may be misleading. Samples of DNA could be left around to frame someone, contamination in the laboratory with stray DNA may occur, or incomplete digestion by restriction endonuclease enzymes in the RFLP procedure may occur. To address the contamination issue most laboratories that perform PCR do so in two different locations on identical specimens and RFLP experiments are duplicated.

(5) Treatment Goals and Techniques

Any discussion of documentation of human rights violations must cover some aspects of treatment goals and techniques. Individuals should begin treatment to attempt to repair physical and psychological damage. If this is not done there are two probable effects. First, increased morbidity and mortality from physical or psychological illness, social decline and unemployment are likely to occur. Second, intergenerational psychological effects may occur. While this area has not been systematically studied in recent survivors, it has been well documented in children of survivors of Nazi concentrations camps, in children of Vietnam Veterans and in children whose parents were abused as children.[19] Assistance is also needed for individuals in the community who were also traumatized by directly witnessing violence or by their complicity by being silent bystanders during periods of repression.

Practitioners involved in treatment must realize that normal to highly functioning people have had their lives thrown off by abnormal events. A survivor's situation may be complicated by refugee status, linguistic difficulties, social problems, financial difficulties and the sense of having been uprooted.

Goals and methods of treatment are to:

1. enter into a supportive therapeutic relationship,
2. take a problem-oriented approach beginning with the major problems as identified by the survivor,

[19] R. E. Phillips, "Impact of Nazi Holocaust on Children of Survivors", *American Journal of Psychotherapy* (1978), 32, pp. 370–378.

R. Rosencheck, P. Nathen, "Secondary Traumatization in Children of Vietnam Veterans", *Hospital and Community Psychiatry* (1985), 36, pp. 538–539.

J. T. Freyberg, "Difficulties in Separation – Individuation as Experienced by Offspring of Nazi Holocaust Survivors", *American Journal of Orthopsychiatry* (1980), 50, pp. 87–95.

Y. Danieli, "Treating Survivors and Children of Survivors of the Nazi Holocaust" in F. Ochburg (ed.) *Post-traumatic Therapy and Victims of Violence* (1988), Brunner/Mazel: New York, pp. 278–294, at pp. 282–283.

J. Cohn, L. Danielsen, K. Holzer, M. Inger, L. Koch, B. Severin, S. Thogersen, O. Aalung, "A Study of Chilean Refugee Children in Denmark", *The Lancet* (1985), pp. 437–438.

F. Allodi, "The Psychiatric Effects in Children and Families of Victims of Political Persecution and Torture", *Danish Medical Bulletin* (1980), 27, pp. 229–232.

3. seek reintegration into pertinent social groups,
4. try to put the trauma experience into perspective so that the survivor can look forward toward the future; and
5. help the individual reintegrate into the larger universe so as to establish a feeling of order and predictability.

Many techniques are used to treat survivors. Cognitive psychotherapies help survivors accurately reinterpret and correct misperceptions about events and their resulting chain of thoughts and emotions. The many issues that can be explored include understanding the torturer's goal to destroy the victim's personality and the way the torturer's techniques aim to achieve their goals, who was responsible for the abuses which the victim and others suffered; that the victim made difficult or impossible choices under extreme duress; and exploring the impact of their age and moral development at the time of trauma and how this relates to their current life situation. Other types of psychotherapy may be useful when the trauma occurred in the remote past giving the individual's character, coping mechanisms and defenses a long time interact prior to treatment or when there were pre-existing characterological problems. Behavioral therapies have been used. Allied techniques such as stress reduction, exercise, journal writing and psychodrama may also be helpful. Group therapy for survivors may help normalize symptoms and provide education for their families. Medications have a place in symptom control when the symptoms interfere with treatment or function. Independent therapeutic initiatives such as art, political activities and legal endeavors such as lawsuits are also therapeutic.

2. Conclusion

What will the future bring? In the diagnostic field advances will be made in documenting the physical sequelae of torture through further research on such current techniques as microscopic analysis of skin to detect microcalcifications diagnostic of electric shock torture[20] and chemical and enzymatic assays to document abuse. Improvements in genetic techniques may make identifying perpetrators of human rights abuses easier and will contribute to locating relatives of individuals, both living and dead, who have been abducted. Advances in all imaging techniques are expected. Continued work with positron emission tomography will identify additional neurotransmitters and their receptors, and will investigate the effects of treatment on neurotransmitter levels and brain function. In the future PET scanning may be coupled with provocative stimuli such as sounds or images associated with the trauma to increase diagnostic specificity. Hypothetically, future patients who have been treated with medication or psychotherapy should have PET scans that become

[20] T. Karlsmark, O. Nielsen, H. K. Thomsen, K. G. Nielsen, L. Danielsen, I. K. Genefke, O. Allund, "Tracing the Use of Electrical Torture", *American Journal of Forensic Medicine and Pathology* (1984), 5, pp. 333–338.

progressively more similar to non-traumatized populations. Finally, the use of other sophisticated imaging techniques such as MRI and radionuclide bone scanning may help with the diagnosis of physical problems currently underdiagnosed.

Evaluation of current diagnostic tools and treatment techniques and their outcomes is a high priority. Currently researchers use questionnaires to measure symptoms and their intensity. For example, multiple questionnaires are available to diagnose and assess depression and post-traumatic stress disorder. Some questionnaires are now beginning to measure function, reintegration into family, community and society, and trust. Methodological problems in evaluation include a lack of appropriate control groups and knowledge of the natural history of the problems of survivors. Research is moving toward objective functional measurements of familial and societal reintegration, satisfaction and sense of place.

Data collection techniques concerning human rights abuses and their statistical analysis will improve. This data could then be used by interested parties to help stop abuses or to prosecute the perpetrators of those abuses. Finally, recognition of anatomical, biochemical and functional abnormalities may lead to new treatments, methods of assessment and documentation enabling us to serve these survivors better.

IAN KENNEDY*

Experimentation on Human Subjects

1. Introduction

I suppose one should be gratified that medical ethics and medical law are now recognized as being a significant area of concern for human rights. But I am somewhat concerned about the implication that threats to human rights exist, that new standards are called for, and that the standards are the way to secure human rights.

First of all, one must ask why there is a call for new standards. It could be that the reason is the new factual situations arising in the development of science and technology in the context of medical research, but new fact situations don't really persuade us to create new standards. They merely ask us to apply old standards to new situations. It could alternatively be suggested that there are now much greater dangers posed in the development of science and technology, in the context of medicine, and that is why we need new standards. I'm not entirely sure that this is the case. It may be thought that perhaps in the area of development in genetics there are new or grave dangers posed and it may be that that is an area we should respond to.

I take the view that there may be a ground for arguing for new standards so as to consolidate everything which has gone before. There are a number of international declarations about biomedical research. There may be a case for consolidating these and at the same time seeking to address new issues which are deemed to be important and not yet caught by existing regulations.

In this paper I argue that there may be new threats, and that there may be a need for new standards, but any call for the development of new international declarations is far less strong than the need for structures to operate and enforce the current standards and future guidelines, if any. This is based on the assumption that biomedical research of an appropriate nature is to continue.

I confine my views to biomedical research. I exclude such matters as behaviour modification on prisoners and the sort of matters outlined in

* Professor, Centre of Medical Law and Ethics, King's College, London, England.

K.E. Mahoney and P. Mahoney (eds.), Human Rights in the Twenty-first Century, 853–857.

Professor Scheflin's paper, elsewhere in this chapter. This is not because I think them trivial – far from it – but I regard them as properly dealt with under the topic of state violence.

So I will consider biomedical research, assuming there is an abuse to a certain extent of human rights by exploitation of the vulnerable and by the drive to material gain, especially by pharmaceutical companies, which are the agents, in most part, of biomedical research. I assume, however, that such abuse is at the edges. This is because pharmaceutical companies increasingly need to develop good data. This development takes place in situations where regulatory agencies in Germany, the U.K. and the U.S. license drugs, and before doing so, they will look carefully at the kind of data developed. But I assume at the edges, certain abuse. So in the face of this I would like to play the role of the British pragmatist. I'm less persuaded by rhetoric. I am sure it has its place, but it is arguably of only limited value to the vulnerable, unemployed person who is being dragooned or otherwise persuaded to join a biomedical test on some particular pharmaceutical product.

2. New Developments

The first development I would notice is the activity of the Council of Europe in a meeting in Istanbul in June of this year, in which there was agreed that there be a convention for the protection of the human person with regard to biomedical science. The Council of Europe took the view that, so far, all they had been able to do had been to enjoin member states to adopt legislation. The Council admitted that enjoining them wasn't particularly satisfactory, although some form of regulatory framework was gradually emerging. The Council of Europe took the view, not unnaturally, that it was the leader in the field engaged in pioneer activities, and therefore desired to make certain proposals. There have been a number of proposals made within the Council of Europe over the last few years, particularly about genetic engineering and manipulation of the genetic inheritance. And concern was expressed on these topics. Concern was also expressed about forum shopping. I point this out as being a matter of major specific concrete concern because without some network of international regulation, the real possibility of forum shopping of countries exists. Pharmaceutical companies, which are largely multinational or transnational, can go from country to country to carry out their research, knowing one country is less likely to inhibit their activities, than others. I will come back to that because I think it is important.

The Council of Europe also noticed its own activity in certain areas of high profile, such as research on human embryo. They recommend that an international convention be developed to regulate biomedical research in, "The application to human beings of biomedicine and biotechnology for therapeutic and diagnostic and scientific purposes." They talk of research on humans, on genetic screening, on embryos and on organ transplants. Significantly, they refer to the need to have proper scientific and ethical surveillance, particularly in the knowledge that research crosses borders. The Council of Europe has given itself till 1993 to develop an international convention, the significant feature of which will be some regulatory or supervisory mechanism.

One such mechanism is what is called in Canada, a Research Ethics Board, or in my country, the U.K., an Ethics Research Board or sometimes an Ethical Research Committee. I have some difficulty persuading those who sit on it that whether the research is ethical or not is a matter for others to judge. It should properly be called an Ethics Review Board.

3. The Problems With Review Boards

These bodies are much beloved of States, but why? Because it is a way whereby those who seek to regulate conduct of biomedicine, the conduct of research, particularly by pharmaceutical companies can, by setting up these bodies, appear to have solved the task. Once the surveillance and the regulation of such research to an appropriately constituted body is assigned, the state can thereafter wash their hands of the particular conduct of these bodies.

The recent Canadian study by the National Council on Bioethics in Human Research, the first workshop on biomedical ethics, is illustrative. The report of the workshop describes what is happening in Canada, the medical research council having indicated what should be done for the surveillance and regulation of biomedical research. Although there were guidelines which the Canadians were supposed to observe, the reality was that there was a considerable gap between intention and performance. I take the view that if biomedical research is to continue, if we are to go beyond some international, some generalized declaration to measures of surveillance and regulation, we should achieve visibility of control, and get in at the planning, rather than at the infringement stage. The bodies, which have been set up in the countries in which most pharmaceutical and biomedical research is taking place, are not able to protect the human rights of those who would be the subjects of such biomedical research. For this reason, therefore, there is an urgent need to develop norms at an international level which can then be translated into national law so as to allow the job to be done properly. In my own country, the U.K., her Majesty's Government has decided to dump this, as well as many other matters onto local research ethics committees. The whole conduct of biomedical research is sloughed off to amateurs, who have no training, or particular background, or often to researchers themselves, both of whom bring to their task no real understanding of the need to protect the human rights of research subjects.

I believe that if there is any national regulatory mechanism set up with appropriate rules, those rules must set the minimum standards which all such bodies must observe, while allowing appropriate flexibility. This would avoid both the legalism of the United States and the catastrophic adhocery of the United Kingdom. There must be rules which establish the constitution and composition of such ethics committees. You have all heard of the term "lay people". I'm sure that such bodies must contain lay people. I always think this is a wonderful technique of professionals to define others as lay people, thereby to define them out of competence, "they shall not thereafter presume to comment on what we do because we have categorized them as lay people". In matters of ethical review of biomedical research, no one is a lay person, and I don't see why a doctor, a nurse, or a research scientist is any more qualified than others to speak on the ethics of research or the ethics of human rights.

4. Setting Minimum Standards

Essentially, any mechanism which is worth its salt will purport to protect the human rights of those who would be the subjects of biomedical research and will take account of these sorts of matters. These are the minimum conditions. Ask the question whether ethics review boards are really ever going to be up to that task or whether governments have, by setting up this straw man of regulation, effectively avoided the task. I cannot see how bodies made up of ten or twelve people, drawn from the four winds, can properly assess the scientific value of a pharmaceutical product intended to reduce the size of cancers in elderly people or monitor the research properly. I cannot understand how they will know what a "randomized control is", or what consent, in the context of the confused and the vulnerable, is. But nonetheless, these are the bodies chosen. It is a matter of those who are interested in the subject to think whether it is appropriate or not. When I say there should be minimum standards I mean standards sufficient to ensure the basic principles of human rights are observed. In other words, the ones that are non-negotiable. But to say that one should preserve the non-negotiable isn't of course to solve the problem of what may be negotiable.

Three examples of biomedical research, which tax either committees in Canada as they do in the U.K. and elsewhere, are illustrative.

In any debate on human rights and biomedical research, there is a strong case to say that there is a human right in the progress of such research. Not only in the scientist and the researcher to pursue knowledge, but also in the right of all of us to benefit from the products of such research properly carried out. There is a danger that those of us who are concerned in this area act too paternalistically. We patronize those who would happily take part in research and seek to prohibit research as being too invasive of people's free choice.

That tension I think is no better illustrated than proposals to undertake research on the vulnerable. The vulnerable include prisoners, the elderly, the senile, children, students and employees. I take the view that it is too easy to say that biomedical research, which is non-therapeutic, not intended to benefit the particular subject, must never be carried out on for example, children or on senile elderly suffering from Alzheimer's Disease. Its too easy because it overlooks the fact that generations of children will suffer and continue to suffer from children's illnesses. If we don't do research on children of a non-therapeutic nature, and if we don't find what the normal blood levels are in normal children, we can never develop techniques of understanding when children become ill. Arguably, it is the right of children now and in the future to have such research conducted, while at the same time we must be protective of those children who may be the subjects of such research.

5. Conclusion

I think there is a challenge for us all, once regulatory guidelines are developed, to translate them into law at a national level. But notwithstanding the general guidelines, descending to the particular, we must also wrestle with the permissibility of that kind of research. I could put before you certain criteria, but I won't, which suggests that it is entirely permissible to carry out such research if it is properly supervised. The challenge is not to take a view, what I would call a Ludite view, a wrecking view, a view of putting one's head in the sand, that all biomedical research is *ipso facto*, the product of a conspiratorial organization seeking to make money at the expense of the vulnerable. That I think is just to over-egg the omelette.

On the other hand there are clear dangers. Somewhere in between we have to find some procedure which will solve concrete problems rather than be too general, which will solve problems as they exist rather than merely be exhortatory in general terms.

SHEILA McLEAN*

The Impact of Technology on Euthanasia and the Elderly

1. Introduction

The "right to die" is a fundamental and universal interest, but its linkages with technology makes it peculiar to the so-called developed world. In addition, it must be said at the outset that it is not a problem confined to the elderly. This topic introduces two distinct, or at least separable, sets of rights. The first is the individual "right" to choose when to die and perhaps also how to die. The second is the more narrow issue of rights, notably, in respect of health care provision, both in terms of the allocation of services and in respect of their possible inappropriate use.

There are a number of perspectives from which this might be approached. Modern technology may impact as a result of its availability (or lack of it); it may impact because of its capacity to prolong existence in circumstances wh re otherwise survival would be unlikely, or at least would be for a shorter time. In addition, its impact will, of course depend on how we define technology. Before considering the question of euthanasia it might be well to consider each of these points briefly.

(1)Availability of Resources

According to Jennett:

> "The elderly present special problems for high technology medicine. Persons over 65 years of age already comprise 14% of the UK population, and this figure is steadily rising. They make up 25% of all surgical admissions and up to 50% in urology and ophthalmology. They comprise about a third of all patients in general intensive care units and more than half of those in coronary care units."[1]

* International Bar Association Professor of Law and Ethics in Medicine, Glasgow University, Scotland.

[1] B. Jennett, "Decisions to Limit the Use of Technologies that Save or Sustain Life", Stanley Davidson Lecture, May 9, 1990; See also, H. J. Aaron, and W. B. Schwartz, *The Painful*

K.E. Mahoney and P. Mahoney (eds.), Human Rights in the Twenty-first Century, 859–870.

Leaf[2] notes that in the United States, although the elderly "make up only 11% of the population at present, they consume nearly 30% of the rapidly growing expenditure on health".[3] It is clear, therefore, that the elderly can prove to be a major user of limited health care resources. This raises two interesting questions about resource allocation, both on a national and on an individual basis. From the national perspective, and regardless of the wishes of the elderly for survival, access to technology may well be based on characteristics which relate to age rather than medical or other need. The allocation of resources to this group is a question which logically precedes the issue of euthanasia. Much has been written on this subject,[4] and it is not necessary to restate it here, beyond noting that this is an issue. Leaf[5] amongst others, has criticized the over-ready use of technology in the elderly as ignoring the prospects of success, whilst on the other hand, if age *simpliciter* were to be used as a criterion for access to medical care, then the potential for discrimination is evident.[6]

(2)Prolonging Life

The converse of this is, of course, that the elderly themselves may have different attitudes to what risks, benefits or quality of life they are prepared to tolerate.[7] A recent article in the *New England Journal of Medicine*[8] makes a worrying suggestion on this point. The author says as follows:

> "The very high suicide rate in older Americans is due partly to concern that they will be unable to stop treatment if hospitalized... Some people now fear living more than dying, because they dread becoming prisoners of technology."[9]

Prescription: Rationing Hospital Care (1984), Washington, D.C., The Brookings Institution; S. McLean, and G. Maher, *Medicine, Morals and the Law* (1983), Aldershot, Gower, (reprinted 1985), Ch. 10.

[2] A. Leaf, "Medicine and the Aged", 297 *New England Journal of Medicine* (1977), p. 887.

[3] Ibid., p. 887.

[4] See note 2, *supra*.

[5] Ibid.

[6] J. Avorn, "Benefit and cost analysis in geriatric care: Turning age discrimination into health policy", 310 *New England Journal of Medicine* (1984), p. 1294.

[7] B. Jennett, "High Technology Medicine and the Elderly", Editorial, 3 *International Journal of Technology Assessment in Health Care* (1987), p. 491 at p. 492; See also, B. Jennett, "The Elderly and High Technology Therapies", in N. Wells, and C. Freer (Eds.) *The Aging Population: Burden or Challenge?* (1988), London, Macmillan.

[8] M. Angell, "Prisoners of Technology: The Case of Nancy Cruzan", 322 *New England Journal of Medicine* (1990), p. 1226.

[9] Ibid., at p. 1228.

(3)Defining Technology

The third preliminary issue relates to how we define technology in the context of medicine. Questions relating to its withholding or withdrawing extend both to clinical decisions made by physicians and to requests from patients themselves, and therefore transcend the issue of euthanasia. A straightforward definition of technology is not so easy to come by as might at first appear. Whilst it might immediately be assumed that technology is only the most highly sophisticated aspect of medicine, this is to ignore the fact that definitions may also be contextual. Thus, what is routine therapy in one case may well be regarded as unusual or sophisticated in another. British[10] and American[11] courts have recently, for example, refused to draw a distinction between medical treatment and the provision of nutrition and hydration, and this is also supported by a statement of the American Medical Association.[12] If these are a form of treatment, then arguably they are part of the technology of medicine, and can therefore become the subject of decisions regarding provision, withholding or withdrawal in the same way as more sophisticated technology, such as life support machines.

To conclude this brief introduction, it seems, therefore, that a number of decisions – taken nationally or personally – may contribute to the question of failure to prolong life with or without the request of the patient, and these should be borne in mind as a backdrop to the question of euthanasia itself. Moreover, we would do well to bear in mind the problems which can arise from the medicalization of death, in much the same way as other contributions urge caution in respect of the medicalization of birth.

2. A Right to Die?

Arguably, the basic issue here relates to the question of whether or not we can expect formal and consistent recognition of the individual's voluntary decisions about death, and this inevitably means whether or not we can expect the law to vindicate such choices. Most commonly, arguments concerning euthanasia centre on the question of whether or not individuals have a "right to die", or more properly whether they have a right to ask someone else to assist them to die. Strictly speaking, the common translation of the word "euthanasia" – a "good" or "happy" death – is unconcerned with questions of such rights or choices. In terms of the definition, euthanasia does not depend on request, but relates rather to the *kind* of death experienced. For this reason, euthanasia is

[10] *In re C (Wardship: Medical Treatment)* [1990] 1 Med LR 46 (Court of Appeal); *Re J (A Minor)* [1990] 2 Med LR 67 (CA).

[11] *In Re O'Connor* 534 N.Y.S. 2d 886 (1988).

[12] AMA Council on Ethical and Judicial Affairs, "Witholding or Withdrawing Life-Prolonging Medical Treatment", 256 *Journal of the American Medical Association* (1986), p. 471.

generally further divided into three distinct kinds – voluntary, non-voluntary and involuntary.[13] The proponents of legal reform argue for the legalization of the first of these, whilst opponents are concerned that legalizing one will inevitably lead to the practice of the others.

This "slippery slope argument", however valid, has a peculiarly powerful hold on the minds of many. As the British writer and journalist Ludovic Kennedy has said:

> "...on the one hand [is] the fear that if voluntary euthanasia is legalized, it will in time slide imperceptibly into compulsory euthanasia and we shall all be in danger of being snuffed out before our time; and on the other hand [is] the fear that if euthanasia is not legalized, we may have to face a future of degraded senility, our last days passed wired to machines, unable to control our bodily functions, all love of living gone."[14]

For the proponents of voluntary euthanasia it is the latter part of this comment that generates the most concern. The fear of a lingering and unhappy death is, in their view, as great as is the fear of the "slippery slope". In addition, it is argued, voluntary euthanasia presents fewer ethical dilemmas than its other forms, since the voluntariness of the patient's choice protects and enhances the individual's right to self-determination or autonomy. The law, it may then be argued, as the ultimate protector of individual rights should act to recognize the right of patients to make such choices.

The law in the Netherlands is often pointed to as a good, rational example.[15] There, euthanasia remains a crime but one which will not be prosecuted if the appropriate guidelines have been followed. This approach is also used in the Netherlands with respect to the use of certain "soft" drugs. It seems to many that this strategy recognizes the rights of individuals while maintaining the ethical tone of the law in its general prohibition on active killing.

Although the definition of euthanasia is unconcerned with the question of choice, it is generally from the perspective of a right to make choices that the debate proceeds. But there is also a sub-plot and this relates to the question of how such choices may be carried out, that is, the distinction between withholding and withdrawing therapy. Arguably, if we concede that there is an inherent right to choose death over life, then this distinction is both practically and ethically irrelevant. However, as Jennett notes:

> "The apparent distinction between withholding and withdrawing life-saving and life sustaining technologies provokes much discussion. Whilst ethicists

[13] I use here the distinction drawn by J. Glover, *Causing Death and Saving Lives* (1977), Harmondsworth, Penguin.

[14] L. Kennedy, *Euthanasia: Counterblast* (1990), 13, London, Chatto & Windus.

[15] For discussion, see M. de Wachter, "Active Euthanasia in the Netherlands", 262 *JAMA* (1989), p. 3316.

argue that there is no moral difference between these decisions, doctors and nurses often perceive withdrawal to be more difficult."[16]

This may well be true, but what relevance does this ultimately have if the value to be protected is of sufficient weight? In addition, it must be asked whether the attitudes of health care providers are directly relevant to the underlying values which might be enhanced. This leaves us with the question as to whether or not the law recognizes a value in the right to seek assisted death. Arguably, the fact that suicide, and attempts at suicide, are no longer criminalized demonstrates a legal recognition that there is a right to choose when one dies. Yet there is a crucial difference. In euthanasia, unlike suicide, there is the inevitable involvement of a third party. Thus, assisting suicide remains a crime in many jurisdictions, as does euthanasia. On the other hand, if there is a value attached to the rights of individuals to choose when and how to die, and there is a willing third party, then it might be argued that their involvement is merely a "red herring", unnecessarily distracting attention from the crucial issue – the rights of the individual.

3. The Legal Position

The problem in respect of technology is to reconcile all of the issues raised above. Decisions about whether or not to allocate resources to groups whose prognosis is likely to be less good than others must be taken against a background of non-discrimination. Here there is a genuine human rights issue about resource allocation, although it is clearly not one which is solely of interest to the elderly and to those providing care for them. Whilst there may be some situations where prognosis is instantly perceived to be so poor that its application will not be clinically recommended, there may also be situations where this only becomes clear after the technology has been put in place. The first of these – especially with the agreement of the patient – seems considerably less problematic. The law will seldom interfere with clinical decisions, made in good faith. Care should therefore be taken that technology is not misapplied. As Leaf argues:

> "In our acute-care hospitals, where the elderly are brought frequently with advanced disease, they are too often subjected indiscriminately to the same management that might offer hope of benefiting a younger person with less extensive disease... A preoccupation with the mechanics of medical gadgets has encroached upon the time to reflect and to individualize patient care."[17]

Where laws are concerned about autonomy in health care in general rather than about euthanasia, legal systems concede the right of the competent patient to

[16] B. Jennett, see note 1, *supra*, p. 410.

[17] A. Leaf, see note 2, *supra*, p. 888.

refuse treatment, even where that refusal will inevitably hasten or cause death. Apart from a few situations, for example in the case of *Elizabeth Bouvia*, such a right is protected by the common law, and in some situations is reinforced by statute.[18] Moreover, in some jurisdictions the law will recognize the validity of so-called "living wills" which permit individuals to make a prospective decision about future health care. This recognition seems to suggest that people can choose to die, even with the active participation of others who may have to suspend their clinical judgment or wishes in the face of an expressed desire. What this amounts to is a recognition that death may be preferable to life in some (voluntarily selected) situations, and that failure to preserve existence, with the consent of the patient, will not always be culpable. Those States with natural death acts also may reasonably countenance the withdrawal of life-sustaining treatment. As a result, it is possible to identify some legal recognition of the right to choose death – the right which is central to the whole question of euthanasia. Indeed, even those most opposed to "assisted death" might find it rather hard to argue with such results. This is not to say that there are no arguments against accepting an expressed view by a patient.

What is most likely to be of concern to the elderly – as a group who have had the opportunity of contemplating the arising of situations where choices might be required to be made about life and death – is a) that they may not receive appropriate treatment because of their age, and b) that others may make decisions on their behalf that survival is not to be sought. Both of these issues, in fact, are concerned not with voluntary euthanasia, but with non-voluntary euthanasia. Despite the fact that opinion polls suggest that just over half of Americans believe that "doctors should be allowed to assist a severely ill person in taking his or her own life"[19] and that the view in the UK is much the same,[20] undoubtedly that same group, if questioned, would fear that decisions might be taken for them, particularly when they are legally competent to take these decisions by themselves. This presents a number of issues of particular relevance to the elderly:

1) Does the law, although it does not directly sanction voluntary euthanasia, ever actually countenenance euthanasia in any other form – that is, is there a genuine reason to fear legal support for non-voluntary termination of life?

and

2) If – as may well be more likely with the elderly – the person is legally incompetent, will the law insist on the maintenance of therapy which preserves them in uncomfortable, inhumane or unpleasant circumstances, or give its authority to proxy decisions?

These will be dealt with in turn.

[18] *E.g.* Natural Death Act 1976 (California).

[19] *Bulletin of Medical Ethics* (October 1990), no. 62, at p. 20; C. K. Cassel and D. E. Meier, "Morals and Moralism in the Debate over Euthanasia and Assisted Suicide", 323 *New England Journal of Medicine* (1990), p. 750.

[20] Cf. "The Scotsman", June 3, 1988.

4. Non-Voluntary Euthanasia

Arguably, it is not the "slippery slope" argument that might cause major concern to the elderly, but rather the fact that non-voluntary killing is already sanctioned – however indirectly – by a number of jurisdictions. Although the arguments of those advocating freedom of choice for the concerned individual have so far failed to carry weight in most countries, many of these States have nonetheless been prepared to sanction, or at least not to invest with legal condemnation, killing or letting die without reference to the wishes of the person concerned. Although most of these cases relate to the deliberate failure to treat the handicapped newborn,[21] sometimes even by judicial recognition of the withholding of nutrition and hydration,[22] their logic could easily be extended to the incompetent or senile adult. Just as the fear of the unwanted application of technology might lead to considerable anxiety, so too (presumably) would the knowledge (in advance of serious or hopeless illness, say in the elderly) that one's view might never be sought, depending on mental or physical condition. In the case of the newborn, the law – certainly in the UK – seems, on the one hand, prepared to agree that it might be preferable for the infant not to survive,[23] in other words that death may be preferable to life, whilst, on the other hand, refusing to concede what is arguably the same point in respect of actions for wrongful life.[24] What such ambivalence succeeds in doing might well be to generate fear and anxiety, whilst continuing to deny the validity of a genuine exercise of choice by the competent adult. What is clear is that, whilst voluntary assistance with death is routinely outlawed, non-voluntary assistance is not.

This apparent ambivalence lends little credence to the argument that a right exists to choose when to die, but much credibility to the notion that others may make the decision for you – a conclusion which is surely somewhat bizarre. Most notably it seems to suggest that there is no value in choices about life and death beyond the question of medical prognosis or third-party assessment of quality of life. But if the value is in recognizing people's rights, these issues are scarcely relevant, and certainly not definitive.

5. Enforced Treatment of the Incompetent

The other side of this coin relates to those living in jurisdictions which do not recognize the "living will" or which have no natural death statutes, and also to those living in countries which do have these facilities but where no statement has been made in advance by the individual. Despite the legal position in respect

[21] Cf. *R* v. *Arthur*; *Re B (a minor)* [1981] 1 WLR 1421 (CA); *Re J*, see note 10, *supra*.

[22] *Re C.*, see note 10, *supra*.

[23] See notes 21 and 22, *supra*.

[24] *McKay* v. *Essex Area Health Authority* [1982] 1 Q.B. 1167 (CA).

of handicapped infants, say in the UK, doctors are only permitted to hasten death in other circumstances by the application of the principle of double effect.[25] No previous statement of choice about when and in what circumstances treatment should be withheld or withdrawn will carry legal weight.

However, even in countries which recognize such prospective choices they run the risk of challenge.[26] Where no statement has been made, the courts may be unwilling to apply to the adult the same tests which seem to them unexceptionable when applied to the newborn. That this is so was recently attested to by the sad case of *Nancy Cruzan*[27] in the United States. There is no need to go into the details of this case here, but the initial refusal of the Supreme Court to assume that the views of Cruzan's parents about what she would have chosen were sufficiently weighty evidence to express the likely views of the patient, must also cause concern for those confronting possible legal incompetence. As Annas has said in the wake of this judgement:

> "Although states no longer have the legal authority to make slaves of people, they now do have a new authority to permit medical technology disconnected from any human purpose to make slaves of incompetent citizens. Medical technologies have taken on a life of their own and seem to have been ceded more rights to be used than previously competent patients have rights to have their families make decisions about such use on their behalf."[28]

What seems clear from the above examples is the weight given – not to the rights of any individual, nor to the people who care for them – but rather to the health care providers' fears about legal action or to their own moral position on the distinction – already discounted – between withholding and withdrawing treatment.

[25] Glover, see note 13, *supra*, at p. 87 says as follows: "This doctrine can be summarized crudely as saying that it is always wrong intentionally to do a bad act for the sake of good consequences that will ensue, but that it may be permissible to do a good act in the knowledge that bad consequences will ensue. The doctrine is explained in terms of the difference between intended and foreseen consequences."; McLean and Maher, see note 1, *supra*, at p. 59, also point out that "it should be noted that in the principle of double effect in Catholic theology emphasis is placed on three factors in addition to the requirement that the good effect and not the evil effect is directly intended. These are (1) the action is itself good or morally indifferent; (2) the good effect is not produced by means of the evil effect; and (3) there is a proportionate reason for allowing the foreseen evil to occur". (at p. 59).

[26] Cf. the case of Fred Finsterbach, *Medical Ethics Advisor* (1990) 6(9) 123 – the request to overturn a living will was refused.

[27] *Cruzan* v. *Director, Missouri Dept. of Health* (1990), 110 S. Ct. 2841.

[28] G. J. Annas, "Nancy Cruzan in China", 20 *Hastings Center Report*, Sept./Oct. 1990, p. 39.

6. Euthanasia and the Elderly

The foregoing has sought to highlight a number of issues which can usefully be considered with direct reference to the elderly.

(a) As a group, the elderly are more likely to need active medical intervention, even although, as Jennett notes,[29] they may also be more tolerant of "certain disabilities and they may be less willing to embark on heroic elective treatment".

(b) As Avorn notes,[30] there may be discrimination against the elderly in the allocation of technological resources, based presumably on expectation of success – a kind of cost/benefit analysis based on age.[31] Where such discrimination does exist – and consider the number of specialist geriatricians there are compared to the number of other specialists – the elderly, perhaps more than any other group, may reasonably fear either the inappropriate non-application of technology or its inappropriate application.

(c) The inclusion of hydration and nutrition in our definition of therapy, and therefore possibly of technology, may generate considerable advance concern and anxiety in this group, unlike the handicapped infants in respect of whom this conflation of food and medical care is often used.

(d) Competent elderly persons may fear the continued application of technology – even given their wishes for its discontinuation – because of the legal problems which will be confronted by those caring for them were they to respect the wishes of the patient.

(e) Jurisdictions which do not recognize, or pay attention to, the "living will" place the currently competent in the position of opting for (perhaps unnecessary) suicide in advance of hopeless illness, or of lacking faith that their genuinely and competently expressed choices will be respected.

(f) Legal acceptance of non-voluntary euthanasia raises the very spectres which those who support voluntary euthanasia would seek to avoid – and which are no part of their case – and may well create fear and anxiety amongst those who would choose survival above all else.

(g) Uncertainties about when decisions may competently be taken on behalf of the patient will be of particular concern to the elderly who might reasonably contemplate that legal incompetence is more likely to affect them than any other group. Incompetence may either amount to a death sentence or to the unwanted continuation of unacceptable existence.

(h) The knowledge that some doctors will, and some will not, assist a patient to die does little for patient confidence and nothing whatever for formal justice.

[29] B. Jennett, see note 1, *supra*, at p. 410.

[30] J. Avorn, see note 6, *supra*.

[31] Cf. Fineberg et al., "Care of Patients With a Low Probability of Acute Myocardial Infarction: Cost Effectiveness of Alternatives to Coronary-Care Unit Admission", 322 *New England Journal of Medicine* (1990), p. 1225.

None of these conclusions suggests either that there is a legal right to ask for assisted death, or that any consistent value is attributed to the actual or reasonably presumed wishes of patients. In addition, they point to the very thing that we most seek to avoid; the fear that the patient will be ignored, or abused, by medicine and the law – two agencies to which they might otherwise turn in trust.

7. Conclusions

In September 1990 *The Lancet* carried a report on the Institute of Medical Ethics Working Party on the Ethics of Prolonging Life and Assisting Death.[32] Carefully avoiding the use of the word "euthanasia" the Working Party noted four main arguments against the recognition of assisted death. First, if it were known that doctors would assist in this way, certain groups – including the elderly – might feel under pressure to ask for assistance in dying rather than continue as a burden. The Working Party seemed relatively sanguine that such requests would be screened out by the clinician in charge of the case, and therefore discounted such a suggestion. In addition, refer to point (e), *supra*. Second, the argument that the existence of an option for doctors to assist in death would inhibit the search for new and better treatments and palliatives. The response of the Working Party to this objection was that advances which have already been made will cut down the number of people seeking assisted death, but that the inevitable shortfall in relieving symptoms or providing cures will always provide a stimulus for continued research. Third, they noted the argument that authorizing assisted death would break down the relationship between doctor and patient. This, however, they declared had not happened in the Netherlands, where active euthanasia may be carried out. Again, refer to my points (b), (c), (d), and (e), *supra*. Finally, they addressed the argument from the "slippery slope", discounting it on the basis that revulsion to involuntary killing is deeply rooted in both doctors and the public. It might be added that, in any event, although this form of argument might work within groups, it is less plausible to argue that it works between them.[33] Point (f) *supra* should also be taken into account here.

In conclusion, they argue as follows:

> "The list of possible undesirable consequences... needs to be balanced against strong arguments for prevention of terminal suffering. Without this help, many patients would, as now, suffer persistent mental and physical distress while awaiting natural death. It would be unjust if only some doctors, as at present, continued to relieve terminal suffering by assisting

[32] *The Lancet* (Sept. 8, 1990), p. 610.
[33] McLean and Maher, see note 1, *supra*.

death in the privacy of the home, while others, especially in hospital, did not do this."[34]

Their conclusion was that, where relief of symptoms was not possible, and a terminally ill person requested assisted death, "the balance of the moral argument has shifted towards asking why death should not be assisted".[35] Indeed, it is easier to make a case for this conclusion than it is to make a case for selective non-treatment of the incompetent patient, be they young or old. The majority view of the Working Party is summarized thus:

> "A doctor, acting in good conscience, is ethically justified in assisting death if the need to relieve intense and unceasing pain or distress caused by an incurable illness greatly outweighs the benefit of further prolonging his life. *This conclusion applies to patients whose sustained wishes on this matter are known to the doctor and should thus be respected as outweighing any contrary opinions expressed by others.*[36] (emphasis added)

Whilst begging a number of questions, these recommendations do go some way towards a recognition of the rights of individuals to make choices concerning what they will tolerate and when their life lacks sufficient quality for them to choose not to continue with it. In many ways, it is merely a logical continuation of the legal rules which already validate decisions to discontinue or refuse life-prolonging or life-saving treatment, since it reflects the same values, enhances the same rights and results in the same outcome.

What does seem clear is that there is an urgent need for the law to re-assess and clarify its position on assisted death. Without this, many currently well and competent people will live in fear of the consequences of mental or physical illness – a problem particularly acute for those approaching old age, with all of its apparently inevitable disabilities. It must be recognized that we do not – either as individuals or communities – always prefer life over death. If this is so, legal recognition, coupled with all possible legal safeguards, not only vindicates the rights of those who would make such a choice, but goes a considerable way towards the provision of formal justice. Recognition of the value of the "living will" is also necessary in the event of incompetence, in much the same way as people's expressed views about the use to which their organs may be put after death are currently respected. To pre-empt one of the problems associated with organ transplantation, it may well be that we should in advance consider whether an "opting in" or an "opting out" approach is most appropriate.

There can be little doubt that technology will continue to advance, and that our capacity to alleviate or cure will increase. Many look to the next decades to provide cures for some of today's most common killers. But this will only reduce the number of people for whom assisted death is an option – it will not eliminate the need to make such decisions. Apart from those whose own

[34] See note 32, *supra*, at p. 611.
[35] Ibid., at p. 613.
[36] Ibid.

conscience will not tolerate such decisions being made other than by, say, God, many recognize the need seriously to address these most difficult and sensitive questions. This need is arguably rendered even more urgent by the fact that the groups most likely to be affected by our conclusions are disproportionately made up of the already vulnerable, whose dignity and rights must be protected by those to whom they – or their loved ones – will turn in times of need. Certainty, as Cassel and Meier argue,[37] we would do well to give our doctors greater founding in moral issues, but we also perhaps need – all of us – to address the same questions. But accepting that there is a right to choose assisted death should not blind us to the likelihood that the major problems in respect of technology and the elderly are related to the discriminatory use and/or availability of health care resources, and in this – as in many other areas of medical practice – we should be careful to assess the judgments made about resource allocation. A clinical judgment is not inevitably value-free. A decision not to treat is not only a medical decision, nor is a decision to prolong unwanted existence. The picture, then, is complex and questions about the individual right to die should be separate and distinct from resource problems, since the ultimate values are human and not clinical. The final word will be left to the distinguished Australian jurist, Michael Kirby:[38]

> "To insist upon the prolongation of life, as nothing more than the coursing of blood and bodily functions, and to do so in circumstances of intractable and irremedial pain, is so offensive to the very purpose of human life that it calls out for relief."[39]

Surely it is not beyond the wit of us all to respond wisely and consistently to this plea.

[37] Cassel & Meier, see note 19, *supra*.

[38] M. Kirby, "Bioethics '89: Can Democracy Cope?", 18, *Law, Medicine and Health Care*, 1–2 Spring/Summer, 1990, p. 5.

[39] Ibid., p. 6.

SECTION V (d): REPRODUCTION, TECHNOLOGIES AND HUMAN RIGHTS

MARGARET SOMERVILLE

Introduction

The Universal Declaration of Human Rights proclaims in Article 27 that:

> "Everyone has the right... to share in scientific advancement and its benefits".[1]

The assumptions and optimism underlying this statement can be compared with those articulated in a report on "Human Rights Aspects of Transactions in Body Parts and Human Fetuses", recently prepared for UNESCO:

> "It is likely that the potential for anxiety and suffering in relation to the new biomedical technologies, ... [including] severe emotional conflict (with human rights implications) ... is just beginning".[2]

The difference between these two statements reflects a new insight: it is only relatively recently that we have recognized that there can be breaches of human rights in the health care arena.

Factors which may have blocked this insight in the past include that, traditionally, there was an assumption that medicine was governed primarily by altruism. Altruistic people are not likely to be identified as human rights violators; rather, they are, by definition, the antithesis of those who harm others. There was also an assumption that the factual basis of medicine was not understandable by persons outside the profession. Consequently, outsiders were not regarded as able to judge what was acceptable conduct and what was not, including whether or not certain conduct was in breach of human rights. Moreover, being motivated by altruism and having access to a body of esoteric knowledge to which others do not have access, are the hallmark of claims for self-regulation. Medicine claimed such hallmarks and was almost entirely self-

* Gale Professor of Law, Faculty of Medicine; Director, McGill Centre for Medicine, Ethics and Law, McGill University, Montreal, Quebec, Canada.

[1] Universal Declaration of Human Rights. Adopted and proclaimed by General Assembly Resolution 217 A (11) of 10 December 1948.

[2] Draft prepared by Professor Eugene B. Brody for UNESCO, Division of Human Rights and Peace, Paris, 24 April, 1990, pp. 24–5.

K.E. Mahoney and P. Mahoney (eds.), Human Rights in the Twenty-first Century, 871–874.

regulating. This meant that for medicine to be sensitive to the possibility of breach of human rights in its milieu, it would have needed to perceive itself as acting in breach of human rights. It is not surprising that practitioners of medicine did not recognize this possibility. In very recent times, however, medicine has become more externally regulated. With this came a perception that there could be breaches of human rights in medicine.

The development of this perception was also related to a recognition that medicine has the power not only to benefit but also to harm which in turn caused the power of medicine (what has been called medical imperialism) to be challenged. Furthermore, it was recognized that medicine's power to benefit as well as its power to harm involves major human rights issues. Medicine's power to do good means that people seek access to it, which raises human rights questions of equity and justice in the distribution of its benefits. Medicine's power to do harm means that people demand protection or the right to decide which harms they will accept or risks they will run, giving rise, for example, to situations of conflict between paternalism and autonomy.

The articulation of such insights has meant that "persons in health care" have become sensitized to breaches of human rights in the health care context and to notions and concepts of human rights in general. Development of this sensitivity has also been further promoted by the growth of health care ethics and law. The latter has meant that health care professionals have become familiar, in theory and in practice, with principles such as respect for persons and their rights; non-maleficence (do not harm); beneficence (response to needs); and justice. These principles require adherence to doctrines and practices such as informed consent, confidentiality, ethical review of medical research, non-discrimination in access to health care, rights to refuse treatment, *etc...* Health care ethics and law also require exploration of human rights-related concepts such as personhood, autonomy, inviolability, suffering, death, and individual rights versus collective "rights". Although most health care professionals have always acted in accordance with such principles, they were often not able to "label" them, and usually had no access to a conceptual structure which would enable them to analyze their conduct in terms of its ethical and legal acceptability. This has changed.

Sensitivity to human rights, while important in all contexts, is of particular importance in the health care context. This is true, because there is universal personal identification with breaches of human rights in that context, because everyone identifies as a potential future "victim". Persons' outrage at such breaches can be generalized, allowing them to feel outrage at (as compared with simply knowing about) breaches of human rights in general, which are not breaches of a kind that would be likely ever to occur to them. This is to distinguish two "ways of knowing" about breaches of human rights, both of which are necessary if we are to respond appropriately and adequately – we need both to know about such breaches and to have an appropriate emotional response (to feel) about them.

Correlatively, but more recently, "persons in human rights" have become sensitive to and concerned about human rights issues in health care. This is due, in large part, to high-profile "modern miracle technologies". The technological imperative, that if we have technology, we must use it, raises many new questions which require highly sophisticated and evolved human rights concepts to deal with them. Questions such as:

- Does a child have a right or a claim not to have its grandmother give birth to it, that is, not to have its grandmother as its gestational mother?
- Do persons in a persistent vegetative state have a right not to have their living prolonged (or is it their dying prolonged) by being maintained on artificial hydration and nutrition?
- Are there rights of future generations to be born from an "untampered with" gene pool?
- What are our obligations not to augment female feticide from the use of technology for prenatal sex determination?
- What are the risks of transgenic animals, for example, the proverbial, until now hypothetical, man-mouse?

Other human rights issues raised in the context of medicine are fundamental to personal dignity and well-being, for example:

- Is failure to relieve serious pain, even when the pain relief treatment could shorten life, a breach of human rights? Could it be regarded as equivalent, in some ways, to torture – that is, could it constitute "cruel and unusual treatment"?
- Do people have a right to a basic level of health care, and, if so, what constitutes such a level? Could such a claim give rise to a national or an international obligation to provide such health care, or both?

Yet other situations involving human rights in the health care context pose problems related to governance of our society and the rules on which it is based, for instance:

- Should we prohibit our politicians, who set the rules of the health care system, from opting out of the system they impose on others, by seeking treatment elsewhere?
- What is the proper balance between personal autonomy and social responsibility in the health care context? For example, to what degree, if any, should we tolerate State control of pregnant women in order to protect the fetus?
- To what degree, if any, should "collective claims" (for example, to most efficient delivery and use of health care) be allowed to predominate over respect for individual rights?

Breaches of human rights in the health care context are important, because health care has an important value-carrying function for society, in general, especially with respect to the value of caring and the reciprocal "dis-value", that of not caring. Breaches of human rights in the health care context challenge such positive values, and help to establish the correlatively negative ones, *in society, in general*. That is, breaches of human rights in the health care context are not only important in themselves, because of the harm and suffering they entail for the persons subject to them, but also in their harmful impact on the symbolism that sets the ethical and legal tone of our society itself.

Medical technology gives rise to possibilities "at the twilight of probability" (to quote the poet Blake) that go to the heart of our human identity. When human identity can be changed through use of this technology in ways that could never occur in nature, from an *integrated whole* to one composed of interchangeable pieces – a *modular theory of human identity* – some of the most important and fundamental human rights issues are raised.

Biotechnology is transnational, transcultural and transdisciplinary. Human rights responses to biotechnology need to exhibit the same characteristics. This is not always easy to achieve. This is demonstrated in the papers, two of which will address issues at the commencement of the life spectrum – those raised by the new reproductive technologies. Margaret Eichler seeks to articulate the assumptions which underlie our analytical, policy and legislative approaches to these technologies. As she says, this is necessary to "clarify the discourse". Renate Klein looks at the potential to technologize women in technologizing reproduction and, in the process, to make children a consumer product. She argues that these technologies are another form of power in the hands of a male elite. Sheilah Martin addresses issues involving reproductive control. She argues that when women do not control their own fertility, human rights issues such as coerced sex, involuntary motherhood, imposed medical treatment as well as pervasive and invasive state intervention will continue across culture and over time.

In short, and in conclusion to these brief opening remarks, how the issues raised by human rights in the health care context are dealt with is fundamental to matters ranging from the principles on which our societies are based, to our perceptions of our own personal identity. Such realizations of the gravity and scope of the impact of our decisions regarding human rights issues in the health care context could be paralysing. But if it is kept in mind that the aim of both rights and health care is the reduction of suffering, the common links and goals should form a basis for the resolution of many difficult questions. What constitutes and best achieves the reduction of human suffering in any given case is where we differ from each other. This results either from our having different values or, if we utilize the same values, our giving different weights or priorities to them. It is within a context that recognizes, encourages and displays "active tolerance" towards such diversity that the papers in this section are to be situated.

MARGRIT EICHLER*

Human Rights and the New Reproductive Technologies – Individual or Collective Choices?[1]

1. Introduction

The new reproductive technologies (NRTs) constitute a complex new set of activities with many legal, social, ethical, medical and economic ramifications. One of the many problems that we are dealing with in this area is that the term "new reproductive technologies" is not accurate[2] – some are not new and some are not technologies. Nor does it adequately describe the very diverse areas that are included in the term. Minimally, we can distinguish between four different aspects:

1) technologies of insemination,
2) techniques of artificial fertilization,
3) pre-natal diagnostic techniques, and
4) genetic interventions[3]

Any considerations we engage in need to be repeated for the various technologies and techniques within each of these areas. What holds true for one does not necessarily hold true for another. It is thus extremely difficult to try to engage in a general discussion of the legal implications of these technologies as

* Professor, Department of Sociology, Ontario Institute for Studies in Education, Toronto, Ontario, Canada, and Visiting Scholar, Canadian Research Institute for Law and the Family, Calgary, Alberta, Canada.

[1] I would like to thank Rosalie Abella, Ursula Franklin, Abby Lippman and Louise Vandelac for help in preparing this paper, either through critical comments on an earlier version, or through helpful discussion and suggestion of relevant materials. I would like to thank Denise Fournier for supplying me with copies of relevant briefs made to the Royal Commission on New Reproductive Technologies.

[2] Artificial insemination, which is commonly included in the discussion, has been practised for over 100 years, and contracts for the production of children, so-called surrogacy contracts, indicate social arrangements rather than technologies. In spite of its name, then, not all technologies included under the label of NRTs are new, nor are all practises technological.

[3] This categorization follows the National Action Committee on the Status of Women brief to the Royal Commission on New Reproductive Technologies, *The New Reproductive Technologies: A Technological Handmaid's Tale* (October 1990), Toronto.

K.E. Mahoney and P. Mahoney (eds.), Human Rights in the Twenty-first Century, 875–887.

a complex.[4] For instance, *in vitro* fertilization (IVF), artificial insemination and use of ultrasound in pregnancy require different levels of technology, are used on different populations and are very different in their degree of invasiveness.

In order to obtain some idea as to what are some of the issues that impinge on the NRTs and human rights, I reviewed submissions[5] made by legal experts to the Canadian Royal Commission on New Reproductive Technologies which is currently in progress. One recurrent theme among legal experts[6] (as well as others) is the issue of how to guarantee access to these technologies to women of different backgrounds. For instance, one submission argues that:

> The issue of access by women to the new reproductive technologies is a vital one. Discussion of this issue does not necessarily mean condonation of the provision of services such as IVF or contract motherhood arrangements, but an analysis of accessibility is crucial in determining how women and their reproductive health are being treated by the medical establishment.[7]

[4] Nevertheless, some overview articles *do* exist, see in particular Bartha M. Knoppers, "Reproductive Technology and International Mechanisms of Protection of the Human Person", in *McGill Law Journal* (1987), Vol. 32, pp. 336–358.

[5] As noted, the Commission is presently on-going. I am not sure whether I managed to get copies of all relevant submissions. I asked the Commission to supply me with copies of those briefs which were submitted by legal organizations or were written by a legal expert, no matter on whose behalf. I have accepted their judgement that the briefs were submitted by legal experts even when that was not obvious from the submission themselves. In addition, I requested additional briefs which I knew to have been made by legal experts but where this was not necessarily visible in the brief itself. The first version of this paper was prepared for the conference which took place in November 90, and included briefs submitted until the beginning of November 90. For this revision of the paper, I looked at additional briefs which have since been submitted (up to the middle of January 91). I have noted a distinct difference in the style and orientation of presentations, away from a narrow focus on access towards more consideration of the larger social context within which NRTs are located – possibly due to the fact that the later submitters had more time for preparing their briefs and hence more opportunity to reflect on larger issues. In these later briefs, there is less of an emphasis on access. Nevertheless, the issues raised in this paper remain important. The briefs I looked at, include, besides the ones quoted in various footnotes below, briefs by the Alberta Branch of the Canadian Bar Association, the Alberta Civil Liberties Research Centre, the Canadian Bar Association, Charter of Rights Coalition (Manitoba), Citizens for Public Justice, Egale, Immigrant and Visible Minority Women of British Columbia, Margaret Joe, Sonia Le Bris, National Organization of Immigrant and Visible Minority Women of Canada, Ninon Ricard, and the Yellowknife Association of Women and the Law.

[6] This is not true for *all* legal experts, however. For instance, the brief by Majury and Clement argues for a moratorium on NRTs until we have had time to study the existing technologies and their consequences. Similarly, Deleury argues for a broad examination of all the issues, including the symbolic and psychic ruptures which are created through the employment of NRTs. The brief of the Manitoba Association of Women and the Law recommends a permanent prohibition of the use of IVF. The brief of Immigrant Women of Saskatchewan argues that "NRT's are oppressive, for all women" (p. 2).

[7] Margaret Buist, *Issues of Accessibility to the New Reproductive Technologies in South-Western Ontario*. Brief to the Royal Commission on the New Reproductive Technologies, presented on behalf of the London Status of Women Action Group, Nov. 2, 1990. In a different vein, a very thoughtful submission by the Halifax Lesbian Committee on Reproductive Technologies recommends:

It then emphasises the need for access for single women and lesbian couples, low-income women and for rural women. Another brief makes a similar plea. It argues that:

> ... two measures must be taken to ensure that fairness and justice are served. One, accessibility should be ensured though explicit policy-making. Two, underrepresented groups must be actively informed, involved and accommodated by the policy and program planners.[8]

This plea is supported by references to the Canadian Charter of Rights and Freedoms, and Human Rights Codes, with the Ontario Human Rights Code used as an example. Failure to adopt such a "proactive approach to ensuring accessibility"[9] is predicted to result in:

> ... an unfair allocation of social and medical resources. Family forms desired or utilized by others, such as single parent families, or homosexual families, will face discriminatory treatment. Similarly, without careful planning and sensitively-designed outreach, women who have historically been disadvantaged by race, ethnicity, sexual orientation, poverty, disability and other factors will also have fewer opportunities to obtain access to the new reproductive technologies. These services must be offered to those women (and men) desiring them on an equal basis.[10]

The non-legal complement to this type of argument centers around the issue of choice. B. Jamie Cameron, for instance argues that access to the new reproductive technologies is the inevitable complement when arguing for choice with respect to access to abortion: "the two issues are inextricably intertwined".[11]

> Many women do not wish to have children, and that is their choice. Many women decide to terminate a pregnancy, and that is their choice, too. But they can only exercise that choice with the assistance of medical intervention.
>
> Women who have a reproductive disability are in precisely the same

1. that serious consideration be given to banning the use of all reproductive technologies (with the exception of alternative insemination) at least until long term implications have been determined; and
2. that if reproductive technologies are going to be made available at all, access to them must not be denied on the basis of social and economic factors. (p. ii)

[8] C. Backhouse and L. Greaves, *Brief to the Royal Commission on New Reproductive Technology* [sic] (Nov. 2, 1990), presented on behalf of the Women's Education and Research Foundation of Ontario (WERF), p. 12. In addition, Ann Robinson and Colette Gendron argue in their submission that "... il ne s'agit pas de rejeter globalement les nouvelles techniques de reproduction mais plutôt de les subordonner au choix éclairé de celles qui souhaitent y avoir recours." (last page)

[9] See note 8, *supra*, p. 17.

[10] Ibid., p. 17.

[11] B. Jamie Cameron. "Fighting Infertility: Please Respect My Choice". *Globe and Mail* (Nov. 5, 1990), p. A13.

situation. Equally, they seek to exercise a right of choice. And similarly, they cannot exercise that right without medical intervention.[12]

Such emphasis on access or choice is premised on several assumptions which need to be critically considered. They include the following questions:

1. Do NRTs constitute medical therapy?
2. Is it appropriate to juxtapose access to abortion with access to NRTs?
3. Is it appropriate to regard the development and employment of NRTs as a matter for individual decision-making rather than collective decision-making?
4. Is a human rights approach helpful in devising an approach to NRTs?

In the following, I shall examine each of these questions in turn.

2. Do NRTs Constitute Medical Therapy?

Scholars and advocates who argue for the desirability of providing access to all NRTs to all types of women (or men) tend to take it for granted that what they are arguing for is access to a medical therapy that may benefit (with certain attached risks) those who receive it. But is this assumption valid? I shall argue that this is not necessarily the case.

For example, artificial insemination involves the insemination of a fertile woman by means other than sexual intercourse. It is a simple procedure that can be relatively easily performed by the woman herself who wishes to conceive, without the presence of medical personnel or any medical technology. If performed by medical personnel, at the end of the "treatment", provided it was successful, the fertile woman is as fertile as she was before, and the infertile husband is as infertile as he was before, since he received no treatment at all. Having intercourse with the man whose sperm is being used would have had the same effect. What has happened, then, is the use of medical institutions to avoid the necessity of sexual intercourse between a particular woman with a particular man.

In the case of a lesbian or unmarried woman, it gives her access to male sperm without involvement with a man. In the case of a married woman, it protects her husband against being seen as infertile.

[12] Ibid. In a parallel manner, the brief by the Atlantic Research Centre argues with respect to prenatal genetic testing:

First, the provision of genetic testing should be based on the *choice* of the couple or family concerned ...

Second, ... it is important that all Canadian citizens have appropriate *access* to the availability of genetic prenatal testing ...

Third, it is essential that the concerned public ... should be adequately *informed* concerning all aspects of prenatal genetic diagnosis.

While I have no problems with the procedure itself,[13] it seems inappropriate to classify it as either therapeutic or medical, since the only thing that makes it medical is the involvement of medical personnel.

In the case of preconception contracts for the production of children, exactly the same considerations apply. The same biological effect could be achieved through sexual intercourse of one fertile man with one fertile woman, provided no embryo transfer is involved.

The matter is more complicated with respect to some other techniques. In the case of IVF, it would depend on the reasons for infertility. If a woman undergoes IVF because of her husband's fertility problems, the medical establishment interferes in a *fertile* body for *social* reasons, not *medical* reasons: that the couple have a chance at a baby that is genetically that of the couple, rather than just of the wife, as could be achieved through artificial insemination of the wife or intercourse with a fertile man other than her husband. If the reason is, for instance, blocked fallopian tubes, and presuming that the woman produces viable eggs and her husband is fertile, one could argue that IVF constitutes a medical intervention.

Does it constitute medical *therapy*, though? In general, we would think very poorly of a therapy which exposes the patient to high risks – whether or not the desired goal is achieved – and which carries an approximate failure rate of 90%.[14] However, this is an accurate description of the current status of IVF.[15] It is for this reason that Marsden Wagner of the World Health Organization has recommended that IVF be classified as experimental research with human subjects, rather than as medical therapy. This would mean that funds for IVF would not come from the health care budget but from the health research budget.[16]

To provide an example from the area of prenatal diagnostic techniques: prenatal diagnoses were originally developed for certain high risk pregnancies. They are now used with increasing frequency, and some of them are used almost indiscriminately, such as ultrasound. Lippman has associated them with

[13] I *do* see problems, however, in the way artificial insemination is currently *practised*: that is, with anonymity, thus preventing the child from knowing its genitor, and without compulsory record-keeping, thus making it impossible to either control the number of children generated through one man's sperm or to contact children in the case of a late-appearing genetic illness on the part of the semen provider. Sweden has developed an alternative approach to AI – see Lena Jonsson, "Artificial Insemination in Sweden", in *Sortir la maternité du laboratoire* (1988), Quebec: Conseil du statut de la femme, pp. 148–155.

[14] Indeed, the success rate for women *on the waiting list* for IVF treatments tends to be higher than that for those actually undergoing treatments. This suggests that some of the "successes" are "successes" because the couple was not infertile to begin with.

[15] "... the overall efficacy, or success of IVF, can be summarized as follows: approximately 10% of all stimulation cycles will result in a live birth associated with: a marked increase in multiple birth, pre-term birth, low birth weight and perinatal mortality; a significant increase in neonatal mortality; a certain significant increase in permanent neurological, vision and hearing disability." M. Wagner, "Is *in vitro* Fertilization Appropriate Technology?" World Health Organization, mimeo, 1989.

[16] Pp. 24/24.

three trends: first, prenatal diagnostic techniques are utilized in order to carry out abortions if fetal abnormalities are detected; second, they lead to a growing practice of "defensive" medicine, that is "the tendency of physicians to make clinical decisions based on the likelihood of a future lawsuit should something go wrong as well as – if not more than – on the likelihood some planned intervention will be effective."[17] Third, they may lead to "predictive medicine", "wherein children identified as 'susceptible' *in utero* are subjected postnatally to programmed 'preventive' measures and discrimination ostensibly for their own 'good' ..."[18]

For instance, amniocentesis is used to determine whether a fetus is going to suffer from certain birth defects or not. The intent is to abort the fetus if certain abnormalities are found. Individual women are thus asked to make eugenic decisions. It is hardly a "therapeutic" approach.

Three of the most important NRTs are thus either not medical in nature (artificial insemination including preconception contracts for the production of children) or not therapeutic (IVF and amniocentesis) – existing rhetoric notwithstanding. Obviously, one would have to repeat these considerations for every individual technique in order to make this statement global. However, given the centrality of these three techniques, minimally the global conceptualization of NRTs as medical therapy cannot be accepted.

3. Is It Appropriate to Juxtapose Access to Abortion with Access to NRTs?

The current debate around the NRTs has led to a number of instances in which incomparable matters are treated as if they were symmetrical. Claiming that the issue of access to NRTs is the natural complement of access to abortion is only one of them. Others include the equalization of sperm and eggs,[19] and therefore of sperm and egg donation,[20] and therefore the equation of fatherhood with

[17] A. Lippman, "Conference", in *Sortir la maternité du laboratoire* (1988), Quebec: Conseil du statut de la femme, pp. 229–238, at p. 234.

[18] Ibid., p. 236.

[19] Sperm is produced in much greater quantities than are eggs. Retrieving sperm is incomparably simpler than retrieving eggs. Sperm donation involves masturbation by a man into some receptacle. By contrast, egg donation involves a major operation, usually with full anesthesia.

[20] Genetic fatherhood has always involved a rupture between the act that leads to insemination and the eventual birth of a child. By contrast, until a few years ago, genetic motherhood has always involved a continuous process with *two*, not one, biological contributions: a genetic contribution through the egg and a gestational contribution, over nine months, towards the formation of the child. Pregnancy has never been a part of the male experience, but an integral aspect of the female experience. Egg retrieval therefore disrupts what used to be a continuous process. Egg donation is the most basic revolution in the female birth experience that can be imagined, barring the use of an artificial womb.

motherhood.[21] All of these must be seen as false parallels. A particularly drastic form of such false parallels can be found in John Robertson.[22] He argues that "new genetic, gestational, and rearing combinations, made possible by the technical ability to fertilize eggs externally and transfer them to any physiologically receptive uterus"[23]

> "may not be as novel as they first appear. In many respects, they are not drastically different from existing social arrangements that separate genetic, gestational and social parentage. ... Further variations created through egg donation, embryo donation and surrogacy are not radically different and should be treated accordingly.[24]"

The point of the matter is, however, that there *was no* separation of the genetic and gestational parentage *for women* until the first embryo generated from sperm and the egg of one woman was transferred into a second woman. The consequences *for men* are similar, for women they are revolutionary.

When we are dealing with access to abortion, we are dealing with a technology that is already developed and that is, in its technical aspects, quite simple. Indeed, abortions have been procured for thousands of years, some of them with the help of entirely non-technological means, such as infusions or massages. Furthermore, although abortion is burdened with a large moral concern, it involves the application of a specific technology at the request of one woman to her only. If abortion was used in instances other than at the specific request of the pregnant woman herself, proponents of choice as well as anti-abortionists would join in condemning it.

[21] Fatherhood has always come in three types: (1) a biological and social father (the traditional father); (2) a biological but not social father (father of a child given up for adoption, someone uninvolved in rearing his child); and (3) a social but not biological father (step-father, adoptive father). There have also always been three types of mothers which correspond to these three types of fathers. However, due to the NRTs and their splitting of the genetic and gestational contributions of the mother, we are now faced with seven types of mothers, all of whom already exist: (1) a uterine, genetic and social mother (traditional mother); (2) a social but neither genetic nor uterine mother (adoptive or step-mother); (3) a uterine and genetic but not social mother (birth mother without custody); (4) a genetic but neither uterine nor social mother (egg donor); (5) a uterine and social but not genetic mother (recipient of a donated embryo); (6) a uterine but not genetic and social mother (embryo carrier); and (7) a genetic and social but not uterine mother (user of an embryo carrier). See Margrit Eichler, *Families in Canada Today. Recent Changes and their Policy Consequences*. Toronto: Gage, 2nd ed., p. 259. The effects on motherhood through NRTs have therefore been incomparably greater than on fatherhood. Any supposed symmetry is false. In addition, as time budget studies show, women still do the vast amount of child care, no matter what the circumstances, and no matter whether they are the biological mother of a child in their care or not. Until the social responsibility of fathers and mothers is truly comparable, it is inappropriate to equate motherhood with fatherhood even in strictly social terms.

[22] John A. Robertson. "Procreative Liberty, Embryos and Collaborative Reproduction: A Legal Perspective", in Elaine Hoffman Baruch, Amadeo F. D'Adamo, Jr., and Joni Seager (eds.) *Embryos, Ethics, and Women's Rights. Exploring the New Reproductive Technologies* (1988), New York: Harrington Park Press, pp. 179–194.

[23] Ibid., p. 186.

[24] Ibid.

By contrast, NRTs are in the process of changing the pregnancy and birthing experience of *all* pregnant women, irrespective of whether or not they have fertility problems. A case in point are the pre-natal diagnostic techniques. Originally developed for certain select problem pregnancies, they are more and more frequently used indiscriminately on all pregnant women, thus profoundly altering the nature of the experience of pregnancy.[25]

New fetal monitoring devices have helped define the fetus as a "life" in its own right, rather than as a part of the woman. This is a new development. Until recently, we dealt with women who were pregnant, expecting a child. Now we are dealing with women who have been reconceptualized as an environment for a "New Life" which displaces the woman as the focus of attention.

> "The sonar was invented to sound out submarines. It is now used routinely to sound out body cavities. It is a modern, complex and elegant technology.
> ... When I look at sonar as a tool, it provides so-called information to the gynaecologists which, at least partially, can be translated for the benefit of the pregnant woman. The information serves as a basis for diagnosis and prognosis. But much more important than as a diagnostic tool is the effect which sonar has on the woman's mind and heart. The tool throws a shadow over the woman's future. It publishes her insides. It shamelessly skins her
> ... The hectoplasma of the media which were fed on scientific facts have materialized in her experience as "one new life".[26]

By accepting the image of "New Life", pregnant women are turned into collaborators in their own transformation from a woman into a "female reproductive actor", trained by gynaecologists for compliance in sharing society's responsibility for the "intrauterine patient"[27] for whom they provide temporarily the appropriate niche.

Effects of such reconceptualization include judicial interventions in pregnancies, with third parties defining themselves as safeguarding the "rights" of the fetus.[28] This constitutes a massive threat to the autonomy and right to self-determination of the pregnant woman.[29]

[25] For a graphic account of the effect of prenatal diagnostic screening, see Monika Leuzinger and Bigna Rambert. "'I can feel it – my baby is healthy': Women's experiences with prenatal diagnosis in Switzerland", in *Reproductive and Genetic Engineering* (1988), Vol. 1, – 3, pp. 239–250.

[26] Barbara Duden. "The Pregnant Woman and the Public Fetus", paper presented at the National Convocation of 'Pro Familia' (Dec. 87), Frankfurt a.M., Germany. My thanks to Ursula Franklin who gave me a copy of this paper.

[27] Ibid. The original uses the term "interuterine" patient. I assume that this is a typo and have changed it to "intrauterine" (within the womb) patient.

[28] In a study examining legal attempts to override a maternal refusal of some medical intervention, the next of kin were not given custody or guardianship in any of the cases described. See Veronika E.B. Kolder, Janet Gallagher, and Michael T. Parsons. "Court-Ordered Obstetrical Interventions", *New England Journal of Medicine* (May 7, 1987), Vol. 316, no. 19, pp. 1192–1196.

[29] Cf. George J. Annas. "Protecting the Liberty of Pregnant Patients", *New England Journal of Medicine* (1987), Vol. 316, no. 19, pp. 1213–1214; and Kelly E. Maier, "Pregnant Women: Fetal Containers or People with Rights?", *Affilia* (1989), Vol. 4, no. 2, pp. 8–20. See also Canadian Bar

The NRTs hold out promises that babies can be perfected: they can be of the "right" sex, free of genetic illnesses,[30] possibly improved in yet unimaginable ways. As spokespeople for the disabled have pointed out, such thinking may lead to a deterioration of the position of the disabled.[31] If their disability is seen as preventable, it can then be seen as a consequence of individual choice – here we are back to choice again – rather than a condition that simply is. Of course, this logic is entirely faulty, for the mother did not "choose" to give birth to a disabled child, the only "choice" she had was to abort the fetus or to carry it to term. The process makes the woman a participant in genetic selection.

> "Prenatal diagnosis now forces women to fulfil their eugenic duty. Women who bear children with Down's syndrome can no longer acquit themselves by disclaiming previous knowledge of the fact. For many women this new responsibility to become conversant with the facts has made pregnancy become an anxiety-filled phase in their lives.[32]"

The main predictors of disability and diseases of newborns and young children are not genetic factors but poverty, and extreme youth, or age of the mother.[33] "It makes no sense to be putting resources into learning how to diagnose relatively rare diseases so as to prevent the babies who have them from being born, while we permit potentially healthy babies to be disabled for reasons that are well-understood and preventable."[34]

Association, *Appendix. Judicial Intervention During Gestation and Childbirth* (Nov. 1990). Background paper, Legislation and Law Reform.

[30] Degener has pointed out that we must draw a distinction between abortion in general and selective abortion as a consequence of prenatal testing for genetic defects:

> Selective abortion ... is a matter of deciding to terminate a pregnancy that was originally desired. It becomes undesired because of a potential qualitative characteristic of the fetus, because a possible disability is valued as being worthy or unworthy of life or as a reasonable or unreasonable burden for the woman. Of course, the nonselective abortion of a pregnancy that was undesired from the start views the fetus as a burden, but this evaluation is not based on an individual characteristic of the potential child, but on aspects that are unrelated to the fetus, such as the woman's living conditions and the way she wants to lead her life. The special character of selective abortion lies in wanting to opt for a so-called norm(al) child and reject a disabled child.

From Theresa Degener. "Female Self-Determination and Voluntary Eugenics", *Reproductive and Genetic Engineering* (1990), Vol. 3, #2, pp. 87–99, quote on pp. 92/3.

Likewise, selective abortion on the basis of sex constitutes an entirely different matter from safeguarding women's control of their reproduction.

[31] See note 30, *supra* and Marsha Saxton. "Prenatal Screening and Discriminatory Attitudes about Disability", in Elaine Hoffman Baruch, Amadeo F. D'Adamo, Jr., and Joni Seager (eds.) *Embryos, Ethics and Women's Rights. Exploring the New Reproductive Technologies* (1988), New York: Harrington Park Press, pp. 217–224. See also the Royal Commission submissions by the Canadian Disability Rights Council and by DAWN Canada.

[32] Ibid., p. 89.

[33] R. Hubbard, "Eugenics: New Tools, Old Ideas", in Elaine Hoffman Baruch, Amadeo D'Adamo, Jr. and Joni Seager (eds.) *Embryos, Ethics and Women's Rights. Exploring the New Reproductive Technologies* (1988), New York: Harrington Par Press, pp. 225–231, esp. p. 233.

[34] Ibid.

Being able to assess genetic predispositions towards certain illnesses without the means of curing these same illnesses seems highly likely to result in discrimination (e.g. by insurance agencies, potential employers, perhaps even drivers' licensing offices).

The further application and development of NRTs therefore affect in a profound manner the nature of the pregnancy and birthing experience of every pregnant woman. This contrasts with the decision to undergo an abortion, which intimately affects the woman who makes her decision, but not others in the same way. The NRTs push us towards a genetic rather than social interpretation of social problems. The assumed symmetry between access to abortion and access to NRTs therefore is a false one. This leads us to the next question:

4. Should Decisions Concerning NRTs Be Seen as Issues Involving Individual or Collective Decision-Making?

We have already seen that certain NRTs have already had an irreversible effect on the experience of pregnancy for all women, whether they "choose" to utilize one of the more complicated techniques, such as IVF, or not. The argument that the important issues concerning NRTs are access and the ability to choose are premised on the notion that the choice is – and should be – an individual one. But is it truly sufficient to say, as does Cameron:[35] "Please respect my choice and let me get on with my life", or is there an overriding set of social issues involved?

Here Ursula Franklin's distinction of "divisible" and "indivisible" benefits and costs is very helpful. "Divisible" benefits and costs are those which can be divided up and enjoyed or paid for by some people only, while "indivisible" benefits and costs are those which are enjoyed or paid for by everyone.

The most important indivisible benefit and cost is the state of the environment. "... If you work hard to fight pollution and you and your friends succeed in changing the practices of the battery-recycling plant down the street, those who helped you get the benefits, but those who didn't get them too. What you and your friends have obtained are indivisible benefits."[36] Likewise, the costs of polluting the environment are indivisible.

The question then becomes: are the benefits and costs that attach to NRTs divisible or indivisible?

As to the benefits, it is clear that many (if not all) of the benefits are divisible. For example, one woman may be able to give birth to a child through the use of IVF, while another woman cannot. One woman is successfully inseminated with donated sperm, but this does not give a child to another woman. And so

[35] See note 11, *supra*.

[36] Ursula Franklin, *The Real World of Technology* (1990), CBC Massey Lecture Series. Montreal: CBC Enterprises, p. 69.

on. While it might be argued that further development of the various technologies could increase the options for other women, nevertheless the result will always be a child (or no child) for some particular woman, not for all women who desire one. This is different from, for instance, small pox, which has been eradicated through collective action by inoculation, so that all people are now protected from this terrible plague.

What about the costs? Some of them are divisible as well, to be sure. Undergoing the process of IVF extracts a great emotional and often financial price, and possibly a great physical price, which is borne by individual women or couples.[37] To the degree that women choose to accept such divisible costs, being fully informed what they are, this must indeed be seen as their choice.

However, to what degree are there indivisible costs attached to NRTs?

Beyond those consequences already mentioned, we note a further commercialization of the process of human reproduction. This is most clearly seen in the practise of preconception contracts for the production of children, so-called surrogate arrangements. This practise was, for instance, endorsed by the Ontario Law Reform Commission.[38]

However, this is merely the most visible form of commercialization, and certainly not the most frequently engaged in. Another form of commercialization involves the buying and selling of human gametes and embryos.[39] This, as well, was endorsed by the Ontario Law Reform Commission.[40]

The profit to be made in biotechnology is in the billions.[41] This includes the production and marketing of fertility-related drugs,[42] the production and marketing of machines and devices that are employed in prenatal diagnoses, and through the patenting of new life forms.[43] Drug companies and IVF clinics sometimes have a very close relationship. IVF clinics have been called the "retail-outlets" for pharmaceutical companies.[44]

[37] See Linda S. Williams. *Wanting Children Badly: An Exploration of the Parenthood Motivation of Couples Seeking In Vitro Fertilization* (1988), Unpublished Ph.D. thesis, University of Toronto.

[38] Ontario Law Reform Commission. *Report on Human Artificial Reproduction and Related Matters* (1985), [Toronto:] Ministry of the Attorney General, 2 vols.

[39] note 22, *supra*, provides a comprehensive defense for such practices.

[40] For an example of how egg selling works, see Johanna Riegler and Aurelia Weikert. "Product egg: Egg selling in an Austrian IVF clinic", in *Reproductive and Genetic Engineering* (1988), Vol. 1, #3, pp, 221–224.

[41] See Linda Ivan. *NRTs: The Costs and the Benefits*. Unpublished paper, University of Toronto, 1989, who provides an assessment of some of the profits involved in the various aspects of NRTs. She concentrates on Canada only. If we multiply her calculations into the global context, the sums involved are enormous.

[42] For some information on the subject, see the NAC brief to the Royal Commission, note 5, *supra*.

[43] See Paula Bradish. "Patenting life forms in Europe", *Reproductive and Genetic Engineering*, Vol. 2, #3, pp. 286–287.

[44] This is a phrase used by Jalna Hanmer while giving a guest lecture in one of my classes (fall 89). I am not sure whether the term originated with her.

It is an issue that should give us some reason to pause. Generally, we regard the abolition of slavery as a great step forward in terms of human rights. What, however, is a contract for the production of a child if not a contract to sell a child?[45] Even if the child will be welcomed and loved by its adoptive parents (and we have no knowledge as to how these children flourish or fail to flourish – which in itself should give us reason to pause), it still involves the sale of a human being – something that is explicitly outlawed with respect to adoption.

The NRTs further lead to the use of production logic in the process of pregnancy and birth. This is most obvious in, but not restricted to, the process of IVF, in which women's hormonal cycles are artificially regulated so that they will ovulate at a time when it is convenient for the doctor to perform the necessary interventions, Monday to Friday, between 9 and 5 o'clock. Individual women's cycles are spaced in accordance with an overall production pattern, not with respect to individual needs and preferences. Embryos that are implanted are inspected and subjected to quality control.

Ultimately, the convergence of these trends leads to the industrialization of human reproduction. I would argue that this constitutes an indivisible cost that is unacceptably high.

5. Is a Human Rights Approach Helpful in Devising an Approach to NRTs?

The Canadian Human Rights Act stipulates:

> "the principle that every individual should have an equal opportunity with other individuals to make for himself or herself the life that he or she is able and wishes to have, consistent with his or her duties and obligations as a member of society, without being hindered or prevented from doing so by discriminatory practices based on race, national or ethnic origin, religion, age, sex, marital status, family status, disability or conviction for an offense for which a pardon has been granted.[46]"

This formulation is oriented towards safeguarding individual rights. With respect to NRTs, it can be read as a justification for arguing for equal access to NRTs for women (and men) of all types, and indeed, this is precisely the argument that has been made.[47]

However, it does not lend itself easily to assessing the desirability of continuing to develop NRTs – it assumes their existence and beneficial effects. Let us consider a parallel: What is the contribution human rights legislation can

[45] See Margrit Eichler. "Preconception Contracts for the Production of Children – What are the Proper Legal Responses?" in *Sortir la maternité du laboratoire* (1988), Quebec: Conseil du statut de la femme, pp. 187–204. For an opposing view point see Bernard Dickens' presentation, in the same volume, pp. 178–186.

[46] Canadian Human Rights Act, 1976–77, c. 33, s.2; 1980–81–83, c. 143, ss. 1,28.

[47] See note 8, *supra*. The authors use the Ontario Human Rights Act as an example, however.

make to decide for or against the employment of nuclear power? Is the issue one of ensuring equal access to the power generated through nuclear reactors, or is there some indivisible cost – the pollution of the earth – that supersedes the right to individual access to power? Do we diminish the capacity of individuals in the future "to make for himself or herself the life that he or she is able and wishes to have" through the generation of wastes which will remain highly toxic for incomparably longer than humanity has had a recorded history?

Clearly, proponents for nuclear power and opponents against it do not agree on this issue. The same would probably be true for NRTs if the question was posed to people in a parallel manner.

With hindsight, had we asked ourselves this question with respect to nuclear power, and had we considered the option of investing billions of dollars into the development of alternative, sustainable, non-polluting energy sources, and into reducing pollution from fossil-fuel consumption for the same length of time we have invested in developing nuclear power, what would have been the better choice?

We still have a choice with respect to how far we wish to push NRTs. The indivisible dangers are great. Any calls for equal access and choice for individual women (or men, or couples) are premature, and not in the best interests of future generations. The decisions have to be made in a global context rather than in terms of human rights, unless we are willing to re-define what we mean by human rights. For as long as a human rights approach to NRTs accepts uncritically the assumption that all NRTs constitute medical therapy, and that there is a right to individual divisible benefits even in the face of indivisible costs, this is not an appropriate context within which to consider NRTs.

We need to expand our approach to human rights to include macro-issues such as the state of the environment and other matters which affect the overall condition for human life on earth, such as to be free from compulsory inclusion in technologies that reshape human reproduction. Only such a macro-level approach to human rights would allow us to utilize a human rights perspective profitably with respect to NRTs. As they are *currently* understood, a human rights perspective to NRTs is more harmful than helpful.

RENATE KLEIN*

The Impact of Reproductive and Genetic Engineering on Women's Bodily Integrity and Human Dignity

1. Introduction

As we move towards the year 2000, the advent of the "Gene Age" and its increasing technologization of people's lives is particularly noticeable in the area of reproduction and reproductive health. Those promoting genetic screening and engineering promise to "identify those people at high risk and advise them how to cut that risk"[1], in order to produce "low risk" people endowed with splendid genes. "Technodocs" and genetic engineers set themselves up as the "objective" arbiters over the production and maintenance of life, providing answers to questions such as who should – or should not – be having children?; where in the world should these children be born?; what should they be like?; and of what sex? Women, still the givers of life, are seen to be unsuitable decision-makers. The imperfect bodies of those deemed fit to reproduce – mainly white, middle class and heterosexual women in the West – need "assisted reproduction". Their embryos must be pre-conceptually and pre-natally "quality-checked" and screened, their fetuses monitored, "selectively reduced" or operated on in the womb if the experts deem it necessary. Birth cannot possibly be left to their whims but must become a controlled technological event. Tomorrow's reproduction will be further removed from women through *in vitro* fertilization, (IVF) perhaps the reproductive method of "choice" of the future once the maturation of immature eggs is perfected, and artificial wombs which will rescue "mankind" (sic) from spending nine dark months in that "hostile environment" – a woman's womb. Furthermore, those with "good" eggs and "good" genes but "bad" other parts, such as a deficient womb, might look for a human incubator who, for love or money, under tight medical surveillance and at the risk of her own health and well being, will gestate a child in her so-called surrogate womb.

In this context, women are told to trust our new benefactors who do this

* FINRRAGE/Deakin University, School of Humanities, Geelong, Victoria 3217, Australia.

[1] B. Williamson, "Using Human Genetic Information", *The Lancet* (July 1, 1989).

K.E. Mahoney and P. Mahoney (eds.), Human Rights in the Twenty-first Century, 889–904.

work.[2] Charles Weissman, a Swiss molecular biologist[3] put it this way: "We are the trustees of the germ line. It is our duty to preserve this genetic material in good shape and transmit it to future generations". Others believe the main purpose of analyzing the human genome is "to relieve the burden of disease on humanity".[4] They suggest, "that it might in theory be possible to identify a gene which contributed, say, a third of an individual's intelligence".[5]

Such statements indicate that the research and application of molecular and genetic technologies has come to define health as the result of "intact" genes or an impeccable biochemical "outfit".[6] The definition of health as an interactive process of body, mind and environment which is adversely affected by poor nutrition, inadequate health care, unfairly distributed resources, pollution, stress and violence in all its forms has become unfashionable.

The present paper examines these claims for "a better future" in the context of human rights, specifically women's human rights. I contend that the very existence of reproductive technologies and genetic engineering practices, not just "aberrations" or "abuses", constitute a fundamental violation of women's human rights. I posit that this so-called liberating technological "progress" that is said to open new "procreative choices" for people is really a new form of violence against women. That is, they rob women of our dignity and damage our integrity of body and soul. In so doing, reproductive and genetic engineering contributes to women's ongoing oppression.

The specific questions addressed in the paper are: first, what constitutes the social context which enables such developments to take place?; second, how do these developments affect the lives of women as individuals and as members of the social group of women in a global context?; and third, what is the response of committed feminists and women's health activists internationally to this new assault on women?

(1) The Social Context

A discussion of the social context of reproductive and genetic engineering must begin by examining the live reality of the key players. In other words, what is in it for the promoters of these technologies – scientists, "technodocs", pharmaceutical companies and increasingly lawyers? What is in it for the users?

In the West, users are white, middle-class heterosexual women in so-called

[2] B. Ehrenreich, and D. English, *For Her Own Good: 150 Years of the Experts' Advice to Women* (1978), New York: Anchor Press/Doubleday.

[3] C. Weissman, at a symposium to celebrate the 40th Anniversary of the Ciba Foundation on Human Genetic Information.

[4] B. Williamson, note 1, *supra*, "Using Human Genetic Information", *The Lancet* (July 1, 1989) p.58.

[5] Ibid., p.59.

[6] R. Kollek, "Die molekulare Definition des Menschen. Forschungsstand und Perspektiven", in F. Hansen and R. Kollek (eds.) *Gen-Technologie. Die Neue Soziale Waffe* (1987), Hamburg: Konkret Literatur Verlag, p. 21.

"stable" relationships who have a fertility problem (theirs or their husbands'), or who are "at risk" to give birth to a handicapped child. Other users are poor women who will be used as human incubators. In the so-called Third World, users are millions of women who have become living test-sites through the use of damaging contraceptives. Other users are thousands of Indian women who after an amniocentesis abort female fetuses because daughters are unwanted. Sometimes they are coercively sterilized. The former group represents the elite, the controlling power. They represent Western (capitalist) technopatriachy with the power to dominate globally anything that is "other" which includes women, "foreign" peoples, and in fact all untamed life on earth – and the arrogance to believe that this is their "right".

The reality of life for the users is thus very different from the one of the promoters; how do their human rights compare? The answer is, badly. Again, it is the group in power that decides what constitutes a human right. What becomes classified as a human right often reflects the dominant Western emphasis on individual political rights[7]. Violence against women often deemed "domestic" rather than political falls outside the traditional scope of human rights. Sexual abuse of children, battery, rape, rape in marriage, sexual harassment and specifically gendered torture in war, as well as violence against women in pornography and prostitution, do not constitute human rights violations. Equally unnoticed goes the fact that women as a social group are oppressed by men as a social group, with the result that worldwide, despite some gains, women continue to be second class citizens. Put differently, despite the fact that in some Western countries a small group of women have managed to become "social males", women continue to be the world's poor, malnourished, sick, illiterate and landless. They are coerced (or "encouraged"!) to have children in pro-natalist states and kept from becoming mothers in anti-natalist states. Violence in women's lives is systemic and daily. Yet it is not seen as a violation of human rights. Small wonder then that medical violence against women goes unrecognized and that it is only feminist activists and scholars who have demonstrated its detrimental effects and called it a violation of women's human rights.[8]

In the general media as well as in medical papers and often couched in the rhetoric of "choice", biotechnological cruelty is represented as a promising new drug, or treatment, or procedure. But, in spite of the rhetoric of responsibility and compassion for people with genetic disorders or an unmet desire for a child, technodocs and genetic engineers are not benign prophets of the future. Rather, they are mundane patriarchs involved in increasing control over human as well as plant and animal life, and in developing businesses which have the primary

[7] C. Bunch, "Women's Rights as Human Rights. Towards a Re-Vision of Human Rights", unpublished, (1990).

[8] Feminist International Network of Resistance to Reproductive and Genetic Engineering, FINRRAGE, founded in 1984. FINRRAGE has chapters in 36 countries. The International Coordination is in Germany: P.O. Box 20 19 03, 2000 Hamburg 20.

aim of making a profit from those they deem in need of technological intervention and "betterment".

Another of the social context is what has been termed *masculine* science, and its ambition to control, dominate and exploit nature, rather than co-operating with it.[9] Scientists frequently demonstrate narrow tunnel-vision and an inability to see the need for, or refuse to accept, controls which society endeavours to place upon them. This masculine control exacerbated by heavy doses of misogyny, is particularly obvious in the historical and current relationship between women and medicine. Vexed by the "irrational" nature of women's bodies (especially the hormonal cycles, which not only vary between women but indeed within one individual depending on a combination of external and internal factors), stringent measures are sought to bring us under control. Hormonal contraceptives, for instance, are based on the principle of turning off the "mother machine."[10] From the "Pill" to the injectables Depo-Provera and Net-En, the implant Norplant, and culminating in the development of RU 486 (the abortion pill) and contraceptive vaccines, these "weapons" to control population growth are becoming more aggressive, more dangerous and more damaging. Most importantly, the decision-making process is increasingly being taken out of women's hands.[11]

This masculinist and misogynist science and medical technology is also characterized by its focus on dismembering, fragmenting and dissecting real live women into their body parts. In what American medical ethicist Janice Raymond has called "Rambotechnology", women are depersonalized and reduced to wombs, eggs, and ovaries – to body parts disconnected from the women and their lives.[12] Dr. Robert Winston, a British IVF practitioner, describes so-called surrogate mothers as "endocrinological environments"; Judge Harvey Sorkow, who heard the Mary Beth Whitehead case, called surrogates "alternative reproduction vehicles"; and the American Fertility Society described them as "therapeutic modalities".[13] Losing their identity and personality, women are also seen by researchers as research animals. As Australian IVF specialists Drs. John McBain and Alan Trounson put it, "the human female is capable of having substantial litters..."[14]

Not only are women dismembered – which goes unrecognized by international human rights bodies as an infringement of women's human rights

[9] B. Easlea, *Science and Sexual Oppression: Patriarchy's Confrontation with Woman and Nature* (1981), London: Weidenfeld and Nicolson.

[10] G. Corea, *The Mother Machine. Reproductive Technologies from Artificial Insemination to Artificial Wombs* (1985), New York: Harper and Row.

[11] R. Klein, J. Raymond, L. Dumble, *RU 486: Misconceptions, Myths and Morals* (1991), Melbourne: Spinifex Press/Cambridge M.I.T.

[12] J. Raymond, "At issue: Of eggs, embryos and altruism". *Reproductive and Genetic Engineering: Journal of International Feminist Analysis*, 1(3); pp. 281–284.

[13] G. Corea, *Sortir La Maternité du Laboratoire* (1988), Quebec: Conseil Du Statut De La Femme.

[14] J. McBain and A. Trounson, "Patient Management – Treatment Cycle", in C. Wood and A. Trounson (eds.) *Clinical In Vitro Fertilization*, Berlin: Springer-Verlag, p. 54.

– but at the same time eggs and embryos are accorded a status of their own. They can be 'orphaned' or 'parentless' and may be of "good quality" or "poor quality". They may even be "wayward" if they don't stay where the doctors put them.[15] And they become "personalized" at the expense of women. In an American court case in 1989, the issue was whether frozen embryos belonged to the sperm donor whose physical contribution consisted of one act of ejaculation, or the woman who had provided the egg and wanted to implant the embryos in her body. The unequal sharing in the responsibility for the gestation of the future child was not recognized during the trial. The sperm donor asserted he was being "raped" of his reproductive rights if implantation of the embryos in his ex-wife's womb went ahead.[16] No mention was made of the fact that not only did the woman have to undergo dangerous and painful *in vitro* fertilization, including surgery, to have her eggs collected, but also, that without her whole body nurturing the developing embryo/fetus for nine months there would never be a child.[17]

The artificial separation of women into parts – eggs, embryos and fetuses – is a central feature of male-created "reproductive technologies". It has even led to the creation of a new crime – "fetal neglect". In 1986, criminal charges were brought against Pamela Rae Stewart "for acts and omissions during pregnancy". Stewart, who had a condition known as *placenta abruptio* (a tendency for the placenta to separate from the uterine wall), was told by her physician that if she began haemorrhaging, she should go to hospital immediately. Instead, when she began to haemorrhage she waited at home for twelve hours. By the time she got to hospital, the baby was in fetal distress. It was born with massive brain damage and subsequently died. Someone in the hospital notified the police and Pamela Rae Stewart was arrested for disobeying her doctor's orders.[18]

In another American case, a 28-year-old pregnant woman with terminal cancer was ordered by the court to have a caesarian section in the 26th week of her pregnancy against her own wishes and those of her parents. The operation was performed and the fetus died within two hours. Angela Carter died two days later, knowing that her child was dead. Court-ordered ceasarians on healthy women have also occurred, despite the fact that this is an area of obstetrical care with a wide array of different opinions about its safety and efficacy.[19]

[15] "Low IVF Pregnancy Rate Tied to 'Wayward Embryos'", *Ob/Gyn News* (October 15, 1986).

[16] "Preborn children or blastocytes?", *New York Times* (August 11, 1989), p. A26.

[17] In the end the judge ruled that Mary Sue Davis was to be allowed to have the embryos implanted. However, his reason was that embryos are unborn children and that life should not be destroyed. He also awarded only temporary *custody* to Mary Sue Davis for her embryos: an incredibly patriarchal and fetus-centred decision to give legal status to embryos and 'disown' a woman of part of her body.

[18] E. Goodman, "A California case tests the rights, obligations of pregnant women", *The Boston Globe* (October 7, 1986), p. 17.

[19] G. J. Annas, "She is going to die: The case of Angela C", *Hastings Center Report* (February/March: 23–25 1988), 18(1).

Women's bodies have traditionally been treated by the medical profession as defective machines in need of improvement and control. Reproductive and genetic engineering are merely new examples of a masculine science that is control-hungry, misogynist and conceptually incapable of recognizing women's dignity as whole human beings. Moreover, they are also deeply and intrinsically eugenicist and racist.

The reductionist claim that we are who we are because "it's in our genes" is a resurrection of the theory and practice of eugenics as it evolved over a century ago in Britain in 1883 from the writings of Francis Galton (Darwin's cousin). Since then, it has seen a number of horrific revivals through the passing of sterilization laws and restricted immigration in the United States, the United Kingdom and Germany in the first three decades of this century – to the Nazi genocide of Jewish people and Gypsies and the elimination, or at least involuntary sterilization, of Non-Aryans, Gypsies, people with schizophrenia, feeble-mindedness, manic depressive insanity, genetic epilepsy, Huntingdon's corea, blindness, deafness, physical deformity, or alcoholism.[20] It is crucial to remember that doctors and scientists were the chief proponents behind this practice of "racial hygene" and that they justified their actions as *Helfen and Heilen* (help and heal), whilst in reality they amounted to nothing less than *Auslese and Ausmerze* (selection and eradication). It is also crucial to know that much of the knowledge and many of the procedures used today in modern gene and reproductive technology were developed by Nazi scientists and doctors who performed cruel, often deadly, experiments on "unworthy" women in concentration camps, and who did so because they wanted to improve fertility for "worthy" women.[21]

Disturbingly, some of the same "diseases" said today to be genetically determined such as manic depression, schizophrenia, and alcoholism, are the same as those targeted in Nazi Germany. When the intention of analyzing the human genome is to "relieve the burden of disease on humanity", a need is created for what is called "preventive medicine". By stressing "the importance of early genetic screening in identifying those most at risk for every illness found from hay fever to heart problems",[22] screening not only for genetic diseases but for predispositions to genetic diseases is encouraged. Professor Wood, the famed Australian IVF pioneer predicts that we will have "a much healthier, much longer-lived race in the future".[23]

Emotional and physical problems often put down to stress, or to *menopause*, or something similar, *will also be diagnosed as genetic diseases*,

[20] C. Ewing, "Tailored Genes: IVF, genetic engineering and eugenics", *Reproductive and Genetic Engineering: Journal of International Feminist Analysis* (1988), 1(1), pp. 31–40.

[21] H. Kaupen-Haas, "Experimental Obstetrics and National Socialism: The Conceptual Basis of Reproductive Technology", *Reproductive and Genetic Engineering: Journal of International Feminist Analysis* (1988), 1(2), pp. 127–132.

[22] C. Miller, Disease and Genes, Medical File, *The Herald* (September 15, 1988), Melbourne.

[23] "The next 200 years", *The Australian Women's Weekly* (January, 1988), pp. 75–77.

and treated effectively with chemicals, or gene replacement".[24] (Emphasis supplied.)

Professor Mark Ferguson of Manchester University[25] believes that,

> "in 50–100 years every human will have his (sic) genes mapped at birth and stored on computer. Genetic defects and susceptibilities to diseases will be known. Prevention or treatment tailored to each individual could be started".

He also thinks that, "Individuals may choose to reproduce by IVF so as to have a bank of spare parts for their offspring when the latter begins to suffer from diseases or injuries".[26] In 1982 Robert Edwards, co-lab "parent" of the first test-tube baby in Britain, proposed to divide embryos, freeze half of them for use in later life and implant only half.[27] In 1990, Karen Dawson and Peter Singer, Australian bioethicists, suggest that young women between 20 and 30 years of age in order to pursue their career without interruption,

> "should have the option to have some ova collected during their optimal age for childbearing (perhaps by using the natural cycle), fertilized, and stored frozen as embryos for future transfer".[28]

The ideology of splitting women and controlling our bodies as "living laboratories"[29] has reached epidemic proportions. Medical science reminds us daily that we are so imperfect that body parts, especially our female-body parts, need constant surveillance. At increasingly early ages breasts are mammographed, cervixes are screened, and, upon pregnancy our "conceptus" is screened and scanned many, many times. If we do not obey, we are told that we are "irresponsible" (we cannot just die: who will take care of our families?; do we expect the state to pay for children with disabilities who need not have been born?).

For those of us "at risk" – and the category of risk is quickly expanding – refined technology such as pre-implantation diagnosis or embryo biopsy make it possible to select "worthy" and eradicate future "unworthy" human life at the time of conception, that is before a pregnancy has even begun. In order to carry out embryo biopsy, embryos need to be available outside a woman's womb. In this procedure, one cell is taken from the embryo and analyzed for chromosomal abnormalities. The rest of the embryo develops normally and

[24] Ibid.

[25] "Prenatal test could eliminate hare lip.", *The Guardian* (August, 1987), London.

[26] Ibid., p. 4.

[27] "New U.K. row on embryo research", *Nature* (September 30, 1982), vol. 299, at p. 383.

[28] K. Dawson, and P. Singer, "Should fertile people have access to in vitro fertilization?", *British Medical Journal* (January 20, 1990), vol. 300, p. 167–170, at p.168.

[29] R. Rowland, "Reproductive Technologies: The Final Solution to the Women's Question?", in R. Arditti, R. Klein and S. Minden (eds.) *Test-Tube Women: What Future for Motherhood?* (1984), Pandora Press, London and Boston, p. 356.

can, if the test-results are acceptable, be transferred to the woman's womb.[30] To enable the genetic engineers, so concerned with the production of "healthy children", to do their work, IVF or "lavage" (where naturally conceived embryos are flushed out of a woman's womb before implantation), would therefore have to become the preferred way of conception.

Genetic screening of embryos raises a host of problems. Today a very small percentage of children are born with severe abnormalities which are said to be genetically inherited. World-wide statistics are not available, but according to British embryologist Dr. Anne McLaren, only about one per cent of all babies born are affected by a severe genetic or chromosomal disability.[31] Undoubtedly, having a severely disabled baby and child puts extraordinary stress on the mother. In our profoundly ablist society, she is treated like an outcast, often plummeted into poverty, and a life of her own may be almost impossible. But misconceptions about genetic screening abound. It is a gross misrepresentation to suggest these technologies can reassure parents-to-be that they will have a healthy child, when so much else can go wrong at a later stage of the pregnancy, or indeed once the child is born. Having children, in the same way as living, is a risk that can never be "controlled". The important questions we must ask are: what is a healthy child and what constitutes a woman "fit" to reproduce? What will increasing selection mean for people who are outside the "norm", whatever the norm is? Why is any deviation from that norm seen as such a problem?[32] In pro-natalist Western societies, it is white, preferably married, heterosexual women who are told to produce "good" children "made to order". The reproductive capabilities of poor women of all colours are at best ignored and at worst subjected to involuntary sterilization and dangerous debilitating hormonal contraceptives.

In my view, misogynous, eugenicist, and racist masculine science applied to women in reproductive and genetic engineering is a violation of women's human rights.

In the next section I look briefly but specifically into how reproductive

[30] Incidentally, this is also a form of cloning: if the embryo was divided into, say, four parts and each of them transferred to a woman's womb, four genetically identical fetuses could be produced.

[31] A. McLaren, "Can we diagnose genetic disease in pre-embryos?", *New Scientist* (December 10, 1987), pp. 42–47.

[32] A recent book by German health activist Eva Schindele on the problems of amniocentesis and chorion villus sampling (1990) highlights the enormous emotional pressure on women to 'choose' to undergo prenatal screening– and a traumatic abortion should the test reveal a deviation from the norm. She also discusses the substantial risks involved in the procedures itself. Importantly, Schindele points out that the tests never reveal the seriousness of the deviation from the norm, i.e. *the degree* of the abnormality, but are only able to detect the abnormality itself. In all probability, many if not most people have some slight chromosomal abnormalities which we will never know about and which we were able to compensate with learning. Through these indiscriminate tests, women are forced to abort potential children they very much wanted and many of whom would have turned out to be well within the gamut of 'normality'. See E. Schindele, *Gläserne Gebär-Mütter. Vorgeburtliche Diagnostik – Fluch or Segen* (1990), Frankfurt A.M. Fischer Taschenbuch Verlag.

technologies affect the lives of women as individuals and as members of the social group of women in a global context, using the experiences of women on IVF programmes including some comments on IVF surrogacy.

(2) Test-Tube Women

(a) The Medical Reality for Women on IVF

Increasingly, a woman's difficulty in getting pregnant is magnified to the extent that it sometimes ends up being a life crisis. As a result of the media hype in favour of IVF depicting it as "a miracle cure" and "the last hope to have your own biological child" (whilst in reality it is often another child), women with fertility problems – their own or their partner's – are more and more quickly pushed onto the medical treadmill. Conventional fertility treatments are bad enough in that they usually take years, involve debilitating drug prescriptions and one invasive test or operation after the other. But, once "under the knife"[33], new problems arise. These include problems related to surgical scarring and adhesions and the drug regimen. In the case of fertile women, who are increasingly on the programmes because of their partners' infertility, these procedures can lead to infertility. So the woman moves from one "treatment" to another. Consequently, IVF – that magic crystal ball for scientists and doctors in their "conquest" to gain total control of baby-making in the lab – has led to trials and tribulations for women with a fertility problem and reached an unprecedented high. Encouraged by friends, families and often husbands, they find themselves compelled to undergo IVF. But as IVF is an inhumane, dangerous and, by and large, failed technology, very few women end up taking a baby home. Instead, the overwhelming majority, that is ninety to ninety-five women out of one hundred, finally give up often after as many as ten or more IVF attempts. At that stage, many women are truly devastated and feel like utter "failures". The message they have been given is that not even with the help of technology can they "produce" their own child. Moreover, the experimental and dangerous IVF procedures harm many women's bodies. Even when IVF is stopped their general health and well-being is often affected.

In the past, women with a fertility problem had to grapple with the pain of involuntary childlessness or the pain of not having another child. But under the IVF procedure, after years and years of failed treatments the desperation about the fertility problem often becomes magnified. When "hope" is artificially engendered by IVF doctors and hospital staff no grieving takes place. Meanwhile, other possible options, such as adoption (conducted ethically), may have been closed off because of age. Additionally, after years on IVF the woman may be economically dependent on her husband because she gave up her job. Her marriage may have broken up because of all the trials and tribulations. She may be seriously sick and she is almost certainly emotionally

[33] R. Klein, "Under the Knife: Surgery in Infertility Treatments and IVF", Paper presented at Women and Surgery Conference, Melbourne, (1990), September.

drained: a disturbing outcome of a so-called "beneficial" medical treatment, said to be in the "patient's" best interest. This is especially alarming when the woman, who after the many attempts is declared a "non-responder" – the ultimate failure – is dumped by IVF programmes and thrown by the wayside with no help whatsoever. For the IVF doctors' purposes (that is to be "world-leaders" and reap glory and money as IVF "fathers"), the unsuccessful woman with her "bad eggs", "diseased tubes", "hostile womb" (all doctors' terms!) is a "fertilization failure". She is an embarrassment for the IVF team – a bad statistic. Women are thus badly harmed by IVF: their (and/or their partner's) desire for a child is cruelly exploited.

This is my conclusion after more than eight years of research on the impact of the new reproductive technologies on women, including three years of research with Australian women who left IVF without a child[34] and after editing an international collection of women's experiences with these technologies as well as surrogate motherhood.[35] In the course of doing this work my anger at the exploitation of a vulnerable group of women skyrocketed, especially when the women told me about their infuriating (and often life endangering) experiences based on misinformation, particularly with regard to the dangers of the IVF procedure, or "success rates" (which, in fact, are "failure rates"). A short summary of the IVF procedure will explain the gruesome medical reality.[36]

Once a couple (never a woman alone) has passed the initial *pro forma* inquiries about the stability of their marriage/relationship, the woman undergoes a battery of tests. These include vaginal swabs and tests for Rubella, Chlamydia, AIDS and hormonal blood levels. The man's sperm is tested for low or no motility and low sperm count. The tests may take weeks or only days. Depending on the outcome most women are instructed to begin ovulation stimulation, also called superovulation.

Clomiphene citrate – usually administered as Clomid – is the most frequently used drug. Correctly prescribed, 5O mg (or a maximum of 100 mg) are taken daily for five days (the prescription is often much higher and for much longer). In order to further increase the maturation of multiple follicles, a second drug, human menopausal gonadotrophin (hMG), is administered (usually as Perganol) through painful injections. Monitoring of the follicle growth and blood levels necessitates daily (sometimes twice daily) visits to the

[34] R. Klein, *The Exploitation of a Desire. Women's Experiences with In Vitro Fertilization*, Women's Studies Summer Institute, Geelong: Deakin University Press, (1989). And R. Klein, "Enough is enough: Women's experiences of in vitro fertilization", in *The Healthsharing Reader: Women Speak About Health*, Compiled by Healthsharing Women Publishing and Production Group, Pandora Press, Allen & Unwin, Sydney, Wellington and London; (1990), pp. 215–224.

[35] R. Klein (ed.) *Infertility, Women Speak Out About Their Experiences of Reproductive Medicine* (1989), London/Sydney: Pandora Press/Allen & Unwin.

[36] Full references for statistics quoted in this section can be found in R. Klein, "Resistance: From the exploitation of infertility to an exploration of infertility", *Infertility, Women Speak Out About Their Experiences of Reproductive Medicine* (1989), London/Sydney: Pandora Press/Allen & Unwin, pp. 229–295.

clinic – a serious problem for women with a job. Once the ovulation seems impending, a hormonal shot of human chorionic gonadotropin (hCG) is given and the woman undergoes egg collection. For many women these "hormonal cocktails" bring with them a host of adverse effects ranging from vision problems, nausea, dizziness, weight gain to hyperstimulation, which is a dangerous swelling of the ovaries and/or the production of cysts. If the ovarian hyperstimulation syndrome is not carefully watched, the ovary can burst, and become infected and cause infertility. Women may also suffer from strokes and die.[37] There are also reported cases where the administration of the fertility drugs has lead to the promotion of cancer.[38]

It is important to know – but rarely made public – that up to 50 per cent of all women who begin the fertility treatment either never reach the egg retrieval stage, or the eggs collected have not developed properly, so that no fertilization takes place. This is important because these women rarely appear in the IVF doctors' statistics. If they were represented, the "success" rates of IVF would come tumbling down even further from the currently internationally acknowledged figures of between 5 and 10 per cent of live births per IVF attempt.

Egg collection is risky business too. If a laparoscopy is used, it necessitates general anaesthesia. We have proof of 15 women who have died during this process.[39] But even newer methods of egg retrieval via the bladder or vagina are not without danger: iliac veins can be injured and infected from the invasive procedure which most women describe as very painful. (As a remedy, women are now administered antibiotics prior to the oocyte aspiration. Surely a questionable weakening of the immune system of a woman who is intending to get pregnant!) If "good" eggs are "harvested", they are put together with the partner's sperm in a petri dish (who has in the meantime masturbated often in a room at the clinic where pornography magazines are provided), and fertilization is expected to take place. If embryo development commences, the next day usually 2 to 4 embryos at the 4 to 8 cell stage are transferred to the woman's womb. Next begins the waiting period to see if the embryo(s) "have taken", described by most women as one of the most difficult times in IVF. If the embryos implant themselves (this happens in about 20% of the roughly 50% of women who make it to the egg collection stage) – then a "clinical" pregnancy begins. That is, a pregnancy leading to the birth of a child. Unfortunately, more than a third of these rare IVF pregnancies end in spontaneous abortions, miscarriages, or are ectopics. Most children from IVF are born prematurely and by caesarians. Up to 25% of all women who do get pregnant end up having

[37] A. Solomon, "Infertility as Crisis: Coping, Surviving and Thriving", see note 35, *supra*, in R. Klein (ed.) *Infertility, Women Speak Out About Their Experiences of Reproductive Medicine* (1989), London/Sydney: Pandora Press/Allen & Unwin, pp. 169–188.

[38] M. Carter and D. Joyce, "Ovarian Carcinoma in Patient Hyperstimulated by Gonadotrophin Therapy for In Vitro Fertilization: A Case Report", *Journal of In Vitro Fertilization and Embryo Transfer* (1987), 4(2), pp. 126–128.

[39] G. Corea, Work in progress.

multiple births due both to the effect of the fertlity hormones and the insertion of multiple embryos in their wombs. (Some doctors have been known to implant up to 13 embryos and later use a procedure called "selective reduction" whereby saline solution is inserted in some of the embryos that then stop growing and disintegrate next to the others who are "allowed" to develop.)

The possible effects of clomiphene citrate and "hormonal cocktails" on the developing fetus and future child, as well as the short- and long-term effects on the woman are matters of great concern.[40] Birth statistics show a slight increase of spina bifida and transposition of the great vessels in children born from IVF. Short-term side effects on the women include complaints such as dizziness, nausea, vision problems, enlargement of the ovaries and the development of ovarian cysts. There are a considerable number of studies drawing attention to chromosomal problems in the eggs produced through this stimulation, and some studies indicate a structural similarity between clomiphene citrate and DES. A possible connection between the drug and both ovarian and breast cancer has been reported.[41] The level of risk and danger associated with this drug make its continued use on women both in IVF and in conventional infertility treatment highly questionable.

A new variation of superovulation begins by administering so-called LH-RH analogues (often marketed as Buserelin) as a nasal spray to de-sensitize the pituitary. This induces chemical menopause, including hot flushes. Once the woman's own hormonal cycle has come to a halt, she is put on ovulation induction agents in order to "superovulate" her (that is induce the production of more than one ripe egg). Ovarian hyperstimulation syndrome is a frequent health hazard and may result in cysts, pleural effusion, ascites, decreased blood volume, reduced urine output, and electrolyte imbalance.[42] The long-term dangers of this treatment for women are unknown, but it is feared that this artificially shutting down and starting again of a woman's own cycle may lead to premature menopause and possibly cancer. Nothing is known about adverse effects on future children.

IVF is increasingly used in connection with surrogacy. A woman with "good" eggs but perhaps no womb or fallopian tubes, undergoes superovulation and egg collection. Her egg is fertilized with her husband's sperm and then implanted into the womb of a commercially hired "surrogate" woman, a sister, or friend. It is argued by IVF doctors[43] – that by not using her

[40] R. Klein and R. Rowland, "Women as Test-Sites for Fertility Drugs: Clomiphene Citrate and Hormonal Cocktails", *Reproductive and Genetic Engineering: Journal of International Feminist Analysis* (1988), 1(3), pp. 251–275.

[41] See note 37, *supra*. See also, P. Bolton, "Bilateral Breast Cancer Associate with Clomiphene", *The Lancet* (December 3, 1977), p. 1176.

[42] Serono, n.d. *Treatment of Infertility with Pergonal*, Serono Laboratories (UK) Ltd, pp. 19–20.

[43] A notable example is Professor John Leeton in Melbourne who makes good use of the media's interest in reproductive technology to advertise this idea despite the fact that surrogacy is outlawed in Victoria.

own egg "the risk of the surrogate mother bonding to the child after that pregnancy is less".[44] Leeton insists, "[t]his is the point that everyone is missing, the vital point".[45] I would ask who is it that is missing the point? Only a mind impregnated (sic) by disrespectful "reprospeak" (my Australian colleague Robyn Rowland's term) could in all seriousness posit that in addition to the traumatic procedure of IVF, a woman's nine months of pregnancy, during which she nurtures the future child with her own body and mind, and often difficult labour, would not make an impact, just because it wasn't her egg!

This example, which I believe epitomizes the ruthless and inhumane reduction of women to soul-less incubators and body parts, leads to the next question about the impact of these technologies on women as members of the social group, women, specifically in a global context.

(b) Implications for Women as a Social Group and in a Global Context

The increasing medicalization of women's lives does not bode well for women's future "in our own hands" nor for the recognition of women as human beings with full human rights. Imbued with the liberal notion of "individual choice" it could also reinforce the notion that we "choose" to need an "expert" to tell us what is wrong with us. IVF promoters and indeed people seeking these treatments claim that infertile women and people "at risk" "choose" and have a human "right" to use reproductive technology, regardless of the possible danger to their own bodies and the assault on their integrity. But women's "choices" are structured within a male-controlled political and social framework.

Women do not as yet control abortion, contraception or the definitions of sexuality and relationships within that framework, and will not be in a position of control with respect to reproductive and genetic engineering. Individual "choice" and "rights" as arguments in favour of reproductive technology fail to take into account a crucial element of the feminist value system which is responsibility to women as a social group. There are times when the desires (not rights) of individual women have to be set aside because the fulfilment of those desires not only endanger individuals, but may endanger the lives, integrity and survival of all women. We must not delude ourselves into thinking that by using the word "choice" we create it. I would argue that women who are seeking reproductive technology are merely making a decision between two negative alternatives – and that is not a choice as would be defined by feminism. The decision between involuntary childlessness and infertility in a world where women's worth is regarded only through motherhood or undertaking a dangerous, expensive and failed technology, is not a choice that feminism would create. Only when women are materially, economically, politically, socially and ideologically equal to men – and equality is defined on women's

[44] J. Monks, "I'll have your surrogate baby: Twins' amazing pact", *New Idea* (September 15, 1990), pp. 12–13.

[45] Ibid.

terms taking into account our differing priorities based on race, class, sexualities, etc., – can the experience of "choice" become a reality.

The rhetoric of individual reproductive "rights" and "choices" is especially problematic in so-called Third World countries. The fact that reproductive and genetic engineering is the logical extension of the patriarchal quest to gain total control over women's fertility, becomes particularly evident when women from countries such as India, Bangladesh, the Philippines but also from Africa and South America speak out. They talk about the damaging nature of contraceptives such as injectables or hormonal implants as well as enforced sterilization which, increasingly are the contraceptive "choices" women are offered.[46]

It is very important to realize that fertility and infertility control are increasingly intertwined. Justifying the growing number of IVF clinics in India, Dr. Anand Kumar, Director of the Institute for Research in Reproduction in Bombay, said that "an understanding of these factors [contributing to infertility] may provide clues as to how to induce infertility in fertile couples as a means of family planning".[47] IVF research has thus become linked with the development of new methods of contraception. Contraceptive vaccines, for example, may become very acceptable in the general population of Bangladesh because vaccines in general are seen as "good medicine".[48] It is easy to envisage how a contraceptive vaccine can be promoted as "choice" whilst in reality many of the women may not even know what it does to their bodies. They will become the "living laboratories" to see whether, as the promoters of the contraceptive vaccine promise, it is truly reversible. As embryo research in so called "Western" countries becomes more difficult to pursue because of laws or ethical concerns expressed by the community, the fear is that women in poor countries, in return for a little food or money, will "choose" to give their bodies as test-sites for new IVF procedures as well as drugs.[49] If the contraceptive

[46] F. Akhter, "The Norplant Trial: An Investigative Study on the Methodology and Ethical Issues", *Hygeia* (1988), 3(1 and 2), pp. 19–34. These developments were explored at the 1989 FINRRAGE-UBINIG Conference in Comilla, Bangladesh, March. (Conference Proceedings edited by Farida Akhter are forthcoming 1991; see also Ewing and Klein, 1989). Of particular importance are the many instances where western governments tie economic aid to population control 'targets' being reached: the 'targets' of course, being largely *women* who have to pay dearly with poor health and poor social standing (eg when the injectables cause breakthrough bleeding which renders them 'unclean' which in turn justifies their husbands' to divorce them.). The greed of multinational drug companies to make profits from women's bodies is another topic which was highlighted at Bangladesh.

[47] Sheth, 1987 quoted in L. Lingam, *"Made in India", A Dossier on the New Reproductive Technologies* (1989), Women's Studies Unit, Tata Institute of Social Sciences, Bombay, India.

[48] See note 45, *supra*.

[49] One of the most dangerous research projects currently undertaken in the USA, Australia and Britain consists of trying to mature immature eggs in vitro (in the laboratory). Once this procedure is possible– it has been successfully achieved with egg cells from cows and led to the production of the 'true' test-tube calf in 1987 (See G. Vines, "Calves a la carte", (1987). *New Scientists*, (1987) 3 December, p. 23. and S. Voumard, "Surprise at Move to Apply IVF Technique" (1988), *The Age*, (1988) April 4.)– a slice of an ovary of any woman will do to mature thousands of eggs which can

vaccine is administered on a large scale, IVF may become the method used to reverse this induced infertility for a certain "chosen" few – the "perfect" solution for a worldwide control of population growth. In this scenario, "choice" definitely will have turned into coercion. The violation of women's human rights will be so gross that perhaps more international human rights advocates will see and acknowledge them.

It is the interconnections between "western" and developing countries that must be emphasized in the discussion of the new reproductive technologies and women's human rights. What is advertized as "choice" for privileged white women in western countries is in reality the prerequisite for "control" of ALL women in ALL parts of the world. We need to resist the fragmentation and dismemberment of women's bodies from reproductive and genetic engineering on a global scale. We also must resist believing the "experts" and obeying the "fathers". Concerned feminists, women's health activists and advocates for women's human rights must work towards a world that values women as human beings rather than as human incubators. Such a world would be based on an "ethics of integrity".[50] We do not need a "Gene Age". Unethical technologies are too failed, too cruel and too dangerous to continue. Women are more than just body parts. Women with fertility problems deserve a much

---

then be fertilised with sperm (easily available) and made into embryos. What is needed next is the womb of a woman: available, perhaps for little money and under little surveillance in poor countries. Alternatively, the artificial womb may soon become a reality. Research is certainly continuing to achieve this 'feat' of the production of life in male hands as the following bizarre experiment carried out in 1987 in Bologna, Italy, shows, (C. Bulletti et al., "Early human pregnancy in vitro utilizing an artificially perfused uterus" (1988), *Fertility and Sterility*, 49(6), pp. 991–996) in a womb removed from a woman by hysterectomy and kept alive on a perfusion machine a 'spare' IVF embryo was injected and kept alive in the laboratory for 52 hours– before the womb collapsed. The embryo was said to develop normally (see Klein, 1989c, pp. 278-279 for more details). And what are we to make of research reported from Rome, Italy, on mice, frogs, and sea urchins in which sperm was said to 'soak up' DNA from another species and then, when put together with an egg, install the alien genes in the resulting embryo and later offspring? It sounds so simple that it must be tempting to repeat the experiment with human sperm. See R. Wilson, "It's Designer Genes". *The Sunday Mail* (July 30, 1989), Brisbane, p. 43.

[50] J. Raymond, *The Transsexual Empire: The Making of the She-Male* (1979), Boston: Beacon Press.

more dignified approach to the pain and grief of their unmet desire for a child.[51]

Women have human dignity and a collective right to bodily integrity. These violent technologies contribute to the worldwide oppression of women. They must be exposed internationally and they must be stopped with passion and wild, life-loving determination.

[51] German women were the first to pioneer the establishment of self-help groups, group counselling and feminist therapy in women's health and community centres. *Before* they are gulped up by the medical treadmill, women (and in some instances their partners) with a fertility problem discuss the life crisis that involuntary childlessness can cause with other women who are in a similar situation, and allow themselves to go through stages of intense rage and anger, deep distress, sadness and finally grief, enabling them to put their feet on the ground again and plot a new life scenario. In this way they save themselves years of misery– and no baby at the end. For details see U. Winkler and Traute Schönenberg, "Options for involuntary childless women", in R. Klein (ed.), see note 34, *supra*, at pp. 207–224, *Infertility: Women Speak Out About Their Experiences of Reproductive Medicine* (1989), Pandora Press/Allen and Unwin, Sydney, pp. 207–224. See also note 36, *supra* and R. Klein, "Women with a fertility problem: An increasing group of clients for feminist therapists", *Feminist Therapy Newsletter* (1989), Melbourne 5(5), pp. 12–17.

SHEILAH MARTIN*

A Woman Centered Approach to Laws on Human Reproduction

1. Introduction

The Handmaid's Tale[1], a novel by Canadian author Margaret Atwood describes a totalitarian society in which a toxic environment has rendered so many women infertile that the reproductive services of fecund women are conscripted in the service of the state. In this fictional society, men operate as the dominant class and women are divided into rigidly stratified categories. Wives are at the pinnacle of this repressive hierarchy and their designated role is to care for husbands and await the birth of children. Prostitutes and domestic workers are at the bottom. Women who are Handmaids are made to provide sexual and procreational services in a society where pregnant women are literally applauded in the streets. Handmaids are chosen solely on the basis of their fertility and the force used to enlist their cooperation is both brutal and subtle. The compliance of the Handmaids is encouraged through a process of indoctrination designed to help them "accept" their appointed role and to participate "willingly" in highly ritualized acts of sexual intercourse and birth. In this society, contraceptives are unavailable and abortion is a crime tantamount to treason. Handmaids undergo mandatory drug treatment and are subject to intensive medical supervision and intervention. This story supposedly takes place in a hypothetical and futuristic society.

Contrast Atwood's vision with a hypothetical society based on sex equality. In an egalitarian society, the full amplitude of rights to freedom and equality would be conferred on both men and women. Women would be free to define their own sexuality; women would decide, each time, about their participation in sexual acts; and women would control the circumstances in which they engaged in intimacy. Women would have access to reliable information on the safety of available contraceptive methods and the ability to choose among them. Unwanted pregnancy would be viewed from the woman's perspective. In all cases, the individual woman would be the only one empowered to make

* Professor, Faculty of Law, The University of Calgary, Calgary, Alberta, Canada.

[1] M. Atwood, *The Handmaid's Tale* (1985).

K.E. Mahoney and P. Mahoney (eds.), Human Rights in the Twenty-first Century, 905–918.

decisions which would have life long consequences for her. For the women who choose to terminate their pregnancies there would be timely access to medically safe and publicly funded abortion services. And women who agreed to carry their fetuses to term would continue to be fully capacitated persons with the ability to conduct their lives, select their medical treatment and determine the manner in which they give birth. In such a hypothetical society, coerced sex, involuntary motherhood and imposed medical treatment, would be seen as completely and fundamentally abhorrent. Women would be valued as autonomous individuals and not by their ability to fulfil men's sexual and reproductive desires. Women would have a full range of life choices, real choices which would not be circumscribed by gender-specific role expectations, legal controls or a social context of inequality. Truly volitional action would replace socially constructed will and women would not be systematically subordinated to men. In such a society, biological difference would be accommodated, gender hierarchy eliminated and women would be viewed as free moral agents, full citizens, and completely capacitated legal persons.

A person's reaction to the society depicted in the *Handmaid's Tale* or the egalitarian one just described will depend on many factors, but it will be shaped by that person's evaluation of where his or her society is seen to fit between these two. Each reader can probably recite the litany of limitations and the catalogue of controls relating to human reproduction imposed in his or her country, but what is likely to emerge is an undeniable pattern of pervasive and invasive state intervention. In this paper I argue that a study of legal controls on human reproduction, across cultures and over time, discloses how we are often much closer to Atwood's dystopia than is either commonly credited or morally comfortable.

2. How to Approach State Controls on Human Reproduction

Establishing an approach to an inquiry is the first step towards defining the problem, analyzing the situation, and uncovering the truth. In the past, certain legal controls on human reproduction, most notably abortion and contraception, have tended to be studied as distinct topics, as if they did not have an interrelationship with other topics and as if they were not socially situated. In my view, only a comprehensive and contextual approach to the wide range of legal controls on human reproduction provides the proper framework for analysis. With a comprehensive and contextual approach it is easier to appreciate how various states have invoked almost every type of coercive device and regulatory incentive to control human reproduction. For example, governments have created crimes, prohibitions, regulations, ordinances, articles, statutes, tax incentives, administrative policies, and bureaucratic requirements in pursuit of allegedly "collective" reproduction related goals. Only with such an approach can one outline how most nations have sought to control almost every stage of human reproduction, from sexual intercourse to birth. One topic cannot be studied in isolation as if it qualified as a discreet phenomenon. A comprehensive and contextual analysis is needed to parallel this span of the biological process and should include a review of laws on sexual intercourse, contraception, abortion and pregnancy.

Although there are many different laws which touch on human reproduction, these subjects represent the major areas in which the state has imposed norms of conduct. When the topic is human reproduction the proper starting point is laws on sexual assault, especially laws concerning marital rape, because despite technological achievements, sexual intercourse is still the most common cause of pregnancy. Understanding forced sex in the context of the pronatalist marital union, where husbands often benefit from legal privileges like a marital rape exemption, exemplifies the extent to which women do not control access to their own bodies. A review of legal controls on contraception is also necessary because contraceptive devices allow the separation of sexual intercourse and pregnancy. Similarly, laws on abortion must be included because this procedure permits the separation of pregnancy and motherhood. Increased state intervention into pregnancy and the birthing process also merit scrutiny. Each and every one of these subjects must be incorporated into an analysis of laws on human reproduction because they correspond with significant points in the process of procreation and they provide a sufficiently wide inquiry to illustrate the special pattern of legal regulation which emerges concerning women and human reproduction.

A comprehensive and contextual review of past and present legal controls suggests that most laws which address human reproduction are not directed primarily towards women's reproductive health. Whether the proffered justification for legal controls is public morality, population control or the sanctity of human life, the reality is that women are effectively controlled in the name of regulating reproduction.

An examination of the real life situation of women and an appreciation of how these various laws combine and compound and impact on women's lives illustrate how fundamental legal protections have been withheld from women in the reproductive context. Because women experience these legal limitations cumulatively, these controls must be studied together, as they really exist and how they truly operate; otherwise, the extent and impact of legal controls on women's sexual and procreative lives may be grossly underestimated. To study laws on any one of these issues in abstract isolation is to run the strong risk of skewing the analysis. A particular provision studied alone may be dismissed as aberrant or more easily justified as somehow necessary in a named or unspecified "public" interest if it is abstracted out of its historical social and legal context. The challenge is therefore, to uncover and understand the social context and actual circumstances in which women have sex, become pregnant, seek abortions, or give birth.

A comprehensive and contextual analysis suggests that many legal controls on human reproduction can only be understood if they are approached as political statements in a fundamental arena of gender conflict. If we acknowledge that historically men and women have competed for the control of women's bodies, the concept of competition conveys that there are divided interests and winners and losers. Men have often used their ability to make laws to protect their appropriated interest in women's reproductive potential. Sometimes the real story is about men controlling women in an attempt to expropriate women's sexual and reproductive labour.[2] Laws have been used to construct women's inequality and condone a social structure in which pregnancy and motherhood are not mere potentials for women – they have often become their divine duty, their imputed natural state and their highest and best use.[3] Women's biological *capacity* has been and continues to be redefined and experienced as a limitation and women's lives continue to be circumscribed by a narrow view of their biological destiny.

If gender conflict over human reproduction is acknowledged one can better appreciate that there is no disinterested, objective or universal perspective on these complex issues and that men are just as politically interested in maintaining the status quo of male privilege as women are in changing it. One uncovers that not only have male interests been protected and packaged as law, men have also simultaneously denied that their self selection is a political choice. Realizing that there is a power struggle between women and men also explains why "allowing" women to assert rights to physical inviolability so threatens many men and many of the patriarchical social orders they have created. A woman writing in 1855 conveys the long-standing urgency of reproductive control for women, "It is very little to me to have the right to vote, to own property, etc., if I may not keep my body, and its uses, in my absolute right."[4] The sustained resistance to women's claims for reproductive control underscores the constancy and centrality of this gender struggle and explains why most women see the ability to control their bodies and regulate their fertility as a core entitlement, among the most fundamental of rights.[5]

[2] See generally M. O'Brien, *The Politics of Reproduction* (1981); R. Petchesky, *Abortion and Woman's Choice* (1984); Clark and Lewis, *Rape: The Price of Coercive Sexuality* (1977).

[3] For a general review of the role of law see C. A. MacKinnon, *Toward a Feminist Theory of the State* (1989); S. Gavigan, 'Law, Gender and Ideology' in A. Bayefsky (ed.) *Legal Theory Meets Legal Practice* (1988) pp. 283–295; K. O'Donovan, *Sexual Divisions in Law* (1985); S. McLean and N. Burrows (eds.) *The Legal Relevance of Gender* (1988); J. Rifkin, 'Toward a Theory of Law and Patriarchy', (1980) 3 Harvard W.L.J. pp. 83–95; D. Polan, "Toward a Theory of Law and Patriarchy", in D. Kairys (ed.) *The Politics of Law* (1982), pp. 294–303.

[4] Lucy Stone in a letter to Antoinette Brown, 1855.

[5] For perspectives on abortion which are sympathetic to the needs and experience of women, see R. P. Petchesky, *Abortion and Woman's Choice* (1984); W. W. Watters, *Compulsory Parenthood: The Truth About Abortion* (1976); K. McDonnell, *Not an Easy Choice* (1984); A. Collins, *The Big Evasion: Abortion, the Issue That Won't Go Away* (1985).

3. LAWS ON HUMAN REPRODUCTION

This section addresses the various subjects which should form part of a comprehensive and contextual approach to legal controls on human reproduction. It includes a discussion of laws on sexual assault and the marital rape exemption, contraception, abortion, and pregnancy and birth.

(1) Laws on Sexual Assault and the Marital Rape Exemption

There are many reasons why the legal treatment of sexual assault, especially any form of marital rape exemption, must be studied when considering laws on human reproduction. First, any right not to be forced to procreate must necessarily include the right to be free from unwanted sexual invasions. For many women, true sexual liberation means the freedom to say no to sex. Second, even though laws against rape and sexual assault may not adequately protect women, they at least remind us that women do not always control the circumstances in which they engage in intercourse and become pregnant. Sexual intercourse and pregnancy must therefore be understood as part of a sequential process which occurs within a social context of inequality.

Third, a marital rape exemption is a blatant example of how the law can be used to protect predominantly male interests.[6] By granting statutory immunity to sexually coercive husbands, Canadian law expressly supported the expropriation of women's sexual and reproductive services, the exemption gave a legal basis to men's assertion of control over women's sexual and reproductive labor.[7] It allowed men to control the bodily integrity of their wives and substituted male desire for women's decision making autonomy. The marital rape exemption operated directly on women's lives by making a wife's experience of nonconsensual intercourse a legal impossibility. By giving husbands these rights over wives, it also operated symbolically to establish a legally sanctioned norm of gender hierarchy for all men and women. It reinforced and fuelled gender stereotypes and illustrated how easily women could be excluded from even the most basic legal guarantees of physical integrity. Through the legally constructed fiction of deemed consent, the sexual violation of wives was made invisible and the wife was deprived of fundamental

[6] See generally M.D.A. Freeman, 'But If You Can't Rape Your Wife, Who(m) Can You Rape: The Marital Rape Exemption Re-Examined' (1981) 15 Fam. L.Q. pp. 1–29; R. Hall, S. James & J. Kertez, *The Rapist Who Pays the Rent* (1984); C. Boyle, 'Married Women Beyond the Pale of the Law of Rape' (1981) 1 Windsor Yearbook of Access to Justice pp. 192–213; G. Geis, 'Rape in Marriage: Law & Law Reform in England, the United States & Sweden' (1978) 6 Adelaide L. Rev. pp. 284–303; D.E.H. Russell, *Rape in Marriage* (1983); D. Finkelhor & K. Yllo; *License to Rape: Sexual Abuse of Wives* (1985).

[7] *The Criminal Code*, R.S.C. 1970, c. C-34, s. 143 defined rape as nonconsensual sexual intercourse "with a female person who is not his wife".

freedoms in the name of the marriage contract.[8] The harms, violence, and physical invasion involved in marital rape were denied on the tenuous basis of imputed agreement. Sex was defined as the wife's self-imposed duty and the law condoned the violation in circumstances where women did not. The same gender-based power imbalance encapsulated in relation to wife rape is reiterated in laws on contraception, abortion and pregnant women.

(2) Contraception

The legal regulation of contraceptives is an important element in a study of laws on human reproduction and it illustrates how even a gender neutral formulation cannot conceal a gender-specific reality. Although most provisions concerning contraceptives appear to apply with equal force to members of both sexes, it is clear that restrictions on the availability of contraceptives disproportionately affect women. As the group which physically reproduces the species, women have always had a special and immediate interest in controlling their fertility and taking steps to counter conception. Even though contraceptives can be employed by either sex, it is generally women who take 'precautions' and are seen to have the primary responsibility, because it is always and ultimately women who pay the price for contraceptive failure. Women take the pill, go under the knife, live with the I.U.D., insert the foam and cross the border to find some technology which may be denied them in their own country. In each case, women's health and physical security is at stake and women's autonomy is in issue. Women must therefore be the focus of such an inquiry because women are members of the group which experience pregnancy, carry the burden of the onset of parenthood and fulfil the socially created and exacting role of motherhood.

In Canada, until 1969, there was a criminal prohibition which outlawed the sale and advertisement of contraceptives[9]. The state was prepared to use its most powerful regulatory weapon, its criminal law power, in an attempt to restrict women's ability to manipulate their fertility. The introduction of a criminal prohibition was supposed to protect the public from sexual immorality and promiscuity[10]. The Canadian government realized that it probably could

[8] The marital rape doctrine was justified in many common law countries on the unsubstantiated claim by Lord Hale in his 1736 *History of the Pleas of the Crown*, Vol. 1 (1971) at 629: "But the husband cannot be guilty of a rape committed by himself upon his lawful wife, for by their mutual matrimonial consent and contract the wife hath given herself in this kind unto her husband, which she cannot retract."

[9] The Criminal Code, 1892, (Can.), 55 & 56 Vict., c. 29 s. 179(1)(c) made it an offence to offer to sell, advertise, publish an advertisement or have for sale or disposal any medicine, drug or article intended or represented as a means of preventing conception or causing abortion.

[10] See generally A. McLaren & A.T. McLaren, *The Bedroom & the State: The Changing Practices & Politics of Contraception and Abortion in Canada 1880–1980* (1986); L. Gordon, *Woman's Body, Woman's Rights: A Social History of Birth Control in America* (1976); J.R. Reid, *From Private Vice to Public Virtue: The Birth Control Movement and American Society since 1830* (1978).

not effectively police what happened in the bedrooms of the nation, but it tried to limit what contraceptive devices could be purchased and what contraceptive information could be commercially communicated. This criminal prohibition had profound consequences for how women experienced and expressed their sexuality and lived their daily lives. The criminal law treatment of contraceptives also played a symbolic role. It sent the clear message that there was a perceived danger to 'society' if women were free to control their own fertility, such that the stigma associated with criminal conduct attached to the whole topic of birth control for many years.

The fact that legal controls on contraceptives either targeted women or disparately affected them was largely absent from the analysis or lost in the debate, until recently. If women were visible at all, they were often perceived as a threat to the social fabric. The fear of a female sexuality not restrained by the natural coercion of unwanted pregnancy or not tethered to one man through marriage, often lay at the foundation of repressive state policies on available contraceptive information. Even the repeal of the Canadian Criminal Code prohibition was justified on the basis that a "married couple" should have the right to control the timing and spacing of their family[11]. It is interesting to note how the woman was seen only as an aspect of something else, of something deemed to be larger and more important than either herself or the group to which she belonged. Rather than being treated as a fully capacitated member of an equal group, she became a mere part of the protected and valued family unit. The emphasis on a collective, shared and marital responsibility may mask the woman's own individual autonomy and physical integrity. Locating decision making on contraceptive use within a unit like the family, a primary site of patriarchal relations, may also make private and individualize the oppression of women. It is only when the story becomes about women and women as a group that patterns of subordination can be uncovered. In this way, the criminal prohibition on contraceptives shows just how fully women did not control the social circumstances in which they became pregnant. Women, both individually and as a group, suffered the burdens of contraceptive failure even though they did not determine the sexual, reproductive or contraceptive conditions of their lives. Women were burdened with responsibility, without the benefit of power and were made to experience the consequences, without exerting the control.

(3) Abortion

Most legal controls on abortion evidence an underlying and deep-seated belief that pregnancy is a women's natural state and primary destiny. The "naturalness" of pregnancy is exaggerated to divert attention from the fact that it is man-made laws which mandate that an unwanted pregnancy will evolve into involuntary motherhood[12]. The emphasis is strategically placed on what is

[11] See *Health & Welfare Committee Hearings* (November 18, 1966).

[12] See generally J. Mohr, *Abortion in America* (1978).

constructed as a biological imperative: that pregnancy must lead to birth for the universe to unfold as it should. Within this ideological framework a woman who wants to terminate a pregnancy is defined and treated as exceptional. Her actions are often classified as selfish, against nature and so contrary to imposed social norms that pregnancy termination must be justified before it can be permitted.[13]

Whatever else is wrong with this assumption, and there is plenty, its effect is to place women who need abortions on the defensive. It requires women to explain why they should be able to assert bodily integrity rather than placing the burden of justification on those who seek to restrict their rights and impose continued pregnancy. By calling for an explanation it establishes a hierarchy, one which implies that someone else both can and should supervise women's procreative decisions. In short, it places the pregnant woman in the position of a suppliant rather than a rights bearer. In different parts of the world women are forced to tailor their life situation to imposed norms which outline when they are allowed to have abortions[14]. Individual decision making is undermined when women are required to prove to a third person that they are sick enough or sufficiently crazed to qualify for an abortion.

Not only are women made to explain why they need abortions, they are required to do so in an overall context of inequality. How abortion is regulated by law is therefore another example of how women are made to take responsibility for matters they do not always or ultimately control. For example, laws on sexual assault show how women do not always control the circumstances in which they engage in sex and laws on contraceptives explain how women do not control accessibility to safe and effective contraceptive devices. As we proceed along the biological and social continuum of human reproduction we see that women also do not control access to abortion. The extent of women's loss of control becomes apparent when one realizes that even women who find themselves pregnant as the result of sexual violence or failed contraception are also called upon to justify why "nature" should be interrupted by abortion.

The social reality is that people engage in sex and contraceptive devices are unavailable or fail. There will, therefore, be many women who will be victimized by an accidental and unintended pregnancy. These women should not be treated as morally blameworthy. A woman "caught" by an unwanted pregnancy should not be required to submit to some form of third party review over her decision to terminate it. If accidental pregnancies are seen as statistically inevitable, abortion is better viewed as a need, something basic like food, rather than something volitional and discretionary.

Abortion will also remain a particularly acute need as long as men forcibly

[13] See R. Cook & B. Dickens, *Abortion Laws in Commonwealth Countries* (1979).

[14] R. Cook & B. Dickens, 'A Decade of International Change in Abortion Laws', A.J.P.H., July 1978, Vol. 68, No. 7, p. 637. See also J.L. Jacobson, *The Global Politics of Abortion* (1990). See generally F. Colin, *Abortion Freedom: A Worldwide Movement* (1984).

impregnate women, as long as women do not control the circumstances in which they become pregnant and as long as mothers live in a social situation of relative disadvantage[15]. Thus, any gender inclusive legal norm must take into account that abortions are required and are performed in a context of women's cumulative inequality. The act of abortion cannot be separated from the social conditions in which impregnation occurs and pregnancy is experienced. Legal controls on abortion should only be analysed after considering matters like sexual aggression, inadequate or unavailable contraception, special legal controls on the conduct of pregnant women, and the patchwork of provisions which deal with related matters such as maternity leaves, pregnancy discrimination and childcare. In my view, women should not be abandoned to their constructed natural biology and their legal rights should not be subordinated because some people endorse or benefit from involuntary motherhood.

A women-centered perspective on abortion would downplay the view of pregnancy as an objective statement of biological fact and replace it with a view which recognizes that pregnancy is a process which derives its meaning from the pregnant woman who experiences it. If pregnancy is seen as a process, its continuing, sequential and ongoing aspects are highlighted. Such a viewpoint conveys that just because a woman is pregnant today does not make it inevitable that she will be pregnant either tomorrow or for nine months. If pregnancy is seen as a process, abortion may be easier to understand or justify because it may appear to take less to interrupt a process than reverse a fact. When pregnancy is seen as a process there may not be the same attenuated cause/effect relationship under which consent to sex becomes deemed consent to pregnancy. A separate act of autonomy should be required to confer the continuing pregnancy with the consensualism it requires to prevent it from being experienced as a violation. Pregnancy would derive its meaning from the women's ongoing consent to maintaining that state. Although there are many problems with any consent-based model when it operates under conditions of social inequality, at least conceptualizing pregnancy as a process focuses attention on the post-pregnancy phase and the key issue becomes whether or not the woman will remain pregnant, and not whether or not she is pregnant.

An experiential and process-based approach to pregnancy would also suggest a legal paradigm in which the legal value to be conferred on fetal life would be determined by the woman who sustains it. The woman's response to her pregnancy would become the defining legal characteristic. Her experience of her pregnancy could not be ignored and women, not doctors or legislators, would become the only legitimate decision makers. An experiential standard would mean that the determination would be made on a case by case basis by the party most intimately involved, instead of allowing the dilemma of an

[15] See C.A. MacKinnon, *Feminism Unmodified* (1987), p. 93.

unwanted pregnancy to be objectified and decided in the abstract by third parties.[16]

(4) Legal Controls on Pregnant Women

Legal controls on women's reproductive lives do not end when a woman decides to carry her fetus to term. Recently in Canada and the United States there have been alarming attempts to dictate how pregnant women conduct their pregnancies and deliver their children. A new arena of gender-based struggle has emerged as pro fetal activists seek many profound limitations on the activities of pregnant women. These attempts to regulate the conduct of women who carry their fetuses to term constitute the most recent assertion of a governmental interest in human reproduction which burdens women's bodies and curtails women's rights.

The proposals to increase the supervision of pregnant women contained in some Canadian and American legal literature are nothing short of frightening.[17] The number, nature and magnitude of suggested interventions illustrates how far certain people are prepared to go to promote their view of fetal health and suggests how easily the fundamental rights of women are subordinated, or even ignored, in reproduction related matters. The dominant theoretical paradigm relied upon to support these wide ranging restrictions on pregnant women is to redefine certain forms of the woman's conduct as giving rise to a "maternal/fetal conflict". It is then suggested that the noted conflict can only be resolved by recognizing "fetal rights" and creating new legal

[16] In *Morgentaler, Smoling et al. v. The Queen*, [1988] 1 S.C.R. 30 at 171 Madame Justice Wilson explained why a woman's decision to terminate a pregnancy merits constitutional protection. She stated:

> It is probably impossible for a man to respond, even imaginatively, to such a dilemma not just because it is outside the realm of his personal experience (although this is, of course, the case) but because he can relate to it only by objectifying it, thereby eliminating the subjective elements of the female psyche which are at the heart of the dilemma.

She also stated:

> This decision is one that will have profound psychological, economic and social consequences for the pregnant woman. The circumstances giving rise to it can be complex and varied and there may be, and usually are, powerful considerations militating in opposite directions. It is a decision that deeply reflects the way the woman thinks about herself and her relationship to others and to society at large. It is not just a medical decision; it is a profound social and ethical one as well. Her response to it will be the response of the whole person.

[17] For a review of Canadian and American authors who seek various forms of criminal liability see J.A. Robertson, 'Procreative Liberty and the Control of Conception, Pregnancy and Childbirth' (1983) 69 Virg. L. Rev. pp. 405–464; 'The Right to Procreate and In Utero Fetal Therapy' (1982) 3 J. Legal Med. 333; 'Fetal Abuse' (1989) 75 A.B.A. Journal 38; J.E.B. Myers, 'Abuse and Neglect of the Unborn: Can the State Intervene?' (1984) 23 Duq. L.R. 1; E.W. Keyserlingk, *The Unborn Child's Right to Prenatal Care* (1984) Montreal: Quebec Research Center for Private and Comparative Law; Law Reform Commission of Canada, *Crimes Against the Foetus* Working Paper 58 (Ottawa: L.R.C., 1989). For a synopsis of the case against criminalization see: Note, 'Maternal Rights and Fetal Wrongs: The Case Against the Criminalization of Fetal Abuse' (1988) 101 Harv. L. Rev. pp. 994–1012.

responsibilities for pregnant women. This paradigm has significant implications for all pregnancy related issues and the legislative proposals derived under it would impact upon almost every aspect of a pregnant woman's life.

Suggested legal controls on how women manage their pregnancies include the creation of new criminal penalties and tort liabilities for women's conduct which may harm the fetuses they carry[18]; the introduction or use of child protection powers to apprehend a fetus thought to be in need of protection, both after birth and while *in utero*[19]; and the forced medical treatment of the pregnant woman for the sake of the fetus, even over her express objections and including such dramatic and physically violent interventions as mandatory caesarean sections[20]. It has been suggested that state intervention could take many forms: crime, compensation, compulsion, prior restraint, restriction and limitation. New laws would involve post-birth sanctions and pre-birth seizures, span the entire biological process of pro-creation from sexual intercourse through birth and be justified on the basis of the state's police power and its jurisdiction *parens patiae*.

Legal prescriptions intended to dictate the conduct of pregnant women postulate and once again exaggerate the danger to "society" which would result if pregnant women were the legally empowered caretakers of the fetuses they carry. Although women are obliged to be the literal and legal "keepers" of their fetuses, and women are the primary caretakers and nurturers of children, they are often prevented, sometimes forcibly, from exercising their rights to control their own body and determine their course of medical treatment. Certain forms of legal controls effectively deny that women remain fully capacitated legal persons and morally responsible decision makers throughout their pregnancies. Whether the lexicon is that of "fetal rights" or "doctor knows best", it is clear that pregnant women are often placed in a separate category where their rights are frequently denied. Many types of regulation also ignore biological reality and intentionally obfuscate the fetus' complete dependence on the pregnant woman by presenting the fetus as a distinct entity, a separate patient and an independent legal person invested with and capable of enjoying and exercising competing rights.

[18] J.A. Robertson, 'Toward Rational Boundaries of Tort Liability for Injury to the Unborn: Prenatal Injuries, Preconception Injuries and Wrongful Life' (1978) Duke L.J. pp. 1401–1457; J.E.B. Meyers, 'Abuse and Neglect of the Unborn: Can the State Intervene?' (1984) 23 Duq. L.R. 1; R. Beal, 'Can I Sue Mommy? An Analysis of a Woman's Tort Liability for Prenatal Injuries to her Child Born Alive' (1983–84) 21 San Diego L. Rev. pp. 325–370.

[19] For a review of the cases in Canada see S.A. Tateishi, 'Apprehending the Fetus en ventre Sa Mère: A Study in Judicial Slight of Hand' (1989) 53 Sask. L. Rev. pp. 113–141; I. Grant, 'Forced Obstetrical Intervention: A Charter Analysis' (1989) 39 U.T.L.J. pp. 217–257.

[20] For a good argument against this emerging practice see J. Gallagher, 'Prenatal Invasions and Interventions: What's Wrong With Fetal Rights' [1987] 10 Harv. W.L.J. pp. 9–58; Rhoden, N., 'The Judge in the Delivery Room: the Emergence of Court-Ordered Caesareans' (1986) 74 Cal. L. Rev. pp. 1951–2030; D. Johnsen, 'A New Threat to Pregnant Women's Autonomy' (1987) Hasting Center Report 33.

At this time in Canada the myriad forms of direct intervention into pregnancy which have been attempted have been largely unsuccessful. Even though the number of cases where prenatal invasions have been legally sanctioned may appear small, the threat they pose to women is real, existing and systemic. The issues raised by legal interventions into pregnancy are extremely important and have ominous and far-reaching consequences for all women.

4. Gender Bias in Legal Norms

Laws on human reproduction discussed in the previous sections raise serious questions about the extent to which women have been excluded from the principles of freedom and equality believed to be fundamental in our free and democratic society. The justifications offered to support these pervasive legal restrictions on women's sexual and reproductive conduct are not convincing and are often advanced as a "state" interest to diffuse attention away from the fact that men are attempting to control women's bodies. For example, although the marital rape exemption is the classic illustration of male privilege packaged as law, it was said to be necessary to promote spousal harmony and marital privacy. Prohibitions on the sale and advertisement of contraceptives were intended to protect family life. Abortion was prohibited to show respect for human life and to protect the state's interest in the birthrate. Legal controls on pregnant women are said to promote good medicine and prevent fetal death or abnormalities.

These legal controls conflict with generally accepted principles because women are not treated as individuals, they are not free to choose between alternatives, nor to act as autonomous moral agents empowered to plan for their view of the good life. These laws are too numerous and similar to be dismissed as isolated exceptions which do not threaten the basic principles themselves. These limitations on women's reproductive conduct are also so invasive that it is difficult to justify them on the basis of some supposedly higher order principle or to attribute them to women's biological capacity. This type of deprivation is so profound and the incidence of its occurrence is so prevalent that the better question is to inquire whether principles of so called human rights are really only reserved for men.

Many of the reasons given for the disadvantageous legal treatment of women have centered on the biological differences between men and women[21]. Women's unique physical capacity to gestate, bear and breastfeed babies has been used as the pretence for special regulation, and submitted as the proof of women's inferiority. Sometimes the sexism takes the form of confusing the naturally mandated with the socially constructed. The obfuscation of nature and nurture takes many forms and, even when it is not intentional, it is certainly

[21] See generally C.A. MacKinnon, 'Difference and Dominance: On Sex Discrimination' in *Feminism Unmodified* (1987), p. 32; C. Smart, *Feminism and the Power of Law* (1989).

ideologically convenient for men. Attributing difference and disadvantage to the natural order means that, short of technological intervention, women remain powerless to change it. It places those who call for change in the role of those who rail against nature, as unaccepting, bitter, slightly crazy and not to be taken seriously.

Other times sexism takes the form of penalizing women for the ways in which they are physically and socially different from men. The biological duality of male/female becomes a hierarchy of difference where what is male is more highly valued. In our society, biological differences do not exist in an atmosphere of mutual acceptance and accommodation. We live within an ordering of values where being different generally means having less than those who establish the standard. Men, especially white, middle class, able bodied men, have operated as the dominant class with the power to name, define, ascribe or deny value. To men in positions of power, women physically represent "the other". The issue has been defined as the ordering of women's real and constructed differences *from* men rather than starting from a premise of equality such that biological diversity, symmetry, and accommodation would replace gender hierarchy. Instead of using women's "different" procreative potential as a reason why the law may deny fundamental protections or impose additional burdens, an egalitarian response to the "naturalness" of pregnancy would be to empower women with expansive and strong rights not to procreate. To the extent equality is about redressing disadvantage, it should not matter that the exploitation of women has been based in part on their biological capacities. When the focus is on the social context of biological difference, it becomes impossible to justify legally sanctioned examples of gender bias on the basis of natural diversity.

5. Conclusion

What unfolds after a review of legal controls on human reproduction is a lengthy history of pervasive and invasive state intervention which effectively defined, devalued, and exploited women. In Canada, these laws operated on women directly by restricting their life choices and indirectly as a symbolic statement that women were not equally valued. A contextual analysis of these laws, seen over time, illustrates how many laws on human reproduction and much of our legal doctrine accepted, validated and perpetuated the socially constructed incidents of difference as the reason why women could be excluded from the enjoyment of basic legal protections and privileges. Although it is women, both individually and as a class, who have been and continue to be the primary targets of legal controls on human reproduction, women's needs and perspective have rarely been incorporated at the center of legal norms and have barely been acknowledged at the periphery. For the most part, the law has been used to protect and promote the appropriated interest men have traditionally asserted over women's sexual and reproductive labour. Many ideological devices have been invoked in an attempt to justify women's imposed disadvantage, and to distract attention away from the privileges these laws confer on men and the burdens they create for women. The exclusion of women, because they were women, was one of the primary ways in which gender bias was made manifest, but gender bias has also taken many indirect and subtle forms.

In most societies women are not in the laboratories or legislatures in sufficient numbers to ensure that women's perspective is acknowledged and women's rights respected. It is frightening that most scientists and lawmakers who control the conditions of human reproduction will never menstruate, be pregnant, give birth or experience menopause. Men have been making laws for women where the role of pregnancy and the proper position of women is defined from the distanced perspective of "the other". It has been a history of one group imposing role expectations and legal obligations in circumstances in which there is no chance they will ever be called upon to personally bear the burdens they create. It is a distressing instance of objectification and it has promoted a special form of tyranny. A recognition of women as full rights bearers, especially within the reproductive context, will be an important step in overcoming this entrenched and prevalent form of sex discrimination.

SECTION VI

Achieving Human Rights Goals

SECTION VI(a): IMPROVING PRESENT STRUCTURES

THOMAS McCARTHY*

Introduction

This section addresses the issues of prevention of human rights violations. All the authors agree that a good basis to proceed in the twenty-first century toward avoiding conflicts is by strengthening respect for human rights. Not all agree, however on the best specific methodology to employ to protect them within existing structures. One thing we have learned in the United Nations is that it is really on the national level that all your efforts have to be focused. In order to strengthen, and make a human rights culture on the national level, international effort is important. The United Nations has a very elaborate and relatively effective system of dealing with human rights violations. Mr. Martenson's paper describes that system. We have to think of some other methods as well. For example, Theo van Boven argues that prevention is the best model of dispute resolution. He sets out a number of preventative strategies which could be developed to avoid the occurrence of gross violations of human rights. He presents the argument from three different perspectives – that of international structures; actions; and international law and standards.

Changes to unjust social and economic structures will help to prevent human rights violations but he believes these alone are not enough. Fact-finding, anticipatory diplomacy and early warning systems are essential to prevent critical situations from reaching catastrophic proportions. He argues that international law and standards must address preventative measures as well as situations and potential situations of civil strife and that preventative action and preventative policies should have a central place in supervision procedures involving the accountability of governments.

Practical assistance to governments or to people not connected to governments in order to strengthen a human rights culture, is another essential methodolgy. One important method stressed here is the strengthening of human rights defenders on the national level. We have to find ways in the international community to protect them, to strengthen them and to help them because they are sort of the antibodies, the social body which will give us warning of impending diseases. Aryeh Neier discusses remedial strategies in the

* Senior Advisor to the Director General of the U.N. at Geneva.

K.E. Mahoney and P. Mahoney (eds.), Human Rights in the Twenty-first Century, 921–923.

context of military conflicts. He says that trying to provide a remedial strategy in the catastrophic circumstances of even one of these conflicts taxes the capacity of the entire world community, yet there are more than 30 such conflicts going on at the present time. He says the capacity of existing human rights institutions are taxed to the limit and cannot do more than they are presently doing. He says if the framework of human rights is broadened, as some papers in this volume suggest, the human rights structure may collapse under it entirely. At the very least, new institutions must be formed and new resources applied to them if the call to broaden the framework of human rights is heeded. Mr. Neier also discusses the basic human rights strategy of accountability, where it has been applied and what results have been achieved.

The United Nations has very recently discovered the important role that human rights has in resolving existing conflicts. One example was in Namibia, where the United Nations played a big role in ensuring that a wide range of human rights were respected in connection with the elections legislation. Similarly in Nicaragua, the international community had a great element of respect for human rights in its efforts to resolve those conflicts. The United Nations agenda now has conflict resolution exercises in Cambodia, El Salvador and Western Sahara. In each one of those you will find a large chapter based on the respect for human rights as an integral element in achieving a peaceful solution.

Secondly, the role that existing U.N. human rights mechanisms, committees, special rapporteurs, and the Secretary-General can play in resolving not the conflict itself but those elements of the conflict that have human rights implications, must be discussed.

There are many ways these roles can play out. For example, the preventative approach can be taken by dealing with the electoral process. We have been involved in helping governments draft electoral laws in such a way that there was no cause for confrontation over the terms of the election, or the way the election was taking place. Election observance, another U.N. function, has the same effect. Recently, the Secretary-General sent a mission to South Africa to deal with the changing situation. It was quite interesting to observe the perceptible effect the mission had on the dialogue between people involved in the situation. Some people who had been frozen in a confrontation mentality after discussing possible internal dialogue options with the Secretary-General's team began to accept the need to at least talk with other people about how to deal with their situation. I was in one meeting in which for two hours through questionings, a clear evolution in thinking of the leaders of one group took place. At one point they asked for a ten minute break. After about 15 minutes they came in and you could see that just the exercise of dialoguing with impartial individuals helped them come to positions where they could advance their search for a resolution to the conflict. I think there may be some ways that the United Nations can help in that.

Other mechanisms need to be explored too, including existing mechanisms which are never used, that is, international human rights treaties procedures for interstate complaints. If a conflict gets to the level of a dispute between states, the United Nations, at least theoretically, could engage in some sort of conciliatory move. The basic challenge is to depoliticize the conflict. If people agreed that resorting to the treaty mechanisms was a non-political act then it may be possible to use them. If however, it was seen as another step in their political confrontation it would be quite dangerous because it could lead to the potential poisoning of all United Nations Human Rights systems. So that is something that we will have to think about in the future.

JAN MARTENSON*

The United Nations and Human Rights Today and Tomorrow

1. Introduction

Forty-five years ago the international community embarked on a new adventure of promoting human dignity for every person on earth through concerted international action. The impetus for this direction was provided by the Charter of the United Nations. It may well be that human rights is one of the areas in which international law has made the most far-reaching progress.

While in human rights one must never be complacent but rather strive for greater progress, we must recognize as did the Secretary-General, in his 1990 report on the work of the United Nations that the "past year has seen the conversion of human rights from a subsidiary theme of international discourse to a dominant concern". In this coming of age of human rights, one important element has been our improved understanding of the place of human rights in today's conceptual framework of international affairs. Of the interrelationship between the three principal objectives of the United Nations the Secretary-General in his report said "resolution of conflicts, observance of human rights, and the promotion of development together weave the fabric of peace; if one of these strands is removed, the tissue will unravel".

The central role of respect for human rights to success in the peace-making and peace-keeping operations of the United Nations is also clearly reflected in the aforementioned report. It recognizes that what distinguishes the handling of a dispute by the United Nations is that full expression of all relevant interests and viewpoints be permitted. The United Nations does not seek to abridge any vital aspect of a situation, including that of justice and human rights. The future challenges to national and international security also have a distinct human rights component and in our approach to them, in the words of the Secretary-General, "the principles of international ethics and human rights articulated by the Charter still hold". One of the significant threats to the stability of nation-states and thus, to international security, lies in lack of respect for human rights.

* United Nations Under-Secretary-General for Human Rights.

K.E. Mahoney and P. Mahoney (eds.), Human Rights in the Twenty-first Century, 925–936.

At the same time, the relationship between economic and social development and human rights has become increasingly clear. As the Secretary-General also noted, "the dysfunctions in the international economy are also reflected at the national level where parallel societies are growing apart, one rich and privileged and the other poor and dispossessed". He drew attention to the very serious consequences such developments have in both developing and industrialized societies.

Human rights must also be an important element in economic development. We must underline the need to measure it but not just in monetary terms. It must be measured by improvements in human lives. National economic development policy must ensure that economic and social progress are shared by all. The 1986 Declaration on the Right to Development laid a basis for the integration of human rights concepts into the planning, execution and evaluation of development projects so that respect for human rights and the effectiveness of these projects are both strengthened and secured. Concern for respect for human rights in the development process and the contribution human rights can make to successful development was reflected in the General Assembly's resolution adopted at its special session on international economic development (May 1990) in the Programme of Action adopted by the Second United Nations Conference on Least Developed Countries at Paris (September 1990), and in the International Development Strategy for the Fourth United Nations Development Decade.

On the national level, we have come to see democracy and development as closely linked. The Secretary-General in his statement to the November 1990 Paris Summit of the Conference on Security and Co-operation in Europe stated, "while democracy is a necessary condition for the recognition of basic human rights, it is not in itself sufficient to ensure the actual enjoyment of those rights. Indeed, genuine political democracy has little chance to survive, and stability is bound to prove elusive, without social justice. Such justice, to be consolidated, needs the help of those who can rightly encourage it, though too often, they abandon it just after it has been brought about".

The international community, in setting standards for human rights, must recognize its obligation to assist in creating conditions within which these standards can be fulfilled. With direct relevance to this, article 28 of the Universal Declaration reads:

> "Everyone is entitled to a social and international order in which the rights and freedoms set forth in this Declaration can be fully realized".

In creating those conditions we must remember the universality of human rights: every person has the right to the full enjoyment of human rights be it the right to life, to adequate food and shelter or the right to take part in government and the right to be free from torture irrespective of where that person lives or the particular history of his or her country; there are no second class citizens for human rights, and no people should be made to sit in the back of the human rights bus.

2. THE STATUS OF HUMAN RIGHTS IN TODAY'S WORLD

The reality of the human rights situation in the world today is a picture of stark contrast; on the one hand, undeniable progress and on the other, the painful reality of widespread violations. Over the last few years amazing changes have taken place in many parts of the world. In Eastern and Central Europe, Latin America and Asia, democratic movements have enabled the people to regain control of their own destinies. Namibia is now an independent Member State of our Organization. We also have reason to believe that a new South Africa will, in spite of difficulties and setbacks, become a reality in the near future. As the Secretary-General said in June 1991, "the process which has begun in South Africa will be difficult and complex. A number of obstacles remain to be overcome, of which intercommunal violence and the release of all political prisoners are but two examples".

It is a matter of deepest concern that while international tensions have eased there appears to be a resurgence of expressions of racial hatred, intolerance and discrimination. Renewed appeals have been addressed to the United Nations regarding the plight of indigenous peoples and attention has been focused on such vulnerable groups as migrant workers. Each day brings its report of torture – some practised in a widespread and institutionalized manner – of killings and arbitrary or summary executions of people who disappear, of the violent suppression of dissent, of the firing on unarmed demonstrations and of discrimination and deprivation. The basic necessities of life as described in the Universal Declaration are out of reach to many millions of our fellow human beings. We learn of denials of religious and cultural freedoms, foreign occupation and the use of mercenaries to attack the basic right of peoples to self-determination.

Last year our attention was focused on the "Rights of the Child". It has provided the occasion to learn more fully the plight of children in developed and developing countries. UNICEF has documented the death, disease, malnutrition and the lack of educational opportunities of millions of children and has pointed the way to affordable solutions.

Reports by the Centre for Human Rights paint a sombre picture of millions of children subjected to forced or bonded labour, to slavery or slave-like conditions, to prostitution, exposure to hazardous or debilitating working conditions, or who are separated from their parents to be sold. Children are forced into armed forces and are often the first to be killed in combat. They are subject to disappearances – cut off forever from their real families – and tortured and executed. Many children suffer, as do their parents, from apartheid, discrimination, foreign occupation or because they belong to minority groups, indigenous peoples, or are children of migrant workers. The fate of children trapped in extreme poverty is often worse than that of others; they are the most vulnerable of the vulnerable.

Faced with the gap between international human rights norms and the actual conditions of life of many of our fellow human beings we cannot but conclude that the challenge to the international community to promote and ensure respect for human rights is no less essential today than it was in 1945, nor is it any less relevant to the preservation of peace; rather to the contrary.

If in some areas of the world we have seen a lowering of international tension, a reduction in the sterile ideological confrontation of the past and of increased international co-operation, we must not forget that failure to ensure respect for human rights could well ignite renewed discord and conflict. Our objectives in the immediate future must be to see that respect for human rights everywhere forms an integral part of the cement of better international understanding and that violations do not become the sparks of future conflagrations.

3. Past, Present and Future: The United Nations and Its Human Rights Programmes

The United Nations human rights programme is carried out in an action-oriented, factual and objective manner and is founded conceptually upon the triangular relationship between legislation, implementation and information/education. This approach has served to guide us in determining the underlying priorities and will be pursued further as we endeavour to extract the maximum and most effective use of our finite and insufficient resources. We have also placed emphasis upon the third element mentioned, namely information/education, since the maxim "to know your rights, you must first be aware of them", remains undeniable. Accordingly, we have undertaken to highlight the importance of the Universal Declaration of Human Rights and to spread the human rights message throughout all regions and all communities. We are striving to be in a position to respond effectively and efficiently to the growing need for information coming from governments, groups and individuals in all Member States. We are now witnessing the undeniable relationship between a growing awareness and a growing number of ratifications, requests and action in this field.

To achieve our aims in the field of human rights as we approach the beginning of the next century, we must maintain and reinforce the existing international machinery for the protection of human rights. Our efforts in the field of public awareness and information must touch every corner of the globe to create a truly universal culture of human rights. Our programmes of technical assistance must be developed so that all countries have the opportunity of strengthening national laws and institutions. Of course, we must remain ever vigilant to violations of human rights and especially to the dangers of racism. The United Nations must further develop its capacity to identify human rights violations at an early stage and to act effectively to bring them to an end. We may also wish to explore ways in which governments can be encouraged – when necessary – to be more responsive to the requests, suggestions and recommendations of United Nations human rights bodies so that the activities of these bodies result in concrete and perceptible changes in the way people live.

With the Child Convention coming into force and the adoption of the Convention on the Rights of Migrant Workers and Their Families, the United Nations human rights programme will embark on the implementation of a new type of human rights instrument; that is, one which covers all or almost all the range of human rights focused on a particular group in the actual situation in which that group is found. This will present a major challenge to all concerned. The work done under the Convention on the Elimination of All Forms of Discrimination Against Women will be a valuable precedent.

Our organization has also recently recorded achievements with regard to particular human rights. Here we may refer to the adoption of the Second Optional Protocol aimed at the abolition of the death penalty which reinforces the cardinal principle of respect for the right to life.

Another important element for our future work will be to enlarge the participation of people in decisions affecting their lives. Over the last two or three years, democratic political institutions have been restored or established in a number of countries. Along with this, calls are being made to increase participation by the people of these countries in matters affecting their lives. Non-governmental organizations are instrumental in encouraging participation. We should explore ways of assisting people from regions where the development of such bodies has lagged behind. This may be achieved by establishing or strengthening non-governmental organizations where needed and by facilitating their participation in the United Nations human rights process.

The fight against racial discrimination and racism is at the very foundation of our organization's work in the field of human rights, and since the first session of the General Assembly the issue of discrimination has had high importance. The abhorrent system of apartheid, the most clearly institutionalized form of racism, has from the very beginning attracted the United Nations' attention.

The Charter itself insists upon "the equal rights of men and women and of nations large or small" and further urges respect for human rights "without distinction as to race, sex, language or religion". Indeed, the elimination of racism and racial discrimination is central to the achievement of today's objectives of the United Nations in preserving world peace and providing improved living standards. As everyone is aware, racial discrimination gives rise not only to internal tensions but also to conflicts between States which may escalate and endanger international stability. And within society, discrimination denies the full participation of all groups and all citizens in the economic, political and social processes and rights to which they are entitled.

The United Nations system has enacted a series of cardinal documents aimed at eliminating racism and apartheid. The international community, however, realized that the adoption of human rights instruments was not sufficient to eradicate racism and racial discrimination from the world-wide perspective.

Additional measures were needed. Thus, the General Assembly proclaimed 1973–1983 the United Nations Decade for Action to Combat Racism and Racial Discrimination and proclaimed 1983–1993 the "Second Decade to Combat Racism and Racial Discrimination". The basic objectives of the Second Decade have been:

- to promote human rights and fundamental freedoms for all, without distinction as to race, colour, descent or national or ethnic origin.
- to eliminate prejudice and racial discrimination.
- to abolish régimes and policies based on racism.

With these objectives in view, the Assembly approved a broad programme of activities for the entire period which is supplemented by detailed plans of action for the periods 1985–1989 and 1990–1993. The activities foreseen are numerous and varied. They include action against apartheid, education, teaching and training, dissemination of information, protection of minorities, migrant workers and indigenous populations, and implementing international conventions and action through national legislation, institutions and recourse procedures.

Under the Decade programme two seminars took place in 1989. One focused on the effects of racism on the social and economic relations between indigenous populations and states, and the other on cultural dialogue between countries of origin and the host countries of migrant workers. A further seminar took place in Geneva in December 1990 on the political, historical, economic, social and cultural factors contributing to racism, racial discrimination and apartheid.

One subject of particular concern for the future is finding ways of promoting the peaceful and constructive solution of problems involving minorities. For approximately ten years the Commission on Human Rights, through a specially established Working Group, has been preparing a draft declaration on the rights of persons belonging to national, ethnic, religious and linguistic minorities. At its 1990 and 1991 sessions, the Working Group completed the first reading of the draft declaration. The Commission and its Working Group will continue their consideration of the draft declaration during their next session in February and March 1992. Conflicts and tensions involving the rights and sensitivities of ethnic, religious, national, linguistic and other minorities can have a very destabilizing impact both nationally and internationally. Should efforts to identify ways of helping resolve these conflicts and tensions be successful, we may see long-term dividends in the avoidance of much struggle and conflict. Investments in this area today may well bring considerable peace dividends later.

Since the adoption of the Universal Declaration of Human Rights, the United Nations has put into place a true international code of human rights. The International Bill of Human Rights – the Universal Declaration of Human Rights, the two International Covenants and the Optional Protocol – forms the centrepiece of this code. Not only do we have a code of international standards protecting human rights, but we also have a system of committees of independent experts charged with critically examining State compliance with their international undertakings, encouraging improved respect for human rights and dealing with individual complaints.

Three other methods of implementing United Nations human rights norms have evolved over the years:

1. the consideration by the Commission on Human Rights through special rapporteurs or a working group of individual reports of particularly serious violations of human rights, such as arbitrary or summary executions, torture, disappearances, arbitrary detention and instances of intolerances based on religion or belief;
2. the study by the Commission and the General Assembly of the human rights situation in specific countries or territories; and
3. the consideration by the human rights organs of petitions from individuals and organizations which tend to show patterns of serious violations of human rights.

Under these procedures the United Nations sends numerous urgent action cables to governments in response to allegations of violations of the physical integrity of individuals.

The United Nations in its standard-setting and international implementation of human rights has certainly had a significant impact on the way people live throughout the world. National legislation norms in human rights have been raised for millions of people and the United Nations has helped place recourse procedures in their own hands, enabling them to protect their own human rights. United Nations interventions in particular cases have saved individual lives, prevented torture and resulted in the recovery of disappeared persons. Patterns of such violations have been curbed through the spotlight of United Nations attention and that same attention has contributed to the favourable evolution of situations in specific countries, including the restoration of democratic government.

Each one of these human rights procedures required the Centre for Human Rights to carry out a wide range of activities and it may be instructive to reflect a moment on what it takes in practical terms to keep the United Nations human rights programme in operation. With regard to the four expert committees serviced by the Centre for Human Rights, in 1990 it translated into 27 weeks of meetings (the equivalent of seven months), the preparation of some 100 State Party Reports, the preparation and analysis of the discussion of those reports and the preparation of four reports to the Assembly.

If we turn to the area of scrutiny of reports of disappearances, torture, or summary or arbitrary executions we find in 1990 that some 1,000 cases were transmitted by urgent cable to governments and many more cases were transmitted by letter. Several thousand communications were screened in connection with those cases, as were numerous replies from governments. Ten sessions of meetings were organized in connection with committees or groups dealing with theme or country specific situations and over 22 rounds of consultations by special rapporteurs were organized. Overall, some 23 specific mandates of groups, special rapporteurs or the Secretary-General were being serviced giving rise to 17 separate reports to the 1990 session of the Assembly and 21 reports to the 1991 session of the Commission on Human Rights. In preparing reports for these bodies, a total of 16 field missions to 19 countries were organized.

In 1990, the equivalent of 20 weeks of sessions were held by the Commission on Human Rights, the Sub-Commission on Prevention of Discrimination and Protection of Minorities and their subsidiary bodies or working groups. Reports prepared by the Secretariat or by special rapporteurs with the help of the Secretariat for these bodies – excluding the reports violations of human rights – totalled just under 100.

The handling of communications concerning alleged violations of human rights has in 1990 meant processing tens of thousands of communications under the well-known procedure governed by resolution 1503 of the Economic and Social Council. Another fast growing component in the human rights programme is the procedure for the examination of individual complaints under the Optional Protocol to the International Covenant on Civil and Political Rights. At present, 55 States have recognized the competence of the Human Rights Committee to engage in an in-depth examination of individual cases and several other States have publicly announced that they will become parties to the Optional Protocol in the near future. There is no doubt that the serious work done by the Committee under the Optional Protocol has already yielded an impressive body of jurisprudence in international human rights law. This is, indeed, a most important component in the ultimate United Nations goal to respond effectively to individual human rights concerns in all parts of the world.

Important though international standard-setting and implementation are, in the final analysis it is on the national and local levels that human rights are enjoyed. Thus, over the past few years there has been a marked expansion of human rights programmes aimed at fostering conditions on the national level propitious to the enjoyment of human rights.

The first requirement of effective national protection is widespread knowledge among the country's citizens of their basic human rights and the procedures available to ensure that they are respected. With this objective in mind, in 1988 the General Assembly launched the World Public Information Campaign for Human Rights to disseminate knowledge of human rights in easily accessible forms throughout the world. This was intended to foster a truly universal culture of human rights. Under this programme, a human rights newsletter is currently published four times a year bringing to a wide audience up-to-date information on human rights activities within the United Nations and the work of non-governmental organizations. Further, significant studies prepared by the United Nations are published as are the results of important meetings, such as that on Human Rights and AIDS. In addition, the African Charter on Human and Peoples' Rights, a manual on Human Rights Reporting under United Nations Treaties and a Global Compilation of National Legislation against Racial Discrimination have been published. Further, some 15 human rights Fact Sheets have been published on such diverse subjects as methods of combating torture, the rights of the child, indigenous populations and the United Nations procedure for individual complaints.

A second requirement for effective national protection of human rights is the existence of adequate national laws and institutions. The United Nations Advisory Services and Technical Assistance Programme in the field of human rights provides the services of experts in *inter alia*, legislation and constitutional law to assist countries in the revision of their legislation and in the establishment of national institutions. As a result of United Nations assistance, national human rights commissions have been established, and penal and other laws revised.

Our advisory services and technical assistance programme has thus furnished the funds and the required expertise for national training programmes and regional workshops to help governments all over the world with the creation or the further development of national human rights infrastructures. In this endeavour we have been greatly helped by the recent creation of a Voluntary Fund for Advisory Services and Technical Assistance. As one example, since mid-1988 when the Voluntary Fund began operations, the Centre has organized some 30 regional or national workshops or training courses in all parts of the world. In the process, over 2,500 administrators of justice, government officials, law enforcement officials, etc. have been trained by highly qualified international experts. The Centre has also assisted in establishing law libraries, in providing translation into local languages and printing basic human rights instruments. It has also undertaken other *ad hoc* forms of technical support.

In 1990, national or regional training courses or workshops were held in Kiev, Manila, Ottawa, Montevideo, Asunción, New Delhi, Caracas, Brasilia, and Lisbon. In March 1991, a training course on human rights and the administration of justice was organized in San Remo (Italy) for French-speaking African countries. We hope to organize a follow-up for English-speaking countries of Africa towards the end of 1991.

In July 1991, the Centre organized a high level regional human rights seminar on international human rights standards and the administration of justice. This was done in co-operation with the African Commission on Human and Peoples' Rights and with the support and co-operation of the Government of Egypt. Representatives from over 40 African countries took part along with members of the African Commission, United Nations agencies and non-governmental organizations.

The Centre has a long standing programme of co-operation with the African Commission going back to mid-1988. It has assisted members of the African Commission in becoming familiar with the work of the Human Rights Committee and has jointly organized training courses with the Commission. Just recently, an agreement was reached for providing various forms of assistance to the African Commission.

One focus of the Advisory Services and Technical Assistance Programme is providing support for the democratization process in Eastern and Central Europe. Expert assistance has been provided to Romania and Albania in connection with the technical and legal aspects of democratic elections. In addition, in December 1990 a seminar was organized in Geneva for Romanian parliamentarians dealing with the drafting of the new constitution. In February, a mission of experts travelled to Bucharest to discuss the draft with those involved in its preparation. Further, agreements for assistance under this programme have been concluded with Bulgaria and Poland and discussions are under way with other countries in the region.

Most recently a seminar was organized in Geneva by the Centre for Human Rights and the World Council of Churches for experts from South Africa on international human rights norms and constitutional law. The purpose of the seminar was to discuss international human rights standards and their expression in constitutional law. The participants, who took part in their personal capacity, came from a broad spectrum of South African society. This seminar was seen by the participants as a positive contribution to the understanding of basic international principles and how they relate to national law and constitutions. Finally, in June of this year, a mission of experts went to Mongolia to assist in the drafting of their new constitution.

Our next activity under this programme includes a workshop on the implementation of international human rights instruments and reporting obligations which is scheduled to take place in Moscow in August 1991. Over 150 government officials, university professors, judges and others from across the Soviet Union are expected to take part in this workshop which is being organized by the Centre with the support of the U.S.S.R. Government. In addition, a seminar on international human rights standards will be organized by the Centre in September 1991 for the judges of the Romanian Supreme Court. Also scheduled at the same time shall be a meeting of experts to review the experiences of countries in the operation of schemes of internal self-government for indigenous populations (Nuuk, Greenland). A further meeting of representatives of national institutions for the promotion and protection of human rights is scheduled in Paris for October 1991.

For many years the United Nations has been promoting the establishment of regional systems for the promotion and protection of human rights and seeking to co-operate ever more closely with the existing systems. Our strong support now goes to helping the African Commission on Human and Peoples Rights in its demanding tasks. On a number of matters, particularly regarding individual complaints, fruitful co-operation has been established between the European and Inter-American Commissions and the Centre for Human Rights.

Regionally, much progress has been made in promoting human rights and fundamental freedoms. New approaches are now being developed and new structures discussed. It is important here, as in other areas, that the regional and universal systems work hand in hand, upholding high standards and implementing them in an efficient manner well aware of the global context.

4. Towards 1993: A World Conference in Human Rights

The momentous changes in international relations over the last few years, the growing prominence of human rights and the establishment of democratic governments in many parts of the world made the time ripe, in my view, for the international community to take stock of the achievements in the field of human rights and of the evolution that has taken place in this field since the International Conference on Human Rights held in Teheran in 1968. Thus, in 1989, I suggested to the General Assembly that a World Conference on Human Rights be organized. It appeared to me at that time that the challenges we face in human rights and the potential for far-reaching human rights advances, which may well transform the course of human history, rendered the holding of such a meeting particularly compelling. The General Assembly has decided to convene such a conference for 1993.

The objectives of the Conference, broadly speaking, are to review and assess progress in human rights since the adoption of the Universal Declaration; to identify obstacles to progress and how they may be overcome; to examine ways to improve the implementation of human rights; and to make concrete recommendations for improving the effectiveness of United Nations activities and mechanisms and for the resources needed to that end. An important element is the examination of the relationship between development and the enjoyment of all human rights and creating the conditions necessary to the enjoyment of all human rights.

Some issues come to mind for eventual consideration by the World Conference. For example, the reaffirmation of United Nations standards in the field of human rights, their universality, and the need to ensure the continued high level of United Nations standards along with the consistency and harmony of new norms with those already established. In addition, we might consider in what way international monitoring activities, both treaty and non-treaty based, could be structured so as to have a more direct impact on national efforts for the promotion of human rights; the role of human rights organs and procedures in conflict prevention and resolution; and how to mobilize all sectors of the United Nations system in the effort to promote human rights.

Although over the last 45 years many steps forward have been taken by the international community to protect human rights, much remains to be done. We cannot relent in the endeavours to bring the beacon of the Universal Declaration to shed its light in the darkest refuges of violations and abuse. We cannot disappoint the hopes of those millions who are coming to learn of the existence of their fundamental rights and freedoms. We must ensure that the potential of respect for human rights in securing peace and universal well-being is truly realized and implemented. And finally, we must also look to our own instrumentalities and procedures. The World Conference on Human Rights will be an appropriate occasion for this review. The academic community and non-governmental organizations will have a key role to play in the preparation of the World Conference and their contributions will be important to its success. The results of this International Conference on Human Rights in the Twenty-First Century will be of utmost significance to that endeavour.

THEO VAN BOVEN*

Prevention of Human Rights Violations

1. Introduction

In the history of international relations and international law, the protection of human rights is a relatively new phenomenon. It was only some 45 years ago that the Charter of the United Nations laid the foundation for a global system of international promotion and protection of human rights. Since then, major accomplishments have been achieved in that international standards have been drawn up which enshrine fundamental rights of individual persons and collectivities and set out obligations of States. Mechanisms and procedures have been developed to monitor compliance with international standards and to provide relief and redress to persons and groups whose rights have been violated.

A growing sense of human rights awareness has been built up largely as a result of activities of the non-governmental sector since World War II. Recently, the spirit of human rights has been strengthened by widespread recognition that pluralistic democracy, the rule of law and full respect for human rights and fundamental freedoms are vital elements for sustainable national societies as well as prerequisites for a lasting international order of peace, justice, security and cooperation.

Thanks to sustained efforts by the United Nations and its specialized agencies, regional organizations and institutions such as the Council of Europe, the Organization of American States, the Conference on Security and Cooperation in Europe and the Organization of African Unity, the framework of an international system for protection of human values and human dignity is now in place. However, this framework does not in itself constitute a sufficient guarantee that human values and human dignity will be universally respected and enhanced. In fact, gross violations of human rights continue to occur on a wide scale, particularly in situations of armed conflict and civil strife and in societies which are characterized by major economic and social disparities. It is one thing to devise and develop policies with a view to putting

* Professor, University of Limburg, The Netherlands.

K.E. Mahoney and P. Mahoney (eds.), Human Rights in the Twenty-first Century, 937–949.

a stop to such gross violations, and to provide means for relief and redress. It is another thing to frame and implement strategies designed to prevent such gross violations of human rights from occurring in the first place, thus sparing people from great suffering. *Prevention versus cure* has always been a prevalent motto in the world of medicine. This motto has undoubtedly the same validity in relation to the safeguard of human rights.

This prevention-versus-cure approach is discussed in this paper from three different perspectives, namely, from the perspective of international structures; from the perspective of actions; and from the perspective of international law and international standards.

2. International Structures

In 1968, on the occasion of the twentieth anniversary of the Universal Declaration of Human Rights, the United Nations organized an international conference on human rights at Teheran in order to review progress made since the adoption of the Universal Declaration and to formulate a programme for the future. One major result achieved at the conference was the adoption of the Proclamation of Teheran.[1] This Proclamation is often quoted because it describes the Universal Declaration of Human Rights not only as "a common understanding of the peoples of the world concerning the inalienable and inviolable rights of all members of the human family", but also as "an obligation for the members of the international community".[2]

The significance of the Proclamation of Teheran is not so much the specific reference to the Universal Declaration as an obligation for the members of the international community but rather its whole thrust. The document is innovative in the sense that it relates human rights to major political, economic and social phenomena which have an incidence upon the welfare and the well-being of large numbers of people. Thus, the Proclamation refers to gross denials of human rights caused by policies and practices of racial discrimination. It speaks of massive denials of human rights arising out of aggression or armed conflict, and resulting in untold human misery. The Proclamation also states that gross denials of human rights arising from discrimination on grounds of race, religion, belief or expressions of opinion outrage the conscience of humankind. It designates the widening gap between the economically developed and developing countries as an impediment to the realization of human rights, and adverts to the existence of over seven hundred million illiterates throughout the world. It highlights the discrimination of which women are the victims in many parts of the world and it emphasizes the

[1] United Nations, *Human Rights – A Compilation of International Instruments* (1988), pp. 43–46.

[2] Proclamation of Teheran, Article 2.

imperative needed to fulfil the aspirations of the younger generation for a better world.

The Proclamation of Teheran sought to elevate human rights beyond the narrow constraints of legal definition and to identify human rights as a relevant factor in relation to major problems of a global nature. The underlying concept was that unless policy-makers are able and willing to tackle the root causes of gross and massive denials of human rights, measures to prevent and prohibit such violations of human rights will have limited or no effect. The same conceptual approach was part of the philosophy which in the seventies inspired the non-aligned countries to put forward a land-mark resolution in the UN General Assembly. Resolution 32/130, like the Proclamation of Teheran, stated that all human rights and fundamental freedoms are indivisible and interdependent. For present purposes the especially significant part is paragraph 1(e,) which reads:

> "In approaching human rights questions within the United Nations system, the international community should accord, or continue to accord, priority to the search for solutions to the mass and flagrant violations of human rights of peoples and persons affected by situations such as those resulting from *apartheid*, from all forms of racial discrimination, from colonialism, from foreign domination and occupation, from aggression and threats against national sovereignty, national unity and territorial integrity, as well as from the refusal to recognize the fundamental rights of peoples to self-determination and of every nation to the exercise of full sovereignty over its wealth and natural resources."

The basic assumption underlying this approach was that unjust international structures prevailing in the world are a major obstacle to the full enjoyment of human rights by large numbers of peoples. Against this background the Secretary-General of the United Nations prepared, at the request of the General Assembly with special reference to Resolution 32/130, a report on existing international conditions affecting human rights. This report presented to the thirty-sixth session of the General Assembly[3] highlighted in particular:
- patterns of inequality: racism, racial discrimination and apartheid;
- patterns of alien subjugation, domination and exploitation perpetuating ties of dependency dating from the past;
- threats or use of force to establish new ties of dependency or to extend existing ones;
- existence of the unjust system of international economic relations;
- obstacles to the establishment of the new international economic order;
- the arms race.

In his conclusions the Secretary-General suggested that periodic reviews of the world human rights situation should be undertaken. He further stated:

[3] UN doc. A/36/462, dated October 8, 1981.

"As the legal basis for a more humane order based on freedom, justice and peace already exists in the International Covenants on Human Rights and other international instruments in the field of human rights adopted by United Nations bodies, the time has come for all States, irrespective of their economic and social systems, to work together for the establishment of such an order. Correcting inequalities, redressing injustices, and accelerating economic and social development would help to eliminate massive and flagrant violations of human rights and the rights of peoples and to underscore that the primary aim of international cooperation is the well-being of the peoples of the world and the realization of their inalienable human rights".[4]

The recognition that human rights violations are more effectively tackled by coming to grips with the root causes of violations rather than merely by dealing with symptoms has been an important concept in the United Nations human rights programme. This same theme also provided the central topic of discussion at the Conference of the International Commission of Jurists on *Development, Human Rights and the Rule of Law*, held in The Hague on April 27 – May 1, 1981, where Philip Alston presented the basic working paper entitled *Prevention Versus Cure as a Human Rights Strategy*.[5]

The fundamental idea behind this strategy is that policies directed at changing and redressing unjust economic and social structures of society and the realization of a new international economic order are essential for the effective promotion of human rights. The same idea was prominent in the minds of all those who pleaded for a new structural approach in order to solve human rights problems. It was the driving force behind the efforts to examine and give concrete meaning to the concept of the right to development.

These efforts eventually resulted in the adoption in 1986 by the UN General Assembly of a Declaration on the Right to Development.[6] The Declaration states that the human person is the central subject of development and should be the active participant and beneficiary of the right to development (Article 2). The Declaration is based on the assumption that the realization of civil and political rights as well as economic, social and cultural rights is an indispensable ingredient of a comprehensive and sound development process and that it is incumbent upon all members of the international society to cooperate with each other in ensuring development and to formulate international development policies with a view to facilitating the full realization of the right to development.

The structural approach to human rights with its important focus on the right to development is a constructive long term strategy with a view to ensuring on a broader scale the enjoyment of human rights and preventing human rights

[4] Ibid., para. 101.

[5] International Commission of Jurists, *Development, Human Rights and the Rule of Law*, Report of a Conference held in The Hague on April 27 – May 1, 1981, Pergamon Press 1981.

[6] Adopted by General Assembly resolution 41/128 of December 4, 1986.

violations. However, this structural approach did not prove to be fully adequate in three respects. First, it is stronger in its analysis than in its implementation. The right-to-development debate and the right-to-development declaration have as yet not been followed by or translated into substantial policy measures. A United Nations Global Consultation on the Realization of the Right to Development as a Human Right, held in Geneva in January 1990, did not change this general pattern.[7] Second, the structural approach with its emphasis on international relations and the international economic order did not pay sufficient attention to patterns of injustice at domestic level and to the need for good governance and the rule of law within national borders. Third, the structural approach ignored the fact that persistent violations of human rights are not only the result of economic and social injustice and disparities, but are also the corollary of religious, national and ethnic divisions between people. Therefore, a preventive strategy aimed at forestalling human rights violations also requires policies and measures of another nature, entailing more immediate and tangible effects.

3. International Action

The awareness is growing that preventive or anticipatory measures are urgently required in order to stop critical situations from reaching catastrophic proportions. The Secretary-General of the United Nations, in recent annual reports on the work of the Organization, repeatedly stressed the importance of preventive action and anticipatory diplomacy in situations where an armed conflict may be impending. He stated: "Experience has shown that it is far more difficult to stop hostilities after their outbreak than to restrain Governments from heading towards the point of no return."[8] The Secretary-General suggested in this connection that the Security Council should hold periodic meetings to survey the political scene and identify points of danger where preventive or anticipatory diplomacy is required.[9] In fact, the United Nations has at its disposal, as part of a progressively accepted and implemented peace strategy, a variety of means, in particular fact-finding and monitoring devices, to prevent possible conflicts. The UN Secretary-General also observed that the need for international solidarity in preventive action is by no means limited to political crises. In this context he pointed to the global threat of environmental

[7] See the Report on the Global Consultation on the Realization of the Right to Development as a Human Right, UN doc. E/CN4/1990/9/Rev.1.

[8] Report of the Secretary-General on the Work of the Organization, September 1989, UN doc. A/44/1, section IV, p. 11.

[9] Report of the Secretary-General on the Work of the Organization, September 1990, UN doc. A/45/1, section III.

degradation and to the food crisis in Africa as areas requiring preventive action.[10]

The views expressed by the UN Secretary-General are being echoed in position papers elaborated by a number of States from East and West within the framework of the Special Committee on the Charter of the United Nations and on the Strengthening of the Role of the Organization. In one of these papers submitted by eight States, the role of fact-finding by the United Nations in the field of the maintenance of international peace and security is strongly advocated.[11]

For present purposes two notions are highlighted. First, the early use of fact-finding capabilities so as "to contribute to the prevention of disputes and situations which may threaten the maintenance of international peace and security".[12] Second, the need for a systematic survey of the world-wide state of international peace and security and the development and strengthening of early-warning and information gathering capabilities.[13]

Another paper submitted to the same United Nations Committee by the USSR appears to go a step further in its plea for the strengthening of the preventive functions of the United Nations. The USSR paper would like to see the sphere of application of preventive UN activities not only focused on situations involving the maintenance of international peace and security but extended to "potentially explosive situations which are caused by internal socio-economic and other factors".[14]

An early proponent of preventive action was Sadruddin Aga Khan who, as a Special Rapporteur of the UN Commission on Human Rights, undertook a Study on Human Rights and Massive Exoduses. A former High Commissioner for Refugees, Prince Sadruddin was particularly mindful of the validity of the notion that an ounce of protection is worth a pound of cure. In 1981 the Special Rapporteur submitted a series of imaginative recommendations aimed at prevention of massive exoduses which did not lead to immediate follow-up action at the time. Nevertheless, his recommendations undoubtedly had a marked influence on the views expressed by the UN Secretary-General and his associates.

Prince Sadruddin recommended *inter alia* "the introduction of an early-warning system based on impartial information gathering and data collection concerning potential mass exodus situations, leading to expeditious reporting to the Secretary-General of the United Nations and competent intergovernmental

[10] Report of the Secretary-General on the Work of the Organization, September 1987, UN doc. A/42/1, section II.

[11] Special Committee on the Charter of the United Nations and on the Strengthening of the Role of Organization, Working Paper submitted by Belgium, Czechoslovakia, German Democratic Republic, Federal Republic of Germany, Italy, Japan, New Zealand and Spain, UN doc. A/AC.182./L.66.

[12] Ibid., para. 29.

[13] Ibid., paras. 35 and 36.

[14] UN doc. A/AC.182/L.65, para. 2(d).

organs for the purpose of timely action if required".[15] In a similar vein, the Special Rapporteur launched the idea of establishing a corps of "humanitarian observers" entrusted with the task of monitoring situations and contributing through their presence to a de-escalation of tension.[16] The same preventive approach informed the Report of the Independent Commission on International Humanitarian Issues entitled *Winning the Human Race?*[17]

While international opinion increasingly favours anticipatory diplomacy and preventive action in crisis situations and conflicts which have international dimensions, such a preventive approach does not seem to have the same degree of support when the issue at stake is mainly perceived as a domestic matter. In fact, violations of human rights have traditionally been treated as a matter pertaining to the internal domain of a State. Only in more recent years have gross and systematic violations of human rights become a subject of legitimate concern in the practice of international relations. However, this tendency is not as yet firmly established. Numerous grave human rights situations, affecting the lives and the physical integrity of thousands of human beings, remain for various reasons ignored by the international community. The tension between international concern for human rights and the principle of non-intervention in domestic affairs has not been overcome. As a result, in spite of the fact that contemporary international law heavily bends towards the duty of the international community to respond effectively to human rights violations, the political threshold regarding preventive diplomacy and action in the area of human rights remains high. A convenient wait-and-see attitude prevails over the readiness to have resort to preventive diplomacy and intercession.

This reluctance to take preventive action with a view to alleviating potential or actual human rights crises has also been noted by B. G. Ramcharan in relation to current United Nations practice:

> "While the Secretary-General of the United Nations and his senior officials regularly engage in preventive diplomacy with regard to differences between states, this preventive machinery has never been put to use systematically with regard to violations of human rights. There is a kind of institutional gap here. True, the Secretary-General does occasionally exercise his humanitarian good offices, but this is used spasmodically and largely as a palliative for failure to make more methodical action."[18]

Nevertheless, as was noted by Ramcharan, a variety of mechanisms and tools have been developed as part of a strategy to cope with human rights

[15] Aga Khan Sadruddin, *Study on Human Rights and Massive Exoduses*, UN doc. E/CN.4/1503, Recommendation (7).

[16] Ibid., Recommendation (9).

[17] *Winning the Human Race?*, The Report of the Independent Commission on International Humanitarian Issues (Foreword by Sadruddin Aga Khan and Hassan bin Talal), 1988, p. 196.

[18] B. G. Ramcharan, *From Peace-Keeping Forces to Humanitarian Forces?*; A comparison of the United Nations peace-keeping and human rights activities, in R. C. Hingorani (ed.) *Humanitarian Law* (1987), pp. 55–64, at p. 59.

violations.[19] Working groups, rapporteurs, envoys and special representatives have been appointed with broad fact-finding mandates in order to deal with country situations or with special phenomena involving gross violations of human rights, such as enforced and involuntary disappearances, summary and arbitrary executions, torture and incidents of religious intolerance. While these mechanisms were devised with a view to responding to human rights violations, their very existence, their presence and their activities, if carried out in an expeditious way, are also bound to entail preventive effects.

For instance, it is fair to assume that, partly due to the active concern of the international community for human rights in Chile during the military dictatorship, the adverse and unacceptable human rights situation in that country was prevented from growing worse. Once authorities are aware that they are being closely watched and monitored, they doubtless observe more restraint than when they know that they are not subject to any scrutiny.

In today's world many situations involving gross violations of human rights are marked by emotions and expressions of deep ethnic, national, racial and religious conflict. Building confidence is an essential condition for conflict prevention. It is an indispensable element for setting forth a human rights strategy based on effective protection.

At a recent meeting in the framework of its Conference on the Human Dimension (Copenhagen, June 5–29, 1990) the Conference on Security and Cooperation in Europe (CSCE) agreed that appropriate new measures should be adopted which "should contribute to achieving further effective progress, *enhance conflict prevention and confidence* in the field of the human dimension of the CSCE" (emphasis added)[20]

In the Charter of Paris for a New Europe, signed on November 21, 1990 by the CSCE Heads of Government, further steps were agreed upon in principle for the prevention and resolution of conflicts among the participating States. Thus, it was decided to create a Conflict Prevention Centre in Vienna in order to assist in reducing the risk of conflict. While in international practice tentative efforts are focused on prevention as a means to meet urgent needs and requirements, the preventive approach is more firmly anchored in international law and in international standards.

4. International Law; International Standards

Under international law there is clearly a duty on the part of States to prevent violations of human rights. The most forceful legal declaration to this effect can be found in the judgment of the Inter-American Court of Human Rights in the

[19] Ibid., p. 60.

[20] CSCE Copenhagen Document, para. (43), 8 *Netherlands Quarterly of Human Rights*, No 3, pp. 323–324. A. Bloed, "Successful Meeting of the Conference on the Human Dimension of CSCE", 8 *Netherlands Quarterly of Human Rights*, No 3, pp. 235–260.

Velásquez Rodríguez Case, July 29, 1988,[21] which concerned the disappearance of Angel Manfredo Velásquez Rodríguez in Honduras. The Court was requested to determine whether Honduras had violated Articles 4 (right to life), 5 (right to humane treatment) and 7 (right to personal liberty) of the American Convention on Human Rights, and to rule that "the consequences of the situation that constituted the breach of such right or freedom be remedied and that fair compensation be paid to the injured party or parties."[22] This case was of tremendous importance: it was the first contentious case before the Inter-American Court and it dealt with one of the most evil plagues inflicted upon the peoples of Latin America during the last two decades, namely the practice of disappearances. In a landmark judgment on state responsibility for violations of human rights, the Inter-American Court addressed the duty of States to prevent violations of human rights. The Court stated:

> "The State has a legal duty to take reasonable steps to prevent human rights violations and to use the means at its disposal to carry out a serious investigation of violations committed within its jurisdiction, to identify those responsible, impose the appropriate punishment and ensure the victim adequate compensation".[23]
>
> "This duty to prevent includes all those means of a legal, political, administrative and cultural nature that promote the safeguard of human rights and ensure that any violations are considered and treated as illegal acts, which, as such, may lead to the punishment of those responsible and the obligation to indemnify the victims for damages. It is not possible to make a detailed list of all such measures, as they vary with the law and the conditions of each State Party. Of course, while the State is obligated to prevent human rights abuses, the existence of a particular violation does not, in itself, prove the failure to take preventive measures. On the other hand, subjecting a person to official, repressive bodies that practice torture and assassination with impunity is itself a breach of the duty to prevent violations of the rights to life and physical integrity of the person, even if that particular person is not tortured or assassinated, or if those facts cannot be proven in a concrete case."[24]

It is clear from the Court's judgment in the *Velásquez Rodríguez* case that the duty to prevent human rights violations implies a wide range of measures with a view to forestalling, or at least limiting, breaches of human rights standards. The duty to prevent also requires that, if such breaches occur, all necessary steps be taken to investigate, identify and punish those responsible and to indemnify the victims. It is taken for granted that the responsibility of the State

[21] Judgment of July 29, 1988, Inter-American Court of Human Rights, series C: Decisions and Judgments No. 4. Also reported in 11 *HRLJ* (1990), pp. 127–133.

[22] Ibid., para. 2.

[23] Ibid., para. 174.

[24] Ibid., para. 175.

is involved in so far as acts or omissions can be attributed to it. In that respect, the State is under a duty to prevent. But in its landmark decision the Inter-American Court went a step further. It stated:

> "An illegal act which violates human rights and which is initially not directly imputable to a State (for example, because it is the act of a private person or because the person responsible has not been identified) can lead to international responsibility of the State, not because of the act itself, but *because of the lack of due diligence to prevent the violation* or to respond to it as required by the Convention".[25]

While the duty to prevent must be considered an integral part of human rights law in general, a review of international human rights instruments reveals that the duty to prevent, and more generally the preventive approach, is an explicit and prominent element of human rights policy and strategy. The titles of a number of international instruments bear eloquent testimony: Convention on the Prevention and Punishment of the Crime of Genocide, European Convention for the Prevention of Torture, Inter-American Convention to Prevent and Punish Torture, Principles on the Effective Prevention and Investigation of Extra-Legal, Arbitrary and Summary Executions.

Other international instruments that do not carry the word "prevention" in their title contain in their provisions important preventive prescriptions. Examples of such instruments are the International Convention on the Elimination of All Forms of Racial Discrimination, the Convention for the Suppression of the Traffic in Persons and of the Exploitation of the Prostitution of Others, the Convention against Torture and Other Cruel, Inhuman or Degrading Treatment or Punishment.[26]

It is clear from the object, nature and purpose of these international instruments that the preventive approach and the duty to prevent are particularly envisaged in relation to the protection of human life and the physical integrity of the human person.

It is also in the same vein that the Document of the Copenhagen meeting of the CSCE Conference on the Human Dimension referred to preventive measures. Under the terms of the Copenhagen document, the participating States "will keep under systematic review interrogation rules, instructions, methods and practices as well as arrangements for the custody and treatment of persons subjected to any form of arrest, detention or imprisonment in any territory under their jurisdiction, with a view to preventing any cases of torture."[27]

Perusal of these various documents makes it evident that the duty to prevent is most clearly and explicitly expressed with a view to precluding gross

[25] Ibid., para. 172.

[26] The texts of these international instruments can be found in: United Nations, *Human Rights – A Compilation of International Instruments*, New York 1988, Sales No. E.88.XIV.I.

[27] CSCE Copenhagen document, para. (16.5), see note 20, *supra*.

violations of human rights and serious breaches of human rights and humanitarian standards.

There is a wide range of preventative means, methods and measures which States have undertaken to implement on the basis of their acceptance of international instruments. They include legislative measures, including criminal legislation and law enforcement; inquiry, investigation and punishment; regular review, control, inspection and reporting; remedies, compensation and rehabilitation; information and education; social measures, development assistance; and international coordination and cooperation.

International instruments differ as to policy approach, choice of preventive means, and emphasis put on preventive action. For instance, the European Convention for the Prevention of Torture is designed to serve an almost exclusively preventive purpose by means of a non-judicial machinery involving visits.[28] On the other hand, the UN Convention against Torture and Other Cruel, Inhuman or Degrading Treatment or Punishment requires the provision at the domestic level of legislative, administrative, judicial and other measures (Article 2), criminal legislation (Article 4), inquiry into the facts (Article 6), measures of information and education (Article 10), systematic review of interrogation rules, instructions etc. (Article 11), recourse and redress procedures (Articles 13,14) etc. In addition, the Convention provides for a series of measures at the international level.[29]

A document of quite another nature, the Programme of Action for prevention of sale of children, child prostitution and child pornography, adopted by the UN Sub-Commission on Prevention of Discrimination and Protection of Minorities, places emphasis on different preventive means. They include information and education, social measures and development assistance, rehabilitation and re-integration but also preventive legislation and law enforcement measures.[30] In sum, a variety of preventive devices are employed. They form an indispensable component of any human rights strategy, in particular within the framework of wide-ranging policies aimed at suppressing and combating grave offenses and evil practices which threaten human life and human dignity.

[28] A. Cassese, "A New Approach to Human Rights: The European Convention for the Prevention of Torture", 83 *AJIL* (1989), pp. 128–153.

[29] J. H. Burgers and H. Danelius, *The United Nations Convention against Torture*; A Handbook on the Convention against Torture and Other Cruel, Inhuman or Degrading Treatment or Punishment, 1988.

[30] UN doc. E/CN.4/Sub.2/1989/39.chap.VII, annex A. See further resolution 1989/43 of the Sub-Commission on Prevention of Discrimination and Protection of Minorities, and Resolution 1990/67 of the Commission on Human Rights.

5. Concluding Observations

Human nature and human inclination tend to be shortsighted. There is a tendency to tackle calamities only after a crisis situation has arisen. Suffering must have reached a high degree of intensity before there is readiness to alleviate and to remedy. Many find it convenient to close their eyes in the face of imminent dangers and imminent disasters. The attitude of *laissez-faire, laissez-aller* appears to have great attraction. However, what is now required is a greater degree of wisdom; a heightened sense of care and responsibility; and a good deal of commitment and morality. These virtues will enable us to look ahead, invest in the future, widen the limits of our immediate, self-centred horizons and to transcend the boundaries of our own clan and generation.

The preventive approach is not easy. In the 70's, blueprints were projected, principles formulated and action programmes devised for the establishment of the new international economic order which was supposed to do more justice to the underprivileged and the destitute. The UN General Assembly declared that the realization of the new international economic order was an essential element for the effective promotion of human rights and fundamental freedoms and should be accorded priority.[31] Regrettably, the lack of political will and of moral conviction rendered the new international economic order ineffective and now largely obsolete.

There may be a new potential in the early 1990's. The détente between East and West opens up new possibilities of confidence-building and international cooperation. The present climate may create conditions conducive to the framing of preventive policies and anticipatory diplomacy. Nations are more willing to rely on multilateral mechanisms and institutions than they were in the recent past. Fact-finding and early warning projects as means to avert and defuse serious conflicts are receiving broader support.

The Secretary-General of the United Nations recently observed,

> "Today, in a growing number of cases, threats to national and international security are no longer as neatly separable as they were before. In not a few countries, civil strife takes a heavy toll of human life and has repercussions beyond national borders."[32]

Preventive measures with a view to the maintenance of peace and security should no more remain within the traditional limits of Chapters VI and VII of the UN Charter. They should also address situations and potential situations of civil strife. As was noted earlier, no systematic machinery is as yet in place to cope with such situations which deeply affect human life and human dignity. Vigorous efforts have to be made to fill this gap.

The most basic and most precious of all human rights is the right to life. The

[31] General Assembly Resolution 32/130, para. 1 (f), adopted December 16, 1977.

[32] Report of the Secretary-General on the Work of the Organization, September 1990, UN doc. A/45/1, section IV.

Human Rights Committee that monitors the compliance with and the realization of the International Covenant on Civil and Political Rights stated in a general comment[33] that the right to life enunciated in article 6 of the Covenant is the supreme right from which no derogation is permitted and which should not be interpreted narrowly. It is most significant that the Human Rights Committee in its authoritative interpretation of the right to life repeatedly stressed preventive duties. As the Committee observed in its general comment 6:[34]

> "... States have the supreme duty to *prevent* wars, acts of genocide and other acts of mass violence causing arbitrary loss of life" (para. 2);
>
> ... States parties should take measures not only to *prevent* and punish deprivation of life by criminal acts, but also to *prevent* arbitrary killing by their own security forces" (para. 3);
>
> ... States parties should also take specific and effective measures to *prevent* the disappearance of individuals, something which unfortunately has become all too frequent and leads too often to arbitrary deprivation of life" (para. 4). (emphasis supplied)

One may conclude from this approach adopted by the Human Rights Committee that preventive action and preventive policies should have a central place in supervisory procedures involving the accountability of governments. Moreover, following the line and the spirit of the preamble of the Universal Declaration of Human Rights, all organs of national and international society carry a responsibility in this regard.

[33] Human Rights Committee, General Comments under article 40, paragraph 4, of the International Covenant on Civil and Political Rights.

[34] United Nations, Report of the Human Rights Committee, Official Records of the General Assembly, 37th session, supplement No. 40, UN doc. A/37/40 (1982).

ARYEH NEIER*

Remedial Human Rights Strategies

Unfortunately catastrophes take place with startling frequency worldwide. Today we have some 30 military conflicts underway around the world. By far the largest number of victims of those military conflicts are not the combatants but the civilian population. They are often the deliberate targets of the parties to those military conflicts. That is, governments and rebel forces attack the presumed civilian supporters of their antagonists as a way of trying to prevail in various military conflicts.

To cite one example of the catastrophes that we must deal with today: a country that had been largely spared military conflict until relatively recently was Liberia. Long regarded as a rather peaceful African country, it was victimized by 10 years of the brutal dictatorship, by Sergeant (then General) and President Samuel Doe. For the last year or so there has been an internal military conflict underway in that small country of 2 1/2 million people. At this moment, approximately three quarters of the entire population of the country has had to flee its homes. Those people are in the most desperate circumstances imaginable. Approximately one quarter of the entire population of the country has fled to neighbouring Cote d'Ivoire Guinea or Sierra Leone. Untold numbers of killings, rapes and mutilations have taken place. Several of the West African countries have sent a peace keeping force but I am afraid that has not helped greatly. Trying to provide a remedial strategy in such catastrophic circumstances taxes the imagination, taxes our creativity, taxes the capacity of the entire world community. Yet this is just one of 30 or so such military conflicts worldwide. Many countries which have not been victimized by military conflict have also suffered catastrophes.

As I have listened to the discussion at this conference, I have heard over and over again calls from various speakers to broaden the framework of human rights. The difficulty I have with those calls, some of which I sympathize with individually, though not all of them, is that most existing institutions that try to protect human rights lack the capacity to do more than they are presently doing. They cannot cope with a larger number of issues than at present. The Africa

* Executive Director, Human Rights Watch, New York, New York.

K.E. Mahoney and P. Mahoney (eds.), Human Rights in the Twenty-first Century, 951–956.

Watch component of my organization for example, is trying to monitor perhaps a fourth of all the countries in Africa. We neglect the other three fourths because we lack the capacity to monitor human rights in them as well. When we hear calls to broaden the framework of human rights, the question is what resources does one divert to try to deal with the other issues that people say should be part of the human rights agenda?

At the very least, one ought to turn back the call to those who say that the framework of human rights should be broadened and say you must create separate institutions, new institutions, if you are going to be effective, if you are going to try to cope with the concerns that have been expressed at this conference. I think the framework of human rights could collapse quite readily if it were broadened to the degree that has been suggested. The framework of human rights is so broad at this stage that the various institutions that operate in the field are not capable of dealing with those matters which fall within the present framework as human rights is most narrowly defined.

Dealing with the catastrophes of the past decade or two or three or four is extraordinarily difficult because, when the catastrophe is at an end, it is often the case that those who were the perpetrators of the catastrophe continue to control substantial power. In many cases the catastrophes have been created in the context of military conflict, or they have been created by military regimes which have exercised power. When civilian democratic governments come into place in various countries where there have been military regimes, or where there has been military conflict the guns generally remain in the hands of the armed forces. Those civilian democratic regimes that try to engage in remedial strategies have enormous difficulties. They are weak and the armed forces are strong.

The catastrophes for which they seek remedies would not have occurred in the first instance had there been the strong civilian institutions that are required to prevent them. Civilian institutions built in the wake of catastrophes tend to be very fragile.

In some circumstances, persons of goodwill who are eager to build democratic societies that are respectful of the rights of their citizens ask that bygones should be allowed to be bygones. They call for national reconciliation. They assert the need to end the cycle of vengeance followed by further conflict. Yet all calls for reconciliation are made with an eye on those armed forces that continue to control the military power of various governments.

What is to be done in such extremely difficult circumstances?

I think by now a consensus has emerged in the human rights community. The most important thing that a civilian, democratic government should try to do as a remedial strategy in the wake of a catastrophe is to provide some form of accountability. This accountability may be divided into at least two phases. One phase is the truth phase. In this phase, the level of victimization is made known. The identities of the victims are made known. The character of the abuses that they endured are made known. The identity of the victimizers is made known. This is the truth phase.

The other phase is the justice phase. In the justice phase one tries to see to it that at least those who have committed the most egregious abuses are punished for their abuses.

Unfortunately, the record thus far in achieving accountability, either in the truth phase or in the justice phase, is extremely poor world wide. As I have suggested, the principal reason is the fragility of civilian democratic governments.

Probably the country which has done best, and it has obvious shortcomings, is Argentina. Argentina had an exemplary truth phase. The Sabato Commission, established by President Alfonsín within days of his assumption of office in December 1983 was an essential part of the truth phase. It published a report which detailed fully and as fairly all the elements of what transpired during the period of military dictatorship in Argentina from March, 1976 to December, 1983.

Truth in Argentina was also served because the Alfonsín government instituted prosecutions against the nine members of the first three military juntas that governed that country following March, 1976. Five of those nine members of the junta were convicted and sentenced to prison terms. This was a scrupulously fair trial. What was most extraordinary about the trial was its supplementary role to the work of the Sabato Commission in making known the extent of the abuses, the nature of the abuses, and the responsibility for those abuses during the period of military dictatorship.

While that trial was underway in Argentina a special newspaper was published which simply reported what was going on in the trial. For the period of the trial, it became the best selling newspaper in the country. Unfortunately, the possibility of further trials was largely circumscribed by a series of military revolts. These military revolts are immensely interesting. The armed services did not rebel against the trial of the members of the three military juntas. Rather they rebelled when prosecutions were being launched against middle ranking members of the armed forces in Argentina.

The argument of the middle ranking members of the armed forces was, "we were following orders, therefore we should not be prosecuted for these crimes." This is not a rationale that can be accepted by those who are concerned with human rights and yet the strong feelings aroused on this question are instructive. That is, the armed forces were able to tolerate the idea that the people with the highest level of responsibility for gross abuses of human rights should be prosecuted. They were not willing to tolerate the idea that the middle ranking members of the armed forces should be prosecuted even though those middle ranking members of the armed forces committed horrendous crimes during the period of military dictatorship.

Another country where a drama was played out with respect to accountability for past abuses was neighbouring Uruguay. In Uruguay the military turned over power to a civilian government in 1985. But, apparently there was a secret arrangement that the civilian government would adopt an amnesty law that would prevent prosecution of members of the armed forces for the crimes of the Uruguayan military dictatorship from 1973 to 1985. Once this was discovered, there was a popular call for a referendum to determine whether or not the public supported the amnesty law.

Under Uruguayan law it is possible to have an issue placed on the ballot for a referendum if 25% of the entire electorate of the country signs a petition for such a referendum. Amazingly, 25% of the entire electorate did sign petitions for a referendum, but when the referendum was held it upheld the amnesty law. One of the factors in the outcome was that the military revolts in Argentina had suggested to many Uruguayans that if amnesty was not granted to the military, they might face another period of military dictatorship. To what extent that weighed in the decision making, it is impossible to know, but it clearly was a factor.

This issue of how to deal with past abuses has arisen in the Philippines; it has arisen in South Korea; it has arisen in the Soviet Union; it has arisen in the various countries of Eastern Europe. In general, the experience is poor everywhere.

The one East European country which has had trials from those responsible for past abuses is Romania, but the trials provided neither justice nor truth. If anything, they seemed like part of an attempt to cover up what took place in the Ceausescu era. Those trials included not only Ceausescu and his wife who were executed by the military, but also members of the Securitaté, the Secret Police under Ceausescu. The charges against the Securitaté however, were limited to the period of the Romanian revolution, December 17 to December 22, 1989, when the Securitaté fired on the civilian population. The Romanian public's desire for retribution against the Securitaté was satisfied by putting them on trial and sentencing them to life imprisonment for what took place during those five days. Everything that had transpired during some 20 years of the Ceausescu dictatorship was excluded from those trials. Consequently, there were no revelations about the nature of abuses during that era, and the victimization and collaboration – perhaps by many who still held power – during that entire period.

One of the countries that has been more successful than most that I can think of in dealing with the question of accountability for past abuses, has been Uganda. A National Commission was established to inquire into the abuses of the Idi Amin and Milton Obote periods. It has held hearings over a period of years, on a weekly basis. The hearings are broadcast in Uganda on television, and more importantly on radio, and are listened to by much of the Ugandan population. The entire life of the country and the entire victimization of the country is canvassed in the hearings. I think hearings such as this are enormously important. They insure that those who suffered are not nameless or faceless persons. Each person has individual worth and individual dignity. An inquiry to determine what happened to those persons at the hands of brutal dictatorships pays them tribute. The suffering of their families is acknowledged and recognized. For these reasons above, the truth phase is terribly important.

The question of whether this kind of remedial effort should take place has been especially controversial in many Latin American countries. I have mentioned Argentina and Uruguay, but a number of other Latin American countries have debated the issue, often resolving it by adopting amnesty laws that prohibit the possibility of prosecutions or inquiries which would deal with the truth of what took place.

Among the countries that have adopted amnesties, usually while the regimes that engaged in the abuses still held power, have been Brazil; Chile, which adopted an amnesty which covered the first five years of the Pinochet dictatorship, during which the largest number of abuses took place; El Salvador, which adopted a general amnesty in October, 1987, which excluded only one crime, the murder of Archbishop Romero; Guatemala, which has adopted repeated amnesties; Nicaragua, which adopted an amnesty before the Sandinistas left power in order to make sure that they could not be prosecuted by the successor regime; and Honduras. Indeed there has been reference here to the *Velasquez Rodriguez* case. I think it is important to add one point with respect to that case.

As Mr. van Boven writes, the Inter-American Court on Human Rights in general called for punishment of those who engage in gross abuses. However, when it came to issuing the order in the particular case before it, the Court refrained from calling for punishment of the soldiers who had engaged in the disappearance. The reason was that the government of Honduras had adopted an amnesty law and the court did not want to challenge it. As a result, the reparations were limited to monetary damages paid to the members of the family, and to injunctive relief against the government of Honduras.

The issue of dealing with past abuses is now at the top of the agenda in Chile. After 17 years of the Pinochet dictatorship, the President of Chile, Patricio Aylwin, appointed a truth and reconciliation commission last April 24. The very name of the commission is interesting. It is not a truth and justice commission. It is a truth and reconciliation commission.

The Aylwin government recognized that while the truth phase is possible in Chile, the justice phase is not. In part this is because of Pinochet's self amnesty and his continuing role as commander and chief of the army which has the power to appoint members of the Chilean Senate. The Supreme Court in Chile also remains intact, the court which upheld the amnesty law. This constitutional arrangement also leaves military court jurisdiction intact, allowing the military to rule on many of the matters which ordinarily belong in civilian courts. One other hurdle in this extra-constitutional case, is Pinochet's public threat that if any of his men are touched, the state of law would end in Chile. For all of these reasons, then, the Commission is called a Truth and Reconciliation Commission rather than a Truth and Justice Commission.

The commission will issue its report by January. I have no doubt that it will be comparable at least to the Sabato Commission Report in Argentina in identifying the victims and identifying the ways in which they were victimized. The Chilean Commission also has the authority to recommend reparations for the victims and their families. I expect that will be a very interesting aspect of the report because, in Chile, families of the disappeared have universally resisted monetary compensation for disappearances. They say they don't want money, they want the truth of what happened to their family members to be acknowledged.

The Commission's authority explicitly excludes finding individual responsibility for the abuses that took place. Nevertheless, if we look to the future with respect to remedial strategies, much will depend upon that Chilean Commission. Even if it cannot recommend that justice should be done in particular cases, it is important that it say something to the world about what is required in dealing with catastrophe. At the least, it should say that while it may not be able to render justice, it is necessary nevertheless that justice should be done in such matters. It should call on governments elsewhere in the world, not only to engage in truth telling but also to provide justice for the victims of the abuses of human rights. Ultimately, that is the only way that the world community has of recognizing the worth and dignity of all those who have suffered the grotesque human rights abuses that characterize our era.

SECTION VI(b): SHIFTING THE PARADIGM*

Introduction

The final section of the book, in many ways, is a microcosm of the entire volume. Addressing the future achievement of human rights goals, the authors represent a variety of constituencies, – the grass-roots, the feminists movement, liberals, non-governmental organizations, academia, and regional and international human rights bodies. Some are radically critical of the *status quo* seeing it as unable to achieve human rights goals while others argue that significant gains can be made by improving present human rights structures, institutions and methodologies. While all differ in their approaches to human rights and their achievement, none are complacent, satisfied, cynical or without hope. In this chapter, the predominant view is that the definition and scope of human rights must change before meaningful achievement of human rights goals will occur.

Peter Leuprecht argues for fundamental change in the ideology of human rights. He says this will not occur unless we re-think the prevailing concept of a "man" and the definition of human rights. "Homo-oeconomicus", the dominant "western man", with his typical attributes of individualism, selfishness, egocentricism, lust for possession, profit and power, unwillingness to share with others is and will be a disaster for human rights. He stresses that in order for the world to achieve human rights goals in the twenty-first century, a much broader definition of human rights is required, capable of limiting and attenuating not only state power but political, economic, social, media, scientific, technological or spiritual power and its violence. At the same time, countries and continents must accept international law and jurisdiction to avoid force and violence in the resolution of disputes. He foresees serious problems in an increasingly smaller, more interdependent world unless greater universal respect for international supervision is forthcoming. The growing inequality and unequal distribution of wealth in the world, extreme nationalism, xenophobia and racism, religious fundamentalism and increasing North/South polarization are serious threats to human rights the world community acting together must resolve. In the last section of his paper, Leuprecht discusses some

* Summary prepared by the editors.

K.E. Mahoney and P. Mahoney (eds.), Human Rights in the Twenty-first Century, 957–958.

strategies for the next millennium including a global responsibility for human rights which he stresses must transcend states and national authorities. He calls for solidarity between individuals, groups, non-governmental organizations and states to share in the responsibility to prevent and remedy human rights violations.

Charlotte Bunch particularizes many of the principles in Peter Leuprecht's paper by focusing on the human rights of women. She explains how a gender consciousness, if brought to civil and political as well as social and economic rights, would strengthen, enrich, energize and bring new insights to the human rights movement. She too argues for an expanded definition of human rights, questioning the prerogative of any group to be human rights gatekeepers denying legitimacy to concerns, they may not appreciate or understand. Taking issue with male perceptions of the very positive effects of the "human rights revolution", she points out the net decrease in the achievement of female human rights on a global scale – a prevailing example of this being violence against women which she discusses in all its shocking ramifications.

Beverly Keene and Adolfo Perez Esquivel write about non-violent solutions in the midst of profound suffering and day-to-day violence experienced in Central and South American states. They posit that the safeguarding and promotion of human life must be the starting point of peaceful solutions to human rights violations. "Active" non-violence means discovering new methodologies and strategies to reinforce people's capacity to transform societies through political action.

William Warden picks up the Leuprecht thread in a different way than Bunch when he writes about the often phoney human rights "activism" of elites and how often they lack sensitivity and authentic concern for the disadvantaged and abused. Warden sees some quantitative progress, however, particularly in the institutionalization of human rights. He says this indicates that governments are beginning to realize the inter-connectedness of human rights and development. This, in turn, increases the global capacity for analyzing the political, economic and social forces and how they bear on human rights.

Warden sees the globalization of economies, democratization and the environment as a major concern for the future of human rights. He wonders whether these trends will empower people at the grassroots or if they will simply provide new structures within which wealth and power can be more effectively concentrated. As global forces put the economically deprived at risk of being totally abandoned, Warden sees a need for global education and global protest as the new human rights activism. He sees the struggle for human rights entering a qualitatively new era which will require the human rights movement to change, just as everything else is changing.

PETER LEUPRECHT*

Conflict Prevention and Alternative Forms of Dispute Resolution: Looking Towards the Twenty-First Century

The brief given for this paper was to look towards the twenty-first century. Although we are approaching the turn of the century and the millennium, this is an extremely difficult task, particularly for somebody who claims no expertise in futurology.

The task may, however, be slightly facilitated by the fact that we are looking to the future from the point of view and in terms of human rights, which like democracy, is a process, a movement, rather than a state of affairs. Let us therefore look to the future on the basis not of a static, but of a dynamic concept of human rights! I am encouraged to do so by the fact that human rights have been at the heart of the recent upheavals in various parts of the world, in particular in Central and Eastern Europe. In terms of thinking and values, these upheavals and positive changes signify a decisive comeback of the human being, the responsible human being, member of a democratic society and possessed of inalienable rights and dignity; at the same time they have been a swinging, heartening rejoinder to those who, in East and West, North and South alike, had announced once again (like the proponents of Nazism and Fascism before them) the death of man, the death of the individual and the end of human rights. In Central and Eastern Europe we have seen the aspiration to democracy, rule of law, justice, freedom and human rights make a powerful surge. It may be that the world has now and will have in the coming century a historic chance to build its unity on these values.

The following statement will, after two preliminary observations, first indicate some of the problems, threats and challenges liable to confront the human rights movement in the coming decade and then set out some principal lines of a possible strategy for the future.

* Director of Human Rights, Council of Europe, Strasbourg, France.

K.E. Mahoney and P. Mahoney (eds.), Human Rights in the Twenty-first Century, 959–965.

1. Preliminary Observations

(1) Human Rights, Violence, and Dispute Resolution

Historically speaking, it is striking to note that the main human rights proclamations were adopted against a background of violence which they attempt to exorcize. At the same time, they aim at the containment and control of violence.

Human rights and national and international systems for their protection are means of prevention of conflict and violence. Conversely human rights violations, especially systematic and "structural" ones (such as poverty, social exclusion, under-development), are often the root cause of violence and upheavals.

National and international systems and machinery for the protection of human rights are also means of non-violent dispute resolution. Finally, the defence of human rights can be a non-violent form of resistance against the violence of power. Many human rights movements aim at countering the violence of those holding power by the strength of the non-violent.

(2) Human Rights versus Power

Human rights always have to be affirmed and defended against power – not only the power of the State, but any political, economic, social, media, scientific, technological or spiritual power. The human rights approach implies a detached and critical attitude towards all kinds of power; in a world where the centres of power have shifted and are shifting, it should encourage us to be constantly on the look-out for all kinds of sources of domination.

Human rights are aimed at limiting, domesticating power and attenuating its violence. In contrast to a utilitarian vision of power, human rights offers an ethical approach setting constraining limits on authority.

2. Looking Towards the Twenty-First Century: Problems, Threats and Challenges

Every period of history and every social system raises particular problems and produces particular threats and challenges to human rights. What might be those of the coming century?

(1) Problems

There are two questions the answer to which will affect decisively the future of the human rights movement.

(a) What Concept of Man?

What concept of man will prevail? A concept of man more and more reduced to a *"homo oeconomicus"*, which is certainly not the only and, in the author's view, not the most interesting variety of the species of *"homo sapiens"*?

This is an absolutely fundamental question. When we talk about human rights and try to define and codify them, it is essential to know what kind of human being we have in mind since human rights are about and for human beings.

The concept of man which is more and more dominant in the West, particularly in the USA, and which the West is trying to promote in other parts of the world is that of *"homo oeconomicus"*. Typical features of this concept of man are selfishness and egocentrism, lust for possession, profit and power, and unwillingness to share with others. His emphasis is on having rather than being. This type of man perceives rights, even human rights, as his rights, not as rights of the others. The human rights approach of *"homo oeconomicus"* is essentially self-centred, individualistic and petulant.

"Homo oeconomicus" shows insufficient respect not only for other human beings and their rights, but also for his environment in the broadest sense of the term. He is indeed a disaster for the environment. The French philosopher Michel Serres is probably right when he says in his recent book *"Le contrat naturel"*[1] that, like the social contract, the Universal Declaration of Human Rights forgot the world. He proposes to complete the social contract by a "natural contract". The law should prevent not only abuses between human beings, but also abuses of man with regard to nature and the environment. It is interesting to note that similar ideas are advocated by the Dalai Lama who, in a Buddhist perspective, considers human rights as just one, though essential, aspect of a broader harmony we should aim at and which should include man's relation with nature.

If the concept of *"homo oeconomicus"* were to prevail this would be extremely harmful to the cause of human rights.

(b) The Future Importance and Impact of International Law and International Human Rights Law

Are we moving towards a world in which relations between States will be increasingly based on law and not power, force or violence, a world in which disputes and differences will be settled by peaceful means according to the rules of law?

There are some encouraging signs pointing in that direction, but unfortunately also some worrying signs to the contrary.

Among the encouraging signals are those coming from Central and Eastern Europe. It can be said that nowadays virtually the whole of Europe recognizes that human rights are central to national and international society and that international protection of human rights takes priority over an out-moded

[1] Michel Serres, *Le Contrat naturel*, Paris 1990.

concept of national sovereignty and of non-interference in domestic affairs which was traditionally dear to the "socialist" countries. Central and Eastern Europe's change of heart on international protection of human rights must be seen in the broader context of a much more receptive and constructive attitude to international law and international jurisdiction generally. This applies also to the USSR. Can the same be said of the other super-power? Interest in and respect for international law should not be limited to situations where it serves political or strategic aims.

In a shrinking world where continents, countries and human beings are more and more interdependent, a growing impact of and respect for international law as well as States' willingness to accept international supervision would contribute decisively to the global progress of the cause of human rights.

(2) Threats and Challenges

What are the threats and challenges which we are facing and might increasingly face in the international human rights movement in the years and decades to come?

One is the *growing inequality* and the *unequal distribution of wealth* in the world and within national societies, including affluent ones. Underdevelopment and mal-development, extreme poverty, misery and social exclusion should be recognized as structural violations of human rights. It is essential to approach these problems not only from the economic and social angles or in terms of assistance, but also and above all from the point of view of law and human rights. People living in extreme poverty and economic and social precarity (and the word "living" is used with some hesitation) are in fact deprived of virtually all human rights, economic and social as well as civil and political rights. They demonstrate the factual indivisibility of human rights. First and foremost we should, as Father Czerny stated in his paper, think in terms of the right to life.[2] Many, and especially many jurists who are often accomplices or prisoners of the established system, have long tried to circumscribe the right to life within its merely "negative" dimension, namely as the right not to be arbitrarily deprived of life. Admittedly, this dimension of the right to life is of major importance. But there is another equally important "positive" aspect: not only the right not to die (and this includes dying of hunger), but also the right to live (and not merely to vegetate, subsist or survive), to live in dignity. That is the full meaning of the right to life. Like other human rights, it can be violated by action or by omission: one may actively put people to death or simply leave them to die.

The *upsurge of extreme and aggressive forms of nationalism and of intolerance, xenophobia and racism* poses another threat to the progress of human rights. Also in our Western, democratic countries we are witnessing the

[2] Michael F. Czerny, S. J., "Liberation Theology and Human Rights", *Human Rights in the Twenty-First Century: A Global Challenge*, 1992, Martinus Nijhoff Publishers

resurgence of certain theories and practices which might have been thought to have disappeared forever and which are based upon denial of the fundamental principle of the equal dignity of all human beings.

Still another threat to the cause of human rights is *religious fundamentalism*. It would be wrong to limit the issue to muslim fundamentalism. The phenomenon is unfortunately much more general. Various religions are being resorted to by regressive forces as a factor of division and exclusion. God, religion and so-called rights of God are once again being used against human beings and human rights.

Looking at the international scene, there is a danger of the East/West rapprochement going hand in hand with *increasing North/South polarization* on human rights. It may be feared that the world-wide struggle for human rights will be lost if we do not succeed in effectively involving the countries of the Third World. The human rights approach risks being irrelevant if it does not take into account the burning problems and legitimate aspirations of the Third World.

The foregoing discussion speaks about a number of threats to the cause of human rights. At the same time, the global and truly universal nature of a growing number of problems and challenges confronting humanity calls for a global and universal response.

3. What Strategy?

What strategy should we adopt on the eve of the next century and millennium?

First of all, human rights will be relevant and will contribute to the prevention and non-violent settlement of conflicts in the world if, and only if, we adopt a *global approach to human rights*.

What is meant by that? What is meant is that human rights have to be truly universal and indivisible.

Universality should not be confused with "Westernization" or universal promotion of capitalism or market economy. This is not the time to discuss the advantages and disadvantages of this form of social system. History might soon be able to judge dialectic materialism and what was called "really existing socialism"; it is too early to say what history's judgment will be about historic capitalism and really existing materialism.

What is dangerous is the way in which the pan-economic ideology invades the human rights discourse. Paradoxically, it produces a kind of Marxist doctrine in reverse, making the market economy the necessary and sufficient prerequisite of enjoyment of human rights. Past and present experience shows how false this assumption is.

What is meant by universality is inclusiveness of human rights as opposed to exclusiveness, respect for cultural diversity without falling into cultural relativism, regional efforts supporting the world-wide effort in favour of human rights.

A global approach to human rights also means that we have to accept, not only in words, but also and above all in deeds, the *indivisibility* of human rights. We will have to reconcile civil and political rights with economic, social and cultural rights, and individual with collective or group rights. And we should pay greater attention to cultural rights which are in fact the most seriously neglected area of human rights.

Human rights call for an unblinkered view without any dead angles. No individual, group, country, region or human situation should be excluded. Contrary to Mr. Neier's paper, what is being advocated here is the broad concept of human rights already recognized by standards of international law.[3] It is of course regrettable that certain States do not adhere to these standards. The author's personal conviction is that the human rights approach will not be of relevance in the real world of tomorrow unless it is based upon the concept of universal and indivisible human rights. This implies an increased responsibility of the international community and all its members.

What we need for universal and indivisible human rights to prevail is solidarity in action.

Action by whom? Who is responsible?

In the last few days it has repeatedly been said that the primary responsibility lies with States and national authorities.

I would go beyond this statement and advocate a *global responsibility*: everybody, individuals, groups, non-governmental organizations, States and the international community, all have a shared responsibility in so far as possible to prevent and where necessary to remedy violations of human rights.

We should also aim at changing the very nature of what we call the international community, to make it more democratic. It should more and more become a community of peoples and of human beings, instead of being exclusively a community of States. After all, the United Nations Charter was drafted in the name of "the peoples".

We might well witness in the years to come a certain demystification and demythologization of the State and the traditional inter-State system. In the name of human rights the State will increasingly be challenged from above, by the international community, and from below, by citizens, groups, non-governmental organizations. It would then be no more than one *"polis"* among others.

When talking about global responsibility and responsibility of the international community, we should think these concepts through to the end and fully accept their consequences, particularly when it comes to problems such as under-development, poverty, malnutrition and hunger in the world. We are talking about collective guarantee of human rights by the international community. Why should responsibility stop at the level of individual States when the enjoyment of economic and social rights and even the survival of

[3] Aryeh Neier, "Redmedial Human Rights Strategies", *Human Rights in the Twenty-First Century: A Global Challenge,* 1992, Martinus Nijhoff Publishers

millions of fellow human beings are concerned? Is it not surprising to see that even the Declaration on the Right to Development[4] does not refer to the responsibility of the international community or of the rich countries with regard to the poor? How could we possibly deny and escape this responsibility?

Solidarity requires us – all of us, individuals, groups, non-governmental organizations, States and the international community – to pay special attention to those regions, countries, groups and individuals who are weak, exposed and vulnerable. We must strongly assert this principle against those in our midst who are harking back to a sort of neo- (or paleo-) social Darwinism, a supposed process of natural selection – in other words, the law of the survival of the fittest, which is nothing other than the law of the jungle.

Finally, just a word about the fundamental importance of human rights education, which is dealt with in another section.[5] Human rights education at all levels should and can make an essential contribution to moving from a culture of violence to a culture of human rights.

It is apt to conclude with the following quotation:

> "The Universal Declaration of Human Rights, the United Nations Charter, the International Covenants on Human Rights, the Helsinki Final Act – all of these can either be worthless pieces of paper or very real and binding instruments of guidance, a true standard. Whether these documents will be one or the other does not depend on governments alone. It is up to all of us to determine how seriously these guidelines will be taken, how they will be implemented and made real. We believe that the time is ripe for us to recall these truths urgently again and try with new energy to act in their spirit. If we wait until social conflicts assume such catastrophic proportions that some changes will have to occur, we will be acting against ourselves. We will all pay dearly for an escalation of conflicts and for the consequences of an explosion that might one day result."

These prophetic words were written in and about Czechoslovakia by the human rights group Charter 77 to commemorate its first decade of existence three and a half years ago. One of the writers of these words, Vaclav Havel, is no longer persecuted for uttering them, but is now President Havel of Czechoslovakia, which has admirably managed its revolution without an explosion of violence. But the words written by our Czech and Slovak friends apply to the world as a whole, and should be taken as a pressing appeal and warning to all and each of us. It is up to all of us to make human rights real. Otherwise we will all pay dearly, humanity will pay dearly for an escalation of conflicts and for the consequences of a terrible explosion.

[4] United Nations General Assembly Resolution 41/128.

[5] Clarence Dias, "Rural Development, Grassroots Education and Human Rights: Some Asian Perspectives", *Human Rights in the Twenty-First Century: A Global Challenge,* 1992, Martinus Nijhoff Publishers

CHARLOTTE BUNCH*

Feminist Visions of Human Rights in the Twenty-First Century

Feminist visions of human rights both add to previous human rights thought and transform it. We must add the specifics of women's experiences into existing categories of human rights, bringing a gender consciousness to civil and political as well as social and economic rights. But we are also transforming human rights concepts so that they more fully address the reality of the daily abuse of women's rights to life, liberty, physical and mental integrity. The ensuing discussion will focus more on the task of transforming concepts because it is often resisted and offers the greatest challenges to and possibilities for human rights in the 21st century.

The latter part of this article discusses four approaches to bringing women's rights and feminist perspectives fully into human rights. But first, it would be useful to comment on attitudes observed at this conference and elsewhere that interfere with a productive dialogue between traditional human rights advocates and those of us called "new actors" in the field. Even the term "new actors" reveals a bias because many of us have been active in racial civil rights, women's rights and other social justice struggles for decades, yet this has usually not been perceived as "human rights" work, creating a division from the start.

Critical questions must be raised about the definition of human rights and who defines it. Who owns the concept of human rights? The U.N. Universal Declaration of Human Rights is the closest we have to an agreed statement, and that is a very broad document. While it does not spell out all the issues brought up here, I believe that they are within the spirit and intent of that document and that it, not any of our organizations, should be the reference point for discussing what are human rights.

Some lament that many groups not previously defined as such now want "human rights" and identify their struggles with that term, claiming that this will dilute the meaning of human rights. While this fear needs to be dealt with in practical terms, it should not stifle the vitality of the concept of human rights.

* Director, The Centre for Global Issues and Women's Leadership, The State University of New Jersey Rutgers, New Brunswick, New Jersey, USA.

K.E. Mahoney and P. Mahoney (eds.), Human Rights in the Twenty-first Century, 967–977.

The success and strength of the vision of human rights is reflected in people's growing identification with it and the desire to extend it to meet their basic needs for human dignity. The concept of democracy began as something for white Western propertied males, but the continuous struggles by the rest of us to extend that concept to include us has given democracy continued importance in the world for several centuries. So too, expanding human rights to address the dignity of all people strengthens, not dilutes, the human rights movement. A feminist vision sees human rights as a powerful moral concept that can address the right to life, liberty, and bodily integrity not only for women but for all regardless of race, class, sexual orientation, religion, age, physical ability, etc. It is a dynamic vision that continually brings allies to the human rights struggle since as new actors define their own human rights, they bring new energy and insights to that movement. For example, often women, people from Third World countries, or lesbians and gays have felt alienated from the human rights movement because the fundamental threats to their daily lives are not recognized as human rights issues. Why should any group fight for others' rights if there is no acknowledgement of their rights as well? If we are to build a truly universal concept of human rights that responds to new situations and consciousness, it must continually bring in new actors and concerns that will make it grow stronger.

It is important to respond to the fear of some human rights groups that women are suggesting that they must take up every human rights issue that we raise. However, this is not what we are asking. Every organization has its practical limits and must define which aspects of human rights abuse it will work on. What we are questioning is the prerogative of any group to be the gatekeepers who say what is and is not a human rights issue and thereby attempt to deny legitimacy to other concerns. What women are asking for is serious consideration of our analysis of human rights as it applies to groups like women and inclusion of our perspectives in the dialogue of the human rights community.

1. Gender Conscious Perspectives on Human Rights

Feminist analysis begins with the recognition that each of us views human rights through a different set of lenses depending on our place in society. In order to understand how others see human rights violations, we must look through the lens of their experiences. An illustration here is the comment made by several men during this conference that 1989–90 has been a time of revolution in human rights. I would suggest that from a woman's lens, this has hardly been a positive revolutionary time; rather it has been a period which has seen a net decrease in the achievement of female human rights. The growth of religious fundamentalism in all the major world faiths has curtailed women's freedom in almost every sphere over the past few years. Violence against women has escalated from the Montreal massacre to the increase in numbers and percentages of women with AIDS around the world, particularly in Southeast Asia, the USA, and Africa. The population now most at risk is women and the fastest growing affected group are girls infected with AIDS as a result of the violence of rape, incest, and prostitution. In 1990, more women sank deeper into critical poverty as the class and gender gap widened internationally with structural adjustment policies that punished the poor. Even in Eastern Europe, where women enjoy new civil and political liberties, they are losing their socio-economic rights to jobs and childcare, seeing an increasing threat to their reproductive rights, and a growth in crime and violence against them in the streets. An assessment of what has been happening with human rights over the past year cannot be singular: it depends on who you are and whose rights and violations you look at. If we are to build a movement that respects all peoples' struggles for human dignity, then we must look through the lenses of many diverse groups to see the total picture.

Looking at human rights through a gender conscious lens, we see that women experience violations of their rights in three broad ways. First, some violations of women's human rights are more or less the same as those experienced by men, caused by women's politics, race, religion, etc. In these cases, the problem is usually one of visibility since men are more often seen as the political actors and made the focus of human rights advocacy. A second type of human rights abuse that women experience is where gender exacerbates other forms of human rights violation such as sexual torture of female political prisoners or rape in jails or refugee camps. Here women may be under attack because of factors such as politics or race, but they experience further violation based on their femaleness. Another variation on this situation is those women whose rights are violated because of their association with powerful men; there human rights are abused because of their gender position as the "property" of men. The third type of human rights violation that women suffer is that directed against them because they are female, such as infanticide or spousal battery and homicide. This area has been the most overlooked in human rights discourse.

Women's rights are too often seen as secondary or trivial in relation to other human rights. Not only is the abuse of women's rights the cause of much death and suffering to women but also it is fundamental to human rights abuse in other forms as well. The abuse of women is central to all cultures and the endemic violence is reinforced by and rooted in the violence that we tolerate against women at an every day level on our streets, in our media, and in our homes. If children view this human rights abuse against women, their mothers, and often themselves as a regular part of life, it is little wonder that many of them are prepared to accept other forms of human rights abuse as natural. Yet such abuse of women is often separated from human rights considerations as the "private" sphere, ignoring both the connections between the public and the private and the State's responsibility for human rights even in non-public spaces. The prevention of gender violence is a crucial aspect of addressing human rights abuse and violent conflicts throughout the world.

2. Gender Violence: The Global War Against Women

One problem in looking at conflict resolution in relation to the prevention of female human rights abuses is the lack of recognition of the large scale gender war on women's rights to our bodies, mobility and life that is occurring today. We are still in the truth-telling phase of this issue. We are only beginning to quantify the magnitude of gender violence and to acknowledge the ways that being female is life-threatening. For example, the Indian social scientist, Amartya Sen, in his study of sex ratios in the world estimates that 68 million women are missing – in India (30 million) and China (38 million).[1] These disappearances or femicide are a result of the abortion of female foetuses; of female infanticide; of malnutrition which the World Health Organization finds afflicts more girls than boys since males get fed more where there is poverty in most regions of the world; of neglect of women's health as children and in childbirth; and of the murder and maiming of women by their spouses and in-laws.[2]

Gender violence afflicts women worldwide in these and other forms. Maternal mortality claims many more lives than it should because health care is inadequate and complications from illegal abortions performed in unsafe health conditions is the leading cause of death for women aged 15–39 in Latin America.[3] Where there are studies of domestic assault, figures range from 40 to 80% of women experiencing it regularly and over 50% of female homicides are committed by family members. In the US, for example, there is a rape every 6 minutes and domestic battery is the leading cause of injury to women accounting for more harm than rape, car accidents and muggings combined, and a study of urban victimization in seven major Canadian cities found that 90% of the victims were women.[4]

Such violence is not random: the risk factor is being female. Like racial-bias crimes, the objective is subordination of the group. If we are to stop such gender violence, we must also recognize that it is political – that it is the result of systematic political, social and economic structures that have been constructed to dominate women. Understanding that it has been politically constructed and is not innate or inevitable enables us to see that it can also be de-constructed. Looking at the statistics on violence against women, one

[1] Amartya K. Sen, "Gender and Cooperative Conflicts", in I. Tinker (Ed.) *Persistent Inequalities: Women and World Development* (1989), New York: Oxford University Press, pp. 123–149.

[2] Sundari Ravindran, *Health Implications of Sex Discrimination in Childhood* (1986) Geneva: World Health Organization; G. Ashworth, *Of Violence and Violation: Women and Human Rights* (1986), London: Change Thinkbook II.

[3] D. Taylor, (Ed.) *Women: A World Report, A New Internationalist Book* (1985), Oxford: Oxford University Press.

[4] C. Everett Koop, M.D., "Violence Against Women: A Global Problem". Presentation by the Surgeon General of the U.S. Public Health Service at a Seminar of the Pan American Health Organization, Washington, D.C., May 22, 1989. Linda McLeod, "The City for Women: No Safe Place", *Women and Environments*, Vol. 12, No. 1, (Fall 1989 – Winter, 1990), pp. 6–7.

becomes pessimistic about men unless this behaviour is seen as socially constructed as a part of society's concept of maleness. Change must come from recognizing its political nature and de-constructing messages about masculinity and femininity that contribute to the perpetuation of gender violence.

Violations of women's human rights have a profile similar to other human rights abuses. Women are imprisoned and tortured in their homes and in brothels. They are held in involuntary slavery in prostitution, for pornography, and even as domestic servants. Compulsory pregnancy kills women; arranged marriages and enforced heterosexuality have led women to suicides or prostitution to escape forced marriages. Women face terrorism on the streets and in jobs in places like the Free Trade Zones where sexual harassment is often a condition for receiving a paycheque. Women are denied their right to assembly and freedom of mobility when husbands beat them or lock them in their homes in retaliation for participating in development projects or simply for going outside the home without permission.[5] Even women's right to education is threatened in villages where boys frighten girls away from schools or in Montreal where 14 women were murdered for seeking to enter a male profession. Gender violence or the threat of it shapes the contours of every woman's life daily, it limits her freedom of movement, speech and assembly, and undermines her sense of human dignity and rights in the world.

If our attitude toward human rights shows who we are as a people, then surely the treatment of women's human rights and the minimal attention to them reveals much about what we are lacking at the core of our societies in terms of fundamental appreciation for the dignity of every human being. The State is explicitly or implicitly involved in this violence at all levels both by the laws it passes that encourage or discourage women's freedom and by the efforts it exerts to implement these laws. The division between public and private has largely been used to uphold a double standard *vis à vis women*. We accept that the State has a duty to intervene to counter human rights abuses even when privately committed, such as slavery or racial segregation which is not accepted by human rights advocates as a cultural practice in South Africa or in the South of the USA. So too, we must cease to dismiss the violation of women's human rights on the grounds of culture, family or religion and affirm the universal human right of all to dignity and freedom from violence in all its forms.

3. Linking Women's Rights to Human Rights

The classification of human rights is more than semantics because it has practical policy consequences. Human rights are considered to be more important than women's rights. The distinction perpetuates the idea that the

[5] R. Carrillo, "Violence Against Women: An Obstacle to Development" (1991), study done for the United Nations Development fund for Women (UNIFEM) and published as a pamphlet by the Center for Women's Global Leadership, New Brunswick, NJ.

rights of women are of a lesser order than the "rights of man", and, as Eisler describes it, "serves to justify practices that do not accord women full and equal status".[6] In the United Nations the Human Rights Commission has more power to hear and investigate cases than the Commission on the Status of Women, more staff and budget, and better mechanisms for implementing its findings. Thus it makes a difference in what can be done if a case is deemed a violation of women's rights and not of human rights.[7]

The determination of refugee status illustrates how the definition of human rights affects people's lives. The Dutch Refugee Association, in its pioneering efforts to get acceptance of sexual persecution and violence against women as a basis justifying refugee status, found that some European governments would take sexual persecution into account as an aspect of other forms of political repression, but none would make it the grounds for refugee status *per se*.[8] The implications of such a distinction are clear when examining a situation like that of some Bangladeshi women who, having been raped during the Pakistan-Bangladesh war, subsequently faced death at the hands of male relatives to preserve "family honour". Western powers professed outrage but did not offer asylum to these victims of human rights abuse.

Four basic approaches can be observed to linking women's rights to human rights. These approaches are presented separately here in order to identify each much more clearly. In practice, they often overlap, and while each raises questions about the others, they should be seen as complementary. These approaches can be applied to many issues, but they will be illustrated primarily in terms of how they address violence against women in order to show the implications of their differences on concrete issues.

(1) Women's Rights as Political and Civil Rights

Taking women's specific needs into consideration as part of the already recognized "first generation" human rights of political and civil liberties is the first approach. This involves both raising the visibility of women who suffer general human rights violations as well as calling attention to particular abuses women encounter because they are female. Thus, issues of violence against women are raised when they connect to other forms of violation such as the sexual torture of women political prisoners in South America.[9] Groups like the

[6] R. Eisler, "Human Rights: Toward an Integrated Theory for Action", *Human Rights Quarterly* 9 (1987), p. 291.

[7] S. Coliver, "United Nations Machineries on Women's Rights: How Might They Better Help Women Whose Rights Are Being Violated?", in E. Lutz, H. Hannum, and K. Burke (Eds.) *New Directions in Human Rights* (1989), Philadelphia: Univ. of Penn. Press.

[8] M. Meyer, "Oppression of Women and Refugee Status", (report to NGO Forum, Nairobi, Kenya, 1985) ® unpublished; Ministry of Social Affairs and Labour, "Sexual Violence Against Women Refugees" (June, 1984), The Netherlands.

[9] X. Bunster describes this in Chile and Argentina, "The Torture of Women Political Prisoners: A Case Study in Female Sexual Slavery", in K. Barry, C. Bunch and S. Castley (Eds.) *International Feminism: Networking Against Female Sexual Slavery* (1984), New York: IWTC.

women's task force of Amnesty International have taken this approach in pushing for Amnesty to launch a campaign on behalf of women political prisoners which would address the sexual abuse and rape of women in custody, their lack of maternal care in detention, and the resulting human rights abuse of their children.

Documenting the problems of women refugees and developing responsive policies are other illustrations of this approach. Women and children make up more than 80% of those in refugee camps, yet few refugee policies are specifically shaped to meet the needs of these vulnerable populations who face considerable sexual abuse. For example, in one camp where men were allocated the community's rations, some gave food to women and their children in exchange for sex. Revealing this abuse led to new policies that allocated food directly to the women.[10]

The political and civil rights approach is a useful starting point for many human rights groups; by considering women's experiences, these groups can expand their efforts in areas where they are already working. This approach also raises contradictions that reveal the limits of a narrow civil liberties view. One contradiction is to define rape as a human rights abuse only when it occurs in state custody but not on the streets or in the home. Another is to say that a violation of the right to free speech occurs when someone is jailed for defending gay rights, but not when someone is jailed or even tortured and killed for homosexuality. Thus, while this approach of adding women and stirring them into existing first generation human rights categories is useful, it is not enough by itself.

(2) Women's Rights as Socio-economic Rights

The second approach includes the particular plight of women with regard to "second generation" human rights such as the rights to food, shelter, health care and employment. This is an approach favoured by those who see the dominant Western human rights tradition and international law as too individualistic and identify women's oppression as primarily economic.

This tendency has its origins among socialists and labour activists who have long argued that political human rights are meaningless to many without economic rights as well. It focuses on the primacy of the need to end women's economic subordination as the key to other issues including women's vulnerability to violence. This particular focus has led to work on issues like women's right to organize as workers and opposition to violence in the workplace, especially in situations like the free trade zones which have targeted women as cheap, non-organized labour. Another focus has been highlighting the feminization of poverty, or what might better be called the increasing impoverishment of females. Poverty has not become strictly female, but

[10] Report given by Margaret Groarke at Women's Panel, Amnesty International New York Regional Meeting, February 24, 1990.

females now comprise the highest percentage of the poor.

Looking at women's rights in the context of socio-economic development is another example of this approach. Third World peoples have called for an understanding of socio-economic development as a human rights issue. Within this demand, some have sought to integrate women into development and have examined women's specific needs in relation to areas like land ownership or access to credit. Among those working on women in development, there is growing interest in violence against women as both a health and development issue; if violence is seen as both a health and development issue; if violence is seen as having negative consequences for social productivity, it may get more attention. This type of narrow economic measure, however, should not determine whether such violence is seen as a human rights concern. Violence as a development issue is linked to the need to understand development not just as an economic issue but also as a question of empowerment and human growth.

One of the limitations of this second approach has been its tendency to reduce women's needs to the economic sphere which implies that women's rights will follow automatically with third world development, which may involve socialism. This has not proven to be the case. Many working from this approach are no longer trying to add women into either the Western capitalist or socialist development models, but rather seek a transformative development process that links women's political, economic and cultural empowerment.

(3) Women's Rights and the Law

The creation of new legal mechanisms to counter sex discrimination characterizes the third approach to women's rights as human rights. These efforts seek to make existing legal and political institutions work for women and to expand the State's responsibility for the violation of women's human rights. National and local laws which address sex discrimination and violence against women are examples of this approach. These measures allow women to fight for their rights within the legal system. The primary international illustration is the Convention on the Elimination of All Forms of Discrimination Against Women.[11]

The Convention has been described as "essentially an international bill of rights for women and a framework for women's participation in the development process... (which) spells out internationally accepted principles and standards for achieving equality between women and men".[12] Adopted by the UN General Assembly in 1979, the convention has been ratified or acceded to by 104 countries as of January 1990. In theory these countries are obligated

[11] Convention on the Elimination of All Forms of Discrimination Against Women, G.A. Res. 34/180, U.N. Doc. A/Res/34/180 (1980).

[12] "The Convention on the Elimination of All Forms of Discrimination Against Women" (1988), Summary of CEDAW prepared by the International Women's Rights Action Watch, Minneapolis: Humphrey Institute of Public Affairs.

to pursue policies in accordance with it and to report on their compliance to the Committee on the Elimination of Discrimination Against Women (CEDAW).

While the Convention addresses many issues of sex discrimination, one of its shortcomings is failure to directly address the question of violence against women. The CEDAW Committee passed a resolution at its eighth Session in Vienna in 1989 expressing concern that this issue be on its agenda and instructing States in their periodic reports to the Committee to include information about statistics, legislation and support services in this area.[13] The Commonwealth Secretariate in its manual on the reporting process for the Convention also interprets the issue of violence against women as "clearly fundamental to the spirit of the Convention", especially in Article 5 which calls for the modification of social and cultural patterns, sex roles and stereotyping that are based on the idea of the inferiority or the superiority of either sex.[14]

The Convention outlines a clear human rights agenda for women which, if accepted by governments, would mark an enormous step forward. It also has the limitations of all such international documents however, in that there is little power to demand its implementation. Within the United Nations, it is not generally regarded as a convention with teeth, as illustrated by the difficulty that CEDAW has had in getting countries to report on compliance with its provisions. Further, it is still treated by governments and most non-governmental organization as a document dealing with women's (read "secondary") rights, not human rights. Nevertheless, it is a useful statement of principles endorsed by the United Nations around which women can organize to achieve legal and political change in their regions.

(4) Feminist Transformation of Human Rights

Transforming the human rights concept from a feminist perspective, so that it will take greater account of women's lives, is the fourth approach. This approach raises the question of how women's rights relate to human rights by first looking at the violations of women's lives and asking how the human rights concept can be changed to be more responsive to women. For example, the GABRIELA women's coalition in the Philippines simply stated that "Women's Rights are Human Rights" in launching a campaign last year. As Ninotchka Rosca[15] explained, coalition members saw that "human rights are not reducible to a question of legal and due process... In the case of women, human rights are affected by the entire society's traditional perception of what is proper or not proper for women". Similarly a panel at the 1990 International Women's Rights Action Watch conference asserted that "Violence Against Women is a

[13] UN G.A. Res. A/44/38, CEDAW Newsletter, 3rd Issue, April 13, 1989.

[14] "The Convention on the Elimination of All Forms of Discrimination Against Women: The Reporting Process – A Manual for Commonwealth Jurisdictions" (1989), London: Commonwealth Secretariat.

[15] Speech given by Ninotchka Rosca at Amnesty International New York Regional Conference (February 24, 1990), p. 2.

Human Rights Issue". While work in the three previous approaches is often done from a feminist perspective, this last view is the most distinctly feminist with its woman-centred stance and refusal to wait for permission from some authority to determine what is or is not a human rights issue.

This transformative approach can be taken toward any issue, but those working from this approach have tended to focus most on abuses that arise specifically out of gender, such as reproductive rights, female sexual slavery, violence against women and "family crimes" like forced marriage, compulsory heterosexuality and female mutilation. These are also the issues most often dismissed as not really human rights questions. This is therefore the most hotly contested area and requires that barriers be broken down between public and private, State and non-governmental responsibilities.

Those working to transform the human rights vision from this perspective can draw on the work of others who have expanded the understanding of human rights previously. For example, two decades ago there was no concept of "disappearances" as a human rights abuse. However, the women of the Plaza de Mayo in Argentina did not wait for an official declaration but stood up to demand State accountability for these crimes. In so doing, they helped to create a context for expanding the concept of responsibility for deaths at the hands of para-military or right-wing death squads which, even if not carried out by the State, were allowed by it to happen. Another example is the developing concept that civil rights violations include "hate crimes", violence that is racially motivated or directed against homosexuals, Jews or other minority groups. Many accept that States have an obligation to work to prevent such human rights abuses, and getting violence against women seen as a hate crime is being pursued by some.

The practical applications of transforming the human rights concept from feminist perspectives need to be explored further. The danger in pursuing this approach only is the tendency to become isolated from and competitive with other human rights groups because they have been so reluctant to address gender violence and discrimination. Yet, most women experience abuse on the grounds of sex, race, class, nation, age, sexual preference, politics, etc. as interrelated. Little benefit comes from separating them as competing claims. The human rights community need not abandon other issues but should incorporate gender perspectives into them and see how these expand the terms of their work. By recognizing issues like violence against women as human rights concerns, human rights scholars and activists do not have to take these up as their primary tasks. However they do have to stop gate-keeping and guarding their prerogative to determine what is considered a "legitimate" human rights issue.

These four approaches are overlapping and all of them contain aspects of what is necessary to achieve women's rights as human rights. However, the mood of women's groups working in this area today is increasingly that expressed by the transformative approach which starts by declaring that women's rights *are* clearly human rights. We are going to work on these issues as violations of human rights. Women are and will increasingly be doing this work in the name of human rights. It is our hope that others in the human rights community will see this transformation as a growing partnership in the struggle for human rights. But we are not conceding the power to someone else to say whether the violations of our human dignity are or are not real human rights issues. If we are not accepted as new actors in this field, we will continue to do the work anyway. We hope to work with others to create a broader vision of human rights that incorporates the feminist understanding of human rights as the struggle for dignity and hope of all people. If the human rights concept and community can be responsive to human need and the ever expanding definitions of people's struggles for their human dignity, then it can remain at the center of hopes and visions for what the 21st century can bring.

ADOLFO PÉREZ ESQUIVEL* and BEVERLY KEENE**

Active Non-Violence in the Process of Liberation

1. Introduction

The decade of the 1980's will long be remembered as a time of profound political transformations the world over. In most of Latin America, a shift from military dictatorships, notorious for their human rights violations, to popularly-elected civilian regimes raised expectations in the recovery of democratic processes, which would be capable of confronting the structures of economic, political and social injustice, which had given rise to such violent social conflict in the past.

As Latin America enters the decade of the nineties, however, a fundamental dilemma, which characterizes these transitions, has become increasingly apparent: the contradiction between the re-opening of the political arena and the re-establishment of democratic institutions and procedures premised on notions of "freedom" and "equality" on the one hand, and the consolidation of economic and social realities marked by stagnation, at best, and the growing misery and marginalization of vast sectors of the population on the other. The economic and social exclusion of the poor majorities in turn leads to the circumscription of their possibilities for meaningful participation, as the reins of power are held ever tighter in a desperate attempt to prevent the whole system from spinning out of control.

This reality of profound injustice and growing frustration is also marked by the continuation, in some cases, of systematic policies of State violence and extermination. The ending of the dictatorships in countries such as Argentina, Uruguay and Chile has brought a virtual conclusion to the policies of State terrorism, which dominated there in the 1970's. But in other instances, including most notoriously Guatemala, Colombia, El Salvador and Perú, the existence of so-called democratic regimes has been used diplomatically outside the country much more effectively than inside, where disappearances, torture,

* Peace and Justice Service, Argentina.

** Director, International Affairs Department, Fundación Servicio Paz y Justicia, Buenos Aires, Republic of Argentina.

K.E. Mahoney and P. Mahoney (eds.), Human Rights in the Twenty-first Century, 979–983.

extra-legal detentions and assassinations are perhaps as serious, or more so, than at any other moment in recent history.

To this level of violence, shielded from prosecution and sanctioned across the continent through the proliferation of diverse mechanisms of State-legitimized impunity, must also be added the growing violence and distinct forms of savage social control directed against the very victims generated by the consolidation of these economic, social and political models characterized by their capacity to exclude. In Brazil, for example, this phenomenon is registered in the faces and ages of the current victims of police and para-state violence, numbered in the thousands last year: street children, the homeless, slum dwellers and landless peasants.

It is here, in the midst of this reality of profound and acute human suffering, of day-to-day violence which takes on and is expressed in countless forms, that we must situate any discussion of non-violence. Here, where the poor, the marginalized, the excluded and oppressed wage their daily struggle for survival: seeking to insure the triumph of life over death. This must be our starting point; and the safeguarding and promotion of human life, the measuring rod of the success, or failure of our actions.

2. What Is Non-Violence?

To begin, we must categorically reject any notion of similarity between non-violence and passivity. There is, indeed, nothing more contradictory. We prefer, in fact, to speak of active non-violence: a means of actively confronting the injustice which surrounds us and which conditions the most fundamental human right of all, the right to life.

Active non-violence is not a utopian dream, as some would argue, but rather a day-to-day effort to transform structures of oppression and to liberate the power of human dignity and creativity, beginning with and building on the real-life sufferings and aspirations of men and women everywhere.

Gandhi called it *catyagrapha*, the force of truth; however, he did not like the word non-violence. Martin Luther King, Jr., preferred to speak of the force of love. In Brazil, our friends and colleagues prefer the name *firmeaza permanente* – relentless persistence – underscoring the union of strength and permanence, which characterizes any form of non-violent action.

Whatever it is called, it can be clearly seen that this active non-violence is not neutral. It parts from a fundamental and unequivocal affirmation of life – of all human life – and from a faith in people's capacity to understand their oppression and to act to transform it. It is a way of life, and a way of struggle, which posits popular participation, the active engagement of those whose life is threatened and cut short by the structures of violence, which pervade their reality, as the determining factor. As such, it constitutes a preferential arm of the poor and dispossessed, building on their numbers and capacity to organize and create, rather than a technological and financial superiority in the race to destroy.

Active non-violence also parts from a conviction that to overcome injustice and dignify human life, both victim and perpetrator, must be challenged and their attitudes and behaviours radically altered. Unless the reality of domination is confronted in its many dimensions, we are in danger of repeating the Sisyphusian task of winning countless skirmishes, but losing the battle.

Celso Furtado, a Brazilian economist and astute observer of Latin American reality, has observed that all relationships of domination, of exploitation and oppression are by their very nature violent. It is not necessary that the violence be expressed in a drastic way: through the barrel of a gun, the dropping of a bomb or the wielding of an electric cattle-prod in a midnight torture session. In as much as both those who dominate, as well as those who suffer domination, are inhibited and dehumanized – one through an excess of power, the other through a lack of power – the relationship is one of violence. Yet, generally speaking, when the oppressed legitimately rebel against this relationship of violence, they are accused of being violent, barbaric, inhuman, etc. We can see that among the countless "rights" that the oppressor or system of domination reserves for him or itself is also the right to define violence: to characterize its nature, locate its perpetrators, determine its legality.

The conscience of domination takes on the role of determining values and of distorting them: manipulating them or simply emptying them of their contents.

So often in Latin America we have experienced this mode of domination. In the name of freedom, people are persecuted and imprisoned and freedoms are suppressed. In the name of justice, all kinds of injustices are committed. In the name of democracy, popular participation is thwarted out of fear that it will threaten the status quo. The system of domination has sought to instil an order in which passivity and domestication are the norms.

It is at this point where active non-violence seeks preferentially to break through the spiral of violence and dehumanization, clearly taking sides with the victims, clearly confronting the injustice, but seeking also to transform the system of domination in which both victim and oppressor are enmeshed and thus, paving the way for lasting alternatives.

Lest there be any doubt, however, we must underscore that even while active non-violence can and should be understood in this sense, to define a kind of spirituality of struggle, based on respect for the oppressor as well as the oppressed and a profound desire to achieve reconciliation, in the midst of our reality of structural violence it is not possible to undertake non-violent action without immediate political consequences for those who want social change, or those who want to impede it. As Nelsa Curbelo, coordinator of the Peace and Justice Service in Latin America, an organization committed to the promotion of active non-violence, has observed, "If we are not effective in this sense – in producing social change – then it is nonsense".

3. Where Do We See Active Non-Violence at Work?

In our continent, we can see and appreciate the force of active non-violence in our people's quest for liberation in many distinct situations. Latin America is an amalgam of people who have experienced a long history of violence and domination, and through that process they have discovered forms and methods which have enabled them first of all to survive, and also to overcome specific instances of oppression and conflict through organization and mobilization.

Some will soon celebrate the 500th anniversary of the "discovery" of Latin America. Many others, including the indigenous peoples of America, but also Latin Americans in general, will seek to commemorate 500 years of resistance to the continuing conquest.

This resistance has taken on multiple forms in the history of our people, responding as it must to the particular moment and circumstances. It is an existential resistance: a cultural, linguistic and religious resistance. It springs from the grass roots, and is manifested, preferentially, through the diverse forms of popular organization that express the relentless persistence of the people to overcome all odds and to pay the price of seeking to transform a reality of great suffering into one of human dignity.

We could speak of the struggle of landless peasants in El Salvador for a parcel of land; of the Alagamara cement factory workers to prevent plant closings in Brazil; of the women of the mines in Bolivia, who with their children and their hunger brought down the dictatorship of General Banzer; of the indigenous of Ecuador, who just months ago paralysed the country for three days in their struggle for recognition, for land, for survival. In Argentina, the Mothers of the Disappeared, with their white kerchiefs and grievous pain, placed the value of human life in the forefront and forced a regime of terror and death to surrender.

The struggle for human rights in Latin America, in general, is a struggle that has grown as a force for human liberation and dignity, and which has discovered in active non-violence the transforming power of people's unity and solidarity, of projecting truth and eroding the pillars of fear and impotence which enable oppression to continue. The examples could be continued at great length. And there is a need to share even more, as this experience of non-violent struggle, the experience of relentless persistence, is the history of the oppressed, and the history we are generally not taught in school or in our history books. The above examples suffice to underscore the fact that in Latin America, active non-violence as a force for people's liberation exists not as a theoretical exercise, but as a dynamic, ever-present historical practice of popular organization and mobilization.

4. The Challenge of Active Non-Violence for Latin America Today

As we observed earlier, despite the significance of the transition from military dictatorships to constitutional democracies, the peoples of Latin America are subjected to extreme levels of violence and dehumanizing injustice in a perversely routine fashion. In the context of our continent, "give us this day our daily bread" becomes neither a prayer for divine sustenance nor a plea for charity. It is, rather, the recognition of a fundamental human right and of the power of human solidarity.

The challenge facing Latin America, as well as other parts of the poorly-named "Third World" (we are all one world, badly distributed), is that of creating life out of the forces of death which seem to prevail at all levels. Whether we refer to the foreign debt, the rise in hunger and infant mortality, the legacy of the military dictatorships, the revival of national security criteria in the so-called "war against drugs", or the consequences of impunity for societies marked by such grievous lawlessness, the odds seem stacked against us.

Gandhi used to say that democracy consists in the weakest having the same opportunities as the strongest. Today, in Latin America, we say that democracy must mean that no child goes to bed hungry, that no man or woman is denied the right to a job, an education, health-care and a sane environment. This radical transformation of the structures of injustice which condition people's livelihood, and indeed life itself, can hardly be achieved except through a process which involves the active participation of the victims: a process which speaks to and from their needs and is organized toward concrete objectives in the struggle for human liberation.

It is here, in the midst of this struggle, where the peoples of Latin America experience the force of active non-violence. Its power lies in the spirit and unity of those who are marginalized and suffer great misery. Its strength grows from their creativity and persistence in the pursuit of liberty and justice – for all people.

To be engaged in active non-violence means to listen and reflect. It means discovering new methodologies and strategies and reinforcing people's capacity to project toward, and through political action to transform our societies. The challenge we face is to understand and deepen the full significance of non-violent struggle, integrating more profoundly its rich, spiritual dimensions with its practical, political expressions, in the process of resisting injustice and contributing to the creation of a more humane society.

WILLIAM WARDEN*

From Analysis to Activism

In the context of the world situation today, it is evident that overall awareness of the issue of "human rights" is increasing. From San Salvador to New York to Phnom Penh to Montreal, the mention of "human rights" generates recognition and emotional response. In the deliberations of regional and world bodies from the United Nations to NATO to the newly emerging Commonwealth of States in the old Soviet Union, human rights are invariably cited as a factor to be taken into account.

True, focus on human rights remains by and large the preserve of the elites. In a world where the primary goal of the great majority of the people is to eke out a subsistence-level existence, human rights activism is regarded as a "luxury" affordable by the more affluent and the few. The poor and deprived understandably see the sustaining of life as their first priority.

It is equally true that lip-service to human rights by the elites does not in any way equate automatically to authentic concern. Commitment rather tends to be generated in direct proportion to the extent to which the interests of one's group will be served. In other words, the elites of Western countries may support human rights in Eastern Europe or South Africa, because by doing so they advance their own interests or protect their positions – but not necessarily because of an interest in promoting human rights *per se*.

Thus, it is evident that the elites are by no means in their totality, sympathetically disposed. On the contrary, in many instances it is clear that elites are addressing the issue of human rights for the purpose of co-opting the movement, or because it is seen as a threat to their position of privilege and power. In other instances, the elites are attempting to narrow the scope of human rights and to obstruct the movement's attempt to deal with broader issues such as gender and class.

Moreover, for some human rights are conceived as an issue in the wider world "out there" – and not one for "me" in the here and now. Treated in this fashion, the result is more likely to be a dulling of sensitivity to abuses on one's own doorstep. Canadians, for example, prefer to focus on apartheid in South

* Executive Director, International Centre, The University of Calgary.

K.E. Mahoney and P. Mahoney (eds.), Human Rights in the Twenty-first Century, 985–990.

Africa, rather than confront burning problems in their own relations with the aboriginal peoples.

Thus, while one speaks of increasing human rights awareness on the part of the elites, there is at the same time a disturbing quality of "immuneness", of insensitivity, of indifference to the plight of the disadvantaged and the abused. These characteristics increasingly mark the outlook of many of the elites.

Yet if one compares the situation of today with that of even a decade ago, we have – again at a certain level – made considerable progress. There are certainly more institutions now focusing on human rights. There is a process of "institutionalisation" taking place in the process of promoting human rights.

The new International Centre for Human Rights and Democratic Development in Montreal is a case in point, as are various institutes and watch-groups established in other parts of the world.

Moreover the Montreal Centre, funded by the Canadian International Development Agency, is illustrative of the fact that governments in a growing number of countries are belatedly coming to the conclusion that development, prosperity and human rights are inextricably linked. Genuine respect for the individual and dignity cannot exist without development; nor can development have a substantive and fundamental impact without parallel progress in human rights.

When measured in quantitative terms, the global capacity for analysing the political, social and economic forces which shape societies and which have a bearing on human rights is indeed increasing in absolute terms. This is all to the good.

Unfortunately, "quantitative" improvement has not necessarily led to a qualitative amelioration in the global situation. It would be difficult, if not impossible, on the basis of the available evidence to state categorically that in human rights terms we are globally better off today than we were a decade ago.

There is a tendency to be blinded to a certain extent, at least in the West, by the changes which have taken place in the Soviet Union and Eastern Europe, or by changes of government in places such as Nicaragua. The assumption is that these changes will automatically translate into long-term improvements in human rights.

The long term, however, holds no guarantees. Looking at the situation from a global perspective, one is struck by the significantly increased stresses and strains created by the accelerating pace of global change. The rapidity of change is such that more often than not one has the impression of living in a kaleidoscope whirling out of control. This is true in both North and South: no one is immune.

In the circumstances, a major concern for human rights activists as they contemplate the next decade and century has to be the now emerging dominant global trends. These include the globalisation of the economy, so-called democratisation, the focus on the environment – and so on. Will globalisation be an instrument for distributing wealth more equitably, or rather a licence to put more money in the pockets of the "haves"? As for "democratisation", will it serve to empower people at the grass roots, or simply to provide a new structure within which wealth and power can be more effectively concentrated? Situated as we are at an environmental watershed, will the current focus on environmental threats move us away from the brink, or is the planet being propelled into a downward spiral from which recovery is highly problematic?

These are all issues with direct implications for human rights, issues with which the human rights activists of our era must grapple, and issues which are addressed in this volume.

Analysis of these trends does not produce encouraging results. There is as yet little concrete evidence to show that globalisation of the economy is bringing substantive benefits to the chronically underprivileged. Even in a so-called developed country such as Canada, globalisation and its accompanying phenomena, such as free trade with neighbours, has so far had only effects which are perceived by the economically under-privileged as negative.

Similarly, an examination of the democratisation process does not necessarily generate optimism. While the collapse of totalitarian rule in a number of countries and the attempt to dismantle its accompanying abuses may be welcomed, serious questions remain as to the structures which will emerge to replace the fallen regimes. Concern derives not the least from the processes observable in the United States where, despite the benefits of "democratic" processes, the past decade has seen a distinct concentration of wealth in the hands of those at the top, and a corresponding diminution in real income in the bottom third of the population. This does not augur well for social harmony or the future prosperity of the corresponding elements of the populations in the newly "democratised" nations.

With respect to the environment, the most one can say at this point in time is that the chances for further degradation over the next two decades are greater than, or at least as great as, the likelihood of improvement.

In this context, a major concern for human rights activists has to be the way in which a continuation of the above trends will almost certainly have a negative impact on human rights. If these trends remain unchecked, one might expect by the year 2000 to see indicators pointing to a serious regression – simply because where the elementary means for sustaining life are put in jeopardy, human rights concerns are pushed into the background.

So far, the North has paid at least lipservice to the concept of development in the South and to bridging the gap between the "haves" and the "have-nots". One should, of course, be under no illusion as to the depth of this commitment; but at least the idea has been intellectually palatable.

The concern is that the world is on a threshold, that even the hitherto shallow commitment of the North is in danger of collapsing. As the global economy slows, as debt increases, as international trade stagnates, as protectionism rises, as the affluent of the world come face to face with the prospect of a "no-growth" future – or even of negative growth – the charade will stop; the thin veneer will fall away and the poorest may in effect be completely written off by the affluent. Even the pretence of "one world" may be dropped.

As what some refer to as the post-war "spirit of generosity" declines, the economically deprived stand in risk of being totally abandoned. The so-called Iron Curtain that has disappeared between East and West may well re-emerge as an impenetrable barrier between the "haves" and the "have-nots". This new barrier will not demarcate the border between North and South, but rather is more likely to be global in nature. It will have the effect of uniting the global "haves" against the global "have-nots".

Again, the impact on human rights can only be negative. The cause of human rights can only be set back and, as part of the vicious circle, development itself will reach an impasse.

In sum, we can say that while much has been done, we are in no way within sight of the target of a world where the scrupulous upholding of the Universal Declaration of Human Rights is the rule rather than the exception. Without the investment of vastly increased resources into the development of human rights consciousness on a global scale, the likelihood is that deprivation and abuse will become more pronounced rather than less, and that dignity and respect will be the preserve of the small elite even more in the future than it has in the past.

The challenges for those promoting human rights are indeed formidable. Consider, for example, the fact that from the perspective of those of us who live today, the struggle is in effect a permanent one. History suggests that the "oppressed" when they come to power invariably become the "oppressors". If this is true, the implication is that in the struggle ahead, there are only milestones. No destinations are in sight.

Consider too that in the struggle for human rights the principal agents of protest and progress will not be governments and institutions. By their very nature they are unsuited to these roles. Rather the main instruments will be individual activists moved to action by the abuses of the oppressors and energised by the grassroots.

These considerations are just as applicable in the North as in the South; they are as applicable in Canada as in Guatemala. In the final reckoning, we ourselves may excel – or our institutions may excel – in the process of analysis, in the process of researching the causes and predicting possible outcomes. The crux of the matter, however, lies in our ability as individuals to move from "objective" observation to personal involvement, from a detached relationship to the issues to a position where we can scarcely separate ourselves from them. In other words, if governments cannot lead and if progress is indeed to be made in the struggle for human rights, this can only occur insofar as we as individuals move from analysis to activism.

How do activists become activists? This question lends itself to no definitive response. One does not know if they are created or born or "called" in the Biblical sense. One does know that they come from across the broad spectrum of human society. India produced her Gandhi and Yugoslavia her Mother Teresa; Nazi Germany gave birth to a Niemoeller and El Salvador had her Romero. One also knows that a prerequisite for activism is a clear awareness of the issues. Activists have always emerged in all ages and systems and societies, and they have provided the necessary leadership.

One senses that the struggle for human rights is entering a qualitatively new era. Just as the world is changing, so the nature of activism will have to change. Just as the "opposition" is assuming new and more sophisticated forms, so there is a need for technological updating of the tools used by the activist. One will have to fight fire with fire.

Principal instruments in the period ahead will be *global* education and *global* protest. Individual action in the sense of action on one's own or action in isolation, effective as it may have been in the past, is unlikely to produce results in our new and globalised world.

This is not to deny the critical role of the individual activist. The starting point for activism will still be the consciousness that "I" as an individual share the guilt of those who abuse others, as well as the pain of those who are abused. It will still be this consciousness and sharing which compels "me" as an individual to action. Activism to have meaning will still have to spring directly from the grassroots victim groups.

The difference in the changing world, however, will be the realisation that "I" am but one link in a global chain and that "I" must act in concert with others. Just as governments and corporations create their global alliances and as the economic elites join forces on a supranational basis, so the human rights activist must aim at creating a global critical mass drawing its objectives and energy from the grassroots. Networking, alliance-building, conferences, electronic communications – the whole gambit of global instruments – will be of the utmost importance in the struggle.

Probably the most formidable challenge today for the human rights community of activists is that of education. On the one hand, there is a fundamental need to translate the growing consciousness of human rights issues to the entire spectrum of human society. The objective should be to ensure that within, say, a period of ten to twenty years virtually every individual on the planet will be fully aware in a practical and personal sense of the provisions of the Universal Declaration.

On the other hand, the need is for a concerted parallel educational effort aimed at key institutions and structures. Targets would be the judiciary, law enforcement agencies, educators, legislators.

Education will be the instrument for breeding and nourishing activism and fresh generations of activists on a much larger scale.

Such an undertaking by human rights activists can clearly only be accomplished to the extent that resources are pooled and global momentum is established. At the Conference there has been some discussion relating to the launching of a massive campaign, global in its vision. The idea is superb; the execution will be difficult in the extreme. Activists do not have a particularly good track record when it comes to working together. At the same time, the challenge was never greater than it is today nor the stakes higher.

The question confronting us is not so much one of "if", but rather one of "how" we can move from theory to action; how we can mobilise the energy that is out there; how we can exploit the opportunities available today; how we can initiate a process which will at the same time be both participatory and effective.

The present Conference has provided an excellent platform for the building of new structures and the concertation of more massive efforts. If it were to provide the launching pad, the motivational power for a far-reaching global educational effort, this would be an enormous achievement.

The cause is noble: the aim is no less than a fundamental change in human relationships.

RICHARD DEVLIN*

Solidarity or Solipsistic Tunnel Vision? Reminiscences of a Renegade Rapporteur**

1. Introductory Comments[1]

Given the approximately ninety seven presentations by activists, government officials, NGO representatives, politicians, sociologists, philosophers, lawyers and many others, what I want to do is briefly highlight some of what are, in my opinion, the key themes and tensions of the Conference and to play them out. However, my approach is not simply descriptive or synthetic, but critical and visionary. It also oscillates between pessimism and optimism. Thus my contribution follows the exhortation by feminist poet and writer, Adrienne Rich, when she calls for:

> "imagination, not merely for changing institutions but for human relationships; not merely for equal rights, but for a new kind of being".[2]

I should also add that given the status of those who have already presented and the quality of some of the papers I am quite nervous in giving these closing comments. But here goes.

2. The Need for Conceptual Clarity: The Nature of Human Rights

To some extent, I was disappointed that few of the presenters directly or expressly addressed the question of the nature of human rights. This may be

* Associate Professor of Law, The University of Calgary, Calgary, Alberta.

** This was the Rapporteur's speech at the closing of the Conference.

[1]This report is, to a significant degree, the end product of a collective effort. Given that for a large part of the Conference several presentations were happening simultaneously, it was necessary that I gained the assistance of David Dzidzornu (LLM candidate, University of Calgary) and Rebecca Johnson (Third Year LLB student, The University of Calgary). Their support was invaluable, although what follows does not necessarily represent their opinions.

[2] A. Rich, "Toward a Woman Centre University" in *Lies, Secrets and Silence* (1979) pp. 125 at 155.

K.E. Mahoney and P. Mahoney (eds.), Human Rights in the Twenty-first Century, 991–1003.

because most people assume that they (and everyone else) knows what they mean by human rights. However, I believe that this is a false assumption, that many of us have differing conceptions of human rights and that in the presentations given there appear to have been several not necessarily compatible assumptions. In short, human rights is "an essentially contested concept".[3] I think it is important to be clear right from the beginning as to what we mean by human rights, because that assumption will determine the remainder of our analysis. Two conceptions, in particular, tended to surface in the Conference and it is important to spotlight them because they underpin, concretize and reflect many of the other tensions of the last couple of days. These I shall call "the essentialist" and "the critical modernist" versions of human rights.

(1) The Essentialist Version

The idea underpinning the essentialist conception of human rights is that there is something about us as human beings, something that goes to our very nature, that inherently suggests that we have an entitlement to basic rights. The core theme is that human rights transcend the contingencies of politics.

At first blush, this version of human rights is attractive. The very universalizability and generalizability of this viewpoint makes it desirable. But it is, unfortunately, pervaded by a variety of problems. First, its very abstraction and lack of specificity while being its greatest strength in one sense, is also its central weakness. It is simply too vague and there is a fundamental lack of consensus as to what the nature and parameters of these basic rights might be. This becomes particularly apparent when the human rights dialogue is cracked open to the perspective of those who have traditionally been excluded from the conversation. This leads to the second problem. As several of the presenters at the conference have indicated, the universality ascribed to human rights discourse is false in that it incorporates Eurocentric and male assumptions. Restated, the white male perspective is the hidden but determinative norm of the dominant tradition in human rights. Third, the essentialist version is based upon a pre-modern concept of the person. In the spirit of the ancient Greek philosophers, it assumes that there is a core/essential subject, whereas a modern viewpoint comprehends the subject as a construct of a multitude of influences.

(2) The Critical Modernist Perspective

The critical modernist perspective refuses to essentialize human rights in this way. It conceives of human rights as an ideological discursive practice, that is, as a way of thinking, talking and knowing that facilitates, structures and

[3] W.B. Gallie, "Essentially Contested Concepts" (1955) lvi Aristotelian Society Proceedings N.S. pp. 167–198.

underpins the ways and means of social interaction. The key idea is that human rights are not distinct from politics, but an element of politics. Therefore, human rights are a contestable terrain of political struggle. By filtering discourse of human rights through the prism of politics, we then get particular, contextual and concrete angles on human rights debates. Because politics is about domination and subordination, power and powerlessness, the question can now be reformulated: "Can human rights as a discursive practice be utilized to break the hierarchy of domination and subordination?"

The significance of the "critical modernist view" is threefold. First, human rights cannot be ossified, reduced or restricted to any pseudo-determinative idea, like for example, "Liberty". To do so is ahistorical and unnecessarily enthrals us to liberal origins of the discourse of rights. Rather, I want to argue that human rights discourse should be conceived of as open-ended and revisable. Second, and more specifically, the critical modernist approach posits that human rights be developed to respond to and facilitate the achievement of the *needs* of people. Thus it does not mire itself in abstractions, but focuses on subordination and powerlessness in their diverse, specific and particularized forms. Third, this refurbished human rights discourse then provides us with an opportunity to not only challenge power, that is, domination and subordination which is "power over" or what Ursula Franklin called "control", but perhaps it also allows us the possibility to reconceptualize power as "power to", as "empowerment". Therefore, human rights can be developed as a strategy of resistance to help us articulate, and to give effect to another form of power, "power to".

2. Key Concepts of Conference

I was also a little disappointed at the looseness of the terminology used by a significant number of the participants and, more particularly, by the failure of some of the papers to address themes specified by the coordinators. In order to fill in this lacuna, let me briefly, though perhaps belatedly, attempt to trace for you my conception of the key concepts of "solidarity" and "interdependence", and the correlative and implicit ideal of "equality".

(1) Solidarity

In my opinion, the concept of solidarity was bandied about with a disturbing amount of imprecision. Let me offer two angles on it. The first draws on the work of the Latin American jurisprude and social theorist, Roberto Mangabeira Unger. The second comes from the work of some North American feminists, in particular, Carol Gilligan and Joan Tronto.

Unger, in his more visionary moments, offers us a substantive, normative vision for social interaction. He posits that "[solidarity is] love struggling to move beyond the circle of intimacy ... The kernel of solidarity is our feeling of responsibility for those whose lives touch in some way upon our own and our greater or lesser willingness to share their fate. Solidarity is the social face of love ..."[4]

Carol Gilligan and Joan Tronto have, along with many other North American feminists, suggested that we need a new social morality, what they call an ethic of care.[5] The central insight of the ethic of care is a consciousness of the constitutive interconnection of self and other. It encourages an enthusiasm for and understanding of the needs of others. It engenders a willingness to respond compassionately and responsibly to those needs. The ethic of care is, I suggest, a cognate of solidarity.

(2) Interdependence

Interdependence was more directly invoked by the presenters but it too has had a chameleon character, so let me attempt to introduce, once again, a little precision. Several layers of meaning were invoked for the purposes of this conference, but I want to suggest that the preferred emphasis should be on the third. The first level of meaning is descriptive, that is, the commonplace – now trite – idea that we live in a global village. One direct consequence of this is that we co-exist in economic mutual reliance. The second level of meaning might be described as "existential", that is, that as people we need each other for our mutual survival beyond material provisioning.

The third layer of interdependence I would describe as "ethical". As persons and communities, our identities are based upon the paradox of a need for, and yet a distance from "others".[6] Solidarity, as an ethos, proposes that we should reject "the fear of the Other"; a fear which I believe lies at the heart of subordination of the other one, for example, the basis of race, gender, class or sexual orientation.[7] Interdependence encourages the recognition that we need the other to be ourselves. This would suggest that we need to embrace and foster a radical diversity and to reject the repressive impulses of the ideology of sameness. For example, I would suggest that those who claim to be human rights supporters and proponents of interdependence and solidarity should concur with Ovide Mercredi's proposition that Canada must recognize and proactively support the "self-determination of First Nations" in Canada. Those of us who have power have nothing to fear from the other except,

[4] R. Unger, *Law in Modern Society* (1975) 207,208.

[5] C. Gilligan, *In a Different Voice* (1982); J. Tronto, "Beyond Gender Difference Towards a Theory of Care" (1987) 12 Signs 644–663. For a significantly more nuanced discussion of the ethic of care than can be offered here see my "Nomos and Thanatos Part B: Feminism as Jurisgenerative Transformation, or Resistance Through Partial Incorporation" (1990) 13 Dal.L.J. pp. 123–210.

[6] See generally, Roberto Mangabeira Unger, *Passion: An Essay on Human Personality* (1984)

[7] See my "The Rule of Law and the Politics of Fear: Some Reflections on Northern Ireland" N.I.L.Q. (forthcoming).

perhaps, our loss of "power over", our socially constructed and conferred ability to dominate.

(3) Equality

If we revision human rights as being about "power to", and are hospitable to the ideals of solidarity and interdependence, we will also require a reconceptualization of equality. We can no longer accept "formal equality" or "equality of opportunity" as adequate to the task of a progressive praxis of human rights. Instead, human rights must aspire to "equality of condition". The focus of this approach is not solely on those who are disadvantaged, for it also factors in the structural conditions in which people exist so that they can have a real existential chance to pursue and direct their own destinies. As Margrit Eichler has pointed out, equality would transmute from an abstract concept to a concrete challenge to eliminate the hierarchical, socially constructed differences between people.[8] This would mean a reformulation of the human rights agenda towards what might be called "shrinking the disparity".

3. Towards a New Human Rights Norm: Self-Reflexivity

Having identified and developed some of the underlying concepts of the Conference, I now want to address and reflect upon some of the emotions that I went through the last couple of days. Stated briefly, as I have sat through the sessions I have oscillated between optimism and pessimism, usually in inverse proportion to the tone of the presenters' thoughts.

First, there were those who talked about the human rights conventions, institutions, decisions etc.. By and large theirs was a tone of reserved optimism, progress was being made, and problems were gradually being ironed out. My personal response to this type of presentation was much more pessimistic. To a person, it seemed to me that they all assumed the narrow and essentialist vision of what human rights might mean. Several went out of their way to emphasize that their work was beyond the contaminating crassness of politics. Their presentations indicate that, at least at this level, human rights has become mired in a legalized proceduralism, that it cannot even fathom the necessity for substantive transformation.

However, there were also many participants who talked about: the existential reality of domination and subordination; how perhaps things were getting worse rather than better; and how traditional and mainstream definitions of human rights were inappropriate for contemporary social relations. Examples might include: Charlotte Bunch, Ursula Franklin, Rozenna Maart, Mona Makram Ebeid and Catharine MacKinnon. Despite the genuinely

[8] Margrit Eichler, "The Elusive Ideal – Defining Equality" (1988), 5 C.H.R.Y.B. pp. 167–188.

and generally pessimistic tone of their analyses, I felt their work to be energizing. Although still marginal to the malestream of human rights discourse, they have problematized and destabilized the traditional human rights bureaucracy; they are acutely conscious of the political nature of human rights; they have disconnected it from its seventeenth century roots; and they have attempted to reconstruct the practice and definition of human rights so as to suit the needs of the twenty first century. Through their efforts human rights are become prospective, not retrospective.

These reflections on optimism and pessimism lead me to tentatively suggest a new norm for a modernist practice of human rights: the "Principle of Self-Reflexivity", the "Principle of Self-Revisability". As human beings, we have an emotional self-interest in believing that we are doing the right thing. However, we need to be more conscious of the particularity and partial nature of our self-perception and consequently to proactively seek out the gaps and failures of our analysis. In other words, we need to build into our analyses a process of critical self-recognition, a disposition for humility and an openness to critique.

The principle of "self-reflexivity" becomes particularly poignant and especially crucial if we are in a position of power and influence: whether it be at the micro or macro level. To provide a few suggestions of the utility of the principle in relation to situations of micropower that surfaced at this conference, consider some of the following illustrative examples. As a progressive white heterosexual male what are you doing in relation to issues of race, of gender, of sexual orientation? or, if you are a Black male struggling against racism, are there times when you perpetuate the domination of women? And if you are a privileged white woman, are you excluding the perspective of the working classes or people of colour?

On the level of macro power, the "self-reflexivity" principle also generates a series of problematics. Are the international human rights systems premised upon Euro-American ideologies that force the assimilation of other cultural worldviews? Or, are they driven by a male conception of the human condition and social structure? Or again, as Kevin Hamilton asks, is our worldview essentially imperialist in that our "well intentioned" attempts to "civilize" what we arrogantly call "primitive" or "third world" societies fail to recognize the richness and sophistication of such cultures? Moreover, we must consider our legal systems' complicity – directly and indirectly, coercively and ideologically – in the entrenchment and perpetuation of abilism, classism, sexism, racism and homophobia.

Of course, this process of "self-reflexivity" is not easy. It is painful to be told that you – individually and institutionally – are sexist and racist and abilist and homophobic. It is disturbing to be told that you are part of the problem when all along you thought you were part of the solution. You may want to resist. You may want to trivialize the critique. You may ridicule your detractors. You may want to lash out. However, the principle of "self-reflexivity" services as counterbalance to these knee-jerk reactions and demands that we respond to the critiques with care, and responsibly.

Moreover, the principle of "self-reflexivity" acts as a counterfoil to one of the most pervasive and nefarious strategies of domination, that is, the silencing or occlusion of oppressions. "Self-reflexivity" helps us to avoid creating new exclusions. For example, as Svend Robinson pointed out, homosexuality and lesbianism have been accorded a relatively low level of priority at this conference. The same is true of children's rights. There has been no discussion of the victims of global economic liberalization – also known as free trade – or the impoverishing activities of the World Bank and the western dominated International Monetary Fund. I am sure there are others, but self-reflexivity demands that human rights discourse be open-ended, inclusive, pro-active, and forward-looking.

The obvious answer to these criticisms is that it is not possible to deal with everything at once, that choices have to be made on the basis of a finite budget. Undoubtedly, this is true. However, the more interesting question is by what criteria will these choices be made and what ultimately will be the results of such choices? This type of question cuts, I think, to one of the fundamental dilemmas of progressive human rights practice: vision constrained by structure. Put simply, this conference could only have happened with the support of what are in essence elitist and conservative structures of power; they provided the credentials, they provided much of the funding, and they provide the space. Yet they also had to be heavily represented, taking up a lot of space, and frequently saying little that is of progressive value. The act of speaking is, of necessity, a monopolization of the channels of discourse and thereby excludes the voices of others. I think that given these constraints the organizers have done quite well in creating deviationist space for some of those who have been excluded by the mainstream of the human rights community. But we must be careful about the excesses of self-congratulation for a great deal more needs to be achieved. The obstacles are structural not just individual.

(1) Public/Private Dichotomy

The principle of "self-reflexivity" has also helped me to get an angle on another of the tensions of the conference: the subterranean but pervasive influence of the public/private dichotomy. The public/private dichotomy like the essentialist conception of human rights invokes closure; it presupposes that there are certain spheres that are naturally "unchangeable", or are "beyond the mandate". However, critical theory and feminism have exposed the "lie" of the public/private dichotomy and have demonstrated the constructed, contingent nature of that ideology, though all the time recognizing that it is a particularly pervasive one.

I want to challenge the public/private dichotomy as it tends to manifest itself in human rights discourse, not to deny that there is State violence, but to highlight the incompleteness of an analysis that goes no further. There is absolutely no doubt that there is extensive State violence, that it is pervasive and systemic and that, in spite of all our self-perceptions of progress, perhaps that we have reached that stage where State violence has become normalized and therefore seemingly legitimate.

Consider the following brief examples. In my native British occupied Northern Ireland, there have been "shoot to kill" policies carried out by RUC/SAS death squads; speeches made by members of the Thatcher government that, in my opinion, have led to the execution of lawyers who defend Irish freedom fighters [the parallel with the Rushdie affair seems to have been missed, the real difference being that Pat Finucane is dead and Rushdie is alive]; and the incarceration of political prisoners whose only "choice" is death by hunger strike. Then, of course, there is my current country of residence, Canada, the so called "peaceable kingdom", with its phenomenally high incarceration rates of First Nations peoples and violations of human rights at Kanesatake and Kahnawake this past summer. And how could we forget the United States, with its covert and overt violence, domestically and internationally. Nor must we ignore the activities of the Israeli state against the Palestinian people, nor forget the historical repression by the Soviet Union against Jews in particular, and more generally the citizenry of other nations.

These are important criticisms and should remain a component of human rights activism but, even in this sphere, particularly in societies that are so numbed by consumerism, the tendency is to only look at the spectacular disasters, the most extreme examples. The principle of self-reflexivity demands that we look at the normalization and legitimization of human rights abuse everyday via domestic law. I would argue that we have become desensitized to the horror of law, that law, and we who work in the legal system, have constitutionalized violence; and that we have imbricated within our laws what Hannah Arendt has called "the banality of evil".[9]

Though all of these fears of State violence, and a vast amount more, are true, to cease one's analysis of human rights abuses at this point would be to leave us with a dramatically incomplete picture. If human rights are to be understood as a challenge to power, as a mode of resistance to domination, then we must confront power in all its manifestations.

Human rights have a contingent history. Specifically, they can be traced to the origins of the liberal democratic tradition. Central to this tradition was the ambition to control and limit the power of the Nation State. Even if it was true at the time, it is no longer true that the State is the sole or even primary agent of domination in the late twentieth century world community. Only those who espouse what Asbjorn Eide has iconoclastically termed "fundamentalist liberalism" could believe this. Power over, power as domination, is not just centralized and statist. It is also pervasive, systemic, localized, individualized, privatized and technified. Rephrased, there are countervailing and complementary dominating powers to that of the State. Therefore, the public/private dichotomy, in this context, is best understood as an ideological

[9] H. Arendt, *Eichmann in Jerusalem: A Report on the Banality of Evil* (1976).

construct and social practice that simultaneously obscures and legitimizes private domination. Consequently, we need a reconceptualization and expansion of our conception of human rights if it is to be an effective strategy in the pursuit of equality of condition.

Examples of the "private" abuses of human rights are legion and were pointed out in a number of papers. One example is the forum shopping by multinational pharmaceutical corporations either to dump or test drugs on humans. Another is the violence against women perpetrated in patriarchal societies. Specifically, pornography, as produced by an economic empire and consumed by individual men, subjects women to sexual assault, or as MacKinnon has powerfully portrayed, torture. Another example of private and novel forms of private human rights abuses are the practices around and uses of the New Reproductive Technologies. Private corporations in the pursuit of profit, and for no other reasons despite their humanitarian rhetoric, have joined what Renate Klein has described as an "unholy alliance of sexist, racist and eugenicist technodocs" which results in commodification and objectification of women. Or again, the media, under the banner of the liberal fundamentalist principle of freedom of expression, propagate misogyny, racism, homophobia and xenophobia, frequently via the insidious strategy of blaming the victim.

Cumulatively, this expanded conception of the domain of the human rights, engendered as it is by a rejection of the public/private dichotomy, is depressing because it highlights much more intangible and complex forms of abuses that simply cannot be fully fathomed within the fishbowl that is called malestream liberalism. Ursula Franklin nicely captured the problem through her discussion of what she called "control technologies", that they are a "headless tyranny", a paradigm of "power over" because they are routinized and normalized. Consider, in this light, Rhoda Howard's discussion of the self-mutilization of North American women, for example, by plastic surgery or by dieting to fit with the male image.

But slowly, I think, the first steps are being taken to combat the problem. By the process of naming, by fighting from the margins, the destabilization of the hegemonic view has begun. Perhaps those who refuse to listen to these alternative conceptions of human rights, those who invoke the silencing strategy of definitional closure, those who control the international human rights agenda should get out of the way. Then they would be part of the solution, or at least not part of the problem.

4. Individual and Community Rights; Universalism and Particularism

Another precept of fundamentalist liberalism and the essentialist conception of human rights is that the individual subject is the core, and frequently exclusive, focus of the analysis. However, the hegemony of this liberal *weltanschauung* reflects an impoverished vision of "the self", severing her interdependence with "the other" and is blind to our mutually constitutive nature. Moreover, it may be premised on ethnocentric assumptions that fail to incorporate the needs and/or visions of subordinated cultures. This, in turn, has tended to generate a fetishization of rights ideology within international human rights circles thereby underplaying the importance of duties or other normative desiderata. What is required, I think is greater responsiveness to community needs and collective rights. Examples might include the inability of the Canadian Government to even comprehend, let alone recognize and affirm, the collective rights of the First Nations. Consider also the discomfort of many within the international human rights field with the African idea of duties not just rights. Perhaps we require, for example, the duty of the State to provide food, or the duty of private corporations to distribute wealth.

The inability of mainstream human rights discourse to fully come to terms with the concept of collective rights is, in fact, symptomatic of another of the tensions that has pervaded the Conference: universalism and particularism. As I tried to make clear earlier, the traditional essentialist conception of human rights espouses universalistic assumptions and visions, premised upon generic, abstract, acontextual and transhistorical conceptions of the person, society and culture. I want to suggest, however, that this is a false universality because its very abstraction renders it pragmatically anaemic. More nefarious though, is that the pretension to universality obscures the partiality and uni-dimensionalism of the underlying norms. To be clear, it seems to me that contemporary mainstream human rights discourse is premised upon a privileged, white male interpretation of the meaning of rights.

What is required is much greater sensitivity to existential, specific reality of differently situated people. Rephrased, we need to work on conceiving and developing a contextualist practice of human rights, one that forgoes the mendaciously idyllic, one that comes to terms with the messiness, specificities and complexity of the multiplicity of realities. Let me provide a few examples. Environmental security may mean very different things depending on whether you live in a rich North Atlantic society, whether you are an Inuit, or whether you are an Indigenous person in a South American rain forest. Human rights activists should be sufficiently self-reflexive to recognize the diversity of these realities and to respond accordingly. This may require fundamental reinterpretations of the source and nature of the problems, the types of questions asked and the answers sought. Or again, refugee rights, rather being premised upon some prototypical norm, must recognize the multiplicity of reasons for actually becoming a refugee including, for example, gender or sexual preference. This is very different from asking, does this person fit within the traditional legalized definition of "refuge status"? Similarly, if the right to be free from torture, inhuman and degrading treatment was reconstructed to accord with a contextualist approach then we would recognize the specific and particular harm that pornography causes to women even though there is no parallel for men.

5. Responsibility and Solidarity: An Integrative Theory of Human Rights

What I am trying to grapple with in this paper is the articulation of what might be called an Integrative Theory of Human Rights. In this approach, concepts of solidarity and interdependence are dovetailed with the dream of equality of condition to provide us with a discursive ideological practice that empowers us to go beyond liberal essentialism; assuage the seeming contradiction of the individual and community; and recognize the mutuality of 'self' and 'other'. Moreover, an integrative vision helps us to resist the subdivisioning (and therefore hierarchicalization) of human rights into civil, political, economic, social and cultural ghettoes because that, as Shelly Wright points out, fractionalizes and does violence to our existential reality.

In particular, this Integrative Theory of Human Rights, because of its emphasis on solidarity, shifts the frame of analysis. Traditionally, the focus of human rights discourse has been on the victims of abuse. This is, of course, vital but at times it ironically results in a sort of structural 'blaming the victim' syndrome. Moreover, we must not forget that human rights abuses do not just happen. Somebody abuses somebody else; there is agency involved. This suggests that we must shift our focus. Therefore, we must look to the cause of the abuse, to seek out who or what is responsible. More specifically, it is necessary to self-reflexively inquire as to whether we who have privilege and power are complicitous in the subordination.

Again some examples might help. Over the last couple of years one question that I have been asking myself is: What is my responsibility as a white male in relation to the domination of women? At this point, part of the answer is that I consider it one of my responsibilities to help make institutional space for women in the environment where I work and to facilitate the emergence of conditions of equality that would engender womens' empowerment. Note that this is very different from doing it for women, for that would be appropriate or masculinist ventriloquism. Rather, the project should be to surrender power over, to encourage power to. Alternatively, I would ask: What is the responsibility of the conference organizers in relation to, for example: the mentally or physically challenged; or the homosexual, lesbian or bisexual members of our societies; or Canada's linguistic minorities?

A starting point and a central responsibility, I would suggest, is that we begin to learn to listen to others. One particular problem is that we of the western culture have constructed a hierarchy of communicative modes, that is, we priorize the written over the spoken word. By way of illustration, consider the preoccupation of the international human rights organizations with conventions, declarations, protocols, and judicial decisions compared to their almost total disregard of oral traditions of, for example, the African verbal tradition or First Nations. Perhaps modern technology could be put to some constructive use here, particularly the visual media. But listening is not enough. As Spike Lee has suggested we must "Do The Right Thing".

Although I have been critical of the international human rights bureaucracy, I also believe that it is too important, too powerful, too influential, to ignore. It too must be rendered vulnerable to the principle of self-reflexivity and the politics of progressivism. Therefore, it is perhaps time for us to name and espouse a new conception of rights: what might be called Solidarity Rights. Roberto Mangabeira Unger has tentatively identified these as being "the domain of the half-articulate relations of trusting interdependence", as giving "legal form to social relations of reliance and trust".[10]

It seems to me that several advantages might accrue from adopting the concept of Solidarity Rights. First, through the power of naming, we provide an entitlement concept that can be drawn upon by the victims of human rights abuse in the plethora of forms that have been identified in this conference. Second, when conceptualized and touted as a right then solidarity might just be understood (and perhaps even responded to) by those who are in positions of responsibility and power. Third, as a strategy, perhaps solidarity rights can be understood not as a complete break with the mainstream tradition of human rights discourse but as an emancipatory leap forward drawing on the already existing precedents of economic, social, cultural rights but casting them in a significantly new light.

However, as my concerns about universalism make clear, insofar as the current international human rights community remains entrenched, other terrains of social struggle need to be developed. Therefore, the environmental slogan, "think globally, act locally", can perhaps be drawn upon in developing a critical practice of human rights activism. Viewed in this light, human rights must be fought for from the bottom up, as well as from the top down. By this I mean, rather than waiting for the sclerotic institutions to play catch up, those who are interested in the praxis of human rights must continue their efforts to reinforce the struggle against racism in South Africa and for self-determination by the First Nations of Canada; recognize the work of women in sexual assault centres as human rights work; and support the mobilization of Blacks in the United States, the intifada by the Palestinians, and the development of anti-sexist and anti-racist refugee policies.

This might all sound just too much, too removed from the traditional ways of "doing human rights". However, the old essentialist ways will not serve the needs of the twenty first century. As the quote from Rich suggests, we need imagination but we do not need to re-invent the wheel for there are models of solidarity practices upon which we can build. Consider, for example: the feminist modes of alternative dispute resolution; the strategies of judicial education; the Waitangi tribunal; and the Rainbow Coalition of Jesse Jackson. However, I think that we need to look beyond the myopic confines of western society: to the non-violent action of the dispossessed in Latin America; to empowerment at the grass roots level in Asia; and the base communities and the

[10] *False Necessity: Anti-Necessitarian Social Theory in the Service of Social Democracy* (1987) pp. 535–536.

preferential option for the poor and the oppressed as developed and practised by the traditionally conservative Catholic Church.

6. Closing Comments

It seems to me that a theory and practice of human rights appropriate for the needs of the twenty first century requires a new critical modernist approach; one that challenges "power over" and pursues "power to"; one that highlights our responsibilities and our opportunities. The options are optimism or pessimism. As I have indicated there have been tensions and controversies in this conference. People have been angry, dismayed, hurt, frustrated. But part of the reason why this is so is because people who have traditionally been excluded have gained some space (though certainly inadequate) to articulate their vision of human rights. The debate has been painful and, I think that the human rights community have begun to hear them. The task that lies ahead is to invoke the standard of self-reflexivity; to turn critique into reconstruction; for those who have power to help transform rage into solidarity; and, for all of us to imagine and put into effect a new relationship, between life, law and love.

Index